D0983005

THE GREAT
CONTEMPORARY
ISSUES

THE CITIES

THE GREAT

CONTEMPORARY

ISSUES

OTHER BOOKS IN THE SERIES

DRUGS
Introduction by J. Anthony Lukas
THE MASS MEDIA AND POLITICS
Introduction by Walter Cronkite
CHINA
O. Edmund Clubb, *Advisory Editor*
LABOR AND MANAGEMENT
Richard B. Morris, *Advisory Editor*
WOMEN: THEIR CHANGING ROLES
Elizabeth Janeway, *Advisory Editor*
BLACK AFRICA
Hollis Lynch, *Advisory Editor*
EDUCATION, U.S.A.
James Cass, *Advisory Editor*
VALUES AMERICANS LIVE BY
Garry Wills, *Advisory Editor*
CRIME AND JUSTICE
Ramsey Clark, *Advisory Editor*
JAPAN
Edwin O. Reischauer, *Advisory Editor*
THE PRESIDENCY
George E. Reedy, *Advisory Editor*
POPULAR CULTURE
David Manning White, *Advisory Editor*
FOOD AND POPULATION: THE WORLD IN CRISIS
Sen. George S. McGovern, *Advisory Editor*
THE U.S. AND THE WORLD ECONOMY
Leonard Silk, *Advisory Editor*
SCIENCE IN THE TWENTIETH CENTURY
Walter Sullivan, *Advisory Editor*
THE MIDDLE EAST
John C. Campbell, *Advisory Editor*

THE GREAT
CONTEMPORARY
ISSUES

THE CITIES

The New York Times

ARNO PRESS

NEW YORK/1976

VOID

RICHARD C. WADE
Advisory Editor

GENE BROWN
Editor

Library of Congress Cataloging in Publication Data

Main entry under title:

The cities.

(The Great contemporary issues)
"Articles which appeared in the New York times."
1. Cities and towns—United States—Addresses, essays, lectures. I. Wade, Richard C. II. Brown, Gene. III. New York times. IV. Series.
HT123.C495 301.36'2'0973 76-29702
ISBN 0-405-09849-9

Manufactured in the United States of America

The editors express special thanks to The Associated Press, United Press International, and Reuters for permission to include in this series of books a number of dispatches originally distributed by those news services.

Book design by Stephanie Rhodes

Contents

Publisher's Note About the Series

It would take even an accomplished speed-reader, moving at full throttle, some three and a half solid hours a day to work his way through all the news The New York Times prints. The sad irony, of course, is that even such indefatigable devotion to life's carnival would scarcely assure a decent understanding of what it was really all about. For even the most dutiful reader might easily overlook an occasional long-range trend of importance, or perhaps some of the fragile, elusive relationships between events that sometimes turn out to be more significant than the events themselves.

This is why "The Great Contemporary Issues" was created—to help make sense out of some of the major forces and counterforces at large in today's world. The philosophical conviction behind the series is a simple one: that the past not only can illuminate the present but must. ("Continuity with the past," declared Oliver Wendell Holmes, "is a necessity, not a duty.") Each book in the series, therefore has as its subject some central issue of our time that needs to be viewed in the context of its antecedents if it is to be fully understood. By showing, through a substantial selection of contemporary accounts from The New York Times, the evolution of a subject and its significance, each book in the series offers a perspective that is available in no other way. For while most books on contemporary affairs specialize, for excellent reasons, in predigested facts and neatly drawn conclusions, the books in this series allow the reader to draw his own conclusions on the basis of the facts as they appeared at virtually the moment of their occurrence. This is not to argue that there is no place for events recollected in tranquility; it is simply to say that when fresh, raw truths are allowed to speak for themselves, some quite distinct values often emerge.

For this reason, most of the articles in "The Great Contemporary Issues" are reprinted in their entirety, even in those cases where portions are not central to a given book's theme. Editing has been done only rarely, and in all such cases it is clearly indicated. (Such an excision occasionally occurs, for example, in the case of a Presidential State of the Union Message, where only brief portions are germane to a particular volume, and in the case of some names, where for legal reasons or reasons of taste it is preferable not to republish specific identifications.) Similarly, typographical errors, where they occur, have been allowed to stand as originally printed.

"The Great Contemporary Issues" inevitably encompasses a substantial amount of history. In order to explore their subjects fully, some of the books go back a century or more. Yet their fundamental theme is not the past but the present. In this series the past is of significance insofar as it suggests how we got where we are today. These books, therefore, do not always treat a subject in a purely chronological way. Rather, their material is arranged to point up trends and interrelationships that the editors believe are more illuminating than a chronological listing would be.

"The Great Contemporary Issues" series will ultimately constitute an encyclopedic library of today's major issues. Long before editorial work on the first volume had even begun, some fifty specific titles had already been either scheduled for definite publication or listed as candidates. Since then, events have prompted the inclusion of a number of additional titles, and the editors are, moreover, alert not only for new issues as they emerge but also for issues whose development may call for the publication of sequel volumes. We will, of course, also welcome readers' suggestions for future topics.

Introduction

In the past twenty years the phrase "urban crisis" has crept, indeed galloped, into our public vocabulary. To many the phrase suggests that something new has entered the life of the metropolis that had not been there before. Behind this perception is the notion that urban conditions today are much worse than they were twenty-five, fifty, or a hundred years ago. It assumes that the long litany of city ills—spreading slums, massive poverty, increasing joblessness, inadequate education, rampant crime, and endemic disorder—are somehow the function of very recent times. More importantly still, present public policy is often based on this premise.

Actually, in almost all these categories the modern American city is better than it has been in the historic past. The percentage of poor is less, the proportion of substandard housing has diminished, employment is generally higher and more stable, even the incidence of crime, vice, and disorder is probably less. Yet why this near panic today? One explanation is that Americans know so little about their urban past. It is only recently that scholars have begun to add an urban dimension to their concerns with more conventional history. Hence the public knows little about conditions in New York, Chicago, or New Orleans in, say, the 1870s. At the same time, the media provides them nightly with dramatic details about the contemporary crisis. Secondly, the very scale of the modern metropolis requires new approaches and new tools. Yet there are few precedents either here or abroad that seem appropriate. Perhaps the beginning of wisdom is to see how we got to where we are.

From the colonial period until about the 1840s, American towns were "walking cities." People went to work, to shop, to visit, and to play on foot. Some of the wealthy lived outside the municipal limits and commuted to their businesses by carriage, but most people, rich and poor, walked. Hence they lived closer together than they ever would again. To be sure, the affluent appropriated the high land and the most desirable locations and the poor huddled in shacks along the waterfront or were tucked into alleys and lanes. Yet no great spaces separated mansions from hovels. In addition, commercial and manufacturing facilities were mixed with housing. In small retail shops, owners or clerks lived above the store, and tanneries, meatpacking plants, and breweries were often within sight—and smell—of the most elegant residences. Railroads and freight yards cut through the heart of the city, the tracks often moving along major streets. The compactness of the "historic city" created a mixture of land uses which would be generally unknown in the twentieth century.

Into this restricted urban center was introduced one of the most revolutionary agents of modern society. Called an omnibus, it provided an alternative, though not always a comfortable one, to walking. Operating first in New York in 1829, the system was quickly adopted in other large cities. Soon the omnibus was placed on tracks to become the horsedrawn streetcar. Then the cable car was invented, followed by the electric trolley, the elevated and underground railways, and finally the automobile.

Mass transportation broke the confinement of the "historic city" and created the conditions necessary for the "modern city" to develop. For now it was possible for residents to work downtown and yet live quite removed from it. A person walks at about three miles an hour; the horsedrawn streetcar went about six miles an hour. When electricity replaced horses, the rate of speed of mass transportation was doubled. And, of course, the elevated and subway carried passengers at an even faster pace, to which the automobile added still another dimension.

The "historic city" had been confined to a few square miles. But with the ease of movement brought by mass transit, American towns quickly spread outside their old limits and covered the surrounding country. Land that lay within an hour's commuting time to the job was opened up to settlement. Municipal boundaries were everywhere greatly extended, and even suburban development grew up beyond the city line. In 1876, St. Louis more than tripled its territory; in 1829, Chicago annexed 126 square miles. By 1920, most places, except in the South and West, had reached their present geographic limits; by 1970 over half of the people in metropolitan areas lived in suburban communities and towns.

The second consequence of the introduction of mass transit was the sorting out of people within the city. As soon as new forms of transportation made it possible to live at the edge of the city and work downtown, the wealthy began to move away from the central area.

Soon the familiar social geography of the modern city appeared—with the rich at the outer edges and the poor huddled in the inner section. There were, of course, exceptions to this pattern, but it prevailed in most large cities by the end of the nineteenth century.

The third consequence stemming from the transportation revolution was an accelerating mobility in the entire urban structure. Everyone was in movement—not only those already in the city who continually changed residences, but also those coming in from the outside. In addition, industrial facilities were moved away from high-priced downtown land. Commercial location, of course, still favored the central district. Yet as cities grew and expanded, business too began to move out to serve outlying neighborhoods. Thus, change and instability became the central characteristics of the American metropolis. City planners later complained that the growth was disorderly; local officials found it difficult to control the process; church and civic leaders struggled to maintain community in old neighborhoods. But the decisions of thousands, indeed tens of thousands, of citizens created the shape and social texture of the modern city.

This urban expansion came about because the immense flow of immigration commenced during the period when mass transit made possible the accommodation of large numbers. A few statistics can convey the magnitude of the change. New York's population jumped from 515,000 in 1850 to 3,437,000 in 1900 and to over 7,800,000 in 1950. Figures for Chicago were at least as startling: 29,900; 1,690,000; and 3,621,000. Nor was the increase confined to bigger places. Omaha, not even founded in 1850, reached 102,555 at the beginning of the century, and moved over the 250,000 mark in 1970. The South joined the sweepstakes with Miami's residents numbering 1681 by 1900 and 249,276 fifty years later. And Los Angeles broke most records when its population soared from 102,479 in 1900 to 1,970,358 in 1950.

But the most visible effect of the first urban explosion was the transformation of the central part of the city. Although immigrants and their children accounted for most of the rapidly growing urban population, the American countryside also contributed. Rural areas had always sent sons and daughters to the city, but hard times on the farms after the Civil War accelerated the historic process. From the wheatlands of the plains, from the cotton Black Belt, from the cornfields of the Midwest, from the declining agricultural backlands of New England, the surplus population, mostly young, headed for the burgeoning cities and towns.

Most of these newcomers arrived with few or no resources. They settled in the central city and took what housing they could get. Some occupied small apartments carved out of mansions left behind by the wealthy; others jammed into makeshift conversions of large commercial facilities; still others sheltered in tenements erected especially to meet the rudimentary requirements of low-income families. With congestion came all the resultant problems—disease, delinquency, vice, crime, and hopelessness. In every city, these densely populated sections were marked as trouble spots by local authorities.

This new urban structure produced its own political institutions, for the process of growth had created a divided city. The newcomers, strangers in a new environment, afflicted with congestion, irregular jobs, and persistent poverty, struggled to find some kind of social organization or identity. None of their old institutions seemed wholly relevant to their predicament, but they utilized what they could and through voluntary associations met some of their needs. Still they remained economically weak and socially insecure.

Though their very numbers were in most cases a curse—the job market was flooded, the breadwinner had too many mouths to feed—in politics this liability could be turned into an asset. Their combined strength could accomplish what none could do alone. Soon the political "boss" and the "machine" rose to organize this potential. Feeding on the vulnerability of the neighborhoods and the hostility of the outside, the boss system became a distinctive feature of American politics. It succeeded because it was rooted in the realities of block life—the clubhouse, the saloon, the cheap theaters, and the street. The boss helped recent arrivals to find housing and jobs, mediated with public authorities, helped families through bad times, and somehow gave newcomers a sense of belonging. To be sure, the cost was high in laws bent and broken, officials corrupted, funds embezzled, and the franchise sullied. Essentially, however, the boss system was simply the political expression of inner-city life.

As slum-dwellers found an economic footing, some of them moved away from the central city to outlying residential areas. Irish, Germans, and Scandinavians, who had come in the first wave, began the flow; people from Eastern Europe followed. By the 1920's many sons and daughters lived far from the scenes of their parents' struggle. But others remained in the inner city, investing the neighborhoods with a kind of warmth and stability and welcoming new arrivals from the old country. This process of concentration and dispersal characterized all the groups which had settled in the city with the important exceptions of blacks and Hispanic immigrants.

Those who moved out found conditions very different on the tree-shaded streets of the residential areas ringing the city. They lived in detached houses on large lots or in two- or three-story apartment dwellings. Men took the trolley to work; women dominated the daytime society of schools, churches, shopping, and clubs. Political organization in the white-collar districts was as much an expression of these neighborhoods as the boss system was of the congested center. "Reform" associations sprang up to protect and advance the concerns of the middle-class constituents of outlying wards. Thus the characteristic instrument of reform was the "Committee of One Hundred" or the "Committee of Seventy-five", etc. Since neighborhoods were scattered and interests diverse, unlike the more compact and socially unified center, the outer regions found the broadly based committee more appropriate than the "boss."

Both inner city and outer fringes were profoundly influenced by the introduction of the automobile. At first a monopoly of the rich, by the twenties it had become a middle-class necessity and after World War II essential to blue-collar workers as well. Though designed for individual use, the vehicle was easily converted into the bus, and soon this form of mass transportation began to push the trolley off the street. Communities outside municipal limits were now freed from dependence upon commuting rail lines. New suburbs sprang up all around the cities, and those already in existence expanded. Near Cleveland, the population of Shaker Heights increased tenfold between 1920 and 1930. Beverly Hills, near Los Angeles, jumped from 674 to 17,429. In the same decade, Westchester County, New York, added 176,511 to its previous total of 344,436.

For three decades into the twentieth century, metropolitan growth sustained the economic development of the nation as a whole. Prosperity, broken by occasional reversals, characterized the nation between 1900 and the Great Depression of the 1930's. But it was essentially an urban prosperity; the countryside did not share in the "good times." Most of the economic activity flowed from the cities where housing construction, the building of new schools, streets, and sewers, industrial expansion, and population growth provided the primary impetus to national prosperity.

It all came to an end in 1929 with the stock market crash. Since prosperity had been largely urban based, the Depression had a severe impact on the cities. As unemployment rates rose to over 25 per cent, the relief resources of local governments soon were exhausted and authorities called on Washington for help. The Hoover administration moved reluctantly and cautiously. By 1935 conditions had worsened so much that President Roosevelt initiated massive assistance plans. New Deal programs dealt largely with human salvage; relief payments; creation of jobs; measures to promote individual and family security. The Public Works Administration began construction of public buildings and facilities. Yet despite the unprecedented involvement of the federal government in their affairs, the cities remained stagnant through most of the 1930's.

Indeed, the revival of urban economies did not come until World War II intervened. The cities were the major beneficiaries of military spending, which began even before Pearl Harbor. Jobs became plentiful, relief rolls dropped quickly, and industrial construction boomed. To be sure, new troubles accompanied the economic upswing. The influx of black workers heightened racial tensions that sporadically spilled over into violence; the conversion of automobile factories to military production put a great strain on urban mass transit systems; and scarcity of materials prevented even the adequate maintenance of public facilities.

The postwar period saw the urban age become the metropolitan age. The census of 1920 had indicated that for the first time more Americans lived in "urban places" than in "rural places." This fact symbolized statistically the supremacy of the city over the countryside. In 1970 the census showed that for the first time more people lived in the suburbs than within city limits. The nation had entered the era of the metropolis. Beginning almost with the peace treaty following World War II, American urbanites headed for the suburbs in larger numbers than ever before. Housing shortages in the cities, federal subsidies for residential building through veterans' programs, and general prosperity combined to impel a whole generation to seek homes in suburbia.

For over two decades, this movement was the most powerful influence on metropolitan growth. Developers flocked to vacant or sparsely used land around every city; great numbers of houses were quickly built, often on small plots, with little concern for design or individuality. Shopping centers, schools, and churches rose—the process of "instant community" produced new towns all around old municipal boundaries. As people and commercial activity moved out, so did manufacturing. In the 1950's and the 1960's most cities were losing factories and jobs to the suburbs, especially to those developed along the new expressways.

As tax producers left the city, tax consumers—the poor and elderly—remained behind where they were joined by Southern and Hispanic migrants. This demographic revolution profoundly altered the nature of urban life everywhere. The demand for services mounted as the revenue base declined. Even large infusions of federal and state funds could not conceal the fundamental fact; American cities could no longer afford expected urban services with only the traditional sources of revenue. By 1975 this was patently true in the older and larger ones; it will become increasingly true for the newer and smaller.

The problem was further complicated by the fact that newcomers were mostly black and Hispanic as well as being poor. The central city had always been a staging ground for newcomers from the countryside and overseas. They gathered there under the most wretched conditions, suffering from high densities, dilapidated housing, poor schools, and unsafe and unsanitary neighborhoods. But slowly they discovered their numbers, got an economic footing, received a rudimentary education and moved into better housing and more pleasant residential communities.

From the start, municipal officials assumed the immigrant analogy, that the blacks would go through the same process. And, in fact, they did congregate at the center. But the new black ghetto was fundamentally different from the old immigrant ghetto. Far from loosening and dispersing, it simply spread block by block, overwhelming old neighborhoods and occupying every available space. Soon nearly every city had large areas almost wholly black and afflicted with the entire range of urban ills. Worse still, as time passed, their inhabitants came to the conclusion that the ghetto, which had been temporary for immigrants, was permanent for them. Out of this despair and hopelessness sprang the demonstrations and riots of the sixties, and the desperate resignation of the seventies.

Hence, two new divisive elements have entered the modern metropolis—the division between city and suburb and the division between black and white. The regional metropolis today is as viable as the smaller one of the past, but the struggle between city and suburb and the issue of race frustrates every attempt to deal rationally with its problems. Though the seriousness of the urban crisis varies from place to place and region to region, it is the common heritage of all American cities. New York's brush with bankruptcy simply revealed in a dramatic fashion the underlying national malaise. Unless all concerned—cities, states and federal government—understand this elementary fact, the country will begin its third century with a crisis of a larger dimension than any since the Civil War.

Richard C. Wade

THE GREAT

CONTEMPORARY

ISSUES

THE CITIES

GRANT CO.
W.T.GRANT CO.
BLUMSTEIN
Ride The Surface Way
191

CHAPTER 1

The Cities Mature

Three generations of urban transit (from left to right): bus, horse-drawn streetcar, and electric trolley.

Courtesy The New York Times

The Growth and Prosperity of New-York.

The growth of this City within the present century is one of the marvels of our country. The little town in which many of our older residents were born, has before their death taken rank among the great capitals of the world, with but a few ahead of it. The reminiscences of Mr. WEED, which have been published in our columns, carry that part of our population under forty years of age back to a period which seems to them centuries away. To read of the society and life, the commerce and industry, the ways and habits, the ideas and prospects, the theatres, the coffee and cake saloons, the evening walks and social talks of our immediate ancestors, who but lately inhabited the lower end of this island; and then to contemplate the City in its present proportions, its commercial and industrial development, its appliances of civilization and its intellectual position—it seems as if we had passed across a space in which generations had lived and died, instead of a period so brief that hundreds of men now living and enjoying the present order of affairs, spent the years of their boyhood and early manhood amid the older and primitive condition of things.

The geographical position and local advantages of New-York have unquestionably had much to do with its unparalleled growth. Of all the seaports on the North Atlantic it is the most inviting, and has the most facilities for commerce. Points by the Gulf of St. Lawrence may be nearer to the great commercial nations of Europe: but nature having made them available only half of the year, they are thereby rendered of little account the whole of it. The commercial points on the Gulf of Mexico are not only, as compared with New-York, a thousand miles out of the direct line of travel between the two civilized continents, but the geology of the region around the Gulf places almost insurmountable obstacles in the way of the establishment there of a city of the greatest pretensions; and the geology of the country bank of the Gulf is such as to render impracticable the building up of these varied industries, and the growth of these populous rural communities which are the necessary adjuncts and supports of all great cities. As for the rival cities nearer to us, if New-York can be said to have any rivals—as for Philadelphia on one side and Boston on the other, Portland in the North and Norfolk in the South—one has but to look at the map to see their inferiority to New-York in one or other of the characteristics which lie at the foundation of a great commercial city.

Not less forward has New-York been in the character of the stock which constitutes the basis of its population. It is not overrating our old Dutch element to say that the historical qualities it illustrated for centuries in Europe, and which it brought to this country, have contributed in a very high degree to the establishment of the City in that supremacy which it now enjoys. It is true enough that the Dutch were here for a couple of centuries before the City gave any astonishing signs of activity or growth; and it is possibly true that without an infusion of the qualities of the English stock we should never have developed into what we now are. But it is equally certain that without their broad-mindedness, their impassivity, their perseverance, their conscientiousness, their industrious habits and their commercial proclivities, New-York City would not have displayed these distinguishing traits today in the high measure that she confessedly does. It is a vital question in the history of a city who were its founders, and New-York was equally fortunate both in her founders and her foundation.

When about 1820, the City first gave intelligible indications of its subsequent greatness—when the astute and enterprising class of merchants (many of whom are still with us, reposing amid their wealth and laurels,) first came upon the stage—none fancied that the rapidity of the City's growth could in any measure approach what has since then been our experience. But the high swell of emigration which began to roll in from Europe, and whose volume has since then been magnified year by year, told beyond belief upon the growing little City. It brought with it new crafts and old experiences; it gave us new labor, and established among us the customs of an older civilization; much capital came with it, and much more followed in its wake. It amalgamated easily and solidly with our native element, and from the twain sprang the product of the present day. It concentrated largely in the city in which was its first experience of America, and which held out to them such unequaled attractions and opportunities. Capital, too, concentrated itself here for essentially the same reasons, and every shilling that found among us profitable investment was a lodestone to attract others to the same locality. Those who left the City for other parts of the State, or for the West, contributed hardly less to its growth and prosperity than those who remained in it. For the former first made a necessity, and then built that wonderful work, the Erie Canal, which has had such an untold influence in building up our City in population, wealth and power. They first made a necessity, and then built the vast system of railroads which find their termini in New-York, and which bear to us the wealth of half a continent, and distribute in return the products of the civilized world. They first made a necessity, and then built those thousand towns in our State, and in adjacent States, and throughout the great West, which now play the part of tributaries to their imperial and natural chief.

In all respects, New-York has thus the most solid basis for the present and the future. Its growth has been quick as that of a mushroom, but solid as the granite are its foundations. Its growth may be retarded and its prosperity impeded by such short-sighted cupidity as some of its land-holders and property-owners have lately displayed; but nothing short of absolute idiocy on their part can even temporarily prevent its march to a position where it will find its only rival in London.

February 20, 1866

ST. LOUIS.

The Growth of the City—Lost Opportunities—Chicago's Foresight—The Wealth of the City—Building of the Bridge.

From Our Own Correspondent.

ST. LOUIS, Mo., Wednesday, June 22, 1870.

The rapid increase of our country can scarcely be estimated by ordinary statistics. The statement that we have so many millions of people and are increasing in a certain ratio, may excite admiration and a general indefinite astonishment; but the real rapidity of our growth can only be properly estimated by an actual inspection of the cities which have sprung up as if by magic in the newer sections of the country. Here upon the banks of the great Mississippi, twelve hundred miles from the Atlantic and an equal distance from the Gulf of Mexico, stands a city which contains a greater population than New-York did forty years ago, and is further advanced in all the elements of social greatness than was the Metropolis at that day, having a greater number of commodious and imposing ware houses and counting-rooms, more avenues of travel and business open, connecting it with a wider extent of territory, and larger and more flourishing social institutions.

THE GROWTH OF ST. LOUIS.

The growth of this city was scarcely perceptible till 1840. Ages ago it was founded by the sagacity and enterprise of the French, during the era of their colossal colonial achievements. The greatness of the distance from the father-land, and the difficulty of reaching such a remote point, together with the long-continued struggles between the rival nations of France and England, prevented any rapid growth of the Louisiana colony. After the transfer of this colony to the United States, the growth of population for many years was too slow to influence this valley. Hence it resulted that, as late as 1830, St. Louis was still a village of no great size. But when the great wave of population from the Eastern States and from Europe poured into this great valley, its influence upon the growth of this city was felt. Her growth until the war was marvelous, and the territory which became tributary to her commercial enterprise was constantly enlarging. The multitude of steamers touching at her levee traded from New-Orleans upon the south to the remote north in Minnesota, and the far off regions of the Upper Missouri. The vast valley of this network of rivers seemed destined to pay tribute to the enterprise of the merchants of this city, and they reposed so securely in the confident assurance that this vast traffic was certainly theirs, that they were indifferent to the efforts made to divert it to other channels.

CHICAGO AND ST. LOUIS.

The construction of railroads created a new era in the tendencies of trade. Chicago early saw the advantages she would acquire by the development of her railroad system, and gave all her strength and influence in this direction. Every iron road brought population to the section of the country of which Chicago was the center, and increased its trade; so that almost before St. Louis became aware of the fact, her northern rival had beaten her in the race. The occurrence of the war increased these tendencies. The disturbances in this neighborhood isolated St. Louis and almost cut off its trade, and thus left Chicago free to enlarge her commerce, an opportunity she was not slow to use. After the conclusion of the war the padlock which had been imposed upon this city was removed, and things returned to their natural course. St. Louis gradually regained her former elevated position, and is rapidly moving to the front.

TENURE OF PROPERTY.

One of the peculiarities impressed upon this city by its early French inhabitants is seen in the tenure of property. A large portion of the real estate of the city belongs to the estates of the old inhabitants. These have generally refused to sell, and have adhered to the system of leases. From this system it has resulted that nearly all the business houses are built upon leased ground. Whenever these leases are renewed the property is estimated at fabulous prices. A marked case of this is furnished in a large block of elegant stores now building on Fourth-street. The ground belongs to the Glasgow estate and comprises eleven lots, having a total frontage of 225 feet by a depth of 120 feet, the rear resting upon a broad alley. This piece of ground was purchased about twenty-six years ago, by Mr. GLASGOW, for $3,000. Now it is considered worth $1,000 a front foot, and is leased at that valuation, the lessees paying six per cent. annually upon the valuation; and at the expiration of the lease of thirty years, surrendering the building. In fact the two lots on the corner of St. Charles-street are leased by a dry-goods firm at an annual rental of $5,000, and the magnificent store they are erecting is to be given to the owner at the expiration of the lease. Upon the same liberal terms nearly all of the business property of the city is leased. The wonder is that any persons are to be found who are unwilling to be the owners of real estate in fee simple, and also that any persons are to be found who are so ambitious to build up the interests of landlords as to assume and fulfill such obligations, especially as this little spot does not comprise the whole frontage of the Mississippi River. But the unsophisticated observer will find in this Western region much more to surprise him, not the least of which is that notwithstanding the greatness of this country and the immense territory appropriated to the site of its numerous cities, ground appears exceedingly scarce, and that the smallest portion can only be obtained by the payment of fabulous prices.

THE FUTURE OF THE CITY.

The position of this city, at the gateway of the trade of this immense inter-continental valley, and upon the direct route to the Pacific, and one-third the distance to San Francisco, gives it a commanding importance. This is being constantly evinced by the network of railroads which the intelligent enterprise of the citizens of this State is constructing, nearly all of which have their ultimate terminus in this city. What it may become in the future, none can predict. But all anticipate for her a career of great success.

THE BRIDGE.

Work upon the bridge is progressing with regularity, although the eyes of mundane spectators behold little of it as yet, because it is entirely sub-aqueous. The work of building up these piers from the solid rock, 117 feet beneath the surface of the water, 90 feet of which are occupied by the sands deposited by the current, is a great labor. It has already cost the lives of several men, but human life, in this progressive age, is not allowed to stand in the way of the achievement of any great enterprise. When this gigantic work shall be completed, it will be a convenient means of crossing this great barrier to travel, and will increase to a wonderful degree the amount of travel and freight by all the various routes concentering here.

OCCIDENT.

July 9, 1870

THE LOUISIANA MO. RAILROAD BRIDGE.

ST. LOUIS, Mo., Dec. 24.—The great iron bridge of the Chicago, Alton and St. Louis Railroad Company, crossing the river at Louisiana, Mo., was completed yesterday, and a train of cars passed over it to-day. This bridge consists of nine spans, ranging from 160 to 260 feet in width. The draw, which is 444 feet in length, is the longest in the world. The total length of the bridge is 4,052 feet, and in it are 5,000 cubic yards of masonry, 50,000 cubic yards of rip-rap, and 250,000 cubic yards of earth embankment. Its superstructure is all iron of the best quality. The whole work has been done in less than six months. A dyke, half a mile long, is being built from the Illinois shore so as to insure a permanent channel through the draw. The officers of the railroad and the bridge company reached Louisiana to-day, and there will be a formal opening of the bridge to-morrow.

December 25, 1873

BOSTON.

CHARLESTOWN, WEST ROXBURY, AND BRIGHTON ABSORBED—BROOKLINE REFUSES.

Special Dispatch to the New-York Times.

BOSTON, Oct. 7.—Boston to-night is much bigger and broader and richer than she was this morning. By popular vote, the City of Charlestown and the towns of West Roxbury and Brighton are added to her territory, and their population and valuation transferred to her credit. Brookline, the fourth candidate, refused to join, though the city voted quite generously to take her in. By the accession of these places, the area, population, and valuation of the city will be represented as follows:

	Taxable area in acres.	Population, 1870.	Valuation, 1873.
Boston............	9,583	250,513	$693,831,400
*Charlestown.....	520	28,323	34,942,120
Brighton..........	2,370	4,967	14,548,531
West Roxbury....	6,627½	8,683	22,148,600
Total..........	19,100½	292,486	$765,470,651

* Valuation Charlestown, 1872.

Boston voted strongly in favor of the annexation of all the candidates. The vote in the case of Brookline was the strongest, more than four to one, and from that the proportion became less down to Brighton, for which there were almost three to one in favor. The vote in Boston was not half as large as the average vote cast at a Gubernatorial election. In Charlestown the contest was quite close and exciting, and the vote cast very large. The party of union was, however, victorious by the decisive majority of 293. In West Roxbury and Brookline the excitement was also intense, but in Brighton everything was pretty much one way, and though the interest in the voting was strong, there was no contest. The vote of West Roxbury was 720 yes against 613 no. In Brookline the majority against was about 400, and in Brighton, out of a vote of 755, 622 were in favor. The provisions of the act of union do not take effect until the first Monday in January next, except so far as they relate to the election of municipal and ward officers. The new wards will elect their ward officers and School Committee men, and will vote for municipal officers in Boston at the city election in December, under the same warrant and regulations that apply in the old wards of Boston; but for all other purposes the tenure and duties of the local officers remain unchanged for the full terms for which they were chosen.

October 8, 1873

KANSAS CITY'S GROWING TRADE.

THE EMBRYO WESTERN METROPOLIS—ITS IMPORTANCE AND ADVANTAGES AS A TRADING DEPOT.

KANSAS CITY, Mo., Feb. 3.—The City of Kansas, in the State of Missouri, presents a spectacle scarcely to be seen just now in any other city of the Union—the spectacle of rapid growth in population, steadily-increasing values and active demand for property, and general commercial enterprise and prosperity. With many natural disadvantages to overcome, this little town, in a few years, has taken rank among the most important cities of the West, and in some respects has taken a generally-acknowledged lead. The situation of Kansas City, like its name, can only be accounted for by the perversity of human nature, and the extreme perversity of that particular phase of human nature which flourished westward of the Mississippi River 15 or 20 years ago. The country round about for many miles, both in Kansas and Missouri, offers nearly every variety of topography for the site of a city—upland plateaus, lowland plains, and gentle hill-side slopes—but the wayward jayhawkers paddled across the muddy Kaw and found this extraordinary combination of hill and valley, towering bluff, and yawning chasm, and forthwith they christened it a city, because of the apparent impossibility of building houses there, and called it Kansas because it was Missouri. Rome, with her seven hills, was a level plain by comparison with the mountainous corruscations of Kansas City.

Later settlers of this embryo metropolis have called attention to the fact that the geographical centre of the United States coincides with that of the North American Continent, whose hub and lynch-pin will be found in Kansas City. The area of North America, extending from Cape Race, at longitude 50°, to Mount St. Elias, at 140° west from Greenwich, and from Franklin Bay at the seventieth, to San José, at the tenth, parallel of north latitude, finds its centre at the confluence of the Kansas and Missouri Rivers, a little east of the ninety-fifth meridian and north of the thirty-ninth parallel. The territory of the United States, stretching from Bishop's Head, at about 66°, to Cape Mendocino, at 124° west longitude, and from Southern Texas, at 27°, to Northern Dakota, at nearly 50° north latitude, has the same central point. In climate, in the character of their productions, and the local characteristics of their citizens, the several States find at this point the intersection of the lines of demarkation between East and West and North and South. Whether the founders of this city were sages or philosophers in disguise, who went forth, armed with theodilites and tape lines to measure off the universe and find this pivotal point, or whether they stumbled upon it by blind chance, may never be known, but certain it is that this unsightly town, with its knee-deep mud, its throat and eye destroying clouds of dust, its precipitous streets and perpendicular building lots, has become the gate through which the manufactures of the North and East are carried to the farmers and grazers and miners of the great Western and South-western States, and through which come back in return the cattle, grain, and mineral products of New-Mexico and Texas, Kansas and Colorado. The grain and cattle markets thus established are surpassed by few in the whole world for the volume and importance of their operations; the packing-houses of beef and pork exceed those of any other city in their size, and the amount of groceries, agricultural implements, and dry goods sold at Kansas City for consumption throughout the vast territory, west and south, of which this is the emporium, is very great, and rapidly increasing with the increase of population throughout those regions.

As early as 1840 the "Kaw Mouth" was an Indian trading point of considerable importance, and it soon became a busy depot for the Mexican trade, in the days of the old overland service. During the war it was occupied as a military post, and business deserted it. No other city is so dependent upon the harmonious intercourse of the several States for its own prosperity as Kansas City. After the war, for many years the revival of its trade was slow. But within the past few years it has taken a new start, and is shooting up with great rapidity.

The traveler steps from the cars at Kansas City into as handsome and commodious a depot as any city of the East can boast. He is hailed by as enthusiastic a chorus of hackmen as could have been produced in any quarter of the globe, and, passing them calmly by, he takes his seat in as substantial an omnibus as any Broadway stage. As he looks from the stage window he finds himself in the heart of a thickly-built and busy town, hemmed in by a high and apparently insurmountable bluff to the east and south, and by the Kansas and Missouri Rivers on the west and north; engines shriek and pant about the plain on every side, dragging cars of lumber, grain, and cattle, while in and out among the stores and houses all the streets are covered with a network of iron rails. At the top of the bluff, 300 feet above, human habitations can be seen, and as the coach begins its journey it gradually clambers upward by a circuitous route, and leaves the city below. Far off, to the north and west, the Kansas and Missouri Rivers wind their separate ways through rolling wooded knolls and waving fields of vast extent. The eye follows their course by glimpses here and there until they meet almost beneath your feet. Across the Kansas lies the City of Wyandotte, nestling under the lee of a gently-sloping hill, and southward, Rosedale, with its furnace smoke and scattered cottages; northward, on the sandy bars of the Missouri, is the little settlement of Harlem, with about 20 houses, and a trustworthy Democratic majority of 400 votes.

Kansas City proper is found to be a rambling, oddly-built collection of houses, clambering up and down the broken surface of the hill-tops, one house a dozen yards above its neighbor, streets running plumb against a perpendicular bluff, or scampering down a precipice into a yawning gulf, to come up on the other side amid a block of well-built and substantial stores or houses. At this point, during nine months in the year, a small simoom, laden with heavy dust, comes swooping down from the crest of an overhanging mountain. Amid gasps and sputterings, and with blinded eyes, the traveler is dropped at the door of the principal hotel. It has cost a dollar to bring him the half mile of ascent from the station. He is then installed in a small, neat, but rather dingy room up three pairs of stairs, with one small window opening on a court, all at a cost no greater than room and board at any first-class hotel in New-York City. In front of the hotel is a great open square, with a pond in the centre, whose surface is some 30 feet below the level of the street. This inland lake is one of many which abound here, having no outlet, and prevented from becoming stagnant only by the constant stirring given them by the cattle, geese, and pigs of the vicinity. The drainage of the city is bad in nearly every quarter, yet, strange to say, there is little malaria of any kind, and "positively no chills and fever."

Kansas City has a population now of somewhat over 50,000. About 10,000 of these have come in during the past year. Over 1,000 houses have been built within the year, all of brick, which is made of excellent quality from the very clay removed from the cellars, and many of these new houses have much pretension to size and even elegance. The supply is totally inadequate to the demand as yet, and many houses built at a cost of $2,000, or less, rent easily at $500 and $600 a year. Stores are less in demand than dwellings, yet none are vacant, and rents are high.

The growth and importance of Kansas City has always depended, and will probably depend in the future, more on its position as a market and railway centre than upon any local element of greatness. There are as yet few manufactures here of much significance, although the rolling mills, car factories, and flouring establishments are of considerable size and employ many men. The "natural highways" of the Missouri and the Kaw are practically neglected, although at times spasmodic efforts are suggested to revive the barge lines and "release the merchants and farmers from the iron grasp of the railway monopolists." These latter have indeed made Kansas City what it is. The Missouri Pacific, the St. Louis, Kansas City and Northern, the Chicago and Alton, Chicago, Burlington and Quincy, Kansas City, St. Joseph and Council Bluffs, and the Hannibal and St. Joseph Railways from the north and east, and the Kansas Pacific, the Atchison, Topeka and Santa Fé, the Missouri River, Fort Scott and Gulf, the Leavenworth, Lawrence and Galveston, and the Missouri, Kansas and Texas on the west and south, make Kansas City a terminus of their lines, and a point of transfer for the really wonderful quantity of freight and number of passengers which pass over their several lines. The meeting here of the various interests represented by the routes and connections of these great railways has, of necessity, established Kansas City as a market for a large portion of the continent, and has given it a cosmopolitan air and character. The capitalists and manufacturers and merchants of the North and East meet here the miners of New-Mexico and Colorado, the cattle kings of Texas and Kansas and the Indian Territory, and the farmers of those great garden States. The sale of agricultural implements throughout these States is very large and centres here. Dry goods are not represented among the jobbing houses here as largely as they well might be, nor in anything like their due proportion to the groceries and drugs, agricultural implements, and hardware sold from this market. One reason for this is undoubtedly to be found in the frugal habits of the people West and South who make the jobbing trade here, but it is also largely due to the fact that the merchants here have not made any very serious efforts to supply the market at low rates; so that the dealers in the smaller towns of Kansas have preferred to buy directly from St. Louis, Chicago, and New-York. They are about to establish a Custom-house here now, and it is likely that some of the dry goods houses of the East will find a profitable addition to their business in a branch at Kansas City.

At the present moment a considerable agitation is being made by the newspapers and politicians of Kansas and Missouri about the question of annexing Kansas City to the State whose name it bears. In many respects this move would be a natural and apparently a desirable one. The principal business of Kansas City is with Kansas people. Its inhabitants are mainly Kansas settlers who have tarried on their way. Successful Kansas merchants have returned to Kansas City to open there establishments, more general and imposing for their Kansas trade, than they could have supported in the smaller towns where they first settled. Most of the prominent corporations organized under Kansas laws, and carrying on their business within her borders, have their general offices, or else an agency which practically transacts their principal office business, at Kansas City. In many respects it is the real capital and metropolis of the State, and must be so for a long time to come. The lawyers say there are serious constitutional questions in the way of annexation or sale of the city from Missouri to Kansas, and it may be that the present notion will never be carried out.

In any event, it may be safely said of Kansas City that for many years to come it will continue among the most growing and most important of the Western towns, and will continue to offer the best opportunities for the employment of Eastern money and Eastern grit and enterprise.

February 10, 1879

CALIFORNIA REVISITED

THE GROWTH AND IMPROVEMENTS OF SAN FRANCISCO.

WHAT THE VISITOR SEES AFTER MANY YEARS —A BEAUTIFUL AND THRIFTY CITY— CERTAIN LOCAL CHARACTERISTICS.

SAN FRANCISCO, Oct. 1.—After an absence from California for more than 12 years, it is with absorbing interest that I have revisited San Francisco, recalling again with curiosity and delight once familiar scenes. The first impression that the old-timer revisiting this city gets, I think, is one of surprise mingled with disappointment. Nobody, especially no old fellow, likes to find the ancient land-mark removed and the once-familiar face changed, even although these mutations come in the form of "improvements." The bane of our new and rapid life is the improvement so dear to the average American. I must confess that I do not know San Francisco in its new garb. The change is simply wonderful. We used in the old times to plume ourselves greatly on the fact that real houses, with handsome furniture and fine paintings, that real business blocks and real pavements covered the sandy, wind-swept slopes that had been mere wastes within the memory of young people. But that era of innocent gratulation has long since been forgotten. Montgomery and Kearney streets, the principal thoroughfares of San Francisco 12 years ago, were lined with what were then thought to be very handsome and even imposing structures. These are replaced by business buildings that are as elegant and massive as those of any city on the continent, so far as my observation goes. The growth of the city has been in all directions. Viewed from any one of the heights with which its suburbs are surrounded, San Francisco looks like a young giant sprawling among the seven or eight hills over which it is built. In old times we had Happy Valley, The Willows, Hayes Valley, The Mission, and many another petty title to distinguish the village-like localities that were hitched to borders of the city like the ragged fringes of a garment. These names sufficiently indicate the rural character of the old San Franciscan suburbs. Now everything is urban. The names of the old resorts exist in the daily speech of men and on the lines of street cars. It is noticeable, too, that the various communities strung along the lines that lie out among the hills have an individuality that marks each as being a settlement by itself. Nevertheless, these different towns, if I may use the word, are all compactly and solidly built together. They form one substantial city where before were scattered settlements, with diverse interests separated from each other by wastes of sand and unbuilt spaces.

The builders of this new city seem to have given over all fears of an earthquake. They defy heaven with their cloud-capped towers and gorgeous palaces. What would the old-time architects have thought of such lofty structures as the Nevada Bank Building and the new Stock Exchange, I wonder? In those elder days it was thought only discreet to build of wood, lath, and plaster; an earthquake could not lay such a city in a heap of ruin. With sublime audacity the San Franciscan rears his modern structure as far above the old-fashioned sky-line of the streets as that line was above the pavement. But the revisitor, pensively prowling about for old landmarks, may find a few in the northern end of the city at the base of Telegraph Hill. By common consent, as it would appear, the march of architectural progress has been southward. The north end of the city has been left to its own picturesque shabbiness. From Clay street to the foot of Telegraph Hill, a distance of some half-dozen blocks, San Francisco, on Montgomery and Kearney streets, remains as it was 12 years ago. And when I add that this portion of the city is mainly given up to the Chinese, the reason for the movement in the other direction may appear. But if one would realize what changes have been wrought in the general appearance of San Francisco, he must ascend one of the hills on which some of the most substantial portions of the city are built. The stranger must be reminded that many of these hills are well nigh precipitous. They are so steep that they were long considered inaccessible for building purposes. Even the valleys nestled in and around them were difficult of access. All back of the range, with a few exceptions, was a howling wilderness, peopled only by hard-faring goats, fugitive and vagrant dogs, and sprinkled sparsely with the cabins of squatters. The cable railway has transformed this waste into a handsome and substantial city. Of all the changes in San Francisco this is certainly the most marvelous. It is like taking a glimpse of Aladdin's palace for the returning San Franciscan to mount one of the cable cars, and, with bated breath, to be whirled up a steep hill which he remembers as a desolate declivity, and now finds covered with costly and tasteful dwellings. The pavements are good, and the streets on these long neglected hills are lined with the most ornate architecture on which the sun ever shone. San Francisco is bulbous with bay windows. The climate is so peculiar that everybody wants all the sunshine that can be drawn from the variable sky. Therefore, each builder throws out as many bay windows as his space will permit. The big Palace Hotel is an example of what may be done on a large scale with bay windows. The architect probably had directions to give every lodger a bay window. The vast structure is knobby with excrescences, and looks like a building afflicted with an acute disease of the skin.

This city should be the paradise of architects. Nobody seems to think of building a sober house. The prevailing style is what might be called the delirious Queen Anne. Of all the efflorescence, floriation, bulbousness, and flamboyant craziness that ever decorated a city I think that San Francisco may carry off the prize. And yet, such is the glittering and metallic brightness of the air—when it is not surcharged with fog—that I am not sure but this riotous run of architectural fancy is not just what the city needs to redeem its otherwise hard nakedness. Certainly under no other sky in the world would so much luxuriance of wood wrought in every shape be tolerable. Nevertheless, the houses have, for the most part, a home-like and comfortable look. This is partly due probably to the wonderful beauty, variety, and vigor of the climbing plants, shrubs, and flowers that one sees in every direction. Nobody knows what the geranium, the passion-flower, the fuschia, and the Australian gum is capable of until he has seen these in San Francisco. As for roses honeysuckles and calla lilies, these grow nowhere else so defiantly as in San Francisco gardens. The rage for extravagant house-building seems to have pervaded all ranks of society. None so poor that he may not have a jig-sawed fret-work, or at least a bay-window to his house. But the sum of local elegance and pretension is reached when one's inquiring gaze falls on the stately palaces of the railway magnates crowning Nob Hill. There is a shoddyite insolence about these great houses that may well rouse the ire of the Sand Lotters and the Kearneyites. For the most part, these palaces, which are built of wood and are very ornate, have no air of habitation. They are dark and forbidding, and the general effect of the whole group is depressing. Fabulous stories are told of the splendors of some of the interiors of the Nob Hill palaces, perticularly of the Hopkins house, in which one stingy old woman is hid in solitary grandeur. Regarding these gorgeous dwellings, built out of spoils of Government and people, one need not be surprised that Communists have threatened to raze them to the ground.

I have just said that the pavements of San Francisco are good; the statement should be qualified. Like Jeremiah's figs, the good are very good indeed, the bad are very bad indeed, and would be disgraceful to any city. One drives suddenly from a smooth and handsomely laid pavement full upon a street full of holes, gullies, and mantraps. The wharves, too, are positively dangerous after dark, so broken and dilapidated are the floorings. There are no street signs at the corners, and the wayfaring stranger must wander in a maze of unnamed thoroughfares, or wait for the unfrequent policeman to guide him in the darkness. The policy of San Francisco local government is to avoid incurring any debt that shall be provided for by long bonds. The people are more generous to posterity than wise for themselves, it seems to me. Nothing can be done until there is money in the Treasury to pay for it, and as there are rings here just the same as in other and more wicked cities, there is not always money in the Treasury when it is very much needed. The City Hall is a monument of this mistaken policy. The city owned a triangular plot of land, then well out of town, when it was decided to build. The land was ample enough to hold the proposed building and leave a handsome surplus for sale. So it was decreed that the outer lots on the triangle should be sold and the avails used for building the new City Hall. In this way the projectors succeeded in surrounding the rising structure with insignificant blocks of houses, from the midst of which emerges the incomplete City Hall, an imposing mass of brick and mortar. The central idea of the building is good. It proposes a large interior mass from which, on either side, are thrown out two widely extended wings. One of these is finished. It contains the Hall of Records, and it is certainly the handsomest and best adapted to its uses of any similar structure of which I have any knowledge. The wings are connected with the main mass by light corridors and colonnades. The front is, or will be, imposing and harmonious. At present two or three lofty towers lift their heads over the dark walls, but the general appearance of the building is that of ruin rather than of arrested development. The bricks are black and dusty, and the addition of a few broad sheets of ivy and woodbine would give to this odd-looking pile the appearance of a first-class mediæval château in the last stages of decay. The original estimated cost of this structure was $1,500,000. It has already cost about $4,000,000, and it is thought that $3,500,000 more will be required to finish it. How much of this large sum represents "stealage" it is impossible to tell.

The Californian is an optimist. He has a grim sense of humor, and he laughs at the short-comings and the dishonesties of his Government. But it must be said that in San Francisco, at least, the

Californian pays his taxes and bears his burdens like a man. The voting population of the city is about 44,000, and the tax-payers number 32,000. I do not believe that many other cities in the land can show so large a proportion of tax-paying voters. In purs[illegible]nce with the financial policy above mentione[illegible] funded debt of San Francisco is small. The October statement shows that the amount of outstanding city bonds—bearing an interest of 6 per cent. per annum—is $3,134,500, while the sinking fund contains $1,095,031, leaving a bonded debt of small proportions. The rate of taxation for city and county purposes this year is 1.20, and that for State purposes is .497. When the various funds fill up, work goes on, and in this way the building of the unfinished City Hall is to be continued, probably, until the last syllable of recorded time. The municipality and citizens of San Francisco are dependent on a private corporation for their water supply. There has been for many years much and acrimonious discussion of various plans for securing city control of a water supply. But as the purchase of the private water company's works and plant would involve the issuance of bonds the project has not yet met with any favor. The price of the proposed purchase also stands in the way, and as the company is continually taking up whatever additional sources of supply that may be accessible to the city the water problem annually grows more difficult. It is an amazing thing that a city like this, boasting a population of 250,000 or 300,000, should be obliged to pay tribute to a private concern for the water consumed for public purposes. I was told, while driving through the Golden Gate Park, (a magnificent addition to the city's pleasure grounds, where the ingenuity of man has redeemed a barren waste of sand and has created a beautiful park of 1,000 acres where before was nothing but the abomination of desolation,) that the annual cost to the city of water to support all this lovliness was $30,000. The park is worth the money that it costs, but the situation seems humiliating, even to a New-Yorker, who knows that his own city enriches a horde of thieves under pretense of supplying the people with pure water.

San Francisco people adhere with great tenacity to specie currency. Bank-notes are used to some extent in large commercial transactions, but in the course of retail dealing one meets with nothing but gold and silver coin. I have not seen any notes of small denominations in circulation since crossing the Rocky Mountains into Oregon. Tender a dealer a five-dollar bill in payment for a fifty-cents' purchase and you will receive in change four standard dollars and a "four-bit piece." Small gold coins are sufficiently common, but the market appears to be glutted with the "dollar of our fathers" to a troublesome extent. It is the custom of the country to regard with a certain contemptuous pity the "tender-foot" who is not glad and thankful to receive a load of silver and gold in exchange for his "rag money." N. B.

October 21, 1883

REVIVING FROM A "BOOM"

LOS ANGELES IS NOW ENJOYING A NATURAL GROWTH.

NEW-YORK MEN INTERESTED IN LARGE STOCK RANCHES IN SOUTHERN CALIFORNIA—A GOVERNOR AND POSSIBLY A UNITED STATES SENATOR.

LOS ANGELES, Cal., Feb. 21.—The "burst boom" of Los Angeles has become proverbial. The boom was unparalleled in its inflation; its collapse was overwhelming. For months men and enterprises sank, tottered, or led a precarious existence. There were persons who predicted that the City of the Angels had received a death blow. But the "boom" has receded into history. It is a thing of the past. Los Angeles, on the contrary, is healthier and stronger than she ever was before. There is a steady and normal demand for real estate, and the city, its suburbs, and the surrounding country are becoming more and more the scenes of beautiful homes and productive enterprises. In the year ending Nov. 30, 1890, there were 12,355 transfers of real estate in this county, the aggregate consideration being $19,344,187.

But the "boom," notwithstanding all the consequent miseries of collapse, had its bright side. It found the city a pile of unbaked clay buildings, with muddy streets; it left it a handsome metropolis of brick, stone, and iron, with smooth, paved thoroughfares. Excepting Denver, no city of corresponding rank is so advanced in its architecture and so well paved as this.

In the minds of many this city, as indeed all Southern California, is associated mainly with the idea of health. Unquestionably, this is one of the great health resorts of the world, but the country, in common with other countries, has resources of its own which account for its growth. First, are its fruit and hay ranches. Think of 185 peach trees yielding a net profit of $1,056.80; six acres of prune trees yielding a net profit of $2,734; seven acres of oranges yielding a net profit of $7,000; 150 acres of potatoes yielding a net profit of $13,500, and 4 acres of alfalfa (hay) yielding a net profit of $240. It is evident that there is a "back country" tributary to this city which is contributing in its money and in its business to the rapid development of Los Angeles. But it is not wholly upon agriculture that the city depends. Natural oil and asphaltum are creating important industries. Within thirty miles sugar manufacturing from beets is about to add largely to the business prosperity of the community. Fruit canning is one of half a dozen other extensive industries which are helping to build up Los Angeles upon a substantial basis.

Last, but not least, three great transcontinental railway routes, with a fourth soon to be added, connect this region with the Eastern world. This city is on the line of the shortest distance across the United States from ocean to ocean. If a ship canal were built across Northern Florida, permitting vessels to reach Galveston without going around the peninsula, a connection could be made at the Texas Gulf port with the Sunset route, and by way of that freight could reach the Pacific by the most direct route practicable through the United States. Something like this is sure to come about in time. As it is, the Southern Pacific already practically affords an all-rail direct highway at the narrowest point between the seaboards of the Atlantic and of the Pacific.

The Baldwin stock ranch has made Southern California famous among horsemen. Richard Gird's great fifty-thousand-acre ranch at Chino is adding lustre in the same line to the fame of the State. Mr. Gird is a native of New-York, having been reared in the east central part of the State. Horses are only a feature of his ranch, but they are a feature which will be heard from when the several hundred colts, from blooded sires and dams of record upon the turf, get before the public. He owns the brother of Mr. Bonner's Sunol, and has had the pleasure of declining an offer of $40,000 for him.

At Burbank, in this county, ten miles from this city, another stock ranch has just been established by New-Yorkers—Messrs. Hackett, Carhart & Co. The ranch is beautifully situated, and the scale upon which the 500 acres purchased are to be operated may be inferred from the statement that a handsome, unfinished "boom" hotel at Burbank has been bought by the firm, which will complete and furnish it to use for the accommodation of its own families when visiting Southern California. Three carloads of fine brood stock were recently received from the East. In the same section are already two other stock ranches, one owned by O. H. Lockhart, and the other by the Los Angeles Farming and Milling Company.

Having had the honor of furnishing the State with a Governor, (Col. Markham,) it is not at all beyond the possibilities that Los Angeles will soon have a United States Senator. The death of Senator Hearst is an event so likely to take place in the immediate future that speculation as to his successor is natural. At the present time public opinion is in favor of Major George H. Bonebrake of this city, President of the Los Angeles National Bank and of the State Loan and Trust Company. The Major is a self-made man. He can recall the time when he taught modern and ancient languages for a living, and, like many a teacher, could not see beyond the limits of a meagre salary. But he knew how to save and invest what he earned, and the result is that to-day he is one of the richest men in this part of the State. He is regarded as a man of extraordinary business sagacity. He is an ardent Republican, and it was mainly through his management of the nominating campaign that Gov. Markham was the choice of the State Convention at Sacramento last May.

Some idea of the productiveness of the soil here and of the "growing" properties of the climate may be had from a fact that came under the writer's observation recently. Over eleven years ago a family living in Brooklyn, N. Y., raised an orange tree from a seed. In time the tree was sent to a nurseryman, who budded or grafted it. It, however, never [illegible] above two feet high until it was brought here by the family last September and planted. The tree at once began to put forth new shoots and to push upward, and recently, for the first time in its history, gave signs of blooming. When it is stated that for several years the tree had been Summer and Winter in a Brooklyn greenhouse, the change that has taken place in its condition is worth noting.

February 22, 1891

A CITY OF VAST ENTERPRISE

UNANIMITY OF ACTION THE SECRET OF CHICAGO'S GROWTH.

Civic Pride and Faith in Its Destiny to Make It the Wonder of the Globe—Remarkable Transformation Now Going on in Its Business District—Increase in Ground Values Makes Higher Buildings a Necessity—The Men Who Helped Make the City and Their New Plans.

CHICAGO, Dec. 23.—Outsiders only know half the truth about this city. Notwithstanding all the publicity which came to Chicago when it was chosen as the site of the World's Fair, very little of that which constitutes its real greatness became known to those who read the thousands of columns of description of its people, its buildings, and its business which have been printed in the newspapers of the world. A year ago Chicago was known to the denizens of the Western wilds as the capital of the Mississippi Valley; to that more fortunate part of the American people which lives near the sea, as a big village on a fresh-water pond, with an inordinate amount of breeziness; to Europeans, as a spot on the map of the United States; to dwellers in the remote regions of the earth, as a puff of smoke in a sky filled with clouds. To-day it is known the world over as a city with herculean enterprise, which dug out of the dumping grounds of the past the ruins of the most beautiful buildings ever seen by men to set them up, rehabilitated by the proceeds of a mortgage on the future, on the shores of the great blue inland ocean; as a city which filled these ancient classic temples with the latest works of the god of Mammon and the creations of those sister fates, Art and Science, with a greater profusion than was ever before deemed possible; as a city, above all things, that had accomplished the unaccomplishable.

What the world has now discovered, the city has long been conscious of. What gave it the courage to produce the Columbian Exposition at the cost of a third of a billion dollars was the conviction that it had already done greater things. In setting out upon this prodigious undertaking it was only doing, before the eyes of the world and for the world's benefit, what it was accustomed to do within the privacy of the city limits for itself. What the world looked upon as an impossibility and now praises with extravagant gestures because it seemed to be so unlikely of accomplishment, the city considered relatively as only an additional "piece of business" in the act which it is constantly playing on the world's stage. To create the Columbian Exposition was play for Chicago, because the city was "fit," like an athlete ready for the ring, since it had trained its nerves, hardened its muscles, and plucked up heart by doing many deeds of daring as a preparation for this undertaking, which made its prowess known to the world.

To the born and bred Chicagoan, who can divorce himself momentarily from his surroundings while he looks about him, there are many notable and curious peculiarities in the city of which he is so proud. One of the chief of these is the unanimity of action which characterizes the citizens when any proposition is broached having for its object the welfare or aggrandizement of the city. It does not always happen that action is immediate. The contrary is more often the case. Desultory discussion of the question goes on perhaps for months. Interest in it seems to be languid, and even waning, when suddenly everybody takes hold, the editors cry "All together!" and the thing is done. One reason for this is that each man has his hands full taking care of his own business. He cannot devote much time to public affairs, but when he does find time he insists upon making it count. The parable of the man and his sons and the bundle of sticks is very applicable to Chicago. But the bundle of sticks, which would truly represent the city, would have to be made up of hickory sticks, thick, tough, and well seasoned, each of which alone could not readily be broken.

No better illustration of this characteristic could be given than that furnished by "Chicago Day" at the World's Fair. All the State and other special days were practically decided upon early in the season. There was talk even then of the desirability of having a Chicago celebration, but it amounted to little at the time, and to an outsider it would have seemed as if the Chicago people thought that the fair itself was all the celebration necessary to work off the exuberance of joy that the city undoubtedly felt at having been so successful. But near, the date being Oct. 9, the anniversary of the "big fire" of 1871, signs of the intention of the citizens to make the combined anniversary and celebration noteworthy became noticeable. For a week beforehand nothing else was talked about, and it is doubtful if a man, woman, or child waked up the morning of Oct. 9 without feeling the excitement of the anticipation that the day would be a record breaker, or that any one of the muscle-aching, bone-racked throng went to bed that night without feeling the exhilaration which comes to those who strive and win. There were 716,881 paid admissions and 40,000 free admissions to the fair that day. More than half the people who paid to get in went there to honor the city. One old groceryman out on the west side said, in reply to a question: "I didn't go to the fair Chicago Day, because somebody had to stay here to watch the store. Otherwise I should. But I sent my wife and children, and I gave all my clerks a holiday so they could go." And the man who made a bet that some one of the clerks did not go lost it, as he deserved to do. Chicago people knew that nothing could be seen that day, that transportation facilities would be inadequate, and that the crowd would be so dense that locomotion would be difficult. No comfort could be taken and nothing could be learned, but Chicago people did not go for comfort or knowledge. They went to glorify Chicago.

What Chicago does, it does unanimously, and does with an eye for the future. It was never short-sighted on a large scale, except once, and that was when it rebuilt the city after the "big fire" of 1871. It is not to be wondered at that the minds of the citizens were too much befuddled at that time to be capable of good judgment or farsightedness. What chiefly concerned them then was to get some kind of shelter in which to live and transact business. There was too pressing a need of providing for the present to give much chance for planning about the future. It is not so remarkable that most of the work done then must now be done over again. Rebuilding the city after the fire was a much greater task than building the World's Columbian Exposition. Resurrecting the city twenty-two years ago was not one-half the undertaking that it is to make it over now, so as to meet the requirements of the present era of prosperity. The smoke-begrimed and penniless citizen of 1871, standing on a heap of ashes, with the glare of the fire in his eyes, and feeling the tugging away at his coat tails and heartstrings of his homeless and hungry family, could not be expected to anticipate the wants of the proud and prosperous people of this year, upon whom the world had gazed for six months as the creators of the most beautiful miniature city ever built. It was enough to set about the work of reconstruction on any scale, and it is noticeable that, even in the face of the greatest calamity ever visited upon any city, the people worked together with that unanimity of purpose and abiding confidence in their ability to overcome all difficulties that have continued to be their chief characteristics.

The big fire destroyed 17,450 buildings, valued at $53,000,000. Other property, produce, manufactures, and personal effects, to the value of $143,000,000, was consumed. There were 98,500 people rendered homeless and 300 were burned to death. Nearly one-third of the population was deprived of shelter, and all but a few of the immediate means of making a livelihood. Yet there was no delay in rebuilding. Money was borrowed from the East and from New-York, and the burned buildings were replaced by those double their value. Stocks of merchandise and personal property were replaced on credit. The indebtedness of the city two or three years after the fire probably fully equaled the total loss incurred by the fire, viz., $196,000,000. Since then this debt has been reduced to about what it would have been if there had been no fire. In addition to that, the city's resources have quadrupled. The day before the fire the bank clearings were $4,203,000, about one-quarter of those of the present time. The banking capital of the city is now nearly $60,000,000 and the deposits about $200,000,000.

It is a good thing to remember when one is thinking about the growth of Chicago that it was only about forty years old when this "big fire" destroyed $196,000,000 worth of property. The first map of the city was issued Aug. 4, 1830, and it showed that the area of the original town was about three-eighths of a square mile, the boundaries being Madison, Desplaines, Kinzie, and State Streets. This is almost the same territory now included in the central business district. In 1835, a year before the first charter was granted, there was a population of 3,265. In 1861 the population was 109,263, and Cook County's share of the expense of reducing the rebellious States was $62,000,000. In 1871 the population was 334,270, and the "big fire" destroyed $196,000,000. This year the population is somewhere around 1,500,000, and the raising of $33,000,000 to build a World's Fair seemed like a mere bagatelle to the city which had lost so much by war and conflagration without flinching.

In much less than twenty years the city had more than recovered from the effects of the fire. Then a curious thing happened, which was as strange as the fire was disastrous. The city had outgrown itself, and that part of it in which the larger part of its business must always be transacted became too small, and because it was small and old-fashioned it became useless. So Chicago is throwing away the buildings which were erected only twenty years ago on the ruins of the fire, and is replacing them with the tallest and best-equipped and most costly buildings in the world. In doing this the city is practically undergoing another conflagration. But it is rising from the ashes of this flameless conflagration in regal splendor, and with superb confidence in the future, for it is building now for the future as well as the present. This change to the new third Chicago is more marked in the centre of the city. But it is going on in the other portions as well. Houses which were deemed palatial residences after the fire have given place to stores and flats, as the city grew apace. Rich men now seek sites for homes two to five miles from the Court House. Poor men are either cramped into the narrow quarters between the business district and the residences of the wealthy, or have to go away out to that vast, surrounding prairie included within the 182 square miles inside the limits, which was lately covered with kitchen gardens, and at one time was included in farms, but is now hidden under numberless small cottages.

About five-eighths of a square mile comprises the central business district of the city. There can never be much increase in this area. The lake and the river bound it on three sides, and the fourth is partly hemmed in by immense railroad yards. There is some chance for extension south on three streets—Michigan Boulevard, Wabash Avenue, and State Street. But one side of the Boulevard faces the lake front park and one side of State Street faces the railroad yards, so that only four street fronts are available for building purposes. This narrow neck of land stretching south is very valuable now, but it can never compare with the property which is included in the five-eighths of a square mile in the very heart of the city. Real estate men who have been asked to place a valuation on this small section of land have found it a difficult matter to make even a rough guess as to what it was worth. The value of property varies so much from time to time, and adjoining or adjacent lots have commanded such different prices, that the statistician is confronted with a very involved problem when he tries to figure out what these few acres of land are really worth. For this reason the figures which are here given are not meant to be accurate. They are only used to give some idea of the amount of money involved in the making over of the second Chicago into the third Chicago.

No estimate has ever been made of the value of the buildings which were on this central section at the time of the fire. Altogether, buildings to the value of $53,000,000 were destroyed. Probably $25,000,000 of this represents what was burned on the area under discussion. The value of the land was probably about $35,000,000. Since then there has been a steady increase in land values, while the buildings erected after the fire have deteriorated and become almost useless and valueless.

Recent sales or long-time leases of downtown real estate have fixed the value of this property as nearly as it can be. The following instances are selected to show values of corners at different points in the downtown district:

	Per Square Foot.
State and Quincy	$87
La Salle and Monroe	93
State and Madison	101
Dearborn and Randolph	105
Clark and Monroe	111
Dearborn and Washington	144
Washington and State	147
Michigan Boulevard and Washington Street	145

So many considerations enter into these sales or leases that it is almost impossible to tell whether these prices represent land values alone or whether something is set apart as the price of the buildings which occupied the lots when the transfer was made. In most cases, however, it may be considered that the valuation is upon the ground alone, as the buildings were at once torn down and replaced by others. It will be noticed that there is a difference of about $45 per square foot between the corner of State and Washington and the corner of State and Madison, one block apart. At the corner of State and Washington the building is to be retained, but it will be altered and several stories added. At State and Madison the building has been torn down and another is in process of erection. The valuation at the corner of Dearborn and Washington includes a small old-fashioned building, and at the corner of Michigan Boulevard and Washington Street a comparatively new and commodious building of somewhat inexpensive construction. It may be safely estimated, then, that corner lots average in price about $100 per square foot. As these corners generally extend back to the alleys on the side streets and well along into the block on the main street, it can reasonably be claimed that every square foot of land in the five-eighths of a square mile of territory comprising the central business district is worth, at the lowest estimate, $60 per square foot. Not counting the streets, there are about 6,760,000 square feet in this area. At $60 per square foot, this small plot of ground of about 155 acres net is worth about $405,600,000, or at the rate of about $2,660,000 per acre for the ground actually built upon. This is an increase in the value of the land since the big fire, twenty-two years ago, of about 1,200 per cent.

The value of buildings, old and new, is still harder to get at than land values. Property is worth what it will produce, and some of the most costly office buildings are being run at a loss or very small profit because they are only partially occupied. But this is a feature of the discussion which may be left to the future to eliminate. The day will soon come when all the skyscrapers will be full of tenants. It probably cost somewhere about $50,000,000 to replace the buildings in the central business district destroyed by the fire. With the rapid increase in the population of the city and its enormous increase in business these buildings undoubtedly increased somewhat in value up to a few years ago, when they began to be replaced by the modern skyscraper.

But when a building is torn down to be replaced by another, its value disappears. If all of the area under discussion were covered by "sky scrapers," their combined value would be over $200,000,000, figuring these buildings as costing about 20 cents a cubic foot. This makes the buildings worth about $1,300,000 an acre for the ground actually covered. The ground and buildings together are worth $605,000,000, and each acre, with the buildings upon it, about $3,900,000. At 5 per cent., this means an income of $30,250,000 a year, just about the amount of money it cost to produce the World's Fair.

At the present rate of progress, nearly all the buildings on this space which were built twenty years ago will be replaced before the year 1900, six years from now. These buildings are not being torn down because they are old. Many of them are still beautiful structures, architecturally, and are sufficiently modern in construction and comfortable to insure their owners continuous rentals. But ground values have become so great that the income from the buildings frequently makes a poor return on the amount of capital represented by the present worth of the ground and buildings. Where the land is leased, the enormous increase in its value eats up the rentals from the buildings. Owners or lessees of fees find it profitable to tear down the old buildings and erect new ones with greater earning power, and lose a year's rentals while the improvement is being made.

These figures about the enormous investment in the small portion of the city known as its business centre are given to show what has accustomed Chicagoans to thinking about enormous sums of money in a matter-of-fact way. The unit of value here is $1,000,000, and fractions are not in vogue. Everything is done on a big scale and in a substantial manner. Pettiness and prettiness are outbalanced. There is also a directness or heartiness about the way Chicago handles money which is engaging. The city always seems to be holding four aces, when sometimes the cards are all suits, and run from the deuce to the ten. If the city is ever caught bluffing it takes the discovery merrily. The Chicagoan appreciates more than anybody else jokes about himself. He knows he is open to criticism, and he does not growl at the man who finds fault with him. He likes a good story, even if he is the butt of it. The newspapers here always reprint any criticism of the city or any slur upon it which appears in the newspapers of other cities, and nobody laughs more heartily over them than one of the men who helped to make the city which is held up to ridicule. This spirit of enjoyment which pervades all classes is best illustrated by the way in which everybody but those directly concerned treats the subject of Chicago's "400." The people who make up the "400" are soberly in earnest in being gay. But every man and woman who watches them does so with an amused look, as if a "400" was something which every city had to have, and so Chicago must have one—something to be tolerated, not frowned upon, as otherwise would happen. And so the great horde of people "not in our set" looks on at the farce which the "400" is playing, and is amused as it would be at the theatre. But the "400" is not allowed the privileges which such institutions have in other cities. It cannot override the people who do not get their names into the society columns, because these people get their names into the news columns, and they feel that in figuring in business transactions worthy of public notice in the newspapers they are quite the equal of the people who only figure in cotillions. The families of the men who have made Chicago what it is, and whose names are known all over the country, are not integral parts of that clique known as the "400." The names of the leaders of the swell set are not even known to the great majority of the people living on the west side of Chicago—its biggest section. Information about New-York's "400" is much more prevalent. The reason for this is that the "400" of New-York does things which make good topics of conversation. The "400" of Chicago does nothing but dine and dance in a perfunctory way, because dining and dancing are the necessary requisites to being a proper "400." Chicago tolerates only a proper "400." If it got to doing improper things which would furnish data for after-dinner stories, then the good sense of the city would come to its rescue, and the "400" would be relegated to some other region.

The time which otherwise might be spent in frivolous pleasures the solid business men of Chicago spend in rest or in planning fresh triumphs in the commercial world, or in providing for the city institutions which will add to its fame and its welfare. It is remarkable to see how the attention of the wealthy men has been turned during the last few years to the intellectual and physical needs of the city as distinguished from its commercial needs. For a time after the big fire everybody was engaged in recouping the losses incurred in that disaster. When the rapid growth of the city made it possible to double a fortune in a year, men soon secured enough money to satisfy them, and they sought enjoyment in other ways than in the mere acquirement of wealth. The praise of their fellow-citizens was craved, and it was secured by large appropriations of their easily-secured fortunes to public enterprises. The city itself began the projection of great public improvements on such a scale that, if similar activity is displayed for twenty-five years, it will make Chicago the best-equipped city in the world in those improvements which tend to the comfort and enjoyment of the whole people.

With a fine appreciation of the advantages of a liberal education and the knowledge that such an education is less costly the nearer it is to the home of the student, the citizens have endowed three great colleges. One of these is situated within the city limits. The undergraduate and academic colleges of the other universities are situated in beautiful suburbs of the city, while their allied professional schools are provided for in the city, where there are better facilities for technical work. All these institutions have liberal endowments. The University of Chicago has now an endowment of $7,000,000, although it has only been about three years in existence. Lake Forest University is endowed to the extent of $3,000,000 and Northwestern University, at Evanston, has $4,000,000. Most of this money has been given by Chicago people within the last ten years. These colleges and their technical schools give a young man as good an education as he could obtain at Yale, Harvard, or Princeton, at much less expense. They are all well provided with libraries and apparatus, and their Faculties are made up of professors who are well known as men of ability in their departments of learning.

The history of Chicago University is interesting because of the short time in which a great institution has been founded and grown to such proportions as to make it a formidable rival to the older colleges near by, as well as an offset to the attractions which Yale and Harvard have for all youth.

Although the first contribution to the foundation of the university came from a resident of another city, who has since increased the amount of his gift very largely, the college is a Chicago enterprise. It is the natural successor to an institution of the same name which died some time ago because of the strength of the colleges at Evanston and Lake Forest. With the exception of the money given to it by John D. Rockefeller, its big endowment has come from Chicago men. Mr. Rockefeller gave $600,000 in 1889 on condition that $400,000 should be raised in addition. Following Mr. Rockefeller's generous gift, Marshall Field gave a large tract of land, worth $125,000, fronting the connecting link between Jackson and Washington Parks, which became famous during the World's Fair as the Midway Plaisance. The $400,000 conditional upon Mr. Rockefeller's gift was soon raised, and he gave $1,000,000 more, of which $800,000 was to go to the general fund, $100,000 to construct a Divinity School, and $100,000 to endow it. The next big gift to the university came through the trustees of the estate of the late William B. Ogden, the first Mayor of Chicago. In Mr. Ogden's will he designated a large amount of property, which was to be given to some educational institution selected by the trustees. They turned over the property, which is worth about $750,000, to the Chicago University, to be used for the foundation of the Ogden Scientific School. Then Chicagoans gave another million, the principal gifts being as follows:

Sidney A. Kent, $187,000 for a chemical laboratory; Marshall Field, $100,000; Silas B. Cobb, $150,000; Martin A. Ryerson, $150,000; George C. Walker, $150,000; H. O. Rust, $50,000; women gave $216,000 of this million, those giving $50,000 each being Mrs. Elizabeth G. Kelly, Mrs. N. S. Foster, Mrs. Mary Beecher, and Mrs. Henrietta Snell. Not long after this amount had been contributed Mr. Rockefeller gave another million to the general endowment, making $2,600,000 in all which he had given to the institution. Other large gifts were $250,000 from the Reynolds estate, and $500,000, or such part of it as may be necessary, which was given by C. T. Yerkes for the erection and endowment of a telescope which should be the largest in the world. This instrument is now being made by Clark, the celebrated telescope maker. It is nearly completed. Four million dollars was received by the Trustees of this new university in one year. Dr. E. L. Harper, who was Professor of Semitic Languages at Yale, was engaged at a salary of $7,000 a year as President of the new institution. Extensive buildings on a comprehensive scale were at once projected. Several of these were completed in time for the opening of the colleges, Oct. 1, 1892, when 100 students began attending lectures and classes. The Faculty numbered 119 professors, associate professors, and tutors. This year, the second school year, there are 800 students in the various departments, about 250 being women. The library numbers 350,000 volumes.

The way this university was planned, built, endowed, and put in operation is very like Chicago. There was no long period of struggling growth. When the institution was born it had already grown to mature proportions. In ten years, at its present rate of progress, it will be the most liberally endowed and the best equipped institution of learning in the country. If it is not, it will be disowned by Chicago.

An intense local pride has been engendered by the remarkable history of the city. It is this feeling which makes rich men so generous. Very few of them inherited wealth, and they are not so anxious to leave vast fortunes to their heirs as they might be if they had received an estate from their progenitors. They feel under greater obligations to the city and the body of the citizens which made the amassing of their wealth possible than to those who are to come after them, only to spend the money which they have worked hard to accumulate. These men, predisposed to give their money back to the city which helped them get it, were set a noble example by the will of John Crerar, who died a few years ago, leaving his entire fortune to public institutions. Mr. Crerar came to Chicago in 1862 and became a partner of J. McGregor Adams in the iron business. The firm made money rapidly. Mr. Crerar never married, and had no immediate relatives. But even under these circumstances and with the example of other Chicagoans before them, Mr. Crerar's will was a revelation. Some of the bequests in his will follow:

Monument to Lincoln	$100,000
Second Presbyterian Church	100,000
Mission of the same church	25,000
Scotch Presbyterian Church, New-York	50,000
Chicago Orphan Asylum	50,000
Chicago Half-Orphan Asylum	50,000
Chicago Historical Society	25,000
Presbyterian Hospital	25,000
St Luke's (Episcopal) Hospital	25,000
American Sunday School Union	25,000
Relief and Aid Society	50,000
St. Andrew's Society of New-York	10,000
St. Andrew's Society of Chicago	10,000
Illinois Training School for Nurses	50,000
Chicago Manual Training School	50,000
Presbyterian League	50,000
Old People's Home	50,000
Young Men's Christian Association	50,000
To found a public library	2,000,000

After these munificent gifts the will provided that a plain stone should mark the grave of the testator.

Some of the men who are still living are giving the people as fine an example of how to be great as Mr. Crerar did with his magnificent will. Directly opposed to Mr. Crerar's method of disposing of his property is the way of Dr. Daniel Kimball Pearson. He is seventy-three years old, but he is as vigorous as a man of fifty. He came here in 1857 and made a great deal of money in real estate. In 1875 he was an Alderman. The city got into financial difficulties and Dr. Pearson went East and raised $500,000 for it, pledging his entire private fortune. He believes that every man should distribute his property before his death, if he expects to have it go to the beneficiaries for whom it is intended. So Dr. Pearson has been giving his money away for ten years. He invariably gives with the condition that a certain other amount of money shall be raised from other sources. In this way he stimulates giving by others. During the last few years he has given the following amounts among other gifts of lesser sums:

Beloit College	$100,000
Lake Forest University	100,000
Knox College, Galesburg, Ill	50,000
Chicago Theological Seminary	100,000
Presbyterian Seminary	70,000
Young Men's Christian Association	30,000
Woman's Board of Foreign Missions	20,000
Drury College, Springfield, Mo	50,000
Yankton (S. D.) College	50,000
Colorado College	50,000

This is not intended as a full list of Dr. Pearson's gifts. It contains only some of the largest and best-known of his efforts to help young and struggling institutions. When it is considered th[illegible] the conditions which he invariably imposes secure the donation of two or three times the amount of his own gift, the importance of his contributions may more readily be seen.

Philip D. Armour, the pork packer, and the late Cyrus H. McCormick followed a different plan. When Mr. Armour's brother, Joseph F. Armour, died, he left $100,000 to found the Armour Mission, which is situated in the centre of the great railroad yards. Philip D. Armour has given $500,000 to this mission founded by his brother. In addition to this, he gave about a year ago $1,400,000 for the endowment of a manual training school, to be connected with the mission. This money was expended in the erection of a school building and of 196 flats, from which an income of $75,000 is annually received. Of this, $50,000 is used for the expenses of the Armour Training School, and $25,000 for the Armour Mission. Cyrus H. McCormick had much the same idea of building up an institution himself, unaided by the contributions of others, and of giving it an income from improved city property, when he gave a large tract of land on the North Side to the Chicago Theological Seminary, a Presbyterian divinity school under the management of Lake Forest University. The property Mr. McCormick gave has been covered with choice residences, and it is now estimated to be worth $2,000,000.

Charles J. Hull, whose name is seldom seen in the newspapers, and who is not known to the great majority of the citizens, has another method of fulfilling the obligations he feels to the city. He has helped 6,000 families to build their own homes by lending money at nominal interest on securities which would not be taken by banks, but which count with a man who has faith in human nature and another man's word.

Other munificent gifts which have been made within the last few years are as follows: To Lake Forest University—United States Senator C. B. Farwell, $200,000; William Bross, late one of the editors of The Chicago Tribune, $125,000; Jacob Beidler, $90,000; Cyrus H. McCormick estate, $100,000; J. V. Farwell, $50,000; Henry C. Durand, $75,000; Edward J. Warner, $25,000, and George M. Boque, $10,000.

In her will, Miss Peck left $500,000 to found a home for incurables. Granville S. Ingraham left $100,000 to found a free hospital. Allen C. Lewis left $150,000 to build a manual training school on the west side. Martin Ryerson, who gave $187,000 to the Chicago University, left $225,000 to be divided between eight charitable institutions. Orrington Lunt gave $50,000 to Northwestern University. John V. Farwell, besides the $50,000 previously noted as going to Lake Forest, gave $150,000 to the Young Men's Christian Association. Mrs. Cyrus McCormick gave $225,000 to the Presbyterian Hospital.

The record of the last year, perhaps, is the best indication of the great liberality of Chicagoans. This year just closing has been considered by most people as a pretty hard one. "Financial depression" has been more often on the lips of people than almost any other phrase. But during 1893 the men and women of this city gave nearly $3,000,000 to public institutions, not counting amounts of less than $5,000, and only taking into consideration those made public. The gifts to the Columbian Museum lead in this list. Marshall Field gave $1,000,000 to the museum on condition that $500,000 in money and $2,000,000 of the stock of the World's Fair, which is worth 10 or 15 cents on the dollar, should be given by others. Most of this money and stock has now been subscribed. George M. Pullman, H. N. Higginbotham, and Levi Z. Leiter gave $100,000 each, and Mrs. Sturges and the South Side Street Railroad Company gave $50,000 each.

There are many liberal men in the city whose gifts are just as large and just as praiseworthy as those that have been mentioned. A full list of these men would fill a column. The good deeds of such men as Thomas B. Bryan, N. K. Fairbank, R. T. Crane, John B. Drake, Eli Bates, William B. Hale, and a host of others, would fill a big book.

These and men like them made it possible for Chicago to build the World's Fair with comparative ease. It was, after all, a drop in the bucket for a city which, after spending millions of money to secure pure water, is spending many millions more for drainage. Before the World's Fair was projected the city had decided to dig the great drainage canal which will carry the sewage of the city down to the Mississippi River. This improvement will cost the city $22,000,000 before the end of 1896, and ten millions more before it is completed. Not staggered by such a load, the people of the city are now figuring on building a canal from Lake Michigan to Lake Erie, 140 miles long, which would bring the Western metropolis 550 miles nearer the seaboard by the water route. It is estimated that this canal would cost $50,000,000, and that it would pay 5 per cent. interest on that amount. But it would be a permanent improvement, and it would be of almost incalculable benefit to the city.

Such schemes as this are not vaporous to Chicagoans. They have implicit confidence in themselves and in the city, and they are not afraid to back their opinions and plans with their money, which has come to them so fast.

This civic pride and faith in the destiny of the city, this enterprise, this spirit of philanthropy, this ability to make wise investments, will make Chicago within a decade the most wonderful city on the face of the globe. Its brief history, its almost total destruction by fire twenty-two years ago, its population now of 1,500,000, the transformation which is now going on in its business district, the magnitude and magnificence of its commercial buildings, which are replacing those put up only a few years ago, and which surpass anything of the kind in the history of the world, its universities, churches, and public buildings complete a phenomenal record and foreshadow a still more phenomenal future.

December 24, 1893

THE NEW YORK OF TO-DAY

A Greater City Comes Into Being Without Any Visible Change in Conditions.

MANY NEW FEATURES, HOWEVER

Some Points for the Guidance of the Residents of the New Municipality —Local Improvements and Sanitary Laws—Police, Schools, Parks, Courts, &c.

Any old New Yorker, who, because of the municipal transformation which takes place to-day, looks for altered conditions or wholesale disturbances in civic affairs, will be disappointed. Like the anxious young man who became of age in a single night without anything happening to him; the inhabitants of the several localities which constitute the Greater New York will enter upon their new governmental relations with comparativly few visible signs of a change.

The capitalists and the wage-earners who dwell on Manhattan Island will pursue their daily routine undisturbed by the throes of consolidation; the scurrying trolley cars of Brooklyn will make just as many trips to and from the bridge, and the ebb and flow of humanity over that structure will probably not be affected in the least by the fact that Brooklyn is now a borough instead of a city; the market gardeners and commuters of Queens will find neither increased profits nor reduced rates in the new order of things, and the farmers of Richmond will certainly not base any crop expectation on the Greater New York charter.

Each of the five boroughs of the enlarged metropolis has an autonomy of its own, a President of its own, and a local board of its own. The detailed work of government will go on, along practically the same lines as heretofore, and except a citizen comes into direct contact with official procedure he will not observe any difference between the old and the new method of local government. To the old-time New Yorker the mere idea of bigness will mean but little. It is the brand-new citizen from Hempstead or from New Dorp who will be most deeply impressed with the honor of living in the second largest city in the world. It is unlikely that future distributions of tax bills will diminish the proud serenity of the brand-new citizen any more than they will stimulate the satisfaction of the old-time New Yorker.

There is one thing that all of the residents of this consolidated city should have in mind and that is its correct name. It is not Greater New York, but "The City of New York." The title of the act creating this great municipality actually contains sixty words, but the short title of "The Greater New York Charter" is officially sanctioned. Section 1 of the charter declares that the new city shall be the successor corporation, in law and fact, of all the municipal and public corporations consolidated, with all their rights and powers, and subject to all their lawful obligations.

It need not be expected that because of the consolidation all of the municipal, town, and village officers in the four other boroughs will come to the Borough of Manhattan to-day and seek for recognition and places in the City Hall. All of these local officers will simply stay in their respective boroughs and continue to perform their duties as prescribed by law.

Only One Kind of Police.

The most notable departmental change wrought by the framers of the new charter was the consolidation into a single force of all the police forces of the territory included in the greater city. There will no longer be a separate park police and a separate bridge police. Everything in the nature of police within the boundaries of the new municipality will become a part of the general system, and subject to the control of a Police Board which supersedes all Police Commissioners of New York, Brooklyn, Long Island City, and Richmond County. This new board is to consist of four persons, to be known as Police Commissioners of the City of New York. These commissioners are to be appointed by the Mayor, and no more than two of them shall belong to the same political party, "or be of the same political opinion on State and National politics."

For the protection of the public parks, it is provided that the Police Board shall from time to time detail to the service of the Department of the Parks, upon the requisition of either of the Commissioners of Parks, as many suitable officers and men as in the judgment of the Police Department are necessary. These policemen, although in all respects an integral part of the police force of the city and paid out of the police funds, shall, so long as their detail lasts, report to the Park Commissioner in charge of the parks in which they serve. A similar detail of policemen must be made by the Police Board upon the requisition of the Commissioner of Bridges. While detailed on the Brooklyn Bridge the policemen must report to the Commissioner of Bridges.

The Chief of the Greater New York Police force must be selected from four men—the present Chief and the Deputy Chief of New York, and the present Superintendent and the Deputy Superintendent of the Brooklyn force. Promotions in the Police Department can be made by a majority vote of the board, but only on a written recommendation of the Chief of Police.

How to Secure Local Improvements.

A citizen, or body of citizens, desiring to secure a local improvement in any particular neighborhood must prepare a petition as the first step. There are to be twenty-two districts of local improvements, and one of the first duties of the new Municipal Assembly is to name, or number, these districts. Each district has its local board, which has power to recommend that proceedings be taken to open, close, pave, widen, or repair streets, to construct lateral sewers, to lay sidewalks, and cross walks, and to set lamps, &c., in all cases where the cost of improvement is to be met in whole or in part by assessments upon the property benefited.

Whenever a street or sidewalk improvement is desired, or a sewer connection is needed, in any particular neighborhood, the persons interested are required to state their wants in a petition and send the petition to the President of their borough. It thereupon becomes the duty of the President to call a meeting of his local board within fifteen days, to consider the matter, and he must publish in the City Record, at least ten days before that meeting, a notice when it will be held, and that the petition is on file in his office for inspection. After the hearing, or hearings, if the local board shall decide to recommend that proceedings be taken on the desired improvement, a resolution to that effect is transmitted to the Board of Public Improvements, which must meet at least once a week. No work involving assessment for benefit shall be authorized by the Board of Public Improvements until there has been submitted to it a written estimate of the cost, and the assessed value on the last tax roll of the real estate to be assessed. This board has power to construct, repair, and clean sewers and to repair pavements and readjust grades of streets in connection therewith.

The new charter provides that the expense of all such improvements shall be assessed and be a lien on the property benefited "in proportion to the amount of benefit," and in no case shall it extend beyond the limits of the district benefited. The local board apparently has power, without petition, to cause the flagging or reflagging of sidewalks, the laying or relaying of cross walks, the fencing of vacant lots or the filling in of sunken lots, by resolution approved by the Board of Public Improvements. The Municipal Assembly cannot enter directly into any contract whatever for any public work or improvement. There must first be a report by the Board of Public Improvements, and if that be unfavorable, it takes a vote of five-sixths of both houses and the Mayor's approval to pass it.

Neighborhood Nuisances.

If the residents of a neighborhood or a particular block object to a drinking saloon, gambling place, or other disorderly house, they may take their grievance to the local board in that particular district. Each local board has power to hear complaints of nuisances in streets or avenues, or against disorderly houses, drinking saloons conducted without observance of the necessary licenses, gambling houses or any other places or congregations in violation of good order or of the laws of the State. Each local board is in a measure made the conservator of the peace, comfort, order, and good government in its own district. It may pass such resolutions concerning these matters as may not be inconsistent with the powers of the Municipal Assembly or of the respective administrative departments.

Board of Health's Great Power.

To the Board of Health the charter gives extraordinary powers, and the penalty for violating any order of the Board of Health is a fine not exceeding $250, or imprisonment not exceeding six months, or both, such violation being a misdemeanor. The Sanitary Code now in force is made binding by the new charter, and according to that code the "owner, lessee, tenant or occupant of any building or premises, or of any part thereof, where there shall be a violation of any ordinance or section of the Sanitary Code shall be jointly and severally liable therefor." Any expense incurred by the Board of Health in keeping private property up to the prescribed standard becomes a lien upon the real estate.

Whenever "any building, erection, excavation, premises, business pursuit, matter, or thing, or the sewerage, drainage, or ventilation thereof, shall be in a condition, or in effect dangerous to life or health" the Board of Health may take sufficient proof to authorize declaring it a public nuisance, or dangerous to life or health, and may order it to be removed, or altered, or improved. No offensive trade can be carried on within the Borough of Manhattan. In the other boroughs such trades as bone boiling, bone burning, horse and cow skinning, or the boiling of offal are not prohibited.

A nuisance under the Greater New York charter embraces not only what is known as a public nuisance at common law, or in equity jurisprudence, but also whatever is dangerous to human life or detrimental to health; whatever building or part thereof is overcrowded with occupants, or is not provided with adequate ingress and egress to and from the same, or the apartments thereof, or is not sufficiently supported, ventilated, sewered, drained, cleaned, or lighted in reference to their or its intended or actual use, and whatever renders the air, or human food, or drink unwholesome are also severally in contemplation of this act nuisances, and all such nuisances are declared illegal. Section 1,261 of the charter provides that all proceedings of the Health Department shall be regarded as in their nature judicial, and shall be treated as prima facie just and legal.

Public Charities and Correction.

In appointing three Commissioners to constitute a Board of Public Charities the Mayor is to designate the President of the board, and assign the Commissioners as follows: One to Manhattan and Bronx, one to Brooklyn and Queens, and one to Richmond. The salaries of the two first mentioned are fixed at $7,500 per annum each, and the salary of the Commissioner for Richmond at $2,500 per annum.

There is a single head of the Department of Correction, and he is called the Commissioner of Correction. His salary is $7,500 a year. All of these Commissioners representing the two Departments of Charities and Correction are vested with authority and duties similar to those hitherto held by the heads of those respective departments.

Section 696 of the charter authorizes the removal of the workhouse and penitentiary from Blackwell's to Hart's Island and Riker's Island. The Commissioner of Correction may direct the removal of the inmates of the workhouse and penitentiary on Blackwell's Island as soon as accommodation can be provided for them on the other islands named. As soon as Blackwell's Island is entirel abandoned by the Department of Correction, the buildings and grounds thus abandoned are to be transferred to the care of the Commissioner of Charities for the boroughs of Manhattan and the Bronx.

At the request of any Commission of Charities of the City of New York, the Commissioner of Correction may detail any inmate of any of the institutions in his department to perform any necessary work or service in the Department of Charities.

The Fire Department.

One Fire Commissioner is to be the head of the Fire Department and he will appoint a Deputy Commissioner whose headquarters are to be in the office of the Fire Department of Brooklyn. This deputy will have supervision of the Fire Department in the boroughs of Brooklyn and Queens. The Long Island City Fire Department is by law made a part of the general Fire Department.

One section of the charter provides for the replacing of the volunteer fire departments in Queens, and Richmond by paid firemen as soon as possible.

The Fire Commissioner is also to be the Treasurer of the department, and he is required to file a bond with the Controller in the amount of $100,000. There are to be one Chief and several Deputy Chiefs and Battalion Chiefs. From and after to-day the uniformed members of the Fire Department who are firemen will be in four grades and will receive annual compensation as follows: First grade, $1,400; second grade, $1,200; third grade, $1,000; fourth grade, $800. All new members appointed after to-day must serve one year in the fourth grade. Should they merit an advance they will be advanced one grade in each succeeding year.

Treatment of "Works of Art."

A unique and hopeful feature of the new form of municipal government is that no "work of art" can become the property of the city until the work or design, with a statement of the proposed location, has been approved by an Art Commission. This commission is to consist of six appointed members, with the Mayor, the President of the Metropolitan Museum of Art, the President of the New York Public Library, and the President of the Brooklyn Institute of Arts and Sciences as members ex officio. The six members are to be appointed by the Mayor from a list containing three times the number to be appointed, furnished by the Fine Arts Federation of New York. One of the men selected must be an architect, another a painter, and a third a sculptor. The three other members must not be members of any profession in the fine arts.

In matters where the approval of the Art Commission is necessary if the commission does not decide within sixty days its approval will be deemed unnecessary. No existing "work of art" can be removed or altered without the approval of the commission unless the Mayor thinks that immediate action should be taken, in which case the commission must act within forty-eight hours, or be deemed to approve. In all matters affecting the work of any one Park Commissioner he is to sit with the Art Commission.

The charter furthermore provides that the Art Commission may act in relation to municipal buildings, bridges, and other matters when so requested by the Mayor or the Municipal Assembly.

There are to be three Commissioners of Parks, one to have jurisdiction in the Boroughs of Manhattan and Richmond, one in Brooklyn and Queens, and the third to devote himself exclusively to the Borough of the Bronx.

New Department of Education.

The existing departments of education in the different boroughs expire on Feb. 1, and they will be succeeded by one new department of education for the City of New York. Central authority will be vested in a board of education, consisting of nineteen members, each to serve one year. This board elects its own President.

There are to be no School Trustees hereafter, but each borough (Manhattan and the Bronx being counted as one) will have a School Board. The present Board of Education in Manhattan will continue in power as the School Board for Manhattan and the Bronx. The present Board of Education of Brooklyn will serve as the School Board for that borough. The Central Board of Education will consist of the Chairman and ten other members of the School Board of Manhattan and the Bronx, the Chairman and five other members of the School Board of Brooklyn, the Chairman of the School Board of Richmond, and the Chairman of the School Board of Queens. There will be one City Superintendent and individual Superintendents for each borough.

Section 1,083 of the new charter provides for the retirement of old teachers on a pension by a two-thirds vote of all the members of the Board of Education. Funds for school purposes for 1898 have been provided under the old methods. A new general school fund will be raised by taxation beginning with 1899.

How to Get a Franchise.

A person or a corporation desiring a franchise from the city must make an application in proper form to the Municipal Assembly. All public franchises unless otherwise provided for in the charter will be granted by an ordinance of the Municipal Assembly. In each case the proposed ordinance, with details of franchise and conditions of grant, must be published twenty days in The City Record and twice in two daily newspapers; it must on the first reading be referred to the Board of Public Improvements, and it must have the approval of that board before it can pass the Municipal Assembly. Thirty days must intervene between the introduction of a franchise ordinance in the Assembly and its final passage. The ordinance must have a three-fourths vote on its passage and a five-sixths vote to pass it over the Mayor's veto.

No franchise can be granted for a longer period than twenty years, but the city has an option of renewing for not more than twenty-five years upon revaluation. A grant may possibly provide for the reversion of the plant and property to the city, with or without further compensation, at the end of the term. In case an ordinance does provide for reversion to the city without compensation, the city may either operate the plant on its own account, renew the lease for twenty years, or lease the property for twenty years to other parties. Should a franchise provide for reversion to the city with compensation, payment to be upon a valuation of property, exclusive of the franchise. After making the payment the city must operate the plant for five years; subsequently the city may either continue to operate or lease in the same manner as docks and ferries.

Each franchise granted by the city must provide for efficient service at reasonable rates and for the maintenance of the property in good condition; it must also specify the mode of determining a revaluation.

The Courts.

Every good citizen of the Greater City will naturally want to know to what courts of law he can resort, even if he does not expect to resort to any of them. The City Court is continued, and its jurisdiction is extended over the consolidated city. A Municipal Court is created, to succeed the present District Courts in New York and the Justices' Courtsi n Brooklyn. In this Municipal Court there are to be twenty-three Justices, each to serve ten years, and each Justice must be a lawyer of five years' experience. These Justices will be distributed as follows: Manhattan, 11; Brooklyn, 5; Queens, 3; Bronx, 2, and Richmond, 2.

In the matter of Special Sessions the new city is divided into two divisions—first, Manhattan and the Bronx, and, second, Brooklyn, Queens, and Richmond. For the First Division the present court is continued, and for the Second Division the Mayor will appoint five Justices.

City Magistrates will serve in divisions, the same as for Special Sessions. The fifteen Magistrates now in office will be continued in the First Division. For the Second Division, the Mayor will appoint 11 Magistrates, as follows: Six in Brooklyn, 3 in Queens, and 2 in Richmond. The Brooklyn Police Justices are abolished.

January 1, 1898

MISCELLANEOUS CITY NEWS

EDISON'S ELECTRIC LIGHT.

THE INVENTOR REMOVES TO THIS CITY AND IS READY FOR WORK.

Prof. Edison has removed from Menlo Park to this City with his family and entire staff, with the exception of an assistant, and is now at No. 65 Fifth-avenue. The house, which is a four-story double brown-stone building, was formerly known as the Bishop Mansion and has been leased for a long term of years by the Edison Electric Light Company. The technical department of the business is now carried on here, viz., the engineers, draughtsmen, electricians; house installation, street installation, statistical and law departments, and all arrangements necessary have been provided. The offices of the Edison Luminating Company of New-York, the Edison Electric Light Company of Great Britain and Europe, and the Edison Electric Railway will also be in the building, and the offices in the Boreel Building will also be retained. A neat black sign, with gold letters—"The Edison Electric Light Company"—has been placed in the front of the building at the side of the main entrance, and on the upper side of the building near the roof the name of the company has been painted in black letters on a pale-green ground. Prof. Edison considers his invention complete, and will now devote his attention to introducing the light in cities. His system is to light cities only, and as that field is so vast he will not undertake the lighting of buildings. Vice-President Eaton said yesterday that Prof. Edison's invention was complete, and they were at work getting rights in different cities to put the wires in the streets and to light the street lamps; they had received 3,000 or 4,000 applications to light houses and hotels, but the former business was too vast to undertake the latter; they would devote their entire attention to lighting cities only, and will not contract to light single buildings, as other companies do who have stock to sell or wish to attract attention in order that the shares might be increased. The Edison system was to light whole cities from central stations, thereby affording the best light at a maximum of economy. The company has an application before the Board of Aldermen for permission to use the streets of New-York to lay wires, and he expected the matter would be acted upon at the next meeting of the board. The Board of Aldermen of Detroit, by a unanimous vote, have given the company the right to lay wires in the streets there, and this was the first city in the United States to grant the use of its streets to an electric company. The company would encourage the people to retain the gas in the street-lamps, and to use both gas and the electric light, and, after giving them a trial, to see which they would rather have as a permanent light.

Prof. Edison has, Mr. Eaton said, removed his family and staff to the building No. 65 Fifth-avenue, and has organized here a system of departments which will afford a subdivision of labor so completely that the utmost possible growth of the business of the company in the future is provided for. The building will be devoted to the technical department of the business, while the executive offices will be retained in the Boreel Building. He said it would take time to obtain the right in the different cities, and there was great difficulty in getting the necessary machinery; the machine-shops are all overloaded, and he found it almost impossible to get machines built, especially such machines as had to be originated, and even for such standard machines as steam-engines he found it impossible to get orders filled.

Concerning the lights at Menlo Park Mr. Eaton said there was a wonderful dynamo there of 100-horse power, by which all the lights for eight miles of street mains and 700 lamps were lighted; this single dynamo was attached, without the intervention of any belting, to a Porter engine of 600 revolutions a minute. Mr. Eaton was asked in regard to the recent patent decision in which it was reported that Prof. Edison was beaten. He said the announcement in the newspapers that Prof. Edison was beaten in the Patent Office on an important invention was an advertisement inserted by a rival company in three of the morning papers, all on the same morning, and in precisely the same language, word for word, and was subsequently put in other papers. The invention referred to was that known as the thermostatic regulator, and it was stated that the case was strenuously contested before the Patent Office, and this regulator was an important part of the Edison system. This, said Mr. Eaton, is absolutely false. The case was not contested, except formally, and of the entire board of 13 Directors of the Edison Electric Light Company only one of them, and he by accident, knew anything about it. The regular counsel of the company did not even give the matter his attention. The thermostatic regulator was a part of the platinum lamp which was abandoned two years ago, not only by Mr. Edison, but by all other inventors working in the same line. The platinum lamp itself and the thermostatic regulator are absolutely dead matters, and belong to the cemetery of inventions. Neither Mr. Edison nor any other inventor has any further use of the platinum lamp or thermostatic regulator, or of any of the other devices that were originated and tested in connection with the platinum lamp in the early stages of electrical lighting. When Mr. Edison abandoned the platinum lamp his next experiments were with a silk thread, after which he experimented with paper, and then with card-board, and with various fibres of wood, and finally with a fibre of bamboo, which is used in his present lamp. The thermostatic regulator forms no part of this lamp and no part of any lamp he has used or experimented with since his very first experiments over two years ago, and the statement that the invention known as the thermostatic regulator has any interest or value whatever to him or to any invention in electric lighting is utterly false.

March 1, 1881

THE CITY OF TELEPHONES.

NOBODY IN CINCINNATI NEED BE WITHOUT HIS OWN WIRE.

From the Cincinnati Commercial.

Sixteen young ladies in cool morning costume sat in a line in a Fourth-street office yesterday afternoon. They were all talking in monosyllables to 16 other people in various parts of the city. A young man sitting at a desk in the rear of the line held a microphone to his year, and heard what each of the 32 persons said. It was a strange chorus of voices, and yet the young man did not appear to get tired, for he had held the instrument to his ear for many hours, and would do so for hours to come. The young ladies were the people who answer "Hello!" to you when you go to the telephone. They sit in the Central Exchange, on Fourth and Walnut streets, and answer the requests of 582 subscribers. Each lady has so many subscribers to attend to, and from early in the morning until 6 o'clock at night she listens to the requests of the people at the wires and answers them. There is no time for reading or loafing. The microphone is so adjusted that she can hear all that is said without trouble, and there are few minutes in the day when it is not talking. A messenger boy walks up and down behind the line of young ladies, and when one of them receives a call from the telephone a little check is made out, and this is given the messenger, who carries it off to a clerk, who thus keeps a constant record of all that is going on outside. This office, on Fourth and Walnut, is never closed. The lights in its windows are bright until the sunlight in the morning makes gas unnecessary. There are eight other exchanges in the city, namely, on Front-street, Freeman, Elm, Broadway, the Public Landing, Brighton, Covington, and Ninth-street.

Each exchange has direct connection with all the others. They are also connected with Richmond, Lawrenceburg, and Aurora, Ind., and Hamilton and Eaton, Ohio. Next week a wire will be begun to connect direct with Dayton, Ohio. The Cincinnati City and Surburban Telegraph Association has the reputation in other cities of giving the best service and being the most efficient of any in the country. It has in use nearly 2,000 wires, and employs over 100 operators, to say nothing of its various other employes, such as clerks and electricians. Capt. George N. Stone, General Manager of the association, said yesterday to a *Commercial* reporter that the telephone business has been an experiment with this company, as it has with all others. It took a good deal of time to perfect the arrangements, and they are only now getting their arrangements in the shape they would like to have them.

"At first," said Mr. Stone, "we put as many as 17 subscribers on one circuit or wire. We charged these $3 per month. This was in the early stages of telephony, and there was no microphone. It was difficult to hear well at best and there was so little use for the telephone then that it looked as though one wire would accommodate any number of subscribers. These things soon began to change. The desire for telephones seemed to grow with what it fed on. Each month compelled us to reduce the number of subscribers to the wire. From 17 we came down to five, and increased the rate to $4 per month for each subscriber within a half-mile of the exchange. We were compelled to build new wires all the time, and for each half-mile of distance we charged $1 extra. We found soon that people living several miles from the exchange could not afford the price. About this time the transmitter came into use. Now let me tell you something about this transmitter and microphone. The early Edison telephone did not have them. They were invented by Bell. It was a question for some time whether they would be successful. The National Bell Telephone Company was organized, and the stock ranged down at something like 15 cents on the dollar. Suddenly Mr. Bell, who had been hard at work in his laboratory, completed his invention. From a slight improvement the Bell telephone became a decided success. Stock doubled and then quadrupled. Men who had gone to bed with a few hundred shares of stock worth little or nothing, woke up to find themselves rich. Mr. Bell had his patents complete. His instrument ran everything out of the market, and of course he had the business in his own hands. He determined to place a royalty of $10 on every transmitter and $10 on every microphone, and, of course, he got it. The result is that we pay $20 a year royalty on every telephone in use. This little thing you talk through and the instrument you hear from you can't buy for love or money. Twenty dollars a year rents them, and if we break one we pay $25 to replace it. Of course, this put prices up. We put in special wires for one subscriber with telephone and transmitter at $6 per month to any point within a radius of one-half mile from the Central Exchange, and $1 for every additional half-mile."

"How did that plan work?"

"Very well. All our business men availed themselves of the special wire, but the $1 for additional distance we still found did not do so well. We therefore concluded to equalize the rates, and at present we furnish a business subscriber with a special wire, telephone, and transmitter anywhere in the city of Cincinnati, Covington, Newport, Clifton, or Avondale for $8 33 per month, and residences in the same limits with special wire at $6 per month, or three subscribers on one wire at $4 15 per month. The equalization increased no subscribers more than $2 33 per month, and decreased many from $1 to $10 per month."

"How do these prices compare with other cities?"

"Well, for special wires to business houses, for one-half mile or five miles, in Cincinnati, the rate is $100 per year. In Chicago the price is $125 per year up to one mile, then it goes to $150 for one and a quarter miles, $175 for one and a half miles, $225 for three miles. New-York City is $150 per annum for one mile, $186 for a mile and a quarter, and $222 for anything over two miles. Pittsburg and New-Orleans are cheaper than Cincinnati for one-half mile, being $84 and $75, respectively. For one mile Pittsburg is $120, and New-Orleans $100, and they both increase—New-Orleans to $200 and Pittsburg to $250—for three miles."

It will be seen from Capt. Stone's figures that Cincinnati is supplied at exceedingly cheap rates, and it only takes a little experience in other cities to make Cincinnatians more than contented with the service.

August 27, 1882

TWO GREAT CITIES UNITED

THE BRIDGE FORMALLY OPENED.

THE BUILDING OF THE BRIDGE.

ITS COST AND THE DIFFICULTIES MET WITH—DETAILS OF THE HISTORY OF A GREAT ENGINEERING TRIUMPH.

The idea of uniting Brooklyn with New-York by means of either bridge or tunnel was a favorite one with the Brooklyn folk for years before the scheme was launched which this week will open to the two cities the largest single span suspension bridge in the world. As Brooklyn began to expand and the daily flow and ebb of her population New-Yorkward increased in volume, the difficulties and delays of river travel emphasized with each recurring season of snow and ice the necessity of some shorter and more direct means of communication than the ferries. A plan among the earliest presented for facilitating rapid transit between Manhattan and Long Islands was known as the quay system, diagrams of which are still in existence. This contemplated the construction of a series of quays in the swirling waters of the East River, connected with draw-bridges. The plan of tunneling the river, laborious as it must prove through such a rocky formation as that known to exist beneath the river bed, has always had its advantages, and it is a mooted question even now among engineers whether this would not have been a far more economical and less hazardous enterprise than that which has resulted in the present suspension bridge. Some time before any practical steps were taken in connection with this enterprise the idea of a suspension bridge was discussed by a number of Brooklyn gentlemen, and the elder Roebling's views were solicited. The art of building these airy structures was then in its infancy here, and Mr. John A. Roebling stood at the head of the engineers who had made it a study. The plan to which his attention was directed was the erection of a light bridge exclusively for foot passengers. Such a bridge, he estimated, could be built at a height above the river of something like 185 feet, and at a cost of about $3,000,000. For the reason probably that the gentlemen who proposed it were unable to secure the necessary financial backing, nothing ever came of this particular project. That the later and more elaborate scheme was, however, its outgrowth has frequently been asserted during the many years that have intervened between the beginning and the completion of the mighty span that now unites the two shores. To no one man can be given the credit of this colossal undertaking, although from his connection with it, through years of evil and good report, probably no other person (always excepting the members of the Roebling family) has been so prominently identified with it as William C. Kingsley, the acting President of its Board of Trustees. Himself a contractor and possessed of ample means and of political as well as business shrewdness, Mr. Kingsley as early as 1865 interested himself in the idea of bridging the East River. Capitalists, equally bold, united with him, and upon the assurance of Engineer Roebling that a span of 1,600 feet, such as would be necessary to avoid impeding the navigation of the river, was feasible, the preliminary proceedings in the history of this famous bridge were taken.

One of the moving spirits henceforth became the late Henry C. Murphy, a member of the State Senate when this scheme began to take practical shape. On the 25th of January, 1867, Senator Murphy introduced a bill incorporating the New-York Bridge Company, and giving it authority "to construct and maintain a permanent bridge over the East River." The names of 41 persons were given as the incorporators. The majority of them were residents of Brooklyn. Tweed, Sweeny, and Connolly, who afterward figured so notoriously in the plundering of this City, were among the incorporators living in New-York. In the list of 41 were the names of ex-Gov. John T. Hoffman, ex-Congressman Simeon B. Chittenden, Edward Ruggles, ex-Mayor Smith Ely, Jr., ex-Mayors Samuel Booth, Martin Kalbfleisch, and William Hunter, Jr., of Brooklyn; Judge Alexander McCue, Granville T. Jenks, Henry E. Pierrepont, John Roach, ex-Controller Andrew H. Green, ex-Water Commissioner William A. Fowler, of Brooklyn; Henry E. Stebbins, William W. W. Wood, Ethelbert S. Mills, Edmund W. Corlies, Alfred W. Craven, Arthur W. Benson, Isaac Van Anden, then chief owner of the Brooklyn *Eagle*; J. Carson Brevoort, William Marshall, Samuel McLean, John H. Prentice, Edmund Driggs, John W. Combs, John P. Atkinson, and John Morton. The act of incorporation became law April 16, 1867. Among other powers conferred, it authorized the cities of New-York and Brooklyn to subscribe to the capital stock (which was fixed at $5,000,000, with power of increase,) such amounts as two-thirds of their Common Councils respectively should determine, and to issue bonds in payment of such subscriptions. Under these provisions Brooklyn subscribed for $3,000,000 of stock, New-York $1,500,000, while the remaining $500,000 was distributed among the incorporators. These latter constituted the first Board of Directors, and by them Senator Murphy was elected President, Mr. John H. Prentice Treasurer, and Mr. Orestes P. Quintard Secretary. The President and Treasurer retained their connection with the enterprise until their deaths. Mr. Quintard still holds the office of Secretary. To an executive board of 13 the affairs of the new company were intrusted. Mr. William C. Kingsley at the very outset had secured the position of General Superintendent. His compensation was fixed, according to William M. Tweed's testimony, at 15 per cent., but according to his own statements, at 5 per cent., of the cost of construction. On the 23d of May, 1867, the elder Roebling, who had already achieved fame as the builder of the International Suspension Bridge at Niagara Falls and of the Covington and Cincinnati Suspension Bridge across the Ohio River, two of the greatest works of their kind that had then been attempted in this country, was employed as chief engineer. His plans, submitted to the Directors on the 1st of September following, fixed the cost of the bridge at $7,000,000, exclusive of the land required, (an item itself amounting to $3,800,000,) and the time of building at about five years. Modifications of these plans and changes and improvements of one kind and another have greatly added to these figures. In round numbers, the cost has been $16,000,000 and the period of building 14 years, estimating from the year 1869, when Engineer Roebling began his initial surveys. In March of that year, at the request of Mr. Roebling, a board of consulting engineers was convened to examine his plans and report upon their feasibility. Its members were Engineers Adams, McAlpine, Allen, Latrobe, Kirkwood, Steele, and Serrell, and the result of their inspection was an indorsement of all he had done. So much had been said about the obstruction to navigation which would be offered by the bridge that Congress directed a still further examination of the plans, and Secretary of War Rawlins appointed Gen. Newton, Gen. Wright, and Major King, three Government engineers, for that purpose. They recommended an increase in the height of the bridge of five feet, but otherwise gave the plans their approval. In accordance with this recommendation changes were made in the proposed method of building the roadway, so that the span midway between the two towers is now 135 feet above high-water mark. Mr. Roebling lived but a few months after the appointment of the Government commission. In the Summer of that year, while standing upon the rack of one of the slips of the Fulton ferry, directing the details of a survey, the shock of an incoming ferry-boat caused him to lose his balance, and one of his feet was terribly crushed between the heavy timbers that formed the rack. The injury resulted in lockjaw, from which he died 16 days afterward. His son, Col. Washington A. Roebling, who had aided in drawing the original plans, and who had been associated with his father in the building of the Covington bridge, was appointed his successor. The caisson disease made the son one of its victims within a twelvemonth. Although his physical health has been impaired to such an extent that he is a confirmed invalid, his mental faculties have retained their vigor, and during all these long years he has directed the work from an upper room in his residence on Columbia Heights, in Brooklyn. As the towers grew and the spinning of the web between them progressed, the younger Roebling has watched from his window the movements of the workmen with the aid of a powerful glass.

BEGINNING THE GREAT WORK.

The erection of the bridge proper began Jan. 3, 1870, when the work of preparing a place for the foundation of the Brooklyn tower was commenced by tearing out the spare slips of Fulton ferry. During the next four years the history of the bridge was marred by complaints of fraud and downright dishonesty on the part of the builders, by investigations of accounts, and by attacks upon personal character which have seldom been surpassed in savageness. The construction account was early opened to criticism, and it was discovered that men who were interested in the bridge company had also a heavy interest in the contracts for furnishing timber, stone, &c. Matters reached that point finally that an Investigating Committee of Fifty went to work upon the accounts and all the records of the Directors. In the early part of 1873 they presented their report. This indicated very clearly that there had been laxity in the management and that the interests of the two heaviest stockholders—the cities of New-York and Brooklyn—had not been protected as they ought to have been. The pressure of public opinion was so great that Mr. Kingsley, on the 1st of June, 1873, felt constrained to resign his position as General Superintendent. The Legislature of the following year took the matter in hand and passed a law investing the authorities of the two cities with power to go on and complete the structure, first extinguishing the title of the private stockholders by purchasing their shares in the company and reimbursing them in full. Under the new order of things the bridge became public property, Brooklyn paying for and owning 66⅔ per cent. and New-York 33⅓ per cent. A Board of Bridge Trustees was organized of 20 members, 16 of whom were named by the Mayors and Controllers of the two cities, while these four officers constituted the ex officio members. So far as Brooklyn was concerned, little change was made by the new law, for that city's officers either reappointed members of the old Board of Directors or members who were by them controlled. As the result of this some of the present Trustees have been identified with the work almost from its very beginning. The new legal name given to the structure by this act of 1874 was the New-York and Brooklyn Bridge. Coming more closely within the province of the Legislature, one or more investigations were deemed necessary to determine the status of its affairs and satisfy the public demand for information. The last of these investigations was in 1879, when, if anything at all was demonstrated, it was the necessity of having the bridge completed at the earliest practicable moment. The last appropriation authorized was that of the past Winter, in which the right to acquire certain property to complete the Brooklyn approach was legalized. At least one more appeal must be made to the Legislature for authority to allow expenditures necessary to perfect the structure and add to its value as a means of rapid transit between the two islands.

A statement that the two massive stone towers at the river's edge are standing on a foundation of timber might, by a stranger to engineering methods, be accepted with some misgivings, and even with absolute doubt. Its truth, however, will be recognized after an explanation of some of the most difficult obstacles encountered and successfully overcome in the earlier stages of this mighty work. The caisson plan of laying a foundation for the towers having been agreed upon as the most practicable, the building of one of these caissons was begun. The word caisson means inverted chest. In this case the caisson was a huge inverted box, built on ways and launched like any other wooden vessel that is fashioned by the Greenpoint ship-builders. The first caisson was built for use on the Brooklyn side. It was 168 feet in length, 102 feet in width, and 22 feet in height. It was intended to sustain an enormous weight, and its top was 15 feet in thickness, being composed of layer after layer of solid yellow pine timbers, each a foot in thickness, crossing one another at right angles, and all bolted together in the most compact manner. The four sides of the caisson were 9 feet 6 inches in height and 9 feet in thickness where they joined the top, and, like the latter, were built of stanch timber bound together with similar heavy bolts. The sides tapered off in thickness, somewhat like the letter V, and at their bottom (corresponding to the point of the V) they were only about six inches thick. An iron casting was bolted over this thin edge in order to afford it strength and protection. The interior of this caisson was divided into six compartments by timber partitions two feet thick, strong and well braced. Through each partition were two openings, high and broad enough to permit of the passage of a man with a wheelbarrow. All the inside joints of the caisson were well caulked with oakum and pitched to prevent the escape of air. A sheathing of tin was laid over the outside by the caisson to protect the timber from the attacks of sea worms and as a still further means of excluding water. Over this sheathing was a layer of 3-inch planks saturated with creosote. Such were the precautions taken to insure an air-tight caisson and to guard against its decay. The spare ferry slip having been demolished, dredging to the depth of 18 feet was necessary. Into this berth the caisson was towed on the 2d of May, 1870, and the work of sinking it began. Around three sides of the berth was built a cofferdam of piles and sheathing. The side next the water was similarly protected after the caisson had been floated into position. Derricks were erected, and, on the 15th of June, blocks of granite from the Maine quarries were hoisted upon the top of the caisson. Under their weight the caisson began to settle. Limestone from the quarries of Kingston, N. Y., was added to the mass, and the base of the Brooklyn tower was fully under way. When the weight upon the caisson was such that its iron-shod edges rested fairly on the river bottom, compressed air was turned into it, the water was expelled, and workmen went down underneath with pick, shovel, and wheelbarrow to commence excavation. An air-lock furnished the means of ingress and egress, and into this on the afternoon of May 10, 1870, Col. Roebling, Engineer Martin, and Master Mechanic Farrington entered. Groping their way into the subterranean chamber into which the air-lock opened, the three men spent 20 minutes in an examination, but were glad to beat a retreat at the end of that time, gasping for breath and half roasted by the intense heat. Water was turned in, the atmosphere of the chamber was cooled off, and, preparations having been completed, men were sent down to begin excavations in earnest on the 10th of July following.

In the early part of the work, before the caisson became firmly fixed in the earth, some curious phenomena were exhibited. Under the influence of a strong air pressure the caisson, notwithstanding the constantly increasing weight of masonry overhead, would tilt a little. Some of the compressed air would escape and a column of water, mud, and loose stones would shoot up on the outside to a height of 30, 40, and even 60 feet. This invariably caused a stampede among the workmen in the outer world. A roaring sound preceded these eruptions, and, due warning of their approach being given, the workmen abandoned the spot with quite as much promptness as formerly, but with far less apprehension of serious consequences. Such disturbances as these were known as "blow-outs." The wave of a passing Sound steam-boat would sometimes disturb the equilibrium of the caisson, and that would cause a "blow-out." In time the workmen within the caisson grew accustomed to such interruptions and paid little attention to them. Oftentimes a fog inside the caisson succeeded a blow-out. For every two feet that the caisson was sunk an additional pound of air pressure had to be applied by the air compressors, until at length the men were compelled to labor under the abnormal pressure of 23 pounds to the square inch. Under such a high pressure one could not even whistle, while a candle snuffed out would immediately ignite again. The material to be excavated was so hard and compact that it could not be broken up with pick and shovel, but steel bars prepared for the purpose had to be driven into it by sledges, and in this way small portions were picked off at a time. So slow was this rate of progress that at first the caisson settled only six inches in a week. The effect of blasting in compressed air was at that time unknown, and it was only after some cautious preliminary tests of the effect of concussion had been made that it was resolved to use gunpowder in the submarine chamber. The first experiment in this direction was the firing of a pistol. No damaging effects, either upon the tympanum or the valves and doors in the air-lock being observable, light blasts were tried. The concussion amounted to nothing, and the use of gunpowder for blasts became an every-day occurrence. As the caisson was divided into six compartments, the workmen very readily protected themselves from flying fragments by stepping from one room into another. The material was transferred to the upper world by means of water shafts.

THE TOWERS AND ANCHORAGES.

Previous borings had demonstrated the necessity of locating the foundations of this tower at least 45 feet below mean water mark. To this depth then the caisson had to be sunk. The work was one of the greatest nicety inside and outside the great wooden box. The correct levels had to be maintained so that there should be no uneven distribution of weight. A mistake at this period meant an error in the erection of the superstructure that might possibly be fatal to the whole bridge scheme. Two memorable events occurred in the sinking of this caisson. One was a blow-out, caused by the neglect of the watchman inside the caisson. The compressed air made its escape and a torrent of water and mud belched out from beneath the sides with a roar that startled pedestrians on Fulton-street into a run for their lives. The muddy column rose to a great height, and in its descent bedaubed shipping along the river and houses near the ferry with a coating of yellow mud. The superincumbent weight upon the caisson at this time was about 17,000 tons. The result of this sudden withdrawal of the support of the compressed air was a settlement of the whole mass—caisson and masonry—10 inches, a crushing of the shoe in some places, and a settlement in the centre of the roof of about four inches. These damages were repaired after a considerable expenditure of time, labor, and money. The fire that was discovered in the caisson on the 29th of December, 1870, was far more destructive. One of the laborers had carelessly placed his lighted candle near a joint in the roof. A fire was communicated to the interior of the timber work, which burned over a space 50 feet square. The first indication of its presence was the discovery of a charred hole the size of a man's fist near the joint where the candle had been carelessly placed. It was never known how long the fire had been silently eating its course through the timber. Carbonic acid gas, water, and steam were turned into this hole in the hope of extinguishing it. Augur-holes bored upward into the roof revealed the fact that the fire was still at work. In his anxiety at this threatening danger, Col. Roebling entered the caisson, where he remained for seven hours. He was partially paralyzed the next morning. The result of that night's labors in the caisson are seen in his shattered health to-day. Flooding the caisson with water was the last resort. The Brooklyn Fire Department was called out, the fire-boat Fuller, and a steamer and tug lent their services, and in five and a half hours the caisson was filled with water. Nearly three months were consumed in making repairs to the caisson. When the work of sinking to the requisite depth had been completed, the interior of the caisson was filled with a liquid mixture of cement and broken stone, the whole hardening and affording as compact a foundation as bed-rock itself. Upon it was reared the Brooklyn tower with its symmetrical gothic arches and its capstones, 271 feet 6 inches above high-water mark. The sinking of the New-York caisson was doubly tedious and troublesome. Nearly twice the depth had to be reached, the air pressure was greater in consequence, and its efforts more disastrous upon the workmen. The experience already gained was valuable. All danger of fire, for instance, was averted by having the caisson lined with boiler-iron. The cost of this was $20,000. The cost of the great fire in the Brooklyn caisson was exactly three-fourths of that sum. The Brooklyn caisson rested upon its bed of rock March 11, 1871, and the New-York caisson in May, 1872, the sinking of the latter having required less than a year's work. The construction of the two towers above the water-line was simple enough after the caisson had been laid. The Brooklyn tower was completed in May, 1875, and the New-York tower in July, 1876. The latter imposes a weight of 90,000 tons of masonry upon its timber foundations, against 70,000 tons in the Brooklyn tower.

Next to the towers in importance are the two anchorages, massive piles of stone weighing 60,000 tons each, and situated 930 feet from the bottom of each tower. Their purpose is two-fold. They not only hold the ends of the cables securely, but they also form a part of the approaches to the suspended floor of the bridge proper. To economize material and labor they were built, not of solid masonry, but with arched passageways running through them lengthwise. Their dimensions are 129 feet in length, 119 feet in width, and 85 feet in height at the river ends. Gradually diminishing in bulk, at the top they are 117 feet in length, 104 feet in width, and 80 feet in height at the land ends. Work was begun on the Brooklyn anchorage in February, 1873. At the bottom of an excavation which had been extended below tide level were laid three courses of yellow pine timber, each stick being 12 inches wide and 12 inches in thickness. Being laid in water sources, they will always be covered and saturated with water; and thus protected from atmospheric changes, they can never decay. Upon this flooring was erected the superstructure of limestone and granite. Deeply imbedded in this mass of masonry are the four anchor plates, (one for each cable,) immense moldings of iron with arms like a star-fish; each plate weighing 23 tons. Riveted to the anchor plates are the wrought-iron anchor bars, which are nothing more than the links in a chain of iron extending from the plates upward through the solid masonry to the top, where they receive the ends of the bridge cables. A device known as a "shoe" is the connecting link between the anchor bars and the cables. Around this shoe are wound the wires which compose the cables. After the cables were spun, several layers of granite were placed in position above the shoes, and the impression gathered from a view of the cables at this point is that the latter spring from the solid rock. Chambers were left in the masonry, however, to enable the engineers at any time to inspect the shoes and determine the condition of the wires. It is estimated that the anchorages will stand 10 times the pressure that can ever be brought to bear upon them. On the other hand, an estimate of the strength of the four cables satisfies the engineers that one of the anchorages could be suspended from them without causing them to break. The New-York anchorage is similar to the Brooklyn anchorage. More difficulty was encountered in building it for it is on made ground at an outskirt of the region known as "the Swamp." In excavating for its foundation the tide-water soaked into the pit so rapidly that engines with a capacity for pumping 600 gallons a minute were employed in freeing the excavation of water. With much labor a foundation of piles was laid, and upon this was erected the superstructure.

The elder Roebling's plans provided for iron approaches, in the form of trestle-work, resting on piers of masonry. The change in the plans has resulted in a more solid structure and in one of the finest viaducts of modern times. The New-York approach particularly is admired for its symmetry and the magnificent curves of its arches. Between Chatham-street to the anchorage—a distance of 1,562 feet 6 inches—seven streets are crossed, all of them by stone arches, except Pearl and Cherry streets. Across Pearl-street, at Franklin-square, has been thrown a substantial iron bridge, to which, in due time, will probably extend stairs leading from the elevated station beneath. At the Chatham-street end of the approach is being erected an iron building so planned as to receive, if it is ever desired to use it for this purpose, cars direct from the elevated railroad. The Brooklyn approach is 971 feet in length, beginning at Sands-street. The grade to the anchorage is easy enough for the heaviest team, being only 2 feet 9 inches in every 100 feet. Prospect, Main, and York streets are each spanned with an iron bridge. A building of iron and glass, to be used for railway purposes, is situated near the Sands-street end of the approach.

MAKING THE BIG CABLES.

With the towers and anchorages completed, the stone age, as it may be conveniently called, gave way to the period of steel. A great deal of delay has occurred in connection with the contracts for furnishing the wire for the cables and the heavy steel for the trusses and girders of the roadway. It was contributed largely on the installment plan and installments somehow or other always seemed to come in when the market price of steel ranged very low. The kind-hearted Trustees could not or would not punish the contractor and his contract dragged along months beyond its allotted time for closing it up. Enough wire was in the bridge yards to enable the work of cable-making to proceed with considerable regularity at first. On the 14th of August, 1876, a wire rope, three-quarters of an inch in diameter, was drawn up the water-front of the Brooklyn tower, passed over its top, and let down again on the opposite side, where its end was seized and carried over the houses to the anchorage. The other end of this rope was placed on a scow and, at a time when there were no passing craft in the river, this was towed to the New-York shore, the rope being paid out into the river just as an ocean cable is laid. Then the rope was drawn up over the tower and carried back to the New-York anchorage and fastened. By means of powerful engines this rope, nearly a mile in length, was stretched to the required degree of tension, and the first link of steel was laid between the two cities. A second rope was extended the same day and their ends were united around driving wheels. The endless rope thus formed served as a traveler to carry other ropes and wires across, running in cast-iron sheaves on the tops of the tops of the towers. As many journeys would have to be taken by the workmen on this traveler, Mr. E. F. Farrington, the master mechanic, decided to show his workmen how easily it was done and to inspire them with courage by an example. A boatswain's buggy, which is nothing more than a short piece of board such as is used in a child's swing, with ropes from its four corners fastened to an iron ring overhead, was rigged up and attached to the traveler. In this frail seat Mr. Farrington seated himself on the afternoon of Aug. 25, 1876. At a given signal the drums were started, and the adventurous voyager began his trip from anchorage to anchorage, starting from the Brooklyn shore. He was whirled over the tops of the houses and the river with amazing rapidity. Workmen stood ready to assist him on the tops of the towers, and having reached the New-York anchorage he turned around and sped back again. Exactly 22 minutes, by President Murphy's watch, had been occupied in making the hazardous journey. Word had gone abroad that something of this nature would be attempted that day, and thousands of spectators gathered in the two cities to watch the event. The firing of cannon, the blowing of whistles by the river craft, and the shouts of the spectators went up in a vast greeting, to the man who sat in the boatswain's buggy, waving his hat with one hand and clinging closely to the ropes with the other. Another endless traveler rope was stretched between the anchorages after this, and then a heavier wire rope known as a carrier. By means of these the three small cables for supporting the cradles, in which the work of building the main cables was to be carried on, were put across and secured in their places over the tops of the towers. Then came the foot-bridge from anchorage to anchorage over the tops of the towers, with wooden slats for its bottom and nothing but a steel wire on either side to serve as a hand rail. Across this dizzy structure hundreds of persons passed. People seemed to be crazy to prostrate themselves on top of the towers. One man started on the journey, got out a few hundred feet, and, calmly lying down, declined to budge an inch in either direction. Mortal terror had seized his soul and he clung like grim death to the wooden slats. Workmen were compelled to go out and get him. Another ambitious gentleman fell down in an epileptic fit halfway between the anchorage and tower, and his legs and arms flew wildly about as he lay on the narrow path—about three feet in width—and sympathetic undertakers who had shops in the vicinity gathered in the expectation of doing all the justice possible to a body that was about to fall 140 feet. Again the bridge workmen intervened and the frothing unfortunate was taken to the ground.

The spinning of the cables fairly began June 11, 1877, and the last wire was run over the river Oct. 15, 1878. Sheds had been put up on top of the Brooklyn anchorage and all the machinery was placed there. Eight enormous drums were put up for each cable. On each 10 miles of wire were wound, making 320 miles in all. The wire, which was made from the best steel and then galvanized, had been dipped in linseed-oil several times until it was well coated. As it was wound on the drums, the end of one coil was fastened to that of the next by a steel ferrule, which had inside screw threads to match those cut in the ends of the wire. At the ends of the cables the wires had to pass shoes which were to be fastened to the anchor chains, and these were put above their places while the wire was run around them, and then they were lowered and made fast. The wire, with one end fast to the shoe, was put over a sheave or wheel which was attached to the traveling rope, and it carried the turn of the wire across the river, making two strands. On the New-York side the turn of the wire was put over another shoe. Another sheave carried over two strands more, and so in each cable, wire after wire was carried across until each strand was completed. The sheaves were sent back empty to start anew. Each separate wire had to be regulated to its proper place by men on the tops of the towers and in cradles, the proper catenarian curve being kept after the first one was made right. For each strand 139 circuits of wire were run out, making 278 wires. The strand was then bound tightly every 15 inches of its length, and formed a rope 3 inches in diameter. At the ends it passed around the shoe or eye-piece, which was fixed, as soon as the strand was done, in its place between the ends of two anchor bars, and held in place by a 7-inch bolt. It took about half an hour to lay and regulate each circuit of wire if no delay was caused. But great obstacles were met with in the force of the wind and in the unequal expansion caused by the sun's rays, and storms and cold weather caused many delays. All the wire was galvanized and then it received five coats of oil to prevent any rusting where the galvanizing might get off. These were the first cables ever made of galvanized steel wire. Each joint, where the wires are screwed together, was also galvanized. The wire was run out to its place at a speed of 11 or 12 feet a second. On the top of the towers the cable strands were laid in saddles, one to [illegible] cable, and so called from the fancied resemblance between their deep groove and the Mexican saddle. Iron rollers were placed in position near by, and over these the wires first passed before being laid in the saddle. Any strain on the cables causing them to deflect at one part makes them move in the saddles, while the rollers take up the strain and prevent any wrenching of the masonry of the tower. Each of the four cables having received its allotted 19 strands, the work of binding them together and wrapping them with wire into a compact cylindrical form was next undertaken. All the temporary wrappings were removed, so that the strands were no longer separate, their wires being brought loosely together. With clamps and squeezers and wooden mallets the one-eighth-inch wires were finally compressed together, and then securely bound in that position by the permanent wrapping of steel wire. Each cable was then painted with white lead and oil, and for miles they could be seen glistening in the sunlight of any fair day. Each cable was 15¾ inches in diameter, or nearly 50 inches around. A remarkable accident happened in connection with the running of the wire on the 19th of June, 1878. One of the great strands broke loose from the New-York anchorage, carrying with it the immense iron "shoe" and its ponderous attachments. The shoe left the anchorage with a "whiz," killing two men outright and took a frightful leap of 900 feet over the tops of houses and streets to the foot of the tower. It rested there for only an instant. The weight of the quarter-mile of wire in the river span jerked it like lightning up the side of the tower, over its top and far out into the river, where it quickly disappeared to the bottom. It was a wonder that none of the river craft were struck by it in its meteoric flight and sent to the bottom to keep it company. Three of the bridge workmen were seriously injured by this accident.

FINISHING THE UNDERTAKING.

Following the completion of the cables came the fastening of the suspender bands to them at intervals of 7½ feet throughout their entire length from anchorage to anchorage. These bands were of wrought-iron, five inches in width and five-eighths of an inch in thickness. They were curved to fit round the cables, and the ends terminate in projections. The band was first heated until it could be opened far enough to go over the cable, and after they were in place they were drawn together by a bolt, which also held the suspender socket. When the bands were all in place the suspender ropes were attached to them. These suspenders are steel ropes varying in length from 170 feet close to the towers to 3 feet in the middle of the central span. They are fastened by sockets to the suspender bands, and at the lower end is a stirrup rod to hold the floor beam in its place. The top of each suspender is fastened in the socket attached to the band by pins driven between the wires and then the whole is filled with melted lead. The ends of the wires are turned over in riveting. Each suspender was tested to sustain 100 tons, and the extreme weight which will come upon each will be only 10 tons.

The suspension of the steel roadway from the suspenders was the closing piece of work in this great enterprise. What a bewildering combination of trusses and beams and girders and cords did this roadway present to the passengers who peered upward from the ferry-boats as month after month it stretched itself along with tortoise-like swiftness! Its weight when finally completed was 6,620 tons. Some idea of the weight imposed upon the bridge can now be formed. The cables weigh 3,460 tons, the suspenders 1,180 tons, the timber flooring 2,760 tons, and the steel rails for the car tracks 660 tons, making the total permanent weight of the bridge 14,680 tons. A transitory load of 3,100 tons can be placed upon it with perfect safety. In general terms, the roadway which will be thrown open to the public this week consists of a steel framework 85 feet in width suspended from the four cables by steel suspenders attached to steel floor beams, seven and one-half feet apart. Six longitudinal trusses divide the flooring into five parts. The two outer parts are for the use of vehicles. The two inner divisions are laid with steel rails and provided with endless wire ropes for hauling across the rapid transit cars. Between the two inner divisions and at some distance above them is the space devoted to foot passengers, 15 feet 7 inches in width, a promenade the most elevated and sightly that the world has ever seen. At the Brooklyn end is the machinery which will move the endless ropes and send the cars speeding across the bridge in five minutes' time. The fare on the cars has been fixed at 5 cents. The toll for foot passengers will be 1 cent, while vehicles will be required to pay a toll varying but little from that now exacted on the ferry-boats. Twenty-four cars will be in operation in trains of four cars each. The cost of this system of rapid transit will be half a million dollars.

Although numerous accidents have occurred and many deaths have been noted among those employed on this wonderful bridge, it is recorded as a somewhat curious fact that no break has occurred in the engineering staff since the death of the elder Roebling. Associated with Col. Roebling from the very beginning of the work were C. C. Martin, Col. W. H. Paine, Francis Collingwood, George W. McNulty, and S. R. Probasco, civil engineers, and E. F. Farrington, master mechanic. That these gentlemen share with Col. Roebling in no small degree the honor of its successful completion is not doubted by the newspaper reporters, who, next to the Trustees, have kept the most faithful watch over this vast enterprise. One of the latest decisions of the Trustees was that of lighting the bridge by electricity, and ornamental supports for the glass globes of the electric system were accordingly placed in position for that purpose.

A table of dimensions and of dates that will prove interesting in connection with this great bridge is the following:

Length of river span, 1,595 feet 6 inches.
Length of each land span, 930 feet.
Full width of bridge flooring, 85 feet.
Height of river span above water, 135 feet 6 inches.
Size of New-York caisson, 172 by 102 feet.
Size of Brooklyn caisson, 168 by 102 feet.
Cubic yards of masonry in New-York tower, 46,945.
Cubic yards of masonry in Brooklyn tower, 38,214.
Length of New-York approach, 1,562 feet 6 inches.
Length of Brooklyn approach, 971 feet.
Depth of New-York foundations below high water, 78 feet 6 inches.
Depth of Brooklyn foundations below high water, 44 feet 6 inches.
Size of towers at high-water mark, 140 by 59 feet.
Size of towers at the top, 136 by 53 feet.
Total height above high water, 271 feet 6 inches.
Height of roadway at towers, 119 feet.
Height of arches above roadway, 117 feet.
Height of towers above roadway, 159 feet.
Width of openings through towers, 33 feet 9 inches.
Weight of each anchorage, 60,000 tons.
Size of anchorages at base, 129 by 119 feet.
Size of anchorages at top, 117 by 104 feet.
Their height in front, 85 feet.
Their height in rear, 80 feet.
Grade of roadway, 3¼ feet in 100.
Number of cables, 4.
Diameter of cables, 15¾ inches.
Length of each cable, 3,578 feet 6 inches.
Miles of wrapping wire on each cable, 243 miles 943 feet.
Number of wires in each cable, 5,282.
Number of suspenders from each cable, main span, 208.
Number of suspenders from each cable, land span, 86.
Number of post bands, each land span, one cable, 35.
Strength of a single suspender, 140,000 pounds.
Sustaining power of each cable, 12,000 tons.
Greatest weight on a single suspender, 20,000 pounds.
Greatest weight on a single cable, 3,000 tons.
Number of overfloor stays, 432.
Total length of wire in each cable, 3,515 miles.
Greatest length of cable wire run in one day, 88 3-5 miles.
First wire rope stretched over the river, Aug. 14, 1876.
River first crossed on a wire rope, Aug. 25, 1876.
Foot-bridge finished and crossed, Feb. 9, 1877.
First cable wire run over and regulated in the elevated position for strand making, May 29, 1877.
Cable-making fairly commenced, June 11, 1877.
Last cable wire run over, Oct. 5, 1878.

May 24, 1883

WORKING UNDERGROUND WIRES.

SUCCESSFUL EXPERIMENTS IN PHILADELPHIA AND CHICAGO.

PHILADELPHIA, Penn., Aug. 16.—The Brooks Underground Conduit Company have completed arrangements for a trial of their system for laying electric wires under ground. It has been maintained that telephone and telegraph wires could not be laid in the same trench or conduit together, no matter how insulated, as the click of the telegraph instrument would, by induction, drown out all messages sent over the telephone wire. This new system of laying wires, as far as the test shows, entirely obviates the difficulty. A number of wires are taken which have been wound with cotton and boiled in paraffine. Thus all watery moisture is driven out and the wires are insulated. From the wires a cable is made. Around the cable another wire is wound, which prevents induction. The cable is then led through wrought-iron pipes sunk 18 inches under ground, and at openings in this pipe, two or three to a block, connection is made with houses and lamp-posts. When the arrangements are completed paraffine-oil from an elevated reservoir is forced into the iron pipe, driving out air and surrounding the cable. In the test of the system the company have a cable of 33 telegraph and telephone wires, which extends from a basement at the north-east corner of Third and Chestnut streets to the Kensington railway station, a distance of two miles and a half. Ten of the wires are in constant use by the Western Union Telegraph Company connecting their office at Tenth and Chestnut streets with New-York. The Telephone wires are laid side by side in the same cable with the telegraph wires. At the telephone, although the 10 telegraph instruments in the office kept up a constant ticking, showing that they were in use. Not an induced sound disturbed the voice of the operator at Kensington as he read the Chief Engineer's report on the water supply or the strains of an organette as it murdered "Pinafore." Besides the fact that underground wires are by far less liable to interruption, it is claimed that by that system a cable of 100 wires can be laid at a cost of $40 a mile per wire, while ordinary over-head telegraph wires cost $100 per mile, and telephone wires $50.

CHICAGO, Aug. 16.—An important step toward relieving the city of the pole nuisance was taken to-day when it was announced that the Postal Telegraph Company had been completely successful in its conduit scheme for carrying wires under ground. Speaking of the results one of the stockholders said to-day officially: "The conduit which we laid from Thirty-ninth-street down Wentworth-avenue to Thirtieth-street, and thence to Lasalle and Washington streets, has proved a complete success. It is now in permanent use by the Postal Telegraph Company, which has leased room for two Paterson cables. This company has experienced no difficulty or inconvenience whatever. The Vandepole Electric Light Company has also placed wires in the conduit from Thirty-third-street to Wentworth-avenue, as a matter of test, and the result has been perfectly satisfactory. Telephone wires have been tried in it with like result. Why, Prof. Elisha Gray, the electrician, and other experts, have made tests to their complete satisfaction, and they all unite in saying that a combination of telegraph, telephone, and electric wires in the conduit will not destroy its utility."

August 17, 1883

BROADWAY TRAFFIC.

P. T. BARNUM'S PLEA FOR A SURFACE RAILROAD.

To the Editor of the New-York Times:

I have always been ardently and persistently opposed to a surface railroad on Broadway. When I kept the American Museum, on the present site of the *Herald* Building, I had several consultations with Mr. A. T. Stewart on this subject, and on one occasion I induced my friend John N. Genin, the hatter, to accompany Mr. Stewart to Albany to oppose in the Legislature such a proposed railroad. But circumstances have materially changed since that time. Omnibuses have become obsolete in all Eastern cities, except New-York, the City of quick transit railroads, which make the snail pace of these lumbering vehicles the more objectionable. They blockade Broadway five times more than a double-track surface railroad would. The private carriages which 15 or 20 years ago were driven in great numbers as low down as Canal-street, now seldom appear in that vicinity. From Union-square to the Battery (and especially to Canal-street) a stupor seems to have settled on Broadway, whereas, above Union-square, where Broadway is many feet narrower, the surface railroad makes business lively, and buildings command good rents. I am convinced that a surface railroad on Broadway is an absolute necessity to the public generally, and to every property-holder from the Battery to Fourteenth-street. I am gratified to know that my opinion is shared by such Broadway property-owners and merchants as the Goelets, Lorillards, Brooks Brothers, W. & J. Sloane, the carpet men, Baldwin, the clothier, James A. Hearn & Son, John Daniell & Son, and many others between Bleecker and Fourteenth-street, as well as many among the wholesale houses below Canal-street. I own 110 feet on Broadway, on the north-east corner of Houston-street, 200 feet deep to Crosby-street, and I submit that it is of great interest to the City Treasury that millions of dollars' worth of Broadway property, which is now half paralyzed and can pay but small taxes, should be electrified into life and value by what has proved in all large cities, and in other parts of New-York City, the most effectual method, viz., a surface railroad.

P. T. BARNUM.

BRIDGEPORT, Conn., Monday, Jan. 20, 1879.

January 23, 1879

THE CABLE ROADS IN CHICAGO.

From the Chicago Inter Ocean.

Of all the new methods for shortening time and space in great cities the most perfect hitherto is that of the cable car system. If one horse can supply the place of a dozen, and still more, if a stationary engine two miles away can eliminate horses almost entirely and furnish more and more rapid accommodation, the gain directly in comfort and indirectly in the spread of the population, is incalculable. That the cable system presents the highest degree of excellence yet attained for city travel needs no demonstration. A short experience was necessary to habituate the public to the cable cars. But, now that we are all familiar with them, every one knows precisely how to deal with them. The cable company have done a work that thinking people will not fail to recognize. Abused and villified, as all good things are; denounced, as every step of progress has been; every man, woman, and child in Chicago now points to the cable cars as one of the most valuable and progressive enterprises of Chicago. The citizen enjoys a quiet chuckle as he does homage to his own superior knowledge at the expense of the mystified looks and questions of his country cousin. We all feel ourselves on a higher plane of intelligence from our being a part of the city with its cable railroad, as well as the other institutions that constitute the pride of Chicago. No wonder this system has been a great success. Over 100 grip cars and more than 300 box cars constantly passing, always occupied and in the mornings and evenings crowded, an army of workmen, and a finance system away up in the millions, present the idea of great public usefulness. There is not one man of us who would not be proud to own a slice, notwithstanding all the detraction of the "early days." It is well known not only that the cable road has immensely increased the value of all real property along the route, but everywhere within convenient access of that route. The extension of the same system through those portions of our chief thoroughfares not yet occupied would be hailed with delight by every man owning a 50-foot lot.

No man can contend that the cable company has not provided locomotion good, cheap, and effective. They deserve their success. The rate of speed is far greater than that attained from a motive power of horses, while the condition of the track is infinitely superior. The cable-car system constitutes the finest method of locomotion ever introduced here or elsewhere.

August 16, 1885

THE PASSING OF THE HORSE CAR.

Evidence accumulates from week to week that both horse power and cables are soon to be displaced on nearly all American street railways by electric force. The Boston *Commercial Bulletin* of last Saturday recorded the closing of contracts by one company for the equipment of eighty-three miles of road on eleven street railways in as many cities, and this appears to have been the report of only one week's transactions. The Chicago *Tribune* published two weeks ago a long account of experiments made in Minneapolis, and announced that as a result of these tests a contract for the equipment of 200 miles of road in St. Paul, Minneapolis, and the intervening district had been made. It was shown in a paper read before the American Institute of Electrical Engineers in May, 1887, that there were then in operation in this country thirteen electric railways, carrying about three million five hundred thousand passengers annually, and it is stated by competent authority that there are now in operation or in course of construction 179 such roads, using nearly 2,000 cars and 1,260 miles of track.

Many very interesting facts relating to this substitution of electric force for horses or cable systems are set forth in *Scribner's Magazine* for April by Mr. JOSEPH WETZLER, who traces in an illustrated article the history of the electric railway. The average reader who cares for information on this subject will turn first, perhaps, to what is said about the commercial aspect of the change. The displacement of horse power and cables now going on furnishes some evidence that the use of electric force does not decrease the profits of a street railway company, but there still lingers in many minds an impression that the use of that force increases the cost of operation. Mr. WETZLER says that it has been "completely demonstrated" that "the operation of street railways by electricity" is "more economical than by either horses or cables," but the statistical proof of this does not seem to have been prepared. An investigation recently made shows that the average cost of electric motive power on the roads in Washington, Richmond, Cleveland, and Scranton is about 5 cents per car mile. At the annual meeting of the American Street Railway Association in Minneapolis last September a committee that had been directed to inquire concerning electric railways submitted a report of which the following was a part:

"If it is desired to make a change from horse power, electricity will fill the bill to perfection, no matter how long or short the road or how many passengers are carried. In the investigation of the subject the most satisfactory results have been shown; it not only increases the traffic over the road, but reduces expense, and actually enables us to operate at a profit a line which heretofore entailed a loss."

This committee made estimates of the cost of equipping a railway ten miles long with cables, with overhead electric wires, and with electric storage batteries, respectively, and these estimates were as follows, in the order named above: $840,000, $190,000, $175,000. In each of the electric systems the cost of roadbed and power plant was only $100,000, while in the case of a cable system the cost of these was $825,000.

Mr. WETZLER publishes tables in which the gross and net earnings of a street railway in Davenport, Iowa, while horse power was used, are compared with those yielded in a corresponding period after the substitution of electricity. The average monthly increase of net earnings was 210 per cent., while the increase of gross earnings was 55 per cent. "Other places," he says, "have shown still more remarkable results, but the reticence of the managers of these roads naturally prevents the publication of what might otherwise be regarded as almost apochryphal earnings."

We shall be glad to see complete statistics concerning this question of comparative cost, and we presume they will soon be available. The publication of them would bring nearer that day when, as Mr. WETZLER says, "there will not be a single horse railway in operation, at least in our own country," a day that, in his opinion, may be reached in ten years. The displacement of the horses and the stables now in use should be hastened in the interests of sanitation, if for no other reason.

March 31, 1890

TROLLEYS FROM CITY TO CITY.

Our exchanges contain many paragraphs relating to projected or completed electric railways between cities in various parts of the country, and a map showing all such lines now in operation or soon to be finished would disclose many electric parallels of steam railways. We have recently explained the situation in Connecticut, where the expansion of electric systems has been checked to some extent by the purchase of electric lines in the interest of the dominant steam corporation. In some parts of the West the paralleling of steam roads has been undertaken on a larger scale. For example, it is announced that the electric road from Akron to Cleveland, Ohio, will be in operation in a few weeks. The distance is about thirty miles, and passengers will be transferred in Cleveland to any of the city lines without additional cost. This road practically parallels a steam road, and the city transfers give it a very perceptible advantage. Moreover, an electric road from Cleveland to Elyria, more than twenty miles, and also a parallel, will soon be finished.

In Massachusetts it is the purpose of the Directors of the Conway Road to extend their tracks to Deerfield, Greenfield, Ashfield, and Plainfield, and to make connection with the line from Greenfield to Turner's Falls. While the proposed extensions will lie partly in districts not well served now by steam roads, they will also affect in some measure the passenger traffic of the Fitchburg and Connecticut River Railroads. It may be noted that work has been begun on an electric line between Norwich and New-London, in Connecticut, which will parallel an existing steam road. We mention these new roads and projects simply as examples, without making any attempt to enumerate all of the interesting and significant movements in this field which are noticed in the pr[illegible]s. The growth of inter-urban electric lines promises to be large in the near future.

November 27, 1895

THE GROWTH OF CITIES.

It is unfortunate that the census bulletin showing the growth of cities during the past ten years does not give more fully the reasons for the figures which it presents. The fact that the cities are steadily gaining in population at the expense of the rural neighborhoods is full of interest, but the interest is increased when it is known that the reason for this apparent shifting of population is found in the fact that trolley lines have permitted the cities to annex and make part of themselves suburbs which, until electric railroads were made practical, were as much country as the corn fields of districts still too remote from the centres of population to admit of consideration as even possibly a part of them. The cities which show populations of 100,000 or more are now 38 in number, against 28 ten years ago. Those of 50,000 and over are 78, against 58; those of 25,000 and over are 161, against 124. Cities of 5,000 to 50,000 have increased in number from 566 to 759, and about this ratio is maintained as the scale declines.

The number of cities of 1,000,000 and over is the same as in 1890, and in this class (1) are found New York, Chicago, and Philadelphia. Class 2, of half a million up, also made up of three cities, includes St. Louis, Boston, and Baltimore. Class 3, of 400,000 to 500,000, which had 3 cities ten years ago, has none this year, all of those composing it having been advanced to Class 2. Class 4, composed of cities of 300,000 to 400,000, is wholly made up of cities advanced from Class 5 of 1890, and now includes Cleveland, Buffalo, Cincinnati, San Francisco, and Pittsburg. Class 5 includes New Orleans, Milwaukee, Detroit, and Washington, which were there in 1890, and has gained by promotion Newark, Jersey City, Louisville, and Minneapolis. Class 6, comprising cities of 100,000 to 200,000, 19 in all, has gained 7 since the last enumeration. The next ten years will undoubtedly show great gains in the number of cities of the third, fourth, fifth, and sixth classes. Since 1850 the percentage of urban population to the total population of the country has increased as shown in the following table:

	Per Cent.		Per Cent.
1850	12.5	1880	22.6
1860	16.1	1890	29.2
1870	20.9	1900	33.1

In looking for an explanation of the astonishing growth of urban populations it is not necessary to go beyond the improvement in facilities for communication between centres of population and their suburbs. About 1850 the horse car became in a small way a factor in determining the diffusion of population, gradually building up suburbs to which the leisure classes withdrew when seeking rural surroundings without entire separation from the advantages of nearness to a city. Anything within an hour of the business centre of a town or city was considered as admitting of suburban development, and an hour by the horse car did not take the passenger very far afield. With the passing of the horse car and the advent of the trolley car, the area of accessible suburbs expanded very rapidly. In an hour a passenger is whirled past the utmost limit of horse car service and into what five or ten years ago were farm lands, worth no more by the acre than they are now valued at per villa site, or under exceptionally favorable conditions per front foot. The suburbs were removed five, six, eight, and even ten miles from the former city limits, and the near-by neighborhoods were left no recourse except to annex themselves to, and become wards of, the cities they had formerly surrounded. Chicago furnishes a striking illustration of this in its recent growth by the annexation of outlying territory containing 598,725 residents, thus jumping its population 54½ per cent. What it thus assimilated represented a city larger than St. Louis. The same tendency is noticeable in nearly every large city, and it is encouraged and facilitated by the electric railroad, which is bringing everything within a radius of five to ten miles as near for all practical purposes as neighborhoods within the mile or two mile radius used to be. This means that what under the conditions existing before the era of electric railroads would have been a relatively small city surrounded by a fringe of villages, and having within a given number of square miles a population about equally divided for purposes of census tabulation between the urban and rural classifications, is now a city of steadily widening boundaries and with, say, twice the population which could be comfortably accommodated within its original municipal limits.

Probably the most noteworthy example of this spreading out of cities which will ever be seen will be furnished with the completion of the New York Rapid Transit Tunnel in the building of a radiating system of electric railroads connecting its northern terminus with every part of the country north and east of us available for residence purposes. In these roads we shall see very little in either construction, equipment, or operation suggestive of street railway practice. As showing what is meant by electric railroading at this time, it may be mentioned that the one-hundred-million-dollar syndicate owning the electric roads of Northern Ohio and Southwestern Michigan are now arranging to put on between Cleveland and Detroit a service of sleeping cars and a freight and express system which will bring their line into direct competition with the steam roads for every class of business. With such facilities, combined with high speeds and low fares, New York may very well count upon a rapid northern expansion along as many lines of development as there are ribs in a Japanese fan. Will our esteemed friends of the New York Central, the New Haven, and the Harlem railroads learn nothing until it is taught them in the costly school of experience?

August 19, 1901

BOSTON'S SUBWAY FINISHED

After Many Protests and Complaints Rapid Transit for the Hub Is Assured.

THE COST WAS $5,000,000

Perfection of the Project May Result in the Erection of an Elevated Railroad, Arrangements for Which Have Already Been Made.

BOSTON, Aug. 14.—Within a very short time, by the 1st of September it is expected, Boston's much-talked-of subway will be in partial operation. The completion of the work will not only call attention to a feat of engineering exceedingly expensive—for the subway represents an outlay of over $5,000,000—but difficult as well, for its course has been laid through the business portion of the two principal streets, Tremont and Washington. From the northern terminus at the Union Station, not far from the Charlestown Bridge, to the southern end at Tremont, Pleasant Street, and Shawmut Avenue, this tunnel comprehends a distance of one and one-third miles, and over it are maintained some of the most important business enterprises of the city. Boston will be the first city of the country to have in operation through its centre the European transit system.

That so conservative an American town should happen to be the pioneer in adopting this is viewed as remarkable. This project was not got under way, however, without the most determined objection on the part of Boston's staid citizens, and after it was begun litigation was so interposed that many times the Commissioners who had the work in charge were almost in despair. The idea of Tremont Street being torn up caused widespread complaint, but when the sacred Common came to be disturbed there was dismay. The thought of that iron fence being removed and the graves in the old cemetery situated on the Common, at the southeast corner of Tremont and Boylston Streets, being disturbed was more than the "oldest inhabitants" could bear. Lengthy epistles concerning the "outrage" descended upon the office of the Transit Commission, but that body was obdurate and was not deterred by such comparative trivialities.

The digging kept on, and when a screaming steam engine was set up at the portals of Park Street Church full many a wail was emitted through the Boston papers. For months, while excavating along Tremont Street mall was in progress, one could walk along in front of the stores and hear such remarks as these: "Isn't that a pretty looking sight!" "Well there! if it hadn't been at a time when the best people were away for the Summer they never would have got the franchise for that subway through the City Council!" But as things went along, and the mall, which had been an ugly ditch surrounded by beams and boards, was relaid and as level as of yore, Boston, after the way of a venerable dame who survives the shock of moving from the ancestral cottage to a modern residence, began to look upon the impudent innovation with a degree of complacence.

Now the better informed and more progressive of Bostonians regard the subway as an enterprise calculated to be of inestimable municipal value, one which, with the proposed Boston elevated road, will aid in solving the seemingly insurmountable transit perplexities and give the Hub a footing among the cities that take pride in the present rather than tearfully commemorate the past.

Subway a Necessity.

The subway has not been a matter of money-making enterprise, but one of necessity—necessity for some means of getting rid of the street car blockades on Tremont and Washington Streets. No venturesome desire to evolve a revenue-producing business undertaking actuated those who began this project. It was simply realized that as Boston and her suburbs increased in population the narrow, tortuous, down-town streets were congested with a traffic that in some way must be provided with an outlet. As the result of continued agitation, the Boston Transit Commission was created in June, 1891. This commission was granted full authority by the Legislature to deal with the subject of transit to and in the City of Boston. In considering the subject, among the various plans proposed were the forming of an "alley" line, running north and south between Washington and Tremont Streets, the widening of Tremont Street, and the running of street cars on the Common. All of these, on close investigation, were found to be faulty.

The "alley" scheme would involve an expenditure of over $6,000,000 in acquiring right of way, to say nothing of other obstacles. Finally, the plan of a subway seemed to be the most advantageous, since it would take all traffic from the streets, and little property would be destroyed in constructing it. This was the course decided on. For the purpose of obtaining some accurate idea of the work such an avenue must be called on to serve, on the Saturday before Christmas, 1894, a count was made of the number of people taking and leaving the cars from West Street to Bromfield Street. These are near the Park Street Church, and lead from Tremont to Washington Street. It was found that the total number that got on or off the cars at this point, between the hours of 6 in the morning and 12 at night, was 64.659. The maximum for any one hour was 8,450.

Beginning of the Work.

On March 28, 1895, the first spadeful of earth was removed in the Public Garden at a point opposite the Providence Railway station, just across Boylston Street. The ceremony was attended by Gov. Greenhalge, the Chairman of the Transit Commission, and various city officials. According to the design, when the subway is completed there will exist an underground passage from the Union Station to Boylston and Tremont Streets which will contain four street car tracks, the tunnel being, in general, 46 feet wide by 15 feet in height. From this locality two lines of track extend southward to Tremont and Pleasant Streets, a distance of a half mile, and two westward under Boylston Street to the point, as before indicated, where operations were first commenced, a distance of about a quarter of a mile. In the work of digging difficulties and obstacles were encountered that perplexed the contractors sorely. One of the first was the discovery of a lot of old graves along the Boylston Street mall.

A Commissioner was appointed to take charge of this, and as fast as the remains were disturbed they were removed to a plat in the common burial ground. This proceeding was watched with interest by antiquarians and citizens, and an exuberant crop of advice and reminiscence resulted. Besides the Boylston Street graves, the common burial ground, the Granary burial ground, and the King's Chapel were in the path of the proposed subway. These latter were, by use of great care, but little molested. The most serious obstruction of all was the perfect network of gas and water mains and electric light wires that were laid in the streets to be dug up. It was the gas escaping from mains, supposed to have been injured by the digging, that, coming in contact with the sparks from the wheels of a passing electric car, caused the terrible accident on March 4 last at the corner of Boylston and Tremont Streets, wherein nine persons were killed and several dangerously hurt.

The masonry and iron work of this subway are of as solid and lasting a construction as it has been possible to make, and engineers say that no work of the kind has been undertaken in years that can excel Boston's subway for safety. The roof of this tunnel is 24 inches through, resting on a great framework of steel beams over a foot thick. The side walls are composed first of a layer of concrete a foot deep, next two inches of ribbed tiling, then four inches of brick, next a half inch of cement mortar, a half inch of asphalt water proofing, and finally three feet of solid concrete.

A Comfortable Retreat.

As the subway now exists, that portion from the Public Garden entrance to Park Street Church is completed, and one descending to it observes a series of walls so neatly covered with enameled brick that the place has a most inviting appearance, and it will certainly be a comfortable retreat on a hot day. The entrance stations overhead along the Tremont Street mall have all been erected and are plain, low granite structures, suggesting at first sight a sort of mausoleum. By the first of next month all the cars that run west and southwest of Boston will be sent in at the Public Garden end of the subway, travel up under the Boylston Street mall to Tremont, thence to the loop below Park Street Church, and back over another track out of the tunnel. The passage will be fully provided with pure air at every 600 feet, a fan of sufficient power being arranged to remove the total air contents of its section once in ten minutes. The form of fan chosen is the result of exhaustive tests recently made. That for the double-tracked division is seven feet in diameter, and that for the four-tracked is eight. These fans will be driven by electric motors.

As the labor of building is at present progressing it is almost certain that the entire subway, with terminal stations and all equipments, will be completed within a few months. The old Boston and Maine station, at Haymarket Square, near the northern end of the subway, was purchased by the Transit Commission for $750,000. This station is now being dismantled, and the large terminal station of the subway will be soon erected. This will be large enough to accommodate extra cars, as will also a big terminal station to be built at Pleasant and Tremont Streets, the southern end.

It is estimated that the entire cost of this extensive project will represent $1,500,000 for purchase of requisite real estate and $3,500,000 for construction. The chief method for realizing revenues has been the sale of bonds from time to time, amounts being issued as demanded.

A striking fact in connection with the creating of the subway is that out of this project has grown the prospect of an elevated railroad, something that in all probability never would have arisen in any other event. The actual truth that Boston had set about partly solving her transit problem gave new inspiration to those who hoped to go further. Last Winter, by the enfranchising of an elevated road company, in which the West End Street Railway (the controlling corporation of the kind in this city) was interested, an arrangement was made whereby the West End Company was granted a lease of the subway with the view to using the same in conjunction with the elevated road. It is therefore not unlikely that within a couple of years Boston need not be ashamed of her transit facilities.

August 15, 1897

RAPID TRANSIT IN CHICAGO

Remarkable Facilities Furnished by the Opening Last Week of the "Loop."

CHICAGO, Oct. 23.—When the trains of the "Alley L" began running around the "loop" this week Chicago witnessed the opening of the most unique system of street railway transportation in the country. The three separate cities of which Chicago is practically composed, are now in direct railway connection with each other for the first time. The three elevated roads—and a fourth will soon be running—bring passengers from the north, south, and west divisions to the heart of the city, which is encircled by elevated tracks known as the "loop" and used by all the roads in common. The loop runs around all that part of the city contained between Wabash and Fifth Avenues and Van Buren and Lake Streets, and it is expected that each of the 1,000 trains to make use of it will take twelve minutes for a trip. Passengers from one portion of the city to another can be transferred without leaving the stations; the time for such a trip is reduced fully one half, and the convenience and comfort of the journey are increased immeasurably. However, it will still continue to cost two fares to go from one division of Chicago to another.

Considerable relief of the congested condition of the streets down town is expected from the operation of the loop. But neither this or the other advantages gained by the people suffice to counterbalance the injury done to the streets and property through the erection of the structure on some of the most valuable of the city's thoroughfares. It is estimated that the "Alley L," which runs south, increased its traffic by 11,000 passengers on the first day of travel around the loop.

October 24, 1897

THE DAY WE CELEBRATE.

Among the occasions for strictly municipal celebration which New York has had, in the course of a history so lengthening that it is now becoming, speaking even the language of world history, long, the opening to-day of the Rapid Transit Subway has not been matched for two generations. The celebration of the introduction of the Croton water is the latest that can be paralleled with this, and that was sixty years ago. A quarter of a century behind that was the celebration of the completion of the Erie Canal, the great work which, bringing art to the assistance of the nature which had at once given New York its unrivaled harbor, and broken through, at the head of navigation of the Hudson River, the wall of the Appalachian chain, fixed definitively Manhattan Island as the metropolis of the Western Hemisphere.

It was then, with the completion of the Erie Canal, that, as the destiny of New York was made manifest, the obligation of planning New York to fulfill that destiny became or should have become manifest also. We blame too much the replanners of New York whose labors were deprived in 1807 of the prevision which had become a common possession by 1825, and to which FENIMORE COOPER, at about the latter date, gave expression in forecasting with singular approximation the population and the position of New York at the end of the century of which the first quarter only had elapsed. But the Commissioners of 1807 were blamable all the same. They were providing for a great city, for a city of a million on Manhattan Island alone, and they omitted to take account of the configuration which constituted the very crux of their problem, and made it certain that the need of transit north and south would be the most urgent need of the growing city as it grew toward the confines of their street system. They provided absurdly ample facilities for travel east and west, for a street every 200 feet, as if the chief needs of the coming population were to be for free and unimpeded transit between the two rivers. But for the longitudinal movement of the population of an island thirteen miles long by only two in width they provided only by one longitudinal artery for every four lateral arteries. Madison Avenue and Lexington Avenue were interpolated in their scheme before it had fairly gone into operation, as an urgently necessary corrective, though a very insufficient one, to their faulty dispositions. True, they had no prevision of means of locomotion faster than horse power, and their notions of public conveyance were limited to the application of horse power to the omnibuses which in their time, and almost down to ours, formed the reliance of suburban London. At an early day it came to be recognized that a man doing business in the city would not as a rule endure or consent to live more than three-quarters of an hour from his business. With the omnibuses, that meant a distance of four miles or thereabout. Forty-fifth Street would have been and remained the outer residential limit of Manhattan under the régime of the "stages." The introduction of the car tracks, which many New Yorkers now living can remember, added, by increasing the speed, say, half a mile to the limit of population. But meanwhile steam had come in as an instrument of traction. At the close of the civil war Fiftieth Street was the practical upper limit of residence on Manhattan Island, all beyond being given to market gardens, to the "villas" of residents who did not need to come into town every day, or to the settlements, like Audubon Park and Fort Washington, that were served by steam railroads. Harlem was not so much a suburb as a self-sufficient and self-subsutent settlement, Yorkville was a wilderness sparsely interspersed with cottages and villas. The owners of land north of the southern boundary of Central Park found the tenants whom they regarded as their proper prey slipping away from them not only to Brooklyn, but by ferry and railroad to the Oranges in New Jersey, to Jamaica and Flushing on Long Island, even to Yonkers and Tarrytown on the northern mainland. Their problem was how to bring their land into use as available for residence of men who earned their rentals and their livings down town. That was the municipal problem of the seventh decade of the nineteenth century.

Almost the first movement that was made toward its solution was the grandiose and monumental project of a viaduct road, buying its right of way through the blocks and selling or renting so much of its substructure as it did not need, which commended itself to the judgment, or at least to the imagination, of PETER B. SWEENY, the "brains" of the Tweed Ring, just about a full generation ago. But the scale of the enterprise staggered private investors after the project had been relegated to private enterprise by the collapse of the ring. There were experiments in subterranean transit. A relic of these may still be seen in the form of a section of the "Beach Pneumatic Tunnel" in Broadway, opposite the City Hall Park, by whoso will take the trouble to dive or excavate for it. But the first really practical measures for relief were the elevated roads, of which the practicability was indicated by the fact that they began almost simultaneously under the auspices of three several corporations, that on Ninth Avenue being the first opened for traffic.

The crisis was passed, and the completion of the roads assured, when the Legislature was induced to declare that the building of an elevated railroad in a public street was a "public use" of the street, and therefore could not be enjoined, leaving the aggrieved land owners to their several and private remedies in actions for damages. It was in 1877 and 1878 that the elevated railroads began to be a real factor in the development of Manhattan, that they began to build up a solid "east side" from Cooper Union to Harlem Bridge, and to develop that new "west side" which is to-day one of our proudest municipal possessions. First the substitution of cables, and then the substitution of underground trolleys for the original horse power enabled the surface lines effectively to supplement, and to some extent to rival, the elevated roads. But, until to-day, the elevated roads, gorged and congested as they have become, even since the introduction of electric traction, by a demand beyond their capacity to supply, have formed the swiftest and surest means of communication between the upper and lower halves of Manhattan Island.

October 27, 1904

THE EFFECT OF THE SUBWAY.

In modern city life distance is measured in time, and time is not only money in the old sense—it is health, vigor, education, and morality. That is to say, reduction in the time of transit between home and work opens up great regions where these blessings are possible, as they are not in congested city districts. The essential advantage of the subway system is the extension of the home area, and great as is this advantage from the lines to be formally opened to-day, that which will follow the development of like lines already sure will be far more vast. It is already a question of vital benefit to a population of three and a half millions; it will within a few years be a matter of vital benefit to a population at least half as large again. We are dealing in this system, which has become in a measure familiar, and which we regard with no amazement, with a body of citizens larger than the population of the United States when WASHINGTON was elected President.

It is not generally realized to what degree, even under the imperfect means of transit we have had in the past, the growth of the population working and doing business in New York has been in the outlying districts. Comparing the registration for this year with the vote in 1892 we find that more votes will be cast in the region above the south line of Central Park than were cast a dozen years ago in what was then the entire city. In like manner on the other side of the East River the regions east and south of the old City of Brooklyn will cast three times as many votes as a dozen years ago, and the increase is larger than in the old city. In this brief period there has settled in the "new" parts of what is now New York a population as great as that of St. Louis and Cleveland combined. The effect of actual rapid transit on the daily life of such a community is in all soberness of greater importance than is the result of many a battle famous in history.

Speaking generally, thirty minutes is the limit of real convenience for a journey night and morning, and an hour may be called the maximum limit within which work and business can be reached without a serious impairment of efficiency. Thirty years ago this extreme limit was reached toward the north at Fifty-ninth Street. By the use of the branch of the rapid transit system opened to-day and its connections, less than a half hour will take passengers at least a dozen miles from the City Hall, and an hour to the confines of Westchester County. The terminus of the west side line at One Hundred and Forty-fifth Street is as near in time as the Fifth Avenue Hotel was thirty years ago, while New Rochelle and Yonkers are as near as Central Park then was. But the part of the system made available to-day will in some respects be surpassed in its effect on the life of the city by that which is in process of construction, and the connections that will be made. The old familiar and long desperate cry of "fifteen minutes to Harlem" is now satisfied. In a few years fifteen minutes will place passengers equally far away toward the east and northeast and southeast on Long Island. The tunnel building under the East River at the lower end of the city, the tunnel building by the Pennsylvania near the centre of Manhattan, with the lines already in operation or planned, will open up a region now thinly settled, stretching in semi-circle from a dozen to a score of miles in radius. Within these limits and those extended to the north by the present lines a population of ten millions can be, and we believe will be, housed comfortably, healthfully, and relatively cheaply. That is the future which the rapid transit system has made not the dream of visionaries, but the calculable and reasonable aim of engineers, capitalists, and the Municipal Government.

October 27, 1904

CHICAGO'S SKY SCRAPERS.

THE WINDY CITY PASSES INTO AN ERA OF VERY HIGH BUILDINGS.

CHICAGO, March 8.—Probably the most notable thing about this city at the present time is the enormous amount of building being done in the central portion. A round dozen buildings are in process of erection which will be from ten to twenty stories in height. The Masonic Temple, to cost $3,000,000, will be twenty stories high, and the "Monadnock" office building and the one to be used as an apartment store by "The Fair" will each be sixteen stories high. In the case of the Masonic Temple, five-story stores, paying large returns on the amount of the investment, were torn down to make way for the larger structure.

This may be said to mark a distinct epoch in the history of the city. Heretofore there has been plenty of room for the expansion of trade. New "districts," devoted to dry goods stores, to office structures, and other uses, have been laid out on land outside the lines of the compact business portion of the city. This process of growth will probably not cease. But there seems to have been a reflex action caused by the expansion of the city to inconvenient distances, and in consequence the old buildings hastily erected after the "big fire" of 1871 are giving way to modern structures of from ten to twenty stories and fitted up with every convenience.

This remodeling process has been going on in a small way for two or three years, but lately some of the largest and best paying office buildings in the city have been purchased by capitalists who propose either to tear them down altogether or put in new foundations under the old buildings, add three to six stories to them, and make them over. It is nearly twenty years since the "Big fire." Many of the buildings which were erected then were paid for by Eastern capital. That these buildings are passing into the hands of Chicago capitalists for improvement shows that the city has more than recovered the ground lost by the great conflagration.

March 9, 1891

ALL READY FOR OPENING DAY

CONDITIONS OF THE WORLD'S FAIR BUILDINGS AND GROUNDS.

The White Palaces Completed—Some of the Exhibits Much More Forward Than Others—The Area Under Roof—The Administration Building the Most Beautiful on the Grounds—Decoration of the Dome—The Styles of Architecture—The Positions of the Buildings Described.

CHICAGO, April 29.—From the time when it was decided that the World's Fair was to be in Chicago and the local Board of Directors laid out a scheme of buildings which in magnitude and beauty promised to be grander and more splendid than any ever erected in the history of the world for a similar purpose, there have been the usual number of croakers who have pretended to believe that these imposing plans could never be carried out.

At one time, when the foundations of the buildings were being laid, the work seemed to drag. Even before this there was delay in the choice of a site in this city. But as soon as the work of construction was really under way it went on slowly but surely. Stupendous obstacles were overcome one after another. The men in charge of the general oversight of the work took no chances. They compelled the contractors to keep every contract to the letter.

They were determined that the promise of the Directory to have the fair in readiness for the opening day should be kept. They wanted to make the croakers eat their words. And they have succeeded.

On the day before the opening the buildings and grounds are in almost perfect order. All of the main buildings are completed. Such buildings as are not ready are those which were added to the original number as the demand for space increased, or to meet the requirements of ideas which did not enter into the original plan. If the exposition officials had two weeks more of good weather before the opening, their part of the contract would have been executed so perfectly that there would be no room for criticism. As it is, no fault can be found with them.

The most noticeable inconvenience which the early visitor to the fair will encounter will be found at the entrances, where the roads are in a deplorably muddy condition. The city and fair management have united finally to pave the streets leading to the grounds. This should have been done earlier. Inside the grounds the roads are in a passable condition except in wet weather, when they become sticky with red mud. But the tardiness of exhibitors in sending their displays made it necessary to delay putting the finishing surface on the roads until after the heavy teaming was finished.

Though the buildings are complete, the exhibits are not. Some departments are much more forward than others. It seemed to be impossible to make exhibitors understand the importance of have their material on the grounds early. They all procrastinated. The result has been that for the last few weeks exhibits which should have been here early in the Winter have been arriving at the rate of 300 cars each day. This rush at the last minute has made more work for everybody and has resulted in such a crush as to impede the work of installation still more. For the last two weeks the laborers in the installation department have been working day and night.

Notwithstanding the large number of exhibits which are not ready for inspection, there is enough to keep visitors busy for many days. There are 200 buildings within the precincts of the inclosure of 633 acres. For any one person to see all the exhibits will be impossible, though he should devote his entire time to it from May to November. The mind will be confused and oppressed in the effort to inspect and enjoy such a wilderness of objects of beauty and wonder. The fact is that even a walk around and between the great buildings, with a casual gaze at their exterior and a passing thought of their contents, will prove almost bewildering.

Although so much has been written about "The White City" and its magnificent buildings, the first sight of them never proves disappointing. They are more imposing and more beautiful than the imagination pictured them.

"I had no conception of the extent, variety, or splendor of these buildings" is the exclamation, mental or verbal, of every visitor when he enters the park. The appearance of the magnificent group of main buildings around the lagoons is so different from anything in the United States, is so un-American, that it startles the imagination. Figures can give some idea of the size of these palaces, but the architecture in its infinite detail must truly be seen to be appreciated.

When it is remembered that the area under roof is equal to that of Paris in 1889, Philadelphia in 1876, and Vienna in 1873 combined, that the cost of the main buildings is estimated roughly at over $6,700,000, some conception of the thought, the care, and the labor which they represent may be obtained. The Administration Building is considered the gem of the exposition palaces. It is situated at the west of the great court in the southern part of the site, looking eastward, and at its rear are the transportation facilities. The great gilded dome of this lofty building is one of the most striking architectural features in the grounds.

There is no dome in this country to which this one can be compared. It is finer in every respect than any other on the Western Hemisphere. Richard M. Hunt is the architect. This imposing edifice cost $463,213. It covers an area of 260 feet square, and consists of four pavilions 84 feet square, one at each of the four angles of the square and connected by a great central dome 120 feet in diameter and 220 feet in height, leaving at the centre of each façade a recess 82 feet wide, within which are the grand entrances to the building. The general design is in the style of the French Renaissance. The first story is in the Doric order. It is of heroic proportions, and is surrounded by a lofty balustrade. The great tiers of the angle of each pavilion are crowned with sculpture. The Ionic style of architecture is represented in the second story, with its lofty and spacious colonnade.

The four entrances, one on each side of the building, are 50 feet wide and 50 feet high, deeply recessed and covered by semi-circular arched vaults. In the rear of these arches are the entrance doors and above them great screens of glass, giving light to the central rotunda. Across the face of these screens, at the level of the office floor, are galleries of communication between the different pavilions. The interior of this building exceeds in beauty and splendor even the exterior, imposing as that is. Between every two of the grand entrances and connecting the intervening pavilion with the great rotunda is a hall 30 feet square, giving access to the offices, and provided with broad circular stairways and commodious elevators.

From the top of the cornice in the second story rises the interior dome 200 feet from the floor. In the centre is an opening, 50 feet in diameter, transmitting a flow of light from the exterior dome overhead. The under side of the dome is enriched with deep panelings, richly molded, and these panelings are filled with sculpture in low relief and immense paintings representing the arts and sciences. The sculptor of the Administration Building is Karl Bitter of New-York. He executed the groups on the small domes and, among other subjects, groups representing "Commerce," "Industry," "Justice," "Religion," "War," "Peace," "Science," and "Art."

The decoration of the dome has been done by William Leftwich Dodge, the youn[illegible]t painter commissioned by the exposition. The space covered by Mr. Dodge's painting is 315 feet in circumference, and 40 feet from apex to base. The subject of the painting is "The Glorification of the Arts." On a throne, which is seen in the portion of the dome opposite the main entrance to the building, Apollo is seated crowning the Arts as they approach from either side. There are ninety-five important figures in the composition, and those in the foreground are 25 feet in height.

In this building are the offices of the Director General and his staff, and the headquarters of the newspapers from every quarter of the globe.

Emerging from the east entrance of the building, the visitor will stand on the spot where the dedication ceremonies will take place, and where President Cleveland will touch the button that starts the machinery. Immediately in front of the building is a plaza 200 yards square, and in the distance lies the most enchanting architectural and landscape scene in the exposition. Its central feature is an immense basin of water, probably 300 by 1,000 feet in size, fringed with balustrades, symbolical pillars, terraces, grass plats, and flower beds. In the foreground is MacMonnies's wonderful fountain representing Columbia seated on the ship of state, which is steered by Father Time, and on the prow of which stands the figure of Fame. This vessel is driven through the water by eight girls standing at the oars, four on either side.

Around the circumference of the basin are young men on horses, and mermaids and cherubs disport themselves in the waves in the wake of the boat. On either side of this fountain are two electric fount-

Looking West from the Peristyle. The Platform where the Opening Exercises are to be Held is Seen at the Base of the Administration Building in the Middle Distance. The Agriculture and Machinery Buildings are on the Left; the Manufactures and Liberal Arts on the Right. French's Statue of the Republic is in the Foreground.
(Drawn Expressly for THE NEW YORK TIMES by Its Own Artists.)

ains. Rising from the water in the distance is French's colossal statue of the Republic, and beyond that, in dazzling white, Atwood's peristyle, between the columns of which are seen the deep-blue waters of the lake. At the space of a hundred yards from the water on every side stand in grandeur and beauty the great buildings of the exposition.

Around the north side of the Administration Building the visitor will see the westernmost of the great quadrilateral galaxy, S. S. Bemis's Mines and Mining Building, 700 by 350 feet in size. Its architecture has its inspiration in early Italian Renaissance. In plan it is simple and straightforward, embracing on the ground floor spacious vestibules, restaurants, toilet rooms, &c.

The mining exhibit is in a very backward condition and hardly any idea can be obtained at the present time of what it will be like.

Just to the east of the Mines and Mining Building the visitor will see Van Brunt & Howe's Electricity Building, 690 by 345 feet in size, and yet all too small for its purposes. Its ten Italian spires, 195 feet high, and its immense arched entrance, filled with statues of the fathers of electrical science, are all designed to be turned into a blaze of electric lights by night. Here will be exhibited electric batteries, electric motors, electric lighting, electric heating, electro-metallurgy, electro-chemistry, electric forging, welding, stamping, tempering and brazing; electric telegraphs, signals, surgery, dentistry, and therapeutics, and illustrations of electrical laws and progress.

To the south of the Administration Building, and covering a space corresponding exactly to the two buildings just mentioned, the visitor will see Peabody & Stearns's Machinery Hall, 492 by 846 feet in size, with its front to the east. Built in the shape of three train houses, with a view to subsequent use, it is still a structure of grace and beauty. Here will be exhibited machinery pertaining to textile fabrics, clothing, wood, typesetting, printing and stamping, hand tools of every description, and whole departments of mechanism. The machinery exhibit is well along, most of the large engines being in readiness for work, and the boiler plant, consisting of a battery of sixty of the largest boilers, steaming away at a great rate.

Just east of Machinery Hall a spur of the basin runs southward, terminating in the immense Lion Fountain and Cleopatra's Needle, and just east of the Electricity Building a corresponding canal extends to the north. East of this transverse canal, on the north side of the main lagoon and south of the Agricultural Building, is the Manufactures and Liberal Arts Building. This building is the largest exposition building ever erected or contemplated. It is 1,687 feet long by 787 feet wide, its greatest dimension being north and south. It covers an area of 30½ acres. It is rectangular in form, its central hall being surrounded by a nave and two galleries.

The feature of the building is the great central hall. It has a clear space of 1,280 feet by 380 feet. Its roof rises to a height of 245½ feet at the apex, and the 380 feet space is covered by a single arched span without a supporting column. Twenty-two steel arches support the centre of the roof. Each arch weighs 125 tons, and more than 5,000 tons of steel enter into the construction of the hall. Only by comparison with existing structures can any adequate idea be formed of the size of this building. It is three times as large as St. Peter's Cathedral in Rome, and the largest church in Chicago can be placed within the vestibule of St. Peter's. On the floor of the Manufactures Building could be placed twenty buildings like the big Auditorium. Its central hall, which occupies but one-third of its area, will comfortably seat 50,000 people.

The building is in the Corinthian style of architecture and is severely classic. The long array of columns and arches which its façades present is relieved from monotony by very elaborate ornamentation. To the artistic ensemble at the Manufactures Building almost every artist of note at the fair has contributed. Gari Melchers of Detroit contributes two panels, "Education" and "The Chase." Walter McEwen of Chicago also has two panels typifying "Music" and "The Textiles." Other paintings that ornament the building are by J. Carroll Beckwith, Walter Shirlaw, E. E. Simmons, Kenyon Cox, C. S. Rheinhart, Robert Reid, J. Alden Weir, E. H. Blashfield, and George W. Maynard. The cost

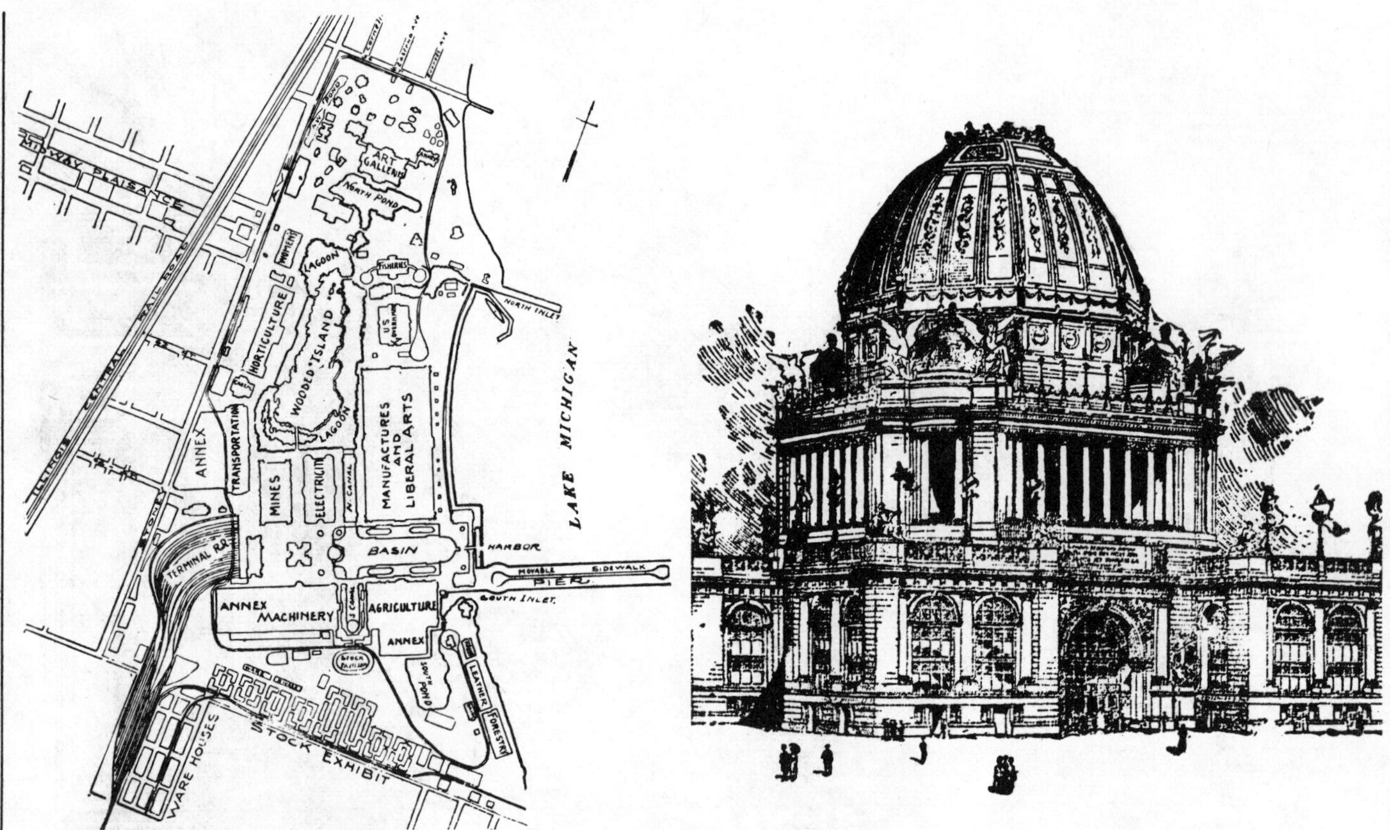

MAP OF THE EXPOSITION GROUNDS.

ADMINISTRATION BUILDING.

of this magnificent building was $1,727,481.

Within this immense structure are myriads of booths and pavilions, where costly wares from every clime are displayed. The appearance of the interior from one of the galleries is like that of a mystic maze. It is comparatively easy to get lost in the avenues, which stretch away almost interminably and are cut at right angles by other streets, cutting the building into little squares, on each of which a miniature exposition building is erected. This building is an exposition in itself. As yet its exhibits are in a chaotic state.

Only a small number of the pavilions are finished, and the work of unpacking the goods and placing them in the cases is just begun. It will be two or three weeks before much can be seen of the wealth of beautiful fabrics and wares which now lie in cases all over the floor.

In making the circuit of the quadrangle the visitor will pass along the south end of the Manufactures Building and come upon the stately Music Hall on the lake shore, and following the peristyle southward, reach its antitype, the Casino, in a commanding position south of the basin. Passing around to the south of the basin he will stand in front of McKim, Mead & White's Agricultural Building. This completes the quadrangle or "Court of Honor," as it has been called.

The Agricultural Building is one of the most magnificent structures raised for the exposition. The style of architecture is classic Renaissance. It is almost surrounded by the lagoons that lead into the park from the lake. It is 500 by 800 feet, its longest dimensions being east and west. The east front looks out into a harbor. The entire west exposure of the building faces a branch of the lagoon that extends along the north side. On both sides of the main entrance are mammoth Corinthian pillars, 50 feet high and 5 feet in diameter. On each corner and from the centre of the building pavilions are reared, the centre one being 144 feet square.

The corner pavilions are connected by curtains, forming a continuous arcade around the top of the building. The main entrance leads through an opening 64 feet wide into a vestibule, from which entrance is had to the rotunda, 100 feet in diameter. This is surmounted by a mammoth glass dome 130 feet high. All through the main vestibule statuary has been designed, illustrative of the agricultural industry. Similar designs are grouped about all of the grand entrances in the most elaborate manner. The corner pavilions are surmounted by domes 96 feet high, and above these tower groups of statuary. The design for these domes is that of three women of herculean proportions, supporting a mammoth globe, by Martiny of New-York.

On the dome is St. Gaudens's gilded statue of Diana which once graced the Madison Square Garden. Within will be displayed all cereals, grasses, tubers, vegetables, teas, coffees, spices, animal and vegetable fibres, fats, oils, soaps, sugars, syrups, foods, liquors, farm buildings, machinery, tools, literature, and many other things that relate to agriculture.

There is a welcome absence of the "corn palace" idea in the decorations of the inside of the building and the pavilions of exhibitors. Farmers and the farmers' friends, the implement makers, have been very slow in getting their exhibits ready. This may be due to the fact that in the busy seeding season it is not expected that many people from the rural districts can be spared from home, and consequently it is not deemed necessary to have that department in which they are particularly interested ready until later in the season. The Agricultural Building covers more than nine acres and its annex about three and one-half acres. It cost $658,687 to build them. Much, however, that is classified under agriculture has demanded and received separate buildings.

To the south of the Agricultural Building is a spacious structure devoted chiefly to live stock and an agricultural assembly hall. Close by the Agricultural Building and its annex is the building for the dairy exhibit. Arranged along the lake front, beginning at the south, are the Forestry Building, devoted to arboriculture, fine woods, and timber; the Dairy Building, containing the illustrations and products of dairy work, and the Leather Building, erected by the leather trade for the display of wares. The Krupp Gun Works, in which the immense cannon that are the wonder of the world will be exhibited, are also to be found here, and on the promontory just east of the Agricultural Building the exact reproduction of the Monastery de la Rabida, which sheltered the footsore and discouraged Columbus.

The "backyard," as this part of the grounds is called, contains many other buildings. Running across the south line of the park will be seen a number of ornamented sheds, where everything that is attractive in blooded horses, cattle, sheep, and swine will be housed. In front of them are the ethnological exhibit, the South American antiquities, the Cliff Dwellers, the White Hart Inn, the Dutch windmill, the French colonies exhibit, the oil exhibit, the Stock Pavilion, the open-air exhibit of agricultural machines, and minor attractions.

North of the Manufactures Building is the United States Building, 345 by 415 feet in size, representing in a general way the National Museum at Washington, but with a dome 236 feet high. The building itself has never excited great admiration, but its exhibits may possibly prove the most interesting on the exposition grounds. They cover all the Government departments, the National Museum, and the Smithsonian Institution. Everything pertaining to the Mint, the Bureau of Printing and Engraving, life-saving stations, and arms and explosives will be seen. The Government exhibit is in a very complete state.

The naval exhibit may be properly classed among the main buildings of the exposition. It consists of a structure that is to all outward appearance a full-sized model of one of the new coast-line battle ships designed by Frank W. Grogan. It is erected on piling on the lake front, east of the Government Building. It is surrounded by water and has the appearance of being moored to a wharf. The structure has all the fittings that belong to an actual ship. Its dimensions follow: Length, 348 feet; width amidships, 69 feet 3 inches; from the main deck to water line, 12 feet.

An inlet from the lake separates the Government Building from the Fish and Fisheries Building, the architect of which is Henry Ives Cobb. The Fisheries Building is one of the most artistic structures in the exposition. It is rectangular in form, 363 feet in length by 163 in width, except in the centre, where the extreme breadth is 242 feet. It has two annexes, which connect with the main building by arcades. Each of these is 135 feet in diameter. The total floor area is 3.5 acres. In the main portion is the general fisheries exhibit. In one of the polygonal buildings is the angling exhibit and in the other the aquaria. The exterior of the building is Spanish-Romanesque, affording an agreeable contrast with the architecture of the surrounding buildings. The decoration of the exterior is unique. Only fish and other sea forms are used as a motif in the designs for capitals, modillions, brackets, cornices, and other ornamental details. The roof of the building is of old Spanish tile and the side walls of pleasing color. The cost of the structure was $217,672.

The exhibit of tackle and boats is ready for inspection, and nearly all the tanks in one pavilion are filled with fish, so that there is already much to attract the visitor to this building.

Beyond the Fish and Fisheries Building are the Art Palace and the National and State Buildings, described elsewhere.

C. B. Atwood's Fine Arts Building, with its two annexes, is already famous for its architecture. The main building is 500 by 350 feet in size, and the style is a remarkably skillful adaptation of Greek forms. It has even been called "the greatest thing since Athens." It is the largest art gallery ever constructed. The height of the building is 125 feet to the top of the dome, which is surmounted by a colossal statue similar to the famous figure of the "Winged Victory." There are in the building seventy-four galleries of varying size, ranging from 30 feet square to 36 by 120 feet.

The situation of the building is admirable. It is in the northern portion of the park with the south front facing the lagoon. Terraces separate it from the water. These are ornamented with balustrades, and an immense flight of steps leads from the building through them to the lagoon, where there is a landing for boats. The north front faces the wide lawn and the group of State buildings, the New-York Building being situated directly opposite the main entrance. In the immediate neighborhood of the Art Palace are groups of statues and replica ornaments of classic art, such as the Choragic Monument, the "Cave of the Winds," and other beautiful examples of Grecian art. The building cost $737,811.

North of the Administration Building, along the west side of the grounds, is the Transportation Building, overlooking the wooded island, forming one of the group of edifices composing the northern architectural court of the exposition. It is refined and simple in architectural treatment. The main entrance consists of an immense single arch, enriched to an extraordinary degree with carvings, bas-reliefs, and mural paintings. It is called the Golden Door. The interior of the building is treated much after the manner of a Roman basilica, with broad nave and aisles. The roof is in three divisions; the middle one rises much higher than the others, and its walls are pierced to form a beautiful arcaded clearstory

The cupola, placed exactly in the centre of the building and rising 165 feet above the ground, is reached by eight elevators. The main Transportation Building measures 960 feet front by 250 feet deep. From this extends westward an enormous annex, covering about nine acres. This is only one story in height. In it may be seen the more bulky exhibits. Along the central avenue or nave, facing each other, are scores of locomotive engines, highly polished. The Transportation Building cost $483,183.

Next north of Transportation Building is Choral Hall, and over its top the Office Building, including the infirmary. North of these is W. L. B. Jenney's Horticultural Building, 250 by 998 feet, with its beautiful dome 122 feet high. A little further north is Miss Sophia B. Hayden's Woman's Building, 200 by 388 feet, and looking directly down the Midway Plaisance to the west. Here will be displayed everything pertaining to the industry and development of women. The roof of the pavilion at each end is covered with an Oriental awning, which shelters at one end a café and at the other a tea garden.

To women, one of the most interesting sights in the grounds will be the Children's Building, which was constructed out of the proceeds of the bazaar given at Mrs. Potter Palmer's residence last Winter. Here mothers can leave their children in the care of attendants while they make the rounds of the exposition grounds.

April 30, 1893

Looking North from the Gallery of the Mines and Mining Building, Showing the Lagoon and Wooded Island in the Foreground and the Transportation, Horticultural, Illinois, and Art Buildings in Order Beginning at the Extreme Left.
(Drawn Expressly for THE NEW YORK TIMES by its Own Artists.)

This Is How the Skyscraper Grew

THE CHICAGO SCHOOL OF ARCHITECTURE: A History of Commercial and Public Building in the Chicago Area 1875-1925. By Carl W. Condit. Illustrated. 238 pp. Chicago: University of Chicago Press. $8.50.

By WILLIAM ALEX

ALTHOUGH the word "skyscraper" appears neither in the title nor subtitle of Carl W. Condit's volume, the tracing of the skyscraper's Chicago genesis, flowering and decline is the major thesis of the book. This is as it should be, for the Chicago School of architects invented and perfected the most spectacular structural system of modern times: the steel skeleton frame of skyscraper construction.

Revising and substantially enlarging his previous "The Rise of the Skyscraper," Mr. Condit, professor of general studies at Northwestern University, has added material both on the Chicago School itself and the following generation of Chicago architects, sometimes called the Prairie School. The sustained technological revolution during which the first truly modern architecture was created in the United States is now placed in a broader social and intellectual context, balancing the thoroughly detailed structural information given on the buildings themselves. Discussion of the Prairie School architects, whose work consisted primarily of houses, schools, churches and small commercial buildings, is limited to the Chicago area.

Before the erection of tall buildings on expensive land in downtown Chicago became an art it was a robust technique born of pragmatic engineering, some of whose practitioners learned their trade in the Civil War. One of these, William Le Baron Jenney, who actually invented the new structural technique, is the book's technological hero, but was not especially interested in the problem of design for height. This unprecedented problem in architecture, the esthetics of a totally new form, was solved by others, men like John Root and like Louis Sullivan who fully grasped these newest concepts of technology and "created a form appropriate to the needs and spirit of the new industrial culture" of the United States. This self-determination came of its own time and place as Chicago's mercantile imperative swept away any need to clothe the shame of commerce in historicist dress.

Chicago was a city like no other in the eighteen-seventies, eighties and nineties. Raw, grasping and booming, it was building and rebuilding itself by the blockfront mile. Out of this constructional maelstrom came the structural techniques that made possible the skyscraper, carefully documented by Mr. Condit; the iron and later steel framing, first layered and then made an integral cage, extensible in any direction, gradually extenuated to permit greater and greater glass areas in Chicago's gridiron street plan.

The author describes the urgent problems of foundations as builders required taller and still taller buildings (Chicago boasted a series of the world's tallest in the eighties and nineties) on shifting sand and clay soil, solved, finally, by the invention of caissons extending far below to hardpan. The economic desirability of natural light for offices forced the development of the Chicago window, the great banks of projecting vertical window bays designed to secure more daylight and to catch the passing breeze but which also seemed to increase the city's visual excitement by presenting the pedestrian with huge undulating building facades.

REMARKABLY enough, in the midst of this busy synthesis of steel technology and art came what is probably Chicago's best historic skyscraper, the Monadnock Building, a 16-story masonry slab designed by John Root. As an architectonic masterpiece born in a milieu of honest design the building is no paradox for Chicago. On the other hand, the architect, whose name is so often coupled with that of Louis Sullivan seems to have become one, as a result of Mr. Condit's careful scrutiny into his subject and his collection into one place of much scattered information.

Serious questions in American architectural history are thereby raised, not only about Root but about Louis Sullivan. Root is shown in the Monadnock to have refined an architectural concept not his own, whose seeming austerity "posed a considerable problem for Root's artistic conscience." As Condit suggests, it was out of character. He also proves that Root had no part in the Reliance Building, thought previously to have been the extension of a design made by Root before his death—the building considered by Siegfried Giedion to be the very epitome of Chicago School design, perfecting the curtain wall in the tradition of the later Mies van der Rohe.

ALTHOUGH the Chicago work of Louis Sullivan is unquestioned as to design, his total creativity is greatly diminished in the opinion Condit quotes in regard to the Prairie School architect, George Elmslie, who joined the Adler and Sullivan office in 1890. "The creative and original design solutions which were expressed in the later buildings of the Sullivan office before 1909," he writes, "were not then an indication of a resurgence of Sullivan's creativity, but rather they demark the architectural development of George Grant Elmslie as a designer in his own right. With this in mind, the work of Sullivan's later years becomes comprehensible, and the later designs of the firm of Purcell and Elmslie assume a new and increased importance in the history of American architecture."

One wishes that the author had broadened the focus of his study beyond the Chicago area, perhaps to Louis Sullivan's series of Midwestern banks which were his swan-song, and delved more deeply into the Prairie School. But one is most grateful for his militant concern with Chicago's unique architectural heritage.

August 30, 1964

Interior light court, Brewster Apartments, 1893, designed by R. H. Turnock.

Glass and iron dome above the light court of The Rookery, 1885-86, designed by Burnham and Root.

"The Golden Door," main entrance to Transportation Building, 1893, designed by Adler and Sullivan.

Second-floor lobby of Auditorium Hotel, 1887-89, designed by Adler and Sullivan.

AN ELECTRIC ELEVATOR

HOW THE POWER OPERATES TO LOWER AND TO RAISE IT.

First Application of Electricity for Hoisting—Elevators That Are Safe and Those That Are Unsafe—Electricity Much Used Because of Its Cheapness and Other Advantages—Starting and Stopping the Machinery—Occasional Difficulties.

The extended use of electricity for freight and passenger elevators will prove surprising to those who take pains to investigate. There are nearly 1,000 in use in New-York City alone, not taking into account a large number that find some of their power in an electric motor, but are not driven by an electric elevator machine. This extraordinary application of power has come about in the last ten years.

The first successful attempt to use electric power for elevators, so far as known, was made in 1884, when a motor for a freight elevator was installed in a Spruce Street building. The arrangement is shown in Fig. 1, in which E represents the elevator platform, B the elevator machine, C a countershaft, and A the electric motor. At present there are probably 700 freight elevators so operated in New-York. The method of operation is as follows:

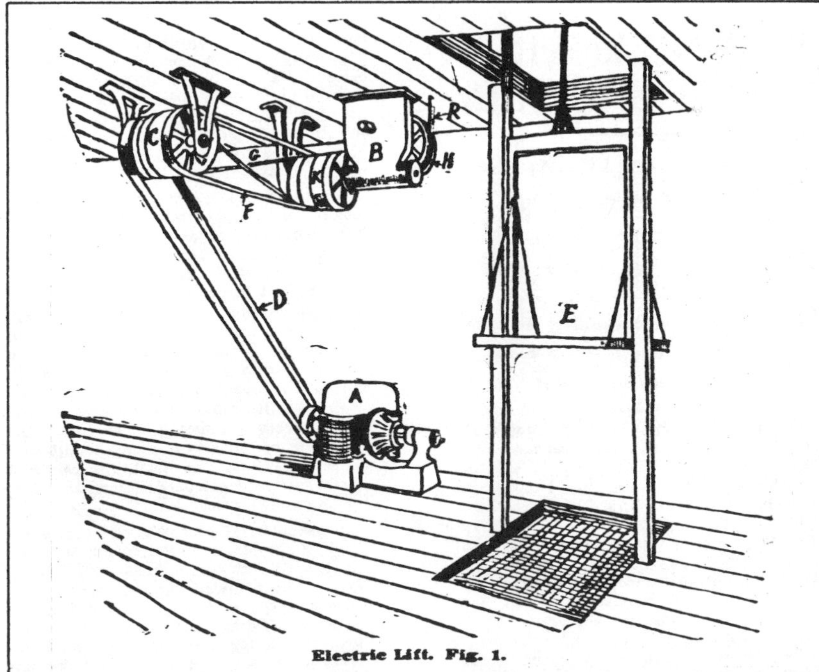

Electric Lift. Fig. 1.

The motor A drives the countershaft C by means of the belt D. The motor and shaft are generally kept running all the time, except when the elevator is not in use. The countershaft C drives the elevator machine B by means of either the open belt F or crossed belt G. On the shaft are three pulleys, shown at K. The centre one is fastened to the shaft. When the belts are on the outside pulleys the elevator will not move. If it is desired to run the car up, a rope which runs up along one side of the elevator well is pulled down. This, by means of a lever, shifts the open belt F upon the centre pulley of the elevator machine B and sets it in motion. The drum H then begins to revolve, and winds up the cable R, which runs up to the top of the building, where it passes over a sheave and descends to the top of the elevator car or platform, to which it is attached. To make the car descend, the starting rope is pulled up, and this throws the open belt off the centre pulley and shifts on the crossed belt G.

Oftentimes operators, when the car is going up and they want to stop, pull the rope up until it will go no further, and the car begins to run down. Then they pull down on the rope, and the car again stops, and begins to run up. After going up and down several times, they succeed in stopping the car. To stop, all that is necessary is to pull the rope midway. Then both belts will be thrown off the centre pulley.

Elevators of this class are used for freight purposes only, and are not as safe as those used for passenger service. They are not very dangerous—in fact, accidents with them are very uncommon. They are provided with most of the safety devices used on passenger elevators, but, as a rule, are suspended to a single steel wire cable. If an elevator car is suspended by two or more cables, the chances of its falling are very small, because any one of the cables is strong enough to hold the weight, and it could not fall unless all the cables broke at the same time, which is next to impossible. People who are nervous about riding in elevators should notice if there are two or more cables.

A class of elevators of the cheaper grade used in small buildings are not even as safe as the freight elevators. They are commonly called grip hoists, or hand elevators. They can be distinguished from the regular power elevators by the heavy hemp cable running down the side of the hatchway. This cable passes over a large wheel attached to the hoisting apparatus at the top of the building, and when pulled by hand sets the machine in motion. These elevators are dangerous, because they are prevented from running down very fast only by the friction of a brake. If this brake should get out of adjustment the car could run away.

Within the last five or six years an attachment has been introduced whereby elevators of this class may be run by an electric motor. This, however, does not make them any safer, as all the motor does is to replace the hand power. Though often run by electricity, they are not electric elevators in any sense of the word.

A type of the genuine electric elevator is shown in Fig. 2. Machines of this class are now manufactured by nearly all the large elevator builders and are very extensively used, New-York City alone having almost 1,000. They are first-class machines and are used in the best grade of buildings and private houses. The designs of the different manufacturers vary somewhat, but in general appearance they are all about as the one shown in Fig. 2. In this cut M represents the electric motor, the shaft of which runs under the casing, S, and engages with a gear wheel, which is attached to the shaft upon which the driver, D, is mounted. R represents the ropes by which the elevator car is moved, and C another set of ropes, to the end of which a counterbalancing weight is suspended. Both these ropes, C and R, run up to the top of the building and pass over sheaves, and thus

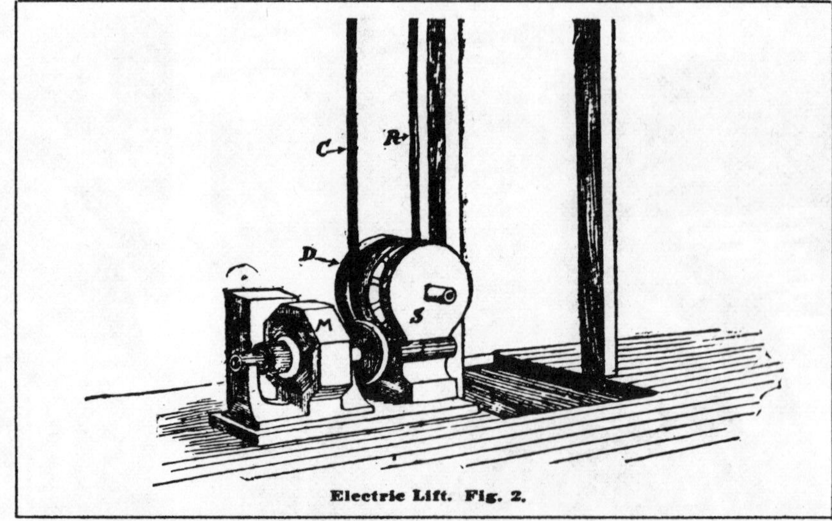

Electric Lift. Fig. 2.

run down and are attached to the counterbalancing weight and car respectively. The box shown back of the motor, M, contains the controlling mechanism by means of which the speed of the car and its direction are regulated.

With these machines, all the most approved safety devices are used, and they are equal to the most elaborate hydraulic elevators. They run the car with a smooth, gliding motion, and can attain the highest velocity.

These elevators are used in first-class office buildings, hotels, theatres, apartment houses, and private reidences. The elevators in the Postal Telegraph Building are electric, as are those in the Sheldon Building.

In most of the new fire-proof buildings that have been erected within the last two years, on Broadway and adjoining streets, above Canal, electric elevators are used.

The current to operate the elevator is generally obtained from the electric light mains, but sometimes an electric generating plant is introduced. In view of the fact that the introduction of electricity into any new field has always been accompanied with a considerable flourish of trumpets, it may be asked, why has it made such great headway in the elevator industry in such a quiet and unobtrusive manner? The reason is just that the machinery which operates an elevator is hidden from view, and a man might ride in an elevator a thousand times without knowing whether it was operated by electric or hydraulic power.

If you want to get a correct impression of the number of electric elevators in use, look at the name plate of the manufacturers whenever you enter an elevator car.

May 10, 1896

PRELIMINARY WORK FOR CONCRETE BUILDINGS

Lofty Tower That Has Mystified 42d Street Neighborhood.

WILL BE 147 FEET HIGH

With Its Aid, New Building on 39th Street Will Rise One Complete Story Every Four Days.

Occupants of the taller buildings in the Times Square neighborhood have had their curiosity aroused lately by a lofty wooden structure rising out of the block bounded by Seventh and Eighth Avenues, Thirty-ninth and Fortieth Streets. In its earlier stages this skeleton of timbers looked much like the "traveler" that is put up on most new building sites preparatory to the foundation work, but day after day men kept adding tier after tier to its height.

The tower is now nearly finished. It is 32 feet square and rises to a height of 147 feet, in the middle of the large plot on the north side of Thirty-ninth Street, just west of Seventh Avenue, where will be erected the new twelve-story building of the McGraw Publishing Company. This structure will be built throughout, from the lowest foundation to cornice, of reinforced concrete, and is, it is believed, the largest building of this type yet erected in Manhattan. This method has been employed within the last year or two in the construction of a number of buildings, but here is to be a huge structure covering a frontage of 198 feet in which not a brick nor a bit of steel such as goes into the ordinary skyscraper framework will be used. The building was designed by Architects Radcliffe & Kelly, and the contract for its erection is in the hands of Frank B. Gilbreth.

The thing that most impresses one in looking at one of these concrete building operations is the vast amount of preliminary work that must be done—the thousands of feet of lumber that must be put in position only to be taken away again when the building is finished. What the builder in concrete must do, practically, is to erect an entire frame structure with an outer and inner shell, fill in the space between the two and then take the frame building down again. The process is such, indeed, that the inexperienced observer finds it difficult to see how it can be much cheaper than steel frame construction, but the fact remains that it is.

In speaking of this phase of the work, J. T. McClellan, Superintendent for Contractor Gilbreth on the McGraw Building, said: "Economy in the handling of materials is the most important feature of concrete building construction. Take that tower there, for example. It rests on concrete piers carried down six feet into the rock and probably contains enough lumber to build a row of small frame houses—a pretty substantial bit of construction just as a preliminary—but from its four corners seventy-five-foot derrick beams will swing, having within their reach every square foot of this whole plot. We also plan to rig intermediate booms on the four sides of the tower, so that the work of placing the concrete in position can be carried forward at a very rapid rate. With the foundations finished and the structure once above the street level we expect to finish an entire story over the whole of the building's area every four days.

"With the increasing use of concrete in building construction have come improvements in the concrete mixing machines. The latest of these, of which we have three here on this work, is almost wholly automatic in its operation. The materials are dumped into a sort of hopper, which, at the pressing of a lever, moves up an incline and deposits its contents in the mixer. Six revolutions and out comes your batch of several yards of concrete all ready for use.

"The concrete building in course of construction," Mr. McClellan went on, "is different from the steel skyscraper in one important particular. In the steel skeleton building the framework always rises ahead of the outer walls. In the concrete building just the reverse order of things must prevail. Men employed on the walls in this structure will work two stories ahead of those on the columns and floors so that the reinforcements can be placed into the solid pilasters of the outside walls.

"Another point to be remembered wherein concrete construction differs from the steel skeleton method, is that in the latter a floor, or even an additional tier of beams, once in position, can be used immediately as a point of vantage from which to carry the building higher. In concrete work, of course, this cannot be done. The concrete columns and floors must be allowed to set for several days before they are subjected to the slightest strain, and it is not until three weeks have elapsed that they attain their full strength. Thus, if the concrete builder figured on using each floor as a stepping stone to the one above, he would find himself compelled to indulge in a swift succession of vacations of three weeks each—perhaps a happy arrangement, but one likely to be rather costly. It is in relation to this feature of the work that our tower here is indispensable. Work can proceed without interruption on the successive floors and without subjecting those already in place to any strain or pressure until they have set thoroughly.

"Samples of the concrete used in a building of this kind are taken at frequent intervals as the work progresses and are molded into bricks 4 by 4 by 8 inches. These are tested to make sure that at every point the artificial stone will be of the necessary strength to stand any strain that may be put upon it. The strength of properly constructed floors of reinforced concrete may be judged from the facts brought out in fire tests. After being subjected to a wood fire for four or five hours—heated red hot—and then suddenly cooled, they have shown no serious defects and have withstood pressure of 600 pounds to the square foot as against the standard requirement of 180 pounds.

"Concrete shows strange characteristics under various conditions. It is a curious fact that while it is setting concrete seems to deteriorate somewhat through exposure to the sun. You will find that the makers of cement blocks are much more anxious to keep them in the shade until they have set than they are to keep them out of the rain. Indeed, concrete seems to thrive in water. I have kept under water for a year blocks made of one part cement, one part sand, and two parts broken stone, and at the end of that time they were as tough as granite. In the construction of buildings, the concrete is, of course, protected from the sun's rays to a large extent by the wooden molds, which are not removed for some time."

The work of building the retaining wall around the new McGraw Building is now in progress and gives a very fair idea of how the reinforced concrete construction is handled. First, the outer mold, or back slab, as it is called, is placed in position and its inner side waterproofed up to grade. Next, the reinforcements, consisting of steel rods seven-eighths of an inch in diameter, are placed in position—those which extend vertically being only three and a half inches apart, while the horizontal ones are two feet apart. At every point where a vertical rod crosses a horizontal one, the two are wired together. Then the inner molds or panels are erected and strongly braced to prevent spreading, after which the space is filled with concrete and carefully tamped so that the reinforcing rods are equidistant from the two faces of the wall. The bracing of the molds is a part of the work which has to be looked after most carefully, for if this is not done the boards will spread and produce wholly unsatisfactory results.

The work on the McGraw Building is a little behind advance estimates, though not as a result of any difficulties in connection with the concrete work. When the excavation had been carried to the proper depth at the front part of the site, plenty of rock was found, but of a very seamy and crumbly variety, all of which had to be removed, for a perfect foundation is fully as essential in the concrete building as in the steel skeleton structure. Five different springs were also found to be in active operation at various points around the site, but these have all been taken care of, and probably within a few days the work of erecting the concrete columns with steel cores and the reinforced floors will be in rapid progress. The distance to be spanned by the floors between columns will be about fifteen feet in one direction and twenty-one feet in the other.

September 30, 1906

GREAT ADVANCE IN CEMENT BUILDING

Superintendent Miller Discusses New Types of Construction Seen in Kansas City.

UNIT SYSTEM ADVANTAGES

Fireproof Requirements Which Should Be Embodied in New York's New Building Code.

Wonderful progress in the use of cement in building construction is being made all over the country, said Superintendent of Buildings Rudolph P. Miller yesterday in discussing some of the practical results of his recent trip to Kansas City, where he attended the convention of the National Association of Cement Users. One of the most interesting features, he said, was the striking object lesson revealed to him of the rapid development that is taking place in the construction of reinforced concrete buildings by the use of separately molded members, called the unit construction.

Supt. Miller examined a number of buildings of this type both in Kansas City and St. Louis. In finished appearance they are hardly distinguishable from the ordinary poured concrete structures. Tests which have been made seem to show that for the same general design the construction by the unit method is the equivalent, so far as strength is concerned, of the ordinary method of construction. Under certain circumstances there is a very marked economy in this unit form of construction.

One of its advantages is well shown in the stack house of the National Lead Company at St. Louis, a one-story structure, 750 feet long and 160 feet wide, especially designed for the manufacture of white lead, which was turned over in part for occupancy while the rest of it was under course of construction without in any way interfering with the use of the finished portion. It is contended for this system that the columns, girders, beams, floor slabs, &c., being cast under factory conditions, can be much better inspected, and there is more certainty of their being exactly correct after being put in place.

In Kansas City Mr. Miller was interested in an apparently unique form of construction used in two buildings of that city, in which the fronts were practically entirely of glass. The columns supporting the front were set back about six feet, and the floor construction was cantilevered out to support the glass and light cast iron facias which formed the two-foot panels under the windows.

In one of the buildings located on a corner, for architectural as well as structural reasons, the fronts were finished at each end with pavilions about ten feet wide of brickwork faced with white glazed terra cotta, which encased the only columns placed on the building line. The pavilions with the frieze immediately under the cornice form a sort of frame for the large window surface. The interior is very light and the tenants seem to be very well pleased with the arrangement. Mr. Miller feels, however, that for a closely built city the construction is not to be commended on account the great exposure hazard.

"A matter that is receiving much attention at the present time," said Mr. Miller, "is the study of the aggregates used in concrete, especially the sand. It has been too frequently assumed that any sand used with cement would make a satisfactory mortar, and when mortars have been unsatisfactory the cement has been generally blamed. It appears, however, upon fuller investigation, that more often the sand was unsuitable. Fortunately the materials used for concrete aggregates in New York City are, generally speaking, above suspicion in this respect.

One of the papers that contained valuable data was on the subject of reinforced concrete grain elevators.

"The adaptability of such material for this purpose," said Mr. Miller, "should be sufficient reason for prohibiting the use of wood for not only grain elevators, but for similar structures, such as coal pockets, icehouses, &c.

"It is to be hoped that any new building code that may be presented for adoption in New York City will require that such structures be of fireproof construction. Numerous examples can be cited showing that this is only a reasonable requirement in this day, irrespective of location. In thickly populated sections fireproof construction should be called for to remove the fire hazard to surrounding buildings.

March 24, 1912

LIMITING BUILDING HEIGHT.

Many Cities Have Already Adopted Ordinances on the Subject.

Here is a list of places where under municipal or State laws a limit is put to the height to which buildings may be erected. The number of these cities is steadily growing, and the question of the legality of the restrictions seems to be settled so far as they are concerned:

Baltimore—Fireproof buildings limited to 175 feet, and non-fireproof buildings to 85 feet.

Scranton—Limit of 125 feet.

Boston—Two and a half times the width of the street; maximum, 125 feet.

Buffalo—No height greater than four times the average of least horizontal dimension of the building.

Chicago—Absolute limit of 200 feet.

Cleveland—Two and a half times the width of street, with maximum of 200 feet. Recesses or setbacks to be counted as added to width of street.

Jersey City—No building or structure, except a church spire, shall exceed in height two and one-half times the width of the widest street upon which it stands.

Los Angeles—Limit of 150 feet.

Paterson—Warehouses and stores must not exceed 100 feet in height.

Denver—Not to exceed twelve stories. Those more than 125 feet to be fireproof.

Portland, Ore.—All buildings, except churches, limited to 150 feet.

Newark—Not to exceed 200 feet, but warehouses and stores shall not exceed 150 feet.

St. Louis—On streets less than 60 feet, two and a half times the width.

April 13, 1913

Bloody Row in Cincinnati—Police overpowered by a Mob.

From the Commercial, 18th.

A disgraceful and somewhat bloody riot and outrage was perpetrated yesterday afternoon, by the riotous Irish population inhabiting the vicinity of Sixth and Culver streets, upon two police officers while they were discharging their duty.

Between 5 and 6 o'clock, Day Policeman KIMBALL, of the First, and GARDNER, of the Thirteenth Wards, arrested JOHN O'BRIEN, for assaulting and beating the keeper of an Irish doggery on Sixth near Culvert street. While they were conducting their prisoner towards the Hammond street Station-house, they were beset by a gang of the riotous inhabitants of that vicinity, who hurled bricks and stones at them, some of the missiles taking painful effect, and then rushed upon the officers in a body and knocked them down with slung-shots and other dangerous weapons. Mr. GARDNER meantime drew his revolver and fired two shots at the ruffians, bringing down one of the number, as he thinks, but has not yet been able to determine the fact. The rowdies, however, who had possession of Mr. KIMBALL, kept him down by force of numbers and stunning blows, until they had beaten him nearly to death. The cry of "police," however, caused them to desist from completing the murder they had half executed, and the savage scoundrels mingled with the dense crowd of spectators of their own class which had assembled to witness the fray, so that they could not be identified. Intense excitement, however, prevailed, and such tremendous uproar agitated the swaying mass that had collected that mere idle spectators were not able for some time to discover the cause of the assemblage. Officer KIMBALL was finally gotten out of the *mêlée* in an insensible condition. His head and brows were a mass of gore, and his body seemed to have been submerged in blood.

During the entire evening considerable excitement agitated the people in the vicinity of the locality where the onslaught was made, and new outrages were anticipated, but a strong police force awed the turbulent elements into subjection.

August 20, 1857

Desperate Riots in Baltimore.

BALTIMORE, Wednesday, Oct. 14.

There were riots here last night. The Turner Hall, a German tavern, was attacked by a political club. Windows were smashed in several other sections of the City last night. The American procession were fired into by Democrats, and the houses from which the shots were fired were sacked. A number of persons were wounded, including four police officers. The election for the City Council is progressing quietly this morning, but warm work is apprehended.

BALTIMORE, Wednesday, Oct. 14—P. M.

A riot broke out this afternoon between the Americans of the Fifth and the Democrats of the Eighth Wards. Muskets and pistols were freely used, and it is said that several persons were killed.

The police captured a quantity of muskets at Jackson Hall, in the Eighth Ward. Police Officer JORDAN was killed, and others were wounded. It is thought several persons were killed.

Another riot is reported as progressing at Lexington Market, in the western section of the city.

The police captured a quantity of firearms from the New-Market Engine-house.

Later.—The election to-day has resulted in the success of the American ticket in every Ward in the city except the Eighth. In many of the Wards the Democrats had no candidates. The vote polled is very small.

The riots have all been quelled. So far only one person is known to be dead, policeman JORDAN. Several are badly wounded, mostly police officers.

October 15, 1857

Firemen's Row in Philadelphia.

PHILADELPHIA, Friday, May 7.

During an alarm of fire this morning the Shiffler Hose Company assaulted the Moyamensing Hose Company, captured their carriage, broke it in pieces, and pitched it overboard at the Reed-street wharf. Many shots were fired, but nobody was injured.

The hose carriage was subsequently towed to the Navy-Yard, and there lifted out of the river with the shears, and restored to the company. All is quiet now, but apprehensions are entertained of retaliation to-night.

May 8, 1858

The Reign of Violence.

There must be some means of checking the lawlessness of New York, which is constantly becoming more dangerous and destructive. There is hardly a day in which the pistol or the knife is not used against human life. Murderous weapons are drawn on the slightest provocation; and whether it be a man shooting down another in a wordy quarrel, a ruffian killing a policeman who attempts his arrest, a person stabbing another on the street for what is called "self-defence," a Sheriff's *posse* firing into a crowd of helpless people to effect an arrest, or a policeman shooting some wretch whom he finds it difficult to manage. They all show a recklessness of life and a defiance of law that are terrible to think of. In all great cities we must expect frequent murders. There are men filled with revenge who will kill their enemy. There are criminals and marauders who will resort to assassination for one end or another—for money or plunder. There are husbands who will kill their wives when their misery has culminated in an uncontrollable passion. There are men fired by liquor, who, in their madness, will butcher a friend or a foe. There are persons who will resort to poison as a means of ridding themselves of some one who stands in their way. Crimes of these kinds occur the world over; and society has not yet been able to discover or apply the moral force or the legal agency that will altogether prevent them.

But the shootings and stabbings that are of such frequent occurrence in our streets, barrooms and public places, are of quite another character. In nine cases out of ten, that which is alleged as the *cause* of them is of an utterly trivial nature. Take, for example, the very last instance we have chronicled. A man, on his way home, goes into a barroom, and, upon being presented with a small bill for an alleged purchase made by his wife, he has a short quarrel with the storekeeper, in the midst of which he draws a revolver from his pocket and shoots his adversary dead. Take, as equally striking examples of the most trivial excuse for murder, the previous case last week. But we prefer not recounting the published circumstances until the offender has been brought to trial. We might mention a score of other cases of recent occurrence, and in nearly all of them it would be seen how petty were the provocations, and how utterly unjustifiable the deadly assault.

It is in criminal assaults and in murders of this character that New-York has become preëminent. We believe that there are fifty such cases of killing here to one of a similar character in London or Paris. We believe they are ten times more numerous here than in Philadelphia or Boston. We have got to be as bad now as New-Orleans was in other times. And instead of growing better we are steadily getting worse.

We have no doubt that the widely prevailing habit of carrying deadly weapons is one cause of the frequency of this class of murders. If in a dispute, or in a rumpus, or at a moment of difficulty, a man finds himself with a pistol or a killing-knife in his pocket, he has an almost irresistible temptation to aggression. Without these, he would be satisfied with giving his adversary the worst in the wrangle, or, at most, he might be satisfied with attempting to knock down the enemy, or to give him a bloody nose or a black eye; but it is hardly in human nature to refrain from drawing a convenient weapon when one has been stung by insult or humiliated by being the victim of the first blow. We believe that no man is at any time safe from becoming a murderer who habitually carries about with him the weapons of murder.

But, above all other causes for the reign of violence, is the way in which justice is administered upon those who are guilty of crimes of violence. A man guilty of murder in New-York has nine chances in ten of escaping punishment altogether, or else of receiving such a slight penalty as is calculated neither to act as a warning to others nor to prevent the culprit from again indulging in crime. Juries are always more ready to find excuses for the deed than to vindicate justice and the order of society. Prosecuting attorneys seem always more anxious to postpone a case than to assert the supremacy of the law. The Courts seem always more inclined to a weak and ruinous leniency than to punish the willful offender. The public seem always more inclined to seek for some justification of the deed than to protect society against the depraved, vicious and reckless classes. At first, when a murder is committed, everybody says of the man guilty of the deed that "he ought to be hung;" but presently he shows the "provocation" he had, and then the offence seems not so bad, and subsequently, after long delay, his trial comes off, and what with the moving appeals and exculpatory arguments of his lawyer, the jury and the public become interested in his behalf, and are altogether pleased when he escapes the "clutches of the law."

It is this looseness in the administration of law, this wicked public disregard of justice, that gives encouragement to the reign of violence. The "terrors of the law" would be particularly effective in preventing the class of crimes now so prevalent. If death were the certain penalty inflicted on those who carry and use weapons to kill, there are far fewer who would render themselves liable to the using of them, and very few indeed who would use them on any such "provocations" as are now constantly urged in defence.

September 6, 1868

THE POLICE OF DIFFERENT CITIES.

WHAT THE ST. LOUIS CHIEF SAW ON HIS TRAVELS.

From the St. Louis Globe-Democrat, Aug. 24.

Capt. Ferdinand Kennett, Chief of the St. Louis Police, has been visiting the large cities of the East and West partly on a trip for recreation, but equally with a purpose of examining into the Police systems of the cities visited. As the result of his examinations we have the following narrative of facts and experiences:

"Cincinnati was the first city visited. The Police there are a fine body of men, and under excellent discipline. It is the municipal system, and Maoor Means takes a great deal of pride in the force. They wouid have killed me with good treatment if I had let them have their own way. After Cincinnati came Pittsburg. They manage Police business there rather curiously. There are only 1₺0 men on the force, and, locking the doors, they leave the station-houses from 11 to 5 without anybody in charge. Each patrolman carries a key, and when an arrest is made the officer takes his man to the station, unlocks the door, and shuts him up. When the Captain comes around he has to go through the station and find out for himself who the prisoners are. It looks like a very loose way of doing things, but the Pittsburg Police seem to give satisfaction.

"In Chicago there is a system of patrol wagons in operation, recently inaugurated. It is the best thing in the way of Police innovation I found while I was away. Chicago is the only city which has it, and the cost is very small compared with the benefits. The system embraces Police wires and alarm-boxes on the lamp-posts. There will be two or three boxes on a beat. All reputable citizens are given keys to these boxes. Thus an officer can open the boxes and call for assistance, or if he is engaged a citizen can do it. The signal for assistance is conveyed to the nearest station-house, and immediately appears the patrol wagon. The horses are kept in stalls as the fire engine horses are, and hitched up at the signal, much of the time-saving apparatus employed at the engine-houses being in use for the Police patrol. Three officers accompany the wagon on the trip. Whenever an arrest is made at any distance from the station-house the patrol wagon is called and the prisoner taken charge of. In this way the officer need not leave the beat. If there is no particular haste for the wagon, the officer gives a second signal, and then communicates with the station by the telephone with which each box is furnished, giving the purpose for which the wagon is wanted. Further than this the officers report to their respective station-houses from different parts of their beats through this system, thus showing just where they are. It serves as a watch on the officer and does much of the work of the patrolling Sergeant. They have had only a short trial of the system in Chicago, but would not be without it. Chicago has 500 men, and about three-fourths of them are on duty at night. Their force is scant in numbers, but the patrol system makes up for that. There is hardly any limit to the benefits derived from the patrol wagon. They go to fires and carry ropes, so that before the engines are fairly at work the street barriers are up and the crowd is kept back.

"In regard to the division of hours for duty, nearly every city has a different plan, but St. Louis is almost alone in not having a reserve at the station-houses. Here officers are on duty 12 hours and then off 12 hours. In other cities they arrange the hours so that there are reserve men at the stations. Thus in one city the men are divided into four platoons, and in another three. In New-York there are three and what they call a dog watch. An officer is on duty eight hours, and then is kept at the station four hours. In Boston they have an all-day platoon on duty 10 hours, and then the 14 hours from night till morning are divided, and during that time the men are off and on by regular relief. In all the station-houses there are comfortable bedrooms. Each officer has his own bed, and usually two sleep in a room. These sleeping quarters in Baltimore are luxuriantly fitted up. They have finely carpeted rooms, marble wash-stands, bath-rooms, and all the conveniences you can imagine. Indeed, of all the places I visited, I think the Baltimore policeman's lot comes nearest to being 'a happy one,' while the Montreal policeman is the worst off by all odds. It's true he is furnished his clothes, but his wages are under $500. He can, however, sleep in the station-house, and thus save his lodging expenses. He is looked upon as the common enemy of all classes of society, and whenever he comes in conflict with the citizen there is a general row, in which the chances are very great that the policeman will get the worst of it. His position is rendered more hazardous by the fact that the Montreal officer is not allowed to carry a pistol. He has his club, and that is all.

"For men of fine physique the West has a higher standard than the East. Chicago has a fine appearing body of men; so has Cincinnati. Further East the men are smaller. I notice this particularly in Boston. The force there is more largely American than in other cities. In Baltimore, in the Central District, they have a gymnasium completely equipped in every respect. The men pay an instructor $100 a month, and take an hour of class exercise every day.

"I looked into the working of the additional rank of Lieutenant, and I believe it is an improvement. The Lieutenant in other cities grades between the Captain and the Sergeant—that is to say, while the Captain commands a district, the Lieutenant has charge of the station-house, and ranks above the Sergeant, whose authority extends over a precinct. I believe the St. Louis force would be improved with the establishment of this additional rank.

"And finally, I find a wide difference in the manner in which the departments of the different cities are managed, a very few being true metropolitan forces, while nearly all are strictly municipal, into the composition and control of which politics enters more or less."

September 30, 1881

A CITY IN RUINS.

The Terrible Devastation of Chicago.

Three Square Miles in the Heart of the City Burned.

Twelve Thousand Buildings Destroyed—Loss $50,000,000.

Every Public Building, Hotel, Bank and Newspaper Swept.

ENGLEWOOD, (seven miles south of Chicago,) }
5 P. M. MONDAY EVENING. }

It is impossible to give in any approach to detail the devastation of Chicago. The fire of Sunday, previously reported, began in the lumber and coal tract, along the west bank of the river, laying in waste several squares, as previously reported, but the total of preliminary destruction among the cheap tenement structures and frame planing-mills of Canal and Clinton streets is lost and inconsiderable in the frightful sequel. The fire, early this morning, crossed the river into the large lumber and coal yards of the South Branch in the South Division, and the work of destruction of the city began in earnest. A violent south-west prairie wind prevailed and filled the air with fiery messengers of destruction before which the cheaper frame tenements of Market, Wells and Franklin streets melted away like wax. The most important city works first to be attacked were the extensive premises of the Chicago Gas Company, on the corner of Market and Adams, and opposite these on Adams-street the large City Armory and Police building, just undergoing repairs. The flames leaped like a prairie fire over the adjacent squares of cheap frame buildings on Wells and Lasalle streets and along the river, and its work, to be calculated only by millions, commenced in earnest after crossing Lasalle-street, where improvements of the best class existed. An area of desolation, of crumbling ruins, of ruined merchandise, the commercial and industrial wealth of Chicago, now extends throughout an extent, to give a sketch of the losses in which would be to reproduce the Business Directory of the city. Throughout the entire day the appalling visitation maintained its unstayed course. At present writing, among the unutterable confusion that reigns, individual loss and suffering is lost in a sea of misery that has overwhelmed more than one-half the population of the city either in their homes or their business.

Writing this at 5 P. M., from Englewood, seven miles south of the city, the junction of the Michigan Southern and Rock Island Railroads, the awful work of destruction still goes on with relentless fury. From Harrison-street, in the south, to Division-street, in the north, and from the river to the lake, an area of four miles long by one mile wide, the flames have swept everything before them. It is estimated that at least 100,000 people are homeless and in a suffering condition. The streets in the district still unburned are lined for miles with such household goods as have been saved from destruction. Most generous offers of assistance in money, food, or anything wanted, are coming in from almost every city and from throughout the country by telegraph. The Mayor has responded to several offers asking that cooked food be provided as soon as possible. Firemen are on their way here from Cincinnati, St. Louis and other cities. The water-works are entirely destroyed. Buildings are now being blown up on the line of the fire to attempt to arrest its progress.

It is now believed that the spread of the fire southward has been stayed at Harrison-street, but on the north side there is no diminution of its fury, and the entire division of the city is evidently doomed to utter destruction. There are grave fears that the flames may spread to the west side of the north branch of the river, and the inhabitants of the streets nearest the river are already moving to places, it is supposed, of greater safety. The Western Union Telegraph Company have now six wires working, each south, running into a temporary office at the corner of State and Sixteenth streets. The North-western Railroad Company are running trains on both its branches, which are crowded with fleeing citizens. It is now positively asserted by some that the water-works are still intact, but the water has been shut off from the South and West Divisions on account of the quantity being used on the north side. A reliable gentleman just arrived from the North Division brings the joyful intelligence that the water-works are uninjured. God grant that it may prove true.

It is impossible now to give even an approximately correct statement of the losses, but a faint idea may be formed when it is stated that every bank in the city, except the small Savings institutions, one on Twenty-second-street, in South Division, and one on Randolph-street, in West Division, are destroyed. All wholesale stores, retail establishments, Post-office, the Court-house, Chamber of Commerce, every hotel in South Division, except Michigan-avenue Hotel, which, standing on the extreme southern limit, escaped, though it is badly scorched; every newspaper office, (the *Tribune*, which was supposed to be fire-proof, having finally succumbed,) every theatre, the six largest elevators, the immense depots of the Michigan Southern and of the Illinois Central Railroad, (both the passenger and freight depots of the latter,) more than a score of churches, and much of the shipping in the river all are destroyed.

Men who were millionaires yesterday morning are nearly penniless today; but more terrible than all is the awful certainty that many human beings have perished in the flames—how many no one can tell. Perhaps no one will ever be able to tell, but it is known that some have perished, and there is only a heart-sickening fear that the victims of the fiery monster may be counted by scores.

Hundreds of horses and cows have been burned in stables, and on the north side numbers of animals, though released from confinement, were so bewildered and confused by the sea of fire which surrounded them that they rushed wildly to and fro, uttering cries of fright and pain until scorched and killed.

Any attempt at a description of the scenes of this appalling calamity would be idle. The simple facts that the once great City of Chicago is destroyed, that hundreds of millions of active capital here have vanished, and that nearly one-third of Chicago's inhabitants are houseless dependents, are enough. Any attempt to embellish would be a mockery. As this awful day draws to a close, thousands of anxious eyes watch the clouds of smoke which still roll over the burnt district, with evident dread that a sudden change of wind may turn the flames upon that portion of the city yet spared.

There seems, however, little cause for apprehensions, and reinforcements of firemen from other cities are constantly arriving. Col. Z. G. Wilson, Superintendent of the Telegraph, is in receipt of dispatches from leading cities, announcing that aid is being provided for the sufferers. Col. Clowry, of St. Louis, telegraphs, that $70,000 have been subscribed by the merchants there. Cincinnati promises $200,000, and Cleveland is proportionately generous. All this and a great deal more will be needed to relieve the immediate pressing wants. Everything is being done by Gen. Stager and his assistants to keep up communications for the citizens and Press with the world outside. Col. Geo. T. Williams, Superintendent at Cincinnati, reported promptly for duty this morning. About three-fourths of the United States mail was saved, and taken possession of by Col. Wood, of the Post-office service.

The Chamber of Commerce occupied the south-east corner of Lasalle and Washington streets, and, with the building attached in the rear, had a frontage of 180 on Lasalle and 100 on Washington-street, owned by Chamber of Commerce Association, and leased to Board of Trade for ninety-nine years. Offices of leading produce-houses on first floor and basement. Exchange Hall above cost, about six years ago, $275,000. North-western National Bank, of Sturges Brothers, occupied the corner office. Insurance offices of Geo. C. Clarke & Co., and Life Association in basement.

The Union National Bank building, a fine marble structure, opposite the Chamber of Commerce, was owned by W. F. Coolbaugh and others, occupied by the Union Bank and the Merchants' National Bank, Yonkers Insurance and other insurance and real estate offices above, 180 by 100; cost of building, $150,000 on leasehold property.

Adjoining and south of the Union building, on Lasalle-street, was the Mercantile building, a fine marble structure; also, the very costly Oriental building and Dr. Bassett's building. In the rear of these James Wadsworth was just completing a large area office building. The Merchants' Insurance Building, opposite the Union Building, owned and occupied by Merchants' Insurance Company on leased ground, cost $175,000 in 1868. The general office of the Western Telegraph Company and Gen. Sheridan's Head-quarters, Bank of Smith Bros.

The west side of Lasalle-street, north from the Merchants' building to Randolph-street, was a line of costly structures, among them the Phoenix building of Messrs. Baird & Bradley, Thomas Haynes' marble building, the State Savings Institution and Savings Bank, and H. H. Magee's Milwaukee brick building occupied by the Home Insurance Company, and filled with offices above. These eight or nine buildings cost from $60,000 to $150,000 each.

The north side of Randolph-street was a continuous front of costly marble buildings from Lasalle to Clark-street. On the corner of the latter, the Sherman House, 180 by 160 feet, five stories high, owned by the heirs of the late F. C. Sherman, built in 1860 and extended in 1868, was occupied by Messrs. Geo. W. & D. A. Gage and John A. Rice, under a lease of five years from 1870, at $55,000 per year. The rentals of the building were nearly $150,000. Total loss in structure and contents, $550,000.

Adjoining the Chamber of Commerce on the east were Nixon's great building and W. S. Johnson's building, the two making a continuous structure 250 feet on Washington, and 180 on Clark, on leased ground, cost $250,000, occupied in officies above, and office of Pacific and Atlantic Telegraph Company in corner office on Ex-change place.

The block opposite the Court-house, on Clark-street, from Washington to Randolph, was occupied by Larmon Block, a five-story marble building, the Fifth National Bank, retail hat and drug-stores, and Bryant & Stratton's Business College above. Next north was Hooley's Theatre, formerly Bryan Hall, recently rebuilt, cost, $100,000. The remaining buildings northward were old and of light value, except the costly block of A. H. Miller, jeweler, on the corner of Randolph, built six years ago, five stories high, cost $90,000; occupied as a first-class jewelry establishment. Riverside Improve-ment Company on third floor, and Baker's engraving establishment. The Washington-street front of this square was brick and marble buildings, the finest being Parker's new block, occupied by the new Bank of Illinois, of George Schneider, and others. Adjoining, on the east, was the *Daily Republican* office, and Judge Otis' building, and King's block on the corner of Washington. The Manufacturers' National Bank of Ira Holmes and others, occupied the corner of Dearborn-street. The Dearborn-street front of this block was a line of retail stores to the alley. Manniere's block, a fine structure, and the McElroy iron building, extended to the corner of Randolph. On the front on the latter street were the beautiful Updike building and a new stone block. Among the principal occupants were J. M. W. Jones' great stationery establishment, Horton & Leonard, printing house, Shober's lithographic establishment, Belden, clothier, and several leading wholesale liquor and clothing houses.

The residue of the square south of the Chamber of Commerce and Nixon & Johnston's building was occupied by a long marble front block on Clark-street, by Pope's block and Pope's new and costly marble front "Open Board," Seeley's building and the costly Boone block of the Union Mutual Insurance Company made up the Lasalle-street front.

The block bounded by Clark, Washington, Dearborn and Madison, contained the costly Methodist Church building on the corner of Clark and Washington, Follansbe's Bank. The entire Washington-street front comprised retail establishments of the best class. The *Daily Times* building was in the middle of the Dearborn-street front of this square, also the marble Manniere block and S. B. Cobb's buildings, extending to the corner of Madison-street, the south frontage of the square along the street containing Cameron, Amberg & Hoffman's stationery and bindery premises and a line of small stores. The Clark-street front of this

The Devastation of Chicago—Map of the Burned District as Far as Heard From.

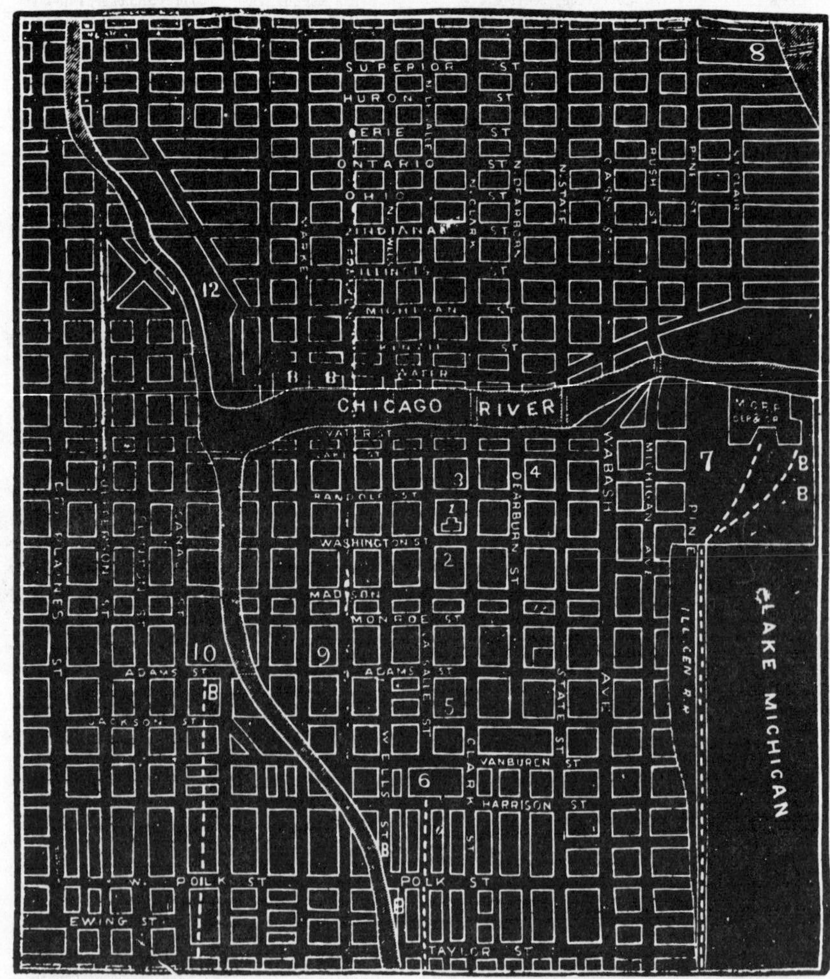

REFERENCES.

1. Court-house.
2. Chamber of Commerce.
3. Sherman House.
4. Tremont House.
5. Pacific Hotel.
6. Lake Shore and Michigan Southern, and Rock Island and Pacific passenger and freight houses.
7. Illinois Central, Michigan Central, and Chicago, Burlington and Quincy freight houses.
8. Chicago Water-works.
9. Chicago City Gas-works.
10. Pittsburg, Fort Wayne and Chicago, and St. Louis, Alton and Chicago Railroad passenger and freight houses.
12. Chicago and North-western Depot grounds.
13. Chicago *Tribune* office.
14. Chicago Shot-tower.

B. B. B. B. Elevators.

square, south of the Methodist block, was occupied by Calhoun's building and Morrison's block, a very large and costly five-story structure, filled with stores and offices.

The square bounded by Madison, Clark, Dearborn and Monroe was probably one of the best built, and most compactly occupied, of any in Chicago. On Madison-street, commencing with the great marble Morrison block, at its north-west angle, and the continuous similar front of Rosenfeld & Rosenberg, among occupants were G. E. Stanton's extensive fine grocery and liquor premises, *Kellogg's Railway Gazette* and *Inside Track* premises, Spalding & La Monte's printing-house, the office of the *Evening Post*, the *Post* job offices, the *Evening Mail* premises, the *Bright Side*, the German *Staats Zeitung* office, in a costly marble building owned by the *Zeitung* Company. The Reynolds' block fronted 180 feet on Dearborn and 80 on Madison, filled with stores and offices. At the south-west angle of the square, on the corner of Dearborn and Monroe streets, stood the solid, detached and now destroyed building, the Post-office and Custom-house. Westward on Monroe was the great Lombard block, fronting 100 on Monroe and 180 on Custom-house-place, one of the most numerously occupied structures in the city. Here was the *Advance* office, the *Little Corporal*, the banking-house of Benjamin Lumbard. West of this, on Monroe, were a line of handsome structures variously occupied, among others by the *Interior*. The square south from Madison-street on the west side of Lasalle contained Judge Otis' block, and his new and splendid block, five stories high. Next this, south on Lasalle, was F. A. Bryan's superb Bryan block, called the best office-building in Chicago, just completed, cost $200,000. West and south of this on Lasalle, and south-westerly and westward on Madison-street, the structures were of a cheaper and humbler class, with no notable values except to the suffering tenants.

Opposite on Lasalle from the Otis building was Major's block, Andrews' block and Farwell Hall, representing a total value of nearly three-quarters of a million dollars, and filling the Madison-street front of this square to the alley. The fire-proof building of the Republic Life and W. K. Nixon's fire-proof office building, on the corner of Lasalle and Madison streets, completed the improvements of this square on the west. Next east of the latter, on Monroe, were the Kent Marble office building and the costly half-completed structures of J. P. Smith and W. A. Lancaster, eighty feet front five stories high. Next east was the extensive type-foundry of Marder, Luse & Co., and the marble Witkowsky Hall, later Olympic Theatre, occupied the corner of Clark. The principal buildings on the Clark-street front of this square were the Henderson block, the costly Arcade building, occupied by Adams, Blackmer & Lyon, Sunday-school publishers; Titsworth, clothing; Lyon & Healy, music; Smith & Nixon, Steinway's pianos. The fine new marble building of Malcom, McNeil & Campbell, and others occupied by wholesale paper stores, shoe and jewelry.

The improvements on South Clark-street, south of Madison, had recently commenced on a magnificent scale, the principal improvement being the great Pacific Hotel, to be completed in May, and to have been leased in this city the present week. The building, receiving its interior finish, covered the entire square bounded by Jackson, Clark, Quincy and Jackson streets; $800,000 already expended. Just north on Clark, at the corner of Adams, the Lake-side Printing Company were completing their costly edifice, 100 by 100.

Improvements of the best class had been pushed along Dearborn-street to Jackson-street. Among the notable structures below Monroe-street were H. H. Honore's splendid buildings, one of them a sumptuously beautiful stone front, just being roofed. The Cook County National Bank was on the corner of Monroe and Dearborn. Next was the beautiful new Bigelow Hotel, 100 by 160 feet, just being furnished, having been leased to W. A. Hughes; hotel owned by G. A. Bigelow, cost, with furniture, $450,000, to have been opened in November. H. M. Shepard's building, marble front, 190 feet on Dearborn, cost last year, $100,000. Among its occupants the *Land Owner*.

On Adams-street, east of Dearborn, the beautiful building of the Academy of Design, the new marble blocks just occupied by the American Tract Society and the American Sunday School Union. These abutted on the Palmer House, an eight story structure on the corner of State and Quincy streets, finished by Potter Palmer last year, W. P. F. Meserve, lessee. Below Quincy, on State, the buildings were of a smaller class.

The block south of Washington-street, between Dearborn and State streets, presented at its north-west angle the large and costly Portland block, with the bank of Messrs. Taylor and others, and the German Savings Bank at the corner of Dearborn and Madison streets. Portland block was 180 feet square, five stories high, of Athens marble, and cost $300,000 before the war. Next on Madison, on the south, Dearborn Varieties, Small's stationery premises, Speed's block, and the Bank of the Merchants Loan and Trust Company and Savings Bank. On the State-street front of this square were Raymond block and Potter Palmer's range of splendid five-story palaces, occupied by Hollister & Phelps, carpets; Downs, dry goods; Carson & Perie, ditto, and the great wholesale dry goods premises of Ross & Gossage.

The buildings on Clark-street, between Randolph and Lake, opposite the Sherman House, were small retail stores, occupying the Kingsbury lease, among the largest occupants, Rand McNally & Co., printers and publishers. Next north was Snow's building, the banking-house of Lunt, Preston & Kean, the bank of J. M. Adsit, the North-western Railroad ticket-office, &c. Opposite, on the west side of Clark-street, were the banking-houses of the Traders' Bank, and the bank of Greenebaum & Foreman. The fine marble building of Wm. B. Ogden, built in 1851, the pioneer of its class of structures in Chicago, occupied the corner of Clark and Lake street. Among its tenants were the National Watch Company of Elgin. On the Lake-street side of the square between Clark and Dearborn streets, were Matson & Hoe's jewelry-store, and a line of elegant retail establishments in four-story brick buildings extending to Dickey's building. On the south-west corner of Lake and Dearborn, opposite the Tremont House, occupied by the Merchants' Loan and Trust Company's Bank of S. A. Smith and others. The basement was the banking office of Wrenn, Ullmann & Co. In the same building on Dearborn-street were the Gas Company's office and J. W. Smith Merchants' Dispatch office. The next building was the *Evening Journal* office and Colby & Wirt's furniture establishment. Next south the marble block of M. O. Walker, adjoining the Matteson House, kept by Hill & Co., built in 1850. Value, with furniture, about $200,000. West of the Matteson, on Randolph-street, was a line of retail stores. B. F. Chase's paper and painting establishment and the Chicago Museum of Col. Wood, recently refitted. Loss, with contents, about $350,000.

The Tremont House was built by Ira Couch in 1850, a model of its class; raised and rebuilt ten years ago; kept by John B. Drake as a first-class hotel; 180 by 180, on Dearborn and Lake streets; five stories high; Drake's lease to expire in 1873; loss, with contents, $500,000. Stores underneath, Michigan Central and Great Western ticket offices: Beers, clothing; Emerson, hatter; Cobb & Pritchard's extensive bookstore. The line of stores east on Lake-street were first-class retail premises—Towne, shoes; Dalton, house-furnishing, and others. On the south-west corner of State and Lake the European Hotel, four stories; loss about $100,000. On the State-street front of this square were Herring's safes Scanlan confectionery, Laflin's paper warehouse and Round's extensive printing establishment. Between this and E. H. Sargent's drug store, on the corner of State and Randolph, were stove, hardware and produce houses, these latter also filling the Randolph-street front to the extensive livery premises, late Rice's, and Eggleston's furniture. Mann's drug-store occupied the south-west corner of Dearborn and Randolph streets. On the Dearborn-street front of this square were the Commercial Exchange Building, owned by George R. Chittenden; a double marble structure, occupied by the banks of A. C. & O. F. Badger, and Eames' Commercial National Bank.

The square bounded by Randolph, Dearborn, Washington and State streets contained the Crosby Opera-house on its central front on Washington, with the music stores of Root & Cady, W. W. Kimball, J. Bauer & Co., and Wright's restaurant under it. The rear building contained Root & Cady's publishing rooms. The cost of the Opera-house, just being refitted at a cost of $50,000, was nearly $600,000, with its extension to State-street, occupied by Spear & Crofut, carpets. The St. James Hotel, owned by Gen. W. L. Stewart, occupied the corner of State and Washington. The Third National Bank of J. Irving Pearce and others was in the costly marble McCormick Building on the north-west angle of the square, fronting on Dearborn and Randolph streets. Next south on Dearborn was the Rice Block, filled with offices and stores. South of this, on the same front, the Masonic Temple, built in 1856, a marble building containing Hardin, Cushman & Co.'s banking office and other banking offices.

To particularise further principal blocks is difficult. The iron-front stores on both sides of Lake-street, the great stores of Keith, millinery; Williams & Fitch, hats and caps; Burley & Tyrrell, crockery, Johnson, Spencer, & Co., cutlery; Hurlbut & Edsall, drugs; Doggett, Bassett & Hills, shoes; Durand, grocer, are a few of these names. South Water-street, east of State, was filled with heavy grocery firms. In this quarter of the city was the Adams House. The block on the east side of Michigan-avenue, from Wabash to Randolph-street, was lined with the great iron houses of Hale & Ayers, Hall, Kimbark & Co., G. C. Cooke & Co., grocers; Hibbard & Spencer, hardware; and the magnificent marble armor building was occupied above by Pullman Palace offices and warehouse. In the rear of these the great depot grounds of the Illinois Central, Michigan Central, Chicago, Burlington and Quinc. Railroad Companies. These buildings were the great Union Passenger House, the freight houses of vast capacity, and beyond these the great elevators.

On State-street, from Washington north to Randolph, stood a line of merchant palaces. On the corner of Washington Potter Palmer's superb white marble building, 180 by 150, was filled through its six stories with the dry goods store of Field, Lester & Co. The loss in building and contents will largely exceed one million. Next Potter Palmer's store, occupied by Allen & Mackey, carpets, the great Thayer & Tobey Furniture Warehouse, and Giles Bros.' costly jewelry-store and stock. Northward, on the corner, Garrett Block, occupied by the Chicago Omnibus Company. On State-street, south of Washington, the magnificent pile of buildings owned by Hale & Bro., Dr. Williams, Peter Page, Sturges Brothers, was known as Book-seller's Row, and contained the great book-houses of Griggs & Co., Keen, Cook & Co., and Western News Company. Boyce's building (in Marquette stone) was in process of construction on the Madison-street corner. On the Wabash-avenue front of this square were a line of costly buildings, owned by Peter Page and others, and occupied by Pardridge, leading dry-goods, and Appleby, picture-frames.

On Wabash-avenue, between Washington and Madison, were the recently rebuilt block of John B. Drake, John V. Farwell and Thatcher Brothers; occupants, Hamlin, dry-goods; J. V. Farwell & Co., dry-goods; F. C. & M. D. Wells, stoves.

On the south-east corner of Wabash-avenue and Madison stood the Clifton House, Mr. Jenkins lessee; value of building and contents, about $150,000.

Below Madison, on Wabash-avenue and Michigan-avenue, the elegant residence section extended, only recently begun, to be invaded by business. On Wabash, north of Madison to the river, on Randolph and Lake streets to the lake shore, was the solidly-built wholesale quarter, a large portion of which was rebuilt in costly style a season or two since.

The Chicago Court-house was a structure extending from Lasalle-street to Clark, 180 feet front on each street, and 325 feet in length, contained the Court rooms, Recorder's and municipal offices, the valable law library, and the jail in the basement. It had been recently rebuilt and enlarged. The structure cost not far from $1,000,000.

October 10, 1871

Report on the Boston Fire.

The report of a committee of five on the causes and management of the great fire which laid the principal business part of Boston in ashes last November, has just been completed. Although it supplies very little new information, its publication at this particular time is calculated to do important service. During several weeks past, applications for permits to rebuild have been sent in considerable numbers to the board having charge of the matter. We have noticed that some of the owners of valuable lots have shown a strong disposition to doubt the advisability of contracting said lots in their depth, so as to allow a greater breadth to the streets. To give way to opposition of this kind, it is needless to say, would be to have the new city as narrow, crooked, and irregular as was the old. The report of the committee of citizens is of value, for the reason that it will be the means of refreshing the public mind by setting forward certain facts in connection with the fire that cannot well be ignored. The statement of the Insurance Commissioner of Massachusetts, to the effect that English underwriters had spoken to him at Liverpool and London of the probable fate of Franklin-street, Winthrop-square, and their surroundings, at the same time proposing to cancel their policies and do no more business with Boston, bears forcibly upon this subject. The streets referred to were narrow, and presented so many difficulties to impede the operations of firemen, that it became absolutely impossible to do anything with them when the flames had got completely under way. That part of the report bearing on proposed changes and improvements in the Fire Department is also of interest. It recommends the purchase of more engines; that the supply of fuel for the same, be methodical; that bridges be supplied for the protection of hose; that water have a better distribution, and that the office of Fire Inspector be created. In directing attention to the causes which so greatly contributed to the spread of the flames, special reference is very properly made to the elevators in warehouses. These elevators, the committee claims, were among the most active agents in destroying buildings, and should, consequently, be forbidden altogether, unless when provided with self-closing hatchings.

The subject of elevators is one that ought not to be lost sight of in our own City. Many of those now in use are not provided with self-closing fire-proof hatches. That they ought to be so is quite obvious. The officers engaged in the inspection of school-houses, hotels, and public institutions could not do better than take a look at the warehouses down-town, and let us have a report upon their condition generally. Most of the great fires that have occurred within the past few years, have been propagated by much more insignificant causes than the draught through the open hatchway of an elevator, and it will, therefore, not be wise to overlook the suggestions of the Boston committee in regard to this matter.

January 29, 1873

Means of Extinguishing Fires.

It was natural that the recent revelations concerning the condition of the Boston Fire Department should be followed by some action upon the part of the insurance companies. The question of taking risks in Boston [illegible] become one of great interest to the insurance companies, and yesterday it came up for formal consideration at a meeting of the Underwriters in this City. There was no denial that the Boston Fire Department is lamentably inefficient, and the suggestion was seriously made that unless great improvements are speedily introduced, it would become necessary to ask whether self-protection would not require the refusal of Boston risks in the future. No one, however, was prepared with a remedy, and finally a committee of twenty-five was appointed to confer with the authorities of Boston upon this subject.

This action of the Underwriters should attract general attention, as the matter to which it is directed is one of vital consequence to every community. Almost unparalleled misfortune has made known the deficiency of Boston in the means of fire extinguishment, but it is well understood that very many other places, in fact nearly all our cities and towns, are badly prepared for a conflagration, which is liable to occur at any moment. At the meeting yesterday attention was called to the peril of Atlanta, where the City Council has just refused to provide a supply of water, but the danger is by no means peculiar to that town. Any one who has taken the trouble to read the newspapers has taken note of the destructive fires which are constantly occurring in all parts of the country. Only a few days ago there were several very serious conflagrations in the smaller towns, and in all these cases it is fair to infer the great loss of property was directly due to the lack of means of fire extinguishment. Our towns and villages are, to a large extent, only immense tinder-boxes, being built almost wholly of wood, and it invariably happens that a fire taking in one of these places must be left to exhaust itself.

It is marvelous that a danger which is so constant as that of fire should excite so little attention. There is hardly a household in the whole land, prepared to meet an emergency that may come at any moment, and we have had many lamentable proofs in this City that even in hôtels, factories, and other public buildings where the pretense of preparation had been made, such private means were wholly insufficient. Even if there is an abundant supply of water in very many cases, fire gains headway on its amateur combatant, as extinguishing flames is a business to be learned by apprenticeship as much as any other avocation. Hence it happens that private apparatus is rarely efficient, and that in the end the building is destroyed or is saved only by the intervention of the public engines, manned by trained firemen. Numerous cases to prove this fact might be cited, but it is so entirely within the experience of every reader, that such evidence is unnecessary.

The great need of the country at large, then, after providing a proper water supply, is the increase and improvement of the public fire departments. In nearly all our minor towns and villages, the fire establishments, where they have any, are provided with the worthless hand-machines, and are based upon the volunteer system, so that they are chiefly useful for propagating ruffians and vagabonds. A community which can afford to have any public fire apparatus —and none can afford to be without one—can support something better than the valueless machines, which is all most of them possess. No compactly-built town, whatever may be its population, should be without steam fire-engines. These machines are now made of any desired size, so that the first cost is but little more than that of the most inexpensive hand-machines, and the subsequent maintenance costs no more.

As the country generally looks to New-York for the model of a fire department, and there is reason to expect that action in this matter will soon become more general than heretofore, it is the duty of our Commissioners to render our department as nearly perfect as possible. We have lately had two quite serious fires, and the warning they contain should not be neglected. We notice that the Commissioners have taken into consideration the adoption of the new aerial ladder as one means of adding to the efficiency of their force. We can readily see how it can be made of very great service, provided it can be made strong enough to bear the strain to which it is subjected, which one did not do on the occasion of a recent trial. Whatever may be done in this matter, as well as in the general management, should be done only upon full consideration. Our Fire Department has attained such great excellence that extraordinary exertion is required to maintain its prestige.

June 19, 1873

GREAT FIRE IN BALTIMORE.

LOSS, ONE MILLION DOLLARS.

PART OF THE CITY IN ASHES—WHOLE BLOCKS IN FLAMES—NUMBERS OF THE FINEST RESIDENCES DESTROYED.

Special Dispatch to the New-York Times.

BALTIMORE, July 25.—For the first time in its history, Baltimore has to-day been visited with a conflagration, the loss from which has amounted to a million of dollars. In the centre of the city is a district of three squares, embraced between Liberty Park, Lexington and Saratoga streets. Between Lexington and Saratoga streets is Clay-street, a small thoroughfare, in which were situated a number of sash and box factories. It was in the large sash-factory of J. Thomas & Son, in Clay-street, that the fire originated. A pile of shavings lying near the mouth of the furnace was ignited by the sparks from it, and although the men on duty made strenuous endeavors to extinguish the rapidly spreading flames, they gained headway with such rapidity that the workmen were driven from the building. On either side of it were similar establishments and rows of small frame buildings, with shingle roofs, upon which the burning cinders fell in such numbers as to speedily spread the fire along the whole street westward to Park and eastward to Liberty. It was at first expected that this would be the boundary of the fire, but while the firemen were working to get it under control, the flames were suddenly seen to extend southward to Lexington-street and northward to Saratoga.

ALARM AT THE SPREAD OF THE FIRE.

So long as the flames only embraced Clay-street the fire was not considered of serious consequence, as the buildings there were small and comparatively worthless; but when the flames extended to the handsome stores and residences on Saratoga and Lexington streets the greatest alarm was visible in the city, and a multitude of people hurried to the scene of conflagration.

CHURCHES DESTROYED.

Spreading in these directions, the flames soon enwrapped the Central Presbyterian Church at the corner of Saratoga and Liberty streets, and the First English Lutheran Church on Lexington-street. The Presbyterian Church was one of the finest buildings in the country, and its destruction presented a most magnificent aspect. The flames wound in fine spirals around its lofty spire, and then burst out into broad flame. The stout walls crumbled under the intense heat, and fell into the burning pile with a crash that resounded for squares around. The handsome furniture of the church and its great organ were entirely destroyed. The English Lutheran Church was not a building of equal pretensions or value, but it was hallowed to the denomination from having had as its pastors some of the most notable Lutheran ministers in this country. It was entirely destroyed, leaving no vestige but its walls.

A BLOCK OF STORES AND ANOTHER OF DWELLINGS BURNED.

The buildings on the north and south fronts of the fire were mainly stores having valuable stocks of dry goods on hand, and most of these were destroyed, either by fire or by water. Solitary among them were the great livery-stables of Stewart & Co., from which, fortunately, all the valuable horses were removed in time to escape death. Just west of the Presbyterian Church on Saratoga-street was a row of fine dwellings, all of which were burned to the ground.

ST. ALPHONSUS SCHOOL AND CHURCH.

On the south side of Saratoga-street was the immense school under the control of the brotherhood of St. Alphonsus Catholic Church. It was burned to the ground. But as there were no pupils within it at the time there was no loss of life. St. Alphonsus Church was in great danger for a while, but the wind suddenly veered to the north-west, and carried the flames back upon the district which was already burning. The efforts to save this church were most heroic. Men mounted upon the outside of its lofty spire, and with buckets of water deluged its blazing roof until the flames were subdued. Immediately adjoining it were the palatial residences of some of the wealthiest residents of Baltimore, and these were only saved from destruction by the most earnest efforts.

CONSTERNATION AMONG THE POOR.

It must be understood that although the exterior boundaries of this district were occupied with handsome stores and residences the interior consisted very largely of the dwellings of poor people. The consternation of these people is impossible to describe. The scene was most terrifying. Men, women, and children were throwing their household goods and furniture into the streets and rushing about in the wildest terror. Their wild scamperings, the screams of the women, the crash of falling walls, the roar of the flames, and the steady pressure onward of the firemen, who were sparing nothing in their endeavor to reach the flames, made up a scene of horror. The sky was darkened with smoke-clouds, amid which the flames leaped up, and created such a heat that men could scarcely live under it. The streets were filled with all descriptions of goods, and cartmen were reaping a harvest in the enormous prices which they demanded. Fortunately, there was no loss of life, although sick persons and children were occasionally removed from houses with scarcely a breath left in them.

THE FIRE LEAPS ACROSS THE STREETS.

Another phase of the fire remains to be told. While it was burning within the district mentioned, the flames had sprung clear across the square between Saratoga and Mulberry streets, and had lighted upon buildings on Mulberry-street. The first edifice on fire in this section was the Maryland University, which had a portion of its walls and roof burned. Next to it was the Maryland Academy of Arts; the walls of this were also burned, but the statuary and paintings were unharmed. A row of fine houses on Mulberry-street were destroyed, but at this point the flames ceased their ravages. The firemen had brought them under control by fighting them from both sides, and by 4 o'clock this afternoon peace and quiet were restored.

TENDERS OF AID TO THE CITY.

Dispatches from here had created an immense excitement, and tenders of assistance from Washington and Philadelphia were freely made. These were only so far availed of as to accept a couple of engines from Washington, which were sent over in thirty-nine minutes, and helped much toward subduing the fire. There was no direct loss of life, except that Sister Rinaldi, a nun in the convent attached to St. Alphonsus Church, died of fright.

July 26, 1873

FOUND FIRE CONDITIONS PERILOUS IN 24 CITIES

Ignorance or Dishonesty Responsible, Says Underwriters' Board.

LOSS IN 1904 BROKE RECORD

Jersey City and Hoboken Said to be Specially Inflammable and Rates Are Raised.

Many attempts at hostile legislation were reported to the thirty-ninth annual meeting of the National Board of Fire Underwriters at the Mutual Life Building yesterday, but it was said that most of the bills had been defeated in the East. Measures to which the underwriters object are still pending in Florida, Illinois, and Michigan. Most of the companies, it was said, have withdrawn from Arkansas rather than incur the heavy penalties threatened by anti-trust legislation.

A membership of 115 companies was reported, three having retired during the year. The Palatine Fire Insurance Company was admitted.

The committee of twenty appointed to investigate fire conditions, reported on twenty-four cities. Conditions were pronounced generally bad, either through ignorance or dishonesty. They were especially condemned in Jersey City and Hoboken. The committee's ideas were approved except in the case of Paterson, where the board has paid $7,000,000 in fire losses, and the water supply is in the hands of a private corporation.

The committee's expenses have been about $10,000 a month, and Mr. Corea of the Home Fire Insurance Company intimated that his concern might withdraw if the inquiry was to be carried on at such a heavy cost. The committee, however, was continued with an appropriation of $104,000 for the coming year by a vote of 48 to 7.

The high-pressure water supply for fire purposes which is about to be installed in this city, the Chairman said, was worth all the money which the board had spent on the committee of twenty. The Chairman said that salt water was not to be used, as it was believed that the necessity for it would never arise, but that if it ever were required provision has been made for it.

President Washburn in his address said that 1904 had been the year of heaviest losses, not excepting the years of the Chicago and Boston conflagrations, and that up to March 1 there had been five fires with damage of more than $1,000,000 each. He declared the suggestions of President Roosevelt as to the National supervision of insurance as embodied in two bills before Congress would not be satisfactory to the underwriters without radical amendments. Smaller rewards were offered and smaller rewards paid for the detection of incendiaries than for many years.

The election of officers resulted as follows:

President—John H. Washburn; Vice President—George W. Burchell, Vice President Queen Fire Insurance Society; Secretary—Charles A. Shaw, President Hanover Fire Insurance Company; Treasurer—Marshall S. Driggs, President Williamsburg City Fire Insurance Company; Executive Committee—George B. Edwards, Vice President Germania Fire Insurance Company; F. O. Affold, Manager Hamburg-Bremen Fire Insurance Company, and R. M. Bissell, Vice President Hartford Fire Insurance Company.

The meeting ended with a banquet at Delmonico's.

It was announced last night that fire insurance rates in Bayonne had been advanced 50 per cent., and in Jersey City and all other municipalities of Hudson County had been raised 30 per cent.

May 12, 1905

OVER 500 DEAD, $200,000,000 LOST IN SAN FRANCISCO EARTHQUAKE

Nearly Half the City Is in Ruins and 50,000 Are Homeless.

WATER SUPPLY FAILS AND DYNAMITE IS USED IN VAIN

Great Buildings Consumed Before Helpless Firemen—Federal Troops and Militia Guard the City, With Orders to Shoot Down Thieves—Citizens Roused in Early Morning by Great Convulsion and Hundreds Caught by Falling Walls.

SAN FRANCISCO, April 18.—Earthquake and fire to-day have put nearly half of San Francisco in ruins. About 500 persons have been killed, a thousand injured, and the property loss will exceed $200,000,000.

Fifty thousand people are homeless and destitute, and all day long streams of people have been fleeing from the stricken districts to places of safety.

It was 5:13 this morning when a terrific earthquake shock shook the whole city and surrounding country. One shock apparently lasted two minutes, and there was almost immediate collapse of flimsy structures all over the city.

The water supply was cut off, and when fires started in various sections there was nothing to do but let the buildings burn. Telegraph and telephone communication was cut off for a time.

The Western Union was put completely out of business and the Postal Company was the only one that managed to get a wire out of the city. About 10 o'clock even the Postal was forced to suspend.

Electric power was stopped and street cars did not run, railroads and ferryboats also ceased operations. The various fires raged all day and the fire department has been powerless to do anything except dynamite buildings threatened. All day long explosions have shaken the city and added to the terror of the inhabitants.

Following the first shock there was another within five minutes, but not nearly so severe. Three hours later there was another slight quake.

First Warning at 5:13 A. M.

Most of the people of San Francisco were asleep at 5:13 o'clock this morning when the terrible earthquake came without warning.

The motion of the disturbance apparently was from east to west. At first the upheaval of the earth was gradual, but in a few seconds it increased in intensity. Chimneys began to fall and buildings to crack, tottering on their foundations.

The people became panic-stricken, and rushed into the streets, most of them in their night attire. They were met by showers of falling bricks, cornices, and walls of buildings.

Many were crushed to death, while others were badly mangled. Those who remained indoors generally escaped with their lives, though scores were hit by detached plaster, pictures, and articles thrown to the floor by the shock. It is believed that more or less loss was sustained by nearly every family in the city.

Steel Frame Buildings Stand.

The tall, steel-frame structures stood the strain better than brick buildings, few of them being badly damaged. The big eleven-story Monadnock office building, in course of construction, adjoining the Palace Hotel, was an exception, however, its rear wall collapsing and many cracks being made across its front.

Some of the docks and freight sheds along the water front slid into the bay. Deep fissures opened in the filled-in ground near the shore, and the Union Ferry Station was badly injured. Its high tower still stands, but will have to be torn down.

A portion of the new City Hall, which cost more than $7,000,000, collapsed, the roof sliding into the courtyard, and the smaller towers tumbling down. The great dome was moved, but did not fall.

The new Post Office, one of the finest in the United States, was badly shattered.

The Valencia Hotel, a four-story wooden building, sank into the basement, a pile of splintered timbers, under which were pinned many dead and dying occupants of the house. The basement was full of water, and some of the helpless victims were drowned.

Fires Start in Many Places.

Scarcely had the earth ceased to shake when fires started simultaneously in many places. The Fire Department promptly responded to the first calls for aid, but it was found that the water mains had been rendered useless by the underground movement.

Fanned by a light breeze, the flames quickly spread, and soon many blocks were seen to be doomed. Then dynamite was resorted to, and the sound of frequent explosions added to the terror of the people. These efforts to stay the progress of the fire, however, proved futile.

The south side of Market Street, from Ninth Street to the bay, was soon ablaze, the fire covering a belt two blocks wide. On this, the main thoroughfare, were many of the finest edifices in the city, including the Grant, Parrott, Flood, Call, Examiner, and Monadnock Buildings, and the Palace and Grand Hotels.

At the same time commercial establishments and banks north of Market Street were burning. The burning district in this section of the city extended from Sansome Street to the water front, and from Market Street to Broadway.

Fires also started in the Mission, and the entire city seemed to be in flames.

The flames, fanned by the rising breeze, swept down the main streets until within a few hundred feet of the ferry station, the high tower of which stood at a dangerous angle.

The big wholesale grocery establishment of Weelman, Peck & Co. was on fire from cellar to roof, and the heat was so oppressive that passengers from the ferry boats were obliged to keep close to the water's edge, in order to get past the burning structure.

It was impossible to reach the centre of the city from the bay without skirting the shore for a long distance so as to get entirely around the burning district.

About 8 o'clock the Southern Pacific officials refused to allow any more passengers from trans-bay points to land, and sent back those already on the boats. The ferry and train service of the Key Route was entirely abandoned owing to damage done to the power house by the earthquake at Emeryville.

There was little dynamite available in the city. The Southern Pacific soon brought some in. At 9 o'clock Mayor Schmitz sent a tug to Pinola for several cases of explosives. He sent also a telegram to Mayor Mott of Oakland. At 10:30 he received this reply to his Oakland message:

"Three engines and hose companies leave here immediately. Will forward dynamite as soon as obtainable."

The town of San Rafael, despite its own needs, sent fire fighting apparatus here.

Mayor Schmitz gave orders to use dynamite wherever necessary, and the firemen and United States soldiers, who assisted them, blew down building after building. Their efforts, however, were useless, so far as checking the headway of the flames was concerned.

The shortage of water was due to the breaking of the mains of the Spring Valley Water Company at San Mateo. The water needed so badly in the city ran in a flood over San Mateo.

The fire swept down the streets so rapidly that it was practically impossible to save anything in its way. It reached the Grand Opera House on Mission Street, and in a moment had burned through the roof. The Metropolitan Opera Company from New York had just opened its season there, and all the expensive scenery and costumes were soon reduced to ashes.

From the opera house the fire leaped from building to building, leveling them almost to the ground in quick succession.

The Call editorial and mechanical departments, in the handsome building at Third and Market Streets, were totally destroyed in a few minutes, and the flames leaped across Stevenson Street toward the fine fifteen-story stone and iron building of Claus Spreckels, which, with its lofty dome, was the most notable structure in San Francisco. Two small wooden buildings furnished fuel to ignite the splendid pile.

Thousands of people watched the hungry tongues of flames licking the stone walls. At first no impression was made, but suddenly there was a cracking of glass and an entrance was effected. The inner furnishings of the fourth floor were the first to go. Then, as if by magic, smoke issued from the top of the dome.

This was followed by a most spectacular illumination. The round windows of the dome shone like so many full moons; they burst and gave vent to long, waving streamers of flames. The crowd watched the spectacle with bated breath. One woman wrung her hands and burst into a torrent of tears. "It is so terrible," she said.

The tall and slender structure which had withstood the forces of the earth appeared doomed to fall a prey to fire. After a while, however, the light grew less intense, and the flames, finding nothing to consume, gradually went out, leaving the building standing, but completely gutted.

At California and Sansome Streets stood the Mutual Life Building, a modern structure of architectural beauty, to which the flames were soon communicated. An attempt was made to save it, but the fire was irrepressible. The flames gained, and in a few moments the big building was beyond hope. The Anglo California Bank was swept by the flames and came down in a rush.

Time and again attempts were made with dynamite to clear a space which should prevent the flames from spreading to other buildings, but freely as the explosive was used the fire crept and climbed from one structure to another.

An unusually loud report showed that a gas house at Eighteenth and Market Streets had blown up. The fire caused by the explosion quickly communicated in various directions. As the gas house exploded a feeling of despair overcame the men who were performing the rescue work.

The Palace Hotel, the rear of which was constantly threatened, was the scene of much excitement, the guests leaving in haste, many with only the clothing they wore. Finding that the hotel was surrounded on all sides by streets, and was likely to remain immune, many returned and made arrangements for the removal of their belongings, though little could be taken away owing to the utter absence of transportation facilities.

The Parrott Building, in which was located the chambers of the State Supreme Court, the lower floors being devoted to an immense department store, was ruined, though its massive walls were not all destroyed.

A little further down Market Street, the Academy of Sciences and the Jennie Flood Building and the History Building kindled and burned like so much tinder. Sparks carried across the wide street, ignited the Phelan Building, and the army headquarters of California, Gen. Funston commanding, were burned.

Still nearing the bay, the waters of which did the firemen good service along the docks, the fire took the Rialto Building, a handsome skyscraper, and converted scores of solid business blocks into smoldering piles of bricks.

Banks and commercial houses, supposed to be fireproof, though not of modern build, burned quickly, and the roar of the flames could be heard even on the hills, which were out of the danger zone. Here many thousands of people congregated and viewed the awful scene.

Great sheets of flame rose high in the heavens, or rushed down some narrow street, joining midway between the sidewalks, making a horizontal chimney of the former passageway.

The dense smoke that arose from the entire business district spread out like an immense funnel and could have been seen miles out at sea. Occasionally as some drug house or place stored with chemicals was reached, most fantastic effects were produced by the centred flames and smoke which rolled out against the darker background.

One of the first orders issued by Chief of Police Dinan this morning was for the closing of every saloon in the city. This step is taken to prevent drink-crazed men from rioting in the streets.

Mayor Schmitz sent out word to the bakeries and milk stations throughout the city that their food supplies must be harbored for the homeless. Provisions were made to place tents in every park in the city, and those who have lost all will be given food and shelter.

Early in the morning the prisoners confined in the city prison on the fifth floor of the Hall of Justice were transferred in irons to the basement of the structure. Later they were removed to the Broadway Jail, and if necessity arises they will be taken to a branch county jail on the Mission Road.

The Mayor also established a base of rescue, and soon had forces out where they could accomplish most. Many men were sent down to the lodging house district near Market Street. There it was found that many frame buildings, packed with people, had collapsed, burying their occupants in the ruins.

The rescuers jumped into the wrecks and pulled out the dead, the dying, and the injured. Practically every physician in the city immediately volunteered his assistance, and soon there was a well-equipped medical corps organized which began ministering to the injured.

For hours bodies were taken out in the lodging house district, and hundreds of men volunteered to go into the ruins to get more.

The pretentious City Hall, bounded by Larkin and McAllister Streets and City Hall Avenue, was badly shattered by the earthquake, and the ruins later were burned. It took twenty years to build the City Hall, the pride of the coast. When the first shock was felt the building rocked and swayed until it cracked. Part of the interior fell and the ruins caught fire. An alarm was turned in and the firemen responded. Chief Sullivan, awakened by the shock at his quarters in a firehouse, hastened to put on his clothes. As he reached for them the tower of the California Hotel dropped upon his building and crushing through the roof killed him.

The firemen arrived at the City Hall, but were helpless. They hitched their hose to the fire plugs, but there was no water supply.

Every possible precaution has been taken to guard property. Immediately after the destructive shocks the police turned out on guard, and the Governor and Gen. Funston, commanding the **Pacific Division of the United States Army, were asked to send troops.**

A thousand men from the Presidio, sent by Gen. Funston, arrived downtown at 9 o'clock to patrol the streets. The Thirteenth Infantry, 1,000 strong, arrived from Angel Island a little later and went on patrol duty at once.

The soldiers were ordered to shoot down vandals caught robbing the dead and to guard with their lives the millions of dollars' worth of property placed in the streets to escape the flames.

The First California Artillery, 200 strong, two companies, was detailed to patrol duty on Ellis Street. Two more companies patrolled Broadway in the Italian section. The Ellis Street contingent of guardsmen were under the command of Capt. G. A. Grattan. Capt. William A. Miller commanded the forces on Broadway.

The city is under martial law, and all the downtown streets are patroled by cavalry and infantry. Details of troops are also guarding the banks.

Early this morning Mayor Schmitz. who established his office at Police Headquarters, named the following citizens as a Committee of Safety:

James D. Phelan, Herbert Law, Thomas Magee, Charles Fee, W. P. Herrin, Thornwell Mullalley, Garret W. Enerney, W. H. Leahy, J. Downey Harvey, Jeremiah Dinan, John J. Mahoney, Henry T. Scott, I. W. Hellman, George A. Knight, I. Steinhart, S. G. Murphy, Homer King, Frank Anderson, W. J. Bartnett, John Martin, Allan Pollock, Mark Gerstle, H. V. Ramsdell, W. G. Harrison, R. A. Crothers, Paul Cowles, M. H. De Young, Claus Spreckles, Rudolph Spreckles, C. W. Fay, John McNaught, Dent Robert, Thomas Garrett, Frank Shea, James Shea, Robert Pisis, T. P. Woodward, Howard Holmes, George Dillman, J. B. Rogers, David Rich, H. T. Cresswell, J. A. Howell, Frank Maestretti, Clem Tobin, George Toumey, E. D. Pond, George A. Newhall, William Watson.

EARTHQUAKE'S AUTOGRAPH AS IT WROTE IT 3,000 MILES AWAY.

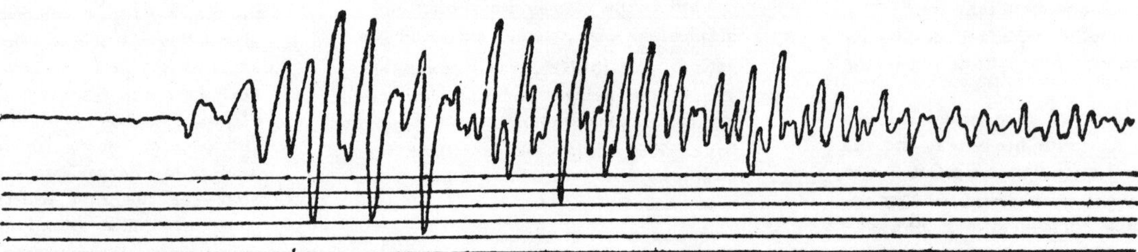

The drawing represents the vibration of the north and south pendulum of the seismograph during the time of the most intense activity, beginning in San Francisco at 5:13 A. M., in Albany at 8:32. In Albany the violent agitation ended at 8:43 A. M. The straight lines at the side of the wavy line indicate the normal condition of the record as the recording drum revolves, and this serves to show the contrast between the ordinary progress of the record and that during a disturbance. The spaces between the dots indicate lapses of one minute each.

The same violent disturbance was noticeable on the seismograph at Washington between 8:32 and 8:35 A. M., thus verifying the time of transit across the continent—19 minutes.

April 19, 1906

FIRE APPARATUS IN GENERAL USE

Over $3,000,000 Invested in Motor Fire Vehicles by 301 Cities and Towns.

Over $3,000,000 has already been invested in motor fire apparatus in this country. A recent census by The Power Wagon showed that 301 cities and towns in the United States have 594 motor-driven fire apparatus of all kinds already in service, each piece being worth anywhere from $3,500 to $10,000, the aggregate value being a trifle over three millions.

In all the history of finance no better investment than this three millions has ever been recorded. And in no other branch of activity has the motor vehicle a more undisputed and proved superiority over the horse. The people whose property is insured by the motor apparatus against destruction by fire, the fire insurance companies who are directly concerned in fire protection, and the Fire Chiefs and firemen whose business it is to put out fires—all these are a unit in declaring the efficiency of the motor from every standpoint, and its unquestioned superiority over the horse.

In the United States, according to the census of 1910, there are 6,225 cities and towns with a population of 2,000 or over; there are 3,553 with a population of 3,000 or over; there are 1,858 with a population of 5,000 or over; there are 842 cities with a population of 10,000 or over; there are 320 cities with a population of 25,000 or more; there are 131 cities with a population exceeding 50,000, and 43 cities have a population of 100,000 or over.

These, then, are the possibilities. Each of these cities and towns, on the average, needs two motor driven fire-fighting machines. The whole country, according to this estimate, which is derived from present statistics, should have a total of 12,450 machines. There are only 594 of them already in service, which leaves a balance of 11,850 still wanted. The value of these is in the neighborhood of $60,000,000.

Present indications show that this business will be absorbed by the motor wagon industry well within the next ten years. But in that time the population of the country will have increased by about 25 per cent., and fire protection will have to increase by a like ratio. Hence, the market for motor fire apparatus for the next ten years is certainly not less than $75,000,000.

All the developments of the last few years are in favor of motor fire apparatus. Improved methods of intercommunication, notably the electric trolley and interurban lines, the telephone, and the increasing radius of the delivery service (by motor wagons) of the great city department stores, have induced people to move out from the congested areas in the cities to the suburbs. The density of city population is decreasing, but the area is increasing enormously. Outlying districts are being built up and the people in them are isolated from fire protection facilities. The horse-driven fire apparatus is thus automatically rendered obsolete, for it simply cannot cover the distance in a reasonably short time. The only alternative is motor apparatus. The people themselves realize this, for in numerous cases have fire motors been purchased by popular subscription, and in several cases even on the installment plan. Public opinion is thus in favor of the motor, and what the public wants it gets, sooner or later.

The economic advantages of the motor

fire apparatus are almost illimitable. It has been calculated that the $3,000,000 already invested in fire motors is paying dividends of hundreds per cent. every year to the American people. Naturally, the total saving is impossible to estimate, but a direct idea of the value to the public of motor fire apparatus is conveyed by the action of the insurance companies, which in numerous cases have voluntarily reduced their rates for fire insurance when motors have been installed. In several cases this reduction has amounted to over 50 per cent.

The saving in fire insurance premiums alone is greater each year than the total cost of all the motor fire apparatus installed up to date. This may sound absurd, but it may easily be verified. A motor hose and chemical engine costing $5,000 will cover an area of twenty-two square miles of average city. A reduction of 10 per cent. in the fire insurance premiums on property covering this area would represent an amount of money sufficient to buy not one but ten machines every year at the price assumed. And in the estimate, which is averaged for the whole country, the most conservative values were taken in arriving at a result.

But this does not even begin to exhaust the economic possibilities of the motor fire apparatus. In the cost of administration and upkeep the motor is very much more economical than the horse, as is amply proved by statistics furnished by fire chiefs in their annual reports.

A very important point in favor of the motor is the tremendous saving it effects in reducing the number of fire stations. To give adequate fire protection with horse apparatus needs three times the number of stations that are required for motors, since the latter have at least three times the speed of horses, even in crowded city streets, and many times their radius. A new fire station costing, say, $25,000, is a serious item to a growing municipality, whereas $5,000 invested in do not end with the purchase price of new station unnecessary. And the expenses do not end with the purchase price of sew buildings. There is rent to pay, besides wages for attendants, telephone bills, and scores of other items, all of which are rendered unnecessary when the fire-fighting radius of existing stations is trebled by the installation of motor apparatus.

These are irrefutable arguments, and although we may love and admire the old-time fire horses, in this case sentiment must give way to business. The fire horse is obsolescent. In ten years he will be extinct. And in the transformation at least $75,000,000 will be needed for motor apparatus.

February 4, 1912

The Necessity of Public Baths—The Example of Boston.

If our Common Council would confer a substantial benefit upon that numerous portion of their constituents who herd in the inconvenient and unwholesome apartments of the fifteen thousand tenement-houses of this City, they ought at once to follow the wise example of the municipal officers of Boston, and provide suitable public bathing accommodations for this class of the population, who would be prompt to appreciate such advantages. The importance of personal cleanliness to the public health, and its bearings upon public morality, make it somewhat startling to know that there are living in this City nearly half a million of poor persons who are utterly destitute of the means of proper ablution at their homes, and who, if they turn elsewhere in search of health and cleanliness, find no conveniences in the shape of free public baths from one end of the City to the other.

We have seen the recently published report of the Joint Standing Committee on Public Bathing of the Boston Common Council, which presents very clearly the operations of their system during the two years it has been in existence. Beginning in 1866 with six salt-water baths, it was at once found that their advantages were fully understood by the class they were intended to benefit. Indeed, it was apparent at the start that all the applicants could not be accommodated, on account of the inconveniences arising from using the same baths at different hours for both sexes. To remedy this defect, and to afford every possible convenience to persons wishing to bathe, the authorities last year increased the number of baths to twelve, of which four were exclusively devoted to women and girls.

These baths are distributed along the water front of the City, wherever they can be placed most economically and conveniently, and are kept open during the months of June, July, August and September. They are each under the charge of a Superintendent, who sees that the simple rules which govern the bathers in regard to the priority of use of the dressing-rooms, the prohibition of profane language, noisy conversation and smoking, are enforced. Each bather is required to provide his own towels and soap, female bathers must furnish themselves with suitable bathing-dresses, and any person who is guilty of defacing the rooms, fences or tanks is excluded from the baths, or arrested, according to the nature of his offence. The popularity of these free baths is shown by the fact that 807,201 persons availed themselves of them during the last season, of which 177,797 were men; 528,176 were boys; 24,376 were women, and 76,852 were girls.

The most surprising feature of the entire system is its economy. The total cost for constructing new bath-houses, altering old ones, repairs, rents, salaries to superintendents, &c., amounted last year to less than $22,000, or an average of .02 3-5 for each bath given.

As a sanitary measure this Boston experiment has received the indorsement of the press, physicians of every school, and all who have given any attention to the subject. The remarkable degree of healthfulness which has marked that city during the two years that these baths have been maintained is attributed, in a great measure, to the daily ablutions of so large a portion of the population.

This excellent example which Boston has set, has been already imitated by Charlestown and Cambridge, in Massachusetts, and by Pittsburg, Cincinnati and St. Louis. There is every reason why the City of New-York should immediately confer similar benefits upon her poor population. The expenditure need not be heavy, and public money devoted to the encouragement of virtue and cleanliness would not be grudged by any class of our citizens. If the Common Council have not the funds on hand for the construction of these greatly-needed conveniences, they might easily obtain them, by inserting a provision in the City tax levy before it passes the Legislature. If there is any humanity and public spirit existing in either branch of the City Government, let it show itself in this matter, without further delay. The Summer season will soon be here, and the wants of the poor denizens of the tenement-houses, in this respect, will be severely felt. There is no good reason why, in the interval between now and the month of June, the requisite preparations may not be made, so that the [illegible] be ready for the use of the public upon the opening of the Summer season.

March 22, 1868

THE POORER CLASSES.

Extent and Increase of Pauperism.

Defects of the Present System of Caring for Paupers and Criminals—Proposed Remedies.

New-York has a right to be proud of the liberal provision which is made by private munificence and public benefaction for the thousands of the poor and unfortunate among her population, but it may well be questioned whether the methods by which this bounty is applied for the relief of the necessities do not display more generosity than wisdom, a disposition to give freely rather than a willingness to do anything to ameliorate the condition of the indigent, the idle and the vicious.

THE EXTENT AND INCREASE OF PAUPERISM.

There is something alarming in the fact that while liberal provision has been made for the care and maintenance of the poor and the helpless, their number has been steadily increasing, until at the present moment one in every thirteen of the inhabitants of this city has been set down in the category of paupers. This exhibits an increase in less than forty years of more than 900 per cent., while the population has not advanced in more than one-tenth of that ratio. In this reckoning are included all those who receive aid from the public, either in the way of permanent support or temporary relief. Startled by such a revelation as this, we naturally inquired whether there is not some radical defect in our system of public charities which contributes to the deplorable result.

WHAT IS DONE BY THE PRESENT SYSTEM.

It has been estimated that not less than $5,000,000 are expended annually in this City for various charitable and philanthropic objects. To say nothing of the large amounts of money and other material aid bestowed by private generosity, or of the liberal endowment of private eleemosynary institutions, the Department of Public Charities and Correction alone disburses about $1,000,000 of the public money through the various institutions under its control. According to the present system any person who is a fit subject for the relief afforded by this department, makes application to the proper officer and is sent to one of the asylums or hospitals, or receives other aid as the case may require. The result is that instead of the disease being driven from the social system it is nursed and fostered at the public expense. The indolent and worthless flock hither to feed on our bounty, while the honest but indigent among our own citizens are not put in the way of bettering their condition, but simply taught to depend on the public institutions as an ultimate reliance.

THE TRUE METHOD

of dealing both with the pauper and criminal classes is one which looks to such an elevation and improvement of their character and condition that they can and will provide for their own wants by the labor of their own hands. The only persons for whom public institutions should be provided or public money appropriated are those who, from physical or mental incapacity, are unable in any situation to provide for themselves, and at the same time have no friends who can assume that duty. Those who are ignorant should have the means of enlightenment, not of support in their ignorance. Those who only need employment which they cannot obtain, should be removed to localities where labor is in demand instead of being encouraged to live in idleness. Those who are vicious and lazy should, under the combined influence of coercion and encouragement, be induced to leave off preying upon others, and devote themselves to their own independent support. And above all, those who are merely in danger of becoming paupers and criminals, should be rescued from that peril and placed in the way of industry and virtue. It would cost much less, both in effort and in money, to furnish the conditions and the facilities to make respectable citizens out of the sons of poverty, than to punish and support them when they have become criminals and paupers.

HOW THE REMEDY IS TO BE APPLIED.

There are two ways of attaining this object, both of which have been greatly neglected while we have been building our asylums and making our private and public donations for the encouragement of want and misery. The first is to provide for the poor the means of improving their condition where they now are, and the other is to remove them to more favorable surroundings in other localities. In other words, we must bring better conditions and more favorable circumstances to them, or take them where better conditions and more favorable circumstances already exist.

HOME AGENCIES NEEDED.

A beginning has been already made in establishing those agencies which are all-important, important beyond all computation in dollars and cents, for the elevation and improvement of those who are born within the purlieus of poverty, ignorance and vice. Of course every effort to render our common school system more complete and effective is an effort in their behalf, and therefore an effort in behalf of the general welfare of the community. The free schools of the Cooper Union and of the mission stations do something for them, and a few meagre libraries and reading rooms have been provided by the contributions of private benevolence, but no adequate means is employed to raise the degraded classes, and to rescue their offspring from the slums of vice and the dens of crime. We make liberal expenditures to punish them when they become criminals, and to support them when they become paupers, but do next to nothing to prevent them from reaching those conditions, where the direct expense which they entail upon the public treasury is but a tithe of the mischief they cause the community. A plan should be devised whereby the powerful and comprehensive workings of public agencies could be brought to bear in this matter, in addition to the restricted efforts of private charity. Libraries, reading rooms and courses of lectures might well become prominent features of our school system, and those structures which are made irksome prisons for children for six hours each day, should be throughout the day and the evening cheerful resorts for the improvement and the real culture of those who must look to the public for those blessings or go without them altogether. And, then, a good general library for the free use of the people of this City is an institution which is yet anxiously looked for. One good library has been founded by the beneficence of a private individual, and rendered practically useless by the policy on which it is conducted. Three-quarters of all the hours in the year, and those including *all* the leisure time of the people, its doors are closed, and hence its volumes stand in goodly ranks as if the building were a dismal catacomb for the works of dead authors, instead of what it should be—a means of diffusing knowledge and education among the people. Libraries, reading rooms, lectures and all the appliances of popular education should be supplied at the public expense on a scale commensurate with the wants of the people.

LABOR BUREAUS.

But the first great want of the indigent is the means of obtaining a livelihood. Thousands are driven to crime, and thousands more to the Almshouse, because they cannot or do not find employment, when all the while there is plenty of work to do. Already a free Labor Bureau has been established in the Department of Public Charities and Correction, and is doing a good work. Still more needs to be done in the same direction. Give the people employment, and then afford them the means of mental and moral improvement, and you transform them from a dangerous and uncontrolable rabble to a body of industrious and respectable citizens. This brings us to a plan which is occupying the attention of some of our most philanthropic citizens, for a

BUREAU OF INFORMATION, STATISTICS AND EMPLOYMENT.

An agency of this kind was proposed some two years ago by a committee of the Citizens Association, to be established by the Commissioners of Charities and Correction for the purpose of forwarding to the labor market of the West the surplus laboring population, or what should be laboring population, of this metropolis. The scheme contemplates the establishment of a Bureau through which communication could be kept up with the officials of the cities and towns of the West, and the names and qualifications of persons here desirous of obtaining employment could be received and recorded. In this way the demand for labor in the new States could be supplied from the superfluous idleness of New-York. Western towns could have their depots for the distribution of labor, receiving constant supplies to order from the East, and the large cities of the Atlantic board could send the streams of population which are too apt to flow into the depths of their lowest slums over the prairies and the valleys of the Mississippi region, there to become independent and self-respecting men and women, instead of criminals and paupers. The great idea of enabling the poor to take care of themselves instead of taking care of them, would thus be realized. This, we are assured, is not merely a visionary scheme, like so many which are talked of and forgotten, but steps are about to be taken to carry it into operation. This whole question of dealing with the classes of our population which make prisons and almshouses, those insults to humanity, a necessary evil, deserves the serious attention of our legislators and philanthropists.

January 9, 1870

LIFE IN THE SLUMS.

Sufferings of the Children of the Poor—The Homes of the Fourth Ward—Sickening Scenes.

On Saturday last we gave the readers of THE TIMES an insight into the homes and daily life of the poverty-stricken and unfortunate in six of the wards of the City. To-day we supplement that account by the researches of our reporters in several other of the tenement-house districts of the Metropolis, including a graphic picture of misery in the notorious Fourth Ward. It will be seen that the field for philanthropic action is indeed wide, and that the demands of the hour are most pressing.

THE FOURTH WARD.

It is but a short distance from the fashionable *quarter* of the Fifth-avenue, and other refined abodes of wealth and luxury, to the opposite extreme of human misery, depravity, and crime. The peasant poet of Scotland has truly said

> "That thin partitions do divide
> The bounds where good and ill reside."

But it should be a cause of congratulation to the citizens of New-York that here the good predominates, and what though the record of the City has been stained with beacon crimes, the innate sense of righteousness, and the broad and munificent charity which are so eminently characteristic of the wealthy citizens, are more than sufficient—doubly armed in a good cause—to combat the hydra of poverty and crime. To explore the depths of the lowest stratum of low life in the City a TIMES reporter yesterday waited on Capt. Ullman of the Fourth Precinct, and requested the attendance of an officer to accompany him through the purlieus of the notorious Fourth Ward. The Captain heartily responding to the spirit which prompted the visit, readily gave the necessary orders, and Sergt. Crow detailed officer Michael Savage, who, he said, best knew the ward, to accompany the reporter. A simple and unvarnished detail of what was seen in that last abode of filth, misery, wretchedness and despair, would be a disgusting repetition of scenes calculated to shock the refined and educated mind. A general description will, therefore, be given introducing such episodes as are most pertinent to the object of the visit.

Accompanied by Officer Savage, the reporter proceeded along Oak, Cherry, Dover, Water, and other principal streets of the ward. In the Fourth Ward the sidewalks are not remarkably wide, nor is the drainage of the first order. The traffic is very heavy along the streets parallel with the river front, and, owing doubtless to this and the insecure foundation, large and extensive ruts are frequent in the streets. The hollows thus formed are the natural receptacles of the overflow of the scanty gutters, and here it is, like so many unfledged goslings, that the little street arabs luxuriate. A thick, black ooze, of the consistency and color of clotted ink, the concentrated essence of the vegetable and other decompositions of the streets here fester in the meridian sun, and insidiously give out its invisible exhalations of disease and death, wrapping the poor little ones in its miasmatic shroud. The sidewalks are encumbered with dust-barrels and coffin-like receptacles for house refuse, but these are so very seldom emptied that the surplus generally forms an extensive cone-shaped mound toward the street. Here and at the margin of the "death pool" are the playgrounds of the children. In all sorts of ragged costumes, in every stage of premature decay, in savage dirt, and impotent depravity revel the youth of the Fourth Ward. Faces frightfully haggard and weird, with indelible traces of want and suffering; old heads on young shoulders, every feature expressive of the bitter maturity of misery; light golden locks fitfully shadowing handsome, though dirty faces; pretty little fellows who yet shrink from contact with the more accomplished youths of the period; chubby little boys, recently transported into this foul abode, who still wear the last trace of rude health on their cheeks; little urchins scarcely able to crawl hover round the skirts of the pool, anxious to have a splash in its odoriferous paste. All stages of childhood, from the babe escaped from its mother's arms to the rising young politician of fourteen years, are to be found in the neighborhood of the filth heaps. Down into the dark and noisome cellars, where daylight seldom penetrates, into the dank and fetid atmosphere of the dens of Water-street, amid scenes of the lowest vice, and through passages and rooms reeking with the sickening fumes of the last night's debauch, went the officer and reporter. Women and men half naked, some reeling about in a state of semi-unconsciousness, some stretched prone on a miserable mattress and almost nude, others comparatively sober, but with faces bruised and scarred, and whose answers to the salutations of the visitors were a flow of low blasphemy and ribald remarks. Little children were to be found in each den, some gaping in astonishment at the visitors, others, more *au fait*, dashed upstairs and announced the domiciliary visit of the officer. The house No. 304 Water-street is the "abomination of desolation." From the cellar to the roof-ridge is a teeming, festering multitude of the most miserable specimens of humanity.

In some rooms in this pandemonium—"apartments" measuring about 9 feet by 9—were no less than six beds, or, more properly, litters, each with two or three occupants; and the invariable adjunct of poor, neglected, and uncomplaining children. One room near the roof was found flooded with some disgusting liquid, in the midst of which a white-headed urchin was playing, while an old harridan hurled volleyed blasphemy at a drunken wretch lying in a corner, as being the cause of the disaster. Anxious to escape from the profane vocabulary of the woman, the officer led the way into another hole, immediately beneath the slope of the roof. The standing-room was two paces by five. There were four litters in the room, and six women and three children managed to find sleeping accommodation within its confined limits. A pretty little girl approached the reporter, and looked at him inquiringly. A flower and some sprigs of myrtle-blossom in his coat attracted her attention, and she appeared anxious to investigate the curiosity. Patting the little unkempt head and toying with the poor faded cheek, the reporter soon established friendly relations with Missy, and ventured to open a conversation. In this, however, he was interrupted by the officer, who had unearthed something extraordinary, and called out to the reporter, "Look at this, Sir! There's a sight!" And it was a pitiful, sorrowing sight. There, on one of those miserable apologies for a bed, exposed to the draft of an open window, lay the emaciated form of a little girl about two years old. Pale and cold it looked, and the damp of death was on its face. Its little eyes were sunken, glassy, and haggard. A heap of old rags, thrown aside by the official club, showed its attenuated body and limbs, denuded of flesh; in fact, a living skeleton. One of the women said the child belonged to her sister, and in answer to the reporter said it had been taken to a doctor. "'Tis only the teeth, Sir," said she, and then turned indifferently away. The eldest little girl followed the reporter, stole her hand into his, and looked in his face so confidingly, that the wretched surroundings were almost forgotten in the remembrance of little ones at home. The stench in this house became so intolerable that the visitors were compelled to seek the less pestiferous air of the street. Here a motley crowd of boys and girls awaited them, and the wildest suggestions were offered as to the object of their visit. One urchin hinted that the reporter was looking for some "stolen swag," another said he was a young doctor, but a young scamp with dilapidated and decayed pantaloons, and gossamer remnant of a shirt, halloed, "He's a reporter, a TIMES fellow; I know him. They're going to get up the picnics again," and forthwith he was surrounded by an admiring crowd, to whom he recounted the pleasant incidents of his last year's excursions. The rumor had gone abroad, and the visitors were followed by an army of ragged and noisy juveniles, who became at last so intolerably attentive that new fields had to be sought for further exploration. In this neighborhood are two or three alleyways, *cul de sacs*, the intervening passage being about three feet, and the houses at each side five stories high. The sunlight never penetrates into the recesses of these loathsome abodes, and the air is hot, reeking, and pestiferous. Nineteen children grovel in the passage and hallways, or bedaub themselves with the fœtid contents of the domestic tubs. Some were stretched on the flags, cooling their feverish bodies, and others lay helplessly gasping for the pure cool air. Up again through the wretched rooms, and again the neglected children are found crowded in each apartment, all exhibiting the effects of the impure air, and want of wholesome exercise. Turning away sadly from the never varying picture of misery, the visitors retraced their steps, this time accompanied by a respectable inhabitant of the ward, to whom was told the object of the mysterious visit. "Ah!" said he to the reporter, "that was the best thing THE TIMES ever did, not excepting scalping Tammany. The subscribers to that Fund little know what good has been accomplished by the picnics and Children's Sick Fund. Why, one day in the open, green country gives new life to the poor children; they are different beings when they get back, and are never done speaking of the fun enjoyed on the trip."

THE TENTH WARD.

The Tenth Ward is densely populated, and almost exclusively by Germans. They are, however, of a better class, and but little poverty prevails, except in the lower portion of Norfolk and Essex streets. The tenement-houses are of the same style as in the other wards, but only a few of the blocks are built through. The every-day life of the inhabitants of the poorer parts of the ward is the same as elsewhere in the City.

About 4 o'clock A. M. the stir of life begins. Work girls and women and men begin to pour out from every tenement to their daily toil. Their pale faces, sunken eyes, and languid steps tell too truly of the poisonous vapors they have inhaled during the hours of the night. To them the hours of sleep, "nature's soft nurse," have brought no strength.

The swarms of children that obstruct one's path at every step have a pallid look, despite sunburn. Their shouts and gambols give an animated appearance to the scene, and make less horrible the wretched squalor and filth of their surroundings. Even the hollow-eyed, slatternly women, basking in the sunshine with babies in their arms, appear for the moment to enjoy life. But it is in the early morning the full effects of the poisonous atmosphere and overcrowding are to be best seen and appreciated. Windows on the north side of the streets are thrown open, and women in a state of semi-nudity seek refuge on the sidewalk from the heated rooms; squalling and puny children lie panting in the mothers' arms, and as the sun ascends the street is soon abandoned, and refuge is sought in the shaded yard, amid the most noisome and deleterious exhalations. There is a style of tenement-house, one of three, crowded into two City lots. It is scarcely sixteen feet clear in the interior by over fifty feet deep. The hall is about two feet six inches in width. A narrow stairway leads to the upper stories, and the landings are generally cumbered with domestic paraphernalia which emit a heavy, sickening odor. As the visitor ascends the passage becomes darker, the air hotter, and is heavily laden with the overpowering stench of the sink in many cases unprovided with a stench-trap—and the feeble gas burning on each landing, "rendering darkness visible," tells of the large amount of oxygen in the atmosphere. Each floor is divided into two compartments, front and rear, and each compartment into two rooms—the family, or general room and kitchen opening on the street or yard, and a dark closet or cupboard, with a loop-hole opening over the sink or the landing, as a ventilator. The closet or cupboard is used as a bedroom, and it is not unusual to have two beds in it. A space for a small chair is all that is left between the bedsteads, and from five to six adults and children sometimes occupy this space of 10 by 10. A lounge in the kitchen

> "Contrives a double debt to pay—
> A bed by night, a lounge or seat by day."

There are five floors in this particular tenement, with four rooms on each floor, and allowing an average of six persons to each family, gives 120 inhabitants to each house, and about 130 cubic feet of air to each person, or 100 feet less than the minimum allowance to sustain average health. In this particular house there is a large number of children, weak, sickly things, tottering about, scarce able to clamber up the steep, dark stairs. Their only enjoyment appears to be to lie off on the stoop or stretch on the roof in the cool of the evening, and strain their glassy eyes to catch a view of the distant country, or a glimpse of the far-off water. Here they lie, many families passing the night on the roof, inhaling large drafts of the cool breeze which springs up in the evening; and here they live, pine, and die, unknown and unpitied by the busy world abroad.

THE ELEVENTH WARD.

That section of the City contained within the Eleventh Ward is bounded on the north by the south side of Fourteenth-street, on the south by the north side of Rivington-street, and on the east and west respectively by the East River and the east side of Avenue A. In that area it would be difficult to find a private family dwelling. The buildings are chiefly four and five story tenements, with here and there a few factories, and along the river front a number of large iron foundries. For its size there is no ward in the City more densely populated. Each tenement-house affords on an average accommodation for four families on every floor, or to speak more correctly, four families are forced to find on each floor of the tenement-houses such accommodation as they can. It is estimated that each tenement-house in the ward gives shelter to from 75 to 100 persons; but in many instances, and this is particularly true of the narrow streets east of Clinton, more than 100 people sleep under the same roof each night. When it is stated that in the district bounded by Rivington and Houston streets, and extending from Clinton-street to the East River, all the blocks are built through—that is, besides the houses facing on the streets there are rear buildings entirely filling up the space in the centre of the blocks, which, in the wealthier districts, is left open for purposes of ventilation—some idea of the crowding may be formed. As the streets for the most part are wider and more regular, and as an occasional health giving breeze from the river finds its way into the noisome courts and alleys, the Eleventh Ward has an advantage over the worst portions of the Sixth. But there the advantage ends, for its sanitary condition could not well be worse than it is.

The narrow stairs running through the tenement building serves as a foul-air conductor. The atmospheric poison of the streets and yards, cesspools and accumulated filth, rushes in through the open doors, and is carried upward through the house, gathering the noxious effluvia of each closet and landing as it ascends, penetrating the recesses of the dark and noisome rooms, and leaving the seeds of disease and death in the lungs and system of the miserable occupants. The strong man and woman, accustomed to life in a tenement-house, are, in a measure, proof against the effects of this death-laden atmosphere, and have become inured to it, but it is on the weak, the delicate constitution, and, above all, on the helpless little ones, that its terrible effects are so painfully manifest. In the morning, after a restless, troubled and feverish stupor, (it cannot be called sleep,) the inmates awake jaded, haggard and borne down with a heavy, enervating lassitude. Windows are thrown open, they are partly so during the night, but the hot and stifling air, laden with impalpable dust, brings no relief to the parched lungs of the occupant. Instinctively they crowd on the stoops, knowing that the lower current is the best air. And here it is that the visitor sees the miseries of tenement life. On the stoop are seated a number of women of all ages, from the gray-haired granddam to the young mother. Children are about, strong in number and noise. Some attenuated specimens of infantile precocity skip about the sidewalk and street with the agility of kids. A pert, old-stylish look, a sort of premature "cuteness," is visible on each little face, and a studied gravity of manner is characteristic of the class. Here is a young mother, with a handsome English face; an unhealthy, hectic blush is on her cheeks, and her eyes are sunken and haggard. She looks completely prostrate, and evidently makes an effort to reply to the feeble little voice at her side. The little invalid is covered with a loose white pelisse, leaving its arms and lower limbs bare. The face is pale and haggard, there is a wild, dreamy longing in the eyes, the lips are pinched and colorless, and the outline of the face is sharp and angular. The little limbs are attenuated, the flesh hanging about the joints like flabby pulp, confined by a pale, sickly, white skin. A nervous play of the fingers, a restless change of position, a heavy breathing and gasping, indicate the condition of the helpless sufferer. The child has been asking the mother a question, and she replies, "Yes, dear, we'll go on Sunday with father and the baby." The little one has relapsed into a state of dreamy unconsciousness, and heeds not the mother's voice. There it is, with its large eyes looking vacantly forward, thinking, perhaps, of the green fields, the beautiful flowers, and the tall shadowy trees, which it saw, perhaps, but once, listening for the rustling of the leaves, or the murmur of the bright and flowing river, and yet gasping for the life giving current of pure air for the lack of which its young life is fast ebbing away. So it is on every stoop along the street, and so it is in every ward in the lower part of the City. Thousands of children passing away, dying of the foul and poisonous atmosphere of the crowded tenement-houses.

THE FOURTEENTH WARD.

The Fourteenth Ward is certainly one of the very worst in this City so far as its density of population is concerned. Crosby, Mulberry, Mott, Elizabeth, Hester, Prince, Spring, and Houston streets are literally nests, and have as many habitations as a well-preserved rabbit-burrow. Go where you will through all this muck and mire and your progress is impeded by children of every age, grade, garb, and color. Dozens of little ones sprawl over the pavement at every corner. In Mulberry, Mott, and Hester streets, children were almost under foot, in the puddles, on the carts, overhead on lamp-posts, in the windows, on the steps, curbs, and even in the garbage-barrels and stable litter, with which, by the way, Mulberry-street is particularly well provided. Every one seemed to be in the street when you looked at it, and in the houses when you looked at them. People! people! everywhere; the very stones and posts were alive with a mass of sweltering, complaining humanity. One could scarcely breathe that warm evening; how, then, can the children live in these places through the fiery Summer months! In short, the Fourteenth Ward furnishes a kaleidoscope of starvation and plenty, tawdry rags and bright-hued dresses, disease struggling with health, and children whose youth declares them innocent, but whose faces are stamped with crime, and is a nursery of all the evils that beset and afflict this great City.

THE FIFTEENTH WARD.

The Fifteenth Ward also contains many poor children. In Thirteenth-street, between Fifth and Sixth avenues, there is a four-story house which shelters eight families; in Eleventh-street there are two of a similar character; in Eighth-street, between Macdougal and Sixth-avenue, there are four front and four rear four-story houses, which accommodate four families on each floor. Fourth-street has one tenement-house between Macdougal and Sixth-avenue, and Bleecker-street two more. The streets running north and south are frequently marked by tenements. Mercer has two; Greene one; Wooster many; South Fifth-avenue many; Thompson-street one, between Bleecker and Amity; Sullivan-street four, front and rear, having from eight to ten families each in them, and Minetta-lane is thronged by colored people. These crowded buildings, as will be seen by reference to the list, are in the narrowest and most unhealthy part of the ward. The sufferings of the children, therefore, while they may not be quite so great as those of others in the densely-populated wards, will be very great, and mortality proportionately large.

June 16, 1873

THE BOARD OF HEALTH.

Death-Rates in Tenement-Houses—Condition of the Streets—The Progress of Cholera.

At a meeting of the Board of Health yesterday the following document in relation to excessive mortality in certain tenement-houses was presented:

The Sanitary Committee respectfully call the attention of the board to the fact that there are certain tenement-houses which annually give a very high death-rate. For example, in 1871 in 1 house there were 11 deaths; in 4 houses there were 36 death, or 9 in each house; in 3 houses there were 24 deaths, or 8 in each house; in 17 houses there were 119 deaths, or 7 in each house; in 37 houses there were 222 deaths, or 6 in each house; in 106 houses there were 530 deaths, or 5 in each house; in 231 houses there were 924, or 4 in each house. This gives 1,866 deaths in 398 houses, or an average of nearly 5 deaths to each house. The mortality in these houses varies but little from year to year, showing either that the population of those houses is very great, or that there are sanitary defects existing, which should either be at once remedied, or if such defects cannot be remedied, the houses should be vacated. Appended is a list of all the tenement-houses which in 1870 and 1871 gave a mortality of six or more persons each. The committee recommended the adoption of the following resolution:

Resolved, That the Sanitary Superintendent be and he is hereby directed to cause an inspection to be made of the houses contained in this list, and report as to the sanitary defects in each, with such recommendation as in his judgment will remedy such defects.

The following is the list referred to above:

Location of House.	No. of Deaths 1870.	No. of Deaths 1871.
No. 31 Allen-street	0	6
No. 14 Baxter-street	4	9
No. 38 Baxter-street	6	6
No. 90 Catharine-street	0	6
No. 38 Centre-street	3	6
No. 15 City Hall-place	6	6
No. 33 Crosby-street	0	6
No. 16½ Downing-street	4	7
No. 141 Duane-street	0	7
No. 144 East Fourth-street	0	8
No. 173 East Fourth-street	0	7
No. 420 East Eleventh-street	3	7
No. 508 East Eleventh-street	0	7
No. 411 East Twelfth-street	0	6
No. 701 East Twelfth-street	0	6
No. 431 East Fourteenth-street	6	7
No. 513 East Sixteenth-street	0	7
No. 405 East Seventeenth-street	0	8
No. 425 East Seventeenth-street	0	6
No. 245 East Twenty-eighth-street	0	6
No. 237 East Forty-sixth-street	0	6
No. 402 East Fifty-third-street	0	6
No. 515 Fifth-street	6	7
No. 317 Fifth-street	0	7
No. 415 Fifth-street	0	6
No. 506 Fifth-street	0	6
No. 525 Fifth-street	0	6
No. 831 First-avenue	0	6
No. 37 Frankfort-street	6	6
No. 32 Madison-street	0	6
No. 186 Mott-street	0	6
No. 9 Mulberry-street	6	11
No. 5 Mulberry-street	0	6
No. 51 Mulberry-street	4	7
No. 55 Mulberry-street	0	6
No. 73 Mulberry-street	0	8
No. 168 Mulberry-street	4	9
No. 154 Norfolk-street	0	6
No. 43 Oliver-street	3	6
No. 153 Orchard-street	0	9
No. 39 Park-street	3	7
No. 47 Park-street	3	6
No. 123 Pitt-street	0	6
No. 246 Rivington-street	0	6
No. 10 Roosevelt-street	7	6
No. 25 Rose street	3	7
No. 396 Second-avenue	0	7
No. 409 Second-avenue	3	6
No. 862 Second-avenue	0	7
No. 514 Sixth-street	0	7
No. 54 Spring-street	4	8
No. 117 Third-street	0	7
No. 119 Third-street	0	6
No. 162 Third-street	0	6
No. 57 Thompson-street	3	6
No. 28 Washington-street	3	6
No. 21 West-street	0	6
No. 447 West Twenty-seventh-street	3	6
No. 510 West Thirty-ninth-street	0	6
No. 423 West Forty-first-street	0	6
No. 68 Willett-street	3	6
No. 119 Willett-street	6	7

In connection with the above subject, Commissioner Vanderpoel offered the following resolution, which was adopted:

Resolved, That the Register of Records be requested to prepare a map designating the mortality which has occurred in each block in the City from July 1, 1872, to July 1, 1873.

A communication was received from a large number of citizens residing in East Forty-ninth-street, complaining of the nuisance created by the slaughter-house in East Forty-ninth-street, between Third-avenue and East River. Referred to Sanitary Superintendent for report.

A remonstrance from the citizens of Harlem against the dumping of ashes, garbage, &c., into McGowan's Creek and the adjacent flats, was also referred to the Sanitary Superintendent.

A petition from Messrs. Kane & Ryan, for permission to dump stable-straw on their lots at the foot of Forty-sixth and Forty-seventh streets, North River, was received and placed on file, the Board declining to grant such permission.

A complaint was received from an anonymous source in relation to the poisonous odors alleged to arise from the works of the Manhattan Gas Company at the foot of Twenty-first and Twenty-second streets, North River. It was referred to Prof. Chandler for examination.

The Board of Police notified the Board of Health that the signatures had been obtained of a requisite number of property-owners in Baxter, Worth, and Park streets, to secure the paving of those streets, and the matter was referred to the Department of Public Works.

The Finance Committee was authorized to purchase twenty barrels of carbolic acid at a price not to exceed $1 75 per gallon, for disinfecting purposes.

Dr. Day, Sanitary Superintendent, presented the following comparative statement of contagious diseases for the two weeks ending 21st inst.

Week ending June 14—Typhus fever, 1; typhoid, 6; scarlet fever, 73; measles, 66; diphtheria, 30; small-pox, 8.

Week ending June 21—Typhus fever, 2; typhoid, 6; scarlet fever, 60; measles, 49; diphtheria, 21; small-pox, 4.

CONDITION OF THE STREETS.

The Sanitary Superintendent presented a partial report in relation to the condition of the streets, as follows: Inspector H. R. Stiles reports that the streets of the Fourth Ward have not been, during the past week, in quite as good a condition of cleanliness as previously. Inspector Post reports the streets in his district in a fair condition, excepting portions of Madison, Monroe, Hamilton, Cherry, Water, Jackson, and Scammel streets, which are more filthy than usual. Inspector Hughes reports the streets of the Eighth Ward in a good condition. Inspector Roberts reports the streets of his district in a better condition than he had ever known them to be before. The rest of the inspectors make similar reports. A copy of the reports was ordered to be sent to the Board of Police.

The tenement-house No. 230 Mott-street, having been reported as being in a condition detrimental to health and dangerous to life, the board ordered the premises to be vacated.

The application of Henry Eisner for a permit to melt and render fat at his premises, at the foot of One Hundred and Sixth-street and East River, was referred to the President of the board.

A permit was granted the Ollomargarine Manufacturing Company to manufacture Ollomargarine or artificial butter at Fifty-sixth-street, between Second and Third avenues.

A number of complaints in relation to the bad condition of the pavement in certain streets, was presented and referred to the Department of Public Works.

THE PROGRESS OF CHOLERA.

Dr. Walter De F. Day, Sanitary Superintendent, presented the following report in relation to the progress of cholera in the South and Southwest:

SANITARY BUREAU, NEW-YORK, June 24, 1873.

I desire to submit the following report upon the progress of cholera so-called during the present year. For many of the facts on which this report is based I am indebted to Dr. A. B. Judson, Sanitary Inspector:

The *Weekly Thibodeaux Sentinel*, Louisiana, of May 17, says: "There seems to be no doubt that cholera is in our midst below Lafourche Crossing. Some fifteen or more deaths, since last Saturday, have occurred." Same journal, May 31, says: "The Parishes of Lafourche, and the adjoining Parish of Assumption, have had, thus far, about thirty deaths from cholera, of which number six were whites."

New-Orleans, La.—From the week ending March 30 to the week ending June 15 the deaths from sporadic cholera were 124; cholera morbus, 81; cholera infantum, 75; diarrhœa, 3; acute diarrhœa, 1; dysentery, 1. (The mortuary reports for the whole year 1872 give cholera morbus 20 and cholera infantum 52.)

Vicksburg, Miss.—From the week ending May 5 to the week ending June 9, out of 110 deaths 19 were from diarrhœal diseases, of which 13 were called cholera.

Jackson, Miss.—The Canton *Mail*, June 17, says: "It is reported on our streets that there have been four deaths from cholera in Jackson;" and the Meriden *Gazette* of June 10 says: "It is reported that the cholera is raging in Jackson." The Louisville *Journal* of June 13 says that "in Jackson and Canton, business is suspended, in consequence of cholera."

At Memphis, Tenn., the whole number of interments for the week ending June 8 were 55, the interments of the corresponding week last year being 26. From June 9 to the 19th, the reported interments were 242; from the 16th to the 19th, inclusive, there were 82 deaths, of which 55 were from cholera and cholera morbus. On the 20th there were 17 deaths from cholera, and on the 22d there were 9.

Nashville, Tenn.—From June 7 to 19, inclusive, there were 233 deaths, the deaths during the last thirty days being 104, of which fifty-nine were called cholera. On the 20th there were seventy-three deaths; on the 21st, fifty-nine; on the 22d, fifty-two. A dispatch of June 18 says: "It is estimated that the exodus of people since the 10th inst. is 10,000." The population is estimated at 25,000.

Gallatin, Tenn.—The Louisville *Courier-Journal* of June 14 says: "Seven cases of cholera have occurred at Gallatin, four of which proved fatal." A dispatch from Nashville, June 11, says: "Dispatches from Gallatin, Lebanon, Greenville, and other points show that the scourge is carrying off a great many in those places." A news dispatch of June 17 reports twenty-three deaths to date, and one of the 18th reports for that day six new deaths—all colored, and several new attacks.

Louisville, Ky.—A dispatch to the *City Press*, dated June 22, says: "The reports of cholera in this city are entirely groundless."

Greenville, Tenn.—A correspondent writing from that place, June 18, gives details of five cases, and adds: "There are several other serious cases in our town, and a great many of lighter form."

Paducah, Ky.—On the 16th inst. four deaths from a disease resembling cholera were reported, and five deaths were said to have occurred on the 20th.

Cincinnati, Ohio.—A news dispatch of June 21 says, "Up to 6 o'clock this evening there were 14 deaths from diseases of the bowels. Six cases classed as cholera were reported for the day at the Health Office."

St. Louis, Mo.—For the week ending June 14, out of a total of 107 deaths from all causes, 8 were from cholera morbus, 4 from cholera infantum, and 2 from diarrhœa.

These deaths, which belong to the larger towns and cities of the South-west, and not to the plantations on the river bottoms, which are reported to have suffered severely, are gathered from Western journals, and are matters of public knowledge. They do not pretend to accuracy, but there is no doubt that a disease resembling Asiatic cholera is approaching us with gradual but certain steps. The greatest mortality has fallen upon the blacks, because in the South-west they are subjected to the wort hygienic conditions.

If the disease reaches this City, which is at present unusually free from diarrhœal disorders, there having been for the past week but thirty-four deaths from such causes, it will attack the same class, those who live in filth, bad air, and misery on streets which are narrow, badly paved, or not paved at all, and where street cleaning is difficult.

I have had the honor to-day to report the condition of the streets, so far as I was able to learn it. The meagreness of the report is due to the recent appointment of many assistant inspectors and the extra duty thrown on the older inspectors in educating them.

From personal observation of some of the water-front streets, and the unpaved streets of the lower part of the City, especially in the Sixth and Fourth Wards, I am convinced that the most thorough disinfection is necessary in those quarters, in view of the not improbable presence of cholera in our midst during the two coming months. I would respectfully recommend that the disinfecting corps be considerably increased.

I have the honor to be, very respectfully,

WALTER DE F. DAY, M. D.,
Sanitary Superintendent.

June 25, 1873

BOSTON'S COSTLIEST RESIDENCES.

THE FATAL DISEASES THAT LURK IN THE MADE LAND UPON WHICH THEY ARE BUILT.

Correspondence of the Salem (Mass.) Gazette.

BOSTON, Jan. 5.—There was a vacant chair in our City Hall to-day, the stately form and fine gray head of Mayor Prince not being visible. The New Year's Day lost him his only daughter, a beautiful girl of 22, by malignant diphtheria. The day following, his eldest son was stricken down with the same dread disease, and was removed, by the doctor's orders, from his father's stately Beacon-street mansion to the City Hospital. The next day, the younger son was attacked with the preliminary symptoms, and also went to the hospital, the afflicted father closing his house and going out of town. Beacon-street, but not the old Beacon-street, which is most healthily and beautifully situated on the high land on the side of the hill which bears the same name. The new Beacon-street, that whose numbers run in the hundreds, has been built up in the later days, on the "made land" which has been reclaimed from the ocean by filling in the bay. Thus the most aristocratic part of Boston is still known as the "Back Bay," and its elegant mansions are famous—or the contrary—for their ill-drainage, and for the foul miasma which rises, when the tide is out, from the Charles River, upon which the back windows of these Beacon-street houses look. Oliver Wendell Holmes's beautiful study and library, which is fitted up with all that wealth and taste can command, has a great bay window from which it had a splendid view of the river, with the City of Cambridge on the western shore, glittering and shimmering under the rays of the setting sun. Truly a poet's dream of beauty, but what a fearful reality is its foundation! Many of Boston's fairest daughters and bravest sons have been done to the death by the pestilential air of their grand homes. Queen Victoria is not the only mother who has had to mourn a daughter lost through the very magnificence of her estate. Many attempts have been made to mitigate this evil in the fairest and newest part of Boston, but any who doubt their utter futility need only sit for an hour at twilight, when the tide is low, in the open window of one of these houses, and, while the eyes are charmed with the rippling water, reflecting myriads of lights, and broken here and there by a boat or a sail, let the sense of smell also have a word in deciding whether you would choose this place for your home and that of your dear ones.

January 10, 1880

DEATHS HERE AND ELSEWHERE.

STATISTICS WHICH SHOW AN INCREASE IN OTHER CITIES AS WELL AS THIS.

In an article on the "Comparative Mortality of New-York," the current number of the *Sanitary Engineer* presents a table of the mortality of New-York, Brooklyn, Philadelphia, Cincinnati, Chicago, and St. Louis from diphtheria, scarlet fever, typhoid fever, measles, and small-pox, for the first three months of 1880 and 1881. Upon the returns of these three months the annual death-rate per 1,000 of population is based, and the result shows an increase of mortality in other cities as well as New-York. The record of deaths from diphtheria upon this basis is as follows: New-York—1880, 0.79; 1881, 1.83. Brooklyn—1880, 1.45; 1881, 2.74. Philadelphia—1880, 0.49; 1881, 0.35. Cincinnati—1880, 0.48; 1881, 0.46. Chicago—1880, 2.18; 1881, 1.31. St. Louis—1880, 0.50; 1881, 0.33. Of scarlet fever, 0.31 out of every 1,000 died in this City in 1880, and 1.58 in 1881; in Brooklyn, 0.45 in 1880, and 1.13 in 1881; in Philadelphia, 0.23 in 1880, and 0.51 in 1881; in Cincinnati, 0.75 in 1880, and 0.30 in 1881; in Chicago, 0.94 in 1880, and 0.40 in 1881, and in St. Louis, 0.15 in 1880, and 0.24 in 1881. For typhoid fever the record shows in this City, 0.15 in 1880, and 0.19 in 1881; Brooklyn, 0.08 in 1880, and 0.10 in 1881; Philadelphia, 0.42 in 1880, and 0.48 in 1881; Cincinnati, 0.43 in 1880 and 0.28 in 1861; Chicago, 0.19 in 1880, and 0.33 in 1881; and St. Louis, 0.30 in 1880, and 0.27 in 1881. From measles there is shown a decrease in the death-rate, except in Cincinnati, the record being as follows: New-York—1880, 0.87; 1881, 0.26; Brooklyn—1880, 0.44; 1881, 0.05; Philadelphia—1880, 0.28; 1881, 0.03; Cincinnati—1880, 0.03; 1881, 0.14; Chicago—1880, 0.55; 1881, 0.06; St. Louis—1880, 0.24; 1881, 0.15. From small-pox the table shows 0.15 deaths in Philadelphia last year, and for the present year 0.32 in this City, 0.05 in Brooklyn, 2.88 in Philadelphia, 0.03 in Cincinnati, and 0.64 in Chicago, no deaths from this cause being reported from St. Louis in either year. The table shows an increase this year in the death-rate from these causes of 2.06 in this City, 1.65 in Brooklyn, and 2.68 in Philadelphia, and a decrease of 0.48 in Cincinnati and 1.12 in Chicago. It will thus be seen that New-York is by no means the only city in which mortality has increased during the present year. The number of reported deaths from small-pox from Jan. 3 to April 2 of this year was, for New-York, 97; Philadelphia, 614; Chicago, 80; Brooklyn, 7, and Cincinnati, 2. During the first three months of the present year deaths from lung diseases were in excess of those from diarrheal diseases in the North-east, while diarrheal diseases were in excess in the North-west. If it is true that diarrheal diseases indicate a tendency to epidemic cholera, it would seem that the West shows a far greater liability to this scourge than the East.

What is known as the "Winter cholera" was very prevalent in Chicago and the West during the severe cold weather of last Winter, but it seems to have had little influence on the mortality rate. On this subject Dr. H. A. Johnson has made a report to the National Board of Health, which gives some very important and interesting facts. The report says: "The epidemic of so-called Winter cholera the present Winter in Chicago is noteworthy as decidedly modifying the usual health condition of the city, and, also, for its own peculiarities. From all that can be learned from conversation with physicians it appears that it became suddenly prevalent about the holidays, though there are records of a rather unusual amount of diarrheal trouble earlier in December. From that time to the present the epidemic has continued with more or less violence, but now seems to be somewhat abating. It is not possible to even approximately estimate the degree of its prevalence with any certainty. The disorder has made no marked figure in the mortality reports, and there are no returns of non-fatal diseases. Judging from the number of cases mentioned to me by physicians as having come under their own observation and treatment, and allowing for the whole number in the City, as well as the very large probable number of cases where no physician was consulted, I should say that at least 15,000 or 20,000 cases have occurred; and perhaps 30,000 or 40,000, of all degrees of mildness or severity, would be more nearly correct. In one of the principal suburbs, where it was easier to make an estimate, and where it was, to all appearances, much less prevalent than in the City, nearly 2 per cent. of the population were more or less affected. Here, too, according to the experience of some physicians, a majority of the cases were adult males, whose business carried them to the City every day. Popular opinion was at first inclined to attribute it to the excessive cold of the Winter, and many physicians were inclined to share the opinion. Bad sewerage and ventilation could not be generally credited with its production, as it occurred equally where nothing was wrong in these respects. It is probable, however, that it was aggravated in some instances by bad sanitary conditions. The fact that the disorder occurred simultaneously in many widely separated localities over the country is against the idea of any local conditions producing it—such as the drinking-water, which was constantly and carefully watched by Dr. De Wolf and the health officers without finding any marked impurities, notwithstanding the fact that the Fullerton-avenue conduit was discharging from the North branch into the lake all Winter. A number of physicians of extensive observation strongly suspected a malarial element in the disorder. In this connection I may state that a well-known physician from the interior of the State, Dr. Howard, of Champaign, has said that in his town he had seen a large number of cases of severe bowel complaint this Winter in children, and very few in adults. In all, or nearly all, cases he found that the sufferers had been eating snow, and that the disease was apparently directly traceable to that. He also favored the idea of its malarial character, at least in part. The facts known are very suggestive, but it will require a much more extensive inquiry at a lator period to justify any positive deductions."

In concluding the article the *Sanitary Engineer* says: "In view of these data, when the efficiency of the New-York Board of Health is under consideration, allowance must be made for the fact that the death-rate of New-York is unduly increased over that of other cities by the arrival of immense numbers of the lower class of foreigners, the mortality among their sick in our hospitals being set against the health of this City, while the pauper poor on Blackwell's Island, and the large tenement house population, present special difficulties in preserving a fair showing."

May 2, 1881

MATTERS WE OUGHT TO KNOW.

HOW THE OTHER HALF LIVES. Studies Among the Tenements of New-York. By JACOB A. RIIS. New-York: CHARLES SCRIBNER'S SONS.

Mr. J. A. Riis has had the fullest experience in regard to the subject he treats, for he has devoted many years to the study of New-York. The title explains itself, for it is true "that one-half of the world does not know how the other half lives." The question is, Does it care?

In 1863 occurred the draft riots. There had been constant increase of crime in the State. Eighty per cent. of the crimes against property and against the person were perpetrated by individuals who had either lost connection with home life or never had any, or "whose homes had ceased to be sufficiently separate, decent, and desirable to afford what are regarded as ordinary wholesome influences of home and family." This was the testimony of the Secretary of the Prison Association of New-York. It was shown then that the younger criminals came "almost exclusively from the worst tenement-house districts." In that earlier stage of inquiry the boundary line of the other half was sharply defined by the tenement houses.

Has New-York City improved since 1863? Mr. Riis says it has grown worse; "to-day three-quarters of its people live in tenements, and the nineteenth century drift of the population to the cities is sending increased multitudes to crowd them." It is not the author's statement that can be challenged, for in his preface he writes of his indebtedness to the President of the Board of Health, Mr. C. G. Wilson, to Chief Inspector Byrnes, and to Dr. Roger S. Tracy, the Registrar of Vital Statistics. When in a former period, not so far distant, there were in New-York City 15,000 tenement houses, to-day there are 37,000, and more than 1,200,000 persons call these tenements their homes. If, then, according to the last census, there are in New-York City something between 1,600,000 and 1,700,000 people, in what minority must be those who do not live in tenements? It was believed that, with increased facilities of locomotion, as represented by rapid transit, the tenement dwellers would have decreased. But rapid transit has shown itself insufficient. Writes Mr. Riis despairingly of this tenement system: "We know there is no way out." The system, "that was the evil offspring of public neglect and private greed, has come to stay, a storm centre of our civilization. Nothing is left but to make the best of a bad bargain."

Is it necessary to expatiate on the accursed life this tenement system entails? Are there not engendered there epidemics which carry death "to rich and poor alike?" They are "the nurseries of pauperism and crime that fill our jails and police courts, that throw off a scum of 40,000 women wrecks to the island asylums and workhouses year by year, that turned out in the last eight years a round half million beggars to prey upon our charities." Worst of all is that deadly moral contagion these tenements breed. Mr. Riis believes that the tenement system in its worst aspect is due to the greed of the owners of such properties. Those who hold such buildings seek too large percentage for their outlay. The place must pay, and questions of salubrity or convenience are secondary ones. Witnesses before a Senate committee declared that the percentage on such hotbeds of disease was expected to pay 15 per cent., that it rarely fell beneath that, and frequently exceeded 30. Instances were given of a tenement which every year paid back in its rental the worth of the property. Let, says the author, "philanthropy and 5 per cent." in the future go toge her.

The genesis of the tenement is a curious study. After the war of 1812 there was an enormous immigration. "In thirty-five years the city of less than one hundred thousand came to harbor half a million of souls, for whom homes had to be found." Those old-fashioned houses along the East River side were abandoned by their former well-to-do owners, and fell into the grip of real-estate agents, and now the evil began. The hands on the docks or in the workshops necessarily sought living rooms near their occupations. At first there was room enough, but very shortly there was not. Then came subdivisions, not of the house alone, but of the rooms. "One large room would be partitioned into several smaller ones." Under such circumstances there could be no provision made for either air or light. Soon these houses were filled from garret to cellar "with a class of tenantry living from hand to mouth, loose in morals, improvident in habits, degraded, and squalid as beggary itself." No such thing as neatness, order, cleanliness, could be dreamed of. Landlords, when found fault with, declared that the filthy habits of the tenants were the excuse for the wretched condition of their property, "utterly losing sight of the fact that it was the tolerance of these habits which was the real evil, and that for this they were alone responsible." In time any open space back or on the side of these houses was built up. Safety and comfort were never thought of. But worse came with new conditions. Barracks were built and spaces devised in which it was barely possible for one or more human beings to live. Middlemen came in and rented whole blocks of ground and built as they pleased. It seems dreadful to be told that to-day there is a tenement house population on the east side which "is still the most densely populated district in the world, China not excluded, for it is packed at the rate of 290,000 souls to the square mi. " In old London the greatest crowding was 175,816. As to rents, they are enormous, for experts testified that as compared with up-town rents they were from 25 to 30 per cent. higher in the worst slums of the lower wards. Once a fire in Mott Street burned down a rear house. Ten families were made homeless "who had paid $5 a month for their mean little cubby holes." The owner declared himself fully insured for $800, though the property had brought him in $600 a year.

In 1879 the first efforts were made to change the order of things and to better them. The Five Points was cleansed. But, as Mr. Riis writes, a stone's throw from there, and conditions are just as they were—even worse, "new centres of corruption always are springing up and getting the upper hand. One overcrowded and filthy tenement is certain to deprave a whole neighborhood." With the air shaft, at least some chance of life becomes possible, that is when to-day new houses are to be built, but "the old remains." In extreme cases horrible rookeries can be cleansed by the authorities, but nothing changes the overcrowding. "All efforts to abate it result only in temporary relief. As long as they exist it will exist with them, and the tenements will exist in New-York forever."

In fifty years, the author tells us tenements "have crept up from the Fourth Ward slums and the Five Points the whole length of the island, and have polluted the annexed district to the Weschester line." What has the future in store for us? If to-day three-quarters of New-York live in tenements and the number of poor, or, what is worse, the illiterate and ignorant, coming from other countries, are to increase these swarms, what is it going to be twenty or thirty years from now? What about "that vast army of workers held captive by poverty," who know not what are the comforts of a home, who have little moral sense. What are they going to do?"

Who are they who live in these tenements, those of the wretched kind, the most crowded? Mr. Riis called it "a mixed crowd." He once discovered the nationalities in a slum in the Fourth Ward. There were 140 families. One hundred were Irish, 38 Italian, and 2 spoke the German tongue. Altogether may be found in one hive of corruption Itali , Germans, Irish, Bohemians, Russians, Scandinavians, and Chinese. Of this ruck they are not all going to remain there. Slowly and in time the German and the Jew will get clear of it all, and so may in a certain sense the Chinaman but he will isolate himself: but as to the rest, they will be likely to stick there. Yo may ask, "Where is the distinctive American colony?" You never will find it. It does not exist. Certainly there are exceptions. The Italian has been here too short a time to show his hand, but there may be a few who will rise. The ragpicker may become a landlord, the Irishman may open a groggery and become in time a landlord and an Alderman. In that case woe betide his tenants. Used and brought up amid such scenes of misery and human degradation, he will not change a whit the character of his tenement. But "the sediment," as Mr. Riis calls it, remains.

Mr. Riis takes each nationality in turn and treats it in a matter-of-fact way. As to the Italian, he writes, "he comes in at the bottom" and he stays there. "In the slums he is welcomed as a tenant who "makes less trouble" than the contentious Irishman or the order-loving German. That is to say, he "is content to live in a pig sty and submits to robbery at the hands of the rent collector without murmur. His ignorance and unconquerable suspicion of strangers dig the pit into which he falls." He not only knows no word of English, but he does not know enough to learn. Rarely only can he write his own language. Because his mind works so slow and acquires few, if any, American ideas, he is at the mercy of a middleman, and is the middleman's prey. He is hired out and remains hired out and is always under contract, and his scant wage is gnawed by the middleman. He comes here mortgaged and remains a chattel, but yet he saves. He always hopes in the future, with the little money he has secreted, to get to his own Italy again. Very, very rarely, let it be said to his credit, is he a thief. He may be hot-headed at times and ugly; but he is not a brigand. If he be an ex-brigand, even of Sicilian stamp, he works honestly now. He will use a knife over a quarrel at cards with his own countrymen. There are exceptions among Italians. The further south you take the Italian the more uncertain is he. All the difference in the world exists between the Northern and Southern Italian. The Piedmontese are among the best men of Europe we can get. Physically he is good; his mental qualities are excellent and capable of improvement. When Mr. W. L. Alden was Consul General at Rome, (1886,) he wrote:

"As to the habits and morals of the emigrants to the United States from the Northern and central portions of Italy, both men and women are sober and industrious, and, as a rule, trustworthy and moral. They are generally strong, powerful workers, and capable of enduring great fatigue. A less favorable view may be taken of emigrants from southern districts and Sicily. These are the most illiterate parts of Italy, and in these districts brigandage was for many years extremely prevalent." During the last ten years (1890 not included) we have received certainly not less than 275,000 Continental Italian immigrants. Sicilians, or those giving themselves out as coming from Sicily, to be added, are stated to be some 1.500 more, but certainly they are in very much greater number, possibly ten times as many.

Mr. Riis's views of the conditions of "the other half" may not be sentimental, but rather the insight of one of a practical turn of mind who describes exactly what he sees. He goes into the slums with his camera and flash light, and in his illustrations he presents what the photograph has produced on the plate. It has been often so black and dark where he has gone that only the magnesium wire would clear up the scene. He gives full credit to those who have devised and carried out better systems of tenement buildings, and he properly lauds the efforts of Mr. A. T. White of Brooklyn, who has devoted a life of beneficent activity to tenement building. Mr. White says: "There is not the slightest reason to doubt that the financial result of a similar undertaking in any tenement-house district in New-York City would be equally good." Returns of an extortionate character are not possible, but 5 or 6 per cent. is—and that is enough.

Do we cry, "Wolf, wolf!" and does the wolf never come? Think of it! Three-quarters of New-York City living wretchedly, breeding epidemics, and training children likely to go to prisons. The muddy tide may rise and sweep for a time all before it. The gap between the two classes, as Mr. Riis writes, "is widening day by day." No tardy enactment of the law, no political expedient can close it. There is but one way to avert a threatening social cataclysm. It is to build a bridge founded upon justice. The curse of New-York is its tenement system. If the poor must forcibly lodge together under one roof, let public opinion be directed toward those who through greed demand extortionate rents and give, and continue to give, horrible accommodation. Mr. Riis has written a powerful book, which deserves careful and thorough reading. The task of remedying the present evils, he confesses, is fraught with difficulties. We are not a paternal Government. We do not want to be, and yet public opinion is strong and acts powerfully in the end, and public opinion should be unceasingly directed toward the owners of these filthy tenements until ameliorations are made, first as to the character of the accommodation offered, and secondly toward the diminishing of the rentals. The first would improve morals, the second permit the poor in time to save money and get themselves clear of these sloughs of despond.

January 4, 1891

THE COUNT OF THE SLUMS

In 1892 the Senate and House of Representatives authorized an outlay of $20,000, this sum to be devoted to the investigation of what was known as "the slums of the cities." This investigation was to be confined to cities of 200,000 inhabitants or more, as shown in the Eleventh Census.

The inadequacy of such an amount as $20,000, when the vastness of the subject to be studied is considered, is at once apparent. Conscious of how little money was available, the Commissioner of Labor used it, however, wisely, as it gave the opportunity to study what were the difficulties of the task, and so suggestions were possible as to how the work, on a large scale, could be carried out. Nevertheless, it is somewhate questionable, as far as cities are concerned, and the particular study of slums, whether the United States Government ever could arrive at the facts with the same precision as could the civic authorities. For a census of the slums, this would be more accurately carried out in New-York City by means of the police. This work might take a year or more to carry out, and might cost, for the additional clerical labor, some $25,000. In London, what is the population of the slums

has been given with a fair amount of accuracy. We doubt whether, so far, the exact facts of slum population in New-York ever have been given.

In 1892 the count of this slum population was said to have comprised "at the least calculation," 800,000 people in Baltimore, Boston, Brooklyn, Buffalo, Chicago, Cincinnati, Cleveland, Detroit, New-York, Philadelphia, Pittsburg, St. Louis, San Francisco, and Washington, the total inhabitants of these cities having been put down at 8,037,485. Ten per cent. as living in the slums must be immensely below the true figures. There has been guess work so far, for the exact data were not procurable.

The Commissioner of Labor presents as the results of his work the examination of the population of slum districts in certain cities, and the table shows in Baltimore the conditions of 18,048 persons. In Chicago there were 19,748 persons thus inspected, in New-York, 28,996, and in Philadelphia, some 17,000. The total was 83,852. Of course this is a mere furrow on the extended soil, for, as the Commissioner writes, according to the estimates, in Baltimore there were 25,000, in Chicago 162,000, in New-York 360,000, and in Philadelphia 35,000 people living in the slums. "These districts," the Commissioner states, "were selected as among the worst in the cities, and may be denominated as the centres of the slum districts. They were outlined and selected in consultation with the city authorities."

Occupying ourselves almost exclusively with New-York, a population of 360,000 living in the slum districts seems, at a first glance, to be exceedingly large. Actually, as those most competent to judge the matter will tell you, the proportion of those living in the slum districts is to-day over 425,000. This seems terrible at first sight, but it is not to be taken for granted that all those who live in the slum districts are either depraved or miserable. Through force of circumstances, habit, accident, there are many who live in the slums who are not bad nor wretched. As often as not, a fair proportion of those living in the slums earn good wages. But, granting that in the slum population there is a fair amount of respectability to-day the student of sociology is right when he says that surroundings have all to do with the status of humanity, and so the correct people who live in a slum are apt to retrograde. If the father and mother of a family can hold their own, their children do not, because they are certain to fall under the baneful influence of their neighbors.

We now look somewhat askance at the Philadelphia figures—35,000 in 1892. We believe that there must be errors in the estimate, though it is well known that the poor have a much better chance of existence there than in any other large city. The 162,000 people living in the slums of Chicago is again, we believe, far under the actual facts.

In the slums in New-York there was one groggery for every 120 persons, and out of the slums one groggery for every 200 persons. Strangely enough, the proportion of groggeries to people in the slum quarter of Chicago was about the same as in New-York. It was very much less in Philadelphia—one "saloon" to every 502 persons. We take here the opportunity of descanting upon that absurd name given to places where drink is sold, whether it be bad whisky or good beer, and calling such places "saloons." The two English words "public house" cover the entire ground, and "liquor saloon," as an absurd Americanism, ought to be relegated to the high-falutin' rubbish of the past. It is nonsense to use the words "liquor saloon," and it is to be trusted that before long "liquor saloons" will find no place in public documents.

Taking the 83,852 people living in the slum districts of the four cities, it was invariably found that there was a larger percentage of males. In New-York it was the highest, 54.61 being males. As to the foreign born, always in relation to the slum districts, there were in New-York, 62.58 per cent. not natives. As to illiterates in New-York in the slums, of native born there were 7.20 per cent.; of foreign birth, 57.69—which latter is a dreadful figure. As to the will of the majority, as punctuated by the votes of the free and enlightened, in the New-York slums, 62.44 per cent. were of foreign birth and could decide the fate of the Nation by means of the ballot box. Think how terrible is this power, when in a population, say, of 1,800,000 or more to-day, in New-York, over one-half of the 350,000 or 400,000 people living in the slums could have a voting power of 200,000 ballots.

Something not suspected is that in the slums the earnings seem to be fair, and "quite up to the general average" of the people in the city living out of the slums.

A really difficult question is to know exactly the number of persons living in each dwelling in a slum district. According to the eleventh census, there were 6.02 persons living in each dwelling in Baltimore, 8.60 in Chicago, 18.52 in New-York, and in Philadelphia 5.60. In the slums, the number in each house in Baltimore and Philadelphia was some 7.71, in Chicago it was 15.51, and in New-York 36.79. Mr. Marshall, in The Century Magazine for this month, (March,) tells us that the density of population in certain parts of London is 373 persons to the acre, and that three wards in New-York City are more densely populated. Of them, the Tenth Ward shows a density of more than 621.

When we come to the question of health, which, with morals, is a vital topic when the slum districts are studied, the Commissioner states that agents and experts were "nearly unanimous" in declaring that no greater sickness prevailed in the slum districts canvassed than in other parts of the city, and that, "while the most wretched conditions were found here and there, the small number of sick people discovered was a surprise to the canvassers." It is worth while mentioning that the canvass took place in the late Spring, and the people lived then with open windows, and were not as much subjected to foul air. We must not here jump at any conclusions. The canvassers saw the live men and women, and their duty being to inspect what was before them, they did not necessarily look into the past history of these families. Infant mortality in all crowded quarters, particularly in these slums, is terrible, as has been shown by Dr. Billings, in his vital statistics. It is here indeed the survival of the fittest, but this is only apparently so, for those who are alive to-day, having struggled through a difficult childhood, are still prone to succumb to the effects of disease. They live an abnormal existence, and, save in some favored races, seem wanting in vitality or the normal power of resistance. We should have to reverse our studies, our comprehension of hygiene, did we accept the idea that there was even an approach to normal health in the slums. When seven persons lived in a room in Baxter Street which was 18 by 20, with 400 cubic feet of air to each individual, no wonder there was present in this vitiated atmosphere .002 of carbon dioxide. This is the slow poison which will kill a mouse under a glass receiver. Every human being ought to have [illegible] cubic feet of air to breathe in, though existence may be carried on with 400, but with distressing consequences. As a preliminary work, with such means as were obtainable, the small sums of money allotted having been judiciously expended, Mr. Carroll D. Wright's report of the slums shows careful study.

March 29, 1896

TENEMENT PROBLEMS IN THE BIG CITIES

Boston, Cincinnati, and Hartford as Bad as New York.

PHILADELPHIA AS A MODEL

Provisions for Wide Air Shafts for High Buildings—Buffalo and Washington Also Have Good Sanitary Regulations.

A comparison of the tenement house conditions in twenty-seven of the largest American cities reveal the fact that, after New York, Boston has the worst conditions of any American city. Hartford, taking into consideration its population, has some very bad housing conditions, in many respects similar to those in Boston.

The comparison is made in the third report of the Tenement House Commission, prepared by Laurence Veiller, the Secretary, and just issued in a book of some sixty pages.

It appears that none of the large American cities, excepting Boston, Cincinnati, Jersey City, and Hartford, have a tenement house problem such as exists in New York. In most of them the poor and working people live generally in small one or two story houses, containing one, or, at most, two families.

With a population of 560,892, Boston has in certain parts of the North End and West End a number of tall tenement houses fronting on narrow alleyways, in which large number of poor foreigners reside. The six and seven story tenements are not so common in that city as in New York, the majority of the buildings not being over four stories high. In the South End the special problem is with the regulation and sanitary inspection of small two and three story houses occupied by several families.

TENEMENT HOUSE LAWS.

The laws in Boston in relation to tenements in many respects resemble the New York statutes, but in several particulars have improved upon them. In 1899 the law passed seven years before, which required that all tenement houses erected thereafter should be fireproof throughout, was so changed as to require that no building thereafter erected should be occupied above the second floor by more than one family, unless it was a first or second class building; a first-class building being defined as one fireproof throughout, and a second-class building being one in which the external or party walls were of brick, stone, or iron, or other equally substantial and incombustible material. The act contained a provision limiting the height of buildings so that they could not exceed two and a half times the width of the street on which they stand.

Cincinnati, with a population of 325,902, after New York and Boston, has the worst conditions of any city. It resembles New York in that it possesses nearly all kinds of bad housings from the large block buildings, with hundreds of occupants, to the small, dilapidated wooden house, occupied by two or three families. As far as can be ascertained, the majority of the poor and working classes live in tenement houses arranged for more than three families each, a considerable number living in large brick tenements similar to those here, but not so high, and in many ways better. Others live in old private dwellings converted into tenements, and many live in ramshackle, dilapidated buildings. The houseboats shelter others. Little has been done to remedy the conditions, a statistical inquiry in 1894 by the Ohio Commissioner of Labor resulting in no practical changes.

IN THE SMALLER CITIES.

Hartford, Conn., with a population of only 79,850, has many of the evils. Not only are there old, dilapidated, wooden, and brick buildings, which were formerly private residences, now occupied by several families, but there are also numerous tenement houses erected for the special purpose of housing a number of people. Lately there have been erected some flats and tenements on the "double-decker; dumbbell" plan, with small air shafts, as in New York. Hartford has practically no special laws on the subject, beyond the general requirements of the Board of Health in regard to light and ventilation.

Pittsburg, with a population of 321,616, is one of the few cities where bad housing conditions have been gradually increasing in recent years. There is a considerable foreign population, and overcrowding has become evident in certain sections, although there are few large tenement buildings. In certain parts of the city there are dark and damp cellar dwellings, and a small part of the population occupies wooden shanties on the outskirts of the city. There are practically no laws in relation to tenement houses.

Although Chicago has no "tenement house problem," it has a number of ordinances on the subject, looking to the sanitary conditions. They are modeled, generally, on those of New York and Boston. Kansas City is one of the cities where housing conditions are gradually assuming a phase which will necessitate legislative action. There are a number of cases where persons are lodged in rooms partly underground, in damp basements, and many persons live in tumbledown shanties.

Philadelphia, with a population of a million and a quarter; St. Louis, with a population of over half a million; Baltimore, with a population of over half a million, and Cleveland, Buffalo, San Francisco, New Orleans, Detroit, Milwaukee, and Washington, each of which cities has a population of over a quarter of a million, have no tenement house problem.

It is pointed out the laws of Buffalo, Philadelphia, and Washington might well serve as a model for New York in many respects, especially in regard to provision for light and air. The Buffalo law provides that "no court or shaft shall be less than six feet wide for one-story and two-story buildings, and at least eight feet wide for three-story and four-story buildings, and one foot wider for each additional story above the fourth story." The Philadelphia law provides that "no shaft or court shall be less than eight feet wide in any part, and that any court or shaft between the wings of a tenement house or between two tenement houses shall not be less in width than twelve feet; and all such shafts and courts shall be open on one side from the ground to the sky."

The present provisions of the New York law permits, instead of wide shafts, mere slits twenty-eight inches wide and sixty feet long, and closed in on all four sides.

December 9, 1900

THE SOCIAL EVIL IN TENEMENT HOUSES

Communication to Gov. Odell by the Committee of Fifteen.

Approves Legislation Proposed by the Tenement House Commission, Making Landlords Directly Responsible.

The Committee of Fifteen has sent to Gov. Odell a letter expressing approval of the legislation proposed by the Tenement House Commission in regard to the suppression of the social evil in tenement houses. The text of the letter is as follows:

New York, March 23, 1901.

Hon. Benjamin B. Odell, Jr., Governor of the State of New York, Executive Chamber, Albany, N. Y.

Sir: At a meeting of the Committee of Fifteen, held March 6, 1901, a resolution was unanimously adopted declaring the adherence of the Committee of Fifteen to the views of the Tenement House Commission in regard to the social evil in tenement houses, and earnestly approving of Sections 141 to 151, inclusive, of the act relating to tenement houses in the City of New York, proposed by said commission. It was also decided to present to you a statement of the attitude of the Committee of Fifteen and the reasons therefor, although the committee is well aware of the cordial support which you are already giving to the proposed legislation of the commission.

That the present conditions are deplorable, if not indeed intolerable, is a matter of common knowledge. And the greatest of existing evils is the intrusion and wide extension of prostitution in the tenement houses, the houses in which the great mass of wage earners are compelled to live. There will probably, for a long time to come, continue to be differences of opinion as to the degree in which it is possible to check social vice in our great cities, but there can be no two opinions as to the necessity of protecting children of tender years from close contact with depravity. An intimate acquaintance with adult vice should, at least, not be forced upon young children by permitting such vice to penetrate into the very houses in which they live. The cry of parents when they ask merely for the opportunity of bringing up their children in an atmosphere free from the pollution of the most degrading forms of moral evil should surely be heeded.

What alarming proportions the condition of affairs mentioned has assumed are shown by an examination of fifty tenement houses, taken at random, in which prostitutes were known to be plying their trade through open solicitation, and which revealed, living in each house, an average of slightly over twenty-eight children below the age of eighteen years. The statistics of diseases due to vice also show that such diseases are increasing at a rapid rate among children in the crowded sections of our city.

The laws at present upon our statute books have not met the situation. The prostitutes themselves when apprehended usually have escaped with a fine which has only served to make greater subsequent activity on their part the more imperative. Their arrest and return have made them more notorious to their tenement house neighbors, and the nature of their business more obvious, both to young and old.

The social evil must be extirpated from the tenement houses. The chief reason why it has been so difficult to accomplish this result hitherto is that the responsible party, the landlord, has enjoyed practical immunity from conviction because the burden of proving his guilty knowledge weighs heavily upon the prosecution. The law holds excused the landlord who wilfully closes his eyes so that he may not see. Furthermore, when hard pressed, he has been able to shift his responsibility by sub-leases and transfers beyond all recognition. The operation of the present statutes has, therefore, tended to intensify the evil, and has allowed responsibility to be evaded.

Under the legislation as proposed by the Tenement House Commission the difficulties of the situation bid fair to be greatly mitigated, if not to disappear altogether. Prostitution will no longer be a paying risk in tenement houses. The landlord, no longer secure from successful attack, will exercise such diligence as will keep his tenement house agent will be highly linwill no longer be able to use his agent as a shield of guilt. Indeed, an irresponsible tenement house agent will be highly improbable, for the landlord will take precautions to save his property harmless from the operation of the law, and the owner's diligence will, in each case, be transferred to the agent in charge.

The committee believes thoroughly that the legislation, as proposed by the Tenement House Commission, is sound and likely to be productive of the result desired. Children of the tenements will thus be given an opportunity to be nurtured in parental care, free from the poisonous influence of degrading examples of vice in their immediate proximity. And the complex social problem of prostitution, if it be not solved, will at least be appreciably simplified. Respectfully yours,

WILLIAM H. BALDWIN, Jr., Chairman;
CHARLES STEWART SMITH,
JOEL B. ERHARDT,
JOHN S. KENNEDY,
FELIX ADLER,
GEORGE HAVEN PUTNAM,
CHARLES SPRAGUE SMITH,
GEORGE FOSTER PEABODY,
JACOB H. SCHIFF,
ANDREW J. SMITH,
AUSTEN G. FOX,
WILLIAM J. O'BRIEN,
ALEXANDER E. ORR,
JOHN HARSEN RHOADES,
EDWIN R. A. SELIGMAN, Secretary.

March 25, 1901

TENEMENT BILLS SIGNED

The Governor Recommends Some Supplemental Legislation.

Extension of Time for Builders and Changes in Minor Features to be Included in a New Bill.

ALBANY, April 12.—Gov. Odell has signed the four tenement house bills which the Legislature passed on the recommendation of the Roosevelt Tenement House Commission. The Governor filed the following memorandum with the bill providing for the manner of construction of tenement houses:

On the hearing before me on this bill it was developed that some hardship would be occasioned by its immediate enactment into law, and also that certain amendatory provisions were proper and necessary. The President of the Tenement House Commission has transmitted to me a letter recommending that certain supplemental legislation be enacted to correct these defects, which is attached to and is to be taken as a part of this memorandum.

In the belief that the Legislature will take this matter up, and in thorough sympathy with the object and purposes of the Tenement House Commission, I have concluded to approve the present bill, leaving to the wisdom of the Legislature the propriety and extent of supplemental legislation on this subject.

B. B. ODELL, Jr.

He made the following letter to him from President Robert W. De Forest a part of the memorandum:

April 11, 1901.

Dear Sir: I have carefully examined the provisions of a proposed amendatory bill intended to meet some of the objections raised at the hearing before you to some details of the Revised Code of the tenement house laws, prepared by the Tenement House Commission. There is, from the point of view of the commission, no objection to them. Permitting builders who have filed lawful plans by April 10, and who have made contracts, but who cannot commence work until May 1, to build under the old law if they progress their work to the setting of the first tier of beams by Aug. 1, 1901, will increase, to be sure, the number of tenements of the old type, but to prevent the carrying out of bona fide building enterprises would work hardship.

The change in the law regulating access to water closets will relieve the better class of tenements from restrictions which in some cases might be onerous. Wood made fire-proof, as is quite possible under modern processes, should stand on a parity with other fire-proof materials. These amendments put in this form so as not to jeopardize other parts of the bill, will meet objections that have been earnestly pressed and will not impair the beneficent operation of the new law.

ROBERT W. DE FOREST,
Chairman of the Tenement House Commission of the State of New York.

Senator Stranahan will introduce the supplementary bill, and it will be passed by the Legislature before its final adjournment and signed by the Governor.

The definition of a tenement will not be changed. Apartment houses will not be exempted from the provisions of the act. Any building wherein three or more families reside will come within the scope of operation of the law. Gov. Odell and the legislators who have the matter in charge fear that the exemption of apartment houses would allow wholesale violations of the law, and they will take no chances. The amendments to be made by the Stranahan bill will cover the points suggested by Mr. De Forest in his letter to the Governor.

April 13, 1901

NEW LAWS' PROVISIONS.

Sweeping Reforms the Creation of the Tenement House Commission Will Bring About.

Chairman Robert W. De Forest of the Tenement House Commission returned to this city from Albany yesterday immediately after he had learned that the Governor had signed the four bills drawn up on the recommendations made in the report of his commission. He said that the new law would make a great change in the tenement house problem in this city and that tenements built in accordance with the law after this would present a great difference to those built under the old law.

"The principal reforms that the new law will bring," he said, "will be more air and light to the dwellers in tenements, the doing away with dark interior rooms and cellar rooms, proper sanitary appliances for every family, proper protection against fire, and a proper enforcement of the laws in regard to tenement houses in the city. This will be accomplished by the appointment of a Tenement House Department which the acts provide for.

"Probably the gravest evils resulting from the present tenement house system arise from a lack of proper sanitary supervision. The number of Sanitary Inspectors is wholly inadequate. The Health Department has plenty to do without inspecting the sanitary conditions in the tenements. The law in regard to the building of new tenements recently has not been enforced. Out of 333 tenements recently constructed only 15 were found, upon examination by the commission, which fulfilled all the conditions laid down in the old law.

"One of the chief reasons why tenement house reform has been a failure in New York for many years is the fact that there was nobody specially charged with the care and oversight of the houses. At present the enforcement of the laws in regard to them is divided among the Health Department, the Building Department, the Police Department, and the Fire Department. The new Tenement Department will have full control of the enforcement of the laws, and the Commissioner at its head will be the one man whom the people of New York will hold directly responsible for any violations."

The bill creating the Tenement House Department provides that the head of the department, who shall be called the Tenement House Commissioner, shall be appointed by the Mayor and shall hold office subject to removal by the Mayor. His salary will be $7,500 annually, and he will be under bonds of $20,000 for a faithful performance of his duties. He will have power to appoint and remove at will one or more Deputy Commissioners, whose annual salaries will not exceed $5,000 each. The Tenement House Department will include a New Building Bureau, an Inspection Bureau, a Bureau of Records, and the Tenement House Commissioner will have power to form other bureaus. The Commissioner will also have power to appoint all registrars, examiners, inspectors, and employes in the department and to fix their salaries.

"All the present power of the Health Department in regard to the sanitary inspection of tenement houses will go to the Tenement House Department," said Mr. De Forest, "as well as those powers and duties now held by the Police and Fire Departments with respect to the prevention of incumbrance of fire-escapes in tenements. The rights and duties of the Building Department with respect to the light and ventilation of tenements and to the equipment of the houses with fire-escapes will also be transferred to the new department. Before the construction of any house the owner will have to submit a detailed statement to the department.

"The new law further provides that every tenement over five stories in height shall be fire-proof, and that fire-escapes consisting of open stairways and balconies shall be built in the front of every non-fire-proof tenement. The balconies must be at least three feet in width and the stairways will have steps of not less than six inches in width and twenty in length with a rise of not more than nine inches. None of the stairways will be at an angle of more than sixty degrees. This will make egress from a building a great deal easier than with the vertical ladder fire-escapes which are on almost all the old tenements. Our report shows that in many cases people were unable to climb down these and were rescued from them by firemen. The public halls and stairs will be at least three feet in width. The stairs in all the buildings must be constructed of fire-proof material, and the floors of stair halls will have steel beams and fire-proof filling, no wooden flooring being allowed."

In regard to lighting and ventilation, Mr. De Forest said that the new law made the narrow airshaft which was a feature of all the old tenement houses a thing of the past. In future no tenement house must exceed in height by more than one-third the width of the street on which it stands. Except upon corner lots, a tenement house of sixty feet must have a rear yard twelve feet in depth, and an additional foot must be added for every twelve feet in the height of the building. What are at present known as airshafts situated between wings or parts of the same building must be at least ten feet wide in a house sixty feet in height, and have an increase of a foot in width for every additional twelve feet in the height of the building. In an inner court surrounded on all four sides the least horizontal dimension for houses sixty feet and under in height shall be twenty-four feet.

No rear tenements can be erected on a lot less than fifty feet in width. The total window area in the rooms must be at least one-tenth of the superficial area of the room, and each room must have at least 120 square feet of floor area. Previous to this, the law has never prescribed any minimum size for rooms. At present one water closet for every two families is required in a tenement. Under the new law there must be one water closet for each family.

One provision in the new law makes any woman who uses a tenement house for immoral purposes a vagrant.

It will be the duty of the Board of Health to inspect each tenement house in the city at least twice before 1902, and for the detailing of a body of sanitary police from the regular police force for the purpose of making inspections.

Mr. De Forest said that the amendment to the new laws permitting builders who had filed plans before April 10 and had made contracts, but were unable to start work until May 1, to build under the old law was only just.

"It will not make it possible for people to get around the law by simply filing plans," he said. "The new law provides that the plans must have been approved and the contracts made."

Abraham Stern, who represented a number of property owners and real estate men who were anxious to have the bill amended in regard to the time it should go into effect, said that he was well satisfied with the new tenement house law.

"We only wanted an amendment that would allow those who had already made contracts to build tenement houses under the old law to go on with them," said he. "That is the amendment that the Governor approved of, and we are satisfied."

April 13, 1901

SETTLEMENT WORKERS HOLD ANNUAL SESSION

Miss Addams of Hull House, Chicago, Praises Immigrants.

Commissioner De Forest Says Danger to Tenement House Reform Is Past Because of Public Sentiment and Not the City Administration.

There was an enthusiastic gathering yesterday afternoon at Sherry's, Fifth Avenue and Forty-fourth Street, on the occasion of the annual meeting of the University Settlement. The announcement that Miss Jane Addams of Hull House, Chicago, was to deliver the principal address brought together a large audience, largely of women, so that a glance over the hall revealed a bewildering scene of millinery and the art of the dressmaker. There were so many attractive bonnets and gowns that it would seem as if the wearers could have no other thought in life than to obtain suitable raiment, but the eagerness of the listeners to catch every word said and the spontaneity with which they caught and applauded the more telling points in the addresses showed that the women were in earnest and had apparently devoted more time to the problems of sociology than to the latest creations of the Parisian modistes.

President Nicholas Murray Butler of Columbia presided, making a brief opening address. In referring to a recent description of Oxford as the home of lost causes, abandoned beliefs, and discredited heroes, he said that there could be no such criticism of the modern university, which to-day looks forward and strives to be of real usefulness in the building up of the social structure and the advancement of mankind in the way of education and the higher civilization.

"The University Settlement work," he said, "is a natural outgrowth of the methods of thought and action inculcated at the modern university. The University Settlement affords the means of developing reciprocal regard among the various classes of society and is of especial importance in a country where there are no artificial lines among the various classes of society, especially important in a country where within a single lifetime one may see many instances of progress from one extreme of society to the other."

"NOT ALMS, BUT A FRIEND."

Robert W. De Forest, Tenement House Commissioner and President of the Charity Organization Society, was the first speaker. He told a number of instances of what had been accomplished by the society and the department, and then said, in part:

"There is a profound desire among both men and women to aid in social service. 'Service' is, in fact, the keynote of twentieth century uplifting, and that it is the right keynote we may know from the emphasis which Christ laid upon it. Social service affords the right means of relief, rather than charity. 'Not alms, but a friend' is a good motto.

"The Settlement, as I understand it, gives the friend. The Charity Organization Society and the University Settlement should co-operate in their labors. I hope that this policy will be continued and that in every case either society will limit its work to what the other is not doing effectively. There is no limit to the good that may be accomplished. I wish to express my appreciation of the good work that the University Settlements in this city have done in the matter of tenement house reform.

"Last January we were face to face with the most dangerous crisis that tenement house reform has encountered since the present law was enacted. Now I believe that I may say that all danger is over, and the fact that the danger is past is due not to the city administration, but to the voice of public sentiment. And in arousing this effective public sentiment, all of the Settlements, both in Manhattan and in Brooklyn, have taken an active and useful part."

Mrs. R. Y. Fitzgerald, manager of the west side branch of the Settlement, 38 King Street, told of the work under her direction.

"When the west side house was opened," she said, "some members of the society doubted whether the location had been well chosen. The streets were wide, the houses old-fashioned and roomy, and there were large back yards, but although the neighborhood was different from the large houses in Rivington Street, plenty of work was found to be done. On one side there was an Irish and Irish-American population, none too thrifty, and with a good capacity to get into troble.

"On the other were Italians, with abundance of thrift, but imposed upon on all sides and needing a friendly hand and very frequently words of advice. The house maintains a kindergarten and a school of carpentry, and will soon introduce some forms of art work such as wood carving, lace making, and rug making. There are a number of families among the Italians near by who are skilled in these industries, but do not know where to find a market, and are, therefore, engaged in work that pays very much less than they could earn, if properly started and aided."

Mrs. James Speyer, President of the Woman's Auxiliary of the University Settlement, was unable to be present on account of the serious illness of a relative. Miss Ella Clark read the report of the Woman's Auxiliary. It dwelt especially on the work in kindergartens and the library. Dickens had proved the favorite author in the neighborhood. It was distinctly stated that a trip through the neighborhood would do away with any notions of race suicide.

Robert Hunter, in charge of the house at Eldridge and Rivington Streets, and head worker of the Settlement, made a short address in which he found warrant for the Settlement in proof of its accomplishment. As an example he suggested the case of a young physician who, having completed his medical course, had opened his office in the crowded section of the east side. Mr. Hunter told of several young men whose education had been started in the Settlement, who, because of this education, were abundantly able to live in other parts of the city, but who held that they were under such obligations that to move elsewhere would be like desertion. They realized what had been done for them and were willing to undergo the discomforts of the crowded district that they might be near by to aid in the work that had done so much for them.

MISS JANE ADDAMS.

Miss Jane Addams was given the heartiest sort of a greeting. Speaking of the work at Hull House, Chicago, she said in part:

"Any list of the achievements of settlements must be pitifully meagre when compared with the needs to be met. Merely to build a great institution is not the main object, for there is a natural distrust of institutionalism. The real object is to get into personal relations with those who need our help, and in spite of their needs we shall find that there is in their lives a pathos, dignity, and worth which is like that of those who are more pleasantly situated.

"It is not so difficult to cultivate relations of friendship with persons who at first are prone to distrust you, because you are better dressed, speak a more refined tongue, and have great advantages. It is not necessary to go to the home of some unfortunate person, seat yourself down, and announce firmly that you have come to make friends. That is not the way to go about it. Friendships are never founded in this way.

"Friendship is a far more subtle thing, something like a growing flower that ripens into beauty, the feeling first a suspicion that you mean well, and have no thought of intrusion, a kindliness in the eyes and in the voice, and an illustration by the hands that you are willing and ready, even eager, to be of assistance. Before long the woman cleaning the ash can and the man tending the furnace, the laborer, his wife and his children come to trust you, and to appreciate you as a friend, the sort of friend, indeed, they can come to when in need.

"A cultured person is the first to avoid giving offense by seeming to see the difference in speech and manner, the last person to force acquaintance on those who are not friends, and it is our effort first to make friends of those we would aid. There is as much in making the friends as there is in afterward trying to help them.

"In our work in Hull House we have steadily grown in tolerance, until we have sometimes had to ask ourselves if we are not in danger of going too far and of reaching that optimism which will accept everything as good, and that is a very useless and dangerous optimism. Yet we are convinced that there is a latent force, a creative power in the people themselves with whom we deal, which will come out if it only has the chance.

"There are few who know how much good these immigrants bring with them, the love of art and useful accomplishments for which they find no market. I know a man in Chicago who was put out of his rooms in a tenement because he had carved his door in the evenings when he came home weary from work, and sought to tell what there was better in him. It was exquisite work, the same he had done in a church in Italy, he said proudly, which is double starred in Baedeker.

"Another had trouble with his landlord because he decorated his ceiling with stucco. This man said that he had been paid for such work at home, but he supposed he ought not to have attempted it here, where the American people like everything smooth and such a queer white. These men were artists, but they were not appreciated in their new surroundings.

"The children are eager to learn, and in many families they have adequate instructors in their parents, from whom they have inherited artistic tastes; but they grow ashamed of it, as they see that it has no reward, and they lose their heritage in our materialistic surroundings. Of course, I meant Chicago when I said that—I don't know about the atmosphere of New York.

"We once had a Greek play in Hull House played by the fruit peddlers, who are laborers in the Summer time. We found that these Greeks knew and had read the stories of Homer, and they were delighted to play before the Americans that they might illustrate and emphasize the fact that they were not barbarians.

"One man always prayed before rehearsing his part, and I asked him the reason for his prayer. He told me that he prayed for power to properly present the honor and glory of ancient Greece to the ignorant people of America, and he was absolutely sincere. We very freely express our opinion of the immigrants to this country, but we don't always stop to think or to question what they may think of us. The answers would be informative and useful. The social gulf that we used to hear so much about is imaginary, but it is deepest in the imaginations that are the most shallow. There is good and great work to be done, and the settlements are trying to do it."

In conclusion Miss Addams said that she could not entirely accept the motto, "Not alms, but friends," as it was often necessary to give alms. She said that it was work and association that were the great thing, and protested against a tendency frequently shown to turn a particular branch of work over to the city as soon as it gave the greatest promise.

W. K. Brice, Franklin H. Giddings, F. J. Goodnow, R. A. Seligman, and Samuel Thorne, Jr., were elected members of the Council of the society, class of 1906.

March 22, 1903

FIFTY YEARS' SOCIAL WORK HAS TRANSFORMED SLUMS

Miss Wald's Report to Coming Conference Reviews Three Periods of Progress—Charles Loring Brace and Jacob Riis Pioneers—House on Henry Street.

THE slums of New York have passed, asserts Miss Lillian D. Wald, head of the Henry Street Settlement, in a report prepared for the National Conference of Social Work in connection with its fiftieth anniversary meeting in Washington, May 16-23.

Miss Wald's study takes the form of an analysis of three books written during the fifty years since the conference came into existence. These are "The Dangerous Classes of New York," by Charles Loring Brace, published in 1872; "How the Other Half Lives," by Jacob A. Riis, published in 1890, and "The House on Henry Street," written by Miss Wald herself in 1915.

"The spirit of the times," Miss Wald now writes by way of bringing her own book up to date, "has expressed itself in many activities that emphasize the dignity of human beings. * * * Beautiful school buildings stand now in former slum' neighborhoods in the place of the old shabby structures; asphalted streets have replaced the broken cobbles of the highways; gone is that strikingly unfair condition which formerly expressed the contempt of the city toward the poor quarters when the trucks were brought from all parts of the city and stalled in the already congested, unswept streets, which were then the only playgrounds for the children.

"Money has been appropriated for small parks and recreation piers; money has commenced to flow in, some day to reach an approximate supply for the needs of recreation of the children. The housing problem is still the sorest blot in the city. But legislation recognizes at least the protection against the dark, unwindowed rooms, the rear tenements and the lack of water supply, conditions that were tolerated before this last era, and specialists employ their energies for protection against landlord exploitation.

"In the lower east side reforms have been initiated that are not only city-wide but world-wide. Medical inspection in the public schools made complete by the school nurse, the introduction into the schools of vocational guidance, the broadening of the curricula, which now include instruction more nearly related to the life of the children, are instances of this conviction.

"Significant, too, is the extension of the city's responsibility for its most pitiful children—the little cripples and defectives—the establishment of children's courts and the probation system for juvenile delinquents.

"Progressive measures for the protection of health now find expression in the Bureau of Child Hygiene in the Department of Health, in efforts to meet the pressing demand for the public health nurse in city, county and State, and, finally, in the apex of the Federal Government through its Children's Bureau.

"Mr. Brace discovered and gave eloquent and moving testimony to the existence of a class labeled Dangerous to Society.' He knew that his discovery would probably be a matter of indifference to prosperous and complacent New York unless he showed that the existence of this 'class' was a menace.

"The establishment of the Newsboys' Lodging House, most identified with his propaganda, was supposed to meet this urgent need, and child-saving agencies were given an impetus in America unknown before the stirring challenge of Loring Brace.

"New York in 1872 was another world. People were not ashamed to call the edges of the city 'slums.' The annual death rate of New York was 28.79 per thousand. For Gotham Court, in Cherry Street, the rate was 195 per thousand. The death rate in New York in 1922 was 11.93. The conditions in New York in 1872, while perhaps no worse than those in London, Glasgow, Naples, Amsterdam or Marseilles, were frightful, though the city was not yet built up.

"The Metropolitan Board of Health in 1866 reported a population of 196,510 per square mile, or sixteen square yards per person, in the Eleventh Ward, and in the Fourth Ward—the section once the home of President Washington, and where Governor Smith was born—were huge barracks, one said to contain 1,500 persons. Underground cellars were crowded with people. Our author tells of a dark, smoky cellar that was home for two men and their wives, a girl of 13, two men and a boy of 17, a mother and two boys of 15 and 10, a mother and two boys of 9 and 11, a total of fourteen persons. He adds that such conditions were frequent.

"The first Tenement House law, passed in 1867, gave discretionary power to the Board of Health, established the year before, and in reality was never enforced. In fact, not until 1895, when the Tenement House act was passed, was provision made for the enforcement of the statute.

"There was no compulsory education law before 1874. The Truancy law of 1853 exempted from school attendance all children engaged in 'lawful' occupations, a term which was very generously defined. In 1856 THE NEW YORK TIMES, speaking of the homeless children under 12, said:

"'Prussia has long practiced a compulsory educational system on the gentle and simple alike. * * * Whether we here in New York, with our jargon of languages in the lower strata of society, can do anything under the same involuntary methods to catch hold of the 30,000 young vagrants that fill our gutters is doubtful. But experiments in our educational, as in our industrial, system will have to be made if we are to hold our rank as an enlightened city.'

"But Mr. Brace saw the need of other reforms, and his program showed prophetic genius. Some of its planks should be posted upon the highways to show what has been accomplished, and also to rebuke the slothfulness of social enterprise. Students need to be reminded that the period of the seventies antedated the tide of immigration. America was the land of opportunity.' The sufferings of the poor were considered due either to misfortune or their own shiftlessness. The Benjamin Franklin axioms were the infallible remedies, to which was added Horace Greeley's 'Go West, young man.' The great idea was to get rid of the elements with supposed criminal inclinations, mixed with the genuine belief that the West gave unlimited golden opportunities. This philosophy is reflected in a farewell speech of a small newsboy to his friends before traveling in to the farmer in the West, which Mr. Brace quotes:

A Newsboy's Speech.

"'Boys, gentlemen, chummies: Perhaps you'd like to hear summit about the West, the great West, the great West where you know so many of our old friends are settled down and growin' up to be great men, maybe the greatest men in the great Republic. Boys, that's the place for growing Congressmen and Governors and Presidents. Do you want to be newsboys always and shoeblacks and timber merchants in a small way by selling matches? If ye do you'll stay in New York, but if you don't you'll go West and begin to be farmers, for the beginning of a farmer, my boys, is the making of a Congressman and a President. * * * How do you know but, if you are honest and good and industrious, you may get so * * * you'll have servants of all kinds to tend you.'

"'Dangerous Classes,' the book, revealed the social measure of the times in its omission of all comment on the frightful sweatshops and very slight reference to the causes of poverty.

"People like Mr. Riis no longer took for granted the necessity for slums or the viciousness of their inhabitants, and in discussing the causes of their bad conditions he gives as the three most important, low wages, bad housing conditions and intemperance. He says there is a closer connection between the wages of the tenement and the vices and improvidence of those who dwell in them than we with the guilt of the tenement upon our heads are willing to admit, even to ourselves.

"The turning point in actual condition in New York, which most influenced social thinking and made the outlook of Mr. Riis (himself an immigrant) upon the world of New York so different from that of Mr. Brace, came with the newer immigration. In the eighties began the inrush of Italians, Russian Jews and other Southern and Eastern European peoples, which continued with unbroken force until the outbreak of the great war. Israel Zangwill coined the phrase the 'melting pot,' and the presence of the multiplying racial groups stirred new thought and helped to develop new methods, but the philanthropists still stressed the need of bringing out from **the different types a single American pattern, believing that disease and sweatshop conditions were due to ignorance. Mr. Riis certainly was a great influence in veering thought to the quality of the children and in broadening and enlarging a conception of their essential needs.**

"Perhaps it would be fair to say that as Mr. Brace is identified with the establishment of the Newsboys' Lodging House, Jacob Riis's name will be most readily identified with the small parks movement and the need of play for little children.

Henry Street—1915.

"Beautiful school buildings are now provided in the neighborhood of the house in Henry Street—in one of the first experiments in the classroom for 'ungraded' children—with space in front of the school marked off in summertime that vehicular traffic may not interfere with the play of the children. On the street is a highly developed school for crippled children where, through the combination of private philanthropy and public educational funds, are given not only suitable education but occupations that insure self-support, and the automobile carries the handicapped children to and from their school and workrooms.

"A little further on in an ordinary tenement is the 'model flat' for instruction in housekeeping under modern educational processes, and on the street the houses of the rich converted into a neighborhood centre that commemorates the name of Jacob Riis. Four or five blocks further down is the House on Henry Street which has been the gathering place of many people who have proved the practicability of their social philosophy, and under its auspices there have been demonstrations continuously made of measures to broaden the culture of children and to emphasize their importance and the importance of their families.

"The best known legislation, perhaps, has been through the creation of the public health nurse, now so universally an instrument of service. Another opportunity which has been used so effectively has been the development of talents so often witnessed in the productions at the Neighborhood Playhouse.

"Schools to train social workers now exist in order that professional efficiency may be standardized and that sentimental, often unwise, though kindly disposed people may be trained into intelligent exercise of their good-will.' The Conference of Charities and Corrections is rechristened 'Conference of Social Work,' as indicative of an altered attitude. Current literature and the conference itself give emphasis to the conviction of interrelationship and the mutual responsibilities between people; 'class' is taboo, and research is directed toward the underlying causes which victimize human beings worthy in themselves, and dignified with 'rights' and obligations."

May 6, 1923

ASSERTS IMMIGRANT IS SCHOOL PROBLEM

Research Director Lays Stress on Education's Part in Work of Assimilation.

CITES OLD PREJUDICES

Albert Shiels Says Critics of the Foreign-Born Are Apt to Generalize Too Much.

The school and the immigrant are the subjects of a report made to the New York Board of Education by Albert Shiels, Director of Reference and Research. Within the last thirty years, he says, there has been considerable uneasiness over the continuous flow of immigration, and the question has been raised as to the power of this country to continue successfully to assimilate so many variant types that might imperil American institutions, customs, traditions, and standards of living.

Whatever justification there may be for this feeling, says Mr. Shiels, its existence is a fact. It has been formulated in magazine articles, books, public discussions, and Governmental reports. It is interesting to note, however, that the present protests affect to be less against immigration, as such, than against the present character of the immigrant laborer, usually referred to in terms of his geographic origin. In the period from 1810 to 1883, 95 per cent. of the total immigration was from countries west of the Russian boundary and north of the Mediterranean and the Balkan Peninsula. From 1883 to 1907 81 per cent. of the immigration was from Italy, Austria-Hungary, the countries of the Balkan Peninsula, Spain, and Asiatic Turkey. Out of the total immigration for the year 1913 the latter type of immigration represents 74 per cent. of the total.

In a discussion of present-day immigration, he declares, we should be mindful that our judgment is always likely to be affected by possible illusions, and that impressions and prejudices may be confounded with fact. One frequent illusion is due to a prejudice derived from familiarity with the newly arrived immigrant, as we may meet him in person—his physical condition and his habits. We are likely here to confound the accidental and temporary with the fundamental and permanent. An immigrant may be unclean in person, repellent in his habits and apparently content to live under offensive conditions. Yet in such matters he may, in many cases, be but a creature of circumstances, perhaps their victim. The real question is whether he is inherently vicious, criminal or indolent, and, on the other hand, whether he may not under favorable conditions develop into a desirable citizen.

Critics Prone to Generalize.

A second illusion, Mr. Shiels finds, is the acceptance of generalizations, which are themselves based on very hasty and superficial inferences. One example is the tendency to repeat what appears on a printed page, without thoughtful reflection. Thus it is frequently stated that recent immigration implies a disproportionate increase in poverty, disease, and crime. Some of the opponents of the immigrant movement affirm this, others are very cautious. There do not seem to be many convincing statistics to prove the validity of all these assertions. Another charge is that immigration displaces native labor, reduces wages, and increases unemployment, or, at least, contributes to under-employment.

A third illusion, and a very real one, in Mr. Shiels's opinion, is a manifestation of what Lord Bacon called an idol of the tribe, meaning our own human tribe. It is the attitude which most persons have against any stranger. To the degree that he differs in nationality, or race, there is always apt to be a corresponding intensity of suspicion and dislike.

Our welcome to immigration, Mr. Shiels says, has been a splendid service to the world; it is necessary to remember, however, that our goodness has not been without reward. When we realize, for example, to what degree the development of mining industries depends upon foreign labor, or remember that three-quarters of all our laborers on railroad and construction work are foreign born, certainly we must hesitate to adopt policies of exclusion, even if we adopt methods so illogical as the imposition of a literary test.

The question, therefore, Mr. Shiels thinks, is not to be solved by personal prejudice, by unprofitable economic theories, nor altogether by the assumption of responsibility for the welfare of the unfortunate of other lands. What we need to know are the fundamental qualities of the immigrant as we are getting him, what promise he and his children hold for good citizenship, what influences, pro and con, he produces on wages, labor and opportunity, and—perhaps the most important question—what we are prepared to do to reap the richest advantage from his coming. What we are doing consciously and purposively is a question the answer to which would scarcely flatter our national pride. If we shall do no more than we have done, if we are content to depend upon the slow process of evolution that has worked fairly well under happier conditions, it is possible that, notwithstanding all the material contributions that the immigrant may make, immigration itself may be a bad thing.

Whatever may be done in the matter of future distribution, Mr. Shiels points out, the immediate problem for teachers is to consider the immigrant, not in the places where we might like to place him, but where he insists on going himself. It is true that many immigrants working in camps or as farmhands go to rural districts. Until State educational agencies evolve a more effective system, however, the main concern of public school teachers will be centred in the interests of immigrants in the cities.

Teachers Need Broad Culture.

It has been doubted, Mr. Shiels says, whether the regular public school teachers are best fitted for this special work. Whatever the merits of the contention for a special school system, the actual conditions are that for some time to come many day public school teachers will continue to do the work in evening classes. Many of them have already done it with conspicuous success. Whatever the system may be, every teacher should have an equipment greater than a mere command of special method, however necessary that is. He should have a real understanding of the questions other than curriculum and teaching technique. The broader understanding brings the deeper sympathy; the foreign pupil should not be a mere recipient for a certain mass of knowledge, or a lay subject for technical demonstration of teaching skill. The foreign pupil, appreciated in all his relations, becomes in the teacher's presence a man like himself, with hopes, aspirations, misadventures, misfortunes; a fellow-being to be aided and encouraged without contempt or patronage.

Our civilization, Mr. Shiels thinks, has indicated a somewhat naïve confidence in the public school teachers' abilities, which, though flattering, is embarassing. The school is assumed to be the exclusive agency in education. Whatever faults the rising generation may have are calmly attributed to it. Such fundamental influences as the home, the street, the newspaper, the differences in individual instincts and experiences are all brushed aside, and the teacher is called upon to assume the rôle of mentor, parent, and inspired prophet. Omnipotence is the prerogative of divinity, and not even public sentiment can confer it on a corps of teachers. There is, however, one duty a teacher is required to perform and to perform well. That is the duty of effective instruction.

Now, in the case of the immigrant, Mr. Shiels says, the whole educational procedure is handicapped from the beginning. The evening school, in which the teaching of foreigners has so large a place, in the words of one teacher, is the stepdaughter of the educational organization. When school funds must be reduced, it is the evening schools that bear the reduction. When other branches of instruction come to require more and more rigid conditions for the training of teachers, it is only among evening classes for foreigners, that in so many communities a place remains for almost any kind of teacher with any kind of license. When elaborate courses in special methods have been evolved in training schools, extension courses, and teachers' colleges, consideration of the critical problem of instructing our immigrants has alone been omitted.

July 11, 1915

CITY NOISES.

The coming in of Summer, with its demand for open windows, brings into prominence a trait of New-York life which is, perhaps, not generally appreciated. We all know that we live in the worst-governed city in the civilized world; we all know that it is the dirtiest place of its size and its pretensions to be found this side of Constantinople, Cologne being clean compared to it. Whoever has a nose, knows also that it is without a rival in the richness and the variety of its stenches, both those which are manufactured within its borders and those which are wafted to it from the surrounding country. From the suburbs of European cities comes the smell of meadows and of flowers, or, if this be lacking, at least that negative sweetness which is the accompaniment of freshness and purity; but from the outskirts and draggled borders of New-York come the odors of the dumping-ground, of the fat-trying establishment, of the bone-boiler's vats, of the petroleum-yard, and others, nameless but not less noisome. But besides these distinctions, we have another: New-York is the noisiest city in the world. The mingled roar and clatter of its streets makes a daily din which far surpasses that of any other city which can justly be compared to it. Only two others surpass it in size and in the amount of traffic carried on within them—London and Paris—but both of these are its inferiors in this respect. The busiest, noisiest quarters in either of them might almost be called silent when compared with any part of New-York below Canal-street, and many parts of it between that street and Forty-second.

The chief reason of the greater noise of New-York streets compared with those of the other great commercial metropolis of the world, London, is the paving of the road-way in our streets. All the principal London streets, even in the city proper, are "macadamized." The difference as to noise thus produced is very great indeed. It is all that could be imagined from the difference between the passage of vehicles over a smooth, soft suface and over a rough, hard one; the diminution of noise in the former case being due not only to the diminution of jar at the point of contact, but to the comparatively undisturbed condition of the vehicles themselves. Carts and carriages in London do not clatter and rattle as they do in New-York; and, besides this, there is the very appreciable difference in noise produced by the tread of the horses, whose iron-shod feet ring out at every step in our streets, but in London are comparatively silent. This difference can hardly be imagined by those who have not made the comparison. Next in noise-producing power come our street railroads, elevated and surface. As to the former, we are yet singular and peculiar in the happiness bestowed by their possession; and even as to the latter, we yet surpass all other cities in the constant traffic through our streets in these strange city vehicles. If old "Commodore" VANDERBILT had only known the blessed innovation in this respect that he was about to introduce to the world, when he obtained the privilege of continuing the Harlem Railroad down through the City, that he might deliver his passengers at the City Hall for an extra six cents a head! For that was the origin of the street railroad, and the railroad in Fourth-avenue was for years the only one even in New-York. The noise of the street railroad cars is a very appreciable addition to the confusion and the din which the inhabitants of New-York are obliged constantly to support. To the rumble and clatter of the car is added a peculiarly noisy impact of the horses' hoofs upon the stones, which is, for some reason, much more obtrusive than that produced by the horses attached to other vehicles; and besides this, there is the ceaseless jingle-jangle of the bells. Now, below Forty-second-street it is almost impossible to get out of hearing of this combination of noises, the sum of which is very considerable. Some parts of Park-avenue and of Fifth-avenue, and only some, are the only places in which it does not form a part of the daily experience of New-Yorkers. Even Madison-avenue is invaded by it. And we are sure that our readers who sit now with open windows in the evening will agree, with few or no dissenting voices, that this combination of rumble, hoof-clatter, and bell-jangle, with the roar and the puffing of steam-trains coming on one side or the other every minute, is a very serious drawback to the tranquil enjoyment of life.

Besides these noises, there are the street-cries, and the hand-organs, and all those other audible nuisances in which we are not peculiar, but which we suffer in their most aggravated form, because of the bad administration of our Municipal affairs and because of our own supineness. There are street-organs, for example, to be heard in most other cities, but in none that we know of are they so incessantly plied in all quarters—in the haunts of business and in the dwelling parts of the City—as they are here. Of this, one reason is that our people "don't like to make a fuss," and they don't tell the organ-grinders to go away, as people in other cities, particularly in England, do; and the consequence is that we suffer, to put money into the pockets of the Italian *padrones*. For, from this noise nuisance, whether musical, so-called, or that which comes from roughly-paved streets, or from cars with horses or cars with steam engines, we do really suffer. It does not follow, because any one of us cannot say that he or she is made appreciably ill at any one time, that our suffering is not worth consideration. The noise nuisance is a considerable addition to the nervous strain and irritation which we are called upon to undergo, and the greater susceptibility of Americans to nervous diseases is increased for the dwellers in our cities, and particularly for those in New-York, by the noisiness of their lives. We cannot be said to be indifferent to this, for we feel it, although like those who live near a cataract or in a mill, we are in a measure used to it. But we are supine about it—we can't take the trouble that would be required to stop it. But in Europe they do take such trouble. There the comfort of people in all respects is considered worth care, and thought and effort. And this matter of city noises is really one of no little serious import. Think, for a moment, what a blessing it would be if the noise of New-York were to stop to-morrow, and we could say, in the words of HOLMES,

"And silence, like a poultice, came
To heal the blows of sound!"

June 6, 1879

CINCINNATI SMOKE NUISANCE.

REPORT OF THE SMOKE INSPECTOR—LITTLE PROGRESS BUT SOME ENCOURAGEMENT.

CINCINNATI, March 7.—The Smoke Inspector to-day made his first official report to the Mayor. The report covers two months' service, and is of a hopeful tone. The Inspector admits, however, that the work of abating the smoke nuisance is one of no small magnitude, and does not promise that the effort to enforce the new law will cause any marked change for some little time. He states that there are over 5,000 boilers in the city in the furnaces of which soft coal is consumed. He has called personally upon 400 of the owners of these furnaces, and has assurances from nearly all of them that they will make reasonable haste to comply with the law. He has examined 23 different smoke-consuming devices, one of which has been perfected. They are all, however, an advantage, and some of them can be depended upon to consume, if carefully tended, from 75 to 90 per cent. of the smoke. It is reasonable to suppose that a perfected device will be an outcome of the attention now being given to the subject. The Inspector is of the opinion that a conservative course should be pursued by the authorities in the enforcement of the law. He argues that inasmuch as none of the devices is perfected they cannot with propriety be forced upon the people. Manufacturers should be urged to give the matter attention and adopt as soon as possible some one of the devices, with the expectation of complying fully with the provisions of the law as soon as a perfect consumer of smoke has been put upon the market. To arrest and prosecute those failing to comply with the law would be easy, but, in the opinion of the Inspector, would not, under the present circumstances, be the wisest course to pursue. He finds the disposition of manufacturers toward the law to be good, and hopes gradually to abolish the nuisance without causing hard feelings.

March 8, 1882

SMOKE ABATEMENT PAYS.

Cleveland Expert Says It Gives a 4,000 Per Cent. Profit.

"Abatement of smoke in this city during 1913 has yielded the city a dividend of 4,000 per cent."

This estimate is a feature of the annual report of the division of smoke issued by City Smoke Commissioner E. P. Roberts of Cleveland, Ohio. He points out that the operation of his division cost $19,000.

The estimated saving of damage from smoke from stationary plants for 1912, 1913 and 1914 is $400,000. This, according to the commissioner's estimate, leaves a net profit of $381,000 and produced a dividend of 2,000 per cent.

The report adds that the plants have an actual life of ten years. Using $200,000 as an average annual saving, and $3,900 as the annual average cost, the annual dividend for ten years is put at 3,600 per cent. By adding the saving from elimination of railroad smoke the total of 4,000 per cent. is produced on a one year's basis, the commissioner asserts.

Another feature of the report is the statement that the damage resulting from the burning of one ton of bituminous coal in cities having a fair degree of smoke abatement is not less than $1.

The total amount of bituminous coal used in Cleveland according to the Chamber of Commerce report for 1913 was 3,500,000 tons. Using Chamber of Commerce data gathered in 1910 as a basis, the Smoke Commissioner says it is reasonable to state the damage is not less than $1 per ton even in cities such as Cleveland and Pittsburgh, where the conditions are much better per ton of coal than would be the case if smoke abatement had not received attention, and very much better than in numerous smaller cities where it has received no attention.

February 1, 1914

VENTILATION IN CITIES.

With the rapid increase of the city as compared with the rural population, it is a matter of great importance that the air holes in the great cities shall be where the population is most dense, and that the ventilation of the streets shall be as manageable as the ventilation of the best houses. The need of this ventilation in European cities has long been recognized, and small spaces have been opened in many densely-crowded sections, so that the breezes can carry away the effluvia of the narrow lanes and alleys and give the people a place where they can have the sunshine by day and the freshness of the evening air on a Summer's night. It has also been recognized by our own Park Commissioners in a very practical way. The wiping out of the notorious "Five Points" by the location of a new park alongside of it shews what may be done to advantage in all densely-populated districts. Crime and filth are as effectually checked by air and sunshine as by more drastic measures, and the opening of these squalid fester sores to the light of day has become one of the most pressing issues wherever the municipal authorities are working to improve the health of the people. Dr. E. R. L. Gould of the United States Department of Labor, who is an acknowledged expert in sanitary matters, has made a careful statement of the comparative advantages of European and American cities in respect of park areas and open spaces in a monograph lately published by the American Statistical Association, and from his tables it is seen that in all the great centres of civilization the increase of breathing places where the population is most dense is receiving attention.

There is but one American city where the people do not believe in fresh air, and that is Pittsburg, where the park area is confined to one and one-third acres. The best ventilated city is Washington, where the open spaces are more numerous in proportion to the population than anywhere else in America. New-York has a park area of 1,213 acres, but 840 of it are in one block, though, with the additions proposed by the Park Commissioners in the annexed district, this area will be increased by 3,808 acres. The most interesting and important section of this enlargement is the six acres which are to be rescued for the people in the vicinity of Five Points, by which the most squalid part of the city will be relieved. Philadelphia devotes 2,491 acres to public uses, but only 48 acres are distributed among the different wards where the breathing places are most needed. Brooklyn has 595 acres of public grounds, but only 89 are distributed throughout the city in small areas. Chicago leads in its number of small parks. Out of an area of 2,000 acres the largest single park has 593. In Boston all the parks have a range of 1,204 acres, out of which 518 are devoted to Franklin Park. Wherever the population is most dense in American cities there is some provision for fresh air and bright sunlight. The leading European cities present a curious study in this respect. London has a park area of 5,976 acres, of which 1,412 are in one lot. Berlin has 1,637, of which 636 are in one inclosure. Paris has 4,739, of which 2,359 are in one domain. Vienna has 2,334, of which all but 344 acres are in one space. Birmingham has 225 acres, with 57 in one area. Leeds has 538 acres, with a single park including 300. Manchester has 169 acres, with a public garden containing 60. This is a fair, general, and comparative exhibit for the two countries. It is seen that the older European cities are those in which the air spaces are best distributed in view of the needs of the population, and that the older American cities are making increased provision for the denser districts, even when it involves the purchase of land at an enormous valuation.

The stress in the ventilation of our American cities is on the increase of the number of air holes in the region of the tenement houses, where the population cannot go to the outlying park and yet needs to disport itself for recreation and refreshment at the end of the day. It is estimated that 1,016,135 of the dwellers in New-York live in the tenement houses and are chiefly dependent on these air holes for what they have in the way of natural life. It is the small spaces near their homes which they need most, and, useful as these are for clearing the atmosphere and clearing out disease and making life wholesome, they are quite as important for recreation. In the Summer months they are indispensable. The working people of the Old World know how to use these breathing spaces better than we do, but, with a difference, their enjoyment of outdoor life in the cities need not be greater than our own. The late Prof. Jevons held that the way to the higher civilization lay principally through the deliberate cultivation of public amusements, and it is the use of the smaller parks in our cities for free or inexpensive amusements and recreations, rendered possible in the Winter as well as in the Summer, which is to make an inroad upon vice and crime with their immense possibilities in a dense population. Dr. Gould rightly urges the development of these small parks on the ground of physical health. City life inevitably leads to physical degeneration. There is practically no third generation in a New-York tenement. The possibilities of a better physical life are closely connected with these playgrounds for the children and breathing spaces for their parents. The great pressure is for the small spaces which the masses of the people can use to advantage, and it is a source of satisfaction that in these, after possibly London, Washington leads the world in the number of spaces of five acres and under for each one thousand of population. Boulevards and broad avenues are enjoyable and the utility of large parks needs no urging, but there is danger in the rapid growth of our American cities that the small air holes shall be overlooked where they are most needed.

January 13, 1889

The citizens of New-York may congratulate themselves, when they consider what they have done to establish public parks, upon the degree of liberality that has been manifested in acquiring and improving land to be devoted to the rest and recreation of its population, and generations yet unborn will look back and bless those who had the foresight to extend the park system and to learn by experience the necessity of anticipating growth and the crowding of dense masses of people.

There is no reason to complain, when New-York is compared with other large cities in this respect, that the metropolis has been slow. We have now in a completed condition the Central Park, with its 840 acres, and the small Riverside and Morningside Parks. But there are also awaiting improvement the new parks in the annexed district, which, together with the Central Park and the smaller city parks, will supply the metropolis with 4,711 acres of park lands, with one park—Van Cortlandt—of 1,070 acres, and another—Pelham Bay—of 1,740 acres.

These look like large figures, and the taking of nearly 5,000 acres of land in a city, or land that will be in the city in a few years, means the subtracting from lands available for building purposes of a great many city lots, representing a vast sum of money. But there are other things to be thought of besides sales of building lots at high prices, and in providing these large parks it is not improbable that an increased value is assured to the neighboring property quite equal to what all the property would be worth if sold to be built upon.

In the chapters given here the readers of The New-York Times are afforded an opportunity to see what public spirit and individual generosity and local pride have done to provide other cities with what are popularly called "breathing spots." A comparison of what has been done by St. Louis, Chicago, and Cincinnati, which have made efforts to improve their parks, makes it plain that New-York has not been too rapid in establishing new parks, or excessive in its appropriations for the improvement of newly acquired tracts.

St. Louis, with a population far less than New-York or Chicago, has 2,126 acres already laid out in parking, and there is no doubt that in natural advantages and in artificial improvement the Forest Park and Tower Grove Park of that city entitle it to be regarded as the leading park city of the country. Chicago, with 1,900 acres of parks encircling the city, is completing a finely designed system of parks under independent commissions in different parts of the city, and its "system" is one entitled to the description, for all of its parks are connected by boulevards paved with asphalting, and providing a continuous drive or bicycle roadway forty-five miles in length.

Other cities whose enterprise is described in the chapters following this introduction have indicated an interest in public parks that is creditable to their citizens, and have supported them with all the liberality the incomes of those cities would justify. St. Louis has the finest botanical garden in the country—excepting, perhaps, only that at Washington. It will take years of time and intelligent direction for New-York to obtain a botanical garden that can be compared with either of those fine collections. And it will be only by the liberal and judicious expenditure of money that New-York will be able to produce a series of drives connecting its great parks that will be as attractive and as extensive as Chicago's park-connecting boulevards.

It will be observed that in the city that has the amplest provision of breathing spots and the oldest parks there are the fewest restrictions upon those who use the parks. The parks of St. Louis are not only the largest, but the finest, the grass being for every one to walk upon, while the greatest liberality of regulations is extended in the sale of refreshments. Of botanical gardens and zoological collections, outside of St. Louis, which has no zoological collection worth speaking of, and Buffalo, which is arranging a botanical garden that will be creditable to the city, there is not much to call attention to in the list of parks of which descriptions are given.

ST. LOUIS.

The public parks of St. Louis embrace an aggregate area of 2,126 acres. The largest is Forest Park, in the central western residence district. Its area is 1,372 acres. This splendid pleasure ground was acquired by the city about twenty years ago, under a special act of the Legislature authorizing the city to purchase the ground, at that time a piece of woodland west of the city limits. The purchase was guarded by restrictions and provisions, the wisdom of which is shown by the present beauty and grandeur of the place. The cost to the city up to date has been close to $2,500,000. There probably is not in the country any similar bit of land more perfectly adapted for a public park for a great city. There are just enough hills and valleys; a beautiful little stream—the River des Pères—winds through it in such a crooked course as to give the impression that there are many streams. When first dedicated it was thickly wooded. The timber has been gradually cut away and the landscape gardener's ingenuity and skill so employed as to leave fully half the territory well covered with grand old monarchs of the forest. Three small ponds and one large lake for boating are in the park. All over the improved part are scattered Summer houses and pavilions of unique or ornate design.

This park is accessible from every part of the city by car line for a five-cent fare, and on Sundays in Summer it is not an unusual thing to see 30,000 or 40,000 people promenading, driving, boating, or otherwise at play. Forest Park is not inclosed. There are very few restrictions to public enjoyment. Three street-car lines run far into the park, and three others reach its confines. There are five picnic grounds, or commons, where the greensward is not considered sacred. Not even a permit is required for the people, singly or by crowds, to enter upon these places and do practically as they please. The flowers and shrubbery, of which there are vast quantities of the finest, are carefully guarded, arrest and a fine being the penalty for despoiling them. The picnic grounds are in the improved half of the park. In the woodlands there is no pretense of restrictions. People throng the woods in Spring and carry away the wildflowers, and it is not an uncommon thing to see a procession of thrifty people carting off wagonloads of freshly cut grass.

There is a small collection of animals in Forest Park, the most notable feature of which is a herd of buffaloes, seven in number. Besides these, there are a score of deer, several elks, some prairie dogs, and a large number of minor animals; two or three eagles, storks, pelicans, swans, and some other rare birds. The park is lighted by a system of electric lights, covering all the improved territory, making the vast network of carriageways and promenades as light as day.

Refreshment privileges are let for ten years. The concessionaire maintains a restaurant and resort at a central point, where he has pretty free swing. Besides this, he has a number of small stands or booths all over the park, but he can sell beer and strong drinks only at the central establishment. His privilege is exclusive. The boating privilege on the lakes is held by another man.

No advertising schemes or gambling devices of any kind are permitted within its precincts. Many efforts have been made to establish various kinds of money-making amusement concerns in the park, and one man has succeeded in getting the right to run a lot of swinging chairs and a flying Dutchman, with steam piano attachment. But sentiment is so strong against converting the grand park into a beer garden that the concessions are not likely to go any further.

A force of special park police keeps order. Tramps are not allowed to loaf or congregate in any of the parks. Forest Park is a great resort for bicyclists of both sexes, one of the regular events of the wheeling calendar being the Forest Park road race. Baseball, tennis, football, cricket, hurling, and all out-door games are provided for in season, and there is always fine skating in Winter. In Forest Park is the half mile track of the Gentlemen's Driving Club, where trotting meetings take place every Saturday afternoon. No admission can be charged; no betting is allowed.

Next to Forest Park in size, but considered superior to any park in the world in artistic beauty, is Tower Grove Park. It contains 267 acres, and was given to the City of St. Louis by the late Henry Shaw. Though a part of the public park system, in that it is entirely open to the public, it is specially provided for. Mr. Shaw devoted the latter half of his life to this park, and his famous botanical garden. When he gave the park to the city he coupled with the gift the condition that the city should appropriate $25,000 each year to improving and beautifying it, and that it should be governed by a special board of three Commissioners. To such a state of perfection has the place been brought that it seems to be folly to spend $25,000 a year on it, or even one-fifth of that sum; but it has to be done, or the Shaw heirs may claim the land. The city has expended nearly $900,000 on this park. The park, though free, is inclosed. There are five entrances, supported by massive granite pillars, with a gate keeper's lodge at each. The drives and walks are magnificent.

Besides these two large parks, there are fifteen smaller ones, most of them so kept as to justify the city's pride in them. In the extreme south end of the city is Carondelet Park, of 180 acres of finely wooded ground. In the extreme north end is O'Fallon Park, comprising 158 acres. These two were purchased and dedicated at the same time as Forest Park, the idea being to have breathing spots in the western, southern, and northern parts of the city.

Nearer the centre of the city are other parks, a chain of them running right through the town. These vary in size from three city blocks, the smallest, to Compton Hill Reservoir Park, with forty acres. Most of them are in the densely populated sections, and are inclosed with iron fences, the gates being locked about midnight.

The parks of the city are under the general supervision of a Park Commissioner, appointed by the Mayor. He selects a head keeper, with assistants, from two to twenty in number, for each of the parks. The keep-off-the-grass rules, and the rules against dogs are enforced with greater or less strictness, according to the vigilance of the watchmen—excepting, of course, as to the commons in the larger parks. The fullest practicable liberty is allowed, and the people appreciate it. And it is worthy of note that the grass is just as green and just as luxuriant on the commons as anywhere else in the grounds. There is no special park tax, appropriations for their maintenance being made from the general revenue. The new appropriation bill, just made a law, provides for maintenance of the parks, and sets apart for the various items of expense a total of nearly $140,000. Of this amount $10,000 is for park police and $6,000 for music during the Summer.

There are many fine statues in the St. Louis parks. Every park has its fountain. Forest Park has four. At the eastern entrance to Forest Park is a bronze statue of Frank P. Blair that cost $9,000. Three statues in Tower Grove Park are world famous. They are Humboldt, Shakespeare and Columbus. The Humboldt statue was provided by the widow of the famous traveler. In Tower Grove Park is a mulberry tree, now of vigorous growth. The late Adelaide Neilson brought here a cutting from the mulberry at the tomb of Shakespeare and planted it with pomp and ceremony. It has flourished beautifully. In Lafayette Park the notable art features are statues of Washington and of Thomas H. Benton, who sat in House and Senate thirty years. Statues of statesmen, warriors and heroes of lesser note are in the other parks.

In addition to the public parks, St. Louis has Shaw's Garden. Next to the Botanical Gardens at Washington this institution is the largest of its kind in this country, and in some respects it surpasses the National Gardens. Its botanical collection is very complete. The late Henry Shaw, philanthropist, after making a vast fortune, devoted fifty years of his life to Tower Grove Park and his garden. The park he gave to the city long before he died. At his death he provided for the maintenance and improvement of the botanical garden for all time, and gave it, not to the city, but to the citizens of St. Louis. He established a fund, to be handled and controlled by a board of trustees. He named the first board and provided for the naming of their successors. Then he said the garden should be open to everybody six days a week, but closed on Sundays, except on two Sundays in the year. Besides this, he provided for the preaching once a year of a sermon on flowers, and that a banquet should be given once a year, to which should be invited famous botanists or lovers of nature to a certain number from all over the world. He died ten years ago.

Shaw's Garden is inclosed by a very high, very thick double stone wall, and has only one entrance. Carriages never enter. No one is allowed to pluck even so much as a leaf; no one can carry a package into or out of the garden. Every plant or shrub or tree that can possibly be made to live in this climate can be seen in the garden.

No works of a scientific character are carried on in the St. Louis parks, unless in that category is to be included the United States fish hatchery in Forest Park.

CHICAGO.

Chicago's parks, or "lungs," as its poetical guide-book writers insist on calling them, are designed upon the same generous plan as the city itself. Chicago now has 1,900 acres of parks, exclusively of the lake front common, and about eighty-five miles of broad, improved boulevards connecting with them. That the Chicagoans appreciate this feature of their city is shown by the fact that they have willingly taxed themselves over $20,000,000 for the purchase and maintenance of parks and boulevards since the creation of the system by legislative act in 1869.

The park system of Chicago is under the control of three separate and distinct boards of commissioners, holding sway in the North, West and South divisions of the city, respectively, and entirely independent of the municipal government. These park boards were all organized under the act of 1869, and two of them have the power, under State control, of levying and collecting taxes. The Commissioners for the North and West sides are appointed by the Governor, and those for the South Side—where the World's Fair was held—are appointed by the Judges of the Circuit Court of Cook County. The South Park Board pays salaries to its President and its auditor, and the other boards of commissioners serve entirely without pay. The South and West Side boards are corporate authorities in their own right and levy their own taxes. Lincoln Park Board, on the North Side, has to depend upon the North Town authorities for its assessment levies, but the rate allowed is not limited, and, though it annually makes a report by courtesy to the Mayor, it is in no wise under city control. The fact that each park board is absolutely independent of the others and of the city is found to have a good effect in promoting both rivalry and diversity in improvements.

The revenues of the parks are secured by annual assessments, varying from 1½ mills on the West Side, to ¾ of 1 per cent. on the North Side. Each board carries an indebtedness for bonds. Most of these bond issues are arranged on the twenty-year payment plan, and are drawing 7 per cent. interest on the oldest, and 5 per cent. on the newer ones. The original land for the parks was purchased by means of special assessments, spread according to benefits on private property. Lincoln Park, which is the oldest in point of improvements, has not only paid the sixteen installments into which its special assessments were divided, but has called in the last of its $800,000 bond issue of 1873, and is now paying off its $500,000 of shore-protection bonds, issued for the construction of a sea wall along its two-and-a-half miles of lake front, and of a fine boulevard and speedway in connection therewith.

The general arrangement of the parks of Chicago shows that the city had already spread out several miles before the people paused long enough in their money getting to think about breathing spots. The six largest parks are arranged in the shape of a broad semi-circle, with a radius of four or five miles—Jackson Park at the south extremity, Lincoln Park at the north, and the lake front common in the centre. This latter immensely valuable tract of thirty or forty acres along the lake shore at the heart of the city still continues in the possession of the municipal government, and if the "boodle gang" in the Council do not take a notion to present it to some of their corporation friends, it may yet be one of the most popular parks in the city. The aggressions of the Illinois Central Railroad, which traverses the edge along the beach, have been checked by a Supreme Court decision, and a project is now on foot to sink the tracks three or four feet, and give the shore to the people again by means of grading and viaducts. The Council also took away the breath of its constituents recently by actually passing an ordinance for extending this park into the lake by utilizing the spoil from the great drainage canal, which, up to this time, has been worse than wasted by being dumped into the harbor in the neighborhood of the waterworks cribs. In its present condition this lake front park is but little used, except for occasional gatherings of strikers, as a camping place for militia, or as a lounging place for tramps, and as the location of the Chicago Art Institute, whose fine building stands upon it at the foot of Adams Street.

It would be difficult to say which is the best park in Chicago, for each of the reservations excels in some special feature. Lincoln Park is the oldest and the most diversified, and, as it is nearest the centre of the city and in the midst of a thickly populated district, it is probably the most generally patronized. The West Side parks—Humboldt, Garfield, and Douglas, enumerating from the north—excel all others by the superior length of the boulevards connecting them. The South Side parks—Washington and Jackson—are larger than all the other parks of the city put together, and the magnificent impetus given this district by the World's Fair is this moment resulting in improvements at Jackson Park which will soon make it the chief of the city's parks for beauty, as it has always been for size.

The South Park Commissioners are Joseph Donnersberger, President; William Best, Auditor; John B. Sherman, James W. Ellsworth, and Jefferson Hodgkins. President Donnersberger gives an idea of the improvements that have been made since the removal of the World's Fair buildings thus:

"By the end of this Fall we shall have spent about $500,000 in Jackson Park and the Midway Plaisance. We have spent $200,000 in the Midway alone, (that always was an expensive place,) and we have completed the lawn surfacing of the north end of Jackson Park, above the Museum Building, at a cost of another $100,000. We are building a bridge at the site of the old battleship which will stand for $40,000 when completed. We are also filling in along the west line of the park, from the Midway down to Sixty-seventh Street, and are working on driveways which we expect to complete this Fall, at a cost of $150,000 more. You would not recognize the desert waste left after the removal of the buildings a year ago."

The South Park Board issued $500,000 of bonds at the inception of the World's Fair enterprise, spent most of the sum in that cause, and was then reimbursed to the amount of $200,000 by the Columbian Exposition Company, and by $100,000 more from salvage. It is these latter sums that the Commissioners are now investing. Mr. Donnersberger estimates that the whole system of improvements projected will cost $1,000,000, but it will be some years before the plans can be carried out. The present tax levy produces an annual lump sum of $300,000 for the maintenance of the parks and also allows an additional tax of half a mill for retiring bonds. The Commissioners are retiring these at the rate of $35,000 a year, and this leaves each year an increasing surplus from this source to apply to improvements.

The Midway Plaisance is indeed a changed thing. The old stamping grounds of the dancing girls and of the leather-lunged capper have been excavated for a wide canal through the centre of its entire length. The plan was to connect the Court of Honor basin with the lakes in Washington Park thus allowing the electric launches, which still ply upon the lagoons, to "do the Midway." Unfortunately, when the canal was nearly dug, it was discovered that the Washington Park lakes were so high above lake level that the new canal would drain them absolutely dry without the intervention of locks. So the canal remains a mile-long meadow, with grass covering the bottom, awaiting the years that shall bring the income necessary for completing the original waterway project. On each side of this waterless canal, however, there are fine drives, graveled walks, trees, and, on one side, a bridle path. The famous street of the nations is therefore more artistic than of yore, although it can never again be quite as naughty or half as interesting.

No scientific work is done in direct connection with any of the Chicago parks, but the magnificent collection of the Field Columbian Museum, the residuary legatee of the World's Fair, now occupies the comely structure remembered by exposition visitors as the Art Palace, in the middle of Jackson Park. The museum daily attracts many visitors, especially on Saturdays and Sundays, when admission is free. This museum is controlled by a Board of Directors, entirely separate from the Park Board, though the two bodies work in harmony.

The South Park Commissioners have no use for "Keep Off the Grass" signs, and allow the people to run all over the 524 acres of Jackson Park and the 371 acres of Washington Park. They draw the line, however, at picnicking on the Wooded Island, where the Japanese temple still flourishes amid a bower of floral embellishments. The German Building stands in its old place, and so does the statue of the "Republic" in the basin. Otherwise there is little left of the great fair.

There are no botanical gardens, so called, in any of the Chicago parks, but almost all the large parks have greenhouses and conservatories, and flowers form the chief element in the landscape gardening of the various tracts. Washington Park probably takes the lead in this regard. Over 300,000 plants and flowers embellish this park and its feeder, Drexel Boulevard. In addition to its conservatory and palmhouse, Washington Park has a remarkable display of water plants, including some magnificent specimens of the Amazon water lily, Virginia Regia.

An important feature of Washington Park is a tract of 100 acres known as the Meadow, which is set aside for sports and for the use of children. Another is the Ramble, a maze of shrubbery planted in thick copses, and interspersed with bits of open ground. Next to Lincoln Park, Washington Park is probably the most popular of all. It has gained rather than lost visitors since the discontinuance of racing on the Washington Park Club track, a few blocks south of the park.

When this park district was created, in 1869, the Commissioners began by issuing $2,000,000 of bonds, which were sold chiefly in New-York. They early gained control of Michigan Avenue and a short space on Thirty-fifth Street, which, in connection with Drexel Boulevard, connected this park system with the down-town district. Half a million dollars' worth of improvements were put upon Michigan Avenue alone, making it one of the most fashionable residence avenues in the city.

Leaving the South Park system, the visitor drives or pedals due west from Washington Park, on Fifty-first Street, otherwise Garfield Boulevard, whose beautiful surface stretches almost as far as the eye can see out into the country, and then turns abruptly north, under the name of Western Avenue Boulevard, until it comes to the big drainage canal. Here a bridge is building, under the joint control of the West and South Park Boards, and beyond this, for about two miles, is the only break in the almost completed circuit of boulevards girdling the city. In a few months the triumphant wheelman can go spinning without a pause from the centre of the city, down Michigan and Drexel Boulevards, to Washington Park; west over Garfield, north over Western Avenue and Douglas Park Boulevard, through Douglas, Garfield, and Humboldt Parks, then east to Lincoln Park, and south along the Lake Shore Drive to the starting point. When he finishes the run, his cyclometer will tell the tale of forty-five miles of smooth rolling.

The West Park Commissioners are Harvey T. Weeks, President; Andrew J. Graham, Carl Moll, John M. Oliver, Edward G. Uihlein, and Charles J. Vopicka. They have provided a pavilion and refectory building in each of their three two-hundred-acre parks, and a band of twenty pieces gives a musical programme in each once a week. There are no scientific buildings of any kind in the West Side parks. These parks are also seriously handicapped by a chronic water famine, and, as they do not possess waterworks of their own, as does Lincoln Park, they are constantly at war with the residents as to the amount of water they may use in sprinkling.

Although there is some complaint about the strictness with which the West Park Commissioners guard their grass, they have at least adopted one feature that meets general approval from all except the "mashers." It is a sign marking as "Children's Commons" certain tracts from which all men are excluded, and where women can resort alone without fear of molestation or annoyance.

The West Park Board issued $1,000,000 of bonds at the inception of the World's Fair boom, and this year the Legislature has again authorized an issue of $600,000. It is with this fund that the Commissioners are completing the fine system of boulevards that is the redeeming feature of this otherwise slighted district. The fact that this board has to divide its funds among three large parks and five small ones, added to the remoteness of all of them from Lake Michigan, accounts for the somewhat less prosperous appearance of these parks as compared with their rivals.

Lincoln Park has band concerts twice a week. It has Charles T. Yerkes's wonderful electric fountain one night in every week. And it has "the animals," the only zoological exhibit in any of the parks of Chicago. The bear pit is well supplied with black, brown and polar bears. The eagle house, the monkeys' quarters, the haunts of the elephant, lions, tigers and wolves, the inclosures of the buffalo and the deer, all have their interested crowds about them day and night. This park, which comprises almost 300 acres, also has generous baseball and tennis lawns, an elaborate yachtsman's harbor, bridle paths and a speedway, a conservatory, a refectory, a fine lake for boating, and, lastly, but not least, it has the Academy of Sciences building. This is a new $100,000 structure of stone, toward which Matthew Laflin, an old Chicagoan, gave $75,000 and the Park Commissioners the rest. The Chicago Academy of Sciences uses the building for a museum and for assembly halls, and the Park Commissioners have their office and their police headquarters in the building.

The Lincoln Park Commissioners are Andrew Crawford, president; Bernard F. Weber, Martin Becker, F. H. Winston, John S. Cooper. They secured the passage by the last Legislature of a law that gives them the right to buy the riparian rights along the shore of Lake Michigan to the north line of Lake View, and are now preparing to extend their sea wall and North Shore drive a couple of miles beyond its present terminus.

Another law has also been passed which allows the formation of park districts anywhere in the State. Evanston, the next municipality north of Lincoln Park, has ordered an election for July 30 to organize a park district under this law for the purchase of riparian rights, and the improvement of the Sheridan road, which is a continuation of the Lincoln Park boulevard system, and which is ultimately to be improved all the way to Milwaukee. The Wisconsin legislators have promised to meet the Illinois people half way in the building of this unique lake shore boulevard.

There is every indication that the botanical features of the Chicago parks will continue to be improved. Despite the extreme popularity of the zoological collection in Lincoln Park, none of the other boards show any disposition to imitate this rather expensive feature. The Lincoln Park authorities settle the grass question by allowing the popular use of spots marked "common" until the grass shows signs of dying, when the signs are removed to other spots.

Are the parks of Chicago in popular use? The almost unbroken processions of the rich in carriages and the poor on foot, that throng all the parks on Sundays and in the evenings, will answer that question decidedly in the affirmative. Bicycles by thousands throng the drives on Sundays. Never have the parks been so thoroughly popular as since the advent of the wheel.

BUFFALO.

When Buffalo planned its park system it set out in deliberate fashion to do it on a broad general plan which would admit of constant improvement in succeeding years. Each of the parks in consequence is connected with all the others by boulevards, so that broad, convenient routes of intercommunication exist between the several parks and the business districts. Frederick Law Olmsted, the landscape architect, conceived the design, and he esteems it as one of his finest works, having exhibited a map of it at Philadelphia in 1876 and at Paris in 1878.

The largest of the parks is the North or Delaware Park, consisting of 350 acres, three and one-half miles north of the City Hall. It is approached by many broad streets of asphalt and macadam. There is a great sweep of undulating turf, 150 acres in extent, and an artificial lake of remarkable beauty covering forty-six acres. This lake is surrounded with splendid shade trees. Groves, picnic grounds and grounds for baseball and football make up some of the attractions. The meadow is a splendid piece of turf, which offers unusual advantages to equestrians. Well-kept roads and bridle paths penetrate every part of the large park and the roads are well shaded by large trees.

Two broad macadam boulevards lead from the eastern end of the park across the city from west to east to the parade, which is two and a half miles easterly from the City Hall, and consists of a smooth, gently sloping lawn designed for military drills, parades, out-of-door sports and large assemblages of the people. This covers fifty-six acres. It has a large grove, and a refectory where liquor is sold, the only place in the whole park system where this is permitted. And it will not be permitted here after May 1, 1896.

Leaving the park at the opposite end, a drive of two miles along macadamed boulevards and broad asphalted park roads leads to the Front, which is on the crest of a steep bluff, sixty feet above the level of Lake Erie, and offers a fine view of the lake and Niagara River, which is just at its beginning here. Miles of the Canadian frontier are in view, and along the Front Fort Potter hugs the cliff and helps to ornament the scene with its soldiery. The Front has fifty acres

The south parks, now in process of beautification, are designed as the ornament of the south side of the city. Recently the city acquired large tracts of land in this section, and has spent hundreds of thousands of dollars in preparing the system of the east side. Three pieces were taken lying along the same line—the South Park of 155 acres, Cazenovia Park, with 76 acres, and Stony Point, with 22½ acres. This gives the city 718½ acres of park lands, without taking into account the many small parks which occur along the connecting boulevards. The south parks are to have an artificial lake, and one of the finest botanical gardens connected with any municipal establishment. They are connected by boulevards with the North Park, the Parade, and the Front, so that one may drive throughout the whole park system without leaving the parkways. Indeed, the park approaches themselves, and there are many others now being added, take in 163 acres.

The botanical garden at the South Park is now the especial object of the Park Board. Propagating houses are being built, and all arrangements made at a large expense to devote the South Park to a botanical garden. David F. Day, one of the best-known botanists in the country, is a member of the Park Board, and this work is being done largely under his supervision.

There is the nucleus of a zoological garden at the North Park, where a large inclosure contains buffalos, deer, foxes, wild cats, &c. Many additions to this feature are planned, but the commission has been cramped for funds of late.

Last year the Park Board spent $250,000. It employed an average of 250 men the year round. The government of the parks is vested in a board of fifteen Commissioners, who have the broadest powers. They employ a Superintendent, who has general charge of the whole system.

The popularity of the parks appeals to the stranger at once. On Sundays, holidays, and on every pleasant night thousands of people may be found at the Parade, the Front, and the Park. Band concerts are given three times a week at the principal parks, and the attendance is astonishing. At the North Park it is not unusual to see 20,000 people gathered around the park lake enjoying the music, the band being stationed at the refectory at the edge of the park lake. All the parks are of easy access, none being more than twenty minutes' ride from the centre of the city.

Perhaps one reason for the popularity of the parks is the absence of "Keep off the grass" signs. Except during certain months in the year, when the Meadow is protected, the people are allowed to go at will everywhere.

CINCINNATI.

Cincinnati suffers from the distinction of possessing one of the most restricted park systems in the country. In fact it can hardly be called a system, so far as the acquirement of the various park lands is concerned. There has been a good deal of hit-or-miss in the purchase of the public breathing spots. A very late appreciation of the value of parks, a scarcity of funds, and a multitude of changes in management have combined to leave the Queen City with very few of these jewels in her crown, and not very large ones at that.

As it happens, the city possesses many natural advantages, which could be easily utilized by park makers. "Cincinnati," says the report of a commission, "as compared with other cities in the United States of like character and importance, has not at present the parks and drives that her citizens require, notwithstanding the fact that the topography of the country presents an opportunity for drives and parks of unequaled beauty and variety of scenery." Local pride and truth are united in this statement. The natural opportunities are at hand, but the city has only about 390 acres of park, with less than five miles of roadway, and about half a mile of bridle path. Connecting boulevards exist only in the hopes of particularly sanguine citizens.

It is estimated that this city has 1,025 persons to every acre of park land. There is one city in the country which is even worse off in this respect; Brooklyn, it is estimated, has 1,061 to the acre. But of cities more nearly the size of Cincinnati, none fare so badly in the statistics. Indianapolis, with about 900 persons for each of the acres in its parks, comes next to the Ohio metropolis, while St. Louis has an acre for every 190 persons, Louisville an acre for 150, and Pittsburg an acre for 337. In respect to driveways, the showing of Cincinnati compares no more favorably with that of the other cities named.

The business portion of Cincinnati and the most densely settled of its residence districts lie between the Ohio River on the south, and a chain of high cliff-like hills on the north, east, and west. In one place there is a break in this chain where the Mill Creek Valley stretches northward from the Ohio River, and along this valley is a district thickly settled, but not to the same degree that prevails in the central part of the city. In the whole of this area between the river and the hills there are but two parks of notable size.

Lincoln Park, the oldest of the city's collection, has been in use since about 1862. It is a West End tract of ten acres, the surface of which is gently rolling. It has a miniature lake, on which boating is possible in Summer and skating in Winter; and its shrubbery, walks, and benches are kept in very good order. It must be said, however, that this little park is a somewhat sombre pleasure ground. The fault does not lie in the arrangement of the place or the care given to it, but in the prevalence of the soot, which frequently falls almost as thickly as snowflakes do in January. And the soot season lasts all the year.

Washington Park is very near the heart of the city. It was a graveyard up to 1864, since which time its four acres have been of use to living Cincinnatians. Like Lincoln Park, it is a distinctly urban tract, and its utility considerably exceeds its beauty. It could be much larger with advantage to the city, for it is very near densely populated districts. It is resorted to by crowds day and night. Some time ago a count of its visitors showed that between 7,000 and 8,000 persons entered its gates in the course of a day. A similar count at Lincoln Park gave figures over 1,000 greater. The attendance on the day of the enumeration was doubtless above the average, but it serves to show the practical popularity of the two lungs of the main part of the city. There are two or three other small areas devoted to public use in this district, but none of them is large enough to meet the demands upon it.

Late in the sixties the business of opening parks in the suburban region on the hilltops was undertaken, what is now known as Eden Park being secured from the Longworth estate. This land is a picturesque stretch of hill and valley which justifies its old name of the Garden of Eden. Sales of part of the property reduced the original area until the park now contains only about 200 acres. From its higher ground magnificent views of the Ohio Valley and of the manufacturing and business part of the city are to be had. A great deal has been done to improve the Eden Park. Among its other structures is the Art Museum, one of the show places of Cincinnati. The land was acquired primarily with an eye to its use by the city water works, and even now a considerable portion of its area is given up to reservoirs. The growth of the city has surrounded Eden Park with enough people amply to justify its use for park purposes, although so far as the residents of the main part of the city are concerned it is somewhat out of the way—not so much in distance as in amount of street car fare. Anybody who can climb the hills is strong enough not to stand in need of a breathing place, while the average Cincinnatian, who isn't quite equal to the task of surmounting the steep grades, is forced to pay tribute to two railway companies to reach the park. It is possible that this difficulty will be ended in a year or two; but so long as it exists it is a very serious drawback to the usefulness of this very beautiful public pleasure ground.

Several years after work had been begun on Eden Park the first steps were taken to secure what is now called Burnett Woods, a tract of 163 acres a mile and a half to the northeast. The city secured from the Burnett estate and W. S. Groesbeck a perpetual lease of the property. The land bore a growth of noble forest trees, and its topography made it possible to open it to the public without a very great amount of labor upon it. Roadways have been laid out and imperatively demanded improvements have been made, but it has been kept as largely as possible a "natural park." A considerable portion of its area has been recently given up to the Cincinnati University, a step which promises to add some fine buildings to the woods, but which is regarded as a serious mistake by many of those who are most active in behalf of the parks.

Various commissions from time to time have reported on the need of enlarging the scope and revenue of the Park Department. Plans have been proposed for an encircling chain of boulevards, with parks of about 250 acres each on the eastern and western borders of the city, but such projects have never progressed beyond their advocates' maps. In fact, there is so much which might be done that it is rather hard to say where the improvement will begin. There is need of small parks in the central parts of the city, and there are excellent sites available for larger parks in the semi-suburban districts. Something, too, ought to be done for a public pleasure ground on the river bank.

"What we need," said R. H. Warder, Superintendent of Parks, to a New-York Times correspondent, "is a proper metropolitan commission to take hold of this matter. It is important to get a large tract of land for future use. We need a considerable extent of valley land, which could be devoted to grounds for athletic sports, lakes for swimming, bathing, and boating in Summer, and skating in Winter. At present the youth of this city must carry on their sports outside the parks. We have no fields for baseball, football, tennis, or the like. There was a croquet ground laid out in Eden Park, but very little use has been made of it, owing to the slope. In fact, as things are now, we haven't enough level ground for any athletic contests.

"A tired city man in search of recreation should have, first of all, a change of scene. Just such a change we would be able to give him in our parks. It is possible for the city to obtain from 1,000 to 1,200 acres at a small cost, which would serve admirably for a park of the kind most desirable for Cincinnati. Until we can get something of the sort we shall have to do the best we can with our present ground. We don't have much money to spend on the parks. In fact, this year we have only about $40,000, out of which we have to pay $12,000 or $13,000 for police. So you see we are not in a position to make expensive experiments. In Eden Park we have the beginnings of a greenhouse. It may serve to help us some day to obtain a botanical collection, although such a thing is not in contemplation at present. We have made no effort to establish a zoological collection. Our reason is that the city already possesses one of the best zoological gardens in the country, which is owned by a private corporation.

"Our first great need, as has been said, is truly rural parks. Such parks must be easily reached by street railway, and the cost of reaching them must be reduced to a minimum. These conditions can be realized, and new parks should be secured and laid out at the earliest possible time. For residents of the hilltop suburbs, Cincinnati's lack of parks does not mean so much, for they have plenty of elbow room in their own neighborhood, but for the thousands who live in crowded quarters on the lower levels it is a very serious matter. Below the hills the population is denser than in almost any other city in the Union. And for these occupants of crowded quarters we have only the park provision offered by the few acres of Lincoln and Washington Parks and the two or three other tiny ones in that part of the city.

"In the way of driveways connecting the parks, much could be done at moderate expense if the Park Department had control of the streets in question, with power to protect them from the wear and tear of heavy travel. But that power is one of the things we can only hope for. We haven't it now."

So far as it is possible for the Park Department to indulge the small boy in his fancy for getting on the grass, the Cincinnati small boy is indulged. In the small down-town parks it is, of course, necessary to keep the children and their elders off the grass. A week of free running over the turf would mean annihilation of the grass. In the parks on the hilltops, however, the rule is to allow as much freedom as possible. When the grass anywhere becomes badly worn, permission to play or picnic upon that particular tract is rescinded for a time, but other parts of the park are still available. An effort is made to deal with this question in a thoroughly common-sense way.

Local conditions have the effect of restricting the open on-the-grass season somewhat. The soil of this region is largely a stiff limestone clay, upon which the grass gets rather a poor start in Spring. Moreover, this soil holds water with a sponge-like tenacity. Hence, for the sake both of the feeble turf and the health of the visitors to the park, the people are not encouraged to wander from the paths until early in June. After that, every effort is made to accommodate them.

The Park Department has some interesting things to show for the money it spends. Among them, in Eden Park, is the first cement bridge of any size built in the United States. It has a seventy-five-foot span. It cost about $7,500; bids for a stone bridge of similar size ranged from $15,000 to $18,000.

Band concerts are a feature of the larger parks. Money to meet the expense involved comes from private enterprise, instead of the public purse. W. S. Groesbeck gave a fund from the income of which music is secured for Saturday afternoon in Burnet Woods. The Cincinnati Street Railway Company, stirred up to mild emulation of Pittsburg, pays for fourteen Sunday concerts in the same park. The Schmidlapp Fund provides twenty Sunday concerts in Eden Park.

MILWAUKEE.

The Milwaukee park system is a paradise for children. They can roam at will over the seven parks controlled by the Park Commissioners. There are a few signs of "Keep off the grass," and they are only used for temporary protection where the sod is not ready to be used for a playground. The rules are few and simple, and meant only to restrain the rough element. The opinion held from the first by the Park Commissioners is that the parks were intended for the use of the people, especially the people who have little opportunity to get away from the city during the hot Summer months.

The system is of recent growth. Seven years ago all the parks Milwaukee had were a few small, widely separated patches of ground scattered about the city. In 1889 a few far-sighted citizens realized that Milwaukee was far behind other cities in its provision for breathing places for its people, and that unless something was done promptly to remedy this lack there was danger that desirable tracts of land could not be obtained. A bill was passed by the Legislature, and the Milwaukee park system was founded. The bill created a board of five Park Commissioners. It confined the Commissioners in their purchase of park property to lands within the city limits. This power was extended by the Legislature of 1891, and the Commissioners were authorized to go beyond the city limits for parks.

The Commissioners purchased in all nearly 400 acres, at a cost of $1,069,644, the payments extending over a long term of years. The size of the parks ranges from 24 to 124.50 acres. The two largest are the Lake Park, on the east side, extending along the lake shore for a mile and a half, and including 123.60 acres, and the West Side Park, on the northwest border of the city, including 124.50 acres. The other parks are River Park, east side, 24 acres; Mitchell, 31 acres; Howell Avenue, 45 acres; Coleman, 26 acres, south side; Perrigo Tract, 24 acres, west side.

The south side parks are about completed. The Commissioners are limited in their expenditures for improvements to about $70,000 each year. This fund, known as the "Park and Boulevard Fund," is raised by a tax of ½ mill on the dollar of all taxable property in the city. This fund will increase each year, and in time will amount to a large sum, but at present the Commissioners find themselves at times badly cramped for money.

With the resources at their command, the Commissioners have done wonders in the few years the park system has been in operation. The heaviest work will have to be done on the Lake Park, which will eventually, owing to its advantageous location, be very handsome. The tract of land included in this park extends along the lake shore for a distance of 7,000 feet. At its southern line it is barely a block in width. At the northern boundary it is about an eighth of a mile wide. The bluff along which the park extends rises 100 feet above the level of the lake. At its foot is a gravel beach washed by the waves of Lake Michigan. The crest of the bluff is a level plateau extending back to the western limit of the park. The northern half of the tract is covered with groves of fine forest trees, principally oaks, which afford a shady and cool retreat in the hot Summer days. To add to the picturesque beauty of the place, the plateau is indented by deep ravines extending back from the lake shore several hundred feet. Even in its present shape, when hardly touched by the landscape gardener, this section of the park has much of picturesque beauty.

West of the Lake Park, less than a mile away, is the River Park, a sequestered nook of 24 acres, extending for about a quarter of a mile along the Milwaukee River, which at this point is shadowed by overhanging bluffs and presents reaches of great beauty. The two parks will be connected by a boulevard 150 feet in width. In time it is intended to extend this boulevard westward to connect with the West Side Park, about three miles to the westward. Eventually all the parks will be connected by a boulevard system.

The West Side Park is the largest of the park system. It is on high ground, its greatest elevation being 180 feet above the level of the lake. It is the intention of the Commissioners to erect here an observatory from which a bird's-eye view of the city and lake can be obtained. The tract included in this park is made up mainly of farm land, with a grove of big forest trees covering about fifteen acres. A great deal of work is needed to perfect the park. A "zoo" will in time be provided for this park, the nucleus of which is a deer paddock, where a few deer are now kept. Animals received by the Commissioners are turned over to the West Side Park. This park is so far outside the street railway facilities, so meagre at present, that it has hardly become a place of popular resort.

The show piece of the park system just now in the Mitchell Park, on the South Side—a tract of thirty-one acres, situated on the edge of the residence section. It is a high piece of rolling ground, overlooking the Menominee Valley, and is dotted by many old trees, in excellent preservation. This park is about completed, and is a favorite resort. There is here an artificial lake covering two acres. Broad-bottomed rowboats are provided, which are let to visitors at 10 cents for each half hour, and on holidays every boat is in almost constant use. In the Winter these lakes are cleared of snow and used for skating purposes, and are as liberally patronized then as when they are open for navigation in the Summer.

On holidays thousands of people cover the sward and haunt the groves. The most of them take with them lunch baskets, and spend the day. Lake Park, on account of its situation, and swept as it is by the cooling breezes from the lake, is the favorite resort on hot days. On any pleasant Sunday, from 10 o'clock in the morning until 3 o'clock in the afternoon, it is almost impossible to get even standing room on the Lake Park cars, unless one goes to the end of the line and takes passage at the starting point down town. Returning, it is the same way. For hours people wait for a chance to get seats.

Although the park system is yet in its infancy, evidence is already supplied to show the great benefit it is to the people. The wonder is that they have got along without parks for so many years.

The Park Commissioners, five in number, serve without pay. The only salaried officer is the Secretary, who is elected by the board. The Commissioners give their time to the work of making their fellow-citizens happy. The original board was made up of Christian Wahl, President; Calvin E. Lewis, John Bentley, Gen. Louis Auer, and Charles Mannegold, Jr. Mr. Bentley died in 1894, and Emil Durr was appointed in his place. With that exception, the board remains as it was first constituted. The board, on organizing, elected C. K. Lush Secretary, who has been continued in that position.

ST. PAUL.

The city of St. Paul began, more than twenty-five years ago, the purchase of land for park purposes, but nothing was done toward establishing a system of parks until 1887, when the Minnesota Legislature created the Board of Park Commissioners. At the legislative sessions of 1889 and 1891 the act of 1887 was confirmed and amended, and the board was permitted to raise a fund of $225,000 to acquire lands for parks by purchase or condemnation, and to maintain them for the use of the public. At a later date $25,000 was added for a boulevard around Lake Como, $25,000 for a boulevard on Summit Avenue, and $20,000 for the purchase of Indian Mounds Park. Owing to the hard times in the last few years, and the consequent protests of the people against being assessed for park purposes, little has been done except on a few of the parks, notably Como Park. In the last eight years $250,000 has been expended on Como and other parks, and the park fund is in such shape that no additional parks or parkways can be secured except by condemnation or donation. Even now the Board of Park Commissioners is depending wholly on such annual appropriations as may be made by the City Council for park purposes. In his last annual report President Wheelock says: "It is highly important that an adequate park fund should be established from some reliable source of revenue. The annual cost of maintaining our parks hereafter may be conservatively estimated at $25,000 at least. An equal sum for improvement purposes will be necessary, and a half-mill tax under our system would just about yield $50,000."

The park system of St. Paul at the present time embraces forty-five different tracts of land. Of these by far the most important is Como Park, which contains 396 acres. The others are, in the main, small breathing spots of from two to nine acres. Of these, two—Smith and Rice Parks—are in the centre of the business district of the city. The great pleasure and play ground of the city is Como Park. This is situated on the northern limits of the city, about three miles from the Court House, and is accessible in a half hour's ride by electric railway. A movement is now on foot for the acquisition of Phalen Park, in the northeastern part of the city on Lake Phalen. This park embraces 586 acres of land and water.

St. Paul's parks have neither botanical nor zoological collections. President Wheelock says in his report: "A botanical garden would serve a highly useful, educative purpose, and it is hoped that the resources of the board may soon permit the necessary expenditures for that purpose." The matter of a zoölogical collection has several times been discussed, but this climate is so severe in the Winter that it is feared that many animals regarded as most valuable in such a collection would not live in it. The nursery at Como Park is five acres in extent. It contains 8,495 young trees and shrubs, deciduous and evergreen. Superintendent Nussbaumer has planted in Como and other parks in the last four years 12,414 trees and shrubs, all except a few hundred direct from this nursery.

The city owns a great greenhouse at Como, and from its prolific propagating beds are drawn all the plants and seedlings used in the decoration of Como and fifteen local parks. Last year there were distributed from this source 124,528 plants and seedlings.

The number of visitors to Como Park during June, July, and August of last year was 475,000. The Park Board is now trying to get the Twin City Rapid Transit Company, which derives most of the revenue for transporting people to and from the park, to bear the whole expense of furnishing music and electric lights. Visitors to the parks are kept off the grass by special park policemen.

The total valuation put upon St. Paul's parks by the Commissioners is $1,430,000. Como Park is valued at $600,000, and the others at smaller amounts. Later in the year, when Phalen Park will have been acquired, the value of the city's parks will reach $2,000,000.

August 4, 1895

LAKE FLOW HELD VITAL TO HEALTH OF CHICAGO

Diversion of Water to Drainage Canal Has Supplied Sewage Outlet Since 1900 for Sanitary District Containing 3,300,000 People

CHICAGO'S sewage disposal problem is a splendid example of the lengths to which a city must go to insure the health of its people.

Changing the course of a river is but a minor detail: bringing down the wrath of neighboring States and the supervising eye of the Federal Government is perhaps a more important one. Today Chicago is virtually in a position of a prisoner at the bar of justice, charged with diverting the waters of Lake Michigan. At present the big city is taking out approximately 10,000 cubic feet of water per second from Lake Michigan, thereby, according to some States, lowering the level of the Great Lakes and endangering lake traffic. Another cause of complaint is that by diverting the waters for home use, Chicago greatly decreases the water power at Niagara Falls used for generating electricity.

Chicago pleads guilty, with reservations, if such a thing is possible, and upholds her position on the ground that the decrease in disease which finds its origin in polluted water is sufficient justification for her act. In the decade before the diversion of the Lake Michigan waters for dilution of sewage in the canal that carries it down the Mississippi, Chicago's typhoid death rate averaged 64.4 per 100,000 people. In the year 1892 it ran as high as 172 for every 100,000 people. In recent years the death rate has gone down to 1.1 for the same basic population figure. During the same period nine other representative large cities of America reduced their composite typhoid fever death rate from 38.5 to 3.5 per 100,000 people.

Perhaps the why and wherefore of this water diversion will be more clearly understood when the fact is stated that before 1900 Chicago's sewage was sent into Lake Michigan and Chicago's drinking and bathing water was taken out of Lake Michigan. Today the 10,000 cubic feet of water per second sends the city's sewage away from the lake, down the river, whose course was changed, and keeps the lake comparatively free of pollution.

To a population like the one living in New York, this situation may be difficult to comprehend. New York gets its drinking water from mountain springs and empties its sewage in rivers and seas surrounding it. The two are not taken from and dropped into the same basin. New Yorkers are hardly aware of the fact that the water supply is of the best and purest.

Chicago, on the other hand, built on the apex of the watersheds of the St. Lawrence and the Mississippi Rivers, stands in an unfortunate position. Her waters naturally drained down to the lake, from which extend the various cribs which lead the drinking water back into the city. Chicago's answer to her sewage problem, and simultaneously her health problem, lay in putting herself on the Mississippi instead of the St. Lawrence watershed. "Let us continue taking our drinking water from the lake," is what the engineers working on the problem said, "but let us divert the Chicago River so that instead of flowing north it will flow south, carrying the city's sewage with it through a canal."

In 1889 this canal, called the Sewage Ship Canal, at the present time the centre of controversy, was authorized by the Illinois Legislature. It reversed the flow of the Chicago River, diverting Chicago's sewage from Lake Michigan; it improved the city's only source of water supply; it ended severe water-borne epidemics; it provided one of the chief links in a waterway from the Great Lakes to the Gulf of Mexico; and it led to development of bathing beaches along the lake, something hitherto impossible because of the condition of the waterfront. At the same time it supplied power for public needs at a point where a decided change in land levels created a waterfall.

Polluting the Water.

In 1856 the first sewers of Chicago were built. They took care of the population of 80,000 by depositing most of the sewage into the Chicago River, which flowed into the lake and succeeded most admirably in polluting the waters and causing typhoid epidemics. The city was not unaware of this danger, and from time to time improvements were made to keep as much of the sewage as possible out of the lake.

As the population grew the condition got worse. By the time the population reached the 800,000 mark, in 1886, it was decided that something had to be done to meet the present and the future needs of the city. An engineering commission was appointed to make a survey and recommend methods of improvement. The three possibilities suggested were a discharge into Lake Michigan, disposal of sewage upon land, or a discharge into the Des Plaines River, a tributary of the Mississippi. After discussing at length the virtues of the three methods, the report recommended the last, proposing the construction of a drainage canal with a capacity of 10,000 cubic feet of water per second, sufficient to dilute the sewage of a future population of 2,500,000, at the rate of four cubic feet per second per 1,000 people, and also sufficient to keep storm flows from flushing the reversed Chicago River back into Lake Michigan.

As a result of this report the Sanitary District of Chicago was organized by the State of Illinois. The original area of the district took in 185 square miles, with a population of 1,140,000 people. Today its area has grown to over 430 miles with a population of 3,300,000. Besides Chicago, it includes about forty-nine other towns and villages. This is necessary owing to the fact that the health of cities near Chicago and along the sewage canal must be considered at the same time that plans are made for the Lake City.

Construction of the canal was started in 1892. It was opened in 1900. It is twenty-eight miles long and connects the Chicago River with the Des Plaines River. Sewage branches lead out to various sections of the city and all the sewage is eventually gathered into the main channel. By the time it reaches a city where the river water is needed for drinking purposes, it has been purified by process of natural oxidation and filtration. There is, apparently, little quarrel on that score.

In 1886, when Chicago's problem was discussed there were two artificial methods of sewage treatment used by large cities. Paris and Berlin used irrigation upon sandy land, London and other English cities treated sewage with chemicals for removal of suspended solids and sent the so-called purified liquid back into the rivers. Chicago's argument against both these methods was that the areas of suitable land within reasonable distance were not available for irrigation or for more intensive land treatment called intermittent sand filtration, and second, that the removal of solids as practiced by English cities was not sufficiently hygienic to warrant the return of the liquids into Lake Michigan to be later used for drinking and bathing purposes. Therefore the dilution method was adopted. Dilution in the Sewage Canal, however, took care only of a population of 2,500,000 people. Chicago's population today is over 3,000,000. Added to that is the industrial sewage of stock yards, packing houses and converting plants. It is estimated that the sewage of Chicago today is comparable to that of a population of 4,800,000.

New Experiments with Waste.

Way back in 1908 the members of the Sanitary Commission of Chicago were aware that the Sewage Canal under the most ideal conditions could adequately dispose of the sewage of only a 2,500,000 population. They knew also that the city was bound to grow beyond that mark. A study of artificial sewage treatment was then promulgated, resulting in the adoption of several experiments in methods of sewage treatment. Since that time, it is declared, Chicago has led all cities in the country in the work on this problem and has been the pioneer on the treatment of trade wastes.

Artificial treatment sewage plants to supplement the work of the canal were started in 1914. Owing to the interference of the war, their completion was retarded until 1922. Meanwhile the State Legislature in 1921 passed an act making obligatory, beginning with 1925, the construction of additional sewage plants each year until a sufficient number were built to take care of the sewage of approximately 1,800,000 people. The rest, it is maintained, will be taken care of by dilution in the canal. One hundred twenty-five million dollars was voted for this purpose.

Already a number of treatment plants have been built in sections of the city where the need is great. The writer visited one of them where sewage of a 300,000 population is taken care of. The sewage, dark with the waste of plants, homes and street flushings, came through the mouth of the sewer and was pumped by electrical power into treatment tanks. In this particular plant the two-story Imhoff sedimentation tank is used. After passing through various tanks which permitted the solids to settle and the fluid to run, the solids were submitted to a sprinkling filter process which further purified them. This stage reached, they were run through a drying machine and packed into bags ready for sale as fertilizer base.

Many Things to Consider.

Opponents of the canal declare that it is in sufficiently good condition to be sent back into the lake, that with chlorination of the lake water it is harmless as drinking or bathing water. Supporters of the canal system, who include practically all of Chicago, will not hear of this and maintain that apart from esthetic and emotional reasons which make treated sewage impossible as drinking water, the liquid that is drained is still not fit for human consumption. At present, and it seems the practice will continue, all the flow from sewage treatment plants is sent into channels connecting with the Sewage Canal. Even at that, however, the lake is not considered safe and the heavy chlorination of its waters is easily recognizable by a visitor to the city.

The charge made by navigation and water power interests that 10,000 cubic feet of water taken from the lake every second lowers its level and that of Lake Huron is admitted by the Sanitary District. The extent of the lowering, it is maintained, however, never exceeds six inches. The question has been asked by many people whether continued abstraction of water for sewage purposes will not eventually drain both these lakes. In answer to that the Sanitary Commission makes reply that a cask is never drained dry if there is as much water flowing in as there is flowing out. More, the inflow to Lakes Huron and Michigan is about eighteen times as much as the flow of 10,000 cubic feet per second which goes out to the Sewage Canal. The effect of the canal is very much the same, it is pointed out, as if there were two holes in the side of a cask, the smaller an inch in diameter, corresponding to the outgoing canal water, and the other eighteen times as large, corresponding to the waters that are constantly pouring into the lakes.

To make up for the five and one-half inch change in the level of the two large bodies of water, Chicago is willing to contribute toward the building of water regulating machinery of the kind erected for Lake Superior on St. Mary's River, and completed in 1916. The water yield at Lake Superior has been about 25 per cent. below normal during the past few years, owing to deficient rainfall on the Lake Superior Drainage Basin. The regulating works, however, have maintained the level of the lake at a nearly uniform high stage equal to that of ten years ago. At present, it is said, Lake Superior is from one to one and one-half feet higher than it would have been without regulating works.

What has been done for Superior, Chicagoans declare, can be done for the other lakes, thus safeguarding lake traffic and the water power at Niagara. Chicago is as anxious that lake steamers be enabled to draw their full cargo as is any port.

Besides serving as a sewage canal, the channel under discussion serves also as a link in the Lakes-to-the-Gulf waterway project. For more than a hundred years both the United States and the State of Illinois have proceeded on a policy of improving the navigation facilities of the country by connecting the Great Lakes through Chicago with the Gulf of Mexico. Construction work on this waterway is now in progress.

While the Chicago diversion of water is made primarily for sanitary and secondly for navigation purposes, the water contains potential power. This power is utilized at Lockport, where there is an appreciable drop in land levels. Most of it is used to run the works of the sanitary district; the surplus is sold to the City of Chicago and other cities in the district for municipal lighting and pumping. A few industries buy what remainder there is. When the sewage treatment works now building and planned are completed, the entire water development will be insufficient to meet the operating requirements of the district. In answer to the complaint of Niagara power interests, Chicago declares that, whether or not she utilizes the potential power of the canal, she needs the 10,000 cubic feet per second to take care of her sewage.

In bringing suit against Chicago, the various interests do not demand that the sewage canal be closed. What they ask is that the amount of water be limited to 4,176 cubic feet per second, which would serve to raise the lake levels about three inches. The method of arrival of their figure entails much legal matter and controversy. According to the Sanitary Commission, this amount of water would be little better than nothing, owing to the topography of the land. Ten thousand cubic feet per second is needed to keep the river reversed.

There is a good deal more to this problem, most of it confined to engineering problems and water litigation. The metering of water used by the consumers in Chicago is included in this. At present Chicago uses 800,000,000 gallons of water daily, equivalent to 275 gallons per person. About one-half of this is wasted and adds to the burden of the sewage system which must dispose of it. The control of this and other waste are details which must be considered. But above all and including all is the 10,000 cubic feet per second which carries the sewage from all parts of Chicago down to the Mississippi River.

March 8, 1925

CHICAGO MUST END DIVERSION OF LAKE

Supreme Court Decides Against Sanitary District in the Drainage Litigation.

VICTORY FOR THE STATES

Hughes as Master Will Determine How Rapidly the Withdrawal Shall Be Decreased.

Special to The New York Times.

WASHINGTON, Jan. 14.—Chicago, or more properly, the Chicago Sanitary District, today lost its fight in the United States Supreme Court in the attempt to assert its right to divert 8,500 cubic feet or water per second from Lake Michigan for drainage and navigation.

Today's decision was a victory for New York, Wisconsin, Minnesota, Ohio, Pennsylvania and Michigan, which fought diversion on the ground that it tended to lower the levels of Lakes Michigan, Huron, Erie and Ontario, their connecting waterways and the St. Lawrence River above tidewater, and on the further ground that diversion had never been authorized by Congress to take care of Chicago sewage.

The States named petitioned that Illinois and the Chicago Sanitary District be enjoined from permanently diverting water from Lake Michigan or dumping or draining sewage into its waterways, which, it was alleged, would render these streams unsanitary and obstruct navigation.

Under today's decision, Chicago must proceed as expeditiously as possible to dispose of its sewage in such manner as to require the diversion of no water from Lake Michigan for purely sanitation purposes. It will be within the power and discretion of Congress, however, to increase the volume of diversion eventually to the present amount, or more, to aid navigation in the projected lakes to the gulf waterway.

Holds Navigation Supply Enough.

Although the decision casts doubt on the power of Congress to authorize diversion for sanitary purposes, the diversion permitted for deep waterways navigation would be sufficient for incidental sanitation, particularly in conjunction with the septic tank sewage disposal now in process of construction in Chicago.

The decision was unanimous and written and read by Chief Justice Taft, who as Secretary of War, refused to permit the increased diversion sought by the Chicago Sanitary District. As Secretary of War, Mr. Taft held the diversion down to the previously permited 4,167 second-feet.

"In increasing the diversion of 4,167 cubic feet a second to 8,500, the drainage district defied the authority of the National Government resting in the Secretary of War," says the court's opinion, "and in so far as the prior diversion was not for the purpose of maintaining navigation in the Chicago River it was without any legal basis, because made for an inadmissible purpose.

"It, therefore, is the duty of this court, by an appropriate decree to compel the reduction of the diversion to a point where it rests on a legal basis and thus to restore the navigable capacity of Lake Michigan to it proper level. * * *

"The Sanitary District authorities, relying on the argument with reference to the health of its people, have much too long delayed the needed substitution of sewage plants as a means of avoiding the diversion of the future. Therefore, they cannot now complain if an immediately heavy burden is placed upon the district because of their attitude and course.

"The situation requires the district to devise proper methods for providing sufficient money and to construct and put in operation with all reasonable expedition adequate plans for the disposition of the sewage through other means than the lake diversion."

The court then gives assurance to the complainant States that though the restoration of their "just rights * * * will be gradual instead of immediate, it must be continuous and as speedy as practicable, and must include everything that is essential to an effective project."

The Court directed Charles Evans Hughes special master, who reported the findings of fact, to hold further hearings and determine, after examining experts, just how rapidly the diversion should be reduced.

While following the general line of the findings of Mr. Hughes as special master, the court rejected his recommendation that the bill of the complainant States be dismissed. The court upholds the complaint, thereby rejecting that part of Mr. Hughes's recommendation that was most favorable to Chicago.

January 15, 1929

JUSTICE AT LAST.

W. M. TWEED CONVICTED.

GUILTY ON TWO HUNDRED AND FOUR COUNTS OF THE INDICTMENT

The trial of William M. Tweed was brought to a close yesterday by the conviction of the prisoner, and it is no exaggeration to say that the result will be received by the honest people throughout the country, irrespective of political affiliations, with feelings of the most unmixed satisfaction. It is not the conviction of the individual which produces this general rejoicing, but the vindication of the principles outraged by his crime, and the restoration of confidence in law and its administration, which very many were induced to think were nullified in the presence of political and moneyed influences. It is now nearly three years since the public mind of the entire nation was startled by the revelation of those monstrous frauds committed by the leaders of the notorious Tammany Ring, and scarcely had it recovered from the shock created by the possibility of such robberies than it found itself confronted with the greatest difficulties which naturally followed their commission. These were a complete and absolute political corruption, a debased public sentiment, the establishment of a despotism which the apathy of the people were unable to overthrow; and, following these causes, came the general distrust and want of confidence in our institutions abroad, which materially affected the condition of trade. The revolt came; the political despots were driven from their high places of power, but when the attempt was made to punish them for their offences, it was found that so complete and thorough was the public mind perverted, and so freely did the accused persons employ the funds stolen from the City Treasury, that convictions were frequently sought in vain. Tweed, the head and motive power of the Ring, insolently defied the people when he uttered the words, "Well, what are you going to do about it;" and the result of the former trial, which failed to convict him, seemed to impart probability to the current phrase that with his money and influence a conviction was an impossibility. With these facts pervading the public mind, the deepest anxiety was felt as to the result of the present trial, and much satisfaction was expressed at the action of Judge Davis in adopting rigorous measures to prevent the jurors from being approached by any outside influences. In these columns the proceedings of the trial have been duly recorded, but with its culmination the interest in the proceedings seemed to have become intensified.

November 20, 1873

BOSS RULE IS EXPENSIVE

What Quay and Martin Politics Cost Philadelphia.

CITY DEBT STEADILY INCREASING

Reckless Extravagance by Councils in Voting Away the Money of the Taxpayers.

THE OLD GAS RING STILL HAS INFLUENCE

The Municipal Government Run Entirely to Suit the Interest of Bosses Quay and Martin.

PHILADELPHIA, Dec. 31.—The system of politics which Matthew Stanley Quay and Dave Martin have adopted is very expensive. That is to say, a government conducted by the politicians which have grown up under Quay's rule is very expensive.

The public moneys are expended in this city by the two Councils, the Select and the Common. The Common Council is made up of one man for every 2,000 voters returned by the election assessors' canvass. The Select Council is composed of thirty-seven men, one from each ward in the city. They pass ordinances ordering improvements and make appropriations to meet the various expenses of the City Government. Within the last five years the general motto of the Councils seems to have been to turn the barrel bung down and let the stream run full head out of the City Treasury.

This policy has been followed with an industry and zeal which has cost the citizens of Philadelphia many million dollars. Great corporations which have wanted rights, franchises, the use of city property, and a monopoly of it, have been able to control the Councils as much as if the members were their own employes and drawing salary from these corporations. Whatever salary they do draw comes from corporations, for the city does not give any salary to members of Councils. Notwithstanding the fact that there is no compensation from the city, there is a great scrambling among cheap politicians, ward workers, and some saloon keepers to hold places in these two legislative bodies. Sometimes men who go into Councils almost penniless, after a year or two of service graduate into positions where they have comfortable, if not extensive, business interests.

The City Councils hold their meetings in Independence Hall, and one of the tablets inlaid in the walls of this ancient building sets forth the fact that in this structure is the meeting place of the legislature which spends the money of this municipality. It is directly over the room in which the Declaration of Independence was signed, and which was the meeting place of the early Congress of the United States, that these ward politicians now meet, at stated intervals, and give away the rights and franchises of the people.

The people of the city have begun to wake up to these facts, and, as in New-York, the ministers were among the first to declare themselves. The petition posted at the very doors of Independence Hall, to which reference was made by The New-York Times on Sunday, was the subject of some remarks by the Rev. Frederick A. Bisbee, a short time after it was posted. He said: "We behold the spectacle of the petition posted about the city and sent through the mails, signed by hundreds of prominent citizens, asking the bosses to nominate a respectable citizen for Mayor. This shows the humiliating depths to which political Philadelphia has sunk. There is, however, one good thing about it. It shows that there is an awakening on the part of reputable citizens in municipal affairs, and this indication of interest is further shown by the action of the Municipal League and of the clergymen of the city, in appealing to the public to save the city from what appears to be an impending crisis.

"As the New-York investigation proceeds it awakens considerable anxiety, not only among officials, but among the citizens of our city. There is felt a desire to avoid the disgrace of an investigation. There is, however, awakening a good deal of interest in the personal character of the candidates for Mayor. This is justifiable and right, because in the matter of the Mayoralty of our city, the Mayor has almost autocratic power. Through his Director he can give us a city of high moral character. It is entirely within his province to absolutely wipe out the disreputable places. And yet, in the face of that, in spite of the fact that our present Mayor is a man of integrity and character, these places, gambling houses, and the like, exist to a shameful extent.

"The fundamental trouble is that politics enters into every department of our city, and it is well known that any attack upon the saloons or the gambling houses or the houses of ill fame, is to cut off political strength, and no Mayor will be free to enter upon a crusade against the violators of the law until a Mayor is elected who is entirely free from political pressure. At present every department of the City Government is put to shame by the presence and influence of the political machine. A prisoner before the magistrate may be condemned or liberated just in accordance with his political influence. A man who has a political pull, who can control a number of votes, can run any sort of an establishment, within or without the limits of the law, with impunity.

"During the last week Councils have voted to give away to the traction company nearly 100 miles of streets, in the face of public protest, and yet these same Councilmen, when they stand for re-election in February will be supported by you voters who are here and other respectable taxpaying citizens and return to their opportunity to give away more of our city."

The politicians who compose the City Councils have been spending money at such a rate that, whereas in 1890 the total expenses of the city were $22,531,381, in 1894 this had increased to the enormous figure of $33,658,704. It will be noticed that between 1890 and 1894 the figures increased at the rate of 46 per cent. This is due in part to a favorite method of financiering which has recently been assumed by the Councils. This is a resort to borrowing. In 1890 the city borrowed $2,300,000. In 1894 it borrowed $7,419,999. In the last five years it has borrowed $16,529,390. The city debt has been growing, although prior to the period referred to there had been a steady reduction. The city debt is now larger than it has been since 1886, and the Councils are said to have in contemplation some more extravagant loans for 1895. The city debt in 1892 was $55,340,614. In 1894 it was $60,678,045. In an extensive article on the city finances, The Philadelphia Record said recently:

"It would be idle to attempt any estimate of the debt for 1895, as it lies within the power of Councils to make such loans as they please, since the city is now well within the limits of its borrowing capacity. How long it will stay there, if the present craze continues for floating loans for all sorts of improvements, it is impossible to say. Of course this rapid growth of the city debt endangers the prospect for the purification of the water supply and improvement of the harbor, for both of which several millions of dollars will be required. Where has all this money gone? Aside from the maintenance of the departments, the great bulk of that remaining for permanent improvement has been scattered over an endless number of small things, without one single really great feat being accomplished. The greatest single consumer of money has been the Water Bureau, whose capacity in this direction seems endless, although Philadelphia is no nearer a purer or more ample supply now than it was when the agitation on this line began, over thirty years ago."

An attack was made upon the department of the city which has to do with the gas-works. Since the great plant of the gas-works, estimated a few years ago to have been worth $25,000,000, came into possession of the city, in 1887, through the abolition of the Gas Trust, nearly $2,000,000 has been spent on improvement and extensions, and yet the amount of gas manufactured last year fell 815,723,000 cubic feet below the amount made in 1887. The deficiency was made up by the purchase of 1,464,197,000 cubic feet of water gas from a private corporation, for which the city paid $570,-449.96.

A Relic of the Old Gas Ring.

The Citizens' Municipal Association has discussed the question of gas and electric lighting, and shown the extravagance which prevails. Notwithstanding the recent reduction in the price of gas to consumers, of about one-third, the association says, there is good reason for believing that the city could make gas at least as cheaply as it now buys it from a private corporation if its facilities were modernized and its roll of employes reduced, regardless of their votes.

There is evidence that a relic of the old "gas ring" which controlled city politics and cost the city and its citizens millions of dollars before it was broken up is still in existence. Strenuous pressure, the Municipal League says, should be brought to bear upon Councils to provide for modernizing the city's gas works in accordance with the suggestion of the Director of Public Works. Any reluctance to make an appropriation would be reasonable cause for suspicion that the retention of the present antiquated and wasteful methods is a piece of the ever-recurring plan by which the city is asked to part with the plant and franchise of the gas works for the huge emolument of private capitalists and the corresponding pillage of the taxpayers. The city now buys nearly one-half of its gas from a private corporation, and, according to the Municipal Association's ideas, the danger of the insidious acquisition of the right to furnish all the gas should shortly be ended by the purchase of this private plant according to the terms of the agreement. In a report which the association has prepared on this subject, it says:

Citizens may watch with suspicion every action of men who have repeatedly voted against the municipal ownership of an electric-lighting system. The vast public advantage assured in this enterprise has been demonstrated by the city's electrical bureau, and the pitiful contradiction offered by Council's Electrical Committee deceives no one. The committee report, however, points clearly to the operation of improper influences, notwithstanding the law requiring Councilmen personally interested in any measure to declare the fact and to refrain from voting. We owe to the sinister influence of corporations and political machines the presence in Councils of men willing to disregard the obvious principles of honor which should govern a representative, even without the necessity of legal enunciation.

Fit Men to Serve Quay and Martin.

The character of the men in Common Councils is not high on the average. Some of these men are honest, decent, and reliable. Many of them are exactly what would be expected under a system of politics of which "Dave" Martin is the boss. This man has filled up the legislative bodies with enough men after his own stripe to give them a somewhat checkered appearance. For instance, Mr. Joseph L. Nobre, who represents the Second Ward in the Select Council, is more a professional politician of the Martin stripe than anything else. He is not only a member of the Select Council, but a real estate assessor, who draws $2,000 a year from the city. Another choice member of the City Council is Mr. Harry Hunter of the Third Ward. He is a professional politician, who devoted considerable time to an attempt to secure the release, without punishment, of the indicted ballot-box stuffers, O'Neill, Kidd, and Thompson. He has also been tried for criminality in election matters himself. Another member of the Council is Mr. William McMullen, generally known as "Bill" McMullen. In the manual of Councils he is put down as by occupation a "gentleman." Another is Samuel F. Houseman, ex-Mercantile Appriaser, who was connected with the scandal in that department some years ago. The Common Council has its quota of ward politicians, some of whom are saloon keepers, and comparatively few of whom are in anywise noted for ability or consistency in their desire to serve the city. The character of the Councils is made the subject of some remarks by the Municipal Association. It says:

"It must be clear that no proper rate and character of municipal advancement can be made by this city until a complete reorganization is effected in the character of the majority in Councils. The action of these bodies is justly watched with suspicion, and it has almost become a matter of expectation that where public interests are opposed by corporations, or where corporation projects are opposed to public policy, the representatives selected by the people will dishonor their oaths and in voice and vote openly appear as agents of private enterprises. This shameless perversion of a high and honorable office will continue as long as the combination of corporations, office holders, contractors, and politicians is able to bind the spell of partisanship upon voters at municipal elections. The corporations and 'combines' which now control us are organized as political machines, requiring political service from their employes."

me comparisons are made which go to r how this choice aggregation of Quay's and Martins' "heelers" serve the people. Twenty-four cities which buy electric light from private companies pay an average of $140 per year for each 2,000-candle power light; twenty-three cities which own their own electrical plants find that the cost of running them is $53.04 per year, and that the addition of charges for depreciation, interest, &c., raise this figure to $86.64 per year. Chicago, with a plant of 1,100 lights, several years old, saves two-thirds of the price formerly exacted by private companies, and finds that it can operate each light for $83 per year. With a plant of 2,000 lights erected at the prevailing lower rates for material, Philadelphia, it is thought, could furnish its own lights for $80 per year, or less.

This city is now parceled out by private agreement among nine companies, and paid $161.61 per light for the average number of lights in operation in 1893. The difference is $81.61, which multiplied by the 3,584 lamps in use at the beginning of 1894, in addition to the number of lamps added during the year, represents a loss of $325,134, to be paid in the shape of profits to electric light corporations which have an influence upon the Councils. In other words the Councils exact $900 a day from the people and give it to corporations. All this, it is well to remember, takes place in Independence Hall, directly over the room in which John Hancock and his associates signed the Declaration of Independence.

In 1890 the city paid for cleaning streets, collecting garbage, &c., $421,112.08. In 1894 the Councils had jumped this figure up to $855,473.75, or a little more than 100 per cent. increase in four years.

Owing to the reckless appropriations made by Councils for all sorts of work this year just past, it is estimated that there will be a deficit, and the amount must be paid by the mandamus process. This will probably be $500,000. One serious result of this will be that the appropriations for 1895 must be tied up until the deficit can be made up by temporary loans or the appropriations scaled down to bring them within the available funds. Before any warrant for 1895 can be drawn for any purpose whatever the Controller must see that the total appropriations are within the amount subject to appropriation. The sum of $700,000 was originally set aside for mandamuses in 1894. When the Controller made up his annual estimate for the Councils in August, the payments had already amounted to $1,271,876.67. He then set aside an additional $700,000, raising the total for mandamuses to $1,971,876.67. Since then the mandamuses have jumped to the unprecedented total of $2,545,999.01, which would indicate an increased deficit of more than $550,000, for which no provision has been made.

All this goes to show the reckless extravagance with which these men whom "Dave" Martin's system of politics has put in charge of the city's funds have conducted themselves.

January 1, 1895

CORRUPTION IN CHICAGO

CHICAGO, July 3.—In this correspondence it was recently remarked that for a body which regarded itself as being so pure as to be above the need of investigation, the Chicago School Board was in the habit of doing some peculiar things. Simultaneously with the appearance of this suggestion in THE NEW YORK TIMES the Chicago newspapers printed, under startling and flaring headlines, stories which confirm the impression that there is reason for criticism and provocation for investigation of the Board's methods and proceedings. Among the general public, however, the blunt charges of fraud created a great sensation. Now that specific details of corruption have been sworn to by responsible parties there may be hopes of an investigation which will bring to light the hidden facts of the School Board's peculiar doings. The exposure consists of affidavits made by the mother and brother of the former wife of Vice President and Acting President Cussack of the School Board. It is evident that family troubles instigated the revelations, but the accusations are none the less serious. The Vice President and Acting President is said by his mother-in-law and brother-in-law to have been in the pay of one of the leading school book publishing houses, from which he received regularly $100 a month for a long time. From a now defunct blackboard firm he is said to have received 10 per cent. on all blackboards supplied the schools, and from property of his held in some one else's name, and illegally rented for school purposes, he also is accused of having netted a comfortable sum. These are ugly charges, all of which Mr. Cussack pretends to attribute to spite, and pronounces unworthy of his august notice. Yet the public feels differently, and even if the affair presented a less serious aspect the people would hail it as a tangible peg upon which to hang their demand for an investigation of the entire School Board management.

There are also some very ugly circumstances surrounding the appropriation of $90,000 for the introduction of filters into the schools, and since last Sunday's developments much light is being shed on that transaction. Indeed, so specific is the talk of a twelve-thousand-dollar "rake off" for some of the members of the board that it does not seem possible to avoid sifting the alleged deal.

Many other suspicious circumstances direct distrustful eyes toward the public schools. Only the most stupid and improbable foolishness or worse causes can account for the imposition on the pupils in the matter of text books. A ring of schoolbook publishers has its grip on all who have anything to do with the books used in the schools. There are some very good men and women on the Chicago School Board, such as President Harper of the Chicago University, for instance, but a few of its members have run the business to suit themselves. It now remains to be seen whether the rich lead which has been struck will be followed up. Judging by the past, there is little cause to hope for anything which will result in permanent good.

Franchises Bought with Bribes.

As was also predicted in this correspondence, it has been impossible to pass through the City Council any ordinances which would protect the people against the gas and street-car legislation which goes into effect July 1, and places the city after that time at the mercy of the various corporations. On the contrary, not only could no favorable action be secured, but the Council actually passed over the Mayor's veto an ordinance which gives to unknown parties a blanket franchise worth millions, and under which not only illuminating, but telephone plants, can be built. This ordinance places the people in the grasp of whatever corporation gets hold of the franchise, as the charges which it permits are exorbitant and the provisions for compensation in return for the privileges granted are absurdly inadequate. The public has not even the consolation of looking forward to a competing company, as the Commonwealth Electric Company, to which this franchise is given, is in all probability nothing more than a mask behind which existing illuminating companies are hidden.

All of this, however, is only a small beginning of the week's revelations of iniquity. Any one who believed that the Aldermen of Chicago had attained the very summit of impudent rascality had little conception of the brazen shamelessness of which those in control of the body are capable. All that had gone before almost sinks into insignificance when compared with what was done in the case of another franchise. Last week reference was made to the revival of an old franchise which granted the right of sixty miles of street on the South Side to the General Electric Railway Company, and by means of which it was hoped that a rival to the existing corporation would be created. This new system, besides being an underground trolley and having all sorts of other improvements and conveniences, was to give the city adequate compensation for the privileges it had received. Last Monday night at the regular meeting of the Council the old ordinance creating this franchise was taken up for a little legislation necessary to its revivification. The Aldermen took advantage of the occasion to strike out every safeguard in the interests of the people and eliminated the provisions for compensating the city. The efforts of the honest Aldermen to prevent this nefarious robbery of compensation already secured to the city were vain. If any other city can anywhere in its history parallel this instance of unabashed defiance of all decency, it might be some consolation to the people of Chicago to be informed of that fact.

The local press goes to the length of stating the exact sum received by the gang from the gas companies for preventing all legislation against the companies before July 1, when the Frontage bill and the bill permitting consolidation went into effect. The amount is stated as $70,000, of which $40,000 was distributed some time ago, and the balance was duly paid at the expiration of the stated time. Considering the vast gain to the corporations and the equally great loss to the city, the sum received by the Aldermen is sadly disproportionate. Unless the new law, by which the consolidated companies will be allowed to buy frontage, can be broken in the courts, Chicago's last chance of securing competition in gas went glimmering when the clock struck 12 on the night of the 30th of June.

At the next meeting of the Council the Aldermen will undoubtedly complete their bargain with the street car men by renewing all old franchises to the limit of fifty years permitted by the recently passed Allen bill. After that there will be no more trouble, for the companies will have secured everything in sight for the next half century without competition, and the Council will have nothing of value left to sell.

Reformers Who Were Treacherous.

As the people of Chicago saw fit to elect keepers of disreputable grogshops, proprietors of gambling houses, and others whose proper place is the penitentiary rather than the Council Chamber, the city has got no more than was to be expected, or than it deserved. There is scarcely a committee of any importance in the Council which has not a Chairman whose daily avocation makes him a violator of the law and an outcast from decent society. Some decent citizens did make an effort to perform long-neglected duties. Civic federations, reform clubs, and like agencies for the purification of politics sprang into existence like mushrooms. As the result of the last two Aldermanic elections it was thought that if a majority of honest men had not been elected, at least a sufficient number of them had won to prevent bad measures passing over the Mayor's veto. The experience of the past two weeks is enough to make a bronze statue smile sardonically, for, as has been seen, the Mayor's veto is no more of an impediment to the gang than is the ambient atmosphere to a cannon ball. The most grievous feature to the reformers is found in the treachery of their pet candidates, the majority of whom have been seduced by the boodlers. Some ten or twelve of these precious specimens of superior virtue gave the reformers written, signed, and witnessed pledges, in which they solemnly promised to vote against franchises without compensation, and with the honest minority generally. It was with the aid of these fellows that the Mayor's vetoes were overridden. It is beginning to dawn on the voters who have been allowing municipal government to go by default that decades of indifference and worse cannot be remedied in a few months.

Another immense franchise has been granted this week. This time it is by the Commissioners of Cook County, and the beneficiaries are the parties composing the Metropolitan Traction Company. The company is allowed to erect surface railway lines propelled by any motive power, except the "dummy" system. The franchise extends over roads covering every point in Cook County outside of the city, where it is or may become desirable to build a street railway line. These 200 miles of roads were given away by the County Commissioners without any sort of return to the county, except the benefit derived by the people from additional transportation facilities. This new grant, no doubt, is part of the gigantic deal by which all the street railways of Chicago and suburbs are to be united in one immense monopoly. Besides passengers, the right to carry freight after dark gives additional value to the franchise. The new road will be a good thing for the suburbs, as it will bring nearly every farmhouse in touch with transportation facilities. But it is the last link in the chain which binds Chicago and its surrounding territory so securely that no hope of escape from the tyranny of a single corporation is possible.

However, the good must be admitted with the bad; while there is no hope for lower fares, 5 cents will give Chicagoans the longest rides in the world. In its own interests the monopoly will have to, and will be able to give, the latest in the way of modern improvements, as the same crowd which controls all the roads has combined all the interests which manufacture the equipments of all sorts. Yerkes, with Widener and Elkins, are the brains of the gigantic monopoly, and the common report is that Pierpont Morgan is to find the money to back them.

The merit system has no better fortune than the rights of the people in their streets. At the request of Mayor Harrison the City Council at one blow knocked out nine long lists of officers from the operation of the civil service law. Yet, Mayor Harrison persists in asserting his inviolate devotion to civil service.

Now that the Aldermen have had an experience of the joys of driving through the law in a cach and six they are not likely to discontinue such pleasing exercise. Mr. Kraus, who was appointed by the Mayor to the Presidency of the Civil Service Commission, is apparently taking the duties of his position seriously, and is opposing his Honor's war upon the merit system—much to the latter's surprise and grief. Between the Mayor's appointees, who are opposing him in his good intentions, and those who are blocking his evil designs, the Chief Executive is making rough weather of it. Mr. Kraus has always been very close to the Harrison family, having been the senior Carter's confidential friend and Corporation Counsel. That the son of his father should now be at loggerheads with his own and his father's friend over such a cause causes some surprise. It will be still more of a surprise if Mr. Kraus is successful in his defense of the law against the combined assaults, of which it is the object.

The Mayor this week let fall the remark that nowhere else was gambling so well regulated as in this good City of Chicago. This is known to be true. There is no doubt that the gamblers are well protected. Nor is it permitted to use violence or induce citizens at the point of a revolver to enter dens and risk their money. The fine point of the regulating is seen in the decision of the Superintendent of Police that only negroes shall be permitted to play "craps," that fascinating game being strictly prohibited to white sports. On the other hand, our colored brother is deprived of the delights of "stud-horse poker" by the order of the same authority. What occult reason may be behind this mysterious order is bothering the world of the green cloth. Every once in a while there is a report that the slot machines have been ordered out of the saloons, cigar stores, and other places where they are so commonly found. But the alarm is usually a false one, or the spasm of virtue is of short duration. It is safe to assert that infinitely more money is daily lost by means of these devices than in all of the regular gambling dens. The saloon without a nickel-in-the-slot machine is a very rare exception, and, as a young man who means business and has a well-developed muscle can drop in nickels at the rate of two or three to the minute, it will be seen that a pretty fair trade can be done. It is notorious that even the little stores frequented by school children are well supplied with this means of making scamps of the young, and the scoundrelly proprietors are by no means backward in encouraging almost infants in years to take the easy lessons in gambling.

July 4, 1897

THE NEW CITY CLUB.

The work of perfecting the organization of the new City Club of New-York is progressing satisfactorily. About 350 men have been elected to membership, and there remains a large list of applicants to draw from. The list of Directors is nearly completed. The charter of the club provides for a board of twenty members.

The following have consented to serve: James C. Carter, Henry E. Howland, Richard Watson Gilder, W. Bayard Cutting, Frederic Bronson, J. Frederick Kernochan, J. Harsen Rhoades, R. Fulton Cutting, W. Harris Roome, Edmond Kelly, William C. Gulliver, James B. Ludlow, John Jay Chapman, Boudinot Keith, J. Noble Hayes, R. W. G. Welling, William Jay Schieffelin.

The purpose of this new club is to maintain a clubhouse having a library, a reading room, and a publication office, for the distribution of the publications of the organization, which, it is expected, will be quite numerous.

The particular object of the club is to promote social intercourse among persons specially interested in the good government of the City of New-York, in securing honesty and efficiency in the administration of city affairs, and in severing municipal from national politics. The organization will also aim to procure the election of fit persons to city offices, and will exert its influence steadily in behalf of an honest, efficient, and independent city government.

March 19, 1892

TO BETTER HOME GOVERNMENT

NATIONAL MUNICIPAL LEAGUE SETS FORTH ITS PURPOSE.

Convention of Good Government Clubs Representing Various Cities in the United States Adopts a Constitution to Band Together Citizens Seeking Improved Rulership—James C. Carter, President, and Other Members Define the Organization's Ideas.

The delegates of the National Municipal League of Good Government Clubs met yesterday at the City Club, 677 Fifth Avenue, to organize and to adopt a constitution, and also to discuss the lines on which the league, whose object is municipal reform, should act.

Delegates were present from nearly all the large cities, and many of the smaller ones all over the land. The following gentlemen, representing the City Club, had charge of the arrangements for the convention:

James C. Carter, Edmond Kelly, J. W. Pryor, R. F. Cutting, Preble Cutler, Alfred Bishop Mason, Charles Taber, J. Noble Hayes, W. Harris Roome, and Alfred R. Conkling.

The following-named sat in the convention as delegates:

Thomas F. Clark, C. Jay Taylor, Robert L. Cochran, Asa A. Alling, Preble Tucker, and George W. McAneny, New-York; H. P. Hull, Milwaukee, Wis.; Claiborn Rogers Woodruff, Philadelphia Municipal League; Henry W. Williams, Baltimore; Augustin Jones and D. M. Thompson, Providence, R. I.; Charles J. Bonaparte, Baltimore Reform League; Dr. L. S. Rowe, Philadelphia; Dudley Tibbitts, Troy; M. G. Curtis, Troy; E. Benjamin Andrews, Providence, R. I.; Charles Richardson, Philadelphia; Herbert Welsh, Philadelphia; Archibald A. Welch, Hartford, Conn.; George G. Mercer, Philadelphia.

Daniel Miller, Baltimore, Md.; George Burnham, Jr., Philadelphia; Nathaniel T. Bacon, Syracuse Municipal Reform League; Datus C. Smith, Yonkers' (N. Y.) Good Government Club; William Potts, Farmington, Conn.; Charles L. Lincoln, West Superior, Wis.; C. Marton Stewart, A. V. W. Jackson, Alexander Laird, I. Osgood Carleton, Dr. A. B. Johnson, Dr. Henry Moffat, Yonkers, N. Y.; John H. C. Nevius, Confederated Council of Good Government Clubs of New-York; [illegible]ph A. Miller, Advance Club, Providence, R. I.

The morning sesison was called to order by James C. Carter, President of the City Club. He said that the complete union of the municipal associations throughout the country was a thing which had long and ardently been wished for by the friends of reform.

"I know of no movement," he added, "so well calculated to purify the whole body of American politics. The object of this league is to establish municipal government on non-party lines, without reference to patronage, or with as little reference to it as possible. With the removal of the patronage system, the principal source of corruption, mischief, and misrule in municipal government will be done away with."

Mr. Carter advised the delegates not to attempt too much, and told them that their main object should be the election to municipal offices of men who would administer offices on non-party lines. He concluded his address by welcoming the delegates on behalf of the City Club.

Charles Richardson of Philadelphia was appointed temporary Chairman, and James J. Pryor of the City Club was made Secretary pro tem.

The following committees were appointed: On Nomination of Permanent Officers—A. Welsh, P. Tucker, C. J. Bonaparte, E. Thompson, and P. Curtis; on By Laws—Henry W. Williams, Augustine Jones, Charles Richardson, Dudley Tibbitts, W. H. Roome, D. Smith, William Potts, Alexander Welsh, and J. W. Pryor.

At the adjourned session in the afternoon the following were announced as elected for permanent officers:

President—James C. Carter of New-York; First Vice President—Charles D. Richardson of Philadelphia; Second Vice President—Samuel B. Capen of Boston; Secretary—Clinton Rogers Woodruff of Philadelphia; Treasurer—R. Fulton Cutting of New-York; Executive Committee—Herbert Welsh, Philadelphia; Dudley Tibbitts, Troy; Matthew Hale, Albany; Louis D. Brandeis, Boston; William G. Low, Brooklyn; Joseph A. Miller, Providence, R. I., and Charles J. Bonaparte, Baltimore.

The following constitution was then adopted, and it was resolved that all associations or leagues desiring to join the National League must first subscribe to it.

The objects of the National Municipal League shall be as follows:

First—To multiply the numbers, harmonize the methods, and combine the forces of all who realize that it is only by united action and organization that good citizens can secure the adoption of good laws and the selection of men of trained ability and proved integrity for all municipal positions, or prevent the success of incompetent or corrupt candidates for public offices.

Second—To promote the thorough investigation and discussion of the conditions and details of civic administration, and of the method for selecting and appointing officials in American cities, and of laws and ordinances relating to such subjects.

Third—To provide for such meetings and conferences and further preparation and circulation of such addresses and other literature as may seem likely to advance the cause of good city government.

The league shall be composed of associations formed in cities of the United States and having as an object the improvenment of municipal government. It shall have no connection with State or national parties or issues, and shall confine itself strictly to municipal affairs. Any association belonging to the league may withdraw at any time.

The league shall be managed by a board of delegates chosen by the associations comprising it. Each association shall be entitled to appoint from time to time as many delegates as it may see fit, and each delegate shall retain his position until he is withdrawn or his successor is qualified or his association becomes inactive.

Whenever a delegate shall demand a vote by associations on any question the vote shall be so taken, and the vote of each association shall be cast according to the preference of the majority of its delegates then present.

Additional associations may be admitted to membership at any time by the Board of Delegates. The said board shall also have the power to terminate the membership of any associations then belonging to the league.

The Board of Delegates shall have power to decide upon the qualifications of its members, to appoint all necessary officers and employes, and to raise funds for all proper expenses, but there shall be no dues or assessments, and no association shall be liable for any sums except such as it may from time to time voluntarily agree to contribute.

The board may delegate any of its powers to such committee, as it may think proper.

In all cases, in the board and in committees, members unable to be present may offer resolutions either by mail or by proxy.

The Board of Delegates may at their discretion, and upon such terms and conditions as they approve, admit individuals as associate members of the league, but such associate memberships shall not confer the right to vote or in any way act for the league.

The Board of Delegates shall have power to make and alter by-laws, provided they do not conflict with the constitution.

The constitution may be amended at any time by the votes of delegates representing three-fourths of the associations then belonging to the league.

The delegates were entertained at dinner in the evening by the City Club, after which addresses were delivered by President Carter and others. President Carter, after speaking on the condition of municipal government, especially in New-York City, said, in part:

"The idea of reform has so taken hold of the public mind that it only needs a few determined men as leaders to put the whole present brood of politicians who now control the fortunes of great commonwealths to rout."

Charles Richardson, of Philadelphia, after speaking of lurking dangers in a failure to supervise local selections for municipal offices, complimented the Christian Endeavor and other religious societies for the class of voters they were producing. He said that they would stand by the course of good, pure government, irrespective of party.

Charles J. Bonaparte of Baltimore, Augustin Jones of the Advance Club of Providence, H. P. Hull of Milwaukee, and Dudley Tibbitts of Troy also spoke. Mr. Tibbitts said:

"In the City of Troy we have suffered, and to-day it is a question of life and death as well as the possession of our property. A citizen of Troy cannot assert his constitutional rights without danger to his life. This is not a theory, but it is a fact. On March 6, the whole city was paralyzed because human life had been taken. Robert Ross had been murdered. When we tried to punish or bring his murderer to justice, we were blocked in all our movements by the Governor of this State."

Mr. Tibbitts said Troy was more in need of municipal reform than any city in the State, and that, unless good men were elected to fill the offices, such occurrences as the murdering of Ross would soon become common.

The league will meet again to-day at 11 A. M., when the question of acquiring a newspaper to represent it will be discussed. This evening there will be a mass meeting under the auspices of the league at the Manhattan Athletic Club Theatre, when the delegates will recount their experiences in the field of municipal reform.

May 29, 1894

MAYORS IN CONFERENCE

United States, Canada, and Mexico Represented at the Meeting in Columbus.

MUNICIPAL OWNERSHIP PAPERS

COLUMBUS, Ohio, Sept. 28.—The first annual conference of the Mayors and Councilmen of the United States, Canada, and Mexico was called to order at 11 o'clock this morning by Mayor Black of this city, about 160 regularly accredited delegates being present in the auditorium. The Mayor's opening remarks were brief, and he closed by introducing Gov. Asa S. Bushnell of Ohio, who delivered an address of welcome.

Mayor C. A. Collier of Atlanta, Ga., responded for the visitors. Mayor Black was made Chairman of the convention, and Editor Gordon of City Government Secretary

Chairman Black this afternoon announced a committee to formulate a plan of permanent organization. A careful count made at the afternoon session disclosed the presence of twenty-seven men wearing the official badges of Mayors and fifty-one men and women with those of Councilmen. New York, Chicago, Brooklyn, Philadelphia, Boston, St. Louis, and other large cities are without representation here.

Joseph W. Stover of New York occupied forty minutes of the time of the convention this afternoon in the reading of a paper on "Telegraphic Systems for the Facilitation of Fire and Police Service." It was technical in character.

Chairman Black, in his opening remarks at the night session, made reference to the importance of street lighting in cities, and called attention to the significance and influence of the National Street Lighting Association, now in session here. In closing he introduced Henry Hopkins of New Haven, Conn., who is Secretary of the association.

Mr. Hopkins read a paper on "The Proper Lighting of City Streets," the chief point of which was an analysis of the reasons why the cost of public lighting is increasing while the cost per light is decreasing.

Mayor McVicar of Des Moines, Iowa, followed with a prepared paper on street lighting by contract and by municipal ownership. In the course of the paper he said:

"While we now generally concede the justice of municipal ownership of waterworks, and are about ready to indorse municipal street lighting, we hesitate at going further and declaring for city ownership of such natural monopolies as gas and street railways. We, however, are rapidly coming to believe in the soundness of this principle. Our newspapers and periodicals are teeming with intelligent information on the subject of municipal ownership. No sentiment should be allowed to stand in the way of utilizing these monopolies for the benefit of the whole people, although it be at the expense of private gain.

"The private lighting company, in its efforts to retain a profitable contract, systematically endeavors to demonstrate that they are furnishing light as cheaply as it is possible to furnish it. They ridicule the estimates of competent engineers and criticise the showing of municipal companies. They argue the impossibility of the city economically or honestly operating a plant because of the element of politics that enters into its management, and the manufacturers of apparatus will frequently substantiate their statements. These statements are plausible to the verge of being convincing, and cause one to hesitate before investing in a municipal plant. But a careful inquiry into the conditions environing these institutions shows watered stock, unproductive investments, and inefficiency of apparatus which will fully explain the high cost of production. Compare such a plant with the results obtained from improved apparatus, judicious selection of machinery which will insure high economy of operation that a properly designed plant with modern appliances can produce, and a very different result will be had."

September 29, 1897

THE PLUNDERING OF CITIES.

Corporation Bribery the Great Evil—Municipal Ownership of Public Monopolies the Remedy.

MILWAUKEE, Wis., Sept. 20.—At the meeting of the National Municipal League this afternoon, the feature was a paper on "The Influence of Public Service Companies on City Governments," by the Rev. Dr. Washington Gladden, who is a member of the Columbus City Council. Dr. Gladden said, in part:

"Some of the relations of public service companies to city governments are open and lawful, but it is generally believed that relations of a subterranean and illegitimate character are often maintained between representatives of the city and representatives of these companies by which the public is plundered. Such illicit relations do not always involve the payment of money by the corporations to the municipal officers; the money is often paid to those who control the Councilmen, and other methods of influence are employed. The election expenses of candidates are often paid. Along with these secret methods there is much direct bribery; many who occupy high positions in society are connected more or less closely with this nefarious business. Mayor Swift of Chicago told the precise truth when he said that most of the bribery of City Councils was the work of 'representative citizens.'

"Those who practice these villainous arts justify themselves on the ground that a man must protect his property. 'Would you sit still,' they demand, 'and see your hard earnings confiscated by robbers?' It seems to be assumed that bribery to prevent the spoliation of properties is justifiable. Just here the public conscience needs toning up. There is really very little distinction between the coward who is bullied into bribery by the public spoilsman and the corruptionist who himself takes the initiative. The one lets the bandits make a tool of him and the other uses the bandits as his tools. Which is the more honorable? On the whole, I have more respect for the aggressive briber. The real criminal is always the man who pays the money.

September 21, 1900

Reform Progress In American Cities

METHODS AND RESULTS OF EFFORTS MADE TO IMPROVE THE CHARACTER OF MUNICIPAL GOVERNMENTS.

By DR. ALBERT SHAW, Editor of Review of Reviews, Author of Local Government in Illinois; Municipal Government in Great Britain; Municipal Government in Continental Europe, etc.

Under the general title of "Municipal Reform in Typical American Cities" THE TIMES has recently published a series of fifteen articles, contributed by as many different writers, each setting forth the methods and results of efforts recently made to improve the character of the city government with which the writer is especially conversant. Most of these articles have been written with commendable intelligence and fair-mindedness; and the fifteen, when re-read connectedly, give a better idea of the present status of so-called municipal reform in this country than anything else that could be found.

Inasmuch as the articles have been written chiefly for New York readers the series has not included a paper upon New York itself. Yet it is here, in the great metropolis of the country, that municipal reform work has achieved the best results, and is deservedly having the most beneficent influence upon good citizenship in a hundred cities throughout the length and breadth of the land.

The articles as published deal with New York's three principal neighbors on the Atlantic seaboard, namely, Boston, Philadelphia, and Baltimore; the great manufacturing city of Pittsburg; the three Ohio cities of Cleveland, Toledo, and Cincinnati; two representatives of a group of Western and Northwestern cities, namely, Detroit and Minneapolis; the two pre-eminent interior centres of population and trade, Chicago and St. Louis; the metropolis of the Pacific Coast, San Francisco, and the metropolis of the lower Mississippi and Gulf region, New Orleans. There is an article about Portland, and, finally, one about the Federal capital, Washington.

INDEPENDENT CITY ISSUE.

Municipal reform in this country has had to exert itself along a number of different lines. In most of our large cities it has had to wage a desperate fight for common honesty, in order to clear the ground for those higher objects of good and efficient municipal administration that concern in a positive way the social well-being of the inhabitants. But in order to assure this great preliminary cause of common honesty it has been necessary to get the city government differentiated from the government of the State, and from the political issues that divide men in National affairs, so that the people might deal consciously and directly with municipal affairs. Abandoning their earlier standpoint—where they manifestly distrusted the people and doubted the possibility of good municipal government at the hands of a democracy like ours—the American municipal reformers have now almost everywhere cheerfully accepted the fact of universal suffrage, and they welcome the chance to fight their cause in the large, open arena.

Instead, moreover, of their old-time reliance upon "checks and balances," and a wide subdivision of authority, the municipal reformers have come to see that complicated machinery is for the advantage of their enemies. Simplicity of organization, with a plan of well-concentrated responsibility, gives the best results. It is true that experienced reformers have ceased to regard the mere framework of the municipal charter as the thing of most importance. They are aware that an indifferent and degraded community will certainly be badly governed under a model charter, while a determined and resolute citizenship may accomplish good results even under an obsolete and ill-advised system of boards and dual chambers and other badly co-related mechanism.

The New York system now gives a chance for the shaping of a square and conclusive issue between those who, for motives of the public welfare, want an upright and intelligent conduct of the municipal corporation, and those, on the other hand, who for reasons of their own private gain or indulgence prefer lax and low standards of administration.

All that is necessary, therefore, with the New York system, in order to have a hopeful fighting chance for good municipal government under the existing charter, is the use of such wisdom, forbearance, and good sense on the part of the leadership of the opponents of bad government as to enable them to act together when the time comes for making nominations. When the anti-Tammany forces unite and a Mayor Strong is elected, with the result that a Waring heads the cleansing department and a Roosevelt controls the police force, progress all along the line is the prevailing rule. But when the opponents of Tammany, through unwisdom or through the intrusion of the party spirit, fail to unite, and a Seth Low, a Benjamin F. Tracy, and a Henry George are all running on rival tickets against a solid Tammany phalanx, the result is quite sure to be the election of a Van Wyck, with the consequent demoralization of the whole municipal service.

Union, once more, on the principle that municipal government has nothing to do with the distinctions of National political parties, defeats Tammany and brings in a Low administration that gives New York its present proud position as one of the best governed of the world's great cities. Separate municipal elections, a charter that focuses responsibility, a disavowal of mere partisan ideals an organization of unselfish workers for good government that never desponds but is alert and busy from one election day to the next, an avoidance of visionary projects, and an adherence to principles of moderation and common sense—such are the means by which New York City has actually achieved municipal reform.

And, in spite of a relapse now and then New York is morally certain by such means in the long run to maintain its place in the list of those great modern cities that are managed in an honest and enlightened way for the health, comfort, and general advantage of their people.

CONDITIONS IN CHICAGO.

Chicago, the second metropolis of North America, has a municipal system that is now and has long been a very different one from that of New York. While the Mayor has an important and responsible position, and is accountable to a large extent for the police administration and the efficiency of the various departments of the municipal life, it is in the elective City Council that the governing authority of Chicago chiefly centres.

Chicago has never suffered from any colossal thefts of public funds or from any such régime as that of Tweed in New York. Its Mayors have done many creditable things, and for a city so young, of such rapid growth, and of such a Babel-tongued diversity of population, it is to Chicago's credit that it has created its great park system, its works for water supply and drainage, its generally effective school system, its public lighting, its fire service, and (with much qualification) its police service.

But the Common Council had gradually sunk to a state of the most scandalous corruption. This had come about through a variety of causes, and had become intrenched in the political system—the corrupt Councilmen being in control of the party machinery for their respective wards or districts. Obviously, great corporations desiring to obtain franchise favors, cultivated the Republicans who controlled the machinery in Republican wards, and the Democrats who were masters of the situation in Democratic wards; while in wards that were closely divided the corporations contributed to the funds of both parties alike.

The chief factor of demoralization in municipal government in Chicago for many years was the street railway system, which had millions of dollars at stake, partly in plans for extension and consolidation, but above all in its need for the renewal of its principal franchises, the terms of which were to expire in the near future.

This bad condition reached a climax some six or seven years ago. Whereupon a group of good citizens got together and formed an association, which took the name of the Voters' Municipal League. It was very fortunate in securing for its executive head a man of dauntless courage and force named George E. Cole, who associated with him as Secretary of the movement a young attorney named Hoyt King. The methods that these men set in motion some seven years ago have grown in power and influence until they have redeemed Chicago, and these methods would seem destined to lead on, from the more negative achievements already gained, to those rewards of virtue that honest municipal government must surely bring in the way of remedied physical conditions and the making of a desirable social environment.

Like the Citizens' Union of New York the Voters' League of Chicago has adopted the plan of being in municipal politics not at election time only, but every day in the year. The Voters' League, in short, has borrowed the "gang's" plan of making a business of city politics. The league publishes the record of every candidate for local office. It submits pledges to all aspirants for office of whatever party. It indorses men of good record, whether Republicans or Democrats, and it denounces and hounds men of bad record. It has finally succeeded in driving out of the Board of Aldermen nearly every man of whom it disapproves.

Its work has been greatly aided by the newspapers of Chicago, just as an intelligent and well-managed Fusionist movement in New York has readily won the support of almost the entire press. The reform of the Aldermanic body has been followed by the establishment of high standards in appointive office. Alongside of the Voters' Municipal League, and made up largely of the same men, is the Legislative Voters' League, which undertakes to see that Chicago is represented at Springfield, the State capital, by men who can be depended upon to oppose measures detrimental to the best interests of the city.

There is another organization, the Citizens' Association, now conducted by men who made the Voters' Municipal League so powerful, and this association has especially devoted itself to the reform of the system of assessing and collecting taxes, and to the toning up of the civil service of the city. The Civic Federation and the Union of Improvement Clubs are organizations which have achieved good results in Chicago.

Thus the great fight for common honesty in Chicago's municipal government has resulted in a very thoroughgoing victory. There will follow, in due time, those improvements in the paving and cleaning of the city, and in other of its services, which in a community as intelligent as Chicago are sure to come where "grafting" has been eliminated. Mr. Peattie's account of this Chicago movement for reform is an inspiring chapter.

REDEMPTION OF ST. LOUIS.

In like manner, Mr. Lemmon's story of the work initiated by two men for the redemption of St. Louis from corrupt administration is the clear account of one of the most notable episodes in the history of local self-government. It should not be thought that St. Louis has no record whatever of honorable and excellent city government in the past. The St. Louis charter, adopted now a good many years ago, was in its day a monument of intelligence and skill, and in its schools and some other departments St. Louis had long ago made a fine record.

But in recent years the city had become an abject victim of the greed for money, and the two branches of its so-called "Legislative Assembly" had fallen under the complete control of rings of men, whose chief business was the giving and taking of bribes. The immediate origin of this carnival of corruption—as without exception in like cases in every other great city of the United States—was the attempt of the street railway corporations to steal valuable public franchises.

In the effort of St. Louis to "clean up" in anticipation of the holding of a world's fair, a reputable young Democratic lawyer, named Joseph W. Folk, was chosen to the office of public prosecutor, locally called the Circuit Attorney. Mr. Rolla Wells, a business man of character, was chosen Mayor. Mr. Folk was fortunate in finding a clue which led to the discovery of the payment of a large sum of money to members of the Council and Board of Aldermen for the granting of a particular street railway franchise. It was a case as clear as that upon which the New York boodlers, many years ago, were exposed and convicted in connection with the Broadway franchise.

A number of men, thereupon, turned State's evidence, and thus laid bare the complete history of boodling conspiracies for a number of years previous. The results that followed in the exposure and punishment of criminals were as sweeping and dramatic as anything in the history of municipal government, excepting the overthrow of the Tweed ring in New York.

Mr. Wells as Mayor has shown character and courage similar to Mr. Folk in cleaning up the executive departments and bringing honesty and efficiency into the general work of the city. These things are recent, and it remains to be seen how well St. Louis will sustain the work of Folk and Wells. It can only be done by the union of honest men for non-partisan good government, under the lead of men like Folk, and with the benefit of all that can be made locally applicable from the experience of New York and Chicago.

Of New York's three principal neighbors on the Atlantic seaboard Baltimore has more hopeful lessons to teach out of her recent experience than either Boston or Philadelphia. At different times in the past Baltimore has given evidence of an ability to carry on municipal government with a considerable degree of honesty and efficiency. It has, however, suffered much through the intrusion of party politics in city affairs, and gross corruption at the polls due to unscrupulous bosses. The Baltimore voters are still too much, by far, under the spell of the Republican and Democratic names, but fortunately for the comparatively small but highly intelligent body of independent voters, the party balance is remarkably close. This gives the independents a chance to turn the scale by favoring the best men.

Such a situation tends to put both parties on their good behavior. They have at length purged their elections of fraud in Baltimore, and in the last municipal contest the independents played back and forth through the party tickets, with the result of electing a reform Democrat for Mayor, a Republican Controller, a Democratic mjaority in one branch of the City Council, and a Republican control of the second branch. Baltimore's new charter was framed by a commission of very able and upright men upon advanced principles. It places municipal elections in the Spring, focuses responsibility upon the Mayor and other officials, carefully guards the finances, and has very many excellent features. With the growth of the independent spirit, and the refusal of an ever-growing number of good Republicans and good Democrats to allow party bosses to govern their action in strictly municipal matters, Baltimore may confidently expect to take a high rank among well-governed cities.

SITUATION IN BOSTON.

While Boston has accomplished a good deal of excellent municipal work within the past ten years it has at present little to report that is definitely instructive to the country. Mr. Talbot's article declares that "petty grafting" is common and municipal extravagance pervasive, but that big and bold instances of public malfeasance are not to be found. In Boston, as everywhere else, he points out that the great public service corporations are responsible directly or indirectly for practically all of the existing corruption. They can get what they want at the City Hall and the State House, and they pay for what they get. They contribute to the campaign funds of Aldermen, and when the campaign is close they make sure of themselves by contributing to both sides. They are in a position to furnish a great deal of employment, and they use patronage as much as they use money.

As respects the cowardice and "conservatism" of the business men and the so-called better elements Boston is in much the same condition that New York and Chicago were a few years ago. Under the present city charter the Mayor has nearly all the powers that formerly belonged to the City Council. He has absolute control over the heads of departments, and many of them are appointed without needing to be confirmed by the Board of Aldermen. Under these circumstances Mr. Talbot holds that the new Good Government Association of Boston makes an obvious blunder in proposing to confine itself to an attempt to elect Aldermen. It is obvious that under the present Boston charter, as under that of New York, the effective thing to do would be to secure a union of all good citizens and good elements for the selection of a Mayor of the highest kind of qualifications of practical ability as well as of character. Mr. Talbot praises the association, however, for securing an enactment by which all the thirteen Aldermen will henceforth be elected at large, while only eight can be nominated by either party.

Boston has had a large experience with charter tinkering with no radical benefit. The Boston reformers have, however, shown by what they have done with their Public School Association to secure control of the school system that their Good Government Association can if it will achieve practical results in the actual field of local politics, apart from its theoretical work in the alteration of charters. The impression one gets from Mr. Talbot's article is that the Boston situation is neither very bad nor very good, and that it cannot be made notably excellent until public opinion has been greatly stimulated by concentrated work on the part of the reformers, and until the press, which is now indifferent, rather than dishonest or corrupt, becomes more zealous in its independence.

The chapter on Philadelphia is written by Mr. Gordon H. Cilley, who devotes himself chiefly to the situation at present existing under the Hon. John Weaver as the new Mayor. Mr. Cilley declares that his close inquiry reveals Mayor Weaver as "a man left heir to a vast estate hopelessly encumbered." He proceeds to draw a swift but vivid picture of an almost unparalleled reign of corruption under the recent administration of Mayor Ashbridge. He finds Weaver honest in his intentions, and persistent in his efforts to stamp out so-called "graft," but not very radical or dramatic in his methods, and unwilling as yet to break away from his close relations to the Republican machine that put him in office.

He quotes Mr. Clinton Rogers Woodruff, however, at great length in eulogy of Mayor Weaver's honesty and strength, and since Mr. Woodruff is eminent as an independent and a reformer, it is to be assumed that Philadelphia has made substantial gain in substituting Weaver for Ashbridge. Mr. Cilley's paper does not, however, set forth any fundamental improvement in the citizenship of Philadelphia, which would indicate that good government is henceforth to be secured as a public right, and by intelligent effort, rather than as a more or less accidental favor from the controlling party machine.

Mr. Carson's chapter on Pittsburg is in the main the story of the rise to power of the Magee-Flinn machine, with its absolute control of municipal government in the interest of street railways and other corporations, and for the promotion of lucrative development schemes in general. It is chiefly instructive by way of warning. The history of successful municipal reform in Pittsburg must begin at some future date, for past efforts have been unavailing.

REFORM IN OHIO CITIES.

The Ohio cities are reorganizing their machinery and adjusting themselves to the new conditions created by the recent enactment of the uniform Ohio municipal code. The articles presented in THE TIMES's series on Cleveland, Toledo, and Cincinnati are interesting in many respects, but do not set forth situations especially instructive to the rest of the country. Cincinnati is more deeply than ever sunk in the mire of the boss rule of Mr. Cox and his Republican machine. Municipal reform there, as at Pittsburg, lies in the future. The reformers are learning that they must go about their work in a business fashion.

Toledo just now presents the picture of an administration divided against itself. Term after term the people of Toledo insist upon re-electing Mayor Sam Jones on his Golden Rule platform. The new Ohio code sets up a series of quasi-independent boards, and most of these, together with the elective Council, are pulling against Mayor Jones. Yet Toledo has made much progress in recent years, and it is almost infinitely removed from the sordid plight of a boss-ridden city like Cincinnati.

Cleveland is one of the most progressive cities in the United States, and in spite of all the criticism brought against Mayor Tom L. Johnson on one ground or on another, it is evident that his administration is one that in the main works for the public welfare, and that it is almost entirely free from those "boodling" and "grafting" propensities that have been the plague of so many American towns. The great struggle of Western cities like Cleveland, Toledo, and Detroit for three-cent street railway fares has had the effect to put the great public service corporations on the defensive, and on this ground, if on no other, those agitations for cheap fares and better service have amazingly helped the cause of clean and efficient public administration.

The chapter on Detroit is the sequel of those things brought about by the ways and works of that strong character and long-time Mayor, the late Hazen S. Pingree. Undoubtedly in the earlier part of his service Pingree brought an amazing force of energy, courage, and integrity to the advancement of the whole work of municipal administration in Detroit. Since Pingree the cause of reform has run a checkered course, but there is to-day a Municipal League at work, very much on the Chicago plan, which bids fair to prevent serious relapses and to uphold the good name of one of the most beautiful of our American cities.

Minneapolis is one of the typical Western cities which in the main have for twenty years shown remarkable efficiency in solving the creative problems of a new centre of urban life. It obtained a wholly ill-proportioned notoriety not long ago through the exposure of corruption in one department, that of the police, through the active participation of a dishonest Mayor. This Mayor came into power by a curious accident in the working of a new and untried system of nomination by primary election. After a few short months in office he left the city a fugitive, and was subsequently indicted and convicted. The chapter on Minneapolis in THE TIMES series is devoted to a recounting of this episode.

The Pacific Coast town of Portland, Ore., has passed through a drastic experience of reform, has been given a model charter, and is at present dominated by the reform spirit. New Orleans is notable for the pluck and persistence of its reform elements, in spite of many obstacles and defeats.

The effective work of municipal reform in San Francisco began some years ago through the efforts of the Merchants' Association, which gradually felt its way to the very heart of the municipal situation. As a result of that association's efforts San Francisco several years ago was provided with a new and excellent charter possessing several features of an unusually progressive character. Under Mayor Phelan and his successor, Mayor Schmitz, the results achieved for good government have not been so satisfactory as the reformers and charter-makers had hoped for. Nevertheless, San Francisco is upon the whole making substantial advance.

November 1, 1903

A City Government Which Galveston Had to Adopt After the Great Flood, and Which Ran Like Wildfire Over the Middle West, Has Now Reached and Conquered the Conservative State Across the Hudson.

GOV. WOODROW WILSON has brought the Commission plan of government to the East. This unostentatious reform, which started in the far South and made its way into the West, might never have invaded the stronghold of conservatism if New Jersey had not elected the human dynamo who became its Governor last Fall.

As it is, two near-by cities, Trenton and Bayonne, have adopted the plan, and very likely other New Jersey towns will do so before long. So we New Yorkers, who up to now have known of the Commission plan only by vague and glowing reports from the South and Middle West, will have a chance to see how it works at our own doors. And if it works well, who can tell but that New York may itself come into line, abolish its Board of Aldermen, and learn of Des Moines?

The Commission form is not so new as its advertisers claim. It has been in force in the City of Washington ever since the early seventies, not quite in the same way in which Galveston and Des Moines introduced it to public attention, but in all essential features practically the same thing. In Galveston and Des Moines the people elect their Commissioners, in Washington they are appointed by the President—that is the only difference.

What is the Commission form? It substitutes for the Mayor and Board of Aldermen a Commission of five men, elected by the people just as they would elect Assemblymen or Aldermen. Each of these five takes special supervision of some department of the government, such as the police, the Fire Department, or water supply. There is no magic in the number 5; any community which wants a Commission of fifteen or of three can have it.

The Commission having been elected, it chooses a Mayor, but the Mayor is one of the board and has very little authority. Virtually, he is simply the Chairman of the Commission, with not much more privilege than the right to call them to order when some Commissioner infringes the rules of Cushing.

Such is the scheme which two New Jersey cities, one of them the capital of the State, have adopted, and which more may adopt before long.

Because it is usually coupled with the initiative, the referendum, the recall, and other nostrums of the modern patent-medicine kind, the impression has grown that there is something very radical about it. Whether it is good or bad, it is not very radical, in the sense in which such a measure as the recall is radical. For example, if cities had always been governed by the Commission plan, and somebody suddenly proposed to substitute for that method a government by a Mayor, a Board of Estimate, and a Board of Aldermen, he might be charged with radicalism. There is nothing much in the radical argument. The only question which really concerns us is, how has the system worked?

It has got far beyond the guesswork stage, having been tried in a large number of American cities. It is apparently no panacea. Still, it is only fair to say that in some of the cities where it has been tried, a better form of government has resulted than that which they had under the old system.

Commission government is only ten years old, and in a way is the result of accident. That is to say, if Galveston, Texas, had not been wrecked by a tidal wave we might never have heard of it.

Galveston, "wrecked both physically and financially by a tidal wave, placed the herculean task of reconstructing its streets, buildings, and finances in the hands of a Commission of five men appointed by the Governor of the State," says an article in The Municipal Journal and Engineer.

But for the total wreck caused by this tidal wave, America might have gone for a long time without knowledge of the new scheme. As it was, however, after Galveston had been forced to adopt it, some other Texas cities followed suit, and finally Des Moines got into line. Now the idea has got to the East.

The Galveston scheme had been in operation four years before Houston was attracted enough to adopt it. In 1907 five other Texas cities placed their government in the hands of Commissions. In the same year the rumor of what Texas had done spread so far abroad that laws were passed permitting the adoption of the scheme by Legislatures of the States of Iowa, Kansas, and the two Dakotas (1907), Mississippi (1906), Minnesota, and Wisconsin (1909), and Illinois (1910). Now New Jersey has come into line, and the thing has come East.

Bayonne voted to adopt it, but Bayonne is a small city. Trenton is different; Trenton is the capital of a State. It is the first State capital, except Des Moines, that has voted to abandon its aldermanic and mayoral government, and Des Moines is so far to the westward that we do not, as a rule, take it as our guide.

Trenton adopted the scheme by a majority of 1,900. The plan was carried through there by an organization known as the Commission Government League, which had Gov. Wilson behind it. Said The Trenton Times on Thursday:

"With a little less than 70 per cent. of the total vote cast, Trenton decided, by a majority of 1,900 to abandon the wasteful, irresponsible, and unsatisfactory system of government, and give the commission plan a trial. The result indicates that a large majority of the people desire a change."

In Washington, in the early seventies, it was discovered that the time-honored way of governing American cities did not work there; and since statesmen from different parts of the country had to go there, and did not wish to be exposed to the caprices of a local and elected administration, they changed the form of government to one in which there was no Mayor and no Board of Aldermen, but three Commissioners appointed by the President. One of these, under the law, had to be an engineer officer of the army, but the other two could be appointed by the President at his own sweet will.

That is Washington's form of government to-day, and it is the best governed city in the United States.

Galveston did not knowingly adopt the Washington plan. But she was in a desperate condition. The tidal wave had wiped out most of the city and all of her government, and in casting about for something which would restore order and sanity she hit, quite accidentally, upon a modification of the plan already adopted in Washington. But she elected her Commissioners instead of having the Federal Government appoint them, and she divided the municipal responsibilities among them in a very definite way. Later on Des Moines imitated her.

Since then the idea has been taken up all over the West and South. In California four cities have adopted it; in Colorado, two; in Idaho, one; in Illinois, eleven; in Iowa, eight; in Kansas, twenty-three, including Kansas City, Leavenworth, Topeka, Wichita, and Emporia; in Kentucky, one; in Louisiana, one, but that one is Shreveport; in Massachusetts, four—Gloucester, Haverhill, Lynn, and Taunton; in Michigan, three; in Minnesota, two; in Mississippi, two; in New Mexico, one; in North Carolina, two; in North Dakota, three; in Oklahoma twelve, including Guthrie; in South Carolina, one; in South Dakota, seven, including Huron, Pierre, Yankton, and Sioux Falls; in Tennessee, one—Memphis; in Texas, seventeen, including Austin, the State capital, Dallas, Fort Worth, Galveston, and Houston; in Washington, two, but they are Spokane and Tacoma; in West Virginia, two, and in Wisconsin, two.

The Commission form is by no means the same wherever it is adopted; the local prejudices and necessities modify it. There is no sanctity about any required number of Commissioners, or about any plan for dividing the work among them. The Galvestonians happened to find it best for their immediate needs to elect five men and to make one of them a Fire Commissioner, one a Water Commissioner, and so on; but in any city of different necessities a different policy can be adopted, and often is.

Prof. Charles A. Beard, in an article recently published in pamphlet form by the Short Ballot Organization, had this to say:

"The phrase 'Commission Government' has, of course, been a misnomer ever since the Galveston Commission ceased to be appointed by the Governor and became elective. The word 'commission' implies appointment, and in the strict sense of the word there have been no cities in the country 'governed by Commission' except Washington, D. C., and Chelsea, Mass. The phrase, however, has been applied in the popular mind to all the new city charters that have been modeled on Galveston and Des Moines. These charters vary from almost exact copies through a twilight zone to charters that are essentially unlike the Galveston plan in all but name. One city changed the title of its Council to 'Commission,' and proceeded to call itself 'Commission Governed,' and is still included in most lists on that slender basis!

"'Commission Plan,' to the average American, means a new plan of city government that seems to be bringing about a substantial and permanent reform in cities where it has been tried. There exists in the popular mind, however, no little confusion as to the precise nature of this new plan, and a variety of definitions are given. Nevertheless, when all incidental features are eliminated, the essential element which accounts for the success thus far achieved is simply this: Conspicuous responsibility- and hence accountability—of all elected officials to the people.

"Another way of expressing it is that a true Commission Plan is one which conforms to the Short Ballot principle, which is defined by the Short Ballot Organization as follows:

"'First. That only those offices should be elective which are important enough to attract (and deserve) public examination.

"'Second. That very few offices should be filled by election at one time, so as to permit adequate and unconfused public examination of the candidates.'

"This excludes Boston, for instance. Under its recent amended charter, Boston has only six names on the ballot, but all except the Mayor are of insignificant authority and uninteresting character, so that they are dangerously obscure. Waco, Texas, is likewise excluded, for although it has the 'Commission' of five members, there are a number of obscure, independently elected officials to get in their way. In neither city should complete popular control be expected to ensue.

"Accordingly a Commission Governed City means to us one that has a 'Short Ballot' according to the Short Ballot principle, which results in popular supremacy with efficient government as a probable by-product."

The Municipal Journal and Engineer, in the course of an exhaustive article upon the Commission form of government, says:

"At least 111 cities have already adopted the Commission form of government, and the number is being added to every month.

"The most apparent danger inherent in this form of government is the possibility that the great powers conferred upon these few officials may be used for selfish ends and against the interests of the people, or at least in a grossly arbitrary way. To meet this, many States and cities have adopted the recall, by which an official can be removed from office by popular vote. The initiative has been adopted by still more, and the referendum by all but a few of the California and Texas cities.

"In about half the cities the board contains five members, while three also is quite common. Five cities have four Commissioners; and six, seven, and nine are each found in one city. In several States five is the number provided for first-class cities, all smaller ones having three only, as their municipal functions are less extensive and complicated. The general idea is to focus popular attention before election, and concentrate responsibility afterward, in as small a number as possible. Another advantage of smallness of number is the probability of more prompt transaction of business. Still another is the possibility of paying salaries adequate to secure competent men.

"There are all sorts of conditions as to term of office, the length varying from two to five years. In some cases the entire board is changed at each election; in others a single member, or one-half or one-third of the members are elected each year, while in still others the Mayor or head of the board serves for a longer or a shorter time than the other members.

"In some cities the members of the board are required to give their entire efforts to the city's affairs, and are paid accordingly. In others they are supposed to give 'as much time as necessary'; while in several the Mayor gives his entire time and the others an hour a day, or such time as is necessary."

When Des Moines adopted the Galveston plan, it was the result of a reaction against a very bad system of city government. "Again and again," wrote Charles Edward Russell, describing the Des Moines situation in Everybody's Magazine, "good men, feeling the sting of these conditions, and upheld by the sympathies of most of the people, set their hands to the task of improvement. Without exception their efforts had one dreary record of failure.

"Good men seemed to become bad when they took public office; wise men to turn foolish; efficient men to become suddenly incapable, and honesty itself to be corrupted. Public service corporations absorbed the highways, the city finances were slipshod, the protection of citizens was often alarmingly inadequate.

"Thus the strange spectacle was presented of able business men yearly investing their money in a notoriously unprofitable venture and supporting an institution so wretchedly mismanaged that it was a kind of public jest. What was strangest of all, while the people had obviously the sense of beauty and the love of adornment, the appearance of the business part of their city was always slovenly.

"In spite, therefore, of what might be called a universal aspiration for good things, the astonishing result was obtained of universally bad things, until part of the people were ready to despair of good government, and another part settled into a cynical acceptance of what seemed to be an irremediable evil."

Mr. Russell alleges that in Galveston the five Commissioners "seemed to develop the sense of service, a sense quite new in the history of American municipalities." He admits that the plan was opposed there "on the ground that it was undemocratic, which it certainly was." He rests his case, not on the compliance of the scheme with the American idea of democracy, but on the success of the way in which the plan worked.

On the other hand, Robert W. Jones, a skilled and competent newspaper man, investigated the Des Moines plan for a Western newspaper and reported adversely. Mr. Jones did not attack the main idea; his complaint was that however excellent that might be, in practical operation it was bound to be warped, and was, in fact, so warped in Des Moines.

His complaint seems to be based chiefly on the reduction of the nominal Mayor to a figurehead. Defenders of the system might reply that such an outcome was contemplated when the system was adopted. But Mr. Jones quotes a Des Moines newspaper as saying:

"The new City Council has sent a thrill of disappointment through the community by its strange and unfair methods in the selection of subordinates and its apparent disposition to rob the Mayor of his legal authority. The attempt to relegate the Mayor to the position of a mere figurehead and to render his office purely perfunctory is not only contrary to the original purpose of the Des Moines plan, but an exhibition of unfairness and audacity on the part of the Councilmen that is not complimentary to them."

Granting that this is true—it is, of course, only an ex parte statement—it is easy to see what might happen in such a town as Jersey City, for instance, if Gov. Wilson's proposed reform should be adopted there. Already it is becoming common talk that if the Commission plan should be accepted by Jersey City, the Commissioners would be Otto Wittpenn, "Jim" O'Melia, Mark Sullivan, and "Johnny" Heavy, or somebody training with them. It is hard to see how such a board would be an improvement on the present government, although, of course, it can be said that such men control the government even now.

One thing the Galveston plan has surely done—it has made possible the beautification of the city, at least in Galveston itself, in Des Moines, and in Cedar Rapids, and towns that had been notoriously ugly under the old system became handsome under the new. Des Moines especially improved its appearance, and Cedar Rapids was made into a new town.

In addition, the advocates of the new system claim that tax rates were reduced, and that life became in every way more livable. In view, however, of Mr. Jones's statements, it is likely to strike most folk as extremely doubtful whether the reform is due to the change in government or to the awakening of a civic spirit among the townspeople, which might have made itself manifest under any form of administration.

In Galveston the city government was given into the hands of five men, three of whom under the original charter were appointed by the Governor and two elected by the people. By a decision of the Supreme Court, the appointment of all the Commissioners was subsequently made elective.

There is a Mayor, or general manager, and four managers of particular departments. All power resides in the Commission. A majority vote of the body is final.

The Mayor is presiding officer and general director of the affairs of the city, but he has no power beyond his vote as Commissioner, except some minor abilities to act in cases of emergency. The Commissioners must also come to the board for all power to act. The Commission at its first meeting divided its departments among its members by vote under these four heads: Commissioner of Finance and Revenue, Police and Fire Commissioner, Commissioner of Streets and Public Property, and Waterworks and Sewerage Commissioner.

In Washington, the engineer officer of the army, who must by law be a member of the Commission, looks out only for engineering matters. The other two Commissioners divide between them such matters as the administration of the police, fire, and health departments.

The plan, as will be seen, easily lends itself to alteration according to the local needs of any community where it may be adopted. It is easy to say that it might work well in a small town, but not in a large one. Des Moines has a population of about 90,000, and is the star exemplar of the system. But Washington's population is close to 300,000. The matter, after all, propably resolves itself into a question of the character of the population not its size.

June 25, 1911

CITY MANAGERS COMING TO FORE

Cincinnati Is Latest City to Adopt Business Management for Municipal Government

BY R. L. DUFFUS.

A MUNICIPAL duel is under way in cities big and little of the country. The fight is between two ideas—an old idea and a new idea. The new and challenging idea is the city manager form of municipal government. In the last notable encounter between the two systems, in the recent election, the city manager form won a victory, and another big city—Cincinnati—is added to the list of those municipalities, now more than 300, which have adopted the idea. Five million citizens are now under the city manager form of government.

What will the outcome be? No man may yet say. Will some one of the great cities of the country try the new system? What have the results been so far where the city manager form is in use? In the little cities? In the big cities?

Among the cities and towns now under this plan, in addition to Cincinnati, are Cleveland, Dayton, Pasadena, San Diego, Colorado Springs, Miami, Wichita, Portland, Me.; Grand Rapids, Niagara Falls, Springfield, Ohio; Knoxville, Beaumont, Texas; Norfolk, Va.; Charleston, Clarksburg and Wheeling, W. Va., and Auburn, Newburgh, Sherrill, Watertown and Watervliet, N. Y. Only four cities which adopted the plan by popular vote have ever discarded it.

Cleveland, the largest of these cities, now has a population of more than 800,000. There is no reason, declare the advocates of city management, why it should not be applied to cities of any size. They believe it would work as well in New York or Chicago, with their millions, as in the little towns of Iowa or Florida, where it has proved both popular and successful. And they are willing to predict that it will be a live issue in New York before many years.

In order to understand what the city manager idea is and why it has spread so rapidly it is necessary to recall a little history. The honor of having the first city manager goes to Staunton, Va., where the idea of having city business conducted by some one who knew how to do it was first put into effect in 1908. Out of this grew the plan in its present form, which was first written into a city charter in Sumter, S. C., in 1912.

Advertised for City Executive.

On October 14, 1912, the city fathers of Sumter published an advertisement which has a historical interest for students of municipal government and which also is as good a description of an ideal city manager as could be found. It read as follows:

"The City of Sumter hereby announces that applications will be received from now till Dec. 1 for the office of city manager of Sumter.

"This is a rapidly growing manufacturing city of 10,000 population and the applicant should be competent to supervise public work, such as paving, lighting, water supply, etc.

"An engineer of standing and ability would be preferred. State salary desired and previous experience in municipal work.

"The city manager will hold office as long as he gives satisfaction to the commission. He will have complete administrative control of the city subject to the approval of the board of three elected Commissioners.

"There will be no politics in the job; the work will be purely that of an expert. Local citizenship is not necessary, although a knowledge of local conditions and traditions will of course be taken into consideration.

"A splendid opportunity for the right man to make a record in a new and coming profession, as this is the first time that a permanent charter position of this sort has been created in the United States."

The successful applicant was Charles E. Ashburner, an English engineer of long experience, now city manager of Stockton, Cal. So successful was he that within two years thirty-two cities had adopted the new plan. Other cities followed, the largest accessions coming between 1918 and 1923. From time to time there were setbacks and disappointments. One city manager in a Southern community discovered that a number of prominent citizens, including the leading banker, who was also one of the City Commissioners, were not paying all the taxes they should. Taking the Chief of Police with him, he invaded the precincts of the bank and demanded $10,000 in back taxes. Public opinion failed to sustain him and he lost his job. But most city managers have had less exciting and more successful careers.

Cleveland Pays $25,000.

Just how successful city management is, from the city manager's point of view, is indicated by some of the salaries paid. Long Beach, Cal., pays $10,000; Pasadena, $12,000; Stockton, $20,000; Dubuque, $10,000; Cleveland, $25,000; Knoxville, $15,000, and other salaries of from $5,000 and up are common. The city manager also enjoys prestige and power in proportion. He is a democratic autocrat—with absolute control, as a rule, over the administrative departments of his city—but usually subject to removal, not only by the City Commissioners but, if necessary, by popular vote.

The city management plan and government by commission go together, although the commission was first worked out in Galveston, Texas, some years before the city manager arrived on the scene. A typical system was that adopted in Dayton, in 1913, after a disastrous flood had called attention to the necessity of increased efficiency in the city government. Dayton elected five non-partisan Commissioners, who proceeded to hire the best city manager they could find, and to turn over to him the administrative control of all the city departments. He could both appoint and remove, subject to civil service restrictions. With this reform went an improved budget plan, an accounting along strictly businesslike lines and other changes designed to cut costs and expedite the city's enterprises.

The basic idea of the new arrangement was its imitation of the manner in which successful private corporations carry on their affairs. The citizen was likened to a shareholder, the Commissioners to a board of directors, and the city manager to the corporation's president or general manager. No one but the professional politicians cared what the manager's politics were, so long as he returned a hundred cents' worth of service, or perhaps a hundred and one cents' worth, for every dollar the taxpayer was compelled to invest.

Before the city manager appeared the commission form of government bad resulted in a number of reforms, but it had been found that expert government could not be expected from boards of five, nine, or even a greater number of men selected by popular vote from private life. The city manager furnished the expert knowledge, experience and executive ability, and the Commissioners then merely determined general policies and supervised the manager's work. They have usually served without pay.

In Cleveland a still further step was taken last year. This was the amendment of the city charter to permit the election of Commissioners on a basis of proportional representation. Ashtabula, Ohio, and Boulder, Col., have adopted a similar provision.

"This means, in Cleveland," said Harold Buttenheim, editor of The American City Magazine, "that any group which can muster one-twenty-fifth of the total vote can have its representative on the City Commission. The result is that the commission, or board of directors, becomes a small reproduction of the different opinions existing in the city. Under the old system many of these opinions, or groups, were totally unrepresented.

"One long-standing evil is done away with. There is no longer a temptation in municipal politics for a major party to offer undesirable inducements to groups or factions whose vote is supposed to be decisive. Nor is every candidate forced to undergo, at every election, the ordeal of a general canvass of the voters. If he can get and hold one-twenty-fifth of the vote he can secure and retain office indefinitely. And this calls into the city's service better qualified men.

"Under this plan racial and other rivalries may reveal themselves in the City Commission's meetings, but it is better to have them quietly discussed there than made the subject of hotly, and sometimes unscrupulously, conducted political campaigns. With this accompaniment the city manager plan becomes more than ever a successful combination of democracy with efficiency."

John G. Stutz of Lawrence, Kan., executive secretary of the International City Managers' Association, also points out the advantages of the non-partisan features of city management.

"The city manager form of city government," declares Mr. Stutz, "stimulates the use of purely city policies in city elections and eliminates unrelated State and national politics. For example, the Democratic and Republican members of the Cleveland Council vote as individuals on city policies, because the people of Cleveland will return them to office for their actions on city affairs, not for their party alignment.

Don't Know Manager's Politics.

"Knoxville, Tenn., is a Republican city. It has a city manager who is a Democrat. His appointments are made without regard to party alignment and very few people in Knoxville know what their manager's national politics is. Some Republican politicians wanted to abandon their city manager charter by action of the State Legislature. The citizens of Knoxville have just defeated the candidates who favored the abandonment by 4,000 and 5,000 majority, a larger majority than they gave the charter a year ago. In city matters Knoxville citizens are now voting for Knoxville, and not for any State or national party.

"The citizens of Dayton voted improvements and tax levies by 65 to 75 per cent. majority, Nov. 4, which was not only a vote of confidence in their form of city government, after eleven years' trial, but much greater majorities than they gave any party candidates."

The only serious protests against the new régime, in most of the cities which have hired city managers, have come from old-line politicians. Obviously, the patronage of the local bosses is greatly interfered with, if not altogether abolished, by the city manager's insistence upon business principles. "Deserving Democrats" or equally "deserving" Republicans do not get jobs unless they can do the work. It is to the city manager's interest to disregard politics, for if he does not he is likely to run up expenses and lose his own job. Moreover, as he is usually not a resident of the city when he is hired he has no local political affiliations and no political debts to pay.

Mr. Kilpatrick believes that the city management plan will work as well in one section of the country as in another, and that it is not necessarily limited to the smaller towns and cities.

In New York City, those familiar with the plan assert, the commission form of government and the city manager system of administration could be installed without difficulty and without breaking down the existing borough divisions. Proportional representation, it is added, might do much to eliminate some of the less desirable features of municipal politics.

Mrs. Rose Barrett, the city manager of Warrenton, Ore., not only manages that city but has been the chief factor in building it. When she started to work, twelve years ago, the site of Warrenton was marked by a few little shacks belonging to fishermen—that was all. Within that time she has done what Ida M. Tarbell calls "one of the most remarkable pieces of constructive work ever accomplished."

"It was twelve years ago," says Mrs. Barrett, who is now in the East, "that I was left a widow and thrown upon my own resources. I didn't know how to do anything to make a living—I had no more than a fifth grade schooling, and no business training whatever—and no money. It happened that I had been interested in the country near the mouth of the Columbia River, and I decided that it had possibilities as a site for a town which should grow into a great port in time. The more I studied it the better it looked. There is unlimited water power, and a supply of water for the use of people up to a million from a clean mountain stream fed from melting snow and rain, soft and fresh. There was the vast forest for lumber, the soil so rich that it needed hardly any labor, and a harbor almost identical with that of Hampton Roads.

"The next thing to do was to get some land there and promote the place. So it wasn't long before I found myself a real estate dealer—and I didn't even know what a promissory note was. I went to night school and studied commercial law. I had to borrow the money, but the idea proved to be worth it, and more, so that soon straightened itself out. I bought on thirty-day options, and then went forth to tell of the possibilities of this site. And now we have a thriving manufacturing town, with a Mayor and three Commissioners to run it besides me, and there are fine roads all around, electric lights, running water, telephones, first-class schools and churches.

"When I became city manager I discovered strife in the Fire Department. Now, even in a small town, it isn't good to have your Fire Department sulking in its tent; so I appointed a new chief, a man who did not like me at all. But he took the appointment and straightened things out—and now he's a friend of mine."

Their Code of Ethics.

At their last annual meeting, held in Montreal in September, the City Managers' Association adopted a code of ethics. Here are some of its clauses:

"The position of city manager is an important and honorable position, and should not be accepted unless the individual believes that he can serve the community to its advantage.

"In personal conduct a city manager should be exemplary and he should display the same obedience to law that he should inculcate in others.

"The city manager is the administrator for all the people, and in performing his duty he should serve without discrimination.

"A city manager should deal frankly with the Council as a unit, and not secretly with its individual members, and, similarly, should foster a spirit of cooperation between all employes of the city's organization.

"No city manager should take an active part in politics.

"A city manager will be known by his works, many of which may outlast him and, regardless of personal popularity or unpopularity, he should not curry favor or temporize, but should in a far-sighted way aim to benefit the community of today and posterity."

The contrast between these ideals of the new profession and those formerly prevalent in hundreds of City Halls, and perhaps still prevalent in many, may be partially responsible for the spread of this new system of city government, for it is spreading, and if the prophets in the field know what they are talking about will be seriously considered before long in every great city in the country.

November 16, 1924

MUNICIPAL RESEARCH AIDING CITY FINANCING

Bondholders Interested in Progress and Accomplishments of Civic Bodies.

Of prime interest to holders of municipal bonds is the progress that is being made along the lines of research by the various municipal research bureaus maintained by large cities throughout the country. Such accomplishments as the development of scientific budget making, modern accounting in city governments, systematic approach to public purchasing, application of standards in public personnel, the short ballot and responsible governmental organization, have been achieved by the various bureaus, in addition to the expansion of American political science to include practical administration and the responsibilities of citizenship.

The Governmental Research Conference, which is affiliated with the National Municipal League, in a brief discussion of the municipal research movement in America entitled, "Twenty Years of Municipal Research," points out that the various municipal research bureaus vary considerably in the manner of financing, in scope of work and in effectiveness.

The bureaus are divided into five groups, viz., those having independent existence, financed by voluntary contributions from public-spirited citizens; those independently organized but financed from community chests; those operating as departments of some larger, parent organization; those financed from city treasuries, and agencies doing municipal work under the name of taxpayers' associations. The bureau in New York falls in the first class.

Two agencies which do not fall in any of these classifications are the Boston Finance Commission, a research organization with a city charter, whose members are appointed by the Governor of Massachusetts and have the power to subpoena witnesses, take testimony under oath and compel the production of any official records, and the Institute for Public Service in this city, which makes surveys and carries on educational work without limiting itself to any city.

November 26, 1927

Exit the Boss, Enter the 'Leader'

By WARREN MOSCOW

IN less than a year, Frank Hague of Jersey City and Ed Kelly of Chicago, both of whom doubled in brass as Mayors and political bosses, have quit one or both of their jobs. In Kansas City, Jim Pendergast, son of the late Tom Pendergast, has pulled out by request and in Hoboken the McFeely brothers' edition of the Hague machine has crumpled like the only slightly older one-hoss shay.

Pendergast and McFeely got out because they had to. As to Kelly and Hague—two of the most powerful bosses of modern times—there is the well-grounded suspicion that they got out while the getting was good, before the electorate began kicking them around, too.

The luxury-loving Mr. Hague turned his Jersey City mayoralty over to his nephew in pretty much the way an eastern caliph would assign his household and perquisites to his favorite son; but it is still much too soon after the event to tell whether the old Hague machine will stand up long against a national trend which has been operating against the traditional big-city political machines.

In general, it is true, all around the country, that the city machines no longer control the vote the way they used to; and that they can no longer elect whom they please, when they please and how they please.

But that the machines are crumbling, that the old-fashioned boss can no longer proclaim and get away with an "I am the law" attitude, does not mean that political parties have become anachronisms. Just as the pot-bellied Alderman has been replaced by the paunchless Councilman, so is the boss being replaced by the "leader" and the machine by the "organization."

POLITICAL organizations, whether known as machines or organizations, will be around as long as we have a two-party system, with nominations for public office to be made by the party members. And there is pretty sure to be some dominant member or group to run the show. It was so in the days of the party caucus, held in the back room of McGillicuddy's saloon, and it is so today as the "boys"—and nobody else—go through the motions of picking candidates in legalized primary elections.

But the difference between organization and machine, between leader and boss, is more than a purely semantic one. It is a difference in methods—brought on by necessity—a difference in respectability, at least on the surface, demanded by changing times.

Because the boss was the product of the machine, even though he may have seemed both its progenitor and copyright owner, it is the change-over from machine to organization that has caused the mutation of boss to leader.

THE old machine *controlled* the vote. It took immigrants, made them citizens, supplied them with jobs, bailed them out in Night Court, kissed their babies and took their adolescents on picnics. It fixed traffic tickets for business men and winked at the violations of building and sanitary codes. It took various racial groups and saw to it that their most aggressive leaders were supplied with reasonably lucrative sinecures on the public payroll. Then, on election day, it took their votes in exchange, the citizenry knowing that their day-to-day destinies—if not their zoning laws and sanitation problems—were in good hands.

Of course, if the citizenry did not respond with a normal vote, just because of some extraneous issue like the tariff or the collapse of the foundations of the new jail, the organization took the votes anyhow. The organization did the counting—sometimes only the weighing—of the vote.

Gradually, over the years, the machine lost its power to do most of these things. The tide of immigration was dammed and the machines had no new crop of rapidly created citizens to help. Government welfare services replaced the clubhouse handout. Probation officers took over from the leader or his deputy in reviewing for the court the background of a youthful offender. Business men, during the depression, became more conscious of the organization "cut," as reflected in the tax rate, than grateful for the favors of the past. And, with the increased use of voting machines and Federal supervision of any election in which a Federal office was voted upon, it became tougher and tougher to steal votes. Those who did, got caught, as witness the recent Kansas City vote scandal.

SO the machine became obsolete and the "organization" slipped quietly in to take its place. The organization does not control the vote, it *influences* the vote. When it goes after racial and religious blocs—and both parties do—it does so by nominating a Negro to a higher office than ever before was offered to a member of his race, or an Italian for State-wide office, or a member of the Jewish faith for a post on the highest court of the State. It sees that its members in Congress vote "right"—for local rather than broad governmental reasons—on allocations of Federal aid abroad or on anti-lynching legislation. Similarly, it sees that its local legislative members petition Congress for action in support of the Vatican or a free Palestine.

It can no longer win the vote by the beer party and the free handout, but it can woo the laboring man by jacking up wage scales or it can increase unemployment insurance payments and prolong their duration.

Naturally the "boss" who sat out on the sidewalk, presiding in tireless and vestless grandeur over a very informal receiving line, has been displaced by the leader—serge-clad, neat and conscious of issues. His alliances may be with the community's entrenched respectability, rather than the underworld, but he is not necessarily more scrupulous—just more careful and much smoother. In most cases, the leader is personally "money honest." This, of course, is not necessarily a recent development. Many political bosses of the past refused to go along with George Washington Plunkett's contention that there was such a thing as "honest graft."

But look at the difference in type today between the old boss and the new leader. The background is different to start with. In the old days a good ward boss, possibly restricted in education to grammar school or less, rose, nevertheless, to be a good city or county boss, and, if hard-bitten, tough, practical and ambitious enough, got to be a State boss whose name was known and whose word was law for miles around. Intrinsically, despite exceptions like Boies Penrose and Mark Hanna, the usual city or State boss was just the best of the ward bosses. He understood his colleagues and preserved most of their characteristics.

Today, the big bosses are not the men who came up as ward bosses or district leaders. They are business men, Governors, United States Senators. Harry F. Byrd's Virginia organization has been called the tightest and best organization in the country today. And Byrd, a Senator and member of an old family, is its active lead-

Richard Croker (1843-1922)
He rose from New York's Gas House Gang to run Tammany like a military machine, hobnobbed with royalty, built his own race track.

T. J. Pendergast (1870-1945)
Overlord of Missouri politics, he was the prototype of boss rule ("I feed 'em and I vote 'em"), went to jail for income tax fraud.

Frank Hague (1876-)
"The last of the barons," he is a political boss of the old city-machine school. His own words: "I am the law in Jersey City."

Edward H. Crump (1875-)
He has held public office twenty-three times. A great political showman, he is still the boss man of Memphis, Tenn.

er. In New York and Indiana, to take two States at random, there are powerful Republican organizations of which the active as well as the titular head is the Governor.

In Indiana, where they play politics for keeps, this writer saw Governor Gates run a recent State convention with an iron hand. The incumbent United States Senator was dropped as the party nominee because the Governor wanted the State chairman in the job. A judge of a high State court was dropped, local reporters said, because he had dared cast a lone dissenting vote in that court in a case in which the organization was interested.

IN New York, Tom Dewey had been elected District Attorney of New York County and had made one unsuccessful though spectacular race for Governor when the Republican leaders of the Legislature—representing the party in the State as a whole—signed and published a solemn declaration that in matters of policy (State-wide politics) they would consult with Mr. Dewey and be guided by his judgment. That was in 1939, and in the intervening years he has consolidated his hold to the point where no one questions his one-man leadership of the party in the State today. Many a loyal Republican would be hard pressed to give the name and initials of the titular State chairman.

In near-by Nassau County, J. Russel Sprague, a popular, efficient county executive—the equivalent of Mayor under Nassau's special charter—is as powerful as Frank Hague was in Jersey City in his heyday. He and his organization make the law, but do not proclaim that they are the law.

HOW do they do it? In the old days there was a political axiom that a boss should not run for public office, but should put his men in office, should be the power behind the throne, able at all times to dictate who should hold what job, either elective or appointive. As the machines went slowly into the discard, the successful remaining bosses were those who paid no attention to the rule. Hague and Kelly, Crump in Memphis, held on longer than the others of their type because they began to dictate policy, too, from the administrative and policy-making public jobs they held.

The new leaders dictate policy and use the patronage whip to enforce their views. Many a balky legislator has given up his objections—founded on whim, prejudice or principle—after a series of phone calls. The Governor's office calls his home county chairman, tells him the legislator's vote is needed and asks if the county chairman will please see that the legislator changes his mind. If the county chairman can't control the legislator, maybe the county chairman is not the proper person to dispense patronage in his county. The chairman gets the idea and the legislator is notified of the trouble he is causing. Of course, if he is just going to be a persistent trouble-maker, interfering with the broad policies of the party in the State, maybe he'll have trouble in the next primary election. The legislator gets the idea.

In one case a legislator who declined to take persistent hints like that, found that his past had been raked into and some disagreeable incidents disclosed, and the next hint was that those might be disclosed to his constituency. This time he saw the light.

TALENTED

One of the most colorful if least known of big-city political bosses was Martin Lomasney, the "Boston Warwick," who was a leader in Democratic politics in Massachusetts for nearly fifty years before his death in 1933. Of him and his brother, also a politician, this election anecdote was told:

A political opponent was making the rounds of Boston polling places in a last-minute effort to recruit supporters. At one he found Joseph Lomasney swinging the vote of a deaf and dumb man by haranguing him energetically with his hands in deaf and dumb language. Despairing of any success there, the opponent went on to another polling place where he tried to outtalk Martin Lomasney in a discussion with several Irish voters. Martin won the day handily by addressing them in their beloved Gaelic.

JOB patronage can't win an election any more, with the extension of civil service, the increase in the size of the electorate and the general lack of interest on the part of the public in low-paying county, city, State and Federal jobs. But it remains extremely important for control of the party organization, indispensable for remaining in power.

So it is not surprising that a systematic, efficient, and comprehensive job-dispensing program exists wherever there is a strong organization in control. In one State, where the Governor was "leader," he had one special secretary whose job was patronage dispensing. To this secretary were referred all requests by county chairmen and city leaders. He would weigh the possibilities, with an eye to present and future party policies, and pass the recommendation up higher—to the Governor, if the job was important enough either in salary or favor-dispensing potentialities. The recommendation also went to the State chairman. When both had approved, the applicant was appointed by the appropriate department head. And, to eliminate any possibility of error or later dispute, the Governor and the State chairman both signed the card of recommendation.

FOR lesser jobs there are certain to be, and in this case there were, local patronage dispensers, for an area in the State, who did the preliminary sifting of possible appointees and forwarded what amounted to final recommendations to the Capitol, even though there they went through an additional processing. The ramifications can best be realized when it is understood that appointees to staff an anti-racial discrimination commission were so selected.

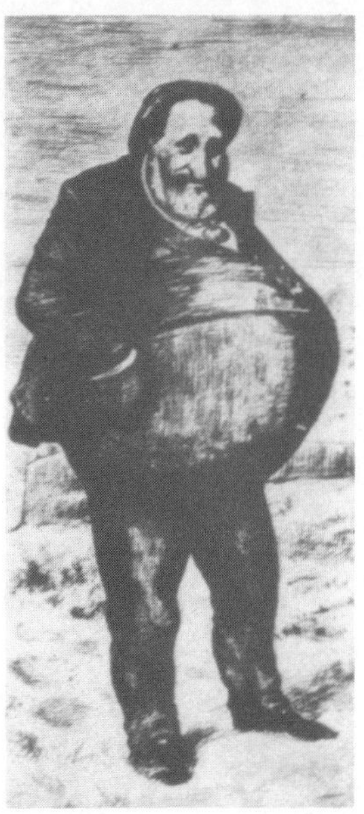

A caricature of Boss Tweed by Thomas Nast, whose crusade against Tammany was famous.

Job patronage can be, and is, defended on the ground that those in sympathy with a governmental policy should be the ones appointed to administer it. But job patronage in policy making or administering posts is also important for the favors patronage it carries with it.

DOING favors has been the way of making friends for political organizations ever since they were started—the old machines or their more modern replacements. Priority on the liquor license list, assignment of a building application to an inspector who will look on it with friendly tolerance, passage of a bill through the Legislature which helps some particular group—such are reasonably frequent demonstrations of favor patronage; and if the man on top is to benefit, either through election support or party contributions, the deputy commissioners, the non-salaried board members, even the legislative leaders, must be men who recognize the paramount importance of the organization and the man who heads it.

They must owe their positions to him, and usually do, or feel that their continuance in those jobs is a matter he can control.

SO the new leaders find public office, high public office, a good place from which to run an organization. Many an old-time leader who did take office contented himself with a non-policy-making sinecure which gave him a headquarters and a secretaryship in which he could place, at public expense, the most trusted of his aides.

Now it is the press secretaries and the ghost writers who, the leader makes sure, are in sufficient supply to do the job of influencing public opinion in order to influence votes and win elections.

Compare the photographs of Dewey, Gates, Byrd and Sprague with those of Croker, Taggart and Bill Barnes and you see the difference that a change in methods from machine to organization has made in the men who rule, the change from bosses to leaders.

Somehow the old-time, big-city machines were never able to achieve respectability, while the new organizations have it as a matter of course. Old Charles Francis Murphy, the Tammany leader who developed Al Smith, Jim Foley and Bob Wagner, as well as others, came closer in his declining years to achieving it for Tammany, but he never actually got there.

And Charles Murphy, knowing that, used to complain that if the Democrats did anything wrong the public cried, "Stop thief," but that "the Republicans can get away with murder in this town."

THE difference, of course, was that the Democrats at one time or another had been caught at thieving, while the Republicans had never been caught at murder, or even at lesser crimes. The old-time machines did steal blatantly and openly. They had the Robin Hood attitude that it was okay to take things from the rich to give to the poor, with a percentage of the take for operating expenses and a good time for the boys.

Those days are gone, possibly forever. Modern improvements have brought big business methods to the field of politics.

June 22, 1947

TWO TROUSER SUITS
BOND
MORE MEN WEAR BOND CLOTHES THAN ANY OTHER CLOTHES IN AMERICA
RIOTOUS RED SKELTON
"WHISTLING IN DIXIE"
ANN RUTHERFORD
RAGS RAGLAND
FIRST NEW YORK SHOWING
F. W. WOOLWORTH CO
Whelan
Whelan
PERFUMES SODA DRUGS COSMETICS

CHAPTER 2

The Modern Metropolis

'he lure of downtown.

'ourtesy The New York Times

CITY POPULATION NOW PASSES RURAL

About 4,000,000 More in Urban Total, Census Estimates Show.

GROWTH 7½ TIMES AS FAST

WASHINGTON, Sept. 30.—Cities are increasing in population seven and a half times as fast as the rural districts, the Census Bureau disclosed tonight in a compilation of figures covering approximately 85 per cent. of the new census. The figures indicated that the completed census would show the majority of the population to be city dwellers.

For the last ten years rural growth was only one-third as great as it was in the previous decade, but the cities almost maintained their rate of growth, getting five new inhabitants from 1910 to 1920 for each six added during the preceding ten years. All population centres, even the county hamlets and towns, showed a greater proportionate increase than the purely rural districts. The greatest increases, however, were in cities of 10,000 or more inhabitants.

While the bureau attempts no explanation of the reasons for the increasing migration to the cities each year during the last decade, presumably higher wages, a shorter working day and home conveniences attracted the rural population, especially during the war, when wages in big industrial centres went up rapidly.

Although showing a check in the rate of population growth for the country as a whole, the bureau's figures indicated that the complete census would place the total number of inhabitants of continental United States at approximately 105,768,100, a gain of 13,795,840, or 15 per cent. Cities will absorb the biggest part of this increase.

Cities About 4,000,000 Ahead.

The movement of the people will place the urban population at approximately 54,796,100 and the rural population at 50,972,000. In 1910 the rural population outstripped that of the cities by almost 7,000,000, there being 49,348,883 in the country and 42,623,383 in the cities.

"For several censuses," it was said in the bureau announcement, "the country has not been growing as rapidly as the city, but the difference appears to be greater at this census than ever before."

The urban population, the announcement added, increased at a rate of 25.2 per cent., while that of the rural districts, including the villages and towns under 2,500 population, was 3.4 per cent. For the strictly farm territory the rate was 3.2 per cent., and that of the villages was 4.7 per cent.

Among the urban centres cities exceeding 50,000 increased 26.4 per cent., those of 10,000 to 50,000 grew 26.7 per cent. and those of 2,500 to 10,000 18.8 per cent. From 1900 to 1910 the percentage rates of increases for these three classifications of cities were 35.6, 33.7 and 27.8 respectively.

Up to ten days ago, according to the announcement, the count of population, estimated at 85 per cent. complete, had reached 92,098,281. For purposes of comparison between city and country the bureau reduced the figure to 90,586,742 by eliminating populations of insular possessions and places in the United States for which comparison was deemed inadvisable because of new boundaries.

Of this total population that classified as urban was reported as 52,494,749, the cities over 50,000 population having 32,533,038 inhabitants those of 10,000 to 50,000 having 11,771,224 and those of 2,500 to 10,000 having 8,190,487. The rural population was 32,025,961 in the country districts and 6,066,032 in towns under 2,500 in population.

Kentucky's population is 2 416,013, an increase of 126,108, or 5.5 per cent. in ten years, while the population of North Dakota is 645,730, an increase of 68,674, or 11.9 per cent., over that of 1910.

These figures, made public today by the Census Bureau, show that Kentucky's rate of growth in the last decade fell off slightly, while that of North Dakota declined 68.9 per cent. as compared with the previous decade.

Other population figures announced by the Census Bureau today are:

Lead, S. D., 5,013; decrease 3,379, or 40.3 per cent.

Deadwood, S. D., 2,403; decrease 1,250, or 34.2 per cent.

Hailey, Idaho, 1,201; decrease 30, or 2.4 per cent.

San Angelo, Texas, 9,392; decrease 929, or 9 per cent.

Douglas County, Nebraska, containing Omaha, 204,524; increase 35,978, or 21.3 per cent.

Jefferson County, Alabama, containing Birmingham, 309,513; increase 83,037, or 36.7 per cent.

Hoquiam, Wash. (revised), 10,058; increase 1,887, or 23.1 per cent.; previously announced, 9,885.

The population of West Virginia will be announced tomorrow.

October 1, 1920

OUR FUTURE CITIES

The Social Aspects of the Trend to Great Centres.

What is the social significance of the continuing drift toward the cities, as revealed in the new census? What does it mean for the future of the nation? These questions are discussed in the following articles. The writer is Professor of Sociology at the University of Chicago.

By WILLIAM F. OGBURN.

Reports from the new census show great increases in our urban population. We have visions of a new civilization of great cities on our continent. The world has always been boastful of its cities—Babylon, Athens, Rome, Florence, Paris, London. And today our census tells us of a larger Detroit, great city erected on the automobile; of a greater Los Angeles, created by seekers of pleasure and Utopian climate; of a new Miami, a tribute to our increasing wealth and the remarkable mobility of our population; of Chicago, transportation centre of the continent, expanding and violent with its tremendous energy; of Atlanta and Memphis, symbols of the new industrialism planted on the plantation culture of the old South.

And so we look forward to great cities on our new continent which will be comparable to the Old World cities, such as Berlin, Munich, Antwerp, Brussels, Vienna. They will not be the same, of course, for each city has its own personality. We cannot have a Rome, or Venice or a Paris, but who shall say that we shall not have great cities with just as much personality?

These are our first impressions and they may be right. But let us look a little more closely into the factors of this great urban growth and see what we find.

Factors That Make a City.

Cities are first of all a result of transportation facilities. Cities are made up of peoples who do not raise their food, but who can get food only by exchanging something else that they make in cities for food. It is railroads that have made cities possible. There were a few cities before the coming of the railroads, but they were on the coast or on rivers, dependent on boats.

The second prerequisite for cities is the possession of skill or machines for making things in these denser areas that can be exchanged for food. This prerequisite was supplied along with the use of steam in the form of tools and machines. And with transportation and manufacture, lo, the city, which so changes our habits, our standards of morality, our family life, the types of our pleasures and recreations, our birth rate and our health, our outlook on life, and really creates a new world.

These twin forces of the industrial revolution show no slackening in growth. Indeed, never before in the history of the world have transportation facilities grown so fast as in the last decade, with the automobile, the autobus, the paved roads, the electric train and the airplane. And we are also told that never before in the history of the world has there ever been so wide and so rapid a diffusion of the use of machines, bringing with their use more power, but more "technological" unemployment.

The horsepower back of these machines is now said to be so great that it is the equivalent of each person having the services of 100 slaves. So with the tremendous growth of these twin forces that make cities it is not surprising that the growth of urban areas has been so great, nor that with new machines like the camera, the gas engine, the electric motor and the airplane we should have cities like Los Angeles, Detroit, Schenectady and Wichita.

Urbanization Goes On.

The curves of these forces show no indications of declining, hence these indexes point to still greater urbanization of the United States. There is one other influence that makes the prophecy of an even larger number of cities almost sure to be fulfilled: the increasing efficiency in the growing of food products on the farm. If the methods of efficiency that come with farm machinery and sciences as now demonstrated in certain farm areas should be extended widely throughout the rural United States we could not find a market for the produce unless the countries around the rim of the Pacific become the buyers. This means that a smaller and smaller percentage of farmers will be able to supply a larger and larger number of city dwellers with food. Perhaps one-quarter of farm population may feed three-quarters of urban population. Here is the explanation of why we are losing farm population, and why there are fewer farmers than at any time in twenty years despite a great growth in total population.

The picture of the situation that we get from histories is that of a swarm of people coming from Europe, overrunning the land, cutting down forests as locusts cut down the leaves, yielding wonderful farms but routing the game animals and leaving rivers that flood their banks. Today this process is being exactly reversed. Having given land to settlers, who cleared away the trees for farming, we are now buying it back in the form of abandoned farms, planting trees on it, and I am told the taxpayers are willing to vote the money because they like to hunt in the young forests.

So the end of the growth of cities is not in sight. The end of the growth of cities in number may not be in sight, but the end of the growth of cities in size may be. I say may be, for there is little evidence from the census returns so far; indeed, the evidence points in the opposite direction. New York is bigger by 24 per cent and Chicago by 25 per cent within ten years, which is a much faster rate than that of the general population, which shows an increase of 16.1 per cent. Yet when the data on smaller places and on the movement of manufactures is analyzed it may be that much manufacturing, such as shoe manufacture, textiles, gas ment trades, printing and others will be shown to have left the larger cities for smaller places where land and labor and living costs are cheaper. So that while the larger cities are growing, they are not growing as fast as they would if there had not been this movement of manufactures to the smaller places.

But why is this movement recent? It has been known for a long time that wages were cheaper in the villages and small towns than in the cities, and it has been shown that the great differences in cost of living are not so much between regions like the South, the West and the East as between large places and small. There is, of course, a lag to be expected before any change of movement. But probably the changes in the transportation and in the transmission of power are the precipitating forces. Modern transportation and manufacture, and hence cities, have been built on power in the form of steam from coal. The only way steam power can be transplanted is through pipes or belting on revolving wheels, never over any great distance. Therefore, large factories or clusters of them.

But now coal makes power available in the form of electricity, which can be transmitted long distances—hundreds of miles—with little loss at low costs. The truck tends to free the factory from the tyranny of railroads, with the different long and short haul rates and their basing point system. A truck can take a load of freight as quickly over a number of miles on paved country highways as it can a few blocks in a congested city. So an analysis of the underlying factors of the truck and electricity point to an accentuation of the growth of the town and small city, and secondarily to a possible decentralization of the very large city.

Power Built the Suburbs.

The dispersion of the big city has been under way for a quarter of a century, but it has never been clearly seen as a possible step in an evolutionary process. About a quarter of a century ago the automobile and electric railroad began to make the suburbs in earnest, so that they have become now huge bedroom cities. The moving picture and the chain store are changing these bedroom cities along the way toward real communities.

Indeed, the large city in a certain sense has disappeared without our knowing it. Early cities were enclosed areas, walled in, so their boundary lines were quite definite. But what is the boundary line of New York or of London? When we asked which was the larger, Los Angeles or San Francisco, the answer depended on a more or less accidental boundary line. The truth is that the large city has been replaced by the metropolitan area, for which as yet we have no name, a creation of modern communication. It is not a political unit, we have no government for it, yet it is an economic and sociological reality. The wall around the medieval city was of the greatest importance. The boundary line of a large city within a metropolitan area is a line on paper.

The decentralizing of cities into metropolitan areas is expected to continue as long as our oil wells hold out or a substitute for present gasoline is found. In this process the telephone should not be passed unnoticed as a contributing factor. Telephone bills for all the conversation necessary will not amount to the differentials in land and labor costs. With the habit of using the long distance telephone growing, rates will be reduced. Differentiation between local and long distance calls will be less significant. The telephone may mean the decentralization of offices as electric power is decentralizing the factory.

Another feature of the city which has been said to draw the moth to the flame has been the attractiveness of its recreation. The city is also more intellectually stimulating in certain ways. But with the radio, the talking pictures and television, the possible social effects of which are not in the least foreseen, who can say what the possibilities of spreading recreation and intellectual stimulation may be? These should also be added to the agencies of decentralization.

Finally, it should be clearly seen that the countryside does not remain unaffected by these forces that are urbanizing the nation, that are building towns and small cities, that are lessening the growth of great cities and that have created that new social unit—the metropolitan area.

Only a century and a half ago all nations were primarily agricultural, nine-tenths or more of the population of these nations living on farms. The city is the new thing. To it were first diffused the effects of steam and the machines. But why should not the effects of steam and the machines spread to the farms as well? So they seem to be.

Farms Are Mechanized Now.

Farms have the combine, the tractor, and now the mechanical cotton picker. Stone roads are being extended and dirt roads closed. There is the truck and automobile, and it is to be expected that the electric wire soon will be in the reach of most farms, putting electric power at the farmer's disposal. Radios, telephones and television are as open to farms as to city homes. A farm may become a sort of factory to utilize the by-products of what the earth and sun produce.

So when we read the returns of the new census of 1930, telling us that Middletown has increased in population 20 per cent in ten years, we note that the implications of the simple statement are far-reaching. These urban percentage increases of which we read in the newspapers from day to day are harbingers of a new era and a new civilization to come. They signify a diffusion of the culture of the large city to the smaller cities, towns and country districts, an urbanized United States.

August 10, 1930

WHY LOS ANGELES GAINED TENTH PLACE

Eastern Observer Tells How Much More Than a Movie Metropolis the City Is.

HOME OF MANY INDUSTRIES

Centre of Rich Oil and Mining Regions—Its Splendid Water and Good Roads Systems.

By CORNELIUS VANDERBILT, Jr.

LOS ANGELES, Cal., Nov. 1.—Why is Los Angeles the largest city in the Far West today? We hear so much concerning the climate, the movies, the boastfulness of Southern California that we are a little loath to believe them when they tell us about Los Angeles. The city is not built by the climate nor by the movies. It was pioneered and constructed by men. It is the community spirit from every other State in the Union concentrated in the space of a few square miles which gives Los Angeles a net population of 576,673 inhabitants, according to the 1920 census. This official figure shows this city to be nearly 70,000 greater in population than the next largest city on the Pacific Coast, and establishes it as the forty-fourth city in the world. Since 1910 Los Angeles has come from seventeenth place to tenth in the United States. This gain in population during the last ten years was nearly five times the average gain for the United States.

The motion picture industry in reality plays but a small part. Of the total city population only 15,000 are annually employed by motion picture firms. True, millions in capital are invested in the plants, and the payroll approximates $30,000,000 annually, but these are small figures in comparison to the totals derived from other industries which are making Los Angeles.

Larger and much richer in resources than many of the duchies and principalities of Europe, and greater in area than Connecticut, is the region of which Los Angeles is the centre. The city was founded in 1781 by a handful of colonists who had been recruited in Mexico. At that time it bore the sonorous title of Neustra Sonora la Reina de Los Angeles. As late as 1880 the census gave it a population of but a scant 11,000. Business was dull and there was no sign that the city was on the eve of a marvelous growth. Five years later, on Nov. 9, 1885, the last spike was driven in the Atlantic & Pacific Railway, thus completing a new overland route from the Atlantic to the Pacific. The great real estate boom of 1886 is a matter of history. The wonderful way in which Los Angeles held up under the reaction that inevitably followed the collapse of the speculative period of 1895 is still another chapter to add to its annals. From this time on the growth of the city has been wonderfully rapid.

A Region of Good Roads.

Twenty-five years ago there was not a single paved street in this area, and today there are 1,236 miles of paved boulevards within the city limits. Millions have been spent on these highways, which radiate like the spokes of a wheel from the heart of the city to all points of the surrounding country. There are more than 400 miles of improved, but not paved, roads within an area of four miles from the heart of the city, which represent the highest development of construction. This is admitted to comprise the best developed county road system in the United States. More than 111,435 Los Angeles automobiles were registered last year. This is an average of one vehicle for every five persons and is said to be the record of the world. The Los Angeles Auto Speedway, open this year, is the finest track for cyclonic motor events in the country. It is an ellipse, one and one-fourth miles in circumference, and has seating accommodations for 104,000 persons.

Industrially speaking, Los Angeles is the growing metropolis of the Southwest. It now has approximately 3,200 manufacturing concerns In the last seventeen years the increase in the products of factories in this area was in excess of 800 per cent. In 1919 the investment in factories here was more than $200,000,000. The product of the factories for 1919 was a little less than $400,000,000. Government figures show that the 1,911 manufacturing establishments in the city turned out products to the value of $103,458,000 in 1919. These figures do not include many plants just outside the corporation limits.

Attractions for Workingmen.

In the last year 313 new industries have located here. The greatest of these will undoubtedly be the Goodyear Tire & Rubber Company of Akron, Ohio, which is now constructing a plant to cost $25,000,000. This company has purchased a tract of 800 acres and expects to employ more than 8,000 in the twelve buildings which are in process of construction. In a conversation with H. Osterlock, general manager of the Goodyear Company, I was informed that the efficiency of its employes was 50 per cent higher in Los Angeles than anywhere else in the country. There are several explanations of this. An employe can for a reasonable amount purchase his own bungalow in as fine a locality as the wealthiest resident of other cities. He doesn't have to buy heavy clothes, for the temperature varies but little the year round. He seldom has to resort to fuel, for heat alone, and when he does it is at his back door. He has schools maintained by the highest per capita rate in the country. The average laborer can get more out of life here than elsewhere. It is, as Mr. Osterlock said, "worth the discount on the pay-check to reside in Los Angeles."

Within a few miles of the city nearly one-fourth of the entire oil supply of the United States is produced, and yet we hear less of these great fields than those of Texas and Oklahoma. The total yield in 1918 was more than 100,000,000 barrels, and half of this was produced from wells within an area of two miles from the heart of the city. The Standard Oil Company operates a large refinery at El Segundo, with a daily capacity of 30,000 barrels. Today the petroleum industry is attracting the attention of the world. The oil produced in the Los Angeles fields differs from that of the more Eastern States being of a heavier grade, with an asphaltum base, and it is used almost exclusively for fuel. Railroad experience shows that four barrels of fuel oil at 75 cents a barrel are equivalent to one ton of coal costing $8 The vast store of oil available is another important factor in contributing to the industrial activities of the city. Identified with it is the increasing production of natural gas. This product is now piped to Los Angeles, and is used as fuel in the manufacture of glass, steel and various clay products.

Centre of Rich Mineral Fields.

This city is also the centre of a number of rich mineral fields. The chief products, exclusive of petroleum, are gold and borax. There are also produced silver, copper, clay, gypsum, cement, lime and other mineral substances. The manufacture of mining machinery and supplies gives employment to a large number of people. There are five large cement mills in operation in the city, and their product is being exported freely. Pumice and talc are now being shipped to the Eastern factories. Large deposits of silica offer opportunities for glass manufacturing. Vast bodies of high-grade iron ore await the coming of blast furnaces. Many chemical establishments have been established within the city in the last few years.

One of the most stupendous enterprises ever undertaken by an American municipality was the building of the Los Angeles aqueduct, which involved the acquisition of the rights to the flow of the Owens River and tributary streams which drain the eastern face of the Sierra Nevada range. Begun in 1904, the aqueduct was formally dedicated and placed in operation in 1913. The total cost was $24,600,000. This aqueduct provides a domestic supply for more than 1,000,000 people and for the irrigation of 135,000 acres of land. In addition, by taking advantage of natural conditions, the city from this source is able to generate hydro-electric energy estimated at 120,000 horsepower. It is the longest aqueduct in the world, bringing the water to the city a distance of more than 250 miles from the snow-clad slopes of Mt. Whitney. The project included the building of six great reservoirs. It carries ten times as much water as all the aqueducts of Rome combined. It is designed to deliver a minimum of 258,000,000 gallons daily to a reservoir twenty-five miles northwest of the Los Angeles City Hall. The system is gravity throughout. No pumping plants are required.

This great water course is constructed entirely of steel and concrete. About 1,250,000 barrels of cement were required for lining the aqueduct. An army of nearly 4,000 men was employed, the work being carried on at forty-five different points at once. The water flows through fifty-two miles of tunnel, twelve miles of siphon, 100 miles of lined and covered conduit, forty miles of open canal, twenty-one miles of open unlined canal and nine miles of reservoirs. Much preparatory work had to be done, including the construction of 225 miles of mountain roads and trails, many of which were cut in solid rock, as well as the installing of a telephone system 350 miles long. In addition, the city caused to be built a broad-gauge railroad from Mojave to Owenyo, a distance of 142 miles across the Mojave Desert. The city also built three hydro-electric power plants to generate power and light for camps and tunnels, which it still maintains. A municipal light and power system for the whole city is about completed.

Los Angeles has a splendid street railway system. The total mileage, all electric, is 591. Most of this has four tracks abreast and operates a car every minute and a quarter. The interurban electric roads radiating from the city have an aggregate of 1,695 miles of double track.

Los Angeles shows a smaller increase in the cost of living than any other of fifty principal cities in which Federal investigations were made, according to detailed figures from the Bureau of Labor Statistics in Washington. Among the cities enumerated in the governmental statement of April 22 were Atlanta, Baltimore, Birmingham, Boston, Buffalo, Chicago, Cincinnati, Cleveland, Denver, Detroit, Indianapolis, Kansas City, Louisville, Milwaukee, Minneapolis, New Orleans, New York, Omaha, Philadelphia, Pittsburgh, Portland, St. Louis, Salt Lake City, San Francisco and Seattle.

The price of land in the Los Angeles district varies greatly, ranging from $50 to $100 per acre for lands adapted to grain, hay, and deciduous fruits, without irrigation, up to $500 per acre for first-class citrus land, with ample water rights. There are bearing orange groves inside the city limits of Los Angeles that pay good interest on $3,000 an acre. A mistaken idea prevails throughout the East, to some extent, that farming is carried on in this section only by means of irrigation, and that without it crops would be a failure. For all grains and Winter crops irrigation is not employed. Corn is irrigated in some localities. On irrigated lands two or three crops a year are frequently raised. With an artificial supply of water the farmer is rendered independent of the season's rains. The production of his land is thereby enormously increased.

The shipment of citrus fruits from this section last season amounted to 47,736 carloads. Deciduous fruits are shipped canned, fresh and dried. An active demand for dried fruit has grown up in foreign countries. Walnuts and strawberries are important crops. Alfalfa, a most valuable forage plant, is cut from six to nine times a year. Quantities of wheat and barley are raised. Corn sometimes grows to a height of twenty feet. Pumpkins have been raised weighing more than 400 pounds. Hundreds of acres are devoted to the cultivation of celery, which is sent East by the trainload. I once saw a freight train of thirty-four cars filled with nothing but celery. The largest olive grove in the world is within the city limits. It consists of over 1,800 acres, with sixty trees to the acre.

San Pedro, the Harbor of Los Angeles.

San Pedro, the harbor of Los Angeles, was discovered in 1542, but it was more than 300 years before any development work was done on it. It did not enter its present phase of improvement until 1909. The Federal Government has expended on improvement work there since 1871 nearly $6,000,000. The city is spending $10,000,000 on further improvement of this great port. Protecting the outer harbor is the massive rock breakwater, more than two miles in length, begun by the Government in 1896 and completed in 1910, at a total expenditure of $3,500,000. It terminates at the seaward end in a magnificent steel and concrete lighthouse with an occulting light of 67,900 candle power. The dredging of the inner channels was completed a few days ago, giving the city one of the finest harbors in the world. United States pierhead lines as now established permit the development of approximately twenty-four miles of wharf frontage. At the present time there are 35,283 linear feet of wharves in the harbor, of which 13,315 feet are owned and operated by the municipality. A six-story reinforced concrete warehouse, containing eleven acres of floor space, fully equipped with elevators, gravity chutes, hoists, scales and sprinkler system, stands on the shore of the inner harbor.

Six transit sheds, each 100 feet wide and totaling more than 4,600 feet in length, have been constructed. All the municipal wharves are on channels having a depth of thirty-five feet of water at low tide. On the shores of the outer harbor there are immense lumber yards, where vessels may discharge their cargoes direct, for Los Angeles is the greatest lumber importing city in the world.

Shipbuilding was born of the war. It is now among the city's new industries. Before the war there was not a yard south of San Francisco which could build a steel ship. So Los Angeles dredged out the swampland and made a record for the United States in turning out a steel ship from the time they started to build their yard to the day it was completed. A city not accustomed to iron and steel went with its own heart to work, and the result astonished America.

Los Angeles is credited with paying a larger per capita tax for education than any other city in the United States. There are now 800 school buildings within the city proper, and even this number is not enough to accommodate the ever-increasing population. The private schools in Los Angeles are many and varied. There are several large business colleges and two universities. The valuation of school property is $18,514,928. The combined salaries of the 5,147 teachers reached a total of $6,765,213 last year. The number of pupils enrolled is about 178,432. Only Massachusetts and Nebraska surpass California in the matter of educational facilities for the very young. Los Angeles leads the cities of the Coast in this most important department.

When we judge the size of a city we must necessarily know some of its financial assets. The bank clearings of the twenty-six Los Angeles banks for 1919 were $2,329,401,197. The post office business for the same year amounted to $3,271,849.96, while the valuation of the building permits was close to $30,000,000. The assessed valuation of the city on Aug. 1 of this year, according to Government figures, was $629,478,343 for the area of 365.67 square miles.

Today I am sitting in our bungalow watching the greatest city on the Pacific Coast at my feet. Thirty miles to the east I can see the snowclad peaks of the Sierra Madres, ten miles west the broad expanse of the Pacific, three miles north the black forests of the high Sierras, and, as far as the eye can reach to the south, the citrus groves for which Southern California is renowned. It is a romantic and interesting sight, and I believe that before the next decade passes this City of the Angels will have passed the million mark, and in doing so will have placed itself as the fifth city of the United States.

November 21, 1920

Bush Terminal Docks, South Brooklyn, Where Vast Quantities of New York's Manufactures Are Loaded on Outgoing Steamships.

New York as Centre of Manufactures

Ahead of All Other American Cities in Output, With Miles of Factories Over Areas Formerly Devoted to Retail Trade or Residences

WITH an increased output of 13.1 per cent. in the Federal census period 1909-1914, New York City is more than holding its own as America's chief manufacturing city, not only as regards the number of new industrial establishments, but in value and volume of finished products as well. Furthermore, this city leads all other municipalities in the extraordinary diversity of its manufactures.

Just what the metropolitan city of the United States measures up to as a manufacturing centre is revealed in a tabulated summary prepared by the Federal Bureau of the Census, giving the results of the census of industries taken here and covering the year 1914. This census, which later will be elaborated into a volume of comprehensive information about New York's manufactures, will serve as the official directory of local industries until the next enumeration is made, which will be in 1919.

In order to visualize New York's commanding position as a manufacturing centre, it should be pointed out that this city surpasses Chicago and Philadelphia combined—the second and third most important industrial centres of the country—in the value of products turned out annually. New York's showing was all the more remarkable because of the fact that 1914, the year to which the Federal census relates, was a period in which industrial activity was somewhat below

normal. As a matter of fact, the period from 1909 to 1914 was not one of great industrial growth. In this connection it is interesting to note that, although industrial initiative throughout the country was below normal, New York in the last census period increased the number of its industrial establishments by 3,700, against a gain of 458 for Chicago, and Philadelphia 79.

All told, New York City contains 29,621 establishments, the output of which amounts to $2,292,831,693, whereas Chicago, the nearest rival, had in 1914 10,114 industrial plants, which produced goods valued at $1,483,498,416. Philadelphia totaled $784,499,633, and Detroit, which ranks fourth in the list, had an output officially returned at $400,347,912. In contrast with the varied character of New York's manufactures, Detroit's production related principally to automobiles and their parts.

The industrial prosperity of New York is also emphasized by the increasing tendency of manufactures to centre in this city, although the tendency throughout the country, as a whole, is toward decentralization. Incidentally, these facts show the incorrectness of the idea, often expressed, that New York City is unable to hold its important lines of manufacture. Further than this, the variety of manufactures here is a guarantee of both stability and prosperity. On this account it is noteworthy that of the twenty-eight important lines of manufacture which show a tendency to concentrate in a limited number of cities New York City is the greatest centre for twelve, the second city in importance for three more, the third city for another two and the fourth and sixth in importance for two others.

These industries are as follows:

PER CENT. OF UNITED STATES TOTAL MANUFACTURED IN NEW YORK CITY.

New York City leads in:	P.C.
Artificial flowers, feathers, and plumes	85.8
Clocks	19.9
Clothing, men's, including shirts	34.7
Clothing, women's	71.7
Dyeing and finishing textiles, exclusive of that done in mills	7.7
Fur goods	66.6
Furnishing goods, men's	40.9
Hair work	50.4
Ink, printing	44.2
Millinery and lace goods	62.0
Pens, fountain, stylographic and gold	68.9
Pipes, tobacco	62.2
New York City is second in:	
Hosiery and knit goods, (not including hand-knit goods)	7.2
Jewelry	25.3
Silk goods, including throwsters	5.9
New York City is third in:	
Automobiles	1.5
Slaughtering and meat packing	6.6
New York City is fourth in:	
Hats, fur, felt	9.6
New York City is sixth in:	
Boots and shoes, including cut stock and findings	4.4

Many of the details regarding the city's pre-eminence in the manufacturing field are highly significant. Since the last census was taken in 1909, for instance, New York has increased its percentage of the country's manufacture of women's clothing by 2.4 per cent., although in the same period the importance of Philadelphia decreased 6 per cent., and that of Chicago remained about stationary. Another increase recorded had to do with the dyeing and finishing of textiles, this city having increased its percentage during the five-year period 5 per cent., although the percentages of Philadelphia and Paterson correspondingly decreased.

Also, during the period New York City increased its share of the production of hosiery and knit goods 1 per cent., although Philadelphia failed to make a gain, while production of these goods declined in such prominent centres as Utica, Amsterdam, Little Falls, and Cohoes. The City of New York made a notable gain, too, in the production of jewelry, showing the largest percentage of increase of any of the important jewelry manufacturing cities. Still another fact developed by the Government's figures was that New York increased its percentage as a shoe manufacturing centre. The important shoe centres of Massachusets, with the exception of Haverhill, have recently manufactured a decreasing percentage of the country's total.

Analysis of the twelve lines of industry which centre principally in New York showed that the relative importance of the city was increased in six during the period, decreased slightly in five, and maintained its position in the remaining industry. Another feature is the steadiness of industry in the city, due in large measure to the great variety of industries. This is shown by the fact that the minimum number of employes in any month during 1914 in all industries was 91.5 per cent. of the maximum number of employes in any month. This was considerably larger than the average for the country and a little higher than the average for large cities. Experts pointed out yesterday that the large cities possessed a strong attraction for industries, owing to the abundance of labor supply. New Yorkers will be glad to learn that the city's increase in industries has been accompanied by a decrease in the number of children under 16 employed. New York children now constitute less than 1 per cent. of factory wage earners.

At present there is considerable shifting of long-established industries to new and more appropriate sites in the city, as in the cases of the factories devoted to the production of women's suits, cloaks, and underwear. These latter are leaving the sections adjacent to the Fifth Avenue shopping districts for better adapted streets in the vicinity of Seventh Avenue, the east side, or Queens Borough. The east side, already a beehive of industry, bids fair, with the expansion now taking place, to be rivaled by both the Seventh Avenue zone and Queens.

Probably the most striking example of New York's most recent industrial growth is shown in the rapid development of the Degnon Terminal in Long Island City, Borough of Queens. In the last four years some of the largest manufacturers in the United States have located their plants there. The terminal now represents an investment of more than $10,000,000, approximately $3,000,000 having been spent in land and improvements and $7,000,000 in buildings. Some idea of the character of the development now going on at this industrial centre may be gauged from the statement that the first building erected there is the largest concrete factory unit in the world, with twenty acres of floor space under one roof. This structure alone cost $2,000,000. Today the demand for buildings is greater than ever before. The inquiries on file at the terminal are for more than 6,000,000 square feet.

Alfred I. Smith, manager of the Industrial Bureau of the Merchants' Association, explains why New York stands in a class by itself as a manufacturing centre.

"There is probably no place in the world where there are so many factories, so many industrial workers, such a volume and variety of raw materials used, and value of manufactured articles produced within the boundaries of a single city as in New York," he said. "The chief appeal of a New York location to many manufacturers is the unsurpassed market situated almost at the factory doors. A city of 5,500,000 inhabitants, with neighboring cities bringing the total up to more than 7,000,000, or almost 7 per cent. of all the people in this country, demands enormous quantities of manufactured goods and must be supplied quickly and steadily.

"In New York the manufacturer can tap an almost inexhaustible labor reservoir, obtaining skilled or unskilled labor of almost every type imaginable. This city's manufacturer rarely has the great difficulties which the small city manufacturer is constantly meeting, namely, a severe scarcity of labor due to competition of new or enlarged factories competing in the same restricted labor market, and the absolute impossibility of obtaining labor with skill of a special or unusual nature."

September 23, 1917

The Lower East Side's Manufacturing Centre, Photographed from the Twenty-eighth Floor of a Broadway Skyscraper.

EVERY NEW YORKER A VILLAGER

By BERTRAM REINITZ

MAPS and airplane views do not show the real divisions of New York City. They do not even yield the merest hint that the big city is actually made up of hamlets, towns and villages.

Of course, it is quite true that, officially, the city is partitioned off into five boroughs, but this doesn't mean much except as far as elections and care of the streets are concerned.

New York is comprised of innumerable distinctive little communities, each as complete unto itself as Ada, Ohio, or Covington, Ind.

This business of telling the world that New York is a mighty mass of milling millions is fine for light Summer reading, but it's pretty poor reporting. Those reiterated charges that New York hasn't any more home life than a traveling salesman are libel per se.

There has been entirely too much said and written about Broadway and not enough about Prospect Avenue, the Bronx. The dazzling fame of Fifth Avenue is international, but it is doubtful if even Yonkers has heard about Central Avenue, Brooklyn. Greenwich Village is known as far east as Baroda, but Washington Heights is or are scarcely known as far east as Quarantine.

This condition may be ascribed to the fact that New York's publicity has been handled, for the most part, by a lot of literary carpetbaggers. They have never alighted from the rubberneck wagon. They seem to be under the impression that the city is composed exclusively of points of interest.

They know of the more prominent squares and circles, but the side streets, where New York lives, just haven't occurred to them.

"The butcher store is the Town Hall."

Through sheer force of repetition they have sold the folks back home the misbelief that native New Yorkers are as scarce in New York as ex-bartenders are at the annual conventions of the W. C. T. U.

According to their version of it, the population of the city runs chiefly to members of the Ohio, Southern and other societies who get together once a year to soulfully sing the praises of their geographical Alma Mater.

The city's chroniclers from the country accredit New York with a complete turn-over of personnel every few days or so, although the 1920 census gave the population as 5,620,048. The hotel registers did not contribute to this total. It covers permanent New Yorkers exclusively. It includes the one and one-half millions of school children here, all of them New Yorkers in the making, even though the world will probably never know of them through the portable typewriters of the transient literati.

New York has been variously described as impersonal, heartless and generally upstage, utterly lacking in that spontaneous hospitality which embraces strangers the moment they hit Hutting, Ark., or Ellsworth, Me.

It is quite true that the deckhands on the municipal ferryboats are called upon occasionally to fish some depressed visitor out of the harbor, but that can hardly be held against New York. The city cannot guarantee success as a motion-picture star to every young woman who deserts the farm and comes here for film fame and fortune. If the girl were willing to do work similar to that which occupied her at home—housework—she would find a warm welcome in at least a thousand homes in Flatbush alone.

Of course, there are many highlights to New York's color, but most of it is of the same shade which tinges any town, regardless of size. For every thirty or forty story building there are ten thousand two and three story structures. For every huge retail establishment, which all visitors are dragged through, there are thousands of small neighborhood stores, where the proprietor knows what grade of coffee and how many eggs a week almost everybody on his block uses.

It must be admitted that in New York every resident doesn't know every other resident. It must also be conceded, however, that all the people in one village are not acquainted with all the people in a village twenty miles away, regardless of how small both the hamlets are. There are sections of the big city separated by more than twenty miles, not miles of fields, but miles of people—miles of other communities.

There aren't any Councilmen passing ordinances for the hamlets which go to make up New York. There is, however, considerable front stoop legislation in the Summer time, and janitors have been known to enact measures to curb the destructive activities of the boys of the neighborhood.

New Yor[illegible]s are imbued with a neighborly [illegible]pirit which is greater even than that permeating small-town residents. The latter usually live in one-family or two-family houses, while most of New York dwells in multi-family houses, where the walls are so thin that even whispers are shared by everybody on the floor.

There are no official statistics on the number of dishes left unwashed in the sinks of New York each evening while housewives gather in hallways and discuss the furniture observed as the new tenants on the second floor moved in. But it is quite safe to say that these unwashed dishes per family in New York outnumber those per family in any town in the world.

Tons of sugar are borrowed annually from each other by New Yorkers after the grocery stores are closed. Dishes are loaned by the cupboardful to aid neighbors overwhelmed with company. Chairs, floor lamps and books to cover over the bare places in the bookcase are freely interchanged.

It is not difficult at all for the New York mother to get a neighbor to mind her children on the night of the banquet of her husband's lodge.

There is more dumbwaiter, airshaft and court conversation on the average city block in a day than there is in Carnegie Hall in a year. Being neighborly is the principal occupation of the average woman of the city, especially those with grown children and housework which doesn't consume more than two or three hours a day.

The block is the communal unit of the city. The butcher store is the Town Hall. It is the local forum where personalities, hats and rich relatives are discussed while the skewers are being stuck into the beef and the cord wound around it.

If the butcher ever took to writing he'd never say that the big city was mystical, insoluble and oppressive. New Yorkers to him are merely people, some preferring the eye of the round, others not content with anything less than the prime ribs, and all of them wanting more fat and bone free of charge than he can afford.

He knows whose husband has got a raise and whose is out on strike. Little boys can be sent to him without notes, and by uttering the word "steak" will be sent home with the proper cut, thickness and weight.

The man who owns the delicatessen store on the block is fully cognizant of the women who begin preparing for the evening repast around 6 o'clock. He is aware of whom to offer chicken salad and who is not interested at all in that expensive wedding of chicken and celery.

The block usually has its tailor, druggist, physician, stationery and candy store and its competing icemen. Each of these servants of the community is intimately acquainted with the preferences of its denizens. They have mental files of whom to trust and from whom to demand cash payment.

Children bring out the neighborhood spirit in an undeniable way. They have their games, friendships and fights on the block. They defend it against invaders coming, for the most part, from a block a little tougher than theirs. Their disputes culminate in controversies of parents as often as do the differences of small-town children. They know who will give them money or fruit or candy when they go visiting in their Thanksgiving Day disguises.

There are thirteen thousand some odd policemen in New York City, but individualities are not lost in this great total. On the vast majority of blocks the patrolman has been there for some little time. He is as much a part of the neighborhood as is the lone constable of a hamlet. The families who stage late and noisy parties are on his black list. He can recite without pause or error precisely how long it takes the various janitors to clear the snow from in front of the premises they look after.

When a window is mysteriously broken he can be counted upon to give a fairly accurate conjecture as to who supplied the power behind the ball.

Co-operation is the keynote of these one-block communities. Preparations for parties find neighbors willing and eager to help, even though they may not be invited to the actual festivities. It is not an unusual occurrence in the poorer districts for neighbors subsisting on modest incomes themselves to give financial assistance to families made destitute through some misfortune. In illness, where nurses are an unattainable luxury, neighbors give freely of their services even to the discomfort of their own families, who do not complain.

Hamlets are not the only unofficial subdivisions of New York City. It has populous towns and villages, too, with brightly lighted main streets. One Hundred and Twenty-fifth Street, for example, might be regarded as the principal business thoroughfare of a city of a hundred thousand. Eighty-sixth Street has a similar aspect. They are little different from Genesee Street, Utica, or Washington Street, Albany. Hundreds nod to one another as they pass along these thoroughfares. They have a certain provincial tone to them. They are boosted by Boards of Trade made up of the merchants, who stage co-operative sales from time to time, when these wide avenues are festooned with colored electric lights and all the windows are ablaze. There is little difference between these events and the concerted "Spring opening weeks" put on by the merchants of Syracuse, N. Y., or even Green Bay, Wis.

It is but necessary to get into the subway at, say, Seventy-second Street and climb out at One Hundred and Sixty-eighth Street or thereabout to obtain the unmistakable impression that New York City is an area of collected communities. The uptown section appears so radically different that it is hard to reconcile it as being part of the same city as the downtown district.

And each section has its schools, its social life, its churches and its cabarets. There are its local celebrations, and some sections even have an unofficial but universally recognized "Mayor."

The closely knit interests of New Yorkers in their separate and innumerable bailiwicks are reflected in the "block parties" which have had a sweeping vogue each Summer. There are those families who contribute the home-made cakes, while others furnish the ice cream and candy. The music and decorations are paid for by donations. Outside of an elderly couple or two who do not like the excitement, virtually the entire block actively pushes these events to success. During the war the proceeds of these parties went to buy things for the boys in the service. Now they go to neighborhood charities.

New York is thoroughly human. The nervous lights of Broadway are somewhat bewildering and visitors, especially writers, are apt to be blinded to the real New York. It should be borne in mind by all tourists in our midst that Broadway is as much of a novelty to most New Yorkers as it is to people from out of town. This also holds true for Coney Island, the Statue of Liberty and the restaurants with the $2 couvert charge.

The average New Yorker hasn't the wanderlust which sends many small town inhabitants out to see the world. He prefers the friendly, familiar setting of his locality. He doesn't particularly crave the excitement of travel, liking quiet home life too much to give it up for uncomfortable journeys.

When he does decide to have a night out and ventures, usually with his wife, down to Broadway, his evening is often spoiled by the raucous roistering of a party from the Middle West seated at an adjoining table.

MILLIONS OF CAPITAL DRAWN TO MIAMI

Florida Community Has Grown From 1,681 Citizens in 1900 to 111,000 Today.

VISITORS COME TO STAY

George E. Merrick Here to Arrange for a $10,000,000 Suburban Development.

NOT A MUSHROOM TOWN

Rich in Tropical Fruits, the Vicinity is Growing Into an American Riviera.

Miami has been misrepresented in a flood of articles which give the impression that it is a boom town, whereas its growth from a population of 1,681 in 1900 to 111,000 in 1925 is the result of the development of the permanent productive resources of the American tropics, according to George Edgar Merrick, who was in this city yesterday at the Hotel Biltmore, arranging with John McEntee Bowman the details of a $10,000,000 suburban development.

Mr. Merrick, who is less than 40 years old, has created a city of tiles, concrete, steel and coral rock out of what a few years ago was his father's orange grove. This is Coral Gables, near Miami. What was an agricultural property a little more than a decade ago is today a varied landscape of lawns and gardens, broken by the white and red of fine residences in the Spanish and Moorish style.

Orange Grove's Transformation.

Mr. Merrick was in New York City studying law and practicing poetry when his father died in 1911. He returned to Miami, which was then a city of about 10,000 inhabitants. The idea occurred to him of turning the grove, which his father called Coral Gables, into a suburb of Miami. As the development began to prosper he called in artists, landscape architects and city planners and they built up a modernized Mediterranean city, in connection with which he and Mr. Bowman are now building the $10,000,000 hotel, country club and bathing casino.

"Just how I came to utilize the Spanish type of architecture in Coral Gables, I can hardly say, except that it always seemed to me to be the only way houses should be built down there in those tropical surroundings," said Mr. Merrick. "I made a trip to Mexico and Central America and was more convinced than ever of the possibilities offered by the adaptations of the Spanish and Moorish type of architecture. The gleaming white coral rock, the palm trees, tropical flowers and verdure seemed to me to provide a natural setting with which Spanish architecture alone would harmonize.

Bryan Employed as Orator.

Mr. Merrick has played an important part in the building in Miami, and his enthusiasm about the place is such that he believes that to sing its praises adequately is a task not unworthy of the powers of the greatest natural orator living. He has employed the services of William Jennings Bryan, who makes a daily address to crowds at Miami on the glories and potentialities of the tropical region of which Miami is the metropolis.

"The recent articles in Northern papers and magazines about Miami have been in many instances so unfair to the real Miami that it seems to me time to bring out the facts behind its great, healthy, substantial growth," he said.

"The 'smart Aleck' writings regarding this great Miami growth, from even financial writers, is akin to the solemn European conclusions reached by some of our near statesmen after a month's visit in Europe. Comparing the steady, healthy and tremendous growth of all Florida but Miami, particularly to Klondike rushes and Texas oil field booms, as done in recent picturesque articles in New York newspapers and magazines, is simply silly, sob-sister, sensational writing.

"Miami merits a more mature consideration and exposition of its remarkable growth and the factors and potentialities which are steadily forcing it more and more into the national limelight.

"I might say here that I am not a promoter just snapping upon a new chance for easy exploitation in Miami. I have lived and worked in the upbuilding of Miami for twenty-six years and I am almost as close to a native son as you usually find in Miami. I have done everything from rubbing the coral rock, clearing pine timbers, planting tomatoes, developing grapefruit and alligator pear groves, and have been in personal contact with most of Miami's principal resources in the actual and manual working of them out. And so on, to the developing and marketing of what is now probably America's greatest realty development, which is Coral Gables.

$21,000,000 Spent in Three Years.

"In Coral Gables there has been expended during the past three years over $21,000,000 in hard, cold cash. There has been nearly $30,000,000 of realty sales made throughout thirty-eight of these United States. There has been close to a thousand Mediterranean-type houses built within three years.

"Such enterprises in Coral Gables as the Miami Biltmore Hotel and the Miami Biltmore Country Club, which, with its golf courses, bathing casino, polo fields, &c., will cost over $10,000,000, are but single phases of this development, which has a definite further ten-year program, involving a $100,000,000 expenditure still ahead.

"Remember, too, that Coral Gables is only one of many great developments in Miami. There is, for instance, Miami Beach, which twelve years ago was a mangrove swamp, but by the genius, energy and millions of Carl Fisher has been transformed into the greatest Winter playground of the nation, and where there has been invested in construction altogether probably $100,000,000.

"It has been said in some of these articles that Miami is in the throes of a wild, fantastic boom. Now, on the contrary, Miami never had a boom, and is not having a boom now. To back up this statement of mine it is necessary to make a further emphatic assertion, which is that should no further persons monly designated as 'tourists' ever again visit Miami it still would steadily become a great city.

The Advantages of Florida.

"My father and my family are examples of what I mean. We went to Florida twenty-six years ago, not as tourists, but to take advantage of the natural resources; the advantage for real and broader living and the potentialities for tremendous profit to be taken out of the ground in Miami. And we found them. Disregarding realty value and enhancements entirely, we found them. Today and every day in Miami, Dade County, in the great Everglade empire to the west and south of Miami, and in that great only American tropics which is the backbone of Miami, hundreds of people are finding and making their own, those same things that drew our family to Miami. And the hundreds of today are healthy, naturally and, just as logically as the endless-chain scheme works, becoming the thousands and hundreds of thousands of tomorrow and the day after.

"From, and because of the establishment of our own faimly at Miami (and also disregarding realty phases entirely), over 300 people have come to Miami in our own single endless chain. Once a Miamian always a Miamian—and the present tremendous growth is largely due to the cumulative effect of these endless chains started by satisfied Miamians.

"Miami has had one continuous, steady growth from the one thousand inhabitants of twenty-five years ago to the hundred thousand or so inhabitants of today. True, it has been growing faster, gathering momentum with each year, and it will continue to grow with still increasing momentum for at least ten more years, into a city of 1,000,000 inhabitants, which we surely expect.

Growth of Bank Deposits.

"The bank deposits of Miami are a fair barometer. They have grown steadily and surely from an aggregate of only a few millions fifteen years ago into about one hundred millions today. The fact that Miami is now an all-year city and not just a tourist resort is shown by the fact that its bank deposits will fall off hardly more than 10 per cent. during the Summer.

"Can you call a city a boom town whose building permits last year were close to $30,000,000 in greater Miami, and whose building permits in the same area this year will exceed $60,000,000, and all of which is materialized in concrete, reinforced concrete and everlasting coral stone? These are surely not the materials of which a boom town is made. Miami has for years been dubbed by architectural and building magazines the 'Concrete City.' In boom cities of the Middle West, of the Southwest and the West you sometimes read of frame schoolhouses burning, sometimes with loss of lives. Througout the entire Miami area there is not a single frame schoolhouse. Literally millions upon millions are invested in the most modern concrete buildings of architectural beauty and ideal arrangements, far surpassing anything else in school building architecture, yet worked out in this country. The same phase is apparent in the churches. An $800,000 Catholic cathedral, a $600,000 Episcopal church, dozens of $500,000 churches supplanting $100,000 ones and in the most beautiful style of ecclesiastical architecture, by national architectural authorities. Does this seem like a boom town?

"A million dollar causeway built only five years ago of stone, concrete and steel, and designed to meet the needs of twenty years is now to be doubled to meet present traffic needs.

Thousands of Miles of Roads.

"Thousands of miles of the most permanent kind of highways gridiron the entire Miami area and make every part of this entire and only American tropical country literally a part of the City of Miami.

"A five million dollar overseas highway is stringing together the 150-mile chain of matchless Florida Keys into a super-Riviera highway which will be the most wonderful motor road in the world.

"A great Tamiami trail costing over a million dollars is being thrown across the Everglade empire to the Gulf Coast, making direct connection with all the Gulf Coast cities and making directly tributary to Miami millions of feet of untouched cypress and the future produce of thousands of square miles of rich lands.

"Nearly $20,000,000 has been spent by the State of Florida in draining and fitting for agriculture that great Everglade empire of millions of acres, the development and exploitation of which will most directly affect Miami. Men who are largely responsible for the sale of the Everglade bonds enabling this great drainage project, and Government men familiar with same, say that the properly developed potentialities of the Everglades alone would make a city of a million people out of Miami.

"Several varieties of rubber are indigenous in this area. American rubber manufacturers are just turning their attention to e xperiments, apparently proving that Everglade rubber culture is a practical thing. Great pulp manufacturers from the North are turning their attention to the Everglades, with its various fibre grasses growing wild and the many tropical fibre plants which would be cultivated thereon, and are actually beginning great manufacturing enterprises based thereon.

"One great sugar company has successfully invested in the neighborhood of Miami over $10,000,000 in the sugar inddstry.

Riches of the Everglades.

"The expensive sea island cotton, finest grade wrapper tobacco, have been proved to grow successfully in the Everglades. Think of millions of acres richer than any other area on this continent, and capable of producing not only the staples of the temperate zones, but all the higher priced commodities of the tropics. Why, many a city in the Middle West has been built into great size on the potentialities of its enveloping corn and grain lands which may make from $10 to $50 per acre per year. Here are millions of acres which will produce crops ranging in yearly profit from $100 to $1,000 per acre.

"Here is the ideal beef-producing section of the United States; with all-year natural forage, capable of growing only the most luxurious tropical grasses twelve months of the year. There are none of the freezes or droughts common to other beef-producing sections to contend with, there is minimum danger of cattle diseases.

"The casual observer sometimes asks, 'How can you expect a great city here at the jumping-off point of Florida?' Havana has been made a great city by reason of the same resources behind Miami. Despite every handicap known to man, and with never in its history any tincture of progressive spirit, Havana, just across the Gulf from Miami, became a great city.

"Great Middle Western cities were built in twenty-five years by farmer migration from the East. Why is it not reasonable for a million people to be drawn in ten years from the congested East and semi-congested West and Middle West to Miami, where the lure, promise and results are a hundred to one more powerful than they were in the Middle West migration?

"A great city, Los Angeles, was brought into being on the far side of the Continent from the congested East, which furnished its population. Economically, should not Miami, which is comparatively a New York suburb, with its vastly greater range of resources and opportunity, grow in vastly greater ratio and extent?

The Factor Which Builds Miami.

"The great factor which is building Miami is that same urge which pulls the Canadian from the place of his birth; which pulled my family from Massachusetts; that is pulling from Mid-Western towns that have reached their limit of opportunity for young men. It is pulling from the great congested centres like New York that offer but really pitiful living advantages for the middle-class family.

"All of these are finding what they want in Miami and are sending back for their friends and relatives just exactly as did the people who have populated other new sections of our country. But in the case of Miami, the pull is stronger. The population building works faster, because there are many many times the resources and potentialities and many times the lure and opportunities of any other new section that has ever been developed in our nation.

"The lure of the tropics is a great and a definite thing alone to build upon. The Miami area and thence on south to Cape Sable (all of which is tributary to Miami) comprises absolutely the only American tropics, and in that great fact Miami owns and will forever hold a priceless American monopoly. We are 600 miles south of the southernmost tip of California. It is the only point in the nation from which the Southern Cross may be seen. It is the only spot in the United States where the royal palm grows wild, where the coconaut naturally thrives and the flowers and vines of the South Sea Islands are as common as roadside weeds."

"In this Miami tropics is grown nine-tenths of all the tropical fruits that are grown in our nation. We have a practical monopoly in the growing of the better types of the alligator pears which mature 12 months in the year in Miami. For six months in the year Southern Florida feeds the nation with all Winter vegetables. Citrus fruits and their by-products are worth millions of dollars annually to the Miami tropics. The alligator pear industry alone is destined to become in the United States a larger business than the banana. This alligator pear growing alone will during the next ten to twenty years give splendid livelihood and even fortune to hundreds of thousands of people that will come to the Miami area. There are in Miami hundreds, yes, thousands, of people who have started in the Winter vegetable business with less than $500 who are now comfortably fixed.

"I know of no other place in the United States where a farmer can take a mule and $10 worth of tools and share crop on a ten-acre piece of ground and usually net from two to five thousand dollars for his season's operations.

"These factors are permanent. The Miami monopoly of the alligator pear industry, the Miami monopoly of the finest all-year climate on the globe—yes, these things are permanent. Miami must continue to grow steadily into a great city, should all tourists (purely tourist type) cease to visit here. But will the tourist cease to visit Miama? You may just as well try to make sparks cease from flying upward!

"Within forty hours of three-quarters of the population of the United States is Miami. Within forty hours of seven-eights of its wealth. Only four days' comfortable automobile ride for the great American family out of snow and ice into everlasting June. Why should a tourist stop going? And a tourist of one year is a Miamian of the next year.

"A James Deering, after traveling the world over to its favorite rest, pleasure and health places, looked in at Miami for several days one year. The second year thereafter you find him building a ten-million dollar estate in Miami. He is typical of hundreds and hundreds, the aggregate of their estates running into hundreds of millions in Miami. In one afternoon in Miami there dropped into my office the president of one of the nation's greatest railroads, the head of one of the nation's greatest chain of hotels, two of the nation's greatest bankers, one of the great writers and one of the greatest living artists. And that was simply a sample afternoon. What other new section of the United States draws so many such men automatically? At a gathering in Coral Gables recently, upraised hands showed thirty-eight States represented. 'Who's Who in America' finds most of its most noted members either living the year round or wintering in Miami.

"Miami was discovered in a large way by the most prominent Americans during the war period when it was difficult to get abroad. Now they don't care to go abroad. Miami is the magnet drawing the most aggressive, progressive go-getting elements from every State west of the Mississippi.

"Miami's port bill has just been approved by Congress and the President, appropriating nearly $2,000,000 for the completion of its wonderful deep water harbor. Despite its poor facilities in the past, its shipping has grown to the point where a dozen large steamer lines and many small freight lines enter Miami, and its shipping has already grown to tremendous proportions.

To Be a Great Pan-American Port.

"With the completion of this harbor Miami will readily take its place as the great Pan-American port of the Atlantic. It is the logical contact port with all of the West Indies, Central and South America, and with a great commercial trade expansion with the United States. Miami's port will grow into something far greater than New Orleans, Galveston or Savannah in the past. Also, with the completion of the deep water program it is likely to mean the throwing across the Everglades, for instance, from the present terminus of the Atlantic Coast Line, 100 miles away, the railroad links which will connect with the great Florida phosphate fields, and the great freight steamers from every port in a short period will be loading phosphate in Miami port.

"All-year business in Miami has grown to the extent that the Florida East Coast Railroad is now engaged in double-tracking its 400 miles, giving us the equivalent of another railroad. It is likely that the Seaboard and one other railroad from the West Coast will shortly be in Miami.

"Industries are springing up with all-year growth of the city. There are now over 150 profitable industries readily expanding. Great natural assets, like our coral rock, are worth untold millions to Miami. Among many other natural industries may be noted the fish and sponge industries.

Run by Five Bank Presidents.

"Miami is today the most cosmopolitan and American of American cities. It is a city and country where, despite its mingling of ultra-conservative stock, no public bond issue has ever been voted down. It is one American city that can boast of having its civic affairs handled for years by a commission of its five bank presidents; where, though in the Far South, sectionalism is never thought of, where the community church idea has been carried to its furthest limits; where capitalism and industry work ideally together; where the crudities of the ordinary new country, the half-baked stage that has been in the development of every other American city, never existed, because national experts in every line are living in our midst and actually working out the future Miami now.

"In Miami the nation has truthfully regained its youth. Optimism is the very air that you breathe—the same air that inspired Flagler in his 70th year to plan the $100,000,000 overseas railroad, which at first his competitors called 'Flagler's Folly,' but by getting Cuban freight traffic is now one of the nicest paying railroad propositions in the United States. It is essentially that life impelling quality of the very Miami air that draws men of great and small affairs back to Miami. It is not, however, a foolish optimism, taking no account of obstacles or wasting time in pipe dreams. It is simply an optimism born of tremendous resources and founded upon a range of potentiality and opportunity absolutely new to American life—an optimism founded on the fact that in a single one of its years of 365 sun-filled working days may be compressed what would ordinarily be a lifetime of effort in the common, starved, older North or Western communities.

"Miami is the minting in America, in one fine, shining piece, of the substantial compound of that very American dream of freedom—Opportunity and Achievement."

March 15, 1925

OUR CHANGING CITIES: DYNAMIC DETROIT

A By-Product of the Factory System, Its Extraordinary Growth in Less Than Two Decades Runs Parallel With the Development of the Motor-Car Industry and the End Is Not in Sight

By R. L. DUFFUS

DETROIT has had three slogans since the twentieth century was young. First it called itself "Detroit the Beautiful." That was in the days when lumber, stoves and nostrums still ranked as its important industries. Travelers coming from the East were ferried across the river, came ashore upon quaint, ramshackle wharves, and found themselves in a city of lawns and tree-lined streets, where life could be lived in leisurely fashion and the old French charm still lingered. This was the end of an era. Eras are always ending in Detroit.

Detroiters, like other Americans, had been riding bicycles throughout the late '90s. The resulting traffic congestion was something frightful to contemplate. But several Detroit youngsters—the Dodge brothers and Henry Ford among them—found even the bicycle too slow. They began, with considerable success, to make automobiles. Before long these machines were as dependable as horses. Sales multiplied. Factories appeared and grew like mushrooms. Detroit, taking and keeping the lead, increased in population from 285,704 in 1900 to 465,766 in 1910. The community now liked to call itself "Detroit, the City Where Life is Worth Living." The trees were being cut down, the lawns built upon. But wages were going up and paving, lighting and sewers and schools were improving.

The real Detroit miracle occurred after 1910. It paralleled the unbelievable — almost grotesque — expansion of the motor-car industry from a production of 187,000 cars in 1910 to one of more than 2,000,000 ten years later. Then everything started to double all over again—industrial output, population, building permits, bank clearings. One grew dizzy watching it. The population in 1920, not counting two completely enclosed but independent cities, with 100,000 inhabitants between them, was 993,678. It is now reliably estimated at a little under 1,400,000.

Building construction in 1925 was nearly ten times what it was in 1910. The number of automobiles owned and operated in the city was about 58,000 in 1917 and about 380,000 at the end of 1926. The entire population can go riding at once, and at times, as it seems, not only can but does. So it now appears reasonable that the city should be described, as it frequently is, as "Detroit the Dynamic."

The end has not come and is not in sight. It certainly will not arrive until America is saturated with automobiles that do not wear out or become out of date, and perhaps not until there are enough airplanes to take the entire population of the United States flying simultaneously. Detroit, to borrow the phrase of an observer who has studied it long and thoughtfully, is Growth. And cities that have acquired the habit of growth are slow to lose it. Their fat years swallow up their lean.

As every schoolboy at one time or another knows, the city has as thrilling a history as any in America. Here, in 1701, Antoine Laumet de la Mothe Cadillac landed to found an outpost of New France. Trade was with the savages, transportation by canoes. The English came in 1760. Pontiac besieged them in 1763. Hull surrendered town and garrison, in 1812, to an inferior force of British and Indians. Detroit was a centre of the fur trade and saw its rise and decline. French was long its principal language and there are still French families who trace their descent to its first settlers. Thus the harshness of Anglo-Saxon pioneer communities was in Detroit a little softened. Like Vincennes, old St. Louis and New Orleans, it mingled two cultures most agreeably.

But if the truth must be told, the history and legends of the past have almost nothing to do with the Detroit of 1927. There is no more intimate connection between the contemporaneous Detroiters and those who lived there fifty years ago than there was between the first French settlers and the Indians. To all intents and purposes Detroit is a new city. All that makes it humanly significant has been added since the present century began. It is a by-product of the modern factory system. Its average man tends a machine—more than 400,000 persons are employed in the plants in and about Detroit.

These workers have put the characteristic stamp upon Detroit. They are, as far as can be ascertained, the most prosperous slice of average humanity that now exists or ever has existed. Detroit pays the highest per capita income tax in the country not because it has a large number of millionaires (though you can hardly cross the street without being run down by one), but because its typical wage rates are high. Mr. Ford, whose great plants at Highland Park and on the River Rouge do not happen to be within the city limits, is not the only large scale employer who has found that good pay is a good investment.

The tradition that something more than a mere living wage attached itself to the automobile industry from the beginning perhaps because the successful automobile manufacturers made so much more than a bare living profit. The spirit of the mining camp was in the air. Men were striking it rich on all sides. At first trained mechanics, who asked and secured a satisfactory compensation, were more numerous, relatively, than they are now. They established a scale from which the unskilled and semi-skilled have benefited.

Thus wages have been consistently high despite the fact that Detroit employers have resisted, with grim determination, all attempts at unionization. Working hours have been steadily reduced. The five-day working week was originated, not in Utopia, but on the banks of the Rouge.

Conditions inside the factories do not, perhaps, come into a picture of Detroit. Whether the worker actually becomes a machine during his working hours is a question that may be wrangled over indefinitely. He is certainly not a free agent. The discipline of the great factories—Mr. Ford's especially—is almost military. But after the 5 o'clock whistle blows the man who has been putting screws in gadgets all day long ceases to be an automaton. He can, if he is fortunate enough to possess one, invite his soul. And so far as he is able he does.

The results show upon the physical map of Detroit. The city has its areas of bad housing, mainly in the region near the waterfront where settlement began. It has not provided adequately for its colored population of more than 83,000—almost 90 per cent. of which has come since the war. But it has no extensive slums, no Shanty Town, no Gas House District.

Its population is distributed with considerable regularity over a large portion of its 139 square miles. The visitor sees block after block of comfortable-looking residences. The more pretentious ones belong to the foremen and skilled mechanics, but a man who is very little above the status of a common laborer may live decently, with some open space about him. Very often he will go to work in his own car, or in a car whose use is shared with neighbors.

The Expanding City

The consequent automobile traffic to and from the industrial district is remarkable. Detroit's fifteen most used streets, the City Plan Commission estimates, carry 4 per cent. more vehicles than do the fifteen most congested streets in New York City. Wayne County, in which Detroit lies, lays claim to more miles of paved highways and streets than does any other equal area on earth. Even California, where almost every hobo now has four rubber-tired wheels and an apology for a gasoline engine, cannot take the palm from Wayne. The intoxicating odor of petrol is ever in the air.

Detroit has expanded as a city on wheels must. It was a great city before any one had planned, not to say foreseen, such a destiny. Again and again the realtors laid our suburban zones and again and again settlement overleaped them. The consequence is that the outlying districts present a rather curious hodge-podge of the humble and the ostentatious, and of all styles of architecture, including the plan North American.

The city has been, one might say, assembled rather than manufactured. The main street, Woodward Avenue, starting at the historic but rather untidy waterfront, carries you through a highly sophisticated shopping and hotel district, which is soon to be dominated by the new eighty-five-story Book Tower. This thoroughfare cuts across a neighborhood where retail shops have been crowding out dignified homes of the older dispensation, passes between the Cass Gilbert Library on the left and the new Paul Cret Art Museum on the right, and then brings you to a region of vast factories.

When Detroit goes to work in the morning the effect is as if some one had poked a stick into an ant hill and had temporarily lost their sense of direction. There is no general stampede toward a centralized workshop district. The traffic flows all ways at once. It is only within factory walls that Detroit becomes passionately systematic.

On second thought this is not quite true. The instinct for order is making itself characteristically felt in city planning. When Detroit stops to consider the matter, it is almost as much distressed to have traffic flowing unnecessarily through its business centre as Henry Ford would be to use two turns of a monkey wrench when one would do. So it produces such projects as the Vernor Highway, which, when completed, will be at no point less than 120 feet wide, and which will be linked up with a system of great boulevards, some of them already in existence, each 204 feet wide. A 204-foot boulevard, with a strip of parking down the centre, is a sight to make a motorist weep for joy.

With the co-operation of surrounding cities and counties, Detroit is working out a majestic series of just such arteries, radiating spokelike from the metropolitan hub. Under the roadbeds, in the congested districts, plans have already been made to run four-track subway lines. Outside the city these will come to the surface and be operated down the centre of the superhighways.

Detroit, like several other cities, hopes to profit by New York City's mistakes. Its Transit Commission is shrewdly mapping out a gridiron that will distribute population instead of concentrating it. It also proposes to build the entire rapid transit system as nearly as possible at one time, or at least continuously, instead of following the New York plan of constructing the lines piecemeal, with a prolonged political fracas between contracts.

These proposals look ahead half a century or so. They may even establish the main traffic channels for as long as traffic continues to run on wheels on the surface of the earth. Ultimately, there is no reason to doubt, the community will be operated with the neatness and regularity so well exemplified in the plants on the banks of the Rouge.

Air traffic as well as ground traffic is being prepared for. There are already four airports in the immediate vicinity of Detroit. It is proposed to make others—one by filling in a shallow area in the Detroit River. A number of Detroit manufacturers have gone into the business of making planes or engines. At the Ford airport you may already see ships arriving or departing, with clocklike regularity, on journeys between Detroit and Cleveland and Detroit and Grand Rapids. For a little more than three times the railway fare you may fly from the Ford field to the latter city. The lines will soon be extended—to Chicago, Milwaukee, Minneapolis, to St. Louis, Kansas City, even to New Orleans.

If air travel gives birth to an important industry, Detroit will be ready for it, as it was ready for the automobile. The future cannot take such a city unawares. In an industrial sense, Detroit is the future. Whatever is about to happen, mechanically speaking, to change American life, will be sure to happen there first. We can count on it for our cogs and wheels as on New York for our plays and on Florida and California for our oranges.

One way of looking at a city is to consider it as a manner of life into which some thousands or hundreds of thousands of people have fallen. It is easier to do this with Detroit than with such communities as Pittsburgh, Chicago or San Francisco, which are under the spell of plains or mountains or the sea. Detroit, as it exists in this year of grace 1927, could be moved a thousand miles East or West without changing its personality. All one would have to do would be to make sure that its mills and factories were taken along, too. Unlike Chicago, it is almost independent of nature and the weather. Give it a little metal to chew and it laughs at the gods of wind and sky—the old gods that men have worshiped for so many plodding centuries.

The machines mold men of many races to the same pattern. The last census listed forty nationalities. Mosques lift their bulbous tops side by side with nine-and-ninety kinds of spires and steeples. The Yugoslav, the Finn and the Mexican Indian line up one after another at the paymaster's window. But they are all, willy-nilly, worshipers at the altar of efficiency. Their ten commandments begin with: Thou shalt not, during working hours, make any unnecessary motions. But their faithfulness has its rewards in security as well as in wages. For Detroit is, in good times and bad, a safe and solid city—by which good fortune it is deprived of some of the vibrant, adventurous quality one feels in Pittsburgh and San Francisco.

Detroit is almost too successful to be thrilling. It hasn't enough struggle, latterly, to make a good motion picture plot. On the other hand, an industrious worker can bring up a family in good surroundings, send the children through high school and probably have enough left to run over to Canada or down to Colorado for a week or so during the slack time in Summer. He can afford to leave high adventure to the bootleggers, whom you can see at almost any time, if you go to the right spot, plying their trade on the waters of the Detroit River.

For many years Detroit was too busy making automobiles and money to be conscious of its privileges and opportunities as a great city. Members of the first generation of the Gasoline Aristocracy, as you will hear them called by their honestly admiring fellow-townsmen, were sometimes better earners than spenders. The second generation, one is told, is keenly alive to public responsibilities. If a good case can be made out for any civic improvement, members of the second generation are for it, even though it may cost heavily.

They support one of the best orchestras in the country, conducted by Gabrilowitsch. Last year they are said to have bought $5,000,000 worth of paintings, many of which will probably find their way in time into the publicly supported art gallery. The cultural urge is being felt, even in the most successfully utilitarian of cities.

Detroit's Debt to Ford

But one always returns, in thinking of Detroit, to the familiar and nevertheless mysterious figure of Henry Ford. Mr. Ford has seemed willing to let Detroit alone if Detroit would return the favor by keeping off his own toes. He has not interfered in the city's politics, nor has he, except in the case of his hospital, made large gifts to its citizens. It is easy to find people in Detroit who think him greatly overrated. Yet the city, as one sees it today, is more his handiwork than that of any other individual.

Mr. Ford made the present city possible thirty-five years ago when he turned out his first practicable motor car in his machine shop at 58 Bagley Avenue, where one of the world's largest motion picture playhouses now stands. Detroit is the incarnation of that optimistic, matter-of-fact, mechanical mind which he so perfectly represents. It may speak forty-odd tongues, and yet one detects in them all the wholesome twang of the Connecticut Yankee.

Detroit is machinery enchaining mankind in order to liberate it—for what ultimate purpose is another question. Perhaps its showers of sparks are stars.

April 10, 1927

OUR CHANGING CITIES: VIGOROUS ATLANTA

Here the North and South Meet and the Old American Racial Stock Predominates

By R. L. DUFFUS

ATLANTA may be described as the triumph of the principle that converging straight lines, sufficiently prolonged, will intersect. It is the result of a masterly solution of a problem in geometry. Its location was as precisely determined by mathematical factors as was the rule that two and two make four—assuming, for the sake of the argument, that two and two really do make four. It was first a dimensionless point on the map and then a city. Its civic traditions go back, not to ships sailing into a harbor under clouds of sails, nor to Indians slipping through the forests laden with furs, nor to a happy portage, nor to the monopoly of a ferry, but to steel rails and locomotives. The same causes which led Sherman to wipe it out and compelled the rise of a greater new city out of the cinders of the old are still operating. Atlanta had its birth in smoke and steam. Its coat of arms ought to be an engine driver whistling for a crossing.

The Atlanta which Sherman did not burn, because it had not then come into being, has a population which is rapidly approaching 300,000; is a centre for fifteen main lines of eight railway systems; had, at the last count, 10,480 business firms and 127,918 persons gainfully employed; has passed the three-and-a-half-billion point in annual bank clearings; entertains the Metropolitan Grand Opera Company every Spring; gives eight weeks of light opera every Summer; has one of the South's best symphony orchestras; is constructing, despite an unhappy degree of political parsimony, one of the country's best school systems, and raises a million dollars at a swoop to advertise its manifold blessings to the rest of the United States.

In Broad Street it has a canyon which shuts out the sun almost as effectively as lower Broadway. Outer Peachtree Street, though it reminds one a little of Mr. Beers's mauve decade, is still one of the most-distinguished thoroughfares in the country; and there are two residential developments, built, respectively, from the proceeds of the sales of a popular drink and the profits of a well-known proprietary remedy, which represent the best that has been done in that line, North or South, East or West. In short, Atlanta is a large city for its section of the country and no mean city, regardless of its size.

All this came primarily from a fortunate intersection of steel rails. It is worth while to glance back some seven or eight decades and see why. If the reader will consult a topographical map of the United States he will observe, roughly paralleling the Atlantic Coast, the Appalachian range of mountains, of which all of us heard while we were in school. The southern wing of these mountains is the Blue Ridge, which, as one goes north from Atlanta on almost any Indian Summer afternoon, still beautifully deserves the name. The first railway builders, and all subsequent ones, found that there were only one or two places at which the Blue Ridge could conveniently be crossed. The best of these points happened to be in the neighborhood of what is now Atlanta.

Whether a railway line started from Washington, from New Orleans, from Savannah or from Chattanooga, or more distant points linked with these cities, the surveyors came to this spot in the rise of land—it has an elevation of 1,050 feet—which divides the waters of the Atlantic from those of the Gulf of Mexico. An Indian trail, laid out by still more ancient pathfinders, already marked the line over which today's limited trains run. In 1833, several years before the Cherokees were elbowed off their ancestral hunting grounds by the whites, a peace-loving citizen named Hardy Ivy built a cabin there.

But if Ivy sought this retreat to dream away his life he must have been disappointed. The era of railway building was beginning. The rattle of shovels, thud of picks and clang of hammers spiking iron strips to wooden rails grew louder as the years went by. It approached Hardy Ivy's cabin. By 1842 the ridge was becoming crowded—Ivy had 200 neighbors. The State of Georgia had already built (and still owns) the line between Atlanta and Chattanooga. In December, 1842, the citizens of Hardy Ivy's town, which then labored under the name of Terminus, borrowed a spare locomotive from the Georgia Railroad, which then ended at Madison, sixty miles east, hauled it through the woods and set it up on the rails leading to Chattanooga. On Christmas Eve it tooted away on its first trip.

Three years later the Georgia Railroad came in from Madison and the same year the Georgia Central bustled into town. Terminus became Marthasville, in honor of a Governor's daughter. It may also have been called White Hall, in honor of nothing in particular. But eventually it became Atalanta, soon shortened to Atlanta, either because the Atalanta of Grecian mythology was, like the railroad cars, an extremely swift traveler, or because the city was now linked by rail with the Atlantic Ocean.

Hardy Ivy faded from the picture, though he left his name on a street. Atlanta erected hotels for passengers who had to change cars. It built stores. It constructed railway shops. It organized banks. It grew It had a population of about

A Flatiron Skyscraper in the Heart of Thriving Atlanta.

Photo by Lane Brothers.

10,000 and was still growing when the Civil War began. Sherman, coming into town after four months of almost continuous and horribly costly fighting, reduced it to very nearly the condition in which Hardy Ivy found it—that is, there were more bricks lying around than in Ivy's day, but few of them were lying evenly on top of one another.

A Story of Growth

But the same laws of mathematics which had created Atlanta restored it. When the railways were rebuilt the city, too, was rebuilt. It struggled through the ghastly period of reconstruction, had 21,789 population in 1870, 37,400 in 1880, 65,533 in 1890, 89,872 in 1900, 154,839 in 1910, 200,616 in 1920, 265,000 at the beginning of 1927. These are not boom figures. But Atlanta grew with the recovering South, and may fairly be said to have led in that recovery. Certainly it outdistanced its own State. In such men as Henry Grady it produced prophets of the South that is yet to be—of what has been called America's last industrial frontier.

Remembering the March to the Sea, Atlanta had no extraordinary reason for loving Northerners. Yet, earlier than most Southern cities, it began to attract Northern men and Northern capital. This tendency has persisted to the present day. Atlanta is not cosmopolitan in its habits or racial make-up. Its foreign-born population is less than 2½ per cent. of the total. Even its negro population, which is a highly important element in its industries, is less than a third of the whole. The remaining two-thirds are substantially all Nordics—whatever that may mean.

It would be difficult to find a city as large as Atlanta in which there is so large and solid a nucleus of the old American stock. Even Boston could hardly compete. The Latin temperament, with its charms, gayeties and weaknesses, is conspicuously absent. The white two-thirds of Atlanta is almost Elizabethan in its racial purity, though not in its uproarious enjoyment of life. Yet it is not parochial. Its leading citizens, as often as not, are not even Southerners by birth. It was a man from Michigan, then President of the Chamber of Commerce, who conceived the idea of pulling the community out of a rut by an ambitious advertising campaign.

Immigration from other parts of the country has given Atlanta a characteristic which helps justify its description as "the New York of the South." It seems to attract the aggressive sort of business man. In this the climate helps, for Atlanta, at a thousand feet or more above sea level, does not share the leisure-inviting Summer temperature which ordinarily goes with its latitude. In fact, if the Atlanta lyre were strummed as loudly as that of Los Angeles has been the Atlanta climate might become as famous as that of Southern California.

At any rate, the city is charged with energy, and its army of high-powered salesmen and executives, permeating the South with a thoroughness Sherman might envy, keep the average income level high. Their wives go shopping in stores which need not apologize to Chicago or New York. Atlanta, except in certain portions of the negro quarter, breathes an air of well-being. And the negro is climbing economically. As a bricklayer, for instance, he earns $7 or $8 a day, or more than many of the paler skinned, white-collar workers. He is beginning to produce his own competent physicians and lawyers.

A Magnet for Many Lads

Atlanta has not only drawn ambitious newcomers from north of the Mason and Dixon line and west of the great rivers. It has also drained its own section of the South. It has been a Mecca for adventurous boys from the sleepy towns of Georgia, Alabama, Mississippi, South Carolina. In Atlanta they found something which seemed to them better than the languorous loveliness of the older South—the romance of achievement rather than of remembrance. For those who like their romance in this form it is here easily to be found.

The Atlanta advertising campaign, for example, was much more than a crude attempt to boost—it was, also, from a business man's point of view, an act of faith. It is no secret that Atlanta was hard hit, some two years ago, by a combination of an agricultural depression and a Florida boom. Florida was draining not only the Middle West but much of the Southeast of men and capital.

The advertising crusade had a double object—to convince outsiders that Atlanta was a promising spot in which to live, work and invest, and to persuade Atlantans that their city had a future. It was partly ballyhoo, but not pure ballyhoo. It contemplated nothing less than an economic revolution. Why should the South pay freight to have its raw materials carried North, pay manufacturers' and middlemen's profits and finally pay freight to have a finished product toted South again? Why should native Georgia clay have to be taken to Ohio to be made into pottery? The cotton mills have been coming South, first into North Carolina, then into Georgia and other States. Why only cotton mills? Why not almost any kind of mill dependent upon native minerals, woods or agricultural products?

The movement was linked up with the natural diversification and industrial expansion of the developing South. It had and has possibilities which may within the present generation break down the old sectional lines. It meant that slavery and the Civil War were at last passing into history. More specifically, it paid immediate returns. Atlanta invested $250,000 in paper and ink and added, during the first year, $8,000,000 to its payrolls. Naturally this is no guarantee of an undeviating prosperity.

But Atlanta has its heart set on quality as well as quantity. It has long been a musical centre, as its orchestra and its grand opera season attest. It fostered the great Confederate memorial on Stone Mountain, which at this writing is fairly under way, under the direction of Augustus Lukeman. It has had no art museum, but it is in process of securing one. Its politicians have done their best to starve the schools, yet they are by way of becoming among the best in the country. Go the rounds with Willis A. Sutton, the Superintendent, and you will find, in native Georgian soil, a surprising reflection of the advanced educational ideas with which such names as John Dewey's are associated.

The South needs, as Mr. Sutton will tell you, a recognition of the dignity of hand labor. There will be no industrial revival until this recognition comes. Mr. Sutton is hammering this principle into the school children and parents of Atlanta. Possibly some of the older conceptions of Southern gentility are going by the board, but the way is being cleared for a more vigorous and prosperous sectional life. The negro, too, comes nearer having his fair share of education in Atlanta than in most Southern cities. At least he gets back in schooling two or three times what he pays in school taxes. The old opposition to negro education is rarely voiced and is undoubtedly dying away.

In some respects the city lags. One does not yet find there a general acceptance of a comprehensive scheme of city planning. Parks excepted, the beautiful sections of Atlanta have been made so by private enterprise. But the planned city, as many indications hint, will come. It will come, if for no other reason, because Atlanta will be obliged to live up to its own advertising. The newly awakened civic pride demands more and more to be proud of. It shouts itself hoarse for Bobby Jones, and behind the shouting may be the knowledge that it is as important to know how to live and play as it is to know how to make money.

The visitor from more heterogeneous cities never ceases to be surprised at the predominance of the Anglo-Saxon type in Atlanta's streets. Here, fresh from towns or farms, are the descendants of the older stock. Turn back the clock for sixty-five years, put them in Confederate butternut, and they would be the images of the men who marched with Lee and Jackson. If they have discarded some of the older traditions they have kept the racial aptitudes. They are face to face with opportunities such as have not existed in the South since Fort Sumter was fired upon.

And they seem to be meeting successfully the competition of the Northern migrant—so successfully that the line between Northerner and Southerner ceases to be remarked upon. The speech of both sections softens to a common dialect, not so crisp as that of New York, but far more hurried and clipped than that of Charleston. And both unite, as well they may, upon a passionate fondness for such articles of diet as corn bread, which reaches its absolute perfection in a certain venerable Atlanta hotel much frequented by politicians.

Here, then, is an experiment in progressive Anglo-Saxondom in an increasingly cosmopolitan country. Economically it is bound to be a successful experiment. Culturally it will be even more interesting. Can it teach the polyglot North something new in the technique of living? Will it draw Northern and Southern cultures together, and combine graciousness with sparkle? In a way that is its largest, and still unrealized, opportunity.

Atlanta's Monument to Her Distinguished Son, Henry W. Grady.

Photo by Courtesy of the Southern Railway.

LESSER CITIES ALSO LIFT THEIR TOWERS

The Skyscraper of Manhattan Becomes the American Expression of Urban Greatness

By H. I. BROCK

SKYSCRAPERS, to which New York was urged by an economic pressure created by the confined and fixed limits of Manhattan Island, have become to the whole of these United States a symbol, a fashion and a heaven-climbing contest. With our square footage of land the single one of our physical assets which was practically constant, and with our business and our population inevitably and rapidly expanding, we here on our narrow neck of earth were forced to pile ourselves up layer on layer and still layer on layer or shortly to stop growing. Therefore, though it was in Chicago that modern steel construction was first invented—at least that is where the credit stands on the books of the experts—it was New York which laid hold of this pre-eminent American contribution to the builders' art as handed down through the ages and made a specialty and a public utility of it.

As a matter of fact, it was only in New York at first that a skyscraper could be made to pay—and the first skyscrapers were baldly utilitarian. Their architectural pretensions went no further, at best, than a false front, an attempt at an ornamental mask for something which it seemed to be assumed had to be in itself ugly. Even so, the fashion of skyscrapers spread, as any number of hideous straight-up-and-down little buildings standing up absurdly and uneconomically out of the general level of our smaller cities are witness to this day. If New York was our biggest city and New York had high buildings, then every city which intended to be big had also to have at least one high building, even if it stuck out like a sore thumb.

Later the bright idea emerged that a skyscraper need not be an eyesore. The head of a chain store concern which had won prodigious success by the popular expedient of selling no single article for more than ten cents grasped the enormous advertising value of associating the name of the concern with the highest building in the world—a building that every visitor to New York was bound to see and everybody outside of New York was bound to hear about.

Thus the Woolworth Building was planned to be just 8 feet short of 800 feet high. Cass Gilbert, who got the job of architect, saw his opportunity and gave the huge pile the outward aspect of a Gothic tower, overtopping all the other Gothic towers and shooting its mass and bright pinnacles at the sun or losing its lofty head in the clouds, according to the weather. It was the first "cathedral of commerce," so called. It set a Gothic fashion in tall buildings which lasted till the present vogue of terraced Babylonian towers displaced it, and it converted visiting Europe to the skyscraper, if not for home consumption at least as a part of the American spectacle.

But the Woolworth Building, for all its imitators, here and elsewhere, did not give the skyscraper fashion the hold upon the popular imagination which has now set the whole country building higher and higher on a scale and at a rate which defies every practical consideration except that of competitive advertising. Chicago, with its business concentrated in the Loop district, got quite a while ago to the point where, with vanity mightly assisting and the pride of competition with New York adding a big boost, it might be hoped at least that real skyscrapers would pay; for notoriously not all skyscrapers pay even in New York.

Raymond M. Hood (the same who designed the gold-topped black American Radiator Building just south of Bryant Park) created in the Chicago Tribune Building another Gothic tower soaring aloft over the Michigan Lake front.

Hood provided the visitor to the city called by outsiders "Windy" with an exclamation point for thrilling admiration matched only by Gilbert's pioneer masterpiece in the transformation of the utilitarian to the beautiful. It is only fair to say, however, that in each case the advertising value of the building was at least as important a consideration as maximum renting space. The architect's problem was simplified to precisely the extent that beauty became a tangible asset. In practice, the advertising value of a skyscraper is always a factor outside of New York and frequently still counts heavily here in spite of the thing itself being a local commonplace. In the smaller cities, where land values do not seem to justify setting half a dozen blocks upright in the space of half a one, in the midst of a not overcrowded horizontal layout, the advertising value—translated into the prestige of doing business in the one and only skyscraper in town—is perhaps the most important factor toward getting such buildings financed, though mere civic pride doubtless gives the initial impetus.

However that may be, it is only since the evolution of the terraced Babylonian tower has given the skyscraper its present distinctive form—since the discovery of the "new American architecture" as the outward and visible form of the new American method of building by setting up steel cages and hanging walls on them—that the skyscraper craze has taken possession of the country.

Everybody knows that the ter-

A Dominant Feature of Cleveland—The Terminal Tower.

Photograph from Bourke-White, Cleveland.

raced tower was originally no architect's invention for art's dear sake. The law in New York City required it, in order to provide "set-backs" from the street as the buildings went higher, so that there might be light both in the street itself and on the lower floors of the buildings, where many tall buildings were set together. Downtown Manhattan with its murky canyons had taught a lesson which was heeded for the future. None the less did the architects, not quite beginning with Ralph T. Walker, create a style, working within the new limitations, as all styles are rightly created by working within limitations toward the form that best expresses the limited thing.

This is the style which you have on a grand scale in New York in Mr. Walker's Telephone and Telegraph Building, which looms so solidly impressive from the Hudson River, and in Cass Gilbert's brand new New York Life Insurance Building, where Madison Square Garden used to be. It is a style in skyscrapers due primarily to a local building regulation of New York City just as the skycraper itself was due primarily to a local limitation of land-footage in New York City. Yet it is a style in skyscrapers which is more and more the accepted model of sky-scrapers even where the problem of preserving the light is not present—as where the building stands in an ample frame of free space like the Los Angeles City Hall, recently completed, with a tower said to be the highest on the Pacific Coast.

Buffalo's Electric Building Overshadows All Others.

***

It may be argued, of course, that every city expects to grow up thickly and sprout skyscrapers on every block—though it might be just as fairly argued that if every city did so sprout skyscrapers and filled them, there would be nobody left in the country to grow the food to feed any city. But the truth is that the simple and impressive forms of the terraced tower or set-back architecture, the broad appeal of the style itself, combined with the label which has been firmly affixed to it, at home and abroad, the label of the "American architecture," are largely responsible for the favor with which it has been received all over the country.

These two considerations sufficiently explain the adoption of the form where no economic or physical pressure exists to enforce it. We may not value excessively the opinion of the foreigner of European habitation and inevitably hampered by the past in which his effete continent specializes. But we are not displeased that our primacy in one art has been admitted by Europeans. There is even a strong impulse to show the foreigner that we can do better and better things with this new architecture of ours, related as it is not only to the Babylonian—which may be accounted accidental—but to the indigenous American architecture of the native red Indians as preserved at Taos and such places.

The pictures on the accompanying pages present tall buildings selected from a large number in cities all over the country, from the Atlantic to the Pacific, from Texas to the Great Lakes, from Florida to Oregon. The types of buildings run the whole scale. They include the primitive block-on-end which was the expression of the

original space-grabbing instinct which undertook to multiply the original square footage of ground the greatest possible number of times that the elevator traffic would bear. They exhibit variant adaptations of the cathedral idea, most of them Gothic, but some betraying a Christopher Wren or Italian Renaissance inspiration—the Metropolitan Tower in New York with its use of the Campanile gives the cue for the latter. And, of course, they exemplify the terraced tower or set-back. This last appears in a number of forms obviously suggested by New York models. But, whereas the base of the pyramid (or the first terrace) is in Manhattan relatively small in proportion to the tower, in some of the Western cities there has been a generous use of ground space, so that the tower rises more slenderly out of a broader base.

In general, the so-called perpendicular principle is used, a device borrowed from the Gothic because, as in case of the Gothic, the idea is to exaggerate the effect of height in all these buildings. That is to say, the architectural emphasis is on the perpendicular lines in the structure itself and in its ornamentation. In at least one case, however, that of a building in Seattle, a building twenty stories high, topped by a ten-story tower, the opposite or horizontal principle has been used, following a style which has lately been considerably exploited in Germany, as for example in the building in Stuttgart, said to be the highest in all the Reich—which if recollection serves runs to well over a dozen stories in height, perhaps seventeen.

A conspicuous example of the perpendicular effect is the Pacific Telephone and Telegraph Building in San Francisco, a twenty-seven story structure with outstanding rib arrangement from base to crown, with the setbacks very high up. Another curious example is a storage warehouse in Hollywood of the movies. This building, which likewise is vertically ribbed in an emphatic manner, seems to stand all alone, with no other tall buildings anywhere about, so that the height is doubly exaggerated.

Oklahoma City contributes an eighteen or twenty story building which is very slightly different from the original block-on-end type. It is called the Petroleum Building—naturally enough in that locality.

Judging from the effect of the pictures, there are still in many cities, where the prevailing arrangement is properly horizontal, ambitious skyscrapers—one or two perhaps—which, whatever their intrinsic merits, serve no right esthetic function in the local urban landscape. Theirs is still the impression of the sore thumb which was the characteristic aspect of those first attempts at imitative skyscrapers about the country in the days when even New York had not discovered the esthetical possibilities of the new machine for concentrating business and multiplying land values by the third dimension daringly extended and subdivided. Much more might be said in general and in particular about our fashion and passion for skyscrapers, but the reader will probably find it more profitable to study the accompanying collection of pictures of the individual buildings which represent the aspirations of cities in many different parts of the country.

May 26, 1929

One of Chicago's Gothic Towers—the Tribune Building.

Photos © Moulin.

The San Francisco-Oakland Bridge Begins to Bestride the Bay—In the Background Is the City of San Francisco.

SEA-BORN SAN FRANCISCO REACHES OUT

The Two Mighty Bridges She Is Building Are A Bold Step Toward Change and Growth

By R. L. DUFFUS

WITH two of the mightiest bridges in the world thrusting out piers northward and eastward, the one across the Golden Gate, the other across the bay to Oakland, the sea-born city of San Francisco will soon have a long-wanted opportunity to stretch.

With water on three sides, the land exit from San Francisco has always been a bottle-neck. For more than eighty years, even while it had plenty of room on its own peninsula, the city has felt cramped and cut off. Its inhabitants could go anywhere in the world by water. They were neighbors to Hawaii, the South Sea Islands, Australia, New Zealand, China, Japan. But by land they could only go south, whereas the main lines of their continental traffic ran east. They had to take ferryboats, which many of them loved, but which could not maintain the tempo deemed essential in modern life.

This war of land and water was also a war in the hearts of the San Franciscans themselves. Their city had, and still has, not only a distinctive topography but a distinctive personality. Drab in many of its details, its total effect is picturesque and even thrilling. It loops over its more than seven hills with a gallant and dashing air, with its white overcoat of fog flowing in the wind.

• • •

THE essence that is San Francisco is hard to define. For one thing, it has conformed to its site rather than dominated it. Even its skyscrapers have not been too conspicuous, placed on the western edge of a huge bowl rimmed with mountains and half filled with water. Its people have been cosmopolitan and provincial, ambitious and lovers of tradition, pugnacious and easy-going, all at the same time.

Change, even growth, might spoil the harmony and upset the balance. Any good San Franciscan would indignantly reject the prediction that his favorite city would ever become a shapeless, sprawling monstrosity such as Los Angeles (in his eyes) already is. But the bridges are a bold and monumental step toward change and growth.

San Francisco could not resist the chance to build them when it came their way through a huge RFC loan in the latter days of the administration of Herbert Hoover. It isn't every city that can have the most majestic bay in the world (a San Franciscan doesn't even except the Bay of Naples), crossed by two of the Number One bridges of the world. But the sentimental San Franciscan sighs even while he cheers. His city will not be quite the same when any automobilist can scoot from Oakland or Marin County directly into Market Street.

Yet the bridges will be in some ways expressions of the city's temperament, just as in other ways they will be negations of it. They are a fling in the face of fate, which San Francisco likes to make.

• • •

TAKE the mighty Bay Bridge, costing more than $72,000,000, four miles long striding on five great piers from its anchorage on historic old Rincon Hill to Goat Island (or Yerba Buena, if one wishes to be poetic), boring a hole through the top of the island, then wading to shore through the Oakland tidal flats. Eleven traffic lanes, two interurban tracks, 16,000 vehicles an hour, all high enough above the channel to let the tallest ships go through—that is the Bay Bridge.

Pier foundations 200 feet below the surface of the water, towers rising as high as 505 feet—who, seeing this spectacle taking shape from the deck of one of the weaving ferryboats (they have to weave nowadays to get around the bridge piers), wouldn't catch his breath.

Take the Golden Gate Bridge, costing the mere pittance of $25,000,000 or so, but suspended on two 740-foot towers, with a span of 4,500 feet from tower to tower—700 feet more than the longest span in the George Washington Bridge. Six lanes, 220 feet above the water, will carry traffic over the Golden Gate, above the masts of ships from all the seas, toward Marin County and Jack London's Valley of the Moon. Any one with a thrill left in him will fetch it out at the sight of that gigantic and—because suspension bridges cannot possibly avoid being graceful—lovely structure.

These engineering visions will be realized in a comparatively short time. After August of next year the motorist who approaches the Bay of San Francisco from the east can keep stepping on the gas; his majestic entryway will be clear. After May, 1937, he can swing to his right as he leaves Rincon Hill, cross the city toward North Beach and spin merrily above the waves toward the bare, brown hills of the Marin shore and the forested slopes of Tamalpais.

San Francisco will no longer be a peninsula somewhat precariously attached to the mainland. It will be for the first time an integral part of the American Continent.

WHAT will happen then? Will there be a Greater San Francisco, with Oakland, Alameda, Berkley and the other bay cities ruled from the San Francisco City Hall? Will the real estate developers, driving stakes, laying out streets, planting rows of geraniums, drain the residential population into the far hills? Will San Francisco become less than ever a city of homes, more than ever a kind of Manhattan Island to which people will go to work, play or dine, but less rarely to sleep the sleep of the just?

The answer is perhaps—and perhaps not. Politically, there are few signs that the bay communities will develop delusions of grandeur and merge their differences and jealousies in an artificial metropolitan monstrosity. Socially, the city will doubtless cling to its old habits. New additions to its population are likely to spill far out beyond its present political boundaries. They have been doing that for years—spreading southward down the peninsula, riding the ferries to Oakland and Sausalito—and the bridges will merely accelerate the tendency.

But doubtless, also, the returned Forty-niner will continue to know the feel of the old city, even though its outward aspects will have altered. The Forty-niner had an imagination which could grasp bigness. He would probably go down to the waterfront, gaze at the startling piers of the Bay Bridge, spit approvingly into the ebb tide that flows toward the other side of the earth, and accept the biggest bridge as he would have accepted the biggest gambling stakes, the gaudiest hotel lobby, or the wickedest street, all of which he himself lived long enough to see.

Something will have departed, of course, just as the sand-hills, the fleas and the mudholes were removed in the interests of previous progress. Lower Market Street, where all the important street-car lines converge at the Ferry Building, won't be as important as it used to be. The whole system of traffic in the heart of town will be revolutionized. Theatres, shops and offices may be pulled eastward, flocking toward the Bay Bridge approach.

And the ferryboats, though they may continue to operate, are perhaps doomed to the romantic obsolescence of those now crossing New York's East River. The ferry tower, the ferry clock—San Francisco's silent Big Ben—will lose most of their significance.

What will become of the gulls, one wonders, that used to wheel and poise and take turns balancing on the tops of ferryboat flagstaffs? And will the commuters miss those morning and evening voyages, past Alcatraz, with the waves rolling in through the Gate, or past Yerba Buena, with the liners coming in from all the Seven Seas? No doubt they will. But a big bridge, as Gertrude Stein might say, is a big bridge.

Atop One of the Towering Piers of the Golden Gate Bridge.

THE AUTO AND THE CITY

WOULD SHIFT CARS TO SIDES OF STREET

Speed of Autos Entitles Them to Trolleys' Place in Centre, Says American City.

CONSIDERS TRAFFIC PROBLEM

Magazine Devoted to Municipalities Suggests Ways of Relieving Present Congestion.

Because automobiles are the fastest moving vehicles on city streets at the present time, street car tracks should be removed from the centre of the streets to the sides, according to an article in the current issue of The American City, a monthly magazine devoted to consideration of municipal problems in this country.

"Because of the many new complications introduced into the use of the streets by the automobile, the time has certainly come to revise thoroughly the traffic methods and regulations of the days of horse-drawn vehicles," the article states. "Some of the older cities which were the first to introduce traffic regulations have now fallen behind smaller places because of failure to recognize the new conditions and to meet new needs.

"With the advent of electricity, the street car became the fastest vehicle in use, and properly belonged in the centre of the street. Passengers were in little danger when getting on and off the cars as long as horses were the only other motive power used. Today the automobile is faster than the electric car, and the tracks logically ought to be removed from the centre of the street to nearer the sides, where cars could stop and passengers could wait and get aboard in safety without the need of safety zones, causing all vehicles coming up behind to stop. As long as car tracks remain in the street centre some kind of safety zone is required at car stops, and the experience of Detroit shows how effectively chauffeurs and drivers can be made to observe such simple things as painted lines on the street pavement.

The Jitney Complicates Problem.

"The recent addition of the jitney to the already excessive street traffic of some cities has greatly complicated the problem of traffic regulation. If automobiles continue to decrease in price and the public shows a growing preference for the jitney to the street car, it is hard to tell where the resulting congestion may land us, in spite of the fact that the increasing speed of vehicles and more skillful use of them tend to offset the larger number.

"The high speed of the automobile has made more urgent than ever the need of abolishing grade crossings of streets and railroads. The increasing delays at street intersections have raised more forcibly than ever the question of abolishing grade crossings of important streets with each other. The Municipal Art Society of New York recently awarded prizes for the best solution of this last grade crossing problem, and many ingenious plans were shown in an exhibition held at the National Arts Club. Grade crossing removal in city streets has long been seriously considered in London, where several notable examples of overhead street crossings already exist. The most striking and far-seeing application of the idea was perhaps the remarkable plan presented to the Royal Commission on London Traffic over ten years ago by Messrs. Meik and Beer, the well-known English engineers. Their exhaustively worked out proposal was to build across London from north to south and east to west two main avenues, which were to have continuous roadways with no grade crossings, with existing streets being connected up with the present street system by means of frequent ramps. This plan, in the opinion of many, would have given London an invaluable backbone of through high-speed highways and rapid transit lines, the scheme being regarded as financially possible if built by means of excess condemnation.

Cost the Chief Drawback.

"The chief drawbacks to most of the proposed plans for overhead crossings of streets, for double-deck streets, and the like, are the excessive cost, the opposition of local business interests, and the doubt if any really substantial increase in street capacity would result, or any increase at all commensurate with the price paid.

"On important thoroughfares in large cities the most hopeful line of approach for reducing traffic congestion appears to lie in more scientific methods of traffic regulation, and hence the importance of the newer methods employed in Detroit, Cleveland, Toronto and other progressive cities. By the use of semaphores, or other improved methods of signaling; by facilities the left hand turn; by instituting safety zones; by removing car tracks to nearer the sides of the streets—by these and other methods, street capacity and speed of vehicles may be increased sufficiently to last for some time.

"If the use of the automobile continues to increase at the present ratio, even these measures of relief will not long prove adequate on certain important streets in the largest cities. But that is a problem for the future to face."

September 19, 1915

FROM A TRAFFIC TOWER

Growing Discipline of New York Crowds to Upraised Arm—Use Psychology's Laws

NEW YORK'S street crowds are rapidly becoming traffic wise. Compared with the crowds of other cities, at home and abroad, they are quick to respond to discipline. An interesting problem in crowd psychology is being worked out in the city streets, more especially on Fifth Avenue, while the crowds themselves are entirely unconscious of it.

A generation ago New York's crowds were wholly undisciplined. The city, and the country as well, looked upon the congestion of the streets as an unsolvable problem. When a few hundred buses and wagons passed up and down Broadway pedestrians were completely baffled, and built a bridge over the street rather than try to penetrate the traffic. When West Street was much narrower than at present, it was often impossible to cross it for hours at a time, and people missed their trains and boats because they could not negotiate its width of perhaps fifty feet. The traffic "jams" often closed streets in the heart of New York for hours.

To appreciate the discipline of New York crowds, and its instant response to authority today, one should look down from the vantage point of a Fifth Avenue traffic tower, a privilege rarely granted. From this elevation one gains an entirely new impression of the Avenue. The tower itself, with its windows closed in this Winter temperature, is a curiously quiet retreat, although surrounded by the busiest stream of traffic in the world. The closely massed vehicles as far as one can see to the north and south, and on the cross streets, move quickly forward, and are checked and again set in motion within a fraction of a second, after the signal is flashed to them. There is absolutely no straggling. The lines at which the traffic is halted are absolutely clear cut.

The discipline of the crowds afoot appears especially remarkable when viewed from this elevation. The traffic tower at Forty-second Street and Fifth Avenue is an especially advantageous point for watching it. The intersection of these two great thoroughfares marks the busiest traffic centre in the world. Before the installation of the present traffic system 115,000 people passed in a day along Forty-second Street and 85,000 up and down Fifth Avenue. The traffic regulations have served to increase this number.

In the old days neither of the great cross streets was ever wholly clear of people, no matter how heavy the vehicular traffic. The crowds constantly bucked the traffic, dodging through the lines of cars. The upraised arm of the traffic policeman only served to check a portion of the crowd. This was the transition period from the old days of street jams and closed streets. Looking down from the traffic tower, it is easy to imagine that the crowd is made up of automatons, in some mysterious way controlled by the switch which the traffic policeman moves back and forth. The lights which flash on and off above the tower are, of course, supplemented by the police on the street below, but the effect of the combination is marvelous.

The red light marking the transition period is only a flash, but it changes the appearance of the broad street as if by magic. One moment the wide pavements of Fifth Avenue are black with people lined up against the sidewalk in a clearly defined line. Few of the hundreds waiting so patiently for the signal to cross overstep the line. At the click of the switch which flashes on the green light the crowd instantly breaks and streams across the Avenue, while the black fringe quickly thickens on the pavements facing the cross street. Occasionally when traffic lets up there are a few stragglers unmindful of the signals, but the discipline of the great majority of the crowd is amazing.

The crowd is responding quite unconsciously to well-known laws of psychology, although it would be surprised to be told so. In devising the present traffic system on Fifth Avenue the mental process of the crowd was all worked out in advance. To some this reasoning might have seemed fanciful, but the results justify the experiment. In the first place, it was conceived that a signal given from a tower would be much more effective than when made by the most ferocious policeman.

Most people resent authority. They may obey the upraised arm of the policeman readily enough, but somewhere at the back of their heads is the feeling that they are being abused in some way. If one is in a hurry the interference of the policeman may cause active resentment. Now, the signal tower is impersonal and its authority is much less likely to be questioned. One stops or starts a car in response to such a signal without reservation. You cannot argue with a traffic tower.

But the great secret of the success of this system of traffic regulation is probably unknown to one in ten thousands among those who obey these signals daily. The remarkable discipline of the New York crowds today is explained by the fact that the system appeals to their sense of fairness. The system of red and green lights, and the alternate starting and stopping of traffic, has been compared to a game of cards. The mental process of the motorist or pedestrian on Fifth Avenue is like that of the player of a game. He plays and then pauses to let his rival play. It is a matter of give and take, each is treated with perfect fairness. The motorist, for instance, who has traveled several blocks uninterrupted, stops, with the best grace in the world, to let the traffic on the cross street pass, knowing that he will have his chance a moment later in his rightful turn.

Few of those who automatically watch the green and yellow signals of the traffic towers are conscious of such reasoning, but the reasoning is undoubtedly sound. New York has responded very quickly to the demands made upon its patience for the new authority of the signal towers. It is believed, as the system is extended and new generations grow up under such training, the public will be more than ever trafficwise, and the problems of congestion will be gradually solved.

The man in the traffic tower is not merely a cog in the machine who turns on and off the lights on a regular schedule. The towers above and below Forty-second Street follow the lead of this master tower, and the efficiency of the system of course depends upon all the signals winking on and off in unison. Emergencies arise, however, which must be met by prompt action. At any moment of the day or night the entire system of signals may be reversed, and each tower must be alert to catch the unusual signal. The exceptional circumstance proves the efficiency of the system.

The great traffic of Fifth Avenue is only held up for more than a minute at a time for the passage of the President, or visiting royalty or distinguished guests, for fire, serious accident or a thief chase. It is a common sight to see the man in the tower telephoning between the time of turning on and off the signal switches. He is in all probability talking with the other towers to learn the traffic situation at another point along the Avenue. If the President, for instance, is expected to pass up or down the Avenue, all the towers are warned in advance, and are on the alert. Should the President's automobile, with its guard of motor cycles, turn on the Avenue, say in the Thirties, the fact is instantly known all along the line. Should the traffic be against him, the red lights will instantly flash from all the towers arresting traffic, and a lane be opened up the Avenue so that the procession will not for a moment check its pace.

The same system is used when fire engines or ambulances are obliged to use the Avenue. The traffic tower nearest the cross street where they turn on the Avenue at once communicates with the other towers. The drivers of all kinds of vehicles are, of course, instructed how to act and make every effort to clear a passage. The red light is also used in rare instances in a thief chase. When an automobile is stolen the number is often sent out to policemen watching traffic along Fifth Avenue. The number of a missing car was sent out recently, with instructions to watch traffic in the Forties. Twenty minutes later a car passed the master tower at Forty-second street, going forty-five miles an hour, and a few moments later crashed into the tower at Fiftieth Street. The traffic policeman closed in on it and discovered it to be the car stolen twenty minutes before. The tower at Fiftieth Street is considered the hoodoo among the traffic squad.

March 12, 1922

MOTOR GROWTH CALLS FOR SUPER-HIGHWAY SYSTEMS

Map for Detroit Suburban Area Provides for Automobile Trunk Lines With No Cross Traffic Interference—Some Roads Would Be 120 Feet in Width

IN anticipation of the need for wide streets and rapid transit routes in the suburban area of Detroit, as the city expands in the future, the Rapid Transit Commission of that city has proposed what it terms a super-highway plan for Greater Detroit.

Basically, the idea is that while land values in the suburban area are low the city shall acquire rights of way for a number of wide streets which eventually may be used for four lines of rapid transit, two roadways for fast motor traffic and two for slow-moving traffic.

The plan presents many factors which may be studied with interest by those working to solve the accumulating traffic problems of New York City and to eliminate excessive congestion in outlying portions of the city by providing traffic facilities suitable for future needs.

The proposed super-highway system, according to The Engineering News-Record, deals with the area between the six-mile and fifteen-mile circles from the centre of Detroit. Consequently it not only is a matter of concern for the present city but also for the counties of Wayne, Oakland and Macomb, and a number of adjacent independent municipalities which ultimately will be included in Greater Detroit. Within the city proper little can be done toward providing wider streets for motor traffic, because the area is already built up, and street widening will require the acquisition of costly property. This is the reason why the Transit Commission has, at this early date, put forward the plan for the acquisition of additional right of way along existing streets and right of way for new streets in the sparsely settled areas before property values go up.

The advantage of this plan, it is explained, lies in the fact that besides providing a right of way for wide streets it also provides space for rapid transit lines in the centre of these new highways, which can be built at grade when they are required, thus avoiding the necessity of building either subways or elevated railways. The cost of such rapid transit lines at grade is estimated at $1,100,000 a mile, as against $5,500,000 for similar four-track subways. Consequently five miles of surface rapid transit can be built for the same money that would be required for one mile of subway if the new streets did not provide this space for rapid transit lines. Of course, within the city proper, rapid transit lines will have to be built as subways under existing streets. The plan recognizes this fact and provides for the transition from 120-foot streets with four-track subways to a 204-foot super-highway near the outskirts of the present city.

The plan does not call for building any or all of the super-highway as a complete unit at the start, as it is recognized that the full width of highway will not be required except as the suburban area develops, and that two-track rapid transit lines will serve adequately until the city passes the ten-mile limit. When that point has been reached, the two additional tracks for express service can be added in the space reserved for that purpose and possibly the inner roadways for fast motor traffic will be added at the same time.

The provision for the fast motor traffic is one of the important features of the plan. These roadways will be so arranged on the radial highways that there will be no cross traffic to interfere with or delay the traffic. This separation of the through from the cross traffic will be accomplished by elevating the two motor speedways as well as the four rapid transit tracks above the cross streets at half-mile intervals. Crosstown traffic will pass under the motor and rapid transit lines through archways which will also provide for access to the rapid transit stations. Thus foot passengers will not be required to cross the motor speedway.

The super-highway district, adds The Engineering News-Record, is generally divided into areas approximately three miles square, or of about nine square miles, bounded on all four sides by super-highways. The super-highway system does not include the thoroughfares through the subdivisions of those areas surrounded by the super-highways themselves, but the plan considers it desirable that the intermediate section line roads located on the mile divisions should be made 120 feet wide and the half-mile streets should be 86 feet wide. If the mile streets are given a width of 120 feet, then it will be practicable, if traffic conditions warrant, to convert them into express motor traffic streets by elevating the express lanes over the half-mile cross streets, as will be done in the case of the super-highways.

The super-highway plan was prepared for the Detroit Rapid Transit Commission by Daniel L. Turner, consulting engineer, and John G. Hallihan, engineer in charge.

June 29, 1924

Thousands of Acres for a New System of Parks and Parkways

Robert Moses, President of the Long Island State Park Commission and Chairman of The State Council of Parks, Outlines Major Features of Big Development Plan

By ROBERT MOSES,

President of the Long Island State Park Commission and Chairman of the State Council of Parks.

THE program for traffic relief through wide arteries and parkways and for recreation areas on Long Island should have been well past the land acquisition stage before the so-called boom in Long Island real estate began. It is futile to consider the reasons why the State and local Governments did not proceed faster in the light of the many signs and figures pointing to the early and rapid growth of Long Island, particularly Queens and Nassau Counties. The City of New York had taken important steps, especially toward traffic relief, to meet the problem within its own borders. The greatest mistake that the city has made on Long Island has been its failure to acquire large park areas in Queens, particularly the wooded natural park areas on the border of Nassau County.

When the Long Island State Park Commission began its work there were practically no recreational facilities open to the general public in Nassau and Suffolk counties except a few inadequate town and village parks and beaches and the more or less inaccessible town lands off the south shore. Practically nothing had been done toward meeting the traffic problem in Nassau County caused by the building of great arteries and widening of roads in Queens. The program developed by the Long Island State Park Commission for park areas on the shore and inland is now fairly well known to the general public. A solution of the traffic problem was worked out at the instance of the Long Island State Park Commission and at the request of Governor Smith by a conference representing the State highway, park and other authorities, county authorities of Nassau and the public works authorities of the City of New York. The solution proposed includes the widening of certain main routes, such as the Jericho and North Hempstead Turnpikes, the establishment of new State highways and the construction of two State parkways. This program will provide over 500 feet of pavement east of the Nassau border to meet some 700 feet being constructed by the city.

Commission Meets With Opposition.

As indicated above, the opposition to this program needs no extended consideration. More and more people understand the source of the opposition, and the public generally is more interested in the results which are being achieved by public officials than in their complaints about the difficulties and obstacles being put in their way. Any public official who expects to make a definite and permanent impression on a problem of this kind in a territory like Long Island without unfair and unjust opposition must start without any idea of the nature and scope of the problem. The opposition on Long Island comes not only from people who are uninformed but also from those who are constitutionally apathetic about public improvements or actually hostile to them, from those who are selfish and want to build a Chinese wall around their communities, insisting that the second best locations are good enough for the public, and from those who have some grudge or argument with public authorities and are able, by hiring a lobby, to influence for a short time political and local public opinion. Other, though less open, sources of opposition are the private or endowed planning groups which slap all sorts of plans on paper without any responsibility for finding the laws, the means or the courage to carry them out.

The problems on Long Island are too great, and the public, when it is informed, is too fair and too sensible to be influenced for any length of time by this sort of opposition. Moreover, the people interested directly in developing the island—in building, transportation and business—know that without intelligent plans and immediate action the growth of the community in an orderly way will be interrupted and conditions will be created which will be permanently harmful.

The recent real estate, housing and related activities on Long Island differ very widely from those in Westchester. Perhaps the most important and most unfortunate single difference between the developments in the two sections lies in the fact that the boom on Long Island has up to recently been practically unsupported by the public improvements without which land at some distance from New York City is inaccessible and relatively worthless for residence, recreation or other active use. You can buy or settle in Westchester and be sure when you go of present and future accessibility and the public conveniences in the section in question. On Long Island up to recently, and even today, you have only promises and often empty promises to guide you on these essential points.

Suffolk and Nassau Counties.

In order to make my meaning clear I should say that by public improvements I mean not only railroads, highways, parkways and parks, but also adequate water, sewerage, garbage, fire, police, zoning and other facilities and protection. This requires not only State plans as to main thoroughfares and recreation areas and other matters of region-wide importance, but also definite county, town and village plans coordinated and tied up with the State program on the one hand and the plans of the greater city on the other. That we are very far from any such program on Long Island every well-informed person will admit. Westchester is way ahead of Long Island in this respect, and the solution of Westchester's problems is much less important to the whole metropolitan community than the future development of the much larger area east of the city on Long Island. So much for the general aspects of the problem.

The specific program laid down by the Long Island State Park Commission calls for the acquisition by transfer, gift, purchase or otherwise of certain substantial areas properly located in Nassau and Suffolk counties. On this part of the plan considerable progress has been made. The City of New York has been persuaded to turn over two thousand acres of the old Brooklyn water works properties in Nassau County, constituting some six strips of parks, with attractive lakes, brooks and ponds. The Southern State Parkway will pass through these properties. The Federal Government has ceded a substantial area at Fire Island adjoining the old Fire Island State Park and also a very small area at Lloyd Neck, now used by the Conservation Department. The State has acquired by eminent domain Deer Range Park at East Islip and a substantial park area on both sides of the Montauk peninsula.

State Buys Belmont Acreage.

The State has recently bought a substantial part of the Belmont Nursery Farm, with the Belmont Lake, through which the Southern State Parkway will pass. Negotiations for a park on the north shore in Suffolk County are practically completed, in addition to the park at Wading River acquired by gift and purchase from the Mitchell estate. Other negotiations for park land are now pending.

The Legislature has also made available out of bond issue funds and current revenues considerable, though inadequate, funds for construction, development and maintenance on the park areas already acquired. The Long Island State Park Commission is proceeding with plans for the expenditure of these funds as fast as the conditions surrounding Government work will permit.

Under an act just passed at Albany the Hempstead Planning Commission has been set up, composed of three nominees of the Town of Hempstead and the three Long Island State Park Commissioners, to work out a program for the development and leasing of over ten thousand acres of town lands on the south shore belonging to the Town of Hempstead. This plan contemplates a causeway constructed by the State and the use of the beach as a State park, the meadow lands being leased by the town and being connected at appropriate intervals with the causeway, thus giving access to them from the mainland.

Jones Beach Causeway.

The causeway to Jones Beach will have a spur leading to Long Beach and with the early connection of the Rockaways and Long Beach, and if the towns of Oyster Bay and Babylon cooperate, there will be an opportunity for a beach boulevard extending from the western end of the Rockaways all the way to Jones Beach opposite Babylon, where it will terminate either at the Cedar Island Inlet or at the Fire Island Inlet. The Fire Island Inlet will for some time constitute a gap, which can probably be bridged by ferry, between this boulevard and a boulevard to the east extending all the way from the western end of Fire Island to Southampton.

So far as parkways and roads are concerned the new connecting links with the city highways in Nassau County, agreed to by the conference referred to above, were all incorporated in a bill at Albany, which is before the Governor for signature. These are the roads connecting with the Grand Central Parkway. Union Turnpike and Hillside Avenue, indicated on the map above. Under another act before the Governor, the re-location of these arteries through the Creedmoor Hospital grounds is provided for. Another act just signed by the Governor and prepared by the State park and highway authorities provides $1,000,000 for widening main arteries in Nassau and Erie Counties, $350,000 of which will go toward paving the first five miles of the Southern State Parkway on a right of way to be provided by the Long Island State Park Commission.

Park funds have also been provided for acquisition of land for rights of way on this parkway, but the sum available will not be adequate unless substantial dedications are made by owners of large tracts who will be enormously benefited by this improvement. A new through route connected with Jamaica Avenue, leading through Brooklyn, has been put on the highway map, leading all the way through Nassau County, and also a continuation of the Pipe Line Boulevard from the Suffolk County line to connect with other State roads through the middle of the island. It will be some time before these new roads can be paved, but they have at least been placed on the highway map and there is nothing to prevent the county from going ahead and acquiring the necessary rights of way, the State being prepared to furnish the surveys almost immediately.

Progress by the State park authorities on the Northern State Parkway has been delayed through local opposition in the Wheatley and Manetto Hills. In the meantime the great Nassau Boulevard leading up to the Wheatley Hills is being constructed by the city and grading work is already going on just west of the Nassau border. This new city artery will bring 110 feet of pavement to the Nassau border, and the traffic over this pavement can be taken care of only through the Northern State Parkway and the Belt Line agreed to by the city authorities in Queens, which will provide for the shifting of truck traffic to other arteries just west of the Nassau border.

Only a Beginning.

In the various plans, developments and legislative measures referred to above which primarily affect Nassau County the State authorities have had the cordial cooperation of county and town authorities in Nassau County.

The above is an outline of the major features of the State park, parkway and highway program on Long Island. While the program is ambitious it by no means does more than fill immediate needs, and it represents only the great metropolitan developments and not the many local improvements which should be coordinated with them. Large sums will be needed to complete this program. Part of the funds for this purpose as well as for the completion of similar developments in other park regions are in sight. Additional State and local highway funds must undoubtedly be obtained. The highway fund problem can be solved in part through special appropriations, like the one this year for Nassau and Erie, but probably nothing short of a gasoline tax will really meet the problem.

Seek Public Aid.

The related problem of park and parkway developments in New York City, particularly in Queens and Kings Counties, can be taken care of under the plans proposed by the Metropolitan Conference of State and City Park Authorities, which have been submitted to the Board of Estimate in general form and which are ready for a decision by the city authorities.

There is every evidence that intelligent people on Long Island are studying this whole problem with increasing interest and sympathy. Owners of property who are interested in its development are beginning to look with favor on cooperation with the State authorities, taking their example from other communities where such cooperation has been mutually beneficial. The recent dedication of the right of way through the Belmont, Guggenheim and other properties on the southern parkway is a case in point. If similar action is taken along the first part of the southern parkway, this great avenue from the city line will be available for public use very soon. Owners of land are beginning to realize that State parks and parkways will benefit adjoining property and that the widening of highways and the establishment of new through routes is a vitally necessary thing which, if delayed, will simply cause great inconvenience and expense in the end.

The public authorities charged with the solution of this problem seek the help of all those who are ready to approach it in a fair way.

Donates 160-Foot Parkway.

Cadman H. Frederick, who last year purchased from Mrs. August Belmont the 1,000-acre Belmont estate at Babylon, L. I., has since sold 200 acres, the mansion, numerous other buildings and the forty-acre Belmont Lake to the Long Island State Park Commission.

Following closely upon the sale, Mr. Frederick donated to the Park Commission the road through the Belmont property, known as Belmont Road, together with sufficient land to provide for a 160-foot parkway for a distance of two and one-half miles, running west and east through the property, for the Southern State Parkway.

Discussing the effect of the new Long Island Park and Parkway system on the future of Long Island, Mr. Frederick said: "The park and parkway system planned by the commission for Long Island should have the unqualified support of Long Islanders in general and in particular of those who have it in their power to facilitate the carrying out of plans for the important improvements already projected and proposed.

"The automobile today is the most important of all factors in the development of the suburbs, and parks and parkways are absolutely necessary to the development of the sections outside of the city limits. The effect of the completion of a comprehensive park and parkway system on Long Island will be the same as it has been in Westchester County and elsewhere, wherever parks and parkways have been scientifically planned and systematically carried out.

"In Westchester County, for instance, where the Westchester County Park Commission, in conjunction with the State Council of Parks, has done such excellent work, millions of dollars have been saved to the taxpayers and the public at large, by the purchase of the lands necessary to the Westchester Park and Parkway system at a time when these lands could be purchased at reasonable prices.

Increase in Values.

"Since the Westchester County parks and parkways were planned and, in some instances, completed, there has been an enormous advance in values along the route of each and every one.

"This increase in values means that there has been a corresponding increase in ratables and that both the State of New York and Westchester County will derive a considerably greater revenue from taxes.

"What has been true of Westchester County is equally as true today on Long Island. The time to buy the necessary property is now, while the necessary land can be had at the present comparatively low levels of value.

If the Long Island State Parkway Commission has to wait a few years to buy the necessary lands, millions of dollars will be wasted and the public will pay the freight.

"It is impossible to over rate the good work done by the Council of Parks, the Long Island State Parkway Commission, and Governor Smith, who has given his most ardent support to the creation of the greatest park and parkway system in the world."

ALL OUR CITIES STRUGGLE IN TRAFFIC TANGLES

Many Are Rushing Work on New Highways and Wider Streets While Experimenting With Various Systems of Control—Only Los Angeles Thinks It Has Found a Solution—A Survey of Conditions

Street traffic in American cities has reached a state of congestion and danger which now holds national attention. At a moment when New York is directing intensive study to the problem it becomes worth while to compare the experiences of other cities. Even casual inquiry shows the increase of automobiles to be the first and evident cause. Concentration of skyscrapers and shopping centres is another reason. But the yearly output of automobiles aggravates a condition almost beyond control. The United States now has 22,000,000 trucks and passenger cars in operation and the total of new cars for 1926 was estimated at about 4,500,000. Fatal automobile accidents are expected to number more than 25,000 when this year's figures are compiled.

Every new automobile does not mean another one added to street congestion, but the ratio is about three new cars to one retired. So great has production become, and so difficult the problem of street regulation, that the motor car defeats its prime purpose of speed in a large measure. In the early days of its introduction it afforded a quick and sure means of transportation. The fact of its success has brought other millions of cars into use until they clutter every street.

While automobiles have been increasing at a rate measured only by the American pocketbook, streets and highways have increased but slowly, at least by comparison. The pressure for room is greatest in the streets. The truth of the matter seems to be that American cities reached maturity too soon. They were designed—when there was any designing—for the day of the horse-car and the horse and buggy. Then came rapid transit in the form of the street car, the elevated road and subway. Old streets were made to serve the new purpose as best they might. Next came the motor car in rising millions and a stalemate that urgently presses for solution.

Causes and Suggested Cures.

Hardly a city in the country except Los Angeles fails to report confusion, injury and discord over automobile traffic. The California city has adopted a plan of control which apparently works. One or two outstanding conclusions seem to be justified in the case of all other cities, including New York:

> It is not speed, but a lack of it, that causes most of the trouble.
>
> Wherever modern boulevards are available the automobile justifies itself as a vehicle for rapid transportation.
>
> Parking under any conditions infringes on the rights of everybody and never should be permitted for more than a few minutes.
>
> The rebuilding of American cities with boulevards in successive circles connected by radial streets is the only ultimate remedy.
>
> Subways and elevated roadways provide prompt and enduring relief.

The rebuilding process has begun in important centres. Many blocks of old buildings are giving way to broad thoroughfares. In such cities as Milwaukee and Chicago it is planned to connect streets and country highways in vast geometrical systems financed by cities, counties and States in a combined plan for action.

New York is about to engage in creating important motor outlets by extending Sixth Avenue to Canal Street, on the west side with a near-by vehicular tunnel to Jersey City and the southern terminus of an elevated automobile roadway close at hand, which will run along Twelfth Avenue to Riverside Drive. Allen Street, on the east side, will be widened and become a thoroughfare for north and south traffic to Delancey Street and the Williamsburg Bridge.

Municipal reconstruction is under way all over the country, offering new opportunities to improve American cities and keep up with the pace of the motor age. A review of conditions in the larger cities outside New York follows:

CHICAGO.

Chicago and Cook County, in which the city lies, have embarked upon a comprehensive plan of traffic improvement. The voters of Cook County at the recent election approved a bond issue of $15,000,000 as their part of $32,000,000 to be spent in the widening and improvement of 535 miles of highways and streets entering Chicago. By voting the expenditure of $15,000,000 on the terminal highway system, Cook County actually will receive the benefit of more than twice that amount from State funds and current county and municipal financing.

As a consequence the widening of congested arteries leading into Chicago to forty feet and the construction of new gateway roads is now assured on a broad scale. Surveys and grading work for thoroughfares to carry traffic through the city will be started at once and the first widened pavements opened to traffic early in the Summer of 1927.

In addition to this $32,000,000 program the Chicago Plan Commission has recommended among future improvements the creation of an eighty-mile boulevard system on the outskirts and an elevated boulevard from the "Loop" or central business district to the northwest side. This encircling boulevard and the diagonal artery are in keeping with a wider plan for the development of boulevards and streets.

The pattern is one of concentric circles, their centre being the "Loop," to meet the lake north and southeast of Chicago with radial roads running from the centre to the circumference like the spokes of a wheel. The proposed outer boulevard would afford a convenient means of getting from the northwest side to the south side without entering congested streets near the centre of the city. But the geometric pattern does not stop at the city limits. It provides for three outer highway belts, enabling through traffic to avoid the city entirely.

The outermost belt highway begins at Milwaukee, curving west at Kenosha, passing through McHenry, Woodstock, Genoa, Dekalb, Millington, Morris, Kankakee and Momence into Indiana, ending at La Porte and Michigan City. The second belt begins at Waukegan, passes through Elgin, Aurora and Joliet and ends at Gary. The inner belt begins at Winnetka and ends at South Chicago and Gary.

Drastic changes in traffic control have been recommended in a report prepared by the street traffic committee of the Chicago Association of Commerce, and now engaging the attention of the municipal authorities. It includes abolition of "Loop" parking privileges, exclusion of horse-drawn vehicles from the business district, the "staggering" of business hours and regulations for foot traffic.

Other recommendations include uniform traffic laws for the metropolitan district, county control or progressive timing system for all stop and go lights, continued efforts to close bridges during the rush hours, the widening and double-decking of heavily traveled streets, additional through streets and arterial highways and wider country roads as gateways to the main thoroughfares of Chicago.

ST. LOUIS.

After two years of diligent effort to solve the traffic problem, St. Louis in 1927 is entering upon a further program of street widening, cutting through new streets and reconstruction work designed to afford quicker movement from the congested districts to the outskirts of the city, which will include 171 construction and paving projects at a cost of about $4,300,000 for paving alone.

Congestion in the downtown district has been controlled by establishment of "no parking" rules throughout the area during the rush hours, morning and night. These rules prevail in a district a mile wide by two miles long, from 7 to 9:30 A. M. and 4:30 to 6 P. M. Other parking restrictions are imposed in certain districts during the hours of heaviest traffic. Many one-way streets aid more rapid movement.

The widening of Olive Street into a main artery 100 feet wide between the business district and the West End has already caused the destruction of eighteen blocks of buildings along one side of the street. Vendeventer Avenue and Enright Avenue are to be widened to relieve special districts, and Cote Brillante will be widened to give better access to the county through Wellston. The Denny Road, in the county, will be made a 100-foot thoroughfare, traversing a wide area.

"Stop and Go" signals operate at many of the corners with satisfactory results. Safety islands have been installed at car stops near schools and new traffic stops are being enforced, as the paving of neglected streets opens up new thoroughfares for the movement of traffic.

Control of the traffic situation is in the hands of a Traffic Council. Its authority to make rules has been challenged several times by attorneys who say that the City Council has no power to delegate authority to the traffic body.

DETROIT.

In an effort to improve traffic facilities Detroit is widening many streets. In three years sixty miles have been widened, and the program calls for fifty more in 1927. The Police Department also has prepared and put into effect a new traffic code governing parking conditions and driving.

Detroit's parking regulations have suffered by the failure of the police to enforce them. Past regulations covered too wide a field, traffic officers being obliged to spend most of their time in ticket writing. The courts could not handle the number of cases, even with 75 per cent. of the "tagged" motorists ignoring tickets entirely. Now offenders go to the Traffic Bureau and pay "assessments," not fines. Otherwise they go before the Judge. This, in a measure, is helping matters.

The new code gives the police power to seize cars illegally parked, such car being classified as "a nuisance." This law grants the police the right to charge "towing fees," but not a right to collect fees for impounding a vehicle. A writ of replevin may recover a car.

Meanwhile, traffic experts have tackled the job of unraveling the maze of traffic light signals installed at corners by the Mayor's committee. Already motorists have found it possible to traverse streets without being halted by red lights at every second corner. The experts are using a progressive timing method. Many of the lights on unimportant downtown corners have been removed and are to protect school street intersections in residential districts.

PITTSBURGH.

Solution of Pittsburgh's problems of street congestion perhaps is more difficult than any of the larger cities of America. Municipal authorities have employed numerous experts, but none has found relief for the narrow streets and irregular intersections in the city's "Golden Triangle."

Subways have been advocated and bond issues voted for the building of an underground system. But as yet no definite plan has been adopted. Pittsburgh has nothing but surface trolley lines at present.

Streets have been widened wherever possible in the last three or four years. The city and Allegheny County authorities are at work on plans to remove the County Jail and other county buildings to permit street widening, thus opening new arteries into the downtown district.

These plans, with the completion of six new bridges over the rivers, are expected to bring relief. The bridges and a new traffic tube just outside the triangle will deliver traffic at scattered points instead of in two or three central routes. Pittsburgh police control traffic by means of officers on crossings in the downtown area. Automatic signals are impracticable because of the many irregular corners and the abundance of left-hand turns. Signal towers are operated in outlying sections. The river front for several years has been used as a public parking place. There are few streets where parking is permitted in the business section.

CITIES TAKE STOCK OF TRAFFIC

STREET hazards and highway congestion in the larger American cities, resulting from the rapid multiplication of motor vehicles, have created extraordinary problems for municipal officials. The very growth of cities has been threatened by the conditions that have arisen.

To overcome this situation drastic measures have been proposed. In some cities huge sums have been voted for widening old streets and cutting new thoroughfares through built-up sections. Ultimately it may be necessary, it is believed, to rebuild some cities with boulevards in concentric circles connected by radial streets. These and other radical plans for relief are being considered in cities where traffic congestion has become so great that no less costly solution seems practicable.

In all cities the problem for the moment seems to centre on the issue of traffic control. Mechanical means such as the system of regulating traffic by lights, as it is done in New York City, are being employed in other cities of the country.

Parking is more and more coming to be recognized as a leading cause of the increasing congestion. City regulations are being enforced more strictly.

The United States, it is now estimated, has about 22,000,000 motor trucks and pleasure cars in operation, and a total output of about 4,500,000 more is expected for the current year, which, it is further estimated, means three new cars for each one retired. The grim estimate of 25,000 fatal motor car accidents for the year is also put forward as sufficient explanation of the immediate and growing necessity of coping with the traffic problem.

In the accompanying article the conditions in eleven of the largest cities are surveyed, and a summary of suggestions for improving conditions is given.

BOSTON.

One of the most serious municipal problems in Boston is the congestion of street traffic. Solution is even more difficult than in many other cities because Boston's streets are notoriously crooked and narrow.

The first step taken to speed the flow of traffic was the widening of a number of main thoroughfares. This policy was first adopted on a large scale in 1920 and is still being followed, although the cost is high, owing to damages for land in the heart of the business district.

In 1920 an east and west artery leading from the Back Bay toward the South station was begun at a cost of about $3,000,000, involving the widening of Stuart Street. This plan is being extended further toward its objective by the widening of Kneeland Street at a cost of $1,225,000. A passage to the suburbs in the north and west was cut through last year by the widening of Cambridge Street at a cost of $4,000,000. A similar line to the south is nearing completion by the widening of Tremont Street at a cost of $1,225,000. In the market district Dock Square has been broadened at a cost of $2,000,000 to facilitate the flow of traffic.

All of the foregoing improvements have been made in the centre of the city. Last year the same policy was extended to three main highways in the outlying southern sections of Boston

A loop highway which would skirt the waterfront and connect the north of the city with the south, avoiding the centre, has been considered by the Legislature for several years, but the plan does not appear to be anywhere near adoption because of the high cost, $35,000,000, and because of divergence of opinion as to the best route. Construction of a bridge over the harbor to East Boston is another project which all leaders agree is necessary to speed northbound traffic.

Traffic is handled by a special traffic police squad of 255 men in two divisions, one with headquarters downtown and one in the Back Bay.

Aside from standards bearing a lantern and "keep to the right" warning, and directional signs, Boston's entire signal system consists of one multiple-light signal pole operated by an officer from the sidewalk, and two multiple light traffic towers operated by an officer on the inside. The former was installed by the city and the other two were gifts from merchants who have large stores in the vicinity.

There is a complex set of traffic regulations concerning parking, one-way streets and turns to right or left. The general parking limit is one hour, but there are a number of streets downtown where parking is allowed for two hours. In still other central areas parking is unlimited after 6 P. M. and in others unlimited during the day.

A proposal for a viaduct to accommodate street cars and motor vehicles has been offered by the metropolitan planning board of the State as a remedy in Governor Square.

SAN FRANCISCO.

Solution of the street traffic problem in San Francisco is still in the formative stage. After trying the plan of a traffic commission named by the Mayor, but without authority to enforce its rules and decisions, the whole plan was abandoned, the commission resigning in a body.

But recognizing that action was necessary, the Mayor named a City Traffic Survey Committee, consisting of leading citizens, who in turn formed a larger body representing every interest directly concerned with traffic, such as retail and wholesale merchants, taxicab concerns, trucking companies, railroads, street car companies, office building owners and hotel men. These, with engineers and city planning experts, decided to make a scientific survey of the city. It is to be completed this month, when the adoption of city-wide traffic rules will be ready for consideration.

In the meantime the Traffic Bureau of the Police Department is enforcing former rules that have gradually grown up as problems became acute. The main features of these rules, which in general have proved successful, are as follows:

No left hand turns in Market Street, the main downtown thoroughfare.

Forty-minute parking rules for all downtown streets where parking is allowed.

No parking in Montgomery Street, the financial district.

Parking generally forbidden in alleys and lanes, in order to give the Fire Department room to operate if necessary.

Automatic signals have been installed at street intersections downtown and are rapidly being extended to all congested points.

Arterial streets also have been designated for thoroughfares in which the main traffic flows at busy periods. Stop signs have been installed, but are not universally observed, because of lack of men to enforce rules.

While the police have a regular traffic division, so many men are needed at the worst corners that 100 regular patrolmen are detailed to aid the traffic squad. Control of pedestrians and jay-walkers is not yet in force, but is under consideration. The most noteworthy aid to traffic was the building of a subway more than 1,000 feet long, on the Embarcadero, in front of the Ferry Building, to take all crosstown traffic off the waterfront. It has proved a great success.

There the main road, or Peninsula Highway, is being widened to 150 feet. Two new highways, the Bayshore and Skyline, are being constructed. Approach from east and north is by ferry only, and privately owned companies try to keep up with demands.

LOS ANGELES.

In the matter of traffic regulation, notwithstanding 590,000 motor vehicles registered in the county, Los Angeles assumes to take a position in the front rank of American cities as concerns the flow of automobiles through its streets.

Up to 1922 traffic laws were of the hit-and-miss kind. At that time a group of business men and civic leaders organized the Traffic Commission, and traffic engineers and city planners were employed. The first real traffic law was drawn by Dr. Miller McClintock, now head of the Erskine Bureau of Traffic Research of Harvard University, and took effect late in 1924. It provided a number of simple rules well understood by motorists and pedestrians.

Pedestrians have the right of way in crosswalks, except at intersections protected by signals, when the mutual rights of pedestrians and motorists are observed. Between crossings the automobile has the right of way and "jay-walking" is a misdemeanor.

Pedestrians are forced to obey traffic signals, either by automatic device or policemen. By education this rule has been successful. Pedestrians observe the "stop" and "go" signals as well as automobile drivers. Approximately 180 street intersections have been protected with automatic signal devices, 150 more of which are to be installed.

At intersections automobiles making a right-hand turn are required to keep close to the curb, and those making left-hand turns must keep to the lane next to the centre of the street.

Several of the main arteries are "boulevard stop" streets, and every automobile must come to a full stop before entering from an intersecting street.

Parking is so regulated as to allow of maximum parking without congesting the roadways. "Double line" parking is forbidden, "loading zones" being provided at frequent intervals for the loading and unloading of commercial vehicles.

No parking is allowed in the downtown district between 4:30 and 6 P. M. From 7 A. M. until 4:30 P. M. parking is limited to forty-five minutes in the congested area.

Approximately 350 policemen out of a total of 2,500 are assigned to the traffic squad. They wear distinctive uniforms.

In seeking a solution of the problem the Traffic Commission decided that the street area should be increased through the opening and widening of arterial highways. City planners were employed who drew up the major traffic street plan adopted by the voters in 1924 as the official plan of Los Angeles.

The major traffic street plan calls for the widening of main arteries to 100 feet, the next class of streets to 80 feet, the bounding of the business district with 120-foot streets and the construction of a parkway system.

MILWAUKEE.

Milwaukee has begun widening streets to relieve traffic congestion, but no comprehensive plan has been adopted. At the northern city limits a street 120 feet wide has been provided, and at the southern limits another 110 feet wide, extending from east to west across the city.

Property is being bought and buildings are being torn down to make way for a street 130 feet wide from east to west through the downtown business district. Initial steps have been taken to provide two north-and-south traffic ways 110 and 120 feet wide, one in the downtown district and another about a mile west. In the outlying district where development is under way a number of streets are to be widened.

Milwaukee County has adopted a system of highways covering the entire county, from 90 to 160 feet wide, the latter being a super-highway to Chicago. These wide county highways lie outside the limits of municipalities and will serve as a basis for wider streets in Milwaukee and other cities.

A graduated system of parking in Milwaukee permits a maximum of thirty minutes in the downtown business area, ranging to unlimited parking in the outer city districts.

A combination of light signals and traffic officers obtains in the city. On the less busy intersections in the downtown area, green and red corner lights guide traffic. At the busy intersections the traffic officer's whistle is the signal to go or stop.

A number of arterial highways cross the city in all directions, starting from the downtown area.

BUFFALO.

A comprehensive effort is under way to end traffic congestion in Buffalo by the use of automatic signal lights, wider streets, one-way thoroughfares and new traffic arteries.

An unusual organization that sits weekly to discuss traffic problems was created here two years ago. The traffic board is empowered to enforce its regulations and has eliminated congestion in the downtown section by the limitation of parking time, one-way streets and the installation of signals.

The parking limit in the crowded sections has been cut to thirty minutes in the densest areas and to sixty minutes in other sections. A system of tagging autos by the police has taken hundreds of motorists into the courts charged with violation of the parking limits and resulted in almost total elimination of abuses.

In two years the City Council has accomplished the widening of Delaware Avenue for two miles. As this street carries the bulk of automobile traffic in Buffalo the improvement has speeded traffic to such an extent that travel flows in unbroken lines at twenty-five to thirty miles an hour. This avenue is the outlet for traffic to and from Niagara Falls and other points along the Niagara border north of Buffalo. The council aided by the City Planning Commission, an independent body, is planning the widening of Delaware Avenue as far as the city line, creating a boulevard 106 feet wide through the park and residential section.

Other streets that have been widened to facilitate movement of traffic in the downtown area are Pearl, Ellicott, Franklin, Eagle and Genesee. Traffic in the past was hampered by the loading and unloading of trucks, but with the wider streets there is less trouble.

In the area outside Buffalo the principal improvement under consideration is the widening of the Lake Shore road, which carries all traffic to and from the West. The Erie County supervisors also are planning a new high speed road from the Erie County line to Buffalo, the highway to parallel the old road.

BALTIMORE.

Legal tangles over the city's parking ordinance complicate traffic regulations in congested sections, but Police Department officials say that conditions are no worse than in other large cities.

A local court declared the Police Commissioner's regulations illegal and the parking ordinance invalid. The case was sent to the State Court of Appeals and the Commissioner asserts nothing further will be done until the parking laws are soundly established. He will try granting permission to downtown business men to control parking space in front of their establishments. While such an arrangement may be satisfactory to merchants, hotels or banking institutions, it increases and aggravates the general traffic congestion.

Parking privileges are liberal in Baltimore. Even under these favorable conditions for motorists 200 drivers daily on an average are haled into traffic court for parking violations. Plans have been suggested and discussed by the city authorities to relieve congestion, but the widening of narrow streets in the retail shopping centre and other business districts is considered prohibitive because of cost. Had not the streets along the waterfront been greatly broadened after the fire in 1904 free traffic now would be almost impossible. In several outlying sections at important junction points of street railways the streets also have been widened to facilitate traffic.

Baltimore began putting up automatic light signals about eighteen months ago. There are only forty-five of these in use in a city of 850,000 population. It is proposed to install forty or fifty more the current year. Two hundred traffic policemen are employed, mostly in the business sections.

WASHINGTON.

Washington has instituted steps within the last year to solve her growing problem of traffic congestion. It has seemed strange to visitors that until recently the national capital never used a system of light control for automobile traffic, but the matter was approached carefully because of the manner in which the city is laid out, with avenues running at angles into circles. However, a complete system of light control has now been installed in Sixteenth Street, one of the principal thoroughfares, and soon will be put into effect in Connecticut Avenue and main arteries.

Virtually all the principal streets leading into the city will have a speed limit of thirty miles an hour until the congested section is reached. Sixteenth Street has been provided with speed light signals, regulating traffic from thirty miles down to twenty-two miles, the authorized speed in the main parts of the city. The outlying sections of Connecticut, Wisconsin and Rhode Island Avenues, Pennsylvania Avenue Southeast, and the Bladensburg Road will have similar high speed limits.

Sections of Connecticut Avenue, Thirteenth Street and E Street have been widened by reducing the sidewalks, affording greater space for parking, and also greater area for moving traffic. An elaborate system of parking has been put into effect. It is prohibited in certain streets during rush hours and only a thirty-minute period is allowed at other times. Outside of a special congested section the parking limit runs through one-hour and two-hour periods to all-day permission. In many instances merchants are allowed to put "no parking" signs outside their places of business, in order that patrons may approach the shops, and also that trucks may have free access.

Heavy penalties and revocation of permits have checked traffic violation within the year.

January 9, 1927

PARKING PROBLEMS IN SUBURBAN TOWNS

Necessary to Provide Facilities Before Difficulty Becomes Too Serious.

Calling attention to the increasing necessity of providing proper parking space in the suburbs, an official of the Homeland Company, which has several subdivisions in Westchester County and New Jersey, points out that before the question reaches the unanswerable stage it should be taken in hand by the local authorities, with the cooperation of planning boards and real estate experts.

He says that the railroads can hardly be expected to turn over large areas of their land for the free use of parked automobiles. It is the duty of the communities themselves to take care of their citizens' needs in this respect, as they do with other common problems. Several of the towns in the suburban district have already started to take this matter under consideration.

Mamaroneck has set aside several acres near the railroad station for parking cars. Bronxville has an elaborately laid out plaza, where, however, all-day parking is not allowed.

The village of Scarsdale has appointed a commission to study the problem. Several solutions have been offered. One suggestion was that for a consideration cars could be left at the station and taken by licensed drivers to the home garage and returned for the evening trains. Another possibility suggested was that a municipal garage be erected of sufficient size to care for the average number of commuters' cars, and that it be operated at cost so that a small monthly fee would cover maintenance.

This would not, it is pointed out, be practical in many towns, since land near enough to the station to be useful is generally zoned for business and commands higher prices, although there are still some communities where land could be purchased at a reasonable figure, and such a garage, being a municipally operated utility, would be free from assessment and might prove a profitable venture.

"Like every other condition which is connected with the acquisition and use of the rapidly diminishing available land in the near-by suburbs," says the Homeland spokesman, "the sooner the difficulty is attacked the less serious will it be in the future."

September 29, 1929

THE 'FREEWAY' SYSTEM EXPANDS

Broader Roads With Grade Crossings Eliminated Are Built and Latest Designs Envision Still Greater Speed and Safety

By E. L. YORDAN.

NEW, fast highways are being announced somewhere almost every week. New York City has just had word of two developments—one a plan of Commissioner of Parks Robert Moses to make direct connections between the city's roadways and the parkways leading through Westchester and beyond, the other Mayor La Guardia's extensive highway program for the city, for which he is seeking PWA funds.

More highways, faster highways, safer highways has been the persistent cry of motorists since they began taking to the road in great numbers. Faster and cheaper automobiles—the motorist also demanded these, and got them. In the mind of the motorist a car is no better than the road it travels on; consequently he has demanded new types of highways to keep pace with the powerful machine at his command.

Today the users of nearly 25,000,000 motor vehicles in this country, for many of whom sixty miles an hour is a cruising speed, must be provided with roadways capable of accommodating a greatly increased volume of traffic and keeping it moving.

The majority of drivers are not content with a spin in the country that will take them 100 or 125 miles away from home; having had a taste of distance, they think little of traveling 250, even 300 miles, in one day, to reach mountain or seashore resorts.

Aims of the Engineer.

Hence the activities of highway planners to provide road systems that will permit present-day car owners to range further afield than ever before. Hence the present efforts not only to speed traffic within large metropolitan areas, but to give outlets to suburban country and, beyond that, express connections with recreational centres, beaches, mountain resorts, as well as between large cities.

Thus at present there are road-building movements in two directions—one toward the extension of parkways, super-highways, express highways and "skyways"; the other toward development of new types of highways—the "freeway," the "limited way" and the "tour way."

Highways being built for the new day in automobiling are aligned almost like railroads, with few curves and the sharper turns super-elevated; with crossing at grade eliminated by means of ramps, "cloverleaves," overpasses and underpasses; with roadsides beautiful and

protected against any encroachment that might endanger or impede traffic, roads bypassing congested business and residential centres and rights-of-way wide enough to provide for future needs.

The improvements in highways demanded by the growth of traffic and the changing habits of motorists have been numerous and rapid, considering, for example, that express or super-highways were a novelty in 1928 and today form an important part in the highway program of every large city.

Growth of Roads System.

It was not long after the introduction of cars at prices millions of persons could afford that the wishes of the car owners made themselves felt. To offer a graphic comparison, in twenty-five years the highway mileage in the United States grew by nearly 1,000,000 miles, and today the system extends over 3,040,000 miles, of which nearly 1,000,000 miles have a high-type surface.

For many years the chief aim was road length: the car owner wanted new places to see, new territories to explore; he wanted to drive up to the mountains, down to the seashore, along lakes and through scented woods. He demanded, and got, roads of varying degrees of efficiency to take him to all those places. The country was made accessible by car.

And then the inevitable happened: as drivers in increasing number answered the call of new roads, the highways grew more congested, and, in the end, ugly. The city motorist, wishing to devote his Sundays to a little touring with his family, found himself traveling through palisades of billboards, along hot dog emporiums, fruit stands and unsightly roadside establishments of every description; he breathed not the sweet air of the country nor enjoyed its scenery, but instead smelled gasoline fumes and saw little else than monstrous posters. The countryside, made accessible by the automobile, was being defaced in its name.

The Parkway Emerges.

The Sunday motorist and his family complained, and gradually, under the impetus of civic groups in Westchester, Long Island and other localities, a new type of highway, where utility did not jostle out beauty, was evolved. Such lovely thoroughfares as the Bronx River Parkway and the Hutchinson River Parkway, to cite familiar examples, are among the finest roads of the parkway type—designed for short, leisurely drives through enchanting landscapes.

When the Sunday motorist became a legion, overcrowding the winding and relatively narrow parkways, and speeding through them with an eye on destinations in the open country beyond, the emphasis shifted to a straight road and a fast one.

The later-type parkway was the answer—broad, speedy thoroughfares such as the Bronx River Parkway Extension and Saw Mill River Parkway in Westchester, Grand Central Parkway and Northern State Parkway and Southern State Parkway in Long Island. These modern parkways, while not losing sight of scenic values, have for dominant motive the handling of vast numbers of vehicles with maximum expedition.

Heit. From Nesmith.

Approach to a Great City. Engineers Are Designing New Highways to Speed the Motorist.

The Super-Highway Built.

As the motor car extended its usefulness in transportation, the business man, the commuter, the truck and bus operator felt the need of highways better suited to fast, unimpeded service—an improvement on the general utility road. The super-highway was provided permitting motorists to drive for long stretches at a rapid pace over surfaces made as straight and smooth as possible. Such highways as New Jersey's Route 25, leading to the Holland Tunnel, and Route 4, connecting with the George Washington Bridge, are super-highways taking motorists to and from the metropolitan district.

How long motorists will be able to use these super roads to the fullest extent is a matter of concern among regional planners. These experts believe that unless protective measures are taken against the growing up of business establishments along the edges of the highways the usefulness of even such express routes will eventually be impaired.

Thus the "freeway," combining elements of both the parkway and the express route, is the new type of road devised to carry motorists swiftly over long distances. It is the best type of road between large centres of population, according to engineers of the Regional Plan Association. On the freeway no parking is permitted, no loading or unloading; there may be no billboards and only a limited number of approved service stations. While commercial traffic is permitted, it is not allowed to interfere with faster passenger cars. The sides of the freeway are permanently protected from marginal developments, and room is allowed for future expansion.

Several freeways are now in use or under construction—part of the Central Westchester Parkway north of White Plains; the Croton cut-off from Bronx Parkway Extension to the Post Road at Croton River; part of the Briarcliff-Peekskill Parkway, and the road between the new town of Norris and the Norris Dam in the Tennessee Valley.

But, with motorists of the nation ever expanding their field of touring, still other roads must be developed—roads that will lead hundreds of miles from cities. It is to meet a new demand that a nation-wide system of broad, landscaped roads, termed "tourways," which would connect the metropolitan centres with the national parks, has been proposed.

The National Construction Council and the American Society of Civil Engineers are among organizations actively fostering the tourways project. Over the tourways, which are an extension of the freeway principle, the motorist would be able to drive at high speed amid landscaped surroundings and safeguarded by every modern road safety device.

But what of the motorists in the cities—for instance, the more than 1,000,000 residents and visitors who daily use their cars in New York City? For him the elevated highways, the tunnels and bridges have been constructed or are planned. Mayor La Guardia's comprehensive plans for a unified city-wide system is a step in the direction of providing a rapid-transit system for automobile traffic in congested urban areas.

The motorist of the future may ride through the city on "limited ways," considered by Dr. Miller McClintock, director of the Bureau of Street Traffic Research of Harvard University, the only permanent solution of the traffic problem of great cities.

A complete system of limited ways for Chicago has received official approval. New York City, with its elevated highways, tunnels and other express roadways, could, with proper coordination and some alterations, lay out a system of limited ways, according to Dr. McClintock. These arteries not only eliminate cross-flow but completely segregate turning movements and the in-and-out actions of vehicles.

February 24, 1935

AT THE WHEEL

By JAMES O. SPEARING

Parking Meters Successful

PARKING meters in the streets of Oklahoma City and Dallas are proving popular with the public and successful as municipal investments, it is reported in the March issue of Public Safety, National Safety Council publication. When the meters were first installed in Oklahoma City last July they aroused some opposition and a temporary injunction was obtained restraining the city from using them. On appeal, however, the District Court dissolved the injunction, holding that "free use" of the streets did not include parking, which was defined as a privilege granted by the municipality rather than an inalienable right of its citizens.

* * *

In Dallas and Oklahoma City the meters are placed at curbs, spaced to permit a twenty-foot parking "stall" for each car. After leaving his car, the driver deposits a five-cent piece in the meter and immediately a flag is raised, indicating by a pointer the time allowed for the nickel in that district. This may be anything from fifteen minutes to two hours. An arrow begins to move gradually toward zero and, when it reaches that point, the flag drops out of sight, indicating that the parking limit has expired. Any policeman or inspector finding a car standing opposite a meter on which a flag is not showing knows that it is illegally parked and may take such action as the traffic regulations provide.

* * *

Commenting on the experience with meters in Dallas, a writer in Public Safety says:

Drivers like metered parking. The ease with which violations are detected reduces greatly the amount of overtime parking and the monopolization of parking spaces. Drivers can go to destinations in the central business district and find places to park where formerly none was available.

The long-period parkers are thus driven to unrestricted zones or off the street entirely. Officials feel justified in running these "parking hogs" off the street because storage of cars is not considered a responsibility of the city.

Metered parking makes getting in and out of spaces easier than is common in other types of parking enforcement. With twenty feet allowed for each "stall" where the parking is parallel, and with the cars parked with the radiator even with the meter, each driver has nearly twenty-five feet of space in which to manoeuvre. Once parked, he need not fear that other parkers will "close in on him" so that he will not be able to get out. Any "pushing around" to make an extra space where it is not warranted is immediately conspicuous and is a violation of regulations governing metered parking.

All motorists, except parking hogs, also like the meters, it is said, because they increase the accommodations of a street.

* * *

In December, 1934, it was revealed by a survey that an average of 4,100 vehicles were parked in the streets of the shopping district of Dallas in a business day, from 1,100 to 1,200 being parked at the same time, making a turnover for the day of about four cars in each parking space. This area is now served by 1,000 meters and last December there were times when daily deposits amounted to $525, indicating that the streets had accommodated at least 10,500 cars during each day. The total was somewhat greater than this because a certain number of motorists obtained free parking by occupying spaces left vacant by cars before the expiration of the time limit.

* * *

It has been estimated that the meters in Dallas will yield $120,000 a year to the city, or sufficient income to pay for their installation in a little less than six months. Nine persons, representing a total payroll of not more than $15,000 a year, are required to service the meters, make collections, mark parking stalls and check violations. This leaves an appreciable profit for the city and reverses the usual experience in the enforcement of parking regulations, eliminating what has been "a source of financial loss to the city and at the same time a source of grief to the enforcement officials."

March 15, 1936

THE LOWLY PARKING LOT THRIVES

Its Spread Has Been Remarkable, and Mayor La Guardia Recently Endorsed It as an Aid to Ending New York's Traffic Jams

By E. L. YORDAN

NOW that Mayor La Guardia has officially endorsed the open-air parking lot, that humble haven of the motorist in a city that offers little other place to park may attain a new respectability more in accord with the essential service it performs. Viewed formerly as a temporary phenomenon, the auto park has become big business and seems likely to stay.

The Mayor recently told a committee studying traffic in Manhattan that New York City needed more parking facilities before cars could be barred from parking in the streets, and he urged the establishment of parking garages and parking lots at congested points. The city, he said, owned one or two places which it might contribute as parking fields.

Time was when the open-air automobile lot had to hide as an outcast behind tall buildings, and was tolerated only as a nuisance in sections jealous of their high-class residential or business heritage. Today it takes its place in the shadow of Rockefeller Center, and, though a skyscraper may some day oust it, it has proved its right to hobnob with giants.

Statistics Tell of Growth

"Truly amazing" is the way the parking-lot boom is described by real estate men. Ten or even eight years ago there were scarcely enough of these areas in most cities to be worth counting. Today, according to the United States Bureau of the Census, 4,341 parking lots are doing business in this country, making $18,000,000 annually. New York City is credited with 255 parking lots. Philadelphia has 156 and Chicago 129. In Washington, D. C., 78 were counted, 52 in San Francisco and 43 in Boston. In almost every case the figures represent sizable gains; they include only the privately owned places, not the hundreds of others municipally operated in scores of communities.

But the most remarkable spread of the parking lot has occurred in Detroit's central district. Ten years ago there were only 110 privately owned lots accommodating 7,700 vehicles. By 1933 the number had grown to 265 lots, with room for 17,-250 cars, and today the total capacity is close to 30,000. Milwaukee a decade ago had open-air parking facilities for 3,000 vehicles, today it can take care of three times that many.

All over the country there has been a wholesale razing of buildings to make room for parking. Many were old structures, but numerous others still had much life in them as "taxpayers," small buildings put up to get a nominal income until replaced by larger edifices. By tearing down the buildings owners avoid paying taxes on them, and assert that they can often get a bigger income by renting the ground for parking.

Big Boom in Detroit

How far this demolition has gone is demonstrated again by Detroit. In 1931 it tore down buildings having total assessed value of $594,000 to make parking lots; the following year it removed fifty-three buildings, valued at $473,000, and the year after thirty-two more, worth $462,000.

Realtors disagree on the effects of such leveling of whole sections of cities. Some call it a bad omen, others find it a healthy toning down of overinflated property values. Many believe that the use of high-priced land in crowded cities for parking is uneconomic and that any widespread upswing in building will wipe out the parking yards. Others are watching possible effects on property tax collections, on zoning and on the use of cars in the city. More people, it seems clear, are again driving their cars into the city, a practice many had discontinued for lack of parking facilities. The result is likely to be more traffic congestion in the streets.

Gradually the parking lot is emerging from its ugly-duckling stage. In some communities, notably in California and Florida, it is putting on trimmings and calling itself an "auto park"; it boasts a neon sign, a neatly painted fence, sections marked off with white lines for varying periods of parking, night illumination and a uniformed attendant.

And the end is not yet. Designers

of communities for tomorrow have evolved plans that will lift the parking lot to the grandeur of a parking plaza or center, with landscaped borders, and with waiting rooms, reading rooms, lounges and refreshment stands. There will be telephone, telegraph, mail and messenger services, and possibly a place where the children may be left while their parents go to the store or the theatre.

The town planner would not shunt such "parking terminals" to back alleys, but would plant them where they are most needed, within easy walking distance of office, shop, entertainment and school. In large cities, where such open spaces would be almost impossible to acquire, he would build storage places beneath existing parks or squares, without damaging their attractiveness or utility. Or he would provide "roof gardens" for parking cars atop buildings.

Service Developed

In the early days the customers demanded no luxuries and were content to use the fields as inexpensive storage places free from fear of the policeman's ticket. But the present clientele—to hear the lot attendant tell it—clamor not only for gasoline and oil, engine and tire repairs, but for sundry other services never contemplated when the parking lot began to spread like a rash.

"We're becoming a parcel-post station," confesses a supervisor at one of the parking areas in midtown New York. "People park their cars here, go shopping, then come back loaded with packages, dump them into the back seat and go off for more shopping or to see a movie."

This used to be confined to women, but business men, too, are sending boys from their offices with boxes, bottles and suitcases to be put in the trunk of the car. On rainy days the parking men could do a land-office business selling or renting umbrellas, raincoats and rubbers, for drivers hate to get out from the dry coziness of their cars into the wet.

Parcel-watching is simple compared with baby-minding. The practice of "parking" children may be rare in Manhattan, but in smaller communities it is not uncommon for the children to stay in the car or play about the parking lot while mother does her marketing. The nursery, too, has taken to the road.

Some places let the driver berth his own car, but, if the yard is crowded or small, the parking directors have learned from bitter experience to perform this delicate task themselves. Too often fenders get smashed, bodies scratched, runningboards bent, headlights or taillights broken.

Aided by Depression

The depression, it is generally agreed, gave a great impetus to the parking field. The yards offered not only stopping places in crowded districts, but at rates generally below those which garages, with higher overhead, could charge. For years opposing interests fought the issuance of permits for sidewalk cuts to parking lots and clamored for enforcement of zoning restrictions which would stem the onrush of open-air places.

Today, with both the roofless enclosures and the garages well filled—thanks in great part to police drives against street parking—the two competitors are on more amicable terms. And, from all accounts, both prosper by adhering to scales set under the old NRA. Parking lots generally charge parkers from 25 to 50 cents and garages from 50 cents to $1, depending on length of stay.

Since the fight with the garages the parking-lot proprietor has enjoyed a measure of peace, despite the growing pains of his trade. But if it is to assume even larger proportions, with service for watchword, and run a nursery lounge room, parcel delivery and similar services as sidelines, he is likely to face more grief than he has yet encountered.

March 14, 1937

MASS TRANSIT

JITNEY BUS WINS FAVOR QUICKLY

Several Thousand of the Nickel Motor Cars Are Now in Operation Throughout the United States.

IN perhaps no country in the world save this could a movement like that of the "jitney" bus have developed from a sporadic experiment to a widespread reality in less than three months. The fact is that the idea of coupling the word jitney, which is slang for a nickel, with any sort of automobile and making the latter do service as a common carrier while the former serves to define the rate of fare, has spread like wildfire from one end of the country to the other. The result is that in scores of cities from the Pacific to the Atlantic the jitney car or jitney bus is running today and making itself popular or unpopular, according to local conditions and the attitude of the street railway interests.

Although there are probably several thousand jitney buses in operation in the country now, the business of jitney busing has not become standardized by any means. For this reason it is somewhat difficult to define it. In the first place, a jitney bus is not necessarily an omnibus at all. To be sure, the bus is being used to some extent and multi-passenger vehicles are being built and converted for the trade. But in its essence the jitney is any kind of automobile in a condition to run. Secondly, it carries passengers for hire, the amount of the fare being strictly limited to one jitney, or nickel. With these two limitations anything on wheels may be, and, if the reports from many parts of the country can be trusted, is a jitney bus.

It is precisely this character which has given the jitney its rapid spread. Anybody who had an automobile, new or old, aristocratic or plebeian, big or little, or anybody with the wherewithal to acquire a car, could at once enter the jitney business if he were so minded. This is why jitneys have sprung up all over the land. It needed but the origination of the idea.

From the fact that the jitney bus is so heterogeneous and so easy to put into operation has arisen the flock of perplexing questions which already surround it. In cities where three or four weeks ago nothing like a jitney was dreamed of, the local authorities are getting their heads together to devise means of regulation for fast-growing fleets. Traction interests in many parts of the country are protesting vigorously against the invasion of their field. Realty associations are backing up the protests of the traction people on the ground that the prosperity and extension of the street car service go hand in hand with the development of real estate, which is not fostered by these jitney men. Taxicab companies and omnibus lines with franchises to protect are ranged against the jitneys solidly, and civic associations, accident lawyers, and safety societies are calling for the supervision and restraint of these newcomers to the city streets.

Instances have already been brought out to show that some of the fears behind the manifold protests are not without foundation. In one Western city a jitney driver who was involved in an accident was found to be deaf and dumb, while in Los Angeles the financial and other irresponsibilty of the drivers has been brought before the City Council in striking fashion. In arguing before that body the other day for the requirement of a substantial bond to be given by any one desiring to operate a jitney, E. B. Drake, an attorney whose practice includes personal injury suits, said:

> I am not against the jitney bus. I am in favor of it. The more jitneys, the more business for me, but there is no use suing some one and getting a judgment unless you can collect. I have here the papers in the case of a client, a lad who was mutilated for life. I was given a judgment against a jitney bus driver who admitted in his deposition that his own negligence had caused the injury. He can neither speak nor write English, hasn't paid for his machine yet and has no property that can be attached. Five thousand dollars is not enough for a bond. If there are ten passengers injured, that $5,000 wouldn't buy peanuts all around, let alone the attorney's contingent fee. The bond should be at least $10,000.

This question of security to protect passengers in case of accident is receiving thought in widely separated parts of the country. The Union and Advertiser of Rochester had something to say on the matter editorially the other day, in part as follows:

> There is one aspect of the jitney bus question that deserves public attention. It is the matter of the solvency of the jitney bus owner when damages are awarded in case of accident due to his negligence. In other cities people have been injured by these buses. Some may be injured here. As most of the owners are not, if we may judge by the appearance of their vehicles, possessed of large assets, where would the victim of an accident due to negligence on the part of the owner or driver of a jitney bus get his money if he were awarded damages in any appreciable sum? A car valued at $150 wouldn't go far toward settling a verdict for $1,000 damages.

In Houston, where jitney service is on an extended scale and where some of the first of the jitneys went into operation, the bonding feature is a prominent part of a new ordinance which is now under consideration for the regulation of these independent knights of the nickel. This ordinance contains a number of provisions which are likely to receive the compliment of imitation in other cities. For instance, applicants for licenses to operate jitney cars are to place their applications in the hands of the Public Service Commissioner with a statement showing the type of car, horse power, factory number, seating capacity, route on which it is proposed to drive, and the name of the driver, in addition to a time schedule.

The amount of the license fee is to be based on the passenger capacity of the car. Cars are not to be allowed to stop save on the near side of the street and within two feet of the curbing. It will be unlawful for one car to attempt to pass another in the effort to get passengers (this provision throws a naïve light on jitney driving) and it will be unlawful for a jitney to block a crossing or interfere with passengers boarding a street car. Passengers may not be carried on the running boards, fenders, or doors of the car. There must be a light inside the car at night.

The Houston ordinance contains a provision that compels the jitney to operate only on a beaten course and on a time schedule. It seems that in Los Angeles unscrupulous drivers have not hesitated to take young girls to other than their desired destination. The City Mothers, an organization of women of the California city, has urged repeatedly that this regulation of route be imposed on the jitneys, giving as a reason that a large number of complaints have been received from young girls who have been taken to places quite different from those advertised on the cars by the jitney drivers.

On this matter of prescribed route, the jitney men, however, have something to say. They claim that they must not be held too strictly to a definite course, since this would mean a big loss of revenue. In one or two cities they have offered a compromise to proposed regulations of this kind, which would allow them to deviate from a regular route by as much as three blocks in order to carry "fares" to their doorsteps.

The whole question, to route or not to route the jitneys, is one of those still in the testing. To force the cars to stick rigidly to one street or series of streets would be to put them in a different category from that in which they began. The earliest jitneys bore the slogan, "Take you anywhere for a jitney"; meaning that the limitations of rails and franchises were to be abolished and that with this twentieth century stagecoach you were to be able to go where fancy willed for the sum of 5 cents.

When Houston decided to put a provision in its pending ordinance to make it illegal for the jitney to carry passengers on the running boards, fenders, or doors it struck a shrewd blow at the pursestrings of the jitney owner. For since the first wheel of these new conveyances turned, it has been the custom to load them not only to capacity but just a bit beyond capacity. In fact, it is from these supernumerary passengers that the owner, in some cases, looks for his profit. As the Vice President of the Los Angeles Auto Bus Owners' Association, the organization of jitney men in that city, puts it: "We figure that every fare on the running board is that much profit. We break even on the load inside the car."

All the questions bearing upon the regulation of jitneys in the many cities in which they are now in operation have brought storms of protest on one side or the other. In Los Angeles, which must be first considered in the jitney matter because with more than one thousand cars in service it has the largest quota of jitneys to date, the City Council is openly charged with framing an ordinance without sufficient restraint on the cars because of political reasons. On the other hand, the papers of many cities are urging fair play for this newcomer in transportation.

In Baltimore the coming of the jitneys has raised an odd situation. It seems that in that city part of the revenue of

Breaking Into the Big League.
From the St. Louis Republic.

the street railway system goes to the city and is for the specific use of the public parks. For this reason the Park Board of Baltimore finds itself intimately concerned with a question of transportation only a small portion of which lies within the parks. It was pointed out at a meeting the other day, at which this subject came under discussion, that for every $100 which the jitneys took in, provided that amount represented an equal reduction in the income of the street railway service, the parks of the city would lose $9. It is now suggested that the Baltimore jitneys may have to bear some portion of the park tax so that loss to the city may be avoided. The jitneys came to Baltimore, by the way, through the energy of a young woman who had seen some in operation on the coast, and promptly went into business on a progressive scale.

The uses of the jitney bus in the cities in which it now is are almost as various as the cities. It carries the business man to and from his work; it serves the purposes of the woman who wants to go shopping; it increases the vogue of the fox trot by making dancing parties more convenient and less expensive to get to; it is possible in some cities for the worker of the family to go home to lunch where time and other considerations used to prevent.

The jitney may be a specially built omnibus, a truck with cross seats nailed on, a limousine that has seen its best days, or a touring car of any quality that has passed through previous conditions of servitude. It may even be new. The history of one small car used for this purpose in Kansas City is not without interest.

It was purchased six weeks ago, new, by one Brown, a locomotive fireman. The car cost him $522.90 and he promptly put it to work. He ran it in all kinds of weather and covered in five and a half weeks of jitneying about 5,000 miles. At the end of that time he sold it for $480. In this period, besides paying for his board and lodging—at a modest rate to be sure—and paying for all the running and upkeep expenses of his five-passenger machine, Brown put $105 in the bank. All of which goes to show that there are more than paper profits in the jitney bus if it is run under fair conditions. Brown had average gross daily receipts of $7.50 to $8, with $12.50 as his best single day.

There are not a few women drivers of jitneys in the Western cities. Houston, Texas, has filled a long-felt want by organizing—not as a civic undertaking, however—a "Jim Crow" line of jitneys for its negro population. In California's exposition cities the jitney has arrived at a fortunate time.

One aspect of the jitney business is interesting the automobile industry deeply. This is its probable effect on the sale of used or second-hand automobiles, which have always presented a problem to the dealer in new machines. Some of the men best qualified to speak on the subject and on the effect of jitneys on general automobile sales are very hopeful. John N. Willys said the other day:

"When the street car interests attempt, through political influences, to deprive the public of the convenience and pleasure of the jitney they are going to have to reckon with the people themselves. Electric street railways, with the congestion and noise, to say nothing of the street dangers such juggernaut cars create in our cities, are not going to be permitted to smother a more desirable, more healthful, and rapid means of locomotion, even if the incomes from inflated capitalization are threatened. It is a question of the survival of the fittest, and the electric line may be doomed to follow into oblivion the horse-drawn cab."

As yet the jitney bus has not invaded New York City. But it is established in New York State. It is at our gates.

NICKEL PSYCHOLOGY.

The nickel fare for urban transportation, says Secretary BAKER, is a "psychological necessity." The words have a constraining sound. One feels forced to the conclusion that, though every traction company in the land were to go bankrupt and be operated to the advantage of politicians at the expense of the taxpayer, the psychology of the nickel would still rule triumphant. In point of mere fact, however, there are communities among us that have resisted this nickel psychology. Boston long ago changed to an 8-cent fare, and the local mind proved so feeble that the fare has now been still further advanced to 10 cents. Of all places Boston should be most subject to psychology, for, as JOSIAH ROYCE discovered, (himself a bit of a psychologer,) Boston is not a city at all but a mental attitude. As it happens, there are some 300 cities and towns in the United States that are charging 8-cent and 10-cent fares. The figures are supplied by Aera, the official organ of the American Electric Railway Association. Shameful as the fact may be, many and many a community among us has not even the cheapest form of psychology.

A radically different point of view is that of Mr. ROGER W. BABSON, who speaks not as a psychologer but as a business expert and statistician. Mr. BABSON says that, except for short hauls in densely populated cities, the nickel fare is doomed. For the vast majority of middling hauls, the 10-cent fare will become universal; and for the longest rides, on subway and elevated lines, the fare will be 25 cents. Theoretically, this zoning system is equitable and involves no serious expense in administration. An exit stub on each ticket would provide a sufficient control. But practically it works a serious hardship upon people who have been lured to live in the suburbs by the prospect of cheap fares. The city, furthermore, loses one of its most effective correctives against congestion. Mr. BABSON is on less contentious ground when he returns to general principles. Commissioners, he says, will do best by the public in inducing transportation companies "to give better service." If they do that, they will have little need "to bother about fares." Where Secretary BAKER talks vaguely of raising the rate only by advice and consent of "the people who are to pay it," Mr. BABSON strikes at the business heart of the situation. This view is corroborated and helpfully extended by Mr. W. O. BLISS, Chairman of the Rhode Island Public Service Commission, who pleads for a unified and thoroughgoing business supervision. "Final solution of the electric street "railway problem will never come "until the power to fix wages is "vested in the same authority which "regulates the rates of fare."

Transportation is not a theory, psychologic or otherwise. It is a basic necessity of the community. The administration that allows it to be deranged or permanently impaired fails in a prime responsibility. It is true that to double the fare, or even to add 2 or 3 cents to it, is to impose a very serious burden upon hundreds of thousands of workers who are already put to it sorely to make ends meet. Nobody will forget that. But, serious as the burden would be, it is less to be considered than the time which the public loses, and the strength it wastes, when traffic is held up or unduly crowded. Transportation is to the civic life what circulation is to the body; when it is clogged, fatigue and coma fall upon every member.

August 15, 1919

URGE COST SERVICE ON ELECTRIC LINES

President's Commission Reports Findings After Studying Trolley Systems.

ADVISES FLUCTUATING FARES

These Would Be Raised or Reduced Automatically as Revenues Rise or Fall.

Special to The New York Times.

WASHINGTON, Aug. 24.—Sweeping reforms in the electric railway industry, designed to restore public confidence and vitally needed credit, are recommended today in a unanimous report made by the Federal Electric Railways Commission to President Wilson. The commission has been investigating the condition of the industry for more than a year, during which time it has covered the field by hearing ninety-five witnesses and examining hundreds of reports and answers to questionnaires.

Outstanding among the recommendations is that for the installation of the service-at-cost plan of operation. This plan, now operative in Cleveland, Cincinnati, Dallas, Montreal (Canada) and other cities will, it is believed, remove the industry from the field of speculative gain, furnish rides at the lowest possible cost and restore credit and public confidence.

Primarily the plan provides for furnishing rides at actual cost, which shall govern the rate of fares, and for protecting the investor by guaranteeing a fixed return on an agreed valuation of his holdings.

Chaos faces the industry unless credit is restored and co-operation between public, managements and employes established, the report insists, and no words are minced in telling the three parties to the situation where their respective duties lie.

Managements are advised that their primary duty is to serve the public with the highest efficiency at the lowest cost, with their cards face upward on the table, and not to use the industry as a means of obtaining profits beyond what may be necessary for upkeep, to pay a fair return upon the agreed value of the property and to secure the investment of funds further required.

The public duty is declared to be the supervision and control of railway properties, with the view of safeguarding the public interest and the allowance of such return upon the fair valuation of the property as may be agreed upon in the contract between the city and the company. By reason of such supervision the future attitude of the public should be one of friendliness and co-operation.

Employes it is said should have a living wage and humane hours of labor and working conditions, and a right to deal collectively with their employers, through committees or representatives of their own selection, but it is added that "all labor disputes should be settled voluntarily or by arbitration and the award of such board should be final and binding on both parties."

"It is intolerable," the report says, "that the transportation service of a city should be subject to occasional paralysis, whether by strikes or lockouts."

Other important declarations of the report are:

That public ownership and operation, generally speaking, are undesirable unless the results under private operation prove unsatisfactory, but the right of the public to own and operate all public utilities should be recognized and legal obstacles in the way of its exercise should be removed.

That extensions into outlying territory benefiting private property should be paid for by assessments on such property in proportion to the benefits received, and that the cost of such extensions should not be added to the valuation of the railroad property upon which a fair return is to be allowed.

That franchises should fix no limit as to the time they shall run nor the fares that may be charged.

As to the present condition of the street railway industry, the commission finds that its financial credit has been lost and that in many localities it is not properly performing its public function. This is considered to be due to increased costs of labor and material, overcapitalization and financial mismanagement, public distrust and antagonism, failure of the fixed five-cent fare to meet existing conditions, extensions into unprofitable territory in furtherance of real estate speculation, and failure of employers and employes to properly co-operate; hence the physical impossibility of giving the necessary assurance of security to investors.

The report estimates that from $175,000,000 to $200,000,000 annually will be required to properly carry out the future needs of the industry, and it emphatically declares that restoration of public confidence is one of the vital necessities of restored credit.

"For rehabilitation, improvements and extensions which are vitally needed to meet the requirements of every growing community," the report says, "new capital at once and in large amounts is imperatively required, and until the force of circumstances convinces those with capital at their disposal that investment in electric railway securites affords safety and fair return it cannot be obtained."

Would End Special Assessments.

The commission declares that the jitney should be regarded as a common carrier and subjected to Public Service regulation.

It recommends the elimination, so far as practicable, of "special assessments for sprinkling, paving and for construction and maintenance of bridges which are used by the public for highway purposes." These are burdens, it is held, which should be borne by the entire community, and should not be shifted from the automobile rider to the street car rider, who is usually less able to bear them.

If, at a given rate of fare, more than a fair return of profits results, it should go neither to the private corporation nor to the city, but should be reflected back by the automatic reduction of the fare paid by the car rider, the report says.

The commission was unanimously of the opinion that, as stated by Secretary Baker at the hearing, the education of the people of a given community and their conviction that the operations of a company are an open book and are under control of a trustworthy representative of the public, are essential to the successful working of the service-at-cost plan.

The commission emphasizes the importance of determining by arbitration or otherwise the fair value of the railway property "as the basis for the financial return of the company," and also as the basis upon which it may, if desired, be taken over by the municipality.

One of the most striking features of this report is that it is unanimous, indicating an agreement among men of strong personality whose interests are so divergent as to cause the belief that they would not be able to agree upon the issues involved.

The Chairman, Charles E. Elmquist, was at the time of his appointment President of the National Association of State Utilities Boards; the Vice Chairman, Edwin F. Sweet, is the Assistant Secretary of Commerce and has served as Mayor of Grand Rapids, Mich.; George L. Baker is the present Mayor of Portland, Ore.; Philip H. Gadsden is President of the Charleston, S. C., Consolidated Railway and Lighting Company, and he represented the American Electric Railways Association; William D. Mahon is the President of the Amalgamated Association of Street and Electric Railway Employes of America, and Charles W. Beall, a New York banker, represented capital investors. Dr. Royal Meeker, Commissioner of Labor Statistics, was appointed as the representative of the Department of Labor, and Louis B. Wehle represented the Treasury Department.

President Congratulates Members.

President Wilson has written the following letter to Chairman Elmquist of the Federal Electric Railways Commission:

The White House, Washington.

My Dear Mr. Elmquist: Will you not accept for yourself and be good enough to extend to the other members of the commission my sincere thanks for the very able and valuable report upon the electric railway situation which you have placed in my hands? I am appreciative of the self-sacrificing efforts of the commission members in so freely devoting their time to the task undertaken at my request, but I cannot but believe that the results achieved will prove to be full compensation for their efforts.

I very much hope that this report will receive the wide publicity which it deserves and that it will be closely studied by all local regulative authorities having to do with the affairs and interests of public service corporations. Sincerely yours,

(Signed) WOODROW WILSON.

Mr. Charles E. Elmquist, Chairman, Federal Electric Railways Commission.

August 25, 1920

Jitneys Leave Salem Streets As Police Back Coolidge Order

SALEM, Mass., Jan. 18.—Motor buses which have been competing with street railway traffic again disappeared from the streets here when Deputy Chief George C. Neale of the State Police served notice this afternoon that arrests would follow their further operation.

The banning of the jitneys was by order of Governor Coolidge, who yesterday directed the Public Trustees of the Eastern Massachusetts Street Railway Company to restore traffic on the local division, after sixty hours' suspension because of jitney competition, and for the jitneys to be taken off the streets.

The Governor said that the jitney traffic was illegal.

January 19, 1920

DECLARES CITIES CANNOT ENFORCE UNJUST FARES

Supreme Court Holds Even a "Contract Calling for Confiscatory Rate" Will Not Stand.

GOVERNOR NOT SURPRISED

WASHINGTON, April 11.—The Supreme Court today affirmed a decree of the Texas District Court enjoining the City of San Antonio from enforcing a 5-cent fare, with universal transfers, over the lines of the San Antonio Public Service Company. In appealing the city asserted that its franchise contract with the railroad called for service at 5 cents and that the courts were without jurisdiction to interfere.

Injunctions obtained by the City of Fairfield, Iowa, in lower courts, restraining the Iowa Electric Company from increasing its rates above those set in its franchise, also were set aside today by the Supreme Court, which reversed the courts below.

The court held that a contract calling for a confiscatory rate would not stand in law.

On the authority of the first case, it reversed Iowa courts which had refused to enjoin the City of Chariton from putting such rates into effect against the Southern Iowa Electric Company and held against the City of Muscatine, Iowa, in a similar case brought by the Muscatine Lighting Company.

April 12, 1921

MOTOR BUS USE GROWING RAPIDLY

By R. E. PLIMPTON,
Member Society of Automotive Engineers.

THE motor vehicle in the form of a bus, stage or jitney, or whatever other name it may be called, has definitely taken its place alongside the electric railway and the steam railroad as a common carrier. With vehicles made to carry passengers in comparatively large numbers, comfortable and regular transportation is being provided over fixed routes by thousands of well-established bus operators.

It is often thought that bus transportation is a small business. Five years ago this might have been justified. Today it is a big business, and growing so fast that it offers one of the most important fields for the use of motor vehicles in the future. In New York City the Fifth Avenue system has been well-established for years, and has set the pace for other bus operators over the country. Of more than 50,000,000 passengers carried each year by the buses on Fifth Avenue it is estimated that about 75 per cent. are persons going to business or to the downtown stores, while the other 25 per cent. are so-called pleasure seekers, that is, those who use the buses Summer evenings or holidays during good weather.

Bus development is equally significant in some of the smaller cities. In Long Beach, Cal., the buses carry about 70 per cent. of all local traffic, while in such towns as Gloucester, Mass., and Middletown, Ohio, they form the only medium of local transportation. In New Jersey bus operation has reached enormous proportions. Newark alone, with some 400 buses in daily service, had a business of at least 75,000,000 passengers during 1922. The number of passengers carried by Newark buses has increased more than sixteen times in six years.

Exit the Horse-Drawn Stage.

California has about 2,500 buses or stages, as they are usually called there, operating between the various cities and to the intermediate villages and the ranches and farms along the wayside. Last year the buses in California carried about 13,000,000 passengers and took $8,000,000 in passenger fares, according to figures given out by the State Railroad Commission. In the mountain States west of the Mississippi, where for years the horse-drawn stage was the monarch of the road, the motor buses have stepped in to carry passengers. Grades are steep, the highways are poor or may be impassable for a considerable time each year, but the service is kept up surprisingly well under these difficult conditions. In practically every State in the Union the bus is an integral part of human existence.

The rolling stock or vehicle used for bus transportation is undergoing a development consistent with the great increase in passengers carried and in number of routes. Originally a light touring car, in which the passengers were packed and jammed to the limit, the one-time jitney has passed through a period of development, to a design consisting of a chassis and body fitted particularly to the large scale movement of human beings.

The demand for motor vehicle transportation grew so rapidly that for a time it was necessary to use the vehicle most quickly available. For city work this was usually the motor truck chassis, to which was fitted a box-shaped body with full-length seats on each side like the older street cars. For work out of town a heavier type of passenger car was used, often with the frame lengthened to give greater seating capacity.

Types of Vehicles.

Out of all this have emerged two well-defined types. The bus of either single deck or double deck construction, with a floor level a foot or so lower than that permitted by the truck, is used for city work where the speed need not be high, but the vehicle must be designed to carry heavy traffic and to make frequent stops. Street car practice is followed to a large extent in the construction of these city buses. Rattan-covered seats are arranged lengthwise of the vehicle or in two rows crosswise with a narrow centre aisle, the particular combination selected depending upon the length of the trip and the number of standing passengers that it is desired to accommodate during rush hours. This city vehicle travels mostly over good pavement, and therefore many of them are fitted with solid or cushion type tires. In the latest design special attention is being paid to passenger comfort by providing illumination so that newspapers can be read, ventilators that work automatically under all weather conditions, and a heating system which keeps the interior at a comfortable temperature by the use of exhaust from the engine.

For service outside the city, either to other cities or through the rural districts, bus construction tends to follow the closed automobile rather than the street car. Instead of the rattan seats we have a heavily cushioned cross seat characteristic of the limousine. The vehicles used are designed for fast long-distance work, where stops are infrequent. The trips are long enough so that riding comfort, as provided by pneumatic tires and shock-absorbing devices, is absolutely essential. Accommodation for light baggage is another characteristic, since the passengers are usually making over-night journeys instead of short business or shopping trips.

There is still another type of bus that is coming into use, the light bus for rural service. Characteristics required are strength and ruggedness, because the bus must often be operated day in and day out over poor roads. Operating economy is essential, for the paseeger traffic offered is not, and perhaps never will be sufficient to justify a heavier and expensive vehicle. Many of these rural lines now are equipped with rebuilt passenger cars or light trucks. Very often the country operators supplement their income from passenger carrying by serving as a mail contractor or by doing a freight business in transferring express and small packages.

Because of the rapid growth of bus transportation its regulation is in a decidedly chaotic condition. There has been no hesitancy, either on the part of the different States or cities, to pass laws and ordinances controlling the operation of bus systems, but they are so unco-ordinated and diverse that their administration presents the most puzzling problem to the authorities, as well as to the operators themselves. In more than half the States the bus operated on regular schedules and over a fixed route is recognized as a public utility, subject to many of the restrictions established by law for the older transportation utilities. A usual requirement is that the bus line must secure a certificate from the State Commission before starting operation. This certificate is granted only after a public hearing to determine whether the service is required and the conditions such that after once being started it can be given permanently and to the benefit of both the operator and the public.

In the past many bus operators have been individuals who entered the business without any great amount of financial backing, and sometimes not even owning the bus they operated. As a result, many States and cities have endeavored to protect the public by requiring a surety bond or indemnity insurance policy. Primarily this is a safety measure to protect passengers in cases of negligence resulting in death or personal injury. For example, the policy may provide for up to $5,000 protection in case of accident to any one passenger, or $10,000 for any one accident. In addition the bonds or policies may also guarantee faithful performance of the service described in the application for a certificate, or cover injury to persons other than passengers.

This insurance is expensive, and often amounts to $600 or $800 a year for each bus. The tendency is to make the careful operator pay for the deficiencies of his less efficient brother. Another grievance of the bus operators is that where the law requires liability insurance or a bond it affects all buses alike, no matter how much each one is or is not used. A spare bus, or one used only during rush hours or on holidays, takes the same yearly rate as one used for heavy mileage, or practically continuous operation.

What Is a Fair Tax?

Just what taxes the buses shall pay, over and above the ordinary license fees they may pay the ordinary license fees other question that is being actively discussed. In New Jersey, all pay 5 per cent. on gross earnings as a franchise tax, and the returns from this tax are distributed among the towns through which the lines pass, according to the mileage covered in each town. In New York State, however, each town is at liberty to levy its own tax or license fee, and in addition the State collects a registration fee based on seating capacity.

There is a widespread movement at present to tax buses according to their use of the highways. In Maryland, the seat-mile is the basis of taxation, and the larger buses are penalized by an increased rate. For example, one weighing less than 3,000 pounds takes an annual tax of one-twentieth of 1 cent for each seat-mile operated. If the bus weighs more than 7,000 pounds net, the rate is increased to one-sixth of 1 cent per seat-mile. On the latter basis a large bus, say of twenty-five passenger capacity, in city operation might often pay $7 or $8 a day, or $2,500 a year to the State in taxes.

The bus transportation industry has reached the point where its members realize the necessity of union, for both its own and the public good. Bus operators are getting together not only in State and national associations but also in so-called pools and in their joint control of terminals or waiting rooms.

Pooling systems, which are usually undertaken on city lines where a number of individually-owned buses follow a common route, are essentially a scheme that provides for equal work and equal pay or revenue. The owners on the same route form an association, with a paid executive, to whom all the income from fares is paid. This income is then divided among the owners, usually in proportion to the passenger capacity of their buses. Schedules are laid out so that each owner does about the same work and gets his share of night and day and of rush-hour and off-peak operation. The executive also may act as a checker, to see that the schedules are followed and proper service given the public. The success of pooling systems, in Jersey cities for example, is leading to other activities, such as the hiring of an association attorney, a joint garage and repair station and the purchase of equipment and supplies.

All signs point to rapid growth in bus transportation. In the cities the bus will be used more and more to supplement the electric railway where passenger traffic is not sufficient to warrant the laying of tracks. Country lines are bound to increase as new highways are built and as bus owners put into practice the lessons in transportation fundamentals they are now learning.

At present public regulation of the bus is largely directed toward the control or prevention of competition. In the future this control is likely to be extended to rates and service. Taxation is an unsettled matter, but the outlook is hopeful because of the investigations being conducted by Government and other agencies. These studies should help to determine a fair basis of taxation, one that will encourage operators to expand and develop their lines and to give service to the public wherever it is needed.

The growth of the industry is also likely to be characterized by larger and more stable operating units. Even now the authorities in many States favor a corporation in granting permits over individuals or partnerships. Economy and other benefits derived from doing business on a large scale are rapidly leading to company ownership of bus systems, instead of the individual operator with his one vehicle. These stronger organizations, combined with more intelligently applied equipment and with fair and sympathetic control by public authorities, should result in hundreds of buses for every one now used in the transportation of passengers.

The vehicles designed for bus service are also proving useful for other purposes. In the cities the new low-floor-level vehicles designed for buses are coming into use for sightseeing work, where they are more attractive and comfortable than the former truck chassis. In rural districts the consolidated schools offer a big field, the school authorities either owning the buses themselves or hiring them from some one engaged in transportation. The intercity bus of the de luxe type is being used effectively by tourists bureaus for long-distance trips. During the last Summer such buses ran from New York to Atlanic City regularly and from Boston to Montreal through the White Mountains. In California and Florida also are provided examples of this sort, where transportation includes not only the actual ride but also hotel accommodations for overnight trips.

January 7, 1923

SAYS PUBLIC PAYS A 7.31-CENT FARE

Dahl Declares B. M. T. Can Live on Nickel Rate, but City Makes It Up.

POINTS TO OTHER CITIES

Cites Failure of Municipal Operation to Keep Fares Down in Detroit and Seattle.

Gerhard M. Dahl, Chairman of the Executive Committee of the Brooklyn-Manhattan Transit Corporation, made public a statement yesterday in which he defined the attitude of that corporation toward a maximum 5-cent transit fare in this and other cities. Mr. Dahl said:

"The posting of a bulletin in our cars quoting a public statement made by Mgr. John L. Belford, D. D., of Brooklyn, coupled with the public demands of the people of the Bronx and Queens for bus and surface car service, even if the fare is more than 5 cents, has inspired a large number of inquiries as to the attitude of the B. M. T.

"Briefly, this company ever since its organization one year ago has maintained that it can live on a 5-cent fare. But there is a vast difference between living on bread and water and living on a square meal. We are today providing a service on our rapid transit lines which, if the taxpayers of this city and the investors were receiving a fair return on the money invested in our rapid transit lines, would cost 7.31 cents per passenger. As long as the taxpayers and investors are willing to hold the bag we can give 7.31-cent service for 5 cents, but we cannot afford to give 7½ cent or 8 cent service. We are today maintaining a maximum service on our rapid transit lines, and there is no possibility of this service being increased until the city completes the Fourteenth Street-Eastern District line and the Nassau-Broad Street extension and builds the new shops and yards which it is obligated to construct under Contract 4.

Says Taxpayers Need Higher Fare.

"To accuse the B. M. T. of agitating for an increased fare is nothing more than an attempt to pull wool over the eyes of the people of this city. This company does not need a higher fare half as much as the taxpayers do. The taxpayers are the real losers in this community. They have $250,000,000 invested in rapid transit lines—investments made by the City of New York. This money is tied up. The city is receiving no return on this gigantic investment. If, however, the car riders today were paying the cost of service the city could borrow all the money it needs to build all the transit lines the people of this city demand, and investors would willingly come forward with all the money needed for the equipment and operation of these lines.

"New York is today practically the only metropolis in the United States where its city officials will not look the facts in the face. In Detroit and Seattle, where the transit lines are owned and operated by the municipal authorities, the fares were increased from 5 cents to 6 and 10 cents, respectively. In Indianapolis, Baltimore and Providence the street railway fares have only recently been increased because the private operating companies could not continue service without an increased revenue.

Fare in Other Cities.

So that today the cash fare rates in nineteen large cities throughout the country, compared to 1913, are as follows:

	1913.	1924.
Chicago	5	10-7
Philadelphia	5	7
Detroit—		
Municipal operation	..	6
Private operation	5	..
Cleveland	3	6
St. Louis	5	7
Boston	5	10
Baltimore	5	8
Buffalo	5	7
Pittsburgh	5	10
Washington, D. C.	5	8
Indianapolis	5	7
Seattle—		
Municipal operation	..	10
Private operation	5	..
Richmond, Va.	5	6
Dallas, Texas	5	6
Omaha	5	7
Kansas City	5	8
Toledo	5	8
Cincinnati	5	9
Providence	5	8

"In September, 1923, Detroit, which up to that time had been one of the exhibition cities of the 5-cent fare, found it expedient to increase the fare to 6 cents in order to keep up with the costs of operation. Detroit was followed three months later by a similar increase in Cleveland. Detroit is the largest city in the United States where street railway lines are operated by the municipal authorities. It is a notable fact that it was only after the lines had been taken over by the city that the fare increase was put into effect.

"Until the lines were acquired by the city in 1922 a private company operated on a 5-cent fare. On May 15, 1922, the city purchased the lines and property of the Detroit Electric Railway Company and operated on a 5-cent fare for one year and four months. In the Fall of 1923 the rate was increased to six cents, despite the fact that under city ownership the company enjoys material advantages in taxes, being exempt from Federal taxation and income taxes; from school, park, franchise and street lighting taxes; from the payment of car and track licenses and any tax for the support of public service commissions or other State regulatory bodies, and is exempted from operating suburban lines that do not pay.

Municipal Operation in Detroit.

"The primary theory of municipal operation—that it will provide lower fares than privately operated companies can give—has failed to work out in practice in Detroit.

"Political interference with fares and the operation of electric railways in Seattle brought about an actual money loss of about $500,000 between March 1 and June 15, 1923.

"Under private operation the street railway lines in Seattle were operated on a 5-cent fare. In order to continue operating and making needed extensions, the company petitioned for a fare increase from 5 to 7 cents. The petition was not granted and the municipal authorities bought the lines. In the following year, under municipal operation, the fare rate was increased to 10 cents. After the lines had been operating for three years at a 10-cent fare and breaking even the same city authorities who had caused the city to refuse the petition of the private owners caused the 5-cent fare to be reinstalled in March, 1923, insisting that a nickel fare was sufficient for any street-car line and that it would attract more business than a higher fare. The losses in three months were so great that in June, 1923, the 10-cent fare was restored.

"In an editorial on the situation The Tacoma News-Tribune wrote:

> Mayor Edward J. Brown of Seattle pledged the people a five-cent fare when he was elected to office. He gave it to them along with an unannounced deficit of $5,000 per day which home-owners must pay in taxes. * * * Mayor Brown's action is frankly dictated by political expediency. His eyes are on the Democratic nomination for Governor, and the five-cent plank was to be the stepping-stone to let him in. The $5,000 deficit unkindly obtruded itself but he hopes to keep his record clear technically and depends upon the notoriously short memory of voters.

"As this is not an era of transit miracles, New York can hardly be expected to escape the experience of the people in other cities."

June 8, 1924

CHICAGO LAGGING IN RAPID TRANSIT

Smaller Proportion of Passengers Carried by the Elevated Lines Than 10 Years Ago.

REVERSE IN OTHER CITIES

Special to THE NEW YORK TIMES.

CHICAGO, Oct. 26.—A survey of rapid transit facilities in New York, Philadelphia and Boston shows a definite trend toward speeding up the mass movement of passengers over the last twenty years. Chicago is the only other city with rapid transit lines. All, with the exception of Chicago, have extended facilities in varying degrees, influenced by physical and financial factors.

The movement toward taking electric cars off the surface and placing them either under or above street level reached the highest stage of development in New York City. Today rapid transit lines handle about 70 per cent of all local transportation in New York. About 20 per cent is carried by surface lines and the rest by buses. The percentage carried by street cars has shown a steady decline in recent years.

These ratios are the reverse of the trend in Chicago. Here 80 per cent are carried on the surface lines with about 18 per cent on the elevated. Contrary to the experience in other cities, the proportion of passengers carried on the rapid transit lines is smaller than it was ten years ago.

In the major cities under survey, as a whole, the proportion of passengers carried in rapid transit lines in 1925 was 37 per cent. It increased to 40 per cent in 1929 and reached 43 per cent in 1934.

While there has been practically no expenditure for the extension of rapid transit in Chicago in more than twenty years, according to a report of the Illinois Commerce Commission, expenditures in New York in that time were $500,000,000 and in Philadelphia $150,000,000.

The first elevated lines in New York were constructed by private capital over sixty years ago. The first subway was built in 1904. Boston went into the rapid transit field early. The first elevated lines were privately constructed, but tunnels and subways have been financed largely by the city. The first rapid transit lines in Philadelphia were constructed in 1907, part subway and part elevated.

All major cities have added bus lines and many smaller centres have substantially or completely supplanted street cars with motorized equipment.

October 27, 1935

HOUSING THE MIDDLE CLASS

A WELCOME RETURN.

What is usually called New-York society is but a small part of what ought to go by that name, and of what includes all the various conditions and classes that decide the social character of our people and enter into our public opinion and life. Is it not true that of late years the most important element has been much slighted and to a certain extent proscribed, and that the great middle class has been far less conspicuous than the two extremes, which are in need of so wholesome a medium and an example? The rich have their place, but it is a limited place, and not sole dominion; and the poor have their rights, but not without the just limitations that are set by sobriety and industry, and not without need of better advisers than sporting politicians or pot-house demagogues. They who have neither poverty nor riches, are not second in dignity and are superior in numbers to either of these two extremes, and it is one of the most cheering aspects of our City at present that so many desirable middle-class people are coming to live here, and are finding homes within their means and to their mind.

Old New-York was famous for its plain, substantial citizens, the men who earned their own living, spoke their own mind, and brought up their children in sound principles and honest industry. Our modern fashions have cut harshly into those good old ways, and they who have traced carefully the social life of New-York for the last twenty years cannot but have noted a marked decline in the numbers and influence of the middle class of our people. It may be that the retreat began in the crash of 1857, when so many mechanics and men of small salaries and of moderate business were thrown out of employment and were unable to pay rents as before, or to live here at all in circumstances near their usual style. The return of prosperity for a time did but, in some respects, exaggerate the mischief. With the opening of the war there came the monstrous inflation of prices, especially of houses and rents, in connection with such a change in the centres of business, that thousands of families were virtually turned out of doors without any available shelter within the limits of this island. Whole neighborhoods were broken up, whole congregations were put to flight, and it was for years not so clear that the new times and homes were to come as that the old times and homes were done away.

The revival of business, the improvement in transit, and the increase of tenements of moderate cost, and other causes, have been lately restoring to us large classes of estimable citizens whose intelligence, sobriety, and industry cannot but tell upon the rising thrift and character of the community. Not only in the newly-peopled districts far up town, but in the old neighborhoods, the change may be seen, and one of the most agreeable sights of our City of late has been the frequent renovation of long-neglected houses down town for the occupation of worthy families, who insist upon having all the essential conditions of health and self-respect at moderate cost. In some cases, the new recruits bring their neighborhood with them, and fill contiguous dwellings with reputable and congenial occupants. There is certainly a great deal to say for such a course, and some of our down-town friends insist, not without fair reason, that they find cheaper rents, more thoroughly-built houses, better drained ground, and more convenient living where they are than many of their more adventurous acquaintances find who insist upon striking into the high latitudes, and who are chafing at the shores of the Harlem River.

But our object is not so much to compare localities as to appreciate and welcome a valuable population, wherever housed in this great City. We certainly need this accession on many accounts, and they can do much to save us from the extremes to which New-York society has been so rapidly tending. Perhaps our richest people are not the most extravagant; there is something in solid capital that carefully counts the cost, and builds more upon character than upon ostentation. Yet, on the whole, our City tends too much to measure dignity by expense, and expense is not content with good taste and reasonable pleasure, but tends to all sorts of excess in hours and dress, entertainments and display, not always within the limits of reason and conscience. Perhaps the persons who suffer most from the contagion of the extravagant example are they who stand just upon the border-ground of high life, and who pay to the shining lights of fashion the tribute of envy which the moth pays to the candle. There ought to be a substantial social life outside of such folly, and it ought to rest upon a solid citizenship which honors thrift, sobriety, and intelligence more than dash and pretension, and which looks to the press, the schools, and the pulpit to be true to the more reasonable and just standards of character. We want more good sense, earnest purpose, kind fellowship, pure taste, frugal and healthful recreation, and these advantages depend to a large extent upon the presence and influence of a powerful class who are not tempted either by poverty or riches. A City like this is full of attractions to such people when they fully and fairly understand it. Thus, let a family of moderate means carefully consider the vast variety of articles and conveniences at their command, and the great gain that they can secure by choosing wisely from whatever is within reach. If you can own a comfortable house, however snug, or if you can pay rent for a proper tenement, what opportunities you here have to get the most and the best for every dollar that you can command. How far you can ride for five cents, and how fast as well as how far for ten cents! With prudence, how much you can buy at low prices for your table or your wardrobe, and for what a trifle you can command the latest and best word from the press or the richest treasures of literature. Too little account has been made of the advantages that this City offers in this way to families of moderate means, and it must be confessed that their welfare has not been sufficiently regarded in the legislation of the City, and in the schemes for enlarging its facilities and magnifying its attractions. But, in spite of corruption in politics and peculation in public works, the City has gained in sightliness, extent, and accommodation, and a new day is now coming to it from the great and goodly company of people who are coming here in search of the essentials of sensible living. The more they are made welcome, the better for us as for them.

January 18, 1880

IS THE FLAT DWELLER "HOMELESS"?

Whether the pronounced tendency in New York to substitute the multiple apartment house for the isolated private dwelling is making this a "homeless" community is worth considering. It is usually discussed in a sentimental or hysterical way which leads to conclusions of very little value. How the idle rich, who may live where and as they please, and who commonly pass a considerable part of every year away from New York, are affected by the change which substitutes the commodious and luxurious apartments for the more commodious but perhaps less comfortable private dwelling, is unimportant. The concern of the student of this particular social problem is neither with the very rich nor the very poor, but with the great mass of the people of New York whose earnings permit them to live comfortably with reasonable economy, and for whom a "flat" is the only home they know for ten or possibly eleven months of the year. There are probably 200,000 families in New York coming strictly within this classification. Twenty or even ten years ago they would have occupied isolated houses. To-day they can do this only by going further from the centres of the city's social and industrial life than they care to go. Would they be any better off if they did?

There is no discoverable reason why living in apartments should be destructive of the home life of a community. As a matter of fact it is not. The possibility of dispensing to a great extent with servants because of the lighter work of housekeeping in apartments brings parents and children closer together, and develops the best elements of the family life. It leaves more time for occupations and pleasures which improve the mind, for reading, and for rest. It has never been discovered that the influence of servants over children was as good as that of parents where the latter recognize their obligations and are fit to perform them. It is probably a safe generalization that the average servant is extremely poor company for the children of a family, and that whatever places children more intimately under the care and constant supervision of their parents makes for good.

The convenience of apartment life relieves the housekeeper of a hundred cares and labors and permits more attention than would have been possible a few years ago to the duties of motherhood in their best sense. If such duties are distasteful to a woman she will probably neglect them, but such neglect is more voluntary than it used to be, and apartment life cannot be held responsible for the preference of frivolous and worldly minded persons for the pleasures which may be had outside of home. The flat dweller is homeless only when he or she prefers to be, and the family life of a great multitude of our citizens thus domiciled is as wholesome and sacred as it could possibly be in any conditions of city residence. Hygienically, the average flat is much better than the average medium-class dwelling house. Probably not 20 per cent. of the isolated three and four story dwellings are or ever were safe to live in. The family life is too near their neglected and unwholesome cellars, the plumbing is defective, and the supply of air for the furnace is drawn from places where pure and clean air cannot possibly be had. Comparatively few of those who live in apartments would go back to the isolated houses of fifteen or twenty years ago, and the fact that last year less than one hundred isolated dwellings for single families were built in New York, and most of these of magnificent proportions and great cost, shows very clearly that the multiple apartment dwelling is the one which in the largest degree meets the public need. Those living in them may properly be objects of sympathy, but not for the reasons commonly given for the sympathy extended to them.

April 25, 1905

RENT OF CITY FLATS IS GETTING CHEAPER

Liking for Semi-Hotel Life Has Brought Figures Down, One Dealer Says.

MUCH DONE FOR THE TENANT

Where Sire Had to Furnish His House Complete, the Son Now Finds It Done for Him.

The oft-repeated cry that the cost of living is constantly rising, that the dollars of our daddies have become, in purchasing power, the cents of their sons, has much to give it cause, no doubt, but those who are conversant with conditions in the real estate business during the last thirty years, in Manhattan and its sister boroughs, are ready to maintain that it is not the landlord who is to blame. Living apartments are the cheapest thing on the market, they contend, and it is only the superficial observer who asserts that a home costs more to-day than it cost his father.

One of the foremost real estate operators in Brooklyn said yesterday that the trouble was that people looked on an apartment as "a ganglion of cells, each with four walls, ceiling and floor, and without considering all that goes with it."

"It is true," he said, "that many persons are paying more for apartments to-day than their fathers paid for houses. It is true the rooms are smaller and sometimes not so light as those in buildings where there are not more than four to a floor. But there the case against the apartment ends—that is, the modern apartment. When the last generation leased a house, that was all it got. The present generation gets an article so greatly improved that there is only the slightest resemblance to the old.

"The problem of housing the ever-growing population is one that is far from being solved, yet we are getting nearer to it every day. One need be little more than forty years old to recall the time when Yorkville and Harlem were dotted with market gardens and the section between Central Park and the Hudson River was inhabited by truck farmers and market gardeners. Squatters' cabins, built of odd boards or rusty tin, were perched on rocky eminences and with the omnipresent goats and geese furnished material for the highly successful plays and songs of Harrigan and Hart, of recent memory. When those conditions ceased to exist, the plays ceased to attract, for it was a phase of old New York life to which the present generation is a total stranger.

"In those days the trip to Coney Island or Rockaway—the latter almost a day's journey, and far more imposing than one now considers a trip to Philadelphia—was a succession of delightfully rural scenes. Wide fields of growing crops spread on either side of the car tracks as far as the eye could reach. Here and there were large patches of woodland. To-day these scenes, common in Brooklyn less than a generation ago, are all but gone. There is only a single spot where farming is carried on to any extent in Brooklyn, down Flatlands way, a section still rather inaccessible. The idea of market gardening in Manhattan is a joke.

"The farms of Flatbush and Gravesend have been converted into building lots by the enterprising farmer or the more far-sighted land-developing companies. Brooklyn, indeed, has always been pre-eminently a city of homes, and it is maintained that a larger percentage of its inhabitants own their own rooftrees than is the case in any other city in America. And this is due to the comparatively low price of land as well as the ever-increasing advantages of quick transportation to Manhattan.

"It was not until about thirty years ago that the convenience of having everything on one floor became known to those who could afford a house. The old-fashioned three and four story, double, cold-water apartment was a step toward the freedom of the housewife from daily labor. Since then many more steps have been taken, and the flat of our fathers has ceased to be an attraction to the builder. Their big rooms, a concession to the old house dweller of earlier times, now are considered too barnlike, for styles in furniture have changed, and few persons have sufficient to equip one of these apartments.

"The tendency nowadays is to do more and more for the tenant, to make his home a place where he may get the maximum of rest and ease and enjoyment at a minimum of effort. To this end a distinct type of building has been devised, and they are being erected in Manhattan and Brooklyn by the score. This is an elaborate structure, capable of housing twenty to forty families, and constructed according to the latest ideas of comfort and elegance.

"As a result of this and the lure of the suburban cottage, now that suburban transit is so good, the rents have fallen materially, and at present those with large holdings of apartments, except in unusual cases, are land poor. As an illustration: On Prospect Park West, the counterpart of Central Park West in Manhattan, facing the park, between Thirteenth and Fourteenth Streets, is an imposing row of limestone apartment houses, steam heated. They are on high ground, command a beautiful view of the park, to which there is an entrance only a block away. Good transit is provided by the Vanderbilt Avenue cars, which pass the door; by the Smith Street line, on Fifteenth Street, a block away, and by the Fifth Avenue elevated road, which has a station at Fifteenth Street, an easy walk. Yet six or seven large rooms and bath may be had for $28 to $30 a month.

"A part of Brooklyn where the demand for steam-heated apartments has held up fairly well is the Bedford section. This is due to its accessibility by many car lines and elevated roads and to the generally high-class character of its residents. As an instance of low prices, on St. James's Place, near Fulton Street, one block from an elevated railroad station and half a block from two lines of trolleys, within easy walking distance of the Subway there are two rows of modern limestone front apartments. The neighborhood is quiet and restricted and in these houses much attention is paid to the home comfortable, yet these apartments with seven light rooms bring only $42 to $48, which is $7 to $10 less than was asked four years ago.

"In the old days houses cost anywhere from $30 up, but all the tenant got was the house. To-day he pays $40 up, but they are heated in Winter and he gets all his shades, window awnings, screens, and hot water, night and day. He has no coal to buy, no furnaces to tend, no ashes to sift, no garbage to put out. In many apartments that may be had for less than fifty dollars he gets the use of a vacuum-cleaner, separate phone service and hall boy; self-draining refrigerators, pier mirrors, sideboards, medicine closets, hat racks and curtain poles are built in. The hardwood floors are furnished.

"Cooking by gas has reduced the cost of living, for a gas bill of $5 is not exorbitant and that will include all lighting and cooking. If it runs to $8 in Winter it will fall in Summer.

April 30, 1911

SAGE FOUNDATION PLANS DISCLOSED

Forest Hills Gardens to be an Object Lesson in Modest Suburban Home-Building.

OBJECT IS NOT CHARITABLE

No "Paternal Control" Over Property Owners, but Each to Have Some Voice in Questions of Proper Use.

The Sage Foundation has at last broken its silence regarding its plans and purposes for its Forest Hills Gardens land development in Queens, a few miles out from Long Island City. John M. Glenn, Secretary of the Foundation, gave out yesterday the first statement on the subject coming from any one connected officially with the Sage Foundation and having inside information of its plans.

Mr. Glenn states emphatically that the Sage community is not in the least degree a charity. He says that it will not be conducted as a charity, or even for people of laboring-class means. It will be the home—a model home, however, the Foundation hopes to make it—for people of moderate means who want a real home, and have now, he says, to choose between a city apartment or a frame house in a suburb built on conventional lines.

The Foundation would offer Forest Hills Gardens as an inspiration to all the people of the city in suburb and home building. Mr. Glenn explains that the Sage Foundation and the Sage Foundation Homes Company are distinct corporations, the Foundation supplying the capital for the purchase and development of the project, but the Homes Company having entire charge of the planning and carrying out of the development scheme.

"The trustees of the Foundation," explains Mr. Glenn, "wished to create a suburb that would combine beauty in the arrangement of grounds with attractiveness and permanency in building. This required the investment of over $2,000,000; that is, over one-fifth of the capital of the Foundation. The maintenance of the work of the Foundation requires that its capital be kept undiminished and that this scheme, like all other investments, must yield a good business profit. The Foundation does not give charitable aid to individuals under any circumstances, its chief function being to inquire into social conditions and to teach effective methods of social betterment.

Chief Aim to Create an Example.

"Failure to make the project a reasonable commercial success would mean that the educational policy of the Foundation would miscarry. Its chief success, if it have any, will be the creation of an example of intelligent and charming use of real estate which will be tempting to other investors in the vicinity of New York and in more distant parts of the country.

"With these aims in view, the Trustees of the Foundation bought the tract of about 140 acres and organized a distinct corporation, the Sage Foundation Homes Company, to hold and develop it, and conveyed the land to this company. The Foundation has loaned the company the necessary capital for the laying out of the land, for the erection of buildings, for the maintenance of a proper force and equipment, and for other incidental purposes. The company is purely a practical business concern, and controls the management and handling of the property."

After stating that Robert W. de Forest is President of the company, and giving the names of its other officers, Mr. Glenn continues:

"The company starts with certain advantages that are not common in suburban development. The company has not had to go into the money market to borrow funds; it has been possible to pay cash for the property and for much of its material. As it is not looking for undue speculative profits, it can afford to move with care and deliberation. It has been able to complete in advance of its buildings an unusually large share of street construction, including the laying of water and gas mains and electric conduits, as well as much of its landscape work and plainting."

Not to Exercise Paternal Control.

Mr. Glenn describes how the suburb will be laid out, giving each house the maximum of light and air, and how the aim will be to make the place attractive as a whole as well as in detail. He then has this to say about the upkeep of the place:

"Streets and other property for general use will be maintained by an agency to be created for the purpose. Each lot owner will contribute his share of the cost and will have a proportionate voice in its expenditure. This plan accords with the desire of the company's officers that the management of the property shall become as democratic as possible, and all lot owners shall have the right and opportunity to express their views on any points that may arise. Each one will be independent as far as may be compatible with the welfare of his neighbors, each one will be able to exercise control over the use by his neighbors of their property in proportion to his interest in the whole property. The company will not attempt to exercise paternal control over lot and house owners.

"It desires to give full value for each purchase and at the same time to dispose of its property at prices that will give it a moderate but fair return for the money and time invested in it. It will not permit lot owners to build unsightly houses nor to establish nuisances, neither will it attempt to control their actions beyond seeing that the general atmosphere of beauty and order is preserved."

September 4, 1911

TWENTY-SIX GARDEN APARTMENT HOUSES COSTING $3,000,000 TO BE BUILT AT JACKSON HEIGHTS

New Structures, Which Will Contain Electric Elevators and Sun Parlors Facing Landscaped Gardens, Will Provide Homes for Several Hundred Families

Three groups of elevator apartment houses, comprising twenty-six buildings of the garden type, are to be erected at Jackson Heights on the Queensboro subway.

These new buildings are the first elevator apartments to be erected at Jackson Heights, where, at the present time, more than 500 apartments, in more than fifty buildings, are co-operatively owned by tenants.

The most important feature of the announcement of this new construction project is the fact that the new buildings are to be erected by Dwight P. Robinson & Co., Inc., which concern has been most prominent in general construction work in all parts of the North and South.

Dwight P. Robinson & Co., Inc., have now decided to enter the apartment building field, and have selected Jackson Heights as the location of their first operation.

The new houses actually will be erected by a new company, known as the Queensboro Apartments, Inc., which is controlled by the Queensboro Corporation and Jackson Heights Apartment Corporation.

The three groups of buildings to be erected, comprising twenty-six buildings, are of four and five story type, to be built around interior gardens, following the general method of construction at Jackson Heights, which has made this section unique as an apartment house community.

George H. Wells, architect, who has designed many of the buildings erected at Jackson Heights, planned the new buildings. The entire operation comprises 234 apartments, of five and six rooms, with one and two baths.

An item of special interest in connection with the construction of these buildings is the installation of automatic elevators. This type of elevator, which is self operated, has been, for many years, in use in Europe, and has been installed in apartment buildings in this country and in privte residences in New York.

This is the first time, however, that the use of automatic elevators has been tried on so large a scale in this section of the country. It is believed that the use of these elevators in the new Jackson Heights apartments will revolutionize the construction of apartment buildings of moderate height, as they give all the advantages of elevator service without the greatly increasing expense of such service required when attendants are employed.

It is proposed, upon the completion of these buildings, some of which will be completed and ready for occupancy early next Spring, to sell the apartments on the tenant-ownership plan, which has been so successful at Jackson Heights, and which has created there, the largest and most select co-operatively owned apartment community in the world.

The Jackscon Heights plan of tenant-ownership differs from many others in that the buildings are 100 per cent. co-operative—the entire equity in each building being owned by the tenant-owners.

The three new groups of apartment buildings are to be financed in part by the Metropolitan Life Insurance Company which has made loans on the three groups in excess of $1,400,000.

E. A. MacDougall, President of the Queensboro Corporation, said:

"These three groups of new garden apartment houses will be erected simultaneously. One group is to be located in Twenty-second and Twenty-third streets, from Fillmore to Hayes Avenue. This group consists of eight buildings having a frontage of 65 feet and 75 feet respectively, and is composed of 64 five and six room apartments, with two baths.

"One unique feature of these buildings, as also of the third group to be described, is the rear combination sun-room and bedroom. This is a large room with three large openings with casement windows looking upon the parked interior court and connected with the dining room by glass doors.

"A ventilated dressing closet and bed closet is part of the equipment, so that at night the room may be used as a bedroom and in the day time can be used as a sun-room. A three-fixture bathroom adjoins this room. The dressing closet is amply large for a clothes press and chiffonier, and the bed closet is ample to enclose any size standard bed during the daytime. The other bed rooms of the apartment are grouped around the bathroom and are separated from the living room and dining room by a foyer hall so as to secure entire privacy.

"This group of buildings is nearest to the Community Clubhouse where are located restaurant, dancing pavilion, bowling alleys and riding academy.

"The second group of buildings is located on the block between Twenty-second and Twenty-third Streets, Polk and Roosevelt Avenues, and consists of four buildings, each having a frontage of 120 feet, each building containing twenty apartments and equipped with two automatic elevators. The apartments are five and six rooms, with attractive garden outlook. The buildings are located nearest to the tennis courts and children's playgrounds, and are only a short distance from the subway station. In fact, there are five subway stations on the property.

"The third and largest group, consisting of fourteen buildings, each five stories high, having 140 five and six room apartments, and occupying the block between Nineteenth and Twentieth Streets, Polk and Fillmore Avenues. One end of these buildings overlooks the Golf Course, and they are within a short distance of the subway station. In addition to the automatic elevators, these apartments will also have the attractive sun-room bedroom feature described in the first group.

"All of the apartments in these three groups have built-in fireplaces, so much needed in this climate, where auxiliary heat is often needed, even in Summer.

"The interior garden between the buildings, which faces Nineteenth Street and Twentieth Street, is 500 feet long and is 83 feet wide at its narrowest point. It will be parked, its entire length with trees, shrubs, flowers, seats, &c., and will constitute the most beautiful of all the garden groups at Jackson Heights, because of its large dimensions.

"Eight of the buildings are 65 feet in width and six are 75 feet in width. They are remarkable because of the small area of the lot covered by the building, which is very little in excess of 30 per cent. By so constructing the building, the large interior park is made possible, as well as parking the fronts of the buildings. This group, when finished, will probably be the most attractive group of apartments of their type ever erected."

In discussing the new operation yesterday F. R. Howe of the company said:

"The industry of building apartment houses, while very long established in New York City, cannot be said to have had any real standard set for advancement, and the progress that has been made in apartment house construction in New York City is only the result of hit or miss methods and not of an intensive study of living conditions or plans of completed projects with the idea of doing better work in the future.

"It might be said that there has been no concerted effort made toward the improvement of apartment houses, except that improvement which has been worked out individually by builders and operators. The idea has been to build to a per-room cost, and lease each room for the largest amount of money rather than to build to an ideal plan and then lease it for a fair return on the then per-room cost.

"Very few operators and builders have taken their tenants into their confidence and discussed their likes and dislikes, and designed with the consensus of these opinions in their mind.

"The Queensboro Corporation might be said to be the first large operators who have made this study and then designed buildings to suit their tenants."

September 25, 1921

3 OF THE 14 NEW GARDEN ELEVATOR APARTMENTS on 19th and 20th STS. JACKSON HEIGHTS

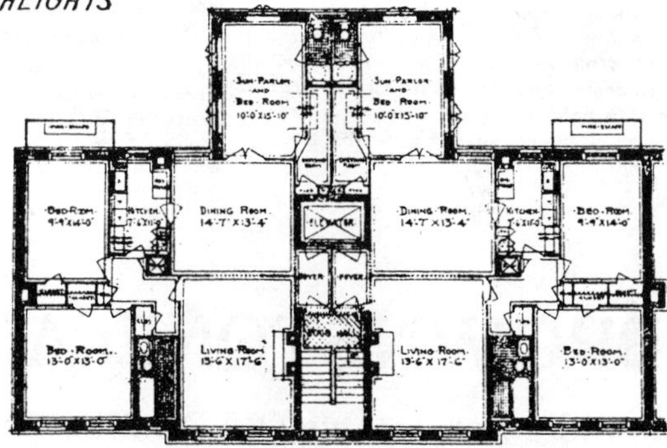

FLOOR PLAN of NEW 6 ROOM ELEVATOR APARTMENTS UNDER CONSTRUCTION at JACKSON HEIGHTS

RAPID GROWTH FOR GARDEN HOME PLAN

Its Success Is Assured in the Next Decade, According to City Planning Expert.

INVESTIGATED IN EUROPE

A rapid growth of the garden home plan of housing in the next decade is seen for American cities by Henry Wright, city planning expert, who recently returned from an extensive tour of investigation in Europe.

Mr. Wright has been appointed city planning consultant to the New York State Commission on Housing and Regional Planning and is just taking up his duties in that capacity.

"Heretofore in the big cities of the United States a garden in connection with the home has been relegated almost entirely to the suburbanites," said Mr. Wright before leaving for Buffalo, where the State commission will take up problems of regional planning for that area.

"We are beginning to learn from England and other European countries that this is not at all necessary.

"In London there are many developments of bright, cheerful flats—eight families to a building—where each family has its own garden plot for the growing of flowers or vegetables. These flats are usually grouped about an open green, a portion of which is assigned each family.

"The whole problem is one of planning. Back yards and their almost unvariable accumulation of waste and scattered outbuildings are being converted into attractive gardens and playgrounds.

"It is entirely practical to build these homes for persons of moderate income. In England and Holland the Government accelerates such construction by furnishing fifty-year housing loans at low interest. The homes are built through public utilities societies, the organization having the same character in both countries. Each Government lends such organizations 75 per cent. of the cost of the house.

"We do not have Government financial aid for housing in America and consequently cannot build the homes as cheaply or experiment in good housing on a large scale. In the absence of that there is the limited dividend company like the City Housing Corporation of New York. Such organizations are not interested primarily in profit but in well constructed homes that can be sold to persons of moderate income on small monthly payments.

"The first unit of the City Housing Corporation's development at Long Island City, which has just been completed, is a fine example of what can be done in garden homes. With a central garden, each owner not only has a garden spot but the use of a playground for the children, a tennis court and a basketball court. The houses are only two rooms deep. A mother can remain at her work in the home and at the same time keep a watchful eye on the children at play in the garden. The youngsters need never romp in the street and, in fact, they have little desire to do so, with all the playground facilities at hand.

"These garden homes are only fifteen minutes from the Grand Central Station.

"I believe Sunnyside will mark a distinct step in pointing the way to better housing in New York. Other builders will take it up when they see the success there. The same plan can be followed in various sections of the city and, at less cost, on cheaper ground."

While abroad Mr. Wright attended the International Conference on Garden City and Town Planning, as the representative of the American Institute of Architects, which was held at Amsterdam this Summer.

September 28, 1924

HOUSING THE MIDDLE CLASS.

A census of Sunnyside, the City Housing Corporation's community of commodious and low-priced homes just over the Queensboro Bridge, reveals highly significant facts as to its composition. The various types of apartments and houses range in purchase price from $4,800 to $17,800; but after an initial payment of 10 per cent. the payment per month averages only $10 a room—which, as the prospectus says, puts them "within the means of the wage earner." Yet most of the people who have applied for these quarters and live in them can scarcely be called wage earners. Out of a total "of about 230," 41, or over one-sixth, are "professionals," the term including lawyers, physicians, engineers and accountants. Eight teachers and three trained nurses are listed separately. Those "in business," presumably as employers, number 29. There are 6 "factory executives," 44 "store and office workers," 14 "salesmen," 4 "municipal employes," 3 "advertising men," 1 "stock broker," 1 "retired," and several "Government employes." Thus upward of 155, or over two-thirds, are professionals, business men and salaried workers. Those employed in "building trades," as "mechanics" and as "chauffeurs," aggregate 43. Adding two cooks, two waiters, an elevator man and a janitor, these compose a little over one-fifth of the total. Figures as to income are to a similar effect. Only eight report $2,000 or less. About half, or 114, report between $2,000 and $3,000. Those who report over $3,000 number 102, of whom 40 report over $4,500.

Evidently such enterprises cannot reach the great body of the laboring poor even though conducted with the utmost economy and good-will, as this one is. Wages are too low and families frequently too large. As to organized laborers who are not poor, the inference seems to be that they prefer other modes of living. Yet to many the Housing Corporation will seem to have achieved a success of the first order, and all the more welcome because it can hardly have been expected. The "new poor" of the middle class—folk of ripely American traditions, advanced education and native idealism—have fared ill through many decades. For the maintenance of their traditional standard of living, and especially for the education of a family to the duties of citizenship and the practice of a profession, $5,000 a year is hardly enough. Such colonies are open to all craftsmen who apply and heartily welcome them, but they can scarcely raise the bars against the struggling professional.

May 10, 1926

COOPERATIVE HOMES IN STEADY DEMAND

Apartment Ownership Principle Growing in Many Sections of the Country.

Sociologists and economists consider that a high percentage of home-ownership is a great stabilizing influence and protection against extreme radicalism, said Roland Feldman, Vice President of Douglas L. Elliman & Co., in discussing city home conditions.

"A few years ago, when Bolshevism was a big everyday topic," he added, "students told us that the United States need not fear Bolshevism because so many families here own their homes.

"According to the 1920 census figures, 10,866,960 homes out of 24,357,676 in this country were owned by their occupants. Obviously, the percentage in small towns and rural communities even higher, because the percentage is lower in the large cities.

"In some large industrial cities, like Akron and Rochester, the percentage is very high—44 and 43 per cent., respectively. In Buffalo, Cincinnati, Cleveland and Philadelphia, the figure is from 35 to 40 per cent. In Chicago it is 27 per cent.

"In Greater New York, 12.7 per cent. of the dwellers own their homes. But in Manhattan, the great apartment and tenement house borough, the figure is 2.1 per cent. That is not a surprising figure. People living in apartment houses have not, until the last few years, owned their homes, except in isolated and unusual instances.

Cooperative Growth.

"I wonder what the Manhattan ownership percentage will be ten or twenty years from now—due to the growth of the cooperative apartment idea. Already more than $200,000,000 worth of cooperative apartments have been erected in New York City. These have not been limited to any one district or financial stratum.

"It is natural that the east side residential district has led the movement. Park and Fifth Avenues and the cross streets east of Central Park are thickly spotted with cooperative projects valued at $100,000,000, while almost every field of human endeavor is represented. As with every great economic movement, the men of wealth and substance must lead the way. People of lesser means and influence follow along until the whole community is traveling in the same direction. Men of moderate means, the salaried classes, labor groups are building and occupying cooperatives, and the momentum of the movement is constantly increasing.

The cooperative apartment idea is not limited to New York. Chicago, Boston, St. Paul, Detroit, Atlanta, St. Louis, Kansas City, Washington, Baltimore, Philadelphia, San Francisco, Los Angeles and many other cities have their cooperative projects.

Causes for Development.

The ownership of a private house is a natural and established condition. But conditions in a large city like New York make a private house an impracticable proposition for the average man. Apartment living has proved to be the economical and convenient method of living.

A cooperative apartment is economical as compared to a private house, because the cost of land and land taxes is shared by many owners, and in like manner the cost of heat, service and general upkeep and repairs.

"Cooperative owners are finding many economies inherent in a cooperative building as compared with a rented building. Any operating profit reverts to the tenant-owners. The permanence of tenure means an absence of vacancies and the resulting losses of income and elimination of costly redecorating whenever a tenant moves in and out. Then there is the absence of income tax on the return from the money invested and the possibility of a considerable speculative profit."

May 16, 1926

BROWNSTONE AGE IS COMING TO A CLOSE

Stolidly Respectable Old Dwelling Houses. Symbolical of a Phase of New York Life That Has Passed Into History, Are Rapidly Giving Way to Modern Apartment Buildings

By JAMES C. YOUNG

THE age of the brownstone front draws to a close. Long blocks of these stolidly respectable houses are yielding to the wrecker. Before long the saunterer who looks for remains of old New York will have to look twice to find a brownstone front. In almost every cross street of Central Manhattan, from river to river, the dignity of brownstone gives way to shining new structures that rise higher. A hundred families come to live where but two or three have dwelt as the panorama of New York moves on.

Of the many institutions pulled down by the hand of the wrecker and offered upon the altar of change, none typified more truly than the brownstone house a definite period in New York social history. Who that has seen a brownstone front in the fullness of its dignity will forget it? Houses have personalities that often equal and sometimes surpass the characters of their occupants. But usually men and the houses they inhabit are much alike. And surely there never could have been a stronger resemblance between men and houses than was reflected in the brownstone front.

The Family Goes to Church

Brownstone and Sunday morning had a special affinity. Thirty or forty years ago a generation of well-to-do New Yorkers opened their front doors regularly every Sunday at 10 o'clock, sniffed the morning air and walked down the brownstone steps in full raiment, bound for church. The frock coat and the glossy silk hat were inevitable. Often a flower in the coat lapel lent color to this austerity. Milady followed in the dignity of silk and satin, and a cab waited at the curb.

In a long block of brownstone fronts, lining the way upon either side with unbroken severity, it was something to see the many doors opened and the many cabs driven off, filled with the good folk of New York bound for worship. In that moment the brownstone front wore its soberest tones and reached the consummation of its destiny.

But the brownstone front also served as a habitat for man on the intervening six days of the week. It appeared upon Manhattan Island in the late '30s or early '40s and reached the flower of its age in the '70s and '80s. Why is it that no historian waited upon the curb, stop-watch in hand, to register the exact hour and day that the first brownstone front reached completion? That was an occasion in the architectural annals of New York without compare, ushering in a uniformity of construction that still strikes the eye with monotonous emphasis in blocks as yet overlooked by the builders.

A brownstone front of three floors, and sometimes four, set back from the street line ten feet, its high stoop reached by eight or nine steps, expressed a phase of New York life with the accuracy of a photograph. That period was prosperous and the brownstone front exemplified substantial comfort. Critics of our social order and the passing parade have called the age of the brownstone front the bourgeois paradise. The brownstone front belonged to the day when servants still arrived by every steamship and did not ask for nights out. It was a token of money in the bank, a pew in the church and a regular Thursday afternoon "at home" in neighborhood society.

There are many accounts of its origin, and the investigator may choose one at random with a fair chance of accuracy. But logic is on the side of a contractor who fell heir to a parcel of lots in the Chelsea district when New York first pushed uptown from Washington Square.

The old village of Chelsea, reminiscent of Colonial times, was undergoing change. New houses of brick rose upon every hand. But it is said that the brick supply of the late '30s fell into the hands of speculators and this contractor cast about for a substitute material so as to profit by the rising tide.

Granite was too costly and fieldstone too difficult to obtain in needed quantities, or perhaps unsuitable for a growing metropolis. Nobody had thought much of the reddish sandstone available in near-by quarries. The story says that the contractor imported from a quarry near Newburgh the earliest brownstone seen in New York and erected a row of houses upon his Chelsea lots. Thus he became responsible for a type of New York building that still endures, though it passes fast.

New York's Great Divide

That story has the semblance of truth. It would be possible to lay down a ruler at Eighth Street, running across the island, and mark the division between brick construction and the beginning of brownstone. In later years the material was used to some extent below Eighth Street on the east side, but only in a restricted measure. It never did find favor south of Washington Square.

Brownstone was the material of a new expansion that began with the opening of Fifth Avenue a hundred years ago. Union and Madison squares were centres of respectability. The old city, from Bowling Green to Greenwich Village, had been a city of brick and stone, especially brick. But the new city spreading northward was largely of brownstone.

The full effect of this movement did not appear until the Civil War ended and New York expanded into blocks of brownstone fronts, all the way from Thirty-fourth Street to Harlem. Just as it is possible to place the southern division at Eighth Street, it also is possible to mark the northern line, running obliquely from Riverside Drive along the high ground of 116th Street and northward across Harlem to the river of that name. But the brownstone front ceased to flourish at Ninety-sixth Street on the west side. It also had a wide vogue in Brooklyn, but was scarcely known in the Bronx.

No one knows how many tons of brownstone were raised one upon another in the heyday of the period. One must be content with the evidence spread wide in so many streets of changing New York. The coming of steel construction and the apartment house banished brownstone and restored brick. It is doubtful whether a new brownstone house has been erected in ten years. The decline began with the first years of the century.

A great many charges might be brought against the brownstone in the name of the arts and culture. But perhaps it would be worth while to look behind one of those impassive fronts before condemning the period. A visitor who mounted the stoop by the correct brownstone steps, his hand laid respectfully upon the brownstone railing, found himself before a door commonly painted black, with a brightly polished brass bell-pull at the right hand. Over the door a graceful fanlight, descended from Colonial houses, sometimes relieved the drab entrance. More often the fanlight was missing.

The brownstone front gained nothing by a wait in its doorway, but the instant that Mary Ann opened the black portal a visitor received impressions more pleasant, though his sense of reverence diminished not a whit. The hallway was austere, like the exterior, meticulously neat, and bore a substantial air. At one side stood a black walnut table with a veined marble top, and on the marble was a bowl of goldfish or a nosegay of waxen lilies underneath a glass case. At the other side a stairway led upward, the handrail of black walnut or some other wood darkly stained, ending in a curved pilaster at the bottom. This handrail was a favored place for the entertainment of small boys, an excellent slide, ending in a grand bounce upon the floor.

An Unchanging Chamber

The stairway was at the left of the entrance and a long chamber opened at the right hand or the order was reversed, but the chamber itself was inevitable and unchanging. A visitor found that two deep French windows looked upon the street and fluffy lace curtains behind yellow shades served to give the chamber a kind of hallowed air. In the centre of the far wall stood a marble fireplace, a mantel above, occasionally touched with gilt and always a bit chilling to the eye. A grilled iron register in the wall permitted the passage of much coal gas and such heat as escaped from the distant furnace.

When a brownstone front reached the perfection of which it was capable this big chamber, first called a drawing room and later the front parlor, was furnished in a manner to match the house. The carpet was red or blue and the furniture was of walnut, covered with horsehair. The centre table bore another slab of marble as a counterpart to the fireplace. Sometimes a gilded French piece, such as a gaily scalloped table, having many curlicues, helped to make the horsehair and walnut more ominous. Perhaps there stood upon the mantel a Swiss clock, distinguished by an involved method of winding which always provided conversation. Not infrequently it was gilded. A piano or organ occupied one corner of the front parlor and a few dark, gloomy canvases hung upon the walls.

But neither the room nor its equipage was used save on great occasions. The family gathered in the back parlor just beyond the folding doors. Both of these parlors had high ceilings from which hung arabesqued gas chandeliers. All in all, the back parlor was a more livable place, where the women sewed by day and looked out into the diminutive yard. A few struggling plants could be seen there in the proper season, but nothing really flourished in one of these yards except a mulberry tree that grew in the far corner despite encroachments. Small boys soon found that the leaves made one's hands smell so badly no amount of washing would remove the odor for hours.

The back parlors of an older New York afforded a not unpleasant scene. A common fence running the length of the block divided the many yards and numerous other fences cut them into small enclosures, forming a kind of inner court. Each house had its own shoebox of a room and a certain privacy out of doors. Here it was that Mary Ann hung the wash every Monday morning. On sunny days the youngsters and their mothers went into the little yards for their games and their discourse. An epic of history has been lost across the rear fences, since, alas! no historian stood by with ready ear.

Underneath the back parlor might be found the culinary branch of a brownstone front, always supplied with a big range, many pots and shining pans. At the front of the house, in a room looking upon the street through an iron grill, the family dined. And a comfortable dining room it was, the one room of the house where severity seldom intruded. The open fire upon the hearth assisted the rickety furnace. Rag rugs were not unknown. The furniture might be stilted and conventional, but this room was a place of welcome, smoking viands and sparkling bottles.

When a sojourner in a brownstone front crawled up the long flight of steps from the parlor floor to the second or even the third landing he found a series of rooms with high ceilings and big windows. The beds were of wood, preferably dark walnut of mahogany, stern in their simplicity. Marble-topped tables and stiff chairs kept company with the beds. Family portraits looked forth from the walls, bearing such names as Hezekiel Smithers and Fanny Smithers, Hezekiel with chin whiskers and Fanny with plastered hair. The sternness of the room was matched by the sternness of the early photographs.

The occupant of such a house could not do otherwise than wear a high collar and cultivate a grave manner. He who belonged to the epoch must wear a brownstone manner. Sentiment was not wholly lacking. Many a brownstone front had a maiden aunt who "lived with" its mistress or its master, a hostage of ill fortune. The small boy knew this aunt exceedingly well and was moved by curiosity when she repaired once a year to the trunk-room high up under the eaves, regularly upon a stated day. Such a boy, with a sharp eye and a sharp ear, has stumbled upon such an aunt kneeling before a worn trunk, her hands filled with letters bound by lavender ribbon. And often she dried her eyes in a shamefaced way as the small boy backed out, mouth agape.

The trunk room was a place of high adventure on rainy days, when a youngster could romp there without annoyance from his elders. It was a great retreat in which to call up pirates from dark corners and Indians from the deep closet, to take fright from the creaking of the window and the howling of the wind and go sliding down the banister at a rate to make the house rattle when the final bounce came.

But the brownstone front, depository of so many memories, the home-place of a generation or two, soon will be a memory itself. In every cross street between Washington Square and Central Park the old houses are disappearing swiftly. Certainly the city will obtain needed room by the change and perhaps gain something artistically, but it also will lose. The brownstone front was peculiarly and essentially the citadel of the home, the stronghold of an old-fashioned era before New York became such a vast hive. In no other city did the brownstone front achieve greatness. It was respectable, prosperous, frock-coated New York at the best.

January 10, 1926

"Brownstone and Sunday Morning Had a Special Affinity."

CHICAGO.

The City Suburbs—The Exodus of City Population—Description of the Towns—Interesting Facts and Statements.

From Our Own Correspondent.

CHICAGO, Saturday, July 8, 1871.

Chicago has a large number of suburban and ambitious little villages, some of which have, however, gradually grown up into respectable towns and even cities. The excessive taxation of the city, the heavy rents and cost of living generally, are driving a large population beyond the corporate limits. The suburban towns are receiving larger accessions than ever this season, and many new towns are springing up. A brief sketch of these suburbs may not be uninteresting. I propose to notice only such as are within a radius of twenty miles from the City Hall, which is about five miles from the northern, western and southern limits of the city.

Commencing on the lake shore, south, we have Calumet, about twelve miles distant. It is an old place, and thirty years ago it was a proposed rival of Chicago. But it never had any growth. It is situated on Calumet River, quite a large stream, which is capable of being made into an excellent harbor. There was formerly a light-house at the mouth of the river; but the project of making a town having been practically abandoned, the light was discontinued about fifteen years ago. But within the past two years work to build up the town there has again commenced in earnest. Congress has made two appropriations of fifty thousand dollars each for harbor purposes, and the Company is expending as much more. It will doubtless grow into a place of considerable importance within the next five years. Back of the town is a system of small lakes, which in time will become an attractive feature of the locality. The Michigan Central and Southern and the Illinois Central Railroads are available for Calumet.

About seven miles out, and beautifully located on the lake shore, is Hyde Park. It is one of our oldest suburbs, and has probably about three thousand inhabitants. Its growth has been considerably retarded by the licensing of whisky and beer saloons, thus introducing a rowdy element, to get rid of which is one reason why families in Chicago with children to bring up prefer a residence in these rural suburbs. Between the city limits and Hyde Park, a distance of about three miles, it is thickly populated with people doing business in Chicago. This is in the region of the new parks and boulevards, and where property has risen from $100 to $300 an acre to from $6,000 to $10,000 within the last five years. Hyde Park is reached by the Illinois and Michigan Central Railroads, which run special trains to connect with the city railways.

About three miles west, near the junction of the Michigan Southern and Rock Island Railroads, is Englewood. It is a newer town, but being pleasantly located in groves of natural trees, it has had quite a rapid growth, and is settled by a good class of people. The county Normal School was located here about two years ago, and an elegant building costing $100,000 erected for its accommodation.

Five miles out is what is now called the "Rock Island Car Works," where a population of several hundred people has grown up around the shops of the Railroad Company, which employs about 700 men at this point.

Something like twelve miles on the Rock Island Road we have Washington Heights, a place which started out two years ago with a great flourish. But the introduction of beer-saloons, and a German population, soon put an end to its prospects as a suburban residence, and it has grown but little.

Still further on—sixteen miles, and we come to Blue Island. This is quite an old and somewhat dilapidated town. Two breweries and their accompaniments, the saloons, have kept people away who are seeking quiet and a safe place to bring up their families. It has a population of about one thousand. Blue Island is so named because it is located on and beside a large hill, which rises to a considerable height, quite abruptly from the prairie.

Lockport, Joliet, and several other towns in this direction, furnish quite a number of men doing business in Chicago with residences, but they are rather too far out to be called suburbs. Over on the Chicago and St. Louis Road, and near the canal, are Brighton and Lemont, containing about one thousand inhabitants. There are two or three other little places. This is the stone-quarrying district, and the majority of the population is rather "hard," and the presence of saloons at these places also causes them to be avoided by those seeking rural homes.

About seventeen miles out, on the Chicago, Pittsburg and Cincinnati Road, we have the new town of Greenwood, beautifully located amid "a forest primeval," or rather a series of groves, which promises to be one of our most popular suburbs. A mile this way is the town of Dalton. The two will probably soon grow into one. They both contain now about five hundred inhabitants.

Passing northward, we come to the line of the Chicago, Burlington and Quincy Road. Men come in from the towns sixty and seventy miles distant to do business in the city, but the only places of note within our twenty miles limitation are Riverside, Hinsdale and Downie's Grove. A little beyond is Naperville, one of the contesting county seats of Dupage County.

Riverside is twelve miles from the city, on the banks of the Desplaines River. Large sums have been expended by the proprietors in all kinds of improvements to render their town beautiful and attractive, and it is regarded as the aristocratic suburb. Its drives and promenades are superior to any in the vicinity of the city, and it is rapidly growing.

Hinsdale is about six miles further west—a beautiful town, situated upon the highest land in all this region, and containing the very best kind of population. It has schools, churches and all the conveniences of life, as, in fact, have all our suburbs, except the very newest, and these enter into the first plans of all.

On the Galena and Dixon branches of the North-western Road are also a large number of towns, which send many men into Chicago daily for the transaction of business. There are twenty, at least, which we may not properly call suburbs.

Three miles west of the city limits is the new town of Austero, which has, within the past year, risen into the dignity of a suburb. It contains probably five or six hundred inhabitants, and is rapidly growing. It is beautifully located on high prairie land, amid beautiful groves.

Two miles further on is Harlem, and just beyond Oak Park; then Cottage Hill, Maywood and Thatcher,—the last two on opposite banks of the Desplaines. At the extent of our limits, twenty miles, is Lombard, a town of four or five hundred inhabitants. Some of these towns have just started out; others have attained to schools, churches, &c., and all contain, probably, about two thousand inhabitants. They are beautifully located, and are destined to have a rapid and healthy growth. Coming upon the Wisconsin branch of the North-western—which is the original road—we find a string of towns, old and new, which have no distinctive features. There are Jefferson, Brickton, Norwood Park, Niles, (a little off the road,) Barrington, Palatine, and some so new that their existence is recognized only on the map. Some of these towns antedate the railroad, while others are the creations of two or three years. We suppose they will aggregate about three thousand inhabitants. Norwood Park is beautifully laid out, and presents attractions which are adding largely to its population this season.

There only remains, now, the list of towns on the Lake Shore, along the line of the Chicago and Milwaukee Road. The largest and most important of these is Evanston. It derives its name from Hon. JOHN EVANS, Governor of Colorado, a while ago. He was formerly a resident of Chicago, and was one of the principal founders of this suburb. It was originally laid out by the Methodists in the interest of education. They founded the North-western University and the Garrett Biblical Institute, and expected to endow them by the rise of the land which they purchased. In this they have been successful, and now estimate the value of the property at $1,250,000, and it is constantly increasing. On the Fourth, the corner-stone of a Ladies' College was laid, under most favorable auspices. Although the town was originated by the Methodists, as a seat of their educational institutions, there are Baptist, Presbyterian, Congregational and Catholic churches in the town—the former of which nearly equals the Methodist Church in membership. The new Trinity building is large and elegant, and it has recently been supplied with a $40,000 library, the gift of W. L. GREENLEAF, Esq., a resident of the town. Evanston is beautifully situated, being located in natural groves, on the bank of Lake Michigan, which is here of moderate elevation. It has a population of about 4,000, and is rapidly increasing. It is eleven miles, or about half an hour's ride from Chicago. The Soldiers' Home is also here.

Ravenswood, Glencoe, Winetka and Willamette are pleasant little towns, lying along the railroad and lake, and are growing satisfactorily. Highland Park rejoices in being a city, with Mayor and Council, with a population of six or eight hundred. The banks of the lake here rise to a height of about one hundred feet, and the site of the town is picturesque and variegated. It is called a Baptist town, as it was principally settled by members of that denomination from Chicago. There is, however, a Presbyterian church recently organized here.

July 17, 1871

THE EXODUS TO NEW JERSEY.

Mayor Gaynor Told That It Is Due to a Lack of Transit Facilities.

A great deal of interest has been aroused in Queens by the publication of a letter addressed to Mayor Gaynor by George W. Pople of the Flushing Business Men's Association. In this letter Mr. Pople states that because of the high taxes, high rents and poor transportation facilities, on an average of 5,000 families a year are leaving New York City and moving to New Jersey.

Mr. Pople reviewed the transit situation in Queens and the heavy assessment under which the people are placed in anticipation of having a share in the rapid transit of the city.

Mayor Gaynor acknowledges receipt of the letter as follows:

> My Dear Mr. Pople: I thank you exceedingly for your letter. It contains many good suggestions. No doubt the city can build all of the subways, but it will take a long time, whereas if we get capital to come in with us we can build those immediately needed at once. Sincerely yours,
> W. J. GAYNOR, Mayor.

Mr. Pople said the figures had been carefully compiled and that he had nothing to add beyond the fact that it was necessary to do something to stem the exodus now under way from New York City to New Jersey.

February 7, 1912

BUILDING UP ATTRACTIVE HOME COMMUNITIES AROUND WHITE PLAINS AND HARTSDALE

Improved Transit Facilities Have Given Stimulus to Development of Many Picturesque Tracts in That Part of Westchester County—Rapid Growth at Greenacres—Van Wyck Estate Cut Up Into Residential Plots—Attractions of Scarsdale Golf Club.

One of the suburban sections of New York which has witnessed a very substantial growth within the last few years is that part of Westchester County in the vicinity of White Plains. Many things have contributed toward making this territory a highly popular one for homeseekers. The locality itself is picturesque, offering many attractions for neat houses, but undoubtedly the most important feature is the excellent transportation facilities. With the electrification of the Harlem Railroad last season to White Plains the running time from Grand Central Station was slightly reduced, while the convenience of travel was materially increased. The building of the New York, Westchester & Boston Road, which, within about a year, will connect the outlying towns of Westchester County, including New Rochelle and White Plains, with the Bronx, has directed greater attention to the desirability of many parts of the county as convenient home communities and the energetic work in pushing the railroad toward completion has resulted in the sale of many large tracts for development. The main terminus of the road will be at White Plains, and from that point branch lines are to extend to Danbury and Brewsters.

White Plains, within the past two years, has experienced a most substantial growth in both business and residential respects. Prices of property in the commercial centre of the town have advanced and some of the recent sales have established high records. New residential districts are being opened, and well built up toward the north, and the proposed building of a new trolley road from Pleasantville to White Plains, running through Kensico Avenue and thus serving the North Broadway and Westchester Park Districts, has brought additional activity to these popular suburban places, which are within a mile of the White Plains station.

On North Broadway some handsome houses have lately been finished. One of the newest is the large stucco house designed by William S. Phillips for Max Levison on North Broadway. It is of the Georgian Colonial type, with terra cotta tile walls and stucco finish. In Clinton Avenue, nearby, about a dozen houses of more moderate cost, averaging $3,000, are now under construction or have just been finished. In the Westminster Park district some of the most artistic homes in the suburbs of White Plains will be found.

Just to the south of White Plains and a trifle northeast of the rapidly growing Hartsdale and Scarsdale sections is another comparatively new residential community known as the Mamaroneck Avenue district, where building operations are particularly active. John Miles and Kelsey Smith are putting up a number of attractive houses, several of which have been sold from the plans.

A small history might be written of the successful development of the Hartsdale and Scarsdale regions. A few years ago comparatively few persons were even acquainted with the names. Now there are scores of artistic houses rendered more attractive by the beauty of the surrounding grounds and the natural charm of the community. The Scarsdale Golf Club with its other amusements has become deservedly popular, and on the Greenacres tract close to the Hartsdale station a tea house is about to be opened in one of the old fine homesteads. In addition to this the Scarsdale Estates, which controls the Greenacres development, is opening a four-acre park with tennis courts, a sunken garden, and other landscape features. Beside Greenacres the Scarsdale Esates is also developing other tracts nearby known respectively as Murray Hill and Scarsdale Hill. The Murray Hill tract is divided into plots of from one to five acres. Greenacres was opened less than two years ago, and there are now twenty-seven houses either finished or under contract, ranging in price from $10,000 to $20,000. Among the owners are A. C. Ayer, E. W. Adams, Edward Bedford, C. N. Bovee, Albert J. Bodker, Douglas H. Cook, S. M. Cauldwell, Harry S. Hamilton, L. Ward Prince, W. Scott Serviss, George P. Ray, C. F. Snyder, Arthur D. Williams, and Dr. Shepard. Wise management has contributed to the popularity of these localities, the development being done along permanent lines with graded streets, sewer, gas, electric light, water, and other attributes of a well-established home community. The Scarsdale Company has also been an active developer in the vicinity.

Another development is the Van Wyck tract, which is being cut up into building lots, and has already shown considerable building activity. It adjoins the Greenacres tract. The old Van Wyck homestead, now occupied by Frederick Van Wyck, is still standing, surrounded by a number of magnificent elms and other trees. Near by is the delightfully situated stucco home of Prof. William T. Brewster of Columbia University. The property is well located, being on a hill, and within five to eight minutes' walk from the Hartsdale Station. The golf links and Country Club are close to the station, and the entire property around the station is restricted.

The northern end of Scarsdale is often erroneously called Hartsdale, because the residents of the locality used the Hartsdale Station on the Harlem Railroad.

Years ago the New York Post Road was the only avenue of travel between White Plains and New York, running through Scarsdale, and there was no road between White Plains and Tuckahoe running west from the New York Post Road until Jesse Fisher, who owned all the property between the New York Post Road and the Bronx River, gave the road from the New York Post Road, where the Scarsdale Town Hall is now located, and running to the Hartsdale Station on the Harlem Road. This was named Fisher Street, and that name remained until a few years ago, when it was renamed Fenimore Road, as it connects with Fenimore Road leading to Mamaroneck.

Near the Hartsdale Station, during the Revolution, there was a skirmish in which some twenty soldiers were killed, and it is the purpose of the residents of Scarsdale to erect a monument to commemorate this fact.

Prior to 1900 there were but four residences on Fenimore Road between the Hartsdale Station and the New York Post Road. The first of these was an old powder house, a picturesque old place under the hill among fine trees. This was so named for the reason that it was built by a Dane who had a powder mill and a number of powder magazines on his farm.

The residence of Jesse Fisher has been purchased by Miss Butler, the owner of the tract of 500 acres called Fox Meadow, on the south side of Fenimore Road, and the old house has been remodeled into a beautiful Colonial residence.

May 14, 1911

Hempstead Tax Rate.

Strong evidence of the extensive suburban growth in Nassau County, Long Island, is furnished by the tax rate in the township of Hempstead, which covers the southern half of the county, where the tax rate is 92 cents on the $100, as compared with the rate of one dollar on the hundred in Oyster Bay Township, and $1.14 on the hundred in North Hempstead Township. Within the boundaries of Hempstead Township are the largest villages in the county, such as Hempstead, Freeport, Rockville Centre, Floral Park, Garden City, East Rockaway, Lynbrook, and Oceanside.

Growth of population in all of these villages has been accelerated by their being linked together by a trolley road that also connects them with the elevated railroad in Brooklyn as well as with points in Queens Borough; and, also by their being served by electric trains of the Long Island Railroad. In other words, improved transportation facilities have caused widespread improvement of vacant property, with a consequent decrease in the tax rate.

Long Beach is within the township of Hempstead, and the reclamation and improvement of that property alone has added hundreds of thousands of dollars to the taxable assets of the township, while the contiguity of Long Beach to Oceanside and East Rockaway has had a beneficial effect on values and improvements in those communities. They are traffic served by the Long Beach division of the Long Island Railroad.

The greater part of the township of Hempstead has become an immense zone of medium priced homes for the middle class, and it is all within commuting distance of New York City.

July 12, 1914

NEW YORK SUBURBS.

Increasing Demand for Homes Outside of Manhattan Island.

The demand on Manhattan Island for more business space is so insistent tnat the whole island will soon become a trading centre surrounded by beautiful suburbs, where people can live and enjoy health, is the opinion of Frank Crowell, President of the Baker Crowell concern.

"Within a radius of fifteen or thirty miles one may leave the office at 5 o'clock, go home and dine and return to the city in ample time for the opera or theatre," he says. "It takes no longer in point of time to go from the Pennsylvania Station to a home in Great Neck or vicinity than it does to get from one's office to upper Manhattan or the Bronx. Nearly every village has its Manhattan department store which delivers merchandise free of charge within a radius of thirty miles.

"Great Neck is the central village of the peninsula that bears the same name and which juts out from the Wheatley Hills into Long Island Sound just east of the city line and fourteen miles from Manhattan. The village is one of the oldest on Long Island, with fine estates near by.

"The effect of the installed third rail electric service over the North Shore section of Long Island has been the medium of increased realty activity. Since 1918 there has been a substantial increase in population. This enhancement is apparent all along the line of the North Shore to Huntington."

January 9, 1921

HOMESEEKERS AND THE SUBURBS.

It is not strange that, according to the figures of the New York Census Committee, 40 per cent. of the schools of the Borough of Manhattan suffered a loss in pupils during last year. In population Manhattan is destined to sink to third and perhaps fourth place before many years pass. In 1920 Manhattan's lead over Brooklyn was only 265,747, the totals being, respectively, 2,284,103 and 2,018,356. In 1900 Brooklyn was 683,511 behind, two years after consolidation; the totals, Manhattan 1,850,093 and Brooklyn 1,166,582. Walter I. Willis, Secretary of the Chamber of Commerce of the Borough of Queens, has estimated that in 1950 the population of Manhattan will be 1,900,000 and that of Brooklyn 2,800,000, while Queens will have passed Manhattan in a canter, boasting 2,200,000 souls. In 1920 Queens had 469,042 people, but there has been a considerable increase in the last three years. Mr. Willis gives the Bronx, which had 730,016 in 1920, a total of 1,500,000 in 1950. Twenty-five years after that Manhattan may be in fourth place, and ultimately, if the waste spaces of Richmond fill up, in fifth place, merely the business hub of the Greater City wheel. It is a fact that the movement of homeseekers to outlying territory is gathering momentum at a rate undreamed of twenty-five years ago.

Although Brooklyn is a fairly close second today, her percentage of the whole population shows only a small gain since consolidation. It is in the Bronx and Queens that the number of residents has gone up by leaps and bounds. In 1900 the Bronx had 200,507 and 730,016 in 1920, while the figures for Queens were, respectively, 152,999 and 469,042. The present development in Queens is now proportionately greater, and the time is not far off when the Bronx may be distanced. Richmond, owing to lack of rapid transit communication, is handicapped and makes a poor showing in the race. Queens began to gain on the Bronx as soon as rapid transit connection with a five-cent fare was made with Manhattan and Brooklyn. In Queens there is an extensive territory to be developed for home building, and land in the latest promotions can still be bought very cheaply. Prices rule higher in the Bronx.

Concerning Manhattan's decline in population, as far back as 1910 flat and apartment rents began to pinch and a movement set in to districts opened up by the subway. It was then that the Bronx and Queens called. The war sent rents still higher. Even in Brooklyn, where a comfortable house could formerly be leased for less than $100 a month, the homekeepers revolted and moved out into Queens and beyond to Nassau. Thousands of families crowded into small flats never knew the privacies of home life until they made first payments for cozy little houses among the fields and trees of Queens and the Bronx.

In 1921 the number of buildings put up for residences along the Long Island Railroad outside of Brooklyn and Long Island City was 19,771. Villages assumed the importance of towns. Flushing became a trading centre. If one who knew by observation the waste places in Queens twenty years ago returns to view them today, he will find them covered with homes and blossoming with gardens. All this means that Mayor Hylan and the Transit Commission must find common ground for the construction of new subways. The pressure of chambers of commerce and home associations for better transportation can be resisted no longer. There must be more main lines and branches to the old ones. Nothing can stop the home movement to the suburbs, not even congestion on the present system of subways and elevated roads, but if something is not done to relieve it, the sufferers will know where to place the responsibility.

June 19, 1923

SUBURBS OFFER GOOD INVESTMENT

Builders Turning Attention to Development Tracts Beyond Metropolitan Area.

COMMUTING ZONE EXPANDED

By JOSEPH P. DAY.

According to Roger W. Babson of the Babson Statistical Organization, suburban land bought at the right price should be the best real estate investment during the next five years.

Further explaining this affirmation, Mr. Babson said, in an interview in The Boston Transcript: "I find that 75 per cent. of the houses built since the war have cost over $6,000; that is, 75 per cent. of the houses built have been available to only about 10 per cent. of the people. Nothing to speak of has been done to relieve the congestion and provide fit housings for those who cannot pay from sixty to one hundred dollars a month in rent or its equivalent in upkeep cost.

"Parallel to this pertinent fact we find the influence of the automobile, and the automobile bus which have broken the barriers, and our cities are spreading out. From the real estate point of view several good automobile roads have the significance of a trolley line. Five miles as a practical limit have been stretched to twenty-five miles. As more people realize that high incomes and high building costs are here to stay we shall trade our slums for wealthy suburbs and suburban properties will enhance in value at the expense of the older residential districts that are too far out for business purposes and not far enough for the new order of houses.

"Statistics would suggest that the great development of the next five to ten years in the real estate markets will be a spreading out into the suburbs. The more astute builders are already planning to go in for small home building as the rush for fancy houses at fancy figures slows up."

Applying Mr. Babson's deductions and conclusions to the real estate and building market in Brooklyn and on Long Island, as we find it, we see his predictions being carried out to the very letter.

Brooklyn, since the construction of the Brooklyn Bridge, 1870-1883, has increased in population from less than 500,000 to more than 2,000,000. This "Borough of Homes and Churches" at the present time rapidly is forging ahead of Manhattan and promises soon to be the largest borough of the largest city of the world.

The older residential sections of Brooklyn, like the older residential sections of Manhattan, gradually, but surely are being transformed into business districts. The old order is changing and the palatial landmark residences of the past are being replaced by the monumental skyscraper apartment houses and hotels of the present. Where one family formerly resided, there are now a score of families, a hundred or more.

The East River bridges, tunnels and subways have eliminated the East River as a barrier and Brooklyn has developed into an integral part of the city at large.

The movement of population East toward the Borough of Queens, Nassau and Suffolk Counties, on Long Island has resulted in the absorption of a very large percentage of all the remaining large tracts of vacant land in the Borough of Brooklyn. Flatbush has been extended to Sheepshead Bay and the ocean front section of Brooklyn is being transformed rapidly by the development of Manhattan Beach and the development that has followed the opening of the Coney Island Boardwalk.

The somewhat retarded development of Jamaica Bay into an integral part of the harbor of New York and one of the foremost industrial sections of the greater city is being discounted in its effect by the push of population in that direction, where the cheaper class of home is strongly in evidence.

All along the dividing line between Brooklyn and Queens the building movement has been most intense since the World War. This significant movement is to be attributed directly to the extension of rapid transit to Jamaica. The movement will be further stimulated by the plans of the city officials for the extension of the existing lines, and the construction of new lines, to the more distant points in the Borough of Queens.

The widening of Queens Boulevard to 200 feet and the projection of a new highway to be known as Nassau Boulevard, together with the improvement of Northern Boulevard (Jackson Avenue) and the extension of Woodhaven Avenue across Jamaica Bay to the Rockaways are a few of the more important public improvements that have tended to stabilize and increase real estate values in Queens and attract capital and population to that fast growing section of Greater New York.

On Long Island as a whole, during 1924, more new buildings were erected than in any single previous year. The total, according to the Long Island Railroad, was 43,567 new structures outside of the old City of Brooklyn and Long Island City.

Counting only five occupants to each of the 31,645 new dwellings erected last year Long Island's population may be said to have increased to the extent of 158,225 inhabitants in 1924. As the new homes built in 1922-23-24 totaled 86,670, the apparent increase in Long Island residents (on the basis of 5 persons to each house), was 433,350 during the brief period of three years.

During 1922-23-24 the total of buildings of all kinds constructed on Long Island, outside of Brooklyn and Long Island City, was 114,047. This is nearly half the total number of structures put up on the Island since 1905.

With the absorption of practically all the remaining large tracts of land in Brooklyn and the steady increase in population, I look forward to an era of higher real estate values in all sections of Brooklyn and to a steady demand for land and lots in the Borough of Queens, where new residential and business districts must develop as the demand increases, and as the transit facilities are improved.

In Nassau County the most decided trend is toward the South Shore, where, along the Montauk Division of the Long Island Railroad, the electrification of which to Babylon will be completed by May 21, there has been remarkable activity in home building in all of the principal villages and towns this side of the Queensboro line and over the the Nassau County line, especially at Babylon and Bay Shore in Suffolk County.

The North Shore of Long Island is still firmly held by the owners of large estates. But the same change that is taking place at Great Neck, where the activity in real estate and building is marked, is taking place further out along the North Shore, this side of Huntington. Eventually there will be the same demand for North Shore properties as there is now for properties along the South Shore, but not to the same extent until the North Shore has better transportation facilities.

March 29, 1925

AMERICA EVOLVING SUBURBAN CITIES

Twentieth Century Communities Are a Distinctive Type in Urban History.

SURVEY SHOWS GROWTH

America is evolving a type of city that the world has never known before, with a manner of living, in its suburban areas, never before possible.

The establishment of this twentieth century type of city community, spreading out into an area five or six times that occupied by cities of its population twenty years ago, will be one of the phases of present tendencies in city growth to be brought before real estate specialists of the United States and Canada, who will meet in Detroit June 23-26 inclusive for the eighteenth annual convention of the National Association of Real Estate Boards.

"The Future of American Cities" will be the opening topic of the convention's general sessions. Dr. William L. Bailey, Professor of Sociology at Northwestern University, will picture this future as it is forecast by a survey he has made covering the present suburban tendencies in every city in the country of over 100,000 population. The survey was made under the auspices of the Institute for Social and Religious Research of the Rockefeller Foundation.

Dr. Bailey's survey bears out the estimate of the United States Department of Agriculture that within the next ten or twenty years American cities will need to add 10,000,000 acres to their urban area to take care of suburban expansion.

Concentration in the City.

Following the age of pioneering and rural expansion, the nation experienced an age of rapid concentration of its population into the cities. But while 6,500,000 people in the last ten years have been drawn from the country regions into the cities, the survey finds that a contrary current of population seeking relief from urban congestion has carried 2,000,000 people outside of city boundaries. The age of big-city development has been succeeded by a nation-wide movement to the zones where city and country meet.

Within commuting distance of the large cities, Dr. Bailey's investigation shows there is now a population equal to nearly half that of the cities proper, and that a dozen large American cities now have more people in their suburbs than within their boundaries. America, the survey indicates, is entering a suburban age.

The general sessions of the convention will deal with the city and its development as that development is affected by real estate conditions and as it is a matter for the concern of real estate boards.

The topics will include comparative city values and why varying values exist; the development of beauty and dignity in American cities, not only in the residential but in the downtown sections; the effect of the automobile on real estate development and values.

April 12, 1925

SUBURBAN AREA EXPANDS.

Now Covers a Radius of Forty Miles, Says Realtor.

Declaring that the pressure of population from within New York has pushed back the suburban frontier to cover a forty-mile radius, L. Ward Prince of the firm of Prince & Ripley yesterday predicted the swift development and expansion of Northern Westchester. Mr. Prince, who has made a complete survey of Northern Westchester following the outstanding success of the Halyan Realty Company's development of Yorktown Heights, said:

"A new frontier for development has been established by the population pressure from within New York. Forty years ago the Bronx with its farms and truck gardens was considered the suburban frontier. Twenty years ago, when I first became active in Westchester realty, White Plains marked the frontier. Today, with the city moving north at the rate of a mile a year, the frontier has been flung back an additional twenty miles.

"The line of this new frontier runs from Peekskill through Yorktown Heights and Katonah to Greenwich and Stamford. Along this line I consider that Yorktown Heights and Katonah occupy strategic positions, and that these communities are destined to become the residential, business and industrial centres of this rapidly developing section of Westchester.

"The signs of this development, which gained so much momentum this year at Yorktown Heights and other sections of Northern Westchester, are unmistakable. Great institutions that require considerable acreage to properly function are rapidly being driven out of Southern Westchester by the mounting value of their land. I have in mind several cases where institutions constructed during the past generation have been able through the sale of their valuable property to erect modern plants with ample acreage further north.

"The same condition prevails to a certain extent in regard to the golf and country clubs. Land values have increased so that clubs by disposing of their holdings can now build finer and more attractive homes in Northern Westchester out of the profits they receive from the increased valuations. Several of the larger clubs have already protected themselves by buying further north. Another strong influence in this movement has been the fact that golf courses lose a part of their attractiveness when located in population centres that surround them with homes and other buildings."

September 26, 1926

SUBURBS EXPANDING FASTER THAN CITIES

Realty Men Call Rapid Growth a Good Omen for Home Ownership.

GAINS SHOWN IN YONKERS

Regional Plan Finds Density of Population Decreasing in Many Towns Near New York City.

A survey of five typical American cities, chosen at random, shows that the suburban areas are growing more rapidly than the cities themselves, and this fact is a favorable omen for home ownership, according to the National Association of Real Estate Boards.

The suburban sections of fourteen smaller towns also surveyed reveals a similar situation, the association reports, offering the figures as evidence that there has been no general decline in the demand for private residences despite the popularity of small apartments in some sections.

The large cities whose suburban communities were shown to be expanding at a faster rate than the urban centres they adjoin were Chicago, St. Louis, Atlanta, Buffalo and Albany.

"The Chicago Regional Planning Association states that while the greater increase in number of people still is inside the city, in percentage the suburban area is growing more rapidly than Chicago itself," the realty organization announces. "Using estimated population figures for next year, the Chicago Planning Association finds that in spite of the rapid growth of the central city its percentage of increase from 1920 to the present time is 23 per cent, as compared to a gain of 83 per cent in suburban territory in a thirty-mile circle around the city. This suburban area covers 125 municipalities.

"The six cities of the Niagara frontier region of New York State, of which Buffalo is one, increased by percentages ranging from one to twelve in the years from 1920 to 1925, while the open territory surrounding these cities increased by percentages ranging from 15 to more than 70 per cent during the same length of time, according to the Niagara Frontier Planning Board The other cities of the Niagara frontier region include Lackawanna, Lockport, Niagara Falls, North Tonawanda and Tonawanda.

"Buffalo increased a little more than 6 per cent in the years from 1920 to 1925, while five townships surrounding Buffalo increased at an average of 46 per cent. Three incorporated villages north of Buffalo increased respectively 106 per cent, 64 per cent and 45 per cent.

"This situation would seem to imply that home owners and renters are moving out into the outlying districts by preference in the Niagara districts, says the planning board, but it is a fact that in some instances the city boundaries have not been moved out for a great many years, and that as a result few vacant lots are available for home sites.

300 Per Cent Increase Reported.

"St. Louis, with a population of 772,000 in 1920 and 856,000 in 1929, has increased 11 per cent in these years, while seven important communities outside of St. Louis, and interdependent upon the St. Louis district, have increased at rates ranging from 98 to 386 per cent in the same length of time. The City Plan Commission of St. Louis in compiling these figures used the estimated population figures for 1929.

"The City Planning Commission of Atlanta, while unable to furnish figures on this subject, states that the suburban area adjacent to Atlanta has been increasing in population very fast in the last five years.

"The Regional Plan of New York and Its Environs, studying this matter from a little different angle, has found decreases in density of population in the built-up areas in many important cities in the New York City area, although all these have increased in population during the period studied, and some of them very rapidly. The fact that in all of these cities the density of population per gross acre has decreased in recent years would indicate that the suburban areas are growing faster than the cities, according to Lawrence M. Orton, secretary of the New York Regional Plan.

"For instance, Yonkers shows an increase of 284 per cent in population but a decrease in density from 43.3 persons per gross acre in 1889 to 32.7 persons in 1925. Albany, which increased 27.5 per cent in population between 1900 and 1925, shows a reduction in density from 22.9 persons to 11.6 persons."

December 1, 1929

CITY PLANNING

MODEL CITY PLANNED FOR ST. LOUIS IN 1903

Municipal Improvement Societies' Scheme for the Exposition.

The Proposals in Detail—A Committee Appointed to Present the Suggestion to the Commissioners.

Within the next ten days a committee which was appointed last evening in the rooms of the National Arts Club, in Thirty-fourth Street, will present to the Commissioners of the St. Louis Exposition a scheme for a model city to be worked out largely in the buildings and streets of the exposition. The plan is simply this—that as certain buildings, streets, parks, engine houses, and the like will have to be erected in any case, they may well embody an idea, that idea to be the exposition of what a model city should be.

In the men who were at the meeting last evening the following organizations, both National and local, were represented: League of American Municipalities, the National Municipal League, the National League of Civic Improvement, the American Park and Out-door Art Association, Reform Club, Municipal Art Society, and the Scenic Society, the latter three organizations being of New York.

The same plan as that which is now proposed to be carried into effect at the St. Louis Exposition was also placed before the Commissioners of the Pan-American Exposition at Buffalo, and had the support of prominent offficals in the State; but for lack of funds could not be carried out.

The committee which will present the plan to the Commissioners of the St. Louis Exposition are these: John De Witt Warner, Charles C. Haight, Charles R. Lamb, and William S. Crandall of New York and Albert Kelsey of Philadelphia. The scheme is outlined as follows:

First—That those departments of the general exposition which are similar in their functions to the same departments in modern cities be incorporated as working models in the general plan of our special exposition. These may include the engineering, parks, and tree planting, fire, police, health, street cleaning, garbage disposal, water supply, and other departments. These might be so grouped as to illustrate the administration of a modern city on the best lines and thus form an object lesson for American and foreign cities without the least interference with their normal functions as necessities of the exposition itself.

Second—There are certain other features which, while not in themselves necessities to the welfare of the exposition, would be valuable educational attractions. Public schools, public library, museum, and similar buildings devoted to educational matters would naturally be included.

Third—My plans of a model city would involve treatment of parks and plaza spaces, street crossings, and other vistas, grouping and architecture of other structures and other lines in which the aesthetic factor is important. To make these practical, however, they must be adjusted to more utilitarian features, (as is the case in actual practice;) hence are thus suggested rather than definitely specified.

Fourth—In order that there might be a place for the assemblage and classification of the smaller concrete objects such as street signs, lamp posts, letter boxes, paper receptacles, park settees, street electroliers, street-cleaning machinery, and a thousand and one other articles employed in the construction and maintenance of a city a building to be called the Municipal Art Building might be erected.

Fifth—To carry out this scheme the committee would recommend the appointment of an advisory board which shall represent various arts, sciences, crafts, and professions involved in the construction and maintenance of a model city. Such a board co-operating with the exposition authorities would insure the unity of the plan.

Sixth—The above suggestions are made with full appreciation of the expense to which any plan for such an exhibit as that proposed must be subordinated to the general plan or scope of the exposition as it shall develop. Hence they must be regarded as tentative only.

Seventh—We believe that effort should be made to have held at St. Louis in 1903 the international convention on municipal art, of which former sessions will have been held at Brussels in 1898, Paris in 1900, and Turin in 1902.

Eighth—Your committee recommends that it be empowered to appoint a sub-committee of not less than three, to be sent to St. Louis at the expense of the Municipal Art Society and kindred organizations, in order to submit this plan to the proper authorities of the exposition at once and secure its adoption.

October 12, 1901

ART AT HOME AND ABROAD—THE MUNICIPAL EXHIBITION OF CITY PLANNING

WILLIAM MORRIS, trained as an architect, saw in all the arts he practiced only the subsidiary features of the house for the furnishing and ornament of which they existed. His imagination or reason went even further, and, like a true artist, rejecting all that should interfere with his picture, he created in "News from Nowhere" an ideal city, a

London small and white and clean
The clear Thames bordered by its gardens green.

Enrolled among the Socialists, and doing his best to play a part for which he was eminently unfitted, he saw life from an artist's standpoint, well proportioned, harmonious, sincere, and beautiful, with art as an expression of that life, an integral part of it, and not an applied ornament.

The Municipal Exhibition of City Planning now on view in the Philadelphia City Hall, indicates that he was as far in advance of his time in his desire for a beautiful city as in his desire for beautiful crafts, and that appreciation of the former as of the latter is even in America beginning to approach his standard. Certainly the exhibition contains a remarkable body of evidence that all over the country the interest of the public is aroused in at least restoring to cities and towns the pleasantness of their beginnings, even where more ambitious considerations are not involved, and is aroused to a sense also that in the laying out of a city art must be kept free from political considerations. The greatest problem to be met in the case of large cities seems to be that of preventing overcrowding and altering the objectionable features of already congested regions. A great deal besides art necessarily enters into this question. The German method of providing a low fare and land protected from speculation for the laboring class in the suburbs of a city is only one of many excellent devices on the part of the German Government for keeping its cities hygienic and beautiful, while the town planners of the new school are following mediaeval models in their designs. England, also, is supplying us with object lessons in the art of city building, which depend chiefly on the interest of the people and the enforcement of good laws as a foundation for the beauty that belongs to art.

As a matter of art, however, and one almost is tempted to say a mere matter of art, in the face of the questions of life and health and morality also involved, the proper spacing of the buildings alone insures a certain amount of ordered beauty in the general effect. The motto of the [illegible] Housing Commission exhibit [illegible] "No city can be beautiful until the homes of the people are clean and sanitary"; and the very conditions that make for cleanliness and sanitation, space and air around the dwelling houses, gardens attached to them and forming in a sense an integral part of them, the suppression of ugly and menacing refuse cans and dump heaps, the planting of trees and shrubs, the tidyness of streets and courtyards—all make equally for civic beauty.

There is no more charming feature of Morris's idyl of London than the long grassy road checkered over with the shadow of tall pear trees, which he caused to run from Trafalgar Square to Parliament House, and it is a very similar road that the city planners show in the model of the proposed parkway in Philadelphia from the City Hall to Fairmount Park, following the French idea of development along vistas with terminal features.

The improvement of cities already extensively built up and populous is, of course, an extremely complicated matter of a nature to tax the intelligence of the most highly gifted experts, especially if the improvements are to conform to the natural conditions of the city's growth and express its complex individuality and special characteristics, and thus insure permanency so far as the inevitable changes in the city's life permit. A definite public opinion as to needs and desires is necessary, also, in order to push plans to the point of performance. This public opinion is much easier to form in smaller cities at the outset of their municipal career than in large ones already in the control of the governing minority, and is more rapid and vigorous in growth in the West than in the East. The City of Denver, Col., for example, has a remarkable exhibit showing that the dignified and stately buildings, fine parks and playgrounds, and handsome monuments already established are only incentives to further action. The pamphlets issued by the Denver Art Commission in favor of a new plaza appeal to the pride of the people in the natural beauty surrounding the city, declaring that the view of the snow-clad range from the Capitol, the sunny skies, and the setting formed by the already beautiful town are reasons for creating a central plaza that no city in the world can excel, and the plaza is almost a foregone conclusion. It is precisely this sort of public pride that found employment for the old bronze founders and iron workers and wood carvers of ancient Nuremberg, where the crafts outdid themselves to add to the city's splendor, and we may be assured that no greater stimulus for all the creative arts can be found than the healthy growth of civic responsibility.

The plans for the town of Corey, Ala., are interesting as showing an entirely different kind of problem, Corey being the model for industrial towns in the South and built for the proper housing of steel mill employes. It may be noted that while strictly economic ideas prevail in these plans, the considerations of health and efficiency lead to the planting of fruit trees, shrubs, and vines about the houses, and to the adoption of wide planting spaces in the residence streets, with narrow roadways screened from sidewalks and houses by shrub hedges, so that the actual appearance of the town will suggest beauty quite as strongly as utility.

In the case of the beautiful buildings at Garden City, and the conscious reminiscence of the famous Plantin printing house, with its air of long traditions sleeping in the vine-draped court, unspoiled by the assaults of tourist armies, there is a more persuasive aesthetic charm. Although such graftings can never have the particular pungent flavor of architecture that has grown up with the life of a people and has become a part of the region through answering its common needs, a peculiarly rich appreciation of the spirit of the past is found in the adaptations of this school of designers and architects, and their work can hardly fail to have that soundness which makes possible true independence and individuality in any age.

A considerable section of the exhibition is given to exhibits of foreign cities, and the briefest possible survey of the material shows that the movement toward town improvement extends practically all over Europe. Among the plans and photographs shown are those of the Hampstead Garden suburb of London, an example of successful development by coöperative societies which is likely to lead to the adoption of certain communal features that will greatly simplify living in suburban towns; a large number of photographs of picturesque German towns, such as Munich and Nüremberg, which have harmonized their modern with their ancient features in such a way as essentially to preserve the character of the city; Paris improvements, and the new Antwerp docks; Port Sunlight, England, a laborers' town planned with its appearance from the point of view of the railway made a prominent consideration; the Garden City of Milan, and the improvements of Amsterdam, Holland.

The cautious observer will feel, indeed, that enough advance already has been achieved and enough zeal shown to make a certain measure of legitimate restraint desirable in order that costly mistakes shall be avoided in the rectification of earlier mistakes, especially in the disturbance of private interests. The wise advice of one of the greatest of modern town planners, Raymoud Unwin, cannot be too often quoted or too closely heeded. At the end of the chapter on "Formal and Informal Beauty" in his book on "Town Planning in Practice," he says:

"Of this I feel very much convinced, that town planning to be successful must be largely the outgrowth of the circumstances of the site and the requirements of the inhabitants, and, going back by way of example to the point as to whether and to what extent the existing boundaries of properties should be regarded in the making of a new town plan, it would seem to me that so long as the sense of property means what it does to the owner and occupiers of land, it would be neglecting one of the most important existing conditions if we were to disregard entirely these boundaries, that to try and carry through some symmetrical plan at the expense of upsetting the whole of the properties and destroying all the traditions and sentiment attaching to these properties would be to give to our plan a degree of artificiality which in the result would probably vastly outweigh any advantage which it might gain from a more complete symmetry. On the other hand, it would be attaching undue importance to one only among the many conditions with which a town plan must comply if we were to refuse to the town planner any powers to rearrange properties or boundaries. It seems to me, in short, that a theoretic preference for formalism or for informalism, while it may find ample scope for expression within the limits of the conditions, in no sense justifies either the neglect to satisfy the requirements of the case or to respect the conditions of the sites. Therefore, while the informalist might welcome the picturesque accidental grouping and the accidental arrangement which would result from respecting in his plan the existing property boundaries, he would probably seriously err should he allow his love for informality to lead him to follow these boundaries to the detriment of the public convenience or to the destruction of all comprehensive planning of his site. The formalist, on the other hand, would be open to the opposite temptation of thinking that the maintenance of a formal character in the details of his plans would justify him in riding roughshod over the property boundaries and the sentiments of the individual owners or occupiers of the various plots of land comprised within his area."

June 11, 1911

CITY PLANNING BOARDS.

New Law Makes Appointment of Such Bodies Compulsory in Massachusetts.

City and town planning boards in Massachusetts must be created by every city and also by every town having a population of more than 10,000 at the last preceding national or State census, according to an act of the Massachusetts Legislature.

These boards are required to "make careful studies of the resources, possibilities, and needs of the city or town, particularly with respect to conditions which may be injurious to the public health or otherwise injurious in and about rented dwellings."

The planning boards are also required to "make plans for the development of the municipality with special reference to the proper housing of its people."

The planning boards are to be appointed by the Mayor of cities or by the commission in commission-governed cities, and in towns they are to be elected by the votes at the annual town meetings. Every planning board is required to report annually to the governing body of its respective city or to the voters of its town, "giving information regarding the condition of the city or town and any plans or proposals for the development of the city or town and estimates of the cost thereof."

The governing bodies of cities are authorized by the act to "make suitable ordinances, and towns are authorized to make suitable by-laws, for carrying out the purposes of the act," and the governing bodies in each case "may appropriate money therefor."

August 24, 1913

CITY FIXES LIMIT ON TALL BUILDINGS

Board of Estimate Adopts Ordinance Which Will Restrict All Skyscrapers.

SAFEGUARD FOR PUBLIC

Light and Air to be Conserved and Manufacturing Zones Kept Under Control.

The Board of Estimate yesterday passed the building zone resolution, a measure which is believed to be the most important step in the development of New York City since the construction of the subways. The resolution, which carried out a State law passed in 1914, became law on its passage at 4:30 P. M., and governs the construction and use of all future buildings for which permits had not been obtained before that hour.

The resolution does not prevent the building of skyscrapers, but requires that they shall not be solidly constructed for a height more than two and a half times the width of the street on which they front. For instance, if this law had been in existence for some years the Equitable Building could have been reared in its present proportions only to a height of 200 feet, or about eighteen stories. On top of that a tower or series of towers could have been erected, the floor space diminishing in proportion to the increase in height.

The restrictions on skyscrapers are only one of many important features of the law which will affect living and business conditions in every part of the city. The law is designed to check the invasion of retail districts by factories and residence districts by factories and business. It is aimed to prevent an increase of the congestion of streets and of subway and street car traffic in sections where the business population is already too great for the sidewalks and transit facilities.

Check on Manufacturing.

It is intended further to prevent the overcrowding by manufacturing concerns of sections where the streets are insufficient for the vehicular traffic, and at the same time to concentrate manufacturing in localities where its products can be handled most efficiently and where its presence will not destroy real estate for residential and retail business purposes.

In addition to preventing congestion of street and transit facilities, which is caused by housing a large population on a small area in a skyscraper, the purpose of restricting the size of buildings is a necessity from the standpoint of light and air, which are impaired by buildings of excess height. The principle of providing for air and light is followed out in building restrictions in all parts of the city.

It is only in the present office building section of lower Manhattan that buildings will be put up in the future two and a half times as high as the width of the street. In the strictly residential sections buildings will be permitted only as high as the street is wide. Tenement and apartment houses can be built one and a quarter or one and a half times as high as the street in front of them is wide.

A height of twice the street width is allowed for the remaining portions of the more intensively developed commercial and industrial sections in a broad belt through the centre of the island from the lower office and financial section to Fifty-ninth Street.

Fifth Avenue Protected.

One of the greatest immediate reforms worked by the law is the protection of the Fifth Avenue retail district from further encroachment by loft building factories, which have threatened to concentrate such a large working population along the avenue as to interfere seriously with shopping. The law protects the entire Fifth Avenue and Broadway section south as far as Twenty-third Street and between Fourth and Sixth Avenues. It achieves the purpose which is set forth as follows in the report of the Commission on Building Districts:

> It is vital to the existence of the city that it maintain such conditions of street traffic that the city's chief hotel, club, theatre, and shopping centre may permanently be maintained in the sole location that is suited to it.

In anticipation of the adoption of the resolution, a great number of permits for buildings which could not be erected under the new law have been filed within the last few days. Two of those filed yesterday were for buildings more than thirty stories in height. Extensive modification of the plans for these buildings would have to be made if they had been filed later than 4:30 o'clock yesterday afternoon.

One of these was for a thirty-nine-story hotel building on the southwest corner of Broadway and Forty-eighth Street. Under the new law this building could have been built solidly to the height of about 200 feet, or about seventeen or eighteen stories high. A tower, or superstructure, covering a smaller area, could have been built on top of that, but probably would not have been feasible on account of the narrowness of the building.

Another was for a thirty-two-story building on the site of the Murray Hill Hotel, on the west side of Park Avenue, between Fortieth and Forty-first Streets. This building would also be allowed 200 feet of solid construction under the new law, and the remaining stories would have to be in the form of a tower, growing smaller as it increased in height.

A Prospective Building.

Another permit was for a twenty-seven-story office building on the site at Broadway and Fulton Street, now occupied by The Evening Mail, which has been purchased by the Western Union Telegraph Company. Just how the plans of this building would have to be changed, had the building permit been filed later, would be a matter requiring considerable study, because it would receive the benefit of being one of the exceptions to the general rule for the so-called "two-and-a-half-times" building. This exception is that in a case where a lot in the lower office and financial section is surrounded by tall buildings, a building may be erected on it to the average height of the buildings adjoining it on either side and the building across the street.

These three tall buildings might have been affected in other ways than in regard to height, had the permits been filed under the new law, as it requires provision for areas and lightwells, and its requirements are modified by the character of the surrounding buildings.

These modifications, which can be made on the existing state of things, run more or less through all of the provisions of the law. There is nothing mathematical about the division of the city into districts. With the exception of the two-and-a-half-times district, which is restricted to the present financial and high office building section, the districts are necessarily scattered about, so that the map of Manhattan and the other boroughs showing the commercial, tenement house, and residential districts resemble jigsaw puzzles.

But, while there was objection right up to the time of the passage of the resolution against the inclusion of certain blocks in certain districts, the opposition to the general principles of the building zone resolution had almost entirely died away during the three and a half years of public hearings and discussions. It passed the Board of Estimate by a vote of eighteen to one, the President of the Borough of Richmond being the only dissentient.

Preliminary Work.

Work on the law was begun with the passage of a resolution by the Board of Estimate on Feb. 17, 1913, creating a Heights of Buildings Committee, with George McAneny, then Borough President, as Chairman. This committee appointed an Advisory Committee consisting of Edward M. Bassett, Chairman; Edward C. Blum, Edward W. Brown, William H. Chesebrough, William A. Cokeley, Otto M. Eidlitz, Abram I. Elkus, Burt L. Fenner, J. Monroe Hewlett, Robert W. Higbie, C. Grant La Farge, Nelson P. Lewis, George T. Mortimer, Lawson Purdy, Allan Robinson, August F. Schwarzler, Franklin S. Tomlin, Lawrence Veiller, and Gaylord S. White.

On June 26, 1914, the present Commission on Building Districts was appointed after the previous one had made its report. The resolution passed yesterday was, with a few exceptions, in the form in which it was drafted by the present commission, whose members are Edward M. Bassett, Chairman; Robert H. Whitten, Secretary; Lawson Purdy, Vice Chairman; Edward C. Blum, James E. Clonin, Otto M. Eidlitz, Burt L. Fenner, Edward R. Hardy, Richard W. Lawrence, Alrick H. Man, Alfred E. Marling, George T. Mortimer, J. F. Smith, Walter Stabler, Franklin S. Tomlin, George C. Whipple, and William G. Willcox.

The height of buildings, which was the subject assigned to the first committee, was found to be only a fraction of the general building problem, which had an important bearing on every matter connected with the welfare and prosperity of the city's population. The Health Department offered many witnesses to tell of the danger to the citys' health in the loss of bacteria-killing sunlight because of high building on narrow streets and the spread of epidemics due to overcrowding on small areas. Fire Chief Kenlon and others described the increased danger from fire in districts where there was not room enough for the emerging population to stand. It was pointed out that hundreds might be killed in a panic in these streets if the occupants of the buildings were stampeded by a great explosion or an earthquake shock. The reduction of elevator accidents was another consideration.

Another momentous consideration was that of taking the best possible care of $8,000,000,000, which is invested in New York real estate, by safeguarding valuable areas from the encroachment of industries or enterprises ruinous to real estate. At the same time it was necessary to recognize that the character of many sections of New York had not yet been determined. For this reason the commission created two vast areas, one known as the "restricted" district, and the other as the "undetermined" district.

The unrestricted district, which can be used for any purpose except that of erecting high office buildings, takes in most of the waterfront and adjoining property in Manhattan and other boroughs and sections in Lower Manhattan, and in other boroughs where the development promises to be industrial. The undetermined districts are areas which may be built up as residences or business districts, and will be subject to future regulation when their character is more fully developed.

In the residence sections of Manhattan the erection of buildings suitable for stores or other uses are confined generally to the avenues, except where they have already a definite residential character, and where the cross-streets already contain stores, garages, or similar business places. The blueprints, which show this complex state of things in the city, are thirty-five in number.

The principal contest before the final passage of the resolution appeared to be between William Waldorf Astor and J. F. Morgan. Charles A. Peabody, representing Mr. Astor, objected to the restriction of the west side of Madison Avenue from Thirty-fifth Street to Thirty-eighth Street to residences, and sought to put the west side of Madison Avenue, from Thirty-fifth Street to Thirty-sixth Street within the business zone. John P. Fox, representing the Murray Hill Property Owners' Association, spoke in favor of the restriction, and said that the association was formed in the library of J. P. Morgan. Mr. Astor lost his objection.

July 26, 1916

MANY CITIES FAVOR BUILDING ZONE ACT

Success in New York Leads to Adoption in Many Parts of Country.

STRENGTHENED BY COURTS

By EDWARD M. BASSETT.

The City of New York was the leader in establishing a building zone ordinance, with official maps showing districts within which certain uses, heights and sizes of buildings are prohibited. St. Louis, Newark, Rochester, Milwaukee, Washington and numerous smaller cities, including Yonkers and White Plains, have followed New York City in adopting zoning regulations and maps. Some cities have made their regulations more stringent than New York, and some have made them more lax, but all have followed the method of three maps, one for use, one for height and one for size of future buildings.

All have followed New York in placing the regulations under the police power after obtaining a grant of the zoning power from the State Legislature. In the early days of zoning in New York many claimed that such restrictions would be unconstitutional, and that the only way that protective restrictions could be applied, if at all, would be under the power of eminent domain, so that each person affected would be paid for his supposed damage.

The zoning went ahead, however, on the theory that the community could prevent chaotic and harmful buildings and uses without making money payment just the same as it can prevent epidemics or lessen fire hazards without making payments. Five years ago there were almost no court decisions on the restrictions of buildings by municipalities.

Restrictions in deeds had been fully and bitterly litigated, but municipal restrictions on buildings were a novelty. It had been decided by the courts in Boston that new buildings could not exceed 125 feet on certain streets and 80 feet on others. In Los Angeles it had been decided by the courts that a brickyard could be ousted from a residential district without making payment to the owner.

The numerous zoning ordinances of the last four years, including that of New York City, have brought about many legal decisions, some of them by the highest courts of the various States. These decisions have uniformly upheld the zoning ordinances and have stated over and over again that, where the regulation was for the health, safety and general welfare of the community, it was not necessary to make payment to property owners.

Building zone ordinances throughout the United States, where passed under a grant of authority by the State and having a relation to the health, safety, morals and general welfare of the community, can now be confidently declared to be constitutional, and they will be protected and enforced by the courts.

The Massachusetts Legislature prepared a law empowering all cities and towns to pass zoning ordinances and, in accordance with a constitutional requirement, requested the opinion of the Supreme Judicial Court of that State before passing it.

In May, 1920, the court handed down a decision in which they said that they were not able to perceive in the proposed law anything contrary to the fundamental law of the Commonwealth.

In April, 1920, the Ohio Court of Common Pleas, passing on a case which arose in East Cleveland, held that it was constitutional to prevent apartment houses in districts of private homes, using the following language:

"It would seem that there could be no two opinions upon the proposition that the apartment house, or tenement, in a section of private residences is a nuisance to those in its immediate vicinity. Under the evidence, and as a matter of common knowledge, of which the court may take judicial notice (16 Cyc. 862), it shuts off the light and air from its neighbors, it invades their privacy, it spreads smoke and soot throughout the neighborhood. The noise of constant deliveries is almost continuous. The fire hazard is recognized to be increased. * * * The light, air and ventilation are necessarily limited from the nature of its construction. The danger of the spread of infectious disease is undoubtedly increased, however little, where a number of families use a common hallway and common front and rear stairways.

"The erection of one apartment house in a district of private homes woudl seriously affect only those persons living in the immediate vicinity thereof, but the common experience is that the erection of one apartment drives out the single residences adjacent thereto, to make way for more apartments. The result is that, in time, and not a very great time, when one apartment is erected, the whole street is given over largely to apartment houses."

The Court of Appeals of New York State in July, 1920, handed down a decision in a case arising in New York City (Lincoln Trust Company vs. Williams Building Corporation, 229 N. Y. 313), unanimously agreeing with Justice McLaughlin of that court, whose opinion in part was as follows:

"The exercise of the police power, within constitutional limitations, depends largely upon the discretion and good judgment of the municipal authorities, with which the courts are reluctant to interfere. * * * I am of the opinion that the resolution in question (the zoning ordinance of New York City) is a valid one."

The above are but a few of the court decisions which are accumulating in support of zoning. Modern cities will not go back to the haphazard, unregulated and chaotic building conditions which formerly injured home owners, apartment house owners and storekeepers alike, and which encouraged the invasion of harmful uses and helped to create blighted districts. Every large city of the United States is today either working under a zoning ordinance or preparing its data and maps for the establishment of one.

November 28, 1920

NEW YORK PORT BILL SIGNED BY HARDING

President Ignores Hylan's Protests and Opens Way for Development Program.

WASHINGTON, July 1.—President Harding signed the Port of New York bill today, which authorizes the States of New York and New Jersey to co-operate for the improvement of the port area.

The bill signed by the President empowers the Port of New York Authority to proceed with its comprehensive plan for the development of the port, which has been approved by the Legislatures of New York and New Jersey and the Governors of the two States. It was said last night that developments in the program might be expected immediately.

It was predicted that the first definite step would be the unification of the terminals on the proposed "waterfront belt line" on the New Jersey side of the Hudson River. Tracks which are to be used in this line are now owned by four railroads, the Lehigh Valley, the Erie, the West Shore and the Central Railroad of New Jersey, with separate terminals. It is proposed to join these tracks and make the tracks and terminals available for all the railroads, as they were during federal operation in the war. Negotiations to bring this about are already in progress with the railroads affected.

This step will not require the expenditure of money, but merely an agreement of the railroads. Management of the waterfront belt line, if the combination is effected, will be by the railroads.

Under the terms of the legislation creating it, the construction of new lines by the Port Authority must be financed by the issue of securities based upon the improvements. The proposed tunnel under the upper Bay from Greenville, N. J., to Bay Ridge, Brooklyn, probably will be one of the first important undertakings. This tunnel will cost approximately $40,000,000, but it was said that no difficulty in financing the project was expected.

Gratification was expressed last night by members of the Port Authority's staff at the promptness of the President in signing the bill, which was only received at the White House on Thursday night. The protest of Mayor Hylan, who has opposed the Port Authority since its inception, was disregarded by the President.

July 2, 1922

CITIES URGED TO GUIDE GROWTH OF SURROUNDING RURAL REGIONS

Present Proper Control Over the Development of New Subdivisions Within Corporate Limits Should Be Extended to Semi-Urban Areas—Realtors Study the Problem.

American cities have realized the importance of controlling the development of new subdivisions of land within their corporate limits, but they have failed as yet to realize the importance of proper plans for guiding the planning of the semi-urban areas outside those limits, which will sooner or later be annexed to the cities, according to study of existing plans for regional subdivision control in twenty-four representative large cities which has just been made by the National Association of Real Estate Boards.

The study was made by the Home Builders and Subdividers' Division of the association. Irenaeus Shuler of Omaha conducted the inquiry.

The information on which the study is based has been furnished by real estate boards, city planning commissions, city engineers and other officials of the various cities.

Good control of subdivision development outside corporate limits was found by the survey in eleven of the twenty-four cities studied, with partial control in three additional cities. Good control of subdivision development inside city limits is reported for seventeen of the cities, with partial control in six additional cities.

The making of a master plan for the whole metropolitan area is held by the report to be the most certain way to insure orderly development of the city into the surrounding rural regions.

Real estate boards are called on to take the leadership in requesting that such master plans be prepared for each large city's guidance.

By the term "master plan" is meant a plan to include the territory within a considerable circle outside the limits of the city, based on a complete topographical survey, showing future street extensions and grades to care properly for both local and through travel and providing for proper drainage.

The report recommends that this circle include territory lying within three miles of the city's limits, that distance having been set aside in many cities for the regulation of plats.

Automobile Brings New Planning Need.

The old country road, planned to accommodate slow-moving horse-drawn vehicles, is now hard surfaced and is alive with rapidly moving motor cars every hour of the day. Therefore, new primary thoroughfares have been required, radiating from congested city areas in all directions, to take care of travel both for business and pleasure.

"In our rapidly growing American cities we find errors made in early planning now being corrected at enormous expense to the community affected," the report states. "In many cases, due to conditions already firmly established, the unforeseen mistakes of the original plat around which grew the present city plan cannot be entirely corrected.

"The plan for the new subdivision, however, whether in the city limits or on the fringe of the city in the suburban area, can and should be under proper control."

Administrative Method Depends on Local Conditions.

Whether the fundamental principles of town planning are put into effect by a local planning board, a regional planning board, a State bureau of planning or by the regularly elected city or other officials is important, but not of first importance, the report finds. The best method of administration would depend on the laws governing such matters in the various States and cities and upon such laws as may be provided where lacking.

The Pennsylvania and Massachusetts plans of State bureaus to give advice and assistance to the local city plan commission would seem the method to adopt in the more or less congested States of the East.

In less densely settled areas of the country this control should be exercised by city officials through local planning boards given the power of planning for the area contiguous to the city through provisions of the charter or by special State legislation as may be necessary

February 15, 1925

SUBURBAN GROWTH EXPANDS CITY LIMITS

Metropolitan Area Includes Northern New Jersey, Western Connecticut, Westchester and Long Island.

The reconstruction of metropolitan districts throughout the entire country is a topic of more than passing interest to the urban and suburban dwellers who live in that district which is known as the New York metropolitan district.

New York home seekers and manufacturers have realized since the housing shortage resulting from the war arose, more emphatically than ever before, that the real New York City is a homogeneous territory, of which the corporate city of five boroughs is merely the nucleus. The City of New York actually takes in the greater part of Long Island, a portion of Western Connecticut, all the counties of New York as far north as Poughkeepsie, and all of Northern New Jersey.

This entire district depends mainly upon New York for its population and its industrial life. Citizens of New York, by the tens of thousands, have been driven into this outer area during the last five years by their inability to find adequate dwelling places in the city. New York manufacturers have been searching out locations in this area for a much longer period. The demand for homes and for factories has brought about a tremendous development throughout this territory and it is still in progress.

The advantages of securing official statistics covering all this district in a comprehensive manner has led the Merchants' Association to participate in the proposed revision of New York's metropolitan district limits. Martin Dodge, manager of its Industrial Bureau, will represent the association in a committee which will work with William M. Steuart, Director of the Census, in defining more accurate metropolitan district lines not only for the City of New York but the other cities throughout the country, both large and small. Many municipal services are based upon the metropolitan district instead of upon the municipality itself.

These often include water supply, sewers, transportation facilities, real estate, planning, &c. City planning and zoning are becoming metropolitan district planning and zoning by extending the power of municipal authorities over areas outside city limits and more recently by proposals to create regional planning commissions, to bring to the plans of different municipalities in a metropolitan district into harmony. Such a commission exists unofficially in New York City in the Committee on Regional Plan and officially in the Port of New York Authority, which takes in not only the City of New York, but also Northern New Jersey. Phases of metropolitan planning will also be taken up by Mayor Walker's Citizens Committee on which the Merchants' Association is represented by the membership of six of its directors.

The present metropolitan district of New York City includes a strip of territory approximately ten miles wide beyond the corporate limits of the city. This takes in a population of about 8,500,000. The plan to redefine the metropolitan district boundaries is of particular moment to industrial development, since it deals with facilities that can be provided for industries outside city borders and with areas to be devoted especially to industrial development.

The metropolitan district has been in use for some time by the Census Bureau, but its exact boundaries are still not very generally understood. Its growing importance warrants a sounder and more accurate definition.

June 27, 1926

ZONING IS UPHELD BY SUPREME COURT

Police Power to Enact Ordinances Is Victorious for the Second Time.

MANY LAWS ARE PENDING

A Number of State Legislatures Are Considering Extension of Policy —Race Case Decision.

With provisions further extending or defining zoning policies now before the Legislatures of a number of States two decisions just handed down by the United States Supreme Court became of special interest to constituent boards of the National Association of Real Estate Boards who are taking an active part in the framing of zoning and planning laws so as best to conserve the real estate values of their communities.

Constitutionality of municipal restriction of land uses under the police power through the enactment of zoning ordinances has been upheld for the second time by the Supreme Court in the case of Beery vs. Houghton, handed down March 21.

The Court here upheld the constitutionality of the zoning ordinance of Minneapolis, in a case involving the right to build an apartment building in a neighborhood that had been restricted to single family residences.

The plaintiff in the case had claimed that the ordinance violated Articles 5 and 14 of the Constitution of the United States.

No written opinion was handed down in the case. The judgment rendered is in accord with the recent clear-cut decision of the Court in the case of the village of Euclid, Ohio, vs. Ambler Realty Company.

Invalidates New Orleans Code Zoning Against Negroes.

Louisiana State and New Orleans municipal codes under which negroes are barred from residence in predominantly white communities where a majority of the white residents have not given their consent in writing have been held unconstitutional by a decision of the United States Supreme Court handed down March 14. The Supreme Court's ruling reverses a decision of the Louisiana State Supreme Court.

The New Orleans ordinance forbids the public authorities "from issuing a building permit for the construction of a residence for negro occupancy in a 'white community,' or for a white person in a 'negro community,' without the written consent of a majority of the persons of the opposite race inhabiting that community."

Further sections make it unlawful for any white person to establish his home or residence in a "negro community" or vice versa except on the written consent of a majority of the persons of the opposite race inhabiting that community.

As ground for the reversal the United States Supreme Court merely cited the case of Buchanan vs. Warley. This case, arising in Louisville, Ky., in 1917, involved an ordinance prohibiting negroes from occupying homes in blocks where the majority of residents were white.

The decision of the Supreme Court is held to remove all restrictions barring negroes from any residential section of New Orleans in which they wish to live.

Baltimore Board Works for State Zoning Act.

A State-wide zoning enabling act for Maryland is urged by the Real Estate Board of Baltimore for passage at the present session of the Legislature.

The enabling act is recommended in preference to the constitutional amendment authorizing zoning, which would be provided in a bill now pending. The board has consulted with a nationally known expert on zoning legislation in preparation for recommending the best means for ultimately bringing about a reasonable and proper zoning system for Baltimore.

The Supreme Court of Maryland has held the previous zoning ordinance of the city unconstitutional.

A State-wide zoning enabling act for Nebraska extending permission for zoning to cities of not less than 5,000 inhabitants is before the Nebraska Legislature.

May 22, 1927

WALKER GETS PLAN TO CHECK HAPHAZARD GROWTH OF THE CITY

Plan and Survey Committee Urges Permanent Board to Guide Future Expansion.

ASKS REVISION OF BUREAUS

TEXT OF THE REPORT.

To the Hon. James J. Walker,
Mayor of the City of New York.

1. Introductory.

This committee was organized on June 21, 1926, and now has the honor to submit a report of its findings. These findings are based on studies made by various subcommittees into matters specified by you for investigation, in your address to the committee at its inaugural meeting. That you accurately conceived what were the predominant problems and needs of the city is proved by the conclusions of these subcommittees. They show agreement with you as to the evils of piecemeal and spasmodic development, and as to the needs of comprehensive and continuous planning. They recognize that the problem of distribution of the population is the most fundamental in connection with the city's growth, that the unbalanced growth which means "overcrowding in some portions and incomplete development in others" is a twin economic and social evil that can only be arrested by some general plan for decent living conditions, such as you visualized.

In appointing a committee of citizens representing so many points of view, diverse interests and strong opinions on civic problems, it was conceivable that the benefits of wide representation would have been obtained at the cost of unanimity in arriving at decisions. Subject to natural differences of opinion on points of detail, the unanimity on general questions of principle has been remarkable. This is pre-eminently so in regard to the need of some permanent body being created to plan the future growth of the city.

The preliminary work of the City Committee on Plan and Survey was divided among eight subcommittees as follows:

(1) Housing, Zoning and Distribution of Population.
(2) Port and Terminal Facilities.
(3) Traffic Regulation and Street Uses.
(4) Sanitation and Harbor Pollution.
(5) Highways and Bridges.
(6) Parks and Recreational Facilities.
(7) Finance, Budget and Revenue.
(8) Departmental Organization.

Summaries of the more important recommendations of each of these subcommittees are included as Appendix I to this report and their reports in full will be found in Appendix II.

Six of the subcommittee reports relate to the physical planning of the city. The subjects they consider are those usually included under the term city planning. The report of the Subcommittee on Finance, Budget and Revenue deals with the questions of financial planning and new sources of revenue. These are very closely related to all problems of physical planning in their economic aspects. The question of departmental organization, however, is not closely related to the remainder of the subjects of study, and is of such a special and involved character that it requires intense and prolonged study by itself.

The recommendations made by the Subcommittee on Departmental Organization are worthy of careful consideration; but this committee feels that the subject should be separately and fully investigated by a specially constituted official body with adequate funds and staff to work out the difficult legal, administrative governmental problems involved.

The six subcommittees whose work includes the problems usually considered in connection with city planning are:

(1) Housing, Zoning and Distribution of Population.
(2) Port and Terminal Facilities.
(3) Traffic Regulation and Street Uses.
(4) Sanitation and Harbor Pollution.
(5) Highways and Bridges.
(6) Parks and Recreational Facilities.

The reports of the above subcommittees contain a mass of valuable data that should be of use in preparing a comprehensive city plan. The recommendations made are, for the most part, general in form. They are not intended to prescribe a definite plan of action, but rather to indicate the subjects for which definite and detailed plans should be made. The subcommittees were not constituted with the thought that they would or could present complete and detailed plans. For such a purpose each subcommittee would have required an expert staff working over a long period of time.

Assuming that each of these subcommittees had been able to work out definite plans covering the various problems assigned to them, it would still have been impractical for this committee to have made such a study of these plans and recommendations as would warrant it in approving them as constituting in the aggregate a fairly complete and coordinated plan for the physical development of the city. The recommendations of the subcommittees, important and well-considered as they as they are, do not constitute a comprehensive city plan but only the first step in the making of such a plan. This limitation is either expressed or implied in the reports of all the subcommittees.

2. The Principal Recommendation—Need of an Official Planning Board.

Several of the subcommittees make as their principal recommendation the establishment of an official city planning board as an integral and permanent part of the city government. The various reports show that such a board is urgently needed to develop a comprehensive plan to guide the physical development of the city. It has been obvious from the outset that this committee could not prepare such a plan. Any complete plan, that would be acceptable to the city government, must be based on detailed engineering, economic, social and legal studies, requiring the continuous application of trained minds for a long period of time. We are of the opinion that the only way to secure this is through an official Planning Board functioning as a permanent city department.

There are today 390 American cities having an aggregate population of 30,000,000 that have appointed city planning commissions. New York City has no central planning authority and no comprehensive plan covering its major public works. Although the need is even more urgent than in the smaller communities, the necessarily complex character of New York City's governmental organization has made the creation of a central planning authority a difficult matter.

At the present time the ultimate control of all details entering into the city's physical growth is vested in the Board of Estimate and Apportionment, but that body, from the very nature of its structure and the great burden of statutory and charter duties laid upon it, is unable to give to general far-ahead planning anything like the adequate attention it requires. Consequently it has to leave most planning and construction of local improvements to be carried out in districts, in a piecemeal fashion so far as the whole city is concerned. We are convinced that the appointment of a planning board would not lessen the present responsibility of the Board of Estimate and Apportionment, but would give much aid and relief in getting an intelligent understanding of projects, and in arriving at decisions with regard to their execution.

As a rule, the city and borough departments acting independently do not develop plans much ahead of actual construction. While effort is made to coordinate such work as may be projected from year to year, real economy and effective results cannot be obtained without a comprehensive plan and the guidance of a coordinating planning board.

As an illustration of the need of a city planning board in relation to traffic alone, we refer you to the decision of the Advisory Committee on Traffic Relief, which was created by the Board of Estimate in December, 1924. This committee, after considering the subject submitted to it for about a year, reported that it was impossible, with the staff at its disposal, to make an adequate study and recommendations in relation to the traffic and highway problem. If, for purposes of dealing with traffic problems only, a permanent board is needed, it is obvious that it is still more needed to deal with all the other related problems, including traffic. Moreover, the city has already suffered much from attempting to solve problems in separate compartments—of traffic, zoning, &c.—when it is apparent that any real solution involves comprehensive and coordinated treatment of all problems together.

Therefore, your committee recommends the creation of a permanent Planning Board.

3. General Functions of Proposed Planning Board.

The proposed board after thorough study, with the aid of an expert staff, should adopt a plan of development for the guidance of the city's future growth. This plan should include the larger projects of physical development covering a long period of years. It should also list these projects according to their relative urgency and indicate the approximate period in which each project should fall. The planning of the city should be a continuous function, and should be constantly studied with a view to its development and adjustment to meet changing conditions.

No attempt will be made herein to outline in detail the organization and functions of the proposed Planning Board. This matter has been considered more fully in the report of the Division on Distribution of Population, in Appendix I. The specific recommendations there contained are commended to your consideration, and should it be decided to create such a board, they will form a useful basis for the legislation that will be needed to establish a Planning Board.

It is clear that the organization and functions of the Planning Board will have to be very carefully studied and adjusted in order not to introduce additional complications in the conduct of city affairs. This is as necessary in the interest of good planning as it is in the interest of the efficient conduct of city administration.

The creation of the Planning Board should afford much relief to the Board of Estimate and Apportionment in connection with changes in the official map and zoning, which now consume much of the time of the Estimate Board.

On matters of detail and routine examination and approval of plans the office of the Chief Engineer of the Board of Estimate and Apportionment should continue to function as in the past, and where feasible its powers extended to approval and authorization, thus avoiding delay and saving the time both of the Estimate Board and the Planning Board.

It is not, of course, proposed that the Planning Board enter into the details of construction carried on by the departments or that it have any authority relating thereto. Its function, in so far as public works are concerned, would be chiefly the preparation and progressive development of the master plan and the correlation of individual projects with such plan. It would have no administrative part in the carrying out of projects.

The Planning Board and its staff should include both architectural and engineering members. This is essential in order that a proper balance may be maintained between purposes of utility and art. The collaboration of the architect with the engineer in the preparation of plans is necessary to secure a well-balanced design.

The Planning Board would be the agency for correlating all separate projects as part of a general plan, and would have to be given some discretionary powers to deal with tentative schemes so as to make its work constructive and not to arrest development.

We anticipate for the Planning Board a great amount of labor in making continuous study of urban growth; in elaborating and changing the city plan; in the work of research into various planning problems that will have to be done; and in dealing with many important projects in course of development by the various departments and authorities. All these will require constant attention, advice and constructive criticism. In addition there will be hearings and decisions on changes in the zoning maps and in the official map. This will have to be considered in deciding on the character and personnel of the board and of its expert staff.

The question of the qualifications of members of the board and whether they should be paid for their services can perhaps best be decided when the legislation fixing their duties has been more fully worked out. It seems clear, however, that the board will head a city department that should be second to none in importance and responsibility. It is simply a question of whether a paid or an unpaid membership will insure a higher measure of ability and of personal responsibility on the part of the members, and also a higher measure of confidence on the part of the other city departments and of the public.

4. Relation of the City Plan to a Regional Plan.

The welfare of New York City is bound up in the proper physical planning of the entire New York region. While New York City has its own interests and problems, it has many interests in common with the areas of adjacent counties. The creation of the Port Authority with the problem of planning harbor and terminal facilities for the Port of New York is an instance of the common interests of the city with parts of the State of New Jersey. The efficiency of the port as a unit is a primary consideration in planning for the future. The location of port, and indeed all transportation facilities in the region, whether within or without the city, will inure to the benefit of the city provided the location selected is the one that will contribute most largely to the efficiency of the port as a whole.

Railroads, highways, bridges and tunnels are other factors of common regional interest. One great advantage of producing or doing business in a metropolitan community is the large local market that can be served by truck and the large population having convenient access by transportation facilities or automobile.

The more complete and adequate the system of regional highways the more fully will each manufacturer and business man, wherever located throughout the region, be able to reap the benefits that should normally accrue from access to a local market of more than ten million people.

The Committee on the Regional Plan of New York and its environs has been actively at work for seven years preparing a plan for the area included within a fifty mile radius of New York. Their work, with the aid of a staff of experts, has included the development of the basic social, economic, legal and physical data needed for the proper planning of this entire region. Their plan will include suggestions for trunk line regional highway and transit lines, large parks and parkways, and the broad apportionment of the land area of the region for docks, industry, commerce, residence and other urban uses.

These studies of the Regional Plan will be available for the use of the proposed Planning Board. It is important to note, however, a distinction between regional planning and city planning. The purpose of the Regional Plan Committee is to study out and suggests the broad lines of regional development—not to make or consider detailed plans and locations for actual construction. The advantage of the Regional Plan is that it will afford the City Planning Board an opportunity to correlate its planning with a general plan for a region comprising the whole of Long Island, the Counties of Westchester, Rockland and Orange in New York, the County of Fairfield in Connecticut, and about 2,220 square miles in the counties of metropolitan New Jersey.

It is not believed to be either practicable or desirable to create an official interstate agency similar to the Port Authority for the purpose of regional planning. If all the area in the New York Region were included within the boundaries of a single State, it would be possible to create an official regional planning commission that would carry on the work of the present unofficial committee, the Regional Plan of New York and its environs. We deem it very important

Principal Recommendations Proposed to Mayor By the City Committee on Plan and Survey

Following are the principal recommendations of the City Committee on Plan and Survey:

Creation of a permanent official City Planning Commission to work out a comprehensive plan for the future growth of New York.

Appointment of a special committee to investigate the necessity for a complete reorganization of the city government.

New sources of city revenue, including a gasoline tax, to meet the cost of the new subway system and other public improvements.

Spread of industries throughout the city to induce a more even distribution of population and relieve the overcrowded tenement districts.

Elimination of the slums, improved housing conditions, and extension of the zoning regulations to provide more light and air for dwellings.

More parks in the outlying sections, especially Queens and Staten Island; more playgrounds in the congested districts.

Relief of traffic congestion by cutting new streets through midtown Manhattan, and establishing express highways and a great loop highway around all centres of congestion.

Better control of pedestrian traffic, more night deliveries of goods, and closer regulation of interurban buses and trucks.

A complete system of airports in different parts of the city.

Additional tunnels and bridges.

More efficient use of waterfront space, especially by industries needing both rail and water facilities.

Garbage incinerators in different parts of city, to obviate dumping of refuse at sea and littering beaches.

to the permanent success of the work of the proposed Planning Board that there should be an unofficial body similar to the present Committee on the Regional Plan permanently functioning to aid in correlating planning work throughout the region. The basic data and plans already prepared by the Regional Plan Committee and the invaluable experience acquired by its staff should in some way be perpetuated for the benefit of New York City and all other communities in this great metropolitan region.

It may be desirable, however, that there be created in time, independent of, and in addition to, the proposed Planning Board of the City or the present Regional Plan Committee, advisory sub-regional planning boards for the counties immediately adjacent to the city. If this were done, it would be further desirable for the planning boards of the city and adjacent counties to have a joint committee.

In course of time, the set-up of a complete planning organization for the region might therefore be as summarized below:

A. An official Planning Board for the City of New York, as recommended in this report.

B. One or two regional planning advisory boards for the New York State counties within the New York region.

In this connection advantages should be taken of the State law permitting the creation by counties of regional planning boards, to establish either a single regional planning advisory board for all of the New York State counties within the New York region, or two such boards, one for Long Island counties and one for the other New York State counties. Onondaga County, which includes the City of Syracuse, has established a regional planning board under the authority of this general State Enabling act. A similar planning board for Buffalo region has been established by special act under the name of "The Niagara Frontier Planning Board." The special conditions existing in the New York region might call for a special enabling act similar to that under which the Niagara Frontier Board has been established.

C. The creation of a similar advisory planning board to correlate planning work in the New Jersey counties that form a part of the New York region may be hoped for as a later development.

D. The foregoing would not render it less desirable for the Committee on the Regional Plan of New York and its environs to carry on planning research and continuously to develop and keep up-to-date the broad features of a general plan for the New York region, for which no official agency can be created.

The matters referred to in the foregoing paragraphs B, C, and D are of general interest, but it is not within the scope of our duties to make specific recommendations with regard to them, because they enter into problems that lie outside of the jurisdiction of the city. We consider, however, that much advantage might be gained were a conference to be held between representatives of the City of New York and of the counties adjacent to the city, in New York and New Jersey States, and we suggest that the question of convening such a conference to consider matters affecting the joint development of these neighboring communities be held at an early date.

5 Recommendations Regarding Specific Problems Referred to Sub-Committees.

Housing, Zoning and Distribution of Population.

Distribution of Population. We concur in the conclusions of the Sub-Committee on Housing, Zoning and Distribution of Population, that the policy of the city should be to encourage the spreading of certain types of industries over wider areas within its limits and thereby first to lessen the distances between homes and places of employment, second to induce a more even growth of activities and population, and third to stabilize the uses of land.

As a means towards the end of better distribution, we also concur in the view that more open spaces be provided within the central areas of the city so far as this is financially practical.

Housing. The importance of the problem of securing improved housing accommodations was stressed in your preliminary address to this committee. The matter has received the serious attention of Governor Smith and has given rise to strong legislative action under his leadership. There is no matter in connection with the city's growth that is so vital to its welfare as the living conditions of the mass of its population. The evils caused by overcrowded conditions of housing accommodations in the city are such as to make it urgent that effective remedies be found. It is equally important and pressing that measures be taken to prevent the recurrence of these evils in suburban areas of the city. The difficulties of correcting established evils show how important it is to prevent their repetition.

While, under present conditions, it may be impracticable to carry out the proposals put forward in the report on housing, we concur in the views expressed as to the needs of securing more light, air and fire resisting materials in dwellings, of preventing the spread of multiple dwellings, of increasing playground space in all areas, and of pressing forward a definite policy in regard to slum clearance. We would also especially urge the need of more stringent regulations over all new construction in suburban areas.

Zoning. The proposals of this committee, which have for their object the improvement of administration of zoning and the establishment of a retail district, should be adopted by the Board of Estimate. We are advised that the administrative changes have been unanimously approved by the Law, Building, Fire and Tenement House Departments, and the Chief Engineer of the Board of Estimate. In general principle we approve recommendations made with regard to height and area and submit them with our general endorsement for the consideration of the city. The time is ripe for amendment and strengthening of the Zoning Resolution which was passed into law eleven years ago. During these years there have been many changes in zoning practice, and the city has gained much valuable experience that can now be profitably used.

In the event of a Planning Board being appointed, it would be desirable to refer the question of changes in zoning restrictions to the board. This would permit a more constructive approach being made to the zoning of the city than has been the case in the past in the absence of a comprehensive plan. In the final analysis the solution of the problems of congestion and of distribution of population will depend on the principles and methods which are applied to the regulation of building uses and densities, and the relation of these to the street and other open areas of the city.

Port and Terminal Facilities.

Among the important matters considered by the Sub-Committee on Port and Terminal Facilities, we especially concur in the recommendations for a reassignment of waterfront accommodations so as to utilize all facilities in the most advantageous manner, for the allocation of definite stretches of waterfronts for industrial development by such industries as require both rail and water facilities, for the establishment of belt line railroad connections to make possible the most complete utilization of the entire waterfront, and for the location and development of a complete system of airports.

We would especially urge the need of coordinated architectural and engineering treatment of the railroad, commercial, park and building uses of the waterfronts of each of the five boroughs. The waterfront of New York is its greatest asset not only from a commercial point of view —but also from that of the opportunity it presents for adding beauty and dignity to the most prominent feature of the city. That so much of the waterfront is occupied by disorderly structures is neither an economy nor a credit to the city's sense of order in the development of its greatest natural endowment.

Traffic Regulation.

We agree with the Sub-Committee on Traffic Regulations and Street Uses that there is need for the careful investigation and study of measures of traffic relief such as the control of pedestrian traffic, the increase of night deliveries for certain classes of goods and materials and the regulation of the operation of interurban buses and trucks. We concur also in this sub-committee's finding that measures of mere regulation cannot begin to cope with the traffic problem. For any real solution we must turn to new street planning and zoning as part of a comprehensive plan, as recommended by this sub-committee.

Sanitation and Pollution.

We agree with the Sub-Committee on Sanitation and Harbor Pollution that the system of garbage and refuse incineration should be so developed as to obviate the necessity of dumping at sea, and that the installation of sewage treatment plants be extended as rapidly as possible, so as to secure the proper treatment of every gallon of sewage discharged into public waters.

Highways and Bridges.

Among the many valuable recommendations of the Sub-Committee on Highways and Bridges, we wish particularly to emphasize the desirability of a great loop highway passing around all centres of congestion in the New York region and permitting the by-passing of those congested centres, the separation of highway grades at important intersections on arterial highways, the provision of off-the-street loading facilities by establishments having a large amount of trucking or passenger car traffic, and the development of a trunk line system of express highways.

The need of study of highway problems on a city-wide scale, of adding to the bridge and tunnel connections within the city, and of creating a planning organization to make a plan for major highway improvements, with which other phases of development in the city should be co-related, stand out as of special importance among the numerous constructive proposals put forward by this sub-committee. Reference is also made to the desirability of controling the erection of buildings in mapped streets. Adequate authority to deal with this important matter is given by Chapter 690 of the Laws of 1926 to any city having an official planning commission. This is another reason for the creation of such a body in New York City.

Parks and Recreational Facilities.

The extension of the city park and parkway system in the boroughs of Queens and Richmond as recommended by the Sub-Committee on Parks and Recreational Facilities is greatly needed. We concur in the sub-committee's recommendation that a complete system of playgrounds adequate to serve existing and estimated future population should be developed without delay. We wish particularly to emphasize the importance both of acquiring new playground sites in densely populated sections not now served by existing playgrounds and of acquiring new playground sites in outlying districts where land is still comparatively inexpensive. The definite suggestions made, as to actual areas suitable for parks and as to changes in administration, should receive immediate attention.

Finance, Budget and Revenue.

The expense incurred and labor done by the Sub-Committee on Finance, Budget and Revenue is reflected in the extensive report it has submitted. It is impossible to do justice to that report in any brief summary of findings, although an effort has been made to indicate the outstanding points in the report in the summary given in Appendix I. We would commend the study of this report and the serious consideration of the proposals it contains, which, generally speaking, must meet with acceptance from those interested in the welfare of the city.

In particular we concur in the recommendation in favor of the preparation and annual revision of a capital outlay program. Certainly a long term program of capital outlay based on the relative urgency of the various projects and the estimated revenues available to pay for them would seem to be a first essential to sound municipal finance. Financial planning is just as important as physical planning. The preparation of a comprehensive city plan would furnish a needed basis for the financial plan. The sub-committee, in considering possible additional sources of revenue to meet the demands that will arise during the next few years, suggests among other sources, a gasoline tax. We believe that a gasoline tax, levied by the State and distributed to the various municipalities, is a most appropriate way of securing a contribution to the cost of highways and bridges from those who are most directly benefited by these improvements.

We would emphasize that retrenchment of expenditures in certain directions may be as important as finding new revenues to meet additional expenditures. The suggestion that the city should pursue methods that would lead to greater economy in acquiring lands for improvements seems to us to be of great importance.

Summary of Conclusions.

Our general conclusions may be summarized as follows:

(1) It is desirable that everything possible should be done, within the legal powers and financial ability of the city, to promote balanced development and even distribution of industry and population throughout the city; to improve the housing conditions of the people; to extend and revise the zoning law; to develop a constructive program for the extension and improvement of port and terminal facilities; to impose further regulations on traffic; to widen and extend highways to a greater extent than hitherto; to construct additional tunnels and bridges; to increase the area of parks and playgrounds; to improve sanitation and lessen pollution of waters; and to develop a constructive program of city finance.

(2) The problem of departmental organization requires special and prolonged investigation by a committee or commission created for that sole purpose. This question is not closely related to the physical planning of the city, and requires more intimate and expert investigation than has been possible for this committee to give.

(3) It was not practicable for this committee to prepare a plan to guide future growth, and the reports submitted are intended only to indicate the nature of the problems requiring to be dealt with and some of the methods and principles that need to be followed, in connection with the preparation of a plan.

(4) The principal recommendation of the committee is that a permanent City Planning Board be created, and suggestions are included in the reports submitted herewith as to the constitution and general functions of such a board. The serious character of the civic problems to be dealt with and the urgency of some effective solutions being found makes it important that this matter receive early attention.

(5) It is desirable that some kind of regional organization, such as the Committee on the Regional Plan of New York and its environs be maintained to collaborate with the city, and any planning board that may be set up on behalf of the City Administration, in dealing with problems affecting the whole New York region. It is also desirable that counties adjacent to the city of New York and New Jersey be invited to form planning boards or commissions to cooperate with the city in respect to matters affecting the city and these neighboring municipalities in common. For this purpose we suggest that a conference of municipal authorities in New York and New Jersey metropolitan areas be held to discuss possible lines of procedure and cooperation.

(6) Without endorsing in detail the various proposals of the subcommittees, we recommend these proposals to the serious consideration of the city. We repeat, however, that the full value, which the city may gain from the adoption of one or any of them, will not accrue unless and until the main recommendation of several sub-committees is adopted; namely the appointment of a permanent planning board, to which all detailed suggestions contained in the reports of this committee should be referred.

Finally, we desire to express appreciation of the opportunity which has been presented to the large body of interested citizens, which constitute the committee, to study the problems connected with the physical development of the city. We believe that the appointment of a large and representative committee was the best step to take, in the first instance, because it has enabled so many citizens to obtain a general understanding o. the complexity and difficulty of civic problems, and of the methods which must be followed and the kind of organization needed, to secure their ultimate solution.

The fact that it was important, for several reasons, to place the responsibility for the preliminary investigations in the hands of such a large grou.. without any expert aid or funds provided by the city, has, of necessity, limited the scope of its work; but no time will be wasted if prompt action is taken to carry out its principal recommendation.

We desire further to place on record our appreciation of the cooperation we have received from the members of the City Administration and the officials of the city; as well as from any unofficial persons and organizations. In particular we are indebted to the Committee of the Regional Plan of New York and Its Environs for valuable aid in furnishing information and for cooperation in analyzing the reports of the sub-committees.

We respectfully submit this report and these conclusions for your consideration and for such action as may seem to you to be fit and appropriate to take in order to achiev.. the general purpose for which this committee was appointed.

MORGAN J. O'BRIEN, *Chairman.*

McAneny Commission Plan.

The following recommendations for the organization of the proposed Planning Commission are contained in a report by George McAneny, Chairman of the Division on Distribution of Population of the Subcommittee on Housing, Zoning and Distribution of Population:

1. **That there be established a commission on the plan of the City of New York, made up of five members of expert qualification, to be appointed by the Mayor, at such rate of compensation as the Board of Estimate and Apportionment may determine.**
2. That such commission have authority to employ an adequate permanent staff, technical and otherwise; and that it also have authority to contract from time to time with engineers, architects, city planners and such other consultants as it may require.
3. That such commission be charged in the first instance, with the assembling and analysis of all existing information and data regarding the city's physical growth and present situation available from any source, and with the consideration of whatever recommendations upon the general subject may be presented to it.
4. That such commission, after appropriate studies have been made, be charged with the preparation of a comprehensive "master" plan, for the future physical development of the city, and, so far as necessary, for the regulation and control of private uses of land areas within the city.
5. That such plan comprehend, among other things:
   (a) The general location and character of the city's major traffic highways, boulevards, parkways, viaducts, bridges and tributary street systems;
   (b) The location and reservation of parks, squares, playgrounds, aviation fields and other public grounds and open spaces;
   (c) The location of public buildings and other public property;
   (d) The relocation, reconstruction, extension or change of use of any of the foregoing public thoroughfares, open spaces or buildings;
   (e) The continued zoning of the city for building purposes, and the continued regulation of the height, size and occupational uses of buildings;
   (f) The relationship and proper adjustment to the City Plan of transit lines, and port and terminal facilities.
6. That after such plan has been adopted by the commission and approved by the city's statutory authorities, all city and borough departments having projects for improvements coming within the scope or definite implications of the plan be required to present such projects to the commission for examination and for acceptance as in conformance with the plan; and. That the formal approval of the commission be required for each such project unless, in case of rejection by the commission, it be thereafter approved by a three-fourths vote of the Board of Estimate and Apportionment.
7. That the commission be required, after careful study, to recommend to the Board of Estimate and Apportionment whatever changes it considers necessary or desirable in the present zoning ordinances and maps;
8. That subsequent to the submission of such recommendations, and action thereon, all changes proposed in the zoning ordinance or maps be submitted to the commission for examination and that no such change, disapproved by the commission, be effective unless thereafter approved by a three-fourths vote of the Board of Estimate and Apportionment.
9. That the commission, whenever requested so to do, either by the established transportation authorities of the city, or by the Port Authority, lend its cooperation in the working out of suitable plans for rail and water terminals within the city, or for the mapping and extension of transit facilities, or in the working out of any other plans within the jurisdiction of these independent bodies;
10. That the commission be directed, through collaboration with the staff of the Regional Plan and with the official agencies of other communities, within the metropolitan area, to promote the harmonious adjustment of the plan of the city, when adopted, to the general planning system of such other communities.

Says Cost Would Be Small.

Mr. McAneny adds that if the general proposal is accepted the subcommittee will draft whatever State or municipal legislation is needed to make it effective. He says the commission would not be a heavy financial burden upon the city, because its cost would be slight, and would be partly offset through the elimination of other existing expense of a similar nature.

Moreover, he argues that the commission would greatly reduce expense through saving the waste of badly balanced planning or construction, as well as the costs of tearing out faulty or inadequate work and replacing it by new work.

He asserts that members of the commission should be selected for their expert or professional fitness for planning work, that they should devote all their time to it, and that they should be well paid.

"It is not believed," he adds, "that reliance for service of the sort that would be required—involving, as such service will, an expert understanding of the city's physical problems and frequent contact with citizens and attendance at many hearings—should be placed upon a group of non-professional citizens, serving without pay and depending for their own guidance chiefly upon staff advice."

Says New York Has Lagged.

Mr. McAneny points out that New York has lagged behind virtually every other city of first rank, here and abroad, in adopting scientific methods of city building and city conservation. Out of the 390 American cities that have appointed city planning commissions, he adds, 176 have already adopted completed plans and are developing under planning rules.

He praises Chicago, saying that it claims with apparent justice that it is one of the best-planned cities in the world. Since 1907, when it adopted the plan prepared by its first commission, he goes on, Chicago has spent $300,000,000 upon detailed improvements which that plan embraced.

The McAneny report also advocates the relief of the congested areas in New York by the definite encouragement of new building to spread out over wider areas in the less congested parts of the city. It suggests the "decentralization of industry" within the city, to lessen the distance between homes and places of employment; more open spaces in the older and more congested sections; new parks and recreation centres in the districts still comparatively open, and the strengthening of zoning regulations to control the character and direction of the future growth of the city.

Ecker Asks Public Support.

Frederick H. Ecker, Chairman of the Subcommittee on Housing, Zoning and Distribution of Population, in his report supports Mr. McAneny's recommendations and urges public support for them.

The Division on Housing, of which Lawrence Veiller is Chairman, recommends that the height of all future dwellings be limited to the width of the street or other open space on which the dwelling abuts, with towers and setbacks permitted if they allow a forty-five degree angle of light.

It urges the creation of private dwelling districts by zoning, in order to prevent the spread of multiple dwellings, and the prohibition of the erection of any dwelling in any part of the city that is not fire-resisting. The Tenement House Department, it recommends, should be changed to a Housing Department, and its jurisdiction should be extended to all dwellings.

Declaring that ordinary window glass shuts out the ultra-violet rays of the sun, the Veiller report urges legislation to prevent builders from using glass which keeps out these beneficial rays.

Would End All Slums.

The report also advocates that the city embark upon a definite program of eliminating its slums, whereby one entire block after another would be cleared of buildings and a strip of land thirty feet in depth around the margin of the block would be leased or sold for the construction of modern tenements two rooms deep. This would leave a small park or playground in the middle of the block to be developed and maintained by the city.

The Division on Zoning, of which Lawson Purdy is Chairman, makes the following recommendations regarding the height of buildings.

"The present height limit within each height district is based on the street width. In a two times district this rule permits a building height at the street line of 200 feet for the 100-foot street, and of 120 feet for the 60-foot street. The division recommends that the height limit now allowed at the street line for a sixty-foot street be made the uniform height limit at the street line for all buildings throughout the district.

"The proposed height limit at the street line is as follows: In a one-times district or in a one and one-quarter times district, 65 feet; in a one and one-half times district, 90 feet; in a two-times district or a two and one-half times district, 125 feet."

To Raise Tower Privilege.

The report also proposed increasing the tower privilege from 25 to 30 per cent. of the lot area in the two-times district and the two and one-half times district. The 30 per cent. tower would be set back twenty feet from the street line, twenty-five feet from the rear lot line and ten feet from each side lot line.

Another recommendation is that all large loft, department store and office buildings erected henceforth shall provide off-the-street loading and unloading space for trucks.

The report urges that larger rear yards be required in the outlying districts of Brooklyn, Queens, the Bronx and Richmond (Staten Island), and that play yards and recreation space be required for each apartment house erected in those sections.

Another Division on Zoning, of which Edward M. Bassett is Chairman, recommends several amendments to the City Charter and the zoning regulation from the administrative standpoint.

The Subcommittee on Finance, Budget and Revenue, of which Herbert H. Lehman is Chairman, with Professors Lindsay Rogers, Howard Lee McBain and Robert Murray Haig of Columbia University as consultants, makes the most voluminous of the reports. It is a volume of 361 pages, with seventy-two pages of recommendations. Only the recommendations are included in the main committee's report.

The report recommends a change in the city's fiscal year, which is now identical with the calendar year. It should be from July 1 to June 30, like the fiscal years of the Federal and State Governments, according to the report.

Puts Budget Up to Mayor.

The Lehman report also recommends that the Mayor should be

made responsible for the preparation of the budget and that there should be created a Department of the Budget under a director appointed by the Mayor. It says that the issue of special revenue bonds should be minimized by making annual appropriations based on average past requirements for snow removal, claims and judgments, Fire Department relief fund, Transit Commission, Board of Transportation, Armory Board and voting machines.

It recommends the adoption and annual revision of a capital outlay program to be included in the annual budget. According to this plan, each department should submit to the Director of the Budget requests for projects to be financed during the coming fiscal year by the issue of corporate stock, serial bonds or tax notes.

Pointing out that the annual budget has doubled since 1919 and has trebled since 1910, the report estimates that it will increase about $20,000,000 a year for the next five years. As interest and sinking fund requirements on new capital outlay will form a large part of the probable budget increases during the next five years, the report says, it has listed the probable future requirements of the city for public improvements during that time. It makes a total of $1,062,000,000, of which $500,000,000 is for subways. Other items are: Schools, $125,000,000; docks, $28,000,000; incinerators, $15,000,000; hospitals, $10,000,000; grade-crossing elimination, $10,000,000; bridges and tunnels, $176,000,000; sewage disposal, $21,000,000; new water supply, $108,000,000.

These projects, excluding subways, the report continues, will require an average increase in the city's debt of 112.4 millions each year, with an annual increase in the budget allowance for interest and mortization of 5.6 millions. It says that the annual increase in the budget for purposes other than subway construction cannot be less than $15,000,000, and is more likely to be $25,000,000.

More Revenue Needed.

As for the cost of subway financing, it reports that the 1928 budget contains a burden of $14,000,000 attributable to the old subways and $25,000,000 to the new system—a total of $39,000,000, representing about 24 points in the tax rate on the 1928 assessment base. Discussing the Board of Transportation's plan to draw enough from the tax budget in the next few years to liquidate more than half of the capital cost of the new subway system, the report questions the Board of Transporation estimate that $76,000,000 will be available for subway projects in the next five years without an increase in the tax rate. The report says this will be impossible unless additional sources of revenue are developed.

Surveying possible new sources of revenue, the report says there may be some relief through a possible reduction of the direct State tax on real estate, which would enable the city to increase its tax on real estate to the extent to which the State tax is reduced.

It also favors the establishment of a settled policy of financing by special assessment all street improvements, including repaving, except in so far as these costs can be more fairly met by a fee system or other special taxes. At present, it points out, there is no such policy as to the character of improvements to be financed by special assessments and no general rule as to the percentages of cost to be borne by property in the immediate vicinity of the improvement, by the real estate of the borough as a whole and by the real estate of the city in general.

It also says that special assessments should be used to recover a part of the cost of subway construction. The location of subway stations, it adds, results in an entirely fortuitous gain to the owners of certain pieces of real estate, who should pay special assessments in return for their special benefits. It suggests that some of the money needed for subway construction might be obtained by a tax on land values alone rather than on both land and buildings.

Citiy services, such as inspection fees and water rates, it adds, should be priced so as to meet their cost. It favors a gasoline tax, to be collected by the State and handed over in part to the city, so that the motorists who use the city streets should help pay for their mantenance. It is estimated that a tax of 1 per cent. a gallon would net the State $10,000,000 a year, and that the city might expect to receive from $1,000,000 to $2,000,000 of this.

The report suggests that a tax on unincorporated business should be established, and that the present personal property tax should be abolished.

The subcommittee on Departmental Organization, of which N. Taylor Phillips is Chairman, recommends the consolidation of various municipal activities where duplication has caused confusion, waste and friction. It also favors a permanent city-planning commission.

The report urges the creation of a department of municipal hospitals, headed by a commissioner and an advisory board, appointed by the Mayor, to operate all municipal-owned and directed hospitals and kindred activities now conducted by the Department of Public Welfare, Department of Health, Board of Trustees of Bellevue and Allied Hospitals and Board of Ambulance Service. It recommends that this department have jurisdiction also over the municipal homes for the aged and infirm and hospitals for contagious and communicable diseases.

It points out that there are now twelve hospitals under the Department of Public Welfare, five under the Department of Health, five under the Board of Trustees of Bellevue and Allied Hospitals, and two institutions for the care of aged and infirm calling for hospital service under the Department of Public Welfare.

The Phillips report also recommends the creation of a Department of Buildings to consolidate all the powers now exercised by the Bureau of Buildings, Tenement House Department, Bureau of Fire Prevention, Fire Department and other city departments with respect to buildings. It says there have been many complaints over the multiplicity and conflict of orders in inspection requirements, permits, &c., because of duplication and overlapping authority under the present system, and the lack of uniformity by various official bodies in the interpretation of the Building Code. The proposed new department would have a commissioner in each borough to be appointed by the Borough President, constituting a board of commissioners with a chairman to be appointed by the Mayor.

It advocates the transfer of authority to examine applicants for permits and licenses from various city boards to the Municipal Civil Service Commission, and the transfer of the Bureau of Weights and Measures from the Mayor's office to the Department of Public Markets.

For the sake of protecting property owners from excessive assessments for public improvements, it recommends an amendment to the City Charter providing that such improvements originating in local improvement boards shall not be carried out if the cost thereof, when the contract is ready to let, exceeds by certain percentages the official estimates on which the improvement has been authorized. If the estimated cost is $1,000 or less the excess in the contract price is to be not more than 50 per cent.; from $1,000 to $10,000, not more than 25 per cent.; more than $10,000, not more than 20 per cent.

The report recommends that the jurisdiction of the Department of Street Cleaning, including snow removal, be extended to cover Queens and Staten Island as well as the rest of the city. It suggests that the City Planning Commission, if established, study the wisdom of creating a Department of Engineering, to assemble all the engineering forces of the city.

It advocates that the custody of all prisoners being taken to and from city prisons be transferred from the county sheriffs to the Department of Correction, and that the county jails in the Bronx and Staten Island be transferred to the Department of Correction. It also recommends that the present city life-saving agencies be transferred to the Department of Parks, and that the collection of water rents be transferred from the Department of Water Supply, Gas and Electricity to the Bureau of City Collections of the Department of Finance.

The subcommittee on Port and Terminal Facilities, of which John J. Fitzgerald is Chairman, urges a City Planning Commission. It says proper study of port and terminal problems is handicapped by the lack of a comprehensive city plan, because such problems are inter-related with the problems of traffic, highways, bridges, tunnels, ferries, transportation and other factors of general and regional planning.

It recommends the gradual rebuilding of the North River waterfront of Manhattan, so as to provide adequate accommodations for large transatlantic liners. Then it would concentrate all transatlantic passenger steamship lines on the North River waterfront, freighters and freight lines on the Brooklyn and Staten Island riverfront, and coastwise and Sound lines on the East River waterfront. Mechanical pier equipment for loading and unloading cargoes is advocated.

The report urges the allocation of definite waterfronts for industrial development by such industries as need both rail and water facilities, including the most complete utilization of Jamaica Bay for such purposes.

It advocates the location and development of airports in different sections of the city.

The Subcommittee on Traffic Regulation and Street Uses, of which Dr. John A. Harriss is Chairman, makes the City Planning Commission its principal recommendation. It says that further measures of traffic regulation will not solve the traffic problem, and that a comprehensive plan for new arteries of travel and new facilities, which can only be brought about by the creation of a permanent City Planning Commission, is needed.

It suggests that such a commission take into consideration the problems of the whole metropolitan area, and that to supplement its work the Governor be empowered to appoint similar commissions to prepare comprehensive plans for Long Island and Westchester County.

The report urges the need of a comprehensive system of express roads or "super streets" in New York City, but says this can only be worked out through the establishment of a permanent planning commission. Other specific problems which should be worked out by such a commission, or in its absence by the Police Department or some other city authority, it adds, are the coordination of the activities of the various city departments in order to minimize the obstruction of traffic in the streets; the control of pedestrian traffic; night deliveries of certain classes of merchandise and limitation of the number of taxicabs.

The Subcommittee on Highways and Bridges, of which Commissioner Albert Goldman of the Department of Plant and Structures is Chairman, recommends that the functions of a permanent city-wide planning commission, if established, include the drawing up of a plan for major highway improvements and its correlation with other phases of the city plan. It points out that there is no existing body authorized to initiate highway projects on a city-wide scale.

The report advocates that the intensely congested section of the city from Thirty-second to Fifty-seventh Street and from Lexington to Tenth Avenue be supplied with new longitudinal highways by the construction of new streets north and south through the long blocks of this section, and that at least three of the east and west streets in the same section be widened from 60 to 100 feet. It also urges a new street along the East River front from Chambers to 125th Street.

It recommends the appropriation of $15,000,000 a year for ten years for carrying out a comprehensive plan of highway improvement. Other recommendations include a new system of highways connecting the city with adjacent States and counties, with provision to move traffic more continuously and at faster speed than now possible in the city streets; removal of all elevated structures, subway kiosks and other obstructions from the city streets; construction of "exterior" streets near the waterfront; underground foot walks at congested places, and extension of the one-way street and traffic control signal systems. Bridges or tunnel connections are recommended between South Brooklyn and Staten Island; Eighth Street, Manhattan, and Metropolitan Avenue, Brooklyn; Thirty-eighth Street, Manhattan, and Long Island City; Eighty-sixth Street, Manhattan, and Astoria, and a triborough bridge.

Urges Single Park Council.

The Subcommittee on Parks and Recreational Facilities, of which George Gordon Battle is Chairman, recommends the creation of a Park Council of nine members with full power to select, acquire and develop new park properties, to be turned over for maintenance to the Park Department. It says administration of the parks and recreation grounds should be centralized under one Park Commissioner for the entire city, with deputy commissioners in each borough, instead of the present system of a park department for each borough. In this it differs from the Subcommittee on Departmental Organization, which favors a continuance of the present Park Board. Creation of a city-wide bureau of recreation under a Commissioner of Recreation responsible to the Park Commissioner is also advocated.

It recommends the development of Riverside and belt line parkways in Manhattan and the Bronx, and the acquisition of new park property in the other boroughs. It also urges the acquisition of new playground sites in various parts of the city and the establishment of two new playgrounds in Central Park, one on the east side and one on the west.

Wants Speedy Incineration.

The subcommittee on Sanitation and Harbor Pollution, of which Dr. Thomas Darlington is Chairman, recommends that all garbage and rubbish collected in New York be disposed of by incinerators to be established in specified zones and that this program be pushed with all possible speed to obviate the further necessity of dumping refuse at sea and littering the beaches.

Asserting that oil in the harbor water constitutes a serious evil, the report says that the Federal Government can control this hazard. It adds that the harbor fishing and shell fishing industries have been injured beyond hope of restoration by any means of water purification that is economically feasible and that it is impossible to purify the harbor waters sufficiently to make them safe for salt water bathing except "at enormous and probably unjustifiable cost." It urges the Board of Estimate to take early action for the installation of sewage treatment plants at the waterfront.

CHICAGO REBUILDS ON A GRANDER SCALE

Super-Highways Are Added to Costly Lake and River Front Improvements

By R. L. DUFFUS.

WHILE gunmen in Chicago lie in wait to pot one another, and charges of corruption in the city and county governments make a perennial scandal, the metropolis on Lake Michigan goes steadily ahead on the most imposing job of city planning ever attempted in the modern world. New York City is soon to benefit by the monumental seven-year labors of the privately-endowed Regional Plan Committee, but Chicago has had a Plan Commission, officially appointed and supported out of public funds, for nearly twenty years. The projects and achievements of this commission must have at least as much weight as the gang killings if we want a true picture of the spirit of Chicago. They are particularly significant to New Yorkers because of their frequent and striking contrasts with what is happening here.

The original Chicago plan, the grandfather of most city planning in America, came out of the World's Fair of 1893, and of the work of the late Daniel H. Burnham and his associates in laying out the buildings for the fair. The question was asked why cities should not be permanently as beautiful as the lath-and-plaster palaces had made the midway. Burnham set out to demonstrate that they could be. The actual lines that he laid down on the map have in many if not in most cases had to be changed.

Not foreseeing the tremendous increase in the uses of the automobile, he plotted a system of streets converging in the Loop—a system which if applied today would probably pile cars several layers deep at the main point of intersection. But he enunciated a policy which was possibly better than any detail of his proposals:

"Make no little plans; they have no magic to stir men's blood, and probably themselves will not be realized. Make big plans; aim high in hope and work, remembering that a noble, logical diagram once recorded will never die, but long after we are gone will be a living thing, asserting itself with growing intensity."

The table of city planning costs to date shows that Chicago took Burnham's advice at its face value. Since the Plan Commission began to function, in 1909, nearly $500,000,000 has been spent, publicly and privately, on projects which it has endorsed. Of this sum nearly $180,000,000 has been expended on street openings and improvements; $162,000,000 on railway terminals, of which the tale is not yet complete; $88,000,000 on lake-front improvements; $17,253,000 on forest parks, and $20,000,000 on a new postoffice. On the program, though funds are not yet authorized in every case, is a further expenditure of nearly $500,000,000. More than $180,000,000 will be spent on streets, $150,000,000 on railway terminals, $105,000,000 more on the lake front, $15,420,000 more on the forest parks and $20,000,000 on airports.

Nor is this total of almost $1,000,000,000, spent or destined to be spent, the last word in city planning for Chicago. New projects come up as old ones are completed. Perhaps more would be on the slate now if the bond issues which were to have helped the super-highway proposals through had not been defeated in the elections of last April. But these defeats reflected Chicago's distrust of the Thompson Administration, not its opposition to city planning. Under good Mayors and bad, the city's pride in the spectacular carries it steadily forward.

Its Street Planning.

Streets naturally come first in any city plan and Chicago's accomplishments and ambitions in this regard are of Roman magnificence. When the city plan was being prepared there were between 600 and 700 streets, of which only twenty-six were through highways. Except for the lake and the Chicago River, Chicago is not hemmed in by natural barriers as New York is. However, Chicago had grown in such a way as to produce a multitude of artificial barriers—a square mile of railroad yards on the south and southwest, the stockyards, markets, cemeteries and poor joinings where former villages, each with a separate street system, had been welded into the greater community. A map of Chicago with the obstructed areas indicated in black made the city look as though it had been having a bad case of smallpox.

Chicago set out to remove this difficulty on a scale for which there is as yet no parallel in the New York region. It planned, and has practically carried out, a twenty-six-mile boulevard running along the lake front for the whole length of the city. A bridge at the mouth of the Chicago River to join the South Parkway with the Lake Shore Drive is about all that is needed to complete the project, and this bridge has already been designed. The lake front itself has been extended by dredging and filling, and there are speedways and parks where once crept the shallow, muddy waters of Lake Michigan. In Grant Park, largely made by filling, there are monumental buildings, including the new Field Museum, the Stadium and the Shedd Aquarium, and here the new Illinois Central Terminal is to be built.

Michigan Avenue, the show street of Chicago, is the product of the Chicago plan. Incidentally the improvement of this thoroughfare showed a neat profit, for it cost $16,000,000 and increased property values by $100,000,000. A half-mile of Michigan Avenue is a two-deck street, with light traffic on the upper level and commercial traffic, street cars and east-and-west-bound vehicles on the lower level. Wacker Drive, completed in 1926, is also a two-deck street. It has already transformed what was a ramshackle and rundown river frontage into one of America's most imposing boulevards, and in the near future it will probably be carried further.

But what Chicago has done with its streets is not half so impressive as what it proposes to do. The projected super-highway system takes one's breath away, unless one is accustomed to thinking in terms of millions of dollars and vast changes in ways of doing things. The super-highways of the Chicago plan are to be elevated roads, substantially and beautifully built, approached by ramps, and wide enough to carry ten or twelve lines of traffic. The speed on such highways will be limited only by the saturation point of the roadbed. There will be no cross traffic.

The Super-Highways.

Of these super-highways five are on the official program and will undoubtedly be built. Construction on one, the Avondale, would already have been started had it not been for the political setback of last April. The system would begin with a new Loop—a super-highway loop around the downtown district. From this would branch a super-highway north along the lake shore, another northwest along Avondale Avenue, another almost due west along Monroe, Congress or Polk Street, a fourth almost due south along South Park and Indiana Avenues, and a fifth southeast along the lake shore. A sixth super-highway running southwest has been suggested

The cost of these thoroughfares will run far over the $180,000,000 mentioned for future street improvements. But this is Chicago's answer to the problem of street congestion. It is, for several reasons, a different answer from New York's. A super-highway is really a railroad, something like those early railroads in our history upon which it was proposed that each customer should furnished his own rolling stock and motive power. The super-highway therefore takes the place of an equivalent amount of rapid transit. It is an individualistic city's substitute for the additional elevated railroads which might be built at about the same cost, or for the subways which could not be constructed through Chicago's mud and sand without enormous difficulty.

No street plan means much without the study and control of the vehicles which run through it. Three years ago the Chicago Association of Commerce made a very thorough traffic survey, some of the lessons of which have already been applied to traffic regulation. But Chicago's system of regulation differs from that of New York in one very important respect. It is administered by the Commissioner of Police, but not dictated by him.

Chicago traffic control is based largely on the recommendations made at the Hoover conference in Washington. Since January, 1928, parking has been prohibited within the Loop district between 7 A. M. and 6:30 P. M. This is construed to mean that a passenger car may have three minutes in which to load or unload and a truck not more than thirty minutes. Left-hand turns are prohibited at most points within the Loop and at sixteen or more congested outlying points. The effect of these restrictions has been to increase rather than diminish the number of cars entering the Loop district. In May, 1926, before the no-parking ordinance went into effect, the total was 92,425 on an average day. On the same day in May, 1928, the total was 109,374.

But Chicago traffic regulation is never dogmatic and never takes anything for granted. Traffic counts and studies at selected street intersections are continually being made. No attempt has been made and none probably will be to fit the whole city or any considerable part of it into a synchronized traffic-light system. The light cycle—the interval from one green flash to another—varies from fifty to seventy-five seconds according to conditions. "We figure in seconds," explains Deputy Commissioner Sorenson. "We clip a second here or add one there whenever we think it will do any good."

The super-highways, if built soon enough, will perhaps save Chicago from the almost hopeless tangle which threatens New York. And besides the super-highways there are other improvements which will relieve the situation. One of them is the straightening of the Chicago River, which was begun in 1926 and is still going forward. This will make it possible to open several new through streets between Polk and Eighteenth Streets.

As yet Chicago has not had to think of high buildings in terms of street congestion, and no ordinances have been aimed, even obliquely, at new towers of Babel. Indeed, the effect of the city's building ordinances has been to encourage towers in contrast to the setback which has become so familiar a feature of the urban skyline of New York.

If present appearances mean anything, Chicago is on the way to becoming, in its show streets, its parks, its skyscrapers and its public buildings, one of the most imposing cities of the modern world. In its vistas and its monumental quality it is undoubtedly outdoing New York. Like ancient Rome, it is making itself a splendid stage for festivals and parades. The defect in its city planning, as some observers see it, is that so far it has done comparatively little to provide adequate housing for the millions of its population, present and to come. In that respect, also, it may bear a certain resemblance to ancient Rome. In contrast, such city planning, public or private, as has been done in the New York region has laid much emphasis upon housing.

If the two cities are to be compared as stage settings, however, there is no doubt that New York must look to its laurels. Unless the greater metropolis awakes to its opportunities, the ruins of Chicago 2,000 or 3,000 years hence may attract more pilgrims than those of Manhattan.

March 10, 1929

MAYOR SIGNS BILL FOR CITY PLANNING

Major Sullivan Will Head New Department to Advise Boards on Changes in Map of City.

After a brief statutory public hearing at City Hall yesterday at which the Citizens Union was the only organization registering opposition, Mayor Walker signed his bill creating a department of city planning. He will appoint Major John F. Sullivan, his engineering adviser, to head the new department. The appointment is expected this week.

R. McGahen of the Citizens Union said his organization was opposed to the bill because the functions it created were not sufficiently adequate. The bill gives the new department advisory powers but does not authorize it to initiate any public improvements. The Citizens Union stood ready to aid the new department in any way possible, Mr. McGahen said, and would help in getting legislation at Albany that would give the city planning department more power.

The Real Estate Board of New York, the United Real Estate Owners, the First Avenue Association and the Regional Plan Association went on record in favor of the bill. Mayor Walker then signed it. Though the bill becomes effective immediately, the new department will not begin to function until the Board of Estimate and Board of Aldermen pass an appropriation for its work.

Major Sullivan receives $12,000 a year in his present position. The salary will be increased to $15,000 on Sept. 1 in accordance with the recent increases voted to high city officials. His appointment will be made effective Sept. 1 for the new position and the position of engineering adviser to the Mayor will then be abolished. Major Sullivan will probably receive $17,500 a year as City Planning Commissioner. He appoints his own secretary under the terms of the bill.

When the city planning bill passed the Board of Estimate branch of the Municipal Assembly by four votes, Borough President Lynch of Richmond was the only one of the five Borough Presidents voting in its favor. The others opposed it on the ground that it would invade their rights to initiate and carry out public improvements. In the Board of Aldermen, Alderman Peter J. McGuinness of Greenpoint cast the only dissenting vote.

The new law authorizes the City Planning Commissioner to construct a topographical model of the city, indicating streets, highways, street grades, public places, bridges, tunnels and their approaches, viaducts, parks, parkways, playgrounds, public markets, public buildings and structures, building zone districts, piers and docks, pierhead and bulkhead lines, waterways, ferry slips and railroads. The commissioner is also to prepare a master plan of the city and coordinate it with plans for the improvement of areas adjacent to the city. He will advise city boards and departments on matters related to city planning upon request. The Board of Estimate will receive reports from the new department before making changes in the map or plan of the city.

July 18, 1930

CITIES THEN AND NOW.

The American City, a monthly magazine ably edited by Mr. HAROLD S. BUTTENHEIM, is celebrating its coming of age. The first number appeared twenty-one years ago this month. The current number is devoted to a review of municipal progress during that time. In more than one respect 1909 did mark the beginning of an epoch. The first national conference on city planning was held in Washington that year. The Massachusetts Legislature having divided Boston into two districts, in one of which buildings were limited to a height of 125 feet and in the other to 80 feet, the United States Supreme Court on May 17, 1909, in the now famous case of WELCH v. SWASEY, declared that this was lawful. In the same year the city of Los Angeles, under a home-rule charter, divided itself into residential and industrial districts, ousted a brickyard from a residence district, and was upheld by the Supreme Court in the Hadacheck case. "No one "sensed the fact that these decisions be-"tokened a new science," Mr. EDWARD M. BASSETT writes in an article covering the great strides since made in zoning, "not any more than that the flying of "the Wright brothers at Kitty Hawk "betokened the birth of the science of "aviation."

Mr. BUTTENHEIM regards city planning and zoning as "perhaps the most significant current movement" in the whole municipal field. Of course, there have been a host of other developments during the two decades. The trained administrator is replacing the ward heeler in many city departments. In some cities—alas! not in New York—the budget system has come into full flower as a means of controlling expenditures. The automobile, that giant just beginning to stretch his limbs in 1909, has brought a demand for better street and highway paving. "This is easier to clean, and "great strides have been made in munic-"ipal housekeeping, including not only "the collection of municipal wastes of all "kinds, but their economical and sani-"tary disposal." Again, unfortunately, New York must push aside the crown. Tucked away in a corner of the magazine there is a picture of scows dumping garbage at sea off Sandy Hook. It was taken in 1910, but it would go for 1930.

Cities have reached out further, and most skilfully, for water supplies, have wrestled—rather feebly—with the housing problem, have given thought to recreational needs. Where there has been an advance, The American City itself has often been found in the lead. But its editor is probably right in dwelling on planning as fundamental to every other improvement. He believes that in the future it calls for bolder handling, "with "much greater emphasis on spaciousness "of development and on departure from "horse-drawn tradition in street and "highway design." This idea underlies our own Regional Plan, though it is still largely on paper—and not official paper at that. The old goal of the "city beautiful" is not inclusive enough. The engineer, the economist, the social worker, the city planner and the architect must work hand in hand.

September 14, 1930

THE DEPRESSION

CITIES SPEND MORE THAN THEIR INCOME

Average Indebtedness Increased $5.56 Per Capita in 261 of Them in 1922.

WASHINGTON, Dec. 28 (Associated Press).—The cities of the country generally—there are exceptions—are not living within their incomes, it is indicated in Census Bureau statistics announced today.

In the fiscal year 1922 in 261 cities having a population of 30,000 or more a total indebtedness was incurred amounting to $5.56 for each resident. The cost of government per capita, including expenditures for permanent improvements, amounted to $57.38 for the year, against revenues of $51.81, the total figures being $2,222,566,519 and $2,007,008,796, respectively.

The total net indebtedness at the close of the year was $3,618,967,272, or $93.42 per capita.

The total cost of government in 1922 was at its highest in the cities having a population of 500 000 or more, with a per capita cost of $66.88. The next highest per capita cost, $64.29, is shown for cities with a population of 300,000 to 500,000. The per capita expenses of cities from 100,000 to 300,000 amounted to $48.71; of cities from 50,000 to 100,000, $44.94, and in the small cities having a population of 30,000 to 50,000, $44.38.

Comparable statistics for 199 of the principal cities show the per capita cost of government has increased from $34.68 in 1918 to $58.07 in 1922.

Of the cost of city government the per capita burden for maintenance and operation of general departments was the principal item and amounted to $33.15. The per capita cost of permanent improvements was $15.95.

New York came through the year with a surplus of revenues of $3.28 per capita over expenditures, but the per capita net indebtedness amounted to $182.72. Chicago's revenues lacked $3.36 per capita of meeting her expenditures, but her net indebtedness amounts to only $46.36 per capita. Philadelphia, third largest city, ended the year with a per capita deficit of $9.95 and a per capita net indebtedness of $103.38.

Among cities with a population of 100,000 or more Seattle had the highest per capita revenue receipts, amounting to $93.85; Boston was second with $80.55, Los Angeles third with $79.81, and New York fourth with $69.94. The four cities with lowest per capita revenues were: Birmingham, $25.38; Reading, $26.13; San Antonio, $26.20, and Nashville, $28.01.

The highest per capita cost of government was in Detroit, where it was $120.30. Seattle was second with $110.71, and Los Angeles third with $99.34. In all of these cities large outlays for permanent improvements were made in the year. The four cities with lowest per capita costs were: San Antonio, $25.65; Birmingham, $28.95; Scranton, $29.03, and Reading, $32.79.

Detroit showed the largest per capita deficit, with $54.77. Norfolk was next with $49.62, Rochester third with $19.10 and Youngstown, Ohio, fourth with $18.05.

St. Louis had the largest per capita surplus, with $4.86. Spokane had $4.61, Boston $4.21 and Cincinnati $3.43.

December 29, 1923

BIG JUMP IN COST OF CITY PROTECTION

New York's Total of $59,976,575 in 1915 Nearly Doubled in Ten Years.

ALL DEPARTMENTS DEARER

Cost of Municipal Courts $4,048,210, Almost Half That for These Courts in Entire Country.

Special to The New York Times.

WASHINGTON, Feb. 19.—Protection of life and property in New York City cost $59,976,575 in 1925, or nearly double the cost in 1915, when the total was $30,256,167, according to statistics just completed by the Census Bureau.

This is one of the outstanding features of an analysis of financial affairs of the city, which shows that the cost of all general departments in 1925 was $265,464,730, or $50.27 per capita, as compared with $133,735,972, or $25.07 per capita in 1915. For the larger cities this increase is exceeded only by Boston, for which the per capita was $58.55 in 1925 as compared with $30.60 in 1915.

Chicago's general departments increased from a per capita cost of $19.76 in 1915 to $40.16 in 1925; Philadelphia from $20.30 to $38.09, Detroit from $21.99 to $39.71, St. Louis from $19.55 to $34.38, Cleveland from $17.31 to $30.68, Baltimore from $16.96 to $31.53 and Pittsburgh from $22.76 to $47.45.

Cost of Courts Doubled.

The cost of municipal and Superior Courts in New York City in 1925 was twice that of ten years before. Municipal Courts, in which criminal actions were tried almost entirely, required in 1925 a total of $4,048,210 as against $2,409,062 in 1915. All the municipal courts in the United States cost $8,779,739 in 1925, showing that those of New York City represented almost one-half the total for the entire country.

The 1925 cost of municipal courts in Chicago was $1,180,294 and in Philadelphia, $1,028,454. The courts in the three largest cities for the trial of criminal cases cost more, therefore, than all the other cities combined.

Superior courts in New York City cost $7,194,321 in 1925, contrasted with $4,380,109 in 1915. For the United States the total expenditure of these courts was $19,729,901 for the same years.

While the increase in court costs has been generally attributed to prohibition enforcement and the postwar backwash, census statistics gave no reasons for them.

Of New York City's expenditure for protection of life and property in 1925 $34,712,587 was for the Police Department. This cost $15,869,755 in 1915.

The Fire Department, not including $202,143 for water service, cost a total of $19,282,236 in 1925, as against $10,128,393 in 1915.

Other costs of protection in 1925 and 1915 included:

Militia and armories, $1,604,714 and $868,132; register of deeds and mortgages, $1,012,791 and $575,987; inspection for buildings, weights and measures, boilers and other things, $2,483,980 and $1,707,426.

The per capita cost of $5.67 for protection in New York City was second only to Boston, for the cities of the country having more than 500,000 population. Boston, Baltimore and Detroit paid more per capita for fire protection than New York, where the ratio was $3.11.

Table of Comparative Costs.

Comparisons of costs for "protection" in 1925 and 1915 are shown in this table:

Cities.	Police. 1925	Police. 1915.	Fire. 1925	Fire. 1915.	All Other. 1925	All Other. 1915.
New York...	$5.67	$2.98	$3.11	$1.73	$0.92	$0.63
Chicago	4.89	2.92	2.11	1.38	.86	.48
Philadelphia..	5.05	2.68	2.15	.91	.77	.48
St. Louis....	5.14	2.90	2.45	1.65	.74	.44
Boston	5.96	3.47	4.62	2.45	.97	.48
Cleveland ...	3.41	1.59	2.62	1.32	.38	.21
Baltimore ...	4.31	2.20	3.44	1.72	.29	.20
Pittsburgh ..	3.57	1.78	3.00	1.82	1.07	.71
Detroit	5.28	2.67	3.30	1.94	.55	.31

The per capita police costs were much larger in some of the smaller cities. Atlantic City, which has a large transient population, had a per capita cost in 1925 of $10.76. In Jersey City the cost was $8.44 and Hoboken $6.97.

"General Government" in New York City, which includes the courts already referred to, cost a total of $30,506,488 in 1925, as compared with $18,348,710 in 1915. This heading covers such expenditures as Board of Aldermen, Mayor's office and other administrative branches.

Holding elections in 1925 cost $1,763,872, not including $16,025 for new booths. This was one of the few items where the cost varied little from ten years ago, for, in 1915, elections cost $1,513,746.

One item, because of its smallness, has attracted attention of census officials to such an extent that they are making a special inquiry. Only $4,000 apparently was spent in 1925 for medical work among school children.

Conservation of health cost $5,117,815 for administration and $138,417 for permanent outlay. For "sanitation or promotion of cleanliness" there was an expenditure of $26,547,487 for administration and $11,776,497 as a permanent outlay. Street cleaning cost $25,307,193.

Highways cost a total of $52,832,182, of which $29,203,770 was in the nature of a permanent outlay. Removal of snow and ice cost $5,625,176 in 1925. Charities, hospitals and corrections cost $22,800,000; education, $151,000,000; recreation, including parks and trees, $19,000,000.

February 20, 1927

LONG-TERM BONDS AS AIDS TO CITIES

Results of Proper Financial Planning for Public Improvements Analyzed.

ST. LOUIS GIVES EXAMPLE

Popular Demands for Increased Service and Decreased Taxes Present Problems.

The advantages of long-term planning in municipal borrowing in determining far in advance the relation between capital expenditures and the reasonable ability of taxpayers to meet the costs is set forth in an analysis made by C. E. Rightor, chief accountant of the Detroit Bureau of Governmental Research, Inc., and Secretary of the Mayor's Committee on Finance. The problem, it is pointed out, is that of two conflicting popular demands: one, for more and better service and physical facilities, the other for relief from taxation and the costs of government.

The city budget, Mr. Rightor is careful to point out, does not offer the solution. The budget, after all, is merely a statement of the public services to be undertaken by the city, their cost and the means of financing them. The funds are to be raised by taxation, and the taxpayers are interested, primarily, in knowing how much they must pay.

"Such budgets do not usually extend beyond a year, and properly so," Mr. Rightor says. "They may, and often do, include such portion of public improvements as the officials plan during the year. But they do not, ordinarily, include the major improvement projects which will require several years for completion. In some cases, if such long-term improvement has received an approving vote of the people, the annual budget ignores any recognition of it.

In general, one result of this budget practice may be substantial fluctuations in the tax rate from year to year, dependent upon the extent of capital projects included. Improvements are generally not of a recurring nature, as are operating costs. And there may be a demand for several projects one year and none the next. The cost of performing ordinary governmental activities in any city is usually financed from taxes, and it may be assumed that their cost would not be so large as to prove burdensome to property owners. But the expense of extending permanent public improvements into outlying territory, if similarly financed, might result in a prohibitive tax rate, as valuations usually follow rather than precede the installation of improvements. The city thus finds it necessary to finance such improvements by loans, which, of course, are gradually repaid out of taxes, and possibly other revenues, during a period of years."

The solution of this problem, Mr. Rightor shows, is through long-term financing. This method requires that every improvement be considered in relation to its necessity to the community. The first city program for general improvements over a period of years to be adopted at the polls was that of St. Louis, in 1923. The program included twenty-one separate projects, for a total value of $88,272,500, to be financed by bonds, and the expenditures to be made during the ensuing ten to fifteen years.

The issue of $7,861,000 City of St. Louis bonds marketed this week represents a portion of this authorization. The original program did not include transportation, which is not a municipal function. More recently the city has prepared a transportation program involving approximately $130,000,000 for rerouting and street car extensions.

Mr. Rightor in conclusion points out that "the preparation of the long-term program, involving as it does varied public improvements and the means of financing them, requires an exact knowledge by the committee, not alone of the city's actual financial status, but also consideration of its general financial policies and economic conditions.

October 1, 1927

Roosevelt Fights R. F. C. Loans to Cities; For Aid by States or by Bankruptcy Law

Special to THE NEW YORK TIMES.

WASHINGTON, May 31.—President Roosevelt is opposed to large loans by the Federal Government to cities to help them sustain their financial structure and meet maturing obligations.

The subject was brought to the attention of the President by Mayors of a group of cities who urged last week that the Reconstruction Finance Corporation Act should be amended to permit the government to grant loans to cities in difficulties.

The President feels that if such a policy were pursued politics in the cities would come under control of the Federal Government, and this would lead to trouble. The Mayors got no encouragement at the White House and took their troubles to Congress.

It is the President's opinion that the States should afford aid to the cities. Recognizing the gravity of the problems facing many of them, however, the President feels that they should be helped by an extension of the bankruptcy laws.

An extension of the laws to apply to cities the same as to railroads, it is argued, would permit them to go into a Federal District Court and get permission to reorganize their financial structure with the approval of a majority of their creditors.

President Roosevelt, it is said, will not go beyond an extension of the bankruptcy laws in proffering aid. He has so informed members of Congress, with indications that such legislation may be passed before Congress adjourns.

June 1, 1933

ECONOMY MEASURES EFFECTED IN TWELVE AMERICAN CITIES

A Survey Reveals That They Include Salary Cuts, Curtailment of Construction and a Reorganization for Efficiency

WHILE New York City has been debating ways and means of reducing its expenses and thus attaining a balanced budget, other important municipalities have put into effect various measures of economy. They have found their receipts considerably lower this year, owing to a reduced tax levy and to other factors, and have planned their expenditures accordingly.

In most of them the first economy undertaken was a reduction in municipal salaries, followed by the abandonment or curtailment of construction and improvements, and consolidation of departments with the subsequent dropping of personnel. It has been pointed out that in New York a general reduction in salaries could not be accomplished without a mandate from the Legislature, since the salaries of certain large groups of municipal employes are fixed by law.

In its study of the New York City budget, undertaken with a view to reducing municipal expenses to meet lower revenues, the Citizens' Budget Committee, of which Peter Grimm is chairman, communicated with the finance officials of a number of large cities, to find out what steps they had already taken. Answers received bore a striking similarity in regard to achievements and plans for the future, while a few made observations somewhat out of the ordinary. The Controller of Atlanta, Ga., for instance, remarked that "the great trouble, as I see it, is that the average taxpayer wants his taxes reduced but does not want the services of the city curtailed in any way." Milwaukee proudly states that "our city has only begun to feel the effects of the depression, but none the less we have seen the troubles of other cities and have planned accordingly."

How twelve American cities have dealt with the crisis is shown in the following:

BOSTON.

Boston has made a thoroughgoing job of reducing its expenses. A system of voluntary contributions out of salary by all municipal employes has been in effect since last November. Money thus realized has been paid into "The Unemployment Relief Fund," and has been used by the Public Welfare Department in alleviating distress. So far contributions have amounted to one day's pay per month, but this is to be increased. Overtime pay for city employes has been eliminated, and the hiring of temporary help cut down to a minimum.

Curtailment or abolition of services formerly performed by the city has brought savings. Practically all municipal automobiles have been sold and automobile service that is absolutely essential is obtained by hiring cars on a mileage basis. Ice-cooling of water in city offices has been abolished. Traffic lights are darkened between 12 midnight and 7 A. M. Resident telephones of officials and city employes, formerly paid for by the municipality, have been discontinued.

When vacancies occur in the various departments, they are left unfilled unless replacement is absolutely essential. Ordinary repairs to public property and buildings have been reduced where possible. City departments have combined in a bulk purchasing scheme to secure the lowest prices for supplies and large printing bills have been brought under rigid control. Attendance of city officials at conventions, at city expense, has been practically eliminated.

PHILADELPHIA.

Here a 10 per cent reduction in the basic wage of city employes has been effected and in several departments the workers take vacations without pay of from two to eight weeks. The number of employes had been cut from 25,825 in December, 1931, to 23,099 in June, 1932. Other current expense items have been cut about 30 per cent.

The city has retired all short-term loan obligations amounting to $8,000,000, carried over from 1931, as well as temporary loans issued in anticipation of cash receipts during 1932, totaling $3,500,000.

Expenditures from loan funds for permanent improvements have been cut about two-thirds, while existing contracts for improvements have been rescinded.

ATLANTA.

Some time ago a group of prominent citizens formed "The Taxpayers' League," which has been active in pointing the way to reduce the city's expenses. At the first of the year, every Atlanta employe, from Mayor to janitor, received a 10 per cent salary cut, while the school teachers suffered a 16 per cent reduction. In addition, all employes are obliged to take a two weeks' vacattion without pay. The municipal personnel has been considerably reduced.

The Atlanta Government determined that each department must keep its expenditures within its budget appropriation, and to this end passed a law that only one-twelfth of the year's allotment could be spent in any month.

Construction work has been practically abandoned.

It is estimated that the salary cuts, personnel reduction and other economies will effect a saving of about $1,000,000.

CLEVELAND.

Here salaries have been considerably reduced, ordinary city employes, including policemen and firemen, receiving 10 per cent less than last year. The salaries of superintendents of departments have been cut, in some cases, as much as 40 per cent. The salaried employes under the Mayor's jurisdiction suffer, in addition, a reduction equal to half a month's pay.

Unnecessary positions have been abolished and 100 employes drawing from $1,500 to $3,800 a year have been dropped.

The buying of supplies has been curtailed; for instance, purchases in June of this year amounted to only $120,000,000, as against $243,000,000 for the same month of 1931.

PITTSBURGH.

Taxes in this city have been reduced, and to meet this decrease in receipts and estimated revenues, and to balance the budget for 1932—which is $3,600,538 less than that of 1931—many positions were abolished, salaries were reduced and enforced vacations of a month without pay for all municipal employes was ordered. Other budget items, as regards supplies and all city activities, were curtailed wherever possible.

On Aug. 1, 1932, it was discovered that estimated receipts for 1932 were running 6 per cent behind schedule, and to meet this situation further reductions in salaries and expenses were ordered.

CHICAGO.

Owing to a large decrease in estimated revenues for the present year Chicago has put into effect departmental reorganizations combining the functions of the various bureaus, and has reduced its municipal personnel considerably. The sums ordinarily spent for construction and improvements have been greatly curtailed.

Salaries are being paid on the basis of the 1931 level less a deduction of seventy-eight days' pay for ordinary city employes, forty-eight days' pay for employes of the municipal court, twenty days for school teachers and one month for school employes.

BALTIMORE.

Municipal employes are required to contribute to the city certain amounts from the 1932 salaries, in proportion to the pay they receive. Salaries of from $1,200 to $1,499 are thus taxed $50; from $1,500 to $1,799, $100; from $3,000 to $3,499, $300; from $5,000 to $5,499, $500, and from $8,000 to $8,499, $800. Those receiving salaries above $8,500 are obliged to contribute 10 per cent of their salaries, while the Mayor is taxed 12½ per cent. Employes of the Department of Education, with the exception of minor workers receiving less than $1,140 a year, must contribute 6⅓ per cent of their salaries.

Members of the Police Department have volunteered to contribute 10 per cent of their 1933 salaries. City officials believe that the same reduction, or a larger one, will be necessary next year.

LOS ANGELES.

Los Angeles has put into effect a five-day week for city employes, with a general cut of 10 per cent in salaries. Some personnel has been dropped and expenses for equipment and construction has been cut to the bone. The assessments on real property and improvements have been reduced about 20 per cent, which amounts to between $300,000,000 and $400,000,000.

ST. LOUIS.

This city has made a large reduction in the assessed valuation of its real property and has cut its expenses accordingly. Thus it spent $22,681,807 in the fiscal year ended April 1, 1932, while its estimated expenditures for the current fiscal year are put at $19,150,151. To meet this situation salaries of municipal employes were cut 10 per cent and money spent for improvements reduced.

PORTLAND, ORE.

Salary cuts have been resorted to in this city. School teachers have accepted a 20 per cent reduction from Sept. 6, 1932. Other city employes voluntarily agreed to pay for relief one day's pay a month from Oct. 1, 1931, to April 1, 1932, and on June 1 accepted further salary cuts.

MILWAUKEE.

Although Milwaukee has suffered little from the depression, it has nevertheless effected some reduction in the budget and the tax rate, has reduced assessed valuations and eliminated many bond-financed projects. The bonded debt has been decreased by about $3,000,000. City employes voluntarily accepted a 10 per cent salary cut, to operate from Aug. 1, and the working hours are reduced wherever possible. The school teachers are expected to take action in regard to a salary reduction soon.

JERSEY CITY.

All persons receiving compensation from the city, including officials, judges, school teachers, firemen and policemen, in fact, all municipal employes, have voluntarily authorized a deduction from their salaries. Those receiving up to and including $4,000 are cut 10 per cent; those drawing over $4,000 are cut 20 per cent.

All positions becoming vacant remain unfilled unless replacement is absolutely necessary for the functioning of the department in question.

Up-State Municipalities.

In addition to the reports from the above municipalities, cities of up-State New York recorded various economies which, for the most part, took the form of salary cuts. In Elmira, policemen and firemen suffered a 12½ per cent salary reduction, while department heads lost from 10 to 30 per cent. Syracuse ordered a donation of 10 per cent from all employes earning more than $1,200. Rochester employes agreed to salary reductions ranging from 4 to 10 per cent. In Albany, a voluntary reduction of [illegible] per cent was agreed on.

August 28, 1932

PHILADELPHIA FAILS TO PAY

City and County Employes Go Without $1,400,000 Salaries.

Special to THE NEW YORK TIMES.

PHILADELPHIA, Nov. 15.—Pay day arrived today for the 23,000 employes of Philadelphia city and county, but there was no money on hand to met the semimonthly payroll of about $1,400,000.

Controller Will B. Hadley, at a conference with Mayor J. Hampton Moore and City Solicitor David J. Smyth, reported that practically every dollar being collected from taxes was reserved for payment on city debt charges due on Dec. 31.

It was expected that a bank loan of $1,500,000, payable before the end of the year, would be negotiated tomorrow to meet salary needs. Similar action was taken two weeks ago, but because of the big shortage estimated in tax receipts by the end of the year city officials have been hesitant of incurring new obligations.

November 16, 1932

FUNDS READY FOR CHICAGO.

Bankers Prepared to Lend Money to Meet Jan. 1 Maturities.

Special to THE NEW YORK TIMES.

CHICAGO, Dec. 9.—Following Mayor Cermak's conference with Eastern financiers, it was learned here tonight that Chicago banks, possibly with the aid of New York institutions, are ready to advance money for the $23,489,190 in bond and interest maturities which the city and school board must meet the first of the year.

Furthermore, the banks are willing to buy enough tax warrants to give every city and school employe a Christmas pay check. The pay checks will certainly be for two weeks and may be for a month.

The city employes and those of the municipal tuberculosis sanitarium have been paid up to Aug. 15. School employes have had only a month's pay since the schools opened in September.

December 10, 1932

SEE AID FOR DETROIT FROM BANK PARLEY

Conferees End Long Session Here—Hope of Financing for City Expressed.

The conference between Detroit industrialists and bankers and New York bankers on the finances of the city of Detroit, which began on Friday morning and was concluded yesterday afternoon, led to the hopeful expression that the city's $5,000,000 bond and interest payments due on Jaan. 1, Jan. 15 and Feb. 1 next would be met promptly. B. E. Hutchinson, vice president and treasurer of the Chrysler Corporation, acted as chairman for the Detroit group.

Advices from Detroit yesterday said a quorum was expected at the special session of the State Legislature called for Tuesday to act on authorizing an issue of $20,000,000 Detroit tax-anticipation bonds due in from one to four years. Some doubt had been entertained previously concerning the attendance of sufficient legislators to form a quorum because many were defeated for re-election on Nov. 8.

All or most of the bonds are expected to be taken by Detroit taxpayers, who may use them for tax payments in lieu of cash. Many large enterprises in Detroit have been helping the city by paying their taxes in advance. New York and Chicago banks have extended aid to the city through short-term loans of about $15,000,000, which have been renewed periodically. Detroit banks have subscribed to approximately $11,000,000.

Detroit, according to comparative tax rates of leading cities of the United States compiled by C. E. Rightor, Controller of Detroit, has a total tax rate of $35.21 per $1,000 of assessed valuation, which is lower than that of Chicago, Los Angeles, Boston, Pittsburgh or San Francisco, all of which are among the thirteen cities of the United States that have populations of 500,000 or more. The legal basis for Detroit's tax rate is apportioned as follows: City, $20.15; school, $7.28; county, $4.35; State, $3.43.

The city's taxes are collected semiannually, July 15 and Dec. 31. The fiscal year begins on July 1. Assessed valuation for 1932 is officially reported as $2,648,326,070, with realty 80 per cent and personal property 20 per cent of the total.

Detroit, which ranks as the fourth largest city in the United States in both population and assessed valuation, has been active for months in effecting economies. Owing to its rapid growth, it embarked on extensive programs of municipal improvements, which were encouraged by the taxpayers when times were prosperous. Now tax collections are slow, so that it has become necessary to study ways and means of assisting the city in dealing with its temporary difficulties.

No formal statement was issued yesterday on behalf of the interested New York bankers, but it was believed that the financiers stood ready to cooperate with the Detroit taxpayers in aiding the city.

December 25, 1932

MAYORS PETITION CONGRESS FOR AID

They Warn of Wide Defaults Unless Federal Help Is Speedily Authorized.

Special to THE NEW YORK TIMES.

WASHINGTON, May 25.—The plea of the Mayors of fifty large cities for legislation providing for Federal loans and for municipal participation in the construction program contained in the public works section of the National Industrial Recovery Bill, was carried to Congress today when a petition was presented to Vice President Garner and Speaker Rainey.

In the Senate, where reading of the petition was asked by Senator La Follette, Senator Copeland supported the Mayors, declaring they had called attention to a serious condition.

"There has not been very hearty cooperation on the part of the banks," he said, "although we have gone to great lengths to assist the banks."

Senator Harrison, chairman of the Finance Committee, invited the Mayors' committee to appear before his committee tomorrow to state the case.

Three Plans Proposed.

At that time, according to Paul Betters, secretary to the Mayors' conference, amendments to the Reconstruction Finance Corporation Act and the National Recovery Bill along the following lines will be presented:

1. That the Reconstruction Finance Corporation be authorized to purchase tax anticipation warrants of the municipalities.
2. That the grants of Federal funds for construction work by municipalities, approved by the President, be increased from the present maximum of 30 per cent of the total.
3. That the Federal Administrator of Public Works to be named under the National Recovery Act be authorized to provide for advances of Federal funds for the remaining percentage of the cost on bonds of the municipalities, and that no amortization or interest charges be made payable until Jan. 1, 1936.

Of the $3,300,000,000 set aside under the National Recovery Bill for a construction program, it has been estimated that about $1,000,000,000 would be devoted over a two-year period to Federal construction, and the remainder to such State and municipal projects as received approval from the Federal Administrator.

According to officials, no definite program has been worked out as to just how the funds shall be apportioned, but the theory has been that by sanctioning certain types of work which would give employment quickly and by putting up around 30 per cent of the funds necessary, the Federal Government would put municipalities in a position to market bonds for the remainder.

Petition Warns of Defaults.

The petition stated that a "grave crisis" threatened the very foundation of all credit in the United States and that municipal credit, because of the inability of citizens to pay taxes and because no market existed for tax certificates, permitted of no further borrowing. So far, it added, more than 1,000 local units had defaulted on their bonds.

"We have in many cities already cut our police and fire service and crippled our schools," the petition declared. "Within a relatively short time a large additional number of cities will be forced to default on their bonds for the first time in history.

"The Reconstruction Finance Corporation is designed to loan money to private corporations except only for partly or wholly self-liquidating projects that are so few as to be inconsequential.

"We assert that if Congress will do for municipal corporations what you have done and are doing for private corporations we will need to ask no other consideration. The advancement of not to exceed $1,000,000,000 a year for not to exceed two years will meet all our needs.

"We therefore recommend that the Reconstruction Finance Corporation Act be amended at this session to authorize the purchase of or loans upon tax anticipation or tax delinquency certificates or notes of municipalities and public bodies, issuing the same in the ratio of 75 per cent of the 1933 or current taxes and 50 per cent of past due outstanding taxes or delinquencies, and on such plans as State debt limitations will not be exceeded."

May 26, 1933

DETROIT DEBT PLAN READY

Michigan Commission Approves Refunding $368,000,000.

The plan of the city of Detroit, Mich., to refund approximately $368,000,000 of its outstanding bonds has been approved formally by the Michigan Public Debt Commission, bankers here were advised yesterday. The plan, designed to relieve the city of burdensome maturities during the next few years, was worked out last Spring by the city officials in cooperation with bankers here and in Chicago and Detroit.

The bondholders' committee, formed in July, is headed by B. A. Tompkins, vice president of the Bankers Trust Company of New York. The committee is accepting deposits of bonds through the following depositories: Bankers Trust Company, Chase National Bank, City Bank Farmers Trust Company and Detroit Trust Company, and the Michigan Trust Company of Grand Rapids, Mich.

September 24, 1933

BANKRUPTCY BILL SIGNED.

WASHINGTON, May 24 (AP).—President Roosevelt today signed into law a measure which grants bankruptcy relief to cities, and at the same time rounds into shape a debtor relief program that extends aid to virtually every type of debtor in the country.

One measure of the broad program that was started in 1933 remains to be completed by Congress. This is a Corporation Bankruptcy Bill which would extend relief similar to that which already has been granted individuals, farmers, railroads and municipalities.

In general, the plan allows these types of debtors to scale down their obligations with the consent of two-thirds of their creditors and Federal court approval.

Under the measure signed today, a little town or a metropolis may, with the consent of 51 per cent of the holders of its outstanding obligations, take a refinancing plan to the district court.

If the court finds it equitable and 75 per cent of the creditors then agree, the refinancing or scaling down of the municipality's debts may be carried out.

May 25, 1934

ROOSEVELT RAISES GRANTS TO CITIES FOR RELIEF WORK

Outright Bounty Is Increased to 45% of Allotments, Interest Is Cut to 3%.

Special to THE NEW YORK TIMES.

WASHINGTON, May 24.—An increase in outright Federal grants for public works projects from 30 to 45 per cent of allotments and a cut in interest rates on public works loans from 4 to 3 per cent were approved today by President Roosevelt in order to encourage cities to partake to the fullest extent in the $4,000,000,000 work relief program.

The President approved the plan assuring "cheap money" to cities after Mayor La Guardia had insisted at the meeting of the Advisory Committee on Allotments yesterday that cities could not undertake "self-liquidating" public works projects, which it had been stated must form the base work for the entire program, under the prevailing PWA arrangement of 30 per cent grants and 4 per cent interest charges on loans.

Relief officials had been worried that major cities of the country, where the unemployment problem centres, would be unable or unwilling to make applications for loans and grants, thus forcing the government to bear the entire cost of the vast program. Taking the 45 per cent grants into account, cities will, under the new arrangement, be enabled to obtain the entire sum required for needed public works projects at "the enticingly low rate" of slightly over 1¼ per cent.

Relief Wage Scale to Stand.

President Roosevelt made clear today that he would stand by the relief wage scale he has approved despite criticism of the $19-to-$94 monthly rate by labor leaders and others.

Asked at his press conference whether any adjustment of the relief wage scale was contemplated, the President replied that adjustments would be made only within the limitations prescribed in his Executive order establishing relief wages.

Coincidentally, Harry L. Hopkins, Works Progress Administrator, announced the geographical limitations of the 307 "work districts" into which the nation has been divided for administrative and operating purposes, and approval of "Federal" projects running into millions of dollars.

New York City, including Kings, Queens, the Bronx, Manhattan and Richmond, constituted one "work district," and there were twelve such districts established in New York State.

The difficulty of fixing upon a proper loan and grant basis for the $800,000,000 public works and the $450,000,000 low-cost housing portions of the work-relief program engrossed President Roosevelt and his advisers yesterday.

A plan calling for a 50 per cent outright grant and a 3 per cent interest rate was tentatively approved by the Allotment Committee yesterday and referred to the President, who is reported to have felt that this arrangement would be too costly to the government.

The agreement finally approved is understood to represent a compromise between the committee and the President.

It had been the belief of some relief officials that interest rates should be left at 4 per cent, thus encouraging cities to supplement grants with loans from private bankers. This system would have left some $200,000,000 to $300,000,000 more available for Federal Work Relief.

The danger that time would be lost in this process, and that unexpected difficulties between some cities and their bankers might tie up the program, is understood to have been largely responsible for shelving of this plan.

Mayor La Guardia had indicated that he would place supplemental public works loans with New York City bankers but had indicated that the lowest interest rates he could get on such loans from private bankers would be 3½ or 3 per cent. Since the Federal Government is offering 3 per cent rates, he is expected here to obtain most of his loans direct from the Public Works Administration.

Step to Aid Bankrupt Cities.

It was provided in the agreement approved by President Roosevelt that Secretary Ickes "after careful investigation of the financial condition of any applicant" may recommend to the advisory committee "a variation in the amount of the grant."

This step was taken, it is understood, to permit larger grants to some bankrupt cities. It is frankly admitted in an official statement that the loan and grant system was liberalized to make it "possible to loan more money instead of making 100 per cent Federal grants to achieve the reemployment objectives."

"Localities with plans completed for construction of schools, hospitals, water works, buildings, sewers and similar types of projects," the statement said, "thus would be encouraged to proceed with such reemploying construction at once."

In another statement explaining the basis on which the 307 "work districts" were established, Mr. Hopkins remarked:

"Each of the States, with the exception of four, have been divided into work districts to facilitate efficient and economical administration of the works program under the State Works Progress Administrators. Delaware, New Hampshire, Vermont and Rhode Island each constitute a single district.

"The districts comprise, in most instances, a group of counties within a State. None of the districts cross State lines. Chicago is a work district separate from Cook County. In some instances, single counties have been made separate work districts.

"Three chief considerations controlled the laying out of the work districts: The number of families on relief in a given area, quick and adequate transportation and communication, and economy and efficiency of central headquarters.

"Under the Work Progress Administration, State Works Progress Administrators will be responsible to Harry L. Hopkins, the Works Progress Administrator. In turn, the district works progress directors will be responsible to the State works progress administrators in their respective States. The works progress functions will be carried out in specific communities within the district by local works progress managers."

May 25, 1935

CITIES' FINANCES GREATLY IMPROVED

National Survey Reveals a Decided Betterment as Compared With Year Ago.

CREDIT RATINGS ADVANCED

Gains Reflect Business Recovery and Rise in Payrolls and Farm Income.

Reports from the leading cities of the country show a decided improvement in municipal finances compared with a year ago. Even those cities which have had a slower recovery are better off than they were, and their remaining difficulties to a large extent are attributed to the unusually heavy blows they suffered at the depth of the depression.

Cities which have adopted a pay-as-you-go policy in financing relief expenditures and have struggled to balance their budgets through economies and emergency tax levies appear to be setting the pace in the restoration of high credit rating and par values for municipal bonds.

Generally speaking, all cities have been materially helped back to financial stability by the nation-wide business recovery, together with the increase in cash farm income and workers' payrolls, all of which have been reflected in better tax collections from holders of city real estate, increases in other tax revenues and large payments of past-due taxes which were defaulted during the depression.

Curbs on political spending, such as the one imposed upon New York by the bankers' agreement also have helped restore strength to municipal finances in the cities where they have been exercised.

New York City is one of the most impregnable financially in the country, with its fiscal condition excellent, its credit rating higher than in years, and its bonds selling at par or better. Other cities which have shown especially marked improvement are San Francisco, Denver, Kansas City, Mo., and Baltimore.

Despite danger spots here and there, practically all cities look forward to an accelerated improvement in municipal finances during 1936, and they anticipate that continued business recovery will further increase tax collections and decrease relief loads. Naturally, uncertainties for the future exist which may cause a revision of municipal plans, especially with respect to the relief problem in the cities if the Federal government should abandon its work-relief program and turn all relief responsibilities back to the States and localities.

Following are the reports from individual cities:

NEW YORK CITY.

New York City starts the new year with its financial house in excellent order, with its credit rating higher than it has been in years.

In 1935 the city made the best financial record since predepression days. Tax collections, especially the all-important real estate levies, improved substantially as compared with 1934, the percentage of the 1935 levy uncollected at the end of the year being only 15.77 per cent, as compared with 21.22 per cent at the end of 1934. It was the best showing since 1930.

During the past year the financial rehabilitation of the city which followed the enactment of the bankers' agreement was more marked than in any other year. Controller Frank J. Taylor, the city's fiscal chief, working in close cooperation with Mayor La Guardia, so improved the city credit standing that in the latter months of the year the city was able to borrow short-term money in the open market at an interest rate of less than 1 per cent.

The funded debt of the city was reduced in 1935, the chief item being the retirement of a $52,000,000 issue of transit construction bonds. Controller Taylor also successfully carried through a refunding operation which will save the city $11,000,000 in interest charges over a term of years. In this operation he called in an issue of 4¼ per cent bonds and replaced them with 3½s.

The city's pay-as-you-go relief policy had much to do with the general credit improvement. Through its special relief taxes, notably the 2 per cent sales tax, expected to bring in at least $42,000,000, and its public utility tax which is figured to bring in $18,000,000, it has not only been able to pay its share of relief during the year but will probably have a small surplus for 1936 needs.

In all, including the relief taxes, the city took in $629,155,396 in 1935, as against $579,827,927 in 1934. Its share of various State taxes, such as the income and bank levies showed a substantial increase in 1935, an increase which local fiscal officers considered proof of general improvement in business.

Another move which improved the city financial picture was a substantial reduction in the city's outstanding short-term debt, consisting of revenue notes and bills sold under the bankers' agreement in anticipation of real estate tax collections. Substantial payments of realty taxes in arrears enabled the city to reduce the amount of these securities from $183,436,500 at the start of 1935 to $105,140,500 at its close. And of this sum an additional $39,987,000 will be redeemed this month.

PHILADELPHIA.

Special to THE NEW YORK TIMES.

PHILADELPHIA, Jan. 4.—This city ended 1935 with a budget deficit estimated $4,500,000, compared with $9,300,000 for 1934 and $11,500,000 for two years ago. Receipts from real estate and personal property taxes and water rents all exceeded the official estimates.

City officials were especially elated because, contrary to custom, it was unnecessary to use last-minute tax receipts and bank borrowings to meet interest requirements on the city's outstanding debt of $555,145,300 this week. There was enough cash on hand several days ahead to pay the $11,874,207 semi-annual interest.

The city has continued to follow Mayor J. Hampton Moore's avowed policy of reducing the debt instead of enlarging it through capital expenditures.

Philadelphia bonds are slightly higher than they were a year ago. The tax rate for 1936 has been cut 5 cents to $1.70 per $100 of assessed realty valuation, exclusive of school taxes.

There is little change in the numbers on Philadelphia's direct relief rolls from a year ago, although 20,000 cases have been removed since the start of WPA projects. The present total of 79,800 families, representing more than 235,000 persons, compares with the April all-time peak of 106,000 families.

BALTIMORE.

Special to THE NEW YORK TIMES.

BALTIMORE, Jan. 4.—The city starts 1936 with a surplus of $1,500,000 in its treasury. The sum represents savings and unspent moneys from the 1935 budget.

This record, made under Mayor Howard W. Jackson, was attained in spite of demands for relief.

A surplus of $400,000 remained in the city's treasury as of Dec. 31, 1934.

While the city found it necessary to increase the tax rate for 1936, assessments on thousands of homes and other real estate have been reduced. Reductions have been made in assessed value of real estate amounting to more than $11,000,000.

The budget for 1935 was fixed at $43,200,000, while the budget for 1936 is $44,796,000, an increase of $1,596,000. The tax rate per $100 on real estate for 1936 was fixed at $2.49, against $2.33 for 1935.

Relief expenditures during 1936 will be met by a gross receipts tax. This tax, which became effective April 1, 1935, already has produced $3,100,000. Proceeds are earmarked for relief and old-age pensions.

Mayor Jackson has maintained a pay-as-you-go policy.

BOSTON.

Special to THE NEW YORK TIMES.

BOSTON, Jan. 4.—Boston enters 1936 with the brightest financial outlook in several years. The city expects a budget reduction, less borrowing for maintenance, no increase in tax rate and a reduction in welfare disbursements.

The worst feature of the situation, about $23,000,000 in uncollected taxes, is somewhat offset by a definite improvement in tax collections in the past year.

Revenue both from the city and the State showed an increase in 1935; tax collections were 72 per cent of the total as against 70 in 1934; the funded debt of the city shows no increase despite borrowings for maintenance due to the fact that many heavy maturities were paid off during the year.

Welfare disbursements have declined sharply in recent weeks and further reductions are in prospect.

Tax refunds have been appreciably lower in the past year.

City authorities expect a budget of about $40,000,000 for 1936, as compared with $42,200,000 in 1925; continuance of the same tax rate, $3.07 per $100, and a welfare appropriation of about $12,000,000, as compared with $13,000,000 in 1935.

The city will be forced to continue borrowing for maintenance in 1936, but the amount raised in this manner will be about half that of 1935.

PITTSBURGH.

Special to THE NEW YORK TIMES.

PITTSBURGH, Jan. 4.—Municipal finances here are much improved. A year ago there was a heavy carryover of delinquent taxes. Today, through the operations of the new law which revokes all penalties on taxes unpaid before the year 1935, a heavy increase in payment has been noted.

At the start of 1935 the relief problem was a serious matter. Today more than 12,000 persons have been restored to employment rolls.

CLEVELAND.

Special to THE NEW YORK TIMES.

CLEVELAND, Jan. 4.—The city government faces the necessity in 1936 of asking voters to authorize a special tax levy to meet an operating deficit estimated from $4 000,000 to $8,000,000.

The city in 1935, under the administration of Mayor Harry L. Davis, faced an operating deficit of about $7,500,000 for the year and accumulated deficits and unpaid obligations from 1931, 1932, 1933 and 1934, years in which sketchy emergency financing was done.

The city chose to ask voters for a special tax levy of 4.4 mills, which raised about $5,333,000, and left an operating deficit of about $2,000,000. The other accumulated obligations were left for financing in 1936.

The new administration of Mayor Harold H. Burton, which took office in November, has not yet announced its financial program, but it is certain there will be a special levy submitted to the voters late in January, or early in February, at a special election.

The administration hopes to submit proposals with the proposed tax levy to issue about $7,000,000 of funding bonds to take care of accumulated obligations and to service about $20,000,000 of bonds outside of the 10 mill limitation imposed last year by amendment to the Ohio Constitution.

DETROIT.

Special to THE NEW YORK TIMES.

DETROIT, Jan. 4.—This city, whose position has shown a consistent improvement since the low point of 1932-33, has started the new year with prospects of increased revenues and determination to restrict its expenditures so far as possible.

Thus far in a fiscal year which started July 1, 1935, there has been collected more than $40,000,000 of a $54,840,000 tax levy. Financial officers estimated an 80 per cent collection. It now seems likely that the estimate will be conservative. On Jan. 3 of 1935 about 65 per cent of a comparable levy had been collected. On Jan. 3 of this year over 72 per cent of the 1935-36 levy has been collected.

The city's gross debt of $384,525,445 has not been reduced in principal since the refunding agreement of June, 1933. Debt service, however, has been consistently met under this agreement and further refunding has been arranged during the past year to obtain more favorable interest rates. This policy of refunding callable bonds will be continued.

The welfare rolls list 16,925 families as of Jan. 3, 1936. Over 20,000 are employed under WPA. This compares with a welfare case load of 48,455 families on Jan. 3, 1935.

CHICAGO.

Special to THE NEW YORK TIMES.

CHICAGO, Jan. 4.—The city of Chicago is entering 1936 paying part of its bills on a cash basis and the remainder in sixty-day periods, Robert B. Upham, City Controller, said. Mr. Upham pointed out that all tax warrants held by the public have been retired with the exception of 1934 corporate warrants now in collection and $21,000,000 worth of 1935 warrants recently sold to local banks.

The city sold no 1935 warrants to the public for 1935 financing. The $21,000,000 in warrants recently sold will provide funds to meet current expenses for the first four months of this year. During 1935 warrants were purchased by the city, with the city's aggregate of funds operating as a working cash fund. The City Council has approved a $122,-142,082 budget for 1936. The 1935 budget was about $130,000,000.

Provisions in the school board budget, now under consideration, provide for the payment of teachers' salaries throughout the year. The teachers' salaries were paid clear through 1935, following a series of broken payments in 1934. Under the school budget Chicago schools will continue to operate on a nine-month basis.

ST. LOUIS.

Special to The New York Times.

ST. LOUIS, Jan. 4.—With some economies effected and an improved collection of taxes certain, Mayor Diekmann is hopeful of balancing this city's budget when the current 1935-36 fiscal year ends next April.

Trends during the present fiscal year are generally more favorable than they were in the preceding period. Budget appropriations for municipal purposes aggregate $19,-289,442 with little likelihood of substantial additional requests. Appropriations in the year before totaled $19,808,208. The budget for bond interest and sinking fund this year is $7,259,665, however, as compared with $6,193,447 for the preceding year.

Real estate and personal property tax collections have been above estimates. Current tax payments for the calendar year of 1935 are $22,346,359 out of a levy of $29,-113,720, leaving only 23 per cent of current taxes delinquent at the present time. This is $1,397,160 more than had been collected at this time last year when $20,949,198 of 1934 taxes had been paid out of a levy of $28,218,616.

It is expected that collection of license and other taxes will increase. Authorities estimate that liquor licenses will yield an increase of $500,000.

The tax rate of St. Louis is $2.77 on each $100 valuation.

St. Louis is contributing $147,000 monthly toward direct relief. Funds are derived from bond issues which are being retired by toll revenue from the Municipal Bridge over the Mississippi.

KANSAS CITY.

Special to The New York Times.

KANSAS CITY, Jan. 4.—Kansas City closed 1935 with no current obligation due and unpaid, according to H. F. McElroy, City Manager. The same condition has existed at the end of each fiscal and calendar year for the last nine years.

However, the city has not furnished any funds for relief by taxation, due to a lack of charter power to levy taxes for such purposes.

The city has been responding to relief needs the last five years by furnishing employment on improvements for which $32,000,000 in bonds were voted in 1930. The city has been issuing $3,200,000 of the bonds a year.

In 1935, $2,700,000 worth of new bonds were issued and sold. The rate ranged from 1¼ to 2¾ per cent, each issue being sold at a premium.

At the close of 1934 the city's bonded debt was $39,660,000. In 1935 the $2,700,000 issue made a total of $42,360,000, but bonds maturing in the year totaled $5,102,000 and were paid, leaving the bonded dept at the close of 1935 at $37,258,-000.

Mr. McElroy said that in the current fiscal year ending April 30, all current outstanding obligations will be paid.

DENVER.

Special to The New York Times.

DENVER, Jan. 4.—Denver was in a sound financial condition at the close of 1935 with a general fund surplus of $44,362, according to the report of City Auditor William H. McNichols. This compares with a general fund surplus of $344,599 in 1934.

During 1935, a total of $1,350,423.07 was expended for relief purposes, independent of Federal and State relief, as compared with $1,772,-825.67 in 1934.

The total expenditures of the Denver municipal government in 1934 amounted to $5,557,513.41 as compared with $6,348,889.39 in 1935.

Denver's credit rating is A1. General obligations bonds sold in 1935 with a 2¼ per cent interest rate, the lowest in the history of the city.

The city's tax collections for 1935 were 96 per cent compared with 94½ per cent in 1934.

SAN FRANCISCO.

Special to The New York Times.

SAN FRANCISCO, Jan. 4.—San Francisco is in a strong financial position, due to a balanced budget and low tax delinquency. The city's strength is reflected in low interest rates on bonds and tax notes.

Bonded debt is $168,016,900, compared with $168,415,000 a year ago. Redemption payments during the last year exceeded bond sales. Issues of 1933, the last authorized, have been selling under 3½ per cent.

The city-county tax rate is $3.68, against $3.86 a year ago, though the general assessment roll dropped again slightly.

The budget of $62,872,102, compared with $59,600,400 the year before, includes $1,000,000 for indigent relief. The same amount in the preceding year was supplemented by $2,500,000 from employe pay cuts, now restored.

Cash reserve to finance the city during tax-dry periods, grew from $2,015,070 to $2,570,103. For the first installment tax in 1935 the delinquency rate was 3.33 per cent, in contrast with 5.35 the year before. This indicated final delinquency will be about normal this year.

January 5, 1936

LAW TO HELP CITIES IN DISTRESS IS VOID; COURT SPLIT 5 TO 4

Municipal Bankruptcy Act of 1934 Is Declared to Invade States Rights.

McREYNOLDS IS EMPHATIC

Sees 'Interference' as End to Sovereignty, With Will of Congress Prevailing.

HUGHES WITH MINORITY

Cardozo, Writing Opinion, Recalls 'Mischief' Which Needed Cure When Measure Was Voted.

Special to The New York Times.

WASHINGTON, May 25.—By a five to four decision the Supreme Court struck down today the Municipal Bankruptcy Act under which Congress two years ago empowered municipalities and other political subdivisions of the States to readjust their indebtedness in the Federal courts.

The majority opinion, written by Justice McReynolds, was shared in by Justices Van Devanter, Sutherland, Butler and Roberts. The dissent, prepared by Justice Cardozo, was supported by Chief Justice Hughes and Justices Brandeis and Stone.

Justice McReynolds held that the law invaded the rights of the States and was thus unconstitutional. He said:

"If obligations of States or their political subdivisions may be subjected to the interference here attempted, they are no longer free to manage their own affairs; the will of Congress prevails over them; although inhibited, the right to tax might be less sinister. And really the sovereignty of the State, so often declared necessary to the Federal system, does not exist."

Sees "Balance" Not Upset

Justice Cardozo was equally emphatic, saying:

"To read into the bankruptcy clause an exception or proviso that there shall be no disturbance of the Federal framework by any bankruptcy proceeding is to do no more than has been done already with reference to the power of taxation by decisions known of all men.

"The statute now in question does not dislocate the balance. It has been framed with sedulous regard to the structure of the Federal system."

The case dealt with a water improvement district in Texas, but it was conceded that the finding would apply to all State subdivisions. Both justices implied as much by their references to municipalities and other units.

The measure was introduced in Congress in June, 1933, as an amendment to the bankruptcy statutes, became law in May, 1934, and was recently extended to 1940.

Agreements to readjust debts of municipalities had to be sanctioned by a Federal court and a majority of creditors ranging from 66 2-3 per cent to 75 per cent.

Very few political units have availed themselves of its provisions, it is said.

Nature of the Appealed Case

Bondholders of the Cameron County Water Improvement District No. 1 of Texas challenged the law. Holders of about one-tenth of $800,000 in bonds outstanding, they opposed a plan to offer them only 49.8 per cent of the face value of the obligations.

The Southern District Federal Court in Texas rebuffed the bondholders, holding the law constitutional, but the Fifth Circuit Court of Appeals reversed this decision, and the bondholders brought the suit to Washington.

In their appeal to the Supreme Court, the opponents of the water district's bankruptcy readjustment asserted that through the law the government usurped the powers reserved to the States because there was an effort to extend the national Bankruptcy Act to political subdivisions of a State.

Representatives of water districts in California, Missouri, Arkansas and other States joined in asking the review.

Government "Interference" Barred

Justice McReynolds, speaking for the majority, said it was "plain enough" that the water district was a political subdivision of the State, "created for the local exercise of her sovereign powers," and that the right to borrow was essential to the district's operations.

"Its fiscal affairs are those of the State, not subject to control or interference by the national government unless the right so to do is definitely accorded by the Federal Constitution," he added.

The opinion then quoted some previous Supreme Court opinions to prove that the government could not invade the powers of the States.

"Notwithstanding the broad grant of power 'to lay and collect taxes,' opinions here plainly show that Congress could not levy any tax on the bonds issued by the respondent or upon income derived therefrom," it continued.

"So to do would be an unwarranted interference with fiscal matters of the State—essential to her existence. Many opinions explain and support this view."

Justice McReynolds asked why, if Federal bankruptcy laws were extended to the water improvement district, they could not be extended to the States themselves. He departed from his written opinion to remark that a "great city" might be brought into court to contest with its creditors.

"If voluntary proceedings may be permitted, so may involuntary ones, subject, of course, to any inhibition of the Eleventh Amendment," he went on. "If the States were proceeding under a statute like the present one, with terms broad enough to include her, apparently the problem would not be materially different."

The justice said the court was concerned with the exercise of such a power in the future.

"The statute undertakes to extend the supposed power of the Federal Government incident to bankruptcy over any embarrassed district which may apply to the court," he added.

Mr. McReynolds remarked that States might voluntarily consent to be sued, but he added:

"Nothing in this tends to support the view that the Federal Government, acting under its bankruptcy clause, may impose its will and impair State powers—pass laws inconsistent with the idea of sovereignty."

Concluding, Mr. McReynolds stated:

"The difficulties arising out of our dual form of government and the opportunities for differing opinions concerning the relative rights of State and National Governments are many; but for a very long time this court has steadfastly adhered to the doctrine that the taxing power of Congress does not extend to the States or their political subdivisions.

"The same basic reasoning which leads to that conclusion, we think, requires like limitation upon the power which springs from the bankruptcy clause."

Justice Cardozo called attention to the Congressional hearings which "exhibit in vivid fashion the breadth and depth of the mischief" the law was designed to remedy. He said that in January, 1934, 2,019 municipalities, counties and other units were in default; they were large cities as well as tiny districts.

The situation, he said, affected forty-one of forty-eight States, and out of $14,000,000,000 securities issued by units smaller than States, $1,000,000,000 was in default.

Accentuating the word, Mr. Cardozo spoke of the "assumptions" of the majority opinion, and added:

"To overcome an act of Congress invalidity must be proved beyond a reasonable doubt."

"No question is before us now and no opinion is intimated as to the power of Congress to enlarge the privilege of bankruptcy by extending it to the States as well as to the local units," said Mr. Cardozo. "Even if the power exists, there has been no attempt to exercise it.

"There is room at least for argument that within the meaning of the Constitution the bankruptcy concept does not embrace the States themselves. In the public law of the United States a State is a sovereign or at least a quasi-sovereign.

"Not so a local governmental unit, though the State may have invested it with governmental power. Such a governmental unit may be brought into court against its will without violating the Eleventh Amendment."

The Securities and Exchange Commission in a recent report to Congress on municipal defaults recommended a strengthening of the Municipal Bankruptcy Act if it was upheld by the Supreme Court.

It added, however, that should the high court's decision be adverse, there would remain the problem of effecting control over protective committees rather than over the municipalities in the bankruptcy proceedings.

It is indicated that as a result of the court's decision a complete reconsideration of the problem will be necessary, and that such a situation precludes the probability of comprehensive recommendations, in time for action by the present session of Congress, on dealing with protective committees in connection with municipal defaults.

Members of the SEC had not had opportunity today to make a careful study of the court decision and there was no formal comment as to future moves. The intimation, however, is that a new approach must be made to the problem, to find a machinery that would exercise control over the committees themselves without exercise of Federal control over municipalities or other State subdivisions.

Counsel for the Reconstruction Finance Corporation began today a study of the decision to determine to what extent its activities would be affected. The RFC has authorized about 500 loans aggregating $120,000,000 to aid in reorganizations of the affairs of drainage districts. Only about fifty of these, however, involve bankruptcies.

Actual disbursements by the RFC have been $54,800,000, these having been made, however, only in instances where the readjustments had been completed by consent of 90 per cent of more of the bondholders.

The principal question facing the corporation is the extent to which it will be able, within the court's decision, to make additional disbursements.

May 26, 1936

REVISED LAW AIDING DEBT-RIDDEN CITIES WINS IN HIGH COURT

Justices, by 6-2, Uphold Act Allowing Readjustments —Old Law Lost 5-4

WALLACE IS REPROVED

Hearings to Set Commissions at Kansas City Stock Yards 'Fatally Defective'

Special to THE NEW YORK TIMES.

WASHINGTON, April 25.—Three decisions of import to the New Deal were handed down by the Supreme Court today as the justices returned from a two weeks absence from the bench.

By a six to two division, with Justice Cardozo again not participating in any court business, the tribunal upheld the constitutionality of the new Municipal Bankruptcy Law passed last August after invalidation of the original statute in 1936.

Splitting six to one, with Justices Cardozo and Reed out of the case, the court rejected as invalid maximum rates proposed by Secretary Wallace, under the Packers and Stockyards Act, for livestock sales commissions at the Kansas City Stock Yards. The court said that Secretary Wallace had accepted as his own the findings of the "active prosecutors for the government," and had not given the packers the right to a full and fair hearing.

In a per curiam opinion the tribunal dismissed the appeal of the Tennessee Electric Power Company against a $4,300,000 PWA loan and grant for a municipal power system at Chattanooga. The court's action was based on its decisions of January, rejecting challenges by the Duke Power Company and Alabama Power Company of the government's policy of financial support to municipal electric plants in competition with private enterprise.

About fifteen formal opinions and many orders were issued by the court, now in the final stages of its term.

Finding on Bankruptcy Law

The new Municipal Bankruptcy Law, Chief Justice Hughes ruled, adequately meets objections uttered when the court in a five-to-four division wiped out the original measure.

He said that the substitute measure "is carefully drawn so as not to impinge on the sovereignty of the State," and that the "formation of an indestructible union of indestructible States" did not "make impossible cooperation between the nation and the States through the exercise of the power of each to the advantage of the people who are citizens of both."

His opinion reversed a ruling by the Southern California District Court rejecting a fight in behalf of the new law by the Federal Government and the Lindsay-Strathmore Irrigation District of Tulare, Calif.

A short note attached to the Hughes finding asserted a belief of Justices McReynolds and Butler that the 1936 decision should have controlled in the present case and that the new law should also be held unconstitutional.

The law permits composition or readjustment of debts of political subdivisions and other taxing agencies if two-thirds of the agency's creditors consent to the plan.

Justice Black was the lone dissenter in the packers decision, also rendered by Chief Justice Hughes, and which reversed a ruling against the livestock men by the Western Missouri District Court, with three judges sitting.

No comment was made by the court upon the maximum rates set for the market agencies at the Kansas City Stock Yards; the Hughes opinion merely said that the hearings by Secretary Wallace were "fatally defective" and thus his rate order must be reversed.

Mr. Wallace was credited by the court with "full and candid testimony" that the evidence was taken before he assumed office, that he "dipped into it from time to time to get its drift," and that in the end he accepted the findings of officers in the Department of Agriculture.

But the court held that "a full and fair hearing" required more than was done. It criticized specifically the failure to let the livestock men examine the findings, saying that those contesting with the government in a quasi-judicial proceeding "are entitled to be fairly advised" of what is going on.

"The maintenance of proper standards on the part of administrative agencies in the performance of their quasi-judicial functions is of the highest importance and in no way cripples or embarrasses the exercise of their appropriate authority," the Chief Justice remarked.

"On the contrary, it is in their manifest interest. For, as we said at the outset, if these multiplying agencies deemed to be necessary in our complex society are to serve the purposes for which they are created and endowed with vast powers, they must accredit themselves by acting in accordance with the cherished tradition embodying the basic concepts of fair play."

Dismissal of the Tennessee Electric suit was a victory for Secretary Ickes, who had already won against the utility in the District of Columbia Appellate Court. The six-line finding of the Supreme Court merely cited the Duke and Alabama Power Company decisions as its precedents.

Through a per curiam opinion Eureka Productions, Inc., lost its battle to enjoin New York State officials from interfering with exhibitions of the film "Ecstacy." The exhibitors contended that the State license law clashed with the government's consent to import the film from abroad.

An opinion delivered by Justice Stone reversed a Second Circuit Court of Appeals decision which had awarded the United States Government about $5,000,000 in Kerensky Russian government deposits left with the Guaranty Trust Company when the Soviet Government came into power in 1917. Mr. Stone held the government had no right to say the suit was barred by the statute of limitations. The case was sent back for further consideration on its merits.

Eleven States joined Georgia today in asking the court to rule that intercollegiate football in State universities is an "essential governmental function" of the States and that the government cannot put a 10 per cent admissions tax on tickets to the games.

April 26, 1938

Ruling May Aid Many Cities

By The Associated Press.

WASHINGTON, April 25.—The Supreme Court, by declaring constitutional the Revised Municipal Bankruptcy Act, opened the way for 3,000 distressed cities, towns and other political subdivisions to seek adjustment of their debts.

The revised law provides a bankruptcy system under which debts can be scaled down under certain conditions, if courts approve.

The earlier invalidating decision was written by Justice McReynolds. Justices Butler and Roberts, among the present court members, voted with him. In the minority were Chief Justice Hughes and Justices Cardozo, Brandeis and Stone.

April 26, 1938

Fewer Cities Adding New Territory; Suburban Trend Seems Slackening

Many Communities Turning Attention to Consolidation and Orderly Growth for Areas Already Absorbed—Vacant Lands Zoned for Business May Become Home Centers Again

By LEE E. COOPER

Taking a lesson from the book of "boom-year" excesses, cities in all parts of the country are proceeding more cautiously today than in the past in annexing new territory.

In the days when every neighboring farm was visioned as a potential suburban business or residential community with hundreds of new taxpayers, municipal authorities overstepped the bounds of reason many times in extending their corporate limits.

They set up business districts, sometimes at the behest of ambitious developers and subdividers, in neighborhoods which had no need and no immediate prospect of supporting the imaginary trade centers.

Land Still Is Idle

Today some of these municipalities are reaping the whirlwind for their ill-considered action. Land on which large sums were spent for municipal improvements and utility services still is largely unoccupied, and the few stores and business places which have been set up within zones which more properly should have been restricted for homes have spoiled the attractiveness of the neighborhood for residential development.

The hectic movement to the suburbs seems to be subsiding at least into orderly expansion, and municipalities are waiting for signs of established growth before seeking to take in outlying areas, Census Bureau reports indicate. Last year only forty cities reported annexations, as compared with sixty the year before and an annual average of eighty territorial expansions during the last decade.

Commenting on these statistics, Herbert U. Nelson, secretary of the National Association of Real Estate Boards, says it looks as if the emphasis is beginning to be placed on consolidation and orderly growth for the territory already absorbed.

"Certainly the prime challenge of our day and the task of the future is replanning and rebuilding within our urban areas, rather than continued expansion," he states. "Only in this way can we salvage the enormous investment that expansion has entailed.

Returned to Home Zones

"Memphis, for example, recently called back the man who drew up its city plan, Harland Bartholomew of St. Louis, for a conference with city officials as to the need of revising that plan in the light of changed conditions."

In his conferences Mr. Bartholomew pointed out that the advent of the automobile touched off an explosion of our cities into the countryside, and that "the too-liberal principal we adopted when we undertook zoning is 'kicking farther downhill' the districts we mistakenly opened to commercial and industrial use that found no such market, and now find themselves harmed for residential use."

He predicted that legislative action for re-establishing residential values will be as widely adopted in the next ten years as zoning has been in the last ten.

Mr. Bartholomew was consultant of the National Association of Real Estate Boards in the drafting of a model neighborhood planning statute which has been brought to the attention of authorities in nearly every State.

October 3, 1937

6,195 Municipal Defaults Tallied in U.S., And in Most Cases Creditors Got Paid

By ROBERT D. McFADDEN

During the Great Depression 45 years ago, the town of Fall River, Mass., defaulted on a snowballing debt. Its credit vanished, its citizens refused to pay their taxes, its officials were humiliated, and state receivers took over the reins of local government for a decade.

No one is sure if these things would happen should New York City be unable to meet its vast obligations in the coming weeks. It would not be a unique case in dimension and detail, experts agree, but hardly a unique event.

Fiscal failure by the city would write only the latest chapter in an unillustrious history of municipal defaults in the United States that date to the failure of Mobile, Ala., in 1838.

Since then, at least 6,195 municipalities—cities, counties, villages, school districts and other local government units—have defaulted on obligations, according to a study by the Advisory Commission on Intergovernmental Relations, a panel of Federal, state and local government officials.

Most Creditors Paid

Of these 6,195 defaults, the study noted, a total of 4,770—about 77 per cent—occurred during the Depression era from 1930 to 1939.

It also pointed out that despite a dearth of Federal and state laws on the subject at that time, most of the municipalities that defaulted eventually paid their creditors every cent of principal and interest due them.

The study, entitled "City Financial Emergencies: The Intergovernmental Dimension," was published in 1973, but many of its data seem more pertinent now in view of New York City's deteriorating fiscal position.

In addition to providing nationwide statistics on defaults, the study analyzed a variety of causes and summarized the case histories of eight cities that defaulted during the Depression.

Hundreds of defaults were associated with other depressions in the eighteen-seventies and nineties, it said.

About two-thirds of the defaults from 1870 to 1879 were on debts used to finance railroad facilities, which ultimately failed to live up to optimistic earnings predictions. Many defaults in the South were a result of thieving Carpetbagger regimes, the study said.

Real estate booms that collapsed, floods and hurricanes that devastated municipalities and the poor quality of local government financial planning and administration were among the many causes of default.

Municipal defaults became a national problem during the economic slide that followed the 1929 stock-market collapse. The maximum indebtedness of insolvent municipalities was reached in 1933, when more than 1,000 local units were in default by nearly $2.6-billion.

The number of municipalities in default during the Depression rose to a peak of 3,251 in 1935, but the total amount of their indebtedness actuallly dropped from the 1933 high.

Despite the dire outlook in 1933, the study said, the ensuing years brought a "high incidence of repayment of defaulted principal and interest"—and in a relatively short time, too.

The 48 cities with populations over 25,000 that were in default during the Depression were out of default by 1938, The study said. This recovery was nearly matched by smaller locales.

In the mid-nineteen-thirties many states passed laws establishing administrative bodies that proved "generallly effective in assisting troubled municipal units," the study said. The Federal Municipal Bankruptcy Act became law in 1937, after a 1934 version was found unconstitutional; it then underwent various amendments and did not emerge in its present form until 1946.

Since that time, the number of bankruptcy cases filed by municipalities has been relatively small—somewhat more than 500. Most of these have pertained to revenue bonds or authorities that operate as revenue-producing enterprises.

Eight Case Histories

Some details of the study's eight case histories follow:

FALL RIVER, MASS.

The basic causes of default were the departure of many textile factories from what was essentially a one-industry town, the failure of the community to broaden the economic base and unsound management of the city finances.

With a population of 130,000, Fall River was prosperous in 1920, but more than half of its assessed valuation was in 121 textile mills. By 1932, there were only 20 mills left. With the sharp drop in revenues, the city failed to make corresponding cuts in expenditures. Trying to preserve the tax rate and an illusion of normalcy, city officials juggled individual property valuations to raise more taxes, but succeeded only in speeding industry's departure.

Borrowing more each year against taxes that proved uncollectible, the city let its debt double, then triple. Finally, banks refused to provide more loans and default occurred in November, 1930. With no credit and a taxpayer revolt under way, the town turned to the State Legislature, which set up a 10-year receivership with absolute control over the city's finances.

The study noted: "Because any of these conditions may occur in a city during the nineteen-seventies, what happened to Fall River is not merely an interesting example of Depression history but can also be a rather chilling lesson concerning the consequences of unsound financial management in today's environment."

DETROIT

Also a one-industry town, Detroit was hard hit when the auto industry faltered during the Depression. Faced with declining revenues and rising demands for expenditures, Detroit —like Fall River—was slow to react and persisted in unsound financial practices, the study noted.

Though acting reluctantly and under pressure from citizens and businesses, Detroit moved in 1931 and 1932 to solve its crisis. Hundreds of city employes were dismissed, vacancies were unfilled, salaries were cut, services were curtailed, and property owners were asked to prepay their taxes. The city even tried to reform its short-term borrowing policies.

The study said the city "did all that could reasonably be expected in its efforts to meet the emergency," but its last stroke—a huge issue of tax-anticipation notes—was concluded on Feb. 14, 1933, the day the banks were closed by Federal Government proclamation, and the city had to default.

A refunding plan was quickly agreed to by the city and representatives of many creditors, who were all ultimately paid without state intervention.

ASHEVILLE, N. C.

A booming resort whose population rose from 28,000 in 1920 to 50,000 in 1930, Asheville discouraged manufacturing to preserve its attractiveness and was swamped by the Depression. It tried to recover from crushing unemployment and dwindling revenues by issuing large amounts of short-term notes, but bank failures cut off the funding supply and the city was forced to default in 1931.

Afterward the population declined, tax delinquencies increased, operating expenses were cut in half and the state had to take over relief, school operating and road maintenance costs. Eventually creditors allowed the town to scale down its debt payments, and a sembance of fiscal balance was restored.

JACKSON, MICH.

Heavily dependent on the auto industry, Jackson's revenues fell by half early in the Depression. The city successfully cut expenses by 48 per cent from 1930 to 1933, but banking failures restricted short-term borrowing, and the city defaulted in 1933 when cash reserves ran out and it was no longer possible to borrow.

Later that year, employment and production began to improve, some relief costs were taken over by the state and Federal Government, and the town had a small operating surplus the following year.

FORT LEE, N.J.

Fort Lee defaulted largely because it lost 40 per cent of its assessed valuation through land condemnation for the construction of the George Washington Bridge and its network of approaches, and for the creation of the Palisades Interstate Park, all between 1928 and 1932.

After default in 1933, committees of resident and non-resident bondholders were formed, a state commission took over the borough's fiscal affairs, and in 1939 a debt-refunding plan was filed under the Federal Municipal Bankruptcy Act. The last of the refunding bonds issued then mature in 1979.

AKRON, OHIO

Primarily dependent on the rubber industry, Akron was severely hurt by the Depression. Encountering increasing operating deficits each year, it did not cut expenses quickly enough and was finally unable to obtain financing. It defaulted in 1932. The next year it cut city employes' salaries by 25 per cent, laid off many workers, reorganized its debts and by 1936 was out of default.

GRAND RAPIDS, MICH.

Grand Rapids responded to soaring Depression relief costs and a loss of one-third of its tax revenues by slashing expenditures by one-third. But mounting tax delinquencies, increasing debt service costs and finally bank closings that tied up all of the city's cash brought the furniture-manufacturing town into default in 1933. The next year the state assumed most relief costs, tax collections improved in 1935 and a refunding plan was set up to ease the pressures.

ASBURY PARK, N. J.

The economy of Asbury Park was based on the summer resort trade, so it was particularly vulnerable to the Depression. Early in the Depression the town's auditorium and casino burned down; with insurance insufficient to rebuild, Asbury Park issued temporary notes to finance new structures. It defaulted on part of these notes in 1933 and, in the next two years, on practically all of its obligations. The city and its creditors were at loggerheads over a refunding plan until 1938, when one was worked out with state help.

September 2, 1975

CHAPTER 3

Big Cities, Big Problems

al view of New York City's Stuyvesant Town
ing project.

rtesy The New York Times

THE CHANGING PATTERN OF AMERICA

Fairchild Aerial Surveys, In

The census shows that America's big cities have almost stopped growing—New York grew only 6 per cent during the decade.

By WILLIAM FIELDING OGBURN

THE zero year of each decade is the time for learning about ourselves as a people, for it is the year when we take the Census. The Domesday Book of William the Conqueror, one of the first great inventories, has evolved now to the point where the Constitution of the United States decrees that such a record be made every ten years. Hence, 1940 is a year for recording our progress in population, in wealth and in a thousand different characteristics. It is a huge undertaking, costing $53,000,000 and requiring an army of statisticians working three years to complete the count. But the results are worth the money and time. The story will not be fully told for several years, but it is being revealed to us item by item for the different population centers as soon as the additions are ready.

The first big news is that the total population of the United States is 131,000,000, as contrasted with 123,000,000 ten years ago. We are larger by only 8,000,000, whereas from 1920 to 1930 we grew 17,000,000. That we would grow only about one-half as fast in the decade between 1930 and 1940 as we did in the decade between 1920 and 1930 was forecast by sociologists quite accurately, which gives added confidence to their prediction that in another thirty years we shall have ceased to increase.

The Far West, where nature is lavish with its beauties, grew the fastest, largely owing to the fact that we continue a 300-year-old practice of moving West. The South was next in growth, because of the high birth rate in that region and because Southerners have not been leaving the South as they did in former years. This latter situation is due to the fact that unemployment in urban areas reduced the incentive for migration. Several States in the Dust Bowl area—the Dakotas, Nebraska, Kansas and Oklahoma—lost population, and New England grew only slightly. The center of population will move still further west.

Somewhat unexpected is the knowledge that the big cities have almost stopped growing. New York grew only 6 per cent during the decade and Chicago's population remained stationary, whereas the growth of each city during the previous decade was about 25 per cent. Philadelphia lost population, as did also Pittsburgh, St. Louis, San Francisco, Boston and Cleveland. Buffalo remained the same, Detroit and Milwaukee grew 3 and 2 per cent and Baltimore 6 per cent, while Los Angeles increased 21 per cent. The total growth of these cities of a half million or more population in 1930 was only a sixth of their growth a decade earlier.

DOES this fact mean that the big cities are too big? Many sociologists have thought so for some time. There is not much play space in the cities for children and the birth rate is too low to maintain the population. The death rate is larger than in the country. Rent is high, the streets are crowded, and speeding automobiles are a menace. Even from an economic point of view the costs of production for industry are lower in the small towns.

The people would be expected to find better and more comfortable living conditions elsewhere than in the big cities, but habits are slow to change and buildings last a long time. The expectations of the sociologists that big cities would cease getting bigger did not come true by 1930, but they are being realized by 1940. For the Census does show that people are not flocking to the large cities as they once did and suggests that some are moving away. Perhaps the Census of 1950 will show an actual decrease in all cities of over a half million. If so, they will not dwindle rapidly, they will hardly become the ghost towns one sees more and more frequently in traveling over the land—towns with deserted buildings and streets, echoes and whistling winds, where once were hustling miners and lumbermen.

FURTHER, all cities, large and small, did not grow as fast as the remainder of the nation. All cities which had 25,000 or more inhabitants in 1930 grew only 4.7 per cent, whereas the nation's total population increased 7 per cent. This is the first time in the history of the United States that cities have not grown faster than the farms, villages and towns. For the past two centuries not only the United States but the *(Continued)* whole civilized world has been characterized by the astounding mass appearance and growth of cities. Does the Census of 1940 tell us that we are witnessing the reversal of a trend that has been an outstanding phenomenon of the Age of Steam? Can it be that we are returning to the farm and village and turning our backs on the urban way of life? Such an important indication needs to be examined more carefully.

The failure of cities to grow as fast as the rest of the country may be merely a temporary phenomenon due to the business depressions of the Nineteen Thirties and not the reversal of centuries-long trends. These hard times meant ten million unemployed, many of whom were in cities. Hence, during the Nineteen Thirties the cities were not so powerful as magnets in attracting the country boys and girls who wanted to get away from the drudgery and low incomes of the farms.

IF the hard times of the past decade did not favor the growth of cities, then they must have meant more people for the farms and small communities. But the Census Bureau has not yet computed the figures to show whether the farms or the small communities grew the faster. An estimate, not an actual count, of the farm population in 1940 has been made by the Bureau of Agricultural Economics. The figure is 32,000,000, an increase of 6.9 per cent over the farm population of 1930. This gain of the farms in population is surprising because the farms had been losing population for twenty years. The farm population was 2,000,000 smaller in 1930 than in 1910. The farms are growing again.

Does this increase of farm population mean a reversal of a trend? Or is it merely a result of the business depression? It is probable that the bad times of the past decade have favored the growth of the farm population. Many families returned to farms generally to the poorer or abandoned ones—in fear of an economic collapse or to dig in until the economic storm had passed. However, the major increase in population of the agricultural areas comes from their high birth rates. The farm population would double in forty-five years if there were no migration and the present birth and death rates remained the same, while, in the same period under the same provisions, the large cities would lose population and be reduced to 68 per cent of their present size. Farms are the breeding ground of the nation, while the cities are the consumers of the population.

THESE differentials of urban and farm growth have led some observers to think that perhaps a peasant class would grow up in the United States. This speculation is reinforced by the disparity between urban and rural income, which had been increasing until counteracted in part by the efforts of the United States Department of Agriculture. The very low income of the sharecropper is also supporting evidence of the view that we are likely to develop a class in the rural regions comparable to the peasants of Europe.

The rural poverty of peasants is found where the farm lands are overcrowded, where the ratio of arable land to farm hands is low. It does not seem probable that we shall reach that condition in the United States, for the reason that the farmers are taking up machines driven by mechanical power.

Tabulating the results of the 1940 census.

One farmer now feeds eighteen persons. With more machines and more science, he may feed thirty-six. But there will not be thirty-six persons for him to feed, with the population of the United States stationary and possibly decreasing twenty-five or thirty years hence. Machines raise the per capita income, but they will also mean technological unemployment on the farms. They are an invasion of iron men taking away jobs from the farmers and farm laborers. Unemployment on the farms is likely to push along the fall of the birth rate on the farms, which is still high.

IF the big cities grow less rapidly and if there is to be less need for farmers, may not the greatest increase be found in the communities of medium size? Indeed, such is one of the most interesting findings from the data so far released. Towns grew at a faster rate than did the cities and faster than the villages and farms combined. Places from 10,000 to 25,000 increased by 9 per cent, while cities beyond this size grew only 4.7 per cent in population, and the smaller communities were larger by only 6.8 per cent.

Why the towns grow at a faster rate is not clear. Perhaps the town dwellers did not migrate to the cities, as in previous decades, while the high birth rate of the farms forced some migration to the towns. The course of migration is not from the farms directly to the big cities, as is supposed. The farm youth generally go first to the towns. In any case, because "our town" is being favored, it should not be concluded that we are all going back to live at Grover's Corners, for the great majority of us still live in rural communities and in the cities.

Is this recrudescence of the town an indication of a trend that will continue through other decades? Perhaps so. A clue to the answer to this question is found in another curious discovery from the Census figures of 1940. It is this: the big cities grew less rapidly than did the counties in which these big cities are located. For instance, the population of cities of over 250,000 population increased by only 3.4 per cent, while the counties surrounding the cities grew by 17 per cent, or five times as fast. Why should the county area surrounding a city grow faster than the city? This county area surrounding the city is the place of fine residences, of factory sites, of small family homes, of satellite towns, of bedroom communities.

COUNTY territory surrounding a city grows faster than the city because of the automobile, though the electric car and steam railroad have aided the trend. The telephone, moving-picture theatre and chain-store have also favored the growth of the suburbs. The truck and paved highway have enabled light industries to move out from the city to regions of lower rents and wages, while manufacturers can at the same time truck their products to ships and railroads which connect with distant centers. The Census of 1940 shows a remarkable growth of this metropolitan area around the great city.

What the Census records regarding large cities is the population of only a political unit, of an area around which there has been drawn a political boundary line. But a city is not merely a political unit. It is also an economic entity. In fact, the raison d'être of a city is economics. Cities were largely created by steam, used in the factories and on the railroads.

There were cities before steam, but only a small percentage of the population lived in them. The multitude of cities of modern times are made by the railroad. The legislators have drawn lines around these economic areas and they are called cities. Quite compact they are, for people needed to live near where they worked, since local transportation was poor or non-existent.

The electric street cars became widely used only at the close of the last century. Dwellings were piled on top of one another. Then the gasoline engine was invented and gave us excellent local transportation, as the railroad steam engine had given us excellent long-distance transportation. The invention of abundant and speedy means of travelling short distances and then its wide adoption is spreading the city outward, and extending its area greatly. This means that economically the city has spread over a great deal of surrounding territory. But the political boundary line has not been redrawn to make it synonymous with the economic boundary.

IF the political boundary of cities had been changed to keep pace with the new economic boundaries, then the Census of 1940 would have shown a greater growth of cities. Instead, this great growth of the metropolitan area is shown in terms of smaller political units—villages, towns and small cities.

A few cities have changed their boundaries to make them fit more nearly the economic area. Los Angeles has extended its limits to include 448 square miles, which is a little less than the area of New York and Chicago combined. Yet the population of Los Angeles is only 1.5 million, while that of New York and Chicago is 10.8 million. Los Angeles grew 21 per cent, while New York and Chicago grew only 4 per cent. Similarly, the area of San Diego encompasses ninety-five square miles, while Cleveland has left her boundary unchanged at seventy-three square miles. The density of San Diego is 2,100 per square mile and Cleveland's is 12,000.

Obviously, the population of political areas, when some cities have widened them to include the economic area and others have not, means little or nothing with regard to the population of the economic area of the city. What does it mean that San Diego grew 37 per cent and Cleveland lost 2 per cent? If they both had included the same per cent of economic area, then the comparisons would be valid. The figures for 1940 merely compare rates of growth between boundary lines of a map.

The less dense the population of the city—that is, the bigger its boundary line—the more likely it is to show large gains in population between 1930 and 1940. The correlation for sixty-five cities over 100,000 in population between density and increase of populations is —.5. It is well for those who fight over the comparisons of the growth of San Francisco and Los Angeles or of other rival cities to remember the lack of economic significance of the political boundary lines.

But the fact that the county outside the city has grown five times as fast as the city does show that the automobile is dispersing the city dwellers outward. It is really destroying the old city as we have known it, the city which the railroad created, and is giving us something else, for which as yet we have no suitable name, but call the metropolitan community.

The growth of the metropolitan community has a good deal of significance for American life. It means the loosening up of the city, the lessening of the overcrowded conditions of the city blocks and the precipitation outward of the city population so that they may have both the advantages of the town and the attractions of the metropolis.

It should be a better world for children, with green lawns and fresher air. It will be a region of wider and faster highways and more parking space for automobiles. It will provide a wonderful opportunity for planning, an opportunity which the cities of the railroad era missed.

Now another opportunity is offered for planning—planning the location of factories, of express highways, of the placing of schools, of the whole metropolitan region, the new economic city, in order that we may have a fuller and a better life. The coming of the helicopter, the autogiro and other steep-flight aircraft will accentuate this whole movement.

October 13, 1940

259 CITIES ANNEX SUBURBAN REALTY

A new high mark in expansion of urban areas was reached during the past year, when 259 cities extended their boundaries to include additional suburban territory.

The records showed a 70 per cent rise over the previous year in the number of municipalities annexing land to control metropolitan "fringe" growth and gain new tax ratables. During 1945 only 150 cities expanded in size.

Among the cities taking in new territory last year, 152 were in the population class above 10,000, according to the International City Managers Association. Statistics from the 1947 Municipal Yearbook showed that twenty-three cities added at least one square mile.

Increased annexations last year reflected efforts to adjust municipalities to record growth during the war and in anticipation of a continuance of suburban building activity.

Forth Worth took in the greatest additional area last year, annexing thirty-five square miles of land by charter amendment election December 17. This triples the city's topographic size, from 17.1 to 52.1 square miles. In the previous year, biggest annexation was made by near-by Dallas, which annexed thirty-nine square miles.

Other cities over 10,000 annexing at least one square mile of territory in 1946 were Beaumont, Borger, Dallas, Lubbock, San Antonio, Tyler, and Waco, in Texas; Wilmington, N. C.; Salem, Ore.; Reno, Nev.; Columbus, Ga.; Denver, Colo.; Marion, Ohio; Fresno and Pasadena, Calif.; Kansas City, Mo; and Fairmont, W. Va.

Annexation generally provides for equalized local tax rates and uniform public services, and facilities long-range community planning. Suburbs usually resist annexation to their parent city because it often means more taxes for suburban residents. Recent singular exception to this resistance is Westwood, an incorporated suburb of 7,000 which recently voted for annexation to Denver. Most annexations are of unincorporated territory.

To clarify for new residents just what annexation means, Kansas City, Mo., recently distributed a booklet entitled "A Message of Welcome From Your City Government" to residents of a newly annexed area containing a population of 10,000.

The pamphlet outlined briefly the major municipal services, contains a chart showing percentage distribution of revenues and expenditures of the city, and gives a detailed list of services available through the public works department. In addition to this new area, Kansas City voters last fall annexed nineteen square miles in Clay County north of the city, effective in 1950.

Among cities of less than 10,000 population annexing land last year, biggest area increase was scored by Tupelo, Miss., with annexation of 4.3 square miles. Other smaller cities annexing areas of one square mile or more in 1946 were Clinton, Ill.; Midland, Texas; Gallup. N. M.; Logan, Ohio; Miami, Okla.; and Russelville, Ark.

Recent annexation increases mark continuation of a long-term trend. While 152 cities over 10,000 population added land last year, and eighty-seven the year before, only twenty-five cities over 10,000 annexed new area in 1935. Forty-five cities in this population class annexed land in 1936, fifty-two in 1937, and forty-five in 1938.

May 25, 1947

Rise of the Urban Region: A Study of New Way of Life

Overlapping of Metropolises, Fostered by Auto in U. S., Is Creating Commerce, Home, School and Road Problems

By CHARLES GRUTZNER

The United States is undergoing the growing pains of a new pattern of settlement—the urban region.

Ways of life are changing for millions of Americans as metropolitan areas lose their familiar identities. New ways are bringing new problems for individuals, communities and central government.

Once there were great cities ringed by quiet suburbs beyond which stretched farm and woodland. This was the classic metropolitan area, which survives in some parts of the country. Beyond its horizons began a distant cluster of suburbs, rimming the central city of another metropolitan area.

Now metropolitan areas overlap. Cities and suburbs, having grown into one another, sprawl in vast complexes of homes, factories and commerce known as urban regions.

Eighteen such urban regions—conurbations as the English would call them—darken the map of the United States. The largest extends almost unbroken along the East Coast for more than six hundred miles—from north of Boston to below Alexandria, Va. It requires no superior visions to look to the time when much bigger areas will be as thickly populated as the older "citified" lands, such as Belgium and the Netherlands.

A study of what is happening to America's cities and the rapidly urbanizing regions about them has been made by a group of reporters of The New York Times. A series of their reports will deal with different aspects of this urbanization, including problems of government, commerce and industry, housing, schools and transportation. There will be reports also on how certain cities and metropolitan areas in the United States and abroad are attempting to meet the problems.

Regional urbanization has been brought about by sharp increases in population, new highways, mass housing extending far beyond city lines, huge shopping centers on former farmland, and expansion of industry with breathless technological advances.

Tying all these together is the automobile. None of this could have come about without America's amazing output of automobiles. Yet, that output has been something other than an undiluted blessing.

Many suburbs are no longer suburban in the popular concept of them as residential retreats from the city's daily bustle, with trees and perhaps hills or a near-by stream.

Bulldozers have nudged down trees. Power shovels have levelled natural contours. Developers have thrown up maximum numbers of mortgaged homes on former farm and woodland. Industry has pushed its flat factories to newly populated communities.

King-sized shopping centers have been built between outlying subdivisions. Most big-city department stores have established suburban outlets; some have pulled out of central cities altogether.

Faraway roads are being clogged by the automobiles of those who have fled the crowding of city buses or subways. Some city dwellers migrated to the outlands because of crowded schools. They have found in many cases that a wave of like-minded newcomers has so inundated the village or district school that crowding and part-time sessions are as bad as in the city.

The Price of Growth

This type of development has grown monstrously since World War II. Some city planners call it "suburban sprawl." Others call it "scatteration" or "regional urbanization."

Under any name, it spells headaches for public officials from the Village Hall level to the White House. It is a cause of worry also for industrial executives, for taxpayers in miles of modest homes whose picture windows stare into the picture windows of their neighbors, and for sociologists and architects who fear it is breeding environmental monotony or worse.

The problems, big now, will become much more serious. The country's population, now 169,600,000, is expected to grow by 1975 to at least 215,000,000 and possibly to 228,000,000. Two-thirds or more of the increase will be in metropolitan areas but less than 5 per cent within the central cities of these areas. Some cities are already losing population.

One hundred million Americans are now living in metropolitan areas, including their central cities.

Will the new pattern of settlement result in eventual dwindling of great cities like New York, Chicago and San Francisco? Will they be just islands of national business headquarters, financial clearing houses and other specialized functions within great flat seas in which the other activities of our national life will mingle?

Or will our historic cities sparkle brighter by contrast with the sprawling urbanized regions that they will serve as centers of culture as well as commerce?

Will the vast program of urban renewal—on which the Federal Government is spending a billion dollars and local communities hundreds of millions more—clear out enough city slums and prevent blight in other sections so that a back-to-the-city movement may develop in some suburbs where the seeds of new slums are already germinating?

The only answers to such questions lie in the opinions of planners who are as sharply divided as Giant and Dodger fans and equally vociferous.

What About New York?

Frank Lloyd Wright told a recent conference of mayors that the doom of central cities was inevitable because of the decentralization fostered by the automobile. In an attention-arresting oversimplification, the famed architect said: "The modern city is a place for banking and prostitution and very little else."

Robert Moses offers a fervent rebuttal to the Wrights and others who see the cities of the future only as modest-sized entities. Mr. Moses is now planning a $186,000,000 cultural, residential and commercial center on a Manhattan slum site as the high point of more than twenty years devoted to rebuilding New York. He offered this prediction:

"Long after the last cowboy has disappeared into the sunset and the last cubic foot of natural gas has dried up in the bowels of the Panhandle, there will be cities with minarets and spires assaulting the heavens, gleaming in the dawn and beckoning to ambitious prairie youth. In them will survive the shrines of Moloch, the smithies of Vulcan, the faces that launched a thousand ships, the topless towers of commerce, the Helens who will make the country yokel immortal with a kiss."

New cities will be created as suburbs fuse into one another and population density requires ways of providing municipal services. Other cities, perhaps with original planning, will grow on what is today open country.

The shapes the new cities take will depend on controls of land use now under study by planning boards, interstate conferences, universities and other experts all over the nation, and upon other factors. The possibility for variety is great in a nation whose present cities run to such extremes as New York, with its skyscraper core, and Los Angeles, a horizontal monster crawling almost endlessly from the sea to the desert and mountains.

But, the development patterns in the urbanized areas outside these central cities will affect even more Americans than those living in the cities.

Before the turn of the century, Sir Patrick Geddes, British sociologist and biologist, predicted that one day the entire Eastern seaboard of the United States would be one continuous city.

Fantastic as that seemed, the nation has come so far along the way that, today for the first time in this hemisphere, more than 27,000,000 people are living under urban conditions in a continuous area stretching more than 600 miles from Boston to the far tip of Fairfax County Virginia. This is a 1950 census figure; estimates of the current population reach 32,000,000.

Luther Gulick, head of the Institute of Public Administration, offers this prediction for the next fifty years:

There will be a solid settlement extending from Boston perhaps as far south as Newport News, Va. It will sprawl westward at least to Chicago, possibly to Kansas City, with manufacturing centers in what are now forests of Kentucky and Tennessee.

Dr. Gulick also foresees other vast urbanized areas in the Southwest and West.

The great urban regions, present and future, will not quite cover every square mile with buildings, highways and other construction.

Even the subdevelopers' steam shovels won't remove the mountain ranges. Some woodland will be preserved within the developed regions for recreational use and as watersheds. Patches of farmland will remain. The point is that over-all settlement of vast areas will be as uniform and dense as in the older urbanized areas of Europe.

A motorist driving from Boston into Virginia will find a few lonely stretches of road although he will seldom be in a county that is not part of a metropolitan area.

In New Jersey, there is a twelve-mile run between New Brunswick and Princeton where there are scattered farmhouses. But few of the residents are commercial farmers reaping as much as $500 a year from agriculture. Living in the farmhouses are scientists, factory workers and others who travel by car to their urban workshops or offices.

A mile-front plot along that lonely stretch of Highway 1 has been bought by a pharmaceutical company that is erecting a large plant. Also within the continuous urban region is a pine-barren of 100,000 acres between Atlantic City and Camden, bought by New Jersey as a potential watershed.

The foregoing are examples of the patchwork in large metropolitan areas. But the open spaces are shrinking, year by year.

The earlier, well-defined metropolitan areas were like fried eggs, each with a central city as its yolk.

When the New York, Newark and Jersey City metropolitan areas crowded together and then spread about other cities, the new metropolitan area became

Urban Regions Take In Many Millions

The great urbanized region of the Eastern Seaboard is made up of the following standard metropolitan areas (populations are 1950 census; the estimated 1957 figures average 15 per cent higher):

Lowell-Lawrence-Haverhill, Mass.	340,906
Boston	2,558,581
Fall River-New Bedford, Mass.	278,247
Providence, R. I.	775,985
Worcester, Mass.	332,261
Springfield-Holyoke, Mass.	407,255
Hartford, Conn.	358,081
Waterbury, Conn.	154,656
New Britain-Bristol, Conn.	146,983
New Haven, Conn.	264,622
Bridgeport, Conn.	258,137
Stamford-Norwalk, Conn.	196,023
New York-Northeast New Jersey	12,911,994
Trenton, N. J.	229,781
Atlantic City, N. J.	132,399
Allentown-Bethlehem-Easton, Pa.	437,824
Philadelphia, Pa.	3,671,048
Reading, Pa.	255,740
Lancaster, Pa.	234,717
Harrisburg, Pa.	292,241
York, Pa.	202,737
Wilmington, Del.	268,387
Baltimore, Md.	1,337,373
Washington, D. C.	1,464,089
Total	27,510,067

An urban region is defined as an expanse in which two or more standard metropolitan areas overlap or adjoin. A standard metropolitan area consists of a county containing at least one city of 50,000 or more population or several adjoining counties containing such cities.

As defined by the Census Bureau, it includes also "contiguous counties if according to certain criteria they are essentially metropolitan in character and socially and economically integrated with the central city." An exception is made for New England, where the Census Bureau defines metropolitan areas in terms of towns and cities instead of counties.

Under these terms the great Eastern Seaboard region is technically two urban regions, with the Boston-centered cluster of metropolitan areas, from Haverhill to Worcester, a separate urban region. For all practical purposes, the Eastern Seaboard's 600-mile strip is regarded as a single region.

The seventeen other urban regions, in order of size, are:

Chicago, Kenosha, Racine, Milwaukee	6,551,234
Cleveland, Lorain-Elyria, Akron, Canton, Youngstown, Wheeling-Steubenville, Pittsburgh, Johnstown, Altoona	5,833,593
Los Angeles, San Diego, San Bernardino-Riverside	5,376,407
Detroit, Flint, Saginaw, Bay City	3,529,136
San Francisco-Oakland, Sacramento, Stockton, San Jose	3,009,204
Cincinnati, Hamilton-Middletown, Dayton, Springfield	1,620,599
Seattle, Tacoma	1,008,868
Dallas, Fort Worth	976,052
Houston, Galveston	919,767
Kansas City, St. Joseph	911,183
Wilkes-Barre-Hazleton, Scranton	649,637
Syracuse, Utica-Rome	625,981
Norfolk-Portsmouth, Hampton-Newport News-Warwick	589,427
Greensboro-High Point, Winston-Salem	337,192
Lansing, Jackson	280,866
Raleigh, Durham	238,089
Springfield, Decatur	230,337
Total	32,686,572

Adding the population of Urban Region No. 1 to the total of the seventeen other urban regions gives a population total of 60,196,639 (1950 census). The urban regions include seventy-seven of the nation's 174 standard metropolitan areas.

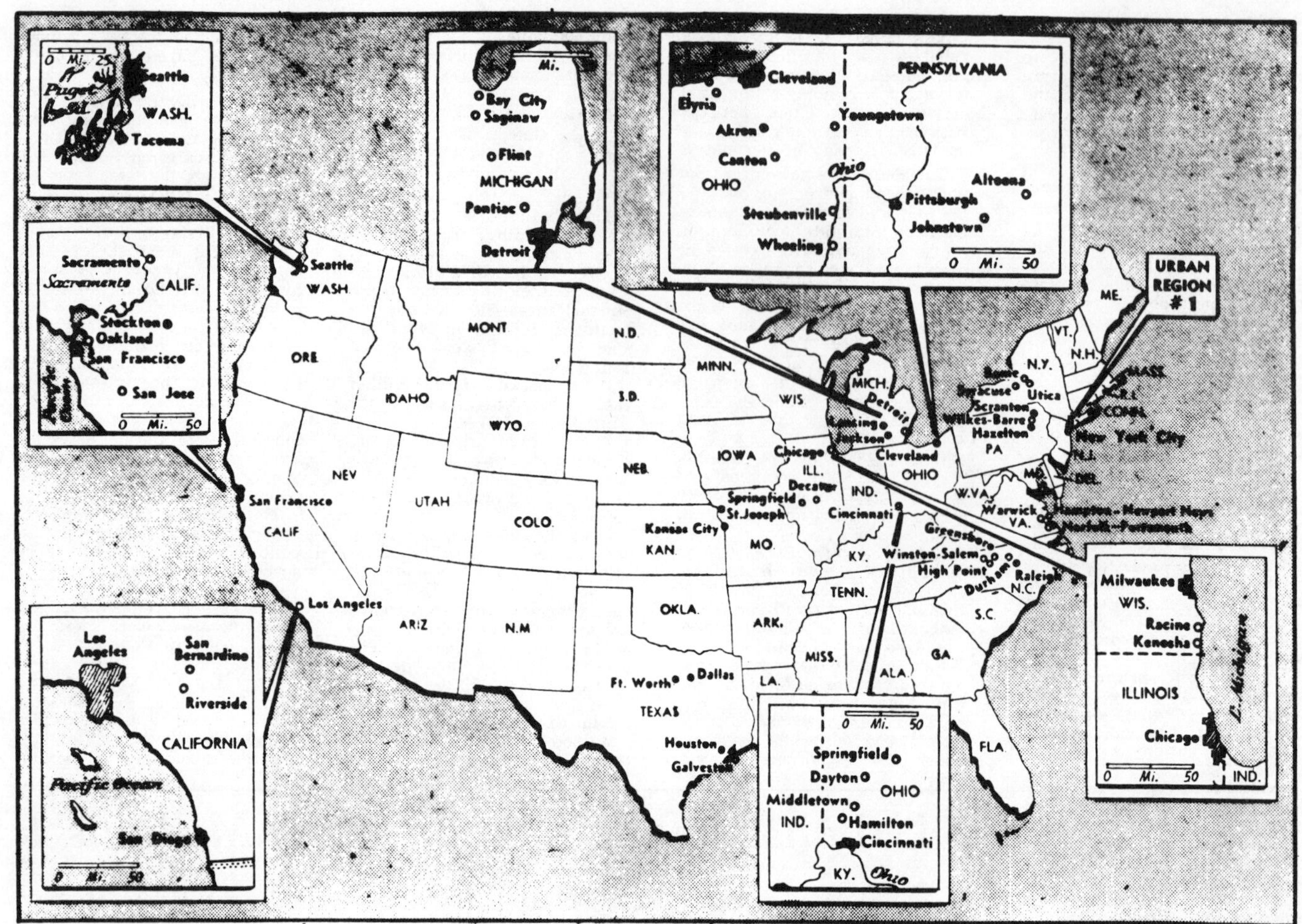

The New York Times — Jan. 27, 1957

POPULATION CENTERS: Pointers lead to detailed insets of largest urban regions in the nation. Key cities in other areas are in heavy type.

a giant pan of fried eggs. The yolks were of different size. among them Paterson (population 140,000) and Passaic in New Jersey. Yonkers in New York, Glen Cove and Long Beach in Long Island.

The great urban regions created by the bursting of metropolitan areas into one another have now become gargantuan scrambles. Solving some of their problems will be no easier than unscrambling scrambled eggs.

The diffusion of orientation of many suburbs is typified in Bucks County, Pa. Some residents work, shop and seek entertainment a few miles north in Trenton, N. J. Others go south to Philadelphia. Still others center much of their activity to the east in Burlington, N. J. An increasing number find most of their needs served right in Bucks County, which is becoming more urbanized by the day.

The eighteen urban regions in the United States had, in the 1950 census, a population of 60,196,639. They had within them seventy-seven of the nation's 174 standard metropolitan areas. But these seventy-seven areas—45 per cent of the number of metropolitan areas—had 71 per cent of the population of all metropolitan areas. The country's population in 1950 was 150,697,361, of whom 84,500,680 lived in metropolitan areas.

Since 1950, the population increase has been more than three times as large in metropolitan areas as outside of them.

The current population increase is at the rate of 1.3 per cent a year. Since World War II, American women have been bearing babies as never before. The average married woman has 2.03 children, but the number of women with three or more children has doubled in the last twenty years.

Older citizens are steadily increasing their life span over that of their forbears. More of them, financially independent now, have their own apartments instead of a room in a relative's home. This has resulted in the design of special apartments for the elderly in some developments, with layouts requiring a minimum of stooping, stretching or stair climbing. Pensioners and other retired oldsters constitute a majority in some Florida communities. Other areas in the South are also attracting the older citizens in large numbers.

Protests have arisen in connection with the housing projects that are planned solely for the elderly. Isolation, it is suggested, blunts any feeling of participation in the total community and deepens the sense that they are being segregated.

There are other factors in the suburban spread. More families have been fleeing from the older cities than a head count within city limits discloses. The exodus of young, white families has been counterbalanced by a strong migration of Negroes from Southern rural districts into cities of the North and West and an influx of Puerto Ricans from their native island to New York and a few other cities.

New York, St. Louis, Detroit, Chicago and other industrial cities are changing racially. It is estimated that nine out of ten Negroes who leave the South move into cities.

The law against discrimination in housing that receives any form of Federal aid has been generally circumvented by suburban developers even though more than half of all homes built in the last ten years were covered by Federal mortgage insurance.

Suburban builders, with few exceptions, have excluded Negroes or limited them to token quotas. Some developers extend the discrimination against other racial minorities.

In the cities it is different, especially in public housing, where eligible families get low-rent apartments regardless of race or nationalities.

This has resulted in Negro concentrations in cities encircled by suburbs almost uniformly white. It is one of the obvious imbalances of regional settlement. A break in the color barrier has been reported in a few communities but a widely integrated suburbia is unlikely for many years.

While there are many reasons for the centrifugal whirl of people and business from the older cities, the automobile has been the greatest factor in the scatteration. Industrial workers and others who formed car pools in World War I got the idea that the motor vehicle would permit them to live beyond the city line.

The flight to the suburbs gained force in the Nineteen Twenties, subsided to a dribble in the early years of the depression when many families lost house and car, and became a surging tide after World War II.

Industries, like their workers, shifted base because of rubber tires. Growing use of trucks made factories less dependent on sites near railroads. The Government's policy of permitting war industries to write off the cost of new plants in a short five years spurred many corporations to build outside congested cities.

This, in turn, led to new patterns of travel.

Instead of flowing radially between homes in the suburbs and jobs in the city, traffic now crisscrosses over wide areas. The Long Island suburbanite, who quit a New York factory job to work in an aircraft plant near home, might, if he lost that job, find employment further

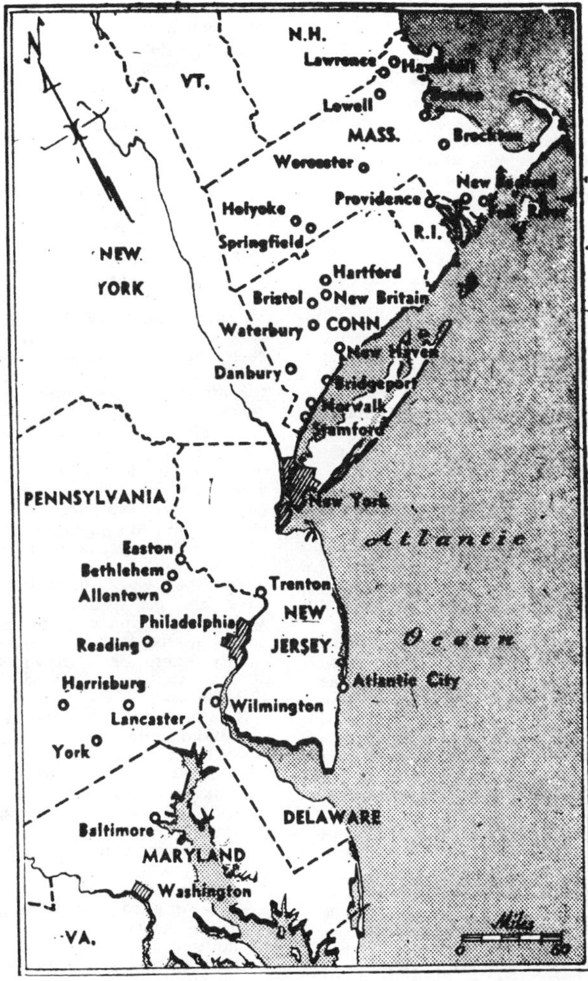

The New York Times — Jan. 27, 1957

EASTERN AREA: This is Urban Region 1 as indicated on large map. It extends from Massachusetts to Virginia. Area marked New York includes a cluster of surrounding cities such as Newark, Jersey City, Yonkers, White Plains.

out on the Island or in New Jersey, with no more time needed for daily travel than when he had worked in the city.

But the same cars and trucks that made possible such far-flung urbanization are now creating congestion in some of the new communities. They also are taking great chunks of open land out of productive and recreational use by coating them with concrete.

In the last ten years, car registration in the United States increased by 26,000,000. By 1975, according to conservative estimates, the number of automobiles will grow from the present 69,000,000 to 100,000,000 or more. The $33,800,000,000 Federal highway program will bury 1,000,000 acres under paving in the next ten years.

Government experts estimate that 1,100,000 acres—about the area of Rhode Island—are lost to crop use every year by urban and suburban development, industry, airports, military establishments and new highways. The nation now has 409,000,000 acres.

With productivity loss of another 700,000 acres a year through soil erosion, tree planting, waterlogging, salt deposits and other contamination, it is estimated that by 1962 all the nation's farms will produce no more food than is needed by the increased population.

This will solve the economic and political problem of farm surpluses, but what will it bring in the years of more population and more conversion of open land to urbanization and to industry, which now builds horizontally instead of vertically?

The amount of water the earth will give up and what it will again absorb has become of tremendous importance as families have settled close together on former farmland. It has created problems that bring discomfort and threat of disaster if their solution is too long deferred.

New Jersey, the most highly urbanized state in the nation, has ignored its water supply problem and now has bubblings of warning. In Atlantic City and other shore communities that rely on wells the amount of water withdrawn for household and industrial use is so great that from time to time the kitchen taps yield salt water.

Jersey legislators offered the citizenry in 1955 a chance to vote $100,000,000 for a dam and reservoir for northern Jersey and southern Jersey. The proposal was voted down. The state is using 10 per cent more water than its long-term average annual yield. Good luck has given New Jersey bonus rainfall in recent years, but a return to average or less could bring serious trouble for many of the state's 5,000,000 inhabitants.

Sanitary drainage causes an equally serious threat. Many subdivisions have become costly messes because septic tanks, though meeting requirements written when one farm family worked forty acres, are unable to take care of a hundredfold load.

In Henrietta Township, N. Y., one of the new suburbs ringing Rochester, a developer sold 640 homes. Almost as soon as the buyers flushed toilets and drained the detergent-laden run-off of dishwashers and home laundries into their new septic tanks, the neat little gardens began flooding.

Local officials insisted that sewers be dug at once. Home purchasers, mortgaged to the hilt, cried that additional costs would ruin them. Finally the developer paid half the sewer costs as a rebate on the worthless septic tanks and the home buyers put up the other half. No one was happy.

Such happenings are repeated over wide reaches of the nation.

The foregoing problems are largely physical—traffic congestion, water supply, sanitation, land use, homebuilding, dispersal of trade and industry.

The problems of government in the sprawling, often amorphous new communities, and in the older cities from which they have siphoned taxpayers, are as serious as any of the others and more complicated than most.

Some communities are trying to meet them by erecting "invasion" barriers. Some have increased the size of plots upon which a house may be built. Two Connecticut towns, Greenwich and New Canaan, have increased the minimum size of building plots in some areas of those towns from two to four acres.

In other townships, zoning and planning boards are arbitrarily trying to direct the course of development by "opening up" only certain sections or refusing to approve building permits until developers make promises such as setting aside acreage from their own property for parks or future school needs.

Some of these devices could not survive a court test, but they have served as stopgap blocks or have won concessions from builders eager to start construction. One suburban official has said: "Most of what we do is illegal, but it's popular."

Who Is to Pay?

The new urbanized regions straddle the boundaries of villages, boroughs, towns, townships, school districts, cities, and even spread across state lines.

How to apportion the costs of services among overlapping units of government? How to prevent provincial differences from cutting sharply through an urbanized region, as in the case of liquor laws that in New York permit service to youths of 18 while New Jersey and Connecticut insist that drinkers be 21 years of age? The liquor law inconsistency has brought out-of-state teen-agers to New York taverns near the state lines.

Nor do fumes from industrial plants recognize village or city lines as they blight vegetation, discolor house paint or choke lungs in neighboring communities. Nor do factory wastes that pollute streams turn about and float upstream when they reach a state line.

Airport development, rapid transit, sanitation, public health, civil defense, traffic control, and fire and police protection are among the problems that have spread beyond the bounds of existing government in many parts of the nation.

Some cities have tried to solve the problems of suburban sprawl by extending their corporate limits.

Los Angeles, whose 455 square miles make it the nation's biggest city geographically while it ranks third in population, got that way by cannibalizing suburbs. New communities were willing to become part of it because Los Angeles had cornered the water supply for the whole arid area.

Houston in 1949 doubled its municipal area by annexing suburbs.

New York, on the other hand, has not annexed any territory since 1898 and is not likely to. A suggestion—not likely to be followed—was made recently that its fiscal and governmental difficulties might be eased by splitting it into five separate cities.

Miami is working now with its neighboring communities to write a charter for a federated form of municipal government covering those functions that are essentially regional without depriving any of the Dade County municipalities of home rule over local matters.

Toronto is the only city on this continent that has adopted a metropolitan area form of government, but the concept of municipal home rule does not exist in Canada to the extent it does here.

The problems of exploding cities and sprawling urbanization are not confined to this continent. Stockholm is seeking to reduce overcrowding in the inner city's fourteen square miles by creating five satellite residential communities in the additional fifty-four square miles of the outer city.

In the United States, the problems of metropolitan areas and urban spread are as important as any domestic question confronting the nation.

The weight of thinking seems to be that these problems will not be solved by drawing a whole new set of geographical lines for governmental units. The answers may lie somewhere between a series of compacts among existing units of local government and new roles for Federal and state government.

January 27, 1957

4 Cities Marshal Agencies To Ease 'Growing Pains'

By GLADWIN HILL

Special to The New York Times.

LOS ANGELES, Feb. 1—A survey last year indicated that 15 per cent of the adults in Los Angeles did not know the name of the Mayor.

This might seem to betoken frightening ignorance in the nation's third largest city. Actually, the statistic reflected the complexity of Los Angeles' growth into the nation's third-ranking metropolis.

There is no compelling reason why most people *should* know the name of the Mayor. (It is Norris Poulson.) The community's development has reduced the Mayor to a ribbon-cutting figurehead, while the job of staving off civic chaos is in the hands of a hired professional administrative officer.

Of the more than 5,000,000 inhabitants of metropolitan Los Angeles—a sociologically, economically and topographically integrated area consisting chiefly of Los Angeles County—only about 2,000,000 live within the city limits. This is a legalistic distinction; it means little geographically.

The county covers 4,000 square miles, from the sea bordering one side of the metropolitan semicircle to the mile-high mountains fifty miles inland rimming the rest of it. It includes the nation's principal center of airplane manufacturing, one of the top-ranking agricultural districts of the nation and a little of everything else from atom-smashers to yoga retreats.

In the county—in addition to the 450-square-mile municipality of Los Angeles—are forty-nine other incorporated communities, aggregating about 335 square miles.

The rest, 3,215 square miles, is unincorporated territory, parts more densely populated than some formal cities. The residents have resisted incorporation to save taxes.

Los Angeles' far-famed city limits have surrounded other autonomous communities, such as Beverly Hills. Amid the incorporated areas, there are about thirty small completely surrounded "islands" of unincorporated county territory, indistinguishable in appearance from their environs, but under the jurisdiction of county rather than municipal government.

In this crazy pattern ,"urban," "suburban" and "exurban" are meaningless. Thirty miles from the Los Angeles City Hall, there are sections as densely populated as Yonkers. Yet within ten miles of that same City Hall, you may encounter rattlesnakes and wildcats.

The area's growth — which proceeds unabated at a rate of 4,300 additional inhabitants in the county every week—has tended to defy efforts of the County Regional Planning Commission and its counterpart, the Los Angeles City Planning Commission, to shape an orderly metropolitan area.

A prime reason for Los Angeles' helter-skelter municipal growth has been the desire of satellite settlements to participate in the city's precious water system.

This system, in an area endowed with less than 2 per cent of the state's natural water supply, brings 69 per cent of the city's water from as far away as 338 miles, in the Sierra Nevadas. Two additional sources are the local underground basin (24 per cent) and the Colorado River, 200 miles away (7 per cent).

Within fifteen years, it is expected that the city and its environs will need water from the Feather River, 500 miles away, in northern California.

This explosive growth has produced the usual array of metropolitan problems — traffic congestion, inadequate public transportation, "blighted" downtown districts, and radical shifts of retail trade to outlying areas—along with the extraordinary problem of smog.

But the most notable, although least publicized consequence, encompassing all these specific problems, has been to pose a challenge in public administration that bewilders experts and with which the Los Angeles metropolitan community has hardly come to grips.

Both the Los Angeles county and city governmental structures are of the horse and buggy model. The county governing body is an elected five-man Board of Supervisors, often amateurs in public administration. The City Government is headed by a City Council of fifteen members—each representing, in theory, the interests of 133,000 people, most of whom don't know their Councilman's name. Efforts to create a modern structure, such as a borough system, have been resisted by entrenched interests.

There are in the county, in addition to the Los Angeles city school system, more than 100 other school districts. Each has its own curricular standards, teacher salary scales and tax rate.

There are four systems for public services such as fire protection, libraries, etc. These are the respective municipal systems; the county system for the 3,000-odd square miles of unincorporated territory; a system called "the Lakewood Plan," under which incorporated communities buy services from the county under contract; and a complex of some 200 special-assessment "districts" serving limited areas with specific services they cannot get otherwise.

When the smog problem became severe more than a decade ago, it took several years just to decide on a way to attack it. This finally was done by persuading the State Legislature to create a county-wide air pollution control authority.

Millions of dollars have been spent on research and purported enforcement of air pollution regulations. But the smog remains, jeopardizing the health of people throughout most of the metropolitan area.

One reason is that the Los Angeles municipal administration has been too ineffectual to take a fundamental step toward alleviating smog: elimination of home incinerators, now necessary under law to dispose of combustible rubbish.

Municipal collection of rubbish was officially proposed more than a year ago. But, in the face of threats and obstruction by private rubbish collectors, city officials temporized. The matter will finally come before the voters as a question on the municipal ballot this spring.

If the automobile were abolished tomorrow, Los Angeles would cease to exist also. It is the most motorized community in the universe, with about two cars for every five people. The question in Los Angeles is not whether a car is a family necessity, but whether a second car is.

Public transportation is a skimpy network of privately owned bus lines that have slipped into the familiar economic tailspin of mounting costs, higher fares and decreasing patronage.

Los Angeles' major prospect for decent public transportation is that public sentiment, or vehicular congestion, may force the institution of comprehensive bus service under public auspices.

Being the metropolis most closely wedded to the automobile in its development, Los Angeles was in the forefront of this generation's great shift in retail trade.

Even from the lips of civic boosters, the terms "blight" and "plight" have become common in reference to downtown Los Angeles.

To revitalize it, attacks are being made on "Skid Row" and other slum centers. Dreary business buildings, a half-century or more old are finally collapsing, figuratively, under their own economic weight.

The old earthquake-born thirteen-story city limit on buildings was voted out last November. A $250,000,000 program of public-building construction, pointed toward an impressive civic center, is materializing. The problem of parking space is under extensive study.

The prospect is that the downtown district will continue, in modernized and perhaps amplified form, as a commercial and governmental center. But its heyday is gone.

Like strange sea creatures that ingest by turning themselves inside out, Los Angeles has attained urbanism, suburbanism and metropolitanism concurrently without ever leaving home.

Miami

By CLAYTON KNOWLES

Special to The New York Times.

MIAMI, Feb. 1—The inability of Miami city fathers to cope with a lion, legally free to roam the streets, helped to spark Dade County's pioneering drive for effective metropolitan government through federation.

Miami, largest of the twenty-six cities in Dade, had no local ordinance to deal with a loose lion, even if it was just a supposedly harmless pet. Public protest forced passage of a Miami ordinance to deal with the lion.

But the owner, unwilling to have his pet penned, moved across the Miami city line into an unincorporated area of the county where again there was no law applying. So the lion still ran free.

E. Albert Pallot, chairman of the Metropolitan Miami Municipal Board—known locally as the 3-M Board—tells the story to make a point. He says it shows how far more serious problems, area-wide in impact, defy solution under piecemeal attack by a multiplicity of local governments.

There was only one lion reported on the loose, but Mr. Pallot notes:

¶Each of the twenty-six cities, as well as the county, offers police protection but standards vary widely. Alarms are broadcast over five different wave lengths within the county, so that a community at times is unaware of serious crime in the very next city. Similar confusion exists in fire protection.

¶Seventy-one sewers, tied in with the various municipal systems, emptied into the county's two rivers and Biscayne Bay even after construction of a county sewage treatment plant.

¶Six bus lines serve the area but there is no coordination either in scheduling or routing.

¶A six-lane road in one city narrows to a two-lane strip in another, pointing up a lack of arterial plan that has produced traffic bottlenecks.

¶The city of Miami furnishes water at cost to other areas of Dade County but some communities, such as Miami Beach, resell it at sizable profit to others.

¶Conflicts in laws and regulations as between cities and county have impeded business. In construction trades, for example, a plumber or electrician may need as many as twenty-seven different licenses to operate in the county.

¶Certain cities are known as "liquor license towns," because they were incorporated to free saloons from county regulation.

Problems such as these are more or less common to the nation's metropolitan areas, but upon Greater Miami they descended like an avalanche in little more than a decade.

Phenomenal post-war growth was paced by former service men who, having trained in Florida, found the Miami area a good place for a family to live. Year-round tourism and new industry opened wide job opportunities.

Dade County covers the 40-by-50-mile southeast corner of the Florida mainland. The Everglades morass on the west channeled growth into eastern Dade along Atlantic coastal waters. Population, 5,000 in 1900, now tops 750,000.

Miami has less than thirty-five square miles of area but it has a third of the county's population. The twenty-five other cities have another third and unincorporated areas have the rest. Miami Beach and Hialeah rank second and third population-wise. Coral Gables and Miami Shores stand at the top as suburbs. Homestead and Florida City dot rural country to the south.

Community leaders early saw the need for metropolitan government. Consolidation efforts failed in 1947 and 1953. In one balloting just 908 votes saved Miami from voting itself out of existence.

Then Miami set up the 3-M Board with a $50,000 appropriation to find a better solution. The League of Municipalities, dubious at first, came to cooperate. The University of Miami was placed in charge and hired the Public Administration Service to make the actual study. It proposed metropolitan county government, federal in concept.

Two measures were pushed through the Florida Legislature by the Dade County delegation, headed by Senator R. B. Gautier. One set up a Metropolitan Charter Board with $50,000 in funds to draft a charter. The other initiated a constitutional amendment conferring home-rule power needed to proceed.

The amendment swept county and state by better than a 2-to-1 margin when submitted to the voters last fall. Strong support from The Miami Herald and The Miami News helped to counter charges that the reform was a step toward socialism or Dade's move for school integration. Actually the schools, like the courts, already were county-operated.

Now a reconstituted Charter Board, another $50,000 in hand, is drafting the metropolitan charter.

The only compromise to date has come on the make-up of the county commission, the governing body under the proposed metropolitan set-up. Many had hoped that members would be elected by area-wide vote. Instead, it was agreed that five would be nominated by district and elected at large. Five others would be chosen solely by district vote.

An eleventh seat would go to Miami by virtue of having a population in excess of 60,000. Miami Beach and Hialeah, within striking distance of the 60,000 mark, seem likely to qualify for additional representation on this basis in the near future.

Policy set by the commission would be executed by a metropolitan manager named by the commission.

Retaining the identity of present cities to deal with purely local problems and to supplement county services, where desired, is the key to federation. The new metropolitan county government would deal only with problems "essentially regional."

Areas of exclusive metropolitan jurisdiction, as defined by the Charter Board, would be these:

¶Arterial highways and off-street parking; traffic engineering; air, water, rail and bus terminals and public transportation generally.

¶Metropolitan land-use zoning; housing, renovation and conservation programs; uniform building and technical codes, and licensing of contractors.

¶Primary flood control, surface drainage; water supply; sewerage and sewage disposal; refuse collection.

¶Health and welfare programs; police and fire standards; county park and recreation facilities; libraries.

The charter is to be submitted to county voters for approval this spring.

St. Louis

Special to The New York Times.

ST. LOUIS, Feb. 1—Far-reaching proposals are in prospect to revise the governmental structure on the Missouri side of the St. Louis area.

Besides the usual irritations common to metropolitan areas, St. Louis has some peculiar to itself and its situation at the confluence of the Missouri and Mississippi Rivers. Within the spread-out metropolitan district are many industrial areas and a railway network rivaling Chicago's.

The St. Louis metropolitan area embraces 2,500 square miles, roughly one and a half times as large as Long Island. The area as a whole has a population of 1,904,000, according to an estimate on Jan. 1, 1956. Of this total, 1,465,000 persons live on the Missouri side of the area and 439,000 across the Mississippi in East St. Louis and other Illinois communities.

Community growth is influenced by accessibility and the location of new plants or other employment opportunities. Almost all the industrial growth in recent years has been outside the city of St. Louis. This is in part attributed to the effect current architecture has on the location of industrial plants.

Most plant designers now prefer horizontal expansion or development to vertical expansion or development. The tendency is to place as many operations as possible on a single floor. Necessarily this enlarges the land area covered. Employe parking space further increases the need for land.

A new Dow Chemical Company plant at Riverside, south of St. Louis, covers 120 acres. If it had been located within the City of St. Louis it would have covered sixty blocks. Another chemical company has taken 200 acres, an aluminum company 120 acres.

But the labor force to operate these plants is not available in the communities where the new plants are located. A large part of the labor force is being drawn from St. Louis and from other communities in the area. The result has been an enormous increase in automobile traffic to and from work over highways and nine bridges that were never planned for such a volume.

Population growth in St. Louis and St. Charles Counties has led to a proliferation of local units of government. With the sole exception of Cook County in Illinois, which includes Chicago and its suburbs, St. Louis County has more separate divisions of government than any other county in the United States.

The City of St. Louis, as other large cities, is suffering from a wholesale migration of middle and upper income families to suburban areas. This has meant that it has been forced to increase proportionately its welfare and other civic expenditures. It has also meant that the city has suffered a loss of leadership material for civic activities and a loss of taxables.

A city earnings tax has enabled St. Louis to offset some of its loss of taxables. This tax is levied against all those who work within the corporate limits of the city, regardless of where they live, and on all residents of the city employed outside the city. It is deducted at the source.

It may seem strange to New Yorkers, but the imposition of this earnings tax was approved at a referendum. One explanation for the favorable vote is that St. Louis has a high percentage of home owners. The earnings tax, one-half of 1 per cent of gross earnings of individuals and of net profits of enterprises, was presented as an alternative to higher real estate taxes.

With the imposition of the tax, the City of St. Louis embarked on a huge slum clearance and public improvement program.

The initiative for the St. Louis face-lifting project and for the current program of revising the governmental structures in the city and in the separate County of St. Louis has been provided by a private organization known as Civic Progress, Inc. This consists of public-spirited citizens and is modeled after the Allegheny Conference on Community Development in Pittsburgh with some adaptions to local conditions. It was organized by former Mayor Joseph M. Darst of St. Louis in 1953 and is now headed by Powell B. McHaney.

The Ford Foundation and a local foundation jointly put up $300,000 to finance a metropolitan St. Louis survey. This is making an analysis and inventory of governmental units in the City of St. Louis and in the County of St. Louis. The survey is being directed by Prof. John C. Bollens of the University of California.

The survey, scheduled for completion this winter, is expected to provide the incentive for utilizing a special section of the Missouri State Constitution to set up a charter revision commission. This group would plan and suggest changes in the charters of both the City of St. Louis and of the County of St. Louis.

Toronto

By H. W. PATTERSON

Special to The New York Times.

TORONTO, Feb. 1—Until three years ago, Toronto and its twelve suburbs were in a typical metropolitan quandary. Each community, pushed by post-war expansion, went its own haphazard way.

Today Toronto and its suburbs—five thickly settled townships, four smaller towns and three villages — are living together as Metropolitan Toronto, often called Metro.

The area's 239.7 miles contain 1,400,000 persons. Premier Leslie Frost of the Province of Ontario believes Metro has cleared the way to a 1970 population of 2,000,000.

The arrangement has critics, of course, but since its inception in January, 1954, Metro's planners point to these achievements: Equalized assessment among industrial, commercial and residential properties; a water system already fifteen times greater in capacity than in 1954; an improved sewage system; construction of arterial roads and expressways; planned school expansion; and a credit rating that provides high borrowing power at interest of 4 per cent, lower than each community could get for itself.

The post-war economic boom, spurred by sharp increases in immigration and the birth rate, has raised the suburban population from 100,000 to 700,000, equaling Toronto's present population. The city stopped annexation thirty-three years ago, and, with the suburbs burgeoning, had no room to expand.

By the early Nineteen Fifties some outlying communities were pushed close to bankruptcy by demands of education, water supply and sewage disposal.

At this point, the Ontario provincial government, which has the power to regulate municipal affairs broadly, enacted Bill 80. This established a federated system of local government, short of amalgamation. The municipalities retained autonomy in local matters and received representation on a new Metro Council responsible for area services.

Metro levies no taxes directly but establishes a uniform rate collected for the central government by member communities, along with the varying local rate.

The ratio of Metro debt to assessment is about 7 per cent, reflecting a solid financial position.

The Toronto Transit Commission has a monopoly on public transportation within the Metro area. With one of the lowest fare structures on the continent —12½ cents for a ticket or token and 15 cents in cash—the T. T. C. recently completed a $60,000,000 north-south subway, and a start on a $150,000,000 crosstown subway is tentatively set for 1958. Metro meets the deficits caused by debt service, although operating revenues are excellent.

When Metro was organized, it was decided to delay unification of the Police and Fire Departments. On Jan. 1 of this year, the thirteen separate police forces were joined, providing greater liaison and communications. Similar merger of fire departments is expected by 1958.

Other joint operations by Metro are the planning board, which seeks to curb undesirable fringe developments; the parks board, which is acquiring parklands and has opened an eighteen-hole golf course; and a lisensing commission with sole control of licenses in the entire district.

Some aspects of Metro have been attacked, particularly the basically undemocratic set-up of the Metro Council. No member of the twenty-five-man body is directly elected. Toronto has twelve members (the Mayor, two Controllers and nine Aldermen), and the twelve surrounding communities send their Mayors, or Reeves. The chairman, appointed annually by the Council, has the twenty-fifth, or tie-breaking, vote.

In the council, Toronto has equal representation with the rest of the Metro community, but a chronic sore spot is the fact that the largest suburban unit (North York, pop. 150,000) has the same single vote as the smallest (Swansea, pop. 9,000).

What may drive Metro closer to outright amalgamation is the increasing urgency of a new financial arrangement. It is designed to enable Metro to plan for a huge capital expansion of $750,000,000 in ten years, without forcing tax increases.

Some insist Metro is already too large and is losing respect for the rights of citizens. They cite residents in suburban Leaside who woke one morning to find road-widening crews staking out portions of their lawns. Only fast action by local councillors **forced Metro to retreat.**

Toronto settled for the Metro arrangement only after its effort for amalgamation through annexation had failed against determined suburban opposition.

But there remains wide support in the city for a full merger. At least half of the Toronto Board of Control favors such a move because Metro is "cumbersome, duplicates government, and is expensive."

Provincial and Metro officials maintain that duplication is being eliminated as authorities find their proper spheres.

February 2, 1957

COUNTIES TAKING URBAN AREA ROLE

Coping With Growth, They Assume Civic Functions From Water to Airports

County governments are meeting the challenge of urban expansion by assuming a larger amount of administrative responsibility.

In its 1958 Municipal Yearbook, the International City Managers Association says that seven out of ten persons now live in urban areas in the United States.

Counties are providing facilities for a greater amount of water supply, planning, airport operation and hospital administration, according to Bernard F. Hillenbrand, executive director of the National Association of County Officials, of Washington.

Mr. Hillenbrand reports that a survey conducted by his organization indicates that counties in metropolitan areas also are taking over duties in civil defense, election registration, property tax assessment and health and welfare activities. He adds that urban renewal, previously a municipal function, has become a county activity in Yollo County, California, and Davidson County, Tennessee.

Mr. Hillenbrand cites Dade County in Florida, which includes Miami, as having recently instituted a plan of federated urban services. He notes that efforts are being made to strengthen county government in Harris County, Tex.; Sacramento County, Calif.; Davidson County, Tenn., and Fairfax County, Va.

May 25, 1958

Nashville Area Approves New Metro Government

NASHVILLE, Tenn., June 29 (AP) — A consolidated government for Nashville and Davidson County has been approved in a referendum. It is scheduled to begin operating next April.

The count from all 121 precincts was 36,978 for the new government set-up, called Metro, and 28,113 against. **Four years ogo a similar plan for consolidating the two governmental units was defeated by a small margin.**

The city administration of Mayor Ben West had opposed Metro.

June 30, 1962

'CONTRACT CITIES' MARK FIFTH YEAR

Coast Communities Buying Services From County Will Hold Seminar

By GLADWIN HILL

Special to The New York Times.

LOS ANGELES, April 23—A group of pioneering communities that have cured a nation-wide municipal headache will celebrate five years of urban bliss this week.

They are California's score of "contract cities" in Los Angeles County, which have no worries about police departments, fire departments, libraries, dog pounds, or other municipal services whose operations burden thousands of conventional communities.

The contract cities buy such services, on a cash-and-carry basis, from the county. They pay their own way, including their share of the county overhead. But they avoid the expense, inefficiency and aggravation of maintaining a bevy of bureaucratic departments duplicating those of every surrounding community.

Their example is regarded by many as a promising key to the management of the country's growing array of metropolises, hampered by archaic municipal boundaries and evermounting overhead.

The contract plan preserves and intensifies community identity and home rule.

The limitation of the system is that it cannot be applied to an isolated municipality. It calls for a sizable cluster of cities, organized under a county or some other super-government **agency that can provide the community services on a sort of supermarket basis.**

The so-called Lakewood Plan has worked so well that its exponents will hold what amounts to a three-day jubilee at Palm Springs starting Friday. The California Contract Cities First Annual Seminar will examine their achievements and problems.

Los Angeles County covers 4,085 square miles, with a population of some 6,000,000. It comprises sixty-eight incorporated communities.

But a sizable portion of its population has inevitably settled in unincorporated areas. These were dependent for community services on county agencies paralleling those of ordinary municipalities.

Incorporation was encouraged by a desire for community identity, but discouraged by the prospect of higher takes to establish, on a municipal basis, the services being received from the county.

Then Lakewood, a Levittown type of suburb of 60,000 people covering 7.5 square miles, which had sprung up as a subdivision on pre-war bean fields, conceived a plan for community identity. Some incorporated cities were buying specialized services from the county; why not buy all of them?

Today Lakewood has 75,000 people. It gets about everything from the county except parks and recreation facilities and water supply, which have been kept under community control. Its annual budget is about $2,000,000, against an estimated possible overhead of $7,000,000 to $10,000,000 under a conventional structure. (Its municipal tax rate is 24 cents per $100 assessed valuation. It has a mayor, a four-man City Council, a city administrator and an aggregate governmental staff of 90.

April 24, 1960

NORTHEAST CITED AS WORLD CENTER

Study for 20th Century Fund Calls Seaboard Megalopolis 'Pioneer' of Modern Society

LEADER IN MANY AREAS

Region Described as Hub of U.S. Decision Making and of International Relations

By MARTIN ARNOLD

The "pioneer area" of modern society stretches from southern New Hampshire to northern Virginia, and from the Atlantic to the Appalachian foothills, according to a study released today.

In this huge complex of cities, suburbs and rural sections, the survey finds, are the major "decision making" centers of the nation and the "dynamic hub of international relations."

It is called the megalopolis—for a city-state planned in the Peloponnesus, in ancient Greece.

The megalopolis study, which took four years and cost $200,000, was made for the Twentieth Century Fund by Jean Gottman, a French geographer. It was published by the fund in a 777-page book entitled "Megalopolis: The Urbanized Northeast Seaboard of the United States."

Dr. Gottman calls the area "the cradle of a new order in the organization of inhabited space" and finds that within it the old distinctions of urban and rural no longer apply.

Loosely Organized Unit

Rather, he says, it has a "personality of its own." It is a loosely organized unit, mainly white-collar populated, containing city centers, decentralized manufacturing areas, suburban belts and ever-increasing areas of parks and woodlands.

Megalopolis has developed a supremacy in the policies, arts, communication and economy of the United States, Dr. Gottman says.

Its [illegible],500 square miles have become "a new stage in human civilization," he says.

"How this great area solves its problems and meets the challenges of a new mode of life is going to be very important to the United States and the rest of the world," Dr. Gottman believes.

He says he does not foresee that the entire area will become one great city, or that present political boundaries within it will be changed. But he does predict that railroads will regain their importance as a means of rapid transit in the megalopolis, and that manufacturing will be pushed to the fringe areas.

Population of 37 Million

The population of megalopolis is 37,000,000, according to the 1960 census.

"The main axis of the region is about 600 miles and the width varies between 30 and 100 miles," Dr. Gottman notes. The chief population and power centers on the axis are New York, Washington, Boston, Philadelphia and Baltimore.

Dr. Gottman holds that other megalopolises will, in time, grow in the industrial Midwest between the Great Lakes and the Ohio River, on the California coast and in Western Europe.

The northeast megalopolis, he writes, is the great experimental center, and "new programs are needed to conserve the natural beauty of the landscape and to assure the health, prosperity and freedom of the people."

Dr. Gottman is a professor at the School of Higher Studies in Paris, associated with the Institute of Advanced Study at Princeton. He is the author also of "A Geography of Europe" and "Virginia at Mid-Century."

November 27, 1961

A New Level of Government Emerges in the Nation: Regional Councils to Attack Areawide Problems

By JOHN HERBERS
Special to The New York Times

WASHINGTON, April 18—While the Federal system in the United States has been undergoing severe strain in recent years, an important new level of government has sprung up almost unnoticed by the public.

More than 140 councils of government—voluntary organizations of municipalties and counties—have been established across the country to attack areawide problems. Most have been established since 1966 under the incentive of Federal grants, and most are in metropolitan areas, which have scores and sometimes hundreds of separate governments, each with its own tax base, ordinances and services.

The only powers the councils have are those delegated by the member governments and increasing authority from Washington to review Federal grants flowing to the local governments, and to decide whether the funded projects are regionally beneficial.

As a result, the councils or COG's as they are called, have been involved more in planning than action and have been reluctant to come to grips with the more controversial forces that are afflicting metropolitan areas.

But they have emerged as the chief regional instrument for preventing chaos and waste. Some of them are beginning to move into social action, and there is a vitality and enthusiasm among the membership that is rare on the current American scene.

Further, there is the possibility that as urban problems grow, the council's may assume power and authority approaching that of the areawide metropolitan government. In the Minneapolis-St. Paul area, for example, the Minnesota Legislature has given the Metro Council taxing authority and the power to plan and carry out anti-pollution measures, solid waste disposal, zoning and noise abatement in a seven-county area.

The typical metropolitan area consists of a central city and a proliferation of suburban municipalities and county governments. The central cities have encountered a declining tax base, due to the movement of wealth outward, and an inability to impose uniform standards for the police, utilities, transportation, pollution control and health and welfare services.

In the mid-Nineteen sixties, the enactment of Federal grant-in-aid programs ranging from sewage treatment plants to antipoverty programs, further increased the confusion. At that time there were only a handful of councils, and there was little movement toward establishing metropolitan - wide governments.

In the Housing Act of 1965, Congress provided for direct Federal assistance to the councils. In the Model cities Act of 1966, Congress required areawide reviews of Federal grants to avoid conflicts, duplications and harmful effects. This task fell largely to the councils, which increased rapidly after

Federal funds had been made available.

The Nixon Administration has further strengthened them by requiring more reviews. The Nixon policy of strengthening the role of the states in domestic affairs has helped the organizations in some instances In Texas, the state government has joined with Washington in providing direct financial assistance, and the council there are flourishing.

But there is fear within some councils that cut across state lines that strengthening the state role in regional projects will harm the organizations.

For example, Walter A. Scheiber, director of the Metropolitan Washington Council, one of the oldest and most innovative of the councils, said that his group was increasingly concerned that Richmond and Annapolis, the Virginia and Maryland capitals, which have jurisdiction over the Washington suburbs would fail to give the council the support it needed.

"Their interests simply don't lie here," Mr. Scheiber said.

The Metropolitan Area Planing Council in Boston, which represents 100 governments in Massachusetts, provides a case study in the problems and promises involved. Each government has one representative on the council. In addition, the Governor appoints 21 members from the area at large, and the chairman of state and local agencies are ex-officio members. Each of the 131 members has one vote.

A staff of 30 persons includes planners, economists, lawyers and designers. Recently, the council has become involved in social issues. It provides technical assistance to low and moderate income housing projects and does some work in manpower training and education.

"There were a lot of people who questioned us at first," said Richard M. Doherty, director of the council. "They thought of us as a monster who would eat up local boundary lines. But we don't have enough power to be controversial. We don't take property or spend their money."

In almost every city, there is a fear on the part of the small governments that the councils will become a government superstructure and fear among blacks that their strength will be diluted by the suburbs.

Robert Farley, deputy director of the Southwest Michigan Council, which represents 105 governments in the Detroit area, said that 18 governments had pulled out of the organization since it was formed in 1968 and 11 others had joined.

'Too Many Cooks'

"Some of them don't want anything to do with inner city problems," he said, "and then some of the militant persons from the inner city see us as a plot to give control to the lily-white suburbs."

One of the critics of the council is Mayor Orville Hubbard of all-white Dearborn who says, "We already have too many cooks in the kitchen, and one more would only further gum up the works. Cities need more home rule, not more regional control."

Nevertheless, the council has brought about a central water system in which Detroit leases water to 60 surrounding communities, is involved in a number of social programs to help the inner-city poor and is currently trying to persuade the state to enact uniform building codes to lower the cost of housing.

The councils cite a wide range of accomplishments. There are the elementary ones: The East-West Gateway Co-Ordinating Council in St. Louis stopped plans of two jurisdictions to build an airport runway and a highway in the same place.

And there are the more sophistiacted examples: The Metropolitan Washington Council was responsible for the member governments adopting a uniform ordinance against air pollution rather than waiting for Federal directives.

The relations between the council and member governments can be quite delicate. Eugene G. Moody, director of the council in St. Louis, said that the council did not try to intervene in certain disputes.

He gave as an example a current dispute between St. Louis and St. Louis County on whether funds under the Federal Crime Control and Safe Streets Act should be used for building juvenile detention facilities, as the city wants, or for helicopters and police equipment, as the county wants.

"The council will not act until it is required to review the final proposal for the funds," Mr. Moody said.

The councils are represented nationally by an organization called National Service to Regional Councils, which also represents economic development districts and regional planning commissions. At the organization's national convention in Atlanta last month, the president, Thomas Bradley, a Los Angeles City Councilman, urged the councils to move beyond planning to action.

Because of public pressures for better services, he said "local governments may very well find it necessary to give of themselves in order that their citizens may receive the level of services to which they are entitled."

A common thread running through the conversations of the people who work with the councils is that they are evolving into something different and meaningful, but no one is sure what that is.

Homer Chandler, director of the Columbia Regional Association of Governments in Portland, Ore., expressed doubt that the people would support a powerful regional government. Officials of the Metropolitan Atlanta Council held up the Minneapolis-St. Paul Council with its limited governmental powers, as a model.

Mr. Moody of the St. Louis Council said, "It's too early to tell whether the council is a success. It is in an evolutionary period. It has done what it can. Conceivably, it may be a bridge to something better."

April 19, 1970

Nation's Cities Fighting to Stem Growth

By GLADWIN HILL

On March 21, the city of St. Petersburg, Fla., adopted an ordinance requiring the last 25,000 people who had settled there to move out.

This extraordinary edict was rescinded only a fortnight later as manifestly unconstitutional and impractical.

But the incident epitomizes rapidly changing attitudes toward community growth: Countless communities around the country, far from welcoming growth in the traditional bigger-is-better vein, now fear they are being overwhelmed by it and are moving hastily to stop it.

Limitations on growth, ranging from population ceilings to moratoriums on building permits, are proliferating by the day. Each place has its own reasons. Water supply and sewage treatment are overloaded. Open space or other environmental values are threatened. Taxpayers are outraged at the prospect of big new capital investments needed to provide community services for soaring populations.

But whatever the reasons for growth controls, however logical they may seem on a local basis, collectively they are confronting the nation with a difficult tangle of questions, questions perplexing to the real estate and construction industries, the legal world, civil rights advocates, demographers, planners, politicians and millions of people simply looking for homes. For example:

¶Upward of 50 million people are going to augment the nation's population in the next 25 years. If growth-limitation becomes general, where are these people going to live?

¶Does a community have a right to "pull up the gangplank" and shunt future population elsewhere?

¶Granting that many communities have real growth problems, who is to decide which ones should be allowed to adopt limits?

¶If states undertook to apportion growth equitably among communities, who would then decide on equitable apportionment of population among the states?

¶How can community constraints on expansion be reconciled with people's right under the Constitution to travel freely and settle where they please?

In sum, growth controls are aggravating this country's traditional philosophical tension between private initiative and public regulation.

And in practical terms, in the view of some observers, they are tending to price a large portion of middle-income people out of the housing market.

The first rumblings of what land use experts are calling the growth-control "explosion" came as far back as the 1960's, when the Pennsylvania courts began getting suits from subdividers whose projects had been rejected by communities on the ground that they just didn't want more people.

By 1970, District of Columbia suburbs in Maryland and Virginia were becoming so overbuilt in relation to sewage treatment facilities that state and county officials were impelled to impose moratoriums on building permits and sewer connections — measures that have continued and been extended ever since.

In 1971 the City of Boulder, Colo., made headlines when its 70,000 residents voted on whether to adopt a population ceiling of 100,000. The proposal was narrowly defeated. But a year later, residents of the plush resort community of Boca Raton, Fla., did take substantially the same step by adopting a zoning plan with a limit of 40,000 residential units—a measure that is still in litigation.

Meanwhile, growth controls have erupted elsewhere at a rate that has reached epidemic proportions. Marin County in California invoked growth controls on the ground that its water supply could not serve many more people.

Palo Alto, Calif., zoned 10 square miles of undeveloped land into 10-acre parcels to thwart building.

Southampton, Long Island, with a population of 39,000, adopted a zoning plan with an ultimate limit of 127,000.

Keyed to Pupil Space

San Jose, Calif., last year voted a two-year freeze on any new residential zoning that would reduce pupil-space in schools.

Orange County, Calif., with 1,500,000 people, has cut back its population ceiling for the year 2020 from 4 million to 2.9 million.

Only a few days ago, Loudoun County, Virginia, a Washington suburban area, refused to approve a $112-million, 4,200-unit "new town," even though the developer promised to reimburse the county for installing the necessary public services.

By last year, according to the Environmental Protection Agency, sewer-hookup moratoriums were in effect in 160 cities in Ohio and Illinois alone, and in 40 communities in Florida.

As of mid-April this year, 30 of the 112 communities in New Jersey's Passaic basin had building moratoriums of one sort or another.

All told, according to the latest survey by the Department of Housing and Urban Development, some 226 cities have imposed moratoriums on building permits, water or sewer connections, rezoning (to permit development), subdividing, or other essentials of growth.

In some cases growth-control measures have been only temporary, pending construction of facilities to serve new residents. But in many if not most cases, communities' avowed reason for growth controls has been to curb unending influxes of new residents.

Population Density Down

Virtually never has the demonstrable cause of such moves been actual exhaustion of physical space.

Contrary to a widespread impression, urban population density in the United States has been steadily declining for half a century, from 6,580 people per square mile in 1920 to 4,230 now — a reflection of "urban sprawl."

Dr. Kenneth E. F. Watt, University of California ecologist, has calculated that the 25,000 people now typically spread over 10 square miles in tract housing could be comfortably accommodated in six 13-story apartment towers covering only 1/50th of a square mile—1/500th of the tract space — with even more pleasures of "the great outdoors" provided immediately at hand. While perhaps only a minority want to live in apartments, the huge space differential in Dr. Watt's figures is considered to reflect spatial economies possible in communities generally.

Studies of relative population pressures on many cities, according to Dr. Judith Blake, University of California demographer, indicate that in many cases growth controls are simply a reactionary "pull up the gangplank" syndrome on the part of established communities resistant to any change in accustomed amenities.

This outlook was typified in a housewife's exhortation at a public hearing in Orion, Mich.: "Don't change Orion or it will become just like so many of the cities we've moved away from. We paid dearly to come out here."

In many other cases, however, growth controls are conceded to be a natural response to inadequate community planning and to belated realization that additional population does not always pay its own way.

While some surveys sponsored by real estate people have indicated that big new developments can be an economic plus, many communities have made contradictory findings, and either blocked developments or concocted heavy surcharges on developers to defray costs of facilities such as streets, water, sewer, and electric lines, schools and parks.

A 1972 Denver study indicated that each new residence would cost taxpayers $21,000 for community services. A Stanford University study at Half Moon Bay, near San Francisco, indicated that a 1,262-unit subdivision would cost the community $400,000 a year by 1982 in indirect subsidies for public services.

Palo Alto's zoning came after a study indicating that a $17,000 surcharge would have to be imposed on a $45,000 home, in addition to regular taxes, if it were to pay its share for the additional public services it occasioned.

Beyond moratoriums, the repertoire of growth controls includes a variety of zoning practices — sequestration of open land, from which development is excluded; large-lot zoning, making home sites too expensive for anyone but the wealthy, and restrictions on commercial development and apartments or other multiple housing.

Another set of devices is special levies on large-scale developers — high permit fees, extra charges of schools and the other community services a new development entails; requirements that developers deed a sizable portion of their land to community facilities such as parks; imposts to pay for parks in other parts of a community, or simply fees — in the name of helping out with community overhead — that go into a city's general treasury.

Controls as Scarcity

Blending these measures in various combinations are "phased-growth" plans, which in effect ration building permits and other development over a period of years.

Last January Fairfax County, Va., a major Washington suburb, adopted a 20-year program banning all building that did not qualify under a point system covering its need and feasibility from the standpoint of costs to the community.

Growth controls so far have not taken the form of uniformed officers heading off newcomers at city limits. Even in communities with building moratoriums there is a turnover in population. There are always residences to be had — at a price.

Instead, controls have taken the subtler form of making buildable land and residences scarcer, automatically pushing prices steadily upward.

The Advance Mortgage Corporation of Detroit estimated that growth constraints deprived the country of at least 50,000 housing units last year.

The National Association of Home Builders says that the median price of a home has jumped in just two years from $25,000 to $35,000—more than can be attributed to normal price components — and that home construction is dropping 40 per cent, from 2.4 million units in 1973 to a projected 1.4 million this year.

In Petaluma, Calif., scene of a major growth control controversy, there have been as many as 1,600 applications for the annual "ration" of 500 building permits.

The Home Builders Association of Westchester County, N. Y., estimates that a home in the area of Purchase that could have been bought for $40,000 five years ago would be priced at around $70,000 today.

Since sewer-connection moratoriums became widespread in the Washington suburbs of Montgomery and Prince Georges counties in Maryland, home building has dropped between one-third and one-half, building industry spokesmen say.

'Overriding Obstacle'

"While the crucial questions of financing, energy conservation and land and labor costs continue to plague the building industry," Ray Lehmkuhl, president of the Pacific Coast Builders Conference said a few days ago, "the overriding obstacle to providing adequate shelter for our citizens continues to be restrictive land use policies by municipalities."

The effects of growth controls have been pronounced enough to convince many responsible people that they constitute an infringement on citizens' legal rights of mobility.

The right to travel among the states and settle where one pleases is not mentioned in the Constituion. But it was set forth in the Articles of Confederation, precursor of the Constitution, so explicitly that the United States Supreme Court has held repeatedly that it is an inferential part of the Constitution.

Opposition to "exclusionary" land use measures has created an odd alliance between the development industry, which an occasion has been accused of discriminatory practices itself, and civil rights organizations.

The National Association of Home Builders, while eschewing litigation itself, has established a $200,000 fund for legal assistance to its regional and local affiliates, which have been plaintiffs in many key lawsuits challenging certain kinds of zoning and other practices aimed at growth control.

Also involved in such challenges are such organizations as the National Association for the Advancement of Colored People, the American Civil Liberties Union, the Suburban Action Committee of White Plains, N. Y., and the National Committee Against Discrimination in Housing.

In some cases courts have agreed with them; in others not. Over-all, the basic issue of constitutional validity, like many other aspects of the growth control movement, remains undecided.

Nevertheless, says James Rouse, mastermind of the celebrated "new town" of Columbia, Md.:

"It's very clear that we are in the midst of probably the most radical change in our concept of private property rights that we have ever seen in this country.

"The notion that a developer has a right to develop because he owns a piece of land, and that the public must let him, is rapidly changing."

Petaluma: The Evolution of a Landmark Growth Controls Case

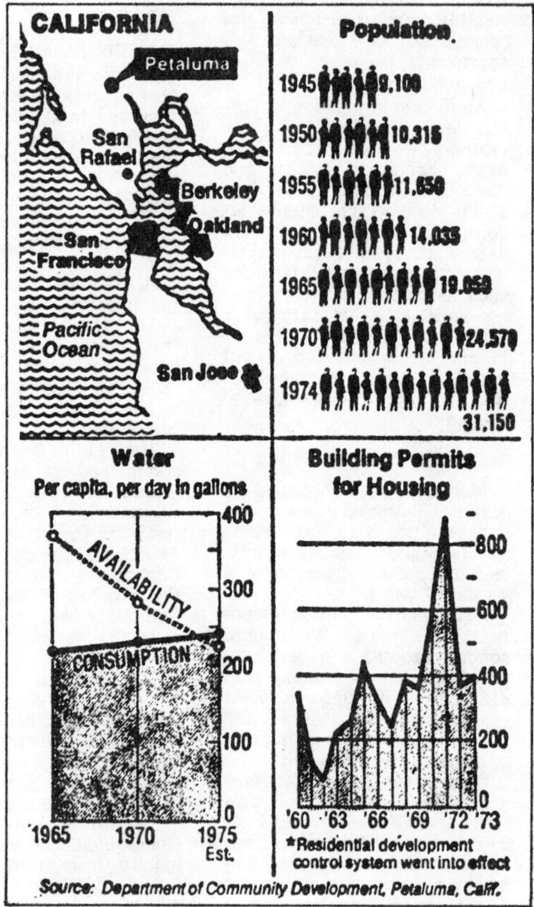

The population of Petaluma, Calif., a 100-year-old farming center involved in a landmark growth controls case, never exceeded 10,000 until recent times.

Then in 1956 U. S. Highway 101 running along the eastern edge of town was widened to a freeway. This, along with suburbanization in the San Francisco Bay area, began a process of explosive growth — 14,000 people in 1960, 25,000 by mid-1970, 30,000 by the end of 1971.

Most of the development was tract housing east of the freeway, with only two freeway crossovers linking the new area with the "old town."

A 1962 "master plan" of development produced by outside consultants had projected an ultimate growth to 77,000 by 1985.

However, even before the 1970 census tally of 25,000, the city public works department warned that the sewage system could handle only one more year of growth at the current rate.

Meanwhile, the city approached the limit of its water supply, schools went on double sessions, and there was a prospective scarcity of open park land east of the freeway.

All these factors impelled citizens in June, 1973, to approve by 4 to 1 an ordinance instituted in August, 1972, "rationing" growth for the ensuing five years to 500 dwelling units a year. A United States District Court has ruled that this "rationing" is invalid. The city is now appealing.

July 28, 1974

THE AUTO STRANGLES THE CITY

LAYS CITIES' 'ROT' TO TRAFFIC JAMS

AAA Official Cites New York and Cleveland as Examples of Deterioration

By BERT PIERCE
Special to THE NEW YORK TIMES.

WASHINGTON, May 14—All of the major cities in this country are "rotting at the core" due to the lack of essential route development and adequate parking facilities, William H. Stinchcomb of Cleveland, chairman of the National Highway and Legislative Committee of the American Automobile Association, said today at the annual meeting of the executive committee of the organization here.

New York and Cleveland were cited by him as examples of deterioration attributable to failure to provide accommodations for motor travel. The far reaching cost of this neglect will mount to billions of dollars before remedies are put into effect, "if they ever are," he added.

Mr. Stinchcomb emphasized that the urban centers are the "bottlenecks" for traffic as more than half of the motor vehicle miles traveled annually throughout the United States is in these areas.

Decentralization Is Underway

"A process of decentralization of population in many cities is underway as business and industry are finding out to their loss," he said.

"With too few thoroughfares to meet travel demands and only a small percentage of necessary parking space, the purchasing power is being forced outside of urban limits and this movement rapidly is increasing."

By-passing large centers is not a practical solution for congestion, he asserted, as the ultimate effect is merely the diversion of traffic seeking to go from one designated location to another.

"New York offers an excellent picture of a city that is fast getting nowhere with its mounting traffic problems," he said. "The basic concepts of orderly and economically sound travel movement are all awry. One anomaly is putting a ban on parking in several of the most important sections of Manhattan when the mass transportation systems are entirely inadequate to carry travel volume thrown upon them. There is just one answer to such tactics and that includes tremendous losses in business and property values."

Mr. Stinchcomb pointed out that the same pattern applied to Cleveland, and the longer the delay in bringing about relief the greater the expense.

To obtain an intelligent program of street and road improvements in large metropolitan areas was termed "an uphill fight" by Mr. Stinchcomb, who pointed out that it is difficult to get local governments to assume responsibility.

"Some cities have made progress in physical programs," he added, "but all are inadequate in financial plans. What I fear is that some day we will wake up and find an emergency of such magnitude that we will not be prepared to meet it."

So serious is the over-all parking situation viewed that a resolution seeking relief was presented under American Automobile Association auspices and offered for country-wide consideration.

It stressed the acute need for parking facilities and urged that until the required space is available that cities adopt regulations which will protect motorists against loss and against exorbitant charges when utilizing privately owned facilities.

May 15, 1947

380 CITIES NOW OWN AUTO PARKING LOTS

Three hundred and eighty cities in the United States, each with a population of more than 10,000, now own and operate municipal parking lots, according to a survey made by the International City Managers' Association. The 380 cities represent almost 40 per cent of the 961 cities that replied to the association's 1950 Municipal Year Book questionnaire.

The survey found that sixty-three cities opened parking lots in 1949. One hundred others opened additional lots during the year.

Among the larger cities which opened parking lots for the first time last year were St. Paul, Minn.; Dayton, Ohio; Gary, Ind.; Syracuse, N. Y., and Trenton, N. J.

Parking meters are used by forty-one of the fifty-nine cities that reported their parking charges. The 5-cent fee for one hour is the most popular.

Hourly rates are used by thirty-three cities, ten cities use daily rates, two use monthly rates and one requires minute rates. The two cities with monthly rates both charge $2.50. All day parking rates range from 25 cents in Akron, Gary and Wheeling to 15 cents in Pittsburgh and Battle Creek, Mich.

Five cities own and operate parking garages. They are: Ann Arbor, Mich.; Bluefield, W. Va.; Kamath Falls, Ore.; La Grange, Ga., and South River, N. J.

May 14, 1950

GROWTH AREA SHIFT TO AUTOS INDICATED

Two significant changes in the distribution of population in the New York-New Jersey-Connecticut metropolitan region should be of "special interest to city officials concerned with the mounting parking problem," the Regional Plan Association reported yetserday.

In a study of population distribution in the decade from 1940 to 1950, the association said that a substantial proportion of the growth in the city's outer boroughs occurred more than one mile from subway stations, while two-thirds of suburban growth took place within one mile of arterial highways.

The two facts indicate that "more and more people in the metropolitan region may be turning from rail to motor vehicles as the principal means of getting to work," Henry Fagin, planning director, said.

"The changing pattern should serve as a sharp warning to state and local officials that improved rapid transit, rail and bus service are essential to maintain the economic prosperity of older centers such as Manhattan, Brooklyn, Newark and Jersey City," he declared.

The planning group also issued a map of the exact geographical distribution of the region's 14,000,000 inhabitants (an 11½ per cent gain over 1940) that, M Fagin said, made it possible for the first time to determine the number of residents within any specified geographical area, however irregular its shape.

January 19, 1953

CHICAGO TO OPEN 'LARGEST' GARAGE

Facility Beneath Grant Park to Hold 2,359 Cars—Part of 50-Million Program

By RALPH KATZ

Special to The New York Times.

CHICAGO, Aug. 14—An underground public garage, described its builders as the world's largest, will be opened here on Sept. 1.

A multi-million-dollar facility that will provide parking space for 2,359 cars on two decks and a mezzanine, it is under Grant Park and Michigan Avenue on the fringe of Chicago's business section. It is the result of more than thirty years of planning, much legal wrangling and long arguments involving financing, location and practicability.

Chicagoans hail the garage as a milestone in the city's plans for construction of five large publicly owned parking garages in the Loop area and hundreds of smaller garages and parking lots in outlying business and residential areas. The cost is expected to be $50,000,000.

The Grant Park garage was built at a cost of $8,300,000, which included moving and replacing trees, fountains and other water mains, sewers, utilities, police and fire alarm systems and other subsurface equipment on Michigan Avenue, Chicago's main thoroughfare.

The city has already announced rates for the garage. 40 cents for the first hour, fifteen cents each for the next eight hours and five cents for the next fifteen hours. These fees will be used to pay off the bonds issued to build the garage.

History Goes Back to '21

Back in 1921 an assistant corporation counsel first sought to remove legal barriers to construction of the underground facility in the park. Three years later, the Chicago Association of Commerce approved plans for ten underground garages, each for 306 cars.

It seemed that the project would get under way immediately when the Chicago Motor Club approved the plan and agreed to underwrite a $1,000,000 bond issue.

The Chicago Tribune reported on June 29, 1924, that "a commission was appointed to prepare a definite proposal to present to the South Park Board at its next meeting July 17. From all indications it will be accepted and work will start at once."

But the underground garage plan seemed doomed in September, 1925, when it was announced that Grant Park surface parking facilities, then accommodating 1,500 cars, would be doubled in size and depressed to sixteen feet below ground level. This was regarded as an adequate substitute to the underground plans.

In May, 1931, the underground garage plan was revived and a bill was prepared for introduction in the State Legislature to lease land in the park for the garage and an exhibition hall to private interests. Nothing came of this and there is no record of the bill's having been introduced.

By 1946 the city recognized "a crippling shortage" of parking facilities and plans for a $5,000,000 underground garage on two levels were submitted to an Association of Commerce committee. But it was not until November, 1951, that plans for the present facility actually were drawn up. In June, 1952, the plan was expanded to two garages that would hold 4,000 cars.

Before any further action could be taken a test case was brought to determine the right of the Park District to construct garages and finance them through the sale of bonds. On May 22, 1952, the Illinois Supreme Court upheld the validity of the operation.

The expanded program for $50,- of city garage construction was approved by the City Council in July, 1952. It was estimated then that the entire project could be completed in five years.

On Jan. 13 last year the John Griffith & Son Construction Company received the contract to construct the Grant Park-Michigan Avenue garage on a bid of $6,539,539. The company agreed to pay $500 for each day it required more than the 325 days for construction and in return would receive the same amount for each day saved. The company will get a bonus of $83,000 for early completion.

The garage has 840,000 square feet and extends 1,200 feet along Michigan Avenue. It also runs from the west curb line of Michigan Avenue to the right of way of the Illinois Central Railroad about 400 feet. The garage runs under that part of Grant Park bordering on Michigan Avenue from Randolph Street to Monroe Street, a distance of three blocks. Entrance and exit ramps are on Michigan Avenue just south of Randolph Street and north of Monroe Street. A pedestrian entrance with escalator stairways is on the west side of Michigan Avenue between Washington and Madison Streets.

August 15, 1954

CITY TRAFFIC RISE CUTS LAND VALUE

Federal Survey Points Up Cost of Parking Problem in Urban Areas

The automobile parking problem in urban America, already bumper-tight, is becoming steadily worse. And as automobile congestion grows, land values in the large cities decline.

Such a connection between the progressive clogging of city streets and the deterioration of land values is pointed up by the Federal Bureau of Roads.

In an analysis of the national parking problem issued last week, the bureau reported "an almost universal decline in land values within the older and larger commercial centers."

The bureau says that an important contributing factor to the decline is the inability of such centers to handle transportation efficiently, and that if street congestion is not relieved, compact business districts will lose their advantages.

Volume of Traffic

The report cites many factors that are responsible for the increasing congestion in large cities. The principal element is the huge volume of traffic thrust upon cities in the postwar years—in cities with antiquated street systems that have been unable to do anything about their inadequacies, particularly in the central business districts.

While populations continue to increase, the number of vehicles entering the business districts remains small because the parking facilities have long been overtaxed. The report found no evidence of a change in the pattern.

Thus motorists are driving out to the less-congested districts where business is reported to be on the increase.

Aggravating the downtown situation further, as populations increase the available curb space for parking shrinks. The explanation found in the bureau's survey lies in the municipalities' expansion of utility services.

After analyzing the parking problems, the report suggests solutions: More parking lots, more meters, more garages. One or the other, and sometimes all three solutions are practicable, depending on the location, the availability of additional space for development as a parking section, and the availability of money.

An approach to implementing

these methods would rest in cooperation between local governments and private enterprise. A survey of such efforts was made by the bureau in 100 cities in thirty-five states, and the findings indicate that some localities can solve the problem by cooperative action. The extent of the problem is apparent in the number of passenger cars now on the road: 55,000,000.

But the bureau also finds that efforts to reduce the problem "too often are left to private enterprise," and adds:

"Once it has become evident that there is a parking problem, responsibility for guiding the solution should be placed in a centralized authority, since no satisfactory solution can be expected from piecemeal and uncoordinated private and public action.

"The need for this integrated effort is emphasized by the problems arising in congested areas."

The report cites at length seven of these problems:

¶A lack of efficient mass transportation.

¶High daily and seasonal parking demand.

¶The use of curb space for parking and loading.

¶A lack of trained traffic-engineering personnel.

¶Reluctance of merchants and property owners to accept financial responsibility for improving the parking situation.

¶Inadequate street systems.

¶Improper location of existing parking facilities in relation to street traffic movement and building usage.

Most Critical Problem

The report lays heavy emphasis on what it considers one of the most critical problems—off-street parking. It reveals that 555 cities operate 1,700 off-street parking lots—with an average capacity of 232 cars. A fee is charged for parking in 541 of the lots; no fee in the rest. However 80 per cent of such facilities are operated by commercial parking concerns or individuals.

An observation of financial interest to municipalities is that the parking meter is growing in popularity as a source of revenue. The bureau estimates that the total annual revenue from parking meters exceeds $100,000,000.

While use of the parking lot shrinks the privately operated parking garage is gaining in popularity. Most of them are ramp-type garages four or five stories high. There are also mechanically operated garages involving the use of elevators and dollies. The latest type of automatic garage uses elevators that carry cars to twelve and fourteen floors — and then swing them horizontally or diagonally into a stall.

Traffic engineers and experienced off-street garage operators are looking with increasing interest into the latter type of garage as a possible solution to the problem. The main attraction here is that elevator garages can be installed in high buildings. There is now so little space for expansion groundwise that there seems to be no place to go but up.

The report, released last week, may be purchased for fifty-five cents (no stamps) from the United States Department of Commerce field office, 110 East Forty-fifth Street, New York 17, New York.

November 4, 1956

Study Finds Cars Choking Cities As 'Urban Sprawl' Takes Over

By HARRISON E. SALISBURY

Many New Yorkers have long cherished a secret dream. Some day at high noon all traffic in the city will halt, choked in its own excess. Every street will be filled to the brim. Not a vehicle will be able to move.

The realization of this dream—or nightmare—is still at least a few years distant in the case of New York. But it could happen tomorrow in Los Angeles.

Los Angeles now has such a number of motor vehicles that if all were brought onto the street at the same moment they would take over every roadway in the whole sprawling area. The city has 12,500 lane-miles of streets. This includes sixty miles of freeway—the largest total of any metropolis in the world.

But it also possesses more than 1,500,000 passenger cars. Traffic engineers calculate that, allowing twenty feet for each car, appropriate footage for 36,000 intersections and a reasonable interval between cars, every street in town would be jammed.

Sometimes, as the engineers struggle with the 5 P. M. automobile jam, they wonder if it has already happened.

New York's problem of moving people and vehicles in, out and through the metropolitan area differs from the problems of Los Angeles, San Francisco, Chicago, Cleveland, Philadelphia, Boston or any other American metropolis.

But in each case there are more similarities than differences. By surveying conditions in other metropolitan cities light can be cast on New York's problems, clues can be gathered to future trends and ideas of what to do and what not to do can be assembled.

No city in America possesses richer, more varied, more exotic experiences in moving people and vehicles than Los Angeles.

Here, nestled under its blanket of smog, girdled by bands of freeways, its core eviscerated by concrete strips and asphalt fields, its circulatory arteries pumping away without focus, lies the prototype of Gasopolis, the rubber-wheeled living region of the future.

Los Angeles is no longer a city as the term has been conventionally defined. Sam S. Taylor, general manager of Los Angeles traffic, calls Los Angeles "a mobile region."

For anyone looking toward the future, toward the end results of full autofication of the American metropolis, Los Angeles is the phenomenon to analyze most carefully.

When Lincoln Steffens went to the Soviet Union just after the Bolshevik Revolution he proclaimed, "I have seen the Future—and it works!"

Today's visitor to Los Angeles might paraphrase Steffens and say: "I have seen the Future—and it doesn't work."

Los Angeles today is confronted with the radical consequences of total reliance upon the gasoline combustion engine. What forty years ago was the world's best interurban transit system—the "big red cars" of Henry Huntington's lines—long since has been consigned to the scrap heap. The cult of the automobile has saturated a vast metropolitan area. Expert after expert has examined the Los Angeles picture and backed away shuddering.

Every transport problem that New York and other big American cities cope with today exists in Los Angeles in nearly insoluble form.

It is from Los Angeles that the most anguished cries are heard for rescue from the rubber-tired incubi. It is Los Angeles that threatens to prohibit new cars unless they are fitted with devices to prevent the discharge of smog-creating hydrocarbon fractions.

It is Los Angeles that sends its officials to plead with the grand viziers of Detroit not to put longer fins on the cars, not to widen the machines because there just is not room on the streets or in the parking spaces.

It is in Los Angeles that serious officials say that the system is exhausting the elements necessary for human life—land, air and water.

And it is in Los Angeles and other motor-oriented West Coast cities that the cry rises clearly that no solution will be found solely in freeways, grade-separated facilities and other devices for multiplying the mobility of private cars.

No matter what the cost, public transit facilities must be provided. Otherwise chaos lies just ahead. That is what the West Coast Cassandras—often yesterday's prophets in the freeway temples—are saying today.

The End of Room

Los Angeles provides a classic example of the Malthusian principle applied to the automobile. As cited by Dr. Lyle C. Fitch, first deputy administrator of New York City, this is the law:

"Today's automobile population continually outruns its lebensraum."

Metropolitan Los Angeles expects to have 900 miles of freeway and 300 miles of expressway by 1980. A freeway is a grade-separated roadway. An expressway is a limited-access street-level roadway. Even with this program, Mr. Taylor says that Los Angeles in 1980 "may well have worse traffic conditions than exist today"—unless public transit is provided.

The building of motor facilities on the scale already carried out by Los Angeles has given the community an anthill aspect.

So much land has been allotted for automotive use that the center of Los Angeles—despite recent public and private building projects—more and more resembles a Swiss cheese, tunneled at the core and gnawed at the edges. About 28 per cent of the 3,300 acres of downtown Los Angeles is occupied by streets, freeways and service ways. About 38 per cent more is occupied by off-street parking garages, loading facilities and other institutions dedicated to rubber-clad wheels.

Thus, about two-thirds of downtown Los Angeles is already in thrall to the gods of gasoline.

Good-by, Walkers

The pedestrian is regarded as an anachronism. Found on the street at night in a residential area he is liable to arrest as a suspicious character.

In fact, the next step calls for elimination of the pedestrian completely in downtown Los Angeles.

Special free-walks, overcrossings, second-story-level sidewalks, and moving platforms are to be provided so that the streets can be turned over exclusively to motor use. Helicopters and "convertiplanes" may ultimately be provided to transfer the obsolete foot traveler to areas where he can be appropriately installed in a four-wheeled vehicle.

The drawback to this, as Mr. Taylor notes, is that as more and more space is allotted to the automobile, the goose that lays the golden eggs is strangled. Enormous areas go from the taxrolls and are rendered unsuitable for productive economic purposes. The community's ability dwindles to foot the ever-multiplying costs of freeways—$10,000,000 a mile in some Los Angeles areas; as high as $50,-000,000 a mile in heavily built-up Eastern cities.

At the same time traffic movement becomes more and more random as concentrated business and special-purpose areas disappear.

But what of the clover-leafs and double-eights of the freeways—do they at least move traffic more rapidly in and out of the city?

The answer is surprising. At peak traffic hours it makes virtually no difference where you drive in Los Angeles—freeway, expressway or ordinary street. Your maximum speed will still be in the range of twenty-five to thirty miles an hour. Time and again freeway movement is impeded by accidents. So chronic is the problem that the engineers propose to remove stalled cars from the highways by helicopter.

The truth is that a horse and buggy could cross Los Angeles almost as fast in 1900 as an automobile can make the trip at 5 P. M. today.

Nowhere are the problems that arise from spongy half-urban half-rural settlement—the kind so rapidly expanding around New York—better studied than in the Los Angeles area. Here what sociologists call "urban sprawl" has been carried to extremes that bring infinite complication to every rational plan to transport people.

Bursting Out of Bounds

No way of life is so greedy and wasteful of space. To accommodate a population of 5,-000,000 in Los Angeles-style single-story ranch homes on average plots requires at least 500,000 acres for homesites and about 1,000,000 acres for homes, churches, schools, shopping centers and recreation facilities. This is 1,560 square miles of residential area. Even now Los Angeles has a population density only one-tenth that of New York.

So diffuse a residence pattern requires lavish land expenditures on highway and traffic facilities.

Some measure of these expenditures can be grasped from the fact that by 1975 the United States highway system will occupy 17,000,000 acres. The new 41,000-mile interstate system alone will require more space than the state of Rhode Island.

Free use of bulldozer-cleared areas, coupled with similar land expenditures for one-level shopping centers and one-level factory sites, is typical of the Los Angeles pattern.

"Our people thus far have continually preferred private conveyance and we have endeavored to accommodate them," Mr. Taylor says. "This cannot go on indefinitely, however. We will run out of space."

It is this realization that has impelled Los Angeles to take the first faltering steps toward re-creation of a mass transit system. A Metropolitan Transit Authority has been set up to take over surviving bus and street-car lines. It is preparing plans that almost certainly will be based on buses with priority on freeways and expressways.

Los Angeles simply has neither space nor funds for a new and separate rail system. However, certain rail links may be built if a recent tendency to reconcentrate office facilities in parts of downtown Los Angeles and the Wilshire Boulevard area proves lasting.

More than one-third of the Los Angeles urban area is occupied by transportation facilities. A single freeway interchange consumes eighty acres of land. Each mile of freeway utilizes twenty-four acres. This means that by 1980 the city will have turned 21,600 acres over to freeway use — thirty-four square miles.

Ultimately, as planners see the future, Los Angeles will have a freeway network forming a giant grid. It will take up one-mile square blocks in the central area and two to four-mile quadrangles in the outer region.

What remains inside the giant motorized checkerboard?

Already Mr. Taylor has noted that the business of downtown Los Angeles is "more or less stagnant." How could it be otherwise when concrete ribbons and asphalt plazas replace stores, offices, hotels and apartments?

Banking Has Moved

So extensive has been the destruction of the Los Angeles core that a major segment of finance banking has shifted to San Francisco. There is no longer a sufficient concentration in Los Angeles to support metropolitan finance.

As the city core disintegrates fewer people are attracted there. A 1941 count showed a maximum accumulation of 173,000 persons in downtown Los Angeles between 6 A. M. and 10 P. M. Of the total 90,000 came by transit; 67,000 rode in 43,000 cars. There were 16,000 pedestrians.

In 1955 maximum accumulation was only 149,000 persons. Transit passengers dropped to 78,000, auto passengers to 65,000 in 39,500 vehicles and pedestrians to 6,000. This was a 15 per cent fall at a time when population rose about 33 per cent.

In 1950, in a twenty-four-hour period, a total of 700,000 persons entered downtown Los Angeles, 85 per cent in private cars. By 1980 the total will be down to 600,000.

A City Like New York

If Los Angeles provides a laboratory in which to examine the end effects of the motor age, San Francisco offers a more direct parallel to New York.

Like New York, San Francisco faces specific limitations of space. It also has the special problems that arise from its harbor, from the water barriers between its areas and from other topographical peculiarities that constrict access to different parts of the region. And like New York, San Francisco has certain cultural and esthetic standards.

It also has a large, well-defined commuting population. In Los Angeles the area is so diffusely settled that it is difficult to define commuters, let alone count them. Everyone drives to work. There is no other way of getting there.

San Francisco now has about 216,000 commuters to the core areas of San Francisco, Oakland and Berkeley. Outside of the Peninsula, where first-class rail commuting service is provided by the Southern Pacific railroad, about 75 per cent of commuting is by auto or bus.

The city has 800 miles of streets in a forty-two-square mile area. It ultimately will have about forty miles of freeway.

Adequate for 50%

But it is calculated that these facilities would handle only 50 per cent of San Francisco's peak traffic loads. The area today has a population of 3,300,-000 with 1,300,000 automobiles. By projecting the statistics, the totals in ten years could reach 5,000,000 people and 2,600,000 vehicles, and by 1980 about 7,-000,000 people and 3,500,000 cars.

Like New York there just isn't room for so many cars in the central city. San Francisco notes that if twenty square feet were allotted to each car, an area of 30,000 acres would be required. This roughly equals the total area of the city. The city would be one vast parking lot.

The San Francisco position is identical with that of New York. If all the Jerseyans now using public transit across the Hudson shifted to automobiles it would take all of Manhattan island below Forty-second Street to park their cars.

John M. Peirce, general manager of the San Francisco Transit District, says:

"Space does not exist to build freeways sufficient to handle the population of 7,000,000 estimated in twenty years."

Comparison Made

As San Francisco experts calculate the figures, a rail facility like the Southern Pacific peninsular service can move 40,000 seated passengers an hour. It would take forty lanes of freeway to move an equiva-

Rock Island Lines

'JET ROCKET' is the name given by the Rock Island Lines to this fast, low-gravity train assigned to Chicago commuter service. The train has a capacity of 500 passengers.

lent number by private car. Freeway capacity by private car is estimated at 2,000 to 2,400 an hour. Or by bus at 6,000 an hour.

The problem grows steadily worse as average occupancy of automobiles drops and drops. Los Angeles studies show the average number of riders declining from 2.4 a car in 1950 to 2 in 1953, 1.8 in 1957 and 1.4 today.

Mr. Peirce points out that with the steady deterioration of public transport the automobile has been transformed "from a willing servant into a Frankenstein monster—a master that has saddled us with congestion that is costly and critical today but will be chaotic and intolerable tomorrow."

The San Francisco populace is concerned not only by the practical aspects of this problem. John C. Beckett, Marin County member of the San Francisco Transit District, believes that residents of the area "want to preserve values and beauty, regardless of the buck."

"Freeways destroy property," Mr. Beckett says. "That is why we are opposed to turning them loose in the metropolitan area."

Set Up Transit Unit

Impelled by practical and esthetic considerations San Francisco after more than six years of study has set up its Metropolitan Transit District.

This body, embracing five San Francisco counties, will present, probably later this year, a plan for financing an integrated transit system. The scheme involves interurban transit and tunnels. They ultimately would cost $800,000,000.

"Our job," in the words of Mr. Peirce, "is to protect urban America against economic disintegration. Our hope is to provide mass transit facilities more characteristic of the jet age than exist elsewhere in America. We do not propose to idolize the automobile to the extent that we are strangulated."

The San Francisco plans are a long distance from realization. The metropolis faces conflict between the inferior governmental units that subdivide the area. These conflicts become acute when questions of finance are involved.

There are also divergencies of viewpoint between the Transit District and the operators of the great San Francisco bridges. These conflicts echo those centering on the Port of New York Authority in the East.

But San Francisco still stands as a shining example of advanced thinking in the sphere of metropolitan circulatory problems. And the projected revival of rail transport has solid public support. Each public opinion poll has shown substantial backing for any system that would enable harassed drivers to trade the daily buck-the-traffic grind for a forty-five-mile-an-hour, comfortable and economical trip via public transport.

Chicago Moves Forcefully

Like every big American city Chicago has been plagued with

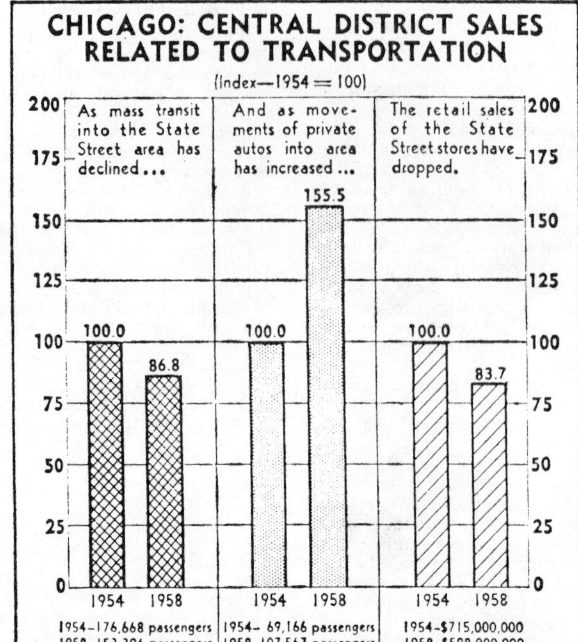

The New York Times March 3, 1959

EFFECT ON STORES: Studies indicate that many shoppers reach the Loop by mass transit—those who come by car are passing through or have come just to look. Likewise in New York, there is evidence that it is the commuting trains and subways that bring customers to Fifth Avenue rather than the cars that fill midtown streets.

commuter problems. But characteristically the big, gusty prairie metropolis has moved aggressively—both in the public and private spheres of transport—to meet the challenge of the motor age.

The Chicago Loop is no exception to the tendencies noted in Manhattan. Volume of movement into the core has declined. But the Chicago pattern differs sharply from the popular concept that more and more people are going to work by car and fewer and fewer by train.

Here are the figures of the Chicago Transit Authority on traffic leaving the Loop during maximum hour movement:

	1948	1951	1954	1957
Sub. railroads	71,136	76,708	73,179	77,094
C.T.A. Rap Tran.	67,268	67,576	70,425	75,126
C.T.A. Surface	73,270	52,990	43,284	36,092
Priv Autos, Taxis	39,017	36,920	34,452	37,444
Other	1,499	1,570	1,328	1,443
Total	252,190	235,764	222,668	227,203

The Chicago figures reveal a modest but well-defined gain in passengers riding suburban railroads and the Chicago subway and right-of-way transit. Buses and automobiles decline in popularity. There is, moreover, an over-all decline in Loop traffic of about 10 per cent.

The increasing patronage of rapid transit appears to be linked directly to the vigorous efforts made in the last decade to improve these facilities.

The extent to which public transportation moves peak traffic out of the Chicago Loop is disclosed in another set of Chicago Transit Authority figures.

In the peak fifteen minutes—from 5 to 5:15 P. M.—72 per cent of the 74,191 persons leaving the Loop go by suburban railroad or C. T. A. rapid transit. Thirty-nine per cent go by rail, 33 per cent by rapid transit. Only 14 per cent go by surface bus and 13 per cent by private car and cab.

At the peak hour of accumulation of persons in the Chicago Loop, 86 per cent had been brought in by public transportation, 14 per cent by private car. In contrast downtown Los Angeles had moved 54 per cent of its peak accumulation by public transport and about 45 per cent by private car.

Changes in Loop

The Chicago area is no stranger to the trends of population settlement and social habits demonstrated in other metropolitan regions. The Loop, for example, is becoming more an office area and relatively less important in retail trade.

The automobile has proved no substitute for mass transit in maintaining the economic health of the Loop shopping center. In fact, there appears to be a direct correlation between decline in mass transit use and decline in retail trade, even though motor traffic may increase.

Taking 1954 as a base, the business of the State Street department stores dropped from $715,000,000 to $598,000,000, or 16.3 per cent, by 1958. In the same period the number of passengers entering the area during shopping hours by mass transit dropped 13.2 per cent from 176,668 to 153,396. The volume of automobile passengers entering the Loop rose 55.5 per cent, from 69,166 to 107,567.

Apparently, many persons who come to the Loop by train or C. T. A. stay to shop. Those who come by car either are passing through or have just come to look.

Comparable figures for New York are not available.

The Fifth Avenue Association declines to make public a breakdown showing business done by the great midtown stores. There is every reason to believe, however, that it is commuting trains and subway that bring Fifth Avenue its paying customers rather than the hordes of cars that choke the midtown streets.

Two in One Package

Chicago has broken through the endless discussions of freeway versus transit. Characteristically, it has combined the two in one package—the Congress Street Expressway.

On a single 650-foot right-of-way, high speed rapid transit has been incorporated with an eight-lane freeway. The eight lanes of expressway carry 6,000 persons an hour at peak travel. The transit line carries 9,000 at about 27 miles an hour.

Some design features of the expressway have been criticized—the length of the access overpasses to the transit stations, for one thing. But it represents the first step toward a combination of rubber-and-steel transit

The combination ends competition for public funds between rival facilities. The tracked system will be integrated with public garages and parking plazas in the city's outskirts so motorists can shift from the freeways for a fast trip to the heart of the city.

Chicago is also the home of the most vigorous and able railroad executives in the country—men who are convinced that the iron rails are here to stay and who believe they can earn dollars for the stockholders by providing efficient, comfortable and rapid commuting service.

The contrast between the Chicago railroad leaders, both in psychology and achievement, and the panic of some of their Eastern counterparts is striking.

Scores Attitude in East

One Chicago railroad executive said:

"I just wish the New Haven or the New York Central would turn their commuting business over to me. If I couldn't make money and provide good service on that kind of volume I'd shoot myself."

Another Chicago railroad chief, commenting on the pleas of some Eastern roads for commuting subsidies said:

"The subsidy is the last refuge of a bankrupt management. To grant a subsidy is to put a premium on inefficiency and obsolescence. Once the subsidy principle is established management no longer needs to think.

Whatever happens they can just send the bill to the public treasury."

Typical of the tough-talking aggressive Chicago railroad executives is Ben W. Heineman of the Chicago and North-Western Railroad, which transports 43,000 commuters daily to Chicago.

Mr. Heineman's commuting business is up 20 per cent in five years. It brought the North-Western $7,272,309 in 1956—about 4 per cent of the road's revenue.

Mr. Heineman is convinced that the road not only can break even on commuting service but also can earn at least 3 per cent on its investment.

He has backed this opinion with substantial sums of money. The road has already forty-eight new double-decked 161-passenger commuter cars. It has ordered thirty-six more at a cost of $5,600,000. He intends to build his fleet of double-deckers to 200 and retire all conventional coaches from service. Thereafter he will order ten new cars a year to accommodate the expected growth in the service.

"We believe strongly," Mr. Heineman says, "that rate or cost is not the determining factor in suburban service. The factors in suburban service are safety, reliability, comfort and speed."

Mr. Heineman believes that commuter railroads can attract and maintain their business at rates higher than those they actually wish to charge

With the cooperation of state and local authorities, Mr. Heineman recently obtained a 26 per cent increase in commuting fares—backed by his pledge that with the new money he would give his customers the service they want.

If he can make good his promises—and few in Chicago doubt his ability to do so—he expects that a $2,000,000 annual red ink item on the North-Western's books will be transfigured into black.

A similar spirit animates Downey Jenks, president of the Rock Island, which transports 30,000 commuters daily. Mr. Jenks' commuter service is about $1,000,000 in the red at this point. But he expects to put it on a profit-making basis soon. He expects fare and tax changes will rapidly improve the economic side of the picture and he is bringing in new equipment to satisfy commuters' desires for comfort and convenience

Mr. Jenks has placed two new types of trains into Chicago commuter service. One is the Jet Rocket, a Talgo type of lightweight low-gravity unit with 500-commuter capacity. The other is the General Motors Aerotrain, ten-car units powered by futuristic 1,200-horsepower Diesel engines. Two of these units have been put into service.

Other Cities Cited

Other North American cities add little more than bits and pieces to the over-all picture presented by Los Angeles, San Francisco and Chicago. Cleveland and Toronto have put new rapid transit systems into operation in the last four or five years. Both are chalking up successful records, providing acceptable service to patrons and relieving the ever-pressing automobile burden.

Toronto's system carries a peak-hour load of 30,000 passengers, but it is only a four-mile system. Cleveland's is a thirteen-mile system, utilizing an old railroad right-of-way.

Boston and Philadelphia are experimenting with subsidy and cooperative rail-municipal kick-back systems. Neither seems likely to prove more than a temporary poultice.

One thing the survey of American cities makes plain. New York's transport circulatory problems are not unique. They arise from the same pattern of social and economic transition observable in all big cities. Universally the changes are linked to new habits stemming from the ease of random movement via automobile.

One other thing is equally plain. Out of the collective American experience ample evidence may be winnowed on which to postulate the future course of New York's development. Evidence may also be found on the available mechanisms, plans and devices that can be called into play to resolve the great crisis of moving New Yorkers hither and thither at something approaching the price, the pace and the means to satisfy their aspirations.

March 3, 1959

'29 REGIONAL PLAN IS PAYING OFF NOW

Dozens of Bridges, Roads, Tunnels and Terminals Have Been Constructed

RAIL PROGRAM IGNORED

Concepts Given Credit for Averting Chaos—Lack of Central Authority Scored

By DAVID BINDER

The Regional Plan of New York, a bold set of recommendations for the comprehensive development of the metropolitan area put forth more than thirty years ago, has in large part been realized today.

Throughout the tri-state region of 7,000 square miles dozens of bridges, express highways, tunnels and parkways envisioned in the plan have been built. Park lands, civic centers, airports, zoning laws, neighborhood units, industrial parks and bus terminals called for by the planners of the Nineteen Twenties have also become reality.

While many of these diverse endeavors were undertaken without coordination by a supra-regional authority, the plan provided an integrated framework for the region's development.

Plan Prevented Chaos

Indeed, those familiar with the plan, which was presented in 1929, are convinced that it has been mainly responsible for preventing the region's present 16,000,000 residents from living in chaos.

They remark that the very parts of the Regional Plan that were not adopted, such as the proposals for an integrated railroad network and for commuter transportation, have left the New York area its only major problems—congestion in the central business district and aimless urban sprawl in the outlying areas.

Regardless of these gaps, the makers of the 1929 plan who are still living and their heirs, the regional planners of today, are certain that the original recommendations had a profound influence not only on New York but on other metropolitan regions throughout the country.

The group that conceived the plan consisted of men who were dreamers as well as realists. They include Charles Dyer Norton, a banker; Frederic A. Delano, a railroad man; George McAneny, a newspaper executive and civic official; Nelson P. Lewis, an engineer, and Lawson Purdy, a public official.

Work Began in 1922

With financial backing from the Russell Sage Foundation, the group began work on the plan in 1922. During the following years, the planners obtained the aid of many prominent engineers, lawyers, architects and economists.

After seven years of research, the group published the plan in ten volumes. Eight of these were surveys covering economic growth factors, population, transportation, recreation areas, highways, building and zoning, neighborhood planning concepts and public services.

The ninth and tenth volumes contained summaries of the surveys and broad proposals for regional development, as well as suggestions for building projects.

Among the many projects recommended in the 1929 plan that have since been built are the following:

¶The George Washington, Triboro, Bronx-Whitestone and Throgs Neck Bridges.

¶The Brooklyn-Battery, Lincoln and Queens-Midtown Tunnels.

¶Manhattan Island's circumferential expressway.

¶The Belt, Garden State, Henry Hudson, Merritt, Northern and Southern State Parkways.

¶The New Jersey Turnpike and the New England Thruway.

¶The region's four major airports.

Other projects anticipated in the plan and now in the process of construction are the Lincoln Center for the Performing Arts, the Cross Bronx Expressway and the Verrazano Bridge across the Narrows.

Reflecting on the role of the plan last week, Lawrence M. Orton, a City Planning Commissioner, remarked that the authorship of these projects could not be attributed solely to the regional planners.

Product of Many Minds

"It is easy to go credit-grabbing," he said. "But the fact is that many of the elements of the plan had been incubating in other minds as well. The inclusion of these proposals in the plan, however, made them more desirable."

Mr. Orton, who assisted the technical director of the plan from 1923 until 1931, added, "The striking thing about it was that a mere suggestion in certain fields such as highways or parks seemed to have a far-reaching influence once it had been recorded in the plan."

Another of the original planners, Harold M. Lewis, said that one reason why so many of the plan proposals were adopted was the fact that projects had been drawn up in cooperation with local authorities of the various governmental jurisdictions.

"We worked very closely with the engineers in the cities and counties in order to get their thinking on roads and parks," he explained. "By the time the plan came out in published form it already had the endorsement of many of these engineers."

Pessimistic Note Intrudes

Mr. Lewis, the son of the late Nelson Lewis, who helped organize the plan, was executive engineer on the Regional Plan staff. He is now a consulting engineer in private practice.

Mr. Lewis and Mr. Orton said that the impact of the 1929 plan went far beyond the specific project proposals. "Consciously or unconsciously, the city administration adopted the spirit of the plan," said Mr. Orton. "And that helped to stem haphazard growth."

He was echoed by C. McKim Norton, executive vice president of the Regional Plan Association, which was formed in 1931 to follow up on the original plan.

Mr. Norton, who is the son of Charles Dyer Norton, one of the originators of the Regional Plan, said, "Most of the 1,400 governments in the region today have zoning laws that derive from the 1929 plan."

Yet, in reviewing the history of the plan, these men also struck a pessimistic note.

"The failure of the region to develop an adequate rail system was probably the greatest tragedy," said Mr. Orton. "To have done so would have laid the foundation for avoiding the crisis we are now in."

"We would not have had quite so much of a sprawl in the suburbs," added Paul Windels, former president of the Regional Plan Association, "because the towns would have developed along the railroad lines instead of indiscriminately."

A spokesman for the Regional Plan Association said that one explanation for the regional railroad situation was the Depression. While the economic decline led to great public works programs such as highways, he said, the privately run railroads had been crippled.

Other plan proposals that have failed to achieve realization include a vehicular bridge across the Hudson River at 125th Street, a crosstown expressway connecting the Lincoln Tunnel with the Queens Midtown Tunnel, a park development along the Harlem River and a railroad passenger terminal at 178th Street and Amsterdam Avenue.

New Study Under Way

The 1929 plan was designed to cover the region's development up to 1965. It dealt with an area of about 5,000 square miles inhabited by about 10,000,000 persons. Transportation was largely by rail, and the nation's transition from track to tire was still in the future.

With this in mind, and realizing that the New York region had altered in other ways, the Regional Plan Association decided in 1956 to inaugurate a new study that would project the growth of the metropolitan area until 1985.

The association asked the Graduate School of Public Administration of Harvard University to undertake the analysis. Last week the final book of a nine-volume set of studies was published.

Mr. Norton said that on the basis of these studies and others, the association was preparing a new regional plan that would provide "broad regional alternatives for development."

Then, with a glance at the large crimson volumes of the 1929 plan, which his late father helped conceive, he added, "It is really much the same type of plan."

July 23, 1961

Expressway Construction Lags As Officials Heed Urban Outcry

By DONALD JANSON

Special to The New York Times

PHILADELPHIA, Feb. 14—Interstate 95 was designed a decade and a half ago as a 1,866-mile-long "Main Street" of the East Coast from Maine to Florida. But on a map today it looks like a mortally wounded snake, severed in such places as Boston, Philadelphia, Baltimore and Washington.

The faltering pace of construction of I-95 through metropolitan areas is matched by that of other expressways in city after city across the country as urban dwellers give voice to social and environmental objections with increasing effect.

Some 133 miles of the interstate system alone are being held up in 16 cities. The 42,500-mile network of superhighways, with 90 per cent Federal and 10 per cent state financing, was established in 1956 as a keystone of the Eisenhower Administration. Two-thirds of the network is open now and most of the rest is under construction, but the achievement of the recently extended completion goal of 1974 has become extremely doubtful.

Here in Philadelphia the expressway is stalled by apparently successful demands of residents that part of it be depressed and covered with a landscaped lid and by the insistence of conservationists that it not damage a wildlife refuge.

For similar reasons I-95 has been delayed in Boston, Baltimore and Washington, while in many other cities, such as San Francisco, New York, New Orleans and Milwaukee, other highways considered essential by engineers and planners have been scuttled althogether in response to protests.

Roadbuilders are finding it more difficult even to route expressways through parks and poor neighborhoods, for long the line of least resistance. And increasingly vocal protesters are buttressed now by requirements of the 1968 Federal Highway Act that insist upon through consideration of human needs, such as adequate relocation housing.

The New York Times Feb. 15, 1970

Major Slowdown

Francis C. Turner, Federal highway administrator, said in a telephone interview from Washington that the result has been a major slowdown for expressway building in urban areas.

"Now we have to change people's minds and sell them on a relocation plan," said Mr. Turner, a highway engineer in the Bureau of Public Roads for 40 years. "Before, we just bought property and relocation was their responsibility.

Because of inflation, Mr. Turner said, delays are sharply increasing the cost of construction.

The 19 miles of I-95 through Baltimore originally were to have cost $200-million. A year ago Federal and state highway officials increased the estimate to $750-million. Opponents contend that the figure may be soon $1-billion.

Delays are also pouring heavy traffic into city thoroughfares from available exits of stalled expressways further clogging the streets and bringing complaints about air and noise pollution.

Here in the nation's fourth largest city, all the passions that have exploded in opposition to highways through densely populated neighborhoods in the rest of the country are seen in microcosm in a revolt of residents against the Crosstown Expressway.

Dividing the City

The eight-lane, 2.8-mile Crosstown would divide South Philadelphia from the City Center, running along shabby, commercial South Street from the Delaware River and the uncompleted I-95 on the east of the Schuylkill River and the planned Cobbs Creek Expressway on the west.

But residents of the old, stable Negro community in the path of the highway and south of it complain bitterly that it would also divide the races, becoming Philadelphia's Mason-Dixon Line between Negroes and the town houses of Society Hill and Rittenhouse Square.

They charge racial discrimination in the selection of the route, failure to prove a need for a road that would bring more cars to the traffic-glutted center city, and failure to provide an adequate plan to relocate several thousand people who would be uprooted.

They appear to be winning, despite the contention of the State Highway Department that the expressway is vital to the region's expressway system. As long ago as 1967 Mayor James H. J. Tate, heeding complaints of the residents and most of the city's civil rights and liberal forces, declared the expressway "dead or dying a slow death."

But the Chamber of Commerce persuaded him to reopen the 25-year-old controversy once again with a study committee that has been meeting since last April. Opponents have used it as a public forum. Militants and radicals have joined in the cause.

Depth of Bitterness

"It is impossible to overstate the depth of bitterness among black people around South Street," R. W. Tucker of the Philadelphia Quarterly Meeting of Friends said in an interview.

George T. Dukes, a member of the Mayor's committee and founder of the Citizen's Committee to Preserve and Develop the Crosstown Community, noted that a 1964 engineering report commissioned by the expressway planners found the road would serve as an "effective buffer" between town houses redeveloped or the affluent to the north and the "incompatible land uses to the south."

"Negroes never raised their voices in the early days," Mr. Dukes said quietly. "Now we do. If the planners can prove a need for a superhighway along South Street they should put a cover on it and build on the cover the homes and parks and things that would bind people together rather than create an open ditch that would keep people apart."

Planners rejected such a covered highway as exorbitant in price. And city officials have said there is now no adequate housing for relocating residents.

"Let the people have a victory," Mayor Tate said when three of his cabinet members, City Managing Director Fred T. Corleto, Planning Director Edmond M. Bacon and Streets Commissioner David M. Smallwood tried to insist in 1968 on pressing ahead with the crosstown.

Construction on the $450-million Delaware Expressway,

Philadelphia's segment of the East Coast's "Main Street," inched ahead throughout the 1960's until it approached the beautifully restored neighborhood of colonial homes just north of South Street called Society Hill.

Residents formed the Gateway Committee to Preserve Our National Heritage. They rallied nationwide support for the argument that an elevated expressway would cut off Independence Hall and other historic treasures from the river and a planned Penn's Landing for historic and cruise ships.

They won. The plan now is to put the superhighway underground past Society Hill, at a cost of $60-million a mile.

Prof. Anthony R. Tomazinis, director of the transportation studies center at the University of Pennsylvania, said in an interview that "one of the major improvements in the field of transportation in the last 10 years" was the requirement of the 1968 Highway Act that more attention be paid to social and environmental considerations in planning expressways.

"This is bound to cause more and longer delays in urban areas," he said. "Some highways will have to be eliminated. Mayors are paying more attention to well-organized protests. Minority voices have been elevated in the decision-making process. All this even raises the risk that center cities might get no more new highways."

"Consequently," he continued, "we are likely to see a trend to more rapid transit for moving people in large cities. But we still need both roads and rapid transit, and the roads that do get built should be better ones because of the legislation that encourages people to scrutinize every proposal much more closely than before."

Such scrutiny has generated donnybrooks in numerous cities. In New York, Mayor Lindsay has declared the much-debated Lower Manhattan Expressway dead "for all time," In San Francisco, Mayor Alioto has said that all future freeways will have to be tunneled underground. In Milwaukee, Mayor Henry Maier has said that all expressway construction should be halted until a housing relocation program is set up. Transportation Secretary John A. Volpe has vetoed a New Orleans highway because it impinged upon esthetic values in the historic French Quarter.

Moreover, in Massachusetts last week, Gov. Francis W. Sargent declared a moratorium on most highway construction in the Boston area pending another in a long series of studies.

And in Ohio, Gov. James A. Rhodes declared I-290, the long and bitterly contested Clark Freeway through Cleveland and the wealthy, Republican suburb of Shaker Heights, officially dead.

The last interstate expressway through the capital city of freeways, Los Angeles, is slowly coming into existence in southern sections of the county. It has encountered the usual resentment against noise, noxious fumes and destruction of neighborhoods. But the 17-mile, $300-million century freeway through Watts and other depressed neighborhoods is not blocked.

Planners have capitalized on experience. Nine municipalities and unincorporated areas on the route have been given a voice in planning the freeway to make it compatible with neighborhood needs and goals, and relocation housing is being provided.

At a recent meeting of Philadelphia's Committee on the Crosstown Expressway, Benjamin Loewenstein, president of a health and welfare organization, expressed a theme now receiving greater priority across the country than ever before:

"When we consider the problem of transportation the expressway hopes to solve, we must also consider the human equation. What happens to the people living in that area?"

February 15, 1970

The New York Times (by Edward Hausner)

END OF THE ROAD: Interstate 95 in Philadelphia, parallel to Delaware River, halts abruptly, its completion blocked by protests. Area at left is Society Hill. Increasing public outcry has slowed numerous road-building projects in many parts of the country.

Cities Show Interest in Traffic Bans As Love Affair With the Auto Wanes

By WAYNE KING

America's love affair with the automobile, a torrid romance for decades, appears to be cooling off in a number of cities. While divorce isn't imminent, some trial separations are already under way.

Encouraged in part of experiments like the one here last week along Madison Avenue, the cities are shutting some of their prime downtown streets to traffic, banning on-street parking and turning the areas over to pedestrians.

Initial reaction among people on the street would seem to be all but unanimous: They like the relief from traffic and want to see it expanded. Merchants tend to be opposed, although many agree that predictions of a slump in trade have not materialized. Urban officials are cautious but interested.

In fact, while most of the traffic bans are limited and tentative, interest in experimenting with them is clearly growing around the country. A check of major cities a year ago indicated little but apathy toward the idea, although it is not a new one.

In St. Louis, for instance, the concept has been considered off and on for over a decade without action. Now, city planners are seeking funds to dust off outmoded plans and update them for renewed consideration.

Other cities have already taken steps to curb downtown traffic, or have set dates to begin doing so. Among them are the following:

PHILADELPHIA. On May 26, between 6:30 and 10 P.M., a seven-block area in the mid-city shopping district will be closed to vehicular traffic. The theme of the event will be "Take a Walk," and a layer of artificial turf will be laid on one street for use as a picnic area. If successful, the experiment will be tried in other areas of the city.

WASHINGTON — Despite strong opposition from merchants and parking interests, the Rev. Jerry A. Moore Jr., a city councilman who is chairman of the transportation committee, said the council was "committed to banning as much traffic as possible in Washington." A council meeting on April 20, however, ended with Mr. Moore suggesting that further study was probably warranted. Ten of 19 businesses in one area suggested for a traffic ban appeared at the meeting to oppose it. Only one of three environmental groups backing the proposal appeared to support it. The city experimented with closing streets last fall.

SAN FRANCISCO. In several steps, the city has gradually moved to prohibit parking along about 30 city blocks, converting others to one-way. The parking ban has had the effect of sharply reducing traffic.

BOSTON. According to William T. Noonan, the city traffic commissioner, the city plans to ban traffic on a one-day basis sometime in May along four blocks of a major downtown street in an attempt to create the setting of a suburban shopping center. The area includes the city's two largest department stores, Jordan Marsh and Filene's.

CHICAGO. Although resistance to any traffic ban here has been strong among many merchants, James J. McDonough, city commissioner of streets and sanitation, said a traffic-ban study was under way and that "something definitive" was expected in about a month. "We're enthusiastic that this can be done and will be successful, despite all the problems," he said. State Street, the major downtown shopping thoroughfare, is among several major streets being evaluated for a trial closing.

In New York, the local chapters of the State Society of Professional Engineers called for a sweeping ban on private cars, taxis and city buses in midtown Manhattan 11 hours every working day.

Reaction to the traffic bans has not all been favorable, and in many cities there is still resistance to tampering with America's primary mode of transportation.

In Los Angeles, Burt Lieper of the City Traffic Department said, "We want the traffic to flow if it can, and the pedestrians to walk if they can." There are no plans to ban traffic on any city streets, he said, and to do so the city would have to obtain the permission of every property owner on the street. A member of the City Planning Commission said, however, that increased density might bring consideration of a traffic ban.

Detroit, the motor capital of the world, also has taken no steps to ban traffic, although several other Michigan cities, including Kalamazoo, Lansing, Pontiac and Jackson, have limited downtown traffic and created pedestrian malls, some of which have been in existence for several years.

In Washington, downtown merchants asked that the pilot project banning traffic from a seven-block area of the main shopping district every Thursday evening last fall be discontinued, at least temporarily, so that there would be no interference with pre-holiday deliveries. Some smaller shops complained that the streets were packed with pedestrians but their stores were empty.

April 25, 1971

MASS TRANSIT VERSUS THE AUTO

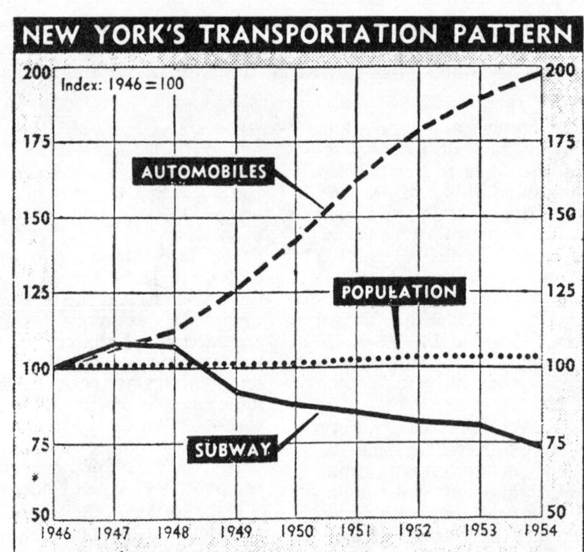

Theodore W. Kheel, impartial chairman of the New York private transit industry, reported last week that a shift from mass transit to private automobiles is hurting the industry and creating traffic congestion, and may lead to a 20-cent subway fare unless the trend is checked. In the chart, the "automobiles" line represents the number of tolls paid on Hudson River crossings; the "subway" line is based on the number of passengers per year.

June 19, 1955

MANY CITIES SING COMMUTER BLUES

Other large cities besides New York have commuter problems.

The general pattern is the same. The operation is essentially unprofitable; a large amount of equipment and manpower, required to meet rush-hour needs, is virtually useless during the balance of the day. Competition from the private automobile is an ever-increasing bedevilment.

Commuters complain about ancient equipment, which the operators say they can't afford to replace. When air conditioning is introduced, it generates heat every time it fails. The better the normal service, the louder the protests when it declines.

A drop in patronage impels an increase in fares; this promptly brings a further drop.

Almost nobody is happy. Yet there are exceptions to the general pattern.

In Chicago commuters on the Burlington Lines are so fond of their railroad that when a 27 per cent increase in fares was sought two years ago not a single voice was raised in objection.

Old Coaches Serve Boston

In Boston commuters on the Boston and Maine travel in coaches reported to have played a vital part in the Civil War, but no one ever does anything more drastic than write a letter to the newspapers. In San Francisco the Southern Pacific carries twice as many commuters as in 1940. It gives them free parking lots, too.

In London the steam locomotive is far from an anachronism, but the sooty old trains provide service that everyone acknowledges is fast, efficient and usually on time.

For a quick look-around:

Boston commuters, like those in New York, depend somewhat on the New York, New Haven and Hartford Railroad. It carries about 21,750 of the 835,600 persons who go into the city to work each day.

The Boston and Maine, which seems to be approaching a union with the New Haven, carries another 25,500. The Boston and Albany, whose rattan-seated commuter coaches never have been exposed to air conditioning, accounts for another 8,150.

Some 360,000 persons commute by private car, the rest by buses of the Eastern Massachusetts Street Railway Company and by Street cars, buses and rapid transit trains of the Metropolitan Transit Authority.

All three railroads operate commuter service at a deficit. The Boston and Albany has figured that it costs $2.34 to take in $1. The deficit for the Metropolitan Transit Authority, which serves fourteen communities, runs about $9,000,000 annually.

Commuter complaints against the railroads are mostly about old equipment and failure of air conditioning, where it exists. On-time performance generally is regarded as good. There never has been any suggestion of organized commuter complaints, or petitions, as in New York.

In Philadelphia, 150,000 commuters arrive each day by trains, buses and high-speed transit lines. Many more—nobody knows exactly how many—arrive by private car.

Of those using public transportation, the Pennsylvania Railroad and the Reading Company carry 39,500 daily in each direction. Buses from New Jersey bring an additional 27,000.

The remaining 85,000 use Red Arrow and Philadelphia Transportation Company buses and trolleys to outlying terminals of the Broad Street subway and the Market Street-Frankford elevated-subway line.

The Pennsylvania operates 325 electric cars on six commuter lines; the Reading, 247 cars, also on six lines. Both provide parking spaces at most stations.

Except for the railroads, the commuter services manage to operate in the black.

All strive to provide a seat for every passenger, but they do not always succeed. In recent years the Pennsylvania placed fifty additional coaches in suburban service at a cost of $4,000,000, and rehabilitated fifty other electric cars at a cost of $3,100,000. Nearly all coaches have ceiling fans.

From 1921 to 1947, railroad commuter fares were unchanged. Since then, however, four rate increases have raised prices more than 100 per cent in some instances.

Nevertheless, the Pennsylvania computed last April that it was spending $1.78 to take in $1.

Various inducements have been offered to increase travel during the off-peak hours. Additional service has been provided during these periods and special "shopper tickets" are sold at reduced rates.

Commuter complaints are principally about high fares, delays, the inadequacy of facilities at some suburban stations and the lack of air-conditioned coaches.

In comparison with New York, commuter service in Philadelphia has the advantage of being separated from through express services. The midtown suburban station is a modern eight-track terminal below street level, entirely for commuter trains.

Chicago's 2,000,000 suburban dwellers are served by eight railroads, reaching out in a radius of fifty miles north, west and south.

Commuter complaints are regional, dependent on which railroad is involved. But generally they center on possible rate increases, old equipment and infrequency of nonrush-hour service. Riders to the north and northwest, especially, say they are tired of traveling in coaches retired years ago from through service.

Things are relatively good for commuters who live south of Chicago. The Illinois Central, with an average daily load of 135,000 commuters, is second in passenger load only to the Long Island Rail Road. Completely electrified in 1926, the Illinois Central reaches twenty-nine miles south. It recently increased its fast morning and evening rush-hour service.

Other suburban railroads serving the area south of Chicago include the Chicago South Shore and South Bend Railroad, the Gulf Mobile and Ohio road and the Chicago, Rock Island and Pacific Railroad.

The South Shore is also electrified, and, like the Illinois Central, offers reasonably fast and frequent service. Rock Island is completely dieselized. South Shore has 2,500 commuters and Rock Island 33,000.

A Rock Island official said that, although the annual passenger deficit in suburban operations is approximately $1,500,000, the road recently bought twenty lightweight cars for $1,988,161. Some of the Rock Island cars are air-conditioned; others have forced draft cooling.

West of Chicago, the picture varies. Because of its excellent operation, the Burlington Lines is a constant source of embarrassment to other managements. Its 19,500 commuters have a high regard and affection for the Burlington. Since 1948, it has spent $15,000,000 in fully dieselizing its suburban service and providing double-decked, air-conditioned coaches seating 148 passengers in roller-bearing comfort. The Burlington also has modernized its "flat top" coaches and equipped them with air-conditioning and roller bearings.

Also operating in this area are the Chicago and North Western Railway, the Milwaukee Road and the Chicago, Aurora and Elgin Railway.

The history of the North Western goes back more than 100 years. It operates three suburban lines that come together just outside its Chicago passenger terminal. On the debit side, as far as commuters are concerned, is the use of ancient coaches and some steam locomotives.

Operating to the North Shore suburbs are the Milwaukee and the Chicago and North Western. The latter, which carries 72,000 persons daily, has succeeded in reducing some commuters' complaints by partially dieselizing its service.

The San Francisco Bay area is in the midst of a $750,000 study of rapid transit problems and what to do about them. The New York consultant engineering firm of Parsons, Brinckerhoff, Hall & Macdonald expects to have recommendations ready late this fall after a two-year survey.

Rising costs, leading to increased commuter fares, have resulted in patronage losses and reduced revenues for some of the mass transit lines. Increasing use of the automobile by commuters has added to the acute traffic and parking problems.

The number of persons who travel from outside to work in San Francisco each day is estimated by the New York engineers as 99,300. The percentage of commuters using mass transportation is placed variously at 40 to 45 per cent.

The Southern Pacific Company opened the first rail commuter service in the San Francisco Bay area in 1864. Twenty-seven or twenty-eight commuter trains operate daily on the run between San Francisco and San Jose to the south.

The density of rush-hour travel has made it necessary for the company to add double-deck coaches to its commuter equipment. Although it sometimes fails, the Southern Pacific tries to give every commuting passenger a seat. It provides free parking lots at the peninsula stations. And it hauls 16,000 commuters in each direction five days a week, as compared with 7,000 in 1940.

The Southern Pacific in 1946 made its first request in twenty-six years for an increase in commuter fares. It received one of 20 per cent. One of 12½ per cent followed in 1948, another of 24 per cent in 1950 and one of 20 per cent last May.

A typical monthly commuter ticket, good five days a week, costs $19.95 for the thirty-mile trip between San Francisco and Palo Alto. The cost was $10.77 before 1946.

The Southern Pacific maintains that it operates commuter service at an out-of-pocket loss despite rises in fare. The same story comes from the Key System, which runs electric trains and buses over the San Francisco-Oakland Bay Bridge. It also applies to the Pacific Greyhound Lines, which operate buses on the peninsula that comprises the city and its suburbs to the south, and to and from Marin County, beyond the Golden Gate Bridge.

Despite complaints about old equipment and lack of a midtown terminal, the Southern Pacific seems to have succeeded better than other transit lines in keeping patrons relatively happy.

While Southern Pacific business continues to rise, the Key System reports it carried 11,000,000 over the bay bridge last year, as compared with 35,000,000 in 1945.

London's mass transportation system carries 1,125,000 persons into the business districts every day. The service is generally held to be efficient and convenient. Like mass transportation elsewhere, it does not pay.

Private cars, estimated to have increased by a third in central London since 1951, cannot replace the red double-decker buses, but the traffic has slowed them down considerably. Most of the decrease in riding public conveyances during the last four years has been on the buses.

About 400,000 rush-hour passengers move by "underground," the equivalent of New York's subways; 270,000 by bus; and just under 400,000 by suburban trains that terminate in London, rather than crossing it.

Most of the underground lines run deep, with elevators or escalators to the platforms. This limits the subway convenience for short trips. There is little effort to "pack 'em in."

The "underground" is slower than the New York subways and there are no expresses. But it is cleaner and quieter. One big drawback is that it stops running about midnight and does not resume until early morning working hours. So do the buses. Nighthawks must use taxis.

As for the railways proper, the 400,000 suburbanites who use London's eleven main passenger stations every morning have a fast, efficient service that is usually on time. The equipment on the lines, like all British railways' rolling stock, is conspicuously aged.

A serious shortcoming is the fact that only one sector of the systems radiating out from London, the Southern, is electrified. Engines bring soot and grime into the heart of the city from the other three quarters of the compass.

The number and central location of London's railroad stations are an advantage. The stations are disposed on an oval about four miles long and two miles deep that circumscribes the business area of London. A drawback is the enormous amount of London property preempted by railroads, estimated at one-third as much area as is devoted to public parks. Considerable areas are blighted by viaducts.

It costs a suburban season ticket buyer in London just about 1.49 cents a mile, as compared with the standard rate of 1.86 cents in third class. The first class rate is 3.29 cents.

Neither the London Transport System nor British Railways makes money out of the commuter business. London Transport did better financially last year, thanks to a fare increase, but it fell $3,640,000 short of meeting its capital charges.

August 15, 1955

SUBWAY IS URGED FOR WASHINGTON

Kennedy Offers Program, Opposing Freeway Lobby

By BEN A. FRANKLIN
Special to The New York Times

WASHINGTON, May 27 — President Kennedy asked Congress today to authorize a $793,000,000 rapid transit system, including a subway, for the District of Columbia.

In doing so, he placed the authority and prestige of the White House in the path of a well-organized lobby for a massive automobile freeway system, which critics have charged would do serious damage to the classic design of the national capital.

In a message to Congress, the President indicated that the Administration, which has been playing an increasingly active role in the local affairs of this voteless city, was postponing controversial portions of the urban freeway program here in favor of the rail system.

Termed Less Costly

Administration spokesmen said the rail system would be "more efficient, less costly and far less damaging to the esthetic and social structure of the city."

Specifically, they said the freeways and interchanges that the Administration opposes would displace 33,000 persons, largely low-income Negroes, in a city without plans for relocating such numbers and with "potentially explosive racial tensions."

In March, it was reported, eight officials of the National Highway Users Conference, a major highway lobbying organization, called on the President. It was understood that the officials urged him not to curtail the Washington freeway system.

The Highway User, a magazine published by the National Highway Users Conference, recently said the President's decision regarding Washington would be a choice "of national significance."

"It could set the stage for depriving other urban areas of their share of highway development, of freeways planned and needed," the magazine said.

A spokesman of the National Capital Transportation Agency, which drafted the subway plan, said that the Administration's overall proposal excluded some of the expressway projects called for in a $2,500,000,000 mass transportation program put forward in 1959.

The agency said that the Washington area had completed or had under construction 205 miles of freeways and parkways. It contended that 50 more freeway miles should be built by 1980 to complement the rapid transit system.

If Congress approves the subway proposal this year, rapid transit service connecting downtown stations could begin in 1968. By 1973, high-speed air-conditioned trains would run on 83 miles of track to major suburban communities in Maryland and Virginia. Outside the downtown area, tracks would be constructed on the surface or in depressed rights of way in the center of major roadways.

The subway system would "dramatically reduce" both traffic congestion and commuting time, the transportation agency said. A trip from suburban Alexandria, Va., to the Capitol would be cut from 60 minutes by present bus routes to 17 minutes by subway.

Running time from Silver Spring, Md., to the Capitol would be 13 minutes, compared with 45 minutes on the present bus system.

The downtown portions of the subway system would have stations within an eight-minute walk of 94 per cent of office buildings and employment centers expected to exist in 1980.

No additional appropriations are needed for the highway portions of the President's plan.

The subway system would be financed through more than $600,000,000 in 4½ per cent private loans on the public bond market, $180,000,000 in grants from local governments and the balance from operating revenues. The President said the system would pay for itself "even under adverse conditions" in 50 years.

May 28, 1963

Chicago Gets Transit Grant

CHICAGO, March 14 (AP)—Mayor Richard J. Daley announced today Federal approval of grants totaling nearly $46-million toward construction of rapid transit lines in the median strips of the Dan Ryan and John F. Kennedy Expressways. The Dan Ryan Expressway serves the South Side and the Kennedy the Northwest Side.

March 15, 1967

PRESIDENT SIGNS TRANSIT-AID BILL

Says $375 Million Program to Help Commuters Shows U.S. Concern for Cities

GRANTS LIMITED HERE

By WARREN WEAVER Jr.
Special to The New York Times

WASHINGTON, July 9 — President Johnson signed into law today the nation's first program to give massive Federal aid to urban transportation systems.

At the ceremony in the White House, Mr. Johnson said the measure to help commuters was "only one of several that this Administration is prepared to take in the days ahead to face up to the problems of the urban areas of this country."

"We are determined," the President told a group of Senators, Representatives, Governors and Mayors, "that we will provide the vision and the leadership necessary, and that they [the cities] will no longer be a stepchild and be neglected by their Government in Washington."

The law will provide $375 million in Federal grants over a three-year period for the construction and rehabilitation of commuter bus, subway and train facilities.

Cities Must Contribute

The money will cover two-thirds of that part of the capital costs of reviving transit facilities that cannot be financed out of prospective fare revenue. The other third must be contributed locally.

Mayor Wagner, who went to Washington for the ceremony, had a mixed view of what the legislation may mean for New York City.

The Mayor listed some major transit projects that he said could be assisted, but later said "there won't be too much for us" in the program.

Under limitations in the law, no single state can receive more than about $47 million of the $375 million in the three years. But New York City could only get as much as that if no other city in New York State received any grant money at all.

Mr. Wagner expressed the hope, however, that "in the years ahead, the amounts available will be more."

This is precisely what opponents of the transit program had predicted on the floor of Congress: that the bill would ultimately involve multibillion-dollar Federal spending.

To Extend Subway

The Mayor said the Federal money would be used "for further extension of our subway system in Queens and possibly other boroughs as well" and to assist in construction of an East River tunnel.

Mr. Wagner predicted the program would also provide "much needed assistance" to the commuter railroads serving New York City—the New Haven, the Long Island and various lines in New Jersey.

The President made it clear he knew the transit bill was not going to solve the nation's urban transportation problems overnight.

"All of us recognize that the curses of congestion in commuting cannot be wiped away with the single stroke of a pen —or the 50 pens we have here," Mr. Johnson said, "but we do know that this legislation we are coming to grips with faces the realities of American life and attempts to put in motion a movement to do something about it."

Mr. Johnson called the new law "by any standard one of the most profoundly significant domestic measures to be enacted by the Congress during the nineteen-sixties." Yet, he said, it was in the tradition of Federal support for railroads, canals, highways and airways.

The impact of the program will not be felt for some time. Because of the length of time required to plan and approve transit programs, the 1964-65 budget only includes $10 million to finance the effort in its initial stages.

Among the guests at the signing ceremony were the chief sponsor of the bill, Senator Harrison A. Williams, Democrat of New Jersey, and its floor managers, Senator John J. Sparkman and Representative Albert Rains, both Alabama Democrats.

Others included Gov. Richard J. Hughes of New Jersey, John J. Gilhooley of the New York City Transit Authority, Edwin G. Michaelian, the Westchester County Executive, and Dr. Robert Weaver, Administrator of the Federal Housing and Home Agency, which will administer the program.

July 10, 1964

Cities Shunning Express-Lane Plan

WASHINGTON, Nov. 9 (AP)—The idea seems simple: set aside a freeway lane for buses only; then whisk commuters nonstop at high speeds between the suburbs and downtown.

Unfortunately, according to Government transportation specialists, it has turned out to be a terribly complicated concept.

Since Federal officials started pushing the idea more than a year ago, which included offering Federal funds for much of the cost, not a single city has adopted the plan.

The main obstacle is that other motorists, jammed bumper-to-bumper on a freeway are not expected to look kindly on a special bus lane that does not have a bus going by every minute, or perhaps every 30 seconds. And attracting that many bus riders has proved an enormous task.

Bus Ramps Needed

The buses so the argument goes, take full advantage of a freeway lane if they have to wait in the frequently long lineups of vehicles to use entrance and exit ramps. So, to make the concept most effective, exclusive ramps have to be built for the buses.

Finally, the specialists say, people do not want to take a bus to work in the city unless they can get adequate public transportation once they are there. And few cities have excellent systems to move people around downtown.

The express-bus impasse typifies the trouble officials have found in pursuading people to leave their cars—an effort they say must succeed if the cities are to be saved from congestion.

"We're beginning to see that you have to look at the whole city as a system," says Paul Sitton, newly named director of the Department of Transportation's Urban Mass Transportation Administration.

Mr. Sitton, whose division this year was transferred from the Department of Housing and Urban Development, says one of the next steps will have to be development of whole new networks to transport people around the centers of cities.

He foresees transfer centers on the edges of downtown areas, where people would leave their cars or disembark from buses or trains. Then they would transfer to one of several modes of travel such as monorails, moving sidewalks or an individually-operated network of taxis that would carry one or two people on guideways above street levels.

Pedestrians would have walkways separated from other vehicles. Trucks would operate on another level, preferably underground.

Mr. Sitton says such systems would be especially feasible in cities such as Dallas, Denver, St. Louis, Atlanta, Seattle, San Francisco, Pittsburgh and Minneapolis and St. Paul.

It would take about 10 years, to demonstrate such systems and prepare them for broad use, according to a recent Federal research study. The development cost was put at $110-million.

The 18-month study has provided what Federal officials call the first clear picture of what can be done about the nation's urban transportation mess.

The next step, Mr. Sitton says, is to "focus public attention on the fact that there are solutions."

H. W. Merritt, director of research for the transit agency, says most people endure the horrors of city travel in relative silence because they do not know what could be done. But he says the average commuter is beginning to realize that more freeways alone are not going to solve the problem.

Among measures recommended by Federal officials and by the research study were:

¶Use of computers and other electronic equipment to control the rate at which vehicles are allowed on freeways, thus preventing freeway jam-ups. This has been done successfully on freeways in a few cities for several years.

¶Automating traffic lights so they change to provide maximum traffic flow and give priority to buses over cars.

¶Providing direct home-to-work premium bus service, such as began this year in Flint, Mich.

¶Adding more cross-town bus service so people can get around better within cities.

¶Providing rental agencies for small cars in suburban areas. The vehicles would be rented for a trip, a day, or longer; for shuttles to and from such places as shopping centers, transit terminals and schools. The idea would be to convince the consumer that such a system would be cheaper than owning a second or third car.

November 10, 1968

Increase in Fares Is Found in Major Cities Across the Nation

By WAYNE KING

Bus and subway riders in major cities across the country are experiencing sharp rises in fares that, in some cases, are headed toward the 50-cent level.

The general pattern of fare increases, which sent New York City fares from 20 cents to 30 cents earlier this month, appears to have accelerated lately. Passenger volume, meanwhile, is continuing a decline that is aggravating the financial deficits in many cities.

Last week, bus riders in Kansas City, Mo., began dropping 50 cents into the fare box, the highest basic fare in the country. But the city is not apt to remain alone.

Other cities, including Chicago, are also considering 50-cent fares.

The pattern in many big cities is the same: Costs are going up swiftly while service and passenger volume are on the decline.

Cleveland's city-owned lines have increased fares three times since 1960, the last time in March to 35 cents, plus 5 cents for a transfer. The increases were coupled with a reduction in service and each was followed by a noticeable decline in passengers.

Lowest Basic Rate

In Washington, the D.C. Transit Line, the largest of four privately owned lines, has increased its bus fares seven times in the last 10 years to a current level of 32 cents, set in October, 1969. Four of the increases were within the last two years. There is talk of another increase—to 40 cents.

In Denver, the Denver Tramway Corporation's fares increased from 10 cents to 15 in 1956, to 20 cents in 1960, to 25 cents in 1964, to 30 cents in 1967, and to 35 cents last June.

In a message to stockholders last year, a company executive said that without "significant relief," other than continued service cuts, direct subsidy or tax relief, the only solution seemed to be "some sort of public ownership."

Even in New Orleans, where the basic fare has been 10 cents for the last 10 years, bus riders begin paying 15 cents today. The fare is still the lowest basic rate in the country, but for New Orleans residents, the rise represents a minor civic tragedy, something like the passing of the nickel beer.

Virtually alone among the nation's larger cities, New Orleans had held the line on its bus fares since 1960, when officials added 3 cents to a fare that had been 7 cents for 28 years.

Passenger Dip Noted

Reports from other cities and industry statistics reflect a different picture. The American Transit Association reports that the average cash fare on both private and publicly owned mass transit systems in the nation rose from 18.94 cents in 1960 to 23.60 cents in 1968, with the recent series of sharp increases not yet compiled. Other studies show a threefold

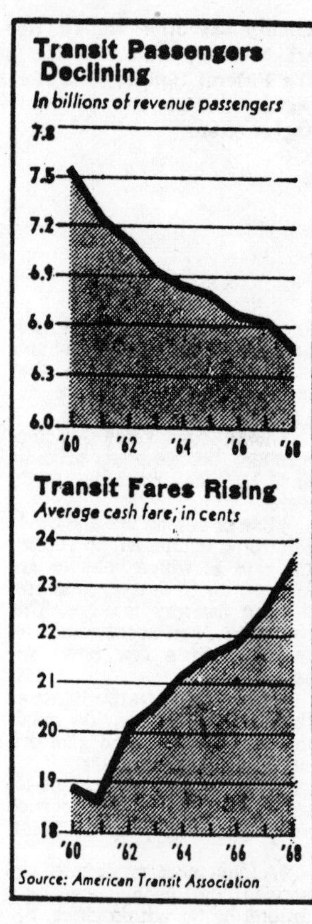

The New York Times Jan. 26, 1970

increase in the last 20 years.

At the same time, the number of fare-paying passengers dropped from 7.65 billion in 1960 to 6.49 billion in 1968, with the downward trend continuing. The number of passengers carried last year is only one-third that of mass transit's boom year of 1945, when almost 19 billion passengers were carried.

In the face of the passenger decline, officials of the Department of Transportation are arguing that the need for efficient mass transit is greater than ever.

Secretary of Transportation John A. Volpe said in Atlanta Friday that development of an effective means of transporting large numbers of people effectively was necessary to revitalize the cities.

Mr. Volpe, who spoke to a group of businessmen, discussed the Nixon Administration's $10-billion long-range plan to assist public transportation in the cities. Hearings on the proposal are expected to resume in the House of Representatives next month.

Although Mr. Volpe has expressed optimism about massive Federal aid to transit systems and has identified himself with the effort to earmark certain taxes for a multibillion-dollar transit program, the White House has insisted that the needs be met by annual appropriations at a somewhat lower rate.

The plan for Government subsidies to mass transit is not based primarily on the desire to keep fares low, according to a spokesman for the Urban Mass Transportation Administration, part of the Department of Transportation.

The agency cites studies indicating that poor service, dirty cars and stations, noise and crowding, not fares, are the prime reasons that riders abandon mass transit.

A report by the Senate Banking and Currency Committee on the mass aid bill noted that "public tansit users are willing to pay somewhat higher costs if the quality of service is improved."

Reports from the cities indicate that the reverse is often the case: Service declines before a fare increase as officials try to cut costs and hold the line on fares—usually a losing battle. The result is more lost passengers.

A disgruntled Washington switchboard operator voiced a common complaint. "The bus system is lousy," she said, "and the fares keep going up and the service gets slower and slower."

At the same time, officials at both the local and Federal levels are looking to subsidies to break the cycle of soaring costs, declining quality and fleeing passengers, they are also conscious of the fact that public transportation has been losing the contest with the automobile for passengers.

Mr. Volpe said in his Atlanta address: "The one thing I've been trying to preach is that we can no longer depend on the automobile as the No. 1 mode of transportation."

Making public transportation attractive enough to woo Americans away from the highways can be done, Federal officials say, but it must be done while maintaining fares that can be paid not only by those who can afford it but also by those who cannot.

A trend toward reduced fares for the elderly and school children is growing in the cities, but so far no universal way has been found to ease the burden on economically depressed inner-city residents.

The Senate Banking Committee noted in its report: "There is little doubt that a lack of adequate transportation has been an important factor in the growing unrest in our cities."

January 26, 1970

Nixon Signs Transit Bill, Terming It a 'Landmark'

Special to The New York Times

WASHINGTON, Oct. 15 — President Nixon signed today legislation he proposed last year to commit $10-billion for new and improved bus and subway systems in urban areas over the next 12 years.

In signing the measure at a White House ceremony, the President said:

"This bill, I think, when we look at the record of this Congress and of this Administration, will be one that will be one of the landmark pieces of legislation."

Surrounded by Congressional leaders and transportation officials, the President described what the new law could mean for urban life in the next few years.

Recalling that the railroads had opened the Western frontier for the nation in the 19th century, he said that the "urban frontier is the challenge of America in the last third of the 20th century."

The bill is designed to halt the deterioration of existing transit systems, provide for the construction of new and faster systems, and ease pollution and traffic congestion by taking automobiles off the highways.

"This, we believe, is a historic step to meet that challenge," Mr. Nixon said.

"It isn't going to be met in a year, not in two years, not three years, not four or five, but the action this Congress has taken and by the action that the Secretary of Transportation will take to implement this bill means that, within five years, 10 years, as we move over the next decade, that we are going to see a significant breakthrough in mass urban transportation."

The transit legislation, known as the Urban Mass Transportation Assistance Act of 1970, was approved by the Senate in February and by the House last month and was forwarded to the President on Oct. 5.

Because of budget restraints, the Nixon Administration had insisted that funding of the legislation be gradual, and Congress complied.

The act authorizes $80-million in the current fiscal year. This increases at a graduated rate to an aggregate amount of $1.86-billion in the fiscal year 1975 and to $3.1-billion thereafter.

Under the act, a formula is established under which the Federal Government pays up to two-thirds of the cost of transit projects as well as the purchase of land, equipment and other facilities.

The act contains a controversial financing provision called "contractual authority." The Secretary of Transportation will be authorized to sign agreements with local communities, pledging the Federal share of the cost. The money may not actually be spent until later, but the cities will be assured the money will be there when needed.

This removes much of the Federal control, in that Congress will be obligated to liquidate the Federal pledges made by the executive branch.

Public Hearings Required

Private transit systems would also be eligible for some assistance under the act. There is a provision for loans to local governments for acquiring property that would be held and used for transit purposes up to 10 years in the future.

The act requires public hearings and other safeguards before a commitment of funds to insure against any harmful social, environmental or economic impact on the community.

When the bill was under debate, Mayors and other urban officials had doubts as to whether the amounts authorized would come close to meeting the cities' needs. Mayor Lindsay of New York had said that his city alone needed at least $5.2-billion for transit development in the nineteen-seventies.

October 16, 1970

Illegal Jitneys Busy In Slums of Cities

By ROBERT LINDSEY

The jitney—a mode of mass transportation that requires only an automobile and a spirit of free enterprise on the part of its owner—is enjoying a resurgence in some American cities.

Jitneys are private cars or small vans that their owners use to carry passengers for a fee. They flourished in many cities in the nineteen-twenties, when "jitney" was a slang term for nickel, the fare in those days.

They are experiencing a revival largely in the slums of major cities and often in violation of local laws.

Transit specialists attribute the revived popularity to rising taxi and transit fares; the national shortage of jobs, which has prompted some unskilled, jobless automobile owners to seek a living with their cars, and the growing number of poor blacks in some cities.

Outlawed in U.S.

Jitney-like conveyances are very much a part of transportation in many foreign nations, particularly in Latin countries, from the Publico of Puerto Rico to the Colectivo of Argentina.

Most American cities outlawed the jitney in the nineteen-thirties after bitter clashes between rival jitney associations and protests from companies that operated taxis and transit lines. Jitneys are legal today in only a handful of cities, including San Francisco, Miami, Atlantic City and Daytona Beach, Fla.

But, according to current reports from around the country, jitneys are illegally thriving in a number of cities, often with the tacit approval of local officials who tolerate them as essential services to the low-income blacks.

In Chicago, scores of the cars can be seen daily. They travel along King Street between 22d and 63d streets, stopping at street corners or in mid-block, to pick up housewives with shopping bags, youths, and other people. For a quarter, they ride a few blocks through the black South Side.

Providing a Link

In Pittsburgh, new and old Cadillacs, Chevrolets and Buicks shuttle passengers along Fifth Avenue, providing a link between the city's Hill District and the downtown business district.

In Winston-Salem, N.C., Boston's Roxbury District, Newark, Watts and in other cities, black entrepreneurs are using their cars to carry passengers for a small fare.

Transit specialists who have studied these operations believe the concept could be applied in other cities to improve transportation between slum communities, suburban job centers and other destinations. But, for the most part, they say, introduction of jitneys has been severely limited by Federal and local policies that are largely rooted in opposition from transit and taxi interests and organized labor.

An Invaluable Service

In Chattanooga, where the black community is served by 87 jitneys, John Russell, the city taxi inspector, conceded that they were illegal under city ordinances. But he said:

"They perform an invaluable service. The bus company couldn't operate in the areas served by the jitneys and make a profit."

Richard J. Solomon, a Boston transportation consultant who studied the jitney industry while at the Urban Systems Laboratory of the Massachusetts Institute of Technology, is among a growing number of transit specialists who support the use of jitneys to serve black communities.

"Because of their smaller size, lower overhead and nonunionized workers," he said, "jitneys are less expensive to operate than buses. Since they need lower revenue per mile than buses to cover costs and make a profit, they can be viable along less densely traveled routes."

To many urban transportation authorities, there is a thin line between the illegal jitneys that have sprung up in many cities and the "gypsy" cabs that also flourish in cities with large black populations.

New York City is estimated to have more than 5,000 gypsies, operating mostly in Harlem and other black sections of the city. Such cabs do not have a city permit (called a medallion in New York) that would allow them to pick up people who hail them from the street. If they have any legal authority at all, it is usually restricted to transporting people who request a cab by telephone.

This rule is widely flouted in parts of New York and elsewhere, largely because drivers of the licensed cabs often refuse to enter the ghetto areas and they willingly forfeit the business.

The main difference between jitneys and gypsy cabs is that the jitneys generally stick to a single boulevard and maintain a scheduled service. They usually charge 25 cents to 40 cents for a ride of a few blocks up to several miles.

The Urban Mass Transportation Administration has considered sponsoring experimental jitneylike services in a San Francisco black community and in other cities to test whether self-employed jitneymen could help provide better transportation between slum areas and employment centers outside the slums.

But the proposals have always been shelved. One transportation researcher said:

"The way the Urban Mass Transportation Act of 1964 is written, organized labor, working through the Department of Labor, can veto almost any kind of concept like this.

"The law prohibits use of Federal funds if the unions say the system would compete with transit workers on existing services, or if it would pay less than prevailing local wages for transit workers. When you have a system where a guy works for himself, the unions don't like it."

Transit and taxi operators who oppose jitneys and gypsy cabs argue that the absence of government regulations similar to those under which they operate encourage cut-throat competition and unsafe operations. They also complain that the vehicles undermine their services by siphoning off customers.

Many transit experts expect the recent popularity of the jitneys to continue, although the growth will be limited by opposition. In St. Louis, they note, efforts are being made to revive a jitney operation that was ended five years ago, but it is being strongly opposed by the local bus line.

Mr. Solomon of Boston remarked: "If we don't make use of the jitney legally for disadvantaged urban residents, it's going to come anyway."

May 30, 1971

Cities Say U.S. Reneges On Rapid-Transit Funding

By ROBERT LINDSEY

What urban leaders contend is a turnabout in Nixon Administration policies regarding mass transportation has thrown plans of more than a dozen American cities to build modern rapid transit systems into a state of confusion.

Officials in Atlanta, Denver, Los Angeles, Miami and other cities assert that they were led to believe by the Administration that Federal aid would be available to pay for up to 80 per cent of the cost of their transit systems, and they planned accordingly. Tax measures were approved by voters in several cities to raise local funds to qualify for Federal grants.

The city leaders contend that the Administration is now backing away from earlier assurances, raising the prospect of unrealized civic dreams, unfinished transit systems, angry local voters and possible continued dependence on the automobile.

"We stuck our necks out," said Mayor Maynard Jackson of Atlanta because the city received "not only the go-ahead but actually the aggressive encouragement of the Federal Government" to build a transit system.

Administration Denial

Now, Mr. Jackson added, Atlantans are told Federal aid may not be forthcoming — a situation tantamount to "our being out on the limb, and the Federal Government behind us sawing it off."

Administration spokesmen deny reneging on previous commitments, although they concede that some local leaders may have been misled into expecting more largesse from Washington than they now appear likely to receive.

Saying that Federal transit programs are at a "crossroads," Frank C. Herringer, who heads the Federal Urban Mass Transportation Administration, says that Federal funds to help cities build subways, commuter lines and other projects are limited and must be spent where they can do the most good.

Mass transportation, which in Washington in recent years grew into an issue that ranked with love of the flag, appears to be losing some of its automatic, unchallenged cachet.

Cost overruns on new transit ventures, troubles with San Francisco's $1.6-billion new rapid transit system, and the limited success so far of federally aided programs in luring motorists from automobiles are prompting harder questioning.

Hearings Under Way

Unhappiness over the Federal Government's success so far in improving urban transportation was reflected in a comment this week by Representative William S. Moorhead, a Pittsburgh Democrat, who is holding hearings on mass transportation as chairman of the Urban Affairs Subcommittee of the Joint Economic Committee.

"Since 1965," he said, "the Federal Government has spent almost $3-billion on programs of assistance to urban transportation," although transit ridership around the nation slipped 22 per cent during this period.

A Congressional committee staff aide said:

"U.M.T.A. has spent more than $200-million on transit research and development in the past five years and look what they've got to show for it—practically nothing."

For the most part, transit specialists in the Administration reject such blanket criticism. They point out that Federal grants in recent years helped keep more than 100 local bus lines in operation, that despite technical problems, San Francisco's new rail line is luring motorists out of cars and that other innovations, such as the use of express buses on reserved freeway lanes, are attracting new riders.

Nevertheless, the belief that mass transit is much less of a panacea for solving urban problems that it was once thought to be appears to be spreading.

"There's been too much overselling of mass transit as a philosophy," a White House specialist on transportation asserted in an interview last week.

The Government's new skepticism that grew out of its first experiences with helping urban mass transit appears to have caught by surprise some cities that had begun planning ambitious — and expensive — transit systems following passage by Congress in 1970 of the transit aid program.

Initially, it provided for cities to receive two-thirds of the cost of transit projects; the proportion was later increased by Congress to four-fifths.

Transit aid totaling $872-million is being given cities during the current fiscal year. The Administration has proposed granting $1.2-billion in the fiscal year starting July 1 and more than $2-billion annually within four years.

Even with this proposed increase, Federal officials say, available funds would fall far short of paying for currently proposed transit projects, even if they were justified.

Commuters in only seven cities are served now by rail rapid transit lines — New York, Boston, Chicago, Cleveland, Newark, Philadelphia and San Francisco. Work is under way on a $3.5-billion transit line in Washington, and work is scheduled to begin on one in Baltimore later this year.

The cities now in various stages of initiating similar projects include Pittsburgh, Rochester, Buffalo, Honolulu, Minneapolis-St. Paul, Dallas and San Juan, P.R.

Denver voters have approved a $425-million bond issue to raise the local share for a $1.6-billion transit system; Miami voters have approved a $132-million bond issue to start a $1.5-billion system; Atlanta area voters approved a sales tax now raising about $50-million yearly to help pay for a $1.8-billion transit line.

Officials in several of the cities maintain that their plans are based on the Federal assurances of receiving adequate aid from Washington that now may not materialize.

May 12, 1974

PRESIDENT SIGNS MASS-TRANSIT ACT

Beame Says City's Share of $11.8-Billion Aid Will Save 35c Fare Through '75

By MARTIN TOLCHIN
Special to The New York Times

WASHINGTON, Nov. 26—President Ford signed a six-year, $11.8-billion mass-transit bill today that Mayor Beame said would save the 35-cent fare through 1975.

Transportation Secretary Claude S. Brinegar later said at a news conference that the Federal funds would begin to flow immediately.

The President hailed the measure in a White House ceremony attended by governors, mayors and Congressmen, some of whom had openly despaired only last month of obtaining any such Federal relief.

"This marks a long-term and vital major Federal commitment to mass transportation," Mr. Ford said at the East Room ceremony, during which scores of witnesses were herded behind ropes and stanchions, jammed together like rush-hour passengers on the IRT.

In his five-minute speech, the President touched on some national problems, such as inflation and energy, that had given new momentum to the quest for operating subsidies for mass transit.

"This legislation is significant in our fight against the excessive use of petroleum, in our economic battle and in our efforts to curb urban pollution and reduce congestion," the President said. "It assures that $11.8-billion in Federal assistance will be available to states and to cities to meet transit needs for the rest of the decade."

Under the legislation, New York City will get $170-million of the more than $200-million needed to save the fare this fiscal year, Mr. Beame said. It will give the city $250-million of the $280-million needed through 1975, he said. The city and state are committed to making up the deficit.

The bill-signing was a personal victory for Mayor Beame, who was instrumental in enlisting President Ford's support of the legislation. The Mayor gave Mr. Ford cufflinks made of subway tokens dipped in gold. They were created by Beverly Yunich, wife of the chairman of the Metropolitan Transportation Authority.

"I'm confident that the fare will be saved through 1975," Mr. Beame told newsmen. "This is an historic occasion which ranks with revenue sharing in its importance to urban America."

Today's ceremony also was a personal victory for Senator Harrison A. Williams Jr. and Representative Joseph G. Minish, New Jersey Democrats, who guided the legislation through its tortuous route in Congress.

"Two months ago," Senator Williams said, "we were depressed about the legislation's chances for enactment. We were beset with legislative problems that looked almost insoluble. The elements that came together came together at just the right moments—the President, the Congress, the nation—all within 48 hours."

Representative Minish said that two months ago, if anybody had told him that he would be attending a bill-signing ceremony today, he would have had "grave doubts—to say the least."

"But I'm resourceful, so here we are," he said.

The enactment also was a victory for the United States Conference of Mayors, which had strenuously lobbied for the bill, and which enlisted President Ford's support last October.

"President Ford has now accomplished more than any President of the United States for mass transportation," said Mayor Joseph L. Alioto of San Francisco, the organization's president. "This marks the day when the automobile stops getting a monopoly of favored treatment from the Federal Government."

Mayor Beame noted that the Metropolitan Transportation Authority projected a $420-million deficit through December, 1975. This would be reduced by $70-million in promised state funds, $70-million in city funds and $250-million in Federal funds for operating subsidies.

Uses Administration Formula

The legislation is formally

called the National Mass Transportation Assistance Act of 1974. It represents the first time that the Federal Government has authorized the use of Federal funds for mass transit.

The bill adopted an Administration formula based on population and density, but not riders, which would have favored New York City. Under the legislation, New York City will receive 15 per cent of operating subsidies, Northern New Jersey, 3 per cent, and Connecticut, 1.5 per cent.

The total operating subsidies will come to more than $3.9-billion, awarded on a 50-50 basis. The total capital funds will come to $7.9-billion, and would be distributed by the Secretary of Transportation, with the Federal Government giving 80 per cent and the local government 20 per cent, but only to approved projects.

The new legislation includes $1.4-billion already appropriated for the Urban Mass Transportation Administration. The bill also reflects the administration's requirement that governors be the sole allocators of funds for urbanized areas of less than 200,000 population.

November 27, 1974

Trolley Staging Comeback Over Nation

By RALPH BLUMENTHAL

A desire named streetcars is growing—a desire for the return of one of America's oldest forms of urban public transportation.

Decades after the nation succumbed to the internal combustion engine in city after city, the electric trolley is being called back to service in an advanced form as an answer to demands for cheap, pollution-free mass transit.

Seeking a bright, new image as "light rail transit," the mode combines elements of the trolley car of yore, including on-street boarding and surface passage under overhead power lines, with features of modern rapid rail transit, such as speedy, smooth travel on restricted rights of way that separate the vehicles from other traffic.

A new appreciation of light rail has been evident in the cities that have retained trolley service. Among them are Boston, San Francisco, Philadelphia, Pittsburgh, Shaker Heights, Ohio, Newark and New Orleans, home of the original (and now defunct) streetcar named Desire of the Tennessee Williams play.

In addition, Dayton, Ohio, has become the first city to develop a plan for a comprehensive new light rail system, and Rochester and Buffalo, among other municipalities, are considering installation of such a system.

Heralding the phenomenon, the Boeing Vertol Company has begun turning out, for Boston and San Francisco, 275 of the first trolley vehicles to be produced in this country since 1952. Other smaller cities across the nation are planning on upgrading older street-car service or building new systems. The trend was strikingly evident last month in Philadelphia, where 600 transit planners and officials from around the country, Canada and Europe—twice the number expected converged for a national conference on light rail transit.

"This has to be the largest gathering of trolley-jollies since World War II," Frank C. Herringer, just-departed urban mass transportation administrator, told the participants, drawing a roar of delight. "It's really amazing."

"It might be we are witnessing what someone called the second coming of the trolley," said William J. Ronan, chairman of the Port Authority of New York and New Jersey, in another keynote address.

The conference—sponsored jointly by the United States Urban Mass Transportation Administration, the Transportation Research Board of the federally aided National Research Council, the American Public Transit Administration and the University of Pennsylvania—was not an exercise in nostalgia for the trolley car or faddism, officials took pains to explain. Rather, they said, the meeting represented recognition of the vital role light rail transit could play in cities today.

"This is a technology that currently demonstrates its effectiveness as part of the total urban transport system in more than 300 cities worldwide," said Lee H. Rogers of the Institute of Public Administration, a transit expert identified at the conference as "the James Bond of the light rail vehicle."

Basically, the difference between the streetcar that was driven into extinction by the auto and bus in most American cities more than a quarter century ago and today's evolved, upgraded version is not so much in the car itself but rather in the manner of its use.

The old streetcar wound through the heart of downtown, mostly down the very center of the street. With the growing number of motorists and bus drivers feeling they owned the streets, a confrontation of interests developed in the nineteen-twenties and thirties that ended with the streetcar's demise at the hands of the more powerful auto and bus forces.

In 1917, near the peak of trolley travel in the United States, 80,000 electric streetcars were plying 45,000 miles of track, carrying 11 billion passengers a year. At that time one could travel from eastern Wisconsin to central New York —more than 1,000 miles—on inter-urban street cars—provided he had enough nickels.

Yet by 1939, there remained only 2,700 miles of inter-urban lines in the country, according to a paper presented at the conference June 23-26 by James R. Mills, president pro tem of the California State Senate.

And today, transit experts said, there remains less than 500 miles of operational track.

Under the new concept, the light rail vehicle runs on its own right of way, generally separated from other traffic. It is thus able to maintain a higher and steadier speed than its predecessors and to keep out of the way of other traffic.

However, the system is still flexible enough to allow divergence of the rail vehicles into mixed traffic if desired. Moreover, the vehicles can load both on the street and in stations like conventional rapid transit systems.

But, because a light rail system does not involve tunneling, it is far cheaper to build than a subway system.

According to figures presented at the Philadelphia conference, the construction cost of a double-track light rail route might range from $4-million to $8-million a mile, not including land acquisition. The rail cars cost about $500,000 each. Subway construction, on the other hand, might now run $50-million a mile and in some congested urban areas, may soon approach double that.

"Conventional rail has just priced itself out of the market," said C. Kenneth Orski, associate administrator of the mass transportation agency. "People are beginning to ask themselves: 'Can any city afford that kind of cost?' There will be very few starts of conventional rapid transit systems of the kind Washington and Atlanta are building."

Atlanta's rapid transit system, projected to cost $1.3-billion in 1971, is now priced at $2.1-billion with further upward adjustments likely. Washington's Metro project is now projected at more than $4-billion. New York recently indefinitely put off a planned new Second Avenue subway line because of spiraling costs.

Yet the light rail systems, like the old streetcars, remain dependent on the blighting web of overhead wires carrying the 600 to 750 volts of DC current that powers the vehicle through the overhead pantograph. The old hookup called "trolley" gave the vehicles their name. While the overhead hookup may have been esthetically unacceptable several years ago, the energy crisis has tempered esthetic concerns with economic and other needs.

"It's important to keep the environment in perspective," said Mr. Herringer, who left as mass transit administrator June 30 to take over operation of the mechanically ailing Bay Area Rapid Transit system in San Francisco.

"Sure, it's intrusive," he said, referring to the wires, "but compared to what? What's more intrusive than a highway? Compared to that, a few overhead wires is not much to put up with."

As now conceived by transit planners, the new light rail systems would be most applicable to cities of under a million population with requirements of moving from 5,000 to 20,000 passengers per track per hour. Demands of from 20,000 to 40,000 passengers an hour are considered more appropriate to conventional rapid transit systems running on higher speed exclusive rights-of-way, often underground.

Thus, light rail transit would have little appeal to New York City, for example, where the subways carry 3.7 million people daily. Light rail might, however, prove feasible in carrying riders from the suburbs or other boroughs to certain points in Manhattan, although surface lines criss-crossing midtown would undoubtedly be too disruptive of other street traffic under current patterns and would repeat the jams and controversy of a half century ago.

Among other leading cities, however, Boston is upgrading

its existing light rail lines and has on order from Boeing Vertol for 175 of the first new cars to be produced in America since the St. Louis Car Company manufactured the last new trolley cars in 1952. San Francisco has ordered 100 more of the cars.

The new cars, under construction at the Boeing Vertol converted helicopter plant outside Philadelphia, are 71 feet long with three doors and with a center-articulated joint to facilitate sharp turns. The car, which is air-conditioned, can hold 219 passengers with seats for 52 or 68 passengers, depending on the city's needs.

The vehicle bodies are imported from the Tokyo Car Company of Japan, the brakes are Italian and other systems are manufactured by other domestic and foreign manufacturers.

The first new Boeing Vertol vehicle, destined for San Francisco, is now being tested on the Boston system. The other vehicles are scheduled for delivery later this year.

Other cities that have maintained or recently upgraded trolley vehicle service include Newark, Shaker Heights, Ohio, New Orleans, Pittsburgh and Philadelphia.

Dayton Seekks Funds

Plans for new light rail service are under way in Rochester and Dayton, Ohio, among other communities. Dayton applied in January for a $48-million capital grant from the mass transportation administration to begin building a 12.2-mile model light rail system and has been waiting with increasing impatience for a reply. Mr. Herringer said it was still under consideration and had not reached his desk.

In addition, the mass transportation agency has asked Buffalo to study the feasibility of building a light rail system instead of a far more expensive subway to connect the downtown area with the new campus of the state university about 11 miles away in suburban Amherst.

At the same time, Mr. Herringer said, the urban mass transportation agency can have no bias toward or against any particular type of transport, whether light rail, buses or rapid transit.

Light rail, he said, "is not U.M.T.A.'s latest fad. It's merely something to consider. We can't say it often enough. We don't favor any mode."

Nevertheless, he said, he was "impressed" with the new light rail car. "In the long run though," he said, "it will need exclusive rights of way. This will demand great political courage. The future of light rail," he concluded, "is brighter than it's been in years."

July 9, 1975

Mass Transit Use of Road Fund Lags

By RALPH BLUMENTHAL

Two years after Congress authorized the use of billions of dollars of Federal highway funds for mass transit projects, the results have proved bitterly disappointing to the advocates who hailed the Congressional action as a great victory.

Although the landmark program made available over three years nearly $2.4-billion from the hither-to sacrosanct Highway Trust Fund, no more than $34.6-million has been awarded so far—and that to only two places in the country—New York City and East St. Louis, Ill.

Only a handful of other communities have even applied for money.

"I would have to say the results have been disappointing to say the least," said Frank C. Herringer, the urban mass transit administrator.

In a briefing in Washington last week, he termed the implementation of the 1973 Federal Highway Act, embodying the highway funds breakthrough, "my biggest disappointment." He added that "unless the dollar level [of awards] gets up, very few cities are going to feel it's worthwhile."

Mr. Herringer, a 32-year-old former aide in the Nixon White House, attributed the "poor results" to a lack of information about the program among local transit officials and to what he called "formidable institutional problems" in the states in switching highway funds to mass transit uses.

Reluctant Local Officials

He also cited the requirement that localities underwrite up to 30 per cent of the funds to Washington's 70 per cent share.

"The decision-making process goes through the Mayor or Governor," he said, "and no one pulls it together." In addition, he said, local highway authorities still exercise considerable control over the disposition of road funds and are often less than eager to turn the money over for other than highway purposes.

A number of communities queried reported that they had encountered some initial resistance from their highway authorities on the applications.

The 1973 legislation tapping the Highway Trust Fund for the first time was the culmination of a long and bitter struggle between urban and environmental forces and highway interests. At stake was a share of the $6-billion in Federal gasoline taxes and highway-use taxes levied on trucks that has flowed annually into the fund for highway construction since 1956.

The Highway Trust Fund financed the massive interstate highway program that, to date, has built 36,000 miles of superhighway at a cost of about $55-billion. Another 6,500 miles remain to be built at a projected cost of $35-billion. It has been called the largest public works project in history.

On Aug. 13, 1973, signing into law the bill that authorized the use of part of these funds for mass transit, President Nixon said:

"The law will enable [localities] at last to relieve congestion and pollution problems by developing more balanced transportation systems where it is appropriate rather than locking them into further highway expenditures which can sometimes make such problems even worse."

What the bill did was make available for local mass transit projects $780-million in so-called "urban systems funds" in the fiscal year 1973-74 and $800-million a year for the next two years.

If the money is not fully allocated at the end of each year, it remains available for another two years.

In one of the only two fund distributions made thus far, New York was awarded $33,017,000 toward the purchase of 398 new buses, which are expected to be delivered starting at the end of the year. The other recipient, East St. Louis, was awarded $1,597,000 toward the purchase of 40 buses.

Little Sense of Urgency

In addition, officials of the mass transit administration said that only three other communities—San Francisco, Chicago and Minot, N. D.—have so far even made application for urban systems funds, for a total of $3.6-million in aid sought.

Calls to a number of other cities indicated that applications for funds were now being prepared, but little sense of urgency was evident.

In Minneapolis-St. Paul, Robert LaShomb and John Jamieson, officials of the Metropolitan Transit Commission, said that requests for mass transit funds were now under way. Mr. LaShomb said the agency had encountered some initial difficulties with a highway-oriented Transportation Advisory Board that screened such applications.

In Houston, where aid applications were under consideration, Barry Goodman, the transit administrator, said, "We met resistance at first" from the Texas highway department, "but after we explained the needs, they agreed."

In addition to the urban systems funds drawn from the vast highways treasury, the Urban Mass Transit Administration has a capital grant budget of nearly $1.1-billion this year. For such grants, localities need put up only 20 per cent to the Federal share of 80 per cent.

Transportation officials acknowledged that one reason localities have been slow to apply for the urban systems funds has been the higher share they must pay in comparison to the grant funds. However, all the nearly $1.1-billion in grant money has already been committed.

Mr. Herringer said that he favored easing the terms of the urban systems allocations to the same 80-20 formal as the grants to encourage applications.

There is another source of Federal mass transit funding. The 1974 Highway Act made it possible for communities to turn down segments of local planned interstate highway projects and use the funds allocated for them on mass transit projects.

But so far, only Boston and Philadelphia have taken advantage of this, transportation officials said.

April 21, 1975

Mass transit, little mass

San Francisco's BART system offers luxury to riders from here to there. But too many heres and theres exist in our cities, so the automobile remains king.

By Robert Lindsey

OAKLAND, Calif.—A few days before the sleek, aluminum-skinned trains of the San Francisco Bay Area Rapid Transit system began hauling passengers three years ago last month, Bill R. Stokes, a former newspaperman and public-relations man who had promoted construction of this system, and went on to become its general manager, took a visitor to a huge window in his fifth-floor office and pointed out the Nimitz Freeway a short distance away. As usual in late afternoon, the Nimitz was a glacial stream of bumper-to-bumper cars and trucks, seemingly going nowhere. "What we're trying to do," Stokes said, "is to change the way people live, to get them out of their cars and off that freeway."

These days, the freeway still has those traffic jams, twice a day, and as predictable as the sun. But Bill Stokes is gone, sacrificed to California state legislators who demanded his ouster as the price of approving still another subsidy to keep trains rolling on the troubled mass-transit system that everybody calls BART. Gone, too, these days, are a lot of illusions about urban mass transportation in the United States.

Robert Lindsey is the Western economics correspondent for The Times.

BART's trains are fast, clean, quiet and comfortable; its stations are spacious, modern and architecturally impressive; its 71 miles of track provide San Francisco, Oakland and Berkeley with their first subway system and connects these cities, by tunnel and elevated lines, with a score of smaller cities east and south of Oakland. People *are* using BART, and many of them seem to thrive on it.

Yet, in demonstrating what modern rail transit can do, BART has also demonstrated what it *cannot* do. Three years after the first leg opened, the system that was designed to pay for itself is running heavily in debt and seems unable to get out of it; its record of reliability is atrocious; and it has hardly made a dent in the traffic jams it was designed to reduce substantially. The persistent traffic tie-ups and some of the other complications demonstrate that rapid-transit systems like BART are only a partial answer to America's urban transportation problems. The people who are using it must commute on limited, fixed routes—those that spread like spokes of a wheel, radiating from a city hub into the suburbs. But many of the commuters who continue to clog the freeways say that BART doesn't take them where they want to go. Some say they live too far from a station. Many are not able to travel the old-fashioned suburb-to-city radial way but commute between sprawling suburbs, where the only way to get from one to the other is by car. BART, conceived as the best urban-transportation system that money could buy, was supposed to give the rest of the nation a look at its own future. But so far, for a variety of reasons, the future hasn't quite worked.

In the mid-nineteen-sixties, after racial ghettos in half a dozen cities exploded, liberal academics and politicians, hoping to find the roots of the violence, decided that one seed was a simple lack of public transportation to jobs outside the ghetto. Meanwhile, the sooty haze of air pollution—and the seemingly hopeless race to build more freeways to keep up with wave after wave of more cars—were causing increasing disenchantment with the automobile. In cities such as Seattle, San Diego, and Bethpage, L.I., many of the nation's aerospace companies and related industries could see that the missile boom and the moon boom, so profitable in the nineteen-sixties, were coming to an end. Searching for new markets, they began cranking out technical papers and fanciful art work proposing an armada of commuter systems using the knowhow that was taking man to the moon. At the same time, the handful of American cities that had rapid transit—principally New York, Chicago, Philadelphia and *(Continued)*

The trains are fast, clean, comfortable—yet in demonstrating what they can do, they're also demonstrating what they cannot do in metropolitan America.

Boston — were growing increasingly concerned that their systems would soon be bankrupt, without new sources of revenue.

These forces combined to sound a public-relations chorus in the late sixties, exalting the glories of mass transportation. Depicted as the ultimate weapon against the ailments of America, mass transportation was to be an urban I.C.B.M. that, in a single shot, would knock out pollution, congestion, urban poverty, the exodus of city dwellers to the suburbs, inner city decay and wasteful consumption of energy. Congress, responding to the blitz, began providing billions, despite the demurrers of some dissenters, such as Prof. Martin Wohl of the Carnegie-Mellon University and George Hilton of the University of California at Los Angeles, who were skeptical about equipping every city of any size with a fancy, space-age transit line.

The San Francisco Bay area was ahead of the rest of the nation. A region that prides itself on its sophistication, one that looks down its nose on congested Los Angeles 450 miles to the south, the Bay area began exploring the feasibility of building a New York-style transit system in the nineteen-fifties. Its goal was to head off the "Los Angelization" of this attractive, pleasant-to-live-in corner of the country. In 1962, voters in three Bay area counties—San Francisco, Alameda and Contra Costa — appoved a bond issue of $790-million to build what was to become the nation's first new regional transit system in more than 50 years. Toll bridge revenues would produce another $130-million toward the estimated $920-million total cost. Even at this early stage, BART had had become something of an overstatement; two of the biggest Bay-area counties, Marin to the north of San Francisco and San Mateo to the south, opted out, partly because of opposition from business interests who didn't warm to making it easier for residents of their area to shop in downtown San Francisco.

By the time the first segment opened in 1972, three years behind schedule, the total cost had to be set at $1.6-billion because of inflation, design changes and bad original estimates. Local taxpayers (through property taxes, sales taxes and a share of the 50-cent toll on the San Francisco-Oakland Bay Bridge) raised more than 80 per cent of the cost. Federal taxpayers provided the remainder—a Federal largesse that was soon to prove very troublesome.

The BART tracks, partly underground and partly on the surface, are roughly laid out in the shape of an "X," with Oakland at the center. One leg, 15 miles long, links Oakland with San Francisco and suburban Daly City via the trans-Bay tunnel; another extends 24 miles south to suburban Fremont through an area of bedroom communities; and the final two legs run 21 and 11 miles, respectively, through other bedroom communities east of Oakland, ending at the towns of Concord and Richmond. Fares vary according to the distance, with 25 cents for a short downtown hop to $1.45 for a 39-mile ride between Fremont and Daly City. Magnetically encoded plastic cards, computerized to match price with distance, are sold by vending machines.

For straphangers accustomed to the noisy and deteriorated atmosphere of New York subways, entering the BART system does seem a bit like stepping into the next century. The experience begins in one of the 34 underground or surface stations, most of them stunning, high-ceiling buildings with fine murals and spacious plazas. The trains themselves are delightful to ride in—when they are running correctly. They have huge expanses of tinted windows, wall-to-wall carpeting and upholstery colored in rust, red and orange, and simulated wood paneling; the trains accelerate gently and then gain momentum at a furious pace, to a maximum speed of almost 80 miles an hour, and then gently decelerate a few moments before reaching a station. Each action of the train—its speed, acceleration, deceleration, opening and closing of doors—is designed to be controlled by a silent conversation between electrical sensing devices, transmitters and receivers that are located aboard the train and along the railroad right-of-way. The ebb and flow of trains is directed by these devices but is constantly monitored and fine-tuned—such as slowing a train that might be running too close to another—by a computer located at the headquarters of BART in Oakland. A human attendant sits in the front of each train, to be there in case of an emergency. And there has been no shortage of emergencies.

Glacier, San Francisco style: The persistent traffic tie-ups shatter a dream of urban planners — that rapid transit would "get people out of their cars and off the freeway."

Almost since the day BART opened, the system has been bedeviled by basic design problems and equipment failure. Less than a month after it opened, a train ran off the end of a track, injuring five persons. The system had given a wrong speed code. In the first few months of operation, the controls — built by Pittsburgh's Westinghouse Corporation—detected innumerable trains on the track that weren't there — so-called "phantoms" that prompted the system to halt other trains because of the imagined threat of collisions. Worse, engineers for the California Public Utilities Commission charged, the electronic detection system was not capable of locating all trains all the time; a stalled train, without power, might not be detected, raising the possibility of a real collision. Doors opened and closed mysteriously when the trains were moving, or refused to open in the station; some trains stopped short of the station, or moved at erratic speed, all because of bugs in the computerized controls.

Management was forced to have an attendant at each station who, each time a train passed, could telephone the station behind, saying the coast was clear to send another. This problem, combined with others, delayed opening of the trans-Bay service between Oakland and San Francisco until September, 1974, because the utilities commission feared accidents near the tunnel. Trans-Bay service was finally inaugurated after special safety procedures were developed — but "phantom" trains and other defects continue to plague the system.

Another difficulty has been the malfunctioning of the transit cars themselves. The 450 electrically self-propelled vehicles were built by Rohr Industries of Chula Vista, Calif., an aerospace contractor and specialist in military communications antennae and aluminum engine pods for jet airlines. The company's experience with BART has been a nightmare — and vice versa. Even now, after the more than three years of operation, BART's management says

Boston — were growing increasingly concerned that their systems would soon be bankrupt, without new sources of revenue.

These forces combined to sound a public-relations chorus in the late sixties, exalting the glories of mass transportation. Depicted as the ultimate weapon against the ailments of America, mass transportation was to be an urban I.C.B.M. that, in a single shot, would knock out pollution, congestion, urban poverty, the exodus of city dwellers to the suburbs, inner city decay and wasteful consumption of energy. Congress, responding to the blitz, began providing billions, despite the demurrers of some dissenters, such as Prof. Martin Wohl of the Carnegie-Mellon University and George Hilton of the University of California at Los Angeles, who were skeptical about equipping every city of any size with a fancy, space-age transit line.

The San Francisco Bay area was ahead of the rest of the nation. A region that prides itself on its sophistication, one that looks down its nose on congested Los Angeles 450 miles to the south, the Bay area began exploring the feasibility of building a New York-style transit system in the nineteen-fifties. Its goal was to head off the "Los Angelization" of this attractive, pleasant-to-live-in corner of the country. In 1962, voters in three Bay area counties—San Francisco, Alameda and Contra Costa — appoved a bond issue of $790-million to build what was to become the nation's first new regional transit system in more than 50 years. Toll bridge revenues would produce another $130-million toward the estimated $920-million total cost. Even at this early stage, BART had had become something of an overstatement; two of the biggest Bay-area counties, Marin to the north of San Francisco and San Mateo to the south, opted out, partly because of opposition from business interests who didn't warm to making it easier for residents of their area to shop in downtown San Francisco.

By the time the first segment opened in 1972, three years behind schedule, the total cost had to be set at $1.6-billion because of inflation, that an average of only half of the 450 cars can be used at any one time. The rest are in the repair shop. Consequently, BART's deficit has been inflated by millions of dollars in extra maintenance costs, and it has had to reduce drastically the number of operating trains.

In hindsight, many persons close to BART say many of its problems are rooted in a decision by its directors more than a decade ago to turn over virtually all aspects of over-all design and management to outsiders—to an engineering and construction consortium, Parsons, Brinkerhoff, Tudor-Bechtel. The P.B.T.B., as it is known, has received more than $150-million in BART contracts. A former BART official singles out Bill Stokes, the first general manager, for criticism: "Stokes's biggest mistake was in putting so much trust in P.B.T.B. He knew he wasn't a technical man, but figured he was hiring experts to do this. He didn't sit on P.B.T.B. or really pay that much attention to what they were doing."

Another observer says the problems stem from the planners' blind faith in the infallibility of the aerospace industry. For one thing, they seemed to assume the trains would never break down and so failed to provide for enough track spurs for disabled cars. For another, the cars were designed without maintainability in mind; to repair the brakes, for example, the wheels must be taken off.

Finding out just who is responsible for BART's jungle of technical problems will probably take years to uncover, through the resolution of suits and countersuits involving more than $250-million in alleged damages, between BART and P.B.T.B., Rohr, Westinghouse and the Bulova Watch Company, a subcontractor on the job.

The idea of using outside experts was borrowed from the Pentagon, which brought in private engineers, executives and scientists to manage development of its early ballistic missiles. Although the military is accustomed to massive cost overruns and, frequently, poor performance of a new weapons system, the voters here were not. In fact, they had been constantly bombarded with publicity to expect the opposite: a flawless futuristic system for $790-million. And some of BART's initial breakdowns were no doubt a product of the political process at work. There had been many delays during construction, and pressure began mounting from local politicians and newspapers. Eventually, Bill Stokes was given an ultimatum by the board of directors to open BART by September, 1972. It did open, then, even though Stokes admitted privately that he knew not all of the defects were corrected. When his premonitions proved correct, the roof caved in on him. "P.B.T.B. screwed up," said an associate, "and Stokes had to take the heat." After his departure he became head of a transit lobby in Washington and remains a respected if frustrated pioneer in the field.

Looking into what happened to one of his principal goals—luring Americans out of their cars—one discovers that, according to a recent survey of BART patrons, the system carries about 125,000 one-way passengers daily. (About 400-000 use Boston-area rapid transit; the population is about the same but other factors differ, so exact comparisons cannot be drawn.) One third of the BART patrons who use the system twice a day, the survey shows, commuted previously by car—25 per cent as drivers, 7 per cent as passengers, or about 15,000 people left the highway. But new residents and others who have shifted their commuting patterns have taken their places. About 40 per cent of BART's passengers had already used mass transit—buses. More than 20 per cent of transit riders said they hadn't regularly traveled the route before. This suggested that many of them were on San Francisco shopping treks that they didn't make before—a conclusion that seems to be supported by retail figures.

Wolfgang Homburger, a researcher for the Institute of Transportation and Traffic Engineering at the University of California, says that on the Bay Bridge there appears to have been a decline of about 2 per cent in the number of cars each day, and a decline of perhaps 4 per cent in traffic during the rush hour, compared with last year. BART can take credit for some of this reduction, he said, but the recession and 60-cents-a-gallon gasoline "obviously has had an effect, too."

Another dream, perhaps even less realized, was to create a system that, if it did not run itself, would at least operate with relatively low labor costs. When the California legislature approved the creation of BART, it ruled that operating costs had to come from the fare box. That was one of the first laws to be changed once the BART trains started running. This fiscal year, it will cost $67-million to operate BART, yet it will take in only about $22-million in fares, including a 25 per cent fare increase effective Nov. 1. Wages and fringe benefits account for about 68 per cent of the operating budget.

BART was originally designed to function with a work force of 1,200 persons to handle about 200,000 riders daily, but at its opening, the number was raised to 1,400. However, although it is now carrying only 125,000 passengers daily, its work force is 2,000. One reason is that the electronic system and cars have proved so complex that 1,000 additional maintenance men have had to be hired. These are not old-time shop hands but rather well-paid technicians.

BART might have absorbed this extra personnel more easily, however, if it hadn't had to seek help from Washington during the final days' construction, thereby bringing it under a troublesome 1964 Federal statute. That law requires the Department of Labor to approve transit grants, theoretically to make certain that Federal aid would not result in adverse effects on currently employed transit employes, such as causing layoffs or cutting wages. In practice, however, the provisions have been used more broadly, and the Labor Department routinely sends application grants along to the officers of local transit unions for what amounts to their approval or disapproval. Some Federal transportation officials have contended that some union leaders use the act as a club, knowingly preventing labor-saving innovations but exacting higher wages, benefits and other concessions under the threat of vetoing an aid package. Rather than lose a grant, most local agencies have given in. The San Francisco system came under the terms of the Federal statute when it had to seek help after costs had sky rocketed and local taxpayers said they would pay no more. One ultimate result was that BART had to raise wages substantially. During the current fiscal year, BART will pay maintenance workers an average of $25,300, including fringe benefits, and station agents and train attendants will receive an average of $23,400.

Still another BART hope—the liberals' notion that providing good public transportation would help poor people get jobs—has faded. For the most part, its riders are affluent businessmen, students on their way to school or college, or women on shopping trips. Almost half of BART's riders earn more than $15,000 a year. Blacks comprise about 12 per cent of the region's population, but so far, according to passenger surveys, they comprise less than 8 per cent of the riders on BART. There are hints that a handful of poor blacks from San Francisco poverty areas might be using BART to reach industrial areas south of Oakland. But Joel Markowitz, who is directing a Federal study of BART's impact on the Bay Area, says there is no solid evidence of this. For the most part, he explains, BART's trains haven't helped minority people get jobs because most jobs, when they are available at all, aren't located near a BART station, but far off in a suburban area unserved by the trains. BART's experience seems to prove an obvious point: When the economy is sluggish, and residents of ghetto communities do not have marketable skills, the fanciest of transportation systems won't get them a job.

During the early years of the first Nixon Administration, former Secretary of Transportation John A. Volpe spent much of his time traveling to cities around the country, urging them to build rail-transit systems, and suggesting that Federal aid would pay most of the cost. At least 20 cities began talking seriously about building BART-style systems, and several actually started. But there has been a mellowing of enthusiasm. Denver, for example, made plans for a fancy "people-mover" but is now considering something more along the lines of updated trolleys. It is not only BART's problems that have given pause to urban planners elsewhere. In Atlanta, voters approved a special sales tax to finance, in part, a $1.3-billion transit network that is now expected to cost $2.1-billion. In Washington, a new subway was supposed to cost $2.5-billion. But the projected cost is now close to $5-billion. In general, rapid-railway-construction costs are now up to $60-million a mile.

One of the lessons of BART is that, all things considered, it seems so far to be an expensive, inflexible and relatively ineffective way to reach and serve the low-density, sprawling communities that are typical of American urban expansion since World War II. The thrust has been toward residential development in which there isn't the mass that goes into mass transportation. America, like it or not, has tailored its communities, and its way of living, to the automobile. New York and a handful of other large, densely populated cities have a market for and need rapid-transit systems. But most of America isn't New York. Manhattan's population density is slightly less than 70,000 people per square mile; nationally, the average population of central cities is 4,464, and for urbanized areas in general, it is only 2,627. Most urbanized regions are exploded metropolises more akin to horizontal Los Angeles than vertical New York, where homes and jobs, schools and hospitals, aren't neatly arranged along spokes of a wheel, but are strewn out and scrambled like parts of a kaleidoscope.

Last year, the United States Department of Transportation asked each state to compile a list of everything that it would build and acquire if it had an unlimited budget for improving public transportation — an anything-goes wish list. States were urged to include any type of transportation they coveted, and as many as they wanted, between then and 1990. The result was a list of rapid rail and bus projects costing a total of $58.2-billion and an anticipated annual operating deficit of $2.5-billion. Costs were calculated at the price of things in 1971; given inflation, the ultimate construction cost would probably be closer to $100-billion. Yet, even assuming that all of this money had been spent, and the states and the cities had their transit dreams in place, the effects on traffic congestion and energy consumption would seem to be relatively small. The total number of people using mass transportation in 1990, the department's analysts estimated, would be about twice the current number, but the percentage of total trips (including those by car) each day made by public transportation would remain about the same as it is today—between 5.5 and 6 per cent nationally, and 11 per cent in urban areas. Virtually all the rest would be by car.

Perhaps, if the price of gasoline continues to soar, and it again becomes scarce, values may change and there could be a renewed interest in building high-speed rail lines that are tailored to avoid the kind of technical problems that have hounded BART. For most communities, however, better mass transportation will probably mean buses. With modern appointments and wider seats and more frequent express service, using reserved freeway lanes, perhaps. This will be far from the space-age travel envisaged in the sixties; it will not satisfy everybody, certainly not all commuters, environmentalists or urban planners. What the planners say is fundamentally needed to improve the quality of public transportation is something that doesn't appear likely very soon—a greater congregation of people living together and working together, so that transportation lines can serve more people and therefore amortize the high cost.

To try to cure BART's ailments, its directors brought in a new general manager this summer. He is Frank C. Herringer, who until then headed the Federal Urban Mass Transportation Administration (U.M.T.A.) in Washington, the agency that dispenses about $1.2-billion a year in Federal transit aid to cities. Herringer, who is 32, and is earning $68,500 in his new job, is an intense, forthright former management consultant. In his first weeks on the job he initiated a major reorganization to correct what he described as a "slightly out-of-control chaos," poor morale and an informal way of doing things that stunned his Eastern sense of work ethic.

Herringer knows he's under pressure from BART's directors, who are themselves under great pressure to make the costly railroad work right. He has imported a number of transit experts from New York City and elsewhere to help debug the system and is developing a broad in-house technical capability.

Few people expect Herringer to be able to do very much about BART's runaway operating costs and high labor expenses. But many who know him are betting that he will be able to solve the reliability problem and give Bay Area residents the kind of ride they were promised, if not an urban I.C.B.M. to attack the future. The problems of getting the full complement of trains to run as they are supposed to, however, is not expected to be accomplished for about two years.

Herringer agrees that BART has "tremendous" problems but he believes it's still going to be a "great system. And what a bargain it was—built before all this recent inflation. . . . I bet you couldn't build it for $5-billion now." He says he recently strolled through BART's Embarcadero Station in San Francisco and glanced about him at the vast expanses of marble. "The stuff they used goes for about $20 a foot; people won't be able to afford systems like this any more," he said. New rail rapid-transit systems may be built in a handful of large cities in the future, he said, but they won't be gold plated. "BART is probably the first and last of its kind." ■

October 19, 1975

THE CITY AND THE ENVIRONMENT

3-Day Smog Torments Entire East As Cold 'Lid' Traps Irritants in Air

It wasn't just the heat that caused distress here yesterday; it was the inflexibility.

Three days' accumulation of sulphur dioxide and tar particles from industrial and residential smokestacks hung inert from ground level to about 600 feet up without prospect of moving before tomorrow. It caused physical distress along the entire Eastern seaboard.

The lower air was irritatingly, but not dangerously, charged with smoke-precipitated chemicals, and could not escape because it was trapped between unseasonal warmth at ground level and colder air masses just above 600 feet. The cold mass acted exactly like a stove lid; it would not permit the chemical accumulations under it to drift off.

The air mass inversion, as meteorologists call it, hung over a wide area. It reached from lower New England down to around Virginia. The condition oppressed most of Pennsylvania, too, and was felt as far west as Ohio. The sulphur dioxide and tar-particle irritants trapped by the inversion were most concentrated in cities, especially in industrial areas.

Oddly enough, sulphur and tar content was heavier here on Wednesday, at one point, than it was yesterday. It had been building up since Monday. By 10 A. M. Wednesday the percentage was up to sixty-five parts in a million. It dropped gradually to twenty-one parts in a million at 3:30 P. M. yesterday when, somehow, it seemed thickest.

While the East gasped for breath in the smog, winter had roared in, in full bluster, in the Far West. Snow was sixteen to seventeen inches deep in the Rockies, especially in Colorado and in Wyoming, where it choked the passes.

Foul air stacked in the metropolitan district between the ground and the cold-air lid had ten times more sulphur dioxide and tar particles yesterday than when there is no inversion. It irritated throats, made eyes burn, and caused headaches, nausea, and loss of appetite. The condition was aggravated by the thermometer's climb.

At 3 P. M. yesterday the mercury stood at 70 degrees, or within .8 of a degree of the Nov. 19 record set in 1921. The Weather Bureau believed today might be as warm, or almost as warm, and that not until tomorrow would the slowly crawling cold front from the West cause the warm lower air-cooler upper lid formation to break up.

It was, according to one man at the Weather Bureau, as though the eastward-moving cold front was a solid wall, with temperatures down to the twenties and thirties on one side of it and with summer-like reading beyond its eastern rim. Portland, Me., had 68 degrees yesterday and in Syracuse, N. Y., pussywillows and tulips were alive, as in a second spring.

Five telephone operators working on the thirtieth floor of the Federal Building on Foley Square were overcome by chemically charged atmosphere yesterday afternoon. They found that breath came harshly and with difficulty and that a peculiar kind of twilight reduced their vision. They could barely see across the room. Floods of calls were held up until nurses in the building brought them to with spirits of ammonia and other restoratives.

The very birds in Foley Square—the great hosts of starlings and pigeons that roost in the gloomy County Court portico—dipped and wheeled and gave out sounds of distress as if in flight from some invisible force. Observers thought there was a kind of note of fright in their twittering and piping.

The thickened and trapped lower air put a diaphanous but dark kind of net curtain between New Yorkers and yesterday's sunset. It veiled last night's yellow moon, too. On New Jersey Turnpike, where fog had moved in to make the accumulation even thicker, motorists had to slow down. In areas where autumn leaves were burning it was worse. The air lid would not let smoke come apart as it normally does.

Newark was enveloped in the accumulation and so were Elizabeth and Jersey City, communities that had suffered distress from it on Wednesday. English newspapers seemed highly interested in the phenomenon here. They eagerly soaked up data on it to relay to England, where "killer fog" has become a more or less commen expression.

November 20, 1953

LOS ANGELES SMOG PERSISTS 9TH DAY

Governor Flies to Investigate —Condition Called Factor in Death of Girl, 10

LOS ANGELES, Oct. 15 (UP) —A choking, eye-searing smog blanketed the Los Angeles metropolitan area today for the ninth straight day and brought on a state of near-emergency.

The smog was blamed as a "contributing factor" in at least one death, that of a 10-year-old girl who choked to death.

Gov. Goodwin J. Knight interrupted his campaign for re-election to fly here and join in an investigation into the cause of the plainly visible pall of fumes, the worst in a year.

While the Governor began conferences with Los Angeles city and Council officials, Bernard Caldwell, chief of the State Highway Patrol, ordered his officers to set up roadblocks and cite all vehicles that put excessive fumes into the air.

The air pollution director Gordon P. Larson, summoned before the county grand jury's investigating committee, blamed inefficient combustion in automobiles for 90 per cent of the fumes in the downtown area. He said that when such fumes were combined with a temperature inversion it caused smog.

The Los Angeles area is surrounded by mountains that keep fumes bottled up in the region unless strong sea breezes disperse them. But in the fall of the year a layer of warm air settles over the region, preventing the cooler surface air from rising and dispersing

Hospitals were deluged with calls for advice on the treatment of the eye-searing efect. In adjacent Pasadena, Mayor Clarence Winder called for public prayer "to deliver us from this scourage," while the Los Angeles City Council donned gas masks to demonstrate that the fumes were even entering the Council chambers.

October 16, 1954

The Car and Smog: A Growing Controversy

Auto Industry Says Evidence Does Not Warrant Controls

By DAVID R. JONES
Special to The New York Times

Smog enveloping a section of downtown Los Angeles. Motor vehicle exhaust is said to be a major contributing factor to the condition, but industry sources question this theory.

DETROIT, April 4—A little-noticed controversy involving the family car, which seems destined to have significant influence on the welfare and pocketbooks of millions of Americans in the years ahead, is raging throughout the nation.

The controversy centers on the question of how much the automobile contributes to the nation's air-pollution problem, in which the major metropolitan areas, such as Los Angeles, face the prospect of eventually choking on their own exhaust.

What should be done to control the gases vehicles spew into the air? The question is pitting the automobile industry against Federal, state and local authorities.

This debate over automotive air pollution will be in the spotlight this week as the Senate Public Works Committee's subcommittee on air and water pollution begins three days of hearings Tuesday in Washington Senator Edmund S. Muskie, Democrat of Maine, who is the subcommittee's chairman, has introduced a bill with broad support to impose nationwide exhaust controls on new cars.

Most government officials involved in the question believe the automobile is a growing pollution menace whose emissions must be strictly controlled. The official' attitude was reflected in President Johnson's conservation message, in which he spoke of the need to substantially reduce or eliminate automotive air pollution.

The nation's automobile makers are equally convinced that there is insufficient evidence that cars are a national pollution problem to warrant controls. They urge further research, and say the taxpayer would get far more for his pollution dollar by spending it to expand controls on pollution from industrial plants and homes instead.

Devices Seen Likely

The most interesting aspect of this battle is that although the two sides squabble over the issue, both are coming to the conclusion that some kind of nationwide controls on auto exhaust are likely on new cars within three years—merited or not.

The industry still believes this would be unjust and it continues to resist the prospect. However, most informed auto executives agree with one company's top pollution engineer, who laments:

"It's clear the politicians think this is for home and motherhood and it hasn't got a chance of losing."

This attitude, in fact, will prompt the industry in this week's hearings to take a more positive approach to the subject. Auto executives are expected to indicate a greater willingness to install control devices if Congress insists, although they still will argue that it would be premature to do so.

They may get some support from the Department of Health, Education and Welfare, which is expected to speak out in favor of the devices but to caution about the problems of inspection and the dangers of moving too quickly.

The relative merits of these divergent positions, and the outcome of the controversy, are of significance because almost every American will be touched by the results. A Federal law requiring exhaust-control devices could add $60 to $75 to the cost of most new cars and raise average maintenance bills by $10 a year.

Pollution experts in the United States contend that failure to install such devices would result in even more costly losses in pollution damage, not to mention health dangers.

Interest in controlling automotive pollution more closely has been mounting for several years, but it has gained new impetus in several states since the industry last August agreed to install exhaust-control devices on the 1966 models it will begin selling this fall in California.

"As soon as word came that the industry was doing something for California, there was a feeling elsewhere that if they could do this for California, they could do it for other states," says Donald A. Jensen, executive officer of the California Motor Vehicle Pollution Control Board in Los Angeles.

Alexander Rihm Jr., executive secretary of the New York State Air Pollution Control Board in Albany, discloses that the board last month voted to support legislation that would require exhaust-control devices on all new cars sold in the state. The board has not yet determined any specifics, but it could select elements from among a half-dozen exhaust-control bills already in the Legislature.

A subcommittee of the New Jersey Air Pollution Control Commission recently recommended exhaust controls for new cars in that state. This has led to a bill that has the backing of Gov. Richard J. Hughes.

The General Services Administration, which buys cars for the Federal Government, plans to require exhaust-control devices on Government cars starting with 1967 models.

The direction and pace of any move to control exhaust on a nationwide basis should make itself clearer in the next few weeks.

The Muskie bill, which already has support within the Public Health Service, has 22 cosponsors. There is considerable Congressional sentiment for auto-pollution control. At present, however, there appears to be at least equal reluctance to impose too tight controls on the auto industry.

Talks and Rebuttal

President Johnson is expected to make good before long on the promise in his conservation message to "institute discussions with industry officials and other interested groups" toward reducing or eliminating auto pollution. The industry is already preparing a rebuttal and bracing for what one executive expects will be "a little arm-twisting" from the President to get the companies to install control devices voluntarily.

There is a possibility that the industry would eventually install exhaust controls on a nationwide basis even if Federal legislation and Presidential persuasion failed. The industry will be installing devices on about 10 per cent of its market when it acts in California. If New York and a couple of other big states require devices, the industry could decide to install them voluntarily. Most auto men, in fact, would prefer Federal standards than a wide range of differing requirements in various states.

Until recently, most of the controversy over automotive air pollution has been confined to California, and particularly the sprawling Los Angeles region. There a combination of climate and geography have created repeated instances of photochemical smog, an irritating and damaging condition caused by the interaction of the sun's ultraviolet rays and chemical pollutants in the air.

Los Angeles has been fighting smog for 20 years, and first imposed strict controls on industry and homeowners to cut down on emissions into the atmosphere. California, which in 1953 pinpointed the reaction of sunlight and automotive emissions as the major air-pollution source, set up the state control board in 1960 to restrict auto emissions and bring air quality back to 1940 standards.

Authorities in other cities have begun in recent years to express greater concern about the problems of air pollution, and particularly auto pollution.

Anthony J. Celebrezze, Secretary of Health, Education and Welfare, in a report to Congress last December, called for immediate nationwide controls.

"Photochemical air pollution or smog is a problem of growing national importance and is attributable largely to the operation of the motor vehicle," the report declared. "Manifestations of this type of air pollution are appearing with increasing frequency and severity in metropolitan areas throughout the United States."

"Biological studies of animals show that the photochemical reaction products of automotive emissions produce adverse health effects," the report continued. "There is substantial evidence that these effects may appear in humans after extended exposure to air which is known to be polluted with these same products in many of the larger urban areas."

Nobody knows for sure how much automobiles contribute to the total problem of air pollution, which has been estimated to cost the United States as much as $11 billion annually in agricultural damage, corrosion, soiling and similar effects. Some Government sources have held auto emissions responsible for about half of the national problem, but that is not certain. California studies indicate that about 10 per cent of the 67.3 million gallons of gasoline consumed by vehicles in the United States last year was emitted into the air.

Most cities have inadequate facilities for accurately determining how much pollution comes from autos. Arthur J. Benline, New York City's Commissioner of Air Pollution Control, estimates that cars cause one-third of the region's problem, but concedes this is only a guess.

Walter E. Jackson, Philadelphia's chief of air pollution control, says studies there indicate the auto causes 25 per cent of the city's problem.

James V. Fitzpatrick, director of Chicago's Department of Air Pollution, calculates from fuel statistics that half the organic gases in the atmosphere there come from vehicles.

Authorities concede that nationwide controls on auto emissions would primarily benefit dwellers in metropolitan areas and impose an unnecessary burden on the millions who reside in pollution-free rural areas. However, they point out that two-thirds of the population already lives in 212 standard metropolitan areas having only 9 per cent of the nation's land area. The Public Health Service says that any place with a population of 50,000 has enough vehicles to create a potential problem.

Impact Bound to Rise

The auto's contribution to pollution seems bound to spread. Between 1950 and 1959, the number of cars on the nation's highways rose at a rate double the population growth.

"This problem can easily become more widespread as the number of gasoline-burning vehicles increases — to 103 million by 1970 at the 1950-to-1959 rate of growth," according to the United States Surgeon General's office.

Gasoline-powered vehicles already discharge an estimated total of 92 million tons of deadly carbon monoxide into the air annually, not to mention millions of tons of the smog-forming hydrocarbons and nitrogen oxides that California is striving to control. The daily output of carbon monoxide from vehicles, if confined over one area, would pollute the air to a concentration of 30 parts of carbon monoxide for each million parts of air to a height of 400 feet over 20,000 square miles — roughly the area of Massachusetts, Connecticut and New Jersey combined.

This concentration, for an eight-hour period, has been judged by California health authorities to cause discomfort, eye irritation, plant damage and reduced visibility. The level is often reached in Los Angeles, occasionally reached in Washington, and exceeded for at least an hour on some days in Chicago and Philadelphia, according to the Public Health Service's air-monitoring stations.

The monitoring network's studies also show that an average of 45 per cent of all hydrocarbons and 40 per cent of all nitrogen oxides discharged into the air in six selected cities come from automobiles. These chemical compounds, under the sun's ultraviolet rays, produce a photochemical reaction that creates oxidants, which are chemical substances such as ozone that have more of an oxidizing power than oxygen itself.

Measure of Pain

California health authorities say that when the oxidant level reaches 0.15 parts for each million of air for one hour, discomfort, eye irritation and plant damage can result. The air-monitoring network found that oxidants equalled or exceeded 0.18 parts for each million of air at least once in 1963 in Cincinnati, Chicago, New Orleans, Los Angeles and Washington. The level equalled or exceeded 0.25 parts for each million at least once in the first half of 1964 in Cincinnati, Philadelphia, St. Louis, Los Angeles, and Washington.

Although these levels were reached only a few days each year, most pollution experts say the frequency is increasing. The air-monitoring network already shows that oxidants in the first half of 1964 reached 0.10 parts for each million of air 34.3 per cent of the days in Los Angeles, 15.7 per cent in Chicago, 11.5 per cent in Washington, and more than 8 per cent in Philadelphia and St. Louis.

"Los Angeles no longer has, if it ever had, a monopoly on photochemical smog," according to a recent Department of Agriculture statement, which said the "characteristic symptoms have been found in almost every metropolitan area in the country."

The entire coastal area from Washington to Boston "has come to rival Southern California for extent, severity, and economic loss to agriculture because of photochemical smog," it said.

Dr. John T. Middleton, director of the air-pollution research center at the University of California at Riverside, says ozone plant damage from photo chemical smog has been found in 22 states.

"The injury that was once confined to Los Angeles County now occurs in many states and causes economic loss estimated in excess of $25 million annually," he says.

Most stanch advocates of auto-pollution control believe vehicle emissions are a human health hazard, but they have been frustrated in their desire to prove it. The United States Surgeon General's office has said that years will be required before a definitive answer is found to that question.

However, a Public Health Service spokesman in Washington insists "we have bits and pieces of circumstantial evidence" that make controls desirable without proof.

"We think we must err on the side of caution when it comes to the protection of public health," he says. "If we have good reason to suspect the public is being exposed to a hazard that can be lessened or eliminated, it ought to be lessened or eliminated."

Dr. Dietrich Hoffman, a biochemist and air-pollution expert at the Sloan-Kettering Institute for Cancer Research in New York, has found that auto exhaust contains particles that, when applied to the skin of mice, have caused cancer. This does not prove that auto exhaust will cause cancer in humans, he explains, but he is working with the General Motors Corporation to reduce formation and emission of these particles — just in case.

"We have no evidence," he asserts, but the work with mice indicates this might be a worthwhile effort because "our goal is prevention."

"Nobody claims man will benefit from air pollutants," he says. "Everyone agrees we can only gain when we find ways to control it."

April 5, 1965

SMOG EMERGENCY CALLED FOR CITY; RELIEF EXPECTED

Jersey and Connecticut Join Plea for Voluntary Action to Cut Down Pollution

CLEARING TODAY IS SEEN

Halt in Nonessential Driving and Use of Incinerators Is Recommended by Heller

By HOMER BIGART

The first stage of an air pollution emergency was declared yesterday in the New York metropolitan area, New Jersey and Connecticut as a stagnant air mass continued to envelop the Eastern Seaboard, trapping potentially lethal gases and smoke.

A sweep-out of the foul air after three days of smog was forecast by the Weather Bureau for today, when a cold air mass from the northwest is expected to start dispersing the gray, corrosive pall.

With the clean, cold air, due between 5 and 9 A.M., should come winds blowing in a southeasterly direction at 10 to 15 miles an hour.

Rain that began at 8:40 last night began clearing the atmosphere of fine dust particles.

Despite this relief, however, a spokesman for the Department of Air Pollution Control said that only the arrival of the cold air would spell an end to the smog.

Voluntary Controls Urged

Until the smog lifts, New Yorkers were asked through newspaper, radio and television announcements to comply voluntarily with these emergency antipollution measures:

¶Motorists were urged to use their automobiles only when absolutely necessary. Owners and operators of trucks were urged to curtail the use of their vehicles.

¶Owners of apartment houses were urged to shut down their incinerators.

¶Landlords using fuel oil or coal were urged to reduce indoor temperatures to 60 degrees. These fuels emit sulphur dioxide, the most lethal component in New York smogs. State law requires that between 6 A.M. and 10 P.M. an indoor temperature of at least 68 degrees be maintained if outside temperatures are below 50.

Temperature Sets Record

Heating was no problem, however, since the temperature here reached 64 degrees at 12:40 P.M. The mark broke the old record high of 63 for the date, set in 1946.

Austin N. Heller, the city's Commissioner of Air Pollution Control, made the recommendations at a City Hall news conference a few minutes after Governor Rockefeller proclaimed a "first alert advisory" for the metropolitan area.

The Governor acted on advice from State Health Commissioner Hollis S. Ingraham that air pollution levels in the metropolitan area had reached a danger point.

Similar voluntary first alerts were placed in effect for New Jersey and Connecticut. Residents of those states were asked to curtail the consumption of heating fuel, gasoline and electricity and to avoid burning trash or leaves.

At City Hall, Commissioner Heller said he saw slight chance that the temperature inversion —the lid of warm air that is preventingn the pollution from escapmg — would last long enough to warrant a second alert.

A second alert calls for more stringent "voluntary" restrictions on traffic and on industrial activity.

A third alert, declared only when the sulphur dioxide and carbon monoxide pollutants approach lethal levels, would empower the city to impose a brownout, throttling all but essential industrial activity and public transport.

New Yorkers went to work yesterday morning in acrid, sour-tatsing air that was almost dead calm.

Many had headaches that were not the product, they thought, of holiday over-eating. Their eyes itched. Their throats scratched. But no deaths were attributed to the smog.

Commissioner Heller said he had checked 10 hospitals and

New York City, in a Shroud of Gray, Gasps for Air

This is how New York appeared to Jerseyans looking across the Hudson from Hoboken

was told that four of them had experienced an increase in asthmatic patients.

Deputy Mayor Robert Price, who stood by his side at the news conference, said that he had been in "constant touch with Mayor Lindsay, who is vacationing in Bermuda, and that the Mayor was "deeply concerned" but had decided not to rush home. The Mayor will return Monday as he had planned.

Dr. Aaron D. Chaves, the director of the City Health Department's Bureau of Tuberculosis, checked all the municipal hospitals and reported last night:

"In not one of them is a pattern emerging which would suggest we are dealing with an important health hazard as of this moment."

He said there had been an increase Thursday in the number of bronchial asthmatic patients admitted to Sydenham and Metropolitan Hospitals. But other hospitals reported a decline in asthmatic admissions, and Dr. Chaves dismissed the Syndenham and Metropolitan figures as "random fluctuations."

Warning in 1963

Yesterday's air-pollution alert was not the city's first.

In October, 1963, a stagnant mass of warm moist air hung over the city for five days. On the fourth day, when pollutant counts had approached hazardous levels, the United States Public Health Service issued an "air-pollution warning" for the whole seaboard between Washington and New Bedford, Mass., extending inland to Altoona, Pa.

But the Public Health Service was powerless to enforce the alert and could only urge united action among the local governments in the metropolitan area.

The October, 1963, smog was swept away on the fifth day by a cold air mass from Canada, saving New York from a repetition of the disastrous smog incident of November, 1953, that accounted for more than 240 deaths.

The dirtiest hour yesterday was from 8 A.M. to 9 A.M., a period of dead calm, when the air-pollution index reached 48.9.

The Department of Air Pollution Control does not rec- basis of the index, which is based only on pollutant counts at the department's labratory at 170 East 121st Street. Other sections of the city might have filthier or cleaner air.

Yesterday's alert came after consultation between Commissioner Heller and members of the Interstate Sanitation Commission, which has been trying to clean up the air in the New York-New Jersey area.

Thomas R. Glenn Jr., chief engineer of the Interstate Sanitation Commission, said the first-stage alert had been recommended because of the high level of carbon monoxide and dust-carrying haze during the five-hour period prior to 11:25 A.M.

During this period, the carbon monoxide measurement exceeded 10 parts per million of air, and the haze exceeded 7.5.

The warning level was reached when the air sustained over 9 parts of carbon monoxide and 7.5 parts of haze for four hours. But the third dangerous component, sulphur dioxide, never passed the warning limit of 0.5 for any appreciable period, so action was delayed until after noon.

As a result of the rain last night, the carbon monoxide measurement fell from 20 parts per million at 8 P.M. to 5 parts per million at midnight. In the same four hours, the haze level dropped from 5.9 to 3.0, while the sulphur dioxide count tapered from .38 to .34.

It was bad news from the Weather Bureau—that despite some freshening of winds in the afternoon the stagnation would return in the evening—that impelled Commissioner Heller to urge the declaration of an alert.

Commissioner Heller pointed out that the city had already taken preparatory steps toward stemming the gush of pollutants into the atmosphere. The city's 11 incinerators were shut down, consuming just enough to keep the fires going.

Consolidated Edison said it had cut its emission of sulphur dioxide by 50 per cent on Thanksgiving Day and 40 per cent yesterday by using more natural gas at its power stations instead of fuel oil. The Long Island Lighting Company also voluntarily cut down on its use of fuel oil.

The Sanitation Department, however, faces an early crisis unless it can resume incineration. Commissioner Samuel J. Kearing Jr. said alternative means of disposal were expensive.

Each of the incinerators has a big storage pit, but these were filling rapidly. If the pits fill up and burning is still not permitted, the garbage would have to be hauled to distant land-fill operations in the Bronx, Brooklyn and Staten Island. This would mean long trips for garbage trucks, often more than eight miles.

Refuse for the Staten Island fill at Fresh Kills is carried by barge, and there are only about 40 scows.

Commissioner Kearing said he might put some of them into night duty, for although none of the tugs are radar-equipped, they can navigate safely in the harbor, provided the smog is not too thick.

Some 600 extra sanitation men will be working tomorrow to help get rid of the refuse. Commissioner Kearing said he was worried about the overtime bill.

The department's 11 incinerators are among the worst offenders of the city's air-pollution code.

It was revealed yesterday that something called "scrubbers" will soon be tried out at the incinerator at 74th Street and the East River. A "scrubber" is a device that throws a stream of air into gases as they proceed through a vent before reaching the stack. The air jet supposedly washes dirt particles out of the gas.

It will cost $200,000 to equip each of the furnaces with scrubbers, and the 11 incinerators have a total of 27 furnaces.

Commissioner Heller, who has promised a get-tough policy to clean up the air, has ordered public hearings starting Dec. 9 on proposals aimed at redesigning some 17,000 private incinerators.

He has already applied to the United States Public Health Service for $545,000 in grants to help develop devices to reduce the outpouring of pollutants from these incinerators. The city would contribute $146,000 toward these projects.

A new law effective next May requires all incinerators—private and city-owned—to be modernized to comply with the air-pollution code.

Officials were thankful that the pollution crisis came on a holiday weekend, when fewer cars belch carbon monoxide and industrial activity is slowed. Although yesterday was a work day for most New Yorkers, traffic was abnormally light.

Frightened perhaps by stories of killer smogs, many New Yorkers apparently retired to the country for fresh air. No revival of heavy traffic fumes is expected before Monday morning.

The effects of the smog were felt, to a lesser degree, in the suburbs and along the seaboard from Washington to Halifax, N. S.

Health officials in Nassau County reported no severe problems. "It is nowhere near the critical stage here as it appears to be in New York City," a spokesman said. "We are not alarmed by it."

In Suffolk County, the smog problem was called "almost nonexistent" by health officials, but the county asked the towns to halt all burning. Suffolk hospitals reported no increase in respiratory ailments.

A heavy haze hung over Westchester, but the county's Health Commissioner discounted any hazard.

"We have not received a single report of anyone becoming ill, and I do not consider the smog to be serious at this time," said the Commissioner, Dr. William A. Brumfield Jr.

In Connecticut, State Health Commissioner Franklin M. Foote warned against the burning of leaves and rubbish. He said that some persons with bronchitis, emphysema, asthma or heart diseases were suffering.

The city of Greenwich reported that the smog had had no serious effects. The smog was light there compared with New York and other areas of Connecticut.

In New Jersey, the smog was said to be heaviest in recent years, but there were no reports of an increase in serious illnesses. An 8 A.M. pollution reading taken in Elizabeth showed the level there was only half that of New York's.

November 26, 1966

MAJOR U.S. CITIES FACE EMERGENCY IN TRASH DISPOSAL

By GLADWIN HILL
Special to The New York Times

LOS ANGELES, June 15—An avalanche of waste and waste-disposal problems is building up around the nation's major cities in an impending emergency that may parallel the existing crises in air and water pollution.

Some features of the situation are being described by conservative Federal officials as "a national disgrace."

Experts feel that resolution of the problems may require radical changes in people's patterns of consumption and disposal, major shifts in municipal administration and sweeping revision of the nation's attitude toward its environment.

These are the conclusions and implications that emerge from interviews with leading authorities in the field and a 13-city check by The New York Times of what is becoming known as "the third pollution": the problem of solid wastes and their disposal.

Every man, woman and child in the country, on average, is now generating more than five pounds of refuse a day—household, commercial and industrial—ranging from garbage to iron filings but excluding vastly larger amounts of uncollected trash such as agricultural waste.

Collection and disposal facilities are staggering under the load, and the load is increasing rapidly.

"The major metropolitan areas are standing in front of an avalanche, and it is threatening to bury them," says Karl Wolf of the American Public Works Association, which has been conducting research projects on waste disposal.

Since 1950, the nation's population has increased 30 per cent, but the waste load has increased 60 per cent and is expected to increase 50 per cent more in the next decade.

The increase results from increased population, increased consumption of commodities and affluence, which has brought the regular discard of things that once were saved.

"We used to get few newspapers — people would save them to make money in paper drives," says Detroit's Public Works Commissioner, Robert P. Roselle. "Now we collect them all. The telephone company used to collect old phone books for their paper value. Now we collect them."

In San Francisco, even with no population increase, waste has increased by a third in the last decade. In Chicago it has been rising 2 per cent a year despite a slight decline in population. Cities across the country are also grappling with mounting numbers of automobiles, a physical and fiscal nuisance, although their mass is minuscule in the total waste picture.

"Half the communities in this country with populations of 2,500 or more," said Wesley Gilbertson, the first Federal Solid Wastes Program director, "are not doing even a minimally acceptable job of solid waste collection and disposal."

Once community trash could be disposed of simply by dumping it on the outskirts of town or burning it. Now with cities growing, outskirts have become fewer and farther away.

And incineration can only be a partial answer, because of the 20 per cent ash residue, the large volume of noncombustibles and air pollution problems.

So, from New York to San Francisco, the cry is going up that cities are running out of disposal space. A year's rubbish from 10,000 persons covers an acre of ground seven feet deep.

Philadelphia has been short of space for years and has had to shift largely to incineration. But it now is near the end of its rope because of incinerator obsolescence and high replacement costs.

New York City has been using up many acres of dumping space a year, with little space left. Even Tucson, Ariz., surrounded by desert, estimates that it will run out of disposal space within the next three years.

The problem is economic. Close-in urban land has become too valuable for dumping; other local dump sites are too far away because of trucking costs. And costs are rising.

Boston's refuse collection costs jumped last year from $2.6-million to $3.9-million just because of payroll increases. New York City's sanitation department, concerned primarily with solid wastes, has 14,000 workers, and its budget has climbed to nearly $150-million a year.

In Milwaukee, annual rubbish-removal charges for a household have risen in a decade from $26.40 to $35.25. Albuquerque's rate went up from $30 to $36 this year. In Portland, Ore., the monthly rate goes from $2 to $2.25 next month.

These trends have touched off a scramble for alternative refuse disposal systems somewhere in the range of present costs.

The average community outlay for refuse collection and disposal, according to a survey made in 1968 by the Public Health Service's Solid Wastes Program, is $6.80 a person a year.

But in some Washington suburbs, household rates run as high as $46.20 a year. New York City figures it costs $30 to dispose of a ton of trash.

San Francisco, where the current household charge is $22 a year, is planning to ship its refuse 375 miles by railroad to a desert disposal area in Lassen County.

Philadelphia is close to completing an arrangement for railroading its rubbish to distant abandoned mine pits. Chicago is considering a 250-mile haul.

Milwaukee has a rail-haul plan, but has not been able to find an amenable disposal locality. Philadelphia figures it now costs about $7.50 a ton to get rid of refuse by incineration; under the railroad plan it would pay a contractor only $5.35 a ton.

Chicago and Detroit are experimenting with trash compaction into blocks; Japanese researchers say that the blocks can be used as building materials.

Pneumatic tube waste-dispensing systems have been tried in Europe, and the Walt Disney organization is planning such equipment for its new Florida development.

Some organizations have been working on ways of macerating household trash, in a device like a garbage grinder, and forcing it in liquefied form to treatment centers. However, this would take care of only part of a community's waste.

Similarly, there has been a lot of talk lately about devising more easily destructible pack aging, particularly bottles and cans. But if all packaging were abolished completely, it would reduce the waste load only about 15 per cent.

Despite all the quests for solutions, some experts believe that the most serviceable short-range answer may lie in cities back yards.

Around 75 per cent of the nation's trash, by tonnage, still goes to open dumps, with about 15 per cent going into incinerators.

The Public Health Service found that 94 per cent of the dumps and 75 per cent of the incinerators were inadequate in respect to sanitation and pollution and termed this "a national disgrace."

Only 5 per cent of refuse is disposed of by the "sanitary landfill" method, in which each day's deposit is covered with six inches or more of compacted dirt, making it rodent-proof and odorless. The process, according to the Public Health Service, in a typical situation costs only $1.27 a ton, against 96 cents for obnoxious dumping.

There is no simple answer to the nation's refuse problem, experts say, because it is a composite of myriad problems that hinge on local economics.

These can vary greatly even in different sections of the same city. In New York, scrap metal contractors pay the city from 21 cents to $4.03 to pick up abandoned automobiles in the Bronx, Brooklyn, Queens and Staten Island.

In Manhattan, because of logistic difficulties, they pay nothing.

Across the country, scrap metal prices vary sharply, depending on transportation and the nearness of metal works.

If Milwaukee could find a disposal area, it is estimated that railroad removal would cost from $5.45 to $6.23 a ton, $2 less than its present dumping-and incineration system.

Yet Denver backed off from a plan to haul its trash by train 75 miles to a point near Colorado Springs because estimates were that within a decade it would cost $419,000 more than local disposal.

Apart from such variables, the quest for new disposal methods starts from the most disorderly of economic bases. Across the country, trash systems have evolved from the primitive town dump, and there is no uniformity or consistency in methods or financing.

Roughly half the nation's refuse collection is by public agencies and half by private collectors, either franchised or dealing directly with customers.

In many places, householders are billed specifically for the service; in others the service is financed from general tax funds.

Sometimes the charge is calculated at cost; sometimes it is pegged to yield a profit. Sometimes the service is given below cost with the differential coming from taxes. The profits of franchised collectors may or may not be subject to regular public scrutiny.

Thus, in many cases citizens have little way of knowing whether they are getting their money's worth and whether the cost of an alternative system would be justified.

Inefficient approaches to waste disposal are the rule rather than the exception.

"Most of what is wrong with solid waste management in the United States," says one official, "can be attributed to fragmenting responsibility down to small political jurisdictions which lack sufficient resources for the job."

In Los Angeles County, 70 communities share rubbish collecting depots and disposal sites. But elsewhere in California, Federal researchers found one area where 80 public agencies were running 70 separate disposal systems.

The hazy economics of some municipal systems, experts have observed, provide a field day for officials and agencies to juggle funds—not necessarily into their own pockets, but to the detriment of efficient refuse disposal.

What is being done about the waste problem nationally?

Congress got the word on the impending waste glut as far back as 1965 and passed the Solid Waste Disposal Act. It gave the Public Health Service primary responsibility for a program of research and technical assistance and matching grants to states and localities to help in the development of disposal programs.

Most of these states have availed themselves of these grants, the average being about $50,000. But total appropriations for the solid waste program have remained less than $20-million a year.

While much valuable basic information has been amassed —(nobody knew anything about the national waste disposal picture before)—and a number of experimental projects launched, the program has not yet come up with any cure-alls.

The general line of thinking is that, as with air and water pollution, each area will have to work out a solution fitted to local circumstances and that waste collection and disposal will have to be handled regionally, with localities pooling efforts.

Ultimately, coping with solid waste, it is believed, should be part of an integrated system covering also liquid and gaseous effluents.

"One of the most significant items of progress," says Richard D. Vaughan, current director of the Solid Wastes Program, "is that state budgets are starting to show specific items for waste disposal work.

"There is public concern about this, where three years ago there wasn't any."

Senator Edmund S. Muskie, the Maine Democrat who fostered basic water pollution legislation, has turned his attention to solid waste and has a bill pending that would increase financing of the solid waste program tenfold, to a level of more than $200-million a year.

Seemingly there are only two things that can be done with rubbish—burn it or bury it, in the ground or in the ocean.

But there is an often overlooked third possibility, and some scientists think it is the only one for the long run. That is to reclaim refuse—to break it down into its main constituents for reuse.

That has been the dream of many people, but it has not been realized, except for a small amount of scrap metal and paper salvage, because it has been cheaper to proccure new materials.

So the nation's economy has continued on a "use-and-discard" pattern. But there comes a point where the cost of getting rid of used material gets so high that the cost of renovating it would represent an economy.

That point is already being approached with the commonest commodity, water.

The same tactic is even more applicable to solid waste. Dirty water, if not renovated, disposes of itself one way or another. Solid waste does not; it just piles up. And scientists foresee the day when accumulation of rubbish, and gases from its incineration, will be as troublesome over the face of the globe as are the wastes in a spacecraft.

The latter are systematically "recycled." The same recycling eventually will be imperative with everyday wastes, it is felt, and may as well be undertaken soon as a decisive answer to the refuse problem.

A scientific report prepared for the Senate Public Works Committee last year said:

"It is now evident that the industrial economy of the United States must undergo a shift from a use-and-discard approach to a closed cycle of use and salvage, reprocess and reuse . . . or else faces the alternative of a congested planet that has turned into a polluted trash heap, devoid of plant and animal life, depleted of minerals, with a climate intolerable to man."

Short of this long-range solution, the public is confronted with some early large-scale expenditures just to get relief from current rubbish bugbears.

Mr. Vaughan estimates it will take an outlay of more than $2-million a day—$835-million a year—for five years, just to "upgrade existing collection and disposal practices to a satisfactory level."

This is a sizable sum, but only a fraction of the $4.5-billion a year the Public Health Service estimates is being spent to deal with all types of solid waste.

Relief may be some time in coming. Frank Stead, a former official of California's Department of Public Health and one of the nation's leading environmental experts, said recently that it would take 16 years to bring about basic changes in solid waste management.

June 16, 1969

GOVERNMENT AND HOUSING

Housing Industrial Fighters---Cost $100,000,000

By OTTO M. EIDLITZ,
Director of Housing, Department of Labor.

THE Administration's request of Congress for $100,000,000 for housing war workers—$50,000,000 to the Shipping Board for shipyard workers and $50,000,000 to the Department of Labor for men working on general war products—has brought up very definitely before the country the question of a national war housing policy.

Although there is doubtless more than one way of dealing with the housing situation, the subject is full of pitfalls for the man who has thought of the subject in a general way without going into a detailed examination of the problem as it now exists in America. He is apt to fall into one of two errors. Looking at the vast number of communities in the United States capable through existing industrial plants of turning out munitions of war, and among which war orders may be distributed, he may decide off-hand that any expenditure whatever is unnecessary and that private initiative should be sufficient to provide any additional housing facilities that may be needed. Why not place orders where the labor is already housed? he may ask.

On the other hand, if he knows something of British experience with its story of $700,000,000 invested in war housing, he may decide that the American Government should go into the business of construction on the same wholesale scale. The truth, so far as investigations made by the Council of National Defense and the various Government departments have been able to determine it, lies between these two extremes.

In the first place, the actual situation shows that something should be done at once to relieve the congestion in many of our munition centres. We are dealing with an existing and emergency situation. The proof is at hand through careful studies of such districts as those around Bridgeport; Erie, Penn.; Bethlehem, Sparrows Point, Newport News, Philadelphia, Wilmington, Del., and several other localities, that war work is being very obviously slowed up by the lack of living quarters for men. The lack has shown itself in two ways: First, in an enormous labor turnover; secondly, a falling off in efficiency in labor which remains in those districts.

It is perhaps not too much to say that the productivity of the plants in some of these centres could be increased a hundred per cent. with the rapid construction of proper living quarters for their employes. Men come to these places in response to the call for war workers, remain a week, find, if they are married, that there is no place to house their families, or perhaps, if they are single, that the quarters provided for them are insanitary and uncomfortable, and move on to other fields. The result is that just about the time when the newcomers are beginning to become effective workers they leave and new men have to be educated to the task. In other words, through lack of housing the munitions firms (and usually the cost falls ultimately on the Government) are compelled to pay heavily for this continual re-education of workers. If figured out on a scientific scale, it is undoubtedly true that the cost would build houses for the men many times over.

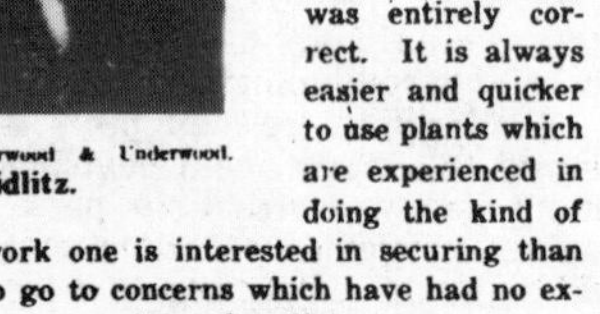
© Underwood & Underwood.
Otto M. Eidlitz.

If the men do not leave but remain, living in inadequate quarters, it does not take long to lower their vitality and thereby their efficiency. In some of the important industrial centres beds are now being used in three shifts; that is, when one man gets up another man is ready to take his place in the bed. It can easily be seen that such conditions are not conducive to good health, physical or mental, and both are essential to efficient production.

The reasons for this congestion, despite the number of munition centres in which war work might with time have been distributed, are simple. Large numbers of firms were engaged in making war products for the Allies before we entered the war. With the commendable idea of utilizing the centres where this work was going on in order to speed up production as rapidly as possible when the war began, the natural tendency of the Government departments was to place war orders with these concerns or with others in their immediate neighborhood. Without considering the labor phases of production, the logic of this plan was entirely correct. It is always easier and quicker to use plants which are experienced in doing the kind of work one is interested in securing than to go to concerns which have had no experience along that line.

The result, however, has been that these centres, most of them east of the Alleghanies, have become swamped with the labor which has rushed in to meet their war needs. Few of these communities had the resources, or indeed have had time, to plan for the reception of these new men. Bridgeport, for example, needed 10,000 new men by the first of January, but the district was already so congested that there was no hope of their being able to handle the men even if they got them. Building and local financial resources alike had already been exhausted in taking care of the surplus they already had.

A similar situation existed in the vicinity of many of the shipyards. The new yards especially were frequently built at some distance from the nearest community. This meant that the men either had to build homes near the shipyard or be transported from the distant community—granting that the community itself had facilities for taking care of them. The contracts which the Government had let usually did not make allowance for housing and the concerns themselves have therefore, in most cases, been unable to advance the necessary funds for this purpose, as such surplus as their contracts provided had to be expended in construction of new plants or the purchase of new equipment.

Even in cases where the need for new housing was apparent from the start the contracting departments of the Government were unable, under existing law, to advance money for housing, and communities, workmen, and contracting firms alike have simply had to make the best of the circumstances. A comprehensive investigation of the situation late last year showed that something would have to be done about the matter shortly or the results would be serious in the extreme.

This, then, was the situation. Granted that the necessary financial aid should come from the Government, the question arose as to how best that aid might be applied. In many cases munitions plants were doing work for several of the production departments, including, for example, ordnance, quartermaster, and the navy. The housing problem, while concerning them all, at the same time obviously should be handled as one problem. This could be done either through co-operation among the departments concerned or, better, by giving to one agency power to deal with the situation as a whole. On Jan. 4 the President authorized the Department of Labor, along with all other phases of the war labor program, to administer the whole question of the housing and transportation of workers.

A bill was therefore planned asking Congress for $100,000,000 for the housing program. As the shipping question was perhaps the most urgent and the Shipping Board already had an organization to deal with housing while it would take some time to build up the necessary agencies in the Department of Labor for its consummation, it was decided in interdepartmental conference to split the amount in two, giving $50,000,000 to the Shipping Board for its needs and $50,000,000 to the Department of Labor for the general program, with the idea of perhaps combining the two under one head after the Department of Labor's organization had got under way. The Shipping Board's appropriation has already been passed by both houses of Congress at the time this article is written, while the general appropriation is now pending in the House of Representatives.

At the time the Appropriation bill was framed the plans had already been worked out for the administration of the funds. There were two ways in which this could be done. The Government, following the example of Great Britain, could enter upon a permanent construction program, building the houses itself with the idea of making a permanent contribution to the welfare of the industrial population; or it could use the money for loans to local agencies, retaining onl, central control of the program and with the expectation that the money would eventually be returned on some proper basis of repayment.

The objections to the first plan were two, one the element of time, the other the extent of territory to be covered. The war emergency program in Great Britain was comparatively simple to the mind of the British Government. Before the war England had entered into a rather extensive program of building homes for her workers. She therefore had the agencies, administrative and financial, ready at her disposal for expansion for war purposes. The Ministry of Munitions has been able to build, with comparative speed, a large number of homes for her war workers, following the lines already mapped out in her pre-war policy. The methods and the means were ready to her hand. To be sure, the results which she has attained in this direction have been striking, but for the American Government a similar accomplishment would have been impossible without the expenditure of a great deal of time and the passage of a great deal of additional legislation.

The need in this country was (and still is) urgent and something had to be planned to relieve the existing difficulties in double-quick time. It seemed neither the time nor the occasion to debate the question of a permanent housing policy. The dominating idea is to do something to speed up production, and that has been retained as the guiding principle throughout the discussion of the matter in the Administration. Industrial welfare has been considered only from this point of view; and while doubtless permanent contribution to the industrial situation will be made by these war developments, they are included only as subordinate to the immediate need of providing quarters which will enable our industrial fighters to turn out at top speed the ships, guns, shells, explosives, airplanes, and the countless other products needed at the front.

If we grant for the sake of argument that such a comprehensive, direct construction program as England's is inexpedient at this time, there remains the other plan which was adopted by the Committee on Housing of the Council of National Defense, of which I had the honor to be Chairman, and which came to its conclusions only after a very thorough study of the problem based on several investigations and consideration of British data.

This plan, in brief, is to utilize every possible existing local agency for the work, with the Government as directing manager and advancing a larger part of the funds. The problem really divides itself into three parts: The community problem, the isolated plant case, and the case of the Government-owned plant. The plan adopted to meet the community problem, which has already been approved by many of the communities interested, contemplates furnishing to the community 80 per cent. of the funds necessary for the work. The communities would organize co-operative limited-profit companies, which would advance the other 20 per cent. The Government must, of course, see to it that the dividend in these housing companies is strictly limited, in order to attract workers by enabling them to occupy the houses at a reasonable rental, or, if they wish, to acquire them outright at a reasonable price. In consideration of the low rate of interest on the Government loan the dividend could and should be cut to the lowest possible margin. The Government's security for the loan, under the proposed plan, would be a blanket mortgage covering the whole of the transaction. The Government's money would be loaned to the communities on easy terms for a fifteen-year period, with a proper amortization scheme, providing for its complete repayment at the end of the fifteen years' period. In other words, the actual work of construction would be placed on the communities, while the Government would, to some extent, control the plans, seeing that they conform to its needs.

In the case of the isolated plant, where the workers in that plant formed the principal portion of the population of the little town, hamlet, or whatever it may be, the individual or people interested would furnish the land and give a blanket mortgage to the Government for the balance of the loan. In the Government-owned plant, operated under agency contracts, in view of the fact that the Government is paying the cost of everything connected with it, including the housing of machinery, it probably would be best for the Government to pay also for the housing of the worker.

With the Government's power to commandeer land and property, the dangers of profiteering in land values could be avoided. This same power of commandeering could also doubtless be used in many cases to cut down materially the amount of new housing construction necessary. The bill now pending is elastic enough in its powers to safeguard the country's interest in all directions.

While in some quarters it is feared that the $50,000,000 asked for is too small for the purpose, it is unquestionable that, with the growing improvement in transportation facilities and the pains now being taken to distribute war orders with the housing question in mind, the funds asked for will go far toward solving the present situation, and the Secretary of Labor has decided that this sum is all that could be effectively utilized during the current year.

As to the character of construction contemplated, it will necessarily vary materially according to local conditions. Wherever time permits and the locality seems to promise a permanent increase in industrial development as a result of the war, care will be taken to make the new houses relatively permanent in character. This might apply particularly to certain of the shipyards. It is especially true of the shipyards that they are usually at some distance from the nearest community, and that where they are likely to remain after the war living quarters will always be necessary in their vicinity. Where emergency towns of this kind have to be built, efforts will be made to give them comparatively permanent construction. Beauty will, of course, have to be subordinated to expediency in their design.

The guiding purpose in all these plans is to provide for an efficient war industrial population. In cases where practically new towns are built, room will be left for schools and churches to spring up; as, if the working population, especially the women, are to be content, they must necessarily have these advantages. This was the plan followed by Great Britain, and results as compared with examples of a different policy have amply justified such measures.

February 24, 1918

TRY MANY PLANS TO AID HOME BUILDING

Cities Throughout Country Are Wrestling with Problem of Housing Shortage.

CREATE BORROWING FUNDS

Labor Department Collects Information of Most Successful Financing Schemes.

Attempts to solve the housing situation have been made throughout the United States, each community evolving its own scheme to cope with the difficulties in its own particular problem. For the most part, there has been no means of sharing information as to the causes of failures or the reasons for success, but the Department of Labor has made a record of the most promising schemes of financing projects, in the interest of the own-your-own-home campaign. Special needs have been taken into account, but the general trend has been toward the establishment of funds from which the small owner might borrow.

In Seattle, Wash., a few weeks before the armistice was signed, the Columbia Investment and Mortgage Company was organized to aid the small investor, and to make possible the proper housing of workers engaged in war industries. Its scope included the buying, leasing, and acquiring of real estate and personal property, the erection of dwellings and other buildings, and the making of improvements on properties. Its powers were comprehensive, and the organization of a company authorized to deal in second mortgages and in real estate contracts where the lien is a secondary lien, was intended to aid house builders who had no market for real estate contracts.

The corporation is enabled to advance to owners of vacant lots the difference between the cost of the house and the amount of money that could be borrowed from insurance companies or other loaning agencies. The capital stock is $200,000, divided into 2,000 shares of $100 each. The company was organized as a patriotic civic undertaking, and arrangements were made with the Metropolitan Building Company to manage the affairs of the new organization.

This scheme is similar in many respects to that advocated and partly carried into operation by the New York State Reconstruction Commission in New York City. Here it was intended that a $5,000,000 fund be raised to supply second mortgage money to those unable to borrow it elsewhere.

In St. Paul, Minn., the Own Your Own Home Financing Corporation was formed to "assist wage earners to the ownership of their homes, and to that end to advance to them not to exceed 80 per cent. of the value of the property" on which the loan is made, such advances to be repaid in monthly or other installments and to be secured either by mortgages, land contracts, or obligations and evidences of indebtedness.

Niagara Falls, N. Y., found a serious shortage of dwellings at the close of the war. According to estimates, 10,000 houses will be needed within ten years. To meet present and future emergencies it empowered its Industrial Housing Committee to study conditions and make recommendations. The committee's report, which was adopted, recommended the organization of a housing corporation, and presented three methods of financing building:

First, by a straight loan from a bank or individual, secured by first mortgage, the corporation taking a second mortgage for the difference between the loan and the cost of the dwelling, the second mortgage to be paid in monthly installments.

Second, a loan from a loan association secured by a first mortgage, payable in installments, on which the company would take a second mortgage payable at the end of a term of years and maturing when the first mortgage is sufficiently reduced to absorb the second mortgage.

Third, a loan for the full value of the building, the borrower giving back a first mortgage for an amount which would render it marketable at once, this mortgage being payable at the end of a term of years, the balance of the loan being secured by a second mortgage, payable by monthly installments.

Under any of these principles the corporation would take up the difference between the first mortgage and the cost of the dwelling. It was recommended that the capital stock of the corporation would be $250,000, all of which would be common stock, with a par value of $100 a share.

A plan devised to stimulate building on a scale sufficient to cover urgent needs, and yet combine simplicity of method and as little interference as possible with regular organized business, whether financial, construction, or real estate, has been outlined in South Bend, Ind. The purpose has been to leave the proposed owners and builders of property free, within reasonable limits, in the design of the houses to be erected, and to advise usual methods of financing as largely as possible through the banks and other institutions.

It is stipulated that homes constructed by this company shall be upon real estate owned by the organization, such real estate to be purchased at fair values or to be accepted at such value in exchange for common or preferred stock in the company. It is the desire of the organization to build houses in lots of approximately twenty, and to borrow approximately 50 per cent. of the total investment upon 6 per cent. first mortgage loans, such loans desirably to run for a period of five years, with privilege of reducing at any semi-annual interest paying period.

Provision is made for the buying and selling of stocks and bonds, directly or indirectly, on commission or otherwise, to the same extent as an individual engaging in such business might do. The company can lend money to individuals, partnerships, and to incorporated societies to assist in the improvement of real estate. It has a capital stock of $500,000 divided into 10,000 shares of $50 each, 4,000 of which are of common stock and 6,000 of preferred.

July 5, 1919

CITY OF PATERSON TO BUILD 200 HOMES

To Meet Housing Evil Municipality Will Rent Buildings at Fair Rate.

Special to The New York Times.

PATERSON, N. J., Feb. 7.—The city of Paterson will erect 200 new homes and will become a municipal landlord just as quickly as work can be started. A committee appointed by Mayor Frank J. Van Noort met today and decided to spend approximately $1,500,000 in building homes in order to relieve congested conditions.

The idea of the city becoming a landlord on a large scale is that of Mayor Van Noort, Democrat, who was elected at the last election. A special committee, consisting of Francis Scott, City Counsel; Henry Marelli, Chairman of the Mayor's Rent Committee, and William R. Meakle, Secretary of the Paterson Savings Institution, will be incorporated as a holding company under the name of The Housing Corporation of Paterson, N. J.

The houses will be of frame of the standard two-family type, with five rooms and bath on each floor and two rooms in the attic. They will be rented at a fair rate, the rental charge to apply on the purchase price. The John W. Ferguson Company will do the work at actual cost, bringing the price down about 25 per cent. The houses will cost about $6,000 each.

February 8, 1920

HOUSING SPEEDS UP AS BILL IS SIGNED

Metropolitan Life Prepares for Early Construction of Block of Fifty Houses.

OTHERS LIKELY TO FOLLOW

Success of Initial Project Will Result in Much Building, Says Halsey Fiske.

Plans for the relief of the housing situation took a quick leap forward yesterday following the signing by Governor Miller of the bill permitting life insurance companies to invest 10 per cent. of their assets in housing for the masses.

Haley Fiske, President of the Metropolitan Life Insurance Company, announced that a group of financiers had approached the company for the purpose of obtaining a $7,000,000 loan to be used to inaugurate a building project similar to that of the Metropolitan.

The Metropolitan Company has completed negotiations for the purchase of four blocks in the Borough of Queens. Within thirty days construction will be begun on fifty houses to accommodate 1,800 families at a rental of not more than $9 a room per month. The site of the project will be made known tomorrow when the contracts are signed.

Both plots are said to be in the 5-cent fare zone. One is described as being within eighteen minutes of Times Square anr the other can be reached from either the Pennsylvania or the Grand Central Station in twenty minutes. All of the houses are expected to be ready by Autumn.

The financial group which has approached the Metropolitan Life for a $7,000,000 loan has stated that it desires to erect a group of 400 houses. The company, it was said, is not only prepared to use the loan for new housing construction but also intends to invest a substantial sum in the project and has given assurances that the rent will be not greater than $9 a room.

Offer to Buy Fifty Houses.

A second financial group, consisting of wealthy men, has told Mr. Fiske that it is ready to buy the Metropolitan's 50-house project as soon as it is completed. If the Metropolitan assents to this proposition, it will be in a position to duplicate the project and to bring into being another group of fifty houses.

"Everything is most encouraging," said President Fiske yesterday. "We are meeting with a great deal of co-operation. We have been assured by Mr. Untermyer that labor will co-operate to the extent of giving one day a week and that concessions may be expected from the material men. But our figures of anticipated costs did not take this into consideration. If it works out in this way, we will be able to come down on our rents.

"All that we expect out of this is a return of 6 per cent. on our investment and a proper allowance for amortization."

The amortization, he explained, had been figured on such a basis that at the end of five years the company would be subjected to no greater risk in the property than would be involved in a first mortgage. The expectation is, however, that when the apartments are completed they will be leased en bloc with restrictions as to rental or sale.

Referring to reports that the Metropolitan would expend $100,000,000 for housing, Mr. Fiske said: "This is a good deal of money and you can't spend it in a night. Our first fifty houses, involving the expenditure of between $5,000,000 and $6,000,000, will be an experiment. It is certainly worth trying. And if it works out and there is still a demand, we are prepared to do it over again."

The houses are to be erected on blocks from 600 to 900 feet long and will have many novel features. The architect, Andrew J. Thomas, has designed plans calling for large playground spaces. Between the houses, at the rear, for the entire length of the block, there will be a space thirty feet wide to be devoted entirely to the children. Between the pairs of houses there will be courtyards 150 feet wide and these also will be used as playgrounds.

To Have All Conveniences.

The houses are to be four stories in height, with hot water, steam heat and every modern convenience. On each floor will be four apartments, with three additional apartments in the basement, so that the project will provide accommodations for about 9,000 persons.

One of the novel features will be stairways so arranged that each stairway will lead to but two apartments on any floor, thus giving some of the privacy of a two-family house.

The savings to be effected by the purchase of the land for cash and by the purchase of materials in large quantities will be a great factor in permitting those behind the project to keep the rents down to the lowest possible figures.

No explanation was forthcoming from Mayor Hylan's office yesterday as to the Mayor's reason for failing to approve the bill which would have permitted the return to tenants of jury fees in untried cases. Under the present law a tenant who contests his rent may go into court and ask for a jury trial. He pays $3 for the privilege of having the jury. In many cases one test case is used by a group of tenants, and as the rent is settled by one trial, the law, suggested by the Lockwood committee, called for the repayment of the jury fee to other tenants who joined in the test case.

April 16, 1922

Nation-Wide Building Survey Of Anticipated 1926 Expenditures

Sound Economic Conditions, With Definite Signs of Stability, Encourage Big Construction Program—Elimination of Waste Space and Better Buildings Strong Factors in New Planning.

A six billion dollar building year in the United States is predicted by The Architectural Forum in its annual survey completed yesterday.

For the past five years The Forum has conducted an extensive survey among architects and builders to determine the amount of building construction contemplated for the ensuing year. The method used includes the obtaining of confidential reports from thousands of sources covering six geographical divisions of the United States in nineteen building classifications. These reports are carefully tabulated and correlated and the totals determined by a careful system of weighting. Thus the final forecast figures are established after months of careful research work.

During this period the forecast has proved to be remarkably close to the actual figures shown at the end of the year; and in all cases conservative, so that the survey has become recognized as an authoritative presentation of probable building activity. The allocation of activity thoroughout the country is an almost certain indication of what will actually take place in the building industry.

Review of 1925 Conditions.

In view of the fact that forecast for 1926 indicates another $6,000,000,000 building year, probably equal to the record-breaking activity of 1925, it will be interesting to review briefly the building activity of the year 1925 in order that later comparisons may be clear.

Up to date the figures for the year 1925 indicate that approximately six and one-half billion dollars were spent this year for new building construction in the United States.

At the beginning of the year 1925 all conditions indicated that this year would probably equal 1924, which established a record up to that time; but no one anticipated completely the amazing volume to which the building totals have climbed. Records were broken everywhere during 1925.

Every one connected with or interested in the building construction industry knows of the phenomenal activity which was apparent during the year 1925. Owing to the limitations of space it is not possible to present here the full details of last year's activity, but the great interest of the building fraternity today is expressed in the question "What will occur in 1926?"

Probable Building Total for 1926.

The survey indicates the anticipated expenditures for new buildings during the year 1926, classified according to nineteen types of structures and divided into six geographical divisions of the United States. This tabulation shows the amazing total of $5,584,782,500, which will pass over the boards of architects and into actual construction during the year 1926. In addition to this vast sum to be spent for building materials and labor there must be considered the fact that in the small house field and that of industrial construction there is considerable building not developed from architects' plans, probably totaling another half-billion dollars.

Thus it is predicted that 1926 will be another six billion dollar building year with certain changes in the relative proportions of activity in building types and districts.

Changes in Public Demand.

Each year the grand total of The Forum forecast is broken up into percentage showing the anticipated activity in new building construction for each of the nineteen building types in the six established geographical divisions of the United States. By comparing these percentages for 1925 and 1926 it is possible to ascertain the changing public demand for new buildings and to establish for each district the relative activity which may be expected.

Character of Anticipated New Building

In the course of the research work involved in establishing this forecast for 1926, The Architectural Forum has had the opportunity to make an interesting series of observations as to the changing character of new building in the United States.

The high cost of building, together with increased real estate values, has, during the past few years provided a forced education for the investing public in this field, indicating the fallacy of poorly considered planning and the use of inferior materials and workmanship.

The great effort in the planning of buildings today is to eliminate all waste space and provide a maximum of rental or utility efficiency, at the same time attempting definitely to reduce depreciation and maintenance cost through good architectural specifications.

Many mortgage companies, having learned the lesson of sound building collateral, are insisting upon better construction and upon a serious review of plans and specifications before building and permanent mortgage loans are made.

The total effect of these conditions is reflected in a constant improvement in the character of new buildings and the placing of greatly increased responsibility upon the architectural profession, which to a great extent controls the expenditure of the building dollar.

Thus it is evident that 1926 will not only show a tremendous volume of new building construction but that these buildings will be in general of better architectural design and better construction.

The American public has learned the lesson of folly in cheap building and poor planning!

A highly important factor in all forecasts of this nature is the background of economic conditions. If business conditions in the United States were not good, with sound promises of so remaining for several years, there might be expected a definite curtailment of building activity—a slowing down of the great momentum established during the past few years. But conditions are good, with definite signs of stability, and as the building industry is the indicator of conditions, so with the entire economic situation favorable, there is little fear of a break in public confidence or any basic business change which will interrupt the anticipated program of another six billion dollar building year during 1926.

The probable "normal" building year of today is four billion dollars or more and on this basis it would take three or four six billion dollar years to meet the still-existing shortage!

All is well with the building industry. It is going about its business seriously, contributing to the wealth and comfort of the nation. Some idea of the magnitude and importance of the construction industry may be gained from a statement recently made by Secretary of Labor Davis in which he said: "More than 11,000,000 of our people are dependent for their living upon the construction industry, and 22 per cent. of all the skilled and unskilled labor of the country is engaged in the building branch alone. Some 250,000 freight cars are required to handle the materials. Our building bill is $200 per year for each family in the United States. It is truly the chief barometer of the business of the country. When construction gains, prosperity is with us. It is the great outstanding influence for good or bad in our financial progress."

Architects are busier than ever before—a sure sign of great building activity to come. The number of plans being filed is constantly increasing—another sign of activity.

December 20, 1925

GOV. SMITH SIGNS NEW HOUSING BILL

He Stresses Need of State Bank in a Statement Approving the Republican Bill.

Special to The New York Times.

ALBANY, May 10.—Governor Smith late today approved the Republican Housing bill, which has been before him since the Legislature adjourned. In an explanatory statement filed with the new statute the Governor more than intimated that the measure was not all that it ought to be.

The bill signed by Governor Smith was enacted as a compromise after the Republicans had declined to pass a bill drafted by Julius Henry Cohen, counsel for the State Housing Commission, who has given years of study to the housing situation and remedial legislation. The principal difference between the Housing Commission bill and the Republican bill is that the latter meaure makes no provision for a State housing bank, as provided for in the commission's bill, but substitutes a State Housing Board with no banking functions.

"Our old friend, Mr. Politics, put his nose in the door, and the majority party in control of the Legislature conceived it to be their duty to have a bill that they called their own. Although left to themselves they initiated nothing, and the Housing Commission's bill was referred to as a socialistic move," Governor Smith said in his explanatory statement. "Of course, nobody took that seriously, not even the men that said it."

The Governor declared that the commission bill would have facilitated the borrowing at a minimum rate of all the money necessary, and that it presented a complete program for quasi-building operations for housing purposes.

Governor Smith's statement, in part, follows:

"The bill as finally enacted leaves some of the financial problems in doubt, but in its main features it recognizes, as I had originally suggested, the limited dividend companies as the basic element, giving to them, under rigid regulation by a State housing board, the right to condemn land needed for large-scale operations, such as are necessary to achieve cheap construction. Rents are regulated and limited. Public aid to those projects is in the form of tax exemptions, positive as to certain kinds of State taxes and permissive in the case of local taxation. Federal tax exemptions for these securities is in doubt, but is to be sought through Congressional action.

The Housing Board which the bill creates has broad powers of regulation and control over the companies operating under the act, and has other responsibilities of study and planning that should prove vitally important in making progress in city planning and general housing development.

"We must make a beginning in the attack on the entrenched system of constructing housing for speculative purposes only, and having reached the conclusion, as evidenced by this bill, that the State has a responsibility in the matter, earnest cooperation between the State and local agencies who can aid in practical ways, and those who can and will finance such undertaking, should soon establish results.

"This legislation is not perfect, nor do I believe we have said the last word on the subject, but honest effort on the part of all those connected with its operation will soon demonstrate in what direction further aid is needed.

"In approving this bill I do so with the sincere hope that it may prove the beginning of a lasting movement to wipe out of our State those blots upon civilization, the old, dilapidated, dark, unsanitary, unsafe tenement houses that long since became unfit for human habitation and certainly are no place for future citizens of New York to grow in."

The approved bill provides for net returns not to exceed 6 per cent. on the capital invested to the limited dividend cooperations, and gives the State Housing Board power to regulate rents and operations of such concerns. In eliminating the Housing Bank, which under the commission bill would have held title to all properties acquired by such corporations for housing purposes, the Republicans maintained that the Housing Commission plan would have had the effect ultimately of involving the State financially in such quasi-public building operations, where the real cure for the situation demanded encouragement of private capital to come forward and supply the needed relief.

May 11, 1926

Many States Press Law Revision To Permit Federal Housing Loans

With plans well advanced for beginning work on the initial model housing projects to be carried out in New York through loans from the Reconstruction Finance Corporation, many other States and cities are reported to be pressing plans to pass legislation which will make them eligible for such aid.

It was reported here last week that the Reconstruction Finance Corporation was likely to act soon upon the first of the New York projects presented for its approval through the State Board of Housing. This State was one step ahead of all others in making requests for loans because the machinery already set up here met the requirements of the $2,000,000,000 Federal emergency relief bill. Eventually the requests for aid on housing work in New York are expected to involve $80,000,000 or more, covering multi-family buildings to represent an investment well in excess of $100,000,000.

A survey by the American Engineering Council, of which William S. Lee is president, shows that considerable progress has been made in mapping out legislation and forming the necessary regulatory bodies in various parts of the country.

Prepare to Pass Legislation.

The legislatures of Illinois and Ohio are now in session and, it is believed, will pass legislation creating regulatory bodies to meet the requirements of the Federal act. The movement for legislative action in Illinois is directed by Alfred K. Stern, director of special activities of the Julius Rosenwald Fund.

In Cleveland, architects have prepared plans for projects based on a survey by the Committee on City plan of the Cleveland Chamber of Commerce, headed by Abram Garfield, president of the Cleveland Chapter of the American Institute of Architects. In Cincinnati a housing project is being developed by the Cincinnati Better Homes Corporation, which, it is said, has been highly successful in providing housing for Negroes. Groups in Cincinnati, Columbus and Toledo have approved the proposed legislation in Ohio, which is sponsored by the Joint Council and Citizens' Committee of Cleveland and which, it is understood, is sanctioned by Governor White.

Mayor Curley of Boston has appointed an advisory committee to study housing legislation. The chairman is William Stanley Parker of the Boston Chapter of the American Institute of Architects. The committee is now working for the passage of a State-wide act setting up a regulatory body in the Department of Public Welfare.

Washington, D. C., expects to participate in the housing loans. It is proposed that the National Park and Planning Commission undertake legislation which will make possible aid for a project to reclaim the alley slum districts of Washington. The commission will decide whether to secure legislation creating a governmental agency to which loans may be made without regulation as to rents and charges, or whether to secure the passage of a regulatory law enabling loans to be made to private corporations.

A measure to establish regulatory machinery failed of passage at the last session of the Pennsylvania Legislature, but, according to present plans, will be reintroduced at the coming session in January. The Philadelphia Chapter of the American Institute of Architects is actively promoting this legislation and has appointed an architects' municipal development council to study the housing situation in Philadelphia.

Conditions Misunderstood.

Misunderstanding exists as to the conditions under which the Reconstruction Finance Corporation can make housing loans. Illustrative of the requirement that a local regulatory authority exists is the corporation's attitude toward the application for a loan from a Mississippi manufacturer for the purpose of erecting homes for the husbands of women employed in a shirt factory. The corporation, in rejecting the application, expressed the view that it was the feeling of Congress in enacting this legislation that the Federal Government could not afford to make loans for housing purposes if it also had to take over the burden of management.

The question of what constitutes a family of low income will necessarily have to be determined in accordance with conditions in the locality where a housing project is to be erected, a Los Angeles company which applied for a loan has been informed. An approach to this problem, however, is contained in the New York State housing law, which provides for a maximum average rental per room per month of $12.50 in New York County and $11 elsewhere.

A bill now before the Illinois Legislature provides that the average maximum rental in cities having a population of over 150,000 for two-room apartments shall be $25; for three-room, $32; for four-room, $39; for five-room, $46; for six-room, $53, and for apartments having more than six rooms, $53 plus $7 for each additional room. Elsewhere in the State maximum figures are $21, $27, $33, $39 and $45 for two, three, four, five and six room apartments respectively. Proposed Pennsylvania legislation provides that the average maximum rental should be $10 per room per month, but that no rental should exceed $11 per room.

No application for a housing loan can be considered by the Reconstruction Finance Corporation until the project has been approved by the local regulatory authority.

October 9, 1932

ICKES CORPORATION TO REBUILD SLUMS

Starting With Large Sum, Probably $200,000,000, It Plans Wide Program.

WILL RENT OR SELL HOMES

Proposes in Next Few Months to Promote Understanding of Housing in 20 Cities.

Special to THE NEW YORK TIMES.

WASHINGTON, Oct. 28.—Incorporation of a Public Works Emergency Housing Corporation to build low-cost apartment houses as slum clearance projects throughout the country was announced today by Secretary Ickes.

The papers were filed at Wilmington, Del., and, although the huge resources of the Public Works Administration will be behind the venture, only three stockholders were listed. Mr. Ickes, Secretary Perkins and Robert D. Kohn, director of the Housing Division of the PWA, hold one share each without par value for the government.

Launched some weeks ago as a move toward improved living conditions for workers of the nation, the Housing Corporation will function as a subsidiary of the Works Administration by "constructing, reconstructing, altering and repair of low-cost housing projects or slum clearance projects, apartment houses, homes and structures of every nature and kind."

Although no amount was named, it was said unofficially today that the initial fund would be about $200,000,000, and be increased as necessary.

Secretary Ickes, in a statement accompanying the announcement of incorporation, said that "our experience of the last three months indicates clearly that we may not depend upon private enterprise or limited dividend corporations to initiate comprehensive low-cost housing and slum clearance projects."

Not to Compete With Business.

Although the corporation, under provisions of the Recovery Act, is empowered to do anything that a private contractor or builder could do, the policy of the Advisory Board will be not to interfere with or enter into competition against legitimate private business of such nature, but rather to supplement and stimulate these activities.

The corporation has broad powers to engage in a general construction business, to perform engineering and architectural work and to conduct and carry on the business of builders and contractors.

In addition to buildings, the corporation has power to locate, lay out, construct and maintain roads, avenues, parks, playgrounds, recreational facilities, sewers, bridges, walls, utilities and incidental improvements in connection with housing projects.

The corporation may equip, furnish, operate, manage and maintain homes and buildings of every nature.

Subject to the approval of the Public Works Administrator or other authorized representatives of the United States the corporation may borrow or otherwise raise money.

The corporation will cooperate in the performance of any of its functions with any private, public or governmental agencies to the end of public benefit.

It is contemplated that all funds with which the corporation will carry out its program will be furnished by the PWA.

In his statement, Mr. Ickes said that on three - or four projects already approved "the land covered with old houses has cost less than $1 per square foot."

He said that elsewhere in the metropolitan areas a higher price would have to be paid, but he denied that the government would pay some of the higher prices proposed in some of our largest cities.

Outlining policy, Mr. Ickes said:

"The formation of this corporation is the outgrowth of our recent experiences in the PWA in attempting to increase building labor employment in the field of low-cost housing. Our experience of the last three months indicates clearly that we may not depend upon private enterprise or limited dividend corporations to indicate comprehensive low-cost housing and slum clearance projects.

"The future financial stability of many of our urban centres depends upon the prompt reclamation of their slum areas. The director of the housing division of the PWA proposes during the next few months to promote a better understanding of the serious nature of housing condition in some twenty cities. In this connection he will make a personal nation-wide survey.

"Relatively few of our cities realize that bad housing has a direct effect on their revenues. To meet this situation more is required than isolated action on the part of individuals. Movements to better conditions must be launched by a body of citizens who realize that action must eventually be guided by a State, county or municipal authority.

"The efforts of the administrator and the corporation will be to encourage the creation of such authorities. Where the municipality lacks or cannot immediately obtain the necessary charter powers it is proposed to proceed along one or the other of the following courses:

"(1)—Through some local group the immediate study of the local situation, including the necessary investigation of available low-cost slum land, will be encouraged. Therefore, the acquisition of the necessary land would be by private contract if possible, otherwise by eminent domain, which power is derived from the National Recovery Act.

"The success of this program depends upon the acquisition of low-cost land in continuous blocks which will involve the destruction of slums. A single clearance and rehousing operation may involv the acquisition of other low-co land than that cleared so as to r duce further land cost per unit an better distribution of the new lo cost housing in respect to industri improvement.

"On three or four projects slum clearance already approved b the Administrator, the land covere with old houses has cost less tha $1 per square foot. Elsewhere metropolitan areas more will hav to be paid, but none will be a proved on such high-price land a has been proposed for certai projects in some of our large cities.

"It is not proposed to standardiz improvements; they will be desig ed to meet needs of each partic lar city. If apartments be used they will be confined to low-typ structures. The building of sky scrapers will not be resorted t under any circumstances.

"(2)—To make available to th State Legislatures information o which they may act to create hous ing authorities in cities or countie so that such authorities may co operate with the government o may act as its agent in the man agement of the properties whe completed.

"(3)—To develop a procedur which will aid a city to work ou a long-term plan on which to con tinue the process which the Fed eral Government has started Eventually each State or large met ropolitan area should have a agency empowered to engage in th rehabilitation of low-cost residenc areas. Through such a body th Federal Government could continu its help and eventually, in a lesse and lesser degree, aid what mus become a local function of govern ment.

"This scheme of Federal ai should produce housing at rental which have never before been at tained. The assignment of thes accommodations to families of lo income must be closely guarded b the organization of agencies in city to control their use so tha those for whom they are built wi really benefit. The housing thu provided will not be competitiv with existing housing of good char acter."

October 29, 193

LEHMAN HAILS LAW TO CLEAR UP SLUMS

Signs Mandelbaum Bill at Once So That Work May Start 'Without Delay.'

ACTION IS BEGUN HERE

Special to THE NEW YORK TIMES.

ALBANY, Jan. 31. — Governor Lehman today signed the Mandelbaum Bill authorizing the creation of municipal housing authorities. The measure provides for setting up authorities of five members in cities, and as it became law the LaGuardia administration began plans for immediate creation of such an authority in New York City to start a program for large-scale slum clearance and low-cost housing, with the aid of $25,000,000 to be allocated by the Federal Government.

The authority will have power to issue bonds to finance housing projects or to finance them with Federal aid and the credit of the city will not be pledged.

In signing the measure Governor Lehman issued a memorandum in which he said:

"I am very happy to give my executive approval to this bill, which provides for the establishment of municipal housing authorities to undertake low-cost housing and slum clearance. For a long time I have advocated such a measure.

Housing Leaders at Signing.

"This bill will give to the cities of the State an opportunity to initiate a permanent program of rehousing within the means of those who are now obliged to live under conditions which are a menace to health, welfare and morals, and moreover to collaborate with the national program of industrial recovery by stimulating production and spreading employment.

"I am informed that the Federal Government has already allocated many millions of dollars for projects in New York. So that work may be started without delay, I am approving this bill at once.

"Low-cost housing and slum clearance through municipal housing authorities is a pioneering program. There is relatively little experience to serve as a guide.

"This measure should not be considered as perfect or final in its provisions. Undoubtedly as more experience is accumulated and more study is given to the housing problem it will become advisable to amend this law from time to time."

Among those present were Senator Samuel Mandelbaum, sponsor of the measure; Mrs. Mary K. Simkhovitch, president of the National Public Housing Conference; Mrs. Herbert Miller of the League of Mothers Clubs, Miss Helen Alfred, secretary of the National Public Housing Conference, and Ira Robbins, its counsel.

Seeks Limit on Pay Assignment.

The Legislature held only very brief sessions today, practically completing the legislative work for the week. Some committees held meetings and a start was made toward a preliminary clean-up of the vast mass of measures referred to them since the opening of the session.

Assemblyman Lipton, Republican of the Bronx, announced that he would introduce a bill to amend the personal property law relating to future assignments of salaries. Under the bill future salaries assigned to secure the purchase price of goods might be assigned only up to 10 per cent. Only one such assignment would be satisfied at one time.

"This bill," said Mr. Lipton, "will

enable wage earners to purchase goods and, as in the past, use their salaries as security for payment, but only to the extent of 10 per cent, so that the family of the wage earner will not be deprived of the weekly or monthly stipend."

2,268 Begin Work on Plans.

With the announcement that the Municipal Housing Bill had been signed by Governor Lehman, the local Civil Works Administration yesterday moved into action 2,268 heretofore unemployed architects, engineers, draftsmen, surveyors, research workers, clerks and others who will take part in a survey of 1,200 blocks in eleven selected slum areas of the city, in preparation for the projects to be developed under the bill.

Detailed charts of the affected areas have already been prepared and prospective field workers had opportunity to familiarize themselves with the territories in which they would work. This preliminary organization has been under the immediate supervision of Major Malcolm Kilduff, staff architect of the CWA here.

"It will be difficult for those not familiar with the purposes of the new legislation to picture the changes that will take place within the coming year," Major Kilduff said.

"Both the people and the city will gain immensely from this undertaking. Hundreds of families will be able to have modernized, comfortable living quarters at a minimum rental and the city authorities will rid themselves of sections that for years have been breeding places of poverty, crime and sickness.

"Moreover, the surveys which we are to make contemplate not only the building of homes, but the building of schools and libraries, and the provision of transportation facilities as well."

The State Temporary Emergency Relief Administration and the State Civil Works Administration yesterday moved their offices from the State Labor Building, 124 East 28th Street, to new quarters at 79 Madison Avenue. The move was necessitated by the recent expansion in work and staff when the State relief administration was made agent in New York State for the Federal Works Administration and other Federal relief activities.

February 1, 1934

Housing Bill Signed, Lumber Prices Cut; Early Building Revival Is Predicted

Special to THE NEW YORK TIMES.

WASHINGTON, June 28.—President Roosevelt signed the housing measure today designed to encourage the expenditure of $3,000,000,000 on the construction or renovation of homes. Simultaneously the National Retail Lumber Dealers Association announced a 10 per cent reduction in the price of lumber and building material, and General Johnson ordered a revision of the "model mark-up" in the Retail Lumber Code to make possible reductions to consumers.

Railroad rates and labor costs, the President indicated also will have to be lowered to carry forward his plan to rejuvenate the building industry.

The NRA "model mark-up" is the percentage which the retail lumber dealer must add to his invoice cost for the expenses of administration, handling and storage. The average for the whole country has been 41 per cent, with a mark-up of 45 per cent in New York City. The average mark-up under the new order is 29 per cent, under 34 per cent for New York City.

The Housing Act makes possible loans of $1,000,000,000 by banks, building and loan associations, and other lending agencies for repairs and renovations with a guarantee of 20 per cent by the government.

It also provides for the insurance up to $1,000,000,000 of mortgages on new homes, provided that they do not exceed $16,000 nor 80 per cent of the value of the property. The President may raise both of these billion-dollar limits at his discretion.

The act also makes possible the exchange of existing short-term mortgages on homes for twenty-year guaranteed, amortized mortgages.

The Lumber Association expects an immediate surge of building as soon as the machinery of administering the Housing Act gets into operation.

June 29, 1934

TUGWELL TO SPEND $6,000,000 ON 'CITY'

'Satellite' Community Near Bound Brook, N. J., Planned to House 3,000 Persons.

OPTIONS ARE BEING SOUGHT

Special to THE NEW YORK TIMES.

WASHINGTON, Nov. 2.—At least $6,000,000 will be spent by Rexford G. Tugwell's Resettlement Administration in constructing the proposed "satellite" city just thirty minutes from Times Square in the "greenbelt" district at Bound Brook, N. J.

That a suburban low-cost housing project would be constructed at Bound Brook was announced by Mr. Tugwell's aides yesterday, but the magnitude of the undertaking was not revealed until today. If plans were executed successfully, more than 3,000 persons would be able to find cheap quarters only half an hour from the heart of New York, officials declared.

This "greenbelt" low-cost housing project, one of four to be undertaken by the Resettlement Administration at a total cost of $31,000,000, is intended by Mr. Tugwell to set a new standard for suburban housing in the New York metropolitan area and to encourage a population trend away from crowded city slums.

When completed, the "satellite" city will be a virtually self-sustained entity, provided with convenient shops and educational facilities. It would provide dwellings largely for persons from Newark, Jersey City, and a smaller number from New York, officials declared, the size of the New York contingent depending upon the number of applications.

Options Now Being Obtained.

There was a reluctance on the part of those directing the project to make known the precise plans. Options were now being obtained on the land required for the project, they said, and the amount of land which can be obtained would determine the exact size of the project. Several thousand New Jersey relief workers will be employed on the project.

Mr. Tugwell's low-cost housing program differs from Secretary Ickes's PWA slum clearance program chiefly in that it is predicated upon the proposition that people should be carried out of the slums, whereas Mr. Ickes would rehabilitate the slum districts themselves.

Meanwhile, approval of a $435,000 PWA low-rent housing project for Enid, Okla., was announced today by Secretary Ickes, who made known, coincidentally, that seven limited-dividend low-cost housing projects financed by PWA have been completed and will receive their first tenants early in 1936.

Secretary Ickes declared officially today that most of the forty-nine PWA slum-clearance projects being developed in thirty-five cities would be operated at the start by the government, but that where local public housing authorities existed "consideration will be given to operating the project through these bodies, probably through a lease agreement."

Mr. Ickes said that he had instructed PWA housing officials to work out detailed plans under either method of procedure.

"Careful consideration was given to this problem," the Secretary said. "Three general approaches seemed possible—either to operate through agreements with local public housing authorities, to operate projects directly by the Federal Government, or to engage private agencies to operate the developments under contract.

"Study developed that it would not legally be possible to engage private agencies under contract to operate government property. That method, therefore, has been discarded, and the developments will be managed either directly by the Federal Government, or through local public housing authorities contingent upon execution of a satisfactory agreement between the local body and the Federal Government.

"Conditions under which the projects will be operated through local authorities or directly by the government will be determined in the near future."

November 3, 1935

GOVERNMENT DROPS HOUSING LAND FIGHT

Suddenly Asks and Obtains Dismissal of Louisville and Detroit Condemnation Cases.

REST OF PWA PLAN GOES ON

But Action Is Seen as Transfer to Local Units of Responsibility on Slum Sites.

Special to THE NEW YORK TIMES.

WASHINGTON, March 5.—A sudden decision by the government to transfer to States and municipalities the responsibility for acquiring land for slum clearance and low-cost housing projects became apparent today when the Department of Justice, without previous warning, obtained a Supreme Court dismissal of two condemnation cases arising in Louisville and Detroit.

The reversal of policy by the administration in the $527,000,000 program is regarded as a victory for Peter Grimm, special assistant to Secretary Morgenthau. Mr. Grimm, coordinator of Federal housing activities, had urged that the question be left to the cities, while Secretary Ickes, Public Works Administrator, had insisted that the government should proceed to condemn land under its power of eminent domain.

Complete secrecy surrounded the government's plans until Solicitor General Reed appeared in the Supreme Court and asked for dismissal of the two cases.

"Let them be dismissed," Chief Justice Hughes said.

Secretary Ickes said later that his first information of the plan to ask dismissal came after the court had answered Mr. Reed's request.

Argument Had Been Due Today.

The Louisville case, in which the government was appealing, was to have been argued tomorrow. It involved condemnation of four city blocks for a $1,618,000 project, but two lower courts had held that the government lacked the power necessary for the purpose intended. The Detroit case had also been appealed by the government after rebuffs in lower tribunals.

In a formal statement, the Department of Justice explained that even if the Supreme Court had ruled in favor of the government, neither of the projects could have been completed because the money originally intended for purchase of the lands had been diverted to other projects not in litigation.

Therefore, the department continued, "it was concluded that it would not be proper to submit for decision cases which, as a practical matter, had become moot."

Reasons for the dismissal, however, went much further than the department indicated. Public works officials conceded that the step indicated that the government would strongly support Senator Wagner's bill for aiding municipalities to construct such housing projects, the cities themselves to acquire the property and carry on construction with the help of Federal funds.

The officials also stated that the cost to the government under the new plan would be relatively small, probably about $12,000,000.

Housing Can Go Ahead, Says Ickes.

"We can go right ahead with a slum clearance program giving municipalities the right to condemn the land," said Mr. Ickes, when he heard of the Supreme Court dismissal. "We shall not try to condemn any land through the Federal Government."

According to Mr. Ickes, twenty-two States and the cities of New York, Chicago, Buffalo and Cleveland now have housing authorities empowered to build housing projects and purchase land for them through condemnation.

While the broad purpose to let the cities handle the basic problem lay behind the government's change of front, some observers asserted that the administration might have feared defeat at the hands of the Supreme Court, where it has won only two cases out of eight New Deal issues. Attorneys opposing the government had stressed arguments that low-cost housing and slum clearance were not really objects of public purpose and thus were not within the power of condemnation under the eminent domain right, that the projects were actually a matter for the police power of the States, and that the renting of buildings and the selling of houses made the government a proprietary landlord in competition with private enterprise.

The Government Arguments.

On the other hand, the government had insisted that it could use eminent domain to take property whenever necessary or appropriate to do so in executing any powers granted to it by the Constitution. Declaring the power sought was essential to its program, the government had argued itself as justified under the general welfare clause of the Constitution, since Congress had held that low-cost housing and slum clearance would promote the general welfare.

Although the Louisville and Detroit projects have been shelved, the rest of the vast Federal plan now under way will go ahead, PWA officials stated. Louisville and Detroit alone were subjects of litigation. The Department of Justice said that in forty-one projects land had been obtained by negotiation and that in eight others it had been obtained partly by condemnation, the only question being the amount of compensation.

March 6, 1936

WAGNER URGES DUAL HOUSING PLAN

A Program to Enlist Both Private and Public Funds Is Advocated as the Solution of a National Problem

By ROBERT F. WAGNER,
Senator From New York.

WASHINGTON, Feb. 29.—In 1933 our new economic program was defensive in temper because the country was on the run. Today it is everywhere apparent that confidence has been bestirred and recovery inspired. The task confronting us has therefore become quite different from what it was in 1933. Instead of merely protecting and conserving, we should seek affirmatively to expand our prosperity prospects.

This critical shift in emphasis must be recognized if we are to place the housing program in its proper setting. Three years ago our housing activities were framed in terms of the immediate objectives of perilous times. Evictions had to be stopped. Dilapidated homes had to be repaired. Investors in real estate had to receive some assurance of realization upon their risks. The industries surrounding the home, as the backbone of our economic system, had to be protected from breaking.

Now the time has come to put flesh upon the framework that we have preserved. In place of saving old homes, we must build new ones. Rather than refinancing old investments, we must develop profitable areas for the operation of new capital.

While many phases of our economic endeavor have already experienced this transformation, the retardment in residential construction is still acute. In 1926, which may fairly be regarded as a normal year, the money lent to build homes for not more than four families each amounted to $2,311,000,000. In 1935, even after two years of general revival, such loans totaled only $280,000,000. During the past year the index of residential construction as a whole trailed at 22 per cent of normal.

"Serious Consequences."

This comparative inactivity is fraught with the most serious consequences for the whole nation. Its effects are clearly written upon the careworn countenances of more than 4,000,000 building tradesmen who are jobless because their normal source of employment is stagnant. And such a source, if flowing freely, would also possess limitless capability of supplying work for thousands of other men who are being stricken constantly by technological unemployment.

Aside from its immediate consequences in shrinking employment opportunities, the housing lag carries foreboding implications for the welfare of all business. Between 1928 and 1929 it was a drop of 33 per cent in the index of residential construction that presaged the depression. The first stages of recovery in 1933 and early 1934, brought on by increasing the purchasing power of the worker and the farmer, were spotty and sporadic because the building trades did not proceed apace. Our industrial history proves conclusively that economic progress may be short-circuited at any moment unless the basic heavy industries are kept alive and active.

The Home Shortage.

The truly vital significance of the housing lag, however, is to be found in a most natural quarter. It is to be found in the shortage of decent homes. Even in 1929, we must recall, the people of this country were inadequately sheltered; statistics indicated that, while one-half of the population had modest incomes, only one-third were comfortably housed. Superimposed upon this so-called "normal" shortage we now have the results of the depression. In 257 cities the number of families provided with new housing dropped from an annual average of 362,000 for the nine-year period beginning with 1921 to 43,000 for the four-year span commencing with 1930. By 1934 only 25,000 new family dwellings per year were being provided.

It is small wonder that at present there are about 10,000,000 families, composing more than one-third of our population, who live in homes that may be injurious to their health and menacing to their safety and morals. These shabby abodes, far from being localized or predominantly urban, disfigure the entire national landscape. They have become a country-wide responsibility.

Slums and Crime.

The true measure of this responsibility can be sensed only by reading the miserable legacy of the slums. Carefully gathered statistics have revealed that in the dark and cold tenement rooms where the sun's rays are unknown, three out of every four babies are afflicted with rickets, the danger of contracting tuberculosis is thirty times intensified, and the infant mortality rate is three times as high as among the well-to-do.

The handmaiden of poverty and disease is crime. In the worst slum regions of Manhattan, the number of arrests per thousand people is two and one-half times as great as in non-slum areas, while women are caught in the clutches of the law four times as frequently. There it is also true that the rate of juvenile delinquency is four times greater than in other sections of the city.

With smug satisfaction we have prided ourselves upon our network of children's courts and reformatories. Until we get nearer to the causes of juvenile delinquency, the supply of these agencies will never equal the demand. It is a hopeless task to attempt to uproot a bitterness that society has implanted in the hearts of the young by its own reckless abandon.

Intimately linked to these humane considerations are the economic aspects of bad housing. A study of a large representative city shows that the per capita cost to society of fire hazards, juvenile delinquency, disease, poor-relief and insanity is seven times as great in the slums as in other areas. In addition there are heavy losses in industrial efficiency when men and women are driven to work weakened in body and spirit, and thus made easy prey to industrial disease and accidents.

HOUSING ADVOCATE

Underwood & Underwood.
Senator Robert F. Wagner.

Finally, we must not neglect to consider the practical undermining of democratic principles and practices when so many of our citizens feel themselves denied the basic opportunities for living free lives.

Advantages of a Program.

These manifold considerations mark out only the minimum of what may be attended to by a large-scale building program. Such a program would blend the most cherished objectives of all those groups to whom recovery has been more a phrase than a reality. It would absorb the major portion of both chronic and technological unemployment in substantial projects that would present unparalleled opportunities for legitimate profits by private industry. It would unite the efforts of industry and labor in a campaign to better the living conditions of the people of the United States.

The release toward this end of approximately $65,000,000,000, almost entirely in private capital, over the next ten years would prove a boon to every calling. It would place our national prosperity on the sound foundation of a healthy condition in the durable-goods industries.

An undertaking of this scope, which must embrace not only slum clearance and low-rent housing, but also the development of better homes for people of moderate means and the replacement of obsolescence of all types, is too big a job for any government.

Work of Private Builders.

There are sizable indications today that industry is rising to meet this responsibility. In thirty-seven States the volume of home building increased from $249,000,000 in 1934 to $479,000,000 in 1935, a gain of 92 per cent; and of this progress over 90 per cent was accomplished by individual initiative.

To the extent that private industry can provide these underprivileged groups with the type of housing that will give them a fair chance to enjoy health and at least a modicum of comfort, well and good. But it has been demonstrated with the conclusiveness of a simple sum in mathematics that most of these people are not able to purchase decent housing. If we admit that every industrious human being is entitled to the protection of his health, we must acknowledge the public responsibility to make up the difference between what the very poor can afford to pay and what is necessary to shelter them properly.

"Competition Not Intended."

This is the whole essence of low-rent housing. It is not designed to compete with private industry any more than the Public Health Service was created to destroy voluntary hospitals. It is intended to cover only that field which industry cannot cover, to serve only those whose low incomes would not permit them to be customers for adequate housing elsewhere.

It is with these fundamentals in mind that I am sponsoring Federal housing legislation, and if public discussion is maintained on this level, I am sure that the measure will be enacted by the present Congress. At that consummation another happy step will have been taken toward assuring further business recovery and toward removing horrible handicaps from the lives of millions of our people.

March 1, 1936

HOUSING BILL SENT TO THE PRESIDENT

Special to THE NEW YORK TIMES.

WASHINGTON, Aug. 21.—The Wagner-Steagall low-cost housing bill was sent to the White House today after both Houses of Congress adopted a conference report which represented concessions by each to give the nation a start toward clearing out its slums.

The Senate adopted the conference report after Senator Walsh had explained it, but some House members who objected to the compromise on the civil service provisions fought for half an hour before the big stick was wielded. Then the House adopted the report on a standing vote, 128 to 48, the opponents being unable to force a roll call.

Representative Fuller of Arkansas led the fight to remove the conference provision on civil service. The Senate had provided that employes of the Housing Authority be engaged under civil service regulations, but the House adhered to its oft-repeated stand against strict classification. The conferees recommended that employes drawing less than $1,980 a year be engaged under the Classification Act, and provided that officers drawing more than $7,500 a year should be subject to confirmation by the Senate.

"They are trying to ram this down our throats," Mr. Fuller said. "It's an insult to 95 per cent of the members of this House who have consistently fought against letting a few people say who are going to get all the jobs."

Republicans Vote Passage

Republicans, many of whom voted against the bill two days ago because it lacked the civil service provisions, joined with their colleague on the conference committee, Representative Walcott of Michigan, to pass the measure. The majority of the votes cast against the report today were those of Democrats.

As finally sent to the White House, the bill provided for the creation of the United States Housing Authority, a corporate body, under the Secretary of the Interior. The powers will be rested in a single administrator. The Senate originally voted for an administrator and two authority members, the House for an administrator and advisory board of nine.

The authority receives a capital of $1,000,000 and is authorized to sell $500,000,000 in bonds, the principal and interest of which is guaranteed by the United States.

Out of this fund, the Authority may lend to public housing groups and make grants for the purpose of financing low-cost housing for families of the lowest incomes. Two methods of administration of the loan provisions are authorized.

In the first, the Authority may lend up to 90 per cent of the cost of the low-cost housing project, the local community contributing 10 per cent. These loans may be made for a period not to exceed sixty years. Originally, the Senate bill provided for full 100 per cent loans by the Authority, but the House cut this to 85 per cent, and the conferees compromised on 90 per cent.

The other method is called "capital grants." The Authority may make an outright grant of 25 per cent to the local group, and the President may allot out of relief funds an additional grant of 15 per cent, to be applied to payment of labor on the projects. If a local community can qualify for this type of loan, it must contribute 20 per cent of the total cost of the project. In that event, the Authority would lend 40 per cent of the total.

"Going Rate" Basis of Loans

In all loans, the rate provided is the "going rate" of Federal interest, plus one-half of 1 per cent. The Federal rate now is 2½ per cent, which would make the interest for loans 3 per cent for at least the first year or so.

The Authority will make annual contributions in the form of subsidies to local public housing groups to assist in achieving and maintaining low rents. The amount cannot exceed 3½ per cent of the total cost of such projects, and such income to the groups must first be applied toward payment of interest to the Authority.

The local group must agree, as a condition to obtaining a subsidy, to demolish in the same area as many slum units as are replaced by new buildings.

These contributions cannot exceed $5,000,000 the first year, nor more than $7,500,000 for each of the next two years.

The bill directs the authority to sell or lease all projects constructed, it being the intent of Congress to decentralize the authority's activities as soon as projects are completed.

No State may receive more than 10 per cent of the total amount available for loans, grants or subsidies.

The bill limits the availability of low-rent units to families whose total incomes do not exceed five times the rental, and in cases of families having three or more minor dependents, to six times the annual rental.

The Authority is prohibited from lending on projects where the cost per room is more than $1,000 or where the family-unit cost exceeds $4,000. It was provided, however, that in cities of more than 500,000 population the cost could run to $1,250 a room or $5,000 for a family. The cost of land and demolition of slums was excluded from the cost of the project, so far as the limitation on construction costs was concerned.

No provision is made for the authority to acquire property by condemnation, it being presumed that the local authorities sponsoring such projects shall have been endowed with the power to acquire through rights of eminent domain, or by purchase or donation, property upon which to erect units.

It was provided that any contract for a loan may contain a condition requiring the maintenance of open spaces or playgrounds where deemed necessary for the safety or health of children.

August 22, 1937

NEW HOME COMMUNITIES THE AIM IN FHA DRIVE

By DELBERT CLARK

WASHINGTON, Dec. 25.—When the new housing law goes on the statute books next month. there will stand ready to administer it a compact, businesslike organization which already, in less than three years, has done nearly two billion dollars' worth of business, business intimately related to the familiar processes of building financing and construction, yet at the same time pioneering in a field unexplored three years ago.

The Federal Housing Administration was created to administer the National Housing Act. It was a new venture in Federal government. It was not to compete with private enterprise, but to assist it. The only private enterprise with which it might be expected to compete was that which subsisted on high rates of interest on home mortgages. Its function was, in brief, to stimulate private construction of dwellings by insuring mortgages at a reasonable cost.

A week ago the FHA had done a gross business of $1,978,947,960, of which about $630,000,000 was transacted during the first eleven months of this year. It had insured 258,066 mortgages, with a value of more than a billion dollars. More than half of this total nad been handled from January to November.

Operating Cost Low

The total operating cost of this giant enterprise during the approximately three years of its existence has amounted to a little over thirty-two millions, or about 1.6 per cent of the gross business.

The principle on which FHA was founded was simple enough. Housing construction had virtually reached a standstill. with a tremendous shortage developing all over the country. If this huge but amorphous industry could be prodded into activity, it would create a large amount of employment, and at the same time provide homes for the nation.

To accomplish this the Federal Government, through FHA, contracted to insure 80 per cent of the value of a home building mortgage within certain cost limits, and with the proviso that the interest rate be below a fixed ceiling.

At the same time, and for a limited period, it agreed to help finance. in similar fashion, modernization and repairs of occupied dwellings. The government itself made no loans. disbursed no funds, except for general operating costs. Banks and other agencies made the loans. and the FHA guaranteed repayment.

Many Jobs Created

The operation of this program, measured in visible employment. amounts to the equivalent of one year's work for more than 200,000 men. In invisible employment—materials, transportation and the like—that figure is multiplied. In housing stimulated by the program but not actually part of it it is multiplied still further.

But insuring private mortgages was not enough. It became apparent at the outset that the FHA must keep a careful and constant check on the work done under its sponsorship in order to assure, first, the construction of dwellings that would still be habitable when the twenty-year mortgage expired, and, second, the construction of dwellings that would be well planned, within the means of their purchasers, and suitable to their environment.

This led to the development of an elaborate and businesslike mechanism of inspection. When an application for insurance of a construction loan is received an appraiser has a look at the site to determine suitable location for the type of dwelling projected. Then the architect's plans are gone over, the credit rating of the borrower investigated. the estimated cost of the structure studied.

Inspection Continues

Once construction has begun, the inspection continues. When the excavation is completed, the FHA man looks it over; when the rough framing is up, he is on the job again, and finally, when the structure is completed, including grading, he gives it a final inspection.

In the case of large-scale developments, the FHA maintains an architectural inspector on the ground at all times. Materials and construction must come up to certain standards or the mortgage is not insured.

All over the country, in villages and in cities, the FHA inspectors are seeing to it that no jerry-built dwellings are erected under the sponsorship of the government, that, indeed, standards of material and construction are elevated from previous minima. The private housing of this decade, officials believe, should represent a decided improvement over that of previous years as a result of this attention to quality-plus cost.

It is, of course, the big developments that catch the public eye and are definitely identified with the FHA. In consequence these are supervised with particular care, since they present a different set of problems from the one-family dwelling.

Many of them are rental propositions, and care is taken that they are desirable for the income groups they are intended to attract; that convenience as well as soundness is a feature of the construction, and that there is plenty of light and air.

With all this, the building industry continues to lag, and the housing shortage is not nearly eliminated. To meet this continuing emergency both houses of Congress, in the last three days of the extra session, passed a bill to extend and liberalize the terms of the National Housing Act. It did not become law because the Senate considerably amended the House bill, and a conference will be necessary to iron out the differences.

The bill as it stands revives Title I of the law permitting insurance of modernization mortgages. It permits insurance of 90 per cent of mortgages up to a certain total, with 80 per cent of the balance. It contains various other sections considerably liberalizing the present law, and it remains a law for the person of small or moderate income. But the Senate bill takes in farm property as well, and permits a twenty-five-year mortgage instead of the present twenty-year limit.

"Prevailing Wage" Proviso

And it also contains what some consider a mortal blow to the whole program—a proviso that the "prevailing wage" in each locality must be paid on work undertaken under the act. Critics of this provision, inserted by Senator Lodge of Massachusetts, just before he voted against the bill, say it nullifies the theory of moderate cost and low financing charges as a stimulant to home construction. They fervently hope that it will be eliminated before final enactment.

While the FHA looks for renewed activity in the building of individual private homes under the liberalized law, it is greatly interested in the provision for increased encouragement of large-scale rental projects. This, they say, is the crying need, since more than 50 per cent of the population lives in rented quarters.

What they hope to see, then, is a really significant upsurge in construction by large syndicates, of whole communities of apartments and individual houses for rent. Such operations to date have constituted only about 3 per cent of the mortgages insured. Pushing them up to a considerably larger proportion of the whole is the real job the FHA now sees before it.

December 26, 1937

FIRST FAMILY AND THEIR FIRST MEAL

A government photo of its initial tenants in a Maryland housing project undertaken to provide both work and new homes.

Private Capital Needed for Building

Removal of FHA Restrictions on Rents Is Regarded as Essential to Broadening of Housing Plans

TO THE EDITOR OF THE NEW YORK TIMES:

It seems fairly clear by now that the anticipated wave of residential construction has failed to materialize. In spite of sharply increasing demand and unprecedented government intervention, the wheels of the industry, for some obscure reason, obstinately refuse to revolve. Opinions differ widely as to the cause, but there is no difference of opinion as to the result. Recovery is being retarded if not checkmated.

We were not overbuilt in 1929, when residential construction ceased, to all intents and purposes. Since then urban population has continued to rise; marriages have increased the number of families; the ravages of time have forced the elimination of thousands of marginal dwelling units. Only a fraction of that number has been replaced by new construction: from 1930 to 1937 only 180,000 units a year, on an average, compared with 800,000 a year between 1923 and 1930. Consequently, we now face a housing shortage which competent authorities estimate at 3,000,000 to 5,500,000 dwelling units.

We all know how much the expansion of residential construction in 1920-1921 contributed to the swift revival from the early post-war depression and to the subsequent era of prosperity. There is no doubt that a similar pick-up today, even on a much smaller scale, would help immensely to pull us out of the present situation.

Federal Agencies

In an attempt to end the stagnation of the building industry, the Administration has set up two Federal agencies. The Federal Housing Administration insures private loans in connection with new dwellings, and thus facilitates financing and marketing, while the United States Housing Authority finances non-competitive low-rent housing by lending directly to local public agencies. FHA may also insure loans on low-rent housing projects approved by USHA. Congress has provided adequate funds and conferred adequate powers on both. The Administration is relying chiefly upon them to prime construction and the related industries, and the President has recommended the appropriation of an additional $300,000,000 for slum clearance undertakings.

In previous depressions construction turned upward only when substantial private operations began. Such operations were invariably financed by institutional loans. Funds for residential construction at all times have been provided principally by the great capital pools represented by institutional lenders. Eighty per cent of the mortgages on residential buildings were owned by life insurance companies, savings banks, building and loan associations and similar institutions. The post-war building boom was possible because these institutions were willing and able to make the necessary building funds available to borrowers, and borrowers found it advisable to build and borrow because the operation gave reasonable assurance of being more profitable than investment in existing buildings.

Money Not Available

Today building operations would clearly be profitable, but in spite of that the necessary financing is not available. The flow of construction loans, interrupted since 1930, remains interrupted, and neither the increasing liquidity of the lending institutions nor the steadily rising demand for dwellings has attracted capital back into building. Until private capital in normal volume enters the construction field directly, or, failing this, until government capital in equivalent volume replaces the deficient private investment in that field, no general upturn in business can reasonably be anticipated. If the two government housing agencies succeed in attracting these private funds, this will be accomplished.

The FHA and the USHA operate upon entirely different principles. The FHA tries to attract private funds by insuring lenders on an actuarial basis against loss of principal. While government credit stands behind the guarantee, government capital is not actually employed to any very significant extent. The USHA, on the other hand, operates with government capital, and private lenders may cooperate with the program only by the roundabout method of purchasing what are practically government obligations.

Purely Business

FHA is a business proposition. It has none of the philanthropic implications which inform the operations of the HOLC or the USHA. It is not constituted to aid the widow or the orphan, the home owner or the slum tenant. The government here acts in its purest proprietary capacity, in the interest of recovery, and exacts a premium from the borrower which is calculated to absorb all probable losses.

Hence the inappropriateness of restrictions on commercial large-scale projects designed to assure that only the "deserving" shall participate in the plan. Here the FHA was intended to stimulate construction, not to provide low-rent housing. Why, therefore, does it hedge about its multi-family insurance scheme with the requirement that profits must be limited to 6 or 8 per cent and that rents must not exceed a stated maximum? Why does it undertake to limit the salaries which the entrepreneur may take from his operation? Why does it prescribe a multitude of rules, regulations and procedures affecting the profit to be derived by the entrepreneur, all of which has nothing to do with the payment of the charges upon the loan or with its security?

Is it the function of FHA to restrict the law of competition? Is there a social purpose in charging a monthly rental of $19 per room rather than $21? Is it an unspoken premise that profits at the going rate are somehow immoral? This policy assumes, in effect, that builders are willing to take all the risks of ownership for a yield of 8 per cent or less, while existing buildings can be purchased to yield twice and three times that. Perhaps builders should. Unfortunately, they will not. If any projects at all are undertaken under these drastic restrictions we must assume that most of them will be monuments to legal ingenuity and financial legerdemain.

The past experiences of the PWA and the State Housing Board with limited dividend applications amply prove the point. If the multi-family provisions are to do more than remain on paper, the limitations on rentals, dividends and profits must, as a practical matter, be abandoned for commercial undertakings. In this way private equity investment will be stimulated. But more than that, the elimination of the rent restriction limitation would remove the danger of competition with existing buildings rented at higher figures. It would put the lenders in a friendlier frame of mind, since most of them with loans on old buildings are reluctant to make new loans, even if insured, on buildings which would compete with the investments they already hold.

Loans at 3 Per Cent

In the case of the USHA I am able to state that lending institutions stand ready to make an initial advance of $250,000,000 or more to local housing authorities. They are willing to make these loans at 3½ per cent interest, for a period of thirty years or more, if secured by first mortgages insured by FHA amounting to 50 per cent or more of the project cost.

Under this arrangement the USHA, instead of lending 90 per cent of project cost, as permitted under the United States Housing Act of 1937, would be called upon to advance only 50 per cent at most. Thus the same amount of Federal financing would make it possible to build about twice the volume of housing with only a slight increase in the annual subsidy or the room rental; and the gainful employment of private funds would do much to promote recovery. Arrangements could be made to preclude any possibility of the projects falling into private hands, and, since FHA would insure the senior mortgage and USHA would hold the junior mortgage, and both these agencies are part of the same Federal Government, there would seem to be no reason for the insistence upon the Federal Government making the whole loan.

Besides this, it would remove one of the greatest difficulties—the requirement that local housing agencies put up 10 per cent of the loan, which many are at present unable to do. Private financing of local housing agencies and the marketing of their bonds is an essential factor for the future, since no one can logically claim that large-scale housing programs can be continuously financed solely through government appropriations and without private funds. Furthermore, private financing, if initiated now on a relatively modest scale and increased in volume later on, would tend to reduce the danger of political pressure against a benevolent government for rent reductions which, while of possible benefit to some tenants, would set back much of the progress so far achieved in the public housing movement.

This private financing would produce under the present appropriation as many low-rent dwellings as could be obtained with the additional $300,000,000 requested by the President. If the $300,000,000 were appropriated it could be made to produce about $600,000,000 in low-rent housing construction.

Well Managed

Both the FHA and the USHA are ably and efficiently managed, but they have operated under a great handicap—the absence of an administrative policy, fixed from above, dictating their relations between themselves and with private capital. If FHA would insure private loans on low-rent housing projects approved by USHA, and USHA would undertake to stimulate private loans to local housing authorities with FHA guarantees, advancing only part of the necessary funds instead of making a 90 per cent loan, a large pool of stagnant capital would be released into low-rent housing operations. If FHA would remove its restrictions on dividends and rents, which have a place only in non-commercial, public undertakings such as low-rent housing, much more commercial housing would be built.

It is essential that in both cases the function of private lending and of private enterprise should be defined and prescribed; that the social be distinguished from the purely actuarial, and that where, in the accomplishment of the social purpose private funds may be drawn in in place of Federal funds, a policy should be devised which would encourage it. In the absence of this definition one is unwarranted in the charge that capital has declared a "strike," at least in this field, it being more accurate to say that governmental policies have made it difficult for capital to function where it is possible for it to do so.

CHARLES ABRAMS.

New York, May 10, 1938.

May 16, 1938

SEARCH FOR A HOUSING POLICY

PRESIDENT SETS UP HOUSING DIVISION

Moves to Coordinate All the Construction for Defense—Charles Palmer at Helm

By FRANK L. KLUCKHOHN
Special to THE NEW YORK TIMES.

POUGHKEEPSIE, N. Y., Jan. 12—President Roosevelt today created by Executive Order a new Division of Defense Housing Coordination with broad powers in a move to assure efficient, adequate and speedy construction in connection with the rearmament and military training programs. He appointed Charles Palmer, who has been housing expert of the National Defense Advisory Commission, as its chief with a salary of $9,000 a year.

The President acted under his limited-emergency proclamation in establishing the new housing organization, which apparently will have powers in its own field equal to those in other defense work of the recently created Office for Production Management, the defense super-council. Mr. Roosevelt made the director, who will have the title Coordinator of Defense Housing, responsible to him only.

At the same time the President made public a letter he had written to Michael Harris of the C. I. O.'s Steel Workers Organizing Committee, praising him for calling off as "unwarranted" a recent strike in the Berwick (Pa.) plant of the American Car and Foundry Company, which has defense contracts. Mr. Roosevelt said he was "even more gratified" to learn that the men had offered to make up without overtime pay eight hours' work lost through the strike. He termed this "in keeping with my request that parties to labor disputes should, during these days, prevent stoppages of work and production."

Duties of Housing Division

The President gave the Division of Defense Housing Coordination power over "all executive departments and independent agencies (engaged in housing activities), including corporations in which the United States owns all or a majority of the stock, either directly or indirectly." These would include not only entities like the Federal Housing Authority and the United States Housing Authority, but Army and Navy agencies involved in building cantonments.

Among the duties outlined for the new division were these:

1. To facilitate "proper coordination of, and economy and efficiency in, the provision of housing facilities essential to national defense."

2. To anticipate housing needs "in localities in which people are engaged, or are to be engaged, in national defense activities, analyze reported defense needs and facilitate the full use of existing housing accommodations."

3. To formulate and recommend to the President "coordinated defense housing projects with the objective of avoiding shortages, delays, duplication and overlapping."

4. To review existing and proposed legislation and recommend such additional legislation "as may be deemed necessary or desirable."

The President issued a set of regulations requiring each government housing agency to furnish the coordinators with copies of its available housing surveys and reports and, for his review and recommendations, the standards for housing which each has established for the development, operation and management of defense housing.

Like the OPM, the new DDHC is established for legal reasons within the Office for Emergency Management of the Executive Office.

Mr. Roosevelt's letter on labor to Mr. Harris read as follows:

"The Secretary of Labor has told me the story of the recent stoppage of work at the plant of the American Car and Foundry Company at Berwick, where materials destined for the defense of the United States are in production.

"I was gratified to learn that you considered the strike as unwarranted under the circumstances; that you immediately recommended and the men agreed to go back to work the next day. This action on the part of you and the employes was in keeping with my request of Dec. 29, that parties to labor disputes should, during these days, prevent stoppages of work and production.

"I was even more gratified to learn that as evidence of good faith the men had also volunteered to make up eight hours' production work without overtime pay in order to make up for any production loss because of the ill-advised walkout.

"I hope you will take occasion to assure the men in this plant of my gratification on this patriotic action."

Roberto Arias, nephew of President Arnulfo Arias of Panama and son of former President Harmodio Arias, was a luncheon guest of the Roosevelts today. Mr. Arias was invited by Mrs. James Roosevelt, the President's mother, according to White House aides.

January 13, 1941

WPB Halts Non-Essential Building; Homes, Highways, Utilities Curbed

By CHARLES E. EGAN
Special to THE NEW YORK TIMES.

WASHINGTON, April 8—The government called a halt today to non-essential building through an order requiring governmental sanction for construction projects whether publicly or privately financed. The order put in jeopardy construction projects which are partly completed, by specifying that such building might be stopped if materials to be used in such projects could be put to more effective use in the war program.

The order, issued by the Division of Industry Operations of the War Production Board, had been forecast by Donald M. Nelson, board chairman, yesterday, at a press conference.

No residential construction, except for maintenance and repair work, may be started without permission if its estimated cost is $500 or more, the order provides. Similarly, no new agricultural construction may be started if the estimated cost is $1,000 or more for the particular building or project involved.

No other construction, including commercial, industrial, recreational, institutional, highway, roadway, sub-surface and utilities construction, whether publicly or privately financed, may be begun without permission if the cost of the project amounts to $5,000 or more.

The figures shown are the limit allowed to be spent in any twelve-month period without previous authorization from WPB.

Effective immediately, the order, known as Conservation Order L-41, prohibits unauthorized construction projects which use material and equipment needed in the war effort. It also places all new publicly and privately financed construction under rigid control, except for certain strictly limited categories.

Official estimates concerning the amount of construction which would be affected by the new order ranged between $2,000,000,000 and $3,000,000,000. The Federal officials said the amount of building falling under the definition of defense construction and of building essential to public safety and health would approach $13,000,000,000 this year.

WPB's action was taken today, officials said, because the war requirements of the United States had created a shortage of materials for war production and construction. It was in the national interest, the board stated, that "all construction which is not essential, directly or indirectly, to the successful prosecution of the war, and which involves the use of labor, material or equipment urgently needed in the war effort, be deferred for the duration of the emergency."

It was added that many of the same materials, such as iron, steel and copper, were used in both essential and non-essential construction, and that the same materials were largely used for war production. Since, it was stated, there were not enough commodities to cover essential and non-essential use, the order, in effect, would allocate these materials away from unnecessary construction and into ships, planes, tanks, guns, defense housing and other essential production.

Exempt Types of Construction

Specific types of construction made exempt by the provisions of the order include:

1. Projects which will be the property of the Army, Navy, Coast Guard, Maritime Commission and certain other listed agencies of the Federal Government.

2. Projects to reconstruct or restore residential property damaged or destroyed on or after Jan. 1, 1942, by fire, flood, tornado, earthquake or the public enemy.

3. Projects of the type restricted or controlled by provisions of the orders of the M-68 series, which cover the production and distribution of petroleum.

Officials emphasized that their order did not affect ordinary maintenance and repair work to return a structure to sound working condition without a change of design.

Consideration, they said, was being given to a plan for devising an emblem which could be issued to authorized projects and be displayed conspicuously on any construction job to show that it had been approved by WPB.

FHA Will Aid the Program

Facilities of the Federal Housing Administration have been made available to the WPB in the administration of this order and applications for authority to start construction will be filed with the local offices of the Federal Housing Administration on forms which may be obtained at any of the district WPB offices or at any local office of the FHA. The public is urged to file only emergency applications during the next month, as it is expected that authorization will be given only for emergency projects.

Authority to begin construction will be granted only when the design and specifications conform with the standards established for the minimum use of critical materials, and no materials will be used on a project which do not conform with those allowed under the authorization.

On the basis of criteria established by the Director of Industry Operations of the WPB, the local officer of the FHA will decide whether the project is eligible for recommendation to the WPB. If the project is deemed eligible, the application will be forwarded by the FHA to the administrator of the order for final consideration.

If the application is denied by the local FHA office, based on the WPB criteria, provision is made for an appeal to an appeals board to consist of the administrator of the order, a representative of labor and a third member who will represent the branch of the WPB within whose jurisdiction the class of project or construction would fall.

April 9, 1942

LACK OF HOUSING IN WAR CENTERS SHOWN IN SURVEY

Work on Temporary Low-Rent Homes Speeded in Busy Defense Districts

REALTY DEMAND HIGHER

Detroit and Portland, Ore., Among Cities Reporting Critical Situation

A critical shortage in living quarters for defense workers in many of the leading war production centers, ready sale of existing homes, increases in rents and a general upturn in the real estate market were shown in reports received yesterday by THE NEW YORK TIMES on conditions in key cities throughout the nation.

While Federal agencies, and in some cases private industry, have tried to meet the sudden demand for more low-rent homes, continued expansion of employment in industries associated with the war effort has kept the need steadily above the supply.

As a result furnished rooms, trailers, temporary and makeshift homes have had to be utilized, and the prospect of still further expansion of the production facilities has brought predictions that by the end of the year the situation will be even more complicated.

The survey gave an indication of the reasons the OPA has seen fit to designate territory in which two-thirds of the nation's families, or about 86,000,000 persons, as defense housing zones in which rents will be stabilized to check profiteering and bring some semblance of order out of the upheaval in population.

Crowded Conditions Cited

Shipbuilding centers such as Portland, Ore., and Seattle; steel production centers like Pittsburgh and Birmingham, and automotive and airplane industrial areas such as Detroit and Hartford, Conn., all report the same story—crowded conditions which threaten to hamper war output or already have done so, and frantic efforts on the part of government agencies to meet the problem.

Conditions in Portland and in Detroit appear to be a greater problem than in most cities. At Portland large units of temporary housing have been started in an effort to provide living quarters as quickly as possible. In Detroit the authorities are wrestling with the problem of transportation to plants as well as the more direct problem of housing. In Atlanta and some other communities difficulties have arisen out of the switch-over from the work of constructing new plant facilities to the actual operation of these facilities.

New York City has not felt the pinch, except for minor difficulties in Staten Island housing, but the situation there has not become acute because many of the workers are able to commute from neighboring points in the city and in New Jersey. Up-State, however, more serious problems have arisen, particularly around Schenectady and Watertown.

The summaries below present an up-to-the-minute picture of the situation in typical production centers.

RENTS STIR HARTFORD

Special to THE NEW YORK TIMES.

HARTFORD, May 2—Real estate activity is seasonally normal, according to the majority of the leading real estate dealers in this vicinity. Some of them are surprised at present conditions, however, because they feel that war production in Hartford County, stiff priorities and extensive governmental defense building should already have seriously affected property transactions.

Within the past few days priorities have had their effect, and at least one large single-family housing development has been suspended for the duration. Many owners, probably because of war dislocations, are seeking to sell their homes in and around Hartford. Many men and women are looking for special residential requirements, something different and better than can be obtained in the defense housing projects, which incidentally are strictly for defense workers.

More than two years ago Hartford established a housing authority and erected a number of low-rental units in various parts of the city. Later New Britain, Manchester, East Hartford, West Hartford and other near-by towns created local authorities, and all of these, together with Wethersfield, Glastonbury and Rocky Hill either have or shortly will have their housing developments ready. Restrictions on tires and gasoline will soon act to compel thousands of defense workers traveling long distances to their employment (some of them at present commuting fifty miles each way to towns in Massachusetts) to live nearer their jobs.

Two months ago Price Administrator Leon Henderson defined the Hartford-New Britain section, with most of the towns in Hartford County, as a defense area for the purposes of rent control and gave the various voluntary rent-control committees sixty days to achieve rent stabilization. Nothing like rent control resulted, and it is now generally expected that the administrator early this month will name a State administrator of rent prices. He will promptly receive more than 150 cases of alleged rent extortion which the Hartford Fair Rent Committee has been unable to solve. As war-production factories continue to enroll more and more workers the housing situation continues serious, despite efforts by the Federal Government to erect additional units, but there have been no intolerable conditions.

PHILADELPHIA HOMES TAKEN

Special to THE NEW YORK TIMES.

PHILADELPHIA, May 2—The current real estate situation in Philadelphia and its environs remains remarkably good and promises to become better if Congress approves the new Title VI amendment to the National Housing Act, authorizing an additional $500,000,000 mortgage insurance of war housing built by private operators.

The Home Builders Association of Philadelphia and Suburbs says passage of the amendment would release plans for work on at least 7,500 home and apartment units in this area.

There is great activity in projects started before the war and now nearing completion, and in the sale and renovation of old properties. Many large old homes are being made over into three, four and five-unit apartment houses commanding good rentals.

The market far exceeds the supply in rentals. The sharp influx of new families attracted here by war industries has absorbed virtually everything available for rent, and new and renovated properties placed on the market are almost always taken within a few days.

OLD BOSTON HOMES SOLD

Special to THE NEW YORK TIMES.

BOSTON, May 2—Recent restrictions in building construction in favor of more homes for war workers have had considerable influence in persuading the average family to buy a home in this area, brokers and real estate agents pointed out.

Because most of Coastal New England is virtually one huge war production area, the influx of workers into this region is beginning to create a serious housing problem.

Many brokers feel that the next few months will witness considerable activity, not only to increase the number of new homes for workers but also in the sale of older homes.

There has been little rise, if any, in residential rents in the Boston area.

A factor increasingly felt in real estate is the reduction in the use of private automobiles. Locations heretofore considered good may suddenly become less attractive, and nearness to public transportation lines and other facilities has developed into an important advantage.

REMODELING IN PITTSBURGH

Special to THE NEW YORK TIMES.

PITTSBURGH, May 2—Although the first three months of the year showed a continued increase in activity, real estate sales shown by deeds record have fallen off in Pittsburgh and Allegheny County.

There were 1,391 "consideration" transfers totaling $6,487,794 in Allegheny County in February as compared with 1,156 consideration transfers and $4,743,164 total consideration in February, 1941, according to the Real Estate Statistical Service.

A number of builders are building in the $6,000 defense housing bracket, and several new developments catering to this price class have sprung up. Several of the low-cost developments are in the South Hills district, long an important factor in realty development in the Pittsburgh area.

The Build for Victory Committee, a voluntary group cooperating with government agencies, has set a goal of 4,000 or more units to rent for $50 per month or less to be provided by conversion of existing properties. Property owners are being given expert assistance in obtaining estimates and priorities for remodeling.

RICHMOND FEARS SHORTAGE

Special to THE NEW YORK TIMES.

RICHMOND, Va., May 2—With the promise of an influx of 14,000 war workers to seek employment in the plant of the James River Shipbuilding Corporation, now under construction in South Richmond, public officials, real estate operators and builders are moving to prevent a serious housing shortage in this city and vicinity.

In an effort to co-ordinate these activities, Mayor Gordon B. Ambler has appointed a Defense Housing Commission, which is now in communication with the Washington authorities to assure adequate rental units for the new workers.

"Unless something is done and done promptly," said William Shands Meacham, chairman of the Richmond Housing Authority, "persons coming to Richmond between now and Jan. 1 will find themselves without shelter."

Gilpin Court, a 301-unit apartment project now being erected by the Housing Authority, already has been assigned to the exclusive use of Negro workers, who are expected to represent about 25 per cent of those employed at the ship yards. The shortage of Negro rental property already has become acute.

The backwash of persons attracted to Richmond by the prospect of war jobs in the Hampton Roads and Petersburg areas already has taxed low-priced housing facilities here to the utmost. Henry Raab, president of the Richmond Real Estate Exchange, said that while there is no shortage yet of the better class of rental properties, neither is there a surplus. "There is going to be a serious shortage of rental property for the laboring man," declared Mr. Raab, "unless the Federal authorities act swiftly to authorize a large amount of public construction."

BIRMINGHAM IN UPHEAVAL

Special to THE NEW YORK TIMES.

BIRMINGHAM, Ala., May 2—This "Pittsburgh of the South" with its blast furnaces and steel mills running full tilt twenty-four hours a day, is undergoing a curious upheaval in real estate due to the change from construction to operational phases of defense industries located from twenty to forty miles from the city.

While prices of homes and real estate built two or three years ago have risen 5 to 10 per cent, particularly in the so-called industrial areas of the city, prices on newly constructed homes have skyrocketed sharply, due to the increase in price of materials and labor. Transactions are brisk but dealers deny anything like a boom.

It is in the rental field where the chief upheaval is taking place. Reaching a peak last September, when 20,000 workers were employed on defense works at Childersburg, Ala., forty miles from Birmingham, with several other thousands engaged at and near Anniston at shell-casing factories, this city was besieged with applications for homes and apartments by transient construction workers.

As the construction workers leave, and the operational staff takes over the plants, there is beginning to be a surplus of houses and apartments here as the permanent workers try to obtain homes nearer their work and as the migratory workers leave.

Apartment buildings still are filled and have waiting lists, but private homes converted into housekeeping apartments are beginning to find the demand slackening and with many an owner wondering where he will find the income source to pay for the alterations and repairs made to convert his home to use by two or more families.

CHICAGO DRAWS BUREAUS

Special to THE NEW YORK TIMES.

CHICAGO, May 2—A survey of real estate trends in Cook County, which embraces the Chicago metropolitan area, showed a sales total of $43,974,653 in March, a gain of 94.60 per cent over the corresponding month of 1941. The number of sales, 9,468, however, showed a decline of 6.97 per cent.

The report, issued by Irvin Jacobs & Co., stressed as noteworthy that the dollar amount of encumbrances was 17.43 per cent less than a year ago and that the total value of building permits increased 99.82 per cent.

According to the survey there exists great uncertainty about the new mortgage business available in this territory. It is possible, the report adds, that the volume of mortgage business will be sharply curtailed for some time to come.

Favorable factors are seen in an increase to 85 per cent in the occupancy of office buildings and a high percentage of occupancy for residential properties. The increase in use of office space is due to the transfer about to be made to Chicago of a number of government agencies.

About 10,000 housing units, exclusive of rooms, are available in the Greater Chicago area, according to the Chicago Real Estate Board, which estimates that about 50,000 rooms are awaiting occupants.

Rents last month, the board stated, were off about .2 per cent from last month. May 1 was expected to show a slight rise. Rent increases during the past year, according to the board, averaged 5.6 per cent.

MINNEAPOLIS SUBURBS BUSY

Special to THE NEW YORK TIMES.

MINNEAPOLIS, May 2—Plans for future building construction took a hard blow in Minneapolis when the WPB freezing order came through, despite the fact the city has been classified as a defense area.

For the past year, with influx of defense workers into four large defense plants—those of the New Brighton Ordnance, Northern Pump, Minneapolis Moline and Minneapolis Honeywell Regulator Company—the ring of hammer and saw could be heard in every block.

That was true not only in the city but in the rapidly expanding suburbs. Building permits within the city proper totaled $10,919,265 last year, the highest since 1929. In St. Louis Park the sum was $2,722,475; in Richfield, $1,730,000, and in Robbinsdale, $620,991.

Building of small homes for defense workers is proceeding at a lively clip. Houses and lots are still changing hands briskly and prices remain up in the lower class field. In St. Louis Park, in particular, which adjoins Minneapolis on the west, you can see, any day, a dozen houses within two blocks under construction.

KANSAS CITY RENTS UP

Special to THE NEW YORK TIMES.

KANSAS CITY, Mo., May 2—New and expanded war industry and military establishments in the Greater Kansas City area have been accompanied by a pick-up in real estate activity and building, particularly in the residential field.

Private builders erected more than 2,500 dwellings in the metropolitan area here in 1941, the greatest number in more than a decade and 50 per cent more than in 1940.

Thus far this year 464 units have been started, 17 per cent more than a year ago. Most of the houses have been in the lower-price range qualifying for title VI of the F. H. A. In additio a 350-unit government defense project is nearing completion in Kansas City, Kan.

The housing situation in Kansas City, a year ago a "high-vacancy" city, is generally considered tight but not yet critical. The transfer of 1,000 employes of the farm credit administration to Kansas City next month and further war expansion already announced may create a scarcity. Rents are up generally to 15 per cent over a year ago, in some instances as much as 35 per cent.

ATLANTA HOUSING AMPLE

Special to THE NEW YORK TIMES.

ATLANTA, May 2—Although both residential and business vacancies in Atlanta are fewer than at any time since the last war, no immediate housing shortage is in prospect and rental costs have turned only slightly upward within the last year and a half.

J. M. Garner, president of the Atlanta Real Estate Board, estimates roughly that only 1½ per cent of residential properties are unoccupied and that, barring unforseen developments, adequate facilities are available to accommodate prospective defense families for at least a year.

When operations of the huge Bell Aircraft bomber plant get underway near here next Spring, however, Mr. Garner said the expected influx of a large per cent of 40,000 prospective workers may create a housing problem unless more building is undertaken. Slightly more than $2,000,000 in private defense housing projects are either under construction or contemplated at the present time. Real estate activity in general here for the first quarter of 1942 showed a considerable decrease as compared with the corresponding period of last year. Fulton County (Atlanta) transfers were down $930,116.55; mortgage and loan deeds decreased $91,431.50; mortgage and loan deeds cancellations were up $696,490.50; building permits fell $1,079,333.

DETROIT IN NEED OF HOUSING

Special to THE NEW YORK TIMES.

DETROIT, May 2—Under the impetus of Detroit's war industry and the influx of thousands of workers, this city finds itself in the midst of a seller's market as far as real estate is concerned.

This applies in the sales and rental divisions of industrial and residential property and in new construction.

In the latter field, there is a

constant demand for so-called low-cost housing in the $6,000 field from war plant workers. This is true not only in the city proper, but also in the suburban areas where many of the new plants are being located.

New projects are announced every few days, some of them up to 1,000 units. Private builders report they have been allocated 30,000 small homes, well above the normal, and they say they expect a tremendous spurt with the adoption by Congress of the FHA amendment to Title VI increasing the limit of mortgage insurance for rental housing.

Dealers report an increasing demand and sale of existing homes in the price ranges exceeding $6,000. There is a definite shortage of this type, however, and dealers are soliciting listings.

A steady rental demand for private homes well in excess of the available supply is reported. This condition has been of recent development. Predictions of a housing shortage in Detroit, made by competent observers more than a year ago, have become fact.

As a result, owners of large single family houses and flats are being urged to convert into smaller units to rent under $50, a field in which the demand is heaviest. Apartments, in which rents have shown a steady upward trend for several months, report few vacancies.

Some relief is in the making, the result of a recent allocation of 18,000 home units under Federal financing in the new Ford Motor Company bomber plant area. Other Federal housing projects in the Detroit area are comparatively small and at best would help take care of only normal requirements.

Unlike some cities, the Detroit rental market it not seasonal, and present demands cannot be attributed to anything but increased industrial activity. Detroit is accustomed to a rental, rather than to a lease basis, so the ordinary turnover is staggered throughout the year instead of rising to peaks in the Spring and Fall.

CLEVELAND ENJOYING BOOM

Special to The New York Times.

CLEVELAND, May 2—Greater Cleveland is enjoying its biggest building boom in fourteen years, despite the recent War Production Board order limiting civilian construction.

Housing shortages in several Cleveland suburbs, particularly Garfield Heights and Euclid, resulted in an expanded building program last Fall and hundreds of units either have been completed or will be finished by early Summer. Contracts for 217 new homes were signed in the last two weeks.

Three large housing groups that will furnish living accommodations for hundreds of war workers also are under way, but officials believe there will be a shortage by next Fall unless additional homes and apartments are constructed, especially in the suburbs where industrial plants are expanding and speeding up production.

Marked decreases in the number of rooms and houses to rent in the advertising columns of newspapers herald a coming shortage of living quarters, according to members of the housing commission.

"The WPB is making surveys on the actual occupancy of war homes built under priorities," J. L. Wadsworth, FHA director here, said. "Chiselers will get caught. With WPB in the saddle I would hate to get caught trying to dodge rules governing use of critical materials."

RENT PROBLEM IN ST. LOUIS

Special to The New York Times.

ST. LOUIS, Mo., May 2—The housing shortage here is critical, and is getting worse due to ever-increasing war population. The last war survey, in October, 1941, showed a vacancy rate of 2 per cent, and a "habitable" vacancy rate of 1.5 per cent. A new survey, just started, will probably show a rate of less than 1 per cent.

Rents have been increasing. The FHA has just sold the city's second largest multiple housing project, 354-unit Manhasseh Village, to a private corporation headed by a real estate man, with only $20,000 as down payment. The same day the deed was filed a 10 per cent increase in rentals was announced. Citizens have been grumbling, holding mass meetings and writing indignant letters to editors and government officials, crying for OPA rent ceiling, which has now been ordered. The St. Louis Real Estate Exchange has asked all members to sign pledges not to "gouge or profiteer." City Hall and County Court House records indicate realty transfers are up to or above normal.

BUY NEW ORLEANS REALTY

Special to The New York Times.

NEW ORLEANS, May 2—The residential market is firm to strong here. Investment properties and single-family homes up to $6,000 are in greatest demand, with prices generally 5 to 10 per cent above a year ago.

Industrial and commercial properties are moving, usually for expansion purposes. Office building space is being satisfactorily absorbed, some of it being taken by Federal agencies. Retail store property activity is spotty, due in many cases to the inability of owners to get priorities for remodeling.

Commercial and industrial leasing is in good volume. Some new commercial building is being noted apart from government contracts, but there is no inflationary trend.

The housing situation is uncertain at the moment. A Federal survey is being conducted to determine the areas best adapted for an estimated 20,000 new homes for war-industry employés, the locations to be fixed with regard to industry sites and minimum extension of utilities, the latter being the local bottleneck.

New Orleans will need some of these homes within ninety days, and, with exception of the extremely low rental bracket which probably will take the form of Federal temporary housing, all can be built by private capital. Applications for slum clearance units here, numbering about 5,000, no longer are being received because of length of waiting lists.

The estimated residential vacancy rate is one-half of 1 per cent, including the highest rental brackets and substandard housing, as against 2 per cent a year ago. Rentals under $20 and above $50 are available, but others are difficult to find. The price trend is upward, from as high as 33 per cent increase for units renting under $20, to 10 and 15 per cent for those bringing between $25 to $40, and from 5 per cent down above $40 monthly. Furnished rentals, where available, are at a premium.

DALLAS HOMES IN DEMAND

Special to The New York Times.

DALLAS, Texas, May 2—Real estate sales have shown a gain in recent weeks in Dallas and other sections of the Southwest, as wartime building restrictions have begun to be felt.

Demand has been noted for duplex homes and apartment houses, farm land and small store buildings, buyers evidently seeking this type of property as a hedge against inflation. Residential purchases have increased as the result of restrictions on building materials.

Outlying defense areas of Dallas where important war plants are located, are enjoying booms from construction of many housing projects. The same is true in other parts of the State where war industries are in operation.

Desirable rental property is in brisk demand in Dallas. Rents have edged upward, but not as much as was expected.

The stoppage of construction of the better type of dwellings is expected to cause an increasing demand for existing residences of this type both for purchase and rent. Completion of defense housing projects is relieving the rent price situation in some sections.

HOUSTON GETS FHA HOUSING

Special to The New York Times.

HOUSTON, Texas, May 2—The War Production Board's orders have stopped practically all building in Houston of a non-defense nature. During the week of April 19 the city issued permits for eighteen alteration and repair jobs costing $6,000 and seven new structures costing $12,250.

The $18,250 building total for the week was one of the lowest in the past fifteen or twenty years.

Last year permits for $19,218,676 worth of new construction and alterations within the city limits were issued. The total so far this year is $4,883,660, the highest of any Texas city. Fort Worth is second with $4,543,674.

There is a shortage of housing quarters for defense workers in and outside of the defense area in the eastern part of the city and the county, but the situation is not acute, Walter Millis, secretary of the Houston Rea Estate Board, reported. The shortage will be partially relieved by the completion of two FHA Title VI housing projects, one of about 350 homes and the other of about sixty homes in the Galena Park Defense area. These projects are well advanced.

There is a fair percentage of vacancies in duplexes and apartments in the South End, Houston's fashionable residential area, and in other strictly residential sections, Mr. Millis said. The price of rents has shown a slight drop from last year's figures.

Real estate brokerage business continues good, particularly in the sale of old homes.

SEATTLE HOUSING TAKEN

Special to The New York Times.

SEATTLE, May 2—Residential realty prices are strong here, with the demand up sharply due to an acute shortage of rental properties. The supply of homes for sale is narrowing steadily as owners cling to their holdings for lack of better homes to buy.

The demand is especially strong along established transportation lines. Prices in near-by suburban communities also are up as buyers are moving outside of the city searching for living quarters.

Residential building is in fair volume on commitments issued before FHA Title VI limit on rental housing mortgage insurance was reached. Several group-housing projects up to 200 units each were suspended or are now being processed pending extension of the loan-insurance limit by Congress. Private industry expects to build 3,000 or more units in the remaining months of this year. The rental situation is bad, with the Defense Housing Commission reporting 2,500 applications for shelter and no supply. Every type of accommodation, including tourist camps, is showing capacity occupancy.

Little apartment construction is evident, the emphasis being on single-family and duplex types. Similar conditions prevail generally in Tacoma, the Bremerton Navy Yard section and at Renton, site of the new Boeing plant, and other war industries.

Commercial property is active, the feature now being hotels of Japanese evacuees in which trading is extraordinarily heavy. Occupancy of large space in several office and specialty buildings by the Army also is contributing to big volume of rentals, generally at good lease rates. Some industrial property sales have been noted, stemming from expansion of war industries.

BUILD IN SAN FRANCISCO

Special to The New York Times.

SAN FRANCISCO, May 2—Current real estate activity in the San Francisco Bay area is largely in defense housing and in central income properties.

The East Bay area in particular, stretching from Lower Alameda northward to industrial Richmond with its mushrooming shipyards, is struggling with an acute housing problem as it faces the prospect of a population increase estimated as high as 40,000 this year.

The Oakland Real Estate Board estimates that housing vacancies in the East Bay section amount to less than one-fourth of 1 per cent. The San Francisco situation is somewhat confusing, with the real estate board here estimating that 7,500 standard units are vacant out of a total of 232,000 housing units in the city.

Land values in San Francisco have always been considered relatively high, with the result that builders of defense housing have gone into other areas to put up small dwellings to sell at $3,850 and upward. Thus, in shipbuilding centers like Vallejo and Richmond building permits in March were higher than for March, 1941, although the figure for the Far West as a whole took a sharp drop.

Despite the establishment of large trailer camps and the provision of much temporary housing, surveys have shown that some workers are required to travel by automobile or bus sixty miles to their jobs every day.

LOS ANGELES ADDS HOMES

Special to THE NEW YORK TIMES.

LOS ANGELES, May 2—Real estate activity in the Southern California area is high despite the war emergency. This has been due in large measure to a steady influx of defense workers, increased earnings and a growing demand reflected in brisk purchases and rentals.

A recent poll showed that seventy-two Southern California localities authorized new construction amounting to $54,240,566 in the first quarter of 1942. Los Angeles proper, with $21,763,709, was more than $2,000,000 ahead of the same period in 1941.

One reason for the fairly adequate supply of housing in Los Angeles and vicinity has been the advance construction of many medium-sized homes, now available for use of defense workers.

Los Angeles has for several years led the nation in the number of building permits issued.

It is believed that new impetus will be given to construction in this territory by national legislation authorizing $500,000,000 additional FHA mortgage insurance on defense housing built by private interests.

Although thousands of workers and those seeking jobs from the East, South and Middle West flocked to Southern California in recent months there thus far has been no actual house shortage or rent skyrocketing in this particular area.

Rents in apartment houses have risen from time to time but it is still possible to obtain a good furnished living unit in a nice neighborhood at between $32.50 and $40 monthly. Unfurnished flats and houses range from $25 to $75 depending on location.

Few large new apartments are being built but the development of tracts and small bungalows and courts continues active.

GETS TEMPORARY HOUSING

Special to THE NEW YORK TIMES.

PORTLAND, Ore., May 2—Expansion of shipbuilding, aluminum, chemical and kindred industries has brought to the Portland area a severe housing problem and a fast-moving residential market.

With an estimated 50,000 newly employed men now at work in shipbuilding and other war industries, the total is expected to reach 100,000 or more by Fall when the Kaiser interests' new yards at Swan Island here and at Vancouver, Wash., across the Columbia River get into full production.

New developments have brought here a half dozen major chemical plants, an Aluminum Company of America ingot plant at Vancouver and an Alcoa aluminum fabrication mill, ship engine manufacturing and airplane parts plants—all further complicated by broad Army and Navy projects whose details cannot be revealed.

The city's homes registration office has appealed for an immediate listing of all dwelling vacancies. A Postoffice survey indicates Portland's residential vacancy approximates one-half of 1 per cent. Home prices are estimated to have advanced an average of 15 to 20 per cent and home rentals from 10 to 15 per cent.

As a result, under Federal funds the Portland Housing Authority has underway a 400-unit project, has obtained approval for 3,100 temporary units, and has applied for 4,500 more units of which 600 would be permanent. The Authority also hopes that private enterprise, meantime, will build 2,000.

Across the Columbia, the Vancouver Housing Authority has under way 5,000 units of Federal housing, including 4,000 demountable and 1,000 permanent, and has applied for 5,000 more.

Dormitories to house 2,000 men near the Kaiser shipyard have also been started. Private construction is expected to contribute 200 more. Kaiser officials have estimated Vancouver will need 12,000 homes to meet its housing problem.

May 3, 1942

U.S. CITY DWELLERS PUT HOUSING FIRST

Survey by Princeton Bureau Shows They Consider It Chief Urban Problem

WANT LOW-RENT HOMES

Transportation Difficulties and Traffic Congestion Are Next in Their Consideration

Special to THE NEW YORK TIMES.

PRINCETON, N. J., Oct. 24—Making public the results of the first nation-wide public opinion survey of American cities and city planning, the Bureau of Urban Research of Princeton University revealed today that most American city dwellers considered the lack of good, low-priced housing to be the outstanding municipal problem of the day. The survey covered a cross-section of the adult white population by the sampling method.

Transportation difficulties and traffic congestion, local wartime conditions, the lack of employment opportunities and the inadequacy or dishonesty of city governments are next in order of importance in the minds of the people who live in cities, according to the report.

The bureau said that the majority of city dwellers believed that city governments should replace the poorest housing with better homes even at the cost of higher taxes for all.

Better streets and street facilities, repair and modernization of homes and buildings, greater neighborhood cleanliness, removal or reconstruction of empty or run-down buildings, and more municipal parks and playgrounds were urged in reply to questions as to what could be done to make cities better places to live in.

The survey reported that twice as many city dwellers desired to own their own homes as were owners now, because they believed home ownership meant security, personal independence, pride of possession and good family environment.

According to the bureau, most city dwellers want to stay where they are, but one-third would like to move, 24 per cent within the same city and 8 per cent to another city. One out of every ten urban residents would like to go to the suburbs, and an equal number would go there if they had to move.

More persons exercise their voting rights and want to remain where they are, the report said, when they are satisfied with their environment and live under favorable conditions.

Declaring that one reason many city plans have been filed and forgotten is that "their technical development has been from the top down rather than from the people up," the report added:

"Although there is a growing acknowledgment of the serious maladjustments confronting American municipalities and a gathering momentum for urban improvement during the post-war era, the vital role of the people is being too largely ignored. Plans are being discussed, studied and framed which involve the fortunes of large segments of the urban population; yet little has been done to discover what people think and want with respect to their own communities. In a democratic nation, plans for city reorganization can be neither realistic nor democratic unless they are based on a foundation of public opinion which accepts the purposes of these efforts and approves the general methods of accomplishment. The alternative is excessive governmental control—paternalistic or arbitrary."

October 25, 1942

1,100,000 Housing Units Started For War Workers Since July, 1940

More than 1,100,000 new housing units for war workers have been started since the beginning of the defense program in July, 1940, National Housing Administrator John B. Blandford Jr. announced yesterday.

Of this total, 813,000 units have been completed and 309,400 additional units are in varying stages of construction. About 180,000 units were completed and 186,000 others started in the first four months of the present year. Mr. Blandford said that 454,000 of the units completed represent privately financed family dwellings. They include those built under local war housing quotas established by the NHA as well as the estimated number of houses built without priorities' assistance in the earlier period of the emergency, but which are serving war housing needs.

Large Building Program

Under the publicly financed phase of the program, units completed up to April 30 included 244,964 family units, 92,069 dormitory units and 21,870 trailers. Practically all publicly financed war housing started during recent months involves temporary structures scheduled for dismantling after the war.

On April 30 a total of 231,777 publicly financed units of all types were under construction and between 75,000 and 80,000 more were scheduled to be started.

All war housing thus far started is designed to meet needs resulting from necessary labor migration to war production centers through July 1, 1943. To complete the privately financed portion of this program private builders had 77,600 family units under construction on April 30, while quotas were established and priorities issued or available for about 123,000 additional units.

Cities Future Needs

Over and above this current program, the NHA has recently completed estimates of the amount of additional war housing which will be required to meet needs resulting from the continued in-migration of war labor during the twelve months beginning July 1, 1943. Forecasts by the War Manpower Commission indicate that about 1,100,000 war workers will migrate to war production areas during that period.

The NHA estimates that these workers can be accommodated in 940,000 dwelling units, considering that some families will have more than one worker.

It also figures that more than 600,000 of these accommodations can be provided in existing housing without alteration, and that 80,000 family units can be supplied through privately financed or publicly financed conversion of existing structures.

Under the proposed program, approximately 250,000 units of new construction will be necessary. These will include 90,000 privately financed family dwellings, 90,000 temporary family units financed by government funds, and 70,000 accommodations for single persons in publicly financed dormitories.

June 6, 1943

Thousands of homes for new war workers are being erected in Virginia by New York builders. Above is view of one of several apartment projects in Norfolk, built by Fred Trump of Brooklyn and James Rosati, contractor. The same builders are engaged on a similar construction job at Chester, Pa.

Metropolitan's Housing Plans Lift Investment to $200,000,000

Insurance Company to Double Outlay in This Field Immediately After War, Adding Three Large Projects in Manhattan

By LEE E. COOPER

Taking the leadership among private investors in plans for additional large scale housing projects at medium rents as soon as war restrictions on civilian construction operations are lifted, the Metropolitan Life Insurance Company had laid plans for new residential communities which will virtually double its present investment in this field.

Heading its post-war program are three major projects for Manhattan—one in Harlem and two on the lower East Side—which will clear away more than a score of blocks of outmoded slum buildings. The company's program also embraces enlargement of some of its residential colonies on the West Coast. The land for all of this construction activity already has been acquired and in some instances the plans have been drawn.

This contemplated expansion of the Metropolitan's holdings has been inspired partly by the success of its operations thus far, and partly by the need for finding a suitable outlet for its money in the face of low returns from most investments. The Metropolitan and all other big institutions have a plethora of funds for which they must find a sound "market."

The insurance company's experience with Parkchester, a residential colony occupying 130 acres in the Bronx, and its housing properties in other cities has inspired further similar projects which await release of materials and manpower.

The company now owns housing for about 19,000 families, and for the first time every one of the apartments is occupied.

Parkchester, with an assessed valuation of about $51,000,000, accommodates 12,272 families and more than 35,000 persons. Built for medium-income families, it is reported to have provided steady earnings, even with moderate rentals.

If the company is able to realize a 6 per cent return on its investment after all charges and expenses, including maintenance, repairs, operation and depreciation, it makes a good showing because a 6 per cent return on sound securities is an exception today, instead of being the rule, as in the past.

The Metropolitan, in addition to its original housing projects in Queens, also owns Parkfairfax, built for 1,684 families on a 200-acre park site in Alexandria, Va., near Washington; Parklabrea in Los Angeles, and Parkmerced, in San Francisco. All of these are filled, and many have long waiting lists.

Parklabrea, occupying 173 acres, originally was designed for 2,620 families in low brick buildings of colonial design. The impact of the war led to delays, but the need for additional housing in the busy Los Angeles brought Government authorization for completion of 1,316 suites which were made available during the spring of 1944 and quickly leased. The remainder of the buildings will be constructed after the war.

Parkmerced went through a similar experience. Priorities were obtained for erection of buildings for 1,687 families, on the 200-acre site, and these have been completed and rented. About 850 more family units are to be added later.

All of these projects were created on vacant or unimproved land, but the three big Manhattan residential communities on the company's construction program will mark the end of about 800 antiquated buildings.

Stuyvesant Town, to occupy the eighteen blocks bounded by First Avenue and Avenue C, Fourteenth and Twentieth Streets, represents one of the first major slum clearance undertakings by private capital. It will house 8,800 families in buildings ten to fourteen stories in height, at rents averaging about $14 a room monthly. The buildings, including tenant garages for 3,000 automobiles, will occupy only 25 per cent of the ground area.

Stuyvesant Town will be built under a contract entered into with the city under the terms of the Redevelopment Companies Law of 1943, with the owner's return limited to 6 per cent. The agreement provides for condemnation and partial tax exemption designed to help keep rents down.

Riverton, also planned under the Redevelopment Companies Law, will occupy six blocks in Harlem bounded by 135th and 138th Streets, Fifth Avenue and the Harlem River, now largely used for industrial purposes. Thirteen-story buildings will accommodate 1,250 families at rentals averaging $12.50 a room monthly.

Peter Cooper Village will occupy the blocks bounded by Twentieth and Twenty-second Streets, First Avenue and the East River Drive, immediately to the north of Stuyvesant Town. It will be constructed wholly as a private enterprise, as in the case of Parkchester, Parklabrea, Parkmerced and Parkfairfax, and will have about 2,000 suites in its thirteen-story buildings. Since it will not enjoy the benefits of partial tax exemption, rents, while not yet fixed, will be somewhat higher than in Stuyvesant Town.

March 11, 1945

PRICE RISE HALTS GI HOME BUYING IN 82% OF CITIES

Veterans Also Finding Rental Houses Scarce, National Realty Survey Shows

REPAIRS ARE NEGLECTED

By LEE E. COOPER

The difficulties encountered by returning veterans in finding suitable homes to buy or rent for their families are a source of steadily increasing concern among city officials and realty men.

The recent upswing in prices and the absorption of virtually all rental dwellings have conspired to make it well-nigh impossible for the average ex-service man to set up housekeeping again under favorable conditions.

After a long absence from his family he has rejoined them only to learn that the changed conditions in the market have shattered at least for a time his hope of buying, building or leasing a comfortable house of the type he needs within his income limits.

Service agencies and other organizations attempting to help him out have been stymied, and the comparatively small amount of new construction permitted thus far under Government order has done little to solve the problem.

Promises of the National Housing Agency and the War Production Board to release enough materials for erection of about 250,000 residences by next spring are contingent upon war needs and have not yet been translated into an apreciable addition of private housing.

Meanwhile the supply of lumber, brick, plumbing equipment and some other products remains scanty. The quota of new dwellings under the so-called H-2 program for the entire New York area during the third quarter is only 3,300.

Few Find Homes Available

The recent survey of the National Association of Real Estate Boards in 348 cities emphasizes the extent of this problem. It shows that in 89 per cent of the cities veterans are having great difficulty in finding homes for rent, and that in 82 per cent of the communities those seeking to buy a home are not finding enough offerings available within their price range.

In 81 per cent of the cities, because of restrictions in the GI Bill of Rights, appraisals made of sound, reasonable, "normal" value are not near enough to the present price levels to make this loan aid available to the former service men.

The association argues that "unless high priority is given to the production of new houses, the current shortage will become increasingly critical for returning vet erans."

The realty group also report that rent levels under present cei ings are insufficient to provide fo reasonable maintenance of a hom in 81 per cent of rent-controlle cities, and in 77 per cent of all re porting cities. Wartime restri tions on expenditures and shor ages of labor and materials als are retarding this work, the ass ciation says, with 47 per cent the cities reporting lack of norm care on roofs, about 75 per cent i dicating houses have plumbing a electrical equipment which is b low par, and structural exterio neglected in 68 per cent of th communities.

Another phase of the surve showed that the most common ra of interest on loans covering dow town business properties now is per cent, with rates as high as per cent listed only for cities less than 100,000 population, 3 a 3½ per cent in a few communitie and as much as 8 per cent in som Western cities.

July 15, 194

MANY FACTORS INVOLVED IN THE HOUSING CRISIS

Skyrocketing Costs Blamed for Failure Of Program to Meet Heavy Demand

By LEE E. COOPER

It is now generally agreed that the emergency housing program, launched seventeen months ago from Washington, has failed to achieve its purpose. The housing crisis is just as acute as ever, and even threatens to become more serious.

From New York to San Francisco, from Milwaukee down to New Orleans, the situation is much the same for veterans and non-veterans. About 40 per cent of the men who were in uniform still are living "doubled up" with friends or relatives, or occupying other makeshift quarters; and nearly 25 per cent of all married veterans are without homes of their own.

In the cities apartment houses are bulging with tenants, and most of the limited number of new multi-family buildings will bring rentals beyond the average pocketbook. In the suburbs, builders and buyers alike are going on strike against inflated construction costs of small homes.

Ambitious residential building programs are being curtailed sharply, and a stalemate is developing in the industry in the face of an unprecedented need. Some experts in the business are predicting that if present conditions persist, the housing shortage may continue indefinitely.

In most communities, the $6,000 post-war dwelling contemplated originally for the "average man" has become a myth. Older houses are scarce at twice their pre-war prices. Veterans are growing restive again over their unhappy plight, and Federal housing executives are concerned over the prospect of declining operations. Housing has become a political bogyman.

I—THE PROGRAM

The experts have figured that this country could absorb a million new family units annually for the next decade without difficulty, because of the backlog of demand created during the depression and war years, when normal building operations were at a standstill.

When Wilson W. Wyatt, former Mayor of Louisville, Ky., was appointed National Housing Expediter by President Truman in December, 1945, he set as his goal 1,200,000 new housing units for the first year of his program and at least 1,500,000 for the second year, to give modern living quarters to 2,700,000 families by the end of 1947.

Mr. Wyatt told builders to concentrate on homes in the $6,000 class because the greatest potential demand was at that price level. For 1946 he wanted 700,000 small homes of the conventional type, 250,000 prefabricated structures and 250,000 temporary units. For 1947 his goal was 900,000 conventional residences and 600,000 factory-built units.

To this end building materials were channeled almost exclusively into homes, the price-ceiling program was supported, and Congress allowed subsidies to increase the output of these supplies and for market guarantees to promote factory-built houses.

Home builders, looking back over the records and finding that their peak production was only 935,000 housing units, achieved over twenty years ago when there were no headaches of reconversion, doubted from the start that the Federal goals could be attained.

A New Goal

When Mr. Wyatt resigned last year he was succeeded by Frank R. Creedon, who set a goal of 1,000,000 homes this year under liberalized regulations.

The National Association of Home Builders also took that figure for its aim as the year started, and leading elements in the industry began talking about a $20 billion to $22 billion construction year, with housing getting the big play.

A few months of rising prices have indicated that even the goal of 1,000,000 houses this year was far too optimistic.

It is even possible that no more than 650,000 residences and apartment units may be added to the supply this year. During each of the first three months of 1947 less than 60,000 homes were completed from the carry-over of more than 350,000 dwellings started, but not made available for occupancy last year. During April only 62,000 starts were made. This number was considered surprisingly small for the season of greatest activity.

II—THE PROBLEM

The causes of the buyers' an builders' strike are not hard t find. In housing, and in relate commercial projects, they revolv about skyrocketing costs, and th general feeling that the value not there at current price levels.

The inflated costs involve dozen factors, but the one mo frequently mentioned is highe wage rates coupled with lower pr ductivity and restrictive practice on the part of labor.

Some veterans' organization led by first World War membe recently have charged building m chanics with inefficiency, citin reports of bricklayers restrictin their output to about 400 bricks day instead of 800 or more; and lathers who handle only thirt three or thirty-five bundles dail instead of fifty-five.

One representative of New Yo contractors estimated that lab efficiency was down 30 to 50 p cent from pre-war levels. As a r sult of this condition the Nation Association of Home Builders an the conservative American Inst tute of Architects came out r cently in favor of the open shop the construction field.

Most of the trades—when the work—now are paid at the rate $2.50 an hour, or $100 a week a forty-hour basis, as compare with $2 an hour in most instanc back in 1940; but the bricklaye recently signed with the Buildi Contractors and Mason Builde Association for $2.75 an hour o the basis of a seven-hour day an five-day week.

High Cost of Materials

Another major factor has bee the rapid rise in prices of buildin materials. Under the price-ceilin arrangement which ended last No vember, many key materials wer into the black market at exorb tant quotations. Recently, however, without controls, hardwood (oak) flooring has been selling in New York at about $260 for 1,000 board feet, which is close to the black-market price. In 1939 it could be purchased readily at about $118 or $120.

The builders have been paying $25.50 for 1,000 common brick, which they could buy in 1939 at $13. Wall plaster has been costing $19 a ton, instead of $12. And so it goes down the line, with lumber and millwork reported up more than 100 per cent since 1941, hardware costing 114 per cent more, and screens, window shades and accessories showing a jump of nearly 300 per cent in the last six years.

Because most material manufacturers insisted on escalator clauses in their contracts, and contractors could not be certain what they would pay for supplies—usually it was more than they expected—the contractor has been forced to take jobs on a cost-plus basis or add a "contingency" item to his estimates to cover these uncertainties. Such items usually have added 10 or 15 per cent to the cost of a project.

Uncertainty in deliveries also has been a costly item in nearly all construction operations since the war. Production has expanded sharply in most lines, but shortage in a single material often would force a builder to suspend work temporarily. The time for erection of a little home gradually lengthened under this handicap, until it was taking nine or ten months to put up these homes. In former days three or four months would suffice.

Land costs, too, have about doubled. As a way out, some developers began taking less desirable and less accessible sites.

In view of all these expensive drawbacks, and with about 2,200 small houses on inaccessible and poorly planned plots in the New York area now standing completed but unsold, the number of idle building mechanics has been increasing here, and in many other parts of the country the outlook is dark.

Unemployed Laborers

About one-fifth of the skilled workers in the building trades are reported unemployed in this area, and nationally there is serious question whether the industry can maintain its recent level of on-site employment at close to 1,200,000 workers.

Insurance companies and other large-scale investors in housing are postponing their projects for more favorable conditions. Although hundreds of rental projects have been scheduled in recent months (under Mr. Creedon's new plan to emphasize this type of operation because he has found so many veterans unable and unwilling to buy) few are proceeding.

The ambitious plan to promote prefabrication by market guarantees never got very far, and few companies have availed themselves of it yet.

III—THE OUTLOOK

Attacks on the housing-cost problem may come from many directions. Labor is being asked by home builders' organizations to desist from further efforts to increase wage scales now, and to bring its production up to prewar basis. Labor leaders assert that a steady flow of materials to the job will be accompanied by increased output on the part of the mechanics.

Government efforts already are under way to bring down the prices of materials, and in some areas a cut of 20 per cent or so is expected by the end of the year. As yet no concerted action has been taken by the manufacturers or dealers to comply with Mr. Truman's plea for price reductions.

A smoother flow of supplies to the builders is necessary. Continued shortages in gypsum lath, hardwood flooring, nails and some other goods must be overcome.

With these improvements in conditions, some experts believe that about 20 per cent of a builder's dollar could be saved.

However, many observers feel that the best hope of producing lower-priced houses in quantity lies with large-scale organizations, buying on a wholesale basis and planning entire communities at one time, either in apartments or single-family units.

"Normal Conditions"

They point to the success of insurance-company projects carried out under "normal conditions" before the war. A few of these experts believe that stock financing might be utilized successfully for soundly planned and expertly managed housing colonies for the average wage-earner who can pay no more than $50 or so monthly.

Others are suggesting revival of tax-exemption plans, such as that under which New York expanded its rental housing after the first World War. This embodied ten-year exemption on the cost of the "improvement," permitting lower rents.

As a further step, talk of an annual wage for building labor has been revived.

The solution of the problem still is to be found. Meanwhile, the average veteran and non-veteran searches in vain for new or better quarters.

May 25, 1947

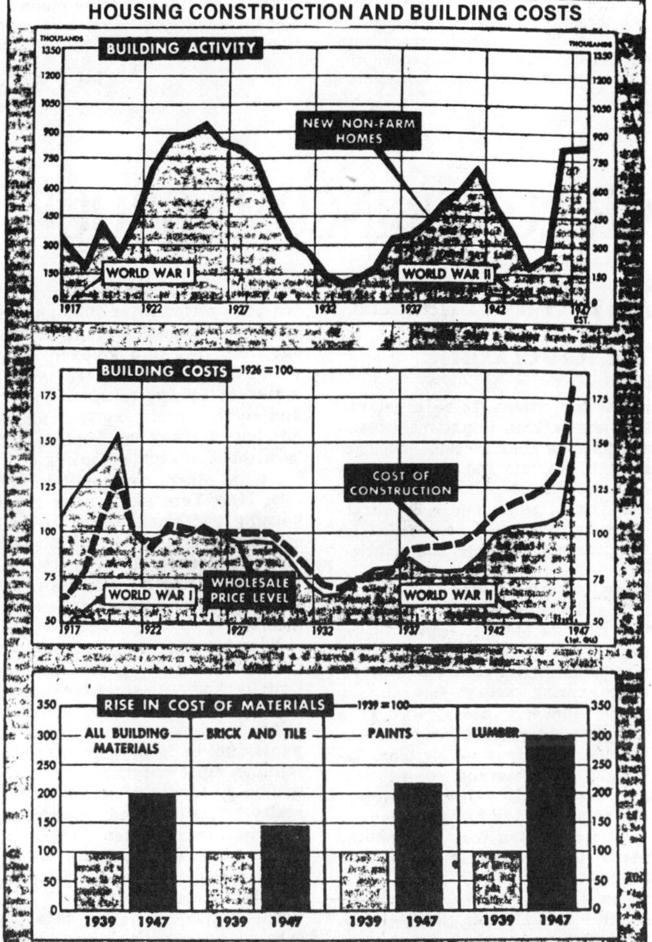

May 25, 1947

Herblock in The Washington Post

N. Y. LIFE'S COLONY WITH 3,000 SUITES IS 50% COMPLETED

Integrated Community Taking Form Rapidly on Golf Club Tract in Flushing

STORE CENTER A FEATURE

By LEE E. COOPER

On a former golf course in Flushing, Queens, a new residential colony which constitutes a veritable city within a city is taking form rapidly.

All over the 170-acre site of the Fresh Meadow Golf Club workmen are busy setting new concrete forms in place, installing equipment and helping tenants to get settled in this integrated community development of the New York Life Insurance Company.

Near the center of the sloping tract two thirteen-story units have been completed and occupied by 600 families, and close by thirty-three of the smaller two-story and three-story buildings already have been finished and fully leased by 550 additional families.

By next spring there will be 140 of these low buildings, spread about among trees and walkways, to provide 2,400 suites and bring the new housing center to fruition with 3,000 living units.

With 1,150 apartments already finished, 400 more to be occupied by the end of the year, and the other buildings in various stages of construction, the project is considered 50 per cent completed.

Big Shopping Center Rising

The houses themselves are but a part of the plan. The community shopping center which is rising on the edge of the tract facing Horace Harding Boulevard is a major undertaking in itself, Gen. Otto L. Nelson, vice president of the insurance company in charge of housing, pointed out in the course of an inspection tour of the property last week.

The tenants will have a branch of Bloomingdale's occupying its own two-story building, with about 105,000 square feet of space; a Food Fair super market, a Horn & Hardart retail shop, a 2,000-seat theatre of the Century chain, a Whelan drug unit, a branch of the Mary Lewis specialty shop, Woolworth's largest "suburban" branch, branches of the Bank of the Manhattan Company and of the Jamaica Savings Bank, and other facilities.

Ample parking will be provided close to these air-cooled shops, and four garages will supply facilities for 1,300 automobiles. The business space rentals are being supervised by James Felt.

To complete the facilities, shaded walkways, playgrounds and other recreational features are being provided. A new public school also is being completed within the housing site.

Close-up view of typical two-story units in Fresh Meadows at Flushing, where 1,150 apartments already are occupied.

Many Suites Leased Ahead

The apartments will range in size from three and one-half to six rooms, with rentals running from $77.50 to $150 monthly. Many leases have been signed in advance, particularly for the smaller units, at the rental office in the former clubhouse on Sixty-fourth Avenue.

Lou Crandall, president of the George A. Fuller Company, contractors, emphasized yesterday the vast amount of planning necessary to keep the work proceeding smoothly in these uncertain times, and cited some of the unusual features, including the great central heating plant which is virtually automatic in operation.

Mr. Crandall explained that stock-piling of some materials and equipment was necessary to assure adequate supplies. Hundreds of electric refrigerators have been bought and stored for use in future units, and a vast amount of pipe, lumber, steel and electrical equipment has been purchased in advance of needs.

Through this advance planning, and by large-scale purchases, work is proceeding without interruption.

August 29, 1948

HOUSING OUTLOOK GRIM FOR LOWER-INCOME GROUP

Public Aid Seems Only Way That the Shortage Can Be Overcome

By LEE COOPER

When the Eightieth Congress convened for the extra session called by President Truman both parties stood committed by their platform declarations to the need for legislation to relieve the nation's acute housing problem.

The Democrats, in their platform adopted in Philadelphia, had promised comprehensive housing legislation, including provisions for slum-clearance and low-rent housing projects "initiated by local agencies," which means Government housing.

The Republicans, in their platform, were less definite, contenting themselves with recommending Federal aid for slum clearance and low rents "only where there is a need that cannot be met by private enterprise or by the states and localities."

The President in his message to the extra session emphasized the gravity of the housing situation and asked for action. The Congress had before it the Taft-Ellender-Wagner Bill—already passed by the Senate—which the President said would do the trick.

The bill which Congress passed last week in the midst of this political controversy was not the T-E-W Bill. It was a much weaker measure. It provided (1) government guarantees up to 90 per cent of loans to builders of apartment houses costing no more than $8,100 per unit, (2) government guarantees up to 80 per cent of loans to contractors building at least twenty-five houses costing $6,000 or less, (3) guarantees to insurance companies of a profit of 2¾ per cent on large rental projects, (4) guarantees ranging from 80 to 95 per cent on loans for houses in the $6,000-$11,000 class.

Need Still Unmet

The bill makes no provision for public low-cost housing. In the opinion of real-estate experts it will not meet the nation's immediate and pressing need.

Three years after the war, where to find a decent place to live remains an exasperating puzzle for millions of people, especially those in the big cities. To both veteran and non-veteran impatiently waiting for new construction—whether built by private industry or Government subsidy—it appears that the desired small house or apartment is hopelessly enmeshed in Congressional debate and politics.

Need for New Units

The housing crisis actually is two decades old. It began during the depression, when comparatively few new dwellings were erected. New housing, except for military or for industry needs, was at a complete standstill during the war because of various restrictions. Returning war veterans, record marriages and birth rates only accentuated an already bad situation.

It is estimated that the country needs new housing at the rate of 1,000,000 to 1,200,000 units (that is, an apartment or house for one family) annually for the next decade. This would make up for the output of only about 264,000 houses built annually during the ten-year period after 1930 and the still lower annual average of 220,000 from 1942 through 1945.

In New York the need is estimated at 150,000 to 265,000 units, and some experts say that almost one out of every ten families here is without adequate housing.

As in other metropolitan centers, New York needs more rental housing and small homes at modest prices. Nearly all of the new homes and many of the apartments today are being built for sale, and at prices beyond the average man's income.

With less than 150,000 rental accommodations being provided nationally, and with some tenants being forced out of their homes by sales to prospective owner-occupants, an unusual percentage of families must purchase homes unwillingly, despite abnormally high realty prices. Indeed, experts say that less than 15 per cent of the new units this year will be for rental, compared to perhaps 40 per cent in normal times.

The problem involves both the dearth of new housing and the absence of living quarters for the

TRENDS IN HOUSING SINCE 1940

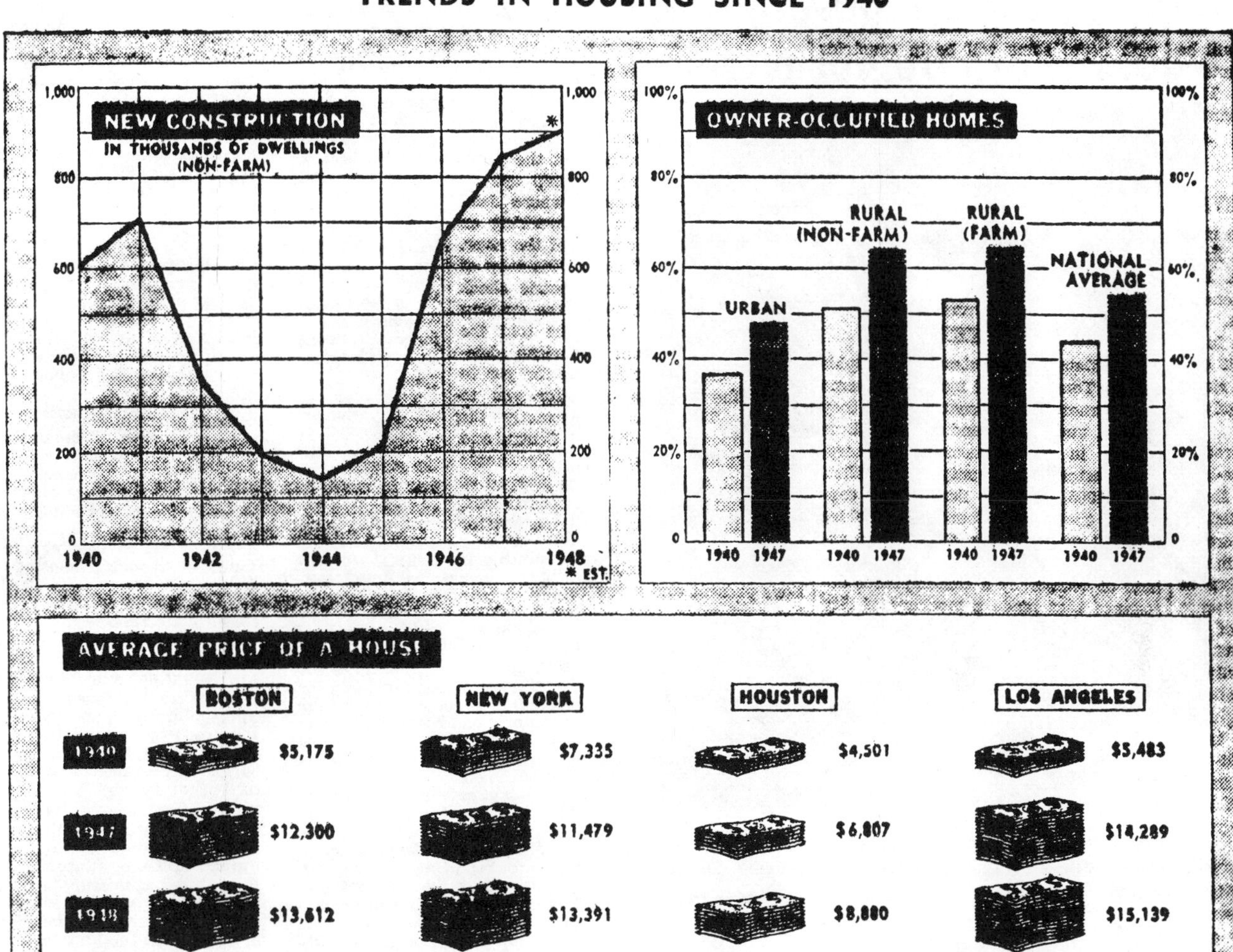

family of modest income.

About 450,000 new dwelling units were started in the country during the first six months of 1948; but there are indications that a decline may take place during the second half of the year.

Decline in Construction

During June builders started only 93,500 dwelling units, as compared with 97,000 in May. In this city the post-war peak was reached last April, when work began on about 4,000 homes, but since then the number has ebbed in the face of slower sales.

Last year about 879,000 homes of all types were completed, and the Commerce and Labor Departments a few days ago issued a revised estimate of $7,100,000,000 as the amount to be spent on housing, but they failed to revise upward their original prediction of 950,000 family units for the year which they made last November. At that time the Federal agencies figured that this number of houses would cost $6,000,000,000.

The situation has caused the President's Council of Economic Advisers to issue a warning that new housing may price itself out of the market "in a few years at most." It has inspired the Federal Reserve Board to give a sharp word of caution over the mounting volume of mortgage loans, which have risen by $2,800,000,000 in the last six months to a new high mark of $32,800,000,000.

At the same time the United Industrial Associates has found the price tag on the average house and lot to be $11,094 in leading cities as compared with $9,749 last summer and $4,599 in 1939. This agency's survey showed an average upswing of 14.5 per cent during the past twelve months, and listed a rise of 16.7 per cent for New York, with the average home here now selling at $13,391 as compared with $6,000 in 1939.

In the suburban districts of New York garden apartments of three to five rooms are being built in large numbers to rent at $80 to $130 monthly, but slower leasing lately has led observers to warn that the saturation point may be approaching for this type of shelter in some neighborhoods. These buildings are free of rent controls, and bring 40 to 60 per cent more than comparable accommodations in the older houses, which still are subject to controls.

Too Expensive for Veterans

Outside of government projects, nothing new is being built for the average veteran who can pay no more than $50 or $60 a month. For such a man the purchase of a modern house is out of the question in most large cities. Here the major part of construction activity now involves residences to sell at $12,000 to $18,000, and scores of builders are working on groups of larger dwellings at $30,000 to $60,000 each. Even in good times the market can absorb only a limited number of such expensive homes.

On the basis of a country-wide survey, the National Association of Real Estate Boards reports that the supply of small homes now is close to normal in about 25 per cent of our cities, but admits that the dearth of living quarters continues in all large centers of population, where the need always has been greatest.

Developments of recent weeks indicate that the country may be losing ground now, instead of gaining, in its efforts to relieve the shortage.

When the year's peak of construction activity is reached in September, contractors may have more than 750,000 workers employed on their dwelling sites to set a new post-war mark, and they may lay the foundations for as many as 100,000 houses during that month. But the average veteran will find most of them beyond his pocketbook.

Rise in Costs

In New York, where conditions are considered typical of metropolitan areas throughout the nation, Thomas F. Farrell, chairman of the New York City Housing Authority, finds that the continued upswing in construction costs already has priced new housing not only out of the low-income market, but beyond the reach of most of the people in the middle-income bracket as well.

Mr. Farrell estimates that the new homes and apartments are too expensive for 90 per cent of the veterans.

The gloomy outlook has led many persons to give up hope that private industry will succeed in tapping the mass market for housing at an early date.

It has led impartial observers more and more to the conclusion that adequate shelter for the vast majority of American families in the income brackets below $2,500 or $3,000 never again can be provided in larger cities without substantial and continuing government assistance.

August 8, 1948

President Signs Housing Bill; Orders Work Begun at Once

The President signing the housing bill. Watching are Senators Maybank, Flanders and Sparkman, and Housing Administrator Foley.

The New York Times (by Bruce Hoertel)

By CHARLES HURD

Special to THE NEW YORK TIMES.

WASHINGTON, July 15—President Truman signed today the public-housing bill in which Congress enacted the initial phase of his "Fair Deal" program.

The multi-billion-dollar measure provides, among other things, for the construction of 810,000 public housing units in the next six years plus Federal rental subsidies on these for forty years, and an ambitious slum-clearance program in cooperation with local authorities.

The President marked the importance he attached to the law by a ceremony in which more than a score of guests saw him sign it. He gave immediate orders for expediting the program, saying:

"This legislation permits us to take a long step toward increasing the well-being and happiness of millions of our fellow citizens.

Absent from the ceremony was one invited guest who was out of town, Senator Robert A. Taft, Republican, of Ohio, a co-sponsor of the housing measure. He sent a letter to the President which read in part as follows:

"I am hopeful that the present act will initiate a program of public and private housing which will lead to a solution of our housing difficulties, and bring about ultimately a condition in which decent housing is available to all."

The bill signed by President Truman contains five major features:

1. A slum-clearance program in which the Federal Government will put up $1,000,000,000 in loans and another $500,000,000 in grants to assist localities.
2. The low-rent housing program, to be handled by local authorities, designed to provide 810,000 units in the next six years and committing the Federal Government to annual maximum subsidies of $308,000,000 over a 40-year period.
3. Broad housing research designed to improve construction while reducing costs.
4. Farm housing aids providing for loans and, in some cases, grants to improve and rehabilitate farm dwellings, with the Federal commitment estimated at $325,000,000.
5. A 60-day extension from last June 30 of temporary authority for the Government to insure loans by private lenders up to $2,500 for repairing and remodeling houses; a 60-day continuation of authority to insure mortgages for construction of small homes up to $5,000, and a $500,000,000 increase in the amount of mortgage insurance that the Government can issue for single-family and multiple-dwelling units.

Foley Issues Estimate

Coincident with signing of the new law, Raymond M. Foley, Housing Administrator, estimated that 50,000 publicly owned dwelling units would be started in the first year of the program. The slum-clearance program, he added, would require more time for a start because of the detailed planning that must be done, as well as presumably new legislation by the States, of which only twenty-four have authorization for joint Federal-State slum clearance projects.

President Truman personally asked that the States and localities "act speedily," and added that he was asking Congress to hurry along appropriations required by the program for the current fiscal year.

In his public statement issued at the signing, Mr. Truman called the law a "far-reaching measure" that "open up the prospect of decent homes in wholesome surroundings for low-income families now living in the squalor of the slums."

Outlines Benefits

"It equips the Federal Government," he added, "for the first time, with effective means for aiding cities in the vital task of clearing slums and rebuilding blighted areas. It authorizes a comprehensive program of housing research aimed at reducing housing costs and raising housing standards. It initiates a program to help farmers obtain better homes. * * *

"The task before us now is to put this legislation into operation with speed and effectiveness."

The President used one pen to sign the measure, and immediately afterward presented the pen to Mayor David Lawrence of Pittsburgh, vice chairman of the Conference of Mayors.

By coincidence, the Labor Department issued today the monthly report on home-building by the Bureau of Labor Statistics, which showed that approximately 100,000 new urban dwelling units were started by private home builders in June. This total was 5,000 units greater than the May total and 2,200 more than in June of 1948.

The first six months of 1949, the report stated, indicated an estimated total of 450,000 new dwelling units placed under construction, compared with 477,600 in the same period in 1948.

July 16, 1949

'MEDIOCRE' HOUSING IS BLAMED ON F.H.A.

Quality Sacrificed for Profits, Says Architectural Forum in Study of Program

In a critical study of the Federal Housing Administration in its current issue, the magazine, Architectural Forum, charges that the FHA rules invite "short cuts" on the part of builders to gain quick profits at a sacrifice in housing quality. The article concedes, however, that FHA Title 6 probably was the only way the building boom could have been started under rent control.

The study lists four major conclusions, as follows:

1. So many apartments are going up under the impetus of FHA Title 608 mortgage insurance that "the housing shortage is more a matter of politics and rent control than a matter of less housing units per thousand population than was considered normal before the war."
2. Probably the only way such a building boom could have been started under rent control was through the "combination of public risk and private profit" exemplified by FHA Title 6.
3. Because FHA has assumed "100 per cent of the risk" for about 70 per cent of the apartment buildings started last year, the Government could become the owner of up to $2,400,000,000 worth of apartments, but
4. Even if the worst should materialize, the cost to the Government would still be "much less than the cost of public housing."

Public, FHA Work Compared

The magazine estimates that public housing to be rented for $35 an apartment to poor people will cost (in high-cost areas) about $10,000 per unit, not counting land. It figures that FHA apartments to house middle-class families at $20 to $25 a room will cost about $2,000 less, and, if Government overhead were included in the public housing costs, FHA apartments would be even bigger bargains by comparison.

"FHA Title 608 must be judged, however, in the light of its effect on the quality as well as the quantity of the housing provided under its auspices," the article continues. "Under the 608 setup most builders are interested only in a quick profit. They find they can add nothing to this quick profit by making their buildings any better than they have to. In fact, since FHA's section 608 guarantees up to 90 per cent of the hypothetical cost of these apartments, builders who can find a way to construct the apartments for less than the cost allowed by the FHA are able to take a substantial cash profit out of the project even before it is completed.

Builders' "Loopholes" Cited

"The builder who wants to turn the FHA 90 per cent guarantee into a 100 or 110 per cent guarantee of his costs has a number of avenues open to him.

"He may save up to 3½ per cent of the 5 per cent architectural fee allowed by FHA.

"He may get a 3 per cent premium from the mortgagee.

"He may build faster than FHA's allowable schedule of twelve to eighteen months (some builders finish in five to six months, not only making a tremendous saving in labor but realizing six extra months of rent).

"Most important, he can cut construction costs below the estimates made by the FHA in setting loan value."

January 29, 1950

SOUTH SEEKING 25% OF PUBLIC HOUSING

65,386 U. S.-Aided Dwelling Units Will Be Built in the Smaller Centers

Special to THE NEW YORK TIMES.

ATLANTA, May 6—In six Southern states applications have been made to the United States Public Housing Administration for a total of 65,386 low-rent dwelling units. For the most part the projects are for small communities, according to figures compiled by the Administration's regional field headquarters in this city.

In many cases the required co-operation agreements between local public-housing authorities and community officials have been signed. It is estimated that actual construction will get under way in the region within six to eight months.

The combined requests, representing the greatest public-housing development in the history of the South, accounts for almost one-fourth of all applications for public housing in this country under provisions of the Housing Act of 1949. As of last month, the Public Housing Administration in Washington had received 592 applications. Of these, 123 originated in Alabama, Florida, Georgia, Mississippi, Tennessee and South Carolina.

Many Small Cities Apply

Especially of significance to the South was the fact that most of the applications involved smaller cities, many of them county seats. In recent years, due to farm mechanization and industrial expansion, there has been a heavy migration to urban areas. As a result, housing has been at a greater premium in county-seat towns than in the big cities. Such projects for small towns were authorized for the first time in the 1949 housing act.

The low-rental projects also are expected to expedite slum clearance programs throughout the region. Authorities pointed out that, under the law, decent and adequate housing must be provided for families displaced by slum-clearance programs. Therefore, they hold, in many cases, as a practical matter, low-rent housing must precede slum clearance.

The 1949 Housing Act authorized the construction of 810,000 low-rent units throughout the country over six years. Congress authorized $1,500,000,000 of loan funds for the program, which would not represent out-of-pocket cost since it would be repaid through bonds sold by local housing authorities.

Annual Subsidy Out-of-Pocket

The out-of-pocket costs would be in the annual subsidy to make up the difference between rental receipts and the cost of operation, and the retiring of bonds. Authorities said that this amount would vary, but that it never had been necessary to use the full amount of the authorized subsidy. By law, the subsidy is limited to $308,000,000 a year for forty years. Authorities hold that on the basis of past experience the anticipated cost would be 58.5 per cent of the annual subsidy.

The cooperation agreements require the payment of not more than 10 per cent of the shelter rent to the local governments in place of taxes. Also, they provide that the respective cities render all necessary service facilities. Once the cooperation agreements are signed, all that remains before actual building is site selection and the letting of contracts.

The Projects by States

The number of low-rent housing units requested in each state follows: Alabama, 15,397; Florida, 11,535; Georgia, 21,065; Mississippi, 2,415; South Carolina, 4,150, and Tennessee, 10,825.

The number of units sought by some of the larger Southern cities, and approved by the Public Housing Administration, where cooperation agreements have been signed, are:

Nashville, 2,400 units; Knoxville, 1,450; Memphis, 1,500, and Chattanooga, Tenn., 1,200; Birmingham, 3,000, and Montgomery, Ala., 1,300; Augusta, 750; Columbus, 800; Charleston, 800; Columbia, 700; Greenville, 600, and Spartanburg, S. C., 400; Biloxi, 200, and Laurel, Miss., 350; Tampa, 1,500; Daytona Beach, 200; Pensacola, 500, and Orlando, Fla., 300.

Other cities with approved applications, but with agreements not yet signed, are Atlanta, 3,500 units; Mobile, Ala., 750; Macon, Ga., 750; Savannah, 800; Miami, 1,500, and Jacksonville, Fla., 1,500.

In Miami, the city commission rejected agreements and a public petition has been circulated to have the commission reconsider, or submit the matter to a citywide referendum.

May 7, 1950

U.S. HOUSING PROGRAM BRAKED BY KOREA WAR

WASHINGTON, Dec. 26 (UP)—The Korean war has put the brakes on the Government's public housing and slum clearance program, and officials are rapidly completing a new program emphasizing housing for defense workers.

Slum clearance projects have been slowed down, and soon may be halted entirely. Low-rent public housing units may be held to 60,000 next year, about half the number planned before the war.

Already the Government has given defense workers first call on Government-owned war housing built during World War II. Housing officials are rushing work on a new billion-dollar defense housing program to be presented to Congress.

The new program will include an estimated $1,000,000,000 insurance fund to encourage builders to construct new housing in defense areas. In addition Congress will be asked to approve $250,000,000 to $300,000,000 for direct Government construction of about 25,000 defense housing units. The first probably will be built at the new Savannah River atomic plant near Aiken, S. C.

Under the low-rent program the Government makes loans and subsidizes rents for projects developed by local communities. The 1949 law authorized construction of 810,000 public housing units by June, 1955. Under the new policy all applications for public housing will be judged by their importance to defense.

December 27, 1950

WORK STARTS IN CHICAGO

New York Life Is the Sponsor of Redevelopment Project

Special to THE NEW YORK TIMES.

CHICAGO, Feb. 9—Construction of Chicago's first big slum-clearance project, planned by the New York Life Insurance Company, is due to begin on Feb. 18, William J. Reardon, project manager for the company, announced here.

Initial construction will consist of two twelve-story buildings with 238 apartments. These will be built on the block bounded by Thirty-third Place, Thirty-fourth Street, and Cottage Grove and Rhodes Avenue in the heart of the South Side Negro district.

Ultimately, the project is to contain 2,000 modern dwelling units. The housing structures will range in size from two-story "garden type" buildings to two twenty-three-story skyscrapers of ultra-modern design. The development will cover more than 100 acres and will be serviced by a modern shopping center and a new school.

The New York Life project is being carried out under a new Chicago housing formula placing the job of slum redevelopment in the hands of private enterprise. Under this plan, the Chicago Land Clearance Commission was established in 1947 for the purpose of using public funds for acquiring expensive slum tracts for resale to private developers at written-down prices.

Ira Bach, executive director of the commission, said acquisition of the New York Life site is expected to cost roughly $16,000,000. The resale price to the insurance company would be about $2,000,000, leaving a net cost in public funds of $14,000,000.

February 10, 1952

REPORT CITES SNAG IN PUBLIC HOUSING

Senate Group Is Told of Fears Sites Will Cause 'Change in Racial Character' of Area

WASHINGTON, April 12 (AP)—The staff of the Senate Banking and Currency Committee said today fears of "a change in the racial character of a neighborhood" were causing difficulties in locating public housing projects.

The view was expressed in one of a series of reports on Government housing programs being made to the committee by its staff. This report said there had been slow progress in completion of public, low-rent housing units under the 1949 law. It added that only 13,500 units had been finished and that 105,000 were under construction on Jan. 31 although 1,125 cities had filed applications to build 500,000 units.

"In a number of cities we found," the report said, "that the local authorities were confronted by organized neighborhood resistance to the location of a particular project.

"The chief opposition seems to arise—and this was true especially in the Northern cities—from what the people in the neighborhood to be selected believed would be a change in the racial character of a neighborhood.

"In some cases, the difficulties created by such fears resulted in rejection of sites, and in other cases long delays.

"The Housing authorities, we found, were not attempting to make any radical change in neighborhood patterns and were attempting in a realistic way to meet their prime responsibility of providing decent housing and respectable and acceptable neighborhoods for those for whom they had to provide the housing."

The report went on to say that a necessity for long negotiations on the projects between officials of local housing authorities, local city officials, and the public housing administration also caused delays.

The staff members said they inspected public housing projects in nineteen cities in preparing the report.

"Our general impression was that the housing was well constructed," they added. "It was designed in terms of light, cleanliness and low operating and maintenance cost, and above average in site planning."

The report said the cost of the projects built so far had been high, running from $9,000 to $13,000 for a family unit with an average of $10,600, but "bids coming in within the last few months have been somewhat lower and the number of bidders for each job have multiplied."

April 13, 1952

12,700,000 ESCAPE END OF RENT CURBS

Federal Controls Lapse Today Except Where Local Action Backs Continuance

WASHINGTON, Sept. 29 (UP)—Federal rent controls expire tomorrow except in critical defense areas and areas in which local governing bodies, by votes before midnight tonight, ask their continuance to April 30.

About 20,000,000 persons in 6,000,000 rental units outside 120 areas designated critical have been under the controls.

The Office of Rent Stabilization announced that up to late today it had received notice that local governing bodies had voted to continue Federal rent controls for at least 12,700,000 persons. These persons live in about 3,900,000 rental units.

In normal defense rental areas hotels, motels, rooming houses and apartments built since 1947 are not covered by rent controls. In critical areas all units have rent ceilings.

Figures released by the rent agency showed that 70 per cent of the major cities in normal defense rental areas have voted to extend the Federal program and that 1,316 communities of 2,400 that could take action had done so. Governing bodies of thirty-six cities with populations of more than 100,000 have voted to extend controls. Seventy-three of 116 cities of more than 50,000 population also voted extension.

The largest cities voting extension were Boston, Providence, New Haven, Springfield, Mass., Worcester, Mass., Philadelphia, Pittsburgh, Scranton, Pa., Erie, Pa., Newark, Jersey City, Trenton, Camden, Paterson, N. J., Chicago, Minneapolis, St. Louis, Duluth, Dayton, Ohio, Youngstown, Ohio, Cleveland, Columbus, Ohio, Cincinnati, San Francisco, St. Pau[l] South Bend, Ind., Baltimore, Memphis and Louisville.

Among the larger cities rejecting rent controls were Atlanta Toledo, Ohio, Detroit, Des Moines Denver, Seattle, Akron, Ohio, Kansas City, Nashville, New Orleans Pueblo, Colo., Portland, Me., and Reading, Pa.

Some of the areas where rent controls would have ended were re-classified today as critical These include Denver, Cedar Rapids, Iowa, Evansville, the Allentown-Bethlehem area in Pennsylvania and Seward, Alaska.

September 30, 1952

HARDSHIP COMMON IN CLEARING SLUMS

Roomers and Large Families Find Plight Worst in Shifts for New Construction

By CHARLES GRUTZNER

Thousands of slum flats and cheap furnished rooms are falling in New York under the wrecker's iron ball. A third of the displaced tenants are moving into modern public housing, where rents are $9 to $16.50 a room. Undetermined numbers of others are finding adequate quarters in private housing within or beyond the city.

Many families and single lodgers are resettling in other slums, as bad or worse than those marked for obliteration in the current slum-clearance programs. Some families, unable to locate acceptable quarters within their ability to pay or turned down by landlords because of color, nationality or number of children, are doubling up with relatives or friends. This increases housing congestion and other evils.

Tenant relocation has stirred controversy within the City Administration and among civic groups, welfare workers, housing experts and realty developers. Dr. Luther H. Gulick, City Administrator, is investigating criticisms of the way the city and private redevelopers are handling the problem. He will report soon to the Board of Estimate on proposals now under study for easing the hardships of the uprooted.

A study by The New York Times indicates that the relocation problem is serious but not of the magnitude some critics have made it appear. Only half the displaced families who are eligible for public housing are availing themselves of it, according to Philip J. Cruise, chairman of the City Housing Authority.

Lone Persons Hard Hit

Some of the eligibles who turn their backs on public housing are unwilling to live in non-segregated projects; some have misconceptions about rules imposed on public housing tenants; some individualists just don't want to live in city, state or Federal housing.

On the other hand, the survey found cases of genuine hardship among persons facing loss of their homes and ineligible for public housing. Hardest hit were lone persons in furnished rooms and families with so many children as to require six-room or larger units. Public housing has relatively few accommodations for single tenants.

The most serious complaints were found in some Title I redevelopments, notably Manhattantown (sometimes called Park West), between Columbus and Amsterdam Avenues from Ninety-seventh to 100th Street, and Harlem Estates (formerly Godfrey Nurse Houses), between Fifth and Lenox Avenues, from 132d to 135th Street. These slums were bought by the city and resold to private realty developers at cut prices, the difference being met by Federal and city subsidies.

These and other Title I projects were laid out by the City's Slum Clearance Committee, headed by Robert Moses, City Construction Coordinator. But the city has delegated to the private redevelopers its legal responsibility for relocating, at rents they can afford, the tenants of the doomed buildings.

Pressure to Move Changed

Interviews with tenants on the Manhattantown and Harlem Estates sites disclosed resentment over alleged pressure, in one form or another, by the developers to get tenants to clear out without the moving expenses, first month's rent for the new quarters or other aid to which the uprooted are entitled in many cases.

Reporter who visited both sites found broken windows, overflowing plumbing, fallen plaster, broken light sockets, flaking paint and other evidences of disrepair in some tenanted apartments. In some cases only a few tenants remained in five-story buildings that were nearly wrecked. Drunken and other unsavory characters slept in abandoned flats adjoining tenanted ones.

Several tenants said that their complaints to the redevelopers' agents brought the suggestion: "Why don't you move out?"

The worst conditions were found in the buildings facing early demolition. Farther back on the sites, where the buildings will not be razed for two or three years, apartments were in much better condition. Some showed signs of recent repairs and repainting.

Some families had moved out, into public housing or elsewhere, from the buildings that will not come down immediately. The redevelopers said those vacant apartments had been repaired and offered to tenants in the buildings marked for early demolition.

Some, unable to find offsite dwellings, had been relocated in the repaired apartments. The developers said those who remained in the buildings slated for early demolition had rejected the offer of free moving within the site.

Some of the "die-hards" said they did not want to keep moving from one doomed building to another. They insisted that it was the developer's responsibility to help them find and move into suitable permanent dwellings.

The Federal Housing Act of 1949, under which the Title I projects are subsidized, requires specifically that there be made available "decent, safe and sanitary dwellings within their financial means" for the present slum dwellers before their homes are taken down. Commissioner Moses certifies at thirty-day intervals to the Federal Housing and Home Finance Agency that this is being done.

The study indicated that these certificates are not based on established facts. If the city's certifications do not wilfully circumvent the Federal law, they interpret it so loosely as to leave huge loopholes in its intended safeguarding of displaced tenants against uninvited hardship.

There is a loophole in the Federal Housing Act itself, in that its protection fails to include, even theoretically, lodgers in rooming houses operated by lessees. In such cases the redeveloper's responsibility is limited to relocating the rooming-house operator but not the individual roomers.

Contradictions Are Noted

The operators of several rooming houses on the Manhattantown site abandoned their lodgers several weeks ago and pulled out owing rent and utility charges. Electricity was shut off. Lodgers scrambled to find rooms wherever else they could, but some are still in the site. Light was restored after Manhattantown got in touch with the utility company.

In several cases there were contradictions between the stories of tenants and redevelopers. Corporation officials contended they were spending large sums for maintenance and repairs, but said some critics seemed to ignore the fact that the buildings were such bad slum structures that they had been selected for the subsidized clearance program.

"We buy brooms and mops by the truckload and paint by the carload," said Samuel Caspert, corporation secretary. "We bring in exterminators. It's maybe the first time there has been an exterminator in some of those old buildings, and they don't stay clean easily."

Jack Ferman, Manhattantown president, conceded that slum clearance had its seamy side. He said clearance of the site had not gone ahead as fast as was anticipated.

Another reporter who visited the Harlem redevelopment site found the same inconsistency between the stories told by redevelopers and tenants. There was visible evidence to support some of the tenant complaints.

Robert Olnick, president of Godfrey Nurse Homes, Inc., said all services were being maintained and repairs were made by the redeveloper's own crews. He said tenants who did not qualify for public housing or find other off-site quarters were relocated in renovated flats in the deferred-demolition section.

Among the tenants who differed with Mr. Olnick was Mrs. Edmonia Tyner, 56 years old, who lives with a daughter in a four-room flat at 40 West 135th Street, where she pays $40.25 rent. She had lived until last August in three rooms in the adjoining building, where the rent was only $28. She h[ad] [t]o move when the wreckers [went] to work on that building. Mrs. Tyner's income is mostly from a pension for loss of her son in World War II.

Mrs. Tyner said services and maintenance were worse than in the building from which she was relocated. She said there was not enough heat, and her gas bills were double what they had been for the same months a year earlier. The building has dirty, poorly illuminated halls through which blasts of cold air blew from empty window frames.

In another flat of the same building Mrs. Ida Burns said she had kept a gas heater burning since November because the redeveloper did not provide enough steam. The paint on the walls was flaked and a rag was tied over a bad leak in the water fixture. Mrs. Burns, an 11-year-old son and a boarder occupy three small rooms, for which she pays $40.25, including a 15 per cent increase the redevelopers put into effect after acquiring from the city the doomed buildings.

April 1, 1954

PRESIDENT SIGNS THE HOUSING LAW

Calls It 'Major Advance,' but Asks More Public Units—Mason Heads F. H. A.

Special to The New York Times.

WASHINGTON, Aug. 2—President Eisenhower approved the Housing Act of 1954 today. Although it fell somewhat short of his requests, he called it "a major advance toward meeting America's housing needs."

The President also witnessed the swearing in of Norman P. Mason as Commissioner of the Federal Housing Administration. Mr. Mason has been acting commissioner during the Senate investigations into housing irregularities.

The President had asked for 35,000 public housing units a year for four years. Congress authorized 35,000 units for one year and inserted provisos that make the attainment of the full number doubtful. The Federal Government subsidizes the rentals of such public housing.

"We shall need to continue our public housing program until the needs can be met by private industry," the President said in a statement. "Also, the Executive should have broader authority to adjust the terms on home loans to changing economic conditions."

On the 'Plus' Side

The rest of the President's statement dealt with the "plus" side of the law, from his viewpoint:

"It will raise the housing standards of our people, help our communities get rid of slums and improve their older neighborhoods and strengthen our mortgage credit system. In coming years it will also strongly stimulate the nation's construction industry and our country's entire economy.

"The new law permits the Government to insure larger home mortgage loans, carrying smaller down payments and longer terms. Millions of our families with modest incomes will be able, for the first time, to buy new or used homes. Families will be helped to enlarge or modernize their present homes.

"Another feature of the law is especially important. Many families have to move from their homes because of slum clearance and other public improvements. This law provides especially easy terms for these deserving people. The new law makes available, for the first time, a practical way for our citizens, in the towns and cities of America, to get rid of their slums and blight.

Modernization Made Easier

"The law strengthens private mortgage credit facilities. It does this by reorganizing the Federal National Mortgage Association. This agency will continue to be a support for the mortgage marke, but later on it will become independent of Federal capital. Under this new law, private financial institutions have a really good chance to mobilize their own resources to supply adequate mortgage credit without regard to race, creed or color to homeowners in every part of our country."

The provisions of the new law include these:

¶It liberalizes the requirement on down payments and repayment periods on homes bought with F. H. A.-insured mortgages.

¶It provides safeguards designed to prevent extra-large profits by builders of Government-backed apartment projects.

¶It contains a clause requiring lenders in the Government-backed home repair loan program to take part of the risk on each loan made.

¶It permits the buyer of a Government-insured home for the first time to take out an increased mortgage for the same terms as the first one if he decides to add improvements. The objective is to encourage modernization.

¶It includes features for expanding slum clearance and urban redevelopment programs operating under Federal-state cooperation.

August 3, 1954

CITY HOUSING RATE STILL BELOW NEED

Despite Mounting Efforts in Low and Middle Income Field, Scarcity Remains

SURVEY SPANS 32 YEARS

127,601 Apartments Added Since 1926, but 388,826 Others Are Substandard

By THOMAS W. ENNIS

Although New York has done more than any other city in the nation to provide housing for low- and middle-income families, the supply is only beginning to meet the need.

This is indicated by a recent housing study by the City Planning Commission, tracing back to 1926 the city's publicly owned housing projects and its privately owned low-cost housing built with city, state or Federal aid.

The study shows that 127,601 apartment units were built here under four separate programs in the last thirty-two years, most of them since World War II. The total figure includes 100,000 apartments in projects of the New York City Housing Authority.

The extent of the city's housing problem is underlined by a Department of Buildings estimate that there are still 388,826 substandard apartment dwellingsin the city. It is also made evident by 70,000 applications received yearly by the City Housing Authority, and by the many families whose incomes are above the eligibility limits for public housing, but too low for privately financed nonsubsidized housing.

Aid to Private Builders

The acute shortage in the middle-income field, which is receiving increasing attention here, has not been alleviated by private builders under the Federal Housing Administration mortgage insurance program. The F.H.A. guarantees to private lending institutions the repayment of loans used to finance construction of the projects.

Under the F.H.A.'s Section 608 program, about 59,000 apartments renting at $22 to $30 a room monthly were erected. The '608' program, an emergency measure, was in force between 1947 and 1952.

About 18,000 cooperatives have been built in the city under Section 213, which authorized Government - insured loans to private developers of cooperative housing. Carrying charges on the apartments were originally $20 to $22 a room monthly. In the 2,100 "213" cooperative apartments now in the planning stage the charges will be about $30 to $35 a room monthly, reflecting higher building costs.

According to the Planning Commission, 40 per cent of the 100,000 publicly aided apartment units now under construction or planned here will be in privately owned, built and managed developments, both cooperative and rental, for middle-income families.

Public Housing Projects

The 100,000 units do not include 40,000 apartments being built or planned by the City Housing Authority. The authority will build 7,600 middle-income units renting at about $23 a room honthly. To date, the authority has provided about 25,000 apartments in middle-income projects, which are entirely supported by the tenants' rents, without cash subsidy from the city or the state.

The private middle-income projects are receiving assistance in land acquisition, tax benefits and direct loans under three separate programs.

One state housing aid is the Limited Profit Housing Companies Law (the Mitchell-Lama Act), which authorizes the state and city to make low-interest loans up to 90 per cent of the cost of a project.

The law limits the sponsors of the housing to 6 per cent profit, but permits a tax abatement of 40 per cent on projects within New York City, and 50 per cent on projects outside the city.

A number of housing officials believe the Mitchell-Lama Act will prove the biggest aid yet given to middle-income housing here. Twenty-three cooperatives housing 8,000 families are either being built or are ready for construction with help under this law.

Two large cooperatives housing 7,368 families are to be built under the State Redevelopment Companies Law, which permits the city to use its condemnation powers to assemble a building site for a private sponsor of medium-rent housing. Stuyvesant Town and the Queensview cooperative are among the large projects already built under this law.

The two new cooperatives will be the 2,184-family Soundview Park cooperative to be erected in the Bronx, and the James Peter Warbasse Houses in the Coney Island section of Brooklyn, with 5,184 apartments.

Altogether, at least 25,000 middle-income families are to be housed in cooperatives built under this state law or with Federal aid under Title I of the National Housing Act of 1949.

Title I permits cities to acquire blighted areas and resell the properties at a markdown to private developers. The Federal Government makes good two-thirds of the resale price markdown and the city one-third.

June 22, 1958

Housing Blight Fought By Code Enforcement

More municipalities are fighting the slum problem by enforcing housing codes today than ever before.

Four years ago housing codes were in force in only forty-four cities. Today at least 260 cities have laws setting minimum requirements for safety and health in housing. There still is a long way to go, since there are about 1,500 cities in the nation with populations of 10,000 or more.

Many proposed codes faced lengthy opposition before they became law. In Little Rock, Ark., a code was debated for five years—and defeated by the city council in 1957—before it became law this year.

In some areas, however, passage is quick. Residents in a Cincinnati neighborhood begged the city to improve housing codes enforcement, and the city council compiled almost immediately.

The Federal Government, which subsidizes part of the slum clearance cost in a city, is now insisting that New York tighten its housing code because housing is deteriorating faster than the city can clear it, according to the National Association of Housing and Redevelopment Officials.

August 9, 1959

Weaver Asserts Disdain for the Poor Hinders Urban Renewal

By BEN A. FRANKLIN
Special to The New York Times

CAMBRIDGE, Mass., March 31 — The head of the Federal Housing Agency says that prejudice and discrimination, not only against Negroes but also against the poor—"white, black, or any color" — are responsible for many of the mounting difficulties of renewal and rehabilitation programs across the nation.

Dr. Robert C. Weaver, administrator of the United States Housing and Home Finance Agency, is among the first high-ranking Government officials to speak publicly about the "class warfare" aspect of the struggle within the cities to improve the lives of millions of aspiring but underprivileged Americans. One of the "great problems of urban housing," he said, is an answer to the question of "where to put the poor."

Dr. Weaver made his comments during a three-part lecture series at Harvard University this week. He said there was hope in a new Federal emphasis on the Government-assisted rehabilitation of existing housing. This, he said, would temporarily ease some of the bitter public controversy that has beclouded and deterred urban housing progress since the basic postwar housing act went into effect in 1949.

Away From Clearance

Dr. Weaver said the rehabilitation program, designed to upgrade existing substandard neighborhoods, would be a move away from huge slum clearance and public housing projects that have been denounced by civil rights leaders and others as part of a "Negro clearance" program creating "storage bins for the poor."

But Dr. Weaver said this change would not end all of the emotionally charged arguments surrounding an urban redevelopment scheme that he described as "conceived in controversy and matured in controversy."

With heavy sarcasm, the Federal housing chief attacked as "intemperate and misdealing" the criticisms of urban renewal contained in recent publications of the Joint Center for Urban Studies—a research group sponsored jointly by Harvard and the Massachusetts Institute of Technology.

James Q. Wilson, director of the joint center and an associate professor of Government at Harvard, wrote in a university publication last January that "there is no urban problem in America except, perhaps, for the problem of urban aesthetics."

Dr. Weaver, in his lecture here this week, suggested that if that was the case, "the joint center might be merged with Harvard's Schools of Fine Arts and Architecture."

'Class Status' Struggle

He declared that almost all urban problems today are directly related to the dual struggle of the economically deprived for civil rights and, at the same time, for "class status."

Most Federal spokesmen have shied away from public comment on the "class warfare" aspects of the civil rights movement of the nineteen-sixties. However, many of them believe that these "class" problems are a major and little-understood force in the "social revolution" now going on in the North and the South.

"Class aspirations" of low-income Negroes, particularly, are believed to provide the basis for continuing demonstrations that will persist long after legislation enforcing basic civil rights has become law.

Dr. Weaver, the first Negro to hold a sub-Cabinet Federal post, was not optimistic about the housing crisis in the cities. "Prejudice is always irrational and illogical," he declared. "Logical solutions do not emerge from illogical problems."

He was less pessimistic about another insistent fact of city life the huge growth of urban populations. Seven of 10 persons in this country now live in cities, he said. The urban share of the total population by the year 2000 may be as high as 85 per cent.

"In the next 35 to 40 years," he declared, "we may have to build as much housing, industrial plants, and as many highways and related developments as we have built in our previous history."

In the process, he said, the amount of land consumed by metropolitan areas will be doubled. He said this growth offered "unparalleled opportunity to achieve a standard and scale of living no society has yet been able to devise."

But "unless we plan more carefully," he warned, "we are in danger of killing off our chance for living decently." He said this warning applied both to the central cities and to the suburbs.

The Federal Housing Administrator also was the first Negro to deliver the Godkin Lectures at Harvard. The 1965 series of three lectures ended Wednesday night. The lectures were endowed in 1903 under a bequest of Edwin L. Godkin, an English and American journalist who was editor of The Nation and of the old New York Evening Post.

The lectures have been delivered over the last 62 years by scores of outstanding Government officials, educators and military and business leaders from this country and from abroad. Dr. Weaver was graduated from Harvard College in 1929. He obtained his master's and a doctor's degree here in 1931 and 1934.

University spokesmen said they believed Dr. Weaver may have been the first Godkin lecturer to be picketed.

50 Come to Picket

A group of 50 angry citizens of the Charlestown, Mass., and the North Harvard area, across the Charles River from Cambridge, paraded outside the university's Sanders Theater on Tuesday and Wednesday nights and then attempted to heckle the speaker during his lecture. They were white but there appeared to be no racial animus in their protest.

The New York Times
Robert C. Weaver

They said they were protesting proposed urban renewal projects that would "enrich real estate speculators" and displace "poor people" to make way for housing units renting at $250 a month. The demonstrators appeared to underline Dr. Weaver's comments on the "class struggle" implications of urban redevelopment.

During a question period, he answered their demands for an end to urban renewal in their communities by declaring that this was a "matter of local decision" over which the Federal Government neither exercised nor sought control.

An audience made up largely of Harvard students and faculty applauded him repeatedly. The bitterness of the hecklers, however, seemed unassuaged. They carried placards that said "Urban Renewal Makes The Poor Man a Pawn of Profit" and "We Want Our Homes."

They were voicing a second major criticism of urban renewal, a complaint less widespread than the "Negro removal" charge leveled by many city civil rights leaders, but nonetheless troubling to Federal and local housing officials.

A Reply to Complaints

The criticism is based on the fact that in many cleared and rebuilt urban renewal areas, the new construction has been for middle-income and even "luxury" tenants, or for commercial and mercantile interests, some of whom are also "slumlords" —owners of dilapidated rental housing occupied by minority groups.

Dr. Weaver answered the harsh complaints about renewal with some hard criticisms of his own. In response to the criticisms, he said the program was taking "new directions."

In describing many of the urban renewal programs already begun, he said they had had a "disruptive impact," had generated "psychological stress,' and had "too frequently complicated rather than eased the "social problems of segregation and slums."

"Tearing down the houses occupied by the poor—and especially the poor who are nonwhite—and rebuilding for high-rent occupancy may accelerate the return of the middle class to central cities," he said, "but in time it generates widespread opposition to urban renewal." He added:

"In retrospect, it seems obvious that urban renewal could never have been simultaneously the economic savior of the central city, an instrument for clearing slums, the means of attracting hordes of upper-middle-class families back into the central cities, and a tool for rehousing former slum dwellers in decent, safe, and sanitary housing."

In outlining the "new directions" in urban redevelopment, he said that the new construction of moderate-income housing and rehabilitation of existing low-income housing in the "gray areas" of cities would be stressed.

'Push for Rehabilitation'

The rehabilitation work, he said, would be "cost-conscious" —limited in the degree and cost of improvement—to "accommodate approximately the same income group as resided in the structures prior to their being improved."

There will be "a push for rehabilitation rather than demolition," he said. His list of urban renewal "priorities" was as follows:

¶Continued downtown commercial redevelopment. Despite criticism that this "enriches the rich" and serves to enhance the investments of banks, real estate speculators, and other large downtown mortgage holders, he said it was necessary to improve the cities' tax base and tax revenues. Without revenue, he said, cities could not provide needed services.

¶Moderate and low-income housing construction on cleared downtown sites, together with "some luxury redevelopment" to "hold in and attract" middle class families. This would involve demolishing some—but not all—substandard buildings in blighted areas.

¶Through rehabilitation subsidies and stricter local enforcement of building codes, upgrade the quality of the existing supply of housing especially in the gray areas.

¶Provide sites for public institutions such as hospitals and universities, and some areas for light industry.

Dr. Weaver's criticism of "suburbia" was largely sympathetic. He foresaw an increasing need for suburban living as urban populations swell. But he said suburban housing must not "have septic tanks that are wet and wells that are dry."

"We must act now," he said, "to discourage the bulldozing away of contours and trees," and to demand adequate mass transportation both for suburban commuters to the cities and for the increasing number of city-dwelling service workers who will be in demand in suburban homes, commerce and industry."

April 4, 1965

OFFICE ON HOUSING SET UP IN CABINET

Johnson Signs Bill but Puts Off Naming Agency Head

Special to The New York Times

WASHINGTON, Sept. 9—President Johnson signed legislation today creating a Department of Housing and Urban Affairs to help the nation's cities solve their mounting problems.

The President did not announce his choice to head the department.

Robert C. Weaver, head of the Housing and Home Finance Agency, which is to be absorbed by the new department, has been called a front-runner for the appointment. He would be the first Negro Cabinet member.

Close observers of the situation said the President's failure to designate Mr. Weaver today might indicate Mr. Weaver would not get the job. Others, however, said the President was delaying such an announcement only because he wanted the extra publicity a separate announcement would get.

Under the law creating it, the department will not come into being for 60 days unless the President establishes it sooner by Executive order.

The department will consist of the programs of the Housing and Home Financing Agency—the Federal Housing Administration, the Public Housing Administration, the Federal National Mortgage Association, the Community Facilities Administration and the Urban Renewal Administration.

In addition, it will be responsible for Federal participation in planning programs to assist metropolitan areas.

The Housing Agency has 13,600 employes in Washington and its regional offices. The department will be smaller than any of the 10 others except the Department of Labor, which has about 9,000 employes.

Thus ended a five-year struggle, which began in the Kennedy Administration, to give the nation's city dwellers a voice in the President's Cabinet.

The department, the first new one since the creation of the Department of Health, Education and Welfare in 1963, was first proposed by President Kennedy in his State of the Union message Jan. 30, 1961. Mr. Kennedy later announced that he would appoint Mr. Weaver to the new Cabinet post. The proposal was defeated in the House largely by Southern Democrats, who opposed a Negro in the Cabinet.

September 10, 1965

Johnson Signs Rent Subsidy Bill and Calls It the Most Important Housing Breakthrough

Special to The New York Times

WASHINGTON, Sept. 7—President Johnson has signed a $13.9-billion appropriations bill containing $22-million for the rent supplement program. He praised the program today as "the single most important breakthrough in the history of public housing."

He also asserted that he had never signed a bill that gave him "greater satisfaction."

"No housing program ever devised by this Government has been so well suited to a nation dedicated to free enterprise," the President said. Later he added:

"It represents everything I have believed in during all my 35 years in public office. It is a clear-cut but compassionate solution to a pressing national problem."

Although Mr. Johnson signed the appropriations measure last night, his statement praising rent supplements was issued by the White House this afternoon.

"I have waited for this moment for 35 years," Mr. Johnson said. "There are many provisions in the appropriations bill, but the most far-reaching—and the one which gives the most satisfaction to me—is the provision of funds for our rent supplement program.

"As a young Congressman from Texas, I helped to secure the nation's first public housing project for my neighbors back home. President Roosevelt signed that bill [the first public housing law] into law almost 30 years ago—and it was a proud moment in my life.

"But this is a prouder moment. What we then sought for poor families in Austin, Tex., we now seek for poor families all over America—and this bill gives us the power to act."

Under the rent supplement program, the Federal Government will pay what amounts to a subsidy for poor families to live in decent housing. The payments will not be sent directly to the tenants but the sponsor-owner of the project. The sponsors must be nonprofit groups, cooperatives, or limited dividend corporations. These are private corporations in which the net return on capital is limited, usually depending on state law, to 6 per cent.

The tenants in rent supplement housing, which can involve either new construction or rehabilitated units, must pay 25 per cent of their income for rent. The difference between this amount and the "economic rent," or what the sponsor needs to pay off his mortgage and pay other basic expenses, constitutes the rent supplement or subsidy.

To be eligible for such a project, a tenant's income must be low enough to make him eligible for public housing. The national median income of public housing occupants on June 30, 1966 was about $2,600, but this figure varies with the locality.

The program, one of the most controversial measures ever proposed by Mr. Johnson, was authorized last year after long and acrimonious debate in Congress. In April of this year Congress—again after bitter debate—gave the program a $12-million appropriation with which to operate for the remainder of the fiscal year 1966, ending last June 30.

In early May, the House voted to provide the program with $22-million for the fiscal year 1967. The Senate concurred in August.

The money in the appropriations bill will support activities of more than a score of Federal agencies in the fiscal year that began last July 1, among them the National Aeronautics and Space Agency, which gets about $5-billion.

September 8, 1966

HOME DESIGN DRAB IN U.S., STUDY SAYS

A Federal Report Deplores Mediocrity in Planning

By ADA LOUISE HUXTABLE

The design of housing and housing sites in the United States was scored yesterday as "of mediocre quality" with "random exceptions" in a 223-page illustrated report sponsored and released by the Department of Housing and Urban Development.

The report is the result of a two-year study of 700 housing sites in 30 cities by Robert D. Katz, an associate professor of the Department of Urban Planning of the University of Illinois. It is a scholarly indictment of current American housing practice in terms of land use planning in both the public and private sectors. Its critical observations are couched in the objective, low-key language of academic research.

Called "Design of the Housing Site, a Critique of American Practice," the study was financed by the Federal Housing Administration, the Urban Renewal Administration and the Mobile Homes Manufacturing Association.

The Urban Renewal Administration has paid for its publication in book form with a demonstration grant. The Federal Housing Administration and the Urban Renewal Administration have since been consolidated into the Department of Housing and Urban Development, headed by Robert C. Weaver.

A flyleaf note states that "the report is the product of the University of Illinois and does not necessarily represent or coincide with the standards or policy of the Federal Housing Administration."

Mr. Weaver's comment on the release of the volume, however, endorses the study at the highest Government level.

"This book provides a much needed new perspective in design of the dwelling environment," he said. "It shows the numerous ways through which sensitive design can add substantially to the quality of housing in areas of multi-family housing."

The report focuses on the connection of design with livability in the American home. Its chief concern is the planning of the complete housing site, or the relationship of buildings to the land and to one another, measured by people's needs. Many experts believe that this is the most valid basis for judging housing design.

In addition to the charge of mediocrity, the report criticizes what it calls the national waste of land through poor open space planning, the low quality of spatial organization of the land that is found in a majority of housing developments, and the missed opportunities for a pleasanter visual and recreational environment.

Group of apartment buildings in Puerto Rico. The report praises variation of facades, underground parking areas and landscaping. Dr. Robert D. Katz prepared document.

Lack of Privacy Cited

Unimaginative landscaping, failure to use open space well, poor relationship of interior to exterior, faulty circulation and inferior solutions for parking and car storage are also cited. Cheap materials, slapdash construction, incorrect placement and inadequate maintenance of buildings are scored.

According to the author, poor site planning also leads to a noticeable lack of privacy in American houses, as well as inadequate provision for differences in family size, type and tastes. Design attention is restricted largely to facade appearance. The result is physical monotony and a lack of focus for social activity.

"Without doubt, there is a serious lack of quality in site planning in the United States today," Professor Katz says. "The challenge of working out a plan that fits the site, climate and special human needs is frequently ignored. The designer falls back on a convenient stack of 'samples.' "

The results, he says, are "leftover space and cut-up little patches of grass, with trees cut down, hills leveled and streams filled to force a recalcitrant merger of building and land."

Where exceptions exist, good practice is attributed to a combination of skillful designers and developers who look beyond short-term profits for a better long-term formula.

The author cites the new town of Reston, Va., with its cluster housing and communal open space, and developments such as the housing for married students at Harvard University, for attractive building-type variety.

He cites mixed residential and commercial use of land as a desirable solution, as well as greater recreational use of rooftops. He also suggests building over highways, piers and parking fields, and more research in industrialized construction.

The report analyzes the causes behind substandard American housing. It states that the emphasis on the single family house, with the multi family house considered less desirable on the American scale of values, has motivated against the development of improved housing types. Building regulations reflect this single house bias. Rising densities and expanding communities, Professor Katz observes, make this a national disaster.

Controls such as zoning and building, housing and sanitary codes, dictated by custom and example, the author says, are rigidly restrictive and have not changed with changing conditions. They are so specific and often so antiquated that there is "virtually no room left for creative design."

He points to protection of property values as one factor promoting this rigidity. Both the Federal Housing Administration and private lending institutions have been hesitant to underwrite departures in housing design that might effect existing neighborhoods.

The housing agency, in its role as mortgage insurer, and the Veterans' Administration, are called the chief forces that have "helped shape suburban America." Neither the public agencies nor the private institutions have a record of encouraging innovation. The burden has been on the designer to "prove" that innovations are desirable.

In recent years, the F.H.A. has considerably liberalized its regulation and procedures. Lately it has introduced incentives to better design.

Broad Planning Urged

It is still common practice, however, to think of building on a traditional block-by-block or lot-by-lot basis, although the reality today is that very large tracts are being developed, often in single ownership.

The more logical procedure, the report says, would be to begin with total, coordinated land or project planning, either by the private developer or by a public agency. An example of wasteful small plot development in the immediate metropolitan region is the whittling away of Staten Island's open land by conventional piecemeal building.

The study takes up one aspect of American housing that is generally ignored, in spite of its rapidly growing popularity. This is the trailer park, which, in its present form, is considered a blighting influence on most communities.

The "mobile home," as its promoters prefer to call it, seldom moves. Mobile home lots are now being sold instead of leased.

The mobile home is the single most economical form of one-family housing being built today. Unlike most other housing, it is being industrially produced. It is cheap, because of its factory production and because building codes, which run up costs, do not apply to it. It also receives the least design assistance in terms of its contributions to the environment.

It is suggested that the mobile home be redesigned to look less like a cross between a car and a house, with an appearance closer to conventional housing. "If the full potential of compact design and flexibility were realized, the mobile home could be a great boon to the residential community," the report concludes.

The study makes these specific recommendations for the improvement of American housing:

¶The role of Government should be to promote operational procedure that encourage good design, and to support innovation and research.

¶In urban renewal, which represents massive amounts of the country's new housing, "land is too difficult to secure and too expensive to develop for design to be a giveaway." Design review by qualified staff or consultants snould be mandatory for all Federally aided programs.

¶A concerted effort must be made to attract talented designers to public service, where the level has been notoriously low. The F.H.A., the Public Housing Administration and the model cities programs of the Department of Housing and Urban Development are cited as critical areas.

¶Sites should be examined before plans are approved, to insure better site development and design.

¶There should be less overriding concern with risks in financing, and more support of site-planning experiments.

¶Code and zoning revisions must be made in favor of "performance" standards. Performance codes set standards for noise, privacy, fireproofing, light and air without giving detailed specifications for setback distances, window openings, roof shapes, and other mandatory or prohibitory requirements. This gives maximum design flexibility.

The report concludes that responsibility for the quality of the American housing environment can be widely distributed among designers, developers, governmental agencies and the public.

It says that housing design has been held in too low professional esteem, developers have been too narrowly profit-oriented, and public expectations have been tool low.

February 13, 1967

Civic Group Fails in Attempt To Make Slum Buildings Pay

By STEVEN V. ROBERTS

After four years as the owner of two tenements on the Lower East Side, a leading civic group has decided that it is virtually impossible for a landlord to maintain decent living conditions in a slum area and make a fair profit.

The group, the Citizens Housing and Planning Council, started out to prove that private capital could make an annual profit of at least 8 per cent by renovating and running slum housing, Roger Starr, its executive director, said yesterday.

Last year the council made a cash profit of slightly more than $1,000 on an investment of almost $300,000. Counting depreciation, it lost $7,335 on the two buildings.

"It soon became clear that you couldn't make anything at all," Mr. Starr declared. "It simply costs more money to keep up your property than you collect from rents at this level of the economic system."

The experiment indicates, Mr. Starr said, that city, state and Federal governments must provide huge subsidies to both landlords and tenants if the city's slums are ever going to be made habitable.

"Without subsidies rehabilitation is a snare and a delusion," Mr. Starr asserted. "No reasonable person would invest money to rehabilitate buildings like the ones we own."

The Citizens Housing and Planning Council is a nonprofit organization that has been concerned with the physical development of the city for 30 years. Its board of directors includes a broad range of civic leaders, businessmen and professional persons.

The council's findings contradict the growing belief in housing circles that massive private investment can, and should be attracted to slum areas to provide new housing and commercial facilities. New York's Senators, Robert F. Kennedy and Jacob K. Javits, are among the public figures who have stressed the importance of private investment in renewing deteriorated neighborhoods.

The findings also differ with the widely held assumption that ownership of slum housing is a highly profitable business, even for landlords who spend money on repairs and maintenance.

Conclusion Disputed

Jason R. Nathan, the Administrator of Housing and Development, said yesterday that the council's experiment "was not by any means the end of the story." He said there was considerable evidence that rehabilitation could be feasible if done over a large area, and not just on scattered buildings.

The more sophisticated technology that is being developed would cut costs and make rehabilitation more profitable, Mr. Nathan added.

The experiment began in late 1961 when Laurence Rockefeller donated $250,000 to a nonprofit foundation established to rehabilitate an old-law tenement at 92 Ridge Street, between Rivington and Delancey Streets.

The council assumed ownership of the building in December, 1962, and bought a second one at 186 East Second Street, between Avenues A and B. Mr. Rockefeller's donation was not enough to renovate both buildings, and the council took out a $45,000 mortgage.

The Ridge Street building is a six-story walk-up built around 1880. It is typical of 43,000 tenements still standing in New York that were built before a 1901 statute required indoor plumbing and other reforms.

$115,000 Spent on Repairs

The council acquired it for $15,500, as opposed to its market value of $16,000 to $19,000 when it was built. In all, $115,000 was spent putting in new kitchens and bathrooms (there had been one hall toilet for every two families before renovation), replacing all electrical wiring and plumbing, replastering the public areas and patching and painting the apartment walls.

Rents were almost tripled from about $23 a month for each apartment to about $65 a month, causing some tenants to move. The building's population, which is largely Puerto Rican, has an annual turnover rate of 80 per cent, Mr. Starr said.

Even so, Mr. Starr said, the building showed a net loss of $565.07 without depreciation, and $4,461.86 counting depreciation.

Walking through the building yesterday, Mr. Starr pointed to broken windows, garbage a foot deep in the air shafts, defaced hallways and new mailboxes that already showed signs of being broken into, probably by narcotics addicts.

"The most discouraging thing," he said, "is that we can't keep the building in very good conditions—and we still lose money."

Vandalism a Factor

The main reasons for the deficit, he said, were vandalism, the high costs of maintenance and materials, and the inability to charge rents that would meet these costs. The deficit exists, he said, even though the building has tax abatement for 12 years, was not thoroughly rehabilitated, and pays a low rate of interest—5¼ per cent—on its mortgage.

The building on Second Street was bought for $27,000, and $123,000 was put into it for repairs that included the refurbishing of apartment walls that was not done on Ridge Street. The building showed a cash profit of $1,647.09 last year, largely because it is in a better neighborhood and rents run about $84 a month, Mr. Starr said.

Moreover, vandalism is much less of a problem on Second Street, which is considered part of the "East Village" and attracts many students and artists.

"The tenants there have a completely different attitude," Mr. Starr said.

Mr. Starr stressed that low-cost mortgages were not sufficient to attract private investment in the slums, and that some kind of outright grant was also needed. Large rent supplements would also be necessary to allow poor families to pay the rents the renovated buildings would require to remain a workable proposition.

Another problem, Mr. Starr said, is that many decrepit slum buildings are not worth saving. "But the city cannot afford to tear them down, and these people have to have some place to live," he added.

Mr. Starr asserted that nonprofit groups snould not get into the rehabilitation business. Many housing experts have said that such groups, such as churches or settlement houses, should undertake massive rehabilitation projects.

Rehabilitation requires expert management that non profit groups cannot provide, he said. Moreover, nonprofit groups would tend to lose interest in a building after "the excitement of doing the work is over."

Another popular proposal—transferring renovated slum housing to the tenants themselves—also won't work, Mr. Starr said.

"Then you just give them all the headaches," he said.

March 9, 1967

Capital Re-Examines Urban Renewal

By ROBERT B. SEMPLE Jr.
Special to The New York Times

WASHINGTON, July 8—Pressures are building here to turn the frequently criticized $750-million urban renewal program into a more effective instrument to help the poor.

In recent weeks the Administration itself has been telling cities that henceforth it will give high priority to projects emphasizing low and moderate-income housing.

Consequently, the projects long favored by mayors and business interests, commercial and luxury residential construction, will get a lower priority.

Nonetheless, several Congressmen—notably Representative William B. Widnall, the New Jersey Republican who has been a long-time critic of urban renewal practices—have been asking the Administration to place even greater stress on housing for the poor.

Similar pleas have been coming from the Office of Economic opportunity, which administers the antipoverty effort. Some officials there have asserted that the Department of Housing and Urban Development, which runs the renewal program, has not been doing all it can to provide housing for low-income families.

Moreover, the administrators, as well as the critics, of the urban renewal program now agree that, given the mounting competition for funds and the worsening plight of the urban poor, both the image and thrust of the program must be significantly changed.

Authorized by '49 Act

Under urban renewal, which was authorized by the Housing Act of 1949, the Federal Government helps cities pay for clearing or rehabilitating blighted neighborhoods.

As a rule of thumb, the size of the Federal grant is about two-thirds of the so-called "net project cost," the difference between what the city pays for buying and clearing the land and what it receives when it sells the land to developers.

The Administration's new policy on applications for funds was detailed in a memorandum to local planning officials on May 19. It said that henceforth applications for funds would receive priority consideration only if they contributed to one of the following three aims:

¶"The renewal of areas with critical and urgent needs," specifically slums characterized by "physical decay, high tensions, and great social need."

¶"The conservation and expansion of the housing supply for low and moderate-income families"—a clear warning that the bulldozing of low-income neighborhoods to make way for expensive high-rise apartments would be frowned upon.

¶"The development of new employment opportunities" through, for example, the creation of industries with jobs for the hard-core unemployed and unskilled.

As a whole, the thrust of the directive is that cities must focus their renewal efforts on residential neighborhoods without depleting the supply of housing for the poor. Thus it places new emphasis on the rehabilitation of existing structures as opposed to clearance.

In a sense, the policy grows from six years of quiet effort by Robert C. Weaver, Secretary of the Department of Housing and Urban Development. Once, urban renewal was almost exclusively a clearance program, but Mr. Weaver has gradually turned it in the direction of rehabilitation.

For example, of 1,329 urban renewal projects in some stage of planning or execution on Dec. 31, 1963, about one-fourth—324—involved rehabilitations.

Three years later, 581 of 1,763 projects—roughly one-third — involved rehabilitation. More significantly, more than half—59 per cent—of the new projects begun in those three years involved rehabilitation.

The trend toward rehabilitation has been accompanied by a rise in the number of low and moderate income units. In a recent interview, Don Hummel, Mr. Weaver's assistant secretary for renewal and housing assistance, said that, of 472 urban renewal projects in the later stages of development, involving 188,109 dwelling units, 68,570 units were designed for low and moderate income housing.

Competition for Funds

Two major factors have reinforced these trends. One is the intense competition for urban renewal funds. Applications for funds pending at the housing agency total $1.3-billion. The backlog has grown in recent years, while urban renewal appropriations have been held to an annual total of $750-million.

According to the memorandum, this competition, plus "the urgent needs of our cities," make it necessary for the housing agency "to adopt policies that will assure that aid is available for those projects which advance national goals responsive to those needs."

The second major factor has been the steady criticism of the program in the academic community and in Congress.

Mr. Widnall, for example, has long objected to what he says is the disproportionate use of urban renewal money to renovate downtown business districts.

Although the law prevents the housing agency from distributing more than 35 per cent of its total funds to commercial projects in any one year, there are no limits on what individual cities can do with the funds.

Accordingly, until last year, some cities—including Boston, Philadelphia, Cleveland and Baltimore—had used between half and three-fourths of their funds for commercial renewal. Atlanta used over 90 per cent of its funds for commercial renewal. The new priorities are expected to change this.

There has been equally intense criticism of the program's tendency to displace the poor through the bulldozer process.

This criticism culminated last year in Congressional approval of an amendment to the Housing Act of 1966. It said that in any predominantly residential renewal project, a "substantial" number of standard housing units must be for low and moderate-income families. The amendment was proposed by Mr. Widnall.

The new priorities established by the housing agency are designed in part to carry out the Widnall amendment. However, Congressional sources say that Mr. Widnall still is not fully satisfied.

The argument concerns the word "substantial." According to another housing agency memorandum, at least 20 per cent of the new or rehabilitated units in urban renewal areas must be for low and moderate-income families.

Mr. Widnall, however, says that "substantial" means more than 20 per cent. He has not publicly stated what he thinks the figure should be, but he appears determined to negotiate a higher one.

He is also said to want additional safeguards to insure that low-income housing for persons in the $4,000-to-$6,000 salary range is constructed, as well as moderate-income housing for those in the $6,000-to-$9,000 bracket.

July 9, 1967

Gain in Use Of Turnkey Plan Noted

By GLENN FOWLER
Special to The New York Times

CHICAGO, Dec. [illegible]—A two-year-old Federal program that could revolutionize public housing is becoming the main vehicle for providing low-cost living quarters to accommodate poor families in the United States.

The program is known as "Turnkey" because its basic concept is to have private industry build and manage public housing projects, turning the key to the completed apartments over to the local housing authority or to co-operative tenant-owners.

Although the program has been in operation for only two years, its initial success has generated considerable enthusiasm among both Government officials and leaders of the private housing field. The consensus is that the Turnkey idea holds promise of superseding the traditional municipally owned public housing project, which has been the standard method of sheltering the poor in large cities in the last three decades.

Critical Assessment

Turnkey housing received intensive critical assessment this week from homebuilders, mortgage lenders and Government officials who attended the 24th annual convention of the National Association of Home Builders at the International Amphitheatre here. More than 35,000 builders, architects, planners, suppliers of construction materials and representatives of related fields attended the week-long meetings.

The Turnkey program has evolved through three distinct stages since it was started two years ago.

The first stage, officially called Phase 1, provides for a private builder to become the developer of a public housing project. The builder supplies the land and erects the apartments, and the local housing authority agrees to buy the completed project for a negotiated price. The builder is permitted a fair profit on his investment. He must obtain his own financing, but he has the advantage of a guarantee that the project will be bought by the local authority with funds partly supplied by the Federal Government.

Existing Units

This method of construction,

according to Robert C. Weaver, Secretary of Housing and Urban Development, saves two to three years in the elpased time between conception and completion of a low-cost housing project. Mr. Weaver contends that it also cuts costs 10 to 15 per cent from the level necessitated by the traditional method of public-housing construction, whereby the local authority invites bids and lets contracts to private builders.

Turnkey projects are not restricted to new construction; builders may rehabilitate existing units, with the housing authority buying them upon completion. There is even provision for single-family houses, new or rehabilitated, under Phase 1 of the Turnkey program.

Under Phase 2, a completed project is not taken over by the local housing authority, but is managed either by the builder or by a private management firm. The authority may also contract for private management for projects already in existence.

Phase 3 of the Turnkey program, the latest innovation, makes it possible for residents of public housing units eventually to become owners of the quarters they occupy. This is done by having the residents handle the maintenance of the housing themselves, and permitting them to pay for the purchase of their units as their incomes rise.

The first project using the Phase 3 approach was announced only three months ago. The project, in North Gulfport, Miss., will consist of 200 single-family houses with three, four and five bedrooms. The development, which will include a community center, will be built by a private contractor under Phase 1 of the Turnkey program, and will be operated under Phase 2 by an interim management firm. Eventually, a permanent homeowners' association will take over the management from the private firm.

U.S. Focuses on Plan

Mr. Weaver said this week that he did not envision the Turnkey program as becoming the sole means of providing low-cost housing for the poor, but he noted that it had already become the Government's prime effort in this direction.

A variety of other tools will continue to be used, he told the builders' convention. Among these are:

¶Rent supplements, with Government money making up the difference between what low-income families can afford to pay for housing in privately owned buildings and what the landlord must receive to achieve a fair return.

¶Financing at below-market interest rates, enabling nonprofit organizations to obtain loans to build low-cost housing without having to pay the high interest charges dictated by the current state of the money market.

¶Experimental programs intended to develop new means of building and operating low-income housing.

It is clear, however, that the Turnkey program has drawn greater interest and support from the private sector of the housing field than any of the other efforts initiated by the Government, though all have been well received by builders and the home-financing industry.

The fiercely independent building industry is perhaps attracted to the Turnkey idea most of all because it contains the absolute minimum of Government participation. Many builders have shied away from public-housing construction because they bridle at the extensive red tape involved—the need for multiple applications, approvals and qualifications that they contend have proliferated over the years.

Builders point out—and Government housing officials are quick to agree—that the Turnkey program's provision for private financing of a project makes the obtaining of a construction loan considerably simpler.

Rugged Individualism

The Turnkey process offers simpler procedures in a number of other ways that builders appreciate. It also places a premium on the ingenuity of the private contractor; he must come up with a proposal for the design and construction of the housing, and once he obtains approval he must adhere to the standards he agrees upon with the local housing authority.

Turnkey housing has its philosophical as well as practical appeal to private builders, as it has to many persons who have no connection with the housing field. By encouraging private operation as well as construction of housing for low-income families, it effectively removes Government from a significant role in the public housing field, without completely abdicating responsibility.

To builders, most of whom profess strong devotion to rugged individualism and private enterprise, this is a salutary trend. But since these same builders do not shy away from massive Government financial aid—as they have long demanded in the form of low-interest borrowing and other forms of Federal subsidy — the Turnkey program pleases them by keeping the Government purse in the housing picture. It represents to most builders the optimum in Federal programs — heavy spending for construction of low-cost housing with the fewest strings binding the private developer.

But perhaps the most important benefit of the Turnkey program is to the many low-income families who are today virtually excluded from access to decent housing in many cities by their inability to pay. With rents rising steadily, and the price of new homes moving upward with equal steadiness, public housing offers virtually their only escape from the slums.

Until now, that escape had to be made into a Government-owned and Government-operated project, and these have earned growing criticism for their monolithic design and their tendency to turn into concentrations of poor families unleavened by more affluent neighbors and increasingly segregated in racial terms.

Turnkey, it is widely hoped, can broaden the horizons of low-income families by bringing them into what amounts to Government-financed private housing in neighborhoods that, if not affluent, are at least being gradually upgraded.

December 10, 1967

DECAYED HOUSING IN CITY REPORTED AT 800,000 UNITS

Widespread Deterioration Is Found to Affect Both the Poor and Middle Class

By STEVEN V. ROBERTS

A group of Baltimore housing officials recently visited Jason R. Nathan, the city's Housing and Development Administrator, to discuss mutual problems.

"To begin with," Mr. Nathan said, "we have at least 800,000 deteriorated apartments in New York City."

The visitors sat silently for a moment before one gasped: "That's almost as much as the number of people in our whole city."

The decay of vast areas of good housing is probably the major problem facing city housing officials—and one of the most important facing the Lindsay administration. The deterioration means that most of the city's poor—especially the Negro and Puerto Rican poor—live in substandard housing with little hope for improvement.

It also means that many middle-class families, especially after they have children, find it increasingly difficult to get decent housing in the city and must seek it elsewhere, usually by migrating to the suburbs.

Since only a limited amount of public money is available to finance new construction, the city government has to run at top speed to stand still.

Last year 12,000 new apartments were built through a variety of publicly aided programs —at least half for middle-income families. But city officials estimate that close to that number of good apartments deteriorated into substandard condition for many reasons: vandalism by tenants and narcotics addicts; the venality of speculators and blockbusters, and above all, the economic difficulties of managing housing for poor families.

Conclusions Listed

These are the basic conclusions of a New York Times study of city housing problems that included interviews with dozens of city officials, landlords, tenants and academic experts.

The study also reached the following conclusions:

¶Housing experts now realize that landlords must make a decent profit if they are going to keep their buildings in good repair, especially in low-income areas.

¶The fear among whites that racial integration will degrade an area both socially and economically has been a self-fulfilling prophecy; it has led to the decay of most areas into which nonwhite residents have moved, and the eventual flight of most whites. Thus nonwhites who can afford decent housing can seldom find it.

¶Programs designed to provide new housing for both low-income and middle-income families have been plagued by rising labor costs, interest rates and taxes. As a result, officials find it increasingly difficult to build housing at rents people can afford.

¶Lengthy bureaucratic delays have slowed down the construction of public housing and made private investors reluctant to become involved in public programs. Moreover, private investors demand such a high return on their money — 6 per cent with government guarantees, twice that without insurance—that authorities generally agree few privately owned projects could ever provide housing for the really poor.

The New York Times (by Edward Hausner)

TENEMENTS: Lower East Side buildings. Officials estimated that last year nearly as many good apartments became substandard as were built—12,000—by publicly aided programs.

Indignities Are Enormous

Above all, the problem of housing in New York is the problem of people. The physical discomforts and indignities the poor must suffer are enormous, but the psychological damage inflicted by life in the slums is perhaps even more critical.

Kathleen Harris grew up in Harlem with her mother and six brothers and sisters. She had the first of five illegitimate children when she was 16 years old, about 10 years ago. There was no privacy, she explained, no escape from the gang on the block.

Arthur Simon, a young Lutheran minister, quoted Miss Harris in his book, "Faces of Poverty":

"Harlem makes you feel disgusted and let down. You feel this way every day. When you get up you don't care any more.

"In Harlem there is too much confusion. People all get to feeling the same. They don't care. They don't try. But most of the people can't move out. They can't afford to. They're trapped there."

Housing for the poor in New York is the rotting tenements on the Lower East Side that Jacob Riis, the social reformer, said were "scarcely fit to shelter brutes" when he viewed the same buildings more than 50 years ago.

Abandoned Buildings

It is the glowering, six-story tenements along Eighth Avenue in Harlem around which junkies and idle youths gather like a flock of birds. It is the dilapidated apartment buildings in the South Bronx; once good housing, most are now abandoned by recent landlords and, from the looks of the streets, by the Sanitation Department as well.

It is the crumbling frame and brownstone houses in Bedford-Stuyvesant. It is the shacks of Arverne on the Rockaway peninsula and Coney Island, the final dumping grounds for the city's largest, most troubled welfare families, who can find housing nowhere else.

Housing for the poor in this city is halls reeking with urine and containing leaking pipes and falling plaster. It is small children crowded into tiny rooms with no heat, and the sharp winter wind cutting through cracked glass.

Most of all, housing is fear: fear of vandals and narcotics addicts, fear of thieves and muggers, fear of the landlord who will throw you out if you complain, fear of being old and helpless in a five-story walk-up, fear for your children in a hundred different ways. Poor housing is the symbol, and the cause, of hopelessness.

In grappling with the housing problem in New York, officials really face two distinct tasks: building new housing, and preserving existing buildings, most of which would provide decent quarters if adequately maintained.

Since it is virtually impossible to quickly replace 800,000 dilapidated apartments, more attention has been focused in recent years on rehabilitation and preservation. For many years the cry of housing reformers was to "take the profit out of the slums." The methods proposed were vigorous criminal prosecution of "slumlords," who would thus be forced into repairing their property. Today virtually every housing expert agrees that purely punitive methods have failed.

"We have to put the profit back into housing for the poor," said Roger Starr, executive director of the Citizens Housing and Planning Council.

Landlords Blame Tenants

"People have to make money or they won't invest," added an official of the Buildings Department. "Nobody will throw good money after bad."

However, most experts, such as Mr. Starr, are pessimistic about the possibility of upgrading existing slum housing. The central reason is that owning and managing decent housing for the poor is just not profitable. Housing experts point out that if an investor can make 6 per cent on his money by buying blue-chip bonds, real estate—with all its headaches — has to provide twice that return to make it worthwhile.

Housing authorities contend that many slum buildings are so abused that they would require enormous investments to be transformed into decent accommodations (investments that usually result in rent increases of as much as 100 per cent). But most landlords would find it extremely difficult to get either mortgage money or insurance in run-down areas. If they did upgrade their buildings, they would run into abnormally high maintenance costs.

There is evidence indicating that tenants themselves sometimes damage buildings. Landlords usually blame tenants for most deterioration. One landlord in Brownsville said: "They're animals, you just don't know what it's like. You can't keep a place decent."

But many academic experts

argue that even if a tenant does damage a building, the roots of his antisocial behavior are deep and complex. "His building is a handy symbol of all the authority in society that oppresses him," said Professor Chester Rapkin of Columbia University. "He just lashes out against it."

Role of Rent Control

Another problem is outside vandalism, primarily by narcotics addicts, who have been known to steal the plumbing from a building in daylight. And good janitorial help, which could keep many minor problems from getting out of hand, is also difficult to find in poor areas.

The rents most families can pay in rundown areas often do not cover the costs of renovation and maintenance. Thus there is no incentive for the landlord to do it. The Citizens Housing and Planning Council tried to rehabilitate two tenements on the Lower East Side last year with a foundation grant and wound up losing money.

Landlords also complain that rent control keeps down their profits and prevents them from investing more money in their buildings. City officials acknowledge privately that in some cases rent control does contribute to deterioration. But they doubt that most landlords would, in fact, put higher profits back into their buildings.

They also note that the lifting of controls would cause tremendous hardship to thousands of families, and is thus both economically and politically unfeasible.

Economics is only half of the problem of upgrading slum housing. The other half is the changing pattern of ownership in low-income housing.

It is generally agreed by students of the problem that the best housing for the poor was provided in the past by resident owners who did much of the maintenance work themselves and took pride in their buildings. But in many areas of the city, close-knit ethnic communities, such as the Lower East Side, have broken up as the immigrants and their children became assimilated into American society and sought better housing elsewhere.

As the number of resident owners dwindled, much of their property was bought up by speculators who were more interested in making as much money as possible than in managing good housing. The poor and unorganized minority groups moving into the old neighborhoods were exploited. Services dropped, profits increased. In addition, a significant amount of slum property fell into the hands of amateurs who either inherited the buildings or bought them for investment purposes.

The speculators are seldom willing, and the amateurs are seldom able, to keep buildings in good repair. The good landlord, who has both the skill and desire to manage decent property, is increasingly rare in poor areas because, as authorities note, he has better investment opportunities, and fewer headaches, elsewhere.

Given these economic problems, and the character of many owners of slum property, most city officials now doubt that private, profit-making ownership can operate decent housing for the poor.

"The historical system of private ownership is just not working," Donald H. Elliott, chairman of the City Planning Commission, said in an interview.

Private Capability in Doubt

The city has tried many programs to make it work. An example is the receivership program, under which the city is able to take over hazardous buildings, make repairs, and bill the owners for the costs.

But out of 120 buildings taken into the program, in only 11 cases have landlords paid the bills and reclaimed their property. It just did not pay for them to do it and the city was left with the responsibility for the properties.

What, then, can the city do? "We have been hearing for years from the easy-answer boys, who have been foisting on the public simplistic answers," Mr. Nathan said. "They say the villain is the slumlord, the Negro, rent control, the city bureaucracy, someone on the take. But there are no answers to these complex questions."

Subsidizing private owners, through rent supplements or other devices, has been suggested as one answer. But Frederic S. Berman, Commissioner of Rent and Housing Maintenance, expressed concern that if many of the landlords who now own slum property were given more income they would not spend it on improving their buildings.

Few housing officials believe widespread public ownership would be a good idea. It would be very expensive, and city-managed public housing has been widely criticized as "sterile" and "institutional," most contend.

City officials have been talking for almost two years about devising some way in which the city could take over slum property, fix it up, and then convey it to either a tenant cooperative or community group. Without a mortgage or real estate taxes, officials believe a building might be able to pay for itself.

While they struggle with the problem of existing slum housing, city officials are also deeply disturbed by the continuing collapse and deterioration of neighborhoods that just a few years ago provided decent housing for thousands of New Yorkers.

It is difficult to measure the spread of deterioration, but every index points in the same direction. As of June 30, 1967, unpaid real-estate taxes had jumped to 5.2 per cent of the total bill, or $169-million. In 1960 arrears amounted to 3.2 per cent. Last year 1,056 properties were foreclosed for nonpayment of taxes as opposed to 629 in 1966 and 535 in 1965.

Prices Cut in Half

Bankers estimate that many millions of dollars in mortgages are in default, and that market prices in many areas have been cut in half. Councilman Robert A. Low estimates there are 5,000 to 12,000 abandoned buildings in the city.

The blight is indiscriminate. In the East New York section of Brooklyn, the city chose a former synagogue to use as headquarters for the Model Cities program — the Federally aided project attacking physical and social deprivation in selected areas. Two weeks later the building was vandalized and burned out.

Why this happens is very complicated. But authorities believe that these areas are faced with a much more rapid version of what happened in the present Negro and Puerto Rican slums about 30 years ago.

As younger generations of Jews, Irish and Italians move out of their old neighborhoods—primarily in the Bronx and Brooklyn—landlords begin to accept minority families who are struggling to escape from the slums in which they are trapped. Often these minority families have a good income and keep their apartments as well or better than their white neighbors.

But fear often begins to pervade a white neighborhood bordering on a nonwhite area. The out-migration of whites accelerates, and more nonwhites move in, perhaps not as well off as the first wave.

Beginning of Decline

As his building begins to fill up with Negroes and Puerto Ricans, a landlord often cuts services, especially if he assumes the neighborhood is going to decline and does not justify more than a minimal investment. His prophecy is self-fulfilling; if he assumes the area will go down, he guarantees that it will.

Blockbusters and speculators move in, and bankers begin to share the assumption that an area is doomed. Mortgage money and fire insurance become hard to get. Deterioration accelerates again, and the flight of whites becomes an unstoppable flood.

The panic, once it hits an area, can be devastating. In the western part of East New York, bordering on Brownsville, city officials estimate that in 1960 the population was 90 per cent white and 10 per cent nonwhite. Today the figures are reversed.

The deterioration of an area like this is not simply a function of racial change. It results from a complex interaction involving the age of a neighborhood, tenant behavior and the venality of speculators. But the most important reason, and the hardest to combat, is fear.

Mr. Nathan and his colleagues believe that while much racial change is inevitable, some whites can be convinced to stay in these turbulent areas. More important, they feel that existing buildings can be preserved so that the new occupants can have decent places to live.

Some middle-class Negroes have moved several times into largely white areas, only to find these sections deteriorating around them in a few years, forcing them to move again.

The most common answer to the problem is that the city must provide special services and show an area that it cares. But often an area seems to suffer a decline in services just as it begins to change.

Study Incomplete

It is problematical, however, whether increased services would make much difference to white residents intent on leaving. In the Crotona section of the Bronx, for example, the East Tremont Young Men's Hebrew Association on Southern Boulevard expanded its program in a renovated building five years ago in a deliberate attempt to keep Jews in the area. But the Jewish population continued to drop so badly that the group is planning to close.

City officials acknowledge that sometimes they are so concerned with the problems of the worst slums that transitional areas tend to get ignored. For example, city officials said almost two years ago that they were deeply troubled about the stability of the Grand Concourse area in the Bronx and would commission a study to find out what to do. The study has never been finished.

When asked specifically what the city's strategy for coping with transitional areas was, Mr. Nathan said: "I don't know, I'm groping. We don't understand the real causes. We're hoping the Rand Corporation [the West Coast research company recently hired by the city] will give us an in-depth analysis so that we can develop a program."

Given the problems of existing slums and transitional areas, the pressure on the city to build new housing has increased enormously. But housing experts maintain that the available resources are in no way equal to the task.

For example, the Federal Government, now the major source of funds for housing programs, has financed only 925,000 apartments in multiple dwellings for the entire country in 30 years—while New York has 800,000 in need of replacement or renovation right now.

President Johnson has proposed the construction of six million new units in the next 10 years. His National Advisory Commission on Civil Disorders has said the country must reach that goal in five years or risk increased violence in the cities. But city officials are gloomy about the prospects for massive new appropriations, noting that Congress last year barely approved tiny appropriations for the Model Cities and rent-supplement programs.

Public subsidy is particularly important because the housing problem is largely a reflection of the poverty problem. The median family income for Negroes and Puerto Ricans in the city — now about 28 per cent of the population — is less than $3,500. Most minority families, and many whites as well, cannot begin to afford new housing on the private market, which costs at least $60 a room a month.

Mr. Nathan said that housing programs have not shown great progress in the last two years, but that the next two would be more productive. He conceded that Mayor Lindsay has lost time by restructuring the city housing agencies under the new Housing and Development Administration and redirecting many old policies.

Moreover, he added, projects usually take several years from the time they are proposed until they are built. Therefore, statistics on how many apartments were started last year reflect more about the Wagner administration than the Lindsay administration, he said.

However, it is possible to get some idea of what the Lindsay Administration has done so far in building low-cost housing. The bulk of low-income apartments are included in public housing, which contains about 525,000 people living in about 144,000 apartment. The average rent is about $18 a room. They were built under a variety of Federal, state and city programs, but since local voters have consistently rejected referendums on new bond issues, most projects today are financed by Washington.

The Housing Authority, which builds and manages public housing, has a waiting list of about 135,000 families. Last year it opened nine projects containing 3,582 apartments, and started another 2,701 apartments, all originally proposed by the Wagner administration.

The city has a four-year allocation for 28,800 apartments from the Federal Government under an appropriation that runs out on June 30, 1969. By its own count, the Lindsay administration says it will have, at most, 16,000 apartments approved on the local level under that appropriation by this summer.

City officials declare that they spent considerable time establishing a new policy of scattering a sizable number of public housing units in largely white, middle-class areas — much to the displeasure of some local residents. In addition, they decided that most public housing within slum areas would be small, well-designed buildings, not the traditional red-brick towers of the past.

Public housing here is also plagued by an apparent rule-of-thumb that Washington will not usually approve a project that costs more than $20,000 a unit to build. Since New York has the highest construction and land costs in the nation, the policy — Federal officials formally deny it exists, but city officials say it does — means that the city has great difficulty building large apartments. But an extremely critical need is for large apartments, especially since landlords have chopped up so many units into single rooms for higher profit.

Moreover, the Housing Authority's rising maintenance costs — coupled with tenants' demands for more protection against crime—could mean a rent rise throughout the city if the Federal Government does not increase its subsidies for operating expenses.

Housing for poor families is also provided by two middle-income programs financed by Federal, state and city sources. For example, the state will provide subsidies for low-income families living in housing built under the Mitchell-Lama law, but only 904 have been financed thus far.

The Federal Government will also provide rent supplements for families living in housing built under a Middle-income program known as 221 (d) (3), which the city hopes to use extensively here.

City housing officials argue that Congress has provided only $40-million for the whole country for rent supplements and has burdened the program with numerous restrictions. A family must pay 25 per cent of its income for rent, which city officials consider far too high for a large family. In addition, a family can make no more than $6,100 a year to qualify—a ceiling officials think is far too low for New York.

These and other programs suffer under another enormous handicap: the difficulty of moving complex technical projects through a tangle of bureaucratic and political decisions that leaves even strong administrations sputtering with anger and dismay.

There are many complex reasons for bureaucratic delay: increasing concern for relocation, detailed checks and audits by timid bureaurats, the fragmented decision-making structure within the city government. Moreover, a large number of well-organized civic and special-interest groups further limit the government's ability to move decisively.

The most vocal and militant groups in recent years have been those representing communities affected by proposed redevelopment plans. These include national organizations such as the Congress of Racial Equality as well as local groups organized by the anti-poverty program. The Lindsay administration is convinced that such groups must play a large role in shaping the future of their neighborhoods, but officials are also aware of some of the problems this policy presents.

The Mayor and his aides have noted that community groups could become platforms for ambitious politicians who do not always speak in the best interests of the community. Local leaders also often lack expertise in technical areas and experience in managing complex bureaucracies.

Moreover, communities often do not agree on what they want. Planning for the Milbank-Frawley Circle urban renewal area in Harlem, for example, has been virtually halted by a battle between Negroes and Puerto Ricans for control of the program.

The prospect of dealing with community groups is one reason why private investors are reluctant to build housing in poor areas.

This is why Governor Rockefeller has proposed, and the Legislature has established, the Urban Development Corporation, which is empowered to act as a sponsor of a housing project in its early stages, when risks from political and bureaucratic delay are enormous for a private investor. The corporation would then sell the building to private interests, which could then avoid these risks.

However, some housing economists believe that private investment is no panacea. A private investor must be guaranteed a sizable return on his money, and without large government subsidies investors cannot build housing for poorer families. The Urban Development Corporation, for instance, will build mainly middle-income housing.

The problem, then, of housing in New York, is many-sided. But the central difficulty is money. Without it, present programs can neither be expanded nor improved to provide housing for the hundreds of thousands of people trapped in the city's slums, and countless others who are forced to flee to the suburbs.

But with city and state sources severely limited, and with the Federal Government shackled by spending for the Vietnam war, city officials are not optimistic. Moreover, the competition for what money there is grows constantly. New York has to fight for every nickel.

Thus experts agree that unless something unexpected happens, the economics and the statistics point to two conclusions. The middle class, particularly families with children, will continue to find it increasingly difficult to afford rents in the city. And generations of poor people, most of them Negro or Puerto Rican, are doomed to live in squalor for the foreseeable future.

May 27, 1968

Johnson Approves 'Massive' Program To House the Poor

By ROBERT B. SEMPLE Jr.

Special to The New York Times

WASHINGTON, Aug. 1 — President Johnson signed today the most ambitious housing bill in the nation's history — a $5.3-billion program for the construction or rehabilitation of more than 1.7 million housing units over the next three years.

The measure, which includes a provision for substantial Federal funds to help the poor buy homes, represents the first installment on Mr. Johnson's goal of six million units for poor and moderate income families in the next decade.

That figure is regarded by urban experts as sufficient to replace all existing substandard dwelling units.

Mr. Johnson signed the bill at a desk placed on a dais on the plaza in front of the curving, modernistic Department of Housing and Urban Development building in southwest Washington. A lunch-time crowd of 2,000, most of them Government workers, gathered for the ceremony in the bright sunshine.

The President called the bill "the most far-sighted, most comprehensive, most massive housing program in all of American history" and said it "can be the Magna Carta to liberate our cities."

In addition to the plan to help nearly 500,000 families buy homes, another key provision provides for 700,000 new housing units for low and moderate income renters.

The essential device in both programs is an interest-rate subsidy, under which the Federal Government reduces the interest rates on monthly mortgage payments to as low as 1 per cent. Most persons now have to pay more than 6 per cent.

Under the home ownership program, home buyers will be required to pay 20 per cent of their income. The subsidy will be the difference between the 20 per cent and the required monthly payment, at market rates of interest for principal, interest taxes, insurance and mortgage premium.

The subsidy will vary with the owner's income, but in no case can it exceed the difference between what the mortgage would cost at the market rate and what it would cost if the interest rate were reduced to 1 per cent.

A family cannot qualify if its income is 35 per cent more than the income ceiling for families in public housing, which is generally restricted to the very poor. These ceilings vary widely from area to area, depending on construction costs and other factors.

Associated Press

AT CEREMONY IN WASHINGTON: President Johnson outside the Housing and Urban Development building, where he signed the bill on home construction and rehabilitation.

Families That Qualify

Government analysts have indicated that a family of four living in Chicago—regarded as a "typical" family in the home-ownership market—can earn as much as $7,080 a year and still qualify for subsidies under the program.

The Administration had sought more liberal income limits that would have allowed a family of four in urban areas earning $8,800 a year to qualify, but these were revised in the House.

However, officials believe that the program will bring home ownership within the range of families earning as little as $3,000 annually if the family does not buy a house costing more than $12,000.

For example, the monthly payment on a $12,000 house is $99.66, at 6¾ per cent interest. A family earning $3,600 a year puts up $60—that is, 20 per cent of its monthly income of $300—and the Government adds $39.66.

Buying the same house, a $3,000-a-year family puts up $50—20 per cent of its monthly income of $250—and the Government provides $45.72.

This is not quite enough to make up the difference between the family's $50 and the total market-rate cost of $99.66, but it is all the Government can pay under the limitations imposed by the bill. If the Government paid a larger subsidy it would be reducing the interest rate on the mortgage below 1 per cent.

The rental program works in much the same way, although the subsidies are paid to the sponsor or owner of the housing project, thereby reducing his payments to the bank. These lower payments are then translated into lower rents for the tenants.

Among the other major provisions of the measure are these:

¶A new Federal-private program under which insurance companies and the states put up most of the money to provide insurance protection for businessmen and homeowners in the slums.

¶The first Government program to protect land buyers against fraudulent interstate land sales.

¶Federal payments for 425,000 new public housing units over three years, thereby vastly accelerating a program that has been building units at an annual rate of 35,000 the last three years.

¶An additional total of 155,000 new or renovated units under the rent supplement program, by which the Government agrees to pay nonprofit landlords the difference between 25 per cent of the tenant's income and what the landlord needs to break even on his project.

¶Permission to corporations to join in partnerships and pool their resources for the construction of low and moderate income housing on a large scale, with or without Federal assistance.

¶Authorization for $1.4-billion more for the urban renewal program beginning July 1, 1969.

¶A program that would give developers of so-called "new towns" Federal backing for loans required to pay the basic capital costs. The principal obstacle to the development of new communities has been the failure of entrepreneurs to obtain adequate financing.

Price Tags Large

The funds for these programs will have to be appropriated in separate appropriations bills, presumably by future Congresses. The price tags are large.

Under the home ownership and rental programs, for instance, the mortgages run for 40 years. The cost to the Government of subsidizing these mortgages over 40 years is estimated at $50-billion.

If, in future authorizations, Congress decides to achieve six million new or rehabilitated units — that is, roughly five times the number authorized in the present bill—the cost over the next four or five decades could exceed $200-billion.

The bill represents the culmination of nearly three years of work. It is an amalgam of ideas that suddenly "fell into place," according to one Government official, and came from sources in and out of Government.

A single guiding thread to the bill appears to be on volume production of low and moderate income units.

The President's associates say the measure illustrates the degree to which he has sought to solve a problem by delegating authority to committees, then pruning what he does not like from their recommendations and defending to the utmost what he does like.

The industrialist Edgar F.

Kaiser, head of the President's Commission on Urban Housing, invented the complex legal mechanism that would enable large corporations to create a common pool of resources for low and moderate income housing while receiving a 12 to 14 per cent return on their investment.

Other Key Panels

Similarly, a panel led by the Secretary of Housing and Urban Development, Robert C. Weaver, worked out the processes whereby six million substandard housing units could be eliminated or replaced through the interest-subsidy principle.

Another group, led by Gov. Richard J. Hughes of New Jersey, devised the plan under which the insurance companies, the states and the Federal Government could provide insurance to owners in riot-torn areas that had not been available.

Not all the ideas came from study groups, however. In early 1967, for example, both Senator Harrison A. Williams Jr., Democrat of New Jersey, and Manuel Cohen, chairman of the Securities and Exchange Commission, had been unsuccessfully pushing a bill to place safeguards on the mail-order sale of land. The President suggested that it be incorporated in the housing bill and thus provided with legislative insulation.

Similarly, White House aides say that Mr. Johnson was the prime mover of the home ownership provision, although it is conceded that the vigorous advocacy by Senator Charles H. Percy, Republican of Illinois, of home ownership for the poor forced the Administration to come up with a plan of its own.

Finally, a television show that Mr. Johnson watched in Texas last year is said by aides to have sparked his interest in the idea of "humanizing" urban renewal, leading in turn to a provision in the measure that allows urban renewal projects to proceed without the immediate dislocation of all neighborhood residents.

There was some bickering over the bill, mainly within the Administration. Some doubted whether six million units could be constructed in 10 years, while others hoped to reduce the timetable to five years.

Meanwile, the Treasury worried about the budgetary impact of the interest rate subsidy program and was mollified only when Mr. Johnson agreed to take the Federal National Mortgage Association, whose purchases of private mortgages had counted as a budget expenditure, and place it in private hands.

August 2, 1968

A Singularly New York Product

By ADA LOUISE HUXTABLE

It is hard to grasp the size, importance and impact of Co-op City. In New York, superlatives bore. This is a city that swallows cities; not, however, without serious urban indigestion.

An Appraisal

But the simple facts of Co-op City stun those trained to think in urban terms. The world's largest cooperative housing community. The largest single apartment development in the United States. A city of 50,000 to 60,000 people in 15,382 apartments piled onto 300 acres—instant new town.

A community of 60,000 was the standard starting point of almost all of the British government-planned, postwar new towns. It was the initial population of those famous Scandinavian planning models, Vallingby and Farsta in Sweden and Tapiola in Finland. But the similarity ends right there.

Co-op City is an example of a singularly American, or New York, product. Its size and scale are monumental; its environmental and social planning is minimal.

The British and Scandinavian new towns are total town-planning concepts. Major preliminary investment in both design and money has been concentrated on providing and integrating those important services and amenities and land-use features that turn houses into real places to live.

In Scandinavia, for example, a great deal of the investment goes into attractive town centers, always a large, focally located and unusually attractive group of buildings, plazas, stores, fountains and recreation spaces that are much more than the shopping centers considered adequate at Co-Op City. The true town center, through its architectural style and quality, creates a community core, a way of life and a special kind of shared environment.

The overwhelming consideration of Co-op City's nonprofit sponsors and builders, the United Housing Foundation, has been to provide livable apartments at an exceptionally low cost, period. This is an unassailable objective in a city that can use all the housing it can get, even if it is producing a bumper crop of human failures through environmental failure.

The United Housing Foundation's philosophy and practice has been to buy relatively inexpensive land and put up uniform, large buildings at high density in a standard cookie-cutter pattern for maximum costs benefits. Beyond the provision of some basic shopping facilities and the space allotment for necessary public services that the city must follow along and provide, everything else is expected to fall into place. Foundation partisans say this pattern, repeated in all their projects, makes the low-cost formula possible.

Certainly, success is on their side. They build good apartments at unbeatable prices.

The foundation has provided this kind of housing in at least a dozen cooperatives to the tune of about half a billion dollars, or half of New York State's investment in low-interest mortgage financing for housing low- and middle-income families.

Why, then, is there any debate about the virtues of Co-op City? Why has the U.H.F., been under constant professional attack for sterile site-planning and uninspired architectural design, for communities that are not communities in the urban expert's sense or according to the standards of the more urbanistically enlightened countries of the world? With so much government financing, are greater sociological and environmental planning the luxuries that the foundation stubbornly contends them to be?

The story of how Co-op City got built provides answers. It reveals the mutually serious faults and failures of the U.H.F.'s planning and design limitations and of the city's sticky machinery for assisting such an undertaking.

The city argues that the full implications of the huge scale of Co-op City were not acknowledged by any significant change in U.H.F. building or planning attitudes. There was no planner involved—only the architect, Herman J. Jessor, who had been producing standard U.H.F. housing since the Forties.

The process that made Co-op City what it is today—a considerably improved version of the foundation formula, if far short of a planner's dream—can be called only planning fence-mending, or a posteriori planning by negotiation.

What the city used for persuasion was its tax abatement powers under the State Mitchell-Lama Law, which provided Co-op City's financing, and necessary mapping and zoning changes. What the foundation used was the promise of all that housing.

Four Bitter Years

"They came in with the usual stereotype that they always build," a city spokesman says.

They went out with the density cut from 17,000 to 15,382 units, a revised plan and street system, consultant site planners and landscape architects—Zion and Breen of Paley Park fame, recommended by the city—tower and V-form variations of their standard buildings, grouped where possible; changes in material and color from endless institutional red brick, and 236 town houses for human scale. While the results will set no world standards, everybody gained.

Protracted negotiations have determined public facilities, transportation, institutional sites for religious and social agencies, garages, schools, open-area treatment and parks, and the relationship of the huge project to its surroundings, including provision for industrial development and jobs.

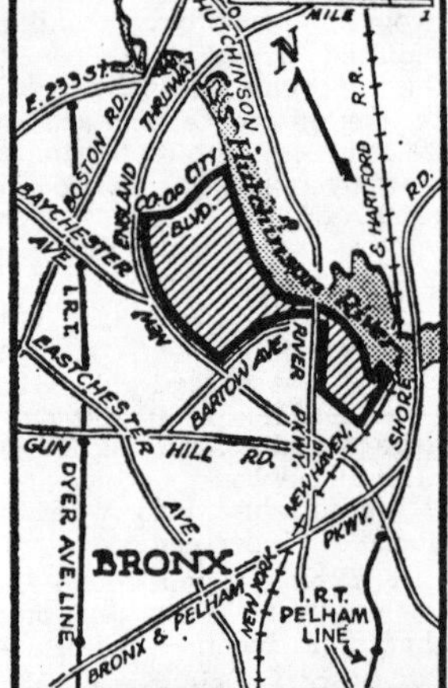

The New York Times Nov. 25, 1968

Two sections of Co-op City will be joined by underpass.

There are 100 pages of street agreements alone. "I can't remember all the gruesome details," one of the city's planning staff says. It took four bitter years.

A city coordinator had to be appointed to pull a dozen bureaucratically mired city departments into coordinated action. Even so, roads are just going in now. Schools will be built by the U.H.F. and repurchased by the city, to get them built at all.

The crippling city zoning that locks big buildings into those desolately spread site plans is yet to be changed to make better planning possible. It will be years before subway lines are extended. Architectural design possibilities remain unexplored.

"Design innovation is not permitted to drive up costs," the foundation insists. That means that New York's most important producer of housing closes the door that might ultimately drive costs down and house more New Yorkers in unaccustomed style. The greatest city in the world stumbles on.

November 25, 1968

Paradox of Big Cities: Houses Are Abandoned Despite Shortage

By JOHN HERBERS

Special to The New York Times

WASHINGTON, Feb. 8—In the District of Columbia, three miles southeast of the Capitol, there is a cluster of two and three-story apartment buildings set on rolling hills and separated by tree-lined streets, lawns, sidewalks and play areas.

The buildings, erected in the ninteen-forties, are made of clean brick, and the design is not unattractive. Yet entire blocks of them are vacant, their windows and doors covered with plywood. In the few that are occupied, people live only on the upper floors because the ground level is considered too vulnerable to burglars, who roam the neighborhood.

On a winter afternoon, the area seems to be a ghost town occupied by children at play. This scene of premature decay and abandonment provides visual evidence of a trend that is evident in large cities across the country.

While the nation is undergoing the most critical housing shortage since World War II, structurally sound dwellings in the inner cities are being abandoned in increasing numbers to vandalism and demolition.

In Detroit, where there are 3,000 empty buildings—1,300 of them abandoned by their owners—Jack Kelley, Deputy Commissioner of the Department of Buildings and Safety Engineering, said:

"People are looking all over for good homes and we have thousands of these empty ones around."

Causes Termed Complex

The causes are complex and are intertwined with all the other factors of urban distress, especially the troubles of poor minorities. A survey of 14 major cities showed that the abandonment of housing that could be rehabilitated at a reasonable cost is occurring almost exclusively in poor minority neighborhoods.

The acceleration of this process, however, seems to be caused chiefly by these developments:

¶The landlord, who has been accused for years of overcharging and underservicing low income families, now finds the slum unprofitable and is withdrawing as fast as possible. "The buildings become harder to rent, and the owners find it more economical simply to walk away," said Albert Nerviani, chief of the St. Louis housing code enforcement office. Tenant strikes and urban violence of recent years also have discouraged investors.

¶Economic conditions that are holding down construction of new housing—high costs and interest rates and scarcity of capital—are also hampering rehabilitation and simple repairs.

¶Whites, and to some extent blacks, when they have the means and opportunity, are migrating to the suburbs or outer areas of the city to escape blighted neighborhoods. For example, Negroes are moving from Anacostia, the southeastern section of Washington, into Prince Georges County, Md., leaving behind vacant units that would be snapped up if they were not in a distressed area.

Federal and local programs of rehabilitation, housing subsidies and demolition programs are barely making a dent in the abandonment process. In the Roxbury section of Boston, 2,700 apartments have been rehabilitated recently under Federal and local effort, but the number of abandoned or vacant buildings in the city has increased from 450 to 800 in the last two years.

In Philadelphia, where at last count there were 24,000 vacant residential structures, Ivan B. Bluckman, assistant housing director, said, "There are thousands of abandoned properties in Philadelphia that are not the responsibility of anyone."

Two Policy Approaches

This raises the question of national policy.

The previous Administration had planned on expanded urban renewal, Model Cities and other Federal programs to help to arrest inner city decay. The Nixon Administration, however, is taking a different approach. For example, the Democrats had projected Model Cities appropriations at about $1-billion for the next fiscal year. Mr. Nixon's new budget calls for half of that, which is the current expenditure.

What the Nixon Administration is promising instead is action and programs that will help the minority poor to acquire more personal wealth and earning capability and opportunity to move into better neighborhoods, as whites have done.

According to the survey, the problem of abandonment is worst in the large cities of the industrial East and Middle West. In New York, officials estimate that 114,000 apartments have been lost since 1965 because of the abandonment of the buildings.

Thieves Move In

The trend is found also, however, in Southern and Western cities where there is a large minority population. In Houston, officials estimate there are 7,500 abandoned dwellings, and New Orleans recently closed part of a five-block area near the center of town because of decay.

In Chicago, where 1,400 buildings were demolished by court order last year, John Hight, chief of the city's building demolition, said that most of the cases fell into a pattern.

"The neighborhood deteriorates, crime increases," he said. "Tenants damage the buildings and may balk at paying their rents. The landlord is hailed into housing court for violations. If he tries to comply, he finds it difficult to get a good contractor to go into the area. He just quits trying.

"Eventually, it gets so bad

The New York Times (by Mike Lien)

A street in Washington, D.C., about three miles from the Capitol, where many apartment buildings are now vacant

people move out. Thieves and vandals come in. Plumbing, heating and electrical services are stripped and sold for salvage. Eventiallly the thieves go through the floor and dig up the lead pipes and sell them.

"A building, which not long before could have been repaired, is wrecked beyond repair. And then it ends up under the ball at the court's direction."

One building in Chicago provides a case study of some of the conflict, sociology and economics involved. The building, at 5801-09 Calumet Avenue on the South Side, was erected in 1901 and contained 24 apartments.

To make more money by packing in more families, the owners converted it some years later to 95 units, in violation of the building codes. The courts in 1962, after a complaint had been filed, ordered it deconverted to 24 units.

Last June, an inspection showed the building to be largely occupied but in a state of neglect and infested with rats and roaches. The authorities said that the building could have been put into shape without major work.

The owners, Cheers Enterprises, Inc., did not follow the orders of the court in correcting code violations, and on Oct. 24 city inspectors found the building vacant and stripped of plumbing and heating facilities. The case was moved to demolition court.

Panthers Occupied Building

Subsequently, members of the Black Panther party occupied the building, and it was there on Nov. 13 that the shooting occurred in which two policemen and a Panther were killed and several policemen and Panthers wounded.

On Dec. 1, the building was ordered demolished, and last week, after several delays caused by cold weather, the structure was gone.

One hopeful sign, housing officials say, is the tax reform enacted last year, which cuts the amount of depreciation an owner can claim during his first few years of ownership. The previous depreciation table encouraged a rapid turnover of buildings and thus their deterioration.

But it is agreed that this does not get at the root causes of the trouble. Stuart H. Brehm, executive director of the Community Improvement Agency in New Orleans, contemplated the thousands of substandard dwellings in his city and concluded, "This is too massive a problem for the city to undertake alone."

February 9, 1970

Inflation and Crime Fuel Public Housing Crisis

By JOHN HERBERS
Special to The New York Times

WASHINGTON, June 3—In cities across the country, thousands of families are on the waiting lists for public housing. Many housing authorities are on the verge of bankruptcy.

A number of the projects, marred by crime and vandalism, have high vacancy rates. Tenants' organizations are springing up and are forming their own security guards and stringent tenant rules.

Construction of much-needed new housing is being slowed by the resistance of middle-income whites and blacks to the new Federal policy of dispersing low-income units outside the slums.

This is the picture that emerges from a New York Times survey of public housing in 17 major cities. Inflation, the slowdown in the economy, the over-all housing shortage, crime and acute maintenance problems are bringing turbulence and a new sense of urgency to the low-income housing crisis that has been building for some time in the troubled centers of large cities.

Probably the most encouraging sign is the formation of tenants' groups that are bringing a feeling of community to neighborhoods where it has long been lacking.

In St. Louis an 11-story high-rise building filled with large families, which is named for the Rev. Dr. Martin Luther King Jr. and run by a newly formed tenant group, is doing well. A few blocks away 33 similar buildings in the Pruitt-Igoe project lie in a state of ruin and abandonment, the nation's foremost monument to the mistakes that have been made in public building.

Despite the failures, authorities in almost every city have been swamped with applications as the national housing shortage has become more acute. Chicago has a waiting list of 21,000, Miami 8,000, Pittsburgh 5,500, Memphis and Louisville 4,000 each, Boston 2,700 and Atlanta 2,000.

"The shortage of housing is so real," said Irvin M. Kriegsfeld, director of the Cleveland authority, "that families may actually begin a squatters' movement in order to find a place to live. It has not come to living in autos yet, but it could happen here."

New public and private housing for low-income families is being built with Federal subsidies, but not nearly fast enough to keep up with population growth and decay of buildings in the central cities. The financial plight of the housing authorities and the scarcity of suitable sites is slowing construction.

Although New York was not included among the cities surveyed, its public housing problems are immense. Vacancy rates in projects are negligible. More than 135,000 low-income families are on the waiting lists, but only 2,000 new units have been built annually in recent years.

The New York City Housing Authority, which manages one-fifth of all the public housing in the country, faces a deficit of $2-million this year because of soaring operating expenses.

One of the mistakes in public housing is that so much of it was built in poverty areas, increasing the distress already there. The Department of Housing and Urban Development, which dispenses Federal subsidies, is now requiring dispersal.

In Memphis, where there are 40,000 substandard homes and 2,000 being added to the list each year, a housing official explained the problem:

"We try to build low-income housing in a white, blue-collar suburb and people out there raise hell. Then we try to build a unit in [predominantly black] South Memphis and middle-class Negroes do the same. People just start panicking over what low-income housing is going to do to their property values."

In Cleveland, an effort backed by Mayor Carl B. Stokes to build 350 single-family, low-income homes in the southeast section was blocked by black residents, some of whom said they had escaped the inner city by hard work and did not want a public housing project that might bring inner-city problems to their neighborhood.

The financial crisis for the housing authorities is caused chiefly by rising costs. Vandalism and crime are contributing factors. In Detroit, where the city authority has used $1.5-million of its $2-million reserve to cover operating costs, Toomark Herley, the assistant director, said:

"It just costs more today because of inflation to keep the places up. We get deeper and deeper in the hole each year. If we raised the rents [$30 to $80 a month a family] then the whole idea of low-cost public housing is defeated."

In St. Louis, where the rents were slightly higher and the incomes of the poor considerably lower, a nine-month rent strike by 700 tenants resulted in a 25 per cent reduction—and additional financing woes for the housing authority.

Federal subsidies to help cover operating costs have helped ease the crisis some, but they have not been sufficient, local authorities complain. They say they do not know how much they can expect in the future.

"We are serving the lower echelon of the lower-income group," said Harold M. Booth Jr. of the Louisville Municipal Commission. "We have got to have additional Federal monies or we will go bankrupt."

The extent of the crisis is suggested by the situation in Miami. There, the Urban League estimates that in the porest sections of the city the inability of the poor to pay rent, in all types of housing, is causing an eviction rate of about 400 families a month.

Crime and vandalism have increased in public housing at about the same rate as in the neighborhoods where they are located.

In Chicago, the housing authority is experimenting with closed circuit television. Cameras in elevators are monitored at a central station which can, by remote control, lock the elevator with a suspect inside until the police arrive.

The most effective and least costly security is being provided by the organizations, which appear to be increasing as housing conditions worsen. In a project in Boston, the tenants take turns manning a security office that has a "hot line" to police headquarters. In Buffalo, male tenants escort the elderly to evening meetings and to pick up and cash their welfare checks.

24-Hour Patrol

In St. Louis, the Cochran Project of high-rise buildings, which has suffered from vandalism, crime and a high vacancy rate, is undergoing a slow restoration due partly to a 24-hour security patrol consisting of men who live in the building. They are paid a small salary out of the revenues from rents, a concession won in the rent strike.

Robberies, burglaries, drug sales, and vandalism have fallen sharply. The patrol has had an important side effect—the creation of community spirit. The patrolmen, who wear work clothes and usually are unarmed, are known and respected by the hundreds of children and teenagers who swarm over the premises.

The patrolmen are an important part of the tenants' groups, which in some buildings enforce strict regulations that have brought destruction of property and littering under control.

In every city, housing authorities now acknowledge that high-rise buildings are best for the elderly and garden apartments or smaller buildings for families. It is largely the high-rise buildings occupied by families that have been disasters.

Clarence L. Swan, a retired white businesesman, and his wife live by choice, not necessity, on one of the upper floors of the Cochran Project in St. Louis, surrounded by black families. "I was in the salvage business until 10 years ago when I retired and decided to try to salvage lives instead," he explained.

In St. Louis, this and other buildings of the Pruitt-Igoe public project are mostly empty

Better Management

Conducting a visitor through one of the tall buildings that had been made to work for families, he said: "Partly it is a matter of management. The people who live here are doing a better job of management than a central authority ever could."

But the vast Pruitt-Igoe project a few blocks away remains in despair. Despite the housing shortage, most of the apartments are vacant. Families who have left feel safe in private slums. Many of the tenants who remain keep dogs who accompany them at all times for protection. There is no sense of community.

The Rev. Buck Jones, an urban priest who was a leader in the rent strike, said, "Average tenants cannot understand why these things have not changed. The vacancy rate is going up. It's a vicious circle.

"You can't attract stable families, like the Federal Government says to do, until we have better conditions and security. But evidently we can't get that until we get stable families to pay better rents.

"I blame the Federal Government," he added. "It should come in and break the vicious circle with funds for maintenance and security."

June 4, 1970

The Case History of a Housing Failure

By JOHN HERBERS
Special to The New York Times

ST. LOUIS, Oct. 29 — In the midst of an acute housing shortage, St. Louis is boarding up 26 eleven-story apartment buildings, part of a $36-million housing project built 15 years ago and not yet paid for.

The 17 remaining buildings in the Pruitt-Igoe public housing complex continue in use, at least for the time being.

But there are officials here who hope for the day when all 43 structures, which rise like great granite cubes on 57 acres of central-city land, will be torn down, the mountains of concrete, steel and brick carted away and the name of Pruitt-Igoe erased forever from the St. Louis map.

For years the housing project has been plagued with rampant crime, vandalism, physical deterioration, accidental deaths and serious injuries.

"It was like building a battleship that would not float," said Thomas P. Costello, acting director of the St. Louis Housing Authority. "The damn thing sank."

Probably no other public housing failure in the nation is as monumental as that of Pruitt-Igoe. Nevertheless, it is indicative, not only of housing problems but also of the web of urban distress that, in varying degrees, grips large cities across the country.

Here the distress is stark and visible and the cause is easily traced.

Pruitt-Igoe was built in 1955 and 1956 on a site that had been cleared of slums. It was proclaimed in architectural magazines as an innovation in high-rise living for the poor, with clean walls of brick and glass providing a sharp contrast to the decayed tenements and row houses a few blocks away.

Yet, almost from the beginning, it was a disaster—socially, architecturally and financially. Various efforts over the years to make it work have failed. It is now a scene of vast devastation. The poorest of the poor would rather live in a dilapidated hut than endure Pruitt-Igoe's concentrated misery. And a destitute housing authority is left with the ruins.

High-rise housing for poor families, although no longer recommended by most planners, can be made to work, as it does in other, smaller projects here and elsewhere in the country. Pruitt-Igoe, everyone now agrees, concentrated too much social disorder and poverty into one place under adverse conditions.

At one time, it was estimated that 12,000 people, all black, lived in the project, counting tenants and all those who stayed there illegally. Most of the tenants were, and are, women and children on welfare. There was no sense of community. The authorities could not, they said, assign enough guards to provide security.

Robbers, burglars, narcotics pushers and street gangs roamed at will through the buildings. Anarchy prevailed. Windows were broken faster than they could be replaced. Under the circumstances, economies that the authorities made in construction made matters worse.

The steam pipes were not covered and children were seriously burned. People fell out of windows or walked into elevator shafts to their deaths.

Elevators stopped only on the fourth, seventh and 10th floors, when they operated at all. The units were built in tiers, silo-like, without corridors to connect all units on a floor. A person living on the end of the 11th floor would have to go down 11 flights and up 11 to visit an apartment on the middle of the 11th floor.

Last winter, with windows out, pipes froze and broke on some of the top floors, sending streams of water through the buildings and forming glaciers on the stairs.

Vacancies Climbed

Tenants moved out as soon as they could find any place at all to go, some who were paying the minimum $20 a month rent. The vacancy rate climbed even as housing for black families became more scarce.

In the late nineteen-sixties, the authority went into debt for $5-million more, which it spent to make some of the buildings more livable and more secure. But Pruitt-Igoe went right on deteriorating. The National Commission on Urban Problems said in a report published in 1968 that the administration of the project had been "benign by intent but vacillating and permissive."

In 1969, public housing tenants throughout the city conducted a prolonged rent strike and won a 25 per cent reduction and a new, democratically selected board of housing commissioners that includes tenants and civic leaders. The chairman is the Rev. Donald Register, a black Presbyterian minister.

Efforts by the new commission to delegate authority to strong tenants organizations to bring about security and a sense of community have worked at some projects, but not at Pruitt-Igoe.

Others in Trouble

The authority has remained solvent only through Federal subsidies, and Pruitt-Igoe has so drained its resources that there is no money for needed improvements at the other projects, some of them also deteriorating.

The New York Times Nov. 2, 1970

The authority has not decided what to do with 26 buildings, or the other 17 that may be emptied soon. It still owes $32-million in construction debt over the next 25 years. No one has offered to buy them.

Some officials want to clear all 57 acres and build townhouses and garden apartments, which have been found to be attractive to families. But the Federal Government would have to assume the debt to provide most of the funds for new construction, and there is no indication as to how the national Administration would respond to that.

"One trouble," said Mr. Costello, "is that Pruitt-Igoe is a cancer within a cancer. You can't cure just a part of it."

The project, a few blocks northwest of the business district, is surrounded by some of the worst slums in the country. The blight extends for acres. Federal programs like model cities have not made a dent. The city, which continues to lose taxable wealth to the suburbs, is chronically without money. Missouri welfare payments are among the lowest in the nation—$134 a month for a mother and four children.

"But out in the suburbs," said one downtown civic leader, "they are hardly aware of Pruitt-Igoe and environs. Unless you count the rash of political statements promising to crack down on crime and disorder that are flooding the television these days."

November 2, 1970

U.S. Now Big Landlord In Decaying Inner City

By JOHN HERBERS
Special to The New York Times

WASHINGTON, Jan. 1—A new and ominous chapter has opened in the decline of the central cities: The Federal Government has begun to come into ownership or control of a large portion of faltering or abandoned inner-city housing.

Many of the subsidized projects built or rehabilitated in recent years with the intent of renewing the cities are in default of mortgage payments or in deep financial trouble; and in one way or another the Government is assuming the losses incurred by urban decay and the excesses and mistakes of developers.

The development has important implications. It is an indicator of accelerated decline for the cities; it is a blow to the mushrooming housing subsidy programs, which have increasingly become a subject of national controversy, and it raises the possibility of the central Government's holding large land reservations in some of the central cities.

Washington officials involved acknowledged that the housing programs have encountered great difficulties in the cities, but said they were being brought under control. In some of the cities, however, there was much less optimism.

In Philadelphia, the name of George Romney, Secretary of Housing and Urban Development, appears hundreds of times on the deed books as the owner of slum housing. In Chicago, where thousands of subsidized apartment units are failing to meet payments, John L. Waner, the H.U.D. area director, said:

"In another year I look to be one of the biggest landlords in the Middle West, second only to Detroit."

In New York, the Federal role is less pronounced for a variety of reasons ranging from the nature of the housing in the city to the existence of programs funded by the city and state. But elsewhere the Federal take-over has been major.

There is a story circulating in the bureaucracy that H.U.D. may soon rival the Department of the Interior, with its millions of acres in parks and forests, as an owner of land—an exaggeration, to be sure, but based on the fact of growing foreclosures in the cities.

Documentation of the emerging trend was obtained over the last several weeks from interviews with various authorities and critics involved, from information compiled by correspondents in representative cities and testimony before Congressional committees.

Federal Role Expanded

In the first three years of the Nixon Administration, the Federal role in housing has expanded to vast and unprecedented proportions. The new subsidy programs enacted by the Democrats during the nineteen-sixties have been implemented and nurtured to maturity by the Republican Administration in its efforts to speed housing construction and end an acute shortage.

Of the more than two million units built or rehabilitated in 1971—a record year—more than 500,000 carried direct Federal subsidies, aside from mortgage guarantees. This compares with 190,000 subsidized units produced in 1968, the last year of the Johnson Administration.

Although construction of the subsidized housing is shifting increasingly to the suburbs, a good portion of that built in metropolitan areas—more than half in some categories — has gone into the core cities. In addition, there has been growing Federal involvement in the older housing programs in the cities. These range from public housing built with Federal help and run by local authorities to guarantees of luxury high-rise apartment buildings.

Main Urban Program

Although much of this was begun by the Democrats, housing nevertheless has constituted the Administration's major move in the cities, which have been losing their middle-class population and wealth to the suburbs while serving as the depository for poverty and compounded social problems.

The Nixon Administration has not expanded the other urban programs that the Democrats enacted to achieve

Associated Press

Representative John Conyers Jr., left, a Democrat of Michigan, and William Whitbeck of Department of Housing and Urban Development, inspect abandoned building in Detroit.

over-all renewal of the cities—antipoverty, Model Cities, urban renewal, for example. It has prescribed remedies, such as welfare reform and expansion and revenue sharing, but these have floundered in Congress.

Whether or not any of these remedies would halt the decline is questionable. In any event, the decline has gone on and the housing that the Government invested in heavily is going down with the cities.

That is a part of it, but not all. There have been in a number of cities scandals of varying degree in the housing programs. "Suede shoe" operators, as they are called in the trade, have been able to fleece both consumers and the Government, and there has been a high incidence of poor construction and dubious site selection.

Subsidies Criticized

Further, the basic structure of the Federal housing subsidies has come increasingly under attack, both by the Administration and its critics as wasteful and inequitable, subject to administrative abuse and with built-in provisions for failure.

The situation varies greatly from city to city, depending on local conditions and the manner in which the Federal programs were applied. In some areas there have been remarkable successes in the housing efforts, and both critics and defenders of the programs agree that they have provided decent housing that otherwise would not have been available for many thousands of families and old people across the country.

Many central cities, especially the newer ones, are not yet in decline and consequently there are fewer housing failures.

But some cities that have wretched conditions have had few failures in the new subsidy programs simply because there has been little construction under them. In St. Louis, some builders said they had stopped trying to build in the central city because they were tired of having wiring, piping and other materials ripped from partially completed structures.

Trend Is Clear

Nevertheless, there is no mistaking the trend. George Sternlieb, director of the Center for Urban Policy Research at Rutgers University and a member of President Nixon's task force on housing, said that there was every indication that the Federal Government through the process of foreclosures, defaults of mortgage payments and overseeing the management of projects on the verge of bankruptcy would "end up owning or operating a high percentage of housing in the central cities."

There are failures in the suburbs, too, but not nearly as many. The suburban ring constitutes the new city and has a stability that can overcome failures in construction and management.

It is difficult to measure the extent of the difficulties and there are indications that the officials in charge do not know the full extent. They have held high-level, emergency meetings on the matter and some have said privately that the situation was grave. Publicly, they are circumspect.

In separate interviews on the over-all housing situation, Mr. Romney, Eugene A. Gulledge, commissioner of the Federal Housing Administration, and Norman V. Watson, Assistant Secretary for Housing Management, acknowledged the problems in the cities, among others, but indicated they were manageable.

Statement by Romney

In a year-end statement, Secretary Romney said that the building boom his department was presiding over was providing better housing and employment opportunities for millions of Americans, but to this he added:

"Millions of central city families still face threatening social, economic and racial strains and tensions. The accelerating decay of our cities, with loss of human and economic resources and continuing rural migration, has not been reversed. Fragmented local governments, weakened state governments and too numerous and complex separately financed Federal programs are not equal to the challenge. Furthermore, the rotting of central cities is beginning to rot the surrounding suburbs."

Mr. Watson said that the department was contracting for the management of 45,000 to 50,000 apartment units that had been foreclosed and were held in Mr. Romney's name, a small number, compared with the four million units of public housing built and operated by local authorities under H.U.D. supervision.

The foreclosures, however, show only a tip of the iceberg. Below the surface are the units in default—no longer making mortgage payments—and the units in trouble that the Government is helping on a temporary basis in a number of ways. This includes extension of the mortgage or suspension of payments.

An indication of what is involved is shown in the apartment program known as Section 236 in which the Government subsidizes interest on the mortgage and provides some of the tenants with rent supplements. The program is only three years old. As of Oct. 31, a total of 179 projects had been completed and one in every 15 was in default.

The situation is much worse in the older apartment subsidy program kown as Section 221 (d)(3). And there are the blocks of single-family homes in Detroit, Philadelphia and other cities to a lesser degree that have been turned back to the Federal Government in the process of abandonment and decay.

Mr. Gulledge pointed out that nationally the over-all foreclosure rate by F.H.A. is less than it was a few years after a period of overbuilding. The circumstances, too, are far different. Then the property was quickly resold at little loss to the Government. Now much of it is concentrated in the central cities in areas of abandonment and there is little market for it, except at a drastically reduced price for long-term speculation.

And mortgage foreclosures are occurring in metropolitan areas where decent housing is in acute shortage.

Situation in Dallas

Even in Dallas, a comparatively new city with a predominantly white, middle-class population, the H.U.D. director foresees massive Federal ownership of residential property if present trends continue.

For racial and economic polarization are taking place there, as elsewhere in the country. Tall new office spires rise in the downtown area where stores and night clubs used to be. On a cold winter night there is hardly any life there.

Most activity now goes on around the outlying expressways and suburbs built for the automobile culture. Dallas is like a big pie spread over the plain, its black population making up a southern wedge of 20 per cent in the old neighborhoods, but struggling to get out where life is better.

There have been intense controversies over school and housing integration in transitional negihborhoods, and middle-income whites are leaving for the suburbs. They have left behind some near-empty apartment buildings, which the poor could not afford and middle-income people shunned. The apartments were not subsidized, but their mortgages were guaranteed by the F.H.A., which was forced to foreclose when payments stopped.

Federal Role Extensive

Dallas is a city that has prided itself on its self-help and independence from Washington, but the Federal Government, nevertheless, has underwritten most of the residential areas in Dallas. About 70 per cent of the housing built there was under Federally guaranteed mortgages, and more than 20,000 units of subsidized housing have been built in recent years.

Overseeing the Government's interests is bearded, 30-year-old Manuel A. Sanchez 3d, a Texas Republican who served in the Washington offices of H.U.D. before being named Dallas area director. He is one of the new breed whom Secretary Romney has imposed over the staid F.H.A. bureaucracy to inject some social thinking into it.

The other day in his 14-floor office Mr. Sanchez pored over a map of Dallas showing the vast Federal investment in the city's real estate and predicted

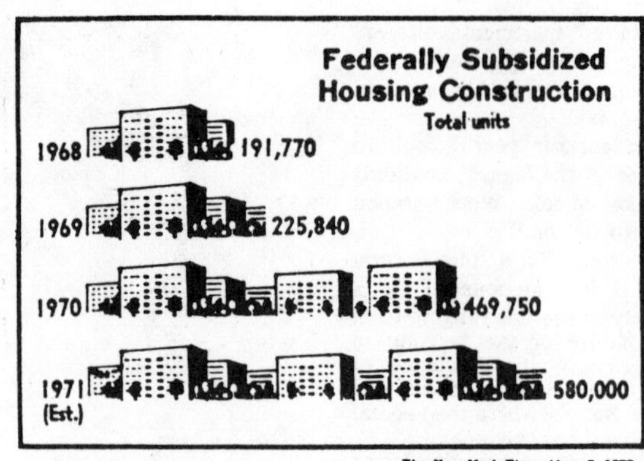

The New York Times/Jan. 2, 1972

that within a few years, as things are now going, Dallas would be predominantly black with whites and their wealth settled in the suburbs.

"If Dallas goes black," he said, his hand sweeping across the map, "we are going to wind up owning all this."

The Government already owns 5,000 single homes in Detroit's inner-city wasteland. There may be foreclosures soon on thousands more and the loss by the Government could be as high as $200-million, according to testimony in Detroit in early December before the Legal and Monetary Affairs Subcommittee of the House Government Operations Committee.

The housing, much of it structurally sound, was caught in the ravages of central city decay, the greed of some real estate operators and laxity of the F.H.A., which made appraisals at prices inflated by speculators. Most of this property, extending for many blocks, now lies vacant and vandalized, abandoned by its owners.

The same thing happened in Chicago on a smaller scale. But the chief problem there is how to keep some 12,000 or more subsidized apartment units, which are insured at about $200-million, from being foreclosed.

"The process already has started," said Mr. Waner, the new Chicago H.U.D. director, a white-haired Republican who ran for Mayor against Richard J. Daley and, of course, lost. "The projects cannot pay the city taxes. Foreclosures are taking place. Reports from our property management section show a bleak picture. Something has got to be done to prevent a calamity."

Ironically, Mr. Waner said, all this is happening while Chicago is under a "fantastic housing shortage."

Many Causes For Failure

As elsewhere in the country, there is a multiplicity of causes for the failures. The apartments were planned and developed by both private interests and nonprofit groups ranging from churches to Community Action agencies. Costs were estimated with little or no margin to win F.H.A. approval, and by the time construction began, labor and materials had gone up in cost.

In many cases economies were made in construction that led to early maintenance problems. Taxes and management costs went up. Some projects were built for a mixture of low- and moderate-income tenants, but for various reasons only the poor would live there and they could not pay the rents required. And a number of the projects were in neighborhoods where crime, drugs, vandalism and disorder take a daily toll in lives and property.

Rehabilitated housing is a particular problem, because it is difficult to put in good condition and because it is frequently in slum or transitional areas.

In Boston, which carried out a widely publicized pilot program in Federally subsidized rehabilitation, some 2,000 of 3,300 units rehabilitated were in default of payments, according to figures several months old. The situation has worsened since, authorities say. At the same time 1,900 of 3,700 new subsidized apartment units were in default.

Reorganization of Offices

H.U.D. offices around the country are staggering under the burden of trying to keep faltering housing afloat at the same time they are undergoing a drastic reorganization ordered by Mr. Romney. In some cities, the problems are compounded by the fact that F.H.A., a former independent agency brought against its will under H.U.D., has had a cozy relationship with the local private interests, including the "suede shoe" operators, who proliferate in the central cities.

An example of this was seen in Philadelphia, where there was gross abuse of a Federal program that provided mortgage guarantees and little down payment for low-income families buying used housing. The Philadelphia Inquirer turned up scores of cases in which a speculator would buy an old row house for, say, $750, make superficial repairs, obtain an F.H.A. appraisal from a private appraiser—hired by F.H.A.—of $6,000 and sell the house for that—a markup of $5,250.

The buyer would soon find the place uninhabitable and stop his mortgage payments. The property would then go to Mr. Romney, with the Government assuming the loss. This was the same kind of practice disclosed nationally by the House Banking and Currency Committee in another home ownership program, known as Section 235, under which the Government not only guarantees the mortgage but also subsidizes the interest. Mr. Romney halted the program in areas until reforms could be instituted.

In Philadelphia, F.H.A. suspended some 160 private appraisers and tightened its regulations.

Even in area offices reputed to have been run with prudence and integrity, critics of the Government programs question whether H.U.D. can handle the responsibilities in its triple role as mortgage insurer, welfare agent and consumer protector.

Baltimore is one of the offices that appears to have remained scandal free. Yet on the day it was visited for this story, Representative Clarence D. Long, Democrat of Maryland, was publicly accusing it of "callousness" and having "a very unhealthy relationship with builders."

What prompted the charge was a rash of complaints about wet basements and other defects from buyers of homes in a 122-unit suburban development on a questionable site that was insured and subsidized by the Government under Section 235.

Allen T. Clapp, the Baltimore director and a veteran F.H.A. officer, seemed exhausted and exasperated, and said, "It is more than my inspectors can do."

As to the cities, the question remains as to what is to be done with the land and property should the trend to Federal ownership come to much larger proportions. The Government does not want it, and the policy is to put it up for sale. The city government or urban renewal agencies buy some of it, but the cities themselves are stuck with large tracts of land on which taxes have not been paid.

In the long run, some authorities believe, Federal ownership could have a beneficial effect, especially if the central cities continue to become a wasteland. If accumulated in large plots the land could be employed for a number of purposes, from building parks or new communities to homesteads. But all of this runs counter to the philosophy of the current Administration and to the present trend against more centralized control.

The situation is filled with ironies. Secretary Romney is one of the few members of the Administration who has, in the opinion of many urban officials, displayed an understanding of the needs of the central cities, and he has battled the White House to save some city programs.

Yet he has put his strongest emphasis, during a housing shortage, on "production, production, production," as one of his area officers put it, an emphasis that Congress also built into the law. Recently, he has instituted moves to preserve the existing housing, to increase the competence and capacity of housing management and to improve quality of construction.

Commissioner Gulledge of the F.H.A., a former president of the National Association of Home Builders, acknowledges that "housing alone cannot do the job" for the central cities.

A few months ago, the department instituted guidelines against building housing that would continue to concentrate minority poor in the central city area. This was in line with court decisions and the general wisdom that poverty in large quantities causes trouble. But the policy also grew out of the difficulties the department is experiencing with the inner-city housing it has approved.

There is a provision in the policy for continuing to build in urban renewal areas or where a massive effort is being made to lift the entire well-being of a neighborhood—a provision some local authorities fear will be slighted. In any event, it is clear that more and more the subsidized housing will be built in the suburbs despite community pressures against it.

Most of this housing is now going for families above the poverty line—up to $10,000 a year—who cannot afford the high cost of decent shelter. President Nixon acknowledged in his housing message to Congress last summer that the building effort was not reaching the very poor. What many authorities expect, then, is a greater migration of the non-poor from the central cities, which would be left with an even greater degree of grinding poverty.

There is no clear policy in Washington for dealing with the larger central city difficulties. The department is using some leverage in its system of grants to move toward metropolitan government in some categories, but basically officials are looking to the reelection of President Nixon in 1972 before formulating any decisive moves in that direction. Meantime, they are encouraging local leaders to take the initiative in improving the central cities.

Dr. Sternlieb of Rutgers, who has documented many of the housing failures, wrote an article in the magazine The Public Interest last fall comparing the old central cities such as Newark and Youngstown, Ohio, with a child's sandbox. The core cities, he said, had simply ost their economic value. Occasionally they are given some trinket or distraction to keep them quiet while the adult world—the real world—goes on around them.

He concluded that a useful economic function for the cities could be found, if policies were designed to insure that everyone had an opportunity for productive employment, even if it involved cost to over-all economic growth and wealth.

"The plight of the inhabitants of our central cities, and the strategy we seem to be adopting to meet that plight, indicate that we are opting for the sandbox," he wrote. "What this will mean for our society in the future we do not fully know; but that the consequences are likely to be cruel and disagreeable has become only too clear."

January 2, 1972

Federal Housing Woes

Officials Criticizing Subsidy Program For Poor Construction and High Cost

By JOHN HERBERS

Special to The New York Times

WASHINGTON, Jan. 31—In the last few months, there has been a dramatic turnabout in many officials' public statements on the explosive subject of federally subsidized housing. Instead of strongly defending the programs and their administration, as they once did, the top authorities are increasingly joining in the criticism. The critics say that the programs have produced a high percentage of poorly constructed housing on questionable sites at an enormous cost to the Treasury.

News Analysis

George Romney, the Secretary of Housing and Urban Development, told the National Association of Home Builders in Houston last Tuesday that in 1969 and 1970, when there was an acute housing shortage and costs were soaring, "the fast-buck artists, the speculators, and the unscrupulous developers moved into the subsidized housing markets."

"The result has been a predictable decline in the quality of housing and a dramatic increase of housing problems of an unprecedented character," he said. "Reports have come back of new or 'rehabilitated' housing with leaky roofs, leaky plumbing, leaky basements, slipshod carpentry work, loose stair treads, paper-thin walls, inoperative furnaces and appliances, inadequate insulation, inferior wiring and a whole host of complaints.

"Shady get - rich - quick schemes abound, involving some realtors, some builders, some developers and even some housing authorities, who line their pockets with the 'sweat money,' yes even the food money of the uninformed, unsuspecting home buyer or renter."

Trend May Get Worse

At a news conference a few days earlier, Mr. Romney said that a recently disclosed trend, in which the Federal Government comes into possession or control of vast amounts of failing, central city housing, was likely to become worse in the months ahead.

This is happening because the Government has guaranteed mortgages on housing that has succumbed to urban decay and abandonment, which is continuing to spread.

An investigation by The New York Times during the last three months, including interviews with officials and housing experts across the country, shows that housing, perhaps more than any other Federal program, is the victim of outdated institutions, insensitive government and excessive influence of special interests.

There is no principal villain in the housing failures, no one political party or administration to bear the major blame. According to a number of critics, a systematic failure spreads from Congress to the lowest Federal Housing Administration office.

The housing laws, vast and complicated, were put together over the years by the Banking and Currency Committees of the House and Senate. These committees have a large contingent of members, both liberals and conservatives, who have been supported in their campaigns by banking and building interests, which nearly always have gotten what they wanted in the law.

The subcommittees that write the housing laws have had little public scrutiny. Because the subject is complex and frequently dull, the national press has given little attention to housing. Most of the laws that were passed were given only superficial coverage, at best, in the mass media.

When the 1968 Omnibus Housing Act was enacted, President Johnson called it "the Magna Carta of housing." Yet it is the programs under this law, extending interest subsidies to mortgages on both apartments and single homes, that have caused much of the criticism.

The 1968 act, along with the Tax Reform Act of 1969, permits a two-way drain on the Treasury—to investors in the form of lucrative tax write-offs and to consumers in the form of housing subsidies. The tax act in effect rewards the rich for investing in housing for people of low and moderate income.

This can be defended in principle, many critics say. It was the contention of the late Senator Robert F. Kennedy, for example, that the slums could be rebuilt only by offering enormous profits to business interests to do it.

Two-Way Drain

But a host of critics of the housing efforts say the public has not begun to get its money's worth. The two-way drain in a few years will rival the cost of welfare. The Government is tied to paying subsidies for 40-year mortgages on much property that, in the opinion of experts, will never last that long.

The litany of complaints includes the following:

¶Because of inflated cost, most of the housing is going not to the poor but to families with incomes of $6,000 to $10,000 a year.

¶The subsidized programs were intended to be a means of getting away from public housing, with all its institutional faults. But public housing, by many accounts, was better built. Although the situation varies greatly from city to city, some local housing authorities have in the last three years constructed more attractive projects on better sites than were built under the subsidy programs.

¶Rapid depreciation and other features in the tax and housing laws permit quick profits for builders and investors and do not require long-range responsibility, thus inviting shoddy construction and equipment that will soon wear out.

¶The Federal Housing Administration has been permissive with the private interests involved, permitting them to take advantage of consumers in many instances.

¶Charges are beginning to be heard that the housing industry is becoming like the defense industry, dependent on Government support and thus less efficient than industries in private competition.

A First Step

Mr. Romney's public recognition of the failures is seen by some as a first step in reforms. Next year, the Administration will authorize fewer subsidized apartments and insist on higher quality, according to officials. Congress is expected to pass legislation this year that may contain reforms and stricter requirements.

In the Senate, Edward W. Brooke, Republican of Massachusetts, and Walter F. Mondale, Democrat of Minnesota, are proposing a revamping of the programs in several respects.

In the House, Representative Thomas L. Ashley, Democrat of Ohio, is proposing setting up metropolitan housing bodies that would oversee quality and site selection. Many officials are looking to housing allowances—subsidies that follow the family rather than the building—as the eventual replacement for all of the subsidy programs.

But the system that created the present programs remains essentially the same. Probably the realistic view is that thoroughgoing reforms are a long way off.

February 1, 1972

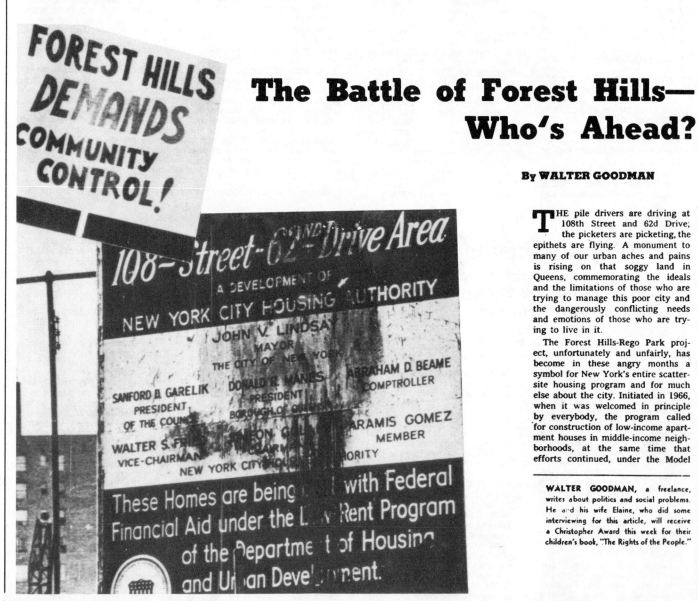

The Battle of Forest Hills—Who's Ahead?

By WALTER GOODMAN

THE pile drivers are driving at 108th Street and 62d Drive; the picketers are picketing, the epithets are flying. A monument to many of our urban aches and pains is rising on that soggy land in Queens, commemorating the ideals and the limitations of those who are trying to manage this poor city and the dangerously conflicting needs and emotions of those who are trying to live in it.

The Forest Hills-Rego Park project, unfortunately and unfairly, has become in these angry months a symbol for New York's entire scatter-site housing program and for much else about the city. Initiated in 1966, when it was welcomed in principle by everybody, the program called for construction of low-income apartment houses in middle-income neighborhoods, at the same time that efforts continued, under the Model

WALTER GOODMAN, a freelance, writes about politics and social problems. He and his wife Elaine, who did some interviewing for this article, will receive a Christopher Award this week for their children's book, "The Rights of the People."

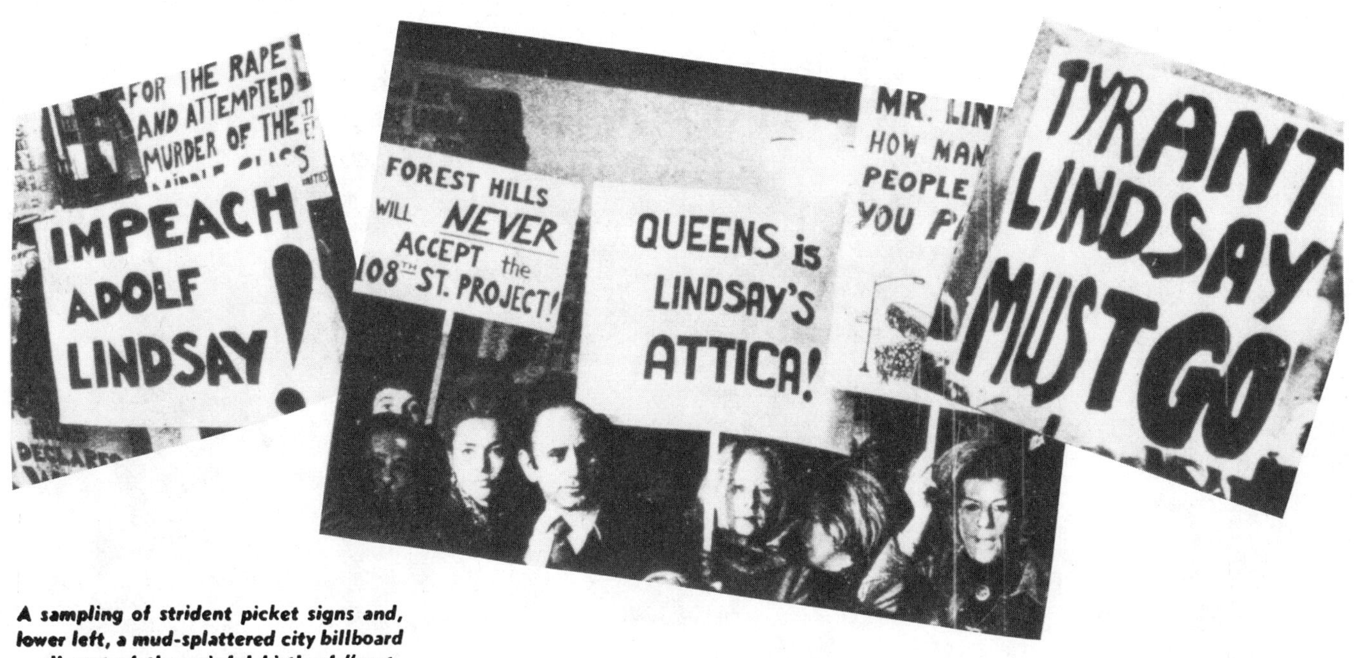

A sampling of strident picket signs and, lower left, a mud-splattered city billboard —all part of the painful birth of "scatter-site" housing in the Forest Hills area.

Cities program, to rebuild the worst sections of Harlem, Bedford-Stuyvesant and the Southeast Bronx. To most people the term "scatter site" suggested fairly small, widely distributed developments, in contrast to the huge buildings that had come to stand for public housing since the nineteen-thirties. The new program was designed to take families out of the slums, sources of infection for so many social ailments, and to move the city toward the objective of racial and, incidentally, economic integration.

In the mid-sixties, racial integration still seemed a good and proper objective to most New Yorkers. To Donald H. Elliott, the young Lindsay protégé named chairman of the City Planning Commission as scatter-site housing began its life of high promise, the program seemed a "moral imperative." It became a legal imperative as well, when the Federal Government (which finances virtually all of the city's low-income public housing) set down rules about locating projects "outside existing areas of minority concentration."

SWITCHING THE PLANS

ONE of the first such areas selected in 1966 was in the Corona section of Queens, a target borough for scatter-site planners attracted by its middle-class character and a relative availability of land to build on. The 5.12-acre site, at Lewis Avenue and 100th Street, vacant except for a swim club, was in a neighborhood of one- and two-family houses whose owners rose up against having four 14-story buildings with some 2,000 inhabitants imposed upon them.

The reaction of Corona's residents was typical of what the city was encountering, and would continue to encounter, wherever a specific site was chosen. "The anti-vote against any public housing is very loud," sighs Mr. Elliott. Of the original 13 projects announced by the Housing Authority in 1966-67, only one has been completed—the Cassidy Place-Lafayette Avenue project in Staten Island, which contains 380 apartments exclusively for the elderly. Two others are under construction; one is "pending construction"; the remainder are "dormant." Reviewing this record not long ago, the National Committee Against Discrimination in Housing charged the Lindsay administration with bowing to "white community resistance." (A second generation of nominal scatter sites seems to be making a better record, in part because some of them are neighborhoods that are already poverty-stricken. Almost 90 per cent of the Housing Authority's building program continues to be focused on ghetto areas.)

Among the numerous steps required before a public housing project can get started in New York, two afford special opportunity for the expression of public opposition—the approvals necessary from the City Planning Commission, which speaks for the Mayor, and from the Board of Estimate, whereon sit the Mayor's friends and enemies. The Corona site was approved by the Planning Commission over community objections on June 21, 1966, with the understanding that a new high school, which everyone agreed was needed in Queens, would be built a few blocks away, across the Horace Harding Expressway, in Forest Hills-Rego Park. During the summer of 1966, while the Corona project awaited Board of Estimate approval, pressure on the administration ran high. Speaking through the Queens Borough President, Mario J. Cariello, the homeowners of Corona at length persuaded Mayor Lindsay to make a radical switch in plans: The high school would be built in Corona, even though that would mean displacing 69 homes because the school needed twice as much land as the project; and the housing would be built in Forest Hills-Rego Park, whose residents were, by and large, unaware of the arrangements which their Borough President was making in their behalf.

"We did not go to the Forest Hills community," concedes Mr. Elliott. The Planning Commission had serious reservations about the change, owing in part to the problem of relocating those 69 Corona families. As Mr. Elliott, who was the Mayor's adviser on housing during the negotiations, explains: "The Mayor acquiesced in that decision. He did not initiate it." The man who did initiate it, Mario Cariello, called the change "a victory for everything that is good and visionary." He characterized the low-cost housing project—in Rego Park, not in Corona—as "important in the planning of our community life." One after another, elected representatives from Queens rose at the Board of Estimate to make known for posterity their pleasure in the compromise. Assemblyman Herbert Miller, representing the affected district then as now, offered no word of criticism.

OFFICIAL approval of the changed site swept through with marvelous speed. On Nov. 30, the Planning Commission held a 5½-hour public hearing—the first of Chairman Elliott's new career—at which area residents, finally alerted to what was intended for them, were permitted to holler their protests. Two days later the site was O.K.'d by the commission, and on Dec. 7 it received the unanimous approval of the Board of Estimate, including Borough President Cariello, sticking by his bargain. Some months later, faced with constituents' protests over a new batch of proposed scatter sites, he would declare himself against all new public housing in Queens until the borough has another subway, more paved streets and improved sanitation and police services. Not long afterward, Cariello went on to the rewards of machine life in New York, a Supreme Court judgeship, leaving behind the consequences of his victory.

Reviewing this history, the uninstructed observer may wonder at the political strategy or simple good sense of switching from a plan that provided a housing site and a school site without the need for evicting anybody to a plan that necessitated the eviction of several hundred people. In his puzzlement, it may occur to him that the city fathers believed that their plans would meet a kinder, or at least quieter, reception from the liberal Jewish apartment dwellers of Forest Hills-Rego Park than from the not-so-liberal Italian homeowners of Corona, especially if the change was zipped through fast enough to keep the opposition from rallying.

TESTING THE SOIL

WHATEVER the impetus for the change, the new housing site, 8.46 unused acres at 108th Street and 62d Drive, where Rego Park begins to deteriorate into Corona, seemed at least as suitable as Lewis Avenue. The immediate surroundings included several seven-story apartment houses, one fancier 15-story building, with rentals starting at $200 a month and going much higher, modest garden developments that were showing signs of running down, a new elementary school and the usual tangle of Queens highways. As the Planning Commission stated in approving the

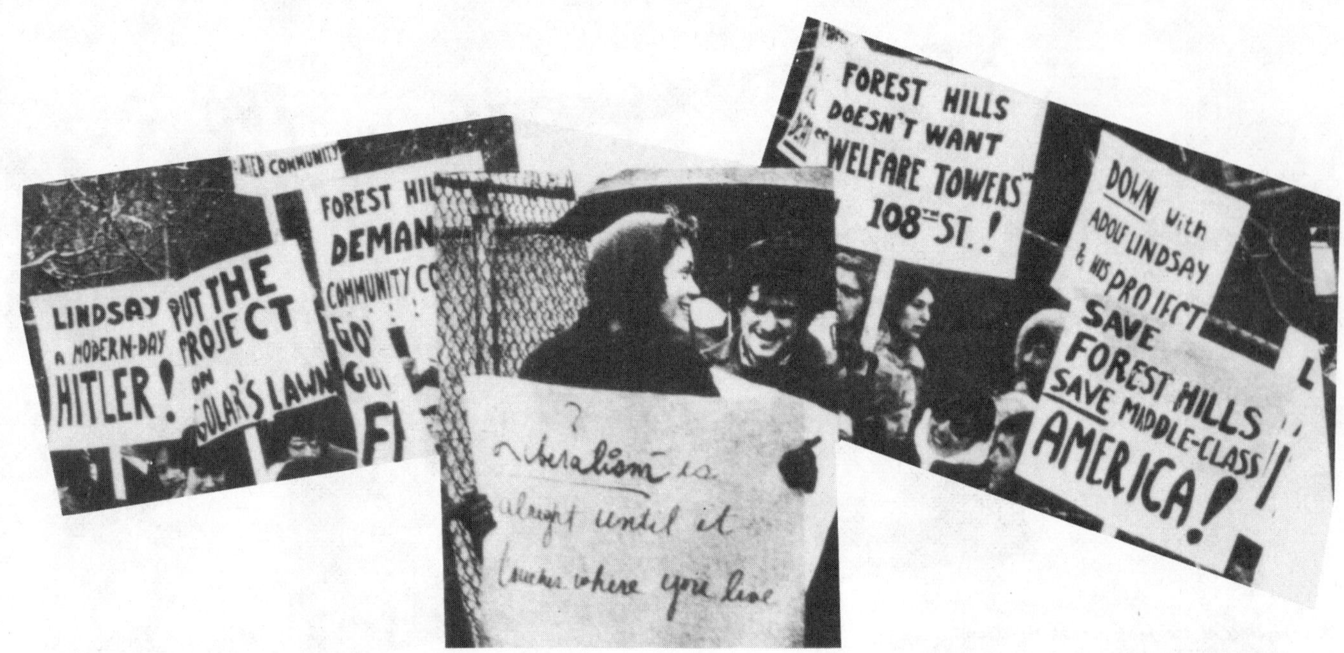

site, it was in "a strong and thriving community," a place where lots of building was going on, where people wanted to live. According to the 1960 census, only 2 per cent of the 55,332 people in the 17 census tracts immediately surrounding the site were non-white, and 1 per cent were Puerto Rican, so it did not seem likely that a low-income project would "tip" the neighborhood into ghettoism. "I really don't think you could find a better site," says Mr. Elliott.

One uninviting feature (not counting the people who live there) was the nature of the land. Beneath the property runs a stream, known as Horse Brook, which makes for a mucky subsoil; the planners understood that pilings would have to be sunk, at unusual expense, for the buildings' foundations. In the early nineteen-sixties, a major developer had been discouraged by the expected foundation costs from construction of two 23-story apartment buildings there, and in 1967, an appraiser for the Department of Housing and Urban Development (HUD) recommended that the site be rejected for housing. Roger Starr, executive director of the Citizens' Housing and Planning Council of New York, who had supported the Corona plan, chided the Planning Commission in December, 1966, for rushing through approval of the new site. He urged the Board of Estimate not to act until the Government determined whether the need for longer pilings than had ever before been used for a project required a reshaping of the entire plan:

"Instead of seven separate buildings, the highest 22 stories high, foundation problems may give us three buildings 35 stories high. Certainly, there is no need for haste so pressing at this moment that the Board of Estimate should be asked to approve one project when a wholly different project may emerge under the pressure of Federal cost limitations and construction problems."

Had the Board of Estimate not been under a political compulsion to ratify the Lindsay-Cariello agreement with speed, it might have saved the Government some time and money. For the original design calling for a total of 828 apartments in seven structures — one 22-story building, three 12-story buildings and three 10-story buildings—was later judged too expensive to put up because of the marshy soil. The cost per apartment would have run over what the Federal Government was prepared to pay.*

The design was altered several times; architects were changed, and in 1969 the plans were finally revised to build three 24-story buildings with 840 apartments — the highest and largest of the city's scatter-site efforts by a substantial margin, with about twice as many apartments as the runner-up. Even its supporters in Forest Hills concede that living space for 2,500 or more people was not what the term "scatter housing" brought to most minds. But there seemed to be no choice: Fewer and higher buildings meant lower foundation costs per apartment.**

Some opponents ascribe the lapse of almost five years between approval of the project in 1966 and the breaking of ground in 1971 to the Lindsay administration's reluctance to upset the voters of Forest Hills, a liberal enclave of Queens, before the 1969 mayoralty election. Perhaps. But it seems unnecessary to search out shrewd explanations for delay in the bureaucracy-ridden world of public housing; it is speed that requires an explanation.

As the plans were finally developed, they contained a number of changes and additions designed for community appeal: 340 of the 840 apartments would be set aside for elderly persons—that is, 40.5 per cent instead of the 30 per cent originally scheduled—and the number of apartments for large families would be cut sharply; a two-story community center would contain facilities for the elderly as well as for others, and there would be a one-story early-childhood center, with seven classrooms for 200 children. (Both would be open to the surrounding community.) The estimated cost of the whole development, except for the childhood center, which is not covered by HUD, is now running at $30-million, or $35,700 per apartment. (Opponents, charging that foundation costs and extras are still being underestimated, put the per-apartment cost $5,000 to $10,000 higher.) The rent will average $21 a room, including utilities.

THE foregoing plans were all made without consulting the people of Forest Hills. That may have been mere self-defense on the planners' part, for residents had made it clear that they were in no humor for collaboration. The local planning board voted against the project unanimously. Herbert Kahn, spokesman for the Queens Council for Better Housing, a sort of conglomerate of liberal groups lending their names to the principle of scatter housing, asks: "What would've been accomplished by waving a flag—'We're coming! We're coming!'?" City officials appear to have assumed or hoped that passions would cool with time and that if they could avoid attracting undue attention, the big buildings would be accepted in the neighborhood as merely another oppressive fact of urban life. Thus, the Housing Authority failed to respond, except with polite thank-yous, to the overtures of a friendly community group, headed by Rabbi Josiah Derby of the Rego Park Jewish Center, which had volunteered to give what help it could on such questions as building design and school facilities.

The secret could not be kept beyond a certain point, however, and early in 1971,

***Washington does not pay directly for low-income housing. It guarantees the principal and interest on bonds put out by the New York City Housing Authority. There are limits as to how much it will guarantee for any given project.**

****A few weeks ago, in response to an inquiry from Congressman Benjamin Rosenthal, whose district takes in the site, the U.S. General Accounting Office advised HUD to get a guarantee from the city that abnormal foundation costs would not run over the estimated 1.72-million. Otherwise, the G.A.O. found that projected costs fit within Federal guidelines.**

The requested guarantee was given. The Housing Authority announced in January that tests showed the estimated piling costs would not be exceeded. The job will require 2,000 pilings made of steel pipe 50 to 60 feet long.

as final plans were approved, protests broke out again at open meetings in Queens of the City Planning Commission. The protestors dominated the proceedings, and now some people who had been against the original idea of putting a high school on the site were calling for the school rather than low-income apartments. By May, when the Housing Authority issued a history of the project which noted that it "does have support in the community (while there is some opposition as well)," it was evident that the parenthesis was misplaced. Whatever support existed was being drowned in the cries of the opponents.

FIGHTING THE CITY

EMOTIONS are running high in Forest Hills, in forms to which America's cities are by now accustomed: meetings, manifestoes and lawsuits, marching and picketing, a bit of stone-throwing, a lot of sloganeering—loud, rude slogans about John Lindsay ("Adolf Lindsay — the middle class will bury you!") and quieter, ruder ones about the prospective newcomers. As elsewhere, the protest has found its spokesman, in this case, Jerry Birbach, a 42-year-old real-estate operator and landlord on the West Side of Manhattan. ("I buy old buildings and renovate them, completely renovate them, rip the entire guts out and put in everything new, and then I rent the apartments out. . . .") Along the paneled walls of his office hang a 1958 diploma from the evening division of City College's School of Business, certifying that he has completed a minimum of 450 hours in real estate studies, and several tributes from District Grand Lodge No. 1 of B'nai B'rith — "BENEVOLENCE, BROTHERLY LOVE, HARMONY."

Birbach is a big man, whose folds of chin turn into a swelling chest without the assistance of a neck. His voice can be loud. He came to Forest Hills 16 years ago as a newlywed, and his inflections betray his Lower East Side and Williamsburg origins. He has headed the Forest Hills Residents Association since its formation last spring for the express purpose of beating back the new project; it claims 3,000 members. None of Birbach's best friends are Negroes, but many of his West Side tenants are, and he invites interviewers to ask them what they think of Jerry Birbach. He knows there are Negroes in Forest Hills because his wife has seen them at Waldbaum's.

Simeon Golar, chairman of the New York City Housing Authority, laments, "Our bad luck was Jerry Birbach." One may sympathize with the chairman, yet recognize in Birbach the kind of community spokesman, representing all that is angry and much that is worse about his community, who has come forward in other parts of the city with the indulgence of the administration and friends of Community Control. As 1,000 residents were doing their usual demonstrating at the project one Sunday morning in December, U. S. Representative Herman Badillo was telling an audience at the Society for Ethical Culture in Manhattan: "No community or group of people has the right to use or consider any part of this city as their private turf—not a middle-income neighborhood any more than the Black Muslims—and if you start giving away turf to one, you'd better be ready to give it to the other." Many who would say "Amen" regret that Representative Badillo did not make the point as forcefully on previous occasions.

"Do they mean that community participation is only applicable in East New York, Bedford-Stuyvesant, Harlem and Brownsville and not for the middle-income people of Forest Hills?" asks Jerry Birbach. To which Simeon Golar replies more or less in the affirmative, observing that middle-class citizens, after all, have never been without an effective voice in their own affairs. There is something to that—yet in matters of protest the middle-class has learned some lessons from the underclass in recent years. "They're aping the street pattern," notes an official of the American Jewish Committee, which has been quietly trying to play the role of conciliator. "They're not waiting on the Establishment. To the black militants, the N.A.A.C.P. was Uncle Tom. To the Jewish militants, we're Uncle Sam."

A CONVERSATION with Jerry Birbach, who goes at first glimpse onto a first-name basis, includes:

Tributes to himself: "I speak from my heart . . . I have one mouth and when I talk to someone I look square in their face . . . no double-talk. . . ."

Compassion for fellow man: "I understand all about poverty and the need for helping fellow man because people opened doors for me on my way up too."

Compassion for the elderly: "In my opinion no high-rise, low-income housing works out. What happens is it becomes a concentration camp for the elderly . . . where eventually you can't go out for a loaf of bread or a bottle of milk. Why don't they build gas chambers for these people?"

Insults for opponents: Mayor Lindsay is a fraud. Donald Elliott is a pompous, arrogant ass. Representative Badillo is a racist. Simeon Golar, too, is a racist, and he is also a liar. The Housing Authority's public-information man is a student of Goebbels.

A pledge or two: "I know one thing . . . those three 24-story buildings are not going up . . . I'll lie down in front of the bulldozers." Or, "If they build those 24-story buildings, I'll sell my home. I'll offer it to the City of New York for poor families."

"If there has to be housing on the site," says Birbach, "I would like to see a garden apartment for senior citizens only, of every race, creed and color . . . a model for the entire world . . . and even have a playground there so when their families come to see them, their grandchildren will have a place to play."

For dealing with the city's housing needs, he favors rehabilitation of abandoned buildings in slum neighborhoods, rather than experiments in "social engineering," a position that has brought him into alliance with the National Economic Growth and Reconstruction Organization (NEGRO), a black "self-help" body of no great membership. "I'm not against scatter-site housing," he says. "Don't misunderstand me." It is difficult to misunderstand Jerry Birbach.

THERE are, to be sure, friends of the project in Forest Hills, some of whom are only beginning to make themselves visible. For the most part, however, expressions of support have come from liberal and civil-rights bodies outside the immediate area—the Urban League, the New York Civil Liberties Union, the N.A.A.C.P., Americans for Democratic Action, peace groups and religious groups, and national Jewish organizations. Whereas the national Anti-Defamation League has come out in support, the Queens branch is strongly opposed. For now, Jerry Birbach seems to speak for most of Forest Hills, and probably for most of the borough.

The objections to the new project are not very different from those raised against virtually every scatter-site project conceived since 1966, from Riverdale to Howard Beach. As gathered from conversations in the immediate area, they concern, in part, what Mr. Birbach likes to call "the amenities," and they warrant varying degrees of attention.

Critics have argued from the beginning that construction costs would be excessive because of the nature of the land. That they had a point was evidenced in the change of plans to fewer, higher buildings. Whatever one thinks of that change, the Federal Government is now prepared to guarantee the bill. But the costs would again become an issue if the proposal of Representative Benjamin Rosenthal and others to cut the buildings in half, to 12 stories, were adopted. For then, there would of course be fewer apartments, and the per-apartment costs would exceed Federal guidelines. (Many opponents find themselves protesting that the cost of the present plan is too high, and then asking that it be increased. If Jerry Birbach's garden apartments were actually built on the site, the price per apartment would mark a peak in the history of Queens County and possibly the nation. Congressman Rosenthal did not inquire into the costs or what might be done about them before advancing his suggestion.)

Pressed to reduce the size of the project, officials have been discovering wondrous

Donald Elliott, chairman of the City Planning Commission: *"The plain fact is that scaling down the project means killing it."*

virtues in 24-story buildings. Chairman Elliott considers them esthetically satisfying in that particular location; the architect, Samuel Paul, calls attention to the "tremendous views" of, among other sights, Flushing Meadows and Shea Stadium, available above the seventh story; Chairman Golar promises that they will be safer because it is cheaper to make security arrangements for three big buildings with only one main entrance each than for seven smaller ones. But the plain fact is that, once having settled on the 108th Street site, planners had no choice but to build high. It was not esthetics; it was not the view; it was not safety; it was Horse Brook and the exigencies of economics.* (The present, fairly standard design replaced a more original, more expensive concept which featured rows of two-story buildings.)

STILL, the population density of about 310 persons an acre, though not inviting to wilderness lovers, is lower than nearby developments such as Park City and Lefrak City. As now planned, 85 per cent of the site will be open space, for playing, parking and sitting, not a meager allotment, as anyone who has strolled along Queens Boulevard can attest, and there is a lot of park land nearby. If somebody had decided to build a high-density, high-rent high-rise there, fewer residents would have rushed to the picket lines.

Will the new inhabitants "overwhelm" the neighborhood, as opponents warn, turning it into another Grand Concourse? Supporters make light of the impact of a couple of thousand newcomers on a "community of a half million people." But the "community" which will feel the project's impact most is much smaller than that—closer to 15,000 than to 500,000. It is not as stable as some advocates contend, and further changes can be anticipated, such as more middle-class black families moving into the garden apartments near the project. But the decline of the West Bronx cannot fairly be laid to low-income projects, and in any case the Bronx need be no model for Forest Hills. The danger now lies in residents' believing their neighborhood's destiny is ordained and acting in ways which will invite what they dread.

Complaints are also heard about the added strain on bus and subway lines from the project. Mass transit in Queens is no better than anywhere else in the city, and in some regards it is worse. Speaking of the Continental Avenue subway station, Jerry Birbach says, "I welcome Mr. Lindsay. I welcome Mr. Golar. You can't get on a platform forgawdsakes." Even a Housing Authority transportation expert concedes that "the Queens Boulevard line suffers some of the most severe overcrowding in the system." Several hundred new daily riders will not improve the situation—nor will they make it much worse. Local bus lines can increase service, and a new Queens subway is being built.

CONCERN over the crowding of subways, however, is as nothing in Forest Hills-Rego Park compared with concern over the crowding of schools. The Board of Education tells us that as of Oct. 30, 1970, there was room for about 280 more children in the regular classrooms of the five elementary schools likely to serve the project—about 70 less than the number of children from 5 to 11 who are expected to live there. If space being used by the district superintendent for offices were made available for teaching, there would be no overload. Moreover, the birth rate in the area has been dropping, and, as the project's anticipated 440 infants and preschoolers reach school age, it might be feasible to reassign some of them to an uncrowded school across Queens Boulevard.

Although the district's intermediate and junior-high schools tend to be overcrowded, the one nearest the building site had 112 empty seats as of October, 1970, enough to take care of the students that the project is expected to add. Nevertheless, new intermediate schools are certainly needed in the area, and plans are afoot to build at least one.

It is at the high-school level that we find the worst overcrowding. Forest Hills High School had 918 students too many as of October, 1970, and has for years been operating on triple sessions. The project is expected to bring in fewer than 100 new high-school students in the fall of 1973; their number will continue to rise steadily after that, and classes will grow ever more crowded until new schools are built. Mr. Elliott and Mr. Golar promise that these schools, already in the budget, will be up "long before the young children from the project reach high-school age"—a way of telling us that they will not be up before then. For now, the long-promised school in Corona remains tangled in Albany's red tape, and the Board of Education indicates that it does not expect a new high school to be built for at least five years.

Jerry Birbach of the Forest Hills Residents Association: *"Does community participation apply to Bedford-Stuyvesant and Harlem . . . and not to middle-income people in Forest Hills?"*

The school issue, of course, goes beyond the figures, for parents are worried less about how many new students will be arriving than about who they will be. Numbers of black youths from the Jamaica section are at present being bused into the Forest Hills-Rego Park schools, and there are complaints about white youths being pushed around and shaken down, and of merchandise being pilfered from local shops. Which brings us to the heart of the matter.

ANTICIPATING THE WORST

FOREST HILLS is by no means a crime-free garden—but it is not the South Bronx either. Many residents, like Jerry Birbach, once lived in places where fear today keeps people behind locked and bolted doors after dark. And their experience tells them that the deterioration of neighborhoods is connected with the arrival of blacks. "They're scared to death," says Haskell Lazere, the American Jewish Committee's New York director. "I have never in my life felt a community to be so in terror."

Loath to concede what all the world knows—that crimes of violence, in New York as in other cities, are committed in disproportionate numbers by poor black youths—city spokesmen have fled into foolishness. At the end of last year, in an effort to rebut Daily News headlines of a "crime wave" in public housing, Mr. Golar released a set of statistics headed, "CRIME IN PUBLIC HOUSING DRAMATICALLY LOWER THAN REST OF CITY, 1971 FIGURES REVEAL." What Mr. Golar's statistician did was to take the crime rate per thousand in each project for the first six months of 1971 and compare it with the rate for the surrounding neighborhood. He discovered that there were more crimes per capita outside the project than inside. No great acuity is required to figure out that many crimes, such as robbing storekeepers, cannot be performed in housing projects, and that muggers and burglars may prefer to choose victims from the well-to-do outside the projects than from the poor within. Unfortunately, the City Planning Commission compounded the confusion by announcing that "the crime rate for public-housing tenants is lower than for the city as a whole"—an ambiguous bit of phrasing which seems to promise that the newcomers will be more law-abiding than the people already in Forest Hills.

We must all hope that Mr. Golar's prophesy that "the bringing of a public-housing population to Forest Hills will not raise the crime rate one iota" will prove accurate. In the meantime, one ought to resist marking down as a racist every parent who is worried about the impact on her children of scores of teenagers fresh from the ghetto. (Black tenants in Baisley Park Houses, a low-income project in Jamaica, expressed many of the same concerns over who will be admitted to a planned scatter-site development near them as white residents of Forest Hills have about the plan for their neighborhood.) Golar's announcement that "less than half of the crimes committed in public housing are committed by public-housing tenants" may not seem reassuring to people who have never known a fellow tenant to be arrested for anything worse than speeding. Yet if officialdom has behaved disingenuously on the delicate subject of crime, some of the project's critics have given way to hysteria. The talk one hears of an influx of criminals betrays a lack of knowledge about the plans for

***Since the Housing Act of 1968, Federal policy has been not to approve high-rise buildings for low-income families with children, unless there is no practical alternative. This act has been judged not retroactive to the Forest Hills project, approved in 1966.**

the project and slanders the families who will in fact be moving in.

To begin with, the 340 apartments for the elderly will contain about 15 per cent of the project's 2,500 to 2,800 people. Most of those in the family apartments will be drawn from the "working poor," employed at jobs that pay less than $8,820 a year. The remainder will be getting by with public assistance of one sort or another, and this group will be predominantly black. According to Mr. Golar, only 10 per cent of the families, upwards of 400 people, will be on public assistance, a far lower percentage than in projects elsewhere in the city. There will be 160 apartments of three bedrooms or more — fewer than a fifth of the total — for larger, often fatherless families, and only 24 of these will have six and one-half to seven and one-half rooms. There will be more whites than blacks and more small families than large ones. The reason for this untypical situation is that the Housing Authority is committed to draw its tenants first from the immediate area and then from the rest of Queens. "We don't expect to go beyond the borough," promises Golar.

Some weeks ago, as the administration tried to calm the neighborhood, Mr. Elliott suggested that a local committee be established to play an advisory role in the screening of tenants. It was one of those "let's-form-a-committee" brainstorms that substitute for ideas at difficult moments. It might mean something or nothing. If it means that Jerry Birbach is going to get his hands on a single applicant's dossier, then it is better if it means nothing. The notion may not be unconstitutional, as the New York Civil Liberties Union maintains, but it is nonetheless deplorable.

Yet the screening of tenants in public housing by responsible officials is essential —not only to the surrounding community, but, primarily, to those who must live there, even though every project has its own housing police. A report written for the Citizens Housing and Planning Council 15 years ago, entitled "The Small Hard Core," stated: ". . . it takes only a very few, very antisocial families to make a floor or a building or a project unsatisfactory to parents who are concerned about their children."

Persons with records of violent crime and known addicts are never admitted to public housing, but the problem of tenant selection is not thereby resolved. In recent years, the Housing Authority has been forced by pressures from welfare-rights groups and antipoverty lawyers to relax its criteria for admission and its eviction procedures, which had been unfair to unwed mothers and others. One result has been a sharp rise in the number of tenants on public assistance. Although, as the Housing Authority emphasizes, its tenantry has traditionally been drawn from the working poor, this has been changing as the city's population has changed. In 10 years, the proportion of households receiving public assistance has risen from 16 per cent to 25 per cent, and more than half of the families being admitted to existing public housing in this recession period are on some form of welfare. It is certain that these families are in need of housing—priority is given to those who have lost their homes because of urban renewal—and it is equally certain that some are sources of antisocial behavior.

Roger Starr wrote recently: "I must admit that I used to inveigh against the Housing Authority for its reluctance to admit female-headed households into the projects unless it had reason to believe that a specific household was relatively stable. My mind was changed, not by any statistics from the authority, but rather by the complaints of the tenants themselves at the way their housing project was being disfigured by the activities of alcoholics, junkies and young delinquents—mostly members of A.F.D.C. [fatherless welfare] families. It became clear to me after a while that only the safe middle class can afford to ignore the distinction which the working poor are willing to draw, between themselves and their poor, nonworking neighbors."

The tenant-screening process is not needed to weed out mischievous children and promiscuous women, but to bar people who cannot, or will not, abide by the rules required for co-existence in close quarters. Ravaged projects throughout the country bear witness to their presence. The choice is cruel—either deny housing to people who now live under abominable conditions or admit them and threaten the tranquillity and safety of the neighborhood. The unsatisfying truth seems to be that there are a sizable number of families in our ghettos whose troubles run so deep that they cannot be helped by public housing, and may in fact destroy it.

Simeon Golar affirms that "The Housing Authority has an obligation to people living in public housing to maintain a decent and stable community," and he promises that the Forest Hills project will not be overloaded with social problems. There is no question of the chairman's commitment to public housing—he grew up in projects—but despite his experience as the city's Human Relations Commissioner he has in recent weeks shown little sensitivity to community feelings. In a role that has called above all for the restraint of a negotiator, he has been provoked to trade insults with Jerry Birbach.

Simeon Golar, chairman of the Housing Authority: *"One fact I have to live with is that I happen to be black and the opposition happens to be white . . . ."*

Golar confesses to an inability to keep his official role separate from his sense of himself: "When all is said and done, one fact I have to live with is that I happen to be black and that the opposition in Forest Hills happens to be white, and some of those good people will find in me the symbolic representation of all that they are concerned about, all that they fear and are angry at and hostile to. I can't help that." He may be indulging in a bit of self-dramatization, for he symbolizes, if anything, qualities which the good people of Forest Hills can, and do, live with and even admire. There would be no picketing if Simeon Golar were to move next door. The fact that he considers himself a central symbol of the controversy, however, helps to explain his flashes of temper at a time when coolness is at a premium.

THE Forest Hills fight has seen much waving of that tattered word "racism," but the fact of race does not explain the resistance to low-income housing throughout the country, unless it is tied in with the fact of class. In 1966, 700 residents disrupted a City Planning Commission meeting to protest the first set of Queens scatter sites, with statements like, "We improved our lot by struggle. The Negroes want everything for free. How much can we take? How much can we pay? We'd be better off on relief." Elinor C. Guggenheimer, then on the Planning Commission, commented: "What has been significant and alarming in the hearings has been the outspoken dislike and fear of the poor, expressed not only by the average residents of the middle-income areas, but by their elected officials. Vituperative references to the poor and to the importance of preserving class distinctions were applauded."

Today Jerry Birbach and many others speak of themselves as people who have worked hard to get where they are, only to see nonworking people moving into apartments ("with air conditioning?"*) which cost more than some existing homes. "I think that when they go back to their old neighborhoods and they see that they were destroyed by low-income families and lack of planning by the city, they have a right to be afraid." Afraid of the poor? Afraid of the blacks? It is not easy to sort out such fears.

The situation is aggravated by the fact that the most prominent protestors against the project are Jewish. To be sure, a number are not—Joseph Devoy, chairman of the local planning board, is a churchgoing man, and there are a couple of Negroes in the Forest Hills Residents Association—but the area is, after all, three-quarters Jewish, and some of the opposition is based on that reality. For the past decade, the large Conservative temples of Queens have been suffering a decline in membership, with younger families moving to the suburbs and older couples retiring to Florida. Some rabbis view the project as an additional spur to dispersal, a concern that Herbert Kahn, friend of scatter housing, dismisses somewhat lightly as "the whole bag of Jewish paranoia." The project represents a special threat to the Orthodox, many of whom have come to Queens from deteriorating and dangerous neighborhoods in other boroughs. Dr. Alvin Lashinsky, outgoing president of the Queens Jewish Community Council, which claims to speak for 53 religious groups, fears that the project will disrupt Jewish life, in particular for those who require a congenial, close-knit setting to carry on their observances, their schools, their traditions. Once settled, the Orthodox find it difficult to move. They grant that they themselves encoun-

***The air-conditioning, an unusual feature in low-income housing, was imposed on the city by the proximity of La-Guardia Airport and by Federal rules for noise levels. During the summer, people who have air-conditioning can shut their windows and keep out the noise. The units for the elderly are to be paid for by HUD; other tenants will be able to have air-conditioners installed for a small monthly fee.**

tered opposition when they first arrived in Queens, but point out that they came family by family; the Government did not plunk them down en masse. They are incensed at what they see as the latest in a series of assaults on New York's Jewish middle class; they speak of teachers intimidated by "community control" and students discriminated against by "open admissions."

THERE are prominent rabbis in the area (including Rabbi Ben Zion Bokser of the Conservative Forest Hills Jewish Center, to which Jerry Birbach belongs) who, despite the feelings of their congregations, have come out in favor of the project. Writing in *Sh'ma*, "a journal of Jewish responsibility," Rabbi I. Usher Kirshblum of the Kew Gardens Hills Jewish Center reviewed the difficulties that Jews had to overcome to find homes in Queens: "We Jews, better than any other people, know what it means to be driven from community to community and crammed into ghettos. We dare not propose the perpetuation of ghetto areas for the poor—be they white or black."

At present, that is a minority view. "We resent the city administration constantly choosing the Jewish population for its experiments in social engineering," says Dr. Lashinsky, alerting politicians from Senator James Buckley to Assemblyman Vito Battista and Councilman Matthew Troy Jr. to the existence of a constituency that can be cultivated.

A few certified liberals, comfortable with neither the Buckley-Birbach alliance nor the city's handling of the project, find themselves in a difficult position. Congressmen Rosenthal of Queens and Edward Koch of Manhattan, both Democrats, have broken with their accustomed allies to oppose the project in its 24-story form. It is not scatter-site housing at all, charges Representative Rosenthal, but "old-fashioned warehousing" which cannot be integrated into the community. Now they must defend themselves against charges of "racism" and of consorting with reactionaries. Even though both have earned A.D.A. liberal quotients of 100 in the House, they must now suffer being put down as "so-called liberals" by Simeon Golar.

The conflicts that have surfaced in Forest Hills will be much with us in this election year. A glimpse of what we can expect was provided a few weeks ago when New York City's Board of Estimate voted down minor zoning changes for a 559-unit low income project near Lindenwood Gardens in the middle-class Howard Beach section of Queens, and thereby stopped it cold—"an outrageous public act," in Donald Elliott's view. The Lindenwood project had already been approved twice by the Board of Estimate—in 1966 and 1970—and no one doubts that final approval would have been routinely forthcoming had it not been for Forest Hills. "The residents of Lindenwood thank the residents of Forest Hills and wish them luck," said the president of the Lindenwood Community Civic Association, which had dispatched several busloads to cheer on the Board of Estimate.

"HUMANIZING" THE SITUATION

THE Forest Hills fight has become a field day for haters of blacks, haters of Jews, haters of Lindsay, haters of the poor and haters of the middle class. It has encouraged posturing on all sides. The administration has managed to be at once moralistic, deceptive and divisive. It has not done all it could to help relatively moderate forces in Queens take leadership away from Jerry Birbach. But even if the city had performed better from the beginning, when it made its bad bargain, this project, like nearly every project, would have met resistance. It was beyond the powers of reasoned discourse to convert the Forest Hills Residents Association.

At present, no one believes that the project can simply be stopped. Opponents are pressing now for an accommodation of some sort, such as reducing the size of the buildings and the number of tenants, especially welfare tenants. (Dr. Lashinsky's group would prefer a breakdown of 70 per cent middle-income, 20 per cent low-income, 10 per cent elderly.) The administration position, its public position at any rate, is that a substantial change at this time would mean the end of low-income housing in Forest Hills. As Mr. Elliott told a State Senate committee in December: "The plain fact is that scaling down the project means killing it. Costs would exceed Federal guidelines. It would need new, all but impossible to achieve, approvals. This would mean further delay and even higher costs. Those who say make it smaller are saying make it vanish."

As I write, closed talks aimed at some sort of understanding are being held "The project will not be built," maintains Seymour C. Samuels, president-elect of the Queens Jewish Community Council. "It will be settled around the table or in the streets." The deadline, he says, is next month's Florida Democratic primary on which John Lindsay's political hopes greatly rest.

There are practical, as well as political and psychological, difficulties in the way of making any major change new. A cutback to 12-story buildings, I am assured, would require city funds to meet the large additional costs. Given the condition of the municipal budget, that is no minor obstacle. To turn the project into something other than a low-income development would also involve changes in funding methods, and no one seems able to say whether such an arrangement could sensibly be worked out for Forest Hills. And even if new approvals would be forthcoming, if the delays would not be excessive, if the additional costs could be met, any change would be strenuously resisted on principle, by the city's black leadership and by liberal groups. Scatter housing in New York has a dim future.

Probably it would have been better to build in Corona. Probably it would be better even now not to build so high. Perhaps it would be better to make all scatter housing small and in part middle-income. One can revel in perhaps and probably. But the one constant in the whole affair is the existence of hundreds of thousands of New Yorkers without a decent place to live. With all its defects, the project due to go up on 108th Street promises to help a few of them.

ALTHOUGH opponents and supporters can find public housing at which to point with pride or dismay, there are no truly comparable projects in terms of size, design, neighborhood and, importantly, the emotions of the period in which this one is being built. It is far from ideal, yet that does not mean it must fail. Unfortunately, the forces operating to make it fail are strong, and they come from the doctrinairism of its supporters as well as from the fears of its opponents. The charges of white racism, the charges of black depravity, might be designed to set people at one another's throats, and the reverberations are being felt beyond Forest Hills.

There are several hundred people on the spot, now getting together in a group called Forest Hills Neighbors, who hold no special affection for this large addition to their neighborhood, yet would like it to work. They are prepared to do what they can—at the least to offer a friendlier welcome than picket signs to the new tenants, who they trust will be chosen from among applicants "who are able and desirous of being absorbed into the community." Paul Sandman, organizer of the group, rejects the notion of direct citizen participation in screening of tenants as "dangerous"; he calls for an immediate start on the Corona high school; he takes a wait-and-see attitude toward Simeon Golar's offers of cooperation. For now, he insists, "the whole situation has got to be humanized." How much such a group will be able to accomplish in the next year or two will depend on whether they can touch the kinder instincts of their fellow residents and on whether the city administration can overcome a habit of basking in its own righteousness and go about devising means to help the people in the project and outside of it to live in safety and comfort and, with time, even amity. ■

February 20, 1972

FORD SIGNS BILL TO AID HOUSING

By EDWARD C. BURKS
Special to The New York Times

WASHINGTON, Aug. 22—President Ford signed the Housing and Community Development Act of 1974 at a White House ceremony today and declared, "The housing industry needs a shot in the arm and this bill can be extremely helpful."

The measure authorizes funding of $11.9-billion over three years, gives communities greatly increased flexibility and control over development programs in low-income areas and provides what Mr. Ford called "significant assistance" to home buyers and home builders.

The President cautioned, however, that the measure, the first omnibus housing and community development bill to become law since 1968, was not expected to bring "substantial immediate relief" to the long-depressed housing market. "But over the long haul," he said, "it should provide the foundations for better housing for all Americans."

New 'Block Grants'

A major new approach in the act authorizes $8.4-billion in funding over three years in single "block grants" to localities for community development programs, sweeping away seven former narrowly defined categories and allowing local officials to decide how to use the money.

Speaking before 200 persons, including Governors, Mayors, members of Congress and of the Administration who were gathered under the glittering chandeliers of the East Room, the President said that the new act "will give a real impetus to local decision-making, local action and local responsibility."

In a statement released just before he signed the bill, President Ford said that "in a very real sense, this bill will help to return power from the banks of the Potomac to people in their own communities."

Governor Wilson of New York and Mayor Beame of New York City, who were present, applauded the concept of the omnibus act, which also includes the biggest change in housing subsidy programs for "lower-income" persons since 1933, according to the Department of Housing and Urban Development.

Governor Wilson said that he welcomed the act because the Federal Government had had a freeze on new subsidized housing programs since early 1973 and "because we have desperate housing needs in New York State, not only in the cities but in nonurban areas, too."

Mayor Beame's comment was more restrained. He said that he was pleased to see that the proposed "block grant" funding for New York City's community development programs in low-income areas would rise by more than 50 per cent — from $101.1-million now to $153.9-million in the fiscal year starting July 1, 1976, according to Federal projections.

But the Mayor emphasized, "We'd like to see the appropriations first." Separate appropriation bills will be needed each year to make the authorized funds available.

'Not Enough Money'

Mayor Kenneth A. Gibson of Newark, who also attended the ceremony, said, "I think basically the bill is good, but my real complaint is there's not enough money in it."

While New York City's block grant funding will rise to $153.9-million by the fiscal year 1977 and then reach a level of $156.5-million for the next three years, under long-range projections, Newark funding will drop slightly in fiscal year 1977 and then plunge steeply in the three following years.

The Newark figures are $20.6-million this year and next, $19.6-million in fiscal year 1977, $13.7-million in fiscal year 1978, $11.85-million in 1979, and $10-million in 1980.

James T. Lynn, Secretary of Housing and Urban Development, said at a news briefing that he would recommend funding of the full $2.5-billion authorized in the act for the first full year of the community development block-grant program. The block grants are replacing such former separate categories as Model Cities, urban renewal, neighborhood facilities and water and sewer grants.

Aid on Mortgages

Mr. Lynn outlined major features that will help home buyers seeking lower-interest mortgages insured by the Federal Housing Administration.

The limit on F.H.A.-insured mortgages is raised to $45,000 from $33,000, and the down-payment requirement slashed in half.

For example, the home buyer who has been paying $3,400 to obtain a $35,000 F.H.A.-insured mortgage will now need only about $1,750 for a down payment, Mr. Lynn said. In addition, the maximum housing loan that a savings and loan association can make is being raised to $55,000 from $45,000.

"We think home builders will be extremely happy with the new legislation," Mr. Lynn added.

August 23, 1974

HOMEOWNERS ASK 'REDLINING' CURB

Senate Witnesses Favor Bill to Force Public Disclosure of Bank Loan Patterns

By WILLIAM E. FARRELL
Special to The New York Times

WASHINGTON, May 5—More than 150 representatives of homeowners in 20 cities and older suburbs that are threatened by "redlining" voiced strong support today for a Senate bill requiring public disclosure of the savings and investment patterns of banks and savings and loan associations throughout the country.

Redlining is the arbitrary process in which lending institutions decline to make conventional mortgages and home improvement loans in areas they deem risks. Another name for the practice is "urban disinvestment."

The term "redlining" derives from lenders' red-penciling a local map, in effect deleting a section of a city from its approved investment areas.

The homeowners — young, old, black and white, from communities as far east as the Bronx and as far west as Oakland, Calif.—crowded into a Senate hearing room for the first of four days of hearings on the bill being held by the Senate Committee on Banking, Housing and Urban Affairs.

With Local Studies

Many of them came armed with the fruits of local research into the growing reluctance of local lending institutions—places where they keep their savings—to make conventional mortgage and home-improvement loans in their aging neighborhoods.

Passage of the bill, sponsored by Senator William Proxmire, Democrat of Wisconsin, is needed as an "essential first step" and as an aid to them in their local struggles to curb redlining, the proponents argued.

Lending institution representatives will testify Wednesday on the proposed Federal disclosure law.

A common thread in today's testimony was a contention that redlining in time becomes a self-fulfilling prophecy—that neighborhoods written off by lenders fall prey to decay precisely because the loans for necessary upkeep are unavailable.

Another theme in the testimony was the contention that savings and loan associations, which attract the savings of homeowners in the areas for which they are chartered, have an investment obligation to those areas.

Need to Preserve

Gale Cincotta, a Chicago housewife, told the committee: "We can no longer afford to destroy the communities our partents have built. We need to preserve our communities for our children and our children's children."

Mrs. Cincotta, a resident of Chicago's working-class Austin section, is the head of National People's Action on Housing, an umbrella group for community housing groups across the nation.

She cited a case where two University of Illinois professors with a joint income of $40,000 a year sought to buy a house near hers and were refused a conventional mortgage.

"Why the redline?" she said. "Because the community is old? My house is 35 years old. If they couldn't get a conventional loan, what about the rest of my neighbors?"

"The saver as consumer has a right to know how his or her deposits are being reinvested," Mrs. Cincotta said. "We are not asking for handouts. All we are asking for is a fair return on our savings into our communities."

Spreading to Suburbs

Paul Bloyd, co-chairman of the Oak Park Community Organization, testified that the practice of "redlining" was no longer limited to inner-city neighborhoods but was spreading to older suburbs such as his.

"The redlining problem is a metropolitan one," Mr. Bloyd said, "joining older, suburbs like Oak Park with the cities as common victims of arbitrary mortgage rejection policies."

Oak Park, which adjoins Chicago, has a population of 62,000. It is a tree-lined, middle-class suburb that boasts 15 Frank Lloyd Wright houses and many other rambling homes from 60 to 80 years old.

"Lenders hold economics as the validifier," said Fran Matarrese, chairman of the East Oakland, Calif., Housing Committee. "But if it is good business to take in small depositors, is it not also good business to loan to small borrowers as well?"

May 6, 1975

The Ivy-Covered Cottage, Nearly an Impossible Dream

One kind of American dream, the rose-covered cottage, the split-level in the suburbs, has been priced beyond the reach of most families in the United States, and there appears to be little chance they can recapture it.

The median price of a new home is up to $41,300. A family must have an annual income of at least $23,300 to afford it, according to a report of the Congressional Joint Economic Committee. The median price of a used house is $35,660, and the income needed is $21,170. Because most Americans don't have that kind of income, a new home is unavailable to 85 per cent of all families, and a used home is out of reach for 80 per cent, the report says.

Inflation and high construction costs and interest rates have pushed the prices up more than $5,000 in the last five years, the report says. In addition, the monthly carrying charges—taxes, insurance, utilities—have risen sharply.

The effect of all this is that the American dream, under present conditions, is realistic only for the rich and the upper middle class. People at lower economic levels increasingly must settle for rental housing, the report says.

Other Dreams Are Shaken, Too

Another fragment of the American dream, reinforced by two decades of relative prosperity, has been that the future will be better. How has the reality of inflation and recession affected that faith?

According to a survey by Yankelovich, Skelly and White, an opinion research organization, while 62 per cent of American families feel they are coping financially, almost one out of two families feels its future will not be determined by its own actions and 45 per cent have begun to accept the idea that each year may not bring financial improvement.

The Protestant Ethic — duty before pleasure, hard work pays off — still dominates American family values. But one out of every two family members now believes that work and a good standard of living is a social right.

The Cost of Owning a Home

NEW HOUSES

	Median Price	Monthly Expense	Minimum Income	Percentage of Families With Minimum Income
1970	$35,500	$373	$17,900	14.9%
1971	36,300	364	17,470	18.0
1972	37,300	375	18,000	20.8
1973	37,100	397	19,060	21.5
1974	41,300	486	23,330	15.0

OLD HOUSES

	Median Price	Monthly Expense	Minimum Income	Percentage of Families With Minimum Income
1970	30,000	319	15,310	21.5
1971	31,700	330	15,840	22.5
1972	33,400	349	16,750	24.8
1973	31,200	348	16,700	29.6
1974	35,600	441	21,170	20.0

Source: Congressional Joint Economic Committee

May 11, 1975

Urban Homesteading Faltering In Fight Against Blight of Cities

By WAYNE KING

Special to The New York Times

BALTIMORE — Urban homesteading, regarded by city planners two years ago as a major solution to urban blight, appears to be losing some of its luster after experience in more than two dozen cities.

Inquiries in cities that have undertaken homesteading programs, including Philadelphia, Baltimore, Newark and Wilmington, Del., and in some cities considering programs, such as New York and Los Angeles, indicate that homesteading has both built-in problems and limited application.

A modern variant of the pioneer homesteading that provided 160 acres of Western land to anyone who would settle on it 100 years ago, urban homesteading offers, free or at low cost, abandoned homes in urban areas to anyone who will renovate and live in them.

The concept, first implemented in Wilmington, Del., almost two years ago, caught the imagination of city officials across the country in urban areas with rapidly growing backlogs of abandoned and blighted housing taken over by the cities primarily for failure to pay back-taxes.

The idea was that the buildings could be given free or at nominal cost to persons who would bring them up to building code standards, thereby saving the city maintenance money, eliminating blight and encouraging other renovations, wiping out havens for alcoholics and drug addicts, and finally, restoring worthless properties to tax-paying status.

Although it is too early to tell if these benefits will all accrue, since very few homesteaded properties have been fully renovated and occupied, it is clear that serious problems have plagued the projects in most cities.

In Wilmington, for example, the first city to undertake an urban homesteading program, only 28 homes have been awarded, eight are occupied and three homesteaders have given up entirely. Mayor Thomas Maloney estimates there are 2,000 abandoned homes in Wilmington.

Initial high interest—more than 100 applications were received for the first 10 houses in Wilmington two years ago, including some from as far away as California—seems to have flagged considerably, and the Federal Housing Administration has warned that homesteaders would likely have to sink more money into repairs than the homes, in their poor neighborhoods, would ever be worth.

Slow in Starting

Elsewhere, projects have been slow getting off the ground, as cities mire themselves in red tape and political in-fighting over control and goals of the programs.

Financing has been a problem, with private institutions generally wary of projects in blighted neighborhoods and public money scarce.

Contractors have shown resistance, although the construction slump now has made many eager to take any jobs they can get. Many homesteaders complain workmanship varies from mediocre to abysmal

As in Wilmington, public response to "dollar houses"—the nominal fee most cities charge for abandoned houses—is extraordinary at first. But many prospects cooled considerably when they saw what was offered—old, decaying buildings, often little more than shells, needing new roofs, floors, walls, plumbing, wiring and fixtures.

Although there are some truly spectacular offerings — leaded glass mansions in almost livable condition — from perhaps 60 per cent to 90 per cent of abandoned housing in most cities is simply not renewable.

Even the good houses are in bad neighborhoods. Moreover, those who administer the programs have had difficulty making it clear that by and large they are not intended for the poor, a belief that became fairly general because the houses were free or extremely cheap.

The poor, they point out, simply cannot afford renovation costs of $10.000 up to $50,000, the expected outlay for some of the grander but more seriously decayed structures. The most successful applicants tend to be young, energetic and middle class—the people who need help the least.

Even where urban homesteading appears successful, as here in Baltimore, there are problems and uncertainties.

Construction in one project has been under way for nearly a year now on some of the houses, which are surrounded by decaying neighborhoods, and a cyclone fence encircles the entire street. It is temporary, but the residents wonder what problems will occur with thieves or vandals when it does come down.

"Everybody is wondering what will happen when the fence comes down," said John Clifford, a young trucking contractor who owns one of the 42 houses in what is called the Stirling Street homesteading project here. "A big problem was getting the contractors to bid, even with the fence. They were afraid of getting ripped off. But it's got to come down sometime."

"The day the fence comes down" seems to be on the minds of at least several of the 25 people who took over the old homes, mostly small, two-story buildings on Stirling Street, joining some of them to make one large structure.

Already, six of the houses being renovated were destroyed when an arsonist set fire to them several months ago.

Mr. Clifford believes the arson was essentially without motive, but that the contrast between what is happening to Stirling Street and the problems in the rest of the area is enough to arouse envy.

Across the street from Mr. Clifford, for example, are two homes being joined and renovated by Robert Hooke, who has taken time off from his job in the antique salvage business to do much of the work on his house himself.

Putting a cassette on the tape machine he plays to inspire him at his work, Mr. Hooke explained that he was seeking the mood of a medieval castle.

"This," he said as Wagnerian music echoed off the aging walls, "will be a great arch leading into the great hall, two stories high, a vaulted cathedral ceiling. Here, it will be Tudor style, white stucco, with darkened beams. This balcony will overlook the great hall."

Most of the renovations on Stirling Street will cost from $25,000 to $30,000, financed chiefly through Federal loans at 3 per cent interest and city loans at 6 per cent. Sixty-four per cent of the Stirling Street owners are single, and the median income is $16,667.

Besides the Stirling Street project, Baltimore has just begun awarding about 100 homes in the Inner Harbor area called Otterbein. The homes, built between 1820 and 1870, provide a view of the waterfront, and will cost from $14,500 to $50,000 to renovate.

Another project involves 12 houses in one area, and 144 more homesteads on what is called "scattered site"—that is, single houses not near other homesteads.

About 50 per cent of the homesteaders are black, with an average age of 32, and average family size of 2.6. The median over-all income citywide is $14,688 for whites and $13,571 for blacks.

The uneven experience so far has made other cities wary of homesteading, although the benefits appear promising enough that as many as 180 are believed to be considering implementing some form of it.

The Department of Housing and Urban Development recently announced it would make available to cities that qualified a total of $5-million worth of properties that could be used for various purposes, including homesteading.

There is no rush to take them over.

In the Los Angeles area, for example, Paul R. Kaup, a H.U.D. official for the region, said:

"We have had very few houses taken. The reason is we have to be extremely careful and give away stuff that is worthless to begin with."

In Compton, Calif., the City Council has been offered 200 properties, but has so far declined to take any. When it does, it will use them for parks, not homesteads.

Los Angeles County at first received numerous bids for homes, until the dilapidated nature of the buildings became known, and the bids were quickly withdrawn.

Some of the county's 14 properties were finally sold to the school system, which will allow students to tear them down as part of a construction training course. Others will be renovated for low-income families.

In Philadelphia, where city officials argued two years ago that they, and not Wilmington, first came up with the homestead idea, only 20 homes are now occupied by homesteaders out of 26,000 that are vacant. Ten thousand are suitable for homesteading, says Aubrey Meyers, director of the city's homestead program.

May 30, 1975

1974 Housing Act Helping Few of the Nation's Poor

By ERNEST HOLSENDOLPH

Special to The New York Times

WASHINGTON, Nov. 1—The $11-billion Housing and Community Development Act, passed by Congress in the late summer of 1974 with provisions that were to create more housing for the poor, has not yet made any impact on their housing supply, according to municipal officials and housing industry spokesmen.

The act, which is a departure from the established approach to housing people who are too poor to compete in the free market, is supposed to replace such programs as public housing, urban renewal, Model Cities and subsidized construction.

So far, however, only about 200 families in the nation have occupied housing under the program. Although the program's defenders say it is too early to judge its effectiveness, some experts say they are convinced that it will never measure up to its promise.

"The 1974 housing act is extremely misguided," said Robert C. Embry Jr., Baltimore's Commissioner of Housing and Community Development. "I cannot understand this Administration's reluctance to admit its failure."

Section 8 of the housing act subsidizes rents of the poor in three kinds of housing—sound, existing housing; rehabilitated housing and newly constructed dwellings.

Under the act the tenant pays from 15 to 25 per cent of his gross annual income to the landlord for rent, with the Department of Housing and Urban Development subsidizing the difference between the tenant's contribution and the going market rent for his unit.

Unlike older housing programs now being phased out, the 1974 act is not a construction program such as public housing or the Section 236 program, frozen by the Administration in January, 1973, which subsidized the financing costs of the builders. Under the 1974 program, builders must get their own financing at the going market rate, using the promise of Government rent subsidies as collateral.

The problem is that investors and financial institutions are uninterested because, in the present economy at least, they consider the program risky and not profitable enough, according to housing industry spokesmen.

Furthermore, Roger Starr, New York City's housing and development administrator, said this week that the Ford Administration's decision to allow New York to default may have sealed the doom of the Section 8 program.

He reasons that local borrowing power across the nation, already weak, will be further undermined by the city's default on its notes and the construction portion of the program will be dormant for an indefinite period.

Not Enough Existing Houses

With the bleak outlook for construction, housing authorities must resort to using existing houses to take part in the Section 8 program—and housing specialists in many areas consider that source to be inadequate to serve their needs.

The city of Chicago, which was proportionally the largest public housing program in the nation, has been able to put in for only 570 housing units under the program. None of them are yet occupied, however.

"We have been unable to find any financing for rehabilitation or construction," said Robert Lefley, a spokesman for the Chicago Housing Authority.

New York has preliminary approvals from the Housing and Urban Development Departent here for 6,600 new units of housing 2,200 units of substantially rehabilitated housing and 4,300 units in existing housing not needing major renovation. So far no units are being occupied under the program.

"The problem is that landlords don't want large families or welfare families," said Mr. Embrey of Baltimore, "and assuming you can find four- and five-bedroom dwellings—and you can't—the landlord can usually get a better price on the market than he can under this subsidized program."

In a check on housing situations in 10 cities, The New York Times has found that most housing authorities are relying on dwindling money in the old program pipelines to build public housing. The fear, however, is that this money will run out before the new law begins to have an effect.

Many housing experts applaud the aim of the 1974 act. With its emphasis on rental assistance for families who might otherwise not be able to afford sound housing and its focus on rehabilitation of older, receding neighborhoods.

In theory it could be the salvation of neighborhoods such as Crown Heights in Brooklyn on East Tremont in the Bronx by halting the deterioration of fundamentally sound buildings.

H.U.D. policy-makers have most often praised the 1974 housing law in concept because of its emphasis on neighborhood conservation, a theme widely embraced by urban planners and city officials, including the National League of cities.

However, the Nixon Administration—and now President Ford—embraced the program because it would get the Government out of the business of financig construction and out of the quagmire of subsidizing the operation of housing projects hit by inflation and questionable management.

The emerging lesson, however, may be that the private sector is even more leery than the Government of getting involved in housing for the poor, or even housing for lower-middle-income people, according to local housing officials.

Concerned about the slowness of the act to get off the ground, the House Subcommittee on Housing and Community Development of the Banking, Currency and Housing Committee held a hearing on Section 8 problems last week. In an illuminating acknowledgement, John S. Rhinelander, Under Secretary of H.U.D., told the committee:

With respect to the use of existing housing, we believe that the problems are essentially manageable. However, with respect to new construction and substantial rehabilitation, the problems are more serious."

Curb on Expectations

He added that because of general economic problems and reduced investor interest in all but the safest long-term investments, "we have to expect that it may not be possible to start a large number of newly constructed or substantially rehabilitated projects under the Section 8 program in the current housing market."

An executive for a large private financial institution that specializes in raising money for municipalities and public bodies was even more pointed in his testimony before the committee.

"Bond investors today want as close to a sure thing as possible; and they are getting very high rates of return on relatively safe investments, so why take a chance!" asked Donald D. Kummerfeld, vice president of the First Boston Corporation.

This new selectivity—and no one knows how temporary it maybe—is an outgrowth of a number of developments, financial specialists say. Part of it has to do with New York City's troubles and the probability of the largest municipal default in national history.

Investors are also increasingly wary of long-term real estate investments in the aftermath of widespread failures among real estate investment trusts. Just this week the Chase Manhatta nMortgage and Realty Trust reported a $166.4-million loss on revenues of $17.6-million for its last fiscal year.

The largest of the real estate investment trusts; Chase Trust, has loans outstanding from many of the nation's leading banks.

According to estimates, it was expected that 40 to 50 per cent of new construction under the 1974 housing act would be financed by state housing finance agencies. But these agencies, particularly in the aftermath of the default of New York's Urban Development Corporation, have had their own problems attracting interest in their bonds.

The bankers and some housing officials want some technical changes in the 1974 housing act, which they say may make the program work, but H.U.D. is resisting them.

H.U.D., has worked hard to be sure that details in the new program will not saddle it with long-term problems, even missing its deadline for issuing regulations for the program by six months. The department is leery of most proposals to change the program.

Pending legislation would change a provision that requires the Government to cut off the rent subsidy for an apartment if it is vacant 60 days. The change would require H.U.D. to keep paying at least a sum adequate to cover the loan interest costs for the dwelling unit.

The idea is that the change would reduce the long-term risk to investors. H.U.D. policymakers believe that the change would reduce the incentive for landlords to keep their buildings in good repair and fully occupied.

Under present law, H.U.D. is obligated to subsidize rents in a Section 8 building for a minimum of 20 years, but it is resisting pressure from the industry to obligate itself for payments for 40 years.

H.U.D. has not been altogether inflexible. In some scattered cases around the nation, housing officials have complained that the amount of subsidy was inadequate for the local cost of living or the limits in individual income of participants were unrealistic. The department has responded by making some changes.

For instance the department, upon request, raised the limit for a New York City family of four that wants to take part in the program from $11,450 to $14,500 a year because of the high and growing cost of living there. Some 14,000 families could take part in the New York City program, based on the city's share of the subsidy money and the projected needs of the families likely to ask for it.

Meanwhile, as bankers and H.U.D. toss the hot financing problem back and forth, there is an accumulating housing shortage that pushes the poor further and further from decent, sanitary houses that they can afford without paying 50 percent of their income.

The City of New Orleans has a fine old stock of housing fit for rehabilitation, but the impasse now has 8,300 families on a waiting list for 14,000 public housing units that are all occupied.

Better off than most cities, New Orleans has an accumulated need that "Section 8 will barely dent," says Robert L. Siegal, who has conducted a housing survey for the city.

Los Angeles has found that it has 370,000 households "needing assistance" based on a survey uncovering large families of low to moderate income paying more than 25 per cent of their income for quarters so inadequate that they often lacked plumbing.

If all works out well, Los Angeles will get 31,000 units in three years of Section 8 operation, according to Michael Salzman, the city's housing director.

Boston, a city hard hit with problems under the old H.U.D. subsidized construction program for poor-to-modest families, needs more than 10,000 more units of housing, the housing authority said in its application. Its allocation of $5.8-million could provide 1,600 units if all works out well.

Atlanta has 4,500 families on a two-year waiting list. Baltimore reports that it has more people on its waiting lists than it has occupying public housing.

Congress, its anxiety rising, has ordered H.U.D. to use at least $50-million for traditional public housing, which should provide about 20,000 units of new construction. But handwringing continues among housing authorities.

The gloomiest statement at the House hearing last week came from Jack H. Shiver, president of the National Association of Housing and Redevelopment Officials, who said:

"The new and still untried Section 8 program cannot by itself respond to the urgency of the housing crisis facing this nation. Projected new construction starts under Section 8 will not, in the near future, significantly reverse economic conditions, reduce construction unemployment or, most importantly, begin to meet the neglected housing needs of lower income families."

The secretary of H.U.D., Carla A. Hills, responded to criticism of the housing program as premature, because the program began only in June, when H.U.D. completed its regulations six months late.

"It's only a baby," she said. "We cannot know how it will turn out."

Other H.U.D. officials struck back pointedly at industry critics. The industry has grown up with construction programs financed by the Government, ever since 1937 when the first public housing measure was passed, they say privately.

"What they have got to learn is that the times have changed and they must change with it," one official said.

November 2, 1975

Housing Agency Assailed As a Chief Slumlord of U.S.

By WILLIAM E. FARRELL

Special to The New York Times

CHICAGO, Dec. 10—The front door of the modest blue frame house at 532 North Leamington on the Northwest Side was open. The cheap metal eye hooks that once held a padlock had long before been pried from the soft wood.

A trespasser entered the single-family house after climbing a flight of rotting steps and passing a faded sign on the door that said: "A theft from your Government is a theft from you."

For the house on Leamington — and thousands like it in cities across the country—is the property of the Department of Housing and Urban Development. It is therefore the property of American taxpayers.

The interior of the house attests to the efficiency of vandals, who had removed plumbing, light fixtures and other items that had resale value.

What remains is a rapidly deteriorating dwelling that, in a time of an acute national shortage of housing for the poor, has almost no chance of ever again harboring anyone but transient hooligans bent on picking it clean.

The accumulation of abandoned and ruined urban housing by the Federal Government began four years ago with the widespread failure of

The New York Times/Gary Settle

Abandoned houses on West 111th Place in Chicago's South Side that now belong to Department of Housing and Urban Development

housing programs for the poor, programs marred by scandal and abuse. Despite repeated efforts at reform, both the scandals and the accumulation of property have continued unabated and given rise to protest community groups in many cities.

Carla A. Hills, who became Secretary of Housing and Urban Development last March, has ordered new regulations intended to end the abuses, but there is skepticism among community groups that they will work.

Her department, according to recent Congressional data, owns more than 65,000 boarded-up and abandoned single-family homes.

The agency owns enough homes to provide for 260,000 people, or roughly the population of Jersey City. In addition the agency owns about 35,000 multifamily units worth more than $2 billion.

Beleaguered Agency

The landlord of these dwellings is one of the most beleaguered agencies in the Federal Government. In recent years, the department has been studied by academinians, investigated by Congress, denounced for its failures by community groups and politicians, and criticized from within.

Data from studies and Congressional testimony, along with interviews ranging from inner-city homeowners to H.U.D. officials, show the following:

¶Multimillion-dollar scandals, dating to 1971, are continuing to plague large cities such as Chicago, Detroit, Philadelphia, New York, Miami and Los Angeles.

¶There has been Congressional inertia, despite detailed hearings and numerous investigations, in making major corrections.

¶H.U.D. and Congress have maintained close links with commercial lending interests, many of whom have profited enormously from the agency's low-income housing programs.

¶The department has failed to supervise the thousands of mortgages, or lenders with whom it does business, and there has been widespread flouting of the agency's guidelines and regulations.

¶The complexity of Federal housing laws has discouraged examination by the public and media.

¶The Federal Government's role in hastening the decline of older urban neighborhoods has contributed to the vandalism of vacant Government-owned housing and the deleterious effect it has on private housing near it.

¶For thousands of low and moderate income families, the national housing goal, enunciated by Congress in 1948, of "a decent home and a suitable living environment for every American family" has been perverted.

Much of H.U.D.'s travails began in 1968 with the National Housing Act. The act, a response to the riots in a number of American cities, set as a goal the availability of home ownership to low-income persons, mostly city dwellers.

High-Risk Program

The program was acknowledged to be a high-risk one. It was placed with the Federal Housing Administration, an arm of H.U.D. and a staid agency considered by many today to have been a most unlikely choice to implement a program with strong social implications.

In effect, the program guaranteed lenders who underwrote mortgages for low-income home buyers that the Government would honor the lenders' claim if the mortgage was foreclosed because the buyer could not meet his modest payments.

The risk to the lender was nil.

Many unscrupulous lenders were quic kto discern the lucrative potential of such a Federal guarantee. Before long, there was feverish activity in many older city neighborhoods by speculators, and the scandals that ravaged portions of cities such as Detroit began.

In some cases, speculators went into working-class white areas, such as the Mattapan section near Boston, and conducted block-busting campaigns by telling white homeowners that blacks were about to move into the area. Frightened whites, convinced that black neighbors meant the loss of equity in their homes, sold their houses for a pittance. They were resold at huge markups, with the sellers safe under the umbrella of the F.H.A. guarantee.

In other cases, old, substandard houses were bought by speculators for a small sum. **They were given cosmetic "repairs" — frequently a coat of cheap paint that for a short while hid major deficiencies.**

Typically, a speculator would seek a "friendly" appraisal of his newly acquired property, often three, four and five times what the place was ever worth. The F.H.A. would often accept the inflated appraisal proffered by persons called "fee appraisers"—that is non-H.U.D. personnel retained to assess a property, often a relative or a friend of a real estate speculator.

$200 Down

The speculator would then seek out a customer; initially, the program permitted purchase of a home for as little as $200 down.

Often the speculator would "lend" the customer the $200 if he did not have it. Often, too, he helped a confused customer falsify employment and other financial data to be submitted to the F.H.A. as proof of his ability to maintain monthly home payments.

The new owner received no counseling on the intricacies of home financing or home ownership. Soon after he moved in, the cosmetic rehabilitation usually wore off, and the deficiencies became apparent. The dejected owner, unable to pay for major repairs, frequently abandoned the property.

After formal foreclosure proceedings, the mortgagee collected the F.H.A. insurance that reflected the inflated appraisal, and the American taxpayer took title to an abandoned dump.

In 1972, major scandals in Detroit, Philadelphia and other cities prompted Congressional hearings into bribery, collusion and the manipulation of the poor for profit while creating boarded-up slums of modest city neighborhoods.

Recommendations for change flowed from committee reports. Little or nothing was done. The department's posture before Congress in those days was that it was "restructuring" itself to be more efficient and to minimize the scandals and the ripoffs.

Meantime, in the inner-city neighborhoods and ghettos, the "suede shoe operators," as the speculators were called, continued unabated. Appraisers continued to make "windshield appraisals," determining the value of older buildings while driving past them.

When a scandal erupted, the **department generally responded that it was peculiar to that place.**

In January 1973, President Nixon froze the program because of the scandals. According to Representative Floyd V. Hicks, Democrat of Washington who is chairman of the House Manpower and Housing Subcommittee, 350,000 active insured mortgages stemming from the program are still held by the department.

A Leading Slumlord

Mr. Hicks says that the department "is one of the largest owners and managers of real estate in the country." Community groups and critics who have studied the agency say it is also one of the nation's leading slumlords.

Mrs. Hills announced last month that $264.1 million fro-

zen in 1973 would be released over the next two years. In addition, she said, the resuscitated program will differ from the suspended one because it is aimed at a higher income group, in the $9,000-to-$11,000 range and will require initial investments of $1,500 to $2,000.

Theoretically, the requirement for a higher down payment will strengthen the owner's commitment to the property.

Mrs. Hills recently sent a department study group to Chicago following articles in The Chicago Tribune that detailed abuses, bribes, destruction of housing and bureaucratic chaos. The report of the group confirmed many of the criticisms made of H.U.D. and the F.H.A. over the last several years. The report, copy of which was recently obtained from sources in Washington, noted that the department dealt with 35,000 lenders and that "H.U.D. has not developed an effective departmental program for monitoring and evaluating mortgages."

"Historically," the report said, "H.U.D. has placed great reliance upon the principle that mortgagees function with great integrity in their operations. In furtherance of this principle, H.U.D. developed many of its systems with limited or no controls. H.U.D.'s experience over the last several years has shown that there are too many mortgagees who have taken advantage of the situation.

"Consequently, H.U.D. and many unsuspecting mortgagors have all too often been victimized through fraudulent origination practices, poor servicing practices, fraudulent billings for assistance payments, false and inadequate recertification submissions, fraudulent bills for property preservation, etc.

Inaction Charged

"Notwithstanding the seriousness of many of the improprieties, H.U.D. has been extremely reluctant to take action against errant and unscrupulous mortgagees."

The report noted that criticism of the department's policy of guaranteeing lenders 100 percent insurance as well as the contention that it "provides an incentive to foreclose rather than forbear for mortgagors in distress because it is more profitable to recover and reinvest the money and that H.U.D. has permitted lenders to do so."

"Because H.U.D. has not monitored servicing practices in a coordinated and comprehensive way, we have no way of knowing how many foreclosures could be prevented," the report said. "The structure of the program and H.U.D.'s liberalized underwriting standards have encouraged the creation of an open policy in large segments of the industry to 'make any loan F.H.A. will take.'

"The present procedure provides no safeguards to assure that mortgagees will make every effort to avoid foreclosure."

The report added that the department "has not administered the program in such a way as to encourage responsibility by the mortgagee."

"Department officials believe there is a need for an overwhelming preponderance of conclusive evidence of wrongdoing before any action should be initiated," the report said. "As a consequence, action is very seldom initiated to withdraw a mortgagee's approval or to suspend a mortgagee from participating in H.U.D.'s programs.

"Generally, the attitude is 'Don't attempt any action if there is the slightest possibility that H.U.D. would not be successful in a hearing.' Additionally, every effort is made to not take action if the mortgagee indicates a willingness to do better in the future.

"Invariably, a mortgagee who has been detected of committing a wrongdoing will express a willingness to correct its practices."

Wait-and-See Attitude

Mrs. Hills has announced a series of detailed agency regulations attempting to curb fast foreclosures and to thwart fast-buck lenders. But many who have followed abortive agency reforms in the past, including increasingly vociferous community groups, are waiting to see if they will be enforced at the local level by the agency's regional and district offices.

One department official recently interviewed in Washington spoke of widespread demoralization in the agency as a major problem facing Mrs. Hills, who took office in March. He felt that many of the best housing personnel had long since left the agency.

Another official, John Waner, director of the department's Chicago area office, told Congressman Hicks's committee that "like any bureaucracy, H.U.D. is resistant to change.

"Yet this resistance has been so solidified," Mr. Waner said, "as to win for H.U.D. in the public mind the unenviable image of the most cumbersome, backward and ineffective of all agencies."

Mr. Waner said that "the administration of some of our programs has contributed to the draining of the economic vitality of entire neighborhoods and communities."

"H.U.D. employees see their future in doubt," he said. "They are worried, uncertain, investigated, criticized, interrogated, lectured, warned and reproached. All too many are disheartened."

December 11, 1975

DOWNTOWN RENEWAL

COMMENDS STUDY OF URBAN DECAY

The encouragement of private corporations under public supervision to enter into the field of "neighborhood redevelopment" is commended by the Federal Home Loan Bank. Attention is called to the fact that New York, Michigan and Illinois have passed laws permitting such urban improvements upon compliance with certain regulations.

The general aim of these acts, explains the current issue of the Bank Review, is to restore property and taxable values and head off the inestimable losses suffered by owners and others every year through the decay of many inherently sound neighborhoods in older communities.

About three years ago, it is pointed out, the Federal Home Loan Bank Board cooperated in a survey of Waverly, a neighborhood area in Baltimore in danger of blight infection. Complete plans were made for its redevelopment including major and minor repairs, remodeling, modernizing and landscaping of all depreciated properties; the formation of interior playgrounds and the revision of zoning and street patterns. This survey and the general conservation projects for Waverly, according to the Review, presents a practical example on which redevelopment corporations in the three States which have adopted enabling legislation may draw.

"Only in recent years have public and private organizations, operating in the fields of real estate, mortgage finance and city planning, made a concentrated effort to study the causes and costs of urban decay and to devise ways by which it can be checked," says the Review. "The new State laws are the result of efforts which have gradually progressed from the realization of the problem, through the experimental planning stages, to the final enactment of legislation.

"The cost of urban decay is of universal interest because of the tremendous portion of the national wealth invested in these problem areas. This wealth consists of the lifetime savings of families who own homes in such districts, of the mortgage investments of financial institutions which represent the primary reservoirs of thrift, and of the public money invested in schools, fire and police protection, power lines, water systems, streets and other municipal facilities.

"Added to the waste of partly used public utilities is the factor that the cost of these facilities becomes increasingly higher in the more decadent areas. For instance, the annual cost of fire protection in Cleveland, according to a recent survey, was $17.50 per capita in the slums as compared with $2.50 in other parts of the city; police protection was $12 per capita as compared with $4 in the balance of the city.

Tax Returns Suffer

"Also, cities are facing financial difficulties because of shrinking tax returns. Property owners in blighted areas are no longer able to meet their tax obligations because their properties cannot yield sufficient incomes. To appreciate the seriousness of the declining tax revenue, it must be kept in mind that the major source of income for most American cities is the real property tax. A loss in revenue from one city district invariably causes an increase in tax rates in other districts."

A redevelopment plan, it is explained, does not necessarily involve demolition of all buildings but may be a combination of remodeling and rebuilding together with demolition for parks and playgrounds. There are no restriction as to types of building to be included in the area. This gives leeway for planners to take advantage of the opportunity to build any type of structure which will be best suited to the needs of the neighborhood.

The Review states that a Californian urban redevelopment measure similar to the New York Michigan and Illinois act, is before the Legislature, and its is reported that plans are under way for future legislation in Massachusetts, Ohio Minnesota and Texas.

September 21, 194

CONGRESS UPHELD ON SLUM CLEARING

Supreme Court Says Federal and State Legislatures Have Wide Redevelopment Power

Special to The New York Times.

WASHINGTON, Nov. 22—The Supreme Court unanimously ruled today that Federal and State Legislatures had broad powers to authorize redevelopment of slum areas.

It upheld the constitutionality of the District of Columbia Redevelopment Act of 1945. This law authorized the acquisition of large areas in Washington for slum clearance and their sale or lease for redevelopment to private interests.

The law was challenged by the owners of seventy-six acres of commercial and residential property in southwest Washington. They asserted that the law authorized seizure of private property for other than public use in violation of the due process clause of the Fifth Amendment to the Constitution.

This amendment says that no person shall be "deprived of life, liberty or property without due process of law."

Justice William O. Douglas, who wrote the high court's opinion, held that Congress, in passing the law, had made "legislative determination" that it was "the policy of the United States to protect and promote the welfare of the inhabitants of the seat of Government" by eliminating injurious conditions by "all means necessary and appropriate for the purpose."

"Once the object is within the authority of Congress," Justice Douglas asserted, "the means by which it will be attained is also for Congress to determine. Here one of the means chosen is the use of private enterprise for redevelopment of the area.

"Subject to specific constitutional limitations, when the Legislature has spoken, the public interest has been declared in terms well-nigh conclusive. In such cases, the Legislature, not the judiciary, is the main guardian of the public needs to be served by social legislation, whether it be Congress legislating concerning the District of Columbia or the states legislating concerning local affairs."

Justice Douglas said that the "concept of public welfare is broad and inclusive," and that it was not the function of the judiciary "to determine whether a particular housing project is or is not desirable."

The decision in the Washington case was regarded as clearing the way for similar programs in other states and municipalities. Such programs have been adopted in thirty-four states and sustained in court proceedings in twenty of them.

November 23, 1954

DETROIT REMAKES DOWNTOWN AREA

Dream of Civic Center Near Reality—City Officials to Move to New Building

Special to The New York Times.

DETROIT, July 16—An eleven-year dream of a beautiful and utilitarian civic center in downtown Detroit is close to reality.

A twenty-story City-County Building and an eight-story Veterans Memorial Building, both constructed of white Vermont marble, already tower above the Detroit river backdrop. The Henry and Edsel Ford Auditorium, built of blue Swedish granite and the same white Vermont marble, is under construction and will be finished next year. A huge convention hall and exhibition center will be started late this year and completed in 1958.

The Detroit Master Plan notes that from the earliest times cities that have reached cultural maturity have sought to arrange their government buildings in orderly, visually effective architectural groups. The idea of a civic center for Detroit, the plan states, arose out of the recognition that this city needed a group of public buildings "symbolic of its social and political democracy."

Detroit officials point out that the $100,000,000 civic center, located at the foot of Woodward Avenue beside the Detroit river, is being built both to beautify a homely waterfront area and to stimulate the entire downtown section to modernization and new construction.

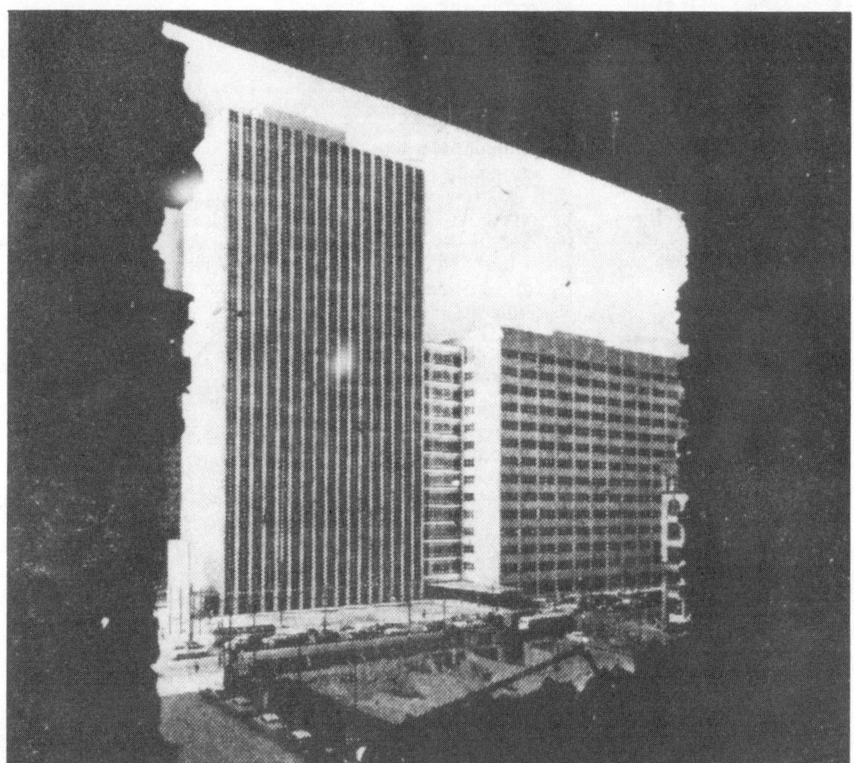

DETROIT CIVIC CENTER NEARS COMPLETION: The new twenty-story City-County Building, which is part of the Detroit Master Plan to beautify and stimulate downtown section to modernization and new construction. The building is made of white Vermont marble.

Other Projects Listed

Charles A. Blessing, director of City Planning, emphasizes also that the civic center development is only part of the over-all planning for the beautification and revitalization of a central area of 800 acres within the developing expressway pattern of downtown Detroit.

"The Mayor [Albert E. Cobo] was convinced," Mr. Blessing said, "that Detroit didn't have to become a ghost city downtown but that by fighting back the central area could be an attractive and advantageous place for business to remain."

Results already are apparent. The Greyhound Corporation is planning a new bus terminal opposite the City-County Building. The National Bank of Detroit has announced its intention of building a $12,000,000 bank a short distance away on Woodward Avenue.

Meanwhile, over-all city planning envisions further development of a cultural center integrated with Wayne University, the Public Library, the Institute of Arts, the Historical Museum, the International Institute and the Rackham Memorial Building.

Plans for the cultural center, along Woodward Avenue at the northwest end of the central expressway loop, call for a Museum of Natural History, a planetarium and a Hall of Man.

Other proposed city projects include the razing of the Skid Row area along Michigan Avenue and building there modern business and housing structures; industrial redevelopment of the Corktown area southwest of the Civic Center and improvement of the huge, market-like Cadillac Square by building a park and, underground, a railway terminal and public garage.

The civic center site, bounded generally by Cass, Larned and Randolph Streets and the Detroit River, was approved by the Common Council in 1944. In 1946, the City Plan Commission published a comprehensive report on the center, showing buildings to be included, a suggested arrangement and cost estimates.

The architectural firm of Saarinen, Saarinen & Associates was retained as consultants on the center. The Saarinens developed general designs for the center and served as consultants to the commission.

General public approval of the center plan has been demonstrated by these developments:

¶Construction of the City-County Office Building was approved by the voters of Detroit and Wayne County.

¶A gift by the Ford dealers of America and the Ford family of $2,500,000 for the construction of the Henry and Edsel Ford Auditorium.

¶Gifts totaling more than $6,000,000 from many Detroit corporations and individuals through the Capital Gifts Committee on the occasion of Detroit's 250th Anniversary in 1951 to be used in the construction of the Convention Hall and Exhibits Building.

The cost of buildings already constructed in the center or now projected is $86,000,000. The entire project when completed and landscaped probably will have cost close to $100,000,000.

The sixty-eight acres representing 89 per cent of the civic center site already has cost the city $14,000,000.

The principal structures in the center are:

The Veterans Memorial Building, started in 1948, was completed in 1950 at a construction cost of $5,074,258. It is used extensively for civic groups' meetings and as a convention center.

The Detroit-Wayne (County) Joint Building Authority began construction of the City-County Building in 1951 with revenue bond financing of $26,087,000. The building is partly occupied at present and will be fully occupied by the end of the year by various city and county departments.

The Henry and Edsel Ford Auditorium, now under construction, will cost $4,770,500. It has seating capacity of 2,800 and will be used primarily as a music hall.

Construction is scheduled to begin late this year on the Convention Hall and Exhibits Building. The cost of the two structures is expected to be $24,200,000. The Convention Hall, a circular edifice, will have permanent seating for 10,000 persons and temporary seating for 4,000.

The Exhibits Building will have 300,000 square feet of exhibit space on its main floor and an additional 100,000 square feet in the basement.

July 17, 1955

LINCOLN SQ. PLAN WINS FINAL VOTE FOR EARLY START

Estimate Board Unanimous in Approving Project for Huge Cultural Center

$205,000,000 COST SET

Condemnation to Begin in 2 Weeks, but Litigation Will Delay Demolition Work

By PAUL CROWELL

The $205,000,000 Lincoln Square slum clearance and redevelopment project was unanimously approved by the Board of Estimate yesterday.

The board authorized the condemnation and resale of a sixty-eight-acre tract north and west of Columbus Circle. It thus took a long step toward the establishment of a cultural and collegiate center and modern housing facilities in an area of thirteen city blocks now considered substandard.

Some minor details of the project will be ironed out at a meeting of the board on Jan. 23. However, condemnation proceedings are expected to start within two weeks, but actual demolition of buildings now on the site may be delayed by litigation to be started soon by opponents of one phase of the project.

Fordham Project Opposed

The litigation will seek to enjoin the demolition pending a court ruling on a contention that a new campus for Fordham University in the project would be a violation of the state and Federal constitutions. This protest charges the alleged expenditure of public funds in aid of a sectarian institution.

The Lincoln Square development is a Title I project under the National Housing Act. The statute enables the city to acquire slum sites and sell them to private developers. Any loss incurred in the resale, together with the cost of community facilities in connection with redevelopment, will be shared two-thirds by the Federal Government and one-third by the city.

The most recent estimates of project cost are $163,000,000 for the private developers, $28,000,000 for the Federal Government and $14,000,000 for the city. The project involves the relocation of 6,500 families now living in the site area and several hundred businesses.

The city's Committee on Slum Clearance, which negotiated the contracts with the Federal Home and Loan Administration and the private sponsors of the housing and cultural facilities, estimated that it wuold take five years to complete the job, provided no new obstacles were encountered.

The housing section of the project will have 4,100 private rental apartments and 400 cooperative units, with provisions for retail stores and offices in the same area. A site has been resreved there for a public school and for church or other institutional development.

The St. Matthew's Roman Catholic Church, originally a sponsor for a new edifice in the area, has withdrawn from the project. The Board of Estimate on Jan. 23 will consider a proposal by the American Red Cross to construct a headquarters building on the 55,000 square foot site that had been reserved for the church.

One of the resolutions adopted by the Board of Estimate yesterday approved a contract with the Lincoln Performing Arts Center, Inc., for the cultural section of the project. That will include a new Metropolitan Opera House, a new home for the New York Philharmonic Society and a ballet theatre—all fronting on a landscaped public square. In the same area there will be a new Juilliard School of Music, a repertory theatre and a public park with a bandshell and seating facilities for 3,500 persons.

The Park Department has plans for an 800-car parking garage under the cultural area.

University Contract Voted

The collegiate center will be the new home for several Fordham University departments for about 4,000 students. A contract with the university for the proposed development was among those also approved by the board.

After the over-all project was approved, Harris L. Present, chairman of the Council on Housing Relocation Practices and counsel for the Lincoln Square Chamber of Commerce, warned the Board of Estimate that he would seek to defeat the project in the courts on the constitutional ground involving Fordham University. He said the suit would include a request for a temporary injunction and a declaratory judgment.

Mr. Present declared that he would carry the litigation to the United States Supreme Court if necessary. He warned the city that it might have to pay heavy damages if it went ahead with the project and was ultimately confronted with an adverse court ruling.

The Board of Estimate gave tentative approval to proposed developments by the Lincoln Guild, sponsor of the coopera**tive housing project, and by the Webb & Knapp Lincoln Square Corporation, sponsor of the private rental housing development. Final approval will await rulings by Corporation Counsel Peter C. Brown on some phases of the agreements.**

The board deferred until Jan. 23 action on approval of an option to buy for $160,000 a five-acre site in the bay shore area of Queens for a National Guard armory now situated in the Lincoln Square area. Residents of the Queens area have objected to the proposed site for the armory.

With Bronx Borough President James J. Lyons dissenting, the board voted not to exercise an option to purchase for $2,500,000 a commercial building in the project area now owned by four of the children of former Ambassador Joseph P. Kennedy. The property, which is assessed for $1,750,000, will be acquired by condemnation.

In voting for the project Borough President Hulan E. Jack of Manhattan announced that he would appoint a watchdog committee to see that the 6,500 families to be removed from the area were relocated in safe, sanitary and adequate housing elsewhere. He said the committee would act as a liaison group between his office and the organizations representing both residential and business tenants to be displaced.

Ample Housing Foreseen

In a recent report recommending approval of the project, the City Planning Commission declared that there was available an ample reservoir of housing to accommodate tenants from the Lincoln Square area as well as from other areas under Title I clearance and redevelopment.

By approving the project the Board of Estimate paved the way for realization of a center conceived about a year ago. The original plan contemplated, in addition to the developments approved by the board, a proposal for a huge theatre center. This was stricken from the over-all plan when the Federal housing authorities insisted that there would not be available enough Federal money to finance it.

The negotiations between the Federal housing authorities and the Slum Clearance Committee over financial details of the project, including the prices at which various areas were to be sold to private developers, included sharp controversies between Robert Moses, committee chairman, and officials of the Federal housing agency.

These were finally resolved, but not before the physical scope and some of the financial aspects of the project were revised downward.

November 27, 1957

FACE-LIFTING — The first stage of New Haven's comprehensive redevelopment program was the complete razing of a 42-acre downtown slum (far left). Now a Southern New England Telephone Co. building is rising to begin the site's renewal.

Urban Ruin— Or Urban Renewal?

The time for decision is now, if we are to save our blighted cities from themselves.

By EDWARD J. LOGUE

"ANY city that does not set in motion by 1960 a comprehensive program to halt blight will be flirting with municipal ruin by 1965."

It is time to heed those words of Federal Housing Administrator Albert M. Cole, for 1960 is here. The Congress which has just been elected is the one that will have to act—and at its first session in 1959—if that deadline against disaster is to be met. Today, the Federal urban renewal program is slowing down because the Congressional session that ended in August was the first in many years to do nothing whatsoever to aid the fight against slums. The nation cannot afford another such lapse if its slum-ridden cities are to be saved from themselves before it is too late.

This is not to say that it is all up to Congress. It is up to everyone to face the hard truth that the American dream is tarnishing, the American way of life becoming a mirage, for tens of millions of our fellow citizens who live in cities.

BUSHELS of statistics have been published to spread the alarm on urban blight, but the response has been slight. Perhaps we need fewer statistics and instead a few good old-fashioned walking tours: walks through the slums, up the stinking stairways into the overcrowded, shabby rooms; walks through the run-down commercial areas, taking care to glance above the first-floor store fronts at the dusty windows of the deserted upper floors; walks through the oil-soaked, dreary factory lofts built before the assembly line was even heard of. The filth, the misery and the danger are all there—easy to see and, once seen, impossible to forget.

Today's slums seem to touch the lives and pocketbooks of the suburbanites and other noncity dwellers lightly, if at all. Not so the slums of tomorrow. The prospects are awesome. If present trends are allowed to continue, 30,000,000 Americans will be living in slums by 1975. Further neglect of the cities now is going to cost taxpayer individual and corporate, untold billions by then. Everybody will be talking about slums then—and everybody will be paying for them.

TOO few people today—even among those who are aware of the problem—are aware that this prospect need not come to pass, that ways to reverse the trend are at hand, if they will only be used. Too many, perhaps, are discouraged by the obvious fact that not one of the various city-saving schemes advanced in the past has even kept us abreast of the spreading blight, let alone helped us get ahead.

For a time we thought that to save our cities we needed to dream what the good city ought to be—and make a plan of that dream. Yet I know of no city where a significant master plan has been carried out; the dreamers' plans were too far removed from the main stream of urban political life. Too many theoretical planners preferred the applause of elegant critics to the earthier appreciation of politicians who had to try to carry out the plans and get re-elected, too.

Then, many felt that the answer lay in detailed zoning ordinances, regulating and restricting the uses which might be made of land, allowing a place for everything and putting everything in its place. But to prevent "hardship," variances were granted, and these—together with political influence on zoning appeals boards—have made a mockery of zoning in one city after another.

The most dramatic approach to the slum problem was the simple physical one—clear the slums and house the slum-dwellers in handsome new buildings on the cleared sites at low, subsidized rents. Hundreds of big projects actually materialized in 900 cities during the past two decades to provide homes for some 1,150,000 families. And for a time many of them did fulfill the purpose for which they were built—housing a cross section of American families who just happened to have low incomes. But now all that has changed. The big projects are there but the tenants are different. In too many cases, communities use these projects as dumping grounds for problems they would like to forget—fatherless families, large families and, particularly, minority families.

Out of the failure of master-planning, zoning, public housing and other one-answer remedies for the ills of cities, a whole new approach has now been developed. It is called urban renewal. It focuses on the city as a whole and treats all urban problems as interrelated, both in their origin and their solution. Solutions are made possible (or were, until Congress failed to renew the appropriation) by the Federal Housing Acts of 1949 and 1954, which provided Government funds for cities to get renewal programs started. So far, 276 cities in all parts of the country have taken advantage of this opportunity and have renewal projects under way; 261 more are in the renewal planning stage.

THE concept of comprehensive urban renewal recognizes that the city is here to stay in essentially its traditional form. The purpose, as the phrase indicates, is the renewal of the city of today, not its replacement by some fanciful city of tomorrow. It is accomplished not by any one method but by combining several:

(1) Total *(Continued)*

RENEWED CITY—A model of the former slum area as it will look when fully redeveloped. Close coordination of slum-clearance and highway planning is a key element of the program.

EDWARD J. LOGUE has been Development Administrator of New Haven, in over-all charge of its urban renewal program, since 1955.

clearance of the worst slums and complete rebuilding.

(2) Humane relocation of displaced families and businesses—the families preferably being integrated into existing neighborhoods rather than dumped into the enormous projects of the past. Where public housing projects are necessary no more than twenty-five or fifty units should be built in one location.

(3) Spot clearance of blighted areas, with rehabilitation of what remains.

(4) Conservation of sound areas—perhaps by organized neighborhood spruce-up campaigns, backed up by vigorous zoning and housing code enforcement—to keep them from slipping into blight.

(5) Coordination of highway building with the city's rebuilding program, to make sure that the new highways further rather than impede the city's plan. The automobile in quantity may be the most important single cause of urban blight; a renewal program which does not provide for an urban highway system to take through and commuter traffic off regular city streets is a waste of time.

(6) Revitalization of the central business district. A city whose central core is not the favored shopping place of the entire region around it, a city whose commerce is fleeing to the residential areas and suburbs, is destroying itself—and is in process of destroying the suburbs, too.

(7) Clearing out old factories to make way for new ones. Cities are the best sites for industry; they offer skilled workers, a variety of suppliers and networks of communications and transportation. But there has been little industrial expansion in cities in recent years because the choice locations are already occupied by factory buildings which are obsolescent, or worse.

MAKING such a comprehensive urban renewal program work requires an intimate partnership of the Federal Government, the city and private enterprise. The Federal Government participates at two stages, first advancing funds for surveys and plans and then underwriting the actual work. After the plans for a given renewal area are approved—and the specifications are strict, to assure that the scheme is workable and can be carried through—the Government loans the city enough money to buy the property, relocate the tenants and demolish the structures.

The cleared land is then sold to private redevelopers for new uses under rigid restrictions—limited land coverage, building setbacks, provisions for off-street parking, and so forth—to insure that the slum or blight will not recur. If, as usually happens, there is a loss between the purchase of the substandard area properties and relocation of families and businesses, and the resale of the cleared land, the Federal Government absorbs two-thirds of the write-down, the city one-third.

THE example of New Haven—where I have been associated with a renewal program that is the largest per capita in the country—will illustrate both how this process works and how it is paid for.

NEW HEART—The second major phase of New Haven's renewal is to be the razing of the old commercial heart of the city on Church Street (above), near the historic Green. Below is an architect's rendering of the new buildings that will rise beside the widened street.

Out of an eventual total of ten slum-clearance and rehabilitation projects for this city of 165,000, six are in varying stages of action or planning; one of the most dramatic is already nearly completed and another is well advanced. These call for the complete razing — at public expense—of two tracts, totaling 140 acres, of slums and blighted commercial structures in the very heart of the downtown area, to be replaced—at private expense — by a striking array of new, modern apartments, office buildings, stores, restaurants, banks and parking facilities. The whole is tied into the new Federal-state highway program to provide ready access to and from the renovated downtown area.

The net cost of buying those 140 acres, relocating the residents (mostly in scattered private housing), razing the buildings and reselling the land to private developers comes to about $22,500,000. Of this the Federal Government will pay about $15,000,000 and the city about $7,500,000 under the Federal Housing Act's two-for-one formula. Thus the city of New Haven is investing nearly $45 per person to get itself an entirely new downtown. This $45, and more, will come back through the greatly increased taxes yielded by the higher valuation of the renovated area—and without any increase in the city's tax rate.

The remaining projects in the New Haven program call rather for spot clearance and neighborhood rehabilitation than for total demolition. When all are completed, within ten years, New Haven believes that it will have become the first city in America to be completely free of slums and blight.

Its flying start is due to the vigorous and versatile leadership of its dynamic young mayor, Richard C. Lee, who is well on his way to doing for city rebuilding what Fiorello La Guardia did for municipal reform — making it colorful, popular and a heavy plus at the polls on election day.

SO far, official delegations from thirty-four other cities all across America have visited New Haven to see what is going on. Mayor Lee and others of us working with him in the New Haven program have also visited many other cities to discuss renewal problems and possible solutions. In the course of those contacts, we have developed four underlying principles of a successful renewal program that we feel are applicable to cities generally. They are:

First, leadership from City Hall. The job cannot be left to ivory-tower planners and volunteer do-gooders. Urban renewal must be a vital part of the down-to-earth political life of the city and its chief spokesman and champion must be the mayor himself. Too many mayors are leery of the disruption, the dislocation and, above all, the decisions required. In cities where responsibility is scattered and the mayor only a court of last resort for bickering bureaucrats and frustrated citizens, urban renewal has little chance to be effective.

Second, organized citizen support. Urban renewal in action causes too much disruption to persons and property to survive without wide and deep community support. The general desire to see good programs succeed must be organized; it does not appear automatically. Here is where the volunteer does have a vital role to play. Whatever its precise form—in New Haven it is the Citizens Action Commission of some 600 business, civic, labor and community leaders—some body of respected citizens should look after the continuing task of rallying support.

Third, a competent and adequate staff. The development and planning staff is no place to cut corners. It should be able, experienced and dedicated, with a budget sufficient to get and keep the personnel it needs. This is a sound and necessary investment in the city's future.

Fourth, coordinated administration. The job of weaving all the varied threads of urban renewal into one workable program cannot be ignored or given to a committee or dumped into the mayor's lap. A single municipal official, with urban renewal his sole responsibility, and with down-the-line backing from the mayor, should be in charge.

THESE four elements—plus money—will make urban renewal work, if New Haven's experience is any criterion. Of course, each city has its own individuality and its own problems. But we believe that New Haven is representative of the 531 cities in the broad population bracket of from 25,000 to 1,000,000, with the 27,000,000 Americans who live in them. For them the present Federal program is basically sound and can provide the impetus for a successful fight against slums, assuming that adequate funds are appropriated—the American Municipal Association has recommended $500 million yearly for ten years.

At the two population extremes, however, there are special problems. The smaller cities of 25,000 or less have a surprising amount of blight, especially in older sections of the country. But they have great difficulty in recruiting redevelopment staffs and organizing effective urban renewal programs. Perhaps there is an opportunity here for the states to offer helping hands. Perhaps they can borrow from the successful precedent of the Federal-state agricultural extension service and establish state renewal departments to help the smaller urban areas. This would lower the costs of project preparation and execution; and it would require no change in the Federal law.

At the other extreme, in the five cities with a population of

THE HUB

Someone is always ready to ask, more than half seriously, "Do we still need cities?"

The answer is simple. The cities are here. We cannot float them downstream. Even bombs—the old-fashioned kind, at least—cannot destroy them. A city is the center of a communications network, the hub of a giant wheel which is part of our social and economic system. Cities are places of exchange, not just of goods but of ideas. They are usually well located, even if poorly laid out and maintained.

If we did not have cities, we would have to invent them or go back to the standard of living of the dark ages. Some of us may live in Westport or Larchmont, but the work of the world still goes on in New York.—E. J. L.

one million or more, the picture is grim, indeed. Their slums are almost unending; slum dwelling units are measured by the hundreds of thousands; they have tremendous concentrations of non-whites who cannot find housing in the suburbs; they are choked by traffic; their industrial districts and downtown shopping areas are losing out to the suburbs; their vital mass transportation systems seem constantly on the verge of bankruptcy.

AMONG them, only New York has a central-city office-building boom to give even an illusion of municipal well-being. New York also has had a huge public housing program and a series of slum-clearance and redevelopment projects which, despite problems with family and business relocation, now being worked out, are the largest, furthest advanced and most dramatic in the United States—monuments to Robert Moses, perhaps the outstanding public servant of our times. Yet New York still seems content to let George do it; and even when George is a giant like Mr. Moses, he is still only one man and one man can do only so much.

The truth is that all that has been accomplished with the $20 to $30 million doled out to New York yearly from limited Federal funds has been far from enough just to keep even in the struggle against spreading blight. For instance, in the time it took New York's sixty-eight-acre Lincoln Square project to get under way, far more than sixty-eight acres slipped into blight in other sections of the city.

NEW York is in the same situation as the other super-cities of America, only more so. These cities cannot possibly dig themselves out. Their problems are too big for them, too big for their states, and far too big for the present Federal urban renewal program. They need a special program of their own—$500 million a year for ten years for just these five cities—and they need it urgently.

Big-city representatives in Congress have, by and large, supported the rebuilding of Europe under the Marshall Plan and the bolstering of undeveloped countries by Point Four. It is time we recognized that the 18,000,000 Americans who live in these slum-saturated cities have a need for Federal help just as great and urgent as any nation of Europe or Asia. There is a large and informed body of public opinion which understands the need for foreign aid. It is time that the need to clear up the mess in our own backyard were equally well understood.

* * *

NONE of us is prepared willingly to accept the consequences, in dollars, delinquency and sh[illegible], of allowing slums and bl[illegible]t to spread unchecked. What are we to do about it?

Locally, cities must take slums seriously and recognize them for the cancer they are. Cities must organize themselves to fight slums as efficiently and matter-of-factly as they now organize to fight fires. Today, leaving slum-fighting to the do-gooder or the planner is as obsolete as leaving firefighting in Times Square to a company of volunteer firemen.

Nationally, we must accept the idea that slum-fighting requires substantial Federal funds *on a continuing basis.* The $500-million minimum proposed by the American Municipal Association is less than one-half of 1 per cent of our Federal budget; even with a special big-city program added it would come to less than 1 per cent—a fraction of what we spend on highways, not to mention agricultural support payments.

Surely we Americans can afford six Federal dollars per year per person for ten years to rid ourselves of slums. If not, the cities of America in the Nineteen Seventies will be festering sores we will be ashamed of before our children. We will long since have refused to live in them ourselves for a day more than we must.

November 9, 1958

New Life in Heart of Minneapolis

Growth Around City Spurred It to Give Core a Face-Lift

By CLAYTON KNOWLES

Special to The New York Times.

MINNEAPOLIS, Minn., June 16—Another big building wave has hit Minneapolis. The main focus is on putting even more vigor in a healthy downtown. And each stage of construction is being carefully plotted and planned.

But it was not that way from the beginning. In fact, it took shock treatment from outside the city to get concentrated downtown planning.

The first jolt came from neighboring St. Paul, the smaller of the Twin Cities. Long dominated by Minneapolis, St. Paul suddenly blossomed forth with a spectacular redevelopment program. It cleared acres of slums and exposed the State Capitol in its full beauty in a parklike setting.

"We suddenly realized," said one Minneappolis business man, "that the good gray lady across the Mississippi River had kicked off her high button shoes, put on saddles and was beginning to run like hell."

The other shocker was the announcement in 1955 by Dayton's, the city's biggest department store and one of the nation's top ten, that it was building a $20,000,000 shopping center called Southdale in the suburbs.

Designed by Victor Gruen, the architect-planner, the vast complex of stores featured, not one, but two department store branches and was completely enclosed and air-conditioned. There was free parking on all sides.

Plans Were Lacking

City fathers and business men were alarmed. They looked around. This is what they found: no master plan for downtown, an outmoded city plan and a city planning commission with an inadequate $65,000 budget and no director.

Reaction was fast. The city's top people, their pride stung and assurance shaken, took a personal hand in matters.

Teaming with local government, they hammered out the hard-headed civic decision that rebuilding at the core was necessary to promote the city's position as regional capital of the Upper Midwest.

The community proudly asserts that $115,000,000 has been spent since World War II in downtown redevelopment and renewal. The boast is that another $85,000,000 in public and private expenditures would be made in the next few years.

Large Outlays Planned

These downtown outlays fall within an estimated total of $92,000,000 in forthcoming annual capital expenditures for the city as a whole. Three-quarters of this spending will be private, the balance public.

Federal aid to cities runs to nine-to-one — nine dollars of Federal money for every one dollar of city investment — on interstate highway links such as will ring the city. Freeway spending is running to $10,000,000 annually.

Federal aid for redevelopment projects averages somewhat better than two-to-one.

The city has raised $105,000,000 in the last five years through bond issues.

Key to the whole downtown refurbishing effort is the $12,822,000 Gateway Center redevelopment project. Here, at the very front door to the main shopping and financial districts, block upon block of skid row and low grade commercial and industrial properties are being razed.

Sixty-eight acres are covered by the project. It is half again as big as New York's Lincoln Center. Only two and one-half acres will not be touched. They house three hotels, a bank and other acceptable properties.

Ample Parking Space

Four new public buildings, including a city library and a Federal court building, already are being built at a cost of $18,000,000. Thirty-five acres still are available for private development.

Extensive landscaping, part of it to be enforced upon developers, and fourteen acres of parking space, chiefly within buildings, are planned.

Construction of hotel and motel, as well as commercial and light industrial buildings, are contemplated. At least two streets will be closed as part of the physical redesign of the area. Land is now being assembled.

History, geography and the human equation make the redevelopment of the old "Lower Loop" highly dramatic.

When completed, it will represent the realization of a Minneapolis dream of the last half century.

The Mississippi River, a city showpiece, lies just to the east. Three of the city's main avenues —Hennepin, Nicollet and Marquette -run through the strip. The two main railroad stations flank it at the river.

Slums Cleared

But even before this project was approved, major steps were under way to impro[illegible]e the downtown climate.

A good deal of it was at the periphery of the central business district. Some of it was done by government but a substantial amount under private auspices as well.

A 180-acre residential slum, a mile west of the downtown section, already has been cleared in the $7,500,000 Glenwood redevelopment project.

Fifty acres have been sold, another seventy-three are available, some for light industry.

Three public housing projects, providing 736 units mostly of the garden apartment variety, are being built at a cost of $12,074,000.

Further west, a 146-acre in-town neighborhood known as Harrison will get a $2,530,000 face-lifting under the city's first rehabilitation project.

Property Deteriorated

Owners of marginal property, meantime, were becoming painfully aware of the changing character of downtown by the steadily deteriorating usage to which their holdings could be put.

They soon came to realize that, if the buildings were razed, taxes would drop and the properties would yield more as parking lots.

Civic Body Formed

Soon a sizable ring surrounding the very downtown core took on a "bombed out" look. A more economic use for the property had been developed but the lots were unsightly. Construction of multi-story parking garages came slowly.

Shocked by Southdale and St. Paul's strides, business leaders moved fast to protect the city's position as the cultural, financial and business center of the Upper Midwest. To mobilize support of the city's 550,000 citizens, they formed the Downtown Council.

Gerald L. Moore, director of this agency which now operates on a $130,000 budget, describes it as a "downtown business pressure group and idea generator."

The council set its sights first on getting City Planning Commission properly staffed and financed. It got strong support from Arnett W. Leslie, an able retired business man who became commission chairman.

He secured approval of a reorganization plan that had been recommended in a study by Frederick T. Aschman of Chicago.

The budget was raised year by year. It now stands at $215,000. Lawrence M. Irvin, who built a national reputation as city planner at Columbus, Ohio, was brought in to direct an enlarged staff.

Just this year, the commission got approval of work objectives ranging from land use to highways. Definitive planning has begun. A program should be ready by 1960.

But much still remains to be done. Minneapolis has a weak mayor-council form of government in which a series of independent boards, like the park and school boards, are at least quasi-autonomous. To effectuate a city or downtown plan, they must be wooed and won over.

The only check on the wide range of varied activities currently is from the Capitol Long-range Improvement Committee, better known as "CLIC."

This group, a citizens' advisory committee, moved in on a void some years back to establish priorities on public projects within the city limits.

The restoration of status to the Planning Commission was welcomed by the Minneapolis Housing and Redevelopment Authority, headed by S. L. Stolte.

This agency, acting for the city in both urban renewal and housing, has independent taxing authority, good for a $380,000 annual budget, under the state redevelopment law through which it was set up in 1947.

9 Projects in Works

Directed by Robert T. Jorvig, the authority has nine projects either completed or, like Gateway Center and Glenwood, in the building.

For lack of city plan, it had to do a lot of supplemental planning that even extended to freeways.

Closer collaboration between Minneapolis and St. Paul has developed through the Twin Cities Metropolitan Planning Commission, a seven-county agency with independent taxing authority headed by C. C. Ludwig. Oddly, the pressure for state legislation that set up the agency came from the suburbs and not the city.

C. David Loecks, who studied planning at the Massachusetts Institute of Technology, is directing the regional inquiry into problems too big for any member city or county.

July 3, 1959

CAMPUS VS. SLUMS

Urban Universities Join Battle For Neighborhood Renewal

By FRED M. HECHINGER

As higher education enrollments grow, the urban universities will play a key role in the expansion. In the total picture of mass-education on the college level, the idyllic rural campus will be the privilege of a few; the city campuses will take care of the many, community as well as resident students. Like the rest of American life, higher education is being urbanized. Unfortunately, this urbanization coincides with the era of the decay of the American cities.

As the cities fight for renewal, the parallel effort of the universities becomes a major battle both of academic and urban society. For the institutions, it is a two-front war: They must contend with lack of space in a crowded setting; and they must halt the encroachment of slums which turn the lack of space for expansion into a straitjacket of physical danger. When Columbia recently took over the mortgage of the run-down, trash-littered Devonshire Hotel at Broadway and 112th Street, it had merely fought another skirmish in this battle.

Key Reasons

It was a skirmish, too, in a battle currently fought by a score of major universities. Key reasons for the battle are:

(1) *The students' safety.* Crime in the slum-belt around urban universities threatens especially undergraduate enrollment. It was a major factor in the decline of the college of the University of Chicago over a decade ago. At a recent lecture for visiting foreign students at Teachers College, Columbia University, a terse announcement warned the guests to keep all dormitory doors locked at all times.

(2) *Holding the faculty.* Since slum-belted campuses offer little, if any, nearby faculty housing and inadequate public school facilities for faculty children, these institutions have lost, or are in danger of losing, valuable faculty members.

(3) *Real estate investments.* The next decade will require the addition of university facilities by the billions of dollars. Such an investment in blighted neighborhoods could be the road to financial disaster.

Fortunately, the battle, though begun late, is now being waged with vigor by a number of universities.

Turning Point

Chicago was the test case and may have been the turning point in the crisis of the urban campus. A spokesman calls the action, which began about nine years ago in the Hyde Park-Kenwood urban renewal program, one of "major surgery." It covers about 900 acres, will take another five years to complete and is estimated to cost $195 million in local, Federal and institutional money.

The United States Office of Education has asked Julian Levi, a Chicago lawyer, urban renewal expert and pioneer in university participation in such efforts, to write a report as a chapter for a nationwide casebook. In this report, "The Neighborhood Program of the University of Chicago," released last month, he recalls that Dr. Robert M. Hutchins, then the university's chancellor, charged in 1945 that Chicago had "the worst housed faculty in the United States."

Bretz in The Miami Herald
Can't keep up appearances much longer."

Problem Not Local

In 1952, the renewal plan began in earnest. By 1957, Chancellor Lawrence A. Kimpton, despite local progress, knew that the problem remained of national scope. He urged Federal legislation and met with the presidents of Harvard, Columbia, the University of Pennsylvania, Yale and the Massachusetts Institute of Technology to consider the problem.

The meeting led to a nationwide study of neighborhoods surrounding universities, eventually involving sixteen major universities from coast to coast.

In 1959, Section 112 of the Housing Act made special Federal aid available for "urban renewal areas involving colleges and universities." The job that faced Chicago may be measured by the fact that it called for the acquisition and "clearing" of 630 buildings and 5,941 living units.

Chicago set the pace. With the acquisition of the old Devonshire Hotel, Columbia was merely continuing a trend that already makes the university the "landlord" of forty-five apartment buildings snatched out of the deterioration of the Morningside Heights area. Morningside Heights, Inc., an improvement organization of twelve educational, religious and medical organizations, is trying to halt the decline of that neighborhood.

New York University is moving fast in reclaiming parts of the region adjoining Washington Square before it deteriorates.

Temple University reports from Philadelphia that, although working in an area "that is one of the wost slums in the city," the renewal success in the first forty acres allocated to the university by the City Planning Commission has encouraged the institution to ask for another ninety-seven acres to be certified for its use. (Under this arrangement the Redevelopment Authority acquires the land for each structure and Temple reimburses the Authority for it.) The city has closed six blocks of streets that are being landscaped as campus area. Eventually, the North Philadelphia slum area will house a modern university with 40,000 students.

Elsewhere in Philadelphia, the University of Pennsylvania is engaged in emphatic renewal.

All Fronts Active

The scale of the battle varies, but it is being fought in cities, large and small, across the country. Harvard is trying to re-establish friendly relations with Cambridge and to stop the deterioration of nearby rooming houses. Yale is benefiting from the imaginative urban renewal program, masterminded by Mayor Richard C. Lee, a former member of Yale's administration.

All of those engaged in this enterprise agree that the battle for institutional survival has only just begun. They point to the need for maximum involvement of key faculty members—sociologists, lawyers, population experts, criminologists, architects, health scientists. A spokesman in Chicago warns that "the universities must believe their own authorities in sociology" and they must realize that the day cannot be won "with a short term sortie from the ivy tower."

October 1, 1961

Vast Urban Renewal Program Is Being Pressed in Baltimore

Model of twenty-three-story office building, designed by Ludwig Mies van der Rohe, on which construction has begun in Charles Center. It is first of six skyscrapers that will be built as part of the $125,000,000 project.

Special to The New York Times.

BALTIMORE

One of the largest urban renewal programs in the country is under way in Baltimore.

Twelve projects — residential, educational, commercial and industrial—involve Federal and municipal aid totaling $113,000,000 and private investments estimated at $350,000,000. Buildings on 775 acres in various parts of the city are being razed or rehabilitated.

The lack of new building in Baltimore has been such that one renewal project, the Mount Royal Plaza, will provide the city with its first apartment house in a decade and only house in a decade, and the second since the Nineteen Twenties.

The largest project in the program will transform the dingy downtown area of Baltimore. This is the $125,000,000 Charles Center, which will consist of six office skyscrapers, two apartment towers, a hotel, a theatre, pedestrian malls lined with specialty shops and parking garages.

The project's site comprises twenty-two acres between the city's financial district on the east and the retail district on the west. Its boundaries are Saratoga, Charles and Lombard Streets, Hopkins Place and Liberty Street.

The project will replace nearly all the structures erected since the Charles Center area was devastated by a fire in 1904. About 150 buildings, many dating to that period, will be razed, and only five will be saved.

The ones that will be kept are the Lord Baltimore Hotel, the headquarters of the Baltimore & Ohio Railroad, the Fidelity Building, the Lexington Building and the Eglin Parking Garage. Some 370 small businesses are gradually being moved to new quarters.

Work has started on the first building in Charles Center. This is a twenty-three-story skyscraper designed by Ludwig Mies van der Rohe, principal architect of the bronze-and-glass Seagram Building on Park Avenue in New York.

The structure will have a facade of gray-tinted glass trimmed with aluminum. It will have 275,000 square feet of office space and 30,000 square feet of retail space. Completion is scheduled for late this year. The building is being erected by Metropolitan Structures, Inc. of Chicago, headed by Bernard Weissbourd. His company is the builder of the Colonnade Park apartments in Newark, and the Lake Shore Drive apartments in Chicago.

Civic Center Plan

Other sponsors of buildings in the development have not yet been selected by the Baltimore Urban Renewal and Housing Agency. However, one of the other office buildings will be a $20,000,000 structure for agencies of the Federal Government.

Charles Center is expected to be the focal point for other developments, such as a new Baltimore Civic Center, expansion of the downtown campus of the University of Maryland, and the Mount Vernon Place and Mount Royal Plaza renewal projects.

The Civic Center, which is going up two blocks from Charles Center, is being built without Federal aid by the City of Baltimore. It will be a combination sports arena and convention hall, with a seating capacity of 10,000 and 100,000 square feet of exhibition space.

The University of Maryland is participating in the renewal program by erecting a hospital, dormitories and buildings for its professional schools on its downtown campus near Charles Center. It will take ten years to complete the university's construction program.

Other renewal projects, either in the planning stage or under construction, in addition to Mount Vernon Place and Mount Royal Plaza, are the Harlem Park projects I and II and the Mount Royal-Fremont development. The last is divided into several sections: Project I, extension of Project I, and Project II.

Apartments and homes of the town-house type are planned for the Mount Vernon Place project, a historic residential section of Baltimore. Mount Royal Plaza is a combined residential and business renewal area. The Mount Royal-Fremont project will be mainly a retail development.

The Harlem Park projects will provide a new elementary and high school for residents of the area and also will involve rehabilitation of rundown houses and apartment buildings.

Work on the first major apartment building in Baltimore in many years will begin soon in the Mount Royal Plaza development. It will be a sixteen-story, centrally air-conditioned structure with 300 apartments. It is sponsored by Renewal Planning Associates of Lindenhurst, L. I., headed by Marvin S. Gilman.

The Mount Royal Plaza project covers seventy-four acres. Three buildings have been completed to house units of the State Office Building, the State Roads Commission Building, and a building for the Department of Employment Security. The Baltimore Life Insurance Company recently completed its own building in the development.

Two industrial parks are included in the renewal program. They are the Camden Industrial Park and the Shot Tower Industrial Park. Both will be adjacent to Baltimore's central business district and will replace rows of rundown homes and commercial structures.

The Shot Tower development will be built around a 150-foot shot tower used in the manufacture of ammunition during the Civil War. Streams of molten metal were dropped from the summit of the tower into water, which hardened the drops of metal into balls of gun shot.

January 14, 1962

CLEVELAND AREA EXCEEDING PACE

20-Year Development May Be Complete in 11 Years

Special to The New York Times

CLEVELAND, March 21—An unusual cooperative plan for redeveloping the University Circle area of Cleveland will end its sixth year of operation far ahead of schedule.

Conceived as a 20-year development involving the investment of $175 million, the University Circle program is likely to reach its goal after 10 to 11 years of operation.

Neil J. Carothers, president of the University Circle Foundation, reported that new structures worth $70 million were completed and that construction valued at $30 million more was under way.

Backed by Church Groups

"We won't be able to maintain this pace," Mr. Carothers said, "but, at the rate we've been going, we may complete the original plans in 11 years."

The University Circle program is supported by 30 organizations and agencies in an area of a square mile, four miles east of downtown Cleveland. In 1957, these groups formed the foundation and hired the planning firm of Adams, Howard and Greeley to draw a 20-year development project.

The best known of the sponsoring groups are Western Reserve University, Case Institute of Technology, University Hospitals, the Cleveland Art Museum, the Cleveland Orchestra, Art Institute of Cleveland, Western Reserve Historical Society, Cleveland Institute of Music and the Natural Science Museum.

In addition, the foundation is supported by seven religious institutions representing all major faiths, a group of welfare agencies, libraries and garden groups in the area.

The foundation was created through donations of $3 million by a group of wealthy Clevelanders interested in building an educational, cultural and medical center for the community. A public drive netted $6 million more.

The final money to operate the foundation came from an unexpected bequest of $2.5 million from the estate of Mrs. Andrew R. Jennings, a widow who had watched the development start from her apartment in nearby Wade Park Manor.

The foundation buys all real estate for member institutions and enforces adherence to the original master plan. It also acquires and operates parking facilities and employs a special police force of 19 men.

Law Was Amended

In cooperation with the University of Chicago, the foundation won an amendment to the Federal housing law, allowing educational institutions to participate in urban renewal projects.

This law has helped University Circle to buy property along its border, protecting it from the spread of an adjacent slum neighborhood.

The development has resulted in new buildings for the Natural History Museum, Institutes of Music and Art, Day Nursery and Maternal Health Association, a new Veterans Administration Mental Hospital and major additions to the Art Museum, Historical Society, and the Cleveland Hearing and Speech Center.

Western Reserve and Case Institute of Technology have been the biggest beneficiaries. They have been able to add new classrooms, laboratories and dormitories and to break out of their tightly confined borders.

March 22, 1964

ARCH SYMBOLIZES ST. LOUIS REVIVAL

Downtown Renewal Giving City Economic Stimulus

By DONALD JANSON
Special to The New York Times

ST. LOUIS, July 31—On St. Louis's drab riverfront, a gleaming stainless steel arch designed by the late Eero Saarinen is beginning to rise.

When completed next year it will soar 630 feet over the 200-year-old city. As a symbol of St. Louis's historic role as a gateway to westward expansion, it is expected to become an international tourist attraction.

It has already become a symbol of hope here for a new economic vitality in the downtown area.

For years much of midtown St. Louis has presented an ugly picture of decay. The city, hemmed in by the Mississippi River and 98 suburbs in St. Louis County, has had no room for expansion.

Exodus to Suburbs

Residents fled to the suburbs, which have rejected all merger proposals made by the city. Inadequate traffic ways and public transit, as well as lack of esthetic appeal, hastened development of office buildings and shopping centers in the suburbs.

Most of the industrial expansion of the last decade has also been outside St. Louis proper. Even with gains in the suburbs, however, there has been no rise in employment in the metropolitan area since 1954, a period that has seen a 13 per cent gain nationally.

St. Louis concerns have expanded, but often in Southern states and elsewhere, largely for tax advantages. With few exceptions the booming space industry has passed the city by.

Population has declined in much of the St. Louis trade area. Although the suburbs took up some of the slack, the central city aged rapidly and was called the "dowager" of the Mississippi.

The conservatism of businessmen and residents here, many of them of Dutch and German ancestry, was said to have contributed to backwardness in developing the postwar potential of a city with all the natural advantages of central location and ready access to transportation, fuel, water and labor.

Slum Area Razed

City planners finally moved into action. Some 450 acres in the heart of the city, a rat-infested residential slum, were razed four years ago in a bold effort to create room for new light industry.

The area, Mill Creek Valley, was also zoned for apartments in a two-pronged program to attract plants and people of means to help improve the city's tax base.

However, the pace of the rebuilding failed to match the speed of the demolition, and frustrated St. Louisans had to become accustomed to seeing a vast weed patch in the heart of their city.

The planners tried again, suggesting a downtown sports stadium. Public approval of a $6,000,000 bond issue for street work was sufficient to stimulate private investment of $20,000,000 and the promise of considerably more.

Edward Durell Stone designed a circular, 50,000-seat sports stadium. Surrounding it will be new parking garages, shops, office buildings and a motel—all part of the $89,000,000 stadium project scheduled for completion by 1966.

Adding to the excitement in the business community is a surge of activity in a long-dormant project to beautify the shabby downtown riverfront.

Arch Becomes Symbol

It is here that the Saarinen arch is beginning to rise on land cleared for a national

Associated Press

NEW ST. LOUIS LANDMARK: Artist's conception of stainless steel arch, designed by the late Eero Saarinen, which is now under construction on St. Louis waterfront.

monument in 1936. Now that its giant legs can be seen, the arch has been adopted in St. Louis as a symbol of progress.

Billboards, brochures and company stationery here bear its likeness. Meantime, developers vying to rebuild the downtown areas that flank the new attractions. Hotels, motels, the first downtown office buildings in 30 years, restaurants, shops and places of entertainment are going up or planned.

Nearby, the Mill Creek Valley is beginning to sprout buildings instead of weeds.

Authorities say that the 10-year renewal project is on schedule. The first of 2,100 planned apartment units are occupied. A number of light industries have erected plants. The rehabilitation is expected to be completed by 1969.

Many credit the impressive Gateway Arch now 72 feet high, with doing most to stimulate action by providing a stunning entrance to the city.

Others say the turning point was the expression of faith in the downtown area in the approval two years ago of the stadium bond issue.

In any event according to Kenneth R. Cravens, chairman of the board of the Mercantile Trust Company, downtown St. Louis "for many years a dying and decaying section has made a complete reversal."

August 4, 1963

CENTER IN BOSTON TO BE DEDICATED

The Prudential Development, a $150 Million Venture, Is in Heart of Back Bay

WORK CONTINUES AT SITE

Planning for 31-Acre Tract Began in 1952 — Lodge and Stevenson to Appear

By JOHN H. FENTON

Special to The New York Times

BOSTON, April 17 — The showcase of the New Boston, a $150 million civic and commercial center in the heart of the Back Bay district, will be dedicated in two days of ceremonies beginning Monday.

Dominated by a 52-story office building, flanked by a 29-story hotel and a municipal auditorium, the Prudential Center represents the agony and the ecstacy of a city striving to rise above the sordidness of its recent past.

The ceremonies will be marked by a forum on "The Free Society and Its Posture in World Affairs, 1965." The participants will include Lord Avon, the former Prime Minister of Great Britain; Adlai E. Stevenson, United States representative at the United Nations, and Henry Cabot Lodge, the former United States representative at the United Nations.

Forum to Follow Foot Race

The forum will be held on Tuesday morning. But other events on the program will begin Monday afternoon, about 2:15 P. M., when the first finishers in the annual Boston Marathon are scheduled to end their 26-mile road race from Hopkinton, Mass.

As a special concession, the start of the race this year will be about half a mile west of the customary line, in order to allow the guests of the center ceremonies to see the finish on the North Plaza.

The marathon has been run annually for 69 years on Patriot's Day, the anniversary of the Battles of Concord and Lexington, signaling the start of the American Revolution, April 19, 1775.

State, city and civic leaders will take part in dedication ceremonies formally marking the opening of the office building, which will serve as the northeast regional home office of the Prudential Life Insurance Company of America, and the newest unit of the Sheraton Hotel Corporation of America, the 1012-room Sheraton-Boston. The auditorium, a war memorial, was dedicated earlier in the year.

Charity Ball Scheduled

Both days, hundreds of notables and less well known will be guests of the Sheraton Boston at a round of receptions and dinners. The two-day event will close with a charity ball under the auspices of the Junior League of Boston in the new hotel's Grand Ballroom.

Within the 31-acre site that takes its name from the towering home office building of the Prudential Life Insurance Company of America, work is continuing on two new tower apartment houses. These represent a downward revision — hopefully temporary—of plans that originally toyed with the dream of six such towers.

To some Bostonians, the unfinished towers signify the uncompleted business of remaking the city in a new image. Only last month, Mayor John F. Collins warned Boston taxpayers to be prepared for an $18 increase in the tax rate on each $1,000 of assessed valuation. The 1964 rate was $99.80.

Moreover, the city has shared some of the shame that has fallen on Massachusetts as a result of the findings of a State Crime Commission. The commission confirmed what had become common knowledge: that corruption was flourishing in state and municipal governments here.

So much concerning the conditions that exist has been published in Boston newspapers and elsewhere that the commission report was something like flogging an already stunned body politic. Before its report, the commission had succeeded in winning 40 convictions against present and past state officials, including two former Speakers of the Massachusetts House of Representatives, one from each party. Some of those indicted have gone to jail. Court action is pending on others.

3 Years—3 Pay Raises

As a measure of the general contempt of the Legislature toward the electorate, the members for the third time in the last three years voted themselves a pay increase early this year. And on April 5, they easily overrode a veto by Gov. John A. Volpe, the Republican Governor who created the Crime Commission in 1962.

The two previous pay rises subsequently were rescinded by referendum. But leaders of the opposition this time appeared to have thrown up their hands. Governor Volpe said he agreed that the legislators were entitled to more than $5,200 a year. But he called on them to enact some of his fiscal reforms before voting themselves a $2,300 increase.

Civil Rights Protests

In another area, nearly 1,000 pickets representing 18 civil rights groups recently paraded in front of the auditorium, a war memorial, to protest inferior schooling for slum-area children, most of them Negroes. The auditorium was dedicated earlier in the year.

The pickets appeared at the opening session of the National School Boards Association representing the 50 states and the Virgin Islands. The Boston School Committee, as host to the association, was the particular target of the civil rights groups. The three-member majority of the committee has steadfastly refused to acknowledge racial imbalance in the public schools.

The slum area encroaches within four or five blocks of the new center. And leaders of the civil rights movement have indicated that with the visit here next Thursday and Friday of the Rev. Dr. Martin Luther King Jr., there may be further demonstrating against building code violations and sketchy inspection of buildings by the city.

Downtown, in what used to be a commercial slum known as Scollay Square, three towering buildings to house Federal, state and municipal offices are rising as part of the rebuilding boom. The area has been renamed Government Center as part of an effort to erase the memory of tattoo parlors, fly-blown bars and transient rooming houses of easy virtue.

A vast urban redevelopment program is underway elsewhere in the city, including Washington Park, a tenement slum in the heavily Negro district of Roxbury. But despite efforts of the development authority to assist in relocating as many displaced families as possible, the new middle-income complexes that are replacing the tenements will fall short by several hundred of providing new living units for those now living doubled up with relatives on the periphery of the area.

But for two days, attention will be focused on the Prudential Center. It represents the fulfillment of a dream that began in 1952 when John B. Hynes was Mayor. Mr. Hynes represented a reform movement that finally ended the dynasty of James Michael Curley, once called the last of the big-city bosses.

City and civic leaders envisioned a gleaming complex of new buildings on the dismal car storage yards of the Boston & Albany Railroad, just two blocks from Copley Square. Mayor Hynes learned that Prudential was contemplating construction of a northeast regional office building in Hartford. Largely through his efforts, the company turned to Boston. Plans for a $15 million building here were announced.

The first of several snags developed when William F. Callahan, the chairman of the Massachusetts Turnpike Authority, made known his intention of running a 12-mile extension of the toll road down through the area. Mr. Callahan, who did not live to see the work completed, was considered more powerful in his heyday than any Governor.

Mr. Callahan held bast patronage power over the Legislature as a result of two terms as State Highway Commissioner and as Turnpike Chairman. And he did not hesitate to use it when bond issues and similar matters were at stake in the Legislature.

When Mr. Callahan agreed to run the turnpike beneath the center, alongside two remaining railroad tracks, Prudential responded by unveiling plans for a center development involving at least $100 million.

A further snag developed when Prudential became concerned over the ability of future city officials to carry out tax agreements. At length, the Legislature amended urban redevelopment statutes, permitting the area to be classified as "blighted."

This paved the way for tax concession. As a result, Prudential this year will pay about $4 million in lieu of taxes to the city. The Boston & Albany

Railroad formerly paid about $50,000 a year.

Richard Cardinal Cushing is credited with at least an indirect assist in breaking the legislative log jam. He and Fred Smith, a vice president of Prudential, longtime friends, discussed the situation a number of times privately. At length, the Boston Roman Catholic prelate publicly asserted that the center would be a great benefit to the city. Shortly afterward, the needed legislation was enacted.

Bond Sale Delayed

Before the way could be cleared to go ahead with the work, the Turnpike Authority ran into a temporary setback in attempts to sell its bonds. This lead to a 14-month delay in the entire program. But eventually, Prudential's patience was rewarded, the bonds were sold and work began.

At first, the center's hotel was to be named the America, as a unit of the Boston-based Hotel Corporation of America. But complications followed the death of A. M. Sonnabend, the founder of the corporation, led to the Sheraton Hotel Corporation of America's taking over management of the hotel. It will be designated the Sheraton-Boston, the 100th unit of the hotel chain that also is based here.

April 18, 1965

HUMAN RENEWAL GAINS APPROVAL

U.S. Redevelopment Officials Make Correction of Social Ills Part of Policy

FEDERAL FUNDS USED

Help for Persons Displaced by Renewal Projects Is Encouraged by Action

Human renewal has been firmly wedded to urban renewal under a recent change in policy by the Urban Renewal Administration.

The realization that correction of social ills must accompany correction of architectural ills has grown upon redevelopment officials and planners over the years as their experience with the urban renewal process has increased.

Now the Federal agency has made official policy of the view that, if slums are to be wiped out, it is not enough to change only the physical environment. The change was announced to the city and state agencies involved in a recent letter from the Urban Renewal Administration.

U.S. to Help in Cost

The agency said that the cost of diagnosing human problems in renewal areas through the use of social and socio-economic surveys and the cost of enlisting and coordinating health and welfare services to meet those problems may now be paid for out of Federal funds allocated to renewal projects.

However, the actual cost of the services cannot be paid for with Federal funds, the agency said.

Since the start of the urban renewal program, communities have been required—at least on paper—to provide relocation assistance and moving expenses for displaced persons, and to offer them decent, safe and sanitary housing within their means.

Studies in New York City and in Pittsburgh, financed in part through demonstration grants from Washington, have tested and proved the usefulness and the efficiency of diagnostic services in both slum clearance and rehabilitation projects, the Urban Renewal Administration said.

New York Test

The New York test was a study of tenants facing relocation from the West Side Urban Renewal area. The study by Greenleigh Associates criticized the city for permitting slum conditions to continue in buildings it had taken over.

The letter warns local agencies that they have a responsibility to minimize the hardships on those driven out by bulldozers or displaced by higher rents, or families who are ineligible for low-rent projects.

This responsibility is crucial, the administration said, when problems of unemployment, poor health, broken families, lack of education, poverty and antisocial behavior are encountered.

The agency cited specifically several problems for which Federal funds can be used in the manner described: alcoholism, drug addiction, illegitimacy, poor housekeeping, criminal records, psychiatric problems, isolation or alienation, and the adverse results of discrimination because of race, religion, nationality, language, age or family size.

The administration said that the diagnostic and referral services should be planned and carried out as a joint effort of the local renewal agencies and the existing social welfare services of the community.

If some of the needed social services are not now available, the agency said, local renewal administrators should work with community groups to develop them.

January 2, 1966

Decline in Skid Row Areas Reported

Skid row residents, including habitues of the Bowery in Manhattan, are rapidly being dispersed by urban renewal and welfare programs to other parts of most cities, according to a study of 29 major skid row areas throughout the country.

"The quality of the data varies from city to city," said Dr. Howard M. Bahr, director of Columbia University's Bowery Project, "but we are confident that the pattern is a valid one throughout the country—skid row is gradually vanishing."

He noted, however, that the decline of major skid row areas gives "little evidence that the absolute number of homeless persons is declining," although "in some places the decline of skid-row populations may represent real attrition of the homeless population."

In such cities as St. Louis and San Francisco, he said last week, the breaking up of major skid row areas has produced smaller skid rows in other areas.

Increase Noted in Tacoma

Of the 29 cities surveyed, only Tacoma, Wash., was found to have an increasing skid row population. Similar areas in Boston, Birmingham and Richmond were reported to have stable skid row populations. All other cities surveyed showed declines of up to 50 per cent.

The Bowery population, which was 13,675 in 1949, has dropped to less than half of that.

In addition to urban programs, Dr. Bahr said, national economic prosperity and the flow of hoodlums into skid row areas may be factors in the population decline.

"The Bowery has never been a particularly dangerous place," he said, "but it is widely believed that there has been a recent influx of Negro hoodlums and, consequently, many older men are afraid to come to the Bowery and walk the streets."

A more obvious factor, he said, is the Department of Welfare's policy of placing homeless men in rooming houses away from the Bowery.

Columbia's Bowery project began in 1964 as a one-year study commissioned by the city. It then received a Federal grant and was extended as a nationwide study, scheduled to end Dec. 31.

The cities found in the survey to have declining skid row populations were: Chattanooga, Chicago, Cincinnati, Cleveland, Detroit, Forth Worth, Houston, Milwaukee, Minneapolis, Nashville, New Orleans, New York, Oklahoma City, Omaha, Philadelphia, Pittsburgh, Portland, Ore., Providence, Rochester, Sacramento, St. Louis, St. Paul, Toledo, Seattle and San Francisco.

On Oct. 31, a new attempt to help the worst of Bowery derelicts is scheduled to begin under the auspices of the Vera Institute of Justice, a private, non-profit organization. Two-man teams, consisting of a plainclothes policeman and a reformed alcoholic or Bowery room clerk, will seek out derelicts and offer them medical help in a 50-bed infirmary.

October 8, 1967

Pittsburgh Renewal Plan Completes Major Phase

By DONALD JANSON
Special to The New York Times

PITTSBURGH, Nov. 28 — A major phase in the revitalization of downtown Pittsburgh was completed this week with dedication of the 10th and final building, a 23-story glass and aluminum office structure, of the Gateway Center project.

The Gateway complex, laced with green plazas, was begun 20 years ago to replace a grimy industrial slum of dilapidated warehouses and small businesses at the historic point of land where the Allegheny and Monongahela Rivers meet to form the Ohio.

At the time of World War II this coal and steel capital suffered from center-city blight and was so polluted with smog and hampered by lack of parking and other facilities that a number of corporate giants with headquarters here were considering moving their main offices elsewhere.

There were cases in which executives could be induced to live here but their wives could not. The air looked like that over Gary, Ind., does today. Motorists only half-jokingly spoke of the advisability of donning gas masks to drive through the city. At times street lights and headlights were necessary at midday.

Threat From Flooding

A recurrent threat, in addition, was flooding. A spring torrent out of the Allegheny Mountains left downtown Pittsburgh mired in muck in 1936.

Pittsburgh leaders marshaled forces for strong action. The Army Corps of Engineers was brought in. Ten upstream dams now regulate the Allegheny and Monongahela. Mills agreed to new smoke regulations that cut smog 88 per cent by 1955.

The state announced plans in 1945 to create a 36-acre park at the three-rivers point where Pittsburgh, named by the British for Prime Minister William Pitt of England, was born more than 200 years ago.

Removal soon of two old bridges to the apex of the park will give Pittsburgh a grassy front lawn with a downstream vista reminiscent of what it was when the British took France's Fort Duquesne in the French and Indian War and replaced it with Fort Pitt. The park is centered on the still-standing Fort Pitt blockhouse.

On the hypotenuse of the park triangle now are the modern high-rises of the 23-acre Gateway Center. Besides eight office buildings, the center includes the city's first new hotel in many years, an apartment tower and a large parking garage under a wooded plaza.

The dramatic change from decay to fountains and pools and skyscrapers sparked other major construction and renovation in adjacent downtown business areas, which with Gateway Center and the State Point Park are now called the Golden Triangle.

With the framework of a new United States Steel Corporation headquarters now at its full 64-story height not far from Gateway, the Pittsburgh skyline has become a miniature Manhattan.

In many quarters the renewal is regarded as a model for the nation. It has brought urban development specialists here for a look from throughout the country as well as from Europe, Japan and Australia.

"It is hard to believe that 20 years ago this area where we stand was a blighted, decaying slum," Mayor Joseph M. Barr said at dedication ceremonies Monday for the final Gateway Center building. "As a result of the equitable program 65 new or renovated buildings have sprung up in the Golden Triangle."

The $150-million Gateway Center was the first major urban redevelopment project in the country to be carried out with private funds. It tested what then was a new concept in city planning, with the municipality using the right of eminent domain to condemn and acquire downtown property and sell it to private enterprise for development.

The Equitable Life Assurance Society of the United States agreed in 1950 to build and operate the center after progress on flood and smoke control was assured and major industries agreed to remain in Pittsburgh and lease 42 per cent of the space in the first three buildings to be completed.

Major credit for the city's master plan of revitalization, including Gateway Center and Mellon Square Park near the new United States Steel headquarters, belongs to the Allegheny Conference on Community Development, formed in 1946 by industrial, business, government and educational leaders here.

After a shaky start amid the debris of renovation, all the office buildings of Gateway Center filled to capacity and remain filled, giving Equitable, as landlord, an annual 6 per cent profit on its investment.

The insurance company completed payment to the city this year of the city's multimillion-dollar investment in acquiring the land.

November 30, 1969

REBUILDING PLANS OF CITIES REDUCED BY NIXON'S CURBS

Larger Municipalities Seem to Be Hardest Hit by Cuts in Renewal Programs

By JOHN HERBERS
Special to The New York Times

WASHINGTON, Feb. 28 — Cities across the country are cutting back their plans for rebuilding blighted neighborhoods because of the Nixon Administration's restrictions on urban renewal and related programs.

Communities of various sizes are affected by the restrictions, but the larger cities, which have severe blight, appear to be particularly hard hit, say housing experts here and around the nation.

Philadelphia, for example, had expected to receive from $40-million to $50-million in "new money" for urban renewal in the next fiscal year, beginning July 1.

"Instead we will receive only $17.5-million and not a dime more," said M. Walter D'Alessio, an official of the city's redevelopment authority. "With this kind of funding we can only work on existing projects. The whole process where we produce new sites for housing and other activities will just dry up."

$15-Million for Chicago

Chicago sought $39-million for new projects for its fiscal year, which starts May 1, but was told by the Department of Housing and Urban Development that it could have only $15-million, or 32 per cent less than it received for the present fiscal year.

San Francisco does not know where it will get the money to finish a 72-block renewal project begun in the nineteen-fifties but only 20 per cent completed.

Justin Herman, director of the city's redevelopment agency, said that, unless more Federal funds were forthcoming, the project "will result in a bombed-out area and, what's worse, there will be a bombed-out credibility as far as the attitudes of the people in the area are concerned towards their government."

Model Cities Hampered

The pinch in urban renewal funds is also hampering model cities projects in a number of communities. In some cities, the model neighborhoods may have to reallocate funds scheduled for services, using them instead for physical improvements that were to have been paid for under urban removal.

In Atlanta, for example, Jim Wright, director of planning for model cities, said he expected urban renewal funds for the city's model neighborhood to be reduced at least 35 per cent from the $8-million budgeted locally for the coming fiscal year.

Urban renewal is a 20-year-old program under which the Federal Government provides money to local authorities for buying and clearing blighted sections and making the land available for new construction, both private and public. Under recent changes, it is being increasingly used for low-income housing and for community facilities.

Changes in Emphasis

Model cities, enacted in 1966, is a program for concentrating Federal and local services in selected blighted neighborhoods in an effort to improve the total quality of life for their residents. Urban renewal is one of the components.

The curtailment that the large cities are beginning to feel stems from two main factors.

First, the Nixon Administration is de-emphasizing certain Federal programs developed by Democratic administrations to improve the core areas of large cities. The increased resources thus made available are being budgeted into welfare reform and other programs. For example, the Housing Act of 1969 authorizes $1.7-billion for urban renewal but the Nixon budget calls for $1-billion.

Second, cities of small and medium size are developing blight and are applying for renewal grants in increasing numbers. Thus, the limited available funds are being dispersed among more cities.

More than 1,200 communities are receiving or have applications pending for urban renewal aid. Last year the Department of Housing and Urban Development initiated two restrictions.

First, it greatly curtailed the neighborhood development program, which is intended to speed revitalization of neighborhoods without red tape. The department froze the funds for several months, then placed a ceiling on the amounts to be allocated and the number of cities to be admitted. Atlanta received $15-million last year and expects to be cut to $7.5-million next year.

A Practice Discontinued

Second, the department has told cities with projects under way for several years that they will not be able to continue the practice of submitting amended applications each year until the projects are finished. Thus, San Francisco sees no way to complete its 72-block project unless new funds are made available.

The National League of Cities and the United States Conference of Mayors are pressing Congress for a $600-million supplementary appropriation for urban renewal for the current year, but this is opposed by the Administration and is likely to fail.

Local disputes, red tape and community pressures are further hampering the renewal of core cities in a number of areas.

Detroit officials said a year ago that the city would receive about $88-million under the neighborhood development program over a two-year period.

Disputes Are Blamed

Edward Prendeville, head of the urban renewal section of the Detroit Housing Commission, said this week that it now appeared the city would receive only about $3-million. The money was to have been used primarily for developing low-income housing and improving poor neighborhoods.

Because of disputes between city planners and citizen groups, there was a delay in filing of applications until "H.U.D. began to change its mind about the importance of the neighborhood development program," Mr. Prendeville said.

Harold J. Bellamy, chief planner for the Detroit Housing Commission, said regretfully, "I thought the neighborhood development program was the best thing to come along in a long time. I saw so much that we could have done for the city."

In St. Louis, 10 major redevelopment proposals, including a $60-million convention center backed by business interests, are in limbo because of the Federal restrictions in the neighborhood development program, according to the local authorities. At the same time, a $30-million project in the West End has been slowed by the disclosure of financial irregularities and protests by citizen groups, which have filed suit to stop the project.

As a result, much of St. Louis "looks like a desert," a city official said.

Cities of medium size seem to be faring better than the large ones. Louisville officials said that the budget restrictions have had little effect there so far. Norfolk, Va., officials said they could live with a 33 per cent cut from what had been expected. Memphis reported only a slight cut, which an official described as "real good in view of what is happening to some cities."

In some cities, there have been charges of political favoritism by Washington.

In New Haven, which has received a drastic cutback, Charles I. Shannoh, director of the redevelopment agency, said, "Since Mr. Nixon has become President, a very popular notion has been that development money was only going to cities that voted for him. I really don't believe this. It's my feeling that at some point New Haven will have its money restored."

March 1, 1970

New Boston Center: Skillful Use of Urban Space

By ADA LOUISE HUXTABLE

Special to The New York Times

An Appraisal

BOSTON — Urban renewal is a lot like pudding; the proof is in the consumption of the finished product. The record of completed renewal projects in American cities is largely one of failure, revelatory hindsight and the learning of a lot of belated lessons about what makes a city work. For those who have been patient enough to wait out one of the country's most ambitious urban renewal schemes, the 60-acre, $300-million Boston Government Center is now virtually complete.

After a decade of planning and construction, and notwithstanding charges of bulldozer clearance and homogenization of function, this huge complex of public and private buildings in the heart of old Boston on the former site of Scollay Square and skid row can be reported a success. Boston has been brought handsomely—and by and large sensitively—into the skyscraper age.

Like most of men's works, the results are imperfect, but it can be said now that the scheme has produced one of the best urban spaces of the 20th century, and that is no insignificant achievement.

Originally conceived in the nineteen-fifties and carried out according to a 1961 master plan by I.M. Pei & Partners under the direction of Edward J. Logue, then head of the Boston Redevelopment Authority and now in charge of the New York State Urban Development Corporation, this is one of the most important groups of urban structures in the country.

Approaching its goal of 30 coordinated buildings through the standard municipal obstacle race of politics, esthetics and economics, it has skillfully united a mixed bag of construction around its stellar attraction, the competition-winning, $27-million City Hall. In this focal building Boston sought, and got, excellence.

In addition to City Hall, the Government Center contains state and Federal buildings and as assortment of official and quasi-official structures, small and large-scale commercial construction, landmarks and a parking garage.

More important than individual buildings and statistics, however, is the successful completion of the vast, nine-acre City Hall Plaza that is the urban and esthetic glue that holds the whole thing together.

This plaza is part of the prize-winning City Hall design of 1962 by architects Campbell, Aldrich & Nulty, and structural engineers Le Messurier Associates.

With the plaza, and specifically because of it, the Boston Government Center can now take its place among the world's great city spaces.

Roughly the size of St. Peter's Square in Rome, it lends a unity and style and sense of logical and rewarding spatial relationships to the complex that are a clear illustration of the best and most basic principles of urban design. It is in the direct tradition of historic Italian plazas and European squares.

These nine acres of red brick paving, stepped and terraced and trapezoidal in shape, are bounded east and west by New Congress and Cambridge Streets and by buildings on its north and south sides.

City Hall itself is placed not at the center of the plaza, but is free-standing at the rear, with the fan-shaped, stepped levels converging on it. The brick paving flows right into City Hall and through the ground floor of the building that is the plaza's calculated climax.

Also not centrally placed, but in a corner formed by the Cambridge Street boundary and the Federal Building, is a delightful, sunken, brick-walled pool and fountain in a kind of minipark.

Where the ground level rises steeply to the north, steps lead to an elevated terrace with trees and benches in front of the Federal Building. Opposite, outdoor cafes spill onto the brick surface from the ground floor restaurants of the restored 19th century Sears Crescent. Between, a pedestrian arcade and shops in the curving Central Plaza office building serve as boundary on the Cambridge Street periphery.

The fountain and City Hall forecourt are the lively setting of Boston's "Summerthing" entertainment and citizen participation programs

Photographs for The New York Times by JOYCE DOPKEEN

In a corner of the Boston Government Center children play in a sunken pool

and much spontaneous activity. In winter, the plaza's New England fate is to be cold and windswept, but the space is handsome at all seasons.

It is the functional and esthetic use of this open space, uniting the disparate and often less than distingushed buildings of the Center, that gives superior design quality to the whole development.

•

This, plus the constructive efforts of the careful design review of buildings by the Boston Redevelopment Authority and its Design Advisory Committee, in relation to the forms, color and scale of City Hall, accounts for much of the secret of the Government Center's success.

Construction was divided into 15 "parcels," all under Redevelopment Authority control. Developers got a "design kit" of generalized specifications, and there were four official design reviews. But it is the urbanistically dramatic use of the open space as theme and connector that is the project's ultimate distinction.

To achieve this, Boston destroyed a lot of its older fabric. Major landmarks, such as Faneuil Hall, were retained, while venerable buildings of less than landmark status were demolished, along with a lot of derelict seediness considered picturesque by some and shameful by others.

Landmarks that have been kept are carefully related to the new construction. The juxtaposition of Faneuil Hall and the new City Hall, the Customs Building seen between City Hall and the new sleek-skinned New England Merchants Bank tower, the Old State House framed in the bank's arcade, are all sensitively calculated vistas. But such historic structures, kept and restored, can be counted on one hand. It has been called token preservation.

It is important to note that there will be more preservation in related areas. Privately sponsored rehabilitation and adaptive use of the superb, adjacent Faneuil Hall market buildings of the eighteen-twenties, one of the most substantial Greek Revival groups in the country and Boston's first urban renewal project, will start soon. This will add considerably to the area's sense of heritage and continuity.

Some new housing, in luxury harbor apartments and the controversial West End development, and the market building rehabilitation, will bring increasing business-residential mix and day-night activity.

Of the Government Center buildings, only the catalytic City Hall is outstanding architectually.

The John F. Kennedy Federal Office Building, a 26-story tower with a four-story lower section, by The Architects Collaborative with Walter Gropius & Samuel Glaser Associates, is distressingly ordinary and already suffering from the American disease of instant deterioration.

Its double tower, which in-

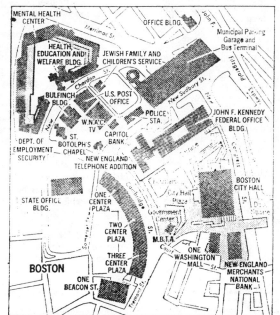

The New York Times/Sept. 11, 1972

creases the number of daylit offices and decreases the visual bulk, is praiseworthy; the fussy, indecisive precast exterior detailing is not. The building's controversial Robert Motherwell mural is to be criticized more for its inept and awkward placement due to inept and awkward architectural transitions than as art.

The Center Office Building, by Welton Beckett & Associates, a critical structure that helps define the space with its long, low curve, does so unpretentiously and well.

The Leverett Saltonstall State Building, by Emery Roth & Associates, is a collection of depressing, pedestrian minimums inside and out, including stale air from sluggish air conditioning.

In an account of the Government Center evolution by Charles G. Hilgenhurst, former director of the Boston Redevelopment Authority's Planning, Urban Design and Advanced Projects, it is pointed out that the building is in an area just beyond the authority's direct design control and that review by the authority's Design Advisory Committee was brief and late.

The State Service Center, three buildings in a single shell on a superblock at Chardon and Cambridge Streets, is an aborted, brilliant tour de force, minus the focal tower and dramatic serpentine stair that were part of the original scheme by Paul Rudolph and a bevy of collaborators. Its truncated version suggests that its drama may have been a little overwrought for its purpose.

The new skyscraper office buildings at the Center's periphery, which proper Bostonians have viewed with articulate alarm, come off particularly well. In large part subject to Redevelopment Authority controls, they are surprisingly sympathetic in scale and design.

Edward L. Barne's New England Merchants Bank is a structure of knife-sharp refinement. Pietro Belluschi's 41-story Boston Building offers a suave, technological display.

Rising now is an impressive tower by Skidmore, Owings & Merrill that has been an object of particular local displeasure. After severe brushes with Redevelopment Authority design review, major compromises by the architects include changes of shape, orientation and cladding. The polished sophistication of its characteristic S.O.M. detailing, tempered by Boston tastes, is creating a powerful presence.

The impression of the new towers, to Boston's credit, is of attention to design and environmental quality.

The Government Center replaces considerable history and squalor. What has been lost by redevelopment are not only those derelict buildings and their occupants that few mourn, but also the virtues of traditional mixed functions and the richness of old streets and structures.

What has been gained is a notable achievement in the creation and control of urban space, and in the uses of monumentality and humanity, in the best pattern of great city building. Old and new Boston are joined through an act of urban design that relates directly to the quality of the city and its life.

September 11, 1972

A Revitalized Cincinnati Blends Old and New Spirit

By GEORGE VECSEY
Special to The New York Times

CINCINNATI, Oct. 8—Huge picture windows on the top of a hillside, rain turning the water-lights into a surrealistic blur, a waiter creates flaming crepes for patrons dressed elegantly for the Symphony. If Tony Bennett strolled into the room singing "I left my heart..." the instinct would be to look for the nearest cable car.

But Cincinnati tore down her last cable car in 1948, much to her current regret, and the shimmering water down below is merely the befouled Ohio River, best glimpsed opaquely from Mount Adams during a romantic fall rain.

In the last decade, while many large cities have lost some of their character through a combination of social, economic and cultural deterioration, Cincinnati has managed to hold firm.

Seemingly abandoned and left for dead a decade ago, this manageably sized city has survived through favorable circumstances and inspired city planning to the extent that Bob Rathgeber, an official with the Cincinnati Reds baseball team, dares call it "The poor man's San Francisco."

Well, maybe. But a San Francisco that was settled by Germans conservative in politics and lavish toward musical culture; where the crime rate ranks 42d, not second as the California city's does, among the 52 largest urban areas, and where antipornography and antiloitering drives pervade like river-valley humidity.

Cincinnati has the lowest cost of living in the North and an unemployment rate of 4.5 per cent that is lower than the national figure of 5.5 per cent. It has a 55-cent bus ride, the costliest in the nation.

It is a place where 30,000 displaced mountaineers live in crowded poverty only a few blocks from three of America's finest French restaurants; whose leaders proudly saved a historic market and river steamboat while refusing to help save Union Terminal, with its stylish nineteen-twenties Art Deco design; a city slightly declining in population but whose downtown surges with life every lunchtime — and will do so when the Reds meet the Pittsburgh Pirates in the National League playoffs at Riverfront Stadium tomorrow.

Hopelessly "hicky" to some natives, the Queen City is a beacon of civilization to others in the region. One Eastern lady, temporarily marooned in nearby Louisville, once returned from a weekend in Cincinnati to report breathlessly: "I saw two men in berets crossing the street."

Middle-American or slightly foreign, Cincinnati has maintained some vibrant leadership from citizens like Charles P. Taft, son of a President, brother of a great Senator, now 75 years of age and still a valuable member of the City Council.

"Cincinnati is small enough that it can't split up, like Cleveland, but big enough that it has continued contact with everything in the country," Mr. Taft remarked. "It's not too big. New York is damn near ungovernable."

This hilly city has its own balkanization problems from tiny municipalities in the surrounding Ohio-Kentucky-Indiana counties. But with a declining city population of 439,000, down from 502,550 in 1960, and a growing seven-county metropolitan population of 1,384,850, Cincinnati is only the 21st largest metropolitan area in the country—although the traffic jam on the bridges to Kentucky at 5 P.M. make it seem much larger.

The smallness of the city is coupled with a conservatism. Cincinnati's industries are steady, like Procter & Gamble, General Electric, Armco Steel, Kroger and Federated Stores with some machine tooling and small auto factories. There is little electronics and little aviation — not much boom, not much bust. Cincinnati was one of the most stable cities during the Depression; people still boast about that. But then it has never had the spectacular growth of Atlanta or Houston.

Cincinnati's biggest boom came in the middle 19th Century when river and rail traffic and a huge migration of Germans made it the sixth largest city for a while.

But then the frontier moved south and west and Cincinnati stabilized. Its vibrant Jewish and German citizens built comfortable homes in the valley and then slowly moved toward the surrounding hills (the official total of hills is seven — just like Rome). These citizens established fine restaurants, music halls and schools and no new waves of immigrants challenged their numbers, save for blacks from the South and mountaineers from Appalachia.

"I think it was somewhat accidental," Mr. Taft said, "but people lived closer to downtown until fairly recently. They kept their roots downtown a lot longer."

The roots were tested after World War II, when Cincinnati began to show her age.

"It was an ugly, dirty old city when I first came here," said George C. Hayward, a city planner who was brought here in 1945 to draw up a master plan for a revitalization. Other committees and plans followed, including one by Victor Gruen in 1962, but there was no progress until the Working Review Committee was founded in 1963.

"We needed a small, powerful group of decision-makers who could get things done," Mr. Hayward recalls. "We had a deadline of 18 months to come up with a plan. We met frequently at all-day sessions. We sent out for sandwiches if we had to. We asked ourselves the most basic questions, like was the city really worth saving."

With 18 élite representatives from government and industry and another planner named Archibald Rogers, the committee issued its plan in December, 1964.

It called for widening and renovating Fountain Square, whose famous gurgling Bavarian statue, the Genius of the Waters, has been the focal point of downtown since 1871.

Underground garages, second-story walkways, improved traffic patterns and brightened designs were planned for a 12-block nucleus at the square—with $20-million of Federal funds matching $10-million of local money. The business community, no doubt operating from financial convictions more than sentimentality for downtown, committed itself to staying rather than fleeing to the suburbs.

Since 1964, at least 24 major projects have been constructed downtown, including a new Stouffer's Hotel, a new Federal Reserve Bank and the DuBois Tower overlooking the rebuilt Fountain Square, whose lunchtime strollers, street people, splashing waters and flower stands give it the vitality of an Italian piazza.

In addition, a $16.6-million bond issue was approved for riverfront land acquisition and new convention center downtown. Later a $25-million riverfront stadium was built downtown with bond money, to house the Reds in baseball and the Bengals in football, ignoring the Reds' former owners who wanted to relocate in the suburbs.

The boost to downtown has been obvious. When the Reds are home during the summer, the antiquated hotels are jammed with joyful, casually dressed families who walk to the ball park, who stroll around the fountain square and who patronize downtown cafeterias and restaurants. Special events like the baseball playoff are said to bring in up to $500,000 while baseball and football are estimated to contribute over $20-million a year to the city's income, more than making up for an annual deficit of $1.8-million at the stadium.

Cincinnati also has a charming art museum and the Playhouse in Eden Park atop Mount Adams, whose old working-class calm has been supplanted by glittering condominiums, leather shops, exotic food shops and music clubs. Johnny Bench, the young super-catcher, and Gov. John J. Gilligan have homes on Mount Adams.

Downtown, the renovated Music Hall houses the Cincinnati Symphony Orchestra, whose annual May Festival attracts top musicians from around the world.

The city is blessed with three fine French restaurants, the Gourmet atop the Terrace Hilton, the Maisonette and Pigall's. The hot slaw and cold beer in many German restaurants here invoke images of another century.

These are the things that visitors notice first. For the residents, the pattern is likely to be a move into Cincinnati's suburbs in the north and west, where school sports, family camping vehicles and shopping centers are the way of life. Blacks, who make up 27.7 per cent of the city population, a figure that is rising, have moved into older white communities like Avondale since the urban renewal and moderate disturbances of the mid-nineteen-sixties.

Another group here is composed of 30,000 former residents of Appalachia who cluster in the former German section called "Over the Rhine," just north of downtown.

"They're not politically conscious," Charles Taft says wistfully. "They vote less than the blacks. They still think they don't belong here, although they comprise 10 or 15 per cent of the city's population."

"This is one of the few American cities with neighborhood identity," said Harris Forusz, an urban planner at the University of Cincinnati. "It's got an ideal college area around Clifton. In my mind it compares with Montreal, Boston, San Francisco and New Orleans among good cities."

A familiar image of Cincinnati stems from the two Kentucky towns, Newport and Covington, just across the river, where gambling, prostitution, after-hours drinking and first rate entertainment flourished until a decade ago, when George Ratterman, a quarterback turned sheriff, closed down much of the vice.

A stringent morality is now being pushed in Cincinnati. The drive is led by Charles H. Keating Jr., a prominent lawyer who gained national attention for dissenting, along with President Nixon, from the liberal findings of the President's Commission on Obscenity and Pornography.

With Mr. Keating as plaintiff, a sex-film theater has remained padlocked since last Jan. 12 by court order as a "public nuisance."

The drive against pornography extended into raids on dirty-book stores and on a warehouse. In a separate incident, the city library briefly removed books by Emile Zola, James Jones and John Updike, among others, following complaints against them by a conservative group. After a long public debate, the books were returned to the shelves.

Alan Brown, a leading civil-liberties lawyer, contends that an "oppressive" trend is being set by Mr. Keating, who has recently become involved in the operation of The Cincinnati Enquirer, the city's only morning newspaper.

As for culture in Cincinnati, Mr. Brown said, "There just aren't many creative people. If you like nineteenth century concerts, this town is better than New York. Sure, we've got summer opera here. But Wagner is avant-garde."

Residents trace Cincinnati's sponsorship of music to Ralph and Patricia Corbett. Some Cincinnatians wish for saviors like the Corbetts in relation to art and architecture here.

The absence of a major boom has enabled many of the older, more stylish buildings to dominate the skyline, from the 49-story Carew Tower and the baroque City Hall to the quaint Bavarian/Appalachian red-brick apartments. (A new columnist in town, David B. Bowes, praised the "Daily Planet" architecture of his newspaper, The Times-Post-Star, noting that he expected to see Superman streaking away from its exterior at any time.)

The conservation of Cincinnati sometimes extends to conservation of landmarks like the Delta Queen, a paddle-wheeler, and the peaked-roof Findlay Market in a quaint square. But nothing saved historic Wesley Chapel after Procter & Gamble bought the land beneath it and leveled the old building one night without notice.

Some residents fear that this will soon happen to Union Terminal. Facing the city skyline from a western rise, Union Terminal was built by the city just before the Depression, employing the Art Deco style that is labeled "a treasure" by Dr. Gabriel Weisberg, associate professor of art history at the University of Cincinnati.

The good gray burghers of Cincinnati were bewildered by the high, sculptured rotunda; the gaudy colors; the integrated design; the powerful Winold Reiss mosaic-murals depicting 14 familiar Cincinnati industries, which dominates the long concourse, where hundreds of trains used to pass every day.

The Last Passenger Train

The station was a landmark during World War II for millions of transients, but now Amtrak is moving to another part of town and the last passenger train will leave Union Terminal on Oct. 29. Southern Railways, which is owned by the city, is apparently eager to destroy the concourse so that it can run its piggyback freight trains underneath. It might take $280,000 to move the Reiss murals in the concourse; the city says it cannot get involved in such a project.

October 9, 1972

Los Angeles, in a Building Boom, Debates Urban Revival

By ROBERT LINDSEY
Special to The New York Times

LOS ANGELES, Dec. 4—In the heart of this city that all but surrendered its soul to the automobile, there is a new vitality these days, the beginnings of a big city skyline and an angry, introspective debate over what kind of future its citizens want for Los Angeles.

New skyscrapers bristle from the western edge of the downtown business district, creating a lean, vertical profile in a city famous for being horizontal—the classic city of sprawl—19 suburbs in search of a city, it used to be said.

A major financial center has sprung up there, a distant and still relatively small reflection of lower Manhattan, but a beachhead in a land of sportshirts and suede shoes where the dark business suit is not only accepted but also expected.

Thus even before the City Council last July 18 approved the largest urban redevelopment project ever undertaken in the United States, part of downtown Los Angeles had been brought back from the grip of urban decay.

Besides new buildings, there are new plazas and malls, colorful underground shopping centers fountains, trees, noontime outdoor concerts and for only 10 cents, a pleasant ride on a minibus that that shuttles around town like an above ground subway.

Yet, not far from the 16 new buildings on the west side that over the last decade have slowly transformed the skyline of the city, there is a skid row of derelicts, $5-a-day hotel rooms and hundreds of old buildings that still look much like those in any big city infected with decay.

It is this area for which after more than five years of discussion the City Council, by a vote of 12 to 1, approved the urban redevelopment project.

The plan called for revitalization of

The New York Times/David Strick

Some of the 16 new buildings on the West Side of Los Angeles that have transformed the once horizontal skyline of the city

virtually all of downtown Los Angeles not already modernized—an area of two and a quarter square miles with 255 square blocks and more than 2,000 buildings.

Thomas Bradley, the city's liberal black Mayor, inherited the plan from his predecessor, Sam Yorty, but he has staked his own prestige solidly on the project.

"It will put a stop to the blight and deterioration that ultimately will destroy the downtown area," Mayor Bradley said in an interview. It will create jobs and, he said, continue a "renaissance" in the center of the country's third largest city.

Financing Plan Scored

But the massive redevelopment project is under mounting and strident attack, largely because of an unusual financing plan: For the next 35 years, all property taxes collected within the 255-block area (which includes most of the recently built new skyscrapers) beyond the level in effect on July 18 will be given to the City Redevelopment Agency to spend on projects within that area.

To Ernani Bernardi, the lone Councilman who dissented on the project, the plan is a "multibillion-dollar tax subsidy to be paid for by all the taxpayers in the county for the benefit of a few major property owners."

His reasoning is that for each dollar invested on the project, taxpayers elsewhere in the county will have to pay an equivalent amount to finance government services. He contends that the diverted tax revenues could reach $4 billion to $6 billion over 35 years, although Mayor Bradley favors putting a limit of $750 million on spending.

Since July, at least five of the 12 Councilmen who voted for the measure have said that they now have doubts about it. Mr. Bernardi has filed two lawsuits challenging the legality of the plan that have not yet come to court. And the government of Los Angeles County has joined him in the suits.

Referendum Next Spring

Alan Robbins, a Democratic State Senator from the San Fernando Valley who is expected to run against Mr. Bradley next year, has embraced the redevelopment controversy as his main campaign issue and introduced legislation in Sacramento that would expedite a referendum election on the plan next spring—on that many political analysts here feel would be lost by the city.

To a large extent, the bitter feud is the end result of Los Angeles's adopted manifest destiny of boundless growth. For decades, the city government, eager for an increased tax base and intent on growth because there seemed to be no alternative for reasonable men, annexed land with the fervor of a blitzkrieg using the freeway as a kind of suture to sew together the sprawling city.

Today, Los Angeles occupies 465 square miles, stretching more than 50 miles wide at some points. To most people, "downtown" isn't the central city, but a local suburban shopping mall.

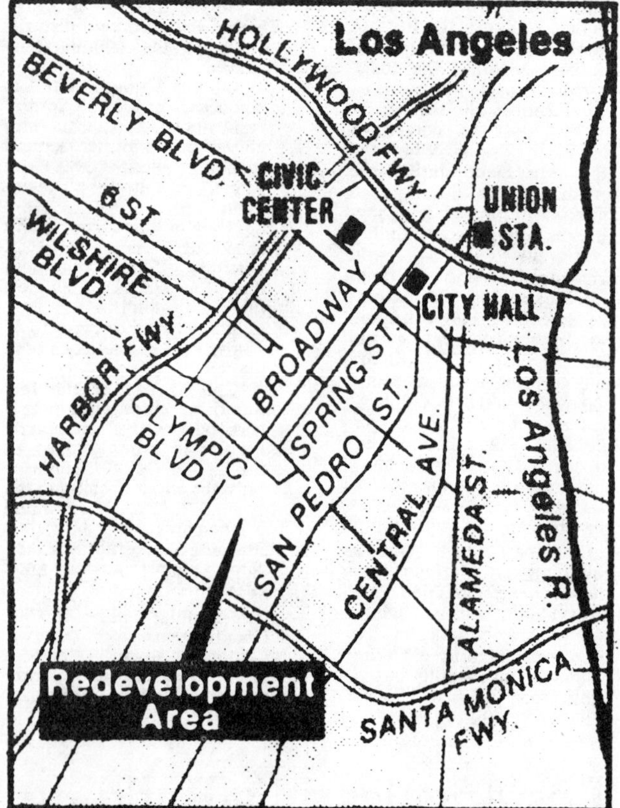

The city establishment is now discovering the obvious—that many if not most of the residents in the San Fernando Valley, the San Gabriel Valley, and many other areas within the city have neither the loyalty nor the inclination to pay for revitalization of the central city.

Without a Solid Core

Los Angeles was the prototype of the city without a solid core, a kaleidoscope of many subcommunities, and like Humpty Dumpty, there is resistance to putting it back together.

It was not always that way. Until after World War II, Los Angeles was in more or less the mold of a classic metropolitan area. It was served by one of the world's most extensive trolley systems, which radiated into suburban areas and brought shoppers to the department stores on Broadway—the city's Fifth Avenue—and customers to the banks on nearby Spring Street. Except for the specially re-enforced 28-story City Hall, buildings seldom exceeded 10 stories or so because of earthquake dangers, and created the city's low profile.

But after the war, the downtown began to go into decline earlier than most central cities, the result of the expansion of mass ownership of automobiles, the freeway, mass production of homes financed with Government-insured mortgages, abandonment of trolley lines and a proliferation of suburban shopping centers.

By the mid-1950's, the downtown had become, in the words of the novelist Raymond Chandler, whose characters often roam Los Angeles, "old and stale—like a living room that had been closed too long."

The Picture Changes

Then a series of events slowly began to change things: In 1957, a revised building code, reflecting advanced earthquake-stressing engineering technology, was passed, and permitted construction of high-rise buildings; in 1960, the Harbor Freeway gave new access to the previously second-rate west side of town; in 1964, the city's Bunker Hill slum clearance project began to make attractive building sites available near this freeway; a year later, a "gentlemen's agreement" of the city's major banks, which had pledged not to leave Spring Street, despite encroaching urban blight from the east side of town, cracked, and that touched off a rush of one-upmanship to build big new buildings.

The largest is the 62-story United California Bank building. Also prominent are the twin 52-story towers built by the Atlantic Richfield Company and the Bank of America, a stunning complex that has six acres of subterranean shopping areas.

Not far away is the Broadway Plaza, a striking development that covers a city block and includes a 32-story office building, a 500-room hotel, a department store, and an airy two-level, glass-roofed shopping mall.

A 500-room hotel designed by an Atlanta architect, John Portman, is rising a few blocks away, not far from where Standard Oil of Indiana is helping to finance a $125 million hotel-commercial development complex.

After years of debate, city officials last month reached accord on a "starter" route for a new rail mass transit system, from a downtown railroad station to suburban Long Beach.

In all, the building boom of recent years has added more than 12 million square feet of office space to the downtown area. Nevertheless vacancy rates are high, with some of the new buildings standing half-empty.

To the disappointment of city boosters, out-of-state corporations have not rushed to relocate headquarters here. And not everybody has been awed by the changing face of downtown Los Angeles.

"The effect is a visual skyline, a stage set, but not a functioning, integrated downtown community," observed John Pastier, former architecture critic of The Los Angeles Times.

"It's plastic, a hodgepodge of projects, largely because of a panic to leave Spring Street; the buildings don't hang together as a unit, because of a lack of planning," he said.

Mr. Pastier was dismissed last month by The Times, which owns property within the redevelopment project, and has been a strong supporter of it editorially. The newspaper says he was discharged because it was unsatisfied with his work. He contended it was because of his criticism of certain elements of the project.

Given mounting unrest among property owners in Southern California over increasing taxes it appears to many persons here that resistance to the redevelopment project will grow, and that eventually voters will be given a chance to decide on the plan. Then, it will be decided whether Los Angeles will recapture its preautomobile past and continue the renaissance of its recent past.

December 5, 1975

Detroit street after the 1967 riots.

ourtesy The New York Times

CHAPTER **4**

An Uncertain Future

THE DUSKY RACE.

Condition of the Colored Population of New-York.

Their Numbers, Avocations and Modes of Living.

The Prejudices and Circumstances that Keep Them Down.

Their Churches and Charitable Institutions.

Scenes in a Colored Dance-house—Statistics of Miscegenation.

What is the present condition of the colored people of this City? This is a question which must be interesting to all classes of the community, not only to those who are infineneced by general philanthropic motives or those who take an especial interest in the well-being and moral elevation of the negro, but also to those lovers of questions of political economy, who consider that the prosperity of each and every section of society is necessary to the national welfare.

THE COLORED POPULATION.

The colored population of New-York which numbered, according to the census of 1860, 12,000 persons, increased during the first years of the war, from the arrival of contrabands and other causes, to 15,000. After the riotous uprising of the Irish against the colored people at the time of the draft, in July, 1863, many of them left the City for fear of future ill-treatment, and a gradual emigration has been since going on which has reduced their numbers at the present time, according to the calculbition of those among them who have the best opportunities of judging, to something near 12,000. This is exclusive of a floating population of seamen, ships' cooks, habitual wanderers, &c., amounting to 2,000 or 3,000. They are thus distributed: In the neighborhood of Mulberry, Crosby, Chrystie, Delancey and Baxter streets, about 1,500; in the Five Points Mission district, about 250; in Twenty-seventh, Twenty-eighth, Twenty-ninth and Thirtieth streets, extending from Fifth-avenue to the North River, nearly 4,300; in the neighborhood of Thompson, Laurens, York, Wooster and Sullivan streets, between Bleecker and Canal streets, and from Bleecker to Eighteenth-street, about 4,500; and some 1,500 scattered indiscriminately over the City. They change their residence so frequently that it is difficult to arrive at a precise estimate of their numbers, but this is believed among their own people to be a fair approximation.

THEIR PURSUITS.

The men are principally occupied as coachmen in private families, waiters in hotels and dining saloons, barbers, whitewashers, bricklayers and kalsominers; while many of them are teamsters and 'longshoremen, and a few work privately as artisans in different trades. In the Spring, Summer and Autumn great numbers of them go as cooks, stewards and waiters on the various river steamers, many more are employed as waiters in the hotels at the different Summer resorts and watering-places; and such is the exodus produced by these causes that it is computed that there are twice as many more colored men in the City during the Winter months, when the hotels are all closed and the steamers laid up, than there are in the Summer time. This latter class are generally compelled during the Winter to subsist upon what they have been able to save from their Summer earnings; and in cases where they have been improvident, or have not had employment during the entire season, very great distress is often experienced by them.

The principal occupations of the women are washing and ironing—for which they seem to have much aptitude—dressmaking and hair-dressing, and a certain number teach in the colored schools. The washerwomen seem, as a class, to be very industriously inclined, and are generally contented with the weekly money they earn. They are compelled of necessity to keep themselves and their places clean, and get up the linen committed to their charge in a style fully equal to their white competitors, and in strange contrast with the dusky color of their skins.

THEIR CHURCHES AND INSTITUTIONS.

In matters of religion, the great bulk of the colored people may be divided into two sections—Methodists and Baptists. The Methodists comprise nearly two-thirds, and the Baptists about one-third, of the whole population; though there are some Episcopalians, Roman Catholics, and Presbyterians. They have two Methodist Episcopalian Churches, each of which has a special section in the cemetery at Cypress Hill for the burial of their people. Zion Church, at the corner of Bleecker and West Tenth streets, of which Rev. WILLIAM F. BUTLER is the pastor, is valued, with the ground on which it stands, at $100,000, and has also real estate belonging to it, in different parts of the City, valued at $100,000 more. There are also two Union Methodist Churches, two Baptist, one Episcopalian, one Presbyterian, and one Methodist Mission. The Roman Catholics are so few in number that they have, as yet, no church of their own, but attend the churches of the whites. The total amount of Church property in this City belonging to the colored people, is valued at $455,000.

Their distinctive institutions are alike various and numerous, and appear to be very well supported by their own people. They have six public schools, an Industrial and Educational School at No. 185 Spring-street, which was opened last Summer, and which is daily crowded with pupils of all ages, from 5 to 30 years, only too anxious to learn something and everything; an Orphan Asylum, capable of accommodating 173 boys and girls, the highest number yet reached; and an asylum for aged people, called "The Old Folks' Home," which contains nearly 200 inmates. They have, moreover, several societies whose objects are relieving the poor, visiting and nursing the sick, burying the dead and reclaiming drunkards. The Society of the Good Samaritan has six lodges, and numbers nearly 600 members; the Society of Love and Charity has 850 members. Then there is the Society of the Sons of Wesley, 120 members; the Saloons' Men Society, 200 members; the Coachmen's Benevolent Society, the Young Men's Christian Benevolent Society, and the Mutual Relief Society. These are all of a benevolent character. But these charitable and benevolent associations are by no means confined to the men. Among the women there are the societies of The Daughters of Esther, a very wealthy institution; The Daughters of Wesley, The Female Perseverance, The Ladies' Mutual Relief, The Ladies' Loyal League, The Daughters of Zion, and Tappin's Assistant Society, numbering altogether nearly 2,000 members. There are fourteen lodges of colored Freemasons, with 750 members, but they have no connection with simlar associations in New-York. The New-York lodges refused admission to all negroes on the ground of their color, but they succeeded in obtaining a charter direct from the Grand Lodge of England, and are governed by the rules of that Order in that country. The Grand United Order of Odd Fellows, which has four lodges with 350 members, also derives its charter direct from England—the white lodges in this city having declined to acknowledge their colored brethren. They have carried their animosity to such a pitch as to sever their connection with the English branch of the Order, in consequence of their having given a charter to the colored men of this and other cities. The Union League Council, which has 1,500 members, is a purely political club, having for its especial object the obtaining of negro suffrage. There is also a Young Men's Christian Association, consisting of 140 members, which has a reading-room and a lending library. A Literary Society is attached to this institution, under whose auspices courses of lectures on various improving topics are from time to time given. The Freedman's Bank, in Bleecker-street, has now been in operation nearly two years, and has received during that period deposits to the amount of $130,000. At the same time, very many others of the savings banks of the City have the names of colored customers on their books.

The *Zion Standard & Weekly Review* is a newspaper edited, printed and published entirely by colored men, for the use and benefit of their own people. It is devoted to religion, news, politics, literature, science and the general interests of the African race in this country—religious but not sectarian. Rev. Dr. JAMES N. GLOUCESTER is the chief editor. The paper, which has correspondents in all parts of the United States, from New-England to California, seems to have a fair advertising business, is very well gotten up, and is altogether very creditable to the enterprise of its promoters.

THE PREJUDICE AGAINST THEM.

Throughout the whole of the exploration which I recently made, accompanied by an experienced officer of the Police force, through the quarters of this City occupied by colored people, I met, in every direction, the most startling evidences of the powerful effects of prejudice. Of all the difficulties with which they have to contend, that of prejudice against them for their color's sake throws all others into the shade, and would seem under present circumstances to be almost insuperable. This is a feeling which is bitterly and intensely fostered by the Irish element, and quietly acquiesced in by a very large portion of native-born citizens. If a colored man applies for work at a new job, he always has to wait till the contractor sees whether he can get enough white laborers for his purpose before he is taken on, and it more often happens that he is at once refused employment, simply on the ground of his color, although the contractor who refuses to employ him, may be at the very moment short of his requisite number of hands; and, when he does succeed in getting work, he has to accept lower wages, and is always expected to work harder than a white man, while his fellow-workmen "put upon" him whenever they get the opportunity, and ceaselessly jeer at him and make him the butt of their jokes. To my inquiries, "Why do you not break up this wretched colony and move into more comfortable quarters," one invariable answer was returned: "We find it so difficult to persuade any one to rent us a decent place on account of our color. Hundreds of us would gladly pay twice the rent to live in some more respectable neighborhood; but the landlords will not accept us as tenants on any terms, declaring that, should they let a couple of rooms to a colored man, all their white lodgers would immediately give them notice to leave." It has happened on many occasions that men, who have succeeded in obtaining work at a long distance from their homes in the negro quarters, and who were naturally anxious to remove themselves and their families to the immediate neighborhood of their work, have actually offered to different landlords much more rent than they could possibly hope to get from white men, and have been curtly told: "I never let my rooms to a nigger." The consequence is that the poor fellow often has to walk three miles to and from his work; and three miles is a long distance after a hard day's labor. Again, many members of the Trades Unions refuse to work on a building job if colored men be employed; and the Irish, especially, have often made combinations to compel the masters to discharge them. Neither will they work for masters who take colored apprentices. I was informed by highly respectable persons, who were by no means desirous of glossing over the faults of their people, that they did not know a single workshop in this city where a colored man could get employment as an artisan, however respectable or however clever at his trade he might be, or where a colored lad would be taken as an apprentice.

But this prejudice against the African people, on account of their color, is by no means confined to the laboring classes. Respectable hotels almost invariably refuse to admit colored people within their doors. The proprietors of ice-cream, oyster and dining saloons, and the keepers of liquor stores, even of a second or third rate class, refuse to furnish them with refreshments. Rev. WILLIAM F. BUTLER, pastor of Zion Church, a man of gentlemanly manners and appearance, and of some considerable education, assured me that one day last Summer he entered, in company with Mrs. BUTLER, an ice-cream saloon, by no means a fashionable one, and requested to be supplied with refreshments; in answer to which request he was informed that they were not in the habit of accommodating colored people, and must refuse to serve him. On another occasion, not long ago,

Mr. BUTLER walked into a dining saloon on Sixth-avenue, about 4 o'clock in the afternoon. The place was empty, and he was readily served with dinner, which he partook of, paid for, and departed without a single remark being made by the proprietor. A day or two afterward he repaired to the same saloon, but on this occasion at midday. The dining-room was nearly full of white people. The proprietor immediately walked across the saloon to him, and informed him that he could not dine there at that hour, but if he chose to come later in the afternoon, after all their white customers had left, he would then allow him to be served with dinner, but not before.

Again, some of the theatres refused to admit colored persons at all, while those who do condescend to do so only allow them to sit in one part of the house—the tier of seats immediately beneath the roof. But perhaps one of the most astonishing instances of this prejudice occurred last Summer; and that in a quarter from whence it might have been least anticipated. The Christian Convention of ministers of all denominations, which was then assembled in this City, thought proper to set the bad example of Christian charity and brotherly love to all the world of not inviting their colored brother ministers to attend their sittings.

The only class in this City who appear to be really uninfluenced by this intolerant spirit of prejudice against the color of the negro are the Germans. They seem, as a general thing, to have no objection to let lodgings to them; they willingly employ them and pay them fair wages—quite as much as they would pay a white man of equal skill and powers of work. Moreover, when they do employ a colored man, they treat him properly, and not simply as *the nigger*.

After making a searching and patient inquiry into the condition, ways and habits of the colored population of New-York, I can come to but one conclusion—that, in spite of all their efforts to the contrary, they are kept back by circumstances over which they themselves have no control; that if they could get rid of this inveterate and all-powerful hostility of the Irish to them, on account of their color, they would soon make rapid progress; but that till that desirable consummation is brought about, they will go on much in the same way as they have done for years past. There are many among them, very intelligent and well-educated men, who are exceedingly anxious to improve the position of their race; but they feel that till this prejudice against color is removed, it is next to impossible to them to achieve any substantial results, and that their efforts are all being wasted. The consequences of this prejudice are daily more and more demoralizing certain classes of them; and many are undoubtedly led into the commission of larceny, and so on to greater crimes, from the evil effect of its influences.

CRIMINAL STATISTICS.

Much stress is laid by some unthinking persons on the unusually heavy proportion of criminals among the colored population of this City. There is no denying that crime does exist among them to a deplorable extent, but not to anything like the amount that is generally supposed. A careful analysis of the official statistics of crime published annually by the Board of Commissioners of Public Charities and Correction, accompanied by a fair and just consideration of all the circumstances of the case, would, I think, lead unbiased persons to considerably modify their views on this head. I find that during the year 1867 there were no less than 47,313 men and women committed to prison from the different City Police Courts—46,144 whites, or about 5 1-5 per cent. of the whole white population, taking it at 900,000, and 1,169 blacks, or 9¾ per cent. of the whole colored population, taking it at 12,000. This would give very nearly two colored criminals for every white one. But, where due allowance has been made for the fact that the colored population, with few exceptions, are all poor, that numbers of them, however willing they may be to work, find the greatest difficulty in obtaining employment, that there is a terrible amount of ignorance among the lower classes of them, and that they labor under social disadvantages to which no other race in the universe is exposed; and, when we consider that those equally poor among the white population are but a small proportion of its total, (there is, perhaps, no metropolitan city in the world where there is so little real poverty as there is in the City of New-York,) and the great bulk of which contributes but a very small quota to the criminal classes, it must be conceded that the proportion of colored criminals is not greater than, if even so great as, that of the whites; certainly nothing like so great as the proportion of criminals among their great enemies, the Irish, who contributed 21,079 persons to the City prisons during the year 1867, against 15,871 native Americans, 7,336 Germans, 1,421 English, 363 French, 410 Scotch, 228 Italians, and 290 Canadians. The criminal classes are, incontestably, recruited from among the poor and uneducated. Of the 47,313 persons committed to the City prisons in 1867, the degree of education of 255 was unknown; 625 were well-educated; 30,390 could only read and write; 12,604 could only read, and 3,439 could neither read nor write. It would then be a fairer mode of making a comparison between the white and colored criminal classes to take a ratio of proportion of the poor and uneducated in each race, and then to work out the percentage of criminals from that ratio. Moreover, the colored people assert that the offences committed among them are by no means of so serious a character as those committed among the whites; and that whereas many whites somehow or other manage to escape the punishment to which they have rendered themselves liable, no colored man is ever allowed to get off.

Another great disadvantage under which many of them labor, arises from the fact that this species of ostracism from respectable neighborhoods compels numbers of them to reside in the Eighth Ward. In that district they are all packed like sardines in a box, in ricketty old houses, whose walls, floors and staircases are begrimed with dirt and where a decent mode of living is almost impossible; some of the houses being actually unprovided with water-closets of any description. It is hardly to be expected where the common decencies of life cannot be observed, that demoralization and degradation can be avoided. Many of the people are so poor that they are compelled to resort to the pawnshops in the Winter time in order to provide food and fuel for their families; and thus, from want of work, their furniture and clothing go, bit by bit, till there is nothing left for them but the workhouse or a prison. However, this is not the case with all of them, and it is wonderful to see how clean and comfortable many of these poor people will make even the miserable rooms in which they live look. But in these instances I generally found that the man or his wife had employment of some kind or another. It is another example of the old saying, that "misery makes men callous."

COLORED GAMBLERS.

I would divide the colored people into two distinct classes—those who are willing to work, and those who would not work if they could get the opportunity. The first and far larger class are quiet, inoffensive and respectable, and remain at home at night; the second are always in the streets day and night, lounging in and out of liquor-stores, policy-shops and gambling-houses, and have mostly got thief written on their faces. They meet at the various bucket-shops about to plan burglaries and robberies from the person; and when they have succeeded in robbing some store or some unhappy wayfarer, and have converted their plunder into money at the "receivers," they go off to the "faro" or to the "sweat" table to get rid of it, for they are just as inveterate gamblers as their white light-fingered brethren. "Sweat," though a very simple game, is extremely popular among them. The proprietor of the place sits at an oblong table covered with black glaze cloth, surrounded by a crowd of eager and excited victims. Six hollow squares are painted in white on the cloth in a straight line, and in the centre of each square are painted the numbers 1, 2, 3, 4, 5, 6. They stake any amount they please, from ten cents to $10, placing their stake on some particular number. They then throw three dice from a box on to the table, and if their number shows uppermost they get back their money and as much more; if not, they lose their stake. I watched the proprietor of one of these tables very narrowly for some time, but could not detect the slightest unfairness on his part. At one of these places a strapping young fellow played till he had lost every cent. He then left the room, but returned in five minutes, saying that he had earned ten cents by helping a man lift a heavy cask into a cart. This sum he also staked, lost it, and again retired, abusing his luck in anything but parlor language. In two or three minutes he returned once more, this time having borrowed ten cents. This he put down on his old number, won, backed his luck, and a quarter of an hour or twenty minutes afterward, when I took my departure, he had several dollar bills in his hand and was still playing. At "faro" they play much higher stakes. The proprietor of one of these tables informed me that on the previous evening he had lost over $300. Nothing seems to put a stop to this gambling. The houses are frequently "pulled" by the Police and shut up, only to be reopened in the nearest alley, or even next door. Not long ago the Police arrested sixty-eight persons in one of these places; the cards, checks, spring-boxes, and all the apparatus for playing, which was beautifully and expensively made, were destroyed, but not the gentleman's business. He has plenty of money, his trade of gambling-hell keeper is sufficiently profitable to stand a loss of this description, and after one of these little accidents, which he looks upon as a part of his business, he obtains a new stock in trade and soon flourishes again. On one of these occasions when one of these houses was "pulled," one of the players, whose occupation was that of a white-washer, on seeing the Police come in, called out somewhat ostentatiously to the proprietor: "Say, boss, where's the old woman gone to; I want to get my money for doing them cellin's and be off." Unluckily, however, for this cute negro, the ceiling happened to be a particularly grimy one, and he had to accompany the rest of them to the cells.

COLORED DANCE-HOUSES.

Of course the colored people must have their dance-houses like the rest of the world, though the women are not costumed in the style of Water-street. I went into one of these places in Laurens-street. Passing through a narrow alley into a dirty court-yard, surrounded by tumble-down houses, I ascended four flights of a ricketty outside staircase, and found myself in a large, low room, something like an empty carpenter's shop, with a bar at one end, and an orchestra, composed of a banjo, a fiddle, and an awfully shrill piccolo at the other. Every one in the room was colored, and nearly all the girls were smoking the filthiest of cigars. They danced a quadrille, a sort of mixture of every dance under the sun, and then a gentleman volunteered to dance a jig for my especial gratification. His performance was decidedly clever. The rapidity with which he moved his feet, and still managed to keep time to the music, was surprising, and yet, when he had finished his performance, he showed no outward signs of fatigue. The whole thing reminded me much of the children's toy—the figure of a black man at the end of a board with a spring to it, which dances when you tap the board with your fingers. This gentleman insisted upon my joining him in a drink at the bar (at my expense.) Of course I was too wary to do more than sip the stuff the proprietor presented to me, although he assured me that it was the finest "Old Rye" to be found in the City of New-York. I can only say that it enabled me fully to account for the fact mentioned to me by my detective, that the people turn out from this dance-house every morning fighting, quarreling and yelling like madmen.

Turning into Wooster-street, I entered a tenement-house only too well-known in that neighborhood as No. 40. If the builder of this house was anxious to erect a place where thieves could play hide-and-seek, and elude the pursuit of the Police, he has certainly succeeded to his heart's content. On entering I was immediately beset by a bevy of the lowest class of negro prostitutes, but on recognizing the detective who escorted me, in spite of his citizen's dress, they soon made off, not feeling quite sure that some of them might not be "wanted." I should think it would be just about as difficult to catch a burglar in that alley, with its many windings and outside staircases, as it would be to catch a wild cat on the house-tops or a pig with a greased tail.

At the corner of Wooster-street my detective called up a tall, powerful, masculine-looking woman, with an arm that would almost fell a bullock, who was standing at the door of a low liquor store known in the neighborhood as "The African Capitol," which is the favorite resort of the refuse of the colored people, and addressing her, said: "Kate, take your shawl off your head and let this gentleman look at you." She did so, and I was astonished to see that she was a red-haired negress—a dark skin, and hair as red as that of any Celt. She was apparently about seven or eight and twenty, but so whisky-soddened that she might have been younger. This woman gets drunk nearly every night, decoys men into dark alleys under the pretence of prostitution and then robs them. She is the terror of the Police, and knows pretty well every nail in every plank in the cells. This corner is the worst part of the district. There is scarcely a night passes without a disturbance of some kind, when these wretched creatures, infuriated with drinking five-cent tumblers or buckets of what is called whisky (!) are turned out from the Capitol at the hour for closing up.

MISCEGENATION.

In the course of my wanderings through the negro quarters, I was particularly struck with the fact that, whereas I found numerous cases of white women living with colored men, (one gentleman I came across luxuriating in two, who happened to be fighting at the moment of my visit,) I did not find a single instance of a white man living with a colored woman; and strange to say, in all the cases of miscegenation which I met with, the women seemed to have picked out the lowest and the most brutal-looking men that they could possibly find.

It is difficult adequately to express the wide margin existing between the highest and lowest class of negroes. They must be seen in their own homes and haunts in order to properly appreciate the difference. The bulk of them, I am inclined to think, have all the elements in them of useful citizenship. Many among them, if they had but a fair chance, would assuredly make a name and a position for themselves, while others are congenitally of so low a type of intellect, and consequently of such low habits, both mental and bodily, as to be little better than mere animals. The more intelligent and thoughtful among the colored people seem to think that little can be done with the present generation, whose better instincts they declare have been ground out of them by tyranny. They centre all their hopes and wishes on the coming one, and spare no pains to improve and educate the children. G.

March 2, 1869

"APARTMENTS TO LET. T."

When the letter T appears in red upon the placards which announce that apartments are to let it means that another "black belt" is to be established in this city. A white owner has had a quarrel with white tenants or with an adjacent landlord, and has handed over his house to negro management. Another prosperous residential block in Harlem is to be depreciated in value and opened to negro tenantry on Sept. 1. That is the threat. Incidentally, the property is for sale at something above its appraised valuation. Will the nearby landlords buy it, thus heading off the negro invaders?

They will either do this, or sell to smart negro speculators their own properties at three-fourths their valuation. Race prejudice in this city is capitalized, and this is the way the colored folk reap the rewards of the prejudice. White tenants move away. Apartments which they vacate must be let at lower rentals and to negro tenants. Only one thing will prevent the planting of the black spots in all parts of the city's residential area and their rapid extension into "belts." That is by voluntary agreements of property holders, similar to that entered into early this year by ninety-eight owners in a certain neighborhood in Harlem, not to allow any part of their premises "to be occupied in whole or in part by any negro, mulatto, quadroon, or octoroon, of either sex, whether as a tenant, guest, boarder, or occupant in any other capacity."

The rigor of this prohibition is somewhat mitigated by clauses permitting the employment of negro servants, and by the careful statement that the property owners do not desire "to preclude or prevent negroes or citizens of African descent from occupying the premises because of their color or race." They wish merely to prevent the depreciation of their property by such methods as that described above. If those methods are legal and do not come within the definition of blackmail, certainly agreements by property holders to resist them are fair and legal. If landlords' covenants of restriction become general, the red-letter placards will no longer hang as disturbing signs of race prejudice, designedly fomented for gain.

August 25, 1911

RACE RIOTERS FIRE EAST ST. LOUIS AND SHOOT OR HANG MANY NEGROES; DEAD ESTIMATED AT FROM 20 TO 75

MANY BODIES IN THE RUINS

Mobs Rage Unchecked for 24 Hours Till Military Rule Is Established.

Special to The New York Times.

EAST ST. LOUIS, Ill., July 2.—Many negroes have been killed in race riots which have been raging here since Sunday night. At a late hour most estimates of the dead range from twenty to seventy-five, of whom three were white men. The negroes were shot down by mobs as they fled from their homes, which the whites had set on fire. The disturbances arose out of the ill-feeling engendered by the importation of negro labor from the South.

State Attorney Schaumloeffel of St. Clair County, in which East St. Louis is situated, drove through the riot district tonight with Police Inspector Walsh of St. Louis, Mo. The State's Attorney estimated that the dead negroes would number 250, but all estimates are conjectural.

Thousands of persons were in the mobs. The rioting is a renewal of race troubles that occurred here a month ago, following the importation of large numbers of negro laborers from the South.

Military rule was proclaimed at 8 o'clock tonight, and at the same time 300 white men were arrested and locked up at Police Headquarters.

Nearly 500 negro men, women, and children are quartered in the City Hall and the police station. At frequent intervals all evening, and until late at night, trucks brought negro refugees from burning sections to augment the cowering groups at these refugee buildings, where a strong guard of troops was stationed. Terror spread among the black men and women at 10:30 P. M., when all the lights in both buildings suddenly went out, due to the destruction of electric wires in the downtown district.

Adjt. Gen. Frank S. Dickson of Illinois arrived and took charge of the situation late tonight. He went into conference immediately with military and civil authorities to outline a plan of procedure. In answer to a question as to why the troops on the ground when the trouble developed did not use force to put down the rioting, General Dickson said the purposes for which the soldiers were sent here had been gained without firing a shot, and that wholesale bloodshed would have been the result of any firing on the part of the troops.

"Five hundred rioters, the ringleaders of the largest mob, I am informed, are now under arrest," said General Dickson. "This was accomplished by surrounding the rioters and forcing them to submit without shooting or employing the bayonet."

General Dickson said after the 500 were taken into custody the disturbance at once took on a less serious aspect.

One of the fires which was started in the negro belt between Third Street and Railroad Avenue spread beyond the control of city firemen, and is threatening the business section of the city at a late hour. Another fire, started by part of the mob in Black Valley, a negro segregated district, between Fourth and Sixth Streets and Broadway and Railroad Avenue, spread until the firefighters admitted that it, too, was beyond their control.

Loss $3,000,000 Already.

The property loss so far is estimated by City Attorney Fekete at $3,000,000. At 11 P. M. another fire had broken out in the extreme northern portion of the city, where there is a negro section. This brought the burning sections to four, lighting the entire city with their glare.

Colonel Tripp, Assistant Adjutant General, stated shortly before midnight that the rioting crowds had for the most part dispersed.

When a report came to military authorities that negroes of Brooklyn, Ill., were moving on East St. Louis, a truck full of guardsmen was sent to the bridge to meet any attack that might be attempted. At the same time another truckload of soldiers was rushed to a corner near the Post Office, where negroes barricaded in upstairs quarters had been firing at soldiers standing guard in the street below.

The worst property damage was done along the tracks of the Southern Railroad Company, where the Southern's warehouse and between 100 and 150 cars, many of them loaded with merchandise, were consumed by flames. The damage there was estimated at between $.00,000 and $500,000.

The Broadway Theatre, valued at $100,000, was destroyed. At night the flames were moving steadily along the tracks, almost unhindered by the feeble efforts of the firemen which were directed toward preventing the blaze from spreading to more important buildings.

Soldiers Ordered to Shoot.

All street railway traffic was suspended at 7 P. M., and theatres and saloons were ordered closed. At that hour, the militiamen were given instructions to shoot to kill in suppressing the white mobs. They at once started a tour of the city, rounding up the blood-mad men, who were out to avenge the death of Policeman Coppedge and William Kayser, a hardware merchant, two of the white men killed.

The third white man killed was Thomas Moore of Granite City. He was standing beside a soldier when a bullet struck him. The shot apparently was intended for the soldier.

Thirty-five houses in Black Valley were in flames within half an hour after the fire started. The blaze spread fast toward the centre of the business district. All fire apparatus in the city was assembled at Third Street and Broadway, where the firemen began a battle to save the town. When the flames reached Broadway a second general alarm was sounded, and apparatus from the St. Louis side of the river was rushed to East St. Louis.

It is estimated that 50,000 men and women were in the streets and that more than two-thirds of this number were armed. Small boys carried revolvers and were shooting at the blacks. Two hundred militiamen were on duty in the zone affected by the fire, but despite fixed bayonets they were unable to control the mob.

Every hospital on the east side is filled with blacks who are so severely injured that many will probably die. Police headquarters is packed with negroes badly beaten and shot. It is estimated that eighty negroes and ten white men have been injured.

One section of the mob gathered around a lone negro on Fourth Street, near Broadway. A rope was thrown around his neck and he was hoisted up a telephone pole, but the rope broke. Men and women in the mob shouted gleefully as the negro fell into the gutter, while half a dozen men riddled his body with bullets. Negroes are lying in the gutters every few feet in some places.

Girls Join the Mob.

Seized with the mob spirit, two young white girls climbed on a car at Broadway and Main Street about 4 P. M. and dragged a negro woman from her seat. As they pulled her through the door of the car to the street, there was a [illegible]eat cheer from men standing on the sidewalk. The negro woman attempted to break away from her assailants, and one of the girls pulled off her shoe and started to beat the victim over the head. The woman flinched under the blows, and was bleeding profusely when rescued by militiamen. The girls were not arrested, and walked away from the scene. There were blood stains on their clothes, and as they passed their friends they told about the part they had played in the riot.

Whenever a white man attempted to drag a negro from the street, intending to give him medical attention, the mob, with drawn pistols, forced him to desist. Several negroes who were killed were thrown into Cahokia Creek.

A mob of more than 100 men, led by ten or fifteen young girls about 18 years old, chased a negro woman at the Relay Depot about 5 o'clock. The girls were brandishing clubs and calling upon the men to kill the woman.

A lone negro man appeared in the railroad yards. The mob immediately gave up the chase of the woman and turned upon the man. He was shot to death.

Militiamen Fire a Volley.

About 8:30 o'clock a mob of more than 500 men, all heavily armed, charged into the negro district on Third Street and set fire to a number of houses. Before these men could start other fires two companies of militiamen, numbering more than 200, charged with fixed bayonets. A volley was fired over the heads of the mob, which then dispersed.

Charles Beach, an ambulance driver for the Deaconess Hospital, was shot and seriously wounded at Tenth and Bond Streets. He was accompanied on the ambulance by John Cange, who was not hit. Negroes congregated at Tenth and Duncan Streets and fired a fusilade into the ambulance. But for Cange's quick action it is likely the automobile would have crashed into a house and turned over. As Beach fell limp from the seat Cange took the wheel and drove with him to the hospital.

While straggling groups of soldiers and police looked on, a large crowd of white men gathered at Fourth Street and Broadway at 7:30 o'clock and captured two negroes who ran from the rear of a burning building. Placing a rope around their necks, the mob attempted to hang them to a telephone pole. The police and soldiers did not offer any interference. Finding the rope inadequate for the weight of the men, they were dragged screaming, to an alley, where many shots were fired into their bodies.

One of the negroes was dragged back to the pole and a new rope was tied around his neck. As two white men attempted to pull him into the air, the rope broke, throwing the white men on their backs, to the amusement of the mob. The negro fell to the ground, dead.

Three more negroes were seen by the mob as the terrorized blacks were trying to escape from a burning building. One of them was strung up to a telephone pole and the other two were shot. The bodies were left in the street.

Colonel Tripp early in the evening figured in the rescue of a negro who was being dragged down Broadway by a rope attached to his neck. The automobile bearing the Colonel and City Attorney Fekete appeared when a mob was in the act of stringing the negro to a telephone pole. Colonel Tripp leaped from the automobile and persuaded the white attackers to desist from their plan to kill the negro.

City Attorney Fekete later in the night saved the life of another young negro who was running from a crowd which had fired a number of shots at him while he was visible in the glare of burning buildings. Fekete placed the negro in his automobile, and, after arguing for ten minutes with the group of men, succeeded in gaining their consent to allow him to take the negro to the City Hall for protection.

Negroes Seized on Street Cars.

The whites began their attacks on street cars shortly before noon, and several negroes were taken from the cars and beaten or pelted with bricks. Eight negroes were injured in this manner before 1 o'clock.

At 1:30 o'clock a crowd of whites pulled the trolley from an Edwardsville car. A mob entered the car and dragged out all the negro passengers. One of them was kicked and beaten by the crowd and then shot. He died in an ambulance on the way to a hospital.

A Bellevue car appeared next. White women as well as men entered the car and pulled out the negroes. Women and girls seized terrified negro women, kicked and clubbed them, and sent them screaming down the street.

Shortly after 2 o'clock the mob pursued a negro down Collinsville Avenue. He was caught and severely beaten. A militiaman stood guard over him and tried to keep the crowd back, but was hustled aside. Fifteen other militiamen who ran to his aid were disarmed. Men in the mob fired the rifles and returned them to the soldiers.

One hundred white men met at Labor Temple Hall, 406 Collinsville Avenue, marched down the avenue, and at Broadway, the most important transfer point in the city, they encountered a negro on a street car. He attempted to run out the front end of the car, but was seized, knocked down, and repeatedly kicked. As he lay on the ground a white man in the mob standing over him fired six bullets into his body.

The mob then turned back down the street, at the mouth of Black Valley, where fifty negroes had assembled. The white men turned again, and in front of the Illmo Hotel came upon a lone negro. He ran, and the white mob hurled bricks at him. Some one fired two shots at the fleeing black, but he managed to escape.

At least 6,000 white men and women paraded through the downtown streets shortly after noon demanding that the authorities force every negro to leave town. Riot calls swept into Police Headquarters, and patrol wagons dashed about the city in what appeared to be a futile effort to stop the growing disregard of the mobs for law and order. In many instances the patrol wagons were bombarded with bricks and other missiles, and policemen were openly jeered.

Negroes Fire on Police.

The disorder began when a mob of 200 negroes fired on an automobile load of policemen last night, killing one. For several days there had been evidences of bad blood, and on Saturday night minor clashes between whites and blacks had occurred. These clashes apparently alarmed the negro quarter of the city, or at least gave agitators a chance to organize the blacks for fighting. When word was telephoned to Police Headquarters that the ringing of a church bell had called armed negroes together, an automobile loaded with police left for the scene to disperse the crowd. The police were met with a volley. Detective Sergeant Coppedge was killed and three policemen were wounded.

C. W. Wallace, editor of a negro religious publication, said the firing on the police was due to a misunderstanding. According to Wallace's account, a negro minister, a negro physician, and himself were returning from St. Louis last night when they saw white "joy riders" ride down a block in Market Street inhabited by negroes and fire into the houses. The neighborhood was aroused and the negroes armed themselves. Wallace did not see the negro mob fire on an automobile filled with policemen, but he said a witness told him that the negroes thought when the police automobile stopped it was the joy riders returning. The shooting began, he was told, before this misunderstanding was removed. It was said that the policemen were in plain clothes.

Race troubles here began late in May as a result of the heavy influx of negro labor. Labor leaders then expressed a fear that the negro labor was being imported to break anticipated strikes during the Summer.

On May 28 a crowd of white men demanded of the City Council that the negro immigration be stopped. Mayor Mollman tried to calm the crowd, saying that an investigation would be ordered. After the meeting had adjourned, white mobs stopped street cars and dragged negroes off and beat them.

The next day State troops arrived. There was considerable disturbance the night of May 29, two white men and three negroes being shot. Within a day or two order was restored, and a few days later the troops were withdrawn.

An investigation by the State Council of Defense was made, and it reported that labor agents had induced negroes to come here from the South. This report was made public last Saturday. Up to that time there had been no serious indications of a renewal of the rioting.

July 3, 1917

More State Troops to Check Rioters; Federal Troops Ready For the Call

SPRINGFIELD, Ill., July 2.—Six additional companies of State troops were ordered to East St. Louis for riot duty tonight, making a total of twelve companies detailed there. Adjt. Gen. Frank S. Dickson left for the scene to take command.

General Dickson said the troops were under orders of the civil authorities of East St. Louis, and only in the event of martial law being declared would they be under orders from the State.

"I do not know whether they have been instructed not to fire on the rioters," he said.

WASHINGTON, July 2.—It was said tonight in an official quarter that Major Gen. Thomas H. Barry, commanding the Central Military Department, with headquarters at Chicago, had authority to act if the necessity arose for sending United States troops to East St. Louis, Ill., to control the situation there due to race riots.

July 3, 1917

14 ARE KILLED AND 76 WOUNDED IN CHICAGO RIOTING; 4,000 TROOPS CALLED OUT TO QUELL NEGRO OUTBREAKS; WILSON IN CAPITOL CONFERENCE URGES SPEED ON TREATY

STREET BATTLES AT NIGHT

Five Negroes Are Killed in One Fight—Rioting Subsides at Midnight

NINE WHITES AMONG DEAD

Negroes Storm Armory in Effort to Obtain Arms and Ammunition.

SOUTH SIDE TERRORIZED

Gangs Stone Vehicles and Beat Up and Stab Lone Whites and Blacks.

Special to The New York Times.

CHICAGO, July 28.—Rioting that ended in looting, arson, and murder broke loose in Chicago's "black belt" tonight. It was the most serious race rioting that has ever stained the history of Illinois. Before midnight fourteen had been killed and seventy-six injured. Of the dead nine were white. Twenty-nine white persons were hurt and forty-seven negroes.

The disorder, which had been going on all day, grew serious at night with the hurling of bricks and the firing of revolvers at Thirty-fifth Street and Wabash Avenue at 7:30 o'clock. Before many hours passed the outbreaks had spread to the Stock Yards district, to Thirty-fifth and Halstead Streets, all through the "black belt" and into the Hyde Park district.

Every available policeman in the city was rushed to the scene; former soldiers and sailors were sworn in; the National Guard and the reserve militia regiments had been called out and were being mobilized; the hospitals were crowded with victims; the street cars and the elevated trains had ceased to run on the south side; telephone wires were cut; scores of white men and black were under arrest.

The Night Victims.

Among the dead in tonight's riots are:

DILLON, OGIST, negro; beaten to death after being dragged off street car.

WARNOCK, NICK, white, 18 years old; shot and killed.

SUNBURG, ALEX., white; killed by bullet at Thirty-seventh Street and Wabash Avenue.

BAKER, HENRY, colored, kneeling in front of his window at 544 East Thirty-seventh Street reading his Bible, as was his nightly custom, shot through the eye by negroes passing in an automobile; died in Provident Hospital.

MARKS, DAVID, white, 509 East Thirty-seventh Street; shot and killed by colored man.

ATANBERG, ALEX., colored; shot through heart and killed in Thirty-first Street, near Wabash Avenue.

GENTLE, EUGENE, white; died at Provident Hospital of stab wounds inflicted by four negroes at State and Thirty-seventh Streets.

DEDRICK, ——, white, motorman; dragged off car at Wabash Avenue and Thirty-fifth Street by negroes and killed.

SIMPSON, JOHN H., colored, policeman, 31; shot through the abdomen at Wabash Avenue and East Twenty-seventh Street; died in Mercy Hospital.

UNIDENTIFIED white man, believed to be Polish; killed by bullet at Forty-third and State Streets.

Unidentified negro, taken off car at Wenthworth Avenue and Root Street and beaten to death.

A Soldier Slain.

Major Frederick Haynes, commanding a battalion of the 1st Reserve, and Corporal Williams of Company C of that unit were among the first casualties. Major Haynes, who lives at 4,050 Prairie Avenue, was found in front of 3,733 Indiana Avenue with the back of his head crushed and his back broken.

Corporal Williams was shot in the shoulder by a sniper as he was going toward the Eighth Regiment Armory, where his company was assembling.

An automobile containing Adjt. Gen. Dickson, First Deputy John H. Alcock, Colonel R. R. Ronayne of the regular army, and Charles Fitzmorris, secretary to Mayor Thompson, was fired upon by snipers in the vicinity of Thirty-sixth Street and Vincennes Avenue, but they escaped injury.

Fierce Fight in the Street.

The fighting at Thirty-fifth Street was the fiercest of the early evening. Here five negroes were killed and scores wounded, two policemen were wounded, one of them after he had made a barricade of his horse and fought, Indian fashion, from the cover of his mount.

The battle started when negroes, in groups of 50 and 100, began firing on isolated policemen. One of these was Policeman William Kross, one of the first to be wounded. Another was Officer Walter Brooks of the mounted squad.

Brooks, when hit, forced his horse to lie down and fired from behind him. Traffic Policeman Otto Newman was reported to have been killed in this battle.

Meantime riot calls went to the Stock Yards Station, the Deering Station, and the Cottage Grove Avenue Station, and patrol loads of police began to pour into the battle.

At the same time a report came in that negroes were breaking into the old 8th Infantry Armory at Thirty-fifth Street and Forest Avenue to obtain rifles and ammunition, and part of the reserve policemen were diverted there, checking the attack.

The Call for the Troops.

The threatening situation early in the evening caused Mayor Thompson and Chief of Police Garrity to apply to Governor Lowden for militia. As a result four regiments, the 11th Illinois Infantry and the 1st, 2d, and 3d Reserve Militia Regiments, comprising 3,500 men, were ordered mobilized by Adjt. Gen. Frank S. Dickson.

The 11th Regiment, under Colonel James E. Burke, with its machine gun company was ordered to assemble at the old 2d Infantry Armory; the 1st Reserve, under Colonel A. F. Lorenzen, in the old 8th Infantry Armory; the 3d Reserve, under Colonel Anson Bolte, in the old 7th Infantry Armory. The 2d Reserve, under Colonel Joseph Wilson, was ordered to hold itself in readiness for assembly at a point to be designated later.

General Dickson said he would remain in Chicago in charge of the military situation. He pointed out that the 11th Infantry and the 1st Reserve Regiments have machine gun companies with experienced machine gunners, and that the line companies of these two regiments and the 2d and 3d Reserve Regiments are armed with new Springfield rifles and Krag-Jörgensen carbines.

"They all have plenty of ammunition," said General Dickson, "and if all the race rioters on the South Side were to combine the militiamen would be able to handle the situation."

One report was that the South Side colored men have 1,500 Springfield rifles of the type formerly used by the Government and placed on sale throughout the city in department stores after their condemnation for Government use. This was denied by colored Aldermen, but it was admitted that many of the negroes possessed arms of one kind or another and were prepared to defend themselves against aggression. The chief fear expressed was that the young hotheads might organize and start a general uprising.

The rioting today was an outgrowth of the fighting Sunday night, which started at the Twenty-ninth Street bathing beach and broke out sporadically at different places in the black belt until midnight.

At noon today five riot calls had been received by the police and all available mounted police were ordered into the South Side districts.

Lone Negro Is Stabbed.

Early in the afternoon white men gathered in groups and stoned, stabbed, or shot at lone colored men wherever they appeared. The negroes in retaliation formed gangs and began to stab, shoot, and throw missiles at automobiles, street cars, or wagons containing white men, and to attack those on the street who were not under actual protection of the police.

The most serious outbreaks today occurred at Thirty-ninth and Wallace Streets, twenty-ninth and State Streets, and Forty-third and Halstead Streets.

Those killed in the early fighting were:

Eugene Cappel, laundryman, white, 3,642 South State Street.

Kaspar Kazzouran, white, peddler, address unknown.

Unidentified negro.

Cappel had operated a laundry at the South State Street address for fifteen years. At 5 o'clock this afternoon, he, with his wife and daughter, closed the laundry and started for their automobile. He had a revolver in his hip pocket, four negroes saw him, rushed for him, and took his weapon from him. He was stabbed in the scuffle, once in the back and three times in the chest. His wife and daughter were severely beaten. All three were taken to the Providence Hospital. Cappel died there fifteen minutes later.

The killing of Kazzouran was witnessed by a large group. He sat on his wagon in front of 3,618 South State Street. A car stopped at the corner of Thirty-sixth and State, a colored man stepped off, ran to where Kazzouran sat, stabbed him in the back, ran half a block further north and boarded a northbound car. No one attempted to stop him.

The unidentified man who was killed was in the riot at Thirty-ninth and Wallace Streets. Thirty whites and nearly as many colored men began by throwing bricks and ended by shooting and stabbing. The negro ran toward Policeman John Condon in front of the Walker Vehicle Company, stumbled into his arms and died. Condon said he had to draw his revolver and threaten to shoot to protect the body from mutilation.

Wayne Dobbins, 3,337 Wabash Avenue, a stock yards employe, was badly beaten at Thirty-ninth and Wabash Avenue by a gang of ten white men.

Mob Gathers About Hotel.

Two unidentifed colored men were walking along Wabash Avenue, in front of the Angelus Hotel at Thirty-fifth Street. White men in the upper stories, it is said, threw bricks at them. A mob of 300 negroes gathered outside. Some shots were fired, but no casualties were reported.

At 7:30 tonight two automobiles, carrying eleven negroes, drove down Wentworth Avenue near Forty-seventh Street. The men were brandishing guns and threatening pedestrians. Policemen Condon and Brennan jumped on to the running board of the first car and Officers Smiley and Corbett on the second. Both machines were taken to the Stock Yards Station. The men in the cars were searched and each found to have a pistol and plenty of ammunition. It was reported that a white man had been shot by them at Forty-fifth Street and Wentworth Avenue, but the report was not verified.

A mob of several hundred white men gathered outside the station and Captain Gallerie ordered ten policemen with shotguns to take posts at the door to prevent an effort to storm the station house.

Marshall Tylus, colored, 3,802 Prairie Avenue, was picked up badly beaten on the car tracks at Forty-seventh and Halstead Streets. He was taken to the Dearborn Hospital.

Wesley Combs, 5,330 Federal Street, was attacked by five white men and badly beaten at Thirty-ninth Street and Emerald Avenue.

John Young, James McLinden and William Smith, all colored, were beaten at Forty-first Street and South Halsted Street by eight white men.

Albert West and Frank Anderson, colored, were set upon at Fifty-first Street and Racine Avenue. Anderson was so badly stabbed that at the Deaconess Hospital it was said he might die. West disappeared.

Willis Smith met a white man in front of 314 Fox Street. They exchanged words and Smith was stabbed in the back as he started to run. He is in a hospital.

Charles Grady, colored, was stoned just as he was about to enter his home, and Charles Plessyenski, white, was arrested, charged with assault.

An elderly colored woman was beaten up at Twenty-sixth Street and Armour Avenue by four white boys not over 15 years old. A police ambulance took her to a hospital.

An unidentified white man was chased for three blocks by a gang and caught just as he attempted to board a State Street car at Thirty-seventh Street. He was badly beaten.

An unidentified negro, during an outbreak at Thirty-sixth and Clark Streets, was slashed across the abdomen by a white man, but he made his way to a drug store where first aid was given and then disappeared.

A crowd of white men stopped an eastbound Forty-seventh Street car at Wallace Street, and after breaking all the windows dragged Grant Jackson, colored, 134 West Thirty-fourth Street, to the street and beat him. His right leg was broken.

Policemen were rushed to Twenty-ninth Street and Wallace Avenue at 8 o'clock, when it was reported that a white woman and her child had been shot and wounded by negro rioters who fired from an automobile. When the police arrived the woman had been taken home by friends.

Six discharged negro soldiers aided the police in stopping impending outbreaks at the same corner when crowds lined up on opposite sides of the street and began throwing bricks.

William L. Brady, white, 1,138 North Hammond Avenue, was severely beaten by negroes armed with stones. He was going south on State Street in an automobile. The mob swarmed around it, dragged Brady out, and began beating him. Detective Sergeant Friend rescued Brady and took him to St. Luke's Hospital.

At Thirty-fourth Street negroes pulled down the trolley of a street car and beat Frank L. Webb, cashier of the Central Manufacturing District Bank, cutting his head with a stone. Webb was taken to the Mercy Hospital.

In the mêlée that followed Raymond Meux, colored, 6,211 South Wabash Avenue, was shot through the body. He was taken to the Bridewell Hospital.

An eyewitness to the riot at Thirty-fifth and States Streets tonight, William Linton, editor of The Chicago Whip, a negro newspaper, said:

"There were 500 or 600 blacks, mostly boys about 16 to 18, gathered underneath the elevated structure.

"Ten police were trying to get them to move on when a colored man shouted an insult at them. The officers fired their revolvers into the crowd, killing five and wounding twenty.

"Alderman De Priest, (colored,) was in the midst of the mêlée. A man was shot dead alongside of him."

To save their employes from danger the Chicago Telephone Company announced tonight that it would allow none of the girls living on the south side to go home and would make accommodations for them.

Street car service was stopped in the "black belt" and the elevated railroads declared that because the negroes were shooting at the trains the service would be abandoned.

Today's riot caused the most complete concentration of the police force in a given district which the city has seen in years.

With four regiments of militia mobilizing, Chief of Police Garrity tonight ordered 1,000 extra policemen into the south side colored area.

Both Chief Garrity and First Deputy Alcock admitted that the "south side situation is dead serious." The First Deputy declared it to be "an unexploded powder mine."

At a meeting of the City Council Alderman John Passmore of the Police Committee declared that both whites and colored men in the affected area must be disarmed if a catastrophe is to be averted.

Politics is to blame for the race rioting in the opinion of State's Attorney MacLayhoyne.

"The present race riots," said the Prosecutor, "are no surprise to me, and I do not believe they are a surprise to the officers of the Police Department. The Police Department is so demoralized by politicians, both black and white, on the south side that the police are afraid to arrest men who are supposed to have political backing.

"I am investigating a case in which it is charged a certain white politician has gone about distributing revolvers and cartridges among vicious colored persons who would be likely to engage in race rioting."

July 29, 1919

Negroes Flocking to Michigan.

LANSING, Mich., June 26—Young negroes are flocking to Michigan industrial centres by the hundreds, according to a report made to the State Administrative Board today. The report, submitted by L. Whitney Watkins, Commissioner of Agriculture, and Carl Young, Labor Commissioner, blames unrest, prevalent among young negroes since the war, and conditions in the South, for the influx.

June 27, 1923

NEGROES TO OCCUPY 12% OF U. S. HOUSING

Their Tenancy Ratio Is Based on 744,000 Dwellings in Current Program

MANY IN OFFICIAL POSTS

WASHINGTON, April 27—Negro tenants will occupy about 88,000 public housing units, representing 12 per cent of a total of 744,000 dwellings, and developed at a cost of more than $360,000,000 when the current public housing program is completed, Herbert Emmerich, Commissioner of the Federal Public Housing Authority, announced.

According to recent estimates, about 42,000 of these dwellings will be provided by the War Housing Program which reached a total of 612,000 units on March 15. Provision for Negro tenants is 7 per cent of this program.

Under the low-rent, non-war program, which made available 132,000 homes, almost 46,000 are finished and occupied by Negro tenants. Many of these low-rent dwellings, in war-production centers now house Negro war workers. The scarcity of critical materials and labor has necessitated the suspension of building under the low-rent program for the duration of the war. Consequently, almost 3,500 of the low-rent dwellings authorized and planned for tenancy by Negroes are now temporarily suspended.

In the development of the total housing program Negro construction workers had earned more than $33,000,000 by the end of 1942. This represented 12 per cent of total payroll expenditures. Negro craftsmen had received $7,000,000 or 4 per cent of the total paid to skilled workers.

About 16,000 of the war dwellings for Negro workers brought into war-production areas have been finished, and 18,000 are under way.

In addition to Negro construction workers, Negro manpower has been utilized in the management and maintenance of public housing projects. More than 1,000 Negroes are currently employed in various capacities such as managers, engineers, clerical assistants and custodial workers. One hundred and thirty Negroes are now in charge of projects.

Approximately 140 Negroes are employed on the departmental staff of the FPHA in Washington, and forty are working in FPHA regional offices. Among these are three lawyers, three architects, an area management supervisor, a project planner and a junior management assistant recruited from the ranks of housing apprentices trained in the agency.

April 28, 1943

23 DEAD IN DETROIT RIOTING; FEDERAL TROOPS ENTER CITY ON THE ORDERS OF ROOSEVELT

INJURED REACH 600

Theatres Closed, Liquor Sales Banned as U. S. Sends Armored Cars

STRICT CURFEW ORDERED

Roaming Bands Loot Stores, Stone Trolley Cars as Wild Fighting Continues in Night

By The United Press.

DETROIT, June 21—Federal troops in full battle regalia, with jeeps, trucks and armored cars, moved into Detroit tonight to help city police, home guards and State troops restore order in the country's worst race riots since the East St. Louis (Ill.) disturbances in the first World War.

[After Federal troops arrived and President Roosevelt's proclamation calling for peace had been received, rioters dispersed and quiet was restored, according to The Associated Press. Mayor Edward J. Jeffries stated at midnight that the situation was much improved.]

The death toll at 10:20 P. M. had reached twenty-three, including twenty Negroes and three white persons. The injured, overflowing hospitals, numbered at least 600 and the number arrested and taken to jails and prisons exceeded that number.

With Detroit and its metropolitan-area population of about 2,500,000 persons—tens of thousands of them employed in Detroit's many war factories—under a state of emergency, Federal troops came from Fort Wayne, Ind., and Mt. Clemens, Mich., near Detroit.

They augmented two battalions of military police from Fort Custer and River Rouge Park as the shootings, beatings and pillaging continued unabated.

Two Hour Battle With Snipers

Late tonight local and State police pumped more than 1,000 rounds of ammunition and dozens of tear gas bombs into an apartment house to rout Negroes sniping from upper windows.

The siege had begun at 9:15 P. M., a few minutes after several Negroes were seen to run into the building with shotguns and revolvers.

The police first used the tear gas, which drove out most of the tenants on the lower floors, but the besieged group held out.

The police began to return fire with fire and the neighborhood rang with shots for more than two hours, the battle ending with the surrender of the Negroes. Two of them had been killed and a policeman, Lawrence Adams, was wounded seriously.

The Federal troops did not take part in the apartment house siege, but assisted other police in patrolling the riot areas, mostly in the downtown Negro section.

The Federal soldiers rode down Woodward Avenue, Detroit's major thoroughfare. They had orders to "clear the streets." With 1,110 assigned here, 1,200 others were held in reserve at Fort Wayne.

Only Workers Escape Curfew

All persons, except those going to and from their jobs in war plants, already had been ordered to stay in their homes under the 10 P. M. to 6 A. M. curfew ordered by Gov. Harry F. Kelly when he declared that a state of emergency existed.

Brig. Gen. William E. Guthner, in charge of military police for the Army's Sixth Service Command, announced that he had been authorized by his headquarters at Chicago to "cooperate with State and city police."

General Guthner said the request for Federal troops was made by Governor Kelly after the mobs had ignored his emergency proclamation. It was learned that 2,000 additional troops would arrive in Detroit tomorrow.

Shootings, stabbings and hundreds of street fights throughout the metropolitan area had led Governor Kelly to declare the state of emergency.

Detroit's municipally owned Receiving Hospital, whose chief surgeon, Dr. Austin Z. Howard, described the riots "as the worst

Crowd pursues a Negro (extreme right) across Woodward Avenue, Detroit's main thoroughfare

calamity in Detroit's history," overflowed with injured. It was necessary to borrow blood plasma from the Red Cross to treat seriously injured victims.

Of the dead, twelve succumbed at Receiving Hospitals. Others died in ambulances en route to the hospitals, and several were found dead in the streets. One white man was found shot to death in the Negro section and a Negro was found dead in a theatre with six bullet wounds. The injured included a policeman who had been shot six times.

Three Counties Under Curbs

Special to THE NEW YORK TIMES.

DETROIT, June 21—Governor Harry F. Kelly tonight imposed his modified form of martial law on three southeastern Michigan counties, comprising the Detroit metropolitan area.

In addition, Governor Kelly ordered the curfew also in the three counties, Wayne, Oakland and Macomb.

All motion-picture houses, theatres and other places of amusement were ordered closed until further orders, and the sale of all alcoholic beverages was indefinitely suspended.

Gatherings and assemblages were forbidden under a separate proclamation issued by Governor Kelly and all persons were banned from carrying firearms except the police and the military.

Governor Kelly was called to Detroit by Mayor Edward J. Jeffries shortly before noon today, when Mayor Jeffries admitted the situation was out of hand. Governor Kelly was attending a conference of Governors at Columbus, Ohio.

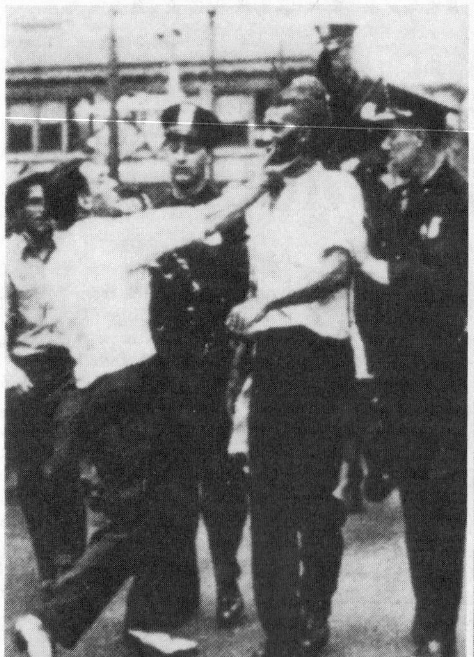

Left: A rioter in the custody of police is attacked by another rioter. Right: Police were kept busy searching for weapons.

Troops Ordered Mobilized

Before flying to Detroit in an army plane Mr. Kelly telephoned Brig. Gen. LeRoy C. Pearson, State Adjutant General, in Lansing, ordering him to mobilize the 6,000 Michigan State troops. He also ordered Michigan State police, to the number of 500, moved into Detroit.

Later in the afternoon the State troops, except for those in the Upper Peninsula, were ordered to Detroit and began arriving early this evening.

Governor Kelly and Mayor Jeffries conferred earlier with military officials, and while no specific request was made then for Federal troops the military police battalion stationed here was put

This gathering at Woodward and Stimson Avenues was broken up by tear gas

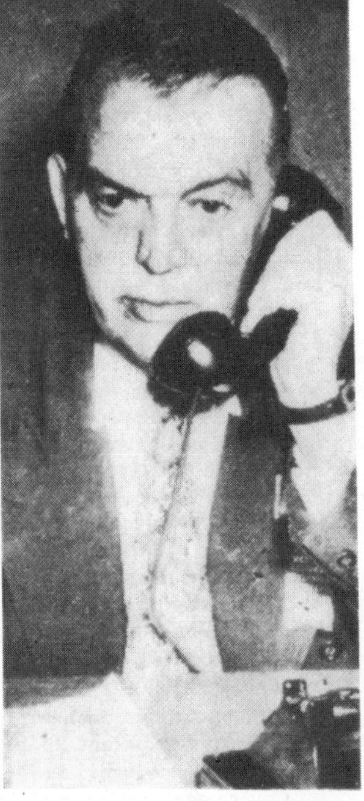

Gov. Harry F. Kelly ordered out the Michigan State Guard to restore order.

on the alert, and a second battalion was ordered in from Fort Custer.

Auxiliary police were mobilized at noon to help out the regular 3,500 members of the Detroit police, most of whom had been on duty since early this morning. It was estimated that all city and State police and State troops on duty in Detroit tonight numbered close to 6,000 men, with more due to arrive Tuesday.

The Governor's Proclamation

The text of Governor Kelly's proclamation was as follows:

"I, Harry F. Kelly, Governor of the State of Michigan and Commander in Chief of the military forces of the said State of Michigan, hereby declare a state of emergency and the necessity for the armed forces of the State of Michigan to aid and assist, but in subordination thereto, all duly constituted civil authorities in the execution of the law of the State.

"The necessity for such aid and assistance is declared to extend to the following counties of the State of Michigan, namely: Wayne, Oakland and Macomb.

"In witness whereof, I have hereunto set my hand and caused to be affixed the great seal of the State of Michigan this twenty-first day of June, 1943.

Although Governor Kelly referred to his action as marital law, it was pointed out that it in no way interfered with the operations of the courts, that civil law was not superseded and that the right to habeas corpus was not impaired.

With the Governor when the proclamation was framed were several Wayne County Circuit judges, including Presiding Judge Ira W. Jayne, and Prosecutor William E. Dowling and State and city officials.

Governor, Mayor in Radio Pleas

At 6:30 o'clock both Governor Kelly and Mayor Jeffries went on the air with a plea for observance of the law and asking people to remain off the streets.

Most downtown Detroit stores were closed early this afternoon at Mayor Jeffries' request. Ordinarily Detroit stores remain open until 9 P. M. on Mondays.

Street car service was stopped in several sections of the city where the trouble was most acute.

At 8 P. M. a crowd of more than 500 persons gathered in front of the City Hall and in front of the Postoffice. Buses were stopped, trolleys were pulled off their wires and squads of police were rushed to the scene. Several persons were arrested befort the crowd was dispersed.

Among the Negroes killed was Mrs. Carrie Hackworth, 29, and one of the dead white men was Dr. Joseph De Horatius, who was beaten this morning by a group which overturned his car on one of the city's main roadways.

Several hundred women, mostly Negroes, were included in the lis of injured.

The rioting began about 10:45 P. M. Sunday, apparently with a fight between a Negro and a white man on Belle Isle Bridge, when large crowds were leaving the island.

The fighting became general as rumors spread through the excited crowds and, as police and sailors from the near-by naval armory cleared the bridge, trouble began out on Belle Isle itself and in Gabriel Richard Park on the mainland side of the bridge.

During the night the rioting spread through the near east and north sides of the city, with both white and Negro crowds roaming the streets.

Workers attempting to go to their jobs this morning were attacked and many of them were injured.

Police received reports in the morning that bands of men had looted pawnshops in Negro districts and had stolen guns and ammunition. All pawnshops and hardware stores were ordered to lock up firearms.

After twelve hours of rioting injured patients were still arriving at the receiving hospital at the rate of one each two minutes. Surgeons said that some of them, apparently still under the influence of hysteria, attempted to knife or injure the doctors and nurses attending them.

On Woodward Avenue, a white band stopped street cars and pulled Negroes from them, stopped and overturned automobiles driven by Negroes and burned them, and chased and beat the drivers.

Thirty of the city's 176 elementary schools were closed at noon, in many instances because only a handful of pupils appeared for classes. Telephone lines were swamped all day as frantic wives sought word of their husbands and children.

No disorders were reported in high schools, but many of the roaming hoodlums appeared to be of high school age.

At noon Commissioner John H. Witherspoon, after a conference with the Rev. Horace A. White of Plymouth Congregational Church and John K. Graham, an attorney, both Negroes, decided to withdraw white police as far as possible from Negro districts and to substitute Negro police and 200 special Negro deputies from the Office of Civilian Defense services.

The afternoon shifts in some Detroit plants engaged in war production were slashed heavily through the absence of workers afraid to come to their jobs. At the Aeronautical Parts Company plant, in the heart of the riot district, company officials reported that a gang of 400 hoodlums stoned street cars without police interference and prevented workers from leaving or entering. Early in the day a company truck driver drove through a Negro crowd to get to the gate, and this touched off the disturbance there.

Montague Clark, head of the War Manpower Commission's Detroit office, said, however, that in large factories out of the riot area only a minor upsetting of schedules had occurred, and that there was no more than normal absenteeism.

The Ford Motor Company reported that hundreds of Negro workers had asked to leave for the day after they received calls from their families saying that they were needed. Mayor Jeffries asked the United Automobile Workers (CIO) to have shop stewards in all plants instruct their members to stay out of the downtown area this evening.

C. M. Bolds, regional labor representative of the War Production Board's labor production division, issued an appeal after he made a survey of major war production plants in the metropolitan area and learned that very few Negroes had reported for work on afternoon shifts.

June 22, 1943

Behind Our Menacing Race Problem

By Turner Catledge

WASHINGTON.

WHATEVER description may eventually be affixed to the riots that flared in Harlem last Sunday and Monday, they did one thing for certain. They helped further to uncover one of the most embarrassing and most dangerous conditions in the United States today. It is the situation, growing tenser by the week, between the Negro and white races. In spots throughout the country, particularly in the acutely crowded industrial centers in Northern and border States, we are witnessing new symptoms of an old sore which has been festering and breaking forth intermittently for four-score years. In all that time we have alternately tried to ignore the basic situation altogether or have treated it in a way that was bound to make it worse.

In the South we looked to the strong arm, to Jim Crow and to physical fear. In the North we turned to the politicians, to Government action and to agitation. In the one case the methods were cruel and inadequate. In the other they proved hollow and unrealistic.

This is no time, in the midst of a war, to make a turn around in these methods, even assuming it could be done. There is too much involved to make that possible within the twinkling of an eye. Public authority, therefore, is pushed up against the last resort in such cases, discipline.

The race problem in the United States tempts one ever to oversimplification, as this correspondent has learned during an investigation made recently in several cities with large Negro communities. Yet the problem is so ramified and runs so deep into the mores of the people as to lead one who attempts simplification into one blind alley after another. In the recent riots in Detroit, for instance, people were able to lay the whole tragedy to almost anything. Those who wanted to find fifth-column or Ku Klux Klan activities—some observers went there with instructions to find such activities—had no great trouble in finding sufficient ground for so simple a conclusion.

Those who wanted to blame the police did so largely with a lot to justify their conclusions. If you want to charge it off to bad housing and recreation, or to selfishness of industrialists, or the influx of new Negro and white workers from the South, or to criminals and hoodlums, as Mayor La Guardia charged off the disturbances in New York, you could take any of these simple outs. You could even blame it on the weather, for the spark that set off the explosion in Detroit was a fight that probably would never have happened had not the night of June 20 been hot and sultry and tens of thousands of people had gone to Belle Isle Park to get a breath of fresh air and got in each other's way.

The truth is that each and every one of the factors suggested as implied was involved in some degree in the disturbance in Detroit. They are present in virtually every other industrial community of the North where the race problem has reared its menacing head.

Backyard: Harlem.

IN the South, where most of the Negro population still lives and where the division between the races is more evenly balanced numerically, the race problem has apparently not become as acute as a general rule as in the North. This is due to differences in social organization in the two sections as related to the races, and to the corollary fact that, even in this time of war, the South has retained its essentially rural characteristics. Many of the conditions which have bred new tensions or intensified old ones have not spread as yet throughout the South, with notable exceptions here and there.

But there are attributes to the problem which are common North and South and virtually in every location in either section where there are large numbers of Negroes (the presence of the two races together makes the problem), and to the extent of these denominators the case can be boiled down to certain general terms.

BEHIND all the immediate trouble, so far as the threat of overt action is concerned, is an impatient, irresistible drive of the Negroes on the one hand for a fuller realization of the equality which has long been promised to them, but just as long denied. And on the other hand, a stubborn, deepening, and in some places broadening, resistance of the whites to that very aim.

"It's the old story of the irresistible force meeting the immovable object," was the way Wilbur La Roe Jr., chairman of the new Inter-Racial Committee of the District of Columbia, put it. "Unless there is a relaxation somewhere along the line, there is bound to be trouble."

Nearly every other major factor connected with the question is a cause or an effect of this basic condition. First among more specific causes of tension is the matter of housing. It is indeed unfortunate that this simple word has been bandied about so much in the fight over social reforms that many people shy from it. But it becomes a stark reality in the race question when it is realized that in a city like Baltimore, for instance, Negroes are crowded into ghettos on an average of ten to the house, or 58,000 to the square mile; that in Baltimore and Chicago and Detroit they live almost altogether in the white man's leavings, in communities rung so completely around by landlord covenants that they are held virtual prisoners in these particular areas.

The crowding has been made more acute by the influx of new workers, both Negroes and whites, into the war factory areas. In Detroit the Negro population has increased more than 50 per cent in five years. In Baltimore the Negro population, already around 200,000 out of roughly 1,000,000, is mounting at the rate of 2,000 per month.

Along with the new Negroes come new whites in many places. For the most part the whites have come from sections which seethed with anti-Negro prejudice. The Negroes in the Middle West call the newly arrived whites "pecks," short for "peckerwood."

Under such crowded conditions, with new provocations over which he has no control, the Negro has become an easy mark for agitators, both the self-seeking and well-meaning varieties. His grievances are easy to exploit. Negro soldiers are growing resentful, as they have shown in many places, when they are told that they are fighting for an empty world so long as "democracy" is being denied to their folks back home, and being denied even to him under the Army's and Navy's policy of segregation.

JUST as housing has proved inadequate, so have the most ordinary recreational facilities. Detroit has only two major parks, only one near enough to the Negro ghetto to be of any use to its inhabitants and it is a constant bone of contention between Negroes and whites. In Baltimore there are said to be only four public tennis courts on which Negroes can play, only one pool in which they can swim.

Crime also has grown under such limitation, adding greatly to the problem on the debit side of (Continued) the Negro. The counterpart of "zoot-suit" gangs is to be found in many Northern industrial centers. In St. Louis there are two rival gangs, known to the police as the "Termites" and the "Counts."

Police in Detroit, St. Louis, Indianapolis, Columbus, Pittsburgh and nearly every mid-Western industrial center are gloomy over the problem. Their gloom is increased by the belief, which is quite well grounded, that the Negroes are being excited to antagonism against the police. The Negroes in many places are being told by their leaders that police are their enemies to all intents and purposes.

The general civilian dislocations of the war; constant crowding of transportation facilities; line-ups at stores, banks and postoffices; general relaxation of civilities and observances of minor laws and regulations—all these can and do easily take on an inter-racial character in times like these. People all too easily blame their irritations on others, and there is a certain added convenience to be able to blame them on persons of another race.

THE pressing necessity for using every available unit of manpower has dissipated one of the trouble sources so far as Negroes are concerned by breaking down the barrier to their employment in war industries. The problem of upgrading has come to take the place of the old barrier, however, and just last week a strike was staged by white riveters in a Baltimore shipyard when the management announced a program of training some Negroes for this type of job.

All these and many more specific elements which enter into the current Negro problem get back sooner or later to the proposition that it is a case, at the bottom, of the Negro taking this occasion to make a determined drive, come what might, for his "rights." One faction of the Negro leaders is insisting not merely on rights comparable or even equal to the whites; they want the "same" rights, which they translate to mean the privilege to use the same facilities as the whites—the same hotels, theatres, night clubs, etc. Segregation, the word and all its stands for, has become anathema to the Negro, so far as he is represented by his more vocal leaders of today.

The whole picture is one in which one can see little hope of avoiding further trouble unless there is more of a spirit of give-and-take on both sides.

There are leaders among both Negroes and whites who are realistic enough to work out a large part of this great human problem. One does not have to look very far to find them. But each group has first to cut through prejudices which have grown up on its own side through the years in which the question has been badly handled, prejudices which now have become active and virulent.

August 8, 1943

SUBSIDY PROTESTED FOR RACE HOUSING

Urban League Charges FHA Is Encouraging Restrictive Areas for Negroes

Lester B. Granger, executive secretary of the National Urban League, appealed yesterday to the National Bar Association to "join forces in a national project to make it impossible for public funds to be spent in what amounts to a practical subsidy of racial ghetto buildings in American cities."

Mr. Granger said that the Federal Housing Authority "not only encouraged the spread of racially restrictive covenants" but had justified them. He added that any revision of the Underwriters Manual, which Mr. Granger calls "the bible for appraisers and financial institutions," would be too late to correct practices "which have distorted housing conditions for Negroes throughout the entire country."

What action the National Bar Association, organization of Negro lawyers now meeting in Cleveland, would take could not be ascertained from officials of the Urban League, who said that Mr. Granger is absent in Washington. It was learned that Lorin Miller of Los Angeles, a prominent member of the NBA, has been in New York for several days discussing with the Urban League action already taken in California on the part of Negro property owners to break restrictive agreements.

Mr. Granger's lette.: to Charles W. Anderson, president of the NBA, said that "about 90 per cent of all privately constructed war housing completed under the War Production Board preference rating orders was financed by FHA insured mortgages."

According to Thomas G. Grace, regional director of the Federal Housing Authority, the Underwriters Manual, to which the Urban League referred, "is in process of being changed." He could not say in what respect changes would be made. The decision, he said, "rests with Washington."

Mr. Grace said he believed that the provision in the Manual describing "harmonious groups" grows out of the fears held by real estate men the "invasion of a neighborhood" by peoples not easily absorbed. When asked if he knew that Negroes felt that rents usually go higher under Negro occupancy, he replied in the affirmative, and added that FHA is trying to prevent "the exploitation of Negroes by unscrupulous builders and speculators."

FHA has no voice in "modernization loans," he said, but was concerned with the "safety of loans" made to an area which was undergoing "the infiltration of unharmonious racial groups." FHA, he declared, has protected Negroes against speculators who are trying to operate on a "too high land value." "We have been guided," he added, "by a desire for economic soundness."

Guichard Parris, assistant to Mr. Granger, said that if housing is badly needed in an area like Harlem, he was willing to accept obviously "Negro housing" as a "needed expedient" although he was opposed to "racially separate housing developments as a principle."

Reginald A. Johnson, field secretary of the Urban League, said:

The urban Negro population is bound to increase. The present Negro ghettoes will not suffice. The Negro will invade new urban territories."

The Urban League has released information gathered by the National Association of Realty Boards in 330 representative cities. Of these, 147 are in favor of immediate housing for Negroes. The rest vary from "no interest" to uncertainty as to the "Negro risk."

The "Negro abuse of property," says the Urban Leage, results from "giving poor or modest Negro families tremendously old 'gingerbread-type houses' or apartments and expecting them to make successful modern homes out of them." Comments in answer to the league's inquiry of realty board members included one from a Detroit builder, who said, "Much can be done if streets are widened, laid and cleaned and dry roofs provided for the homes where Negroes now are." A Macon, Ga., man declared, "There is considerable substandard housing which could be materially improved," and a reply from Columbia, S. C., said, "We should pass an ordinance requiring installation of modern baths and sewerage in all Negro units."

December 1, 1945

ANTI-NEGRO PACTS ON REALTY RULED NOT ENFORCEABLE

Special to THE NEW YORK TIMES.

WASHINGTON, May 3—Covenants to bar Negroes or other racial groups from owning real estate were held legally unenforceable by a 6 to 0 ruling in the Supreme Court today.

Chief Justice Fred M. Vinson handed down two opinions advancing the long fight made by Negroes against such covenants and against their enforcement by courts in the states and federal territory.

One of the opinions, neither of which prohibited the making of such agreements, dealt with cases arising in Missouri and Michigan, while the other originated in the District of Columbia.

The state court issue was decided on that part of the Fourteenth Amendment to the Constitution that forbids any state to deny to any person within its jurisdiction the equal protection of the laws.

In the District of Columbia case, the high court said that it was unnecessary to consider any constitutional question, inasmuch as the Civil Rights Act of 1866 commanded that all citizens, regardless of color, should have the right to "inherit, purchase, lease, sell, hold and convey real and personal property."

Moreover, Chief Justice Vinson said that for the Federal courts of the district to enforce the covenants was "contrary to the public policy of the United States."

Bare Legal Quorum Obtained

Even though the two opinions were unanimous, they were decided by a bare legal quorum. Justices Stanley F. Reed, Robert H. Jackson and Wiley Rutledge did not participate. The assumption around the court was that one or more of them might have owned, or were interested in, property restricted by covenants. They disqualified themselves when the cases were argued in January.

"Because of the race or color of these petitioners," Chief Justice Vinson said in the state cases, "they have been denied rights of ownership or occupancy enjoyed as a matter of course by other citizens of different race or color.

"The Fourteenth Amendment declares that all persons, whether colored or white, shall stand equal before the laws of the states, and, in regard to the colored race, for whose protection the amendment was primarily designed, that no discrimination shall be made against them by law because of their color.

"In these cases the states have acted to deny petitioners the equal protection of the laws guaranteed by the Fourteenth Amendment. We find it unnecessary to consider whether petitioners have also been deprived of property without due process of law or denied privileges and immunities of citizens of the United States."

Negroes buying real estate in the District of Columbia challenged the covenants here as violative of the Fifth Amendment which prevents taking property without the process of law. The Supreme Court "found it unnecessary to resolve" that constitutional issue, however, and rested its finding on the Civil Rights Act.

The Chief Justice said that it was "clear" that Negroes had been denied their rights to real estate through the action of the District Courts in upholding the covenants.

"We hold," he stated, "that the action of the District Court directed against the Negro purchasers and the white sellers denies rights intended by Congress to be protected by the Civil Rights Act and that consequently, the action cannot stand.

"But even in the absence of the (Civil Rights) statute, there are other considerations which would indicate that enforcement of restrictive covenants in these cases is judicial action contrary to the public policy of the United States."

In the Missouri case, Mr. and Mrs. J. D. Shelley, Negroes, bought covenanted property in St. Louis. The trial court said that they had no actual knowledge of the pact. In the Michigan case, Mr. and Mrs. Orsel McGhee, also Negroes, purchased restricted property in Detroit.

The District of Columbia cases started when a real estate operator sold three lots to Negroes, and another lot was sold to James M. Hurd, listed in the legal papers as a Mohawk Indian. The restrictive compacts were respectively sustained by the Missouri and Michigan Supreme Courts, and by the Federal Court of Appeals for the District of Columbia.

Covenants Are Not Outlawed

While the Supreme Court denied state courts authority to enforce the covenants, the tribunal did not question the validity of the agreements themselves. According to Chief Justice Vinson, the six jurists held that "the restrictive agreements standing alone cannot be regarded as a violation of any rights guaranteed by the Fourteenth Amendment.

"So long as the purposes of those agreements are effectuated by voluntary adherence to their terms, it would appear clear that there has been no action by the state and the provisions of the amendment have not been violated. The amendment erects no shield against merely private conduct, however discriminatory or wrongful."

Mr. Vinson also said that the question before the Supreme Court was the "validity, not of the private agreements as such, but of the judicial enforcement of those agreements."

Lawyers took that to mean that property owners breaking the covenants by sale to Negroes might be sued for damages. They quickly added, however, that such suits would amount to little, because the state courts could not enforce the pacts.

"It cannot be doubted that among the civil rights intended to be protected from discriminatory state action by the Fourteenth Amendment," Chief Justice Vinson said, "are the rights to acquire, enjoy, own and dispose of property. Equality in the enjoyment of property rights was regarded by the framers of that amendment as an essential pre-condition to the realization of other basic civil rights and liberties which the amendment was intended to guarantee.

"The Constitution confers upon no individual the right to demand action by the state which results in the denial of equal protection of the laws to other individuals. And it would appear beyond question that the power of the state to create and enforce property interests must be exercised within the boundaries defined by the Fourteenth Amendment."

May 4, 1948

RULING IS ACCLAIMED HERE

It Is Called a Blow to All Discriminatory Agreements

Negro and Jewish organizations and church and labor groups hailed last night the ruling of the Supreme Court forbidding use of the courts to enforce racially restrictive real estate covenants. It was said that more than 75 per cent of the new housing developments on Long Island and in Westchester had such agreements.

Although the decision did not outlaw the covenants so long as they were kept without resort to the courts, spokesman for the interested groups said that it was a blow against the eventual effectiveness of all discriminatory agreements.

As a direct result of the ruling, a motion is to be filed today in the Appellate Division, Brooklyn, to enable Samuel Richardson, Negro chain store owner of Washington, to complete the purchase of a dwelling in Addisleigh Park, St. Albans, Queens.

Supreme Court Justice Jacob H. Livingston granted an injunction in February, 1947, forbidding sale of the house at 112-03 177th Street to Mr. Richardson, and his action was unanimously sustained by the Appellate Division.

The decision was described by the National Association for the Advancement of Colored People as justification of its thirty-one-year fight to outlaw discrimination in housing. Thurgood Marshall, special counsel to the NAACP, said that it gave "thousands of prospective home buyers throughout the United States new courage and hope in the American form of government."

Joseph M. Proskauer, president of the American Jewish Committee, called the ruling "a milestone in the democratic effort to eliminate discrimination in the enjoyment of basic civil and political rights by all groups, regardless of race, color, religion or national origin."

Similar expressions were voiced by spokesmen for other organizations that filed briefs in the Supreme Court cases or locally in the Richardson case. Among them were the Anti-Defamation League of B'nai B'rith, the Methodist Federation for Social Service, the Congress of Industrial Organizations, the Social Action Committee of the New York City Congregational Association, the Jewish War Veterans and the Jewish Labor Committee.

May 4, 1948

HOUSING BIAS CURB CALLED MINOR GAIN

Restrictive-Pact Ruling Held of Little Use Unless U. S. Agencies Can Halt Funds

By GEORGE STREATOR
Special to THE NEW YORK TIMES.

WASHINGTON, April 26—Minority groups can expect little comfort from the Supreme Court decision ruling restrictive housing covenants unenforceable in courts of law unless power is given federal agencies to go a step further by withholding federal funds from housing developments that discriminate, according to officials of the Housing and Home Finance Agency.

These officials said that the decision showed a willingness to help mold public opinion, but was not meant to bestow enforcement powers upon any existing housing agencies.

A recent directive issued by Franklin D. Richards, Commissioner of the Federal Housing Administration, aroused much comment among Negroes, with some taking a position of hope and encouragement, saying that Negroes could look forward to building and buying homes without restrictions.

This directive sought to end a policy of rejecting applicants for federal insurance because this "type of occupaancy might affect the market attitude toward other properties in the immediate neighborhood," and another section of the same report instructed the chief FHA underwriters that federal insurance should not be "precluded on the ground that the introduction of a different occupancy type may affect the values of other properties in the area.

Berchmans T. Fitzpatrick, assistant administrator and chief counsel of the Housing and Home Finance Agency, said that this order meant that a Federal agency could not determine the "class" of housing set-up in an area, especially since such Government-imposed restrictions were equivalent to defining the amount of money a citizen must have to live in certain areas.

Advantages Are Explained

The FHA order read further: "Such residential areas, even though developed with homes having values somewhat lower than adjacent areas, often contribute important factors to sustain or enhance general value levels. They frequently result in providing more schools, better shopping facilities, increased transportation lines, playgrounds, and other desirable community facilities that generally accompany built-up areas."

Mr. Fitzpatrick said that the "improvement" in FHA instructions "mean that underwriters are no longer free to write-down an evaluation because non-white races are involved in the transaction. It means that there must be some concrete, objective set of standards on which a writing-down because of race is permitted."

Under old policies an appraiser was permitted to rule that non-homogeneous groups were poor property risks.

April 27, 1949

HOUSING RACE BIAS EVIDENT IN NORTH

Segregation More Strict in Many Large Cities Than in South, Survey Finds

Racial segregation in housing is more strict in Chicago, Detroit and "many northern cities" than in the South, according to a pamphlet just published by the New York State Committee on Discrimination in Housing.

The pamphlet was produced by the Public Affairs Committee, a non-profit concern that has issued 16,000,000 leaflets on public questions since 1935. This booklet was the result of a personal survey by Alexander L. Crosby, free-lance journalist, and Marion Palfi, photographer, of ten American cities last year.

The cities were New York, Chicago, Los Angeles, Detroit, Denver, Springfield, Ill.; Waterbury, Conn.; Phoenix, Ariz.; Charlottesville, Va., and Sledge, Miss. They were chosen for geographical and special reasons; they were not intended as a "statistical" sampling that would be typical of the United States as a whole.

"Segregation is too often identified with the South," the foreword to the pamphlet says. "Many northern cities enforce housing segregation more rigorously than the South does. The nation's largest ghettos, for example, are not in New Orleans or Atlanta, but in Chicago and New York.

Why the Situation Exists

"The key fact is that urban redevelopment cannot be handled intelligently unless the principle of democratic housing is accepted. Central slums cannot be torn down until decent housing is provided elsewhere for their inhabitants, who are usually minority groups.

"And in nearly every city the only vacant land suitable for relocating these families is outside the segregated districts. The first step is to recognize the right of minorities to live anywhere they choose. Federal funds must not be used to build new ghettos."

Although virtually all cities segregate Negroes as to residence, the situation was found to be comparatively good in New York. The State set an example in 1950 with the Wicks-Austin anti-discrimination law: the city had already enacted similar legislation the year before. Low-rent housing projects in the city, to provide 250,000 dwellings, are wholly interracial. Non-segregated, private housing is needed, the pamphlet asserts, for higher-income Negroes and Spanish-Americans.

Among the bad examples, the pamphlet cited Chicago and Detroit as "powder kegs" of racial antagonism.

"No large city is doing more than Chicago to keep the Negro in segregated neighborhoods," Mr Crosby wrote. "Negro housing is concentrated more rigidly there than in southern cities. In the past decade, the Negro population has soared past 400,000, an increase of close to 45 per cent as against 6 per cent for whites. New arrivals have been wedged into the old slums."

Danger in Detroit Pointed Out

In Detroit, the author said, "the race question is an acknowledged public issue, more so than in any large northern city," especially since the race riots of 1942 and 1943. A trifling spark could touch off "wholesale murder," he declared.

"Public housing is solidly jim crow in Detroit," he concluded. "Negroes, whose housing need is most acute, have been allotted a smaller proportion of dwellings than in many southern cities."

Contrariwise, Denver and Los Angeles were praised for progressive efforts to end segregation. Nnder the administration of young Mayor Quigg Newton, Denver is building 4,000 low-rent dwellings to be occupied without discrimination. The city also is energetically eliminating racial and religious bigotry in public employment, recreation and even private housing.

Denver's largest minority is not Negro, but Mexican and other Spanish-speaking people.

Los Angeles also has a sizable Mexican minority, and many Japanese. However, the biggest minority is 200,000 Negroes, who have "won more freedom of residence than in other large cities," Mr. Crosby said.

Housing Authority Commended

The city Housing Authority, distinguished from the county authority, was commended for a "bright" record in keeping all its twenty-four projects unrestricted. As a matter of fact, the authority threatens to evict anyone who "disturbs the peace with intolerant activity."

Effective segregations against Negroes in almost all phases of daily life were found in Springfield, Ill., home town of Abraham Lincoln, and Charlottesville, Va., where Thomas Jefferson founded the University of Virginia.

The New York State Committee on Discrimination in Housing, which sponsored the pamphlet, is a co-operative of eighteen religious civic, labor and liberal groups headed by Algernon D. Black.

April 15, 1951

Survey in South Emphasizes Need For Better Housing for Negroes

Special to THE NEW YORK TIMES.

ATLANTA, Nov. 10—The urban housing of white residents in the South has undergone "onsiderable improvement" in the past ten years, but that available to Negroes "has scarcely held its own," the Southern Regional Council reported today.

"Unless far more imagination and energy are devoted to solving the South's over-all urban housing problem in the next ten years, the 1960 figures may be appalling beyond belief," the council warned.

Widely regarded as the most effective interracial organization in the South, the council is composed of clergymen, business men, educators, labor leaders, newspaper men and professional people from thirteen Southern states.

The council's regional assessment was based on early reports of the 1950 census submitted from thirteen Southern metropolitan areas to the Bureau of the Census. The cities were Dallas, Houston, Louisville, Miami, San Antonio, Tampa-St. Petersburg, Birmingham, Atlanta, Memphis, Nashville, New Orleans, Norfolk-Portsmouth, and Richmond, the last seven reporting their findings by race.

Taking the thirteen areas together, the council noted, the number of occupied dwelling units had increased by 656,800, or 50 per cent, since 1940. This was explained in part, the council declared, b. new construction and by the division of larger houses into apartments. There was also less "overcrowding" in 1950, the council reported.

During the decade the number of home owners in the thirteen areas increased to slightly more than 50 per cent, as compared to 33 per cent. This following the national trend showing more home owners than renters in 1950 for the first time since the Census Bureau began collecting such information in 1890.

While the South generally was better off in housing than it had been a decade ago, a substantial number of homes was listed as "dilapidated," meaning that they did not provide adequate or safe shelter, the council found. It also noted than 29 per cent of the dwellings in the thirteen areas were without private toilets or baths.

Negro housing as reported separately in seven of the metropolitan areas was "dismally below the average of 1940," the council stated. In these cities, proportionately twice as many Negro houses as white were listed by the council as "dilapidated."

"This disparity in physical condition shows up clearly in the estimated values of the typical white and typical Negro dwellings," the council declared. "In the highest ranking city of the group, Atlanta, the median value was $9,144 for all houses, but only $3,992 for Negro houses."

The South's increase in home ownership has "done little or nothing to bring Negro ownership up to the white level," and a large proportion of Negro housing is overcrowded, averaging from two and one-half to eight times as much as among whites, the council found.

The preliminary census figures "illustrate the inequity of the pattern of housing for the two races which prevails in our large cities, the council said, and the system which requires Negro housing to expand on a block-by-block basis through "changing" residential sections results frequently in interracial tensions that sometime explode into violence.

Consequently, the council held, home ownership is unlikely to increase much among Negroes when they are limited to substandard neighborhoods. The low income of most Negro families is only part of the explanation, the council added, since Negroes of moderate and substantial means also have little incentive to invest in old and dilapidated houses. The council then commented:

"The evil myth that Negroes are slum-dwellers by choice is withering in the light of practical experience. A growing number of private developments have proved conclusively that many Negro families are able and willing to pay medium rents for comfortable, modern apartments.

"Single-family houses, financed with the assistance of the Federal Housing Administration are also finding a ready market. The chief obstacle is acquiring the land for new expansion outside blighted areas.

"These difficulties can be overcome by intelligent cooperation between business and private and public agencies. Still, much will remain that can be relieved only by joint programs of local and Federal Government."

November 11, 1951

NEGRO GAINS SHOWN BY A CHICAGO STUDY

Special to The New York Times.

CHICAGO, Aug. 26—Negroes are in the majority in fifteen of Chicago's seventy-five communities.

The Chicago Commission on Human Relations reported this finding this week. It studied the city's population changes between 1950 and 1960.

In those ten years Chicago's Negro population rose from 492,265 to 812,637. At the same time white population declined from 3,111,525 to 2,712,748.

The commission noted that the Negro area on the South Side expanded substantially during the decade and that Negroes moved into many more areas. More than 250,000 Negroes now live on the West and Near North Sides, the commission reported.

Negroes made up 23 per cent of Chicago's population in 1960, compared with 14 per cent in 1950. The proportion of Negroes in suburban areas, however, remained about the same. Nonwhite population of the suburban area increased from 2.9 per cent in 1950 to 3.1 per cent in 1960.

August 27, 1961

PRESIDENT BARS BIAS IN HOUSING ASSISTED BY U.S.

Order Forbids Any Racial or Religious Discrimination —Pledge Is Fulfilled

By JOHN D. MORRIS
Special to The New York Times

WASHINGTON, Nov. 20—By a long-promised "stroke of the pen," President Kennedy prohibited today racial and religious discrimination in housing built or purchased with Federal aid.

In an Executive order, he directed Federal agencies to take "all necessary and appropriate action" to that end.

Administration officials said that the order would apply principally to housing projects and apartments. When the regulations are drawn, they said, sales of private homes by individual owners will probably be exempt.

Thus, the order is unlikely to affect houses that are not in commercially developed neighborhoods. Officials indicated that F. H. A.-insured loans for home improvements will be excluded, too. And the order itself does not cover "conventional" —that is, purely private—financing at all.

Sanctions Are Provided

The order authorizes various sanctions to enforce its provisions with respect to all future construction. Enforcement with respect to existing housing will depend on persuasion and possible court action.

The President announced his action in an opening statement at his news conference tonight, a few minutes after signing the order. His action carried out a pledge he repeatedly made in his campaign for President in 1960.

Mr. Kennedy said in several campaign speeches that President Dwight D. Eisenhower could and should, "by one stroke of the pen," have prohibited discrimination in Federally aided housing.

Extent Is Uncertain

The order today covers housing financed by direct Federal loans or grants, and by private mortgages guaranteed or insured by the Federal Housing Administration, the Veterans Administration and the Farmers Home Administration, as well as property owned by the Federal Government.

This includes low-rent public housing projects, housing constructed under the urban renewal program, college housing, farm housing, the Federal community facilities program, and housing administered by the Defense Department.

There is no way of measuring how much housing will be affected. Administration officials noted that one-fourth of the new housing being constructed these days was covered by Federal insurance or guarantees. They stressed, however, that in recent years 50 per cent of the housing in suburban developments, or "subdivisions," had been financed with Federal backing. This is where they expect the most effect.

The order is effective immediately. The Federal Housing Administration sent telegrams to all its field offices tonight directing them, at the opening of business tomorrow, to put the President's policy into effect.

Loan agreements on applications received from then on will contain a clause specifying that the Government's aid commitment does not apply to housing denied to a purchaser because of race, creed, color or national origin.

If violations occur, the Government will first try to obtain voluntary compliance. If that fails, the order provides for such sanctions as cancellation of the commitment at issue and of all other commitments extended previously to the violator.

Officials said that court action would be taken "as a last resort."

In a section that applies to existing housing, as distinguished from future construction, the order directs Federal agencies "to use their good offices and take other action permitted by law, including the institution of appropriate litigation, if required, to promote the abandonment of discriminatory practices."

The order also creates a new Cabinet-level group, the President's Committee on Equal Opportunity in Housing, to coordinate and aid the work of Federal agencies in carrying out the anti-discrimination policy. A member of the White House staff will be assigned by the President as chairman and executive director. The President is expected to appoint several members from the public as well as from the Cabinet and the various Federal agencies concerned with housing.

Cites Policy of Equality

President Kennedy told his news conference that it was "neither proper nor equitable that Americans should be denied the benefits of housing owned by the Federal Government or financed through Federal assistance on the basis of their race, color, creed or national origin."

"Our national policy is equal opportunity for all," he declared, "and the Federal Government will continue to take such legal and proper steps as it may to achieve the realization of this goal."

The President's order does not go so far as to cover housing credit extended by all banks and savings and loan associations that carry Federal insurance on their deposits. This would have made the ban virtually all-inclusive with regard to future construction, since nearly all private lending institutions carry such insurance.

By omitting such a provision, the order disregards a recommendation made last year by the Federal Civil Rights Commission.

It was learned that the Justice Department had advised against so far-reaching a step at this time because of what officials said were the "very serious enforcement problems." Some officials had contended, however, that the obstacles were largely technical and should not have stood in the way of broader action.

Since taking office in January, 1961, President Kennedy has been under heavy pressure from anti-discrimination groups to follow up his "stroke-of-the-pen" campaign speeches with a prompt Executive order. Simultaneously, there has been strong political pressure from the South against issuing such an order.

At several news conferences after becoming President, Mr. Kennedy told questioners that he was considering the order and would put it into effect "when I think it would be useful."

A reporter asked today why it had taken so long.

"Well," the President replied, "I said I would issue it at the time when I thought it was in the public interest, and now is the time."

As to whether the order would have an adverse economic impact — by slowing housing construction — the President said there might be "some adverse reactions." But he said he thought the country would be "able to proceed in the development of our housing industry, which is important to our economy."

The main obstacle to issuing the order earlier in the Kennedy term, according to some informants, was the fear of retaliation by powerful Southern members of Congress. There was a feeling, according to these sources, that Southern Democrats should not be unduly antagonized until the President's legislative program was well on its way through Congress.

The order was finally ready for the President's signature before the elections, Nov. 6, but it was decided to wait until after the elections to issue it.

November 21, 1962

Riots Viewed Against History of Clashes Almost as Old as U.S.

By JOSEPH LELYVELD

It was a hot, muggy night in August and racial tensions in Philadelphia had been running high. The mob began milling around early in the evening, rapidly swelling to several hundred men and boys. Alerted, the Mayor rushed to the scene to avert a disaster — and failed.

Then the mob started moving, breaking into homes as it went, beating people who fell in its way. The riots lasted three nights and before they ended one man had been killed and 31 homes pillaged.

That mob was white and its victims black — the year was 1834.

On a hot, muggy night 130 Augusts later — two weekends ago — another mob moved through the streets of Philadelphia. It was black.

Mobs Formed in Cities

This mob was one of a series that suddenly came together in the Negro districts of Northern cities during the summer.

President Johnson has ordered the Federal Bureau of Investigation to report on whether the disturbances that followed conformed to "some particular pattern that will need to be pointed up."

Some observers have seen a pattern in the fact that most of the disturbances began on hot weekend nights and lasted for three nights, and that their immediate causes were often obscure or trivial.

These observers suggest that such a pattern could have been imposed by outside agitators.

But most note that the majority of race riots in this country have started obscurely on hot, summer weekends, have lasted three nights—and have produced suggestions of outside agitation.

From the historical standpoint, however, this summer's outbursts represented something new. Although racial violence in this country is almost as old as the nation, the pattern usually found whites making the first assaults. There had been Negro riots, but never before an epidemic of them.

What lies behind the summer's rioting? How did it spread? Were there common factors in the troubles of Harlem, Rochester, Jersey City and Philadelphia? How did this year's outbreaks contrast with those of the past?

Not all the answers are clear, but social scientists have some clues.

The riots this summer, with the exception of the one in Chicago's predominantly Negro suburb of Dixmoor, erupted at the center of a dense urban ghetto. The riots of the past were usually on borders between Negro and white areas—with the conspicuous exception of riots that took place in Harlem in 1935 and 1943.

In many past riots the toll in human life in a single night surpassed that of all the violence this summer. Almost always, the fighting would be one-sided. The police either stood aside or joined the white mob in its attacks on Negroes. As lae as 1951, in Cicero, Ill., a police chief was convicted on charges of abetting white rioters.

The Swedish sociologist Gunnar Myrdal, in his classic "An American Dilemma" described a race riot as "the most extreme form of extra-legal mob violence used to prevent Negroes from getting justice."

He added: "The breaking point is caused by a crime or a rumor of a crime by a Negro against a white person, or the attempt of a Negro to obtain a legal right."

The most savage race riot in American history took place in East St. Louis in 1917. At least 39 Negroes and 9 whites were killed. Two years later in Chicago, 23 Negroes and 15 whites lost their lives. (In that summer, 26 race riots took place across the country.)

Detroit Riot in 1943

In 1943 in Detroit, in the last of such large-scale bloody clashes in a Northern city, 25 Negroes and 9 whites were killed.

Some students of relations between the races would contend the outburst in Detroit was actually the last race riot. They maintain that the term should be reserved for frontal clashes between the races.

They present a distinction: In this summer's outbreaks one race did not attack the other; it attacked instead the symbols of the "establishment" — the police and property.

Of course, deep in the ghetto the police and the merchants were usually the only whites at hand. But in contrast to previous disturbances, no whites have been deliberately killed and no sallies into white neighborhoods have been attempted.

Prof. Allen D. Grimshaw of Indiana University, author of an unpublished, book-length thesis on racial rioting in this country, said in a recent telephone interview that he was impressed by the fact that the first policeman attacked in Philadelphia was a Negro. He was also impressed because some Negro stores in Rochester were pillaged as well as white establishments.

"These have been much less race riots than expressions of a class aggression," he observed.

The looters, he noted, seem to have concentrated on bulky, high-priced items, such as television sets and sofas, rather than necessities, even though the large items were easier to trace and more difficult to translate into cash. These thefts, Dr. Grimshaw says, suggest the kind of class consciousness that may have impelled the looter.

Precedent for Looting

There is a precedent, he says. In 1943, the summer of the great Detroit riot, there was an explosive outbreak in Harlem. Since it was not a direct clash, social scientists say that it did not have the elements of a race riot. The death toll was small—five persons—but with widespread looting of stores, the property damage was higher.

In the Harlem riots of 1935 and 1943, except for the police and the merchants, the white population was affected only remotely. This presents a paradox Negro writers have often noted: Negro violence is almost always inflicted on Negroes.

This summer's troubles have been cut on the pattern of Harlem, not Detroit. And Harlem was the first ghetto to catch the fever.

As in 1943, the spark this year was the shooting of a Negro by a white policeman. In 1943, the Negro, a soldier, was only wounded but the rumor that he had been killed spread through the community like a prairie fire. This year, the Negro, a 15-year-old student, was shot and killed by an off-duty policeman.

The riot in 1943 broke out at once. The 1964 riot, however, did not come until two days after the shooting. Harlem had been tense all summer — for may summers—but there was no expectation of a riot that particular night—Saturday, July 19.

The explosion came after speakers at a protest rally called for a march on a local police station. Within days, the rioting had spread to the Bedford- Stuyvesant section of Brooklyn and, by the end of the week, to Rochester.

Social scientists take seriously the possibility that the reports of the riots in one place helped to ignite them in another.

Professor Rose said that while he had no way of evaluating suggestions that the disorders were organized, he was highly skeptical of them. Communications between Negro communities, he said, are so fast as to seem almost instantaneous.

Dr. Kenneth B. Clark, City College of New York sociolo gist, said in another interview that the Harlem riot "might well have triggered the others." But it appeared to have taken a significantly different course from those that followed. The Harlem mobs seemed angrier but were less inclined to looting.

Minor Encounters

In the other cities, the explosions were set off by minor encounters with the police, usually the arrest of a Negro—in several instances, a woman—on a disorderly conduct charge. In Rochester and Philadelphia, wild rumors helped to inflame the crowds—in Rochester, that a girl had been bitten by a police dog, and in Philadelphia, that a woman had been shot and killed.

In Rochester, there was considerable anxiety that a full-scale race riot might develop. In the Chicago suburb of Dixmoor, one almost did: A white gang formed and moved off toward the Negro mob. But the police were able to prevent a fatal clash.

The Dixmoor Negroes attacked whites in passing automobiles. There were also such incidents in Harlem. In Jersey City, Paterson and Elizabeth, there was considerable rock throwing.

In Bedford-Stuyvesant, Rochester and Philadelphia, the main riot activity, however, was the looting of stores.

Racial feeling seemed much more conspicuous in Harlem than in the disturbances that followed; the warfare between the police and crowds, more prolonged and bitter. In Harlem alone, of all the riots, this warfare was the central activity, and the looting and throwing of rocks at passing traffic incidental.

Most analysts tend to discount suggestions that the riots were conscious protests. They call these ideas as a form of after-the-fact rationalizations.

"I think they're not only after the fact but independent of the fact," Dr. Clark said.

The deeper causes of the tension and discontent in these communities—poverty, joblessness, discrimination, hopelessness — are notorious. Negro leaders have consistently maintained during the summer that it mattered little whether there have been agitators behind the riots. What matters, they say, is that the ghetto communities have long been deeply agitated.

Whitney M. Young Jr., director of the National Urban League cautioned yesterday that the nation would remain apprehensive of new rioting so long as Negroes are denied equal opportunities.

In a speech at New York University, Mr. Young described Negro ghettos as "smouldering powderkegs of resentment and denial."

"Either we formulate a coast-to-coast blueprint for equal opportunities for all," he said, "or we may find ourselves, as we do today, wondering which extremist group or gang will trigger tomorrow's riots."

September 11, 1964

Fire Still Smolders

Negroes Say 'Nothing Has Been Done' To End Causes of Last Summer's Riots

By FRED POWLEDGE

It is getting cold now in the Northern cities that were racked last summer by racial rioting. A gray winter bleakness is overtaking the low-income housing projects and the ghetto tenements where thousands of Negroes revolted against the white communities and then against the police who were sent to calm them.

News Analysis

There is sparse evidence now of the desperate hatred that filled the air on those summer nights in Harlem and Bedford-Stuyvesant and in Rochester, Paterson, Jersey City, Elizabeth and Philadelphia. But those who have been watching the situation say the fire is still smoldering, and that the white people have done little since then to extinguish it.

Those who exist within the ghetto are aware that officials in each of the riot cities have taken steps to participate in the Federal Government's newly enacted antipoverty bill, which will soon provide $861,500,000 for projects to help the poor. The problems of the poor are, for the most part, the problems of the Northern urban Negro.

Few of the Negroes in the riot areas who were questioned recently expressed more than passing interest in the poverty program. Many sneered when it was mentioned; they said they doubted it would amount to more than a new governmental agency, providing well-paying jobs for a handful of politicians.

Little or Nothing Done

Even those who professed faith in the poverty program said, when asked what had happened since the riots, "Nothing." Not only Negroes gave this reply; some city officials agreed, privately, that little of significance had been done.

One white man, a city official who acknowledged he was a member of the white power structure, said: "Nothing's changed, which is not to say that nothing's being done. A lot is being done. A lot was being done before the riots. But what is being done is not being done on the right scale and fast enough."

When city officials speak of what is being done, they usually refer to the delegations they have sent to Washington; the poverty programs they have started to develop in their own ghetto areas, and the local councils on human relations they established long before the riots, when race relations first became an issue of concern in the North. The human relations groups have been working overtime since the riots, trying to establish communication between the races.

These examples, by and large, have not impressed the Negro leaders or the rank and file. They say they see no change in their living conditions and their employment potential, and only minute change in their ability to obtain quality public education for their children.

To one of the most candid leaders, Cecil Moore of Philadelphia, an important ingredient of last summer's rioting has not yet been touched. Mr. Moore, in a recent interview, dismissed Philadelphia's urban renewal effort and poverty program as the creatures of "limp-wristed social workers and preachers."

'Exploitation . . . Goes On'

"The perpetual exploitation of the Negro, which was one of the big causes of the riots, goes on," he said. "Nothing has changed."

Negroes in the other riot cities agree that the merchants behind the newly replaced plate glass windows in the ghetto still charge more and deliver less than do their counterparts in the white sections.

One reason for Negroes' reluctance to put much faith in the cities' new projects is the way in which some of the cities responded to the riots.

In New York, emergency jobs were promised to 20,000 persons. About 1,100 actually got employment, according to the city.

In Paterson. N. J., three storefront offices were set up in the poorer sections, advertising the city's willingness to provide advice and help. At first the stores were locked. Then, when they were opened, the people who went looking for jobs were referred to the State Employment Service, which had been in Paterson all along.

Arthur Holloway, the Paterson president of the National Association for the Advancement of Colored People, said he knew that the three offices soon would start providing real assistance. But when that happens, he said, "we've got to go back into the neighborhood and convince the people that they really mean it."

There is general agreement among the Negro leaders that one facet of life in the ghetto has changed for the better. The Negro's relations with the police, they say, are better than they have been in a long time.

In some of the cities, the Negroes say the police are more careful now about "pushing people around." In New York, the difference is attributed to the selection last summer of a Negro policeman, Capt. Lloyd Sealy, as commander of the largest police station in Harlem.

"It has made a dramatic difference," said James Farmer, the national director of the Congress of Racial Equality. "It's more difficult for the inhabitants of Harlem to look upon the police as their enemy, when he's the same color they are."

November 7, 1964

Baltimore Negro Births Rise

BALTIMORE, Jan. 2 (AP)—There were more Negro births in Baltimore than whites last year for the first time in the city's history, the Health Department has reported. In its annual report issued this week, the department reported that the number of white births declined to 10,700—close to the 1940 level—while there were 11,300 Negro babies born compared with 3,600 in 1940.

January 3, 1965

LOS ANGELES RIOTING IS CHECKED; TROOPS HUNT SNIPERS; 31 ARE DEAD; POLICEMAN IS SLAIN IN LONG BEACH

CURFEW EXTENDED

Fire Damage Is Near $200 Million—2,200 Under Arrest

By GLADWIN HILL
Special to The New York Times

LOS ANGELES, Aug. 15—Authorities asserted that they had gained "the upper hand" on the fifth day of rioting in the city's southwestern Negro district today, although sporadic looting, sniping and armed conflict continued.

It appeared that the nation's worst outburst of racial violence in many years might be tapering off toward restoration of law and order.

Tonight, however, new racial strife broke out in Long Beach, just south of Los Angeles. One policeman was killed and another wounded in a Negro area when they were ambushed by snipers.

A 24-block area was immediately cordoned off and a curfew imposed.

In the Los Angeles riot district, where about 2,500 of the 15,000 National Guard troops in the city area were deployed, the death toll rose today from 22 to 31.

Seven of the nine killed were Negroes shot in exchanges with soldiers or law officers or while looting. One was a 14-year-old Negro girl killed in a traffic accident while fleeing the scene of a looting. One was a 5-year-old Negro child shot by a sniper.

The total of arrests reached 2,255 and the number of injured 762, as the troops used rifle fire, tear gas, machine guns and bayonets to quell depredations of Negro hoodlums.

Losses from fires approached $200 million. Losses from looting had not been calculated.

The Sunday dawn, following an overnight curfew imposed on

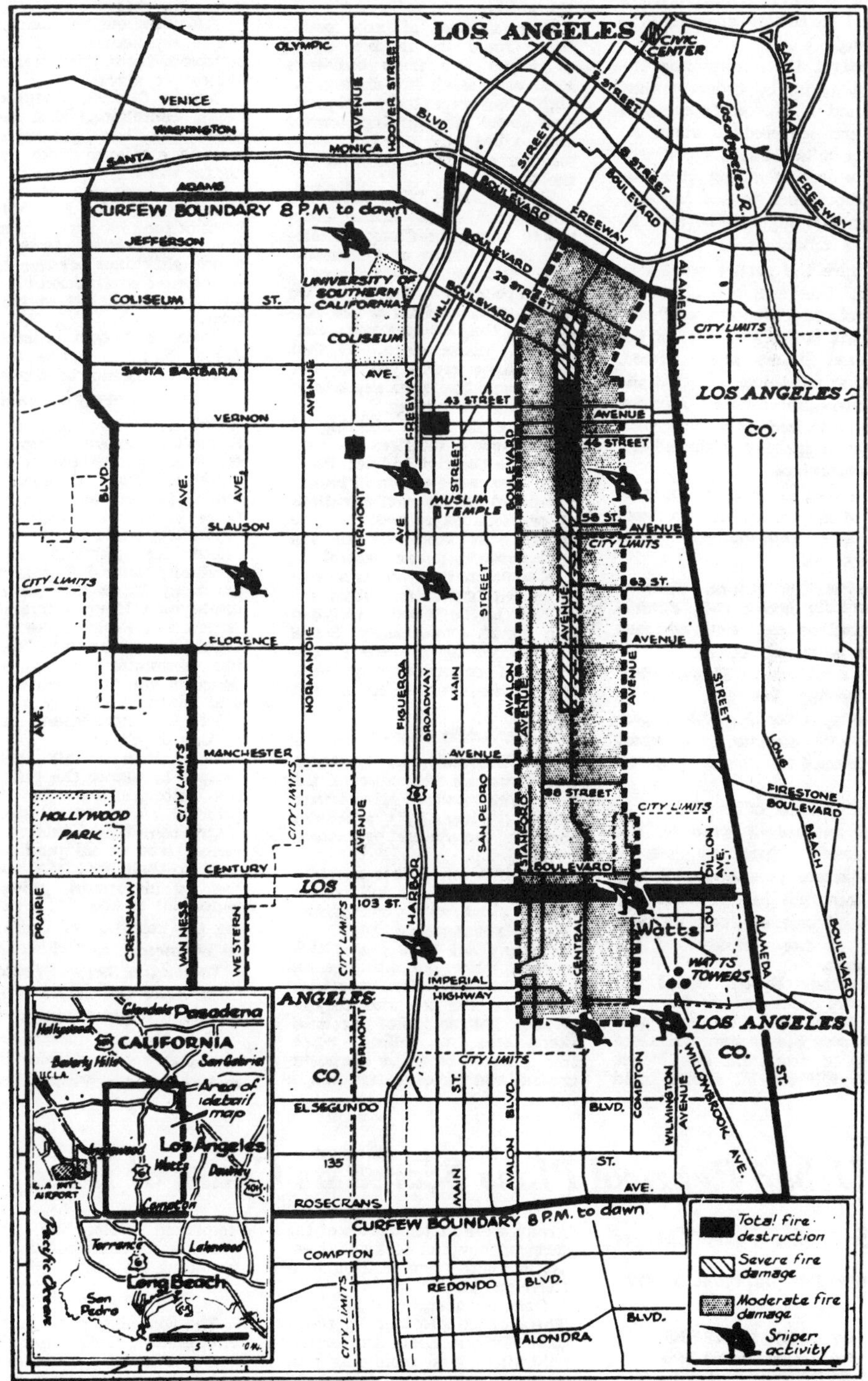

The New York Times Aug. 16, 1965

FIFTH DAY OF RIOTS: Symbols for sniper action and shading for fire damage show the scope of disorders in the Los Angeles Negro district and the surrounding area.

all residents of the riot area, brought an eerily unfamiliar atmosphere of serenity at many points. Amid blocks of devastation centering on the impoverished Watts area, residents emerged from houses to chat amiably with soldiers on guard duty.

Street-by-street sweeps by armed columns to round up suspected malefactors stopped, at least for the time being.

The soldiers' efforts concentrated on halting guerrilla-type sniping.

Tonight the curfew was imposed again, by order of Gov. Edmund G. Brown. He enlarged the area covered to about 50 square miles—about 1 per cent of the area of metropoltan Los Angeles. When the curfew was begun last night it covered 35 square miles.

Before the curfew went into effect this evening, about 25 Negroes appeared at the Lincoln Heights jail, where most of the arrested rioters are confined. They shouted demands that the prisoners be released. Twenty-five motorized policemen with shotguns speedily dispersed the demonstrators.

The jail is on the opposite side of the downtown area from the riot district—five miles away.

Inside the prison, disorder apparently broke out. Sounds of shouting and breaking glass could be heard outside.

On a knoll in Elysian Park overlooking the jail, officers broke up a small crowd of persons who directed small-arms fire toward the five-story building.

The return of a degree of quiet moderated growing apprehension among the metropolis's white population. Stores had reported an extraordinary weekend sale of guns, particularly on the periphery of the riot area.

Governor Brown called the reported gun sales "a very dangerous thing," on the ground that most people were untrained in using firearms. But Police Chief William H. Parker said he would not take it upon himself to discourage people from exercising their legal right to buy guns if they felt they needed the protection.

Heat Wave Continues

No one was sure whether the lessening of hostilities was the end of an outbreak of anarchy or just a lull. As a week-long nerve-fraying heat wave continued with temperatures in the sultry 90's, the emotions and frustrations of the Negro community remained palpable in the air.

Any minute, at any point, there could be another crack of sniper fire from buildings and roofs. Such fire during the night had repeatedly jeopardized even firefighting crews and killed the Negro child playing on the lawn with its mother.

Two hundred "flak suits" of bulletproof mesh armor, borrowed from the Camp Pendleton Marine base at Oceanside, were distributed to firemen.

A spokesman for the Fire Department said three fire stations in the riot area were considered "under siege," in that firefighting crews, rolling out on alarms, had been repeatedly subjected to sniping.

In the 12 hours starting at 8 A.M. today, 103 fires were reported in the riot district. However, they were all small blazes, compared to the conflagrations of previous days, and the Fire Department said they all had been brought under control.

Schools in the riot area will be closed tomorrow. Other facilities to be closed included two Youth Opportunity Board centers set up to relieve substandard economic conditions. Movie theaters decided to shut down.

University Classes Off

The University of Southern California, on the edge of the riot area, called off classes. Public transit schedules through the district remained suspended.

A half-dozen offices of state agencies in the area will remain closed, along with some industrial establishments.

Police Chief Parker said this morning that the situation in respect to the rioters was that "we're on the top and they're on the bottom." But he said there was no telling when things would be under complete control and violence stopped.

Governor Brown, who returned to California last night from a European vacation, announced after a morning conference with law-enforcement officials that he did not think it would be necessary to bring in Federal forces, as some officials had expected.

The Guard troops in the area are from two California Guard divisions, the 40th Armored and the 49th Infantry. The soldiers are on rotating patrol duty in the riot area, along with about 1,000 policemen and other civilian law-enforcement officers.

Under the curfew, persons on the street between 8 P.M. and sunrise without good reason are subject to arrest.

County General Hospital officials complained that curfew roadblocks had prevented 60 nursing employes from reporting for work.

The Congress of Racial Equality appealed for contributions of food for residents of the riot area, saying there were severe shortages because of the widespread destruction of stores and the sealing off of the district.

Governor Brown ordered the State Disaster Office to distribute emergency food supplies.

Meeting With Negroes

Governor Brown conferred this afternoon with Negro leaders in the city about three objectives: The restoration of order; prevention of a recurrence of violence, and avenues to "lasting peace."

But as physical violence gradually subsided, interracial acrimony increased. State Assemblyman Mervyn Dymally, a Negro, said Police Chief Parker should resign, because "the Negro community has no confidence in him and these tensions will continue as long as he is chief law-enforcement officer of this city."

Chief Parker said that attempts to blame the police for the outbreak were "a vicious canard." He spoke of ostensible Negro community leaders "who cannot lead at all" and said it was at their instance that he had, to his regret, pulled the police out of the riot area during the inception of the trouble on Wednesday and Thursday.

The rioting began Wednesday night after the arrest of a Negro on drunken driving charges.

The National Guard forces are now operating under the direction of the Police Department, since there has been no declaration of martial law.

The police chief challenged the idea that the rioters were largely teen-age hoodlums, observing that only some 300 out of the more than 2,200 arrested were juveniles. He said the police were planning to continue their policy of mass arrests.

'Years of Privation'

Representative Augustus F. Hawkins, Los Angeles Democrat, the only Negro Congressman from the West, said the Negro leaders "are down there doing what they can to restore normalcy." He said the outbreak was rooted in the fact that "the Negro is too far separated from the white power structure, and that has resulted in years of privation."

Mr. Hawkins added: "I think a lot of people have been arrested who are not criminals. In many cases the looting is the act of a person who has been deprived all of his life. The courts should consider the sociological factors."

The Rev. H. H. Brookins, chairman of the local United Civil Rights Committee, termed Chief Parker's attitude "bigoted, biased and insensitive."

Governor Brown commented that he thought the riot was "going to hurt a lot of work that's already been done by people of both races" toward ethnic harmony.

Court officials of the state, county and city met here this afternoon to discuss the handling of the riot defendants.

A total of 1,680 were adults charged with felonies; 232, adults charged with misdemeanors; 287, juveniles charged with felonies, and 56, juveniles charged with misdemeanors.

The court officials decided to operate the Municipal Courts in two eight-hour shifts for at least two days to handle arraignments.

Most of those killed over the five days were Negro rioters, shot during depredations. One victim was a fireman, killed by a falling wall, and another a sheriff's deputy.

Of those hurt, 68 were policemen; 32, firemen; four, peace officers of other forces; four, soldiers, and 654, civilians.

August 16, 1965

Urban Renewal Plans Scored as Cause of Decay

U.S. Rights Panel Charges Programs Impound Slums

By JOHN HERBERS
Special to The New York Times

CLEVELAND, April 4—Members of the United States Commission on Civil Rights charged today that urban renewal and other Federal programs were major causes of the despondency and decay that exist in acute form in Hough, a Cleveland ghetto.

One member, of the Rev. Theodore M. Hesburgh, president of Notre Dame University, said all Federal rebuilding programs as administered here and in other cities were "immoral."

The Commissioner spoke out after questioning state and Federal officials who conceded that combined rebuilding efforts could have contributed to "impounding the ghetto."

Focusing on Hough

The commission, an independent research and advisory agency, is conducting five days of public hearings here to find out how Negroes and other minority groups are faring in Northern slums.

One purpose is to gauge the effectiveness of Federal laws on the lives of slum dwellers.

The chief area under investigation is Hough, a rat-infested neighborhood of almost 60,000 people on the East Side near the center of the city.

In 1962, the worst part of Hough was placed in an urban renewal program, whereby the Federal government was to provide most of the funds for buying run-down property, clearing it and making it available for new developments.

In the last three years Hough

has undergone a steady decline. Its streets and alleys are littered with garbage and debris. Most of the buildings are in poor repair and many are vacant and foreboding.

Stores have gone out of business. Gangs roam through the abandoned property and use the great empty houses as vantage points for rape and robbery.

Many of the vacant buildings reflect the signs of urban renewal. Some have been torn down but there is no sign of new development.

As to the remaining buildings, a series of witnesses painted for the commission a picture of falling plaster, broken plumbing, basements filled with sewage, inadequate wiring, rats and roaches.

Charles Sheboy, Housing Commissioner for the City of Cleveland, testified that complaints of violation of the city code were turned over to the Department of Urban Renewal, when they come under that agency's jurisdiction.

"Urban renewal then will work with the property owners," Mr. Sheboy said.

However, James P. Friedman, Commissioner of Urban Renewal, testified that his agency had made no effort to enforce the code because of a policy that had been established in City Hall before he assumed the job.

Erwin N. Griswold, dean of the Harvard Law School and a commission member, asked if the purpose of this was "to keep down the costs" of property later to be bought by urban renewal.

Mr. Friedman replied that he was not clear as to the purpose of the policy but he said costs were involved. He added that the policy had recently been changed and said the code would be enforced.

The commissioners were indignant at what they called official neglect of people living in the area.

Eugene Patterson, editor of The Atlanta Constitution, said apartment dwellers had "been kept in a limbo" between the city and the Urban Renewal Agency.

"So far urban renewal has done only harm," Mr. Griswold said.

Testimony indicated that persons relocated by urban renewal and highway programs were frequently moved to worse surroundings. The commission study also showed that a great majority of Negroes were relocated in Negro areas.

"In these Federal programs to rebuild the cities," Father Hesburgh said, "what has happened is that people in the worst condition find their houses bulldozed from under them. The total program is immoral."

April 5, 1966

TROOPS RESTORING ORDER IN CHICAGO NEGRO GHETTO; 2 DEAD, 57 HURT IN RIOTING

4,000 CALLED UP

National Guard Units Patrol Streets After 3 Days of Strife

By DONALD JANSON
Special to The New York Times

CHICAGO, Saturday, July 16—National Guard troops patrolled the streets of Chicago's Negro West Side last night and early today. For the first time in four nights there was no major violence in the riot-torn ghetto area.

Gov. Otto Kerner called out 4,000 guardsmen yesterday after a third successive night of rioting led to exchanges of gunfire between the police and Negro snipers and roving bands.

Two Negroes were killed and six policemen were wounded by snipers. Fifty-one others were injured by bullets, rocks and flying glass.

A total of 282 persons were arrested.

'We Need Jobs'

Late yesterday the Rev. Dr. Martin Luther King Jr. won a pledge from Mayor Richard J. Daley, after a 90-minute meeting, that the city would put sprinklers on fire hydrants so that ghetto children could cool off on hot summer days. The rioting began Thursday when the police turned off hydrant water Negroes were using.

But comments by Negroes on porches and in doorways early today indicated that there were more basic considerations than sprinklers underlying the riots that left store windows along miles of ghetto business streets smashed and broken.

"We don't need sprinklers," said William Williams, who has a temporary urban renewal job this summer. "We need jobs." The sentiment was echoed by Richard Tidwell, leader of the Roman Saints, one of the gangs that led the rioting.

Only isolated incidents of tossing Molotov cocktails and rocks, along with an occasional sniper's shot, marred the relative calm last night and early today. Police Capt. John Hartnett, deputy chief of patrol, attributed it to the show of force by 800 policemen and 1,500 guardsmen who cruised the troubled area all night.

The guardsmen, armed with carbines and fixed bayonets, patroled on foot and in Jeeps and troop trucks. They moved into the area just before dusk. Twenty-five hundred more stood by at five Chicago armories.

At midday yesterday the police had sealed off some streets, reporting they could no longer control looting from all the stores with smashed plate glass windows.

"The situation has grown beyond the capacity of the police to deal with it," said Police Superintendent Orlando W. Wilson in explaining his request that the guard be called out.

Roosevelt Road and other thoroughfares were littered with glass, stones, pieces of furniture, broken bottles and anything else Negroes had been able to lay hands on to throw at more than 900 policemen who fought to keep order Thursday night and Friday morning.

Killed in the cross-fire between the Negroes and the policemen Friday morning were Rosalynd Howard, 14 years old, and Raymond Williams, 28.

The police said Mr. Williams, of Robinsonville, Miss., had been looting. Dr. James Henry, the coroner's pathologist, said Miss Howard was pregnant and close to giving birth.

2 Shot in Back

Most seriously wounded of the policemen were Capt. Francis Nolan, 43, and Patrolman Donald Ingram 28, both shot in the back.

The rioting reached a peak early Friday. Every police car and passing white motorist was a target for rocks and bricks, snipers aimed at patrolmen. The police fired back with hundreds of rounds of ammunition and clubbed and prodded taunting, jeering youths from the streets.

"This has been coming for a long time," an unidentified Negro man was overheard to say Friday morning.

White-owned stores were the principal targets of the violence. Most white businessmen stayed out of the area Friday.

The mood of the Negroes who roamed the streets Thursday night and of those who stood on the sidelines and cheered them on was summed up by a man who shouted:

"You ain't seen anything yet, you going to die tomorrow night, white man!"

Dr. King's Staff Blamed

At a news conference Friday afternoon, Mayor Daley laid much of the blame of the lawlessness to the staff of Dr. King's Southern Christian Leadership Conference, which has been working in the West Side ghetto for about a year.

"I think you can't charge it to Martin Luther King directly," Mayor Daley said.

"But surely some of the people that came in here have been talking for the last year of violence, and showing pictures and instructing people in how to conduct violence. They're on his staff and they're responsible in a great measure for the instruction that has been given for training youngsters."

Dr. King branded the charges "absolutely untrue." He said it seemed to be necessary to call out the guard, but feared the step might "aggravate" the tense situation.

In his meeting with the Mayor, Dr. King won city agreement to four requests

The city agreed to the following:

¶Install sprinklers on fire hydrants so children in the ghetto can cool off on hot summer days.

¶Request Federal funds to construct swimming pools and other recreational facilities for Negroes.

¶Appoint a citizens committee to make a study of the police department and how its relations with minority groups can be improved. Dr. King has demanded that a civilian review board be established to investigate charges of police brutality.

¶Assign two workers to each precinct in the riot zone to work for an end to the rioting.

No agreement was announced on a King demand for a crash employment program for jobless Negro men.

Accord Called A Start

Dr. King said the steps agreed to did not meet the "basic needs" of the ghetto but were a start.

"We emerged with something concrete to offer the people," he said.

Mayor Daley and Dr. King both said they would continue to work for long-range goals of equality, better housing and job opportunities.

Dr. King and his top aides were in the streets till 4 A.M. Friday seeking to calm the crowds and preach nonviolence.

Dr. King sped from the scene of one battle to another as incidents multiplied, but he remained in his car most of the time.

He said the basic causes of of the disturbances were segregated slum living conditions and police brutality.

But he told a rally earlier in the evening that "our victories" would not come through violence.

"We shall overcome when black and white work together," he said.

Dr. King presented a long list of civil rights demands to Mayor Daley early this week. He said he left a conference with the Mayor and city officials Monday without gaining any commitments for improvements. He added then that "direct action" would be necessary to achieve his program for Chicago.

Mayor Daley asserted angrily Friday that the strife was "planned." Dr. King's aides, he said, were "in here for no other purpose than to bring disorder to the streets of Chicago."

At a news conference Friday afternoon, Dr. J. H. Jackson, president of the National Baptist Convention, the largest organized body of Negroes in the country, blamed "outside interference."

Although Dr. King is not guilty of preaching hate, he said, "there is danger of using nonviolence in such a way that it will create violence."

In his denunciation of the King organization, Mayor Daley said Dr. King's aides "showed pictures" of techniques in violence.

He apparently alluded to activities of the Rev. James Bevel, project director of the Southern Christian Leadership Conference's action program for Chicago. Mr. Bevel has been showing motion pictures of last year's destructive riots in Watts, Calif., to Negroes here.

Dr. King said the movies were used "to show the negative results of rioting."

Six extra courtrooms in the Criminal Courts Building were pressed into service this afternoon for hearings for the scores of persons arrested in the four-day race riot, which began Tuesday when the police turned off a hydrant Negro children were using to cool off in the 98-degree heat.

Chief Circuit Court Judge John S. Boyle said the courts would operate on a round-the-clock basis if necessary. All city magistrates, 10 suburban magistrates, more than 20 court clerks and many bailiffs were ordered to stand by for duty in the special courts. Many persons were jailed on charges of disorderly conduct, and theft and on more serious charges.

Frie Stations Evacuated

Six fire stations in the riot zone were evacuated Friday afternoon to safeguard equipment and protect the lives of firemen. Crews and trucks were moved to stations on the perimeter of the troubled area.

Firemen rushing to blazes, started when Negroes tossed Molotov cocktails, were among the injured Thursday night and early Friday. One fireman, Lieut. Donald Taylor, was hit in the face by a brick as it crashed through the windshield of his fire engine.

Policemen chasing two men carrying cartons of empty bottles found a cache of Molotov cocktails in an alley.

A Molotov cocktail is a bottle, filled with gasoline and containing a fuse, which when lighted and thrown bursts into flames.

The riot-torn zone extends from Canal Street just west of the downtown loop to the western city limits. It is bounded on the north by Lake Street and on the south by 24th Street. The area of trouble has grown considerably from the neighborhood disturbance that started the melees, but does not extend into the big South Side Negro ghetto.

The West and South Side ghettos combined contain nearly a million Negroes, almost a third of Chicago's 3,500,000 population.

Second Call-up in Year

Today's guard call-up was the second in less than a year

United Press International Telephoto

AS NATIONAL GUARD ARRIVED: Youngsters move up to a line of military vehicles as National Guardsmen roll into a staging area near Chicago's riot-torn West Side.

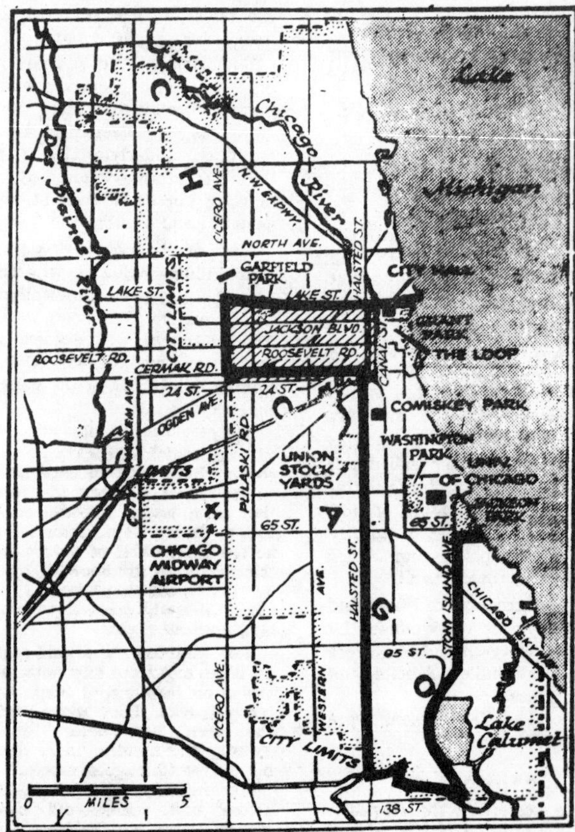

The New York Times July 16, 1966

GHETTO AREA: Heavy line outlines predominantly Negro neighborhoods in Chicago. Violence has occurred in the section on West Side denoted by diagonal shading.

here. Last August Governor Kerner ordered 2,500 troops to duty to keep the peace in a smaller West Side area, West Garfield, also after three nights of rioting.

The violence this week has brought more terror to the West Side because rioters have added rifles to their arsenal. The most vicious exchange of gunfire so far occurred late Thursday night at the Henry Horner public housing project at Lake and Wood Streets.

Within minutes at least a dozen muzzle flashes were counted from an upper-floor window in one 10-story building. The police, about a hundred strong, trained flood lights on the structure and raked the apartment with gunfire. After an hour-long siege, they swept into the building under covering fire but failed to find the snipers.

They had halted an elevated train approaching the scene, and passengers crouched on the floor till the shooting ended.

The pop-pop of rifle fire from dark rooftops kept the police whirling and ducking from doorway to doorway all night. Crowds on nearly every street jeered as policemen ran from one trouble spot to another on sidewalks and alleys alive with gunfire and showers of stones and bricks.

No estimate of the extensive damage and looting loss has been made yet by city officials.

The largest fire in the riot zone Friday sent flames and smoke billowing from a bottling plant and adjacent packing company filled with cardboard boxes. Firemen poured thousands of gallons of water into the building to bring the blaze under control.

Richard Stogin, owner of the packing company, reported that he was told by an employe that his Negro employes had been warned to get out of the building because "it will be burned to the ground this afternoon."

Three hundred firemen and 60 pieces of equipment were used to fight the fire, which caused $100,000 damage. Fire Commissioner Robert Quinn ordered a full investigation of the cause.

Rumors circulated Friday that 12 persons arrested Thursday night in a rain on a basement meeting would be charged with conspiracy to commit treason against the state of Illinois.

The 12 included Frederick Andrews, a leader of Act, a militant civil rights group here. Commander George T. Sims said a gun and leaflets advocating civil disobedience were found in the basement. He said the treason charge had been considered but was changed to disorderly conduct.

Hearings on the disorderly conduct charges were set Friday afternoon for July 28. Arresting policemen had written on the arrest slip of each that "the above subject was arrested at 3838 West Jackson Boulevard for disorderly conduct and conspiracy to commit treason."

State's Attorney Daniel P. Ward, however, said the police had done so without authorization from his office and that no conspiracy charges would be preferred without further investigation.

July 16, 1966

TROOPS BATTLE DETROIT SNIPERS, FIRING MACHINE GUNS FROM TANKS

DETROIT TOLL IS 31

Rioters Rout Police— Guardsmen Released to Aid Other Cities

By GENE ROBERTS
Special to The New York Times

DETROIT, Wednesday, July 26—National Guard tank crews blasted away at entrenched snipers with .50-caliber machine guns early today after sniper fire routed policemen from a square-mile area of the city.

The deadly gun battle, the worst in three days of Negro rioting here, took the lives of a 4-year-old Negro girl, a motel guest and a sniper.

Two others were killed while attempting to crash a police-National Guard barricade, raising the death toll to 31.

"It's worth your life in there," said Lieut. Col. Herman Steenstra of the Michigan National Guard as he helped seal off the West Side riot area to motorists.

"If we see anyone move, we shoot and ask questions later," another guardsman said.

Lieut. Gen. John L. Throckmorton, the 18th Airborne Corps Commander in charge of the 4,700 paratroopers and 3,000 guardsmen here, called a news conference at 2:30 A.M. after some of the fiercest fighting.

4 Policemen Wounded

"The East Side is secure," he said, "and the West Side is under control but not quite secure."

At times snipers ranged out of the major battle area, which lies about a mile from General Motors headquarters, and fired into Receiving Hospital and the Harlan House Motel.

The police said a bullet had smashed through a fourth-floor window of the motel, fatally wounding Helen Hall of Oakdale, Conn.

Several other persons, four of them policemen, were wounded here last night as the gun battles continued in near darkness. Gunfire had shattered almost all of the street lights at the scene.

At least 21 persons—including seven National Guardsmen, four city policemen and a state trooper—were treated at Henry Ford Hospital for gunshot wounds.

The gun battles continued into early morning in near darkness as bullets had shattered almost all street lights.

Meanwhile, Army paratroopers—sent into the city by President Johnson yesterday—shielded firemen during an outbreak of more than 100 new fires.

Before dusk last night, the police and Federal troops had reported progress in controlling the riot that started Sunday morning on 12th Street, in the same area now embattled by sniper fire.

Gov. George Romney, after learning yesterday afternoon that looting and burning were subsiding, withdrew some National Guardsmen from Detroit for possible use in controlling rioting in such cities as Grand Rapids, Flint and Pontiac.

He received approval for the personnel shift from General Throckmorton, 18th Airborne Corps Commander, who is in charge of 4,700 paratroopers and about 3,000 National Guardsmen.

General Throckmorton and the state and city police are coordinating their riot control efforts at a command post on the third floor of police headquarters.

In Grand Rapids, Negroes hurled firebombs and bricks at policemen and firemen and looting spread. Firemen were stoned as they fought more than 35 fires.

In Pontiac, there was relative calm, after two Negroes had been killed early yesterday during a night of violence. In Flint, Negroes who were arrested Monday were released on promises that they would patrol the streets telling others to "cool it."

In Toledo, Ohio, reinforced police units converged on several areas of the city as at least seven firebombings were reported.

The troop losses from Detroit were partly offset late yesterday when the Pentagon ordered a company of 25 helicopters into the area from Fort Riley, Kan. The craft were called in apparently to provide aerial reconnaissance over still smoldering riot areas.

Neither Governor Romney nor General Throckmorton would say how many guardsmen were dispatched from Detroit, or how many still remained in the city.

But the police said that about two or three thousand had remained on duty here in addition to the 4,700 Army paratroopers.

Orders to Shoot

All the troops, along with about 4,000 Detroit policemen,

United Press International Telephoto

NEW FIRES sent smoke rising in Detroit last night. This was scene in 12th Street, where riots began on Sunday.

were under orders to shoot fleeing felons.

"If there's any trouble," Governor Romney said, "these men will take prompt and firm action. Those caught setting fires and looting should be prepared to pay the consequences."

Cyrus Vance, President Johnson's representative at the riot scene, said that the violence in Detroit had ebbed "considerably," but he cautioned that it was still too early to declare the city's emergency at an end.

Encouraged by the presence of the Federal troops, many of the city's white residents were venturing out of their homes yesterday for the first time since rioting began early Sunday morning.

They saw a city that looked —in many areas—as if it were a set for a World War II movie.

No fewer than 950 buildings had been destroyed or heavily damaged by fire, the police said, and at least 1,500 more had been looted for a total property loss of more than $150-million, making it the costliest riot in the nation's history.

Injuries stood at nearly 900 and arrests at 2,700. Of the 31 dead, 5 were white—a woman, a policeman, a fireman, a looter and a sniper.

The police were uncertain about the causes of the deaths but said that at lease one appeared to have resulted from fire.

Seven refugee centers were in operation yesterday to care for families that fled from the hardest-hit riot areas. Most fled out of fear rather than because their dwellings had been damaged by fire and looting.

With the exception of storetop apartments, the fire damage had been sustained almost exclusively by shops, groceries, appliance department and variety stores.

For the most part the destruction followed a familiar pattern. The looters first stripped the stores of all they could carry and then set fire as they fled the buildings.

Major furniture stores and discount houses were destroyed on Livernois Avenue, near Seven Mile Road, a street that contains one of the nation's largest concentration of new and used car agencies.

The University of Detroit is situated only a stone's throw from the scene of one of the street's major fires. Thousands of middle class Negroes and whites live side by side in the area.

Stores in another integrated district of low-income families along Grand River Avenue were also hard hit, but the damage was heaviest along solidly Negro segments of Grand River, Linwood Avenue and 12th Street, where the rioting began on Sunday after the police raided a speakeasy.

Today's outbreaks of looting and fire came mainly on Detroit's East Side, more than 12 miles from the Grand River-Linwood-12th Street districts, possibly because there were few stores left unlooted in the northwest Negro areas.

Negroes, who on Monday were carting off almost everything in sight, milled about the streets yesterday afternoon waving and smiling at the heavily integrated paratroop units.

It was another humid day here with temperatures in the low eighties. Many of the paratroopers were sweat soaked from rushing from incident to incident in jeeps that had been flown here in transport planes from Fort Bragg, N. C., and Fort Campbell, Ky.

The troopers set up command posts and bivouac areas in schoolhouses in the heart of the riot-torn neighborhoods. Some could be seen playing cards, reading paperback novels as they waited for emergency calls.

Some took up positions at street corners in areas still menaced by looters, but most troopers remained mobile, moving in to shield firemen from sniper attacks and to answer whatever calls were channeled to them by the police.

Meanwhile Mayor Jerome P. Cavanagh sharply rebuffed a black nationalist organization, the Malcolm X Society, which said it could end violence by 7 P.M. if a iist of eight demands were met.

Richard Henry, spokesman for the organization, said his group had no direct contact with the rioters but added:

"We think the people involved will respond to our call for cessation of hostilities if our points are accepted as a basis of discussion."

Among Mr. Henry's demands were the immediate withdrawal of all troops and the immediate release of all prisoners.

City judges made it clear that they planned to place snipers on trial. They held two suspected snipers under $200,000 bond after arraigning them on charges of assault with intent to commit murder.

The unusually heavy bond came after a warning by the Wayne County prosecutor, William Callahan, that suspected rioters would be prosecuted to the "fullest extent of the law."

Sniping reached a peak late Monday night and early yesterday when Negroes laid siege to two police precinct stations, temporarily trapping more than 100 National Guardsmen and policemen inside.

The snipers were driven back by guardsmen who arrived at the scene in tanks.

After touring the riot-struck areas again Mayor Cavanagh announced the resumption of garbage collection services for the first time in three days and said he was hopeful that the city's commerce could return to normal soon.

July 26, 1967

URBAN COALITION URGES U.S. SPUR JOBS FOR MILLION

Conference of 800 Leaders Calls for New Priorities—Housing Drive Backed

PRIVATE ROLE STRESSED

Dissatisfaction Is Indicated With Johnson Response to Cities' Difficulties

By ROBERT B. SEMPLE Jr.
Special to The New York Times

WASHINGTON, Aug. 24—A convocation of more than 800 mayors and business, labor, church and civil rights leaders called on the Government today to "reorder national priorities" and develop "an emergency work program" to provide jobs in the nation's riot-torn cities.

The group, which calls itself the Urban Coalition, held a one-day meeting at the Shoreham Hotel here. It sought solutions to the urban crisis and, in the words of its keynote speaker, Mayor Lindsay of New York, sought also to forge "a national coalition of those with a stake in the city and its people."

In a statement of "principles, goals, and commitments," which was adopted by a rousing voice vote shortly before noon, the coalition pledged itself to work for better urban conditions on a variety of fronts.

An Appeal to Washington

The statement also urged Congress and the Administration to do the following:

¶Provide at least one million "meaningful" and "socially useful" jobs immediately, concentrating on "the huge backlog of employment needs in parks, streets, slums, countryside, schools, colleges, libraries and hospitals."

¶Develop a closer working relationship with the private sector and, through incentives, encourage industry to create vast new programs of job training.

¶Undertake "bold and immediate steps" to provide a decent home for every American, "including the goal of at least a million housing units for lower-income families annually."

Although neither the statement nor the speakers mentioned President Johnson by name, the tone of the remarks and the substance of the document strongly suggested that the delegates believed the Administration's response to the urban crisis had been insufficient.

Mr. Lindsay won the day's biggest applause when he stated that the American commitment abroad "should not be allowed to weaken our resolve at home." Later he added:

"If our defense commitment, our commitment to space, or any other commitment made before our urban areas were beset by agony is blocking a vigorous effort to end those agonies, those commitments should be reassessed."

The statement of principles adopted this morning declared:

"We believe the American people and the Congress must reorder national priorities, with a commitment of resources equal to the magnitude of the problems we face. The crisis requires a new dimension of effort in both the public and private sectors, working together to provide jobs, housing, education and the other needs of the cities."

The coalition grew out of a yearlong effort by the big-city mayors to overcome what they felt was "citizen indifference" to city problems.

The participants at the meeting today included well-known leaders from nearly every major field.

'Deal With All Segments'

There were some notable absentees — no governors, no members of the Federal Government, and, with the exception of a small group from Rochester, N. Y., and perhaps some others, very few of the poor.

The absence of the poor themselves was not a matter of public comment until the closing moments of the session when Andrew Heiskell, board chairman of Time, Inc, who was co-chairman of the meeting, invited final comments from the delegates.

The last to speak was Marion Barry, former leader of the Student Nonviolent Coordinating Committee in the capital, who is now active in other civil rights groups here. Dressed in a green T-shirt and wearing sunglasses, Mr. Barry, who said he had not been invited, moved to the rostrum and warned the coalition not to overlook the poor.

Randolph Is Co-Chairman

"You've got to deal with all segments," he said, including those "not accustomed to coming to the Shoreham Hotel and fussing round. They don't understand all this hifalutin talk.

"And when you hold these meetings, please don't have them out her at the Shoreham. Hold them down where the people are, get down there and try to get to the nitty-gritty. When that time comes we'll begin to scratch the surface of the urban problem."

The other co-chairman of the meeting was A. Philip Randolph, president of the Brotherhood of Sleeping Car Porters. Both he and Mr. Heiskell were members of a 32-man steering committee that hammered out the statement of principles in a three-and-a-half-hour session last night.

Other members of the steering committee included Henry Ford 2d, chairman of the Ford Motor Company; David Rockefeller, president of the Chase Manhattan Bank; George Meany, president of the American Federation of Labor and Congress of Industrial Organizations; Walter P. Reuther, president of the United Auto Workers.

Also, Whitney M. Young Jr., executive director of the National Urban League; Roy Wilkins, executive director of the National Association for the Advancement of Colored People; the Most Rev. John F. Dearden, Roman Catholic Archbishop of Detroit; Rabbi Jacob P. Rudin, president of the Synagogue Council of America, and the mayors of several major cities.

In the opinion of many of the participants, the meeting served several useful purposes apart from the fundamental objective of dramatizing the crisis in the cities.

In the steering committee sessions last night and the panel sessions this afternoon, "a lot of plain talking was done and a lot of problems were finally brought out on the table," one participant told a reporter.

Sources reported that at last night's meeting of the steering Committee, which was closed to the press, Mr. Meany and Joseph D. Keenan, secretary of the International Brotherhood of Electrical Workers, agreed to make a serious, sustained effort to end restrictive admission practices in the building trades unions and cooperate in promoting new and perhaps quicker methods of construction.

The convocation clearly illuminated the contrast between the rhetoric of the urban liberals on the one hand and the realities of budget pressures and Congressional caution on the other.

Lunch With Congressmen

Following the adoption of the statement, for example, a delegation from the steering committee drove to Capitol Hill to press its case over lunch with Congressional leaders. No Republicans appeared. The four Democrats who did show up were the Speaker of the House, John W. McCormack of Massachusetts, Representative Carl Albert of Oklahoma, the House Majority Leader; Representative Hale Boggs of Louisiana, the Assistant Majority Leader, and Senator Russell B. Long of Louisiana,the Assistant Majority Leader of the Senate.

Mr. McCormack listed a number of close votes and recent defeats for the Administration and urged the delegates to use their influence to persuade Congressmen to support urban-oriented measures.

But he and the others were cool to bold new emergency measures, leading one disgruntled delegate to remark:

"They didn't really understand what we were talking about."

In a report later to the other members of the coalition, Mayor Jerome P. Cavanagh of Detroit repeated this sentiment publicly.

"A sense of purpose and national goals was lacking in our meeting with the distinguished members of Congress," he said.

Moreover, even as the coalition was calling for a massive job-creating program, reports were circulating that Joseph A. Califano Jr., special assistant to the President, in a private memorandum to some members of the Senate Labor Committee, had attacked sharply a special \$3-billion emergency job program attached to the antipoverty bill by Senator Joseph S. Clark, Pennsylvania Democrat.

Mr. Califano denied that he had drafted the memorandum. Other persons said it was apparently written in the Office of Economic Opportunity.

The point of the memo was that the \$3-billion measure should be considered separately, on grounds that the antipoverty measure was in enough trouble without being weighted down by other costly proposals.

Despite the incident on Capitol Hill, the coalition determined to push ahead. There was talk this afternoon of drafting a bill similar to Mr. Clark's for presentation in the House. And the coalition appointed five separate committees to draw up specific proposals to implement its general recommendations for jobs, housing and industry-government-labor cooperation.

August 25, 1967

Riots in a 'Model City'

By WILLIAM BORDERS

NEW HAVEN — Mayor Richard C. Lee lost seven pounds last week as gangs of Negroes rocked the streets of his model city with looting, arson and violence. The disorders tapered off last Wednesday, and this week, if calm continues and sleep returns, the Mayor hopes to gain back the seven pounds. But the loss to his city and to its reputation as a pattern for urban excellence may be impossible to make up.

The disorder, in which 200 store windows were broken and several fire trucks were stoned, was much less severe than it was in some other cities this summer. But to many, it caused a greater shock, because, as one official put it, "We thought New Haven had already accomplished the things other cities are just beginning to strive for."

The antipoverty program here, which was set up a full two years before President Johnson first proposed his own War on Poverty, has been used as a model from coast to coast. Its annual budget, now over $8-million, has reached the neighborhoods not only through common channels like job training but also through the development of novel ideas, like courses to make shrewd shoppers out of poor housewives, and the community school program, in which public schools are open outside classroom hours for use by the aged.

Spotlight on Lee

The city's elaborate urban renewal projects first put the national spotlight on Mayor Lee more than 10 years ago. To his vast pride, the city—long regarded nationally as no more than a vast unappealing slum one passed through to get to Yale—has become at least as much of an attraction to visitors as the university that dominated it for 200 years. Experts arrive by the busload to study the city's imaginative rent supplement programs for the poor, and in the economic boom of Mr. Lee's renewal, three new hotels, two new department stores and a sleek two-story shopping mall have transformed the downtown area and given New Haven a new face.

Then racial violence struck where the urban experts had least expected it. But some Negroes, long frustrated and bitter about what they saw as the ironic unfairness of New Haven's reputation as a model had been predicting trouble for months. "You can talk all you want about how wonderful Dick Lee has been, but it doesn't impress the guy in the slums whose kid's been bitten by a rat," said one worker on the staff of Community Progress, Inc., the antipoverty program that was so highly regarded that the Federal Government used it as a model.

But for the 51-year-old Mayor, to whom last week brought something close to personal grief, the dream has still not been shattered. "I feel saddened by this whole thing," he said, his voice gravelly from lack of sleep, "but it won't deter me from continuing our programs. We've got a good thing that must be made better, not a bad thing that must be changed."

'I Hate That Term'

The Mayor, who grew up in a cold-water flat on a street where the residents were throwing beer bottles at the police last Monday night, has consistently denied that this is a model city. "I hate that term," he said months ago, "because there's still so much to do. If this is the model, then God help America."

Mr. Lee's severest critics have long agreed that New Haven is no model, but the question they ask is: Why not?

The Mayor has been in office 13 years, with steadily growing local popularity and a Democratic registration edge so large that his party now holds every seat on the Board of Aldermen.

He has attracted dollars at a pace that is not only staggering but self-perpetuating as well: the Ford Foundation, which started the poverty program here with a $2.5-million grant, was originally attracted by the gleaming success of New Haven's urban renewal. Although it has only 140,000 people, New Haven has consistently been among the top cities in the country in grants received from the Federal Government. Its present urban renewal allocation from Washington averages out to $800 for every man, woman and child in town.

That is a statistic that Mayor Lee and his aides quote almost daily. But last week one angry Negro came home from his arraignment hearing, after being arrested in the rioting, surveyed a shabby row of tenements where the rents range up to $150 a month, and said, "Yeah, $800 is my share. But you don't see one dime of it spent on my block."

August 27, 1967

Mayor Charges U.S. Scrimps on City Aid

By STEVEN V. ROBERTS

In some of the harshest language he has used against the Federal Government, Mayor Lindsay accused it yesterday of not providing sufficient aid to the nation's cities.

The Mayor noted that the Department of Housing and Urban Development has not yet designated New York as eligible for aid under the Model Cities program, even though its application was filed last spring. He added:

"Once again, it seems, the bureaucracy has met the rising expectations of the poor, the ill-housed and the oppressed with the empty rhetoric of promises and pledges."

The Model Cities program is designed to provide cities with unrestricted grants to combat problems of physical blight, health, education and welfare in selected poor neighborhoods. About $11-million was appropriated last year for planning purposes, but Congress is still debating how much to allocate for in actual programs.

The Doubts Expressed

The Mayor addressed a hearing of the National Commission on Urban Problems at the Cooperative Auditorium, 551 Grand Street. The commission, headed by former Senator Paul H. Douglas, will hold its final hearing today at the Community Church, 40 East 35th Street.

Many speakers at Wednesday's hearing expressed doubt that Congress would ever appropriate significant aid for the cities and stressed the need to attract private investment in the slums. But Mayor Lindsay emphasized the Federal responsibility:

"We need vigorous national support if we are to redeem the debt the nation has incurred through a century of neglect and oppression. If that support is denied us, all the wind in Washington cannot fill the bag the mayors will be left holding."

Bayard Rustin, the civil rights leader, declared: "David Rockefeller made it very clear to me the other day that the private sector won't provide housing for the hard-core poor, and for one simple reason, there is not enough money in it for them."

Mr. Rockefeller, the chairman of the Chase Manhattan Bank, and his brother Governor Rockefeller have both advocated increased private investment in the slums. But even supporters of this policy acknowledge that enormous financial incentives would have to be offered before the private sector would make such investments.

On Wednesday Senator Robert F. Kennedy, Democrat of New York, urged support for legislation he is sponsoring that would provide tax benefits and low-cost mortgages to private industry willing to build businesses and low-income housing in ghetto areas.

Charles Abrams chairman of the department of urban planning at Columbia University, said the urban commission's major goal should be to make it clear that "the cities can't take care of themselves; the Federal Government has to realize the burden is on it."

Mr. Lindsay also charged that the Federal Government imposes regulations that render existing programs "virtually useless." For example, he said, the city is not allowed to spend more than $20,000 for every unit of public housing. The result is that very few apartments are built for the large families who need them most.

Washington also has a cost ceiling on its middle-income programs called 221(d) (3), which has severely limited its use in New York, Mr. Lindsay said. Limits that are realistic in other cities produce headaches in New York, which has the highest building costs in the nation.

The Mayor stressed that even though New York badly needed money for physical construction, it needed operating revenue even more. For example, he said, "Our backs are to the wall with the pressures of collective bargaining."

Concede Bottleneck

One solution, he said, would be for the Federal Government to assume the entire cost of the city's burgeoning welfare programs.

Mr. Lindsay acknowledged that the city had as many

bureaucratic bottlenecks as Washington. He said: "The delays in the Budget Bureau, in the Controller's office, in all the hearings any project has to go through mean plans can drag on for a very, very long time."

Mr. Abrams also criticized the Federal administration of programs. "The Federal Housing Administration used to discriminate along racial lines," he said. "Now it discriminates on economic grounds — it won't invest in the slums — but the victims are the same."

Mr. Abrams said he would undertake a project this fall in which youths from East Harlem who had participated in the disorders there this summer would work at Columbia on a plan for the development of their neighborhood. "Who knows better what the neighborhood needs?" he asked.

September 8, 1967

63 CITIES CHOSEN TO GET SLUM AID; NEW YORK LISTED

MODEL CITIES SET

Will Share $11-Million in Planning Program, $300-Million Later

By ROBERT B. SEMPLE Jr.
Special to The New York Times

WASHINGTON, Nov. 16— The Administration made public today a list of 63 cities, including New York, that will take part in the first phase of the model cities program.

The program is designed to help cities rebuild slum neighborhoods and is regarded by the Administration as the most important new weapon in its campaign against urban blight.

The 63 communities were chosen from 193 that submitted preliminary applications for funds. The winners will share $11-million in planning money appropriated by Congress last year. The exact amount of each grant will be worked out in negotiations between Federal and local officials.

After the cities have drawn up detailed plans and submitted them to Washington, they will become eligible for $300-million appropriated last month to carry out the rebuilding process.

No Formal Deadline

No formal deadline for the final plans has been established, but Robert C. Weaver, Secretary of Housing and Urban Development, said that "in no instance" would a city have more than a year to complete its plan.

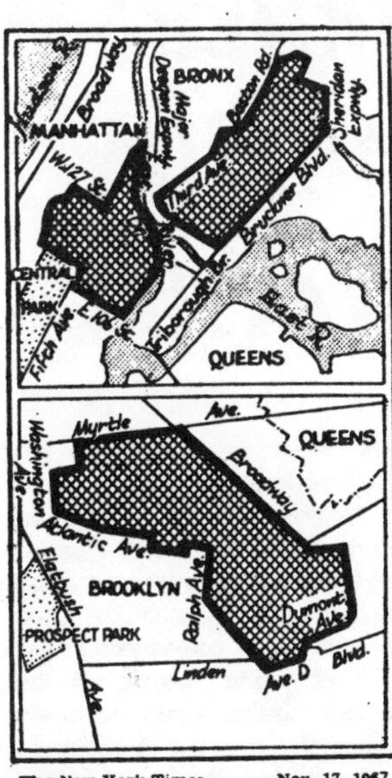

The New York Times Nov. 17, 1967

Harlem and South Bronx, in map at top, and Central Brooklyn, below, have been selected for Federal aid.

Mr. Weaver, who announced the list at a news conference this morning, also warned that cities receiving planning funds were not guaranteed construction funds later on.

"They must successfully complete the planning process," he declared.

However, it is virtually certain that most of the cities named will receive program funds. They have already survived stiff competition, and program funds would be denied only if a city's detailed plans fell short of the promise of its preliminary application.

New York will receive funds to begin planning for the social and physical rehabilitation of three slum neighborhoods: Harlem, Central Brooklyn and the South Bronx. The city asked for $406,340 in planning funds but will probably have to settle for less.

Negotiations Later

According to usually well-informed sources here, the housing agency is prepared to give New York $300,000 to $350,000, although negotiations over the next two weeks with city officials may push this figure somewhat higher. Most other cities will also suffer cuts.

However, the fact that New York has been authorized to begin planning in all three of the areas named in its application is regarded here as a victory for Mayor Lindsay and a vindication of his strategy in dealing with Federal officials on model cities funds.

This strategy called for the submission of all three neighborhoods even though the program was originally designed to rejuvenate a single "showcase" neighborhood in each city. Mr. Lindsay argued that to choose among New York's three worst slums was morally and politically impossible. Apparently officials here agreed. New York was the only city to submit a multiple application.

Today's announcement had been delayed for months by administrative complexities and political pressures. The day after the May 1 deadline for applications, H. Ralph Taylor, Assistant Secretary of Housing and Uurban Development, who is in charge of the program, announced that the list of winners would be announced in "about 60 days," or July 1.

However, the selection process turned out to be long and difficult, partly because of the nature of the program itself.

As stipulated by Congress, the authorizing legislation requires cities receiving model cities grants to coordinate a variety of social and physical programs to achieve a visible and substantial impact on the "model neighborhood."

Accordingly, each application was forced to run a gantlet composed of a half-dozen Federal agencies with urban programs. And most of the applications were several hundred pages long.

Moreover, officials feared that an early announcement of the winners would antagonize Congressmen whose cities had not been chosen and rob the Administration of badly needed votes on a number of appropriations bills, including the $300-million model cities appropriation only a few weeks ago.

This strategy did not command unanimity in the Administration. Some officials believed the early enthusiasm for the program generated in hundreds of communities would dwindle if the announcements were delayed. But the White House counseled delay, and its view prevailed.

Immediate Criticism

Mr. Weaver's announcement of the winners provoked immediate criticism from some quarters on Capitol Hill this afternoon, suggesting that the White House might have had good reason for caution.

The House Republican leader, Gerald R. Ford of Michigan, told a news conference he hoped the model cities had been chosen "on the merits" of their applications but noted that only nine of the 63 were in Republican Congressional districts.

"When Republicans get 14 per cent it must raise a question whether merit was a total factor," he declared.

Representative Robert Taft Jr. of Ohio complained that only three of 11 applicants from Ohio had been chosen, while four out of seven from Texas had been. He promised to investigate the exclusion of Cincinnati.

Representative Samuel S. Stratton, upstate New York Democrat, said he was "keenly disappointed" by the exclusion of Amsterdam, N.Y., his home town, from the list and complained that not enough small cities had been chosen.

"I supported model cities only because of early assurance from the Secretary that small cities would be fairly included and that the bulk of the money wouldn't just go to big cities," he said. "Yet today the announcement discloses that as far as New York State is concerned there is only one small city and everything else goes to the three largest cities in the state."

The New York cities, apart from New York City itself, were Buffalo, Rochester and Poughkeepsie.

Officials of the housing agency said they had tried to achieve the proper "mix" between small, medium-sized and large cities. They added that the competitive nature of the program meant that some cities would inevitably lose and that they had expected an uproar. They insisted finally that despite political pressures they had tried to judge every city on its merits.

Critics of the Administration were also quick to point out what they asserted was a suspiciously close relationship between some of the cities and key Congressmen.

Among the smaller cities selected was Smithville, Tenn., home of Representative Joe L. Evins, a Democrat who is chairman of the subcommittee that handles the housing agency's appropriations and who played a leading role in winning funds for the program in a hostile House; Texarkana, Tex., home of Representative Wright Patman, Democrat who heads the House Banking and Currency Committee, which authorized the model cities bill; Pikeville, Ky., which is in the Congressional district of Representative Carl D. Perkins, chairman of the House Education and Labor Committee, which handles antipoverty legislation.

The list also included several communities hard hit by last summer's riots—including Detroit and Newark—but there were several prominent omissions.

Neither Cleveland nor Los Angeles received grants, even though both had serious racial disturbances. Mr. Weaver told newsmen that Los Angeles had not met the program criteria and that Cleveland had not submitted an impressive plan.

However, he reminded the disappointed losers that Congress had appropriated $12-million more for a second round of planning grants.

"We will soon be inviting applications for this second round," he said. "It is our hope that many of the cities that applied for the first round, and were not selected for planning funds, will join other localities in applying for the second round."

President Johnson originally asked for $2.3-billion to carry the program over a six-year period. Last year, Congress cut this to a $900-million authorization over two years. Then, during the fight over appropriations this year, Congress cut Mr. Johnson's request for $662-million in the fiscal year 1968 to $300-million. Given the change in the balance of power in the House, however, most Administration officials were happy to get even this amount.

November 17, 1967

PANEL ON CIVIL DISORDERS CALLS FOR DRASTIC ACTION TO AVOID 2-SOCIETY NATION

WHITES CRITICIZED

Vast Aid to Negroes Urged, With New Taxes if Needed

By JOHN HERBERS
Special to The New York Times

WASHINGTON, Feb. 29—The President's National Advisory Commission on Civil Disorders gave this warning to Americans tonight: "Our nation is moving toward two societies, one black, one white—separate and unequal."

Unless drastic and costly remedies are begun at once, the commission said, there will be a "continuing polarization of the American community and, ultimately, the destruction of basic democratic values."

The commission said "white racism" was chiefly to blame for the explosive conditions that sparked riots in American cities during the last few summers. But it also warned that a policy of separatism now advocated by many black militants "can only relegate Negroes to a permanently inferior economic state."

As for the civil disorders that ravaged American cities last summer, the commission said they "were not caused by, nor were they the consequences of, any organized plan or 'conspiracy.'"

Broad Proposals

The panel made sweeping recommendations at Federal and local levels in law enforcement, welfare, employment, education and the news media. It made no attempt to put a price tag on these recommendations, but they go far beyond social programs that are now in trouble in Congress because of a tight budget. They would cost many billions of dollars.

"The vital needs of the nation must be met," the commission said. "Hard choices must be made, and, if necessary, new taxes enacted."

The 11-member commission, headed by Gov. Otto Kerner of Illinois, was appointed by President Johnson last July 27 to find the causes of urban riots and recommend solutions.

Its report amounts to a stinging indictment of the white society for its isolation and neglect of the Negro minority. Its pages are filled with findings to bear this out.

"Segregation and poverty have created in the racial ghetto a destructive environment totally unknown to most white Americans," the commission said. "What white Americans have never fully understood—but what the Negro can never forget—is that the white society is deeply implicated in the ghetto. White institutions created it, white institutions maintain it, and white society condones it."

The report was considered remarkable in that it was chiefly the work of white, middle-class Americans, several of them politicians with white constituencies. Most of the commission members are known as moderates.

Some, however, said they were shocked by the conditions they had found in Negro slums during their seven months of work. Some believed at the outset that because of the extent of the rioting there was bound to be some conspiracy involved, some plan for rioting that had been carried out.

But the most exhaustive investigations could find no evidence of this, the report indicated, even though it was clearly established that black militants had created a climate for rioting in their calls for violence. What the commission found over and over was evidence of white prejudice or ignorance that had led to Negroes being crowded into the inner city under a "destructive environment."

New Attitudes Urged

"Reaction to last summer's disorders had quickened the movement and deepened the division," the commission said. "Discrimination and segregation have long permeated much of American life; they now threaten the future of every American."

But the movement can be reversed, the commission said.

"The alternative is not blind repression of capitulation to lawlessness," it said. "It is the realization of common opportunities for all within a single society. This alternative will require a commitment to national action — compassionate, massive and sustained, backed by the resources of the most powerful and richest nation on this earth. From every American it will require new attitudes, new understanding, and, above all, new will."

Although the report was signed by all members, there was a close division on what approach to take. The very strong report, with very broad recommendations, was said to be chiefly due to the consistent pressures of Mayor Lindsay of New York, the vice chairman, Senator Fred Harris, Democrat of Oklahoma, and several others.

They were said to be aligned on most votes with Governor Kerner, Roy Wilkins, national director of the National Association for the Advancement of Colored People, Senator Edward W. Brooke, Republican of Massachusetts, and Herbert Jenkins, Atlanta police chief.

Drive for Jobs Asked

Other members of the commission were Representative James C. Corman, Democrat of California; Representative William M. McCulloch, Republican of Ohio; I. W. Abel, president of the United Steelworkers of

America; Charles B. Thornton, president of Litton Industries, and Mrs. Katherine G. Peden, former Commerce Commissioner of Kentucky.

The following were among the commission's scores of recommendations for bringing about equality and integration:

¶A revamping of the welfare system, with the Federal Government assuming a much higher percentage of the cost—up to 90 per cent—and with changes in administration that would help to hold families together.

¶Immediate action to create 2 million new jobs, 1 million by the state, local and Federal governments and 1 million by private industry.

¶Federal subsidy of on-the-job training for hard-core unemployed "by contract or by tax credits."

¶Long-range approach to a "guaranteed minimum income" for all Americans through a "basic allowance" to individuals and families.

¶Bringing 6 million new and existing dwellings within reach of low and moderate income families in the next five years, starting with 600,000 next year.

¶Decentralizing city governments to make them more responsive to the needs of the poor and placing police officers, with a higher percentage of Negroes, in the slums to act as advocates of the people as well as keepers of the peace.

¶Creation of a privately organized and financed Institute of Urban Communications to train and educate journalists in urban affairs and to bring more Negroes into journalism.

News Media Assailed

Turning to news coverage of last summer's racial disorders, the commission charged that some newspapers and radio and television stations so badly portrayed the scale and character of the violence that "the over-all effect was . . . an exaggeration of both mood and event."

The commission credited news media "on the whole" with trying to give a balanced report of the summer unrest. But, the commission added, "important segments . . . failed to report adequately on the causes and consequences of civil disorders and on the underlying problems of race relations."

"They have not communicated to the majority of their audience — which is white — a sense of the degradation, misery and hopelessness of life in the ghetto," the commission said.

The commission declared that reportorial improvement must come from within the media and not through governmental restrictions. They recommended that newspapers and radio and television stations take the following steps:

¶Expand and intensify coverage of the Negro community and racial problems so that the resulting newspapers and radio and television programs "recognize the existence and activities of Negroes as a group within the community."

¶Recruit more Negro reporters and editors and employ more newsmen familiar with urban and racial affairs.

¶Adopt self-regulating reporting guidelines for racial news and improve coordination with police information officers.

¶Organize an Institute of Urban Communications that will study urban affairs, train newsmen in covering them, recruit more Negro reporters and editors and develop better police-press relations.

The report has deep political implications. The commission is advocating that the nation go much further than the President has recommended in seeking new social legislation. It comes at a time, too, when the nation is deeply involved in the war in Vietnam and there have been reports that the President might send in additional troops, further increasing the cost of the war.

Congress has been reluctant to increase domestic programs while the war is draining so much of the nation's resources —$2-billion a month.

But the thrust of the commission's report is that the nation cannot afford to continue on its present domestic course, even if new sacrifices are needed.

"Large-scale and continuing violence could result," the group said, "followed by white retaliation, and, ultimately, the separation of the two communities in a garrison state."

"Even if violence does not occur," it said, "the consequences are unacceptable."

The commission added that the second choice—"enrichment of the slums and abandonment of integration"—is also unacceptable. "It is another way of choosing a permanently divided country" in which Negroes would continue to have a "permanently inferior economic status," it declared.

The commission also warned that "there is a grave danger that some communities may resort to the indiscriminate and excessive use of force." It went on:

"The commission condemns moves to equip police departments with mass destruction weapons, such as automatic rifles, machineguns and tanks. Weapons which are designed to destroy, not to control, have no place in densely populated urban communities."

Of the black militants who preach separation of their race as a means of advancing, the commission had this to say:

"They have retreated from a direct confrontation with American society on the issue of integration and, by preaching separatism, unconsciously function as an accommodation to white racism."

But the commission said "white racism is essentially responsible for the explosive mixture which has been accumulating in our cities since the end of World War II." It listed the following as the "most bitter fruits" of this racism:

¶Pervasive discrimination and segregation in employment, education and housing have resulted in the exclusion of great numbers of Negroes from economic progress that whites have enjoyed.

¶Migration of Negroes into the cities and movement of whites to the suburbs has created a "growing crisis of deteriorating facilities and services and unmet human needs."

¶In the slums, segregation and poverty converge on the young to destroy opportunity and enforce failure.

The commission devoted one section of its report to other minorities who have worked their way out of poverty and segregation and are now asking why Negroes do not do the same.

"Today, whites tend to exaggerate how well and quickly they escaped from poverty," it said. "The fact is that immigrants who came from rural backgrounds, as many Negroes do, are only now, after three generations, finally beginning to move into the middle class.

"By contrast, Negroes began concentrating in the city less than two generations ago, and under much less favorable conditions. Although some Negroes have escaped poverty, few have been able to escape the urban ghetto."

March 1, 1968

ARMY TROOPS IN CAPITAL AS NEGROES RIOT; GUARD SENT INTO CHICAGO, DETROIT, BOSTON; JOHNSON ASKS A JOINT SESSION OF CONGRESS

MANY FIRES SET

By BEN A. FRANKLIN
Special to The New York Times

WASHINGTON, April 5—President Johnson ordered 4,000 regular Army and National Guard troops into the nation's capital tonight to try to end riotous looting, burglarizing and burning by roving bands of Negro youths. The arson and looting began yesterday after the murder of the Rev. Dr. Martin Luther King Jr. in Memphis.

The White House announced at 5 P.M. that because the President had determined that "a condition of domestic violence and disorder" existed, he had issued a proclamation and an Executive order mobilizing combat-equipped troops in Washington. Some of the troops were sent to guard the Capitol and the White House.

Reinforcements numbering 2,500 riot-trained soldiers — a brigade of the 82d Airborne Division from Ft. Bragg, N. C.— were airlifted to nearby Andrews Air Force Base, to be held in reserve this weekend.

Guard Called In Other Cities

The National Guard also was called out in a half-dozen other cities in an effort to stem disorders or guard against them— Chicago, Detroit, Boston, Jackson, Miss., Raleigh, N. C., and Tallahassee, Fla.

The death toll from the violence stemming from Dr. King's assassination stood at a total of 14 tonight. Besides five deaths in Washington, they included seven in Chicago, one in Detroit and one in Tallahassee.

Mayor Walter E. Washington, who is a Negro, declared a 13-hour curfew, from 5:30 P.M. to 6:30 A.M. The Mayor's emergency order halted the sale of liquor and forbade the sale,

Associated Press

ON DUTY IN WASHINGTON: A soldier with a machine gun and another with a rifle, left, stand guard on the steps outside the Senate chamber. Flag was lowered to half-staff in tribute to the Rev. Dr. Martin Luther King Jr.

transportation or possession of firearms, explosives or flammable liquids.

At midnight, the police reported five dead, all but one of them Negroes, in 28 hours of disorders in this city of about 800,000, 63 per cent of them Negroes. Four Negroes were killed today, including two suspected looters, one of them 14 years old, who were shot to death by policemen in separate isolated encounters across the Anacostia River, far from the areas of general disorders. The two other Negro deaths today were described as apparently the result of accidents.

The white man, George Fletcher, 28, of suburban Woodbridge, Va., died this morning from injuries he received when a gang of Negro youths attacked him and three white companions in a Washington filling station at 2 A.M.

More than 350 persons were treated at hospitals including seven policemen and six firemen. More than 800 persons were arrested.

The police said reports of fires and lootings were diminishing apparently in part due to a sudden drop in the temperature. After a sultry day, the night air was a brisk 40 degrees.

The violence in Washington affected four areas of the city. For hours this afternoon and early evening, disorderly youths roamed most of the downtown shopping district, between 15th and Seventh Streets and F and H Streets N.W.

The three other areas were all Negro sections. There was no precise count of the number of fires or looted stores, but they ran well into the hundreds.

George Christian, the White House press secretary, said the President had acted on the recommendation of Mayor Washington, the Mayor's public safety director, Patrick V. Murphy, and the police chief, John B. Layton.

The 2,800-man District of Columbia police force, after a night of looting and arson set off yesterday by the assassination, lacked the manpower to respond to mounting calls to detain looters and protect motorists and firemen.

The looting and fires continued tonight. The police dispersed crowds as they gathered but made little or no effort to stop scattered looting by individuals and groups of two and three.

The city was abandoned tonight. Buses stopped running at dusk after a midafternoon rush of Government employes to flee the city. The Government workers and other civilians were advised by the police and Federal authorities to go home at about 2:30 P.M., a decision that caused a massive traffic jam and aided the looters. Police and fire vehicles were caught in the jam.

Tourists Affected

Also caught up in the unexpected disturbances were Washington's spring crush of thousands of tourists. Events scheduled for today and the weekend in connection with the Washington Cherry Blossom Festival—a major money-making attraction in this city, where tourism is the biggest industry—were canceled.

The opening game of the baseball season, the American League debut between the Washington Senators and the Minnesota Twins at D. C. Stadium, was postponed from Monday to Tuesday as a gesture of respect to Dr. King.

Both the outbreak of trouble last night and today's renewal of arson and looting followed angry public outbursts on Dr. King's death by Stokely Carmichael, the militant former chairman of the Student Nonviolent Coordinating Committee. He has been active as a committee field representative in Washington since his return from an around-the-world trip last January.

The looting last night followed a protest march led by Carmichael down 14th Street N.W., the center of a principal Negro commercial and shopping area. He demanded that businesses close for the night as a gesture of mourning for Dr. King. Then he urged Negroes to "go home and get your guns."

A Breathing Spell

By dawn 14th Street was a shambles of shattered glass and scattered merchandise. But sunlight brought a breathing spell. Sanitation workers began shoveling up the shards of glass.

At 10 A.M. Carmichael called a news conference at the 14th Street headquarters of the New School for Afro-American Thought. Before television cameras he declared that "white America has declared war on black America" with the murder of Dr. King.

There is "no alternative to retribution," he said.

"Black people have to survive, and the only way they will survive is by getting guns," he said.

Less than an hour after the 30-minute news conference ended, Carmichael was in the street with a following of 50 Negroes. Both newsmen and the police lost track of him as the day progressed.

The police either could not or would not interfere with the looting, and much of it was done brazenly, under the gaze of outnumbered police officers. Loot was hauled away in automobiles and trucks. During most of the afternoon the police dealt only with large groups of looters and a seemingly endless series of fires.

In the downtown shopping area of large department and specialty stores, the windows of such stores as Hecht's and Woodward and Lothrop's were smashed and looted. There were fires at both stores. The police appeared to concentrate their protective maneuvers along F Street, giving the other areas less priority.

In the second area hit, along Seventh Street N.W. from K to P. Streets, looting and fires—the major fires of the day were concentrated there—gradually drained off the scattered police manpower.

In a third area, looters and firebombers struck along 14th Street from downtown F Street as far north as Park Road N.W., nearly halfway to the Maryland line at Silver Spring.

Another less well defined area of looting and arson was across the Anacostia River, in heavily Negro Southeast Washington. Two of today's deaths occurred there.

North and West of the city, the two contiguous suburban jurisdictions in Maryland, Montgomery and Prince Georges Counties, both declared local emergencies during the day, invoking most of the special powers, with the exception of a curfew, authorized in the city. More than 50 pieces of fire equipment from volunteer companies in suburban counties were rushed into the city during the afternoon to aid the overtaxed district fire department.

A rash of major fires broke out in the fourth area hit, along H Street N.E., a section of block-square department store and food warehouses just east of Union Station.

It was the opening of this new front that appeared to convince reluctant city officials that the police could not continue the battle alone. Despite extended tours of duty that had kept some officers on their feet for nearly 24 hours, no more than about 1,000 patrolmen were available to cope with the spreading disorder.

Openly, on the police radio, precinct commanders and other police officials expressed their exasperation.

Once the decision was made to summon Army troops, the deployment came rapidly. Mr. Johnson signed the orders at 4:02 P.M., similar to those he signed in sending Army troops to Detroit last summer during rioting. By the time the White House announced the arrival of military reinforcements an hour later, helmeted combat troops carrying rifles with sheathed bayonets were in position to protect the White House and the Capitol.

A company of trained riot troops was billeted in the White House itself. Outside, other troops took station at the southeast gate.

Troops ringed the Capitol and set up a light machinegun post on the Capitol's west steps, overlooking the Mall.

The precautions were more than routine in the case of the White House. Looting and fires reached within two blocks of it at about the time the troops began to arrive.

Within hours, Army troops and federalized Guardsmen began establishing "a visible presence"—merely standing at parade rest—along 14th Street. As the soldiers arrived, the looting and arson advanced ahead of them into areas nominally still under police jurisdiction.

Tonight, as Guardsmen moved to occupy the upper reaches of 14th Street, as far north as Randolph Street, N.W., besieged residents of apartment buildings—most of them Negroes—cheered from their windows.

The troops fired a rolling barrage of tear gas before them. As they advanced, they passed a small shopping area—a dry cleaning establishment, delicatessen, bar and liquor store—all in flames. There was no fire fighting equipment on the scene.

The troops included 2,000 men of the Army and Air Force National Guard of the District of Columbia, under regular Army command. There were two companies from the Third Infantry Regiment, the Capital's crack ceremonial unit at nearby Fort Myers, Va., and

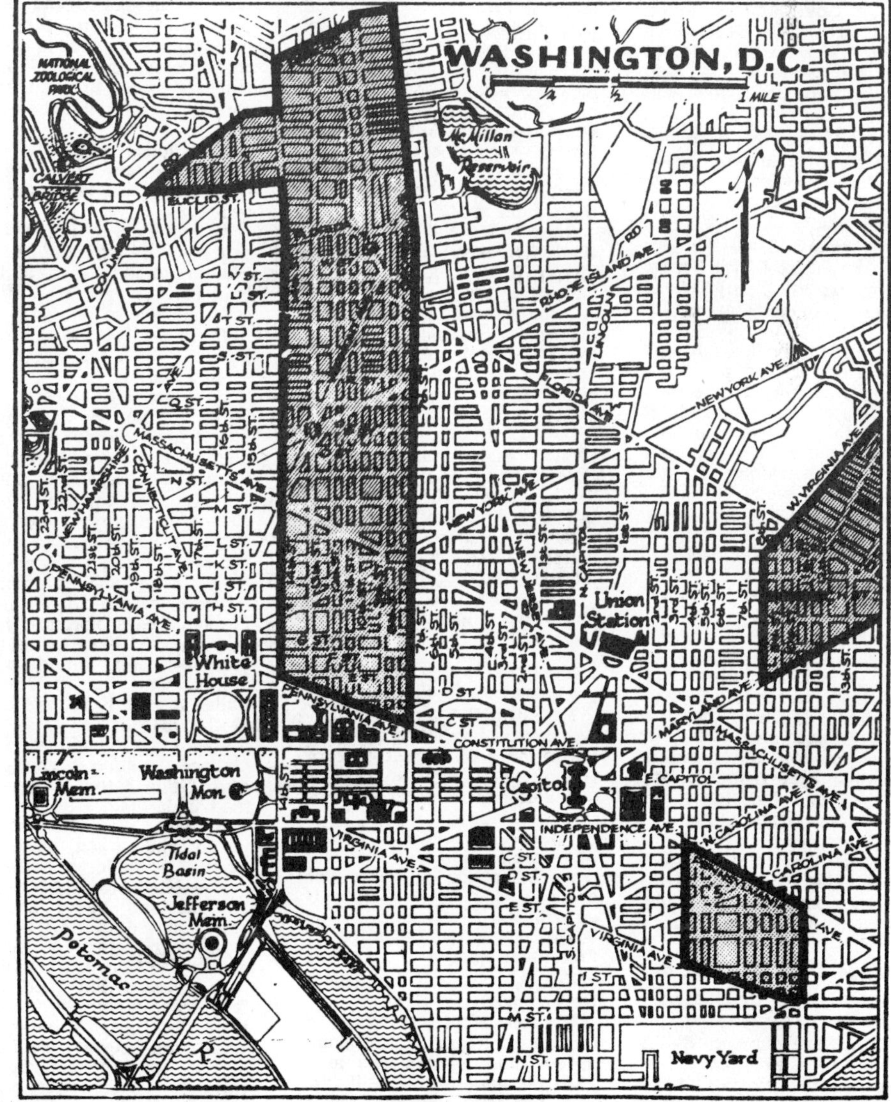

The New York Times April 6, 1968

VIOLENCE IN WASHINGTON: Dark lines enclose the major areas of disorder in the city

a squadron of the Sixth Cavalry Regiment from Fort Meade, Md., the Third Army headquarters halfway between Washington and Baltimore.

The troops also included elements of the 91st Engineering Battalion from nearby Fort Belvoir, Va.

It was the first time regular Army troops had been ordered into Washington for a civil disturbance since 1932, when cavalry under the late Gen. Douglas MacArthur drove hundreds of protesting bonus marchers from a squatters' encampment on the Anacostia River.

Alert in Boston

By JOHN H. FENTON

Special to The New York Times

Boston, April 5—Lieut. Gov. Francis W. Sargent placed several units of the Massachusetts National Guard on stand-by alert tonight as a precaution against possible rioting following the assassination of the Rev. Dr. Martin Luther King Jr.

Mr. Sargent, acting in the absence of Gov. John A. Volpe, who is on a State Department trip to Japan, said the troops would be assembled in their armories and not patrol the streets.

He conferred by telephone with Mr. Volpe and in person with Maj. Gen. Joseph S. Ambrose, commander of the National Guard.

More than 15,000 persons gathered in Post Office Square today to express their grief and outrage at the slaying of Dr. King.

The throng swelled during a march that started at Northeastern University in the Back Bay district and went three miles, through Boston Common and past the Massachusetts State House. Most of the marchers were white.

The group was joined downtown by young people from the Roxbury district, the heart of the Negro slum. The demonstration, aside from tying up traffic, was orderly.

Speakers warned of "bloody violence" if white racism did not soon end. The demonstration, chiefly arranged through telephone calls during the night and morning, was called by the Congress of Racial Equality, People Against Racism and New England Resistance, an antidraft organization.

Mayor Kevin H. White stayed at City Hall through most of the night, conferring with Negro leaders about avoiding destructive demonstrations.

Philadelphia Bars Closed

By MAURICE CARROLL

Special to The New York Times

PHILADELPHIA, April 5—A limited state of emergency, providing for the closing of all bars and liquor stores and a ban on outdoor gatherings of more than 12 persons, was declared here tonight.

There was only scattered disorder in Negro neighborhoods in reaction to the slaying of the Rev. Dr. Martin Luther King Jr. However, Mayor James H. J. Tate said that, "based on intelligence given us," there was a threat that the violence that struck other cities could erupt here.

So, at 9:02 P.M. Police Commissioner Frank L. Rizzo signed a sheet proclaiming a "limited state of emergency in the city of Philadelphia."

At the same time, the city's red painted police squad cars began visiting the 3,900 tap rooms, ordering them to close.

The proclamation, which also prohibits possession of dangerous weapons in public, will run until 6 A.M. Wednesday.

So far, said Mr. Rizzo, "Philadelphia has done a real fine job."

There has been no looting, he said, but some 75 windows had been broken since midnight, a couple of dozen persons had been beaten and there were some instances in which cars stopped for traffic lights had been rocked back and forth by bands of youngsters.

Earlier in the day, the 7,000-member police force was put on 12-hour shifts and all leaves were canceled. At key points through the city about 17 buses—50 policemen in each—were stationed to rush to any potential trouble spot.

State police and the National Guard had been alerted to stand by, Mr. Rizzo said.

But the city weathered without major trouble an incident that had held considerable potential for violence, a memorial rally for Dr. King in Independence Square. It spilled into a march by some 5,000 persons toward City Hall, almost a mile away. "Black, black black," chanted some of the marchers, led by a man who called himself "Freedom Smitty."

But after more oratory the march petered out without major disorder.

About one-third of Philadelphia's two million residents are Negro.

Vandalism in Pittsburgh

PITTSBURGH, April (UPI)—Widespread vandalism broke out in the predominantly Negro Hill district tonight and spilled over into several other areas of the city.

Up to 20 persons were arrested. A white man was shot and wounded seriously. Detectives said the shooting was connected with the disorders.

The city's 1,400-man police force was placed on 12-hour shifts. All days off and leaves were canceled.

Matthew Moore, an officer of the United Negro Protest Committee, said all windows in a 10-block area of the Hill district had been smashed. About 200 policemen were operating in the district. Others investigated window smashings and break ins in the adjacent Hazelwood, Uptown, fringe areas of Oakland, East Liberty and downtown Pittsburgh.

At least two liquor stores in the Hill district were broken into and some looting was reported.

Gangs of 50 to 100 persons roamed the Hill chanting "Dr. Martin Luther King" and smashing windows on white-owned stores on Fifth and Centre Avenues.

Emergency in Detroit

Special to The New York Times

DETROIT, April 5—A state of emergency was declared in Detroit this afternoon because of scattered violence, and 3,000 National Guardsmen were ordered into the streets. One looter was killed in a scuffle with policemen.

The city was placed under an 8 P.M. to 5 A.M. curfew.

By 6:30 this evening, the police said 24 adults and as many juveniles had been arrested. Two Negroes were shot, one by the police and one by persons unknown, the police said. Both were shot in the 12th Street area, the scene of last summer's riots, but neither was seriously injured, the police said.

The police also said there were only two fires that they could connect with the disorders.

A looter was killed "accidentally" by the police, Gov. George Romney said, in Highland Park, a separate city that is an enclave of Detroit.

There are 650,000 Negroes in Detroit, which has a population of 1.65 million.

Governor Romney joined Mayor Jerome P. Cavanagh at police headquarters this afternoon, the main command post for police operations in the city.

A tour of the city tonight showed the curfew completely effective. Police cruised through the areas and guardsmen were visible at marshaling points.

There were incidents all afternoon. Gangs of Negro youths marched in the streets, broke windows and looted a few stores. One cab driver was pulled from his taxi and beaten in the 12th Street area.

Mayor Cavanagh, who proclaimed the state of emergency, said, "It is better to overreact than underreact."

He went on radio and television and urged parents to keep their children home.

The Mayor ordered gasoline stations and liquor and gun stores closed this afternoon.

In Negro areas of the city people lined up in front of grocery stores to buy food, and a few Negroes painted "Soul" on their storefronts. From midafternoon on, freeways leading out of the city were jammed with workers or shoppers going home early.

Gov. George Romney ordered 9,000 National Guardsmen alerted. State policemen were also alerted for riot duty, and 400 joined the 4,500 Detroit policemen.

In the 12th Street area, crowds of young Negroes threw rocks at cars, but squads of policemen, in three-car convoys, cruised the streets dispersing the crowds.

The police wore steel Army helmets and carried shotguns.

Curfew Imposed in Toledo

TOLEDO, Ohio, April 5 (UPI)—Mayor William Ensign imposed a curfew on this city today in the wake of a disturbance involving about 2,000 Negro high school students.

Mayor Ensign said the curfew would forbid persons under 22 years of age from being on city streets and in public places during the hours it is in effect—from 8 P.M. tonight until 6 A.M. tomorrow.

The students had earlier refused to attend classes at predominantly Negro Scott High School in reaction to the slaying of the Rev. Dr. Martin Luther King Jr. The police said the students roamed a square-mile area of the West Side, throwing rocks at windows and passing cars.

Outbreak In Missouri

JEFFERSON CITY, Mo., April 5 (AP)—Some 200 Negro students from Lincoln University marched into downtown Jefferson City today, broke several store windows and, the police said, "stole at least five rifles from a sporting goods store."

The window-breaking took place after the students had gone to a newspaper office and protested an editorial that had criticized the Rev. Dr. Martin Luther King Jr. the day before his assassination. The editorial was published in The Post-Tribune and Capital-News.

The students demanded a retraction, but the newspaper declined.

Five Hurt in Greensboro

GREENSBORO, N. C., April 5 (AP)—Five policemen and National Guardsmen were injured tonight in an exchange of gunfire with snipers near the campus of predominantly Negro North Carolina A. & T. State University at Greensboro.

Two of the policemen were shot. One suffered apparently minor injuries from shotgun pellets. Another policeman and a guardsman were hit by bricks.

About 900 guardsmen and an undetermined number of police were in the university neighborhood. Guardsmen split into two groups and moved toward Hodgin Hall, a dormitory, but were pinned down. Police said sniper fire was coming from a corner of the building.

Police reports said the shooting started when someone passing in a station wagon fired into a crowd of Negroes, but missed hitting anyone. Two white men later were arrested.

Col. Guy Langston, who is commanding the guardsmen in Greensboro, sent his men to the area with orders for selected sharpshooters to return the fire.

Mississippi Guard Alerted

JACKSON, Miss., April 5 (AP)—"The entire National Guard is either on alert or stand-by," Gov. John Bell Williams told a statewide television audience today. He said "troublemakers are fanning the flames of hatred and giving encouragement to lawlessness, anarchy and violence."

Calling the assassination of Dr. King "a senseless atrocity," Mr. Williams said he had given the State Adjutant General authority to call as many National Guardsmen as needed to quell any violence.

Over 1,400 guardsmen were already on active duty, the Governor told a news conference held after his television apearance. The full force of more than 10,000 could be mobilized within minutes, he added.

Three Hurt in Savannah

SAVANNAH, Ga. April 5 (AP)—Three persons, including a fireman, were injured early today as a result of sporadic incidents of violence that broke out in the coastal city, apparently in reaction to news of the slaying of Dr. King.

The police said one white-owned department store in a predominantly Negro section was destroyed after a firebomb was thrown through a glass window of the store.

Kirk Mobilizes Guard

TALLAHASSEE, Fla., April 5 (UPI)—Gov. Claude R. Kirk Jr., mobilized 50 National Guardsmen tonight and alerted 200 others in an attempt to prevent a second night of violence near the Florida A. and M. University campus.

A spokesman for Mr. Kirk's office said that the helmeted guardsmen were being deployed by local law enforcement officials.

Roadblocks were set up in the area and nobody was allowed in or out of the area. Florida A. and M. was closed for a week. One person died last night, five were injured and 14 arrested.

San Francisco Looting

SAN FRANCISCO, April 5 (Reuters) — Gangs of Negro youths began looting stores in San Francisco and the neighboring cities of Oakland and Berkeley today, but the police said that they were "pretty well contained."

Bands of about 50 in number moved through streets here, breaking store windows and taking merchandise from a five-and-dime after an open air memorial service for the Rev. Dr. Martin Luther King Jr. attended by 7,000 persons.

All members of the police force were on duty or standing by here and in Oakland, where Negroes make up almost half the population of 367,000.

April 6, 1968

PRESIDENT SIGNS CIVIL RIGHTS BILL; PLEADS FOR CALM

Acts a Day After Final Vote on Measure That Stresses Open Housing in Nation

FINDS MUCH TO BE DONE

In White House Ceremony, He Calls for Enactment of Rest of His Program

Special to The New York Times

WASHINGTON, April 11—With another plea against violence and for the legal redress of injustice, President Johnson signed today the Civil Rights Act of 1968.

Its major provision is intended to end racial discrimination in the sale and rental of 80 per cent of the nation's homes and apartments.

Mr. Johnson read swiftly but with feeling through a brief speech that invoked the memories of the slaying of the Rev. Dr. Martin Luther King Jr. a week ago and the rioting that ensued in many cities.

But the President also displayed the pride that comes, he said, with the signing of the "promises of a century." Few thought when he proposed it at a White House meeting two years ago that fair housing would "in our time" become the law of the land, he said, "and now at long last this afternoon its day has come."

'Roots of Injustice'

"We all know that the roots of injustice run deep," the President asserted, "but violence cannot redress a solitary wrong or remedy a single unfairness.

"Of course all America is outraged at the assassination of an outstanding Negro leader who was at that meeting that afternoon in the White House in 1966.

"And America is also outraged at the looting and the burning that defiles our democracy. And we just must put our shoulders together and put a stop to both. The time is here. Action must be now."

The action he wants, the President said to leaders of Congress who received a pen symbolizing attendance at the signing, is the enactment of all his domestic programs and appropriations.

These include programs for the accelerated construction of low-cost housing, improved vocational training for the poor, Federal aid to law enforcement, urban development, education and health and for a tax increase to pay the costs.

There is much to do, the President said, and after his program is enacted there will be still more to do.

As he indicated to moderate Negro leaders whom he assembled at the White House last Friday after the slaying, it would be quite an achievement to enact what he had already suggested.

But Mr. Johnson had also scheduled an address to a special joint session of Congress. On reflection and a closer look at the crowded legislative agenda, he postponed the address, apparently indefinitely.

Mr. Johnson seems to believe that new proposals for faster action for the poor will only arouse false hopes in the country while meeting resistance in Congress.

Although some of his aides have wanted him to make an inspiring address to the nation as the rioting subsides, his principal concern, as usual, is said to be with effectiveness on Capitol Hill.

The House passed the civil rights bill yesterday in the same form in which it was rescued from a Senate filibuster last month by a single vote. As the President scheduled the signing ceremony this noon, Federal troops were still on duty in the Capital to help patrol the tenser sections of the Negro slums.

One of the first invitations to the East Room ceremony was telephoned to Mrs. King in Atlanta, but she was out and did not return the call for several hours.

The Rev. Ralph D. Abernathy, Dr. King's successor as head of the Southern Christian Leadership Conference, had still not been reached when the ceremony began at 5 P.M.

Hence, only a few of the better known civil rights leaders were among the 300 guests who were mostly members of Congress and the executive branch, along with staff officers who had worked on the measure.

Present were Justice Thurgood Marshall, the first Negro on the Supreme Court; Sen. Edward W. Brooke, Republican of Massachusetts, the first Negro Senator since Reconstruction; Walter E. Washington, Chief Commissioner of the District of Columbia, and Clarence Mitchell Jr., local director of the National Association for the Advancement of Colored People.

Mrs. Johnson, wearing a bright green dress, was also present for the speech, which was carried live over television, and then she led her husband by the hand to a receiving line. He was introduced to every guest.

The White House said that an effort had been made to reach every group that had participated in the drafting of and the lobbying for the bill.

The act immediately bars discrimination in federally owned housing and in multi-unit dwellings insured with Federal funds.

On Dec. 31, it will cover all multi-unit dwellings and homes in real estate developments except those occupied by the owners with four or fewer units, such as boarding houses.

Effective Jan. 1, 1970, it will extend to all single-family homes that are sold or rented through brokers.

The act provides for Federal conciliation efforts, allows civil suits for damages and permits the Attorney General to seek injunctions against discernible patterns of discrimination.

Other provisions provide heavy penalties for persons convicted of threatening or injuring persons exercising their civil rights; makes it a Federal crime to travel or broadcast from one state to another with intent to incite a riot; makes it a Federal crime to manufacture, sell or demonstrate firearms, firebombs or other explosives for use in riots, and extends broad rights to American Indians in their dealings with their tribal authorities and with local, state and Federal courts.

April 12, 1968

HIGH COURT RULES 1866 LAW BARS COLOR LINE IN HOUSING IN ALL SALES AND RENTALS

NEGROES CAN SUE

Decision Goes Beyond 1968 Act to Ban Bias in Private Sales

By FRED P. GRAHAM
Special to The New York Times

WASHINGTON, June 17—The Supreme Court turned an almost forgotten civil rights law of 1866 into a sweeping fair housing statute today in a 7-to-2 ruling that prohibits racial discrimination in all sales and rentals of property.

The Reconstruction Era statute had been thought by most lawyers only to secure the rights of former slaves to own property It was invoked by lawyers for a St. Louis couple in the case decided today.

The Court, in a paraphrase of the provisions of the Civil Rights Act of 1866, said it provided that:

"All citizens of the United States shall have the same right, in every state and territory, as is enjoyed by white citizens thereof to inherit, purchase, lease, sell, hold, and convey real and personal property."

In breathing new life into the act today, the Court in effect created a fair housing law that goes beyond the newly enacted Civil Rights Act of 1968 in several respects.

The ruling means Negroes can now sue under the law of 1866 to bar racial discrimination in sales or rentals by private homeowners. These transactions are not covered by the new fair housing provisions of the 1968 law.

The 1866 law also covers rentals in units containing fewer than five families. These were exempted in the 1968 law.

The 1968 law's major prohibitions against housing discrimination do not go into effect until Jan. 1, 1969. Under today's Supreme Court ruling, Negroes can sue immediately to bar owners from refusing on racial grounds to sell or rent real property or personal property to them.

However, the remedies available to enforce the old law are weaker than those provided by the statute of 1968. The 1866 law can be enforced by a court order barring discrimination, but it is unclear as to whether those who discriminate can be made to pay money damages.

Under the new law, a Negro can get a court order against discrimination, plus actual damages and punitive damages up to $1,000. There are also provisions for mediation by the Department of Housing and Urban Development, and the Attorney General can bring suits to break up a pattern or practice of discrimination.

Justices John M. Harlan and Byron R. White denounced today's decision as "ill-considered and ill-advised" in a dissent written by Justice Harlan. It chided the majority for wiping out exceptions to the fair housing provisions in the 1968 law that had been worked out as a result of compromises in Congress.

Stewart Writes Opinion

Justice Potter Stewart wrote the Court's opinion. He was joined by Chief Justice Earl Warren and Justices Hugo L. Black, William J. Brennan Jr., William O. Douglas, Abe Fortas and Thurgood Marshall.

The decision was one of 11 handed down by the Court as it met for the final session of the 1967-68 term. It will reconvene on the first Monday in October.

The housing decision grew out of a suit brought by Joseph Lee Jones, a Negro bail bondsman in St. Louis, and his wife, Barbara Jo, who is white. They asserted that the owners of the Paddock Woods subdivision in suburban St. Louis had refused to sell them a home site because Mr. Jones is a Negro.

A Federal District Court dismissed the case, and the United States Court of Appeals for the Eighth Circuit affirmed this decision. Both courts held that neither the 1866 law nor the Constitution banned racial discrimination by private owners in real estate transactions.

Many lawyers felt that the Joneses' lawyers, who are associated with the National Committee Against Discrimination in Housing, had brought in the law of 1866 as a makeweight, or additional, argument.

The 1866 law was passed to enforce the Thirteenth Amendment, ratified in 1865. The amendment says that "neither slavery nor involuntary servitude . . . shall exist within the United States, or any place subject to their jurisdiction."

The law says:

"Be it enacted by the Senate and House of Representatives in Congress assembled, that all persons born in the United States and not subject to any foreign power, excluding Indians not taxed, are hereby declared to be citizens of the United States; and such citizens, of every race and color, without regard to any previous condition of slavery or involuntary servitude, except as a punishment for crime whereof the party shall have been duly convicted, shall have the same right, in every state and territory in the United States, to make and enforce contracts, to sue, be parties, and give evidence, to inherit, purchase, lease, sell, hold, and convey real and personal property, and to full and equal benefit of all laws and proceedings for the security of person and property, as is enjoyed by white citizens, and shall be subject to like punishment, pains, and penalties, and to none other, any law, statute, ordinance, regulation, or custom, to the contrary notwithstanding."

In 1883, in the landmark Civil Rights Cases, the Supreme Court held that the 1866 law could not be interpreted to outlaw discrimination in public accommodations, since the Thirteenth Amendment only gave Congress power to undo slavery.

Since then, as slavery disappeared, the Thirteenth Amendment and the 1866 law fell into disuse. The Supreme Court was not, before this appeal, asked to decide if the law could be enforced as a fair housing statute.

In the only known case in which it was invoked as such—in a Federal court decision in Arkansas in 1903—the judge ordered a white man to lease land to a Negro. But that case was not appealed, and no others were brought.

'Relic of Slavery'

In today's opinion, Justice Stewart said that housing discrimination against Negroes was "a relic of slavery" He said Congress had the power, under the Thirteenth Amendment, to legislate against it.

He cited statements by Reconstruction Congressmen to show that Congress intended the 1866 law to be a fair housing law.

Justice Harlan responded with an equally long recitation of quoted statements intended to show that the statesmen of that day did not dream that they were limiting individuals' right to dispose of their property.

Today's ruling appeared to broaden Congress's constitutional power to pass laws aimed at private discrimination in general, and not just housin bias.

"Surely Congress has the power under the Thirteenth Amendment rationally to determine what are the badges and the incidents of slavery, and the authority to translate that determination into effective legislation," Justice Stewart said.

Samuel H. Liberman of St. Louis argued for the Joneses. Attorney General Ramsey Clark argued on their behalf as a friend of the Court. Israel Treiman of St. Louis argued for the Alfred H. Mayer Company, developers of Paddock Woods.

The fair housing provisions of 1968 are to take effect in three stages. By Jan. 1, 1970, they will cover 80 per cent of all housing sold or rented.

Immediately prohibited by the act is discrimination in the sale or rental of 900,000 federally insured housing units. On Jan. 1, 1969, discrimination will be prohibited in the sale or rental of 19.8 million units of multifamily housing, such as apartment buildings and large developments.

Effective Jan. 1, 1970, discrimination will be prohibited in 31.3 million single-family homes sold or rented through a broker.

The law exempts so-called "Mrs. Murphy" units—housing with two to four apartments, one of which is occupied by the owner—and single-family homes sold by the owner himself without benefit of an agent.

June 18, 1968

STUDY SAYS NEGRO JUSTIFIES RIOTING AS SOCIAL PROTEST

Report Compiled for Panel on Civil Disorders Finds Noncriminals Take Part

INTEGRATION STILL GOAL

Substantial Minority in Black Community Is Said to Have Lost Faith in America

By JOHN HERBERS

Special to The New York Times

WASHINGTON, July 27 — The National Advisory Commission on Civil Disorders released studies today showing that the urban riots of the nineteen-sixties are a form of social protest by noncriminal elements and are justified as such by a majority of Negroes.

The findings suggest that, short of massive suppression of millions, future riots can be prevented only by transforming the Negro slums and the institutions and attitudes that have made them.

One of the three studies purports to repudiate the "riffraff theory" of riots, which holds that only a small fraction of the Negro population participates in disorders, that these are principally the riffraff of the community and that the vast majority of the Negro population deplores the violence.

Militants Gaining Support

The second, an examination of Negro and white attitudes, shows that the majority of Negroes still desire integration and conciliation with whites but a substantial minority seem to have lost faith in the American system and are looking increasingly to militant leaders who advocate violence and separatism.

The third study documents what has come to be a common belief by Negroes and some whites—that businesses, the police and other institutions serving the Negro slums are frequently insensitive to the needs and attitude of the people living there.

Generally, the findings substantiate the conclusions that the Presidential commission itself made in its report last Feb. 29. The commission held that the nation was moving toward "two societies, one black, one white—separate and unequal" and that "white racism" was largely to blame.

However, the studies released today indicated that racism may not be as monolithic as the commission suggested. Massive surveys of urban populations showed ambivalence among both Negroes and whites in racial attitudes and that most whites have some sense of the problems in the cities and are looking for solutions.

The 11-member commission, headed by the former Governor of Illinois, Otto Kerner, was appointed one year ago today by President Johnson to find the causes of the 1967 riots and recommend solutions.

After an extensive investigation it made sweeping recommendations at Federal and local levels in law enforcement, welfare, employment, education and the news media, the vast majority of which are yet to be put into force.

After issuing its report, the commission disbanded its staff but ordered additional studies in areas it believed had not been adequately explored. So comprehensive were the studies that the authors complained throughout the reports about the lack of time in meeting the commission's deadline.

David Ginsburg, executive director of the commission, said at a briefing on the reports that they constituted "the most authoritative presentation of data that is available so far in this country."

Reports Not Endorsed

The reports were made public as the work of their authors and without endorsement of the commission. Two, on racial attitudes and on slum institutions, were financed by Ford Foundation grants.

The most dramatic and probably the most meaningful for the education of white Americans is that dealing with the "riffraff theory," entitled "Who Riots? A Study of Participation in the 1967 Riots." It was conducted by Dr. Robert M. Fogelson, associate professor of history and urban planning at Massachusetts Institute of Technology, and Dr. Robert B. Hall, an associate of the Bureau of Applied Social Research at Columbia University.

According to the authors, the "riffraff theory" has been widely accepted, dating back to the East St. Louis, Chicago and Washington riots of 1916 and 1919. As riots swept the cities in the nineteen-sixties police chiefs, Mayors, Governors and others used the "riffraff theory" to explain what had happened until it became the prevalant view in the land.

A Reassuring Theory

The reason, the authors suggested, was that the theory was reassuring to most white Americans.

"If, indeed, the rioters were a tiny fraction of the Negro population, composed of the riffraff and outside agitators and opposed by a large majority of the ghetto residents, the riots were less ominous than they appeared," they wrote.

"They were also a function of poverty, which, in American ideology, is alterable, rather than race, which is immutable; in which case too, they were peripheral to the issue of white-black relations in the United States."

If the theory were true, the riots could be dealt with without radically changing American cities and thoroughly overhauling basic institutions or seriously inconveniencing its white majority.

Only recently, the authors said, had the theory been challenged, and then on inconclusive studies. To reach their conclusions, the authors studied profiles of Negro communities and 10,000 arrest records from 10 cities—Cincinnati, Dayton, Detroit, Grand Rapids, Newark, New Haven, Boston, Plainfield and Phoenix.

The Major Findings

They found that in six cities that experienced rioting in 1967, about 18 per cent of the Negro residents in the riot areas participated in the disorders and were fairly representative of the Negro community. Here are some of their findings:

¶The overwhelming majority of rioters were employed. About three-fourths of those arrested had jobs.

¶More than two-thirds of those arrested were adults (over 18 years).

Although those arrested were 90 per cent males, the surveys indicated that many females participated in the riots but were not arrested. "The police for one reason or another, are permitting large numbers of female rioters to go unapprehended."

¶Most rioters were native to the area. Older migrants from the South tended to wait until the later stages to join the disorder but when they did they participated in the arson and looting.

¶Although 40 to 90 per cent of those arrested had prior criminal records, the criminal element was not found to be overrepresented. Criminologists estimate that from 50 to 90 per cent of the Negro males in the slums have criminal records.

A Startling Finding

The last finding appears somewhat startling and would lend credence to the widely held belief among whites that pathological behavior is common to Negro districts. But the authors explained that having a criminal record in the United States simply means an arrest and probably no more than one-fourth of those arrested are convicted of a major crime.

"Hence, to label most rioters as criminals is simply to brand most members of the Negro community as criminals," the authors said. "Therefore the criminal element is not overrepresented among the rioters. Since the close surveillance of the Negro community by the police results in a disproportionately high number of arrests among male Negroes, it is to be expected that a majority of the rioters—who are predominantly young Negro males—would have criminal records."

The authors concluded that the the 1967 riots were carried out by a "small but significant minority of the Negro population, fairly representative of the ghetto residents" and "tacitly supported by at least a large minority of the black community."

This, they said, "means that the 1960's riots were a manifestation of race and racism in the United States, a reflection of the social problems of modern black ghettos, a protest against the essential conditions of life there and an indicator of the necessity for fundamental changes in American society."

Their findings were supported at least in part by another study entitled "Racial Attitudes in 15 American Cities." It was conducted by Prof. Angus Campell and Prof. Howard Schuman of the Institute for Social Research of the University of Michigan.

They supervised interviews with more than 5,000 Negroes and whites in Baltimore, Boston, Chicago, Cincinnati, Cleveland, Detroit, Gary, Milwaukee, Newark, New York (Brooklyn only), Philadelphia, Pittsburgh, San Francisco, St. Louis and Washington.

The authors concluded that "riots are justified by most Negroes but they are not recommended."

"Most Negroes see the riots partly or wholly as spontaneous protests against unfair conditions, economic deprivation, or as a combination of the two," they said. "Only a very small percentage of the Negro population define the riots as essentially criminal actions to be suppressed by public force."

The white population, however, has a different view. Approximately one-third of the whites in the 15 cities agree with Negroes that the riots are a revolt against real grievances, but another third regard them as criminal in character and inspired by radicals and they feel that police power is the only answer. The balance of the white population displayed a mixture of the two views.

The authors also examined Negro attitudes toward separatism. Almost half indicated a preference for living in a mixed neighborhood and another third said that the racial character of the neighborhood made no difference to them. Only one Negro respondent out of eight said they favored residential separation.

"It is clear," they said, "that in early 1968 the major commitment of the great majority of the Negro population in these 15 cities was not to racial exclusiveness insofar as this meant personal rejection of whites or an emphasis on racial considerations in running community institutions. Negroes hold strongly, perhaps more strongly than any other element of the American population, to a belief in nondiscrimination and racial harmony."

However, it was found that about 6 per cent wanted a "separate black nation here" and this implies that "200,000 Negroes in these 15 cities feel so little a part of American society that they are withdrawing allegiance from the United States."

In a formal election, the authors pointed out, 6 per cent of the vote means little, "but in a campaign to change minds and influences policies, 6 per cent of a population can represent a considerable force."

Further, a much larger percentage of Negroes expressed a desire for more black identity. For example, 42 per cent said they would like an African language to be taught in the schools, and approximately one-fifth of those interviewed said they believed that stores in Negro neighborhoods should be owned and run by Negroes. The authors saw this as in keeping with American diversity rather than separatism.

However, the surveys showed that partial or complete approval of Negro spokesmen identified with separatism is several times greater than is support for separatism itself.

"This is probably because the discontent these spokesmen express about race relations is approved even where their preferred separatist solutions are rejected or ignored."

35% Back Carmichael

For example, the "stand" taken by Stokely Carmichael, who advocates separatism and the use of violence to obtain Negro rights, was approved or partly approved by 35 per cent of those interviewed.

H. Rap Brown, who is even more militant than Carmichael, won slightly less support than Carmichael in the surveys. The authors found it significant that the names of these and other leaders who were hardly known a few years ago now "seem to be slightly better known than the name of Roy Wilkins, executive director of the National Association for the Advancement of Colored People."

Mr. Wilkins's "stand" was fully approved by 54 per cent of those interviewed. Mr. Wilkins is a moderate who has consistently advocated integration and nonviolence.

Most Negroes believe that their race has made substantial progress in recent years but "the more striking finding is that one out of every three respondents agrees there has not been much real change for Negroes over a period that dates roughly from the 1954 Supreme Court decision on school desegregation.

"The basic assumption of major improvement so seemingly obvious to many white Americans is not accepted by many black Americans," the authors said.

Roughly a third of the Negro males interviewed said they had been refused a job because of racial discrimination. There was no way of telling if this were true but the authors said what was important in race relations was that "a great many Negroes believe that discrimination not only happens but that it has happened personally to them."

On the other hand, 95 per cent of the whites interviewed said they were opposed to discrimination in employment and 75 per cent would support legislation to this effect. There was less support for integrated neighborhoods with about half saying they were opposed to open housing legislation.

Most whites look to the established Government agencies to solve urban problems. About 5 per cent said they would advocate counterriot violence against Negroes, compared to 8 per cent of the Negroes who said they would join a riot.

"If translated into popular terms the numbers of Negroes and whites involved are almost identical because the white population is larger in the 15 cities," the authors said.

The third study, on institutions operating in the Negro slums, was conducted under the direction of Prof. Peter H. Rossi of the department of social relations, Johns Hopkins University.

Six occupational groups — the police, teachers, retail merchants, welfare workers, political party workers and employers—in the same 15 cities were interviewed as to their attitudes and knowledge of life in the ghettoes.

"Our findings strongly suggest that the delivery system of the central institutions of our local communities serve the ghetto poorly and are insensitive" to the plight of urban Negroes, the report said.

"If these are the faces that American institutions present to the ghetto, then the alienation of the ghetto from the main community is scarcely to be wondered at."

The economic system through-the slums, the report said, 'seems particulary to present a stance of denying that the ghetto is really any different than other areas, except perhaps poorer and certainly more troubled."

Policemen pictured themselves as an embatled and harrassed group, the authors said. "Nor do they apparently understand why negroes are resentful, denying that they are discriminated against."

Educators are more sympathetic, the report said, but are too quick to put the onus of poor performance on the characteristic of the students rather than the school system.

July 28, 1968

Avoidance of Slums Defended by Agnew; He Cites His Record

By THOMAS A. JOHNSON

Special to The New York Times

DETROIT, Oct. 18—Defending his campaign for the Vice-Presidency, which has not taken him into the Negro slums, Gov. Spiro T. Agnew declared today that he had been to many racial ghettos and, "to some extent, if you've seen one city slum you've seen them all."

The Maryland Governor spoke to television newsmen at station WXYZ-TV on the interview show "Spotlight."

The interviewers, like most newsmen who get to question the Governor, spent a good deal of time on his views regarding the problems of the cities. If elected Vice President, urban problems will be his primary responsibility, Mr. Agnew has frequently stated. One interviewer asked why Mr. Agnew did not plan to visit any of the nation's slums and he replied:

"I didn't say I wouldn't go into ghetto areas. I've been in many of them and to some extent I would have to say this, if you've seen one city slum you've seen them all. I don't think it's imperative that I showboat [with] campaign appearances through ghetto areas to prove I know something about the cities."

Aides to Mr. Agnew said he had visited the Baltimore slums as well as other Negro ghettos in Maryland on many occasions.

The Republican candidate for Vice President has denied running a white-oriented campaign, maintaining that his speeches are made in public halls where everyone is welcome and that most people, black and white, get their news about candidates through radio and television.

He was asked if there were "greater authorities" on slum conditions than the people living in slums.

"Well I'd say yes there're much greater authorities on slum conditions," Mr. Agnew said and repeated an analogy he often uses.

He said: "Well, I'd say this, that a person who's suffering from an incurable disease doesn't know as much about it as the doctor who's doing the operating." He contended that professionals who have studied ghetto problems were the authorities.

In the area of foreign policy, Mr. Agnew said he did not think Richard M. Nixon or any other candidate "has a plan" for ending the war in Vietnam.

He said: "We have over-all steps that should be taken. We know that new leadership creates a better atmosphere for peace negotiations in Paris.

Questioned about his "qualifications" to be Vice President and his knowledge of international problems, the candidate smiled and told the interviewers to ask him some questions.

"I would love to demonstrate my new-found expertise," he asserted.

Later today Mr. Agnew's campaign manager, George W. White, issued a statement to counter allegations and rumors that the Vice-Presidential campaign was being restricted because the Governor had made errors in the past that could cost himself, and other Republican candidates, votes during the coming elections.

Later today in Washington, Mr. Agnew received the sixth annual testimonial man-of-the-year award from the Adelphia Post No. 38 of the American Legion. This was presented at their testimonial dinner at the Shoreham Hotel.

October 19, 1968

New Negro Mayors Make 'Black Power' Daily Reality

By STEVEN V. ROBERTS
Special to The New York Times

LOS ANGELES, May 22—There is a new campaign button in the Chicago ghettos. It says, "A Black Mayor in '71," and the Negroes who wear it, however outsiders may smile, are not kidding. They are just as serious, in fact, as the hundreds of thousands of others who are forging a new role for black politicians in the nation's cities.

In recent weeks Chapel Hill, N.C., and Fayette, Miss., have elected Negro Mayors. For some time there have been Negro Mayors in Cleveland and Gary, Ind., and a Negro chief executive in the District of Columbia.

Several Negroes, moreover, have won figurehead mayoral jobs in cities run by professional managers as scores of others have gained seats on various municipal governing bodies. And now there appears to be a better-than-even chance that Los Angeles, the nation's third largest city, will elect its first Negro Mayor next Tuesday.

Thus are the nation's Negroes not only gaining greater leverage in urban politics but participating as well in many areas of life that were closed to them just a few years ago.

The reasons for this upsurge in black power are fairly obvious. The migration of Negroes from rural to urban areas has been accompanied by, and partly caused by, the exodus of many middle-class whites to suburbia. Negroes now account for more than one-third of the population in many major cities.

Federal legislation has vastly increased the number of Negroes registering to vote, particularly in the South. And throughout the country, campaigns for civil rights and black power have shaken the apathy of many blacks and convinced them that political success is both possible and necessary.

There are still only a very few cities, however, where Negroes hold a working majority. Thus most black politicians must create alliances with white groups and appeal for white votes in order to win, and this fact strongly influences the shape and direction of urban politics.

The successful black politician must usually appeal to the broad middle section of the community. He must be a moderate and respectable man who poses little threat to the white establishment while forcefully advocating the needs of the poor. As Howard Lee, the new Mayor of Chapel Hill, put it:

"I'll be walking a tightrope. I could be slaughtered from both sides, by the white racists or the black militants."

Here in Los Angeles, City Councilman Thomas Bradley has walked that tight-rope. He has drawn support from conservative Republican businessmen, labor leaders, representatives of the "new politics" and Democratic party officials, as well as from the black community, which accounts for only about 18 per cent of the population here.

His stands for integration and against violence in race relations have drawn charges of "Uncle Tomism" from militant blacks, while his opponent, Mayor Samuel W. Yorty, has accused him of appealing for the "bloc vote" of "black militants and left-wing radicals."

In Jersey City last week,

Associated Press

City Councilman Thomas Bradley of Los Angeles is favored to become Mayor next Tuesday even though black community is only 18 per cent of population.

The New York Times

Mayor Carl Stokes of Cleveland is in middle, between police and black leaders.

Associated Press

William T. Patrick of Detroit is considered strong, but is reluctant to run for Mayor.

The New York Times

Mayor Walter Washington of Washington. Some support blacks as "insurance."

The New York Times

Mayor Charles Evers of Fayette, Miss. Foundations are expected to help him out.

United Press International

Mayor Richard Hatcher of Gary, Ind., said people tend to expect more from a black.

Howard Lee, the new Mayor of Chapel Hill, N. C. "I'll be walking a tightrope."

Julian Robinson, a Negro, was expected to win about 20 per cent of the vote in the mayoral election and finish second or third. He wound up in fourth place with 10.3 per cent, and local observers felt that his failure to disown the Black Panthers and other extremist groups had lost him votes among some middle-class Negroes.

"Liberal fronts" supporting black candidates are also impeded by the disunity and competing ambitions that can splinter a black community as readily as a white one. In both Newark and Baltimore, for example, at least two Negroes seem intent on running for Mayor in the next election, and observers believe they would only cancel each other out.

Black politicians are also thwarted by Democratic party organizations, which in some cities continue to retain the loyalty of many Negroes. In Chicago, for instance, 10 of the 50 aldermen are Negro, but seven belong to the organization of Mayor Richard J. Daley, and could hardly be expected to support an insurgent black candidate against him. Many other Negroes enjoy city jobs they are eager to retain.

Some whites feel that many major cities are "not ready" for black Mayors, and are urging Negroes to stand aside for a liberal white candidates with a better chance of winning. In Chicago, Adlai Stevenson 3d has been promoted as a possible mayoral contender in 1971, at the same time that blacks are talking about running their own candidate.

In Detroit, Walter Reuther, head of the United Auto Workers, has reportedly been urging Negroes to run a candidate for City Clerk on the ticket with the encumbent, Mayor Jerome Cavanagh, in 1970 rather than challenge the Mayor directly.

Supporters of black candidates believe that in many instances, however, a Negro would attract a wider base of support than a white. "A black candidate here could get more than 50 per cent of the black vote, and no white man could get nearly that much away from the machine," said one Chicago labor official. "He could combine that with the liberal white vote and maybe give the machine a scare."

Nevertheless, many Negro leaders are still reluctant to run for Mayor in a number of cities. Some share the conviction that the population is "not ready" to elect a black man; others are reluctant to leave lucrative jobs for the travail and uncertainty of politics.

In Detroit, many observers believe that William T. Patrick, president of New Detroit, an association of community leaders, would give Mayor Cavanagh a strong fight, but he remains reluctant to make the race.

In Oakland, for instance, a widely respected lawyer, Donald McCullum, resisted entreaties to run against the incumbent, Mayor John H. Redding, in last April's election. Lawrence A. Joyner, a relatively unknown official of the antipoverty program, then lost by more than two to one to Mayor Redding.

But whether or not Negroes run for Mayor, the growth of black political power is having a significant influence in many cities. In New Orleans, several mayoral condidates in the fall election are making strong pitches for Negro votes, although four years ago the Mayor was elected on an avowedly segregationist platform.

What if a Negro does win? Mayor Richard Hatcher of Gary has complained that people tend to expect more from a black man. "But there is no reason to believe that a black man has wider feet and can walk on water," said a seasoned observer of Mayor Carl Stokes in Cleveland.

In recent years, the issue of law and order with its corollary debate over the conduct of the police, has probably become the most troublesome and emotional urban question, and it puts a Negro in a particularly difficult position.

On the other hand, the law and order issue can sometimes help a Negro. In political terms, it could bring into the race a right-wing candidate who would draw off support from the major white contender. This is how Mr. Hatcher won the Democratic nomination in Gary.

In several cities, the business establishment has supported black politicians who they feel would provide some "fire insurance" against renewed rioting.

"Ninety-nine per cent of the business men who support Walter Washington here are interested in protecting their investments downtown," said one observer in the nation's capital, where Mr. Washington was appointed mayor. "They think he'll pacify the natives."

Beyond the question of law enforcement is the larger issue of the reconstruction of the nation's urban centers. And at least for a time, perhaps while they are still novelties, black Mayor have been able to attract considerable contributions from the Federal Government, local businessmen and foundations.

Mayor Stokes raised more than $11-million for a redevelopment project called "Cleveland Now!" Right after his election in Fayette, Miss., Charles Evers took off on a fund-raising tour and one of his white opponents said:

"I expect some of those foundations like Ford and Rockefeller will put money in here to help make this a national success and encourage the colored people in other areas to work through the political system."

May 23, 1969

Many Post-Riot Bus Projects to Carry Inner City Poor to Jobs Are Failing

By JOHN HERBERS
Special to The New York Times

BALTIMORE, March 28 — Every day a battery of green and white buses marked "J.E.T. Express" rumbles through the slums of Baltimore and outward to the suburbs, trying to bridge the two separate worlds that make up the metropolitan area.

The experimental transportation project, which carries Baltimore's inner city poor out to where the jobs are, faces an increasingly difficult task as the suburban ring, with its gleaming industrial parks, creeps farther away from the old row houses at the center of town.

And in the dozen other cities receiving Federal funds for similar busing projects, there have been more failures than successes.

Thus urban planners' post-riot hopes of a few years ago that the ghetto could be brought back into the mainstream of economic life have faded somewhat as projects like J.E.T. have encountered, in their small way, the great distractions of American cities.

Distances a Problem

In some instances, the distances between homes and jobs was overwhelming, both in cost and in patience of the passengers. In Boston, when the "Employment Express" began carrying residents of the Roxbury section to the electronics and other industries strung out along Highway 128, the round trip cost per passenger was estimated at $13. Each rider was charged $1.

In Nassau County, L.I., where one of the more ambitious projects is under way with mixed success, Mrs. Lois Blume, Federal and state aid coordinator, said: "People have to travel an hour for a $1.60 an hour job. They're not interested in doing it."

Frequently, the promise of employment at the other end of the line fails to materialize. In Gary, Ind., thousands of steel mill jobs pledged for inner-city blacks have evaporated as the economy has slowed in recent weeks.

Hampered by Conflicts

The busing projects have further been hampered by the entire array of various Government and private conflicts that plague the cities themselves. Projects in St. Louis and Buffalo have been shut down or curtailed prematurely, partly because they could not cope with the system.

Still, in some instances, the bus lines have kept families off the welfare rolls. In the words of an iron worker in St. Louis who regularly rides the curtailed TEMPO bus project there:

"This means bread in my family's mouth. I couldn't get

to my job without this bus or a car. And I haven't got a car."

In some of the cities, those involved say the projects point up graphically that the problems of the cities cannot be handled by a piecemeal approach, although at times, as one transit official said, "A Bandaid is better than nothing." The Baltimore experience shows both the problems and the promises involved.

As has happened in most major American cities, a sizable share of Baltimore's economic base has been moving out past the city limits along with the white residents. Both industries and public institutions have been springing up along Interstate 695, the Baltimore beltway that rings the city, and beside the highways and roads that stem from it.

White Man's Domain

This is a world of golf courses, new housing developments, woods, meadows, lakes and curving country lanes with names like Green Spring Valley Road—the white man's domain.

Whites step into their cars each morning and within minutes spin along the expressways to jobs at such places as the national headquarters for the Social Security Administration and the General Electric Company.

Everything is designed for the automobile, and without one a person can feel impaled.

Because of housing costs and other restrictions, both psychological and real, the poor live largely in the inner city along streets with names like Lafayette and Oliver. These neighborhoods have a high component of unemployed, those with the least skills but most in need of income.

Before J.E.T. started, those who found employment in the suburban ring and who did not have automobiles could spend hours each day shuttling back and forth and transferring between metropolitan and suburban transit lines.

Ads Run on Radio and TV

The project began in January, 1969, with a Federal subsidy of $100,000, since increased to $250,000, to the Metropolitan Transit Authority, a state agency. But it immediately ran into management problems—for one thing it was called the "Ghetto Express"—and in a few months the city took it over under a new plan.

The new management named it J.E.T. for Job Express Transportation, and coordinated it with the complex of Federal, local and state manpower training programs and community action agencies. Public service advertisements were placed on radio and television. Collge students surveyed the neighborhoods and rode the buses to find what was needed in service and scheduling.

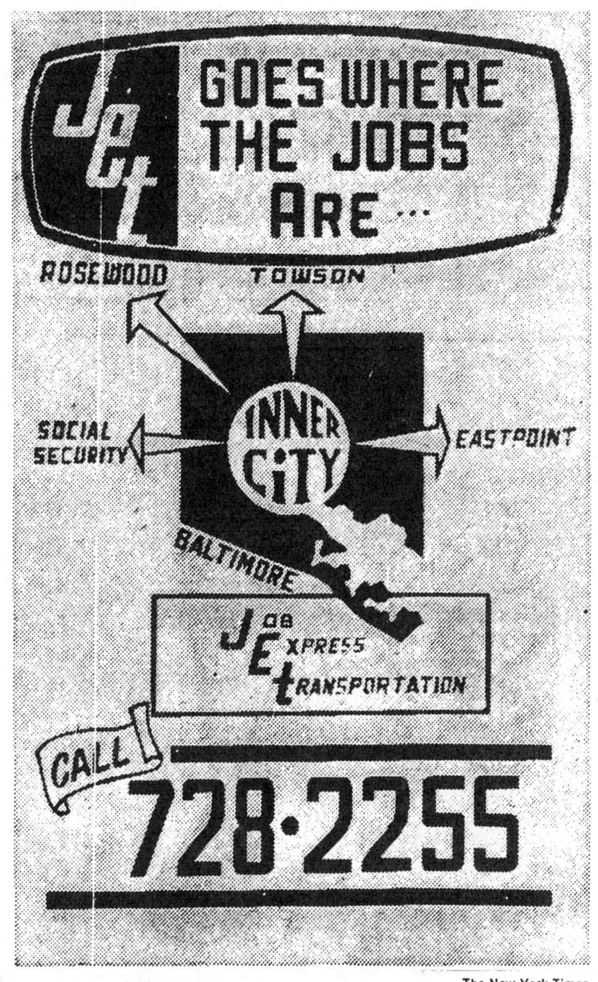

The New York Times

Poster advertising "J.E.T. Express" bus service in Baltimore

The project director is a 24-year-old white, Elliot Dackman, who displays a sensitivity to the social problems involved. Mr. Dackman said the number of riders has gradually increased. In February there was an average of 370 a day.

The fare is 30 cents, plus an additional dime for zone charges, the same rate charged by the Baltimore Transit Company, a private corporation that runs the main bus line. Baltimore Transit supplies all buses and drivers, because Federal law requires experimental projects to pay the prevailing wage.

Mr. Dackman said J.E.T. could do better by providing its own buses and drivers. He said JET cold also do better if it could go to Cockeysville, a giant industrial complex about 20 miles north of the inner city along Interstate 83. But a suburban transit company holds the franchise for all busing in and out of Cockeysville and Baltimore residents have to transfer to get there.

Federal Aid Temporary

The city is currently involved in a legal fight to permit JET to run express routes into the complex.

Mr. Dackman said the fares were now paying between 37 and 41 per cent of the costs. The remainder comes from Federal and city subsidies. For this kind of project such a cost breakdown is not unusual.

In Washington, Dr. Robert Hemmes, assistant administrator for research in the Urban Mass Transit Division of the Department of Transportation, made it clear that the Federal subsidies were temporary and were for gathering information.

The Stanford Research Institute of California is evaluating all of the projects. From its study there will flow a report that will serve to help cities establish permanent projects if they wish.

The St. Louis project provides a study in failure. Started in April of 1968, with $1,147,500 project TEMPO (for Transportation, Employment and Manpower Provide Opportunity) was sponsored with great hope by the St. Louis model city agency under a complicated arrangement involving a number of agencies.

Mayor Alfanso J. Cervantes took the first ride and proclaimed TEMPO "a giant stride toward the solution of one of our greatest problems—unemployment." It had 28 buses running from the inner city to the sprawling Hazelwood industrial complex in north St. Louis County. Now it is down to two buses, and Robert Baer of the Human Development Corporation said:

"It costs about $6 on the average to get a man to Hazlewood [on TEMPO]. A taxicab would be cheaper."

Petty Bickering Blamed

The Department of Transportation blamed petty bickering betwen the local agencies involved for a large part of the failure. Louis G. Berra, who headed the project at one time, expressed the disillusionment of local officials this way:

"In the beginning, we had visions of not one or two lines, but five or more. Obviously, we don't have those visions now. Somewhere along the line, people are failing to get jobs. Maybe we were wrong to think transportation was one of the main reasons. If there's no job at the end, nobody's going to ride the bus."

In Buffalo a half-million dollar project was suspended after a few months because of a combination of bad management and the lack of passengers, according to both local and Federal sources.

But in some cities, the buses are running at capacity and are either paying for themselves or running only a slight deficit.

In Nassau County, nine of 19 routes being assisted by a $2.2-million Federal grant are supporting themselves, according to Richard Andryshak of the Department of Transportation, who oversees the projects.

In the Minneapolis-St. Paul area and in Cleveland, rapid transit projects between the inner city and airports are said to be successful because they also shuttle passengers and employment aides.

Other cities with experimental projects are Los Angeles, Chicago, Omaha, Washington, Detroit and Kansas City.

In Boston, where the "Employment Express" is now down to serving only about 70 people a day, Martin Gopen of the Urban League, one of the sponsors, expressed a typical summation:

"The population changes every few weeks. People just use the buses as a way to tap jobs, then strike out on their own. Community groups are not prepared to motivate the hard core to go out there, to overcome their fear of the unknown, and business and industry is not yet equipped to receive them. Anyway, how can five buses make a dent?"

March 29, 1970

NIXON TO ENFORCE RIGHTS MEASURES FOR U.S. HOUSING

But He Refuses to Impose Low- and Middle-Income Units on Communities

2 TYPES OF SEGREGATION

President Stresses Racial Bars Are Unconstitutional, but Not Economic Kinds

By ROBERT B. SEMPLE Jr.
Special to The New York Times

WASHINGTON, June 11 — President Nixon pledged today to enforce existing prohibitions against racial discrimination in housing, but said he would not use Federal leverage to force local communities to accept low- and moderate-income housing against their wishes.

In a major policy statement more than 8,000 words long, which was the result of nearly seven months of internal debate and discussion, Mr. Nixon clung to and reinforced with elaborate arguments the distinction he made at news conferences this year and last between "racial" and "economic" segregation.

The first, he said, is clearly unconstitutional and "will not be tolerated." At the same time, the President argued, racial and economic segregation are not synonymous, and he insisted that there is nothing in existing law that authorizes, much less mandates, the imposition of low- and moderate-income housing on affluent communities.

Mixed Reaction to Statement

The message brought a quick and mixed reaction from civil rights groups. The Suburban Action Institute, a group that believes only a deliberate policy of dispersing low- and moderate-income housing to the suburbs can break up the growing concentrations of blacks in the inner cities, said it regarded the message with "keen disappointment."

The institute argued that "racial discrimination in the suburbs is the direct and calculated result of economic discrimination," and suggested that Mr. Nixon, by making a distinction between the two, had issued an open invitation to all-white suburbs to exclude blacks through subterfuge.

Meanwhile, however, lawyers in the Civil Rights Division of the Justice Department, some of whom have been awaiting today's statement with considerable apprehension, said they were pleasantly surprised and encouraged—both by the President's assertion that he would vigorously enforce existing laws, and by what amounted to a pledge to make certain that suburbs did not practice racial discrimination by calling it economic discrimination.

"We will not seek to impose economic integration upon an existing local jurisdiction," the President said. "At the same time, we will not countenance any use of economic measures as a subterfuge for racial discrimination."

"When such an action is called into question," the President went on, "we will study its effect. If the effect of the action is to exclude Americans from equal housing opportunity on the basis of their race, religion or ethnic background, we will vigorously oppose it by whatever means are appropriate —regardless of the rationale which may have cloaked the discriminatory act."

On the basis of this and related statements elsewhere in the message, some Administration officials forecast that the Government would finally bring suit against the town of Blackjack, Mo., a St. Louis suburb that changed its zoning laws to prevent construction of a federally subsidized moderate-income housing project.

The city's officials have argued from the beginning that the zoning change was aimed at preserving the economic integrity of the town, but both the Department of Housing and Urban Development and the Justice Department's Civil Rights Division urged Attorney General John N. Mitchell last November to bring suit on the ground that the city's actions were racially motivated.

Some Encouraged

Those who thought Mr. Mitchell would now move against Blackjack were further encouraged by another section of today's statement, which read in part:

"Unlawful racial discrimination in housing extends beyond the barring of individuals from particular buildings or neighborhoods because of race. The courts have also held that, when its reasons for doing so are racial, a community may not rezone in order to exclude a federally assisted housing development. In such cases, where changes in land use regulations are made for what turns out to be a racially discriminatory purpose, the Attorney General, in appropriate circumstances, will also bring legal proceedings."

Much of the debate over the proper role of the Federal Government in securing desegregated housing has revolved around differing interpretations of a clause in Title VIII of the Civil Rights Act of 1968.

The clause not only prohibits discrimination in the sale or rental of almost all housing —whether privately or federally subsidized—but also urges all executive agencies of Government, and particularly the Department of Housing and Urban Development, to administer their programs "affirmatively" to achieve desegragated housing.

A Vital Interpretation

In a sense, therefore, today's statement represented Mr. Nixon's long-awaited personal interpretation of the meaning of the world "affirmatively," and his judgment as to the lengths that the Federal Government might go to promote nondiscrimination in housing.

In sum, as he had in discussing the school desegregation question in a similar public statement last year, Mr. Nixon asserted that he would obey and enforce but not go beyond the legal requirements set forth by the courts and the statutory mandates of Congress in the field of fair housing.

Pledge on Zoning Issue

And, finally, he pledged to move forcefully through the courts against efforts by communities to use their zoning powers to exclude blacks.

He cited as support the recent refusal of the Supreme Court to review a decision by the Court of Appeals of the Second Circuit that held unconstitutional an effort by officials of Lackawanna, N. Y., to block a subsidized low-income housing project in an all-white neighborhood.

Where he departed sharply from those who take a broader view of the Federal Government's powers to act "affirmatively" in behalf of minorities was in his judgment, which he repeated several times in the statement, that while the Government can legitimately approve or disapprove of applications for funds submitted by localities, it cannot go beyond that point and force a community to accept low-income and moderate-income housing against its wishes.

"This Administration will not attempt to impose federally assisted housing upon any community" he asserted, adding elsewhere that his review of the legislative history of the Civil Rights Act of 1968 had persuaded him that the "affirmative action" clause did not authorize "housing officials and Federal agencies [to] dictate local land use policy."

Genesis of Statement

Today's statement had its genesis, not surprisingly, in complaints to the White House over a year ago that various regional offices of the Department of Housing and Urban Development were attempting to force communities to accept low-cost housing by threatening them with the loss of other Federal aid funds.

These efforts reportedly have the tacit backing of George Romney, the Secretary of Housing and Urban Development, who once threatened the city of Warren, Mich., with the loss of some urban renewal funds if the community failed to provide housing for low-income and moderate-income workers who were employed at plants in the neighborhood.

Responding to these complaints, John Ehrlichman, assistant to the President for domestic affairs and now director of the Domestic Council, dispatched a memorandum to all agencies asking them to avoid major policy initiatives in the sensitive area of desegregated housing pending a high-level review of the issue.

Various working groups were established in the fall of last year—one of which included the Attorney General and Mr. Romney—to thrash out the issue.

Mr. Nixon reportedly set forth his views on the issue at what informed sources say was a crucial meeting in the President's office with Mr. Romney and Mr. Mitchell on Dec. 29.

By the turn of the year, according to informed sources, Mr. Romney had come out to the view that neither the "affirmative action" clause of the 1968 act nor the courts had provided his agency with the firm legal basis to use the economic leverage of the Government to force "economic integration."

In March, various materials on the issue were submitted to Mr. Nixon in San Clemente, Calif., and on May 5 he was given a draft message prepared, perhaps ironically, by the Department of Housing and Urban Development. That draft formed the basis of today's final Presidential declaration on the subject.

June 12, 1971

The Cities: The 'Lower Class'

By EDWARD C. BANFIELD

The Problem Centers In a 'Lower Class' Which Defies Reform

The tangle of social pathologies that people mainly have in mind when they speak of "the urban crisis" arises principally from the presence in the inner districts of the central cities and of their larger, older suburbs of a small "lower class" the defining feature of which is its inability (or at any rate failure) to take account of the future and to control impulses.

The lower (as opposed to working) class person never sacrifices any present satisfaction for the sake of a larger future one. He lives from moment to moment.

This is to say, he does not discipline himself to acquire an occupational or other skill, to hold down a regular job, to maintain stable family ties, or to stay out of trouble with the law. His bodily needs (especially for sex) and his taste for "action" take precedence over everything else. The slum is his natural habitat. He does not care how dirty and dilapidated his housing is, and he does not notice or care about the deficiencies of public facilities like schools, parks, and libraries. Indeed, the very qualities that make the slum repellent to others make it attractive to him. He likes the feeling that something violent is about to happen and he likes the opportunities to buy or sell illicit commodities and to find concealment from the police.

For obvious reasons, "lower class" people are always unskilled and usually low income. However, the great majority of the unskilled and the low income — indeed, the great majority of slum dwellers — are not "lower class." It cannot be too strongly emphasized that being "lower class" is a matter of outlook and life style, not one of schooling, income, or social status.

Nor is it one of race. For historical reasons that are familiar to everyone the proportion of Negroes who are "lower class" is relatively large as compared to whites. This has little or nothing to do with race, however. Until a few decades ago the urban lower class was almost entirely white; every ethnic group, including the Anglo-Saxon Protestant one, contributed to it, and its outlook and style of life were strikingly similar to those of the present Negro lower class.

Now that relatively few whites are lower class, it is all too easy for whites (including, unfortunately, many teachers and many policemen) to make the mistake of assuming that a poorly dressed and poorly spoken Negro must be "lower class." This would be an unsafe assumption in dealing with whites but it is a highly implausible one in dealing with Negroes, many of whom have had little or no opportunity to acquire the outward marks of working or middle class culture. Because of their failure to look beyond externals, many whites classify as "Negro" behavior that they should classify as "lower class." Similarly, some of the behavior by whites that Negroes assume to be "racially prejudiced" is in fact "class prejudiced."

It is impossible to tell from Census or other existing data just how many lower class people there are in the cities. To make a count one would first have to decide where to draw the line between the lower and the not-lower classes, and of course any decision about this would have to be more or less arbitrary. Depending on where the line was drawn, it is likely that between 5 and 15 per cent of the population of the large central cities would be "lower class."

The size and importance of the problems that the "lower class" presents to the city are not at all well indicated by those figures, however. In St. Paul, Minnesota, a survey showed that 6 per cent of the city's families absorbed 77 per cent of its public assistance, 51 per cent of its public health services, and 56 per cent of its mental health and correction casework services. Studies in other cities have shown that a very small part of the population is responsible for most of the crimes of violence

So long as the city contains a sizeable "lower class" nothing basic can be done about its most serious problems. Good jobs may be offered to all, but some will remain chronically unemployed. Slums may be demolished, but if the housing that replaces them is occupied by the "lower class" it will shortly be turned into new slums. Welfare payments may be doubled or tripled and a negative income tax instituted, but some persons will continue to live in squalor and misery. New schools may be built, new curricula devised, and the teacher-pupil ratio cut in half, but if the children who attend these schools come from lower-class homes, the schools will be turned into blackboard jungles and those who graduate from them, or drop out of them, will in most cases be functionally illiterate. The streets may be filled with armies of policemen, but violent crime and civil disorder will decrease very little.

If, however, the "lower class" were to disappear — if, say, its members were overnight to acquire the attitudes, motivations, and habits of the working class—the most serious and intractable problems of the city would disappear with it.

If the problems of the city arise more from class cultural than from racial factors, not to recognize that fact may be a tragic error. Misplaced emphasis upon "white racism" is likely to make matters worse both by directing the attention of policymakers away from matters that should be grappled with and by causing Negroes to see even more prejudice than actually exists.

Edward C. Banfield is Professor of Government at Harvard University and author of "The Unheavenly City," from which this first of two articles is adapted.

The Cities: Babies For Sale

By EDWARD C. BANFIELD

Many social scientists are confident that people who live for the moment would soon begin to take account of the future if they were placed in a situation where it would be advantageous for them (in terms of the values that they themselves hold) to do so.

The "lower class" is present-oriented, these social scientists think, because conditions like racial discrimination have made it impossible, or nearly impossible, for them to improve their position by work and sacrifice. Society in effect tells the "lower class" person that he will not be allowed to get ahead no matter what he does.

Very likely there are people who feel, with more or less basis in fact, that any effort to get ahead would be effort wasted. It may be indicative of this that Negro boys are much more likely to drop out of high school than are Negro girls: most of the boys will get the same (poor) jobs whether they graduate or not whereas girls who graduate can count on good office jobs.

To the extent that present-orientedness is a rational response to real or fancied lack of opportunity, the way to eliminate it is surely to open opportunities that are unmistakably good. This is easier said than done however. How is it possible to offer a "really good" job to someone who has no occupational skill and no inclination to learn one and who perhaps very much prefers the excitement of street life to high salaried boredom? Unfortunately, the really-good-job treatment can be given only to those who do not have the disease that it is supposed to cure.

Even if the individual cannot be given a good job he can be given money, and some social scientists think that if his income is raised very dramatically this of itself will cause him to change his style of life. Perhaps it will in some cases. But it seems likely that in a very much larger number of cases the effect of very high welfare payment levels would be to induce people to be more present-oriented than ever.

It may be that in general "lower class" ways are not so much a response to lack of opportunity as they are deeply ingrained habits of the individual or the group. An adult who has been lazy and improvident all of his life is not going to change very much no matter what happens. If he learned in infancy and childhood to perceive, feel, and think in the manner of the "lower class" (as, for example, a Hopi child learns to perceive, feel, and think in the Hopi manner) he may suffer from a kind of psychological blind spot that will persist in later life and prevent him from seeing whatever opportunities are offered him. Insofar as this is the case, the effort of policy should be to protect society from him and him from it.

If "lower class" ways constitute a culture (strictly speaking, a sub-culture) that is learned in childhood, it would seem that the only way to eliminate it is to prevent children from being brought up in it. This means taking the child from his "lower class" parents at an early age and either giving him to adoptive parents who are not "lower class" or putting him in an orphanage. Of course there are obvious objections to this. One is that it is no crime to be "lower class" and a country which values human rights cannot deprive parents of their children on any such grounds. Other objections (if others are needed) are that it is doubtful whether enough orphanages and adoptive homes could be provided and that even if they could be the children might be more severely damaged by being taken from their natural parents than by being allowed to grow up in the "lower class" culture.

The number of adoptions might be increased by permitting the sale of children to persons of good character. This would not involve any violation of parents' rights but it would, if the bidding were active, offer them sizable inducements to hand the children over to persons who are better qualified to bring them up. That a child was offered for sale would be proof positive that its parents were not fit to have it.

Boarding schools and day nurseries are a somewhat more practicable possibility. These might be located in or near slum neighborhoods and staffed with working class women and girls. Even if attendance were free it is doubtful if many "lower class" parents would make use of them; the "lower class" mother sees nothing wrong with the way she brings up her children and she is apt to be very suspicious of social workers, teachers, and their likes.

Perhaps it would be possible to bribe her to send the child to school with an increase of welfare payments but this would be very expensive since the increase would have to go to all welfare recipients who sent their children, not merely to the relatively small number of "lower class" ones who did. Even if ways were found of getting the "lower class" children to the schools it is not at all sure that their being there would do them much good. In an experimental project in Boston, 21 children aged two and one-half to six, all of them from "lower class" families, spent two to three mornings a week in a nursery that was generously staffed with highly trained personnel. After from one to three years of attendance there were some noticeable improvements in the children but these were not such as to offer much hope that the course of their lives would be drastically altered by the experience.

October 13, 1970

Role of 'White Racism'

To the Editor:

Edward C. Banfield's Op. Ed. columns (Oct. 12, 13—"The Cities: The Lower Class" and "The Cities: Babies for Sale.") are insulting, inaccurate and dangerous.

Insulting in that they attempt to create a clinical distance from the real and tragic conditions that surround and restrict the lives of millions of black Americans who inhabit America's ghettos.

For the sake of a reductive, guinea-pig approach that views the problems of the ghettos and barrios as those of the "lower class," Mr. Banfield denies that America's ghettos have become the voice of racial consciousness that even the most impatient observer would recognize to be an indispensable foundation for the evolving cultural, political and economic autonomy of American minorities.

The columns are inaccurate because Mr. Banfield fails to note that present concentrations of racial minorities within urban centers are the result of factors wholly different from those of immigrant minorities of the late nineteenth and early to mid-twentieth century.

Mr. Banfield's attempt to identify the crux of the problem as "class-cultural" without a clear recognition that "white racism" constitutes the penultimate in class-cultural conflicts is dangerous. One would surmise from Mr. Banfield's articles that white Americans should accept a stance of studied insouciance (perhaps more accurate, "benign neglect?) vis-à-vis the problems of the ghetto when he places the solution of these problems almost entirely upon the backs of the ghetto residents themselves.

The fact is that white racism permeates all structures and institutions within America. Any steps minorities in America take to bolster themselves culturally, economically and politically must have a counter-flank in the parallel battle against white racism.

By dismissing the role that the majority of Americans have in confronting their racism, Mr. Banfield does not see that America is not yet ready for the changes and sophistication that will accompany black America's liberation. Insofar as the problems of black America are the problems of all America in the extreme, every American has an equal share in the responsibility of cleaning up America.

Even if whites accept their responsibility, difficult times still lay ahead. If, on the other hand, America accepts to any degree the stance taken by Mr. Banfield and scholars who represent similar schools of thought, America is begging none less than a revolution.

RINKER BUCK
Brunswick, Me., Oct. 14, 1970

November 3, 1970

Inner-City Decay Causes Business Life to Wither

By JERRY M. FLINT
Special to The New York Times

DETROIT, July 18—The weather-beaten plywood board is replacing the gleaming steel and glass skyscraper as a symbol of the American city.

Outside the central city, apartments and air-conditioned shopping plazas and theaters spring up, miles apart but bound together by freeways making anything only a few minutes away from the auto-equipped resident of that outer city, suburbia.

But for those remaining in the central city cores—the black ghettos and the poor and even middle-class white areas around them—it is harder to buy food because the big supermarkets are going and the little stores are boarded up or torn down; it is harder to find a doctor or dentist; harder to fill a prescription or have a suit cleaned because the stores are gone; harder to buy a newspaper; call a taxi; find a pleasant park, a good restaurant or even a good corned beef sandwich.

The traditional commercial services are dying and the old urban cores have not yet been able to adapt to the new commercial pattern.

What is more, years after the racial riots along these same streets and after innumerable pledges to rebuild, the decay has intensified.

Four years ago this week, Detroit's great riot occurred and today the streets, if anything, look emptier with large stretches of dusty cleared land and even larger stretches of shabby boarded-up storefronts. And reports from other citites — Pittsburgh, Chicago, Washington, for example — are much the same.

In a dozen cities examined as the summer began, the scene on these streets is similar: blocks abandoned, storefronts covered with plywood. Open stores are dingy, the fronts bricked up in the architectural style that dominates the ghetto of the nineteen seventies: "Riot Renaissance." If anything new is built on the old commercial arteries, it is probably another gas station or a gaudy drive-in.

A Few Exceptions

There are exceptions. Here and there a bright shopping center exists, not matching the glistening ones in the suburbs but reversing the general commercial decay. And some of the old shopping streets, such as 125th Street in Harlem, are still bustling and bright, with a wide range of stores and throngs of noontime shoppers. But they are not typical.

Some blame a lack of Federal money for the continued blight. Others blame the squabbling of citizens groups, or high crime, or burdensome insurance, or freeze-outs by banks and private investors, or inability to gather large blocks of land needed for modern commercial services, or high costs for the obviously unwanted city blocks. Whatever the reason, the imagination and the will to rebuild the city cores seem lacking.

"We don't need the central city, even as a communications center," said Peter Drucker, the social critic. In Europe, he said, "the city was a desirable form of life. In this country it never was. This is a country of anticities."

Here are reports on the situation around the nation:

PITTSBURGH

The large core ghetto is called the Hill district. After the murder of Dr. Martin Luther King Jr. three years ago 100 stores were looted or burned. Most have not been rebuilt, and where the rubble was cleared away there's new debris: beer cans, whisky bottles, trash.

"After the 1968 troubles we cut our hours. We close at 5:30 P.M., not open at night. Our black employes don't want to go out at night," said Leonard Edelson, a white co-owner of the bustling Hill Pharmacy. His store keeps its windows boarded up and is busy because "four major drugstores in the Hill were burned out" and because the welfare business has more than doubled in three years, he said.

He has to send a driver to pick up drugs each day because the suppliers pulled their men from the routes when they were attacked.

'Nothing to Open Up For'

"There's nothing here to open up for," said Matthew Moore, a Pennsylvania state coordinator for the National Association for the Advancement of Colored People. "Drugs are flourishing so people are afraid to come out. The Hill is full of winos and junkies. People are afraid to carry money."

"Some services are available," he added wryly. "We control the bars, beauty shops, barbers and churches."

BOSTON

The Boston ghetto stretches from the South End near downtown into Roxbury, its heart, and in it live four-fifths of the city's 105,000 Negroes. More than 50 stores along Blue Hill Avenue, a main thoroughfare, were damaged in the 1967 riot and most have not reopened. Some $56-million in pledges of aid for rebuilding never materialized, but some new black-owned or black-run businesses have opened, replacing white ones.

"So many Jewish shop owners got out of deep Roxbury that it amounted to a mass exodus" after the 1967 riot, said a spokesman for the Anti-Defamation League of B'nai B'rith. In one area 100 stores changed hands. Despite some new businesses and improvements the old core area is still "a business desert," said Robert M. Coard, executive director for the city's major antipoverty agency.

"A very bad situation," said Donald E. Sneed Jr., president of the Unity Bank, the largest black-run business in New England. "I think we in the community feel we're an island by ourselves in terms of real progress compared to the surrounding area."

BIRMINGHAM

Although the city says it tries to give the same treatment to the streets and sidewalks of Birmingham's ghetto as to other parts of the city one can see piles of trash lying about. Outside the biggest grocery store boxes, paper, old produce and other refuse lie around for two or three days.

The only new restaurant in the area in five years, a quick-service hamburger franchise, changed management twice and has closed.

DETROIT

Twelfth Street, once a thriving Jewish commercial strip, then a busy honky-tonk black strip and the heart of the 1967 riot, is practically leveled, and residents must travel miles to find a large grocery or drugstore. Even the pimps complain: "I used to make $100 a day on this street. Now I can't make a dime," one said.

On the east side of the city, on Mack Avenue, 127 vacant stores were counted in a two-mile stretch. A west side resident complained: "I called to have milk delivered and they said they don't have any trucks out here."

Detroit's car makers invested almost $10-million to set up black-owned automobile showrooms in inner-city locations abandoned by whites, but now the companies have decided that even blacks can't do much business there.

CHICAGO

"In the past 10 years I would estimate that the attrition rate of ghetto business is 30 to 40 per cent, as high as 50 per cent in areas affected by the riots," said Pierre DeVise, a social scientist at DePaul University. "Madison Street [on the West Side of Chicago] looks like it was hit by a holocaust. Maybe only one-third of the stores operating there 10 years ago are still functioning. A three-block area lined by storefronts before 1968 lies completely vacant."

"See for yourself. Nothing has been replaced. The only new places are the gas stations moving onto some of this cleared land and one Midas muffler store," said Tommy Lee Durham, a black who owns a second-hand refrigerator store on Madison.

Construction of new stores has proved to be a failure in some cases.

Dr. Arthur Falls is a Negro and part of a 16-member syndicate that owns a shopping center in the South Side ghetto. He said $1-million was invested in the center in four years. Now graffiti cover the walls of the stores, four of the seven are vacant, and chicken-wire, plywood or brickwork cover the windows.

There has been fire bombing and thievery and no profits, he said.

TRENTON

In the last five years two large department stores in Trenton have closed and some expect the remaining two to follow. Both downtown hotels are gone. Plans for a downtown shopping mall fell apart, and of the four movie theaters downtown all are expected to be closed by next month.

The seven black neighborhoods in Trenton are serviced by one small and one large supermarket. Bars and liquor stores abound, but a trip downtown is necessary for drugs or hardware, for shoes or to see a doctor.

On the eight blocks of North Clinton Avenue there were 120 businesses in 1950; now there are 60. Every other store window is boarded up; alleys are filled with garbage and broken glass.

In most ghetto areas residents can't buy a newspaper because there are no stands and few stores, and carrier boys are scarce.

"The whites have siphoned off the money and are leaving the city and they try to sell their businesses to blacks like they were doing us a big favor, but it's all because no one else will buy it but a black guy," said Albert Robinson, director of Trenton's antipoverty program.

LOS ANGELES

On Central Avenue in Watts nearly all the stores were destroyed in the 1965 riot and about one-third remain boarded up today. There are no major supermarkets in the business strips, Central and Compton Avenues and 103d Street.

"If I get someone going to Watts in the daytime, and he looks O.K., I demand he pay in

SYMPTOM: Boarded-up stores on West Madison Street, Chicago. Commercial services of the central city are dying.

advance, and I take him. At night I won't go," said a white taxi driver. Services, which were scarce in the area before the riots, have not improved. And jobs and transportation still seem the major concern.

WASHINGTON

Plywood is a big decorating item along Seventh and 14th Streets N.W. and H Street N.E., the old commercial corridors damaged in the 1968 riots. Black-owned stores are increasing but, said Cornelius Pitts, who owns the Pitts Motor Hotel just off 14th and has founded a black businessmen's alliance:

"After the riots when whites were selling out to blacks, the new owners were paying substantially higher prices, based on prior volume, than volume justified afterwards. As a result, many have gone out of business, and a lot of the rest are just hanging on."

"I'm dying for lack of business," he admitted.

"I've been discouraged for the last year and a half," said Rufus A. Isley, owner of two clothing stores and winner of a Small Business Administration award a year ago. His side of the 3000 block of 14th Street looks as if the riots had occurred last month rather than three years ago.

NEW YORK

Harlem is exceptional, both within the nation and within New York City. The density of its mobile but constant population of about half a million people is part of a critical set of variables that set it apart even from Brooklyn's larger Bedford-Stuyvesant section.

"Harlem is different and the negatives are more aggravated than in other cities," said Hope Stevens, a prominent black Harlem lawyer who is also president of the predominantly white Uptown Chamber of Commerce.

It does not have to rebuild structures damaged in civil disturbances. Although there was an outbreak of violence following the death of Dr. King, property damage was not as extensive as in other cities.

But spiraling insurance costs, followed by a rise in prices for inferior goods, have been a source of aggravation. This has been accompanied by a high incidence of crime against property. One study by the Small Businessmen's Chamber of Commerce — a predominantly black group — estimated that crime last year cost the community "more than $2-billion."

"The cost of crime," said Mr. Stevens, "is passed back to the consumer. It doesn't drive the businesses out. They simply raise the prices."

Many of the larger white businesses are said to be "up for sale." But as one black businessman put it. "There are no banks or other agencies willing to give the black businessman a loan."

In all the cities studied, of course, many residents of the core areas, black and white, own automobiles and can drive to the suburban shopping centers. Any visitor to Northland, Detroit's major suburban center, can see that a large percentage of the buyers are blacks from the city.

Dealer Loses Customers

"You don't know what a big thing it is for a black family to get in a car and go out to the suburbs to shop," said a black automobile dealer in Chicago. "That's where half my business goes."

And in some of the central cities, some of the shopping streets are succeeding.

In Philadelphia, not far from Columbia Avenue, a former riot area, there's a striking new shopping center. Progress Plaza opened in 1968 with 17 stores and offices. One of its main backers was the Rev. Leon Sullivan, a leader in the black capitalism effort.

There's an A. & P. supermarket, two banks, shoe stores, a drugstore, appliance store, bookstore and others, all owned or managed by blacks. There have been no failures and the center's stores did $5-million in business their first year, Dr. Sullivan said.

Blight More Common

In most places, however, the blight is widespread and deepening. For millions of people, living becomes a little more inconvenient and a little uglier each year.

Mrs. Anita Watson, a 26-year-old mother and part-time college student who lives in public housing on Chicago's West Side, paints a familiar picture.

There are no large chain stores or cleaning shops within walking distance, she says, nor are there milkmen or licensed taxi cabs.

"The grocery store picture is so ridiculous," she said. "During the day milk will sell for $1.12 a gallon, but at night when only one store is open the price is $1.40. And you've got to pay or drink water. If you decide to travel outside the neighborhood and you don't have a car, it will cost you a dollar round trip on the buses."

July 19, 1971

U.S. Revenue-Sharing Aid To Chicago Halted for Bias

By ERNEST HOLSENDOLPH

Special to The New York Times

WASHINGTON, Dec. 18—The Federal District Court here ordered the Treasury Department today to cut off general revenue-sharing funds to Chicago for having used the money in a way that discriminated against women, blacks and other minorities.

It was the first instance of a city losing its share of funds under the $30.2-billion revenue-sharing program because of discrimination charges since the program began in 1972, according to the Office of Revenue Sharing, which operates as a part of the Treasury Department.

The order to cut off or defer Chicago's funds until it complies with the antidiscrimination provision of the revenue sharing law could be a precedent for similar actions in several other cities, including Tallahassee, Fla., Buffalo and Philadelphia, according to a Justice Department spokesman.

$19-Million Due

Chicago, which has already drawn $184-million in funds

under revenue sharing, was scheduled to receive a quarterly check for $19,195,633 next month.

"I have already given instructions to hold the check that would have been sent to Chicago Jan. 6," said Graham Watt, director of the Office of Revenue Sharing, less than an hour after the ruling by Judge John Lewis Smith.

Several local jurisdictions throughout the country, including Montclair, N. J., have been called into question about alleged discrimination in their expenditure of revenue-sharing funds. But Federal revenue-sharing authorities here have declined to cut funds off without a court order.

A Federal court in Chicago has already found the city guilty of discriminating against women and blacks and other minorities in the hiring and promotion policies in the Chicago Police Department. The court enjoined the city from further relief to correct the effects of poned, pending other developments, the issuing of additional relief tocorrect the effects of past discrimination.

The Lawyers Committee for Civil Rights Under Law, acting for the Chicago plaintiffs here, successfully argued that the Treasury Department should cut off funds immediately. Mr. Watt said the Government had no plans to appeal the decision.

Harold Himmelman, who argued the case for the lawyers committee, said: "The result of the ruling is that any government that gets funds and discriminates could be subjected to the same kind of order. The message is clear — discrimination in the use of general revenue-sharing funds will not be tolerated."

Lawyers for the Government took the same position at the hearing this morning that Mr. Watt and the Office of Revenue Sharing had frequently taken in the past — that discrimination is prohibited by the revenue-sharing law but the office and the Secretary of the Treasury were without specific authority to cut off funds.

Instead, Federal officials — even when they had determined discrimination by local governments — tended to rely on mediation and persuasion first, and then turned the matters over to the Justice Department for prosecution.

The Chicago case was initiated by private complaints, with Renault Robinson, executive director of the Afro-American Patrolmen's League, as the leading plaintiff.

Subsequently, the Office of Revenue Sharing entered the case and turned the matter over to the Justice Department, which sued Chicago under the Civil Rights Act of 1964. The lawyers committee in Chicago also entered the case in behalf of Mr. Robinson.

Judge Preston Marshall of Federal District Court made the ruling last Nov. 7 against Chicago and froze the police recruitment program in the city until complaints against discriminatory aspects of the police test for applicants were satisfied.

Judge Marshall has held off a final ruling in the case until proceedings resume next March, when additional questions will be addressed, according to lawyers here. But the judge has retained tight rein over the Chicago Police Department.

Recently, at the city's request for permission to add 600 new members to the police force, Judge Marshall issued a mandatory quota that included 300 blacks and other minorities, 99 women and 201 whites.

Richard J. Phelan, special assistant corporation counsel for Chicago, termed the action by Judge Smith "an atrocious ruling." He spoke to reporters in Chicago.

Mr. Phelan filed an emergency petition in Federal District Court in Chicago, seeking an order to compel the Treasury Department to continue payments to the city. He also asked for an immediate ruling on the jurisdictional powers of Judge Smith here to pass on the Chicago case.

Judge Marshall promised a ruling on the jurisdictional question by next Monday.

The order signed by Judge Smith this afternoon specified that:

Government lawyers disclosed in court this morning that the Treasury Department was working on new regulations to cut off funds to states and local jurisdictions found to have been discriminatory in the use of revenue-sharing funds. But the process of promulgating the new regulations is expected to take two months or more—too much time to allow the department to act on the Chicago case before the next payment is due.

"This whole experience has shown that there is a gap in our regulations," Mr. Watt said after today's court decision.

Mr. Watt also said there was no pending case that paralleled the Chicago case. Earlier, the office had entered consent agreements with Los Angeles and Milwaukee, satisfying charges of discrimination in the use of revenue-sharing funds in those cities.

A number of cities have legal actions pending with the Justice Department under charges of discrimination, and could suffer a cut-off of funds if the Chicago precedent holds.

In Buffalo, discrimination in the police and fire departments has been charged in Philadelphia, the police department has been accused of sex discrimination; and in Tallahassee, the Justice Department charged last Saturday that there was racial discrimination in 11 municipal departments.

December 19, 1974

In Watts a Decade Later: Poverty in Ashes of Riots

By JON NORDHEIMER

Special to The New York Times

LOS ANGELES, Aug. 6—Ten years after the fires of the era of the long hot summer were kindled in Watts, the black ghetto on the south side of Los Angeles has lapsed into a cold autumn of desperation.

Watts, for a while, became a workshop for new ideas and bold invention—a laboratory for social theory and strategies financed by the foundations and the universities and the Federal Government.

But the money and manpower dried up, and so did the programs and the will of those who felt that individual risk and sacrifice could make the difference. Like a great wave that surged forth in full flood, it eventually retreated under resistance, carrying away with it the elements not irretrievably rooted there.

Compared with the economic and spiritual desolation that exists today, the conditions that sparked six days of looting and burning a decade ago now seem almost salubrious.

For Watts today is a community that has been left behind in the advancement of those who by luck or pluck were able to take advantage of the gains won by black Americans in the intervening years.

Watts today, in the view of those inside and outside the community, is a compendium of urban failure, a nesting place of the social and racial ills that represent the nation's retreat from the challenge of finding effective measures to deal with its most intractable problems.

Like scores of other black, central-city ghettos, Watts in the summer of 1975 has been further devastated by high unemployment and other ills of the national recession, yet so far there has been no sign of a renewal of mass violence.

It is an area stripped of stable leadership, for those who can escape Watts depart at the first opportunity, leaving behind a paralyzed society of welfare mothers, street gangs and the elderly. Unemployment is running about 50 per cent among those who can work, breeding hard-core social dependence and crime.

The white-owned shops and small plants that were burned out or closed by the rioting have never reopened. Houses that were removed by renewal projects were not replaced. Economic conditions that created a recession elsewhere fell with a hammer blow here.

'Designed for Failure'

"This whole environment is designed for failure," says Gregory Welch, a 25-year-old ex-convict, as he stands at the intersection of Central Avenue and 103d Street, the epicenter of the 1965 riots. "Watts is all negative with very few positives."

There are few who dispute that assessment. "What we are seeing today is an overwhelming mental depression, particularly among the young, that life holds no promise of opportunity for them," says Dr. Roland Jefferson, a black psychiatrist who is a consultant at the Watts Health Center.

Consequently, Dr. Jefferson notes, ghetto youths in recent years have moved deeper into self-destructive pursuits, turning aggression inward through a variety of forms such as drug addiction, alcoholism or suicide, a pattern he describes as "ominous."

"The increase in the number of black alcoholics, particularly among the young, is phenomenal," he says. "Even more frightening is the sharp rise in young black suicides, where black males under the age of 25 now have the highest suicide rate of any group in the country."

28,000 Residents

Technically, Watts is a three-square-mile community of about 28,000 residents in the southwestern corner of Los Angeles, a palm-lined ghetto of one-family cottages and sun-splashed public housing projects that appear benign compared to the festering tenements of New York's Harlem or the Chicago South Side.

But emotionally Watts represents the broader, predominantly south-central corridor of the city that fell under curfew during the 1965 riots that resulted in 34 deaths, more than 1,000 injured, and property damage estimated at $40-million.

Median family income in Watts is about $6,000, a figure that includes welfare benefits. Increasingly, it has become a community of welfare mothers and children, unemployed young blacks and the elderly. The group between 25 and 50 has become the vanishing generation of Watts.

Since the riots, Watts has become one of the most analyzed communities in America, yet the only tangible product of all the research and all the reports is a dust-gathering pile of paperwork and the corrosive emotion of failure.

Cycle of Poverty

Watts today is not typical of anything except a community where the cycle of poverty, promises and a new decline has exhausted the energy of change and hope. Conditions are not quite that bad for poor blacks in other areas of Los Angeles, but some other areas come close to Watts.

The city of Compton to the south, for example, is a community with black political control where conditions were recently described by a recent special report of the Los Angeles grand jury as "worse than at the time of the Watts revolt."

As in Watts, unemployment in Compton is running above 50 per cent, and an estimated 60 per cent of the population there is receiving some form of public assistance, compared to 24 per cent in Watts 10 years ago.

And almost no one knows what to do about these conditions. For the most part—with few skills, money or other resources—there is little that the people of Watts can do outside of trying to survive one day at a time. Even the threat of rioting has little support, though each summer day still holds the potential for a spontaneous outburst.

"The cops got all the power," says Robert Searles, a lounger outside a Central Avenue barbecue stand. "Rocks ain't much good against tanks."

Of Faint Meaning

The fact that Los Angeles now has a black Mayor, Tom Bradley, or that black men now hold top state posts as Lieutenant Governor or state School Superintendent, is perceived as only faintly meaningful.

Racial pride takes a back seat to jobs and hope, particularly if the black politicians cannot deliver significant new gains to the black community, according to Ted Watkins, director of the Watts Labor Community Action Committee, a dynamic black man who has fashioned a grant-funded string of community enterprises that provide Watts with its only signs, however faint, of economic vitality.

Mr. Watkins, 50, is a controversial figure outside the community. Some scorn his diamond rings and fancy cars as inappropriate for an antipoverty leader. Others criticize him for the mismanagement of four supermarkets placed under his organization's control in 1969, where losses ran into millions of dollars before the stores were closed.

But it is generally agreed that no one in the community could easily replace him, either as a charismatic leader or as an expert in nabbing what limited grants are available from state, Federal or labor union sources. The committee's activities range from operating senior citizen centers to growing collard greens on power company transmission line easements that run through Watts; without them the community would suffer even more pain.

'Our Last Legs'

"The people with some money say the heck with Watts and its problems, and then run farther away from us," Mr. Watkins remarked in an interview in his office a few blocks from Charcoal Alley, the scarred center of the 1965 rioting. "The rest of us are on our last legs economically.

"Folks in Watts can't even get domestic jobs any more. No one even hires black bellhops these days. Kids come out of high school and can't read or write and even the menial jobs aren't available. They turn off the world like cold water, and there's a buildup in the community of violence against each other.

"All our organization can do is put together a survival kit of stores and foods stamps and wait for a shot in the arm, which has to come from the outside, because the only wealth in Watts leaves at 5 o'clock with the doctors, lawyers and landlords."

Improvements in living conditions are hard to find. One is in transportation services, although the opening of new bus routes to Watts took about a decade to accomplish. Lack of the routes had been identified by the McCone Commission report that studies the causes of the 1965 violence as one of the community's major needs.

Persons living in Watts in 1965 felt trapped because the privately owned local bus company serving the community provided scant routes to outside employment opportunities. The bus line was taken over by the citywide Rapid Transit District in 1971, but it was not until this March that county subsidies enabled the district to

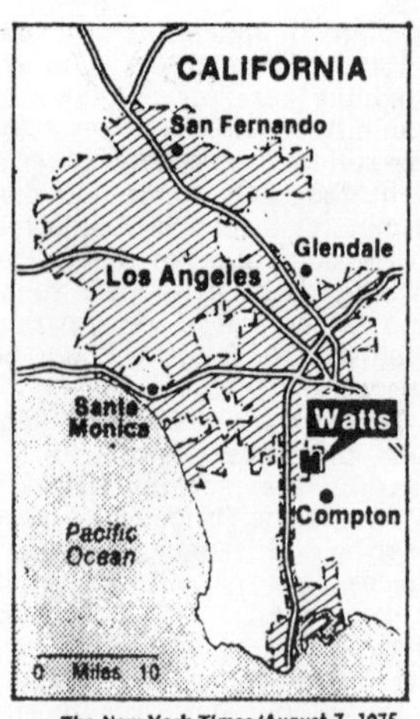

The New York Times/August 7, 1975

radically improve services through a grid system in the black community.

Now bus lines are operating, but there are few jobs to travel to in the recession.

Perhaps the brightest development in the community since 1965 has been improvements in health, although health problems still exceed the norm for the rest of Los Angeles County. The food stamp program has improved nutrition and ameliorated hunger, and for the first time in the history of Watts two publicly funded health care facilities now service the community.

The Watts Health Center was opened in 1967 with antipoverty funds to supply an array of treatment to an area where about half the residents are medically indigent. The funds, however, have been cut every year since 1973 by the Federal Government.

The Martin Luther King Jr. Hospital, a $40-million facility that opened three years ago in the Willowbrook section just south of Watts, has had a far-reaching impact, although the crush of demand for services has limited its goal of providing comprehensive health care to the wider community that it serves.

The hospital has also been jolted by a number of internal disputes between the medical staff and the administration, and allegations of substandard medical treatment, bureaucratic difficulties and problems associated with hospital-community relations have contributed to unrest among the staff almost since the opening day.

Watts historically was the "back door" to Southern California. It was the first address for poor rural blacks landing in Los Angeles from sharecropper origins in East Texas or Louisiana. It was, therefore, always the place the new-arrivals aspired to leave once a job could be secured and enough money saved to escape to those surrounding communities then open to blacks.

But prior to 1965, because of the paucity of opportunity for blacks—a condition that exacerbated frustration and helped lead to the 1965 outburst—many families had lived in Watts for years, giving a cohesion to it and a natural progression of leadership.

The riot not only provided an added incentive to move away from the rubble of Watts, but the period immediately following it provided the opportunity, as the more competent members of the community suddenly found access to education, jobs and neighborhoods that had been beyond their reach before the civil rights gains of the decade.

'There's Nothing There'

"The problem with Watts today," says Stanley Sanders, 32, a partner in an all-black law firm located near Beverly Hills, "is that blacks have given up on it just like the whites did. There's nothing there any more except a lot of very young people and some very old people. There is no vitality there—no stores, no movies, no restaurants and no future."

Mr. Sanders, a Rhodes scholar and a graduate of Yale Law School, tried to keep his home in Watts because, he said, he felt an obligation to preserve "models of success" for the young eople in the community who had an abundance of negative "models." Several years ago he wrote an article in Ebony magazine declaring that he would never move away from Watts.

"Darn it," he sighed over a drink at his Wilshire Boulevard office building, "I was the guy who was going to be different. I had a social commitment to stay because of the advantages that had been bestowed on me. It was pure hell when I had to make the decision to leave, just like the rest of the guys of my generation who had dreamed about a future for Watts after the riots. All the dreamers have left—they're either into cushy jobs or in jail, on dope, dead or political exile."

He said that Watts today was a product of Nixon Administration policies and those in the Administration who urged neglect of black social issues. Shorn of Federal aid, the community no longer clings to the expectations that resulted in the riot a decade ago, he said. Now there is no hope for Watts and no unrealistic expectations held by the people stranded there, he said.

The Watts Summer Festival, founded the year after the riots in a spirit of renaissance, will be held this month on the anniversary of the Watts revolt. But it has become an uneasy summer confrontation chiefly between the black street gangs and the police, where admission is charged because the festival has lost $150,000 in recent years.

August 7, 1975

Urban Crisis of the 1960's Is Over, Ford Aides Say

By ERNEST HOLSENDOLPH
Special to The New York Times

WASHINGTON, March 22 — Urban policy makers in the Ford Administration have concluded, despite vigorous objections from many local political leaders and experts on the condition of the cities, that the "urban crisis" of the nineteen-sixties is over.

Even with the emergence in recent months of the fiscal squeeze between reduced tax revenue because of the recession and rising costs because of inflation, officials here still tend to give the troubles of the cities a relatively low priority.

The Administration's budget for the next fiscal year, which would do little more than hold the line on Federal payments to the cities, is partly a reflection of the dislocations within the economy.

But it is also an expression of the fact that the urban situation, a critical national issue occupying much time and attention in a nervous capital a decade ago, is no longer one of Washington's principal worries.

'Serious Problems'

"There was an urban crisis at one time," says William Lilley 3d, Deputy Assistant Secretary of Policy Development at the Department of Housing and Urban Development. "But that has changed in the past few years. Oh yes, there are serious problems—and some cities are in crisis—but now the picture varies from one city to another."

Indeed, much about the cities has changed in the five years since The New York Times last surveyed them. Most notable is the absence of racial riots and the lingering anxiety they caused, crucial elements in defining the crisis atmosphere of the sixties.

In the minds of Administration planners, racial tensions have been overshadowed, if not replaced, by concerns that cut across lines of race, neighborhood or class—the fiscal pressures, for example, or the concern everywhere about safety on the streets.

At the same time, these officials see signs of hope that the cities are becoming attractive again to the middle class. There is talk of "urban conservation" and less interest in the proposition of the early sixties that the cities should be knocked down and done over.

A main ingredient in the lessening of crisis, the Administration planners say, is the easing of the heavy migration of whites to the suburbs and of blacks and poor whites from the countryside to the cities, a mass shifting of peoples that caused a concentration of poverty and all its attendant troubles in the cities.

Moreover, the theory goes, there has been some turnabout in city finances, despite recent inflation-recession problems, and there has been a migration of more blacks and other minorities to the suburbs.

Census Aides Agree

The staff of the Social and Economic Statistics Administration of the Bureau of the Census agree with the impression that there has been a leveling-off of the influx of poor and rural people into central cities, although the department has no figures to document the proposition.

Figures that are available tend to run counter to the Administration position that urban problems, strictly speaking, are becoming less pronounced, however. Specifically, the socioeconomic gap between the central cities and the suburbs has been growing, according to Larry H. Long, chief of the population analysis staff of the Social and Economic Statistics Administration.

In 1960 the median income of central city families was 89 per cent of the median income of suburban families, he said, and by 1970 it had dropped to 84 per cent, and to 81 per cent by 1974.

The median income among families in central cities grew from $5,950 in 1960 to $11,379 in 1974, according to census figures, but at the same time median income among families in the outlying portions of metropolitan areas grew from $6,707 to $14,056. The gap grew from $767 to $2,677.

"In the past the widening income gap between central cities and their suburbs has resulted partly from a tendency of poor, rural migrants to settle in central cities as opposed to suburbs," Mr. Long said.

'City-to-Suburb Migration'

"But it also results from a pattern of city-to-suburb migration of the more affluent population of central cities," he continued. He pointed out that this trend had caused the suburbs to accumulate an increasingly high percentage of the affluent and educated.

The movement of blacks and other minorities toward the suburbs, leaving poorer members of the minorities behind, has also tended to concentrate the needy in center cities.

The fact that industries have also moved toward more spacious outlying areas, taking their taxes with them, has also weakened the power of cities to finance their needs.

Although some Federal measures have been aimed at mitigating the growing economic gap—especially the $30.2-billion general revenue-sharing program enacted in 1972 to give relatively more Federal aid to poorer jurisdictions than well-to-do ones—cities maintain that they have a worsening income problem.

The Administration view that the urban crisis is over is sharply contested in some quarters. Critics of the Administration say assertions that the crisis has passed are only a justification for inaction and for cost-cutting for its own sake. "What they really mean is that the cities are not burning," says Representative Parren Mitchell, a Maryland Democrat, whose district includes part of Baltimore.

Concentration Continues

As to the migration, Mr. Long of the Census Bureau points out that although it is correct to say that the inflow has leveled off, the concentration of poor, marginally educated people remains. The minority migrants from the center cities to the suburbs are the affluent and better educated, thus depressing the city indicators all the more.

Partly because of their view of the changed circumstances in the cities, Administration planners have embarked on a number of new policies in the last few years, some of them without specific sanction of Congress and most of them, in the spirit of former President Nixon's "New Federalism," meant to reduce the Federal role in local affairs. They include:

¶Reduction in the size and scope of housing subsidy programs, including the summary suspension of two authorized programs in January, 1972.

¶Efforts to cut the cost of welfare—although mostly in the name of rationalizing administration of the program and elimination of unqualified recipients—and initial steps to reduce food stamp benefits.

¶A new housing bill with emphasis on leasing of existing housing rather than the continued construction of new, relatively expensive housing units.

¶Greatly reduced commitment to the last vestiges of former President Johnson's "Great Society" programs, which most Administration planners and many outside critics say were not only costly but no more than minimally productive.

While there has been criticism of the Federal Government's decision to turn down the volume of some aid to urban communities, the Administration shows signs of having picked its timing well.

Staff members on the House Subcommittee on Housing say that mail was running quite heavily against the Government programs for subsidized private houses and subsidized rental units before the Nixon Administration decided to close them down two years ago.

Program Called Unfair

The programs were designed to allow individuals with modest incomes to build houses or occupy new rental units at subsidized rates. Citizens in neighborhoods where the new housing was built complained that the program was inequitable.

"We worked hard to buy our houses," was a typical remark, according to George Gross, who was a staff member on the subcommittee. "Why should these guys get for practically free what we worked for so hard?"

Others complained that the houses looked "tacky" and "destroyed the character of the neighborhood."

"Of course," Mr. Gross added, "a lot of the complaints were racial, from white suburbanites who were afraid the program would bring more blacks into their area."

The subsidized programs also came under fire from some Congressmen because of scandals involving developers and loose management in some urban areas.

"Much of the subsidized program was shut down because of broad discontent," said Mr. Lilley of H.U.D. "It cost too much, actually contributed to discrimination in some instances, and caused too many political problems."

Other critics of the housing program said that the construction programs that were frozen by the Administration in January, 1972, contained little incentive to cut unnecessary costs, mainly because architects, lawyers and others associated with the transactions worked on a percentage basic.

As the planners perceived it, it seemed ill-advised to subsidize housing at the production level. "The real problem was the matter of too little income among the people who needed and did not have adequate housing," Mr. Lilley said.

Forerunner of an Allowance

Housing and community development thinkers within the Administration are now clearly

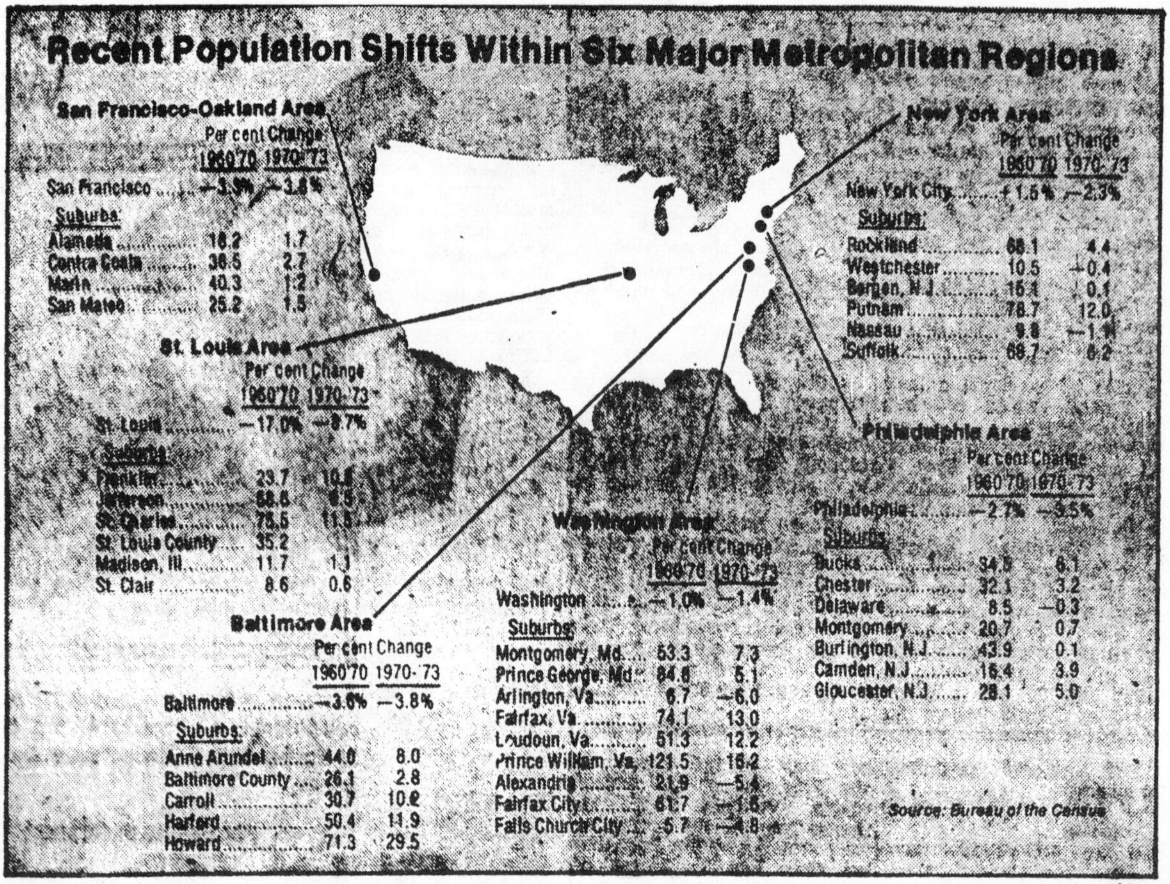

Recent Population Shifts Within Six Major Metropolitan Regions

San Francisco-Oakland Area

	Per cent Change 1960-70	1970-73
San Francisco	—3.3%	—3.8%
Suburbs:		
Alameda	18.2	1.7
Contra Costa	38.5	2.7
Marin	40.3	1.2
San Mateo	25.2	1.5

St. Louis Area

	Per cent Change 1960-70	1970-73
St. Louis	—17.0%	—8.7%
Suburbs:		
Franklin	23.7	10.6
Jefferson	58.6	6.5
St. Charles	75.5	11.5
St. Louis County	35.2	
Madison, Ill.	11.7	1.1
St. Clair	8.6	0.6

Baltimore Area

	Per cent Change 1960-70	1970-73
Baltimore	—3.6%	—3.8%
Suburbs:		
Anne Arundel	44.0	8.0
Baltimore County	26.1	2.8
Carroll	30.7	10.2
Harford	50.4	11.9
Howard	71.3	29.5

Washington Area

	Per cent Change 1960-70	1970-73
Washington	—1.0%	—1.4%
Suburbs:		
Montgomery, Md.	53.3	7.3
Prince George, Md.	84.6	5.1
Arlington, Va.	6.7	—6.0
Fairfax, Va.	74.1	13.0
Loudoun, Va.	51.3	12.2
Prince William, Va.	121.5	16.2
Alexandria	21.9	—5.4
Fairfax City	61.7	—1.5
Falls Church City	5.7	—4.8

New York Area

	Per cent Change 1960-70	1970-73
New York City	+1.5%	—2.3%
Suburbs:		
Rockland	68.1	4.4
Westchester	10.5	+0.4
Bergen, N.J.	15.1	0.1
Putnam	78.7	12.0
Nassau	9.8	—1.1
Suffolk	68.7	8.2

Philadelphia Area

	Per cent Change 1960-70	1970-73
Philadelphia	—2.7%	—3.5%
Suburbs:		
Bucks	34.5	6.1
Chester	32.1	3.2
Delaware	8.5	—0.3
Montgomery	20.7	0.7
Burlington, N.J.	43.9	0.1
Camden, N.J.	16.4	3.9
Gloucester, N.J.	28.1	5.0

Source: Bureau of the Census

The New York Times/March 22, 1975

most excited about the "leased housing" provisions in the Housing Act of 1974, whereby rents in existing housing will be subsidized by the Government.

This limited program is seen as a forerunner of a housing allowance program, or a system of augmenting the income of the poor to allow them to shop for their quarters—a significant departure from the public housing program, under which governmental agencies built quarters just for poor-to-modest income people.

Meanwhile, H.U.D. is running a $230-million experiment in 12 cities around the nation to see if housing allowances may not be the best solution to housing the disadvantaged in cities.

Critics are dubious about the principle of housing allowances at this point, primarily because in many cities there is a shortage of safe, sanitary housing that is free of major code violations. For its part, in the words of one H.U.D. spokesman, the department feels that there is a need "to get more juice flowing through the system to keep the housing stock high."

Whatever the merits of the new housing policy, the traditional public housing concept has been pressed far into the background now. Although public housing has been viewed often as the most convenient way to house the very poor and the elderly, it has been criticized as a "containerization" of the disadvantaged into high-rise ghettos.

Dramatic failures of public housing, one of the most conspicuous being the collapse of the giant Pruitt-Igo development in St. Louis, have tended to underline difficulties caused by large concentrations of people with problems, overtaxing the systems for delivering social and other services.

Public Housing Debated

Over and over again it has been proved that public housing, as built traditionally by big-city public housing authorities, does not work, Administration planners say. But other housing experts, including Philip Brownstein, former commissioner of the Federal Housing Authority, differ.

"There are problems in public housing, of course," Mr. Brownstein says. "We know that high-rise construction does not always work, especially for families with children, but the answer is to build the housing differently," he added.

Just before the latest economic crunch, brought along by the general state of the economy, many cities seemed to be digging themselves out from under financial problems that brought many of them close to bankruptcy.

There were several reasons for this development, including the enactment of city payroll taxes, the coming of general revenue sharing to augment regular operating budgets, revenue-sharing programs between states and their cities, and more economic cooperation between center cities and surrounding suburbs.

In a speech to the League of Cities meeting in San Juan in 1973, Detroit's Mayor Roman S. Gribbs was able to say, "We have moved out of the category of 'destitute' and up to the category of 'impoverished.'"

Productivity a Topic

With the cost of inflation and a drop in income because of growing unemployment, however, that marginal improvement in urban finances is being reversed — very seriously in some cities.

At the annual National League of Cities meeting in Houston last month the subject of productivity in labor management was the hottest subject among the urban politicians, who stood in the workshop rooms to hear labor experts speak on the matter.

City officials were particularly eager to obtain advice on how to deal with public unions, whose efforts increasingly are leading to ever larger contracts and better protection for city workers—and adding to the inflation in municipal operations.

And the current agony of New York City is proof that many cities need better financial-growth management. "They [New York] just couldn't go on indefinitely at such annual growth rates," one observer said. Even Detroit, it was pointed out, now has about half of its public safety budget eaten up by pension costs.

The second hottest subject at the Houston convention was crime, reflecting the growing concern about public safety in the nation's urban areas.

The Federal Government has had a growing part in the financing of planning, training and equipping of law enforcement agencies in cities around the country, as well as the support of other aspects of the criminal justice system. From a standing start in 1965 under the Johnson Administration, the Law Enforcement Assistance Administration's budget has grown to a total of $871-million.

'Guns and More Guns'

At the Houston meeting, some city councilmen criticized the use of L.E.A.A. funds for "guns and more guns" as a means of reducing crime. "Why aren't the funds used for social programs that might reduce the root causes of crime?" was one frequently asked question.

An answer given by one black city official was this: "If I can spend the money in my city to cut the crime in a poor neighborhood, where some poor black women are afraid to walk home after they finish their day's work, that will be a social program well worth the spending!"

The principal social program with a bearing on the nation's very big cities is the $11-billion public welfare system, half financed by the Government's Department of Health, Education and Welfare.

A large, weblike system that tends to grow in fits and starts—but always goes on growing—the welfare system appears headed for some kind of substantial revision.

A leading notion, put forth by H.E.W. Secretary Caspar W. Weinberger most recently, and also by former Representative Martha Griffiths, Democrat of Michigan, has been a proposal for a form of negative income tax, which the Administration is calling an Income Supplement Program, or I.S.P.

In the spirit of the Nixon Administration's push to play down programs and, instead, put cash into the people's hands, I.S.P. would simply send out checks to the needy who qualiffy, theoretically reducing the public welfare bureaucracy and eliminating a large amount of overhead.

The shift in Government urban policy has coincided with a new push by the cities through their own National League of Cities. Absolutely delighted over general revenue sharing, which is now about halfway through its course, the league said in a policy statement some time ago that the $30.2-billion program gives communities a new measure of power.

Promulgated at the annual meeting in San Juan, in 1973, the statement said in part:

"Urban areas contain more than 70 per cent of the citizens of this country. They represent the greater portion of the tangible wealth, of the centers of culture and learning, of the sites of business and industry.

"They elect Congressmen and provide electoral votes all out of proportion to their land mass, and still, they have been largely unheard for all these years despite their terrible plight and undeniable needs."

Metropolitan Planning

Cities are now getting more of their share of power, thanks in some measure to redistricting. There is also a tendency in urban legislation now to require some form of metropolitan planning for the use of urban development funds.

This gradual move toward what Wilfred Owen of the Brookings Institution calls the "systems" approach to urban development, could well result in more metropolitan or even regional planning and some curb on the aimless sprawl of the nineteen-sixties.

Mr. Owen and others are pleased at the "block grant" approach of the Housing and Community Development Act of 1974, which authorizes $8.4-billion in funding over three years in single grants to localities for community development programs.

It is hoped that the new approach will bring to an end the practice of having one independent agency clearing land, another putting up houses and another designing transportation and so on.

Mr. Owen, a student of transportation who has paid special attention to San Francisco's Bay Area Rapid Transit, says he is convinced that too often transportation systems are merely bridges to connect the accidents of urban development. In his view, the less dependence on mass transportation needed the better.

New efforts to do complete community planning should reduce the need for transportation, he says.

But if transportation is necessary, Mr. Owen says, buses usually are a wiser investment than urban rail systems, which tend to be expensive and serve comparatively few people.

"I hope the urban mass transportation department will decide to spend a lot of the new money for buses," Mr. Owen said. "Buses reach the people and take them where they want to go—now all we need are more bus lanes and all-bus highways."

What is recognized in much of the new urban policy is the scope and nature of the "new" city.

Allen E. Pritchard, executive director of the National League of Cities, wrote lucidly about these shifts in his "State of the Cities" report to the league's convention in Puerto Rico in 1973.

The city has come a long way from the role of street paver and garbage collector, he said. Now there is talk of "quality of life" and the "capacity of cities to meet people's needs."

And then he wrote:

"It is also true that these expectations have been reflected in a fundamental transformation of the goals of public policy. Before 1960, public policy emphasized the tangible inputs to problem-solving—if people lived in deteriorating neighborhoods, housing projects were constructed; if they were victimized, 100 additional police officers were hired; if they were sick, a wing or two were added to a hospital.

"By the mid-sixties, we began to understand all this building of things was not an unmixed blessing. Neighborhoods and communities were ripped apart by urban renewal and highway construction. Children in brand new schools were simply not learning any better. We created a surplus of hospital rooms, but health care was not improving.

"Policy responses to these understandings were vigorous but had a peculiar frantic quality . . . Head Start . . . War on Poverty . . . Black Capitalism . . . Citizen Participation . . . Manpower Development and on and on."

"More was promised than could be delivered," he said.

March 23, 1975

. . . Indifferent Uncle

The message that the Ford Administration regards the crisis of the cities as over stands in strange contrast to the realities of mayors staring at growing puddles of red ink on their ledgers and of new recruits added weekly to the ranks of the unemployed.

Officially expressed relief that all's quiet in the slums will not be shared by those who believe that the rise of violent crime is directly related to frustrations aggravated by the alarming level of joblessness among black youths.

Limited gains have undoubtedly been made in some areas. Although statistics are far from conclusive, the migration that in the past decade inundated the cities with wave after wave of rural poor appears to have slowed, as has the middle-class exodus from the urban centers. The conflict between the races also seems at least to be muted—in part, some observers say poignantly, because the threat of unemployment and uncertainty is now more often shared across racial lines.

The cities, and the nation, cannot afford to resurrect the Nixon Administration's doctrine of "benign neglect" under the new guise of a dangerous self-delusion that victory in the war against urban decline is at hand. It would be playing with fire to conclude from the painful lesson of the urban riots in the sixties that the absence of any imminent threat of violence is cause for complacency about the condition of America's cities.

March 25, 1975

SUBURBAN TREND MEANS CITY LOSS

Realty Official Holds Deeper Study Is Urgently Needed in Planning Methods

A warning that the trend of population from cities to suburban areas may result in serious consequences to business conditions and realty values is voiced by Philip W. Kniskern of Philadelphia, vice president of the National Association of Real Estate Boards. He urges that communities study the recommendations of the national body and name nonpartisan groups representing municipal and financial interests, utilities, property owners and others to investigate the causes of urban decentralization and to evolve remedial action.

"If the trend to suburban areas is permitted to continue unchecked," states Mr. Kniskern, "it will, in time, mean a serious loss in central business district property values. Already this change in economic assets has made itself definitely apparent in a number of cities.

"It must be remembered that our central city business district properties are rated at high values. They also carry high assessments and form an important part of a municipality's revenue. Any damage to their value injuries not only the property owner but the community as well. Again, it must be borne in mind that many of these properties are owned by bondholders, and these investment owners come from all spheres and walks of life. Many of them, too, are important parts of endowments of educational and charitable institutions. If their income-producing power is affected, it harms and retards the work of these institutions.

Called Serious Problem

"This move to the suburbs is affecting not only central city properties but residential properties as well. It is evident that when a mass movement occurs in any neighborhood, property values there tend to decline and the section assumes a cheaper tone.

"Traffic and parking problems are playing an important part in the possible deterioration of our central city business districts. The problems to be considered are many. The longer this study is put off, the worse the situation will become.

"There are communities where this condition is still to arise; there are others where it has been felt only slightly. In still others it is beginning to assume serious proportions.

"Formation of non-partisan city planning groups to study and solve this question will help all communities. In those sections where the problem is still to arise steps can be taken, based upon the experience of other cities, to forestall such conditions. In other municipalities, where the situation has developed, a group may be able to check the tendency and effect remedial steps to prevent loss in property values and municipal revenue."

The city of Chicago has taken cognizance of this problem and recently appointed a city planning commission of twenty-six members, fourteen of whom are public officials and twelve are drawn from community leaders. The ordinance states that it shall have powers "to prepare and recommend to the City Council a comprehensive plan for the development of existing property and the rehabilitation of depreciated areas."

Commends Chicago Action

This action, points out Herbert U. Nelson, executive vice president of the National Association of Real Estate Boards, is very encouraging and other cities should take similar steps.

"The automobile and other forms of rapid transit have done much for the American people," says Mr. Nelson. "They have widened our horizons and enriched our experience. But with these possibilities our old concepts of how cities should be planned have been materially changed.

"Our cities have sprawled out to such an extent that they cover, on an average, six times the area of a European city of the same population. Also, practically one-third of the privately owned land within this urban area lies unused, involving a large blighted area which once included high-class residential properties.

"Lying as they do near the business centers, these neighborhoods should be valuable land. In European cities they are the most valuable kind of residential property. But in our cities, despite the costly street and sewer construction and the miles of other public service installations, these regions have been left to molder till they are no longer a source of tax revenue.

"The problem of our city building cannot be solved by constantly running away from our cities. We must learn how to rebuild them. They must be planned for the comfort and welfare of human beings. In pioneer days cities were built for workshops. That had to be done first but now they must be built for living. They must be designed and planned for that purpose, with the same directness and clarity that the engineer brings to his problem of creating a useful and beautiful machine."

January 21, 1940

CITIES WATCHING FACTORY CHANGES

Experts Cite Possible Effects of Movement to New Sites in Outlying Areas

In a symposium discussing the trend toward relocation and modernization of industries in relation to cities, Homer Hoyt, director of economic studies of the Regional Plan Association of New York, takes the view that sites on the fringes of cities are better for factories unless their location within the city is part of a careful plan considering operational efficiency and effect on other land uses.

The problem was raised by the National Committee on Housing in its current issue of Tomorrow's Town and discussed by E. C. Atkins, president of the E. C. Atkins Company of Indianapolis; George H. Miehls, president of the Albert Kohn Associated Architects and Engineers, Inc., of Detroit; Melvin H. Baker, president of the National Gypsum Company, Buffalo, and C. Donald Dallas, president of Revere Copper and Brass, Inc., of this city, in addition to Mr. Hoyt.

While different opinions were rendered on the problem of eliminating industrial blight caused when industries move out of central locations to suburban areas, there was general agreement on the need for a greater degree of planning for the metropolitan district.

Mr. Atkins related that his company had decided not to move its factory from the central location it had occupied for eighty-eight years despite the costs of modernizing the existing plant. The decision, he said, was based on the opinion that "every time a large property owner or business moves out of the central part of the city another and undesirable contribution is made to deterioration and decentralization."

According to Mr. Baker, industry has become too congested and should be decentralized. He recommended the surveying of cities for long range growth. Keeping future trends in mind, he declared, the surveys should include the possibilities of rezoning, revision of building codes and adoption of slum clearance programs to eliminate the present blighted areas and to avoid the development of others in the future.

The continuance of owners moving their factories to city fringes where they can take advantage of cheaper land or lower taxes was foreseen by Mr. Miehls. But he added that this need not be injurious to the cities. He suggested that housing and commercial outlets be developed in the urban areas for those whose labor is marketed there, while industrial workers find other housing nearer their employment as factories move to the outskirts.

Mr. Dallas said that education and stimulation of neighborhood pride and responsibility could prevent industrial blight, and added: "The people at the top of city planing should consider the education of various family units and individuals in the different neighborhoods as one of the prime tasks confronting them."

In the opinion of Mr. Hoyt "there are industrial as well as residential slums, and it is as undesirable to perpetuate a single good plant in an area of obsolete factory buildings where the entire street pattern is poorly designed for the efficient operation of industry as it is to prolong the life of a residential slum by modernizing a few of its structures or by erecting in its midst a few isolated new buildings."

January 27, 1946

LEVITTS SET GOAL AT 30 HOMES DAILY

Levitt & Sons, Long Island home builders, have started production at the rate of twenty houses a day on their largest small-dwelling project.

The new community, known as Island Trees, is near Hempstead. It will consist of 2,000 houses to rent at $60 monthly. The first units will be ready for occupancy by war veterans early in September, and a production goal of thirty a day is expected to be reached about that time. All are due to be completed by early spring of 1948.

All of these homes have been taken in advance, and about 10,000 applications were received before the list was closed. In order to help meet the additional demand, the Levitts expect to acquire additional adjoining land for about 2,000 more.

The house itself has four rooms on the main floor and a stairway leading to an unfinished attic. The houses are built on a solid concrete slab and imbedded in the concrete are copper hot water coils to provide radiant heating and domestic hot water.

On preliminary tests there has been a variation of temperature between floor and ceiling of less than 2 degrees. Levitt ran an experimental job of thirty-one houses through last winter in which all types and kinds of heating were utilized. Radiant heating then was decided upon as the most satisfactory.

Unusual features in the house include the kitchen, which provides space for the automatic laundry, an electric refrigerator and electric range, all of which are standard equipment. Cabinets are of steel.

In one corner of the dinette space is a built-in-cupboard with both open and closed shelves.

Closets have chromium fittings and an accordion-type shutter door permits ventilation tending to overcome the problem of moths. The side of the staircase exposed to the living room has been formed into open bookshelves, providing both a decorative and utilitarian touch in the house. Metal Venetian blinds are standard equipment on all windows. The minimum plot of ground is 60 by 100 feet and will be landscaped.

Under Federal Rules

All houses are being built under Title VI of the National Housing Act. Because of the scope of the job, which covers over 500 acres, the Town of Hempstead has appointed both resident building inspectors and engineers, and the Federal Housing Administration has a resident inspector constantly on the job so as to avoid any slowdown.

In the center of the community the builders have set aside a twelve-acre combination shopping and recreation area. Among the buildings proposed there are bowling alleys, a bank, postoffice, as well as the usual super markets and necessity shops. Another feature will be a large circular swimming pool, which will be set in the midst of gardens and pathways for pedestrians. The builders are sinking their own water wells, permission for which was received from the New York State Water, Power and Control Commission.

Levitt & Sons has scheduled for this year an additional 1,000 houses which are being built for sale. Most of these have already been sold and at the rate sales are proceeding, they may be completely under contract by Aug. 15. Price on these is $7,500 with a nominal down payment of $500 and carrying charges of $52 a month.

July 20, 1947

SHOPPING CENTERS IN NASSAU COUNTY TO STRESS PARKING

Owners to Improve Nine-Acre Site at Levittown With Modern Store Groups

HOME GROWTH IS FACTOR

Additional Retail Facilities Are Provided in New Blockfront Project at Merrick

Blockfront of stores going up on Merrick Avenue between Garfield and Lincoln Streets, in Merrick, under sponsorship of Initial Builders, Inc., from plans by Schulman & Soloway.

By LEE E. COOPER

Outlying communities, already suffering from growing pains, are taking no chances that in later years the traffic in their business and shopping centers will be tied up and realty values threatened by lack of adequate parking facilities.

The new store centers which are springing up in Nassau County close to the vast new stretches of small homes are an example. Only where ample space is provided for automobiles are the new projects receiving approval of municipal authorities or of prospective tenants.

An outstanding illustration of the trend, out in Nassau County which has not yet reached the point of congestion felt in Queens, is to be found in the modern taxpayer group announced for a large site in Levittown. With the first section of this shopping center already in progress, the sponsors announced that upon completion about six acres of parking would be available in the front rather than in the rear of the retail buildings.

Site Covers Nine Acres

Space to handle the automobiles of customers thus will be twice as large as the area covered by the stores themselves. The first section of twelve store units is under way for occupancy about Nov. 1 on the tract at the southwest intersection of Gardiners Avenue and Hempstead-Bethpage Turnpike, in Levittown.

These stores will supplement the modern business districts being developed by Levitt & Sons themselves in other parts of the residential community they have built up on former farmland, which also have stressed easy access.

The latest project is being built by Leonel R. Bauman, Manhattan real estate man, and Samuel Leider, Forest Hills builder. It has been designed by Schulman & Soloway.

The entire project, with two additional sections to go up on adjoining land later, will be known as the Center Island Shopping Park. It will have space for nearly 1,000 cars. The stores will be laid out in the shape of an L along two sides and to the rear of the parking field. A 20-foot-wide pedestrian walk will run along the front of the shops.

The first building, now being roofed in, is 201 feet long and 70 feet deep. The Hempstead Bank has closed a long lease for about 2,100 feet with basement space, and provision for drive-in service, for a branch in a corner location in this initial building.

Other prospective tenants with whom leases are pending are a variety chain store, a drug chain, a food market, a laundry and dry-cleaning groups.

The entire front of the first group of stroes is of glass and stainless steel, with ends and rear of red brick. Ceilings are fourteen feet, and a five-foot overhang extends over the sidewalk to protect the pedestrians.

A smaller Nassau project, but one which also illustrates the trend, is under construction in the blockfront on Merrick Avenue from Garfield Street to Lincoln Street, in Merrick. The 200-foot store center, alsos to be occupied about Nov. 1, is sponsored bn Initial Builders, Inc. (Irving Cooperman), of Brooklyn. The cost is estimated at $150,000.

Parking space will be provided in the rear, and each store unit will have basement space. As in the case of the Levittown improvement, each tenant will have a separate heating plant. There will be eight units 70 fet in depth, with a super-market taking up a space of 70 by 80 feet.

A new shopping center for residents of Alden Terrace, L. I., is being completed by Phoebus Kaplan, builder who has been active in that area, on Central Avenue near the Southern State Parkway, to include a super-market and ten other retail units. Six of the eleven stores have been rented from the plans, Mr. Kaplan said.

September 18, 1949

SUBURBAN GROWTH TOPS THAT OF CITIES

Census Listing of Metropolitan Areas Shows Mass Movement Into Adjacent Communities

WASHINGTON, July 29 (AP)—Suburbs of the country's twelve largest cities outgrew the cities themselves in every case between 1940 and 1950. The Census Bureau disclosed this today in a listing of the largest metropolitan areas on the basis of preliminary 1950 population totals.

The figures confirmed earlier evidence of a mass-scale movement from the cities to the suburbs—to get more fresh air, cheaper land, lower taxes, more auto parking room, and so on.

In some instances, suburban growth during the decade more than doubled the growth in the central city. In the Boston, Los Angeles, San Francisco and Pittsburgh areas, suburban populations outnumber city dwellers—sometimes more than 2 to 1.

The list also showed that metropolitan ranking by size differed considerably from city size rankings. New York, Chicago and Detroit—Nos. 1, 2 and 5 among the cities, respectively, have the same positions as metropolitan areas.

Philadelphia and Los Angeles, 3 and 4 among cities, are in reverse order as metropolitan areas. Boston is sixth as a metropolitan area although only tenth as a city.

San Francisco has the seventh largest metropolitan population although it is eleventh among cities. Pittsburgh is metropolitan area No. 8, though city No. 12.

St. Louis is eighth as a city, ninth as a metropolitan area. Washington, ninth among cities, is eleventh among metropolitan areas. Baltimore is twelfth as a metropolitan area although sixth as a city.

The metropolitan areas consist of whole counties "substantially integrated" with the city's activities. The definition of such areas has been changed since 1940 when it cut across county lines. However, today's figures ignore the old lines and draw their comparisons between 1950 and 1940 in the whole counties which make up the present metropolitan areas.

Here are the metropolitan areas in order of size according to 1950 preliminary population counts, with rankings of cities shown parenthetically:

	1950	1940
New York City (1)	7,841,610	7,454,995
Suburbs	4,996,533	4,205,844
Chicago (2)	3,631,835	3,396,808
Suburbs	1,862,294	1,428,719
Los Angeles (4)	1,954,036	1,504,277
Suburbs	2,376,926	1,412,126
Philadelphia (3)	2,057,210	1,931,334
Suburbs	1,594,520	1,268,303
Detroit (5)	1,837,617	1,623,452
Suburbs	1,159,800	753,877
Boston (10)	788,552	770,816
Suburbs	1,564,816	1,406,805
San Francisco (11)	760,381	634,536
Suburbs	1,453,103	827,268
Pittsburgh (12)	673,700	671,659
Suburbs	1,519,170	1,410,877
St. Louis (8)	852,523	816,048
Suburbs	821,905	616,039
Cleveland (7)	909,546	878,336
Suburbs	548,013	388,934
Washington (9)	792,234	663,091
Suburbs	660,115	304,894
Baltimore (6)	941,809	859,100
Suburbs	384,450	224,200

July 30, 1950

Population Upset in Housing Seen, With Manhattan Middle Class Out

By ROBERT C. DOTY

Manhattan rapidly is being transformed into forbidden ground for middle-income families who neither can afford today's high rents in the free market nor qualify for admission to subsidized public housing.

Post-war residential construction in the city's geographic and traditional heart has set a pattern that threatens to expedite the migration of middle-class families to other boroughs and suburbs and, ultimately, to complete the upset of Manhattan's population balance.

New building has been predominantly of high rental, luxury apartments or of subsidized public housing for low-income groups. Mushrooming acres of garden-type apartments at moderate rentals, and one-family dwellings with federally financed mortgages have found no vertical counterparts in crowded Gotham.

As a result, according to urban planners and real-estate men questioned in a study of rental conditions, the flight of middle-income families that began many years ago now has reached an abnormal rate. If unchecked, it might turn Manhattan into the exclusive province of the rich and subsidized lower income families.

Decentralization of big-city populations has been proceeding for many years, prompted by many factors in addition to high rents, these experts point out. Many middle-income families move to the suburbs in search of greener fields and bluer skies than Manhattan offers, or of newer, less-crowded schools.

But there also is evidence that many families that would prefer the conveniences and cultural advantages of urban living are being forced to leave Manhattan because they can find no suitable living space. As evidence of this, more than 200,000 applications were received by the Metropolitan Life Insurance Company for the 8,755 apartment units in Stuyvesant Town, largest middle-income housing project built in Manhattan since World War II.

The consensus of experts indicates:

1. **Luxury housing—renting for $400 a room a year and more in family-size units is in adequate supply. There even are indications of the beginnings of a buyer's market in this field.**
2. **Very little new housing for middle-income families—priced at $200 to $400 a room a year in two and three-bedroom units—is available or under construction. Moderately priced older apartments under rent controls are solidly occupied.**
3. **Numerically, the shortage probably is still greatest for low-income families but progress in this field is being made by continuing construction of subsidized public housing projects.**

Gloomy Picture Seen

Some experts said these factors combined to paint a gloomy picture of future population trends in Manhattan. Normal decentralization, a long-established and inevitable trend, would in itself arouse no concern. But, when evidence mounts that most families leaving Manhattan are from a single class—the middle-income group—these experts foresee and fear the unhealthy division of the borough's population into upper and lower income families exclusively.

This view was expressed independently by three men who have studied the Manhattan real-estate situation closely. They are James Felt, president of James Felt & Co., Inc., Manhattan real estate concern, and a real estate consultant; Robert W. Dowling, president of City Investing Company, director of Starrett Brothers and Eken, Inc., builders, and chairman of the Citizens Budget Commission; and Ira S. Robbins, executive vice president of the Citizens' Housing and Planning Council of New York, Inc.

"Unless something is done to reverse this movement," said Mr. Felt, "Manhattan may develop into an exclusively high-rent and low-rent town, with nothing in between. The migration may be good for the other boroughs and the suburbs, but it has a stultifying effect on Manhattan."

Mr. Felt and others foresaw grave political and social dislocations if the polarization of the borough's population into economic extremes continued unchecked.

Tax burdens on the remaining residents would be increased. Loss or serious reduction of the contribution of middle-income families to the borough's civic and cultural life would reduce the vitality of these activities. In the political field, block voting by upper and lower income groups would be increased if the power and influence of the economic middle class, which prevents either major party from becoming the exclusive possessor of one or the other of the economic extremes, were to be further seriously reduced.

Nevertheless, the process of squeezing "white collar" families out of Manhattan continues.

Census Analyses Awaited

The experts await the detailed analyses of the 1950 census, providing family income statistics, to measure the extent of the trend. Further light on general conditions in the Manhattan rental market will be cast by a state-wide survey of rent levels, vacancy rates and other factors that is being made by the office of Joseph D. McGoldrick, State Rent Administrator; it will be published in November. The Real Estate Board of New York makes periodic check-ups of the rental field but does not make public its results.

In the absence of detailed data on vacancy rates and other conditions in the luxury apartment field there were these indications:

1. New, luxury apartment buildings, of the type that formerly were 100 per cent rented well before the buildings were ready for occupancy, now offers vacancies up to and beyond completion. Two, now within a few weeks of completion and renting at $720 and $750 a room a year, were 85 and 83 per cent rented, respectively.
2. Volume of rental offerings in classified columns in 1950 has increased by 33 to 100 per cent over comparable days in 1949, and most of these offerings were in the high-rental field.
3. Individual apartments in older high-rental buildings recently have remained vacant for periods of up to three months at a time. Formerly vacant apartments at all price levels were speedily rented.

Mortimer Grunauer, secretary of **Bing & Bing, Inc., owners and management agents for high-rental apartment properties, said:**

"Frankly, we're finding that people are not falling over themselves to lease higher rental apartments. They've become more choosy, more discriminating, more careful. I see no cause for concern about the market at present, but I won't say how far in the future that will hold true."

Others in the same field expressed satisfaction with the market for luxury apartments.

"I don't think the market is saturated—we haven't reached anything like normal pre-war vacancy rates," said David Tishman of the Tishman Realty and Construction Company, owners of extensive Park Avenue and East Side midtown apartment properties.

It's Unimportant to Many

The question of whether a surplus is being born in the numerically unimportant field of luxury housing has only a slight bearing on the plight of Manhattan's low and middle income groups.

Even a deep and general reduction of top rentals—which currently is foreseen by no one—would make only a relatively few apartments available to some upper middle-income families, the experts agreed.

Most new rental housing has been erected by private builders, privately financed in desirable residential neighborhoods. Few of these are offered at rents below $600 a room annually; many cost twice that much.

The City Housing Authority has built, is building or has approved plans for 86,000 apartment units throughout the city, 20,000 of them in Manhattan. Of these, 66,000 receive annual cash subsidy from public funds, and rent at an average of $108 a room a year. The 20,000 other units receive no cash subsidy but have tax and financing advantages and rent for a maximum of $199.08 a room a year. Tenancy is limited to families with cash incomes of not more than $3,100—$4,200 for war veterans—in the cash-subsidy houses; in the nonsubsidy projects, maximum income for tenants is $4,900.

The Housing Authority has 250,000 applications on file for these 86,000 units—direct evidence that supply has not begun to equal the housing demands of these low and lower middle-income groups.

But, however inadequate this program may be to those earning less than $5,000 a year, it offers some prospect of eventually finding housing in Manhattan within their means. For those earning from $5,000 to about $7,000, very little is being done by either public or private housing interests in Manhattan.

These are the families that seek housing at monthly rentals of $18 to $30 a room, willing to pay from $80 to $130 a month for a two-bedroom apartment.

In Manhattan, suitable housing within this rent range is to be found almost exclusively in rent-controlled dwellings. These are solidly rented and pass from friend to friend in the rare cases of vacancy **and never appear on the market.**

The Citizens' Housing and Planning Council directory of large-scale rental housing in the city lists only two major developments built since the war to rent within the range for middle-income families.

One is Peter Cooper Village on the Lower East Side, with average rentals of $28 a room a month; the other is Stuyvesant Town, its neighbor to the south, where average rent is $18 a room a month. Together, they have 11,250 dwelling units. The Metropolitan Life Insurance Company, which built them, had received 200,000 applications for apartments in Stuyvesant Town alone before the company decided to reject more.

Stuyvesant Town was made possible by a combination of indirect subsidy by the city and the large

capital resources of the insurance company. The city agreed to tax the development for a period of twenty-five years on the value of the land and old buildings on the site rather than on the improved value of the project. Even with this advantage, building and maintenance cost increases over original estimates forced revision of rental schedules from a projected $14 a room a month to $17 (or $18 with utilities).

Manhattan land values, building costs, interest rates, and the difficulty of re-locating tenants of existing housing on potential sites, all are factors that make highly unlikely the duplication of Stuyvesant Town by private builders.

Yet, unless Stuyvesant Town is duplicated, or approximated, many times over, urban planners and real estate experts consider it likely that, within a few decades, most of Manhattan's white collar, middle-income earners will be catching the 5:18 for the suburbs.

There seems to be no simple formula for solving the problem but hopeful proposals have been made, involving large-scale urban re-development by combined public and private capital and effort.

October 2, 1950

'Dream Town'— Large Economy Size

Pennsylvania's new Levittown is pre-planned down to the last thousand living rooms.

By PENN KIMBALL

LEVITTOWN, Pa.

THE sparkling vision of new towns in America, graceful and spacious cities with attractive homes and progressive civic planning, has danced on the drafting boards of idealistic young architects for years immemorial. A few tentative experiments in greenbelt living actually advanced beyond the blueprint stage prior to World War II. Some were an esthetic success; most were financial failures. In today's environment of urban catacombs and suburban cell-blocks mankind's inner yearning for reasonable shelter plus tolerable elbow-room flames more fiercely than ever.

How to build the ideal town—on paper — no longer stumps the experts, although individual ideas may clash. How to build a dream town with hard brick and mortar, on the other hand, becomes a knotty question: first of finding economic incentives to bring it to life; then of working out practical ways to amortize twentieth-century luxuries like grass, trees and playgrounds in addition to absolute necessities like asphalt parking lots. Initial cost is the great compromiser of planners' dreams; upkeep is their destroyer.

Yet forces are now being turned loose by an explosive American technology which—potentially, at least—are capable of transforming yesterday's wild dream into tomorrow's commonplace. Building is being revolutionized by assembly-line construction with standardized materials. Geography is being upset by the movement and growth of mammoth new facilities for making aluminum, steel, power, atomic weapons.

THE vital ingredient for the planners' brave new world is finally within reach. Industry, bursting at the seams, is not only creating the demand for new plant sites and new homes for shifting thousands of factory workers; relocated industry, more than that, promises new sources of stable and taxable wealth to support the planners' schemes, an indispensable artery to pump life into the phantom carcass of a model town.

Thus it is that on the Pennsylvania bank of the Delaware River, not far from where Washington crossed to surprise the Hessians at Trenton, an astonishing pattern begins these days to unfold. A fabulous new skyline of masonry and metal soars from the river flats—a half-billion dollars in blast furnaces, stacks, coke ovens, rolling mills for United States Steel's giant new Fairless Works, which last week poured its first molten iron from its first open-hearth. Conveniently close to thousands of new jobs and already starting to fill with married couples, baby carriages, respectability and hopes, (3,250 families will be moved in by Christmas), is the pre-planned new town of the pre-planned frontier.

U. S. STEEL PLANT *going up near by creates new jobs and housing demand.*

The paper dreams of the planners here stir into reality above the reddish-brown loam of the Bucks County landscape. If a little rubs off on the planners' purity of concept, the process is perhaps less drastic than usual wherever shiny hopes rub against the drab facts of life. Here mass production is joined to mass housing by the cord of mutual advantage. Here also mass housing at irresistible unit prices bowls over the old-fashioned values from a more laggard culture—such as the outmatched urge to be original or the stifled passion for privacy.

HERE most any day can be found William Levitt of Levitt & Sons, Inc., builders and merchandisers of new houses in bulk, sitting, quite likely, in the expansive living room of a lovely, old, non-mass-produced, Bucks County farmhouse. The thick stone walls and stout oak beams of the ancient house were painstakingly fashioned by the loving hands of some highly skilled craftsman—built to outlast the ages. Standing alone here, a splendid sentinel on the crest of a wooded hill, the house has both majesty and charm. The house has character. The house is, in fact, obsolete.

"It isn't fair," Mr. Levitt explained, pointing to the old room's ornate moldings and broad baseboards, "to ask the public to pay for things they don't need and can't afford. Imagine asking a modern housewife to clean this place." Mr. *(Continued)* Levitt's lawyer and public relations man nodded quick confirmation. "Imagine sticking your own wife way off in the country like this, all by herself. People like people. That's been our experience."

As long as people continue to like people, Levitt & Sons are prepared to accommodate them. Through the wide window of Bill Levitt's farmhouse headquarters are plainly visible the first rooftops and light poles of a booming new Levittown—the first batch of 16,000 houses to go up on 1,100 streets cut through acreage where but a few months ago local farmers raised only spinach. The view from this farmhouse window three years from now will have erupted into the tenth largest city in the State of Pennsylvania.

STARTING from scratch, the Levitts will have converted eight square miles of open farm country into a densely populated community of 70,000. Paved streets, sewer lines, school sites, baseball diamonds, shopping center, parking lots, new railroad station, factory sidings, churches, trunk arteries, newspapers, garden clubs, swimming pools, doctors, dentists and town hall—all conceived in advance, all previously planned in one of the most colossal acts ever of mortal creation.

"The most perfectly planned community in America," the Levitts say.

Confidence in this ambitious undertaking and its far-reaching results positively radiates from the countenance of Bill Levitt. The 45-year-old builder, organizer and salesman scarcely looks like a planner as he strides about in a royal blue sports coat, light slacks and fawn-colored oxfords. He doesn't talk exactly like a planner either.

"Personally, I don't put much stock in theories or the book. In this business that market research stuff is the bunk, too. People need to be shown. Ask a woman if she wants a door on the kitchen, she says she wants a door on the kitchen. Then you build a kitchen the size she can afford and she complains of claustrophobia. We know that by experience, the hard way. We don't have to take the door off because she complains. We don't put it on in the first place."

Self-confidence is one of the by-products of the fact that customers have been registering faith in Levitt decisions for a quarter of a century, and spectacularly so during the mass migration to Levittown, L. I., after the war. William, his brother Alfred and father Abraham designed, built and sold 17,500 homes there in five and one-half years. The four-room Levitt house, appearing on the market in the midst of a shortage, offered light, air, convenience and value—selling for substantially less than $10,000 with closing fees, landscaping and kitchen appliances thrown in.

Mass production methods right on the building site (Levitt carpenters never touch a hand saw; paint speckled in two colors comes out of one spray gun) made the Levitt price feasible. But they also defined the massive contours of a rather formidable looking city. Like Topsy, Levittown, L. I., just grow'd—and grow'd.

LATE commuters, lost among identical rows of houses along identical street blocks, sometimes reported a sense of panic like bewildered children suddenly turned loose in a house of mirrors. "I got lost there myself looking for street names I never heard of," Bill Levitt recalls. When the lady of the house hung out the wash, the awesome result was 17,500 pairs of shorts flapping in 17,500 backyards. The struggle for identity in these prefabricated circumstances reduced itself occasionally to a pretty fine point—like the tone of a door-chime or a novel idea for a wastebasket.

People liked it, anyhow, were grateful for it, got used to it, grew fond of it. People, it turned out, liked people.

Levittowners, mostly young ex-G. I.'s just getting started, acquired a certain esprit de corps. The crime rate was phenomenally low. By some mysterious process (perhaps some form of mass immunization via mass infection) Levittowners seemed to grow progressively healthier.

THE Levitts learned as they built. When a rash of head lacerations swept over the community, they solved the epidemic by removing a swinging window pane from their original design. They found out, contrary to some social theorists, that their customers resisted a chance to acquire extra-sized lots around their houses at no extra expense. The man of the family proved allergic to mowing more lawn and clipping more hedge.

Levittown lawns must be mowed once a week nowadays and the wash never flaps on Sunday. It's all in the deed.

Luckily, Levittown, L. I., sprang up in a previously settled suburban district where such essentials as fire departments, garbage collection and snow plows were already in supply. But the problem of providing and paying for sudden additions to overtaxed facilities quickly had to be faced. One Levittown school district had thirty-one pupils in its two-room school in 1947. Three thousand school kids inundated the same district three years later.

THE experience, the pain, the knowledge, the frustrations of their pioneering venture in the potato fields of Long Island—all these are being plowed back into the Levitt's latest project on the banks of the Delaware. "Sure, there's a thrill in meeting a demand with a product no one else can meet," Bill Levitt said. "But I'm not here just to build and sell houses. To be perfectly frank, I'm looking for a little glory, too. It's only human. I want to build a town to be proud of."

The Levitts can, for example, put down water mains and sewer pipes just about where they choose to. They have chosen to put them beneath the backyards of houses instead of under the streets—a simple idea which will save Levittowners the future expense of digging up the pavements every time repairs are needed. A town hall, containing meeting rooms and an 800-seat auditorium, is built where the same parking lots which service a shopping center by day can service community activities in the town hall at night.

Nearly everything does double duty at Levittown. A growing gravel pit adjacent to the concrete plant eventually turns into a community lake. It's all in the plans.

"Intelligent planning is just plain common sense," brother Alfred maintains.

The Levitts discovered on Long Island that 2,000 families can make use of a swimming pool, which occupies no more land than an ordinary tennis court, which at most can accommodate only four persons at a time. There will be eight swimming pools and no tennis courts in Levittown, Pa. Growing trees enhance the value of property as the buildings deteriorate. Trees are being planted at the rate of one every twenty-eight feet—two and one-half trees per home.

In the struggle against monotony the same floor plan has been enclosed by four different types of exteriors, painted in seven varieties of color so that your shape of Levittown house occurs in the same color only once every twenty-eight times. Streets are curved gently for further esthetic effect, and to slow down auto traffic.

MOST ambitious of all is the mass builders' solution for what Lewis Mumford has called the need for "a return to the human scale"—a scale small enough to be recognizable, intimate enough to be neighborly, cohesive enough to function.

Levittown, Pa., will be subdivided into sixteen separate "neighborhoods," each bearing distinctive place names like Stonybrook, Lakeside, Birch Valley. (Every street in Stonybrook, for example, begins with "S"—a big help to the postman and late celebrants.) "Birch Valley lies in a little valley where hundreds of birch trees grow," a publicity release idylizes.

Sociologically speaking, the 300 to 600 families in each of

PENN KIMBALL *of The Times Sunday staff has only one complaint about dream houses. Despite persistent searching his is still a dream.*

these distinguishable communities will be encouraged to think of themselves as Lakesiders rather than Levittowners, to create their own garden clubs, Little League baseball teams, veterans' organizations, and neighborhood idiosyncrasies. Thus, it is hoped, tender shoots of friendship, kindness and goodwill can push through the chaos and blight of our machine society.

Two or three of these integrated neighborhoods center upon a single school site, with adjacent recreational and athletic facilities. Children can walk to each hub, away from the circumferential boulevards enclosing each community unit, without ever crossing a through street. No school buses will be necessary, another money-saver.

HOW does all this stack up against professional theory about the ideal town?

Lewis Mumford, a demanding critic of many recent housing developments, has conceded that the Levitt house by itself has a "superior interior design" and offers the public "a great deal of value for the price." After a recent trip to Bucks County, however, he observed that, outside, the Levitts appeared to be using "new-fashioned methods to compound old-fashioned mistakes."

"Most of the open space is in the form of streets instead of gardens," Mumford said. "Endless roads and lengthy sewer lines cost money that might better be spent on reducing the number of houses per acre."

The most pressing requirment of the ideally planned

Each "neighborhood" has a letter helping to locate 1,100 streets.

town, Mumford believes, is diversity. "Levittown offers a very narrow range of house type to a narrow income range. It is a one-class community on a great scale—too congested for effective variety and too spread out for social relationships necessary among high school children, old folks and families who can't afford outside help. Mechanically, it is admirably done. Socially, the design is backward."

"What would you call the places our house owners left to move out here?" Bill Levitt replied. "We give them something better and something they can pay for."

MUMFORD and other experts agree that the Levitts are aimed in the right direction with their plans for identifiable neighborhoods, interior school locations, shade trees, swimming pools and built-in community services. These are ideas which have been set down for years in planning textbooks. The sight of actual earth-moving machines, actual warehouses jammed with crates of home appliances, the sawmills sawing, the trench-diggers digging, the miles of sewer pipe, the miles of brick, the cement plant (worth $165,000), the pumping stations, the forty-eight carloads of material arriving in the rail yards each morning—all this only suggests the immensity of the investment required, the enormousness of the gamble.

"You have to have nerve," Bill Levitt said. "You have to think big."

Experts are also agreed on the difficulties of creating new communities that can be both self-supporting and self-respecting — that is, neither "company towns" nor "government towns" and still boasting all the modern conveniences. There never was an acute need for industrial acreage in the settled suburban tract over which the Levitts first expanded in Nassau

BEFORE the Levitts arrived, open farmland on their Bucks County building site looked like this from air. Chief crop was spinach.

AFTER only nine months of construction, same acres already contain 3,000 new families. Unfilled space is for school and recreation facilities.

County. With U. S. Steel's giant plant only two miles away, however, the demand of suppliers and satellites for industrial sites in the unsettled Levittown, Pa., area is expected to be tremendous.

NEW industry is important to independent communities because factories add to the tax list needed to support municipal services. The Levitts estimate that there is already nearly $1,500 worth of community facilities in the $10,500 price they are asking for their 1953 house. Even so, their plans fall short of the ideal. For instance, to remove one eyesore—row upon row of overhead wires and light poles—would add $500 to the cost of each house, Bill Levitt calculates. Although the builders turn over streets, swimming pools, water mains, sewage lines, and town hall free and clear to civic authorities, local residents are going to have to solve the problem of maintaining them.

The dilemma was graphically illustrated when it came time to turn on the street lights for Pennsylvania Levittown's first completed and occupied neighborhood. The stout farmers of Tullytown, one of the four boroughs in which Levittown's 5,000 acres happen to fall, simply refused to switch on any juice for those city fellows over the hill. There never had been any street lights in Tullytown before. Besides, who was going to put up $4,200 a year to pay for them? The Levitt lawyers stepped in and the lights were lit.

AS far as local government is concerned, Levittown, Pa., doesn't really exist — just Tullytown, Falls Township, Middletown and Bristol. Politically, the new arrivals have thus been gerrymandered in advance. Traditionally, this has been Republican territory, the home bailiwick of Pennsylvania's famous old Joe Grundy. Part-time road commissioners in these places used to handle most of the public issues which ever popped up prior to the arrival of Bill Levitt's bulldozers. Levitt's dream is to incorporate all of his preplanned town under one political roof. "It would cost me a million in capital assets," Levitt sighed. "But what a town, we could make then, what a town!"

December 14, 1952

BOSTON SUBURBS BESET BY ZONING

New Roads Help Migration to 'Bedroom' Towns and the Problems Follow

By JOHN H. FENTON

Special to THE NEW YORK TIMES.

BOSTON, Jan. 16—Easier access to Boston's outlying "bedroom communities" is giving taxpayers of those towns some sleepless nights.

A migration to the suburbs has been accelerated in the last two years by the construction of new express highways, particularly north of Boston. As a consequence, speculative housing developments have sprung up in every available meadow.

This not only has increased tax rates for new schools, utilities and municipal services, but more recently it also has raised the issue of zoning. One view is that semi-rural charm is worth the price of resisting rapid development. Another is that tight restrictions price building lots out of the market at a time when new real estate revenue is needed.

Although the conditions are not localized in the north metropolitan area, residents up that way are particularly concerned with the results of relocating two major highways, Routes 1 and 128.

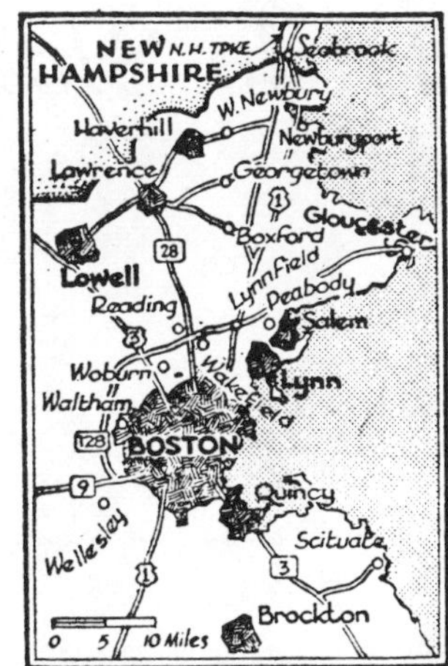

The New York Times Jan. 17, 1954

ZONING PROBLEMS: Communities surrounding Boston face many new problems as new roads encourage migration of many to suburbs.

Part of Coastal System

Route 1 is part of the national coastal highway system extending from Florida to Maine. From Boston to the New Hampshire line, it dates back to stage coach days as the Newburyport Turnpike. The pressure of motor traffic in recent years created the need for widening the turnpike.

The encroachment of valuable property along the original route prompted the Commonwealth to relocate the highway across cheaper land a few miles farther west, through sleepy farming towns that had not been disturbed in 300 years.

As a consequence, the centers of such colonial towns as Boxford, Georgetown and West Newbury are but a short drive from the new six-lane highway that is thrusting north toward New Hampshire's recently opened toll road.

Route 128, a circumferential highway skirting Boston to the west, was a hodgepodge of twists and turns until the first segment of a relocated route was opened two years ago, also through much new territory. It runs now to Gloucester from Route 9 at Wellesley. Eventually, it will be continued south of Boston to Scituate.

Now, sections of Waltham, Lexington, Woburn, Reading, Wakefield, Lynnfield and Peabody have been opened up to those seeking escape from the crowded conditions in Boston and continguous communities.

Within the last few months, at special town meetings, several communities have adopted new zoning laws, largely aimed at increasing the minimum size of building lots. Other communities are considering them for action at the regular March town meetings.

Families Seek More Room

According to the planning division of the Massachusetts Department of Commerce, the move for stricter zoning laws largely is being led by new arrivals in the dormitory towns, many of them veterans seeking more playroom for their growing families.

Older residents, Charles E. Downe, director of the division, said today, have had "voluntary zoning for upward of 200 years." He explained that old neighbors almost always consulted abutters before building garages or adding ells. With increasing populations, written zoning laws were needed, he said.

There was a danger in rushing into zoning laws as a sure cure for "growing pains," Mr. Downe cautioned, for this was a field in which long-range planning was needed. His division, created last year, has spent considerable time in working out a basic formula for town planning that could be adapted to local needs.

Boxford, a village some thirty miles north of Boston that was incorporated in the seventeenth century, has doubled its population to around 1,000 since World War II.

William E. Dorman, a newcomer to town, was among a group that moved for a zoning law increasing lot sizes from half an acre to a full acre to protect the "colonial charm." Trailers, restaurants and gravel pit operations are forbidden.

January 17, 1954

A SCIENTIST LOOKS AT SUBURBANITES

By DAMON STETSON

Special to The New York Times.

DETROIT, Sept. 9—A sociologist from Northwestern University lowered his microscope today on the family in suburbia.

Dr. Ernest R. Mowrer found the species characterized by a child-centered and home-centered life in which the mother was the chauffeur and the father an after-work handyman.

Perhaps the most characteristic feature of life in the newer suburbs, he said, is the loss of class distinctions that function in the city. But he concluded that such class distinctions tended to reappear as the neighborhood grew older.

"In fact," he said, "homogeneity and social integration seem to be characteristic of the initial stages of suburban life succeeded later by diversity and anonymity so typical of the urban community."

Dr. Mower made his observations in a paper presented on the last day of a three-day meeting here of the American Sociological Society. The report was based on a study of the Chicago area.

Children Are Basis

The development of the suburban family, Dr. Mowrer reported, is initially based on a conviction that life in the suburbs will be good for the children and that it can be surrounded with greater physical conveniences than in the cities.

"There is little doubt," he said, "that parents indulge and pamper their children as never before, and that the open spaces of the suburbs seem to offer greater opportunities for such indulgence."

Most suburban couples have lived either in older suburban neighborhoods or in the central cities before moving to the newer suburbia, usually after the birth of the first child, he said. The mean family size of the suburban species, he explained, is 3.8, slightly above the United States mean of 3.6.

The suburban husband is about 40 years old and probably has gone to college. He is most likely to be employed in a managerial or executive capacity.

"The two roles which most eloquently characterize suburban life of adults," Dr. Mowrer said, "are the role of the chauffeur, which the suburban wife plays, and that of the handyman, which the husband plays."

Roles Are Flexible

The sociologist took note, too, of the flexibility of roles, which he called characteristic of suburban life. The husband often performs feminine household functions such as feeding and diapering the children, he said, while the wife performs masculine functions such as shoveling snow.

"There is probably no place in contemporary life," Dr. Mowrer said, "where the equalitarian pattern is more prevalent than in the new suburbs."

Socially, he said, the suburban family is home-centered, employing a sitter on an average of only four hours a week in order to go out. What the urbanite achieves vicariously by sitting in a night club, Dr. Mowrer said, the suburbanite achieves by participating in organizations of his community.

Everybody knows everybody else in the suburban area, he said, and discussion of personal affairs becomes a common interest.

But it is not the gossip heard on the party line of rural life, he observed. Rather, it consists of items about the children on the school bus and almost always has to do with the present, not the past.

At first, suburban communities have a high esprit de corps, Dr. Mowrer said. People share transportation, exchange tools and horticultural know-how. There is an early intimacy and cohesiveness among families.

But, he added:

"The initial stage passes shortly as the individuals become identified with specialized activities of the larger community. The symbols of status reassert themselves and class distinction again appear. Intimacy of association is slowly dissipated except for small clusters, each individual becoming absorbed into multi-differentiated groups of the large community.

"Eventually, even this stage passes into a stage of secondary relations not unlike that in apartment house areas of the city * * * the suburban becomes urban both with respect to the family and the community, although the single dwelling still remains as a symbol of the suburban vision."

September 10, 1956

Growing Suburbs Battle Slum Blight

The New York Times (by Barney Ingoglia)

This is the backyard of a home on Powell Avenue in Southampton, L. I., which is seeking U. S. aid to wipe out slums

By CHARLES GRUTZNER

The village of Southampton, L. I., a landmark of social elegance, is preparing to ask for Federal help in wiping out its patches of shabby housing. It has already applied to the state for funds to complete a master plan to prevent further decay.

Westchester County's semi-rural township of Greenburgh will add $912,500 of its own to the $1,825,000 that the Federal Government will make available for preparing a substandard area of 183 acres for redevelopment.

The downtown business district of Danbury, Conn., where old buildings were knocked askew by floods, is to be rebuilt around the flood-crest area. Municipal parking fields will provide open space in the crest area itself, in case the Still River rampages again.

In New Brunswick, N. J., private capital is developing a $4,000,000 integrated shopping center-hotel-office building on a ten-acre site. It has been cleared of slums with $845,630 in Federal aid and half that amount in city funds.

Glen Cove, Rockville Centre and Huntington, L. I.; New Rochelle, Tarrytown and Yonkers, N. Y.; Stamford and Norwalk, Conn.; Hackensack and Orange, N. J., and dozens of other suburbs of New York City have under way or in planning a diversity of projects to excise their sore spots and halt the spread of blight. They add up to a ferment of suburban renewal on a scale that was never before possible.

Some of these suburbs did nothing for generations to halt the deterioration that accompanied growth. They closed their eyes to shantytowns, overcrowding of older neighborhoods, conversion of family **mansions to rookeries, jerry-built new construction, improper land use and moribund business districts;**

The public housing program

has been responsible for most of the slum demolition in the past. About 20,000 acres in cities and suburbs across the country have been cleared of slums and had low-rent public housing built on them since World War II. But now a newer program is beginning to produce physical results in some suburbs and planning in others.

The newer program, which involves public aid to private redevolpment, was slow in spreading from a few big cities into the suburbs. It is still known in the Housing and Home Finance Agency, which administers it, as urban renewal. Increasing emphasis is being given to it in the suburbs.

Race for Federal Aid

A race has started among the suburbs and between suburbs and core cities for whatever Federal money remains available or will be voted by Congress. Villages, towns and lesser cities that had lagged behind New York and a few other central cities in availing themselves of such aid are rushing to file project applications or are drawing up local workable programs that are a prerequisite for Federal aid.

A survey has been made by The New York Times of what New York's suburbs are doing to remedy the deterioration resulting from age, over-rapid growth, traffic congestion, lack of proper planing or weak enforcement of codes.

The study included Nassau, Suffolk, Westchester and Rockland counties in New York State, Fairfield County in Connecticut and the New Jersey counties of Bergen, Passaic, Hudson, Essex, Union, Morris and Middlesex.

A report on what has been accomplished in suburban redevelopment, some of the problems of the suburbs and a look ahead are contained in this article and others to follow.

Urban (or suburban) renewal is made possible by Title I of the National Housing Law. **This permits cities and suburban governments to acquire blighted properties and resell them at a markdown to redevelopers. The Federal government makes good two-thirds the resale price difference and the local unit contributes one-third.**

Three urban renewal projects for Nassau County are being processed by the housing and home agency. One is on file from Suffolk. Westchester has six, two of them partly constructed. Rockland County has no plans filed, but at least one preliminary official study is under way.

Fairfield County has three projects. The furthest advanced is in Stamford, where the city has cleared an area near the waterfront, Connecticut Turnpike and New York, New Haven and Hartford Railroad for resale to industry.

The count in the nearby Jersey counties of projects that are being processed by the Federal agency or have received grants or gone into construction is: Eight in Hudson, five in Essex, one in Morris, three in Union, six in Middlesex, two in Passaic and one in Bergen.

87 Million in Public Funds

Estimated Federal contributions to the thirty-nine projects total about $58,000,000, with the communities required to put up $29,000,000 of their own. For every one of these eighty-seven million public dollars earmarked for projects already on file, additional amounts will be spent by private developers or —where the site is to be used for public housing—local housing authorities.

The projects listed with the Federal agency represent only a small part of the war against blight that is being waged within commuting distance of Times Square. For every application that has been filed, at least six are on scattered drafting boards and maybe a dozen more are being talked up in village halls and board of trade meetings.

The plans include construction of apartments in a wide rental range. cooperatives, one-family sale homes, rehabilitation of deteriorated dwellings worth saving, remodeling of outdated and traffic-choked business districts, commuter parking lots and transformation of substandard areas into humming industrial or commercial compounds.

Congressional authorizations for urban renewal have totaled $1,350,000,000 since the original Title I was enacted in 1949. **Projects across the country already on file will use up every dollar except $100,000,000 reserved by Congress for the President to make available when he sees fit.**

Most of the available Federal money has been earmarked for big cities, which, for various reasons, got their projects on file first. New York City, for instance, has Federal allocations totaling $127,000,000, to which it must add $63,500,000 in cash or public works benefiting the projects. The largest Federal contribution for a single project is $27,331,325 toward the $205,000,000 Lincoln Square redevelopment.

The amount made available to New York City is more than double that earmarked for all projects in the dozen suburban counties that are about the city.

The growing competition for every dollar of Federal aid will bring strong pressures on Congress to authorize substantially more than the $350,000,000 it voted this year. The National Association of Housing and Redevelopment Officials has already sounded the S. O. S.—Save our Suburbs. It has pointed out that the money voted to date for urban and suburban redevelopment has totaled only slightly more than one-thirtieth of the $30,000,000,000 slated for the Federal highway program.

Private Capital Sought

The land resale markdown was devised to attract private capital to slum redevelopment. It represents the difference be-tween what it costs the city or village to acquire the blighted properties, rehouse the site tenants and tear down the buildings and the reuse value to a developer of the cleared site.

The permitted resale of such tracts for private development has resulted in a surge of renewal plans from some suburbs that had opposed slum clearance for public housing. Other suburbs have combined Title I with public housing, using the latter for relocation of some of the slum dwellers.

In the suburban redevelopment projects, as in every city except New York, the municipality or local authority relocates the tenants and clears the land before reselling it.

The bulldozer and wrecker's ball dominated the early slum clearance projects. In contrast to the complete demolition that had been standard procedure, the suburban approach is to combine spot clearance of the worst buildings with preservation of good buildings. Those that are sound despite some deterioration are repaired or remodeled.

The Federal agency is encouraging the new approach, where feasible, to achieve maximum results within budgetary allowances. Walter S. Fried, administrator of the New York regional office of the Housing and Home Finance Agency, and his urban renewal director, Charles J. Horan, have in recent instances counseled town or village officials to revise clearance plans to let some structures remain.

Original plans for the Rockville Centre project envisioned demolition of every building in a thirty-six-acre area. The Federal men inspected the site, two blocks north of Sunrise Highway, and decided some dwellings could be rehabilitated. The local officials are drafting new plans that are expected to save some structures and raze others. Room will be made for private apartment construction and commercial buildings—maybe a hotel — and recreational facilities.

In an eight-block renewal project for Glen Cove, only one-fourth of the tract is to be cleared. This will be resold to private builders of rental housing for lower-middle-income families. The owners of buildings on 75 per cent of the area will be offered Federal loans to make repairs and to modernize.

Rehabilitation of a large part of the buildings on the Glen Cove site can be enforced if owners do not act voluntarily. The housing agency has advanced $59,500 to the city for studies that will include drafting of Glen Cove's first master plan.

Prevent Recurrence

The master plan and workable program are keys to suburban renewal. They are the barriers against recurrence of conditions that have spotted small cities and former semirustic retreats with decay and squalor.

The Federal Government, refusing to give money to a community without assurances against new blight, has required since 1954 that the locality spell out its workable program before renewal aid is granted. This includes adoption and enforcement of housing codes and other ordinances to prevent spread of blight into good areas. It entails also a comprehensive community program, sound local financing, adequate relocation of site tenants and evidence of citizen participation in rehabilitation.

The words "workable program" have frightened some local officials. That fear is groundless.

In some suburbs, a first spurt of enthusiasm has bogged down in official indifference or community dissension. This became an issue in several local elections this month. In Bridgeport, the defeat of Mayor Jasper McLevy has been attributed to failure to carry out a Federal project.

A bad case of suburban decay in the Inwood corner of Nassau County became a campaign issue in Hemstead Township after Edward P. Larkin, presiding supervisor, scoffed at a survey directed by State Housing Commissioner Joseph P. McMurray. Mr. Larkin insisted that "there are no slums in Nassau County." In this case, the local furor did not prevent Mr. Larkin's re-election to town office.

Riverhead, the Suffolk County seat, has two shameful slums—an old one in the heart of the village and a relatively new one —by far the worse—on the outskirts. Nothing is being done to eliminate either one or to remedy the conditions that created them.

Seven blocks from the county Court House cluster the shanties of what is known in Riverhead as "The Bottom." Three years ago the county Health Commissioner reported extreme slum conditions in a majority of its sixty-seven houses.

Beyond the village, across rickety wooden bridges posted "unsafe," live 500 Negroes in some thirty wretched buildings that lack toilets and tubs. Some of the "apartments" are converted duck brooders. This is **the Hollis Warner colony. Unlike the familiar urban slum, this rural housing nightmare is spread over farmland.**

There are no street lights, no paved roads, no sidewalks. The tenants, who work as domestics and farm hands, would be [illegible]gible for public housing if Riverhead had any. No other private housing is available to them.

One mile north of Suffern, N. Y., as miserable a housing development as has ever defiled a setting of natural beauty is hidden from the New York Thruway by a screen of trees. Nearly a score of weathered, dilapidated, large frame houses with outdoor toilets are grouped in the hamlet of Ramapo, which was settled before the American Revolution.

Some of the tenants are descendants of mountain folk and former slaves. **Many families** moved into the valley when the iron mines in Sterling Forest shut down about thirty years ago. The houses, owned by the Ramapo Land Company, have not been painted since. The road is badly broken.

Application Flood Expected

Federal officials anticipate a flood of new applications involving limited spot-clearance and rehabilitation. In some suburbs where local officials have been inert, the impetus has come from civic groups and merchants in obsolescent business districts who have lost trade to spacious shopping centers a short auto ride away.

Official and unofficial champions of suburban renewal are doing what they can to swell that flow. The New York State Division of Housing has put out a fifty-five-page how-to-do-it booklet, detailing the variety of aids available. It is available without cost at the division office, 270 Broadway.

In this twelve-county suburban area, where public housing has cleared nearly 1,000 acres, the score stands at 100 projects in operation, construction or planning in thirty-seven communities. The seventy-four completed projects house 21,650 families who formerly lived in slums. Three public housing projects are built on slum sites for every one constructed on undeveloped or other nonslum land.

A breakdown of the Federal public housing program in the near-by suburbs shows eleven projects with 3,826 apartments in five Fairfield communities, eight projects with 1,750 units in five Westchester suburbs, a single project of 100 units under construction in Nassau and the following in North Jersey: twenty-nine projects, 6,200 units, in eight communities in Hudson County; seventeen projects, 9,496 units, in three localities of Essex; seven projects, 554 units, in three Bergen localities; eight projects, 2,406 units, in two communities of Passaic County; ten projects, 1,512 units, in six Middlesex communities, and two projects, 150 units, in Morristown, Morris County.

The New York Times

SLUM CLEARANCE IN STAMFORD, CONN.: This area, cleared of sub-standard housing units and condemned business structures, is available for industrial development.

Westchester has, in addition, seven state-aided public housing projects tenanted by 1,793 families. Nassau has four in operation, with a total of 347 apartments. A fifth, of seventy-one units, will be ready for occupancy early next year.

Among the reasons smaller communities, particularly on Long Island, have shied away from public housing are the fear that it will bring in "poor people," including Negroes, from outside. The argument that public housing might depreciate near-by property values has been proved unsound wherever tested.

Port Washington's public housing project was bitterly fought as far as the courts. Now it is widely accepted as a boon to the community.

The Greenburgh urban renewal project in Westchester is one of several in which original plans have been revised to include some public housing along with private redevelopment. First plans called for use of the entire 183 acres for one-family sale houses. The change was made after the Federal agency found that the neighboring communities of Elmsford, White Plains and Scarsdale did not have availabe housing at rentals suited to most of the families who would be displaced.

Much suburban renewal is being accomplished by local governments or private enterprise without Federal aid. One example among dozens is in Rye, N. Y. The city decided that its downtown district needed help after merchants had complained that they were losing trade to the shopping centers of Port Chester, N. Y., and Greenwich, Conn. The city razed some shabby buildings, including tenements, and laid out parking lots.

Federal officials emphasize that local government and private capital must continue the day-by-day work of modernizing the time-worn, replacing the obsolete, cutting out the bad and halting blighting influences wherever they can. The purpose of the Federal program is to give help where renewal would be impossible without it.

November 25, 1957

MAIN CENSUS RISE FOUND IN SUBURBS

By RICHARD E. MOONEY
Special to The New York Times.

WASHINGTON, June 20—Nearly two-thirds of the increase in the population of the United States since 1950 occurred in suburbs, the Census Bureau reported today.

The bureau published preliminary city-and-suburb details for 189 metropolitan areas. All but nine of the areas gained population between the 1950 and 1960 censuses. Six of the nine losers were in the coal mining regions of Pennsylvania and West Virginia.

Within the areas, one-third of the central cities lost population. In twenty-one areas the suburban section lost population while the central city and the over-all area gained. This reversal of the general pattern occurred primarily in the Southwest, and probably could be explained in most cases by annexation of suburban territory by cities.

Four of the five largest cities lost population, but the metropolitan areas of all five gained. The four losers were New York, Chicago, Philadelphia and Detroit. The one gainer was Los Angeles, which has done some annexing in the last decade.

Population Up 18%

The nation's population rose by 18½ per cent, or 28,000,000, since the 1950 census. The metropolitan area growth was 21,300,000, of which 17,100,000 was in the suburbs and 4,200,000 in the cities.

There are 225 central cities in the 189 metropolitan areas described by today's report. Some of the areas have two or three central cities, such as Albany, Schenectady and Troy, N. Y.

The combined population of the 225 cities increased by 8.2 per cent between censuses; their suburbs by 47.2 per cent, and the 189 areas as a whole by 24.3 per cent. Areas outside these metropolitan areas grew by 8 per cent on the average, or slightly less than the central cities.

Of the 225 cities, 153 grew and 72 lost population. The shrinkage was far more widespread than census specialists had expected. In other words, the movement to the suburbs had been underestimated.

Explanations for the movement are many City slums are being torn down and replaced by fewer dwelling units per acre. Parking lots and office buildings are being put up. Cities are becoming more the place to work and less the place to sleep. Suburbs attract young families with children, and the Nineteen Fifties were big family years.

The New York City area is four metropolitan areas by statistical definition. The central cities of the four areas are New York, Newark, Jersey City, and Paterson, Clifton and Passaic, N J. They were reported as one area ten years ago, but have been divided on the basis of a Government analysis of who works and lives where around these cities. The 1950 figures have been divided to make them comparable with the new division.

Today's report showed losses for New York City, Jersey City and its surroundings, Newark and Passaic. The New York suburban area—Nassau, Suffolk, Westchester and Rockland counties—grew, as did the Newark suburbs, Paterson, Clifton and the Paterson - Clifton - Passaic suburbs.

June 21, 1960

Census Totals for Major Cities and Near-by Areas

WASHINGTON, June 20 (AP)—Following is a table issued by the Bureau of the Census today showing the population changes between 1950 and 1960 in the twenty-four United States metropolitan areas with registered populations of 1,000,000 or more. It also gives the changes for all metropolitan areas in New York, New Jersey, Connecticut and Pennsylvania. The figures are preliminary. In each instance, totals are given first for the metropolitan area, then for the city proper, then for the areas outside the central city.

	1960.	1950.	Per Cent of Change (— Denotes Decrease)
Albany-Schenectady-Troy, N. Y.	648,865	588,359	10.1
Albany	125,041	134,995	—6.9
Schenectady	81,284	91,785	—11.4
Troy	69,938	72,311	—3.3
Outside central cities	372,002	290,268	28.2
Allentown-Bethlehem-Easton	490,723	437,824	12.1
Allentown	108,551	106,756	1.7
Bethlehem	75,055	66,340	13.1
Easton	31,872	35,632	—10.6
Outside central cities	275,245	229,096	20.1
Altoona, Pa.	136,026	139,514	—2.5
Altoona	69,083	77,177	—10.5
Outside central city	66,943	62,337	7.4
Atlanta, Ga.	1,014,349	726,989	39.5
Atlanta	485,425	331,314	46.5
Outside central city	528,924	395,675	33.7
Atlantic City, N. J.	157,139	132,399	18.7
Atlantic City	58,006	61,657	—5.9
Outside central city	99,133	70,742	40.1
Baltimore, Md.	1,706,076	1,405,399	21.4
Baltimore	921,363	949,708	—3.0
Outside central city	784,713	455,691	72.2
Binghamton, N. Y.	211,374	184,698	14.4
Binghamton	75,135	80,674	—6.9
Outside central city	136,239	104,024	31.0
Boston, Mass.	2,561,450	2,410,372	6.3
Boston	677,626	801,444	—15.4
Outside central city	1,883,824	1,609,128	17.1
Bridgeport, Conn.	333,773	273,723	21.9
Bridgeport	156,162	158,709	—1.6
Outside central city	177,611	115,014	54.4
Buffalo, N. Y.	1,304,581	1,089,230	19.8
Buffalo	528,387	580,132	—8.9
Outside central city	776,194	509,098	52.5
Chicago, Ill.	6,150,532	5,177,868	18.8
Chicago	3,492,945	3,620,962	—3.5
Outside central city	2,657,587	1,556,906	70.7
Cincinnati, Ohio-Ky.	1,059,026	904,402	17.1
Cincinnati	487,462	503,998	—3.3
Outside central city	561,564	400,404	42.7
Cleveland, Ohio	1,780,263	1,465,511	21.5
Cleveland	869,867	914,808	—4.9
Outside central city	910,396	550,703	65.3
Detroit, Mich.	3,761,220	3,016,197	24.7
Detroit	1,672,574	1,849,568	—9.6
Outside central city	2,088,646	1,166,629	79.0
Erie	246,459	219,388	12.3
Erie	135,057	130,803	3.3
Outside central city	111,402	88,585	25.8
Harrisburg, Pa.	342,039	292,241	10.7
Harrisburg	78,869	89,544	—11.9
Outside central city	263,170	202,697	20.7
Hartford, Conn.	521,810	406,534	28.4
Hartford	160,467	177,397	—9.5
Outside central city	361,343	229,137	57.7
Houston, Tex.	1,232,179	806,701	52.7
Houston	929,991	596,163	56.0
Outside central city	302,188	210,538	43.5
Jersey City, N. J.	602,340	647,437	—7.0
Jersey City	269,621	299,017	—9.8
Outside central city	332,719	348,420	—4.5
Johnstown, Pa.	279,603	291,354	—4.0
Johnstown	53,636	63,232	—15.2
Outside central city	225,967	228,122	—0.9
Kansas City, Mo.-Kan.	1,027,562	814,357	26.7
Kansas City	468,325	456,622	0.3
Outside central city	559,237	357,735	56.3
Lancaster, Pa.	272,899	234,717	16.3
Lancaster	59,420	63,774	—6.8
Outside central city	213,479	170,943	24.9
Los Angeles-Long Beach, Calif.	6,690,069	4,367,911	53.2
Los Angeles	2,448,018	1,970,358	24.2
Long Beach	323,996	250,767	29.2
Outside central cities	3,918,055	2,146,786	82.5
Milwaukee, Wis.	1,186,875	956,948	24.0
Milwaukee	734,788	637,392	15.3
Outside central city	452,087	319,556	41.5
Minneapolis-St. Paul, Minn.	1,477,080	1,151,053	28.3
Minneapolis	481,026	521,718	—7.8
St. Paul	313,209	311.349	0.6
Outside central cities	682,845	317,986	114.7
New Britain, Conn.	128,467	104,251	23.2
New Britain	81,569	73,726	10.6
Outside central city	46,898	30,525	53.6
New Haven, Conn.	308,654	269,714	14.4
New Haven	148,923	164,443	—9.4
Outside central city	159,731	105,271	51.7
New York, N. Y.	10,545,300	9,555,943	10.4
New York	7,660,000	7,891,957	—2.9
Outside central city	2,885,300	1,663,986	73.4
Newark, N. J.	1,726,862	1,468,458	17.6
Newark	396,252	438,776	—9.7
Outside central city	1,330,610	1,029,682	29.2
Paterson-Clifton-Passaic, N. J.	1,180,186	876,232	34.7
Paterson	141,385	139,336	1.5
Clifton	81,696	64,511	26.6
Passaic	53,770	57,702	—6.8
Outside central cities	903,335	614,683	47.0
Philadelphia, Pa.-N. J.	4,081,827	3,671,048	11.2
Philadelphia	1,959,966	2,071,605	—5.4
Outside central city	2,121,861	1,599,443	32.7
Pittsburgh, Pa.	2,394,623	2,213,236	8.2
Pittsburgh	600,684	676,806	—11.2
Outside central city	1,793,939	1,536,430	16.8
Reading, Pa.	271,828	255,740	6.3
Reading	96,462	109,320	—11.8
Outside central city	175,366	146,420	19.8
Rochester, N. Y.	582,777	487,632	19.5
Rochester	316,074	332,488	—4.9
Outside central city	266,703	155,144	71.9
St. Louis, Mo.-Ill.	2,040,188	1,719,288	18.7
St. Louis	740,424	856,796	—13.6
Outside central city	1,299,764	862,492	50.7
San Diego, Calif.	1,003,522	556,808	80.2
San Diego	547,294	334,387	63.7
Outside central city	456,228	222,421	105.1
San Francisco-Oakland, Calif.	2,721,045	2,240,767	21.4
San Francisco	715,609	775,357	—7.7
Oakland	361,082	384,575	—6.1
Outside central cities	1,644,354	1,080,835	52.1
Scranton, Pa.	232,702	257,396	—9.6
Scranton	109,891	125,536	—12.5
Outside central city	122,811	131,860	—6.9
Seattle, Wash.	1,096,778	844,572	29.9
Seattle	550,525	467,591	17.7
Outside central city	546,253	376,981	44.9
Stamford, Conn.	174,146	134,896	29.1
Stamford	89,956	74,293	21.1
Outside central city	84,190	60,603	38.9
Syracuse, N. Y.	562,499	465,114	20.9
Syracuse	215,291	220,583	—2.4
Outside central city	347,208	244,531	42.0
Trenton, N. J.	265,766	229,781	15.7
Trenton	115,014	128,009	—10.9
Outside central city	151,751	101,772	49.1
Utica-Rome, N. Y.	328,255	284,262	15.5
Utica	99,262	101,531	—2.2
Rome	51,131	41,682	22.7
Outside central cities	177,862	141,049	26.1
Washington, D. C.-Md.-Va.	1,968,562	1,464,089	34.5
Washington	746,958	802,178	—6.9
Outside central city	1,221,604	661,911	84.6
Waterbury, Conn.	180,538	154,656	16.7
Waterbury	106,803	104,477	2.2
Outside central city	73,735	50,179	46.9
Wilkes-Barre-Hazleton, Pa.	346,506	392,241	—11.7
Wilkes-Barre	61,971	78,826	—19.3
Hazleton	31,854	35,491	—10.2
Outside central cities	252,681	279,924	—9.7
Wilmington, Del.-N. J.	363,527	268,387	35.4
Wilmington	94,262	110,356	—14.6
Outside central city	269,265	158,031	70.4
York, Pa.	236,723	202,737	16.8
York	53,927	59,953	—10.1
Outside central city	182,796	142,784	28.0

June 21, 1960

PARADOXES FOUND IN SAN FRANCISCO

Families Moving Out Despite Top Facilities in Nation

By LAWRENCE E. DAVIES
Special to The New York Times

SAN FRANCISCO, April 10—The family is deserting San Francisco and is being replaced by the widow or widower, the bachelor and the working girl.

This was one of the conclusions reached in a two-year, $1 million study just completed, with the Federal Government paying two-thirds of the bill.

Arthur D. Little, Inc., management research consultants of Cambridge, Mass., made the survey. In their report this week to the City Planning Commission, the consultants recommended that San Francisco undertake the most extensive improvement program since the 1906 earthquake and fire.

The city learned some things about itself. Some paradoxes like this one were produced in the final report:

"In terms of families with children, San Francisco, more than any other major city in America, has been a victim of the lure of the suburbs even though its percentage of locations suitable to families is probably greater than that of any other city in America."

Lowest in Nation

The investigators pointed to the city as suffering from a dearth of middle-income families, "traditionally the foundation of the economic and social structure of our society."

The study found that in 1960 families with children constituted only slightly more than 23 per cent of the total households in San Francisco, the lowest percentage of any major city in the country.

Despite the family's flight to "more desirable environmental amenities" the staff making the study came under the spell of San Francisco as "the embodiment of charm, beauty, culture and gracious living."

"It has developed this image," the report asserted, "by blending some of the finest attributes of the East and West Coasts within the framework of a cosmopolitan environment . . . to most people San Francisco symbolizes excitement and opportunity."

But the Little organization cautioned that the city was changing — "partly because of national trends, partly from bay area trends and partly from San Francisco's own special quality."

"For example," it said, "like other urban areas throughout the country, San Francisco is losing manufacturing firms and employment to suburban areas and is experiencing an increase in low-income groups."

$45 Million Program

Regardless of this, Dr. Cyril C. Herrmann, a Little organization vice president who is responsible for work in city planning, declared that San Francisco "has the opportunity of surpassing all other cities in the quality of its buildings, its beauty and amenities, and its concern for the economic and social well-being of its citizens."

He said the action called for in the recommended community renewal program would cost $45 million over the next six years.

"Two thirds of this amount," he continued, "will come from the Federal Government. One third comes from the city. Through the use of capital improvements, such as streets, parks, schools and other needed improvements, the one-third input from the city need not involve any cash dedicated solely to renewal."

The analysis convinced the study staff that economic growth and development was an urgent need. The analysts found that manufacturing activities were dwindling and that the city's economy was becoming more and more dependent upon trade, services and finance, insurance and real estate. They said that efforts to upgrade San Francisco's physical plant must recognize this fact.

They found the housing supply in relatively good condition, with deterioration perhaps a serious problem at a future date, and they said that buildings and public officials should focus efforts on providing single-family, owner-occupied and rental structures. Many small apartment buildings would have to be upgraded.

The analysis put great emphasis on the design and operation of a programing computer that Dr. Herrmann asserted "is unique [and] places San Francisco in the forefront of planning activity in the United States."

The computer is described as giving a comprehensive forecast of changes that would occur in the city if certain actions were taken. Spokesmen for the Little organization said that costly mistakes thus could be avoided and the process of decision-making could be improved.

But, Dr. Hermann protested, "the city has not been turned over to a machine."

"The programing model doesn't make decisions in terms of telling you where to build the next building," he explained. "However, for an investor who is going to build in San Francisco, the model will provide him with more and better information to guide his own decision than has been available before."

April 11, 1965

DANGER TO CITIES ISOLATED IN STUDY

5-Year Investigation Finds Problems Behind the Need for Urban Renewal

By LAWRENCE O'KANE

A five-year investigation of urban renewal and related programs, financed by the Ford Foundation, has concluded that Government must do much more than tear down slums if the nation's declining cities are to be saved.

The study, which will be distributed in book form tomorrow, was made by Charles Abrams, head of the city planning department of the Columbia University School of Architecture, former head of the State Rent Commission and the State Commission Against Discrimination and a United Nations consultant.

It was made with the help of a $25,000 grant administered by the Joint Center for Urban Studies of the Massachusetts Institute of Technology and Harvard University.

Cart Before the Horse

The fundamental weakness of the renewal program, Mr. Abrams says in the book, "The City Is the Frontier," is that it assumes that cities are sound for investment, that slum clearance and rebuilding of cities can make them sound if they are not, that the operations can even be profitable if only the land cost is written down and the mortgage money is offered to the builders.

All this, he says, puts the cart before the horse. First, it is necessary to remove the causes of slum. If cities had better schools, recreation and environments, if they cut taxes and were made safer and pleasanter—in sum, if they were made better places for investment—many of the failures that cloud the successes of the renewal program would not occur.

Mr. Abrams declares that the urban-renewal program ignores such other aspects of the city's predicament as poverty, social unrest, school programs, racial frictions, physical obsolescence, spatial restrictions, decline of the economic base and the lack of financial resources to cope with its difficulties.

"The poverty program," he adds, "is only a feeble start toward grappling with a few of these problems."

Congress Is Faulted

The aims and tools of the urban-renewal program both were broadened in the legislative overhauls of 1950 and 1954. Nevertheless, Mr. Abrams contends, Congress has been unwilling to face the real issues, and the program's basic defects still remain.

While overemphasizing slum clearance, he asserts, the program still lacks an adequate housing program for those it evicts. It makes no provision for rehousing relocatees except in cities.

Another defect, in his view, is the almost exclusive reliance of the program on the speculative profit motive for the rebuilding of slum neighborhoods. Some planned projects, he says, cannot show a profit and should be developed for parks or playgrounds.

In outlining a new philosophy to guide the renewal of the cities, the Columbia planner argued that poverty must become a national concern.

The new Federal anti-poverty program, still viewed as subject to state consent, must be expanded from a demonstration to a comprehensive program, Mr. Abrams believes. And because poverty exists mostly in the cities, the well-being of cities as well as the elimination of poverty must be part of the national responsibility.

In seeking these ends, he advocates the Federal Government taking on many obligations that the cities can no longer bear and which the state is no longer posed to do. This would require a re-examination of the nation's tax-system and a redeployment of its revenues, Mr. Abrams pointed out.

Doubtless, the urban renewal program "has done many cities good and some cities more harm than good." Mr. Abrams said. "However, the issue is not whether it has done more harm than good but whether its faults can be rectified so that it can do better."

An Important Tool

In sum, Mr. Abrams considers the urban renewal program an important tool for cities, deserving continuation and expansion. But it must do far more than it has done to date. It must be further implemented and must become more selective in its project authorizations and sufficiently free of pressures to reject applications that are profit-motivated but not socially useful.

Despite his many criticisms, Mr. Abrams concluded that something hopeful could be discerned in the rubble left by the departing bulldozer.

"If urban renewal has accomplished nothing else, he said, it has stimulated a new interest in cities. . . . If Congress can be aroused to keep looking and searching for the real causes and cures of urban erosion, urban renewal and its concomitant programs will be a gain."

The "City Is the Frontier" is published by Harper and Row and is priced at $6.50.

October 24, 1965

U.S. TOLD SUBURBS MUST HELP CITIES

Mayors Seek to Force Areas to Share Poverty Cost

By ROBERT B. SEMPLE Jr.
Special to The New York Times

DALLAS, June 15—A group of mayors asked the Federal Government today to use its powers to force all-white suburbs to bear part of the burden of housing and schooling low-income citizens of large cities.

The mayors urged that the Government threaten to cut off its financial aid unless the suburban areas helped provide a "reasonable share" of meeting the costs of such problems.

In a heated final session of the United States Conference of Mayors, the mayors approved by a sizable margin a resolution by Mayor Henry W. Maier of Milwaukee. The resolution is aimed at spreading the costs of caring for the disadvantaged throughout entire metropolitan areas, thus easing burdens on the central cities.

This was the first time that the mayors' group had ever asked the Government to use its leverage to achieve broader distribution of the poor and their problems.

In other major actions, the conference approved resolutions asking the Administration to put domestic needs on an "equal footing" with the war in Vietnam; urging Congressional passage of the demonstration cities bill, the President's $2.3-billion slum rehabilitation program; and deploring attempts by a House committee to "restrict" the flexibility of local community action agencies by earmarking poverty funds in advance for specific programs.

An amendment to the poverty resolution written by Mayor Lindsay of New York was also approved. The amendment urges President Johnson and Congress to support a $250-million supplemental appropriation for the fiscal year 1966 to bring the program to the level recommended in earlier authorizing legislation.

In one unexpected move, the conference, by a narrow margin and after considerable debate, overturned its own Resolutions Committee and approved a motion supporting an amendment to the Constitution sponsored by Senator Everett McKinley Dirksen of Illinois that is aimed at restoring "voluntary" prayer to public schools.

There was no roll-call, but of the 100 or so officials voting on the issue, more than half cast their vote in favor. Mr. Lindsay, represented at the meeting by a special assistant, Jay Kriegel, voted against.

Commenting on the mayors' liberal attitude toward Mr. Maier's revolutionary proposal and their rather more conservative approach to school prayers, one official commented:

"In one day, the mayors have tried to put God in the central city schools and Negroes in the suburbs."

The Maier proposals, which Mr. Lindsay supported, dominated the day and reflected a widespread feeling here that the mobility and opportunities of the poor must be expanded to avoid serious social and racial disturbances.

Specifically, the resolution calls on Congress to enact legislation that would:

¶Make all Federal grants for community facilities such as water and sewer systems, open spaces, parks and so on contingent upon an agreement by the recipient to provide a "reasonable share" of the low and middle income housing in the area.

¶Make Federal funds to education contingent upon a similar agreement to accept pupils from poor districts—by busing if necessary—to "reduce the social and economic" differences between city and suburban school systems.

¶Revise policies of the Federal Housing Administration and other Government agencies "to favor and encourage the building of low and middle income housing in all municipalities of metropolitan areas."

Some suburban mayors reacted violently to the proposal. Mayor James Clarkson of Southfield, Mich., for example, called the proposals "reverse bigotry," an example of "big-city domination," an invitation to community "disruption," potentially "unconstitutional," and an imposition on the suburbs, which have "plenty of problems of their own."

The mayors appeared to have shifted their views on the poverty program substantially in the year since the last annual meeting, in St. Louis. At that time, many mayors objected violently to what they believed was an attempt by Washington to emphasize the role of the poor in managing the program and to restrict the role of local officials.

Today, an attempt to write language into the poverty proposal—language urging greater control of the program by municipal officials—was soundly defeated.

June 16, 1966

NATION IS WARNED UNREST IN CITIES IMPERILS SYSTEM

Advisory Unit Calls Failure to Solve Issue Greatest Threat Since Civil War

AUTHORS 'PESSIMISTIC'

By BEN A. FRANKLIN
Special to The New York Times

WASHINGTON, Jan. 30 — The failure of government to prevent rioting, despair and "threatened anarchy" in the nation's large cities has brought the Federal system to the brink of its greatest crisis since the Civil War, a Government study commission declared today.

In a report its authors characterized as "pessimistic," the Advisory Commission on Intergovernmental Relations said the historic American system of plural government—local, state and national—was in danger.

The abdication or inability of the states, of city government, and of the Federal Government, singly or jointly, to hold back the deterioration of urban life, the commission said, raises the prospect of pervasive Federal dominance in the name of security.

14-Page Preamble

In a strongly worded 14-page preamble to its ninth annual report to the President and Congress, the commission warned that Federal authority over governmental responsibilities that had traditionally been those of states, counties and cities might be—might have to be—greatly expanded to maintain law and order. It said many cities were "seething" with racial and class revolt and that many were near public bankruptcy.

"The manner of meeting these challenges," the commission declared, "will largely determine the fate of the American political system; it will determine if we can maintain a form of government marked by partnership and wholesome competition among national, state and local levels, or if instead—in the face of threatened anarchy—we must sacrifice political diversity as the price of the authoritative action required for the nation's survival."

The commission is not confident the sacrifice can be avoided. Its report virtually acknowledged that some cities might already be ungovernable, at least without the extraordinary and aggressive efforts of private, nongovernment groups, such as industrial employers and corporations willing to invest in improving the urban environment in which they exist.

The report praised business groups generally for having "crossed the Rubicon" — for ending, for the most part, their rigid view that "the best government is the least government." But it said that among all the wielders of the political power who must cooperate in the cities to avoid a damaging spread of Federal "authoritative action," "progress seems discouragingly slow."

In an interview, the commission's staff director, William G. Colman, singled out the rapidly growing number of suburban voters in the country as "the leadership potential." Both Mr. Colman and the report spoke encouragingly of efforts to form urban-suburban "metro" governments.

"When the question is raised on the survival of our cities—and some of them are on the verge of bankruptcy — the answer always comes back to the Federal Government," Mr. Colman said. "But these problems are all bound up in archaic and restrictive state constitutions and state legislatures, the very areas of government where suburban people now have or are getting control. There must be leadership from the suburban environment if we are to meet these problems without altering our system of government."

The report attributed much of the inaction on urban needs to local and state failures to end "repressive restrictions" on welfare, housing and education funds and on zoning and planning policies that have created "the 'white noose' of the suburbs" around the teeming poor of the central cities.

Asked to justify the "Civil War analogy" of the report, another commission staff official, Eugene R. Elkins, explained it by saying "then it was a matter of some states pulling out of the Union—now it's a matter of the Federal system going down the drain altogether."

January 31, 1968

LINKS TO NEGROES PLANNED BY JEWS

Miami Congress Seeks Halt in Neighborhood Decline

By IRVING SPIEGEL
Special to The New York Times

MIAMI, May 18 — The American Jewish Congress announced today that it had put into action a program designed to reverse what it described as the otherwise "inevitable" decline of middle-class white neighborhoods with a majority of Jewish residents when Negro families move in.

As the first step, the organization — which is holding its national biennial convention at the Doral Country Club—has helped establish in various parts of the country coalitions of local, civic, religious, business and labor groups "to overcome fear, restore community confidence, organize residents and deal with blight and decay."

Murray A. Gordon of New York, chairman of the organization's Commission on Community Interrelations, said the aim was "to avoid the dialogue syndrome — in which Negroes and Jews merely talk to one another — and to concentrate on working together on specific projects of mutual concern."

'To End Panic'

By bringing members of the Jewish community into direct and productive contact with Negroes living or working in the same communities, Mr. Gordon said, "we seek to end panic and thus prevent the deterioration and blight that comes from fear."

For instance, the congress undertook in the Grand Concourse section of the Bronx a comprehensive study of the social and physical conditions of the area. After distributing the study widely, the organization called a meeting of Jewish community leaders to win their cooperation in the establishment of a community council for the area.

Out of this developed the East-West Grand Concourse Council, consisting of 30 local religious, civic, fraternal, social, business and labor organization.

At a meeting earlier this month attended by more than 400 community leaders and residents, including Roman Catholics, Protestants, Jews, Negroes and Puerto Ricans, the council outlined its program. It would establish a children's day care center, open storefront recreation facilities for the elderly, put pressure on the city administration for additional recreation facilities for teen-agers and encourage property owners to use available public funds for improvements and rehabilitation projects.

One problem encountered by the American Jewish Congress in its programs to prevent the "panic flights" of Jews has been the attitude of Jewish communal institutions, such as synagogues and community centers. These institutions, it was said, are often quick to abandon the center city, thus speeding further the flight to the suburbs.

In Detroit, the congress is seeking to persuade the heads of Jewish communal institutions to retain "a Jewish institutional presence" in the city for those Jews who wish to stay."

In Los Angeles, the congress is working with the Community Relations Conference of Southern California in a project aimed at preventing panic selling of homes and encouraging white parents to keep their children in local public schools.

A similar project is under way in Boston in the Mattapan-Dorchester section.

May 19, 1968

PANEL SEES CRIME TURNING THE CITIES INTO ARMED CAMPS

Warns of Violence Dividing Areas Into 'Fortresses' and 'Places of Terror'

CITES NEED FOR POLICY

Urges Change in Priorities and Massive Spending to Curb Growth of Fear

By JOHN HERBERS
Special to The New York Times

WASHINGTON, Nov. 23—The National Commission on the Causes and Prevention of Violence warned today that American cities were on their way to becoming a mixture of "places of terror" and "fortresses."

Under present policies, the commission said in a report on violent crime, the central cities will be unsafe in varying degree, the well-to-do will live in privately guarded compounds, residents will travel in armored vehicles through "sanitized corridors" connecting safe areas, and radical groups will possess "tremendous armories of weapons that could be brought into play with or without provocation."

All this, the commission concluded, will lead to "intensifying hatred and deepening divisions" under which "violence will increase further and the defensive response of the affluent will become still more elaborate."

'Massive Action' Required

The commission said its gloomy prediction will come true "in a few more years" unless the nation alters its priorities and takes "the massive actions that seems to be needed" to build "the great, open, humane city-societies of which we are capable."

What is needed, the commission said, is a national urban policy of the kind recently suggested by Daniel Patrick Moynihan, President Nixon's Counselor on Urban Strategy, but which has not been adopted by the Administration or Congress. Such a policy would require a large expenditure of money.

"If the nation is not in a position to launch a full-scale war on domestic ills, especially urban ills, at this moment, because of the difficulty in freeing ourselves quickly from other obligations, we should now legally make the essential commitments and then carry them out as quickly as funds can be obtained," the commission said.

An important part of the 8,000-word report was a summary of the findings of the most detailed national study made of homicide, assault, rape and robbery. The study was based on reports by the Federal Bureau of Investigation and a commission survey of 17 major cities.

This type of crime, the study showed, is primarily centered in the large cities, is increasingly committed by males between 15 and 24 years of age and stems "disproportionately from the ghetto slums where most Negroes live."

The commission stressed that the causes are sociological, not racial.

"When poverty, dilapidated housing, high unemployment, poor education, overpopulation and broken homes are combined, an interrelated complex of powerful criminogenic forces is produced by the ghetto environment," the report said. "These social forces for crime are intensified by the inferiority-inducing attitudes of the larger American society—attitudes that today view ghetto blacks as being suspended between slavery and the full rights and dignity of free men."

'Most Important' Report

Milton S. Eisenhower, brother of the late President and chairman of the commission, said in a news conference on the report that he considered it "by all odds the most important" of several released by the 13-member commission since it was appointed in the summer of 1968 by President Johnson after the assassination of Senator Robert F. Kennedy.

Several other Presidential commissions and study groups have warned of increased hostilities, violence and deterioration unless a national commitment and new resources were made for the cities. Most of their recommendations have been rejected or ignored for various reasons.

In the commission's view, the nation has neglected not only the residents of the central cities but the entire system of criminal justice. As a result, it said, efforts of affluent citizens to provide for their own safety are "misshaping" the metropolitan area and providing only "precarious" security for themselves in the process.

The commission said that even though available statistics were inadequate to measure the extent of violent crimes, "it is still clear that significant and disturbing increases in the true rates of homicide and, especially, of assault and robbery, have occurred over the last decade."

To obtain a more accurate profile of violent crime, the commission studied 10,000 arrest records in 17 cities — Atlanta, Washington, Philadelphia, New York, Boston, Miami, Dallas, New Orleans, Detroit, Cleveland, Chicago, Minneapolis, St. Louis, Denver, Seattle. San Francisco and Los Angeles.

Among other things, the study showed "dramatic and disturbing increases" in the arrests of children between 10 and 14 years old for violent crimes — a 300 per cent increase for arrests for assault and 200 per cent for robbery between 1958 and 1967.

The commission said that, although crime had a direct connection with the condition of life in the slums, the incidence of crime had increased so rapidly that other explanations were needed.

The commission offered the following "informed judgments" about the reasons for the increase:

¶The rapid social change in the United States has "led to a breakdown of traditional social roles and institutional controls over the behavior of young and old alike, but particularly the young."

¶Law enforcement agencies have not been strengthened sufficiently to cope with the violence.

¶There has been a breakdown in the public belief, found especially in the slums, that rule-making institutions are entitled to rule.

The commission said that a 10-point urban policy recently outlined by Mr. Moynihan merits "careful consideration." This recommendation, which Mr. Moynihan made on his own, includes some of the policies being pursued by the Nixon Administration.

November 24, 1969

Zoning Laws Face Growing Attack in Suburbs That Curb the Poor

By DAVID K. SHIPLER

Zoning laws that tend to exclude poor and working class families from affluent suburbs ringing the major cities are shaping up as a key battleground in efforts to improve the nation's housing.

The head of Operation Breakthrough, the Nixon Administration's program to develop assembly - line construction techniques, says that such zoning patterns must be broken to open up suburban land for apartment buildings if a mass market is to be provided for such prefabricated housing.

Harold B. Finger, Assistant Secretary of Housing and Urban Development, said in an interview in Washington that the Federal agency planned to create incentives for towns to relax such zoning laws.

Opposition Increasing

Meantime, the controversial zoning practices are coming under increasing attack in the courts, from civil rights groups, and from legislators.

Suburban towns, often "bedrooms" for commuters who work in the cities, usually adopt zoning to preserve a certain style of life, to keep school costs down, to protect and perpetuate communities of spacious, single-family homes surrounded in some cases by vast lawns.

The "snob zoning" ordinances, as they are called by their opponents, may require that each lot be a minimum of one, two, three or four acres in size. Or the laws may permit small lots but ban apartment houses.

The result is to make housing in those towns too expensive for families of low and moderate incomes. Some city planners and civil rights groups see in this a disguise for racial discrimination.

A Federal Priority

An examination of the problem around the nation by The New York Times has shown that the decay and congestion of the central cities and the inaccessibility of much suburban land close to blue-collar jobs have produced enormous pressures and bitter fights over zoning in such diverse places as Union City, Calif., a small town with a Mexican-American population, and Philadelphia, where whites have blocked public housing in their neighborhoods.

Among the main developments are the following:

¶The Department of Housing and Urban Development plans to give first priority in sewer, water and open space grants to towns that relax their zoning laws. If that fails, Mr. Finger said, he favors cutting off the agency's aid to communities that keep out apartment houses.

¶A bipartisan bill mandating this harsher penalty has been filed in the Senate by Senators Jacob K. Javits of New York and Hugh Scott of Pennsylvania, Republicans, and Philip A. Hart of Michigan, a Democrat.

¶At least four constitutional challenges to restrictive zoning are in the Federal courts. Last week, the National Association for the Advancement of Colored People announced the preparation of a fifth as the start of a nationwide drive.

¶A Federal court ordered the Chicago Housing Authority last summer to build 75 per cent of its new low-income apartments in white neighborhoods.

¶The Massachusetts legislature recently enacted a law creating a state committee empowered to overrule local zoning upon appeal by a nonprofit or limited-profit developer.

¶Builders, also looking for space, are joining civil rights groups in seeking ways to break down the zoning.

Calls for Effective Use

"State and city action can remedy the effects of unduly restrictive local zoning regulations," George Romney, Secretary of Housing and Urban Development, said in a recent speech. "All too generally, these exclusionary practices foster and perpetuate artificially isolated enclaves, distort the natural and needed balanced development of metropolitan areas and prevent the efficient and effective use of land."

Some civil rights lawyers think their cases will reach the Supreme Court and may result in a landmark decision as important as the 1954 school desegregation ruling, Brown v. Board of Education.

According to Mr. Finger, an objective of the Federal agency in seeking a relaxation of zoning laws is to create a housing market large enough to induce private corporations to invest in factories to turn out prefabricated parts for housing.

New York's Regional Plan Association has estimated that a family earning less than $15,000 a year could not afford to live in most suburbs around New York City, which means that nearly 90 per cent of the metropolitan area's population does not have access to most of the region's land.

Pattern Is Typical

Simultaneously, the plants with blue-collar jobs are moving away from the low-income people who need them but are locked in the central cities, the planners contend. A Census Bureau study found that, from 1952 to 1966, the entire New York region gained 888,000 jobs, of which only 111,000 were in the city.

Many industries in the Chicago suburbs send shuttle buses to the ends of municipal transportation lines to pick up workers from the central city and take them to suburban factories.

In St. Louis during those years, employment dropped by 50,000 while it rose 193,500 in the surrounding suburbs, a pattern typical of other large cities.

"The jobs are in the suburbs, but the unemployed are in the ghetto. It's ironic," said Edward L. Holmgren, head of the Leadership Council for Metropolitan Open Communities, a nonprofit agency in Chicago.

The Federal court order against the Chicago Housing Authority last summer directed the authority to stop concentrating low-income. Government-subsidized housing in the slums.

Suit in Montclair

Although that case did not deal directly with zoning, there are several pending that do. The National Committee Against Discrimination in Housing has filed Federal suits against Union City, Calif.; Lawton, Okla., and Montclair, N. J.

The N. A. A. C. P. Legal Defense and Educational Fund has a case in Lansing, Mich., and the N. A. A. C. P. plans a court test of zoning in Oyster Bay,

L. I., as the first step in its nationwide drive.

Union City, once an agricultural settlement 10 miles southeast of Oakland, has grown quickly in the last few years to a suburban town with a population of 13,550.

Last spring, a group of Mexican-Americans from the town's rundown neighborhoods won from the City Council a rezoning of a 23.4-acre parcel of land for 279 apartments under a Federal subsidy program for low-income and moderate-income families.

But residents of Westview Estates, a new development of single-family houses across a tree-lined creek from the proposed apartment site, circulated a petition and collected 800 signatures requesting a reversal of the rezoning.

Arguing that the project would become "an instant slum" and would overcrowd the schools, the Westview residents persuaded the City Council to hold a referendum on the matter. The rezoning lost, 1,049 to 845, and the project was blocked.

According to Richard F. Bellman, an attorney for the Committee Against Discrimination in Housing, the irony is that the Mexican-Americans have lived in the town much longer than the whites in Westview Estates. And tracts of land, he maintains, have been rezoned numerous times without any referendum as the town has grown.

Federal Funds Used

A suit has been filed contending that the rezoning procedure was a violation of the equal protection clause of the Constitution's 14th Amendment. Mr. Bellman said that because the project was to be financed by Department of Housing and Urban Development, the Federal Government was asked to enter the case as a friend of the court, but it refused.

A spokesman for the department said last week that there had been "some talk" among the department's legal staff about going into court but that only the Justice Department could do it. He said his agency had made no request for action by the Justice Department.

A similar case emerged in Lansing recently, when white homeowners managed to get a referendum scheduled for next month on a rezoning action by the City Council that would permit Government-subsidized apartments. The Legal Defense Fund has filed suit in Federal court.

In Lawton, the Committee Against Discrimination joined in a suit by the Roman Catholic Archdiocese of Oklahoma City and Tulsa, which had been rebuffed in an attempt to build a moderate-income project.

The town of Monclair, Mr. Bellman said, made a zoning change for a builder on the condition that with his garden apartments he erect two single-family houses costing not less than $35,000 each. The committee contends that legislating cost minimums is unconstitutional.

A week ago, the N.A.A.C.P. announced that it had asked the town of Oyster Bay, L.I., to rezone 20 per cent of its vacant land for low-density apartments, the least expensive type of housing now produced. If the town fails to act by Jan. 1, the association plans a broad court test of Oyster Bay's zoning.

Black Population Down

Neil Newton Gold and Paul Davidoff, two planners whose organization the Suburban Action Institute, is acting as consultant to the N.A.A.C.P., say that Oyster Bay is especially vulnerable to a lawsuit. They cited the fact that it is close to large industrial plants such as Grumman Aircraft Engineering Corporation and Republic Aviation Division of Fairchild Hiller, where more blacks could work if they could live nearby.

Furthermore, they cite a Bi-County Planning Board study showing that the town is getting more whites and fewer blacks. From 1960 to 1965, the study shows, the white population rose to 348,000 from 309,000, while the number of nonwhites fell to 3,000 from 4,600. In this period, New York City gained half a million nonwhites, Mr. Davidoff said.

"It's an improper use of the police power of the state," Jack E. Wood Jr., co-director of the Committee Against Discrimination, said in reference to exclusionary zoning.

But whether the courts will think so is another question. Lawyers observe that the Supreme Court has not heard a zoning case since the nineteen-twenties. And lower court decisions have repeatedly stressed that each case must be decided on its peculiar and specific circumstances, that the courts are not supra planning commissions.

Nevertheless, Mr. Bellman and other civil rights lawyers are putting their chips on a Supreme Court decision in 1926, Euclid, Ohio, v. Ambler Realty Company, in which the Court upheld the town's right to zone out industry, but also concluded:

"It is not meant by this, however, to exclude the possibility of cases where the general public interest would so far outweigh the interest of the municipality that the municipality would not be allowed to stand in the way."

View Zoning as Tool

There is some fear among planners that successful court challenges will simply destroy certain aspects of zoning. They believe that zoning is clearly a tool that must be used to give some order to development.

Mr. Bellman believes this, too, and says his court action is aimed to get the judiciary to set standards by which zoning can be measured. In fact, his associate, Mr. Wood, criticized the N.A.A.C.P.'s Oyster Bay action as "precipitous."

The New York State Urban Development Corporation has the power to ignore local zoning ordinances, condemn property and build new structures. It is the only such public corporation in the country, and Mr. Finger, of the Department of Housing and Urban Development, remarked, "We'd like to see that kind of organization in more places."

Timidity Is Alleged

But both Mr. Gold and Mr. Wood have charged that the corporation has been too timid about using its power. Edward J. Logue, who heads it, says he plans to move "quietly and carefully."

The political climate apparently does not permit him to do much more. Nineteen bills were filed in the Legislature last year to dilute the corporation's power. And Governor Rockefeller is running for re-election next November.

Observers in the suburbs say there is no more highly emotional issue than zoning, not only because there are racial overtones to it but also, and perhaps more compelling, because apartment buildings mean that the city and all its problems have come a little closer. There are a little less green and a little less sunlight, more of a burden on the roads and the schools, and a little less place for escape.

December 14, 1969

SUPREME COURT GIVES U. S. JUDGES VOICE IN STATES' REAPPORTIONING; URBAN-RURAL STRUGGLE AT ISSUE

DECISION IS 6 TO 2

By ANTHONY LEWIS

Special to The New York Times.

WASHINGTON, March 26—The Supreme Court held today that the distribution of seats in State Legislatures was subject to the constitutional scrutiny of the Federal courts.

The historic decision was a sharp departure from the court's traditional reluctance to get into questions of fairness in legislative districting. It could significantly affect the nation-wide struggle of urban, rural and suburban forces for political power.

The vote, in a case brought by Tennessee city-dwellers, was 6 to 2.

Justice William J. Brennan Jr. wrote the opinion of the court, joined by Chief Justice Earl Warren and Justices Hugo L. Black, William O. Douglas, Tom C. Clark and Potter Stewart. Justices Douglas, Clark and Stewart also wrote separate concurring opinions.

The dissenters—each joining in an opinion by the other—were Justices Felix Frankfurter and John Marshall Harlan. Justice Charles E. Whittaker, who has been in the hospital ten days for a physical check-up, took no part in the decision.

Summary of Decision

The Supreme Court's action was only a first step into the apportionment field. It left many questions for decision later. In summary, today's decision did the following:

¶It held that the Federal courts had the power, and the duty, to consider the constitutionality of state legislative apportionments.

¶It said that some apportionments could be so unfair as to violate the clause of the Fourteenth Amendment providing that no state shall "deny to any person . . . the equal protection of the laws."

¶It refused at this time to indicate how bad an apportionment would have to be before it was deemed unconstitutional.

While only Tennessee's legislative districts were under attack in the case decided today, many states will probably be forced, as a result, to defend the validity of their apportionment in court.

Suits have already been brought in New York, Michigan, Maryland, Ohio, Indiana and Georgia to challenge some aspect of apportionment. These cases will have to be decided, or reconsidered, in the light of today's decision.

The majority did not say specifically that districts must be based on equal population. Justice Brennan's opinion spoke only of "arbitrary and capricious" districting violating the Constitution, without defining the words.

Despite that vagueness, the decision was generally regarded here as one of great significance — certainly the Supreme Court's longest legal step since the school segregation decision of 1954. Justice Harlan, who came to the court in 1955, said from the bench during his oral dissent today:

"This is the most important decision rendered by this court, in its potential consequences, since I have had the privilege of being here."

The Tennessee city-dwellers who brought the suit, like many urbanites around the country, believed their interests had been frustrated by rural control of the state legislature.

The Tennessee legislature has not been reapportioned since 1901, despite provisions in the State Constitution requiring reapportionment every ten years. Rural legislators have simply refused to change the districts.

Because of vast population shifts in the last sixty years there are great disparities among the Tennessee districts. Many, though not all, of these favor rural voters by failing to credit urban areas with their increased population.

For example, rural Moore County has 3,454 residents and one member of the Tennessee House. Shelby County (Memphis) has eight members for 627,019 residents—about 78,000 persons per legislator.

Thus a vote in Moore County is worth more than twenty-two times as much as a vote in Shelby.

After an unsuccessful suit in the state courts, the urban forces took their case to a three - judge Federal District Court. That court agreed that the plaintiffs' rights had been violated, but it said "the remedy in this situation clearly does not lie with the courts."

The lower court based its refusal to act on a succession of Supreme Court decisions beginning with the landmark case of Colegrove V. Green in 1946.

Close Vote in 1946

A seven-man court at that time refused to get into the question of Illinois' Congressional districts. The vote was 4 to 3.

Justice Frankfurter, writing for three justices, at the time, said the issue was not "justiciable"—appropriate for resolution by a court. It was too "political" a question, he said, and he concluded that "courts ought not to enter this political thicket."

A fourth member of the Colegrove court, Justice Wiley Rutledge, thought the issue was justiciable but agreed for his own reasons that the court should not then intervene.

In about a dozen later cases the Supreme Court refused to get into various kinds of apportionment problems, often citing the Colegrove case as the reason. Thus the general assumption among lawyers has been that Justice Frankfurter's opinion in that case was the law.

This assumption turned out to be false.

Justice Brennan said today that the majority in the Colegrove case, including Justice Rutledge, had actually found the apportionment question justifiable.

He explained the court's refusal to act then, and in the later cases, as resting on circumstances different from those in the Tennessee case. But the actual effect was to overrule what had been the general understanding of the Colegrove doctrine.

The opinion reviewed at length the much-debated problem of what is a "political question" to be turned aside by the courts. Justice Brennan concluded that the Tennessee voters' "allegations of a denial of equal protection present a justifiable constitutional cause of action."

The court sent the case back to the three-judge Federal bench in Tennessee to decide the ultimate question: Do the present Tennessee legislative districts actually violate the Constitution?

Charles S. Rhyne of Washington, who argued the case for the Tennessee voters along with Z. T. Osborn Jr. of Nashville, said today that he expected a quick affirmative answer to that question. He said the lower court had already indicated its feeling that the districts were unlawful but thought it was barred from acting.

The next question will be what relief the courts can give. They cannot, under ordinary circumstances, order the members of a legislature to pass a particular bill.

One possibility is for the lower court to enjoin Tennessee's executive officials from holding an election under the present districts. Or the court itself could combine certain counties into single districts and make some other relatively simple changes to equalize the districts.

Up to District Court

Justice Brennan did not go into the question of possible remedies. He said only:

"We have no cause at this stage to doubt the district court will be able to fashion relief if violations of constitutional rights are found."

Altogether, the six opinions delivered in the case totaled 165 printed pages.

Justice Clark, concurring, said he would like to have gone ahead to pass on the constitutionality of the Tennessee districts. He termed them a "crazy quilt without rational basis" hence plainly unconstitutional.

On the other hand, Justice Stewart made clear that he was intimating no views on the merits. He said that, "as in other cases, the proper place for the trial is in the trial court, not here."

Justice Douglas recanvassed the political question theory and rejected its applicability. He had dissented to the Colegrove decision and to most of its successors, and he made clear that he thought they were wrong the first time.

Frankfurter's Dissent

Justice Frankfurter's dissent rang with deep feeling. It sounded two main themes—that the courts are incompetent to gauge the constitutionality of districts or devise workable remedies, and that the courts will be damaged by getting so far into political matters.

The result, he said, was "a massive repudiation of the experience of our whole past in asserting destructively novel judicial power."

"It may well impair," he added, "the court's position as the ultimate organ of 'the supreme law of the land' in that vast range of legal problems, often strongly entangled in popular feeling, on which this court must pronounce.

"The court's authority—possessed neither of the purse nor the sword—ultimately rests on sustained public confidence in its moral sanction. Such feeling must be nourished by the court's complete detachment, in fact and in appearance, from political entanglements."

Justice Frankfurter warned that the decision "empowers the courts of the country to devise what should constitute the proper composition of the legislatures of the fifty states." He said that would lead judges into a "mathematical quagmire."

"There is not under our Constitution a judicial remedy for every political mischief," he said. "In a democratic society like ours, relief must come through an aroused popular conscience that sears the conscience of the people's representatives."

Justice Harlan's dissent argued that, quite apart from the justiciability of the question, the Tennessee districts were not so "irrational" as to be unconstitutional. He also sounded a warning similar to Justice Frankfurter's:

"Those who consider that continuing national respect for the court's authority depends in large measure upon its wise exercise of self - restraint and discipline in constiutional adjudication will view the decision with deep concern."

The decision was a notable victory for the Justice Department and especially for the Solicitor General, Archibald Cox, who argued the case as a friend of the court last term and again this term on reargument.

The original step to get the Government into the case on the side of those demanding judicial intervention was taken in the last Administration by Mr. Cox's predecessor, J. Lee Rankin.

The case was argued for the Tennessee officials resisting the lawsuit by Jack Wilson, assistant State Attorney General.

March 27, 1962

The Year of the Suburbs: More People, More Power

By JACK ROSENTHAL
Special to The New York Times

WASHINGTON, June 20—One day this year—it may already have gone by unnoticed—the United States passes a major social and political turning point.

On that day, according to census estimates, the nation's suburbs, with more than 71 million residents, become the largest sector of the population, exceeding for the first time both central cities (59 million) and all the rest of the country outside metropolitan areas (about 71 million).

In short order, this turning point will be translated into political power, with reapportionment of Congress and State Legislatures based on the census.

The changes are awaited gloomily by the nation's big-city Mayors, already disillusioned with reapportionment ordered by courts.

Legislators represent people,

not trees or acres, the Supreme Court said in its historic decisions of the nineteen-sixties, and joyful urbanists proclaimed the imminent salvation of the cities.

At last, they believed, the iron grip of rural minorities on State Legislatures had been broken. At last, city residents could command their rightful share of state power, concern, and funds.

They were only half right. The rural grip has been loosened. The principal beneficiaries, however, have not been cities but suburbs. They were both the most badly underrepresented in State Legislatures and the fastest growing segment of the population.

The problem for cities has been that the swelling new crops of suburban legislators has generally been indifferent, even antagonistic, to the calls for help from tormented big-city Mayors.

"Reapportionment has suburbanized the Legislatures," says Mayor Wes Uhlman of Seattle, "and the suburbanites are as hostile to the city as the farmers ever were."

That view, repeated in Denver this week by many Mayors at their annual conference, is strongly supported by a survey made by correspondents for The New York Times in every state capital.

Signs of Urban Gains

At the same time, the survey disclosed, there may yet be an urban center swirling in the heretofore nonmagic lamp of reapportionment.

Once-new suburbs are growing older, more susceptible to urban sympathy and support for urban remedies.

Even before reapportionment based on the 1970 census, suburban legislative power had mushroomed dramatically in every part of the country. The Times survey, which defined suburbs as metropolitan areas outside cities larger than 100,000 population, showed the following:

¶In the 40-member California Senate, suburban representation rose from 18 per cent in 1960 to 47 per cent now.

¶In the Minnesota Legislature, in the same period, suburban representation rose from 4 per cent to 21 per cent.

¶In New Jersey's Legislature, suburban representation was 25 per cent in 1950 and 32 per cent in 1960, and it is estimated to be 46 per cent now.

For the most part, these gains have been at the expense of overrepresented small town and rural areas. In New York, however, it is the cities that appear to overrepresented, an imbalance likely to be corrected as a result of the new census.

Suburban Suffolk County, for example, is still represented in the State Legislature on the basis of its 1960 population of about 600,000. The present population is estimated at 1.5 million.

In state after state, rising suburban strength has meant rising opposition to legislation benefiting cities. The most common victims have been measured to provide new tax revenues, educational support, and assistance for city-operated services like zoos and museums, which benefit an entire metropolitan area.

"The suburbs are where you are finding so much of the opposition to urban legislation," says Haven J. Barlow, president of the Utah Senate.

He cited a legislative proposal last year for an optional sales tax increase, needed by Salt Lake City for increased fire and police protection. The bill died in committee, largely because of opposition from suburban and rural legislators.

Similar Minnesota Issue

Cities suffered a parallel tax defeat in Minnesota in the 1969 legislative session. Suburban and rural legislatures combined to stop a tax proposal arguing that the cities should raise property taxes instead.

Urban observers regard this not so much as hostility as apathy and ignorance. Nonurban legislators, they argue, simply will not recognize that central city populations are aging and that older people are less able to pay property taxes.

In Minneapolis, they observe, about a third of all homeowners are at retirement age.

The setbacks cities have suffered in their efforts to obtain increased state aid for their hard-pressed schools are typified by California's 1969 legislative action.

The Legislature appropriated about $45-million in extra funds for "low wealth" suburban school districts but virtually nothing extra for big-city districts. An all-white Sacramento suburb gained twice as much in increased funds as the city, where 25 per cent of the school children are from minority groups.

Suburban Resistance

Cities in different parts of the country have sought state assistance for facilities used by many noncity residents. For example, a bill was proposed this year in the Missouri legislature to establish a metropolitan area cultural district to support the city zoo and art museum and the suburban science museum.

The city facilities are paid for by city property owners, the county museum by private funds.

Last month, the bill was defeated with 15 of the 26 suburban legislators opposed or absent.

The larger subject of state aid to cities has been the subject of a two-year dispute between Gov. Warren E. Hearnes of Missouri and Mayor A. J. Cervantes of St. Louis.

"I just don't believe in revenue sharing," Governor Hearnes has said. "I don't feel we should tax McDonald County to pay for the problems of St. Louis."

Mayor Cervantes recently retorted that a state tourism booklet portrayed Missouri as "a kind of wildlife preserve peopled by hunters, woodsmen and fishermen.

"Clearly someone is getting robbed and I think you will agree with me that it is the people of Missouri, who, in large part, are not forest rustics but city dwellers."

Dollars are only one of the reasons evident for suburban opposition to urban aid. "What seems destined to become increasingly the gut issue is black versus white. The core cities increasingly are turning black," says Walter de Vries, Michigan professor and former state official.

Signs of Cooperation

"There is latent hostility and resentment," he believes, "merely because the cities have the problems—drugs, crime, housing—and make many of the suburbs' headaches.'"

Urban supporters make precisely the same point in arguing that suburbs should be allies, not enemies, of the city. They cite aging suburban municipalities bordering major cities—in some cases now indistinguishable from the cities.

Such areas, they say, demonstrate that city problems cannot be quarantined within city limits.

There are in different parts of the country signs that suburban legislators are moving toward cooperation with the cities—moving fast enough to make some authorities believe that suburban hostility is not a final result, but only a transitional stage, of the reapportionment revolution. These are some examples:

In Colorado, suburban and rural legislators have combined on several issues to defeat measures sought by Denver. But, says Allen Dines, a Democratic State Senator from the city, "we seem to b a lot less at each others' throats than we were even five years ago."

In Indiana, suburban-rural alliances have defeated revenue measures favoring cities, but in 1969, rural and some suburban legislators supported the successful creation of unified government for Indianapolis and suburban Marion County.

In Georgia, until two years ago, suburban legislators were regarded as enemies of urban legislation. But then city and suburban members joined in an Urban Caucus, the move was motivated at least in part because areas around Atlanta, including Cobb County, began experiencing many of the same traffic, pollution, health and housing problems as the city. On one occasion, the Urban Caucus secured the critical vote of a single rural legislator for an urban measure by giving him all of its 80 votes against a tobacco tax.

In Ohio, the "crabgrass brigade" of suburban legislators is regarded as just as conservative as the "cornstalk brigade" from rural areas concerning social issues like urban blight and welfare. But as elsewhere, the "crabgrass brigade" evidences considerable concern about problems shared by cities and suburbs, notably police protection, housing and mass transit.

Such changes are a result not only of shifts in problems, but also of shifts in the type of legislators elected.

In Ohio, older, conservative members have been supplanted by legislators who "are younger brighter, and more aware," says Charles F. Kurfess, Republican Speaker of the House. They may not be more liberal, but "they are of a higher caliber and have a more progressive outlook," he says.

The combination of contagious problems and progressive suburban legislators may yet, in the view of urban authorities, vindicate the hopes expressed when the Supreme Court first ordered reapportionment.

"Suburban legislators," says Herbert Fineman of Philadelphia, Democratic Speaker of the Pennsylvania House, "are for the most part still identifying with rural areas. They should be aligning themselves with the cities. They will eventually, have to."

June 21, 1970

Change and Fear Mark Ethnic Area in Ohio

By BILL KOVACH

Special to The New York Times

CLEVELAND, Oct. 5—The far end of Buckeye Road in the east end of town is a jumble of shops with names that rely on the last five letters of the alphabet, and their windows are filled with snapshots the owners made on their last trip to the old country.

Talk of Cleveland

It is also an area that the Hungarians and the Slovaks, many of whom came here as children 50 years ago, shun at night. The neighborhood where many of them have spent most of their lives and whose fraternal clubs and churches shielded them from contact with the outer world is changing, and they are confused and afraid.

In each election year, ethnic communities in cities such as this become the focus of campaigns by politicians who hope to find acceptance by identifying with local memories and customs. This year many politicians have been forced by the renewed awareness of ethnic identity to ask themselves if they ever understood the ethnic neighborhoods at all.

A restaurant owner whose face has an Oriental cast that recalls the ancient Mongolian invasion of the Balkans has seen the change.

"I used to have the place full of Hungarian families at night, singing and drinking and remembering the old country," he said. "But now I do all my business at lunch. Many have moved out of the city and the ones who stay won't come out at night."

The neighborhood has always been a shifting place. Newer immigrants have moved in as some of the sons and daughters of older generations of ethnic Americans moved out. Since the early nineteen-sixties, a rising affluence among blacks has allowed them to move from the core of the city to these neighborhoods near the edge of the core.

In 1960, the Buckeye Road area was almost entirely blue-collar ethnics, mostly Hungarians and Slovaks. It is now 40 per cent black. In common with most areas of most cities, it has a rising incidence of crime, especially robberies and assaults.

In every strudel shop or grocery store are leaflets of the Buckeye Neighborhood Nationalities Civic Association. Members of the association have organized a volunteer police force — a group of unarmed men who have received police academy training at their own expense at nearby Case Western Reserve University.

Volume 1, No. 1 of the community "fact sheet" observed that "crime in our community has reached frightening proportions." The leaflet dates the trouble "since 1967," the year Mayor Carl B. Stokes, a Negro, was elected. It ignores the fact that Mayor Stokes has allocated 50 per cent of the total city budget for 1971 to public safety.

"But we're not all hung up just on law and order," said Robert D. Lavdis, an insurance man who recently lost his bid for re-election to the City Council to a Republican in a solidly Democratic district. "We are meeting weekly with community groups, trying to get families to visit new Negroes as they move in to explain our custom, our history and to understand theirs," he continued. "We hope to have a Christmas festival this year for the Hungarians and the Czechs and the Slovaks and the Negroes."

Meanwhile, a restaurant owner who has lost 85 per cent of his evening trade says firmly: "I'm not leaving. We spent too long building this business up; everything we have is invested here. Maybe things will work out, who knows?"

A gulch that roughly follows the north-south course of the Cuyahoga River and is jammed with rail lines and factories billowing black and white smoke into the air sharply divides this city into east and west.

Along Broadway near the gulch, they say you could once spend an entire day and never hear anybody speak English. Catholic churches and their parochial schools conducted services and classes in Polish. This year, the National Alliance of Poles in America has invested $10,000 in Polish language textbooks in the hope that it can begin language classes for a half hour each Saturday for youngsters who cannot communicate with their parents.

Ben Stefanski is president of the Third Federal Savings & Loan of Cleveland, the third largest savings bank in the city. He began the business in 1937 with $50,000. Today it has assets of $225-million.

"This business was built almost exclusively on the habits of thrift, the desire for a home and the neighborhood orientation of the Polish immigrants," Mr. Stefanski said recently.

Located in the heart of what is called Little Warsaw, a community that once had 75,000 Polish immigrants, the bank and its Polish owner were only one part of a close-knit, self-contained community. They borrowed their money at the bank because they were buying older homes, many of which would not qualify for Federal home loans. During the Depression, the area had the fewest number of foreclosures in the city.

"We've branched out now," Mr. Stefanski said. "We've had to follow our people into the suburbs. But we still make a lot of loans here, especially to those who are converting the old Mom and Pop stores into apartments."

One long-time resident of the neighborhood has also noticed these conversions. The children, he said, have moved into the suburbs—mostly to Parma, one of the fastest-growing sections in the suburbs—and when their parents die they convert the property into apartments.

"The only time they come back is on holidays and they look around and say, 'Why have you people let the place change like this?'" the old resident said. "All the time, they're carving the old home place up into apartments and renting them to hillbillys from the South who've come up here."

There are blocks of upstairs-downstairs duplex homes in the southeastern part of town, where the immigrants demonstrate their pride in home ownership with a war on dirt. Home exteriors are washed or painted in the spring, lawns are trimmed and the curbstones are whitewashed every year.

Many of the homes were dilapidated when they were bought. Using skills learned in the old country, the new owners repaired and added to their homes. They neither knew of nor cared for permits from the city to make such alterations. In their old age, a city strapped for money began citywide reassessment programs in which the improvements were first recorded.

As with the blacks who are moving into other ethnic neighborhoods, the Appalachian whites are Protestant and tend to have large families.

"It's the hardest thing in the world to get the ethnic groups to understand the increasing needs of education," says Henry J. Matt, executive assistant to the Mayor. "Every day they read about the exodus to the suburbs—we've lost about 100,000 people in 10 years. They don't understand that the people leaving supported parochial schools and the new ones depend on public schools. The combination of the new immigrants and the closing of Catholic schools—attendance is down 50 per cent in many Catholic schools and many others have consolidated—is a tremendous pressure on the public school system."

October 8, 1970

Many Cities Struggling in Suburban Strangle-Hold

By JOHN HERBERS

Special to The New York Times

WASHINGTON, Dec. 5—When Kansas City, Mo., moved recently to expand its boundaries to provide room for a new international airport, opposition developed from two unexpected sources.

First, the suburban community of Platt City, population 2,000, went to court and quietly incorporated a vast tract of the land in question as its own before Kansas City, population 500,000, knew what was happening.

Second, residents elsewhere in the area filed suit under Federal civil rights laws to stop the expansion of the Kansas City limits. They charged that they were being denied equal protection of the law by being annexed without their permission.

Struggle of Cities

Both cases are in the courts and the city may or may not get its land. The incident illustrates how cities across the nation are struggling to exist and grow amid rings of suburban communities, which in recent years have achieved unprecedented populations and political power and are frequently hostile to the central cities.

In the South, repeated efforts have been made to merge city and county governments. Most have failed.

One that recently succeeded was the joining of Columbus and Muscogee County, Ga., into a city of 234,000, effective Jan. 1. Columbus now has a population of 152,000.

Many cities, particularly in the Southwest, have been able under favorable state laws to annex most of their suburbs.

Phoenix, Ariz., and Houston, for example, have steadily taken in new communities until their city limits encompass most of their metropolitan areas. These cities have to a large extent avoided the financial and governing crises of the cities that have not annexed new territory in recent years.

Little Gain in Northeast

In the industrial Northeast, where the large cities are older, there has been little progress in either annexation or mergers.

A number of other proposals have been under consideration, including "leapfrogging" city boundaries over the suburban ring and establishing two-level systems that would assign some functions of government to local comunities and others to a metropolitan area.

Throughout the country, councils of government have sprung up to coordinate the efforts of county and city governments within a metropolitan area.

But the growth of the suburbs and the loss of people and wealth in the central cities have worsened the governing difficulties.

This can be seen clearly in Missouri, which has two large cities, Kansas City and St. Louis, and a legislature that is dominated by rural and suburban interests and that rigidly controls municipal affairs and finances.

Carroll Tanner, a member of the Kansas City legal staff, which has been pressing for annexation, described in a recent interview there the problems of uniting the city and the suburbs.

"People come here from the country to make a living," he said. "But they don't like the city even after years of working in it. They still like the country. They settle on the outskirts and resist efforts to make them part of the city, even when they would profit by city services."

The 1970 census figures tell another part of the story. Central cities across the nation lost population to the suburbs.

In Missouri, the districts of three central-city Congressmen declined substantially in population since 1960 while suburban districts gained. The three Representatives, Richard W. Bolling of Kansas City and Leonor K. Sullivan and William L. Clay of St. Louis, consistently vote for municipal aid, antipoverty programs and other urban support.

Black District Declines

Mr. Clay's predominantly black district dropped from 439,000 to 379,000.

However the legislature redraws the boundaries for the 1972 elections, another political gain for the suburbs will result.

Kansas City, like most central cities, is undergoing a financial crisis brought on by declining Federal grants, a lack of state support and the refusal of citizens to approve new municipal taxes.

But Kansas City is in much less trouble than St. Louis, and boundaries are part of the reason.

The St. Louis city limits were set before the turn of the century. The city has 607,000 people, only about 27 per cent of the population of the metropolitan area. Its poor neighborhoods extend all the way to the city limits in places. The area around it has become dominant in almost every respect—in industry, in wealth and in political power.

City Left With Poor

The city is left with most of the poor, a declining tax base and little means of spreading the burden. The contrast between the vast areas of desolation in the central city and the gleaming, bustling appearance of the suburban communities such as Clayton is startling.

Kansas City has about three times the land area of St. Louis and about 40 per cent of the population of its metropolitan area, 1.24-million. Although large communities such as Independence and Kansas City, Kan., are still outside its boundaries, the city has been able to annex affluent suburbs of the kind that are independent of St. Louis. More than half of its area has been annexed since 1959.

In Kansas City, unlike St. Louis, there is a feeling that the central city still maintains its leadership role despite the current annexing difficulties. There is less of a sense of alienation and despair, less of a concentration of poverty within the city boundaries.

But future annexations and mergers, in Kansas City and elsewhere, are considered unlikely as the suburbs become more powerful and independent.

The three major consolidations of county and city governments in recent years—in Indianapolis, Nashville and Jacksonville, Fla. — occurred under unusual circumstances. Numerous other efforts across the country to achieve unity failed.

Earlier this year, the Committee on Economic Development recommended a two-level system, under which some functions, such as school administration, would be decentralized, and others, such as transportation and environmental matters, would be centralized.

Joseph F. Zimmerman, professor of political science at the State University of New York at Albany, who has made numerous studies in this field, believes it is unlikely that much progress will be made under present policies. He said in a telephone interview that there was virtually no Federal policy to encourage unity of local government and that few states had moved in that direction.

"Barring a dramatic reversal of Federal policy," Mr. Zimmerman wrote in the September-October edition of Public Administration Review, "it is unlikely that the nineteen-seventies will be a decade of metropolitan reform. . . . If either the Federal or state governments decide to promote a rationalization of the local government system, it is probable that the prescription will call for use of revenue sharing and grants in aid to encourage the creation of the two-tier system."

The two-level system, he said, "is less disruptive to the existing system, allows for uniformity in certain functional areas and diversity in other areas and would not be as susceptible as consolidation to promoting alienation between citizens and their governments."

December 6, 1970

Concerns in Many Cities Leaving for the Suburbs

By RICHARD REEVES

When the General Dynamics Corporation announced two months ago that it was moving its national headquarters out of the city, New York's loss appeared to be St. Louis's gain as the company announced:

"St. Louis is well-located, offers excellent facilities at reasonable cost and provides major living advantages for our people."

But St. Louis gained almost nothing.

General Dynamics has since decided to move to Clayton, Mo., a St. Louis suburb of 16,000 people that has been pulling business out of the Missouri city for 10 years, just as Greenwich, Conn., has pulled business from New York and as Southfield, Mich., has pulled business from Detroit.

The exodus of business from downtown to suburb—a subject much discussed here because of corporate moves in recent months—is not a New York phenomenon, but a national pattern, according to reports from correspondents of The New York Times in 10 cities.

In fact, in Detroit the exodus has reached such proportions that two prime symbols of civic identity, the Detroit Lions football team and The Detroit News, are moving out, the Lions to a new stadium in Pontiac and The News to a new satellite printing plant in Sterling Heights.

With that, a banner at the last banquet of the Detroit Press Club facetiously made one request: "Will the last company to leave Detroit please turn off the lights?"

In St. Louis, which like other cities has a local group—Downtown St. Louis, Inc.—trying to hold or expand downtown business, the number of merchant licenses has decreased from 6,302 in 1969 to 5,608 this year, and manufacturing licenses from 1,270 last year to 1,210 this year.

The suburban business exodus has—and not surprisingly—hit the older cities of the North hardest — cities like Detroit, plagued by older buildings, racial tensions, strikes, school problems, crime and tax increases.

Until the last few years the effects of the suburban moves were mitigated somewhat by expansion of the national economy and growth of many corporations that remained in the cities. New York, for example, was losing hundreds of manufacturing companies and dozens of corporate headquarters, but it was still producing enough jobs to fill new office towers rising all over Manhattan.

The same thing happened in other cities, including St. Louis, which invested hundreds of millions of dollars to rebuild its downtown section. But now, in both New York and St. Louis, businessmen are wondering whether those shiny new towers will be filled with desks and clerks for long.

Some Gains Reported

There are also major breaks in the business-to-the-suburbs pattern, particularly in the newer cities of the West Coast and Southwest. Los Angeles, Portland, Ore., and Houston, are much different places than New York, and their economic development agencies issue glowing reports.

"We are still bringing industry in," said Howard Chappell, president of the Los Angeles Economic Development Board. And John Kenward, executive secretary of the Portland Development Commission, added: "We just have a freshness and vitality in the central city that is refreshing when compared to the Midwest and East."

Kansas City, Mo., has also managed to hold its position as the unchallenged business center of its area, by extending city boundaries into unincorporated suburbs. The area of the city has grown from 60 square miles to 317 in the last 25 years.

Thus, at the moment, Kansas City has something that the Mayors of New York or Detroit will never have again—100 square miles of undeveloped land.

The need for land to expand is a primary factor that drives corporate offices, manfacturing and assembly plants, and even athletic teams, out of central cities.

Space and Costs Cited

"We've contacted firms and asked why they moved," said a spokesman for the Boston Economic Development Industrial Commission. "The prime reason is lack of space and the high cost of space. Only a handful—less than 10 per cent—even list crime, vandalism, congestion or taxes."

But, in other cities—particularly Detroit — city officials and businessmen do tend to talk about the spectrum of urban problems. The vice president of a Detroit insurance company who asked not to be identified, said several major moves had been based on insidious institutional racism."

The insurance executive reported:

"A vice president of [he named a prominent organization] told me that they wanted to move for one reason—to get rid of low-echelon workers, like file clerks and typists. These days in Detroit those workers have to be black."

Some urban spokesmen—New York's Economic Development Administrator, Ken Patton, is one—believe the decisions of companies to move to the suburbs often reflect the feelings of one or two men at the top of the business.

They point to the General Dynamics move and the fact that the company's new chairman, Donald S. Lewis, is moving the headquarters a few minutes driving time from his home near Clayton. When he resigned as president of McDonnell-Douglas, Inc., in St. Louis last year to join General Dynamics in New York, Mr. Lewis's family stayed in the St. Louis suburbs, and now he will be rejoining them.

Clayton itself is an example of what older downtown areas, with all their problems, are competing with. The St. Louis suburb, which calls itself "the Executive City," has aggressively recruited business to its grassy land since World War II. It now has offices with jobs for more than 40,000 people, and its 16,000 residents have not had local taxes increased since 1954. The business that has left St. Louis pays the tax bill.

The situation in other cities surveyed by correspondents of The New York Times follows:

NEW ORLEANS

"This is a very serious problem for us, if for no other reason than because it reduces our city sales-tax collection," says Robert E. Develle, the city's Finance Director.

New Orleans does not compile statistics on its suburban exodus, but it has lost the Elmer Candy Company, the Diebert-Bancroft Machinery Works, automobile dealers and numerous distributors of national products. Most companies have moved to Tangipahoa Parish, which offers tax-exempt bonding for industrial construction.

ATLANTA

Despite the construction of 10 million square feet of office space in downtown Atlanta in the last 10 years, the city has lost many major corporate offices to suburban office parks, including Sinclair Oil, Shell Oil, the Continental Can Company, Avon Cosmetics, the Piedmont Life Insurance Company, and Monsanto Chemical Company.

CHICAGO

"A lot of industries have moved out, but they've been replaced with commercial-type businesses," says Dever Scholes, director of research of the Chicago Association of Commerce and Industry.

The association compiles industrial and commercial development statistics, which show that the number of new industrial projects and industrial expansions have steadily decreased in the city and now total only 24 per cent of similar suburban projects.

But office-building, warehouse and financial-institution projects have increased in Chicago in recent years, and are now growing at about the same rate as similar suburban projects.

BOSTON

The Mayor's Economic Development Industrial Commission reports business loss is a "seious, but manageable, problem." As in many other cities, Boston officials say that they are losing small and medium-sized manufacturing concerns—perhaps 100 in the last five years—but that new office jobs have helped the city "weather the storm."

MILWAUKEE

"We've lost very few companies to the suburbs," says Harvey Hohl, chief economist of the Division of Milwaukee Development. "When we lose them, they normally go to the South or West; they pull out altogether."

Mr. Hohl estimates that his city has gained as much business as it has lost, even though the Jos. Schlitz Brewing Company and other major local companies are building new facilities in the suburbs, because they have run out of space to expand their city operations.

April 28, 1971

The Outer City: U.S. In Suburban Turmoil

By JACK ROSENTHAL

Special to The New York Times

WASHINGTON, May 29—Rapidly, relentlessly, almost unconsciously, America has created a new form of urban settlement. It is higher, bolder and richer than anything man has yet called city.

Transfixed by the image of bedroom towns in the orbit of true cities, most Americans still speak of suburbs. But a city's suburbs are no longer just bedrooms. They are no longer mere orbital satellites. They are no longer *sub.*

They are broad, ballooning bands, interlinked as cities in their own right. In population, jobs, investment, construction, stores, political power—all the measurements that add up to "urban"—the old inner city is now rivaled, often surpassed, by the new.

This is the Outer City.

Vast Changes Noted

And from its massive, centerless development, repeated again and again across the country, spring the most serious implications for the quality of urban life.

In 1940, suburbs contained 27 million people; 2 of every 10 Americans; 19 million

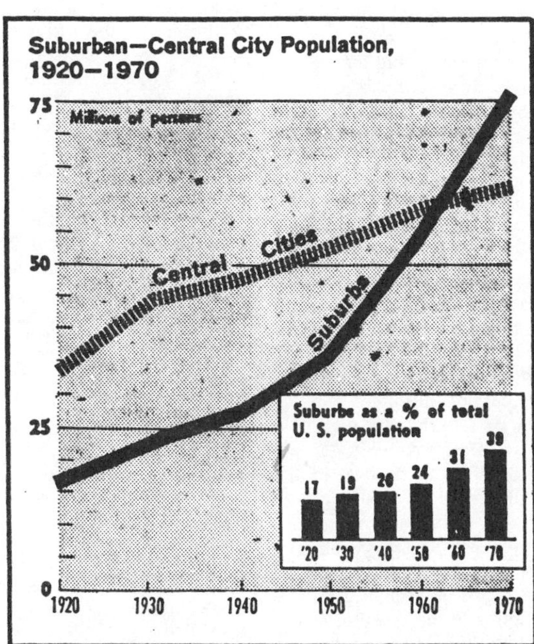

The New York Times/William E. Sauro

In Newport Center, Calif., 49 miles from Los Angeles, an 18-story office building towers over a shopping center and suburban homes near the sea. "Downtown has ceased to have any real relevance," says a political scientist.

fewer than the cities. Now they contain 76 million; almost 4 of every 10; 12 million more than the cities that spawned them.

Once-rustic fringe villages now have their own zip codes, area codes, big league stadiums. They are the sites of luxury hotels and industrial plants, fine stores and corporate offices.

In New York, the population remains about equally divided between urban and suburban. But elsewhere the suburbs are already two, three, four times more populous than the inner cities they surround.

Commonly, 40, 50 and even 60 per cent of those who live in a city's suburbs also work in them. Half, or more, of every retail dollar is spent in the suburbs. More than 8 of every 12 dollars spent on housing construction is spent in the suburbs. About two-thirds of all industrial construction is in the suburbs, in the outer cities of the nation.

Visits and interviews in five geographically representative areas — Baltimore, Cleveland, Los Angeles, Houston and Atlanta—showed that the suburbs are individual, diverse communities with a diversity of problems. In the distant exurban greenery, planners worry about how to channel new growth. In closer suburbs, officials struggle to show that age need not bring decay. In the closest, decay has already begun.

But taken together, the suburbs have, like New York's, become informally federated in many areas. Their residents use the suburbs collectively: as a city, a centerless city.

Mrs. Ada Mae Hardeman is a Californian who says she doesn't really know where she is from:

"I live in Garden Grove, work in Irvine, shop in Santa Ana, go to the dentist in Anaheim, my husband works in Long Beach, and I used to be president of the League of Women Voters in Fullerton."

She doesn't much mind. "I don't miss central city pleasures out here in spread city. Honestly, I have to say I love it."

Now such independence of the city is being massively fortified with concrete. Broad beltways already encircle 10 large cities and will soon rim 70 more — the accidental new main streets of the outer cities.

And the residents of the outer cities have become so independent of the inner cities that it is common to hear people brag that they haven't been downtown in months, even years.

Still, like many inner-city residents who think that the urban world revolves around downtown, they do not concede that the suburban rings constitute an alternate city.

They prize the array of urban facilities of their outer city. But many, as in parts of New York's Westchester County and Northern New Jersey, still identify with the image of the pastoral town.

They are alarmed by the consequences of their own growth, like increasing density and pollution. But they still cling to the governmental forms of isolated villages.

Federal Action Endorsed

They are increasingly willing — even, surprisingly, in the most conservative communities —to endorse *Federal* action to assuage the poverty and blight left behind in the inner cities. But, otherwise, they shrink from these problems, often with indifference, sometimes with anger.

Tormented city officials, like Larry Reich, the Baltimore city planner, may denounce what they regard as unfairness:

"The city of Baltimore makes the suburbs possible because we carry the burdens of the old, poor, black and deviants. Why should we keep carrying the burden?"

But in the suburbs, many people quote with unabashed candor the old troopship cry: "Pull up the ladder, Jack, I'm on board."

See How They Grow

And the new outer cities continue — rapidly, centerlessly — to grow:

¶For all the vitality of downtown Houston, the fashion center is not downtown. Tiffany's in Houston now is a block from the Loop beltway, one small segment of a $300-million retail, commercial and hotel development called City Post Oak. Even in the twilight, the rows of plaza light globes, like luminous pearls, only soften the staggered concrete shapes behind them that stretch outward for eight blocks and upward for 22 stories.

¶It was once second-rate farmland out amid the slash pine and red clay 15 miles from Atlanta's old warehouse district. Now H. C. Pattillo, who calls himself merely a medium-size local builder, has developed an industrial park, serving local and national concerns alike. It contains long, low, attractive plants, 103 of them, on a 2,000-acre tract.

¶Roosevelt Field, the lonely little Long Island airport from which Charles Lindbergh took off for Paris in 1927, is now the Roosevelt Shopping Center, one of the East's largest. In place of the tiny crowd that watched the Spirit of St. Louis disappear into the morning fog are the crowds of housewives shuttling from Macy's to Gimbel's.

¶In Orange County, Calif., once a sprawling bedroom for Los Angeles, Newport Center, a vast alabaster oasis, gleams against the tan foothills near the Pacific. The floor space in the fashion stores and 18-story office towers already nearly equals that of Manhattan's Pan Am Building, and they are 49 miles from downtown Los Angeles.

"Everybody thinks a city needs to have a center," says Richard Baisden, a political scientist at the new University of California at Irvine. "Well, why does it? Downtown has ceased to have any real relevance. Its functions have dissipated and decentralized out to where the people are."

This decentralization, it is evident from the visits to five metropolitan areas, is nearly complete.

A Home at Last

The barges, boxcars and industries that once gave the inner city its pre-eminence, and jobs, have not disappeared. But now they are rivaled by tractor-trailer rigs, beltways and fork-lift trucks that make desirable such low-rent industrial plants as the Pattillo development in Atlanta.

The central cities, their variety of apartments, flats and homes growing old, are no longer the sole, or even the most desirable, location of housing. For millions, the automobile and Federal insurance for new housing in outlying areas have crystallized the American dream.

"The suburban house," says Edgardo Contini, a noted Los Angeles urbanist, "is the idealization of every immigrant's dream — the vassal's dream of his own castle.

"Europeans who come here are delighted by our suburbs, even by the worst sprawl. Not to live in an apartment! It is a universal aspiration to own your own home."

'Ribbon of Gold'

The movement of people, in turn, has sped the outward spiral of shopping, a movement so rapid that in some cities, total suburban retail sales now far exceed those in the inner city.

And now have come the circumferential highways, what Baltimore calls the Beltway, Houston the Loop, Atlanta the Perimeter — and what one developer calls "the ribbon of gold."

Pasadena, Tex., near the Houston Loop beltway, expects to double and redouble its population. This growth will come, says Mayor Clyde Doyal, despite the fact that "we have no bus station, no railroad, no airport; what we've got is a freeway."

In Atlanta, people call the Perimeter the lifeline to development of the outer city. "People are learning to use it, learning to drive faster by driving farther," says Harold Brockey, president of Rich's. "No one says it took me 10 miles to get here; they say it took me 15 minutes."

The beltways are generating yet another level of growth. Suburban development once meant tract homes, schools and flat shopping centers. Now it is typified by monumental complexes like Mario Doccolo's $22-million Hampton Plaza in suburban Towson, Md.

Why did he build this gleaming, round, 29-story tower of tan stone — with offices, fine shops and condominium apartments — in the suburbs?

Because, Mr. Doccolo says, "*This* is the city. They're getting out of Baltimore. People go there to do what they have to do and then — zoom! — back out to the suburbs.

"I could see Mohammed wasn't going to the mountain any more, so I said, 'Let's build the mountain out here'. That's what I bet on."

Thus the outer city: people, houses, plants, jobs, stores, space, greenery, independence.

Not Complete Yet

But it is not, at least not yet, the complete city.

Some functions are still left to the inner city. Rapid high-rise office development in many cities testifies to one. White collar professionals — lawyers, brokers, bankers, government workers — still require frequent face-to-face contact, a central verbal marketplace.

Inner cities also remain culture centers. But many suburban residents are willing to do without downtown museums, theaters and symphonies, satisfying their cultural needs at outlying universities or amateur performances.

Most notably, the inner cities, despite the erosion of their economic strength, are still called on to perform a major social function: caring for the needy and bringing the poor fully into society.

The inner city remains the haven where the rural migrant, the poor black, the struggling widow can find cheap housing, health care, welfare and orientation to the complexities of urban life.

The burden of this function, clear from the straining budgets of every major city, prompts officials everywhere to talk of the swelling new outer cities as parasites.

"The middle class has entirely abandoned the city," says Norman Krumholtz, Cleveland's lean, intense planning director. "Twenty years down the road, it's perfectly conceivable that the city will be just one great big poorhouse."

Where, asks Baltimore's Larry Reich, are the blacks in the suburbs? It is a rhetorical question. He knows the suburbs are less than 7 per cent black, compared with the city's 47 per cent.

Where, he asks, do hippies, many of them children of the suburbs, congregate? Where is the suburban skid row? Where is the fairness?

In Orange County, Calif., the black population is less than 1 per cent. Yet nearly 7,000 of the county's 10,000 blacks are concentrated in beleaguered Santa Ana.

In Cleveland, a suburban-dominated regional council, overriding city protests, voted a new freeway that would chew up more of the city's eroding tax base.

The speaker is a suburban city manager in California, but his words convey the sentiments of outer-city residents across the country:

"Social problems in the city? People here would say, 'Sympathy, yes. But willingness to help? That's their tough luck. That's their problem.'"

May 30, 1971

The Outer City: Negroes Find Few Tangible Gains

By PAUL DELANEY

Special to The New York Times

EAST CLEVELAND, Ohio—A small, growing number of black families is increasingly able to penetrate the new Outer Cities of America, the swelling bands of suburbs that ring the stagnating inner cities.

But for most of the 800,000 blacks who fled, technically, to "the suburbs" in the last decade, the move has been to municipalities like this one, just a political dividing line away from Cleveland's ghetto.

It has meant little more than exchanging one hand-me-down neighborhood for another. If there is improvement over the inner-city ghetto, it is more in the state of mind than in the quality of life.

"They feel that at least they are not living in the inner city," says Gladstone L. Chandler Jr., the stocky black City Manager of this town of 39,600—which went from all-white 15 years ago to 60 per cent black now.

Total Is Slight

Even the total number of Negroes who moved to second-hand suburbs on the inner rim of the outer city has been relatively slight.

In the Cleveland area, as in other inner and outer cities visited for an assessment of suburban growth, the figures appear dramatic compared with 1960. The black population of Cleveland's suburbs increased almost 500 per cent in the decade.

In raw numbers, the black "suburban" population increased from 8,000 to 45,000—but that 45,000 is out of a total outer-city population of 1.3 million.

Meanwhile, the outer city has meant nothing to the far larger number of Cleveland blacks, 300,000, still in the inner city.

Actually, the suburbs may have had an effect that is worse than nothing to inner-city blacks, considering the deep hostility of middle-income whites, and Negroes, toward making any room for those with low or moderate incomes.

There has been one kind of change, however slight, that a black with a good income can now often penetrate the white suburban noose.

"You have to earn at least $10,000 or $12,000 a year to move to the Cleveland suburbs," remarked Gerta Friedheim, young, petite Cleveland Heights housewife who heads the Suburban Citizens for Open Housing, an organization pushing for integration of the outer city.

In the upper-income areas of the outer city, there is salt-and-pepper integration, a sprinkling of Negroes here and there, but it is insignificant.

For example, of 71,000 residents of predominantly Republican and ethnically proud Lakewood, made up of neatly kept neighborhoods and high-rise luxury apartments on Lake Erie west of downtown Cleveland, 21 are Negroes.

In the predominantly Jewish, upper-income bedroom community of University Heights east of the city, there are 88 Negroes out of 17,055 residents.

It's Not Always Easy

Anaheim, Calif., has 170 blacks in a population of 166,701. In nearby Newport Beach, a resort town on the Pacific, there are 41 blacks in 49,422.

Even these handfuls have not found the move to better suburbs easy. Judson Robinson Jr., a tall handsome black realtor and defeated candidate for the Houston City Council four years ago, explained that blacks literally had to have money in hand if they were interested in a house in a white section.

"If blacks attempt to dicker a little, like even wanting to sleep on a price, the house is gone the next day," Mr. Robinson said. "It is very strange, but somehow the houses seem to sell overnight if blacks express an interest."

The Pattern

Upper-income blacks are also victims of the "Ralph Bunche syndrome," according to a white Baltimore County developer.

"Few whites would complain if a Ralph Bunche moved next door," the developer said as he drove visitors through exclusive sections of Dulaney Valley. "Maybe they would if two moved in.

"They wouldn't complain about a Ralph Bunche, but these same whites would oppose low-income housing in their area, and low-income housing certainly does more for blacks than allowing one Ralph Bunche in."

Thus, most outer-city integration has been restricted to areas contiguous to black sections of the inner city, leaving heavier concentrations of poorer blacks at inner-city lines, and a few in middle-income and upper-income suburbs farther away from the city.

Black blue-collar workers replaced white blue-collar residents in East Cleveland, which is a good example of the pattern of black movement from the inner city.

East Cleveland Process

It is repeated in Compton, Calif., with its winding, tree-shaded streets of small houses, populated by blacks who left Watts and East Los Angeles.

It is repeated in the outer city of New York, in Yonkers, New Rochelle and Mount Vernon, as blacks have worked from the Bronx and Harlem.

The move to East Cleveland has merely meant stepping across the boundary lines from the black Glenville section in northeast Cleveland. The homes look exactly alike on either side of the line—two-story and three-story frame homes, most painted white, with detached two-car garages in back and side entrances of the driveway, sitting 20 to 30 feet from the curb, small lawns in front.

The process by which blacks got to East Cleveland was typical and went like this:

Prior to World War II, blacks were relegated to the deteriorating Central section on the near east side around downtown Cleveland, in big two-story and three-story frame houses situated very close to each other on the side streets of Cedar, Central and Woodland Avenues.

During and right after the war, the Hough area, farther eastward, with its bigger and better homes and many apartment buildings, opened to blacks through a combination of block busting and white flight. It immediately felt the tremendous impact of larger families as blacks from the South poured into the city to work in its steel mills and heavy industry. The larger dwelling units were split into smaller units to accommodate the overflow of people.

In the early fifties, Glenville, even farther eastward, became "the" section for middle-class blacks, with its mixture of smaller homes, fewer apartments and grand old homes along East Boulevard, where black lawyers and doctors resided. However, by the late fifties, Glenville had followed the fate of the Central and Hough areas as the poor flooded in. And then, in 1961, poorer blacks began spilling over into East Cleveland, and middle-class blacks moved to the Mount Pleasant and Shaker Heights areas.

Mainly a Transferral

The migration to the East Cleveland bedroom community, one of the oldest in the area, has improved the self-esteem of blacks more than it has their condition. They still work at the same jobs, whether at the Ford plant in the western part of Cuyahoga County or the Fisher Body factory nearby.

Photographs for The New York Times by WILLIAM E. SAURO

Youngsters returning to their home in Compton, Calif., typical in the largely black city

In Compton, Calif., City Manager James Johnson observes that professionals among blacks who make up 70 per cent of population are moving to nearby Carson and other areas, leaving Compton to low-income families.

The deterioration still follows them.

The move to the outer city has mainly meant transferring the inner-city.

"We are an inner-city suburb with all the problems of the central city," remarked Mr. Chandler, the articulate, East Cleveland city manager.

He said that larger and poorer families were moving in, taxing the city's services and schools and reducing its revenue, and thereby causing fast deterioration.

A few blacks whose incomes grow move on to other outer cities, such as Shaker Heights and Cleveland Heights, he said.

The same complaint was registered by the Compton, Calif., city manager, James Johnson, 37 years old, quiet and, like Mr. Chandler, black.

Mr Johnson said that Compton was a town of middle-class Negro professionals—blacks are 70 per cent of the city's 78,611 residents—but that they were moving farther out in the outer city, most to bordering Carson, leaving as replacements low-income families with more children and more problems.

New Terminology

Although middle-class and upper-income white outer cities grudgingly accept a few blacks of similar income levels, the resistance to most blacks, as well as to other minorities and whites who are poor, is probably greater than ever before.

The resistance is couched in new terminology and techniques that still mean "keep out," such as being against "high-density" developments, "low-income" housing and "forced integration" of the outer city.

The fear of blacks' moving to the outer city influences many actions of whites living there and attempting to protect themselves from integration. Dan Colasino, administrative assistant to the Baltimore County executive, noted that the all-white, lower-income, working-class section of Dundalk, in the eastern part of Baltimore County, was quite self-contained.

"Yes, it is its own community," commented Mr. Colasino, a conservative Democrat who wears a key ring with 26 keys on it. "The only thing we need is a swimming pool. But as soon as we did that, the colored'll come in from the city to swim."

The Poor Are There

This fear of migration by lower-income persons does not mean that there are no poor in the outer city, as believed by many residents. New census data show that 53 per cent of the increase in the number of poor families in the country between 1969 and 1970 was in the outer city.

Poverty in the outer city is often invisible. Much of it is camouflaged by greenery. It is harder to see the poor blacks and other minorities in even Santa Ana, Calif., than it is on Chicago's South Side or Atlanta's Vine City.

What is the future for poor blacks in the city and suburban resistance?

"I really do believe this thing can work," Mrs. Friedheim said at lunch in a Shaker Heights restaurant. "I'm not about to bat my head against the wall unless I think it could work."

She believes that race is disappearing as a factor and that people are at least willing to accept well-to-do Negroes into their neighborhoods.

"The big question then is about the poor," she said.

Mrs. Freidheim paused, then sighed, and added:

"There is no political force for them at all, other than Stokes [Mayor Carl B. Stokes of Cleveland]. If it's going to come at all, it has to come from Federal leverage."

June 1, 1971

The Outer City: Growth Turning Into a Menace

By LINDA GREENHOUSE
Special to The New York Times

SANTA ANA, Calif.—Growth, the snowballing, leapfrogging growth that for so long held out to the suburbs the promise of an endlessly prosperous future, has suddenly developed into a shadow across that future.

Everywhere in the new outer cities, politicians, planners and residents of subdivisions that were strawberry patches or orange groves less than a generation ago are taking increasingly worried looks at the growth rates they once welcomed and pointed to with pride.

Here in Orange County, the population doubled in the last 10 years, from 700,000 to more than 1.4 million. But public opinion has turned so decisively against keeping up that pace that the new chairman of the County Board of Supervisors can make a statement nearly unthinkable a few years ago.

"The Chamber of Commerce tells us that growth is wonderful," Robert Battin says. "I see it as a cancer."

In the last decade, the number of people living in the nation's suburbs climbed from 55 million to 76 million. The most recent census figures, still uncompiled, will show that the suburbs contain more apartments, more office parks, more high-rise construction than ever before. A 29-story office tower in Towson, Md., a 103-warehouse industrial park outside Decatur, Ga., a planned city for 430,000 in Orange Conty tell only a fraction of the story.

Thirty years ago, only 2 out of every 10 Americans lived in the suburbs. Now the suburbs claim 4 of every 10. Only recently have these people come to realize that the city they now live in—the new Outer City—is becoming the city they thought they had left behind, with many of the same problems and responsibilities.

They know they cannot turn Santa Ana back into an orange grove, and for the most part they would not want to. People are seeking not to reverse the tide, but to hold it—or at least to channel and direct it, to soften the impact.

But for all the numbers and potential power, the outer cities remain largely masses of little islands, unable to work together to harness the forces shaping the future.

So development continues to accelerate beyond the grasp of a Santa Ana, which fears that apartment construction may soon bring in 50,000 new people, more than it can provide services for. Despite Mr. Battin's fighting words, the outer city is not yet in control of its future.

Ecology Movement

The turn against growth was gaining momentum even before the emergence of ecology as an issue in the last year or two. Suburban residents, like those in New Jersey's Bergen County, as well as California's Orange County, had already begun to worry about the traffic jams, the rising taxes to pay for more schools and public services, the spillover of racial problems, the first signs of what one suburban planner calls "the spreading great central crud."

Now the ecology movement has given these worries a new focus and momentum and, even among conservatives, a new respectability.

"Many politically conservative people want the natural assets of the county preserved for their own use, and don't want other people to come in and glop it up," says Forest Dickason, director of the Orange County Department of Planning.

Houston View

Even in Houston, which its boosters delight in calling a boomtown, one of the city's wealthiest men can muse: "Houston is still not prepared to say no to growth, despite the traffic and pollution. But I personally would like to see the streets rendered passable and the air cleared before I'd invite anyone else to come here."

And in Baltimore County, Dan Colasino, administrative assistant to the county executive, mentioned a proposal to build 25,000 units of low-income housing for blacks and commented: "We don't even have enough for whites. This county is growing very fast—too damn fast."

The rising public wariness toward growth has brought subtle shifts in the balance of power between the private market and the public planners, long the flabby stepchildren of local government.

When 1,700 people crowd into a junior high school auditorium in White Plains, N. Y., on a Saturday morning to hear the Regional Plan Association's presentation of "The Future of Westchester County," there is no doubt that suburban residents care about what planners have to tell them.

When the public outcry on behalf of the Baltimore County Planning Department, which last fall removed large sections of the county's vacant land from potential commercial development, is so great that the County Council has to withdraw the changes it tried to make on behalf of the developers, there is no doubt that the planners have acquired new muscle.

But visits and interviews around the country produced clear evidence that, despite the planners' new leverage, the private market remains by far the most powerful engine of growth, shaping the future of the new outer city as it once gave form to the old.

The new suburban landscape itself—with its growing concentration of high-rise office buildings, sprawling industrial parks, luxury housing in planned unit developments — offers dramatic evidence.

To support "high-density' development is still bad politics in most suburban areas, arousing such negative feelings that most planners are reluctant to squander their credibility by advocating more apartments.

But the private sector is not only building apartments at an astonishing rate; it is both creating and satisfying a rapidly growing public demand for them.

Many Welcome Apartments

While many families still live in apartments because they cannot afford to buy houses, an increasing number of suburban middle-class families welcome the imaginative design, convenience and recreational facilities that the new developments offer.

"A child who has grown up in a typical suburb has had his fill of cutting all that grass," said Clark Harrison, chairman of the board of commissioners of DeKalb County in suburban Atlanta.

Mr. Harrison offers DeKalb as an illustration of the paradox reflected around the country — that suburban residents denounce apartments and seem to rush into apartments at the same time.

"It's the strangest thing," he said. "People around here complain when they can see a high-rise building through the trees." Yet apartment construction in DeKalb is now outpacing single family homes by 2 to 1, and the ratio is certain to increase.

Just as residents of the outer cities are turning to these new forms of social organization, they are looking to new governmental structures to ease the impact of the growth.

Everywhere people talk as if the forms themselves matter. In Cuyahoga County, for example, civic leaders complain that countywide cooperation on planning issues is impossible with Cleveland and 59 other towns and cities to contend with.

But liberals in Baltimore County, 600 square miles without a single incorporated city, make the opposite complaint. They insist that the lack of community governments makes it harder for individual views to be heard.

Meanwhile, many city leaders say that if only they had metropolitan government — to offset the flight of their tax base and middle class to the suburbs—they would have the resources to solve their problems.

No Panacea There

But Houston's experience indicates that structure alone can never be the panacea people seek.

Houston, in effect, does have metropolitan government. A strong Texas law allows it to annex the areas which in other states would become suburban rings.

But instead of using its resources to attack its poverty problems or improve its housing and schools, it chooses to tax itself at the lowest rate of the 25 largest cities.

Its school district, for example, spends $511 a pupil annually, $300 below the national average and less than half of New York's expenditure.

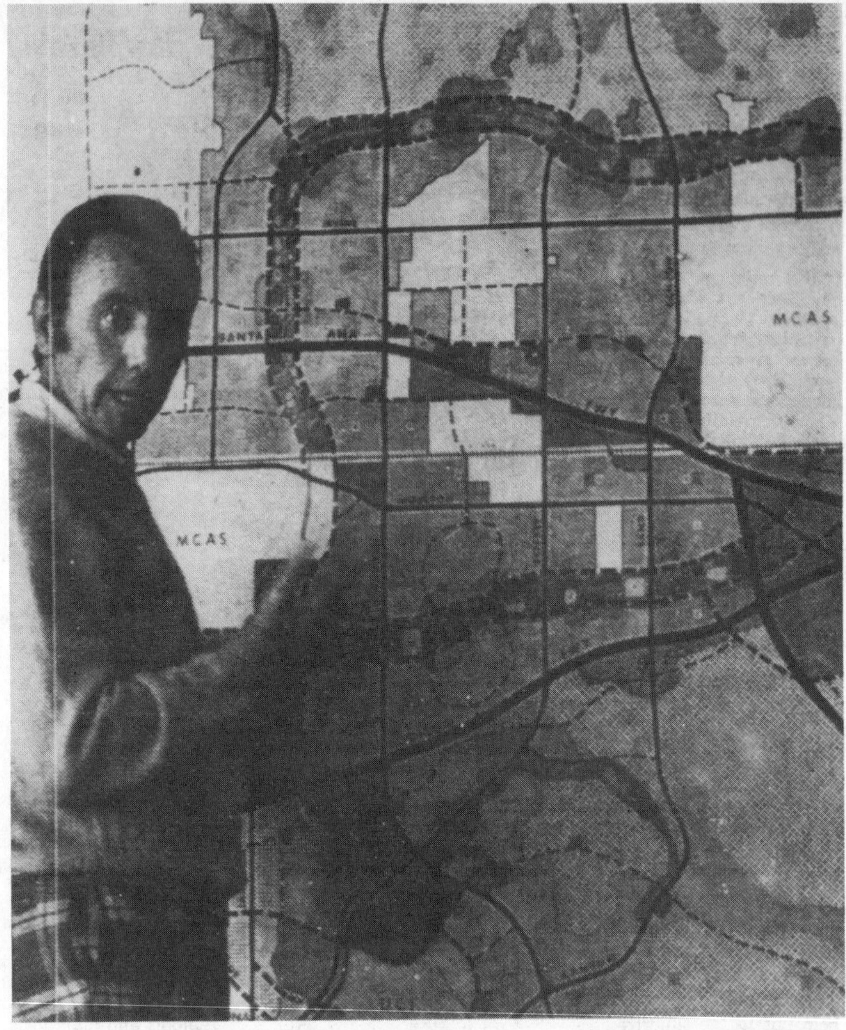

The New York Times/William E. Sauro

Raymond L. Watson, executive vice president of concern that is developing a planned city on the 80,000-acre Irvine Ranch. Santa Ana fears it will lose people and resources to the new community, and seeks to have low-income housing built on the ranch area.

Emphasis on Quality

The new public concern about unlimited development has challenged both local governments and the private market. Government's attempts to channel growth have been largely ineffective. For its part, the private market has responded to the challenge with new attention to quality in planning and design. It does not matter whether that change is born of conviction or is merely a concession to the mood of a public no longer willing to pay for unimaginative urban sprawl. The final product is the same, and it is often stunning.

Builders who admit that they might once have been content to put up rows of identical little houses say now that they are willing to spend the extra money that quality design requires.

"Good architecture pays off fast—and it doesn't necessarily cost that much more," said Gerald D. Hines, whose $50-million Galleria has become a new urban center six miles southwest of downtown Houston. "People now will pay that little extra for quality."

New Problems Created

Nevertheless, the very scale and quality of the new growth, itself a response to problems of the past, is creating a problem that may eventually make the victories over poor design and unmanaged growth look pyrrhic indeed.

Here in Santa Ana, the seat of Orange County, that challenge is already dramatically apparent. While its population is only a tenth of the county's 1.4 million, Santa Ana already has two-thirds of the black population, a third of the welfare caseload and at least a third of the poor Mexican-American barrios.

Even its better areas, like those in much of the older portions of the county, are vulnerable to change. Eighty-five per cent of the housing in Orange County has been built since 1950. "Like the one-horse shay, it will all wear out at once," says Alfred Bell, principal planner for the County Planning Department. "Within the decade, our rehabilitation needs will be massive."

And now change stares Santa Ana hard in the face. The city lies adjacent to the 80,000-acre Irvine Ranch, said to be the single most valuable parcel of undeveloped urban land in the world, which already is being developed into a handsome, planned city for 430,000.

The city fears that the Irvine development will be a magnet, drawing people and resources away from Santa Ana.

Unless the Irvine developers can be persuaded to include substantial amounts of low-income housing in their plans, says Carl Thornton, the Santa Ana city manager, "our city will look like downtown Kansas City, downtown Detroit."

And so the cycle begins

anew. It appears to be a new natural law that even areas that grew up as satellites to inner cities must, as they themselves grow, create their own poor cores, their own repositories for the infirm, the incapable, the unwanted.

Whether through lack of resources or lack of will, if local government remains powerless to guide the form or pace of growth—to make sure there is room for the poor as well as the rich, for people as well as cars—what is the future for the new outer cities?

Will the private market, motivated by the new public desire for quality, be free to create still newer forms, more daring and imaginative than anything we have yet seen—as different from the present as the glass towers of New York's Lexington Avenue are from the four-story, red-brick tenements thtat preceded them a generation ago?

Or, operating without consistent guidelines for balancing public and private needs, are the developers of the new cities bound to repeat the mistakes of the old?

Or will local communities themselves, with or without coherent government, somehow be able to compel virtue from the private sector through zoning or new government forms?

Edgardo Contini, a noted Los Angeles urbanist, is convinced that to rely on local governments to save the new cities from the fate of the old is to insure failure.

"Solutions have to come from a level higher than the problem," he said. "Don't ask for virtue retail. Don't ask local communities to martyr themselves. You are asking them to be noble, and people are not like that. The leadership has to come from the top, from the Federal Government."

The pace of growth this time around is quicker. The scale is bigger, and the stakes, in the Outer City, are vastly higher.

As Prof. Richard Baisden, dean of the extension division of the University of California at Irvine, said during dinner at the resort enclave of Corona del Mar:

"I came here in flight from smog and congestion and I've found relief from both, temporarily. But after this, I don't know where people will go.

"I don't know where we can go from here."

June 3, 1971

Quiet Decay Erodes Downtown Areas of Small Cities

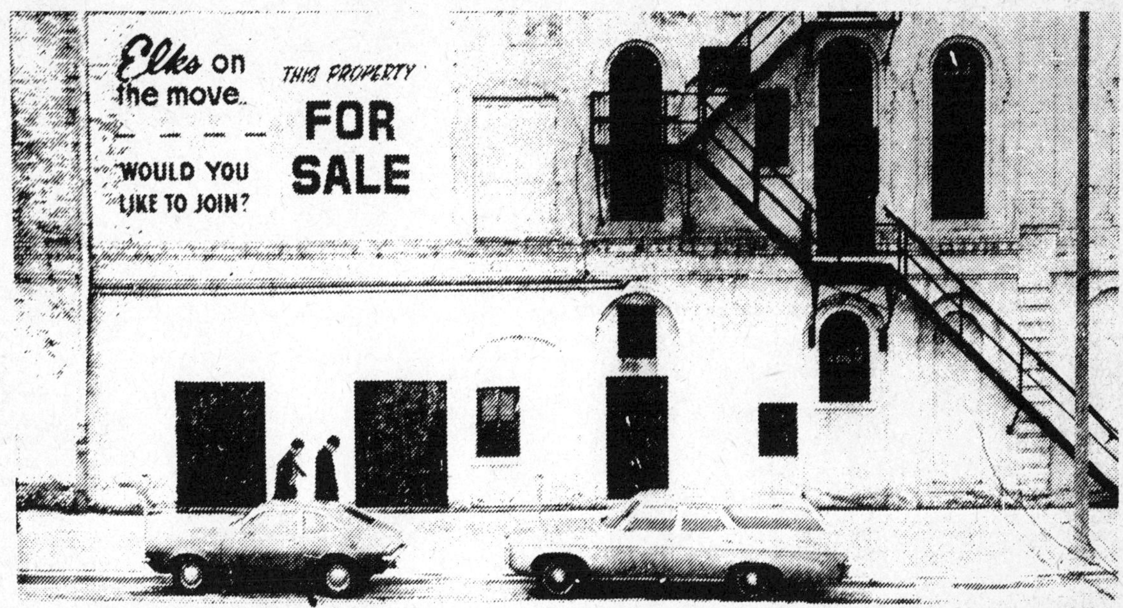

The New York Times/Gary Settle

An aging opera house in downtown Janesville, Wis., is shared by X-rated movie and Elks, who are trying to move

By DOUGLAS E. KNEELAND
Special to The New York Times

JANESVILLE, Wis. — While concern has mounted in the last decade over the plight of the inner cities in vast metropolitan areas, the aging downtowns of hundreds of smaller cities have been quietly deteriorating with little national notice.

Politicians, planners and sociologists have fretted loudly about the urban rot in New York, Cleveland, St. Louis and Detroit. But few have raised their voices about the decline in the downtowns of Janesville, Portland, Me., Selma, Ala., or Rochester, Minn.

Still, the decline is there, more as a result of age than fear and flight. The streets and the buildings in many of the downtowns are antiquated and unable to cope with meeting traffic and merchandising needs.

People do not really flee from the Janesvilles of America. They may leave in search of greater opportunity, more excitement or a different quality of life, but they're not running away from high crime rates, exorbitant rents, and noise and crush of the city or a tide of minority-group immigration. Most of them, in fact, do not leave; they merely spread out a bit.

Nevertheless, the old downtowns in many of the nation's cities of less than 100,000 that were once the primary shopping and service centers for wide areas are losing businesses and office-users just as surely as their metropolitan cousins.

Frequently, the exodus from downtown is going on even as the cities themselves are growing in population. Often the downtowns, because of inflation and the rising number of residents, are continuing to show a slight increase in business receipts despite their problems. However, in most cases, their percentage share of a city's sales and rental income is shrinking fast as new shopping centers and office buildings on the outskirts with easy access, from new or improved highways, and abundant parking draw off more and more of the area's business.

In the smaller cities, suburbs are not as likely to be the villains as they are in the larger ones.

No Janesville Suburbs

Janesville, for instance, has no suburbs. Lying 70 miles southwest of Milwaukee, 40 miles southeast of Madison and 50 miles north of Rockford, Ill., it is the county seat of Rock County, the hub of a rich farm and dairy area.

Like many communities its size that are not caught up in a metropolitan complex, it has been able to keep its spreading housing and business developments within the city limits by annexation. At least partly as a result of this, its population has grown from 24,899 in 1950 to 35,164 in 1960 and 46,426 in 1970. But its downtown business section, straddling the brownish waters of the Rock River, is in trouble.

"Our problem really—and the problem of every downtown—is that they were laid out in the eighteen-forties or eighteen-fifties when people were on horseback," said Roger E. Krempel, Janesville's serious, heavy-set Director of Public Works. "They were cut up in small blocks and by today's standards they're not adequate.

"We're locked into these 1840

The New York Times

IN TROUBLE: Downtown Janesville, Wis.: ". . . the problem of every downtown—is that they were laid out in the eighteen-forties or eighteen-fifties when people were on horseback," said Roger E. Krempel, Public Works Director.

and 1850 street systems. We need to expand the traffic flow around our cities and create tracts of land suitable for development.

"Our major problem is the slipping away of the tax base around our center city. About the end of World War II we checked and found that 17 per cent of the city's tax base was provided by the center city. Today it is less than 5 per cent."

Renewal Need Cited

Pondering the difficulty of convincing Janesville residents that a downtown renewal now being planned is essential to the city's health, he went on:

"Our city center has not hit rock bottom like so many have. This is one of the biggest hurdles toward redevelopment. The cash registers are still ringing, largely due to inflation. But if we went back to 1940, 90 per cent of the sales were in the center city. Now less than 30 per cent is being spent in the center city."

Mr. Krempel spoke mainly for Janesville, but reports on nearly a score of smaller cities around the country indicate that the problems are widely mirrored elsewhere.

Portland, the largest city in Maine, had a population of 75,000 in 1960, a figure that dropped to 63,000 in 1970 as residents left the aging seaport for the rapidly developing suburbs.

In 1958, the year before the first shopping center opened in the area, downtown Portland's sidewalks were so crowded on Saturday afternoons that there was barely room to pass. Gross sales of downtown retail merchants that year were $140-million. Now there are 10 shopping centers in Greater Portland, including the recently opened Maine Mall, an enclosed center with about 50 shops and two huge department stores. Downtown retail sales have fallen to about $40-million annually.

Resignation of a City

Like a number of other cities, Portland seems to be somewhat resigned to downtown's loss of retail dominance to the shopping centers. And like others it is visualizing a new role for downtown as a service center with apartments, office buildings, hotels, restaurants and entertainment.

"We are beginning to see that the strengthening of the economic base is not coming from retail activity, but from service activities," City Manager John E. Menario said.

As evidence, he noted that a new parking garage would soon be opened downtown, that a 300-room Holiday Inn was being built near the shopping district, that the New England Telephone and Telegraph Company was putting up a midtown office building and that a multimillion-dollar high-rise bank and office building was opened a year ago in Monument Square, the heart of downtown Portland. In the meantime, many offices in the older downtown buildings are vacant.

In Selma, Ala., a hand-lettered sign in the window of Tepper's, the city's leading department store since 1875, reads: "It's cheaper to sell it than to move it."

Reference To Merchandise

The sign refers to the store's merchandise, but one person who saw it observed wryly that "it could well refer to the whole downtown area of Selma."

Tepper's will soon be closed and will reopen about two miles away in the new enclosed, air-

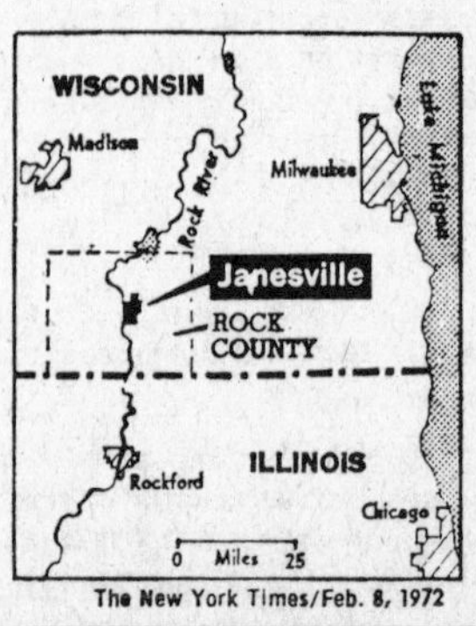

The New York Times/Feb. 8, 1972

conditioned Selma Mall, which will house 40 other stores. Already, Sears and Kress, two other big stores that had been in downtown Selma for years, have moved to the mall, which people in the area expect to become the real retail center of town before the year ends.

The store that Sears vacated is still empty and there are no prospects for renting the five-story Tepper's building, the largest in the city, which stands at the main intersection, Broad Street and Alabama Avenue. "I guess it will be just a pigeon roost," said a clerk in the store.

Frank Shoey, manager of Tepper's, explained the pending move in terms that have been heard again and again in the older cities from one corner of the country to another.

"We decided to move a year and a half ago, just as soon as they announced the mall was being built," he said. "Parking was the main consideration. It is a tremendous problem here. The trend is toward converting.

A Common Complaint

In reply, Joe T. Smitherman, Mayor of Selma, whose population of 27,379 is about evenly divided between black and white, echoed a plaint that is common to the countless cities that have tried to combat the move to the shopping centers.

"We've got four off-street parking lots where you can park all day for 40 cents," the Mayor said, "but people just want to park right in front of the store when they come downtown."

And then he touched on another problem, the fragmentation of property ownership, which has been an obstacle to the rehabiliation or replacement of decaying buildings in the nation's old downtowns.

"Some downtown buildings are tied up in estates owned by as many as 32 people, scattered all over the country," he said. "It makes it almost impossible for them to get together and carry out renovations that are necessary. As a result, the upper floors—the ones which were occupied by lawyers, doctors and dentists—are now all vacant. They're unusable."

Home of Mayo Clinic

Rochester, the southeastern Minnesota home of the renowned Mayo Clinic, is not Selma, whose unwanted notoriety stems from the civil rights strife there in the nineteen-sixties. During that decade, Selma lost 1,000 residents, while Rochester grew from 41,000 to 54,000.

Moreover, registrations at the Mayo Clinic increased from 165,000 in 1960 to 220,000 in 1970 and the 750,000 visitors attracted annually by the famous medical facility help keep Rochester's 25 hotels and 37 motels busy.

All this should make for a booming center-city economy perhaps, but Rochester's downtown, like Selma's, is in difficulty.

Rochester has eight shopping centers, including Apache Mall, which soon will be the third-largest in the state. The J. C. Penney Company and Montgomery Ward have both fled from downtown for shopping centers and Dayton's, the city's largest remaining downtown department store, plans to move in August to Apache Mall.

"No one is discounting downtown Rochester as part of a viable and growing community," Darryl A. Lee, executive vice president of the Chamber of Commerce, said. "We simply have to look for new alternatives."

$21-Million Alternative

One of the new alternatives was a $21-million downtown urban renewal plan that was blocked in 1969 by a record outpouring of voters who opposed a bond issue for the city's $3.2-million share of the redevelopment. Since then, Mayor Dewey Day has encountered difficulty in attempting to win support for even a vastly scaled-down revitalization plan.

The list of small cities with similar troubles could go on and on—Marietta, Ga., Petersburg, Va., Hudson, N. Y., Greenville, Miss., Iowa City—but most of the problems are visible right here in Janesville.

Janesville, like most American cities, was not laid out by planners. It just sort of happened.

When Henry Janes came to the Rock River Valley in 1836, a few years after the Army had chased Chief Black Hawk out of the area, he built a cabin near what is now the east end of the Milwaukee Street bridge. An enterprising man, he followed that with a tavern and then knocked together a ferry to lure more trade from among settlers across the river. Soon he had plotted his land and it is little wonder that when Rock County was formed in 1839, Janesville became the county seat.

Town Prospered

Henry Janes was not without foresight. Janesville, in the midst of some of the richest agricultural land in the world, grew and prospered. Over the years it also attracted industry and even now is the national home of the Parker Pen Company and the site of a General Motors assembly plant, as well as several small electronics companies.

Well-built and attractive frame houses march along elm-shaded streets to the very edge of downtown. But more and more of the people who live in those houses are driving away from the nearby downtown stores to the five shopping centers that have been built on the outskirts in the last decade.

As in others, the interstate highway that bypasses Janesville has proved a mixed blessing, easing traffic pressure on the 19th-century downtown streets, but opening up the fertile farm land of the countryside to shopping centers and strip developers and speeding local residents to even larger centers in Madison 40 miles to the north.

Meanwhile, the old two and three-story brick buildings along Main and Milwaukee Streets have grown shabbier, many of the offices on the upper floors abandoned, the merchants at streets level cramped for space. One-way street patterns have provided a circuit for bored teen-agers to cruise at night, but have done little to ease the discomfort of shoppers circling the steep slopes that rise from the river in search of parking spaces.

Television Has Impact

Again, here as elsewhere, television has long since usurped the old role of downtown as an entertainment center. Where once there were four movie theaters, there now are two, both frequently specializing in X-rated films.

On a recent night, one, the Myers, in an aging opera house shared by the Elks who are trying to sell the building and move to new quarters, was featuring "Dagmar's Hot Pants, Inc." and "The Fountain of Love." There seemed to be few takers, but a sign in the cashier's window noted that for a 50-cent membership fee senior citizens over 60 would be admitted for 75 cents instead of the regular $2 price.

Janesville is a public-spirited city.

In fact, a private group, the Greater Janesville Corporation, has been formed to work with the city and try to save the downtown area. A number of professional studies have been made and a plan has been evolved that calls for assembling several of the tiny downtown blocks into sites that might be attractive to big department stores.

If the proper retail anchors can be found, the plan also provides for more parking, the beautification of the river banks with walkways and trees, the construction of an upper-level pedestrian mall above the traffic and other features to make downtown a shopping center that would outshine all its rivals on the outskirts.

15-Year Plan Backed

A number of cities across the country, such as Grand Junction, Colo., Yuma, Ariz., and Urbana, Ill., have taken similar steps to fight the competition and many in Janesville are confident that their 15-year plan will succeed.

"This downtown hasn't gone downhill as much as some—some of them wait for the crisis stage," said City Manager Robert Bailey. "The merchants here are aggressively taking this thing and putting their money where their mouths are. That's the difference in this town. If people say they're going to do something, they do it here. They don't just say they're going to do it."

Meanwhile, there are those who mourn both the past and the present of downtown Janesville.

"In the old days, the farmers all came to town on Saturday night," Howard Koehn, a long-time resident, recalled sadly. "Not anymore, it's just dead."

And a teen-age girl driving what is locally known as "the Circuit" said bitterly:

"This town is for nothing but old fogeys. It's a bummer."

February 8, 1972

Large Suburbs Overtaking Cities In Number of Jobs They Provide

By JACK ROSENTHAL
Special to The New York Times

WASHINGTON, Oct. 14—The mushrooming suburbs of America's major metropolitan areas, which already have more population than the cities that produced them, are fast approaching an even more striking milestone in urbanization.

They have equaled, and perhaps by now surpassed, the central cities as providers of jobs.

According to a New York Times analysis of new data from the 1970 Census, half of all employment in the 15 largest metropolitan areas is now outside city limits.

And of all the enormous number of workers who live in the suburbs, only one in four still commutes from a suburban home to a city job. The others both live and work in the suburbs, whose headlong evolution into Outer Cities is one of the paramount features of the $200-million statistical portrait of America provided by the 1970 Census.

A Quizmaster's Delight

The first faint outlines of that portrait began to emerge soon after the census was taken on April 1, 1970. But as of today, with publication of the United States Summary of general social and economic characteristics, all the main features have come into focus.

The thick book is a quizmaster's delight. One can learn, for example, that on a per capita basis, Mississippi has four times as many maids as New York but that New York has twice as many policemen. Or that California has many more people in homes for the aged but New York has many more in mental hospitals.

But beyond the mass of detailed specific information in the report's 280,000 statistics—and the thousands of pages of other findings that its publication climaxes—the following major themes stand out:

¶The continuation of deep changes among minority groups. The migration of blacks, Hispanic-Americans and other minority groups to central cities has continued unabated. It has been paralleled by striking gains in education. But even after a decade of passionate attention to civil rights, the economic status of minorities has changed barely at all.

¶The coming of age of the "baby boom" generation that followed World War II. The impact of this outsized generation on schools has begun to diminish. Its impact on politics has just started. And perhaps its most decisive impact lies just ahead. In short order, young couples will be starting their own households in prodigious numbers.

¶Striking changes in the status of women. Increasingly, they are much more interested in becoming workers and much less in becoming mothers. They are getting more—and better—jobs and they are having strikingly fewer babies.

¶Most striking of all is the massive and richly varied development of the one-time bedroom communities and boondocks beyond the city limits. The nineteen-sixties, future historians may one day conclude, was the Decade of the Suburbs.

The Suburbs

It is a time of the suburbanization of almost everything. Potato fields and tract developments have been joined by poverty (for every three poor people in the cities there are two in the suburbs) and wealth (all 50 of the nation's richest counties cover suburban areas); by crime and culture; by pro football and French cuisine.

Still, for all the development and diversity, the conventional view of the suburbs has remained mired in what John F. Kain, a Harvard economist, calls "the monocentric trap." This is that at root, suburbs remain "sub" because their residents commute to cities to earn their livelihood.

The first finding of The Times's new analysis of suburban work patterns—drawn from 1970 and 1960 census reports for each of the 15 largest metropolitan areas—demonstrates that this view is now decisively obsolete.

In 1960, the suburbs of these areas contained about seven million jobs and their cities contained about 12 million. That is, the central cities provided nearly two-thirds of

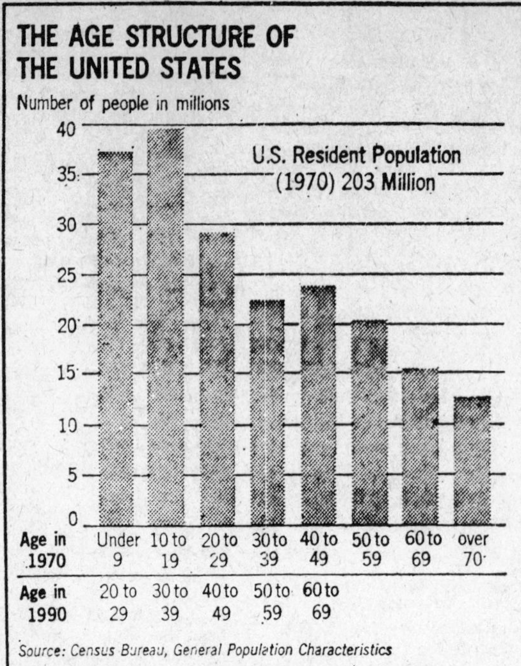

The coming of age of the baby boom generation is indicated by this graph of the population by age. The impact of the postwar surge in children can be estimated. By 1990, what is now a disproportionately large "youth generation" will be entering middle age.

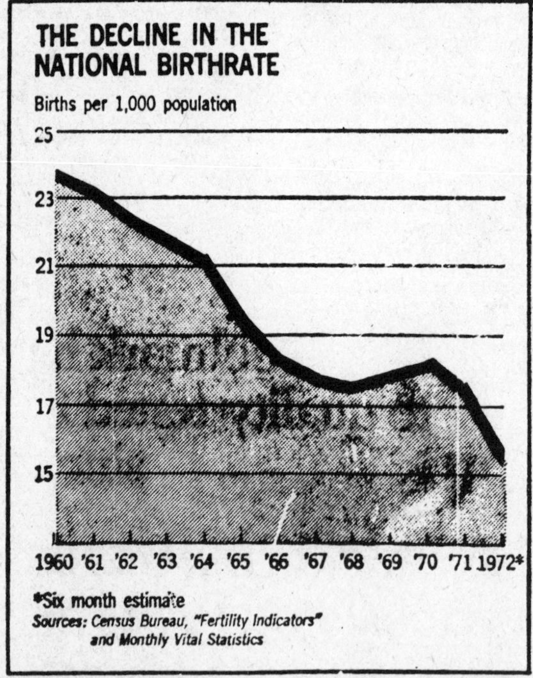

Graph shows both the long-term decline and the recent short-term plunge in the birth rate. The recent drop is so sharp that the total number of births, as well as the birth rate, is lower than it was a year ago.

the jobs in their metropolitan areas.

But during the nineteen-sixties, the suburbs of these areas gained more than three million jobs—a rise of 44 per cent. Meanwhile, the central cities lost 836,000, a 7 per cent decline.

By census day, April 1, 1970, the central cities had only 52 per cent of total metropolitan area jobs—11,224,000 as against 10,158,000 in the suburbs. And if, as is likely, the rates of change of the last decade have continued, one day in the next month or two the suburbs will draw ahead.

New York an Exception

In some individual areas, notably New York, that day may never come. New York City still provides two-thirds of the jobs in its broad metropolitan area. Cities like Houston, which can still readily annex developing suburbs, provide three-fourth of metropolitan employment.

But in nine of the 15 largest metropolitan areas, the milestone has already been passed: the suburbs have already equaled—and even far exceeded—the cities as the principal location of jobs.

The single most dramatic example is Washington, D.C. Even here in the nation's capital, with its heavy city concentration of Government employment, at least 55 per cent of all jobs are now suburban.

In 1960, there were 483,000 city jobs and 274,000 suburban jobs. In 1970, after a momentous 118 per cent jump in the suburban category, there were 492,000 city jobs and 597,000 in the suburbs.

Much of the explanation for such striking changes lies in the development of most new jobs in the suburbs. But there is another explanation more ominous for the economic future of the central cities.

Of the 15 cities covered in The Times's study, only two had significantly more jobs at the end of the nineteen-sixties than at the decade's start. And both of these were in Texas, where state law facilitates city annexation of growing fringe areas.

Total employment in the 15 areas went up 11 per cent in the decade. But nine of the central cities lost jobs. The largest numerical loss was in New York City, whose total dropped 10 per cent to 3,172,000. By far the largest proportionate loss was in Detroit, where city employment dropped 23 per cent.

And the other four cities barely held their own.

Second Major Finding

The second major finding of The Times's analysis is of a massive increase in the number of workers who both live and work in the suburbs.

There was a rise in the number of conventional "monocentric" commuters — from suburb to city. They increased 13 per cent, to 3.3 million. But meanwhile, the number of people who commuted from a home somewhere in the suburbs to a job somewhere in the suburbs shot up 40 per cent, to 8.7 million.

Over-all in the 15 metropolitan areas, 72 per cent of workers who live in the suburbs also work in the sub-

HOW JOBS HAVE SHIFTED TO THE SUBURBS
(In the 15 largest metropolitan areas)

Metropolitan Area		Reported Met Area Workers	Those Who Work in the City	Those Who Work in the Suburbs	Those Who Live and Work in the Suburbs: Number	Per Cent	City's Share of Metro Area Jobs: Per Cent
		Figures in thousands of workers					
New York	1970	4,943	3,172	1,771	1,593	77.7	64.1
	1960	4,929	3,511	1,418	1,267	74.9	71.2
Los Angeles—Long Beach	1970	2,483	1,133	1,350	1,053	78.6	45.7
	1960	2,432	1,270	1,162	947	68.8	52.2
Chicago—Gary—Hammond	1970	2,737	1,438	1,299	1,065	73.2	52.5
	1960	2,460	1,670	790	674	65.4	67.8
Philadelphia	1970	1,597	772	825	744	77.8	48.2
	1960	1,381	870	511	459	69.8	63.0
Detroit	1970	1,393	537	856	695	76.3	38.6
	1960	1,223	693	530	433	65.1	56.7
San Francisco—Oakland	1970	1,113	557	556	500	70.4	50.0
	1960	1,008	555	453	448	73.8	55.1
Washington D. C.	1970	1,089	492	597	544	66.7	45.1
	1960	757	483	274	238	52.8	63.8
Boston	1970	988	374	614	564	74.2	37.8
	1960	920	409	511	467	70.8	44.5
Pittsburgh	1970	786	286	500	465	76.2	36.3
	1960	762	274	488	465	83.0	36.0
St. Louis	1970	809	340	469	426	70.0	42.0
	1960	661	401	260	239	59.9	60.7
Baltimore	1970	723	368	355	282	67.3	50.1
	1960	591	390	201	164	61.4	65.9
Cleveland	1970	726	392	334	273	56.9	54.0
	1960	646	463	183	159	47.7	71.7
Houston	1970	714	537	177	135	76.2	75.6
	1960	427	360	67	53	54.1	84.3
Minneapolis—St. Paul	1970	694	409	285	227	56.7	58.9
	1960	534	408	126	125	51.7	76.4
Dallas	1970	587	417	170	133	50.1	71.0
	1960	401	303	98	89	63.1	75.6
TOTALS:	1970	21,382	11,224	10,158	8,699	72.3	52.4
	1960	19,132	12,060	7,072	6,227	67.8	63.0

SOURCE: New York Times analysis of Census Tract Reports

Chart shows the rapid growth of the suburbs, not merely as bedrooms for city workers but as centers of employment in their own right. In 1960, they had seven million jobs, five million less than the cities they surround. By 1970, they had 10.2 million, about a million less. By now, suburban jobs may even have surpassed jobs in the cities.

urbs. For some areas, the figure is significantly higher. In the New York suburbs, for example, it is 78 per cent. In other words only 22 per cent of suburban workers commute to the city.

The pull of suburban employment is evident also from a sharp rise in reverse commuters, those who travel from homes in the city to jobs in the suburbs. Over-all, the number rose from 845,000, or 4 per cent of metropolitan employment, in 1960 to 1,460,000, or 7 per cent.

Types of Employment

The same pattern of suburban pre-eminence appears in each of the major types of employment covered by a Census Bureau analysis of the economic censuses of 1958 and 1967.

For example, the suburbs accounted for three-fourths of all new manufacturing and retail jobs that developed in this period. As a result, by 1967, they had 45 per cent of all metropolitan area manufacturing jobs and 41 per cent of all those in retail trade.

By now, as with other measurements, the suburbs may have pulled even and perhaps gone ahead. For all these measures are reflections of an "outward movement" in this century that ranks in importance with the Westward movement of the last.

This outward movement overshadows even major shifts of population between regions in the nineteen-sixties. The South, for example, the most populous region, grew by 7.8 million during the decade, to a total of 63 million.The West gained 6.8 million, a 24 per cent increase, reaching 35 million.

But the movement to the outer cities of America was greater still, and it affected every region. As of 1970, there were 76 million suburban Americans, compared with 64 million in the cities and 63 million outside metropolitan areas.

The force of those totals is evident from a comparison with the 1950 census. In the intervening 20 years, cities added 10 million people. Suburbs added 35 million.

Minorities

In Baltimore, St. Louis and elsewhere, people call the suburbs the white ring around the increasingly black city. But that view overlooks significant black, as well as white, movement to the suburbs.

The black population of all suburban areas increased by a million in the nineteen-sixties, bringing the total to about 3.6 million. With fair housing ordinances, even formerly exclusive suburban areas began to open to black home buyers.

But for three reasons, the "white ring" label remained a largely accurate description. One is that white movement to the suburbs was so massive that it far outweighed the black shift. In 1960, 4.2 per cent of the suburban population was black. In 1970, the figure had risen only to 4.7 per cent.

The second reason cannot be found in census data, for they do not specify which are booming, affluent suburbs and which are older, closer fringe communities afflicted with urban decay. And it is to the latter areas that many of the "suburban" blacks have been limited.

The third and most dramatic reason for the white ring view is that the truly massive movement of blacks in the nineteen-sixties, as in the nineteen-fifties, was from Southern farms to Northern—and now, increasingly, also Southern—cities.

In 1940, the South contained 77 per cent of the black population. By 1970, the proportion had dropped to 53 per cent. In the same period, the population of the Northeast and North Central states went from 11 to about 20 per cent black.

The black proportion of the population as a whole is 11.1 per cent—22,580,289. But in cities the proportion is much higher. The figure is 21 per cent for all central cities. In the 12 cities with more than 2 million people, it is 28 per cent.

In nine cities, more than 40 per cent of the population is black, and four major cities have a black majority. The highest proportion is in Washington, whose 538,000 blacks constitute 71 per cent of the city's population.

In total numbers, by far the largest concentration is in New York City, where 1.7 million blacks make up 21 per cent of the population.

The urbanization of the black population has proceeded so strikingly that in 1970 almost three of every five blacks—58 per cent—lived in central cities, compared with 28 per cent of the white population.

The [illegible]ement of blacks to Northern cities strongly appears to be paralleled by an increase in the amount of education for their children.

Even with recent gains, the South as a whole still lags behind the rest of the nation on several educational scales. For example, nationally, the median number of school years completed in 1970 by adults was 12.1—meaning that more than half the population had finished high school.

In the South, the median was 11.3 years—the beginning of senior year in high school. And even that region-wide figure masks lower ones in some states. In Kentucky, the median was 9.9 years, and in South Carolina and Arkansas, 10.5.

(By contrast, the median in the West was 12.4 years and in Utah, the highest-ranking state, it was 12.5.)

Rural blacks, most of them in the South, had a still lower median education level—7.2 years. But for blacks in urban areas the figure was notably higher—10.2 years.

Only 13 per cent of rural blacks over the age of 25 had finished high school, according to the 1970 findings. For urban blacks, the figure was 35 per cent. For Hispanic-Americans, it was 36 per cent. For all whites, it was 55 per cent.

These figures for the minority groups represented major improvements over those in 1960. But the relative gains were offset by still stronger improvements in white educational levels.

Nearly the same was true of family income. In 1960, half of black families made more than $3,000 and half less. By March, 1972, the figure had risen to $6,440. In the same period, however, white income also advanced rapidly. From about $6,000 it jumped to more than $10,000.

Thus, in terms of dollars, the black-white gap widened, although in percentage terms black families gained slightly. In any event, as of last March, a third of the black population lived below the official Federal poverty income level—compared with only a tenth of the white population. (Whites continue to make up 70 per cent of the total poverty population).

Recent Census Bureau studies show that Hispanic-Americans as a whole earn significantly more than blacks. This general comparison, however, masks wide variations among persons of different Spanish-speaking backgrounds.

The 9.3 million reported Hispanic-Americans are roughly 5 per cent of the total population. But two-thirds are concentrated in five states, and more than half live in California (3.1 million) and Texas (2.1 million) alone.

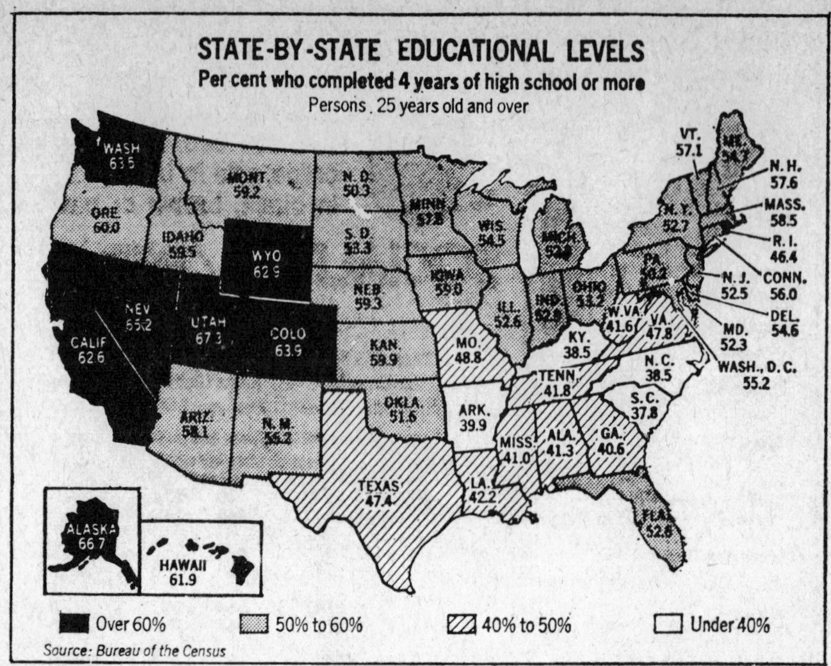

The 1970 Census reported sharp regional variations in schooling. The best-educated state was Utah, where two-thirds of the population had at least finished high school. The lowest-ranking state was South Carolina, where less than 38 per cent of the population had achieved a high school diploma.

Youth

Like a pearl in an oyster, there is a crystal ball of sorts embedded in the endless rows of tiny numbers of the 1970 Census reports. It rests in a category demographers call the age structure.

What they refer to is the differing size of different age groups in the population. The crystal ball possibilities arise from the knowledge that people at different ages have broadly predictable needs.

There are some striking ups and downs, indeed, in the current American age structure. There are now about 12.1 million people aged 47 to 51. But there are only 11.1 million aged 37 to 41—the clear result of low birth rates in the Depression.

Most Striking Bulge

The most striking bulge in the age structure now exists among those between the ages of 6 and 25. This is the baby boom generation, and its size can be illustrated by noting that there now are 2.1 million people aged 38—and 4.3 million aged 12.

The predictable—and unpredictable—impact of this enormous youth bulge on society was one of the major developments of the nineteen-sixties, as it was of the nineteen-fifties. The statistical footprints stand out sharply from a page of figures in the new United States Summary entitled "School Enrollment by Age."

For instance, in 1970, there were nearly as many 18-and 19-year-olds still in school as there were total people of those ages in 1960.

It is not just that there are many more people of school age. It is also that much higher proportions of people are going to school and staying longer.

Thus, almost 90 per cent of 16- and 17-year-olds were in school in 1970. In 1960, it was 81 per cent. In 1920, it was 43 per cent.

'Uncoupling' Phenomenon

There is a future as well as a past side to the age-structure coin. With the leading edge of the baby boom now in its mid-twenties, the impact it has had on education is now starting to be felt in different ways.

One of the first is in housing. A generation ago, for a young unmarried person to move out of the family home provoked raised eyebrows among the neighbors. But now, rapidly, it has become a commonplace.

"Uncoupling" is what demographers call this phenomenon, and they cite figures showing that just between 1964 and 1970, the number of young people setting up housekeeping has jumped by more than 130 per cent.

There has been a parallel, though not quite so dramatic a jump—of 50 per cent—in the number of older adults, over age 65, also uncoupling. They move to apartments, for example, rather than feel themselves to be a burden on their children.

The total effect of such movement, by young and old, has been a huge 50 per cent increase in one-person households. And the almost certain prospect is that such households will increase even more sharply in the near future.

Conrad F. Taeuber, director of the 1970 Census, notes that between 1945 and 1965, about 48 million Americans reached age 20. Between 1965 and 1985, about 78 million will.

Nor will household changes be limited to single persons. Mr. Taeuber, one of the nation's leading demographers, foresees massive rises in total household formations.

Apartments in Suburbs

The annual total has been running at something under a million a year. It is already starting to go up and, he says, "may reach as much as 1.5 million per year before it begins declining again."

The signs are already evident from what once would have sounded like a contradiction in terms: suburban apartments. In the nineteen-sixties, they increased so fast—96 per cent—that there is now one suburban apartment for every two in the city.

The crystal ball possibilities are plain, whether for those who manufacture spatulas or those who make housing policy. And small wonder that George H. Brown, the director of the Census Bureau, believes that the years leading to 1985 will be the "Era of the Young Married."

Women

Women now outnumber men as never before in this century. There are 100 women for every 95 men, 5.4 million more across the country. And the difference is by no means accounted for only by women of older ages.

More boys are born than girls, but with increases in the death rate among younger men, women are now more numerous at every level over age 20.

The most striking change

in the status of women in the nineteen - sixties concerned work. Women of all ages and all family income levels surged into the labor force in massive numbers and accelerating rates.

Among all women over age 14, 13 million—or 26 per cent—were in the labor force in 1940. In 1970, there were 30.8 million working women —40 per cent. Among adult women only, the figure was 43 per cent. And in some age groups, it was even higher.

A considerably greater proportion of black women than white are in the labor force. Among women over 35, the black rate is 60 per cent. But at the same time, three times as many black women support themselves and their families without a husband present. In general, they work more and earn less than their white counterparts.

Their quest for better salaries and work with higher status is clear from the 1970 census findings on private household workers. In all, there are 600,000 fewer maids than there were in 1960. The 1970 total was 1.1 million.

Most of the drop was accounted for by black women. The number working as domestics plunged from 900,000 to about 500,000.

For black women, indeed for all working women, one of the notable findings of the United States Summary is that their job status improved appreciably during the nineteen-sixties. The proportion of working women in factory jobs decreased. The proportion in professional, clerical and service jobs increased.

Thus, in 1960, 2.7 million women worked in professional and technical jobs—13 per cent of the female work force. In 1970, there were 4.3 million women in such jobs, 15 per cent of their total workers. Among black women alone, the shift was even clearer. The number in professional jobs jumped from 197,000 to 344,000.

Men Gaining Even Faster

Despite these gains, however, men are moving up the occupational status ladder even faster. For example, the male increase in professional and technical jobs was half again that of women.

And there was evidence of strong continued discrimination against women in earnings. A study by two Census Bureau analysts found that women who had worked throughout their adult lives averaged only 62 per cent of male earnings in parallel jobs. Even in professional and technical jobs, women earned only 66 per cent of what men did.

A fundamental question is raised by sharp increases in the number of working women: what about the children? One answer offered by American women—with particular force in the last several years—is to have fewer of them.

Fewer young women are marrying—or at least marrying young. After staying stable for 20 years, the median age at marriage for women has started to rise notably. It is now about 21. For men it is a little over 23.

And even those who are marrying are considerably less eager to have children quickly, to have many children, and perhaps even to have children at all.

By every measure, births and fertility have been in decline since 1957. And since 1968, the trend line has moved to what is now a historic low.

More Divorced Women

The increased work rates among women are one possible explanation. So are improved contraception, rapidly rising public approval of abortion and an increase in divorced and separated women. Whatever the reason, the impact is dramatically evident.

With the coming of age of the baby boom generation, there are 3 per cent more potential young mothers this year than last. But the birth rate for the first six months of 1972 is 10 per cent lower than in the first half of 1971.

The decline is so sharp that in the same period the actual number of births went down sharply. In the 1971 period, there were 1,755,000 children born. In 1972, there were 1,604,000.

These low figures translate into an estimated fertility rate of 2.1 children per woman. And that, to demographers, is a symbolic number because it is the rate—if it continued for about 70 years—at which the country would achieve zero population growth.

More Births Than Deaths

Fertility rates, however, are unpredictable, and no reputable authority believes the nation is likely to achieve the widely discussed goal of zero population growth. Indeed, even with the absolute decline in births, the country continues to grow.

In the first six months of this year, there were 600,000 more births than deaths. In the 30 months since the census was taken, the population has increased more than 5 million, from 203,211,926 to more than 208,232,000. Even should low birth rates continue, the population by the year 2000 would be close to 270 million.

But that would be moderate by contrast with some predictions as recent as two years ago that the population then would exceed 320 million.

In any event, the larger problem illuminated by the massive reports of the 1970 Census is not the size of the population, but its concentration. For all its growth, the American population still lives on a tiny fraction of the land. Three-fourths of the population lives in cities and suburbs, and even that high proportion is increasing steadily.

Where will the new households be formed? Some, surely, will be in the cities. But most cities are already full—and are themselves losing great chunks of population.

The nineteen-seventies, in short, are even more likely than the nineteen-sixties to be, above all, the Decade of the Suburbs.

October 15, 1972

Planned Towns as Big Business

The building of new towns is no longer the sole province of the real-estate developer. Now, more and more major corporations are entering the field.

The list includes such giants as the Gulf Oil Corporation in Reston, Va., and the Smithkline Corporation in Franklin Town, Pa.

The business of building planned communities, however, is not without its problems. As Hugh Mields Jr., the author of the recently published "Federally Assisted New Communities," pointed out in an interview last week, there is no way to predict which communities will be financially successful.

He noted that "there usually isn't any profit taking until the seventh or eighth or ninth year" and added that "many developers think you can't make any money."

The costs, Mr. Mields said, can reach into billions of dollars and "no developers under Title VII [of the Housing and Urban Development Act of 1970] have made anything yet."

Under Title VII of the act, the Federal Government was, among other things, to "provide loan guarantees for bonds floated on the private market" and "interest differential grants" for taxable bonds. The Government, however, has never provided funds for the grants, Mr. Mields said.

In January, the Nixon Administration suspended funds for low- and middle-income housing, which had the effect of slowing applications for new towns. Those communities that were already in progress and had received Federal funds, though, appear to be proceeding as planned.

Mr. Mields pointed out that "the practical effect" of the suspension of funds "had been to discourage public involvement."

"Most of the action" he noted, "has been on the private side."

Virginia

Reston, Va., was one of the first of the recent planned communities. Approved by Fairfax County in 1962, it now has 22,000 residents. Plans project 80,000 residents by 1980 and completion by 1982. It was built without Federal assistance.

The town covers 6,750 acres, of which 40 per cent is to be open space It will comprise seven villages, each with its own small shopping center. A major shopping center will serve the entire city. Two villages have been completed.

Reston was founded by Robert E. Simons, who received a $15-million loan guarantee from the Gulf Oil Corporation in 1964. In 1967 when Mr. Simons had financial difficulties, Gulf took over the project and renamed it Gulf-Reston.

According to Gulf spokesmen, the company has about $40-million invested in Reston as of this year. The project went into the black last year.

One of Reston's problems is its image of being restricted to the upper middle class. A survey last year showed that the average adult in Reston has 16.2 years of schooling. Median family income is estimated at $25,000.

Upon completion, Reston is expected to have 25,000 homes and 24,500 jobs, one for every three residents.

Maryland

The first residents arrived in Columbia, Md., in 1967. Now there are 25,000. When the town is completed in 1981, the population is projected to be 110,000.

The city is being built on 15,000 acres in Howard County that were bought by James W. Rouse & Co., Inc., a development and mortgage-banking firm. It was financed by the Rouse company and the Connecticut General Insurance Corporation.

The developers' costs of more than $100-million do not include housing, which is paid for by individual builders. The town was planned and developed by Rouse, which sells plots of land designated for certain types of housing to builders who then construct the houses and sell them.

Columbia was, like Reston, constructed without any Federal aid. However, several hundred row houses and apartments were built with the aid of Government subsidy plans to allow middle- and low-income families to move to the new city.

The Rouse company has also situated a number of light industrial operations at Columbia, including a 1,000-acre regional assembly plant of the General Electric Company.

In Charles County in southern Maryland, 25 miles southeast of Washington, the town of St. Charles Communities is being developed on 8,000 acres. The projected cost is $125-million for the town, which will have a population of 80,000 by 1993, its completion date.

The Interstate General Corporation, which is based in Puerto Rico, is developing St. Charles Communities with funds guaranteed by the Department of Housing and Urban Development. The town is to include its own industry and recreational and shopping facilities, all within walking distance of housing in the town.

H.U.D. has required the developers to provide for low-income families to be able to live there, and 80 per cent of the single-family houses will cost $25,000 or less, according to Mr. Mields.

Pennsylvania

Franklin Town, Pa., a new town to be created within the city of Philadelphia, will be started in late August or early September. The $400-million development of homes, commercial structures, hotels and office buildings will be located on a 50-acre site covering about 22 blocks near the center of the city.

Six concerns and a bank have started the development firm of Franklin Town, Inc., which is not receiving any Federal assistance. They include the Prudential Insurance Company of America, the Smithkline Corporation, the I-T-E Imperial Corporation, the Philadelphia Electric Company, the stock brokerage firm of Butcher & Sherrerd, the Korman Corporation and the Girard Trust Bank.

The project is expected to provide 3 million to 4 million square feet of office space, housing for 4,000 families, 1,400 hotel rooms and recreational facilities.

Franklin Town, Inc., is headed by Jason R. Nathan, who was formerly chief of housing and development in New York City.

"We are, to my knowledge, the only privately sponsored development in the United States which has agreed to match or exceed at its own expense all of the relocation benefits that would be provided if this were a Federally subsidized project," he said.

The City Council has ruled that any homeowners displaced by the development must be relocated within the site. Of 32 homeowners on the site, 17 will move out. Of the remaining 15, 12 will get new homes and three will have their present homes rebuilt at no extra cost.

The value of the existing homes is an average of about $22,900, but the replacement homes will have an average value of $43,000, according to the corporation.

The first apartments will be occupied at the end of 1974. Completion is scheduled in 10 years. Housing is planned in Franklin Town for all income levels.

Minnesota

The total cost of Cedar-Riverside, Minn., a "new-town-in town" in Minneapolis, is, according to its developers, expected to be more than $500-million. The population is expected to reach 30,000 by 1992.

The project's developer, Cedar-Riverside Associates, has planned for five residential neighborhoods bounded by the Mississippi River and two interstate highways. Each neighborhood will have its own support facilities, schools, day-care centers and health centers. Plans call for both subsidized and luxury apartments.

Cedar-Riverside, which is being financed mainly by the Northwestern Mutual Life Insurance Company, received a loan guarantee of $24-million from H.U.D.

Jonathan, Minn., 25 miles southwest of Cedar-Riverside, is in its third year of a 20-year development plan. It is expected to have a population of 50,000 and employment for 20,000 when it is completed in 1990.

Jonathan is privately financed but it received a loan guarantee of $21-million from the Government.

Twenty-four companies have moved to the new town's industrial park and 10 more are expected this year. Robert J. Dahlin, president of the Jonathan Development Corporation, said the company expected to make a profit this year.

"That's earlier than anyone looked for," he noted.

Texas

Flower Mound New Town, Tex., a development covering about one-third of the 20,000 acres of the town of Flower Mound, is scheduled to open in November. One hundred fifty single-family dwellings are to be available for occupancy then.

The Raymond D. Nasher Company of Dallas is the developer of the town, which is 20 miles from Dallas and Fort Worth.

At the end of the first year Flower Mound New Town will have about 700 homes. Eight hundred will be added the second year and about 1,000 each succeeding year. Nearly 50 per cent of the development will be residential.

At the end of the 18-year project, the population of Flower Mound New Town is expected to be 65,000.

Flower Mound, which now has 2,000 residents, is being developed separately. Its developers predict it will eventually have 100,000 residents.

The first homes in Flower Mound New Town will cost between $25,000 and $35,000. Prices will eventually range from $18,000 to $75,000.

Federal grants of $3.4-million from H.U.D. and $1.3-million from the Environmental Protection Agency for water and sewage facilities will be funneled to the city of Flower Mound, not to New Town. However, New Town received loan guarantees on its bonds from H.U.D.

JEAN CHRISTENSEN

August 5, 1973

The Chicago Loop's Decline Is Magnificent Mile's Gain

By SETH S. KING
Special to The New York Times

CHICAGO, Sept. 20—"Put the city up; tear the city down; put it up again; let us find a city," wrote Carl Sandburg, the poet laureate of Chicago, in his poem 'The Windy City."

Mr. Sandburg wrote these lines in 1922. But they are just as apt today, and no two areas of Chicago have been changing as quickly as the Loop — the traditional shopping and entertainment area within or surrounding the ancient elevated railway tracks that loop through central Chicago — or the area along or adjacent to upper Michigan Avenue.

The Loop remains one of the busiest shopping districts in the world—by day. But many attractions that drew Chicagoans and suburbanites to the Loop after dark have now moved northward or gone to the expanding suburbs themselves.

New ranks of elegant stores and luxury hotels are appearing along the 14 tree-lined blocks of Michigan Avenue from the Chicago River northward to Oak Beach, a section promoters are now calling "The Magnificent Mile."

Across the river and beyond Michigan Avenue, northeast of the Loop, the wasteland that once held only the Illinois Central's freight yards has been named "Illinois Center" and is being filled with office buildings, as well as another large hotel and the first parts of a vast apartment and shopping complex.

The Loop still includes the city's largest department stores and many of its older specialty shops.

But in recent years Chicago has been losing an average of 55,000 residents annually to the suburbs, and the State Street department stores within the Loop have themselves been pulling these customers away from their downtown stores with large suburban branches.

Entertainment Center

In the place of these old customers, the State Street stores are now selling to increasing numbers of Chicago's growing black population, drawn to the Loop as more of their traditional neighborhood shopping facilities have been erased by expressways and urban renewal.

By night, the Loop has become an entertainment center for the black community. Within the last year, most of the large old first-run movie theaters within the Loop have changed their playbills, now offering either the new black-made films about blacks, or the gaudiest of the new horror films, or pornography.

At the tag end of the summer season, only one of the old legitimate theaters in the Loop is offering a stage production. But the live theater of Chicago is flourishing in the intimate new dinner theaters in the northern neighborhoods or in the suburbs, and Hollywood's major first-run movies are now displayed in new cinemas in both areas.

It has been years since the younger generation of World War II flocked to the College Inn of the Sherman House hotel, drawn by the swing and jazz of Bob Crosby and his orchestra. But in the last year, some of the Loop's oldest restaurants have either closed or stopped serving dinner.

The night music is now found across the Chicago River on the Near North Side, among the go-go joints and the throbbing singles bars on upper State, Rush, and Division Streets.

And now the Sherman House is being torn down, leaving the Palmer House as the only large luxury hotel still within the Loop itself.

The Loop has always been virtually devoid of permanent residents. But adjacent to the upper end of Michigan Avenue, rows of high-rise luxury apartments have been completed in the last two years. The upper third of the Hancock Center, the city's third tallest building, consists of apartments, anchoring a new nighttime population along Michigan Avenue.

Alongside the Hancock building the steel structure of Water Tower Place is rising. When it is finished next year, this elaborate complex will combine 12 floors of department stores, boutiques, restaurants, bars and offices with 22 floors of a new Ritz-Carleton Hotel and 40 floors of condominium apartments above the hotel.

Two new office buildings have already been completed and occupied in Illinois Center, and the new Standard Oil Building, the city's second tallest, is nearing completion there. Construction has already begun on a new 1,000-room Hyatt House hotel and on an elaborate cluster of condominiums called

Photographs for The New York Times by GARY SETTLE

View looking northeast across Michigan Avenue. The Old Water Tower is in the foreground, and the John Hancock Center is across the street at left. The excavation between them will be a complex of stores, offices and apartments.

Harbor Point Dwellings.

Marshall Field's, which Carl Sandburg called "The Cathedral of Department Stores," sent tremors through State Street last year when it announced that it would open a store in Water Tower Place.

But the store's officers insist that this will be only a branch, like the nine others it has in the suburbs, and that the parent Marshall Field's in the Loop hopes to continue there as it always has.

The forces behind these changes are discussed delicately by the developers and urbanologists.

"It's hard to talk about some of the reasons without sounding racist," one developer conceded. "But there is too much awareness of the black community among Chicago's whites and too many of them who forget that black money is just as good as theirs."

Changes Noted

"Certainly the Loop is becoming a major black shopping area by day and one of the nicest areas of entertainment for them at night," he went on. "This should only be welcome news to the merchants. But you can only hope this change won't mean another polarization of the races in Chicago."

Pierre de Vise, an urbanologist who is a specialist in Chicago's population trends, estimates that the nighttime population of the Loop, the people who shop, work and play on its streets after dark, has dropped from 70,000 in the nineteen-fifties to 23,000 last year.

He attributes this to several forces.

"The Loop has never had a residential population, and when white people began moving to the suburbs and got everything they wanted there, they stopped coming back into the Loop, especially at night," he said.

"A lot of the largest cultural affairs, the symphony, the opera, and the art museum, are still in or near the Loop," he continued. "But there wasn't enough from them to sustain the restaurants and movie houses at night. At the same time, the blacks had been losing their shopping and entertainment areas. They had a need for the Loop, and are satisfying that need."

Chicagoans have often maintained that the intersection of State and Madison Streets in the heart of the Loop was the crossroads of the world and that anyone who stood there long enough would see someone he knew.

"You still may do that," said James Bade, managing director of the State Street Council, the association of merchants that champions the Loop.

"But like all cities, Chicago is seeing social, economic and cultural changes, and the Loop is part of these changes, especially at night," he said.

Within the last five years the financial district on the western edge of the Loop has witnessed one of the greatest commercial building booms in the nation, Mr. Bade noted.

September 21, 1973

Rand Report Calls Future of St. Louis Economically Bleak

Special to The New York Times

ST. LOUIS, Nov. 3—A rather gloomy report by the Rand Corporation on the status and future of St. Louis has brought sharp protests from city leaders, but suburban leaders think some of the observations should be considered as warning signals.

Basically, the year-long study of St. Louis and two other cities—Seattle and San Jose, Calif.—disclosed last month, found St. Louis to be in the worst economic position, with its future bleak and greatly dependent on Federal programs.

The report said St. Louis's position as the economic center of the metropolitan area would be blotted out by continuing suburban development. It suggested that the most plausible solution to the city's problem

Norman C. Murdock, the state and metropolitan tax revenues to be used for the city's needs.

The city's political and business leadership was, for the most part, outraged with the report. "It's made me so mad, it's made so many people damn mad, that it's probably been a beneficial thing," said the president of Downtown St. Louis, Inc., a downtown promotion group, Ethan A. Shepley Jr.

"Be it resolved that the Board of Aldermen records its deep appreciation to the Rand Corporation and its benefactors for choosing to spend their time and treasure in studying the city of St. Louis and fashioning its obituary," began an aldermanic resolution, written by Alderman John G. Roach. He dismissed the report as another manifestation of "crabgrass philosophy." The Board of Aldermen approved the resolution.

Many other local critics accused the California-based research organization of making hand-wringing laments about the city without offering constructive solutions.

would be increased Federal, city's Director of Planning and Development, said, "They didn't follow through with specific policy recommendations."

Suburban leaders had a different view. "The city's leaders have been unwilling to face what's happened to the city," said Gerald A. Rimmel, chairman of the St. Louis County Council. He suggested that the Rand report might be helpful. "Rand didn't say the city is dead, it just said it isn't the same city it was 30 years ago or so."

Many political leaders, from both the city and county, pointed to extensive projected building in the downtown as an indication that things were improving.

November 4, 1973

HARTFORD BLOCKS AID FOR SUBURBS

Federal Judge Enjoins U.S. From Giving Road Funds While Poor Need Homes

By LAWRENCE FELLOWS

Special to The New York Times

HARTFORD, Jan. 28—In a case brought by the City of Hartford, a Federal judge here today enjoined the Federal Government from giving approximately $4 million in community development funds to seven of Hartford's relatively affluent suburbs.

The suit, in which Hartford pleaded that the money was needed more for housing the poor than it was for roads, sewers, parks and other improvements in the suburbs, could have wide repercussions across the country.

The Department of Housing and Urban Development in Washington is dealing with 3,000 applications similar to those from Hartford and its suburbs, many of them involving similar situations of city-suburban competition.

3,000 Cases Vulnerable

Although H.U.D. officials in Washington would not comment on the Hartford case, it was obvious that the 3,000 applications were at least vulnerable to challenge in the courts. There are 25 other applications in Connecticut alone.

"We think it was a momentous decision," said Councilman Richard Suisman of Hartford, who was a prime mover in the suit.

Hartford contended in its suit that more than 90 percent of the poor people in the region had crowded into Hartford because there was no place else for them to go.

Hartford has been awarded $10,025,000 by H.U.D. The city challenged a total of $4,435,000 awarded to West Hartford, East Hartford, Glastonbury, Vernon, Farmington, Enfield and Windsor Locks to force the suburbs to spend the money on low-cost housing and to take some of the burden away from the city.

"We were not looking for that money," Councilman Suisman said. "That was never our intent."

The Councilman referred to the problem many cities encounter when businesses and wealthier residents move to the suburbs and pay their taxes there. The city is forced to try to keep open its hospitals and libraries, and to cope with a smaller tax base, deteriorating housing, a more crowded population and the rising expenses of such things as police and fire protection, education and welfare.

"The question was: Can one city supply all the services?" Mr. Suisman said.

Judge M. Joseph Blumenfeld held in United States District Court that the Department of Housing and Urban Development exceeded its authority by informing towns applying for community development funds that they need not make projections of how many low-income residents they expected to move into their communities, in spite of the legal requirement that these projections be made.

Because the information the

towns needed to make such projections was difficult to get, H.U.D. waived the requirement last May. Tonight it was said by a department spokesman in Washington that the projections had to be supplied.

The projections, Judge Blumenfeld said, were the principal element of the Federal Government's Community Development Act of 1974, which was passed by Congress to help break up the concentrations of poor people in the cities.

Urban Crisis Cited

"The statute clearly has, as one of its objectives, the spatial deconcentration of lower-income groups, particularly from the central cities," the judge wrote in a 42-page memorandum of decision.

"Congress apparently decided that this was part of the solution to the crisis facing our urban communities," he added.

"It's fantastic," said Paul Davidoff, executive director of the Suburban Action Institute, which had been retained by the city to provide technical and legal assistance.

"This will affect the whole movement to have the suburbs share with the cities the burden of the poor," Mr. Davidoff said.

The leaders of the suburban committees were furious when Hartford brought suit and won a temporary injunction from Judge Blumenfeld last Sept. 30, denying the seven suburbs the money they had been awarded.

A movement to boycott Hartford was started in Windsor Locks, but never got off the ground. Several members of Connecticut's suburban-dominated General Assembly said Hartford had, in effect, declared war on its suburbs and thereby insured that it would have trouble in the future with legislation the city wanted.

Judge Blumenfeld, in the last line of his memorandum of decision, said the suburban towns could apply for funds again and include the information the law required about the number of poor people who might be expected to move in.

But he also made it clear that H.U.D. would have to give that information greater weight when dealing with the applications.

"I'm optimistic that regional relations are going to be much, much better," Councilman Suisman said.

"I've found a lot of good will in the suburbs."

January 29, 1976

CRISIS IN MUNICIPAL FINANCE

INCOME TAX LEVIED ON PHILADELPHIA

Measure Affects Resident and Non-Resident Earners, WPA, Relief Workers, Servants

BALANCED BUDGET IS AIM

Special to THE NEW YORK TIMES.

PHILADELPHIA, Dec. 13—In fifteen minutes today, the City Council, acting under a suspension of rules, passed an ordinance imposing a municipal tax of 1½ per cent on earned income and made it possible to give Philadelphia a balanced budget for 1940. Acting Mayor George Connell signed the ordinance immediately.

It is estimated that 1,000,000 persons are liable to payment of the tax, which affects non-residents earning their living here as well as residents and which, under strict application of the law's provisions, would be paid by WPA workers, relief workers under the Pierson act, servants, peddlers and any one else who earns money. Exempt, however, are incomes received from securities.

The final vote of the Councilmen, who had heard only mild protests against the ordinance, was 17 to 3. Acting Mayor Connell hailed it as the most equitable and the least harmful tax that might be imposed and predicted that it would mean "a quickening of business and industrial life" in this city through allowing balancing the budget and the building up of "Philadelphia's confidence in its own future."

Organized labor, however, was considering a three-way attack on the new law. It was preparing a legal test of pay-envelope deductions by employers, as provided in the act, wage increases to compensate for the tax payments and possibly a one-day tax protest "holiday."

Barring a decision holding the law unconstitutional, Philadelphia employers starting next month will be required to deduct 1½ per cent from the wages of their employes, whether or not they live in the city. Professional men and others who earn profits in unincorporated businesses must make a return on or before March 15 next and calculate the tax on the basis of their 1939 earned income.

Incorporated businesses are exempt from the tax but the liability of unincorporated firms, such as some stores which already pay a State mercantile license fee, was still to be worked out.

Also occupying an undetermined status were Philadelphia residents who receive their income from out-of-town sources and whose employers cannot be forced to deduct the tax from their envelopes.

The Council apparently completed its budget-making task by passing an ordinance retaining the present real estate tax rate of $1.70 per $100 of assessed valuation, which has been in effect since 1935. Including the realty tax for school purposes, set at $1.17½, the total real estate tax for next year will be $2.87½.

Slightly less than $17,000,000 was needed to balance the 1940 budget, according to estimates presented early this week. The income tax is expected to yield that and enable the Council to give its final approval to the budget on Friday, the legal deadline.

December 14, 1939

Home Rule of Municipalities Being Sold for Cash Is Charge

D. M. Wood, Finance Expert, Tells Security Traders Change Taking Place Bodes No Good for Our Form of Government

Home rule is little by little being sold by the municipalities for cash just as centuries ago they bought it from the kings of England for cash, David M. Wood, municipal finance expert and senior partner in Thomson, Wood & Hoffman, attorneys, declared yesterday at the annual convention of the National Security Traders Association in New Orleans. Mr. Wood addressed the convention's municipal forum on the subject "American Municipalities in Transition."

"A subtle change is now taking place in our municipalities," Mr. Wood said, "which, in my opinion, bodes no good for the democratic form of government. The sturdy, almost belligerent, assertion of home rule, which reached its peak in the early Nineteen Hundreds, has been replaced by plaintive pleas for aid from the State or from the Federal Government."

This dependency of local governments upon the State and Federal Governments has resulted in the incorporation of local political organizations as subordinate branches of the State or national party in power, according to Mr. Wood, and the municipalities are being subjected to remote control.

Discussing the financial problems of the municipalities in respect to the increasing social service functions demanded of them, Mr. Wood said that the municipalities, to avoid constitutional debt limits, have created separate districts such as school districts, sanitary districts and street improvement districts, for the financing of which bonds are floated. In addition, he discussed the "revenue bond," another device for evading constitutional debt limitation. These evasions, Mr. Wood conceded, have been the results of necessity, but because of them the inhabitants of our municipalities are paying through the nose.

"I believe that an intelligent reexamination of the constitutional and statutory limitations imposed upon our municipalities, in the light of modern conditions, would result in drastic changes in these limitations which would avoid the necessity of resorting to all of the expensive subterfuges now resorted to in order to permit the financing of enterprises which the public demands," Mr. Wood concluded.

September 24, 1941

MANY CITIES STUDY PAY-AS-YOU-GO IDEA

Hope to Become Debt-Free by Programs Being Developed to Go on a Cash Basis

A SOLUTION IS DIFFICULT

Creation of Public Interest in Well-Run Services Termed Essential to Success

By WILL LISSNER

A pay-as-you-go movement, aimed at wiping out the municipal debt eventually, is developing in various American cities. Among the cities in which plans for achieving a cash basis for undertaking public works have become a prime political issue are Milwaukee, Kalamazoo, Buffalo, Syracuse and Rochester.

Freedom from debt among villages and smaller municipalities is not new, although in most cases it is achieved by inequity in taxation, as by levying a hidden tax on utility consumers to achieve profits in publicly owned public utilities which cover the costs of other municipal services. For the larger municipalities the idea is an innovation.

The high level of individual incomes during the war, and its boom in urban real estate values, the basis of municipal revenues, eased the financial positions of many cities and enabled many others to reduce their indebtedness. As a result, the total of municipal debt has declined substantially. Out of this situation the pay-as-you-go movement has arisen.

The saving of debt service charges to the tax-paying real estate owner is being stressed. In Buffalo, where the Common Council approved the plan and authorized setting up of a committee to work out a practicable program, it is estimated that by adopting the principle of a cash basis for public improvements the tax rate could be reduced $6.56 a $1,000 of assessed valuation in the course of twenty-five years. This city reduced its indebtedness from $120,000,000 in 1935-36 to $86,000,000 in 1944. In Syracuse it is emphasized that debt-service charges account for $10.99 of the tax rate of $29.68 a $1,000 of assessed valuation. Its municipal debt of $18,688,001 is half what it was in 1938, when the high point was reached.

Show Skeptical Interest

Dr. Mabel L. Walker, executive director of the Tax Institute, 150 Nassau Street, who is gathering information about the movement, expressed the skeptical interest of students of public finance in the phenomenon by remarking: "We have been looking forward to being rid of poison ivy and mosquitos and if we are also to have debt-free cities it will indeed be a brave new world."

The movement clearly arises from the chaotic state of municipal financing in this country. The late Jens P. Jensen of the University of Kansas, one of this country's greatest experts on Government finance, declared after an exhaustive review of our fiscal practices that in any case where it must be decided to finance a public improvement by loan or by taxation, or forego it, the presumption should always be in favor of operating on a cash basis. This, however, was because he had found that when public bodies undertake a public improvement they do not usually give adequate weight to the burden of deferred tax payments that eventually must meet the cost, if it is not met from current revenues or reserves or if the debt is not pyramided.

Is No Financial Solution

If the policy of operating on a cash basis is the only alternative to running up a perennial, unmanageable and burdensome municipal debt, it well may prove to be a useful practical expedient for many cities. But it is no solution to the financial problems of American cities, and assumption that it is may delay long-overdue reform of the fiscal practices of local governments.

The need for recasting the general property tax, on which municipal financing depends, was pointed out in 1943 by the Treasury Department's Committee on Intergovernmental Fiscal Relations, headed by Harold M. Groves, Luther Gulick and Mabel Newcomer, but its recommendations evoked little response.

Reform of the municipal tax structure is only one part of the problem. The other part, and the most important today, consists of developing in the electorate an interest in obtaining economical and efficient operation of municipal services and in establishing popular, rather than political or bureaucratic, control over public expenditures and public investments in improvements.

Adoption of a pay-as-you-go policy in lieu of municipal fiscal reform amounts to the adoption of a lower standard of living as far as municipal services are concerned. For the interest paid on municipal debt is wasted only when unnecessary and unjustifiable improvements are undertaken, and then its loss is only a small item compared with the principal costs of the projects. The expense of credit represents the cost of obtaining benefits of the service of the projects at an earlier date than would be possible from current revenues. For the city to abjure credit because it has often misused it is a flight from, not an attack on, its fiscal problems.

August 12, 1945

8-CITY COST RISE OUTSTRIPS TAXES

Philadelphia Survey Finds 80% Expense Increase, 69% Revenue Gain

Special to The New York Times.

PHILADELPHIA, Dec. 23—Tax revenues in eight selected Eastern and Mid-Western cities increased an average of 69 per cent between 1945 and 1954, the Chamber of Commerce of Greater Philadelphia reported this week.

In the same period, operating expenses rose an average of 80 per cent in New York, Baltimore, Cincinnati, Cleveland, Detroit, Milwaukee, Philadelphia and Pittsburgh.

The chamber began a study a year ago to improve comparisons of expenditures, receipts and other financial data of large cities.

The report, based on that study, emphasizes the rising trend in operating costs of city governments and the rising expenditures in state governments, the chamber said.

Cincinnati Rise Sharpest

Of the eight cities, Cincinnati had the highest tax revenue increase in the ten-year period, 110 per cent. Pittsburgh reported the biggest increase in operating expenses, 112 per cent.

Tax revenue for Cincinnati advanced from $23.90 per capita in 1945 to $50.15 in 1954. Pittsburgh's operating expenses in 1945 were $24.62 per capita and $52.28 in 1954.

Detroit showed the smallest increase in both tax receipts and operating expenses, 13 per cent ($51.06 to $57.89 per capita) and 8 per cent ($63.34 to $68.25 per capita), respectively.

Tax revenue increases in the other cities showed Baltimore up 67 per cent in the ten years, Cleveland 68 per cent, Milwaukee 29 per cent, New York 97 per cent, Philadelphia 77 per cent and Pittsburgh 107 per cent.

Baltimore showed a 109 per cent increase in operating gains, Cincinnati 111 per cent, Cleveland 98 per cent, Milwaukee 63 per cent, New York 91 per cent and Philadelphia 90 per cent.

Regarding per capita expenditures in cities, including a proportionate share of state funds, New York in 1954 had the highest outlay, an estimated $251.96, with Pittsburgh the lowest at $201.76.

Other per capita expenditure figures in the report are: Baltimore, $221.52; Cincinnati, $244.43; Cleveland, $203.94; Detroit, $241.06; Milwaukee, $247.67 and Philadelphia, $223.34. The average for the eight cities was $229.47.

Average Debt Up

The report showed that during the ten years the average per capita debt for the eight cities increased an average of 54 per cent while state fiscal aid to local governments in the six states in which the cities are located went up 136 per cent.

Six states, Maryland, Michigan, New York, Ohio, Pennsylvania and Wisconsin, also reported that tax revenues had averaged a 105 per cent increase and operating expenses, excluding fiscal aid to local governments, had advanced 190 per cent.

The report was based on statistics of the United States Bureau of the Census and a compendium of city finances gathered by William A. Schellenberg, manager of the chamber's Tax Revision Division and former Director of the Budget of Philadelphia.

Mr. Schellenberg conferred with John M. Leavens, executive director of the Citizens Budget Commission, Inc., of New York, and officials of the Commerce and Industry Association of New York. Both organizations had sent representatives to take part in the study.

Officials of the Chamber of Commerce and other civic agencies from the eight cities and executives from other cities, will meet here on Jan. 19 under the chamber sponsorship to discuss the study.

December 24, 1955

U. S. CITIES SHOW 100% PAYROLL RISE

Census Bureau Puts Costs at $450,000,000, Jump of $244,200,000 in Decade

330,000 INCREASE IN JOBS

Employes Total 1,485,000—Ratio Expands With Size and Scope of Services

Special to The New York Times.

WASHINGTON, Feb. 10 — City payrolls have more than doubled and the number of city employes has increased by more than one-fourth in the last ten years, the Census Bureau reported today.

In the 16,778 cities, towns and villages of the United States that are administered by municipal governments, the report showed, payrolls for October, 1956, aggregated $450,000,000, compared with $205,800,000 ten years earlier.

The municipal governments had 1,485,000 paid employes in October, 1956, or 49,000 more than a year earlier and 330,000 more than ten years earlier.

The most marked employment and payroll increases were in cities with populations of 10,000 to 25,000, according to the report.

In the suburban and commuter towns of metropolitan areas there has been tremendous growth since the end of World War II and additional employes have been needed to furnish the increasing municipal services.

Size of City is Cost Factor

The report showed that large cities had more employes in relation to population than did the others and, in general, had higher pay rates.

The greater relative number of employes in the large cities was ascribed chiefly to more intensive staffing for several important municipal functions, such as police and fire protection.

The large cities also provide some services, such as education, hospitals and public utilities, that in smaller cities are often provided by separate units of government, such as counties or independent school districts, or by private companies.

The figures for October, 1956, showed that of those on municipal payrolls 1,256,000, or 85 per cent, were full-time employes and 229,000 were on a part-time basis.

The part-time employes included paid volunteer firemen and elected officials of small cities.

The report put the average monthly pay of full-time employes of city governments at $349 in October, 1956, compared with $331 in October, 1955, and $295 in October, 1952.

Range of Municipal Pay

In the latest forty-eight months covered by the report the average compensation of city employes rose about 19 per cent, which was in keeping with the trend from January, 1940, the earliest date in the Census Bureau surveys of government employment.

Pay in October, 1956, ranged from $250 for city hospital employes to $409 for municipal transit employes and $444 for city school personnel.

A factor in the school figure is a wide practice of adjusting salaries to the school year, rather than the twelve-month year.

The low average cash pay for hospital work reflects as a common practice supplementation of cash by provision of quarters and meals and other extras not included in payroll data covered by the report.

New York City had 241,644 employes on Oct. 15, 1956, and recorded a major share of all municipal transit employment and payrolls.

Its payroll in October was $97,619,500, more than 20 per cent of the country's aggregate of municipal payrolls.

February 11, 1957

17 U.S. CITIES CITE OWN FISCAL WOES

Survey Reports Budgetary Dilemma Across Nation —Fund Sources Lost

By PAUL CROWELL

The Citizens Budget Commission had a consoling word for Mayor Wagner's administration yesterday. It said the city's fiscal troubles were about the same as those confronting seventeen other municipalities in the nation.

The commission's findings, which were based on answers to questionnaires that were sent to Mayors and city managers, were brief and pointed. The commission found that most of the seventeen officials queried attributed their fiscal plight to Federal and state appropriation or control of revenue sources.

The commission also found that cities that were cores of metropolitan areas were being squeezed between growing populations, including daily commuters, and too few sources of additional revenue.

'Limitations' Are Noted

Harold Riegelman, counsel for the commission, said that the survey showed the principal causes of municipal troubles in raising revenue for operating expenses were "characteristic limitations imposed by the states" on city revenue sources.

"Mayors and city managers of cities other than New York," he said, "wherever they are sorely pressed by revenue problems, almost invariably point to the fact that state and Federal Governments have preempted the best of potential municipal revenue sources."

Mr. Riegelman said the officials had agreed almost unanimously that suburban areas and cities would continue to suffer from business and residential downgrading unless they did some cooperative planning.

Domination Deplored

The commission's study found officials in the cities that were surveyed complaining that Legislatures were dominated by members from rural areas.

The cities covered were Rochester, N. Y.; Baltimore; Seattle, Wash.; Kansas City, Mo.; Chicago; Fort Worth, Tex.; Cincinnati; Denver; Boston; Indianapolis; Norfolk, Va.; Worcester, Mass.; New Orleans; St. Louis; Columbus, Ohio; Long Beach, Calif., and Milwaukee.

The commission declared that the growing acuteness of city-state fiscal conflicts called for "challenge and change." It urged that the coordination of local governmental activities in metropolitan areas be expedited. It also recommended that vigorous steps be taken to install sound standards for measuring services in terms of dollars spent in city governments.

Spokesmen for the commission are expected to refer to survey findings at public hearings next month on the proposed 1959-60 expense budget, which the Mayor will submit to the Board of Estimate Wednesday.

The Mayor's proposed austerity budget was subjected again yesterday to criticism by organizations of city employes.

The American Federation of State, County and Municipal Employes, which has scheduled a one-day work stoppage tomorrow, declared that only caretaker staffs would remain at city zoos, museums and other cultural facilities. Jerry Wurf, regional director of the union, asked parents not to take their children to those places during the work stoppage.

A plea for united action by organizations of school teachers in their fight for pay rises was made by Rose Russell, legislative representative of the Teachers Union.

In letters to the Teachers Guild and the High School Teachers Association, she asked that all teacher organizations end their squabbling and wage a united campaign against proposed cuts in "promised" pay rises.

March 30, 1959

PARADOX IS SEEN IN PROPERTY TAX

The property tax system in the United States has been found by a research study to contain a "great paradox"—it discourages the improvement of land in blighted areas, where improvement is needed most.

The study was made by the Urban Land Institute, which reports that, in rundown areas of most cities, when a property owner makes a major improvement in an old building, the assessment for tax purposes frequently is increased. As a result, a premium is put on neglect, and investment in property is discouraged.

The study was developed in a series of conferences sponsored by the institute, an independent research organization specializing in land use, planning and development.

Federal Tax Influence

The conferences examined the impact of taxation on urban development, on the maintenance of existing properties and on the upgrading of deteriorated areas. The conclusions appear in a research monograph, "Changing Urban Land Uses as Affected by Taxation," edited by Dr. Jerome P. Pickard, the institute's research director.

Boston is cited as having the highest property tax level of any major American city. The monograph notes that, to attract new commercial and industrial construction, Boston has been forced to make special tax arrangements.

Observing that Boston's downtown area has had "unusual stagnation" in building, the monograph points out that, lacking the increased revenue afforded by new buildings, present tax rates are under continuing pressure to increase.

Overassessment of commercial and industrial property within Boston's city limits was found to be widespread, while residential property is underassessed. However, in Boston's suburbs, the reverse situation prevails.

In most of the nation's cities, land uses—the type of improvement and the density of construction on any given site—are determined by investment return, Federal taxes and local property taxes. "Tax angles," usually concerning Federal levies, are often the determining factor in deciding whether or not a specific project should be undertaken and by what kind of investor.

Opinion ranged widely regarding the desirability of coordinating and using taxes to attain planning objectives, according to Dr. Pickard.

The country's best "tax havens," according to the study either are communities of above-average wealth or ones that have recently become industrialized. As a rule they are characterized by stable population and good management of civic affairs.

Communities in the worst tax position, on the other hand, were found to contain densely settled, blighted sections or World War II emergency housing projects.

The study showed that property taxes in urban and metropolitan counties were highest in the Massachusetts-Connecticut-New York-New Jersey area, the upper Midwest extending from Wisconsin to Montana and south through Nebraska, and in Arizona and California. A large low-property-tax region extends from Pennsylvania through the entire South, with the exception of Texas.

April 21, 1963

CITY COSTS SCORED BY BUDGET GROUP

10-Year Summary Notes Surpluses Are Gone

By CHARLES G. BENNETT

New York City was pictured yesterday by the Citizens Budget Commission as a slovenly housekeeper who had begun to spend extravagantly and far beyond its means.

In a new 10-year "Pocket Summary of City Finances," issued annually, the budget commission, a nonpartisan watchdog civic group, found that surpluses of a decade ago had "completely disappeared" and that "even worse, the 1965-66 expense budget ($3.8 billion) is not actually in balance."

"A total of $256 million in borrowing officially admitted as being in the budget, and $56 million in general fund revenues for 1965-66 are actually nonexistent—they have already been spent to balance the budget last year," John M. Leavens, executive director of the commission declared.

Budget is $3.8 Billion

The city was permitted by state legislation to borrow about $256 million in the fiscal year beginning last July 1 for some of the payments to be made to city pension funds. Also, with state permission, the city issued $56.6 million in revenue anticipation notes to be redeemed by collections of taxes after the close of the 1964-65 fiscal year.

Mr. Leavens noted that in the last 10 years, with the budget mounting from $1.7 billion to $3.8 billion, the per capita cost of the budget had increased from $221 to $494.

Similarly, the per capita net debt has increased by more than one-half, from $337 to $500. The city's gross funded debt has soared in the decade from $3.5 billion to $4.7 billion, resulting in an increase in debt service—the amount set aside to amortize and pay interest on the city budget—from $288 million to a current $545 million.

Reflecting in effect obligations incurred to pay for improvements of years gone by, debt service now accounts for about 14 per cent of the city budget.

Ten years ago, $303 million was enough to operate the city's schools. Now $752 million, or 19 per cent of the city budget, are allocated to this purpose. Welfare, up from $201 million to $494 million in the decade, accounts for 13 per cent of the budget.

Mr. Leavens stressed that tax-exempt property — including property belonging to various governmental units and religious and charitable organizations—had jumped from $7.9 billion in 1955-56 to $15.2 billion currently. In this time the assessed valuation of all taxable real estate went up from $21.1 billion to $30.9 billion.

The basic real estate tax rate was found to have climbed from $3.85 for each $100 of assessed valuation 10 years ago to $4.56 in the present fiscal year. Each cent in the 1965-66 tax rate, Mr. Leavens noted, accounts for $3.1 million in tax revenue.

The real estate tax, which according to the budget commission survey brought in $808 million in 1955-56, will account for $1.4 billion in the current budget.

General fund revenues—excise taxes, water rentals and fees—rose from $559 million in the decade to $1.1 billion, the budget group found, while supplemental revenues — largely Federal and state aid and parking meter receipts — went up from $389 million to $1.3 billion.

Despite this apparent affluence, New York City has fallen behind in its bill-paying, Mr. Leavens said, with the result that the expense budget item for borrowing — completely lacking from previous budgets—has appeared in 1965-66 for the first time.

"Transit operations," Mr. Leavens declared, "which showed a $5 million surplus 10 years ago, are expected to result in a $62 million deficit this year, even though the city now provides a $33 million annual operating subsidy which did not exist 10 years ago. And general fund surpluses of $28 million 10 years ago and $48 million five years ago have completely disappeared."

The Citizens Budget Commission will supply copies of the pocket summary without charge, as long as the supply lasts, to those applying by letter to the commission at 51 East 42d Street.

September 8, 1965

The Changing City: A Financial Paradox

The following report was prepared by Richard Phalon and Michael Stern.

New York, says Budget Director Frederick O'R. Hayes, is a "city of two faces, a combination of affluence and municipal poverty."

On its affluent side, the city has never had it so good. The glass and steel of more than $1.5-billion worth of new office construction is being bolted into place; retail sales are pounding along at the rate of more than $12.7-billion a year; Wall Street is all capital gains; more than 70,000 jobs have been added to the work force in the last year alone; unemployment is at an all-time low.

Yet there is evidence of municipal poverty in the explosive growth of the welfare rolls—chilling evidence because their growth reflects society's failure to nurse more than a million blighted lives into the mainstream of its economy; chilling because their growth has compounded the city's chronic budget problems and forced it to reallocate money that might otherwise have gone into cleaner streets, cleaner air, better schools and better hospitals.

The streets will continue to be littered and the air contaminated despite the fact that the city's operating budget will reach $6.6-billion next year—more money than is spent by either the state of California or the state of New York; more money than any Federal budget before Franklin D. Roosevelt's first term.

"Municipal poverty" and a $6.6-billion budget? How can the two be squared?

"In the paradox of this city's wealth and its municipal finances, nothing is mutually exclusive," Mr. Hayes says "We're going broke on $6.6-billion a year."

Moreover, to a large extent the city is molded by a myriad of forces beyond its control—the birth rate, the uncertainties of the Vietnam war, technological developments that simultaneously improve and retard the urban environment, and even out-of-state elections that send to Congress men unattuned to or unsympathetic with the urban crisis.

Added to this is a welfare and antipoverty effort that has proliferated from 10.8 per cent of the budget in 1963 to 26.6 per cent now and the following factors:

¶The growing union militancy of the city's 354,600 employes who have come away from the bargaining table with sizable gains and pushed labor costs to 60 per cent of the budget.

¶The ambitious spectrum of services the city provides—a tuition-free university and a hospital system, for instance—that elsewhere are either paid for entirely by state government or privately run.

¶A "balance of payments" problem that is widening because of the growing number of high-salary commuters who make their money here but pay most of their taxes in the suburbs.

¶The $16.2-billion worth of property here—36 per cent of total valuations—that is exempt from the real-estate tax because it serves religious, educational, charitable or government purposes.

¶A comparatively inelastic tax structure that leaves the city vulnerable to inflation and a complicated tangle of relationships with the state and Federal governments that makes it difficult for the city to retain a larger share of the enormous wealth it generates.

The New York Times (by Don Hogan Charles)

A family can have a good life in New York—it's an affluent place, where retail sales exceed $12.7-billion. There's money to spend, and much to do.

The New York Times (by Edward Hausner)

But people have to put up with litter and other inconveniences because the city, suffering from "municipal poverty," cannot afford adequate services

Taxes Up, Service Down

What all this means for, say, the average householder in Queens is that he must pay higher taxes, but must wait longer to have the pothole in his street repaired, continue to suffer a street-cleaning operation that one city official concedes to be "worse than five years ago," have his children attend improperly maintained schools and see the parks in his neighborhood continue to deteriorate.

The city bears roughly only 30 per cent of all welfare payments (the Federal and state governments absorb the rest), but its tax revenues simply have not grown fast enough to meet the needs of the poor and at the same time keep pace with its other, more traditional services.

The pressures have forced a significant shift in the city's spending mix.

A comparison of the average shares going to vital services in the period of 1963 through fiscal 1966 and in fiscal 1967 through next year's projection shows the following: public schools dropped from 26 per cent of the budget to 21.91; police work from 9.53 per cent to 8.3; firefighting from 4.95 per cent to 3.86; sanitation from 3.54 per cent to 2.87; hospitals from 7 per cent to 6.56.

Deficits Not New

The city has always had a difficult time making municipal ends meet. From 1962 to 1966, for example, it ran deficits that ranged from $45-million to $300-million, deficits that were covered by dipping into reserves, by borrowing against future budgets and by the sale of long-term notes that are still being paid off at the rate of more than $50-million a year.

Not since the days of the Depression, however, has the treasury's plight been so apparent as in the budget for the next fiscal year, which the Mayor presented to the Board of Estimate and the City Council last April 15.

The way the Mayor saw things, the budget—though $597-million more than the $6-billion the city expects to spend this year—fell $668-million short of what it would take just to hold municipal services at the current level, let alone improve them.

Who Pays the Bill?

City budgets are of necessity a blend of economics and politics. Mayors must take into account the fact that much of the city's money comes from the State Legislature.

"The scenario," says Mr. Hayes, "is pretty much dictated by a situation where the city, for more than a deccade, has not been able to see how it was going to finance its next budget without

having some additional revenue from Albany."

Albany did provide more money — state aid will amount to 24.9 per cent of next year's budget compared with 24.7 per cent this year—but unlike the emergency infusions of the past, not enough more money to compensate for the increased cost of running the city.

The result was a squeeze. Threatened service cuts in hospitals, the schools, museums and libraries touched off a wave of demonstrations and sit-ins that set the city looking for more money.

Then the Mayor, employing a tactic used by other Mayors in other years, discovered $79.7-million by reestimating the amount of revenue the city expected to receive next year.

This was enough to stave off the threatened cutback in library and museum schedules and to ease some of the pinch on the hospitals, but it brought a charge from Democratic Councilmen that the Mayor had "needlessly precipitated months of artificial crisis" at a time when threatened cuts in services exacerbated racial tensions.

The juggling of budget accounts has become known over the years in the Budget Bureau as "flimflam." Enough of this has been reported in the current budget—shifting some expenses to the capital budget, for instance, where they could be paid for by borrowing rather than from current income—to suggest to some officials that the city does not have much more room for maneuver.

The chronic problem is where to find more money—a problem that plagues almost every major municipality and an endless succession of mayors everywhere.

As with almost everything else, however, New York has more disequilibrium than almost anywhere else.

Some of that disparity is due not only to the rising costs of welfare, but also to the way welfare costs are financed. In general, New York State provides more over-all local aid than most neighboring states. But in Pennsylvania, for instance, the state shares the entire cost of welfare with the Federal government, leaving Philadelphia to raise nothing through direct local taxes for that purpose.

In New York, on the other hand, the city and the state split the welfare balance about 50-50 after Federal contributions, which means **that the city next year will have to raise a minimum of $300-million on its own for welfare.**

Welfare, of course, is not the only reason why the expense side of the revenue-cost equation has tied the city's finances in knots. New York is a high-cost town. Since 1966 a fireman first grade's salary has risen 29 per cent.

Police pay has matched this rise, and this fall, a first grade patrolman with 20 years experience will be making $11,350 a year, compared with a maximum of $10,974 in Los Angeles.

The arithmetic of generally higher pay scales bites deep because the city, in effect, is a gigantic service organization. A succession of expensive wage settlements has pushed labor costs from 57 per cent to 60 per cent of the budget. The rise in pay and pension costs next year will be $400-million.

Some of those labor costs—in health services, education and welfare — are absorbed by the Federal Government and the state. Their contributions have been expanding — from a combined 24.8 per cent of the budget in 1963 to 40.8 per cent of next year's proposed spending.

"One cannot gainsay the expansion of state aid, nor discount increased Federal aid," says Mayor Lindsay, "but it has not been enough."

It has not been enough because much of the increase has simply paralleled the rise of the welfare rolls and left the city to deal relatively unaided with the demons of inflation generally, and the departments in which the bulk of the big pay raises have come—police, fire and sanitation.

Inelastic Tax Methods

The structure of the city's revenue base has proved unequal to the task. Though New Yorkers are among the most highly taxed people in the nation, the major levies on which the city has traditionally relied (sales and real estate taxes) are comparatively inelastic. They tend to expand no faster than the economy as a whole.

The city income tax, wrung out of the Legislature in 1966, offers more growth potential, but it is no panacea.

Since 1963 the city's needs—as expressed by the budget — have increased 136.5 per cent. Real estate tax yields, however, have risen only 72.7 per cent and the proceeds from all other levies (sales taxes, corporation taxes and the like) have risen only 118 per cent.

The way those yields have lagged helps to explain why New York runs a chronic budget gap — why projected spending always exceeds what the city can expect to take in.

Albany has been having budget problems, too. The Legislature resolved them in the last session by increasing the sales tax one cent on the dollar and by cutting back on welfare payment formulas.

The change in the New York payment formulas, which are regulated by the state, means that three-fourths of the one million people on welfare will be getting less money—in the case of a family of four, as much as $568 a year less.

The cut was not without some popularity in a city where 25 cents of every dollar in the budget goes to the Human Resources Administration. As the welfare rolls have grown so has taxpayer resistance to the higher costs.

But the roots of the welfare problem are not in Albany, or even in the city. Many students of the problem say they lie in Washington and in a national agricultural policy that has promoted and subsidized the grim march of mechanization over the South's cotton fields and tobacco lands.

In the last generation more than 3.5-million Negroes, driven off the farms by the enormous productivity of the tractor and the new agricultural economics, have packed up and headed north to the cities, including New York—traditionally regarded as a city of opportunity.

Federal Action May Help

One reason that at least some came to New York was that welfare payments here average $71 a month for dependent children compared to the national average of $41. Further, unlike 40 other states, New York had no minimum residency requirement for persons seeking welfare.

Two things may help to ease this situation, but since so many of the poor already have moved here they may be too late to have major impact. First, the Supreme Court recently struck down the residency requirements in the other states. Second, the Nixon Administration is considering establishing national standards for welfare.

Many of those who came here were poor, often illiterate and rarely trained in skills that can fetch more than a minimum wage in the cities. Combined with a similar migratory stream from Puerto Rico, they have pushed the welfare rolls up to a point where one of every eight New York City residents now relies upon government for his food, shelter and other necessities.

At the same time, the white middle class has been leaving the city for the suburbs in search of better schools, lower taxes, lower living costs, lower racial tensions.

The result has been a dramatic shift in the population. Between 1950 and 1965 according to the Bureau of Labor Statistics, more than 1.5 million comparatively high-income whites have moved out; more than 1.25 million Negroes and Puerto Ricans have moved in.

The shift has put the city's budget in double jeopardy. **The influx of the poor and the compounded miseries of slum life has meant higher** costs not only for welfare, but also for health services, remedial education, and expanded fire and police protection.

Further, the poorer people do not pay as much in taxes as the high-income people they replaced. Many of the expatriates take a high share of the new white-collar jobs being produced by the city's expanding economy but the **bulk of their local tax bill goes to support government in New Jersey, Long Island and Westchester instead of New York City.**

More Are Accepted

A recent Columbia University study suggests that a distinct change in city policy has also added to welfare costs. In 1965, the last year of the Wagner administration the city accepted only 58 out of every 100 applications made for aid to dependent children. By the middle of 1967, the second year of the Lindsay administration, the figure had climbed to 75 out of every 100.

However, in a recent interview, Mayor Lindsay said:

"It is not right to say that the city encouraged people to go on welfare. Community-action groups did that. They dug out the most severe poverty of all the persons who were festering in sickness and brought the whole stuff up to the surface. The fact that it came up from underneath the mud and could be seen in all of its ugliness may have been an important thing."

Further, he added that since welfare standards are set by the state the city has no right to stand between a poor citizen and his rights to welfare.

Jack R. Goldberg, the city's Social Services Commissioner, while denying that lax procedures have encouraged people to sign up for welfare, adds, "It is not my job to keep people off the rolls who are legally entitled to it."

Some upstate cities have traditionally taken a hard

line with applicants.

"You just ask them a lot of questions about how they managed to get along before and make them come back with proof of their claims," says Joseph H. Louchheim, a deputy commissioner for the State Department of Social Services.

Mr. Louchheim, who served as a deputy welfare commissioner here under Mayor Robert F. Wagner, contends "the city definitely is not discouraging people the way it once did."

One of the most discouraging facets of the welfare problem here is that the rolls have been rising during a period of economic expansion and rising employment.

Why haven't more of the poor been able to find jobs? How many ineligible are there on the welfare rolls?

Both of those questions are being examined in a major study initiated by the Federal Government's Department of Health, Education and Welfare, which has become alarmed by the year-by-year rise in the Federal public assistance contributions required by the poverty cities.

The cities contend that putting more welfare recipients to work is virtually impossible because of the kind of people who are on the rolls.

In New York, a Department of Social Services report says that 59 per cent are children too young to work, 19.1 per cent are mothers kept from work because they must look after those children, 5.6 per cent are too old to work, 8.6 per cent are disabled, 2.7 per cent have jobs, but earn too little to support themselves, and 4.5 per cent are unable to work because of alcoholism, narcotics addiction, emotional instability or other problems.

The high proportion of women and children without husbands and fathers—over 78 per cent of those receiving public help — reflects, not only increasing illegitimacy, but also the high cost of living, comparatively low wage scales and a law that some people say encourages the disintegration of families by providing Federal help to broken families rather than to whole ones.

According to Herbert Bienstock, regional director for the Bureau of Labor Statistics, 48 per cent of all jobs here paid $100 a week or less in 1966—the most recent year for which figures are available—and one-third paid $80 or less. Discrimination, including that in some unions, bars Negroes from many higher paying jobs.

Low-reward jobs that are open to unskilled workers often are the only ones available to black and Puerto Rican fathers in the city's poorest neighborhoods.

Such a father, say a man with a wife and three children filling one of these jobs at the minimum legal wage of $3,328 a year, obviously and desperately can use more money in this city of high-living costs.

One way he can get an immediate "raise" of $3,700 a year is to move away from his family and thus make them eligible for full welfare assistance.

For such a man, Mr. Bienstock notes, "welfare becomes competitive with work" and his choice is to try to get along on an impossibly low wage or to surrender his dependents to a welfare system that can give them more money than he can.

"Because these people are poor, we cannot assume that they are any less intelligent than we are," Mr. Bienstock said. "They can see where their economic advantage lies."

The city has tried to help families achieve self-sufficiency. Last year, it placed 40,000 persons in jobs, and 25 antipoverty agencies offered a variety of services to help people find their way out of poverty.

However, many of those helped came not from the one million on the welfare rolls but from another million who are counted as poverty stricken because, even though they are working, they earn less than the official poverty standard of $3,700 a year for a family of four.

No one pretends that $3,700 a year for a family of four is adequate in a high-cost city like New York. A Department of Labor study issued in March showed that the minimal income for a four-person family here should be $6,021.

How, then, do so many people get by on so little? The answers to that question lie in underground facts that no city officials will acknowledge for the record. Privately, some say it is probably true that much of the domestic and casual labor of the city is done by people on welfare who do not get caught because their employers agree not to report their earnings to the government.

They also say that many of the illicit activities that plague the slums—prostitution, thefts, narcotics peddling, numbers running—have their motivation in the compelling need to supplement inadequate income. The social costs of such activities, and the direct costs to government in trying to control them, are incalculable.

Mayor Lindsay summed it all up recently when he said that "welfare is resented by those who receive it," derided "by those who administer it" and hated "by those who pay for it."

There is some hope that the rise in the welfare rolls is beginning to taper off. The evidence so far is meager, but mildly encouraging. The rate of increase dropped from a monthly average of 21,164 individuals in the third quarter of last year to 14,220 in the fourth quarter to 8,663 in the first quarter of this year.

At the moment, city officials do not understand the reasons for the decline. Some think the great in-migrations have finally begun to run out of steam. Others think that the flood tide of the economy has finally begun to trickle down to some of the bedrock poor.

If all those believed eligible apply for help the city will have no alternative but to squeeze still more money out of other operating departments, according to Mr. Hayes, because the city is not likely to get any more major taxing power out of the Legislature.

It would like very much, for instance, to have the income levy on commuters raised to a par with the income tax on city residents. The possibility of Albany's going along with such a move is considered remote because the commuters are represented by a powerful bloc in the Legislature.

Similar opposition from suburban and upstate legislators has blocked city proposals for a higher liquor tax, for off-track betting and for basing a part of state aid to cities on the amount of money the cities raise themselves.

As a "creature of the state," the city gets its taxing powers only from the Legislature. And as a panel of experts noted in a recent issue of Nation's Cities, a publication for municipal planners, the states "have seen fit to limit the cities' taxing powers, partly because the states do not want the cities dipping deep into the same tax sources the states depend on for their own support; partly because some state legislators still do not trust their cities, and partly because state legislators do not always understand their cities' problems."

Even if the city had unlimited taxing power of its own, it could not use it freely. High taxes are one of the reasons why a number of manufacturers have left the city, taking with them in the last 19 years almost 200,000 blue collar jobs—jobs that might have helped to take some of the pressure off the welfare rolls.

High taxes are also one of the reasons why so many comparatively high - salaried former New Yorkers now call the suburbs home—an economic exodus the city cannot afford to accelerate.

Yet if the city cannot tap new revenue sources it faces what Mr. Hayes calls a "decay in the quality of urban life."

"If we're going to maintain the kind of life we want to have," he says, "it is going to take a lot of money."

Where is the money to come from? Washington, the way the city sees things. It calls for the Federal Government to take over all welfare costs and an extended system of revenue sharing in which Washington would automatically make sizable outright grants to the cities every year.

The premise is pegged to the enormous elasticity of the Federal income tax, which, because of its progressive rate structure, yields a 15 per cent increase in revenues for every 10 per cent increase in the total output of the nation's goods and services.

Federal spending, on the other hand—heavy military demands such as Vietnam aside—tends to rise at a slower rate than national output. The result, many economists argue, is a "fiscal dividend" that could mean salvation for the cities.

The Federal deficits of the last several years, however, have left the implementation of revenue sharing as remote as when the concept was voiced in 1964 by Walter W. Heller, then chairman of the Council of Economic Advisers. An end to the war in Vietnam might get the concept back on the rails, but critics of the industrial-military complex have their doubts.

The Nixon Administration does have some welfare reforms in the works that could take some of the load off the city, but it is too soon to tell how much. For the short term at least, the city will continue in the squeeze Mr. Micawber described a long time ago:

"Annual income twenty pounds, annual expenditure nineteen, six: result, happiness.

"Annual income twenty pounds, annual expenditure twenty pounds, six: result, misery."

June 1, 1969

CITIES CUT BACK JOBS AND SERVICES IN FINANCIAL PINCH

Action Is Forced by Inflation and Declining Tax Base—Many Confront Crisis

By PAUL DELANEY

Special to The New York Times

WASHINGTON, Nov. 26—The combined pressures of continued inflation and a declining tax base are forcing many of the nation's major cities to lay off workers, trim services and adopt other belt-tightening measures.

Reports from cities around the country this week showed that those city officials who had earlier complained of financial troubles are now warning that the situation may be reaching crisis proportions. And even in those cities where the picture is less bleak—such as Atlanta, Milwaukee and Houston — municipal leaders say they fear a change for the worse in the near future.

The financial problems of the cities were exemplified in New York last week when Mayor Lindsay laid off 500 employes to save the city $2-million a year. And the Mayor and 25 top officials agreed to take $1,000-a-year pay cuts as their personal response to the budget crisis.

Running Out of Fuel

Baltimore's Mayor, Thomas J. D'Alesandro 3d, likens the money supply for his city to fuel for Gen. George S. Patton's tanks:

"You run as far as you can, but when you run out of gas you've got to stop."

Boston's budget director, Richard E. Wall, said that next year "is going to be a bad year; our expenses are very great and rapidly increasing." And Richard Clark, budget director of Denver, commented:

"The basic situation is that over a period of at least 10 years our expenditures have increased at a rate of from 10 to 12 per cent, while revenues from the existing tax structure have increased about 3 or 4 per cent a year."

The National League of Cities reports that while local governments have raised their tax collections by 499 per cent since World War II, city costs have risen by almost 550 per cent.

The cities are caught in the crunch of increased operating costs, added to the exodus of higher income groups and industry, leaving the inner cities to lower income residents, which results in a lower tax base.

To meet the growing problems, city officials have taken a number of steps, as follows:

¶Cuts in city service, programs and budgets are becoming widespread. San Diego reduced downtown rubbish collections from twice weekly to once a week, the same as the residential schedule. Because of the defeat of a tax proposal, in the Nov. 3 election, trash collection and snow removal in Cleveland will be sharply cut this winter.

Dallas has shelved the planned construction of a $50-million city hall and cut expenditures for equipment for the fire and police departments, for street resurfacing, traffic control programs, land purchases and community health programs.

"The curtailed capital expansion program is at the expense of the future," George Schrader, the assistant city manager, remarked. "The curtailment of planning efforts in a community such as Dallas is a reduction of services."

No Money For Trees

In Kansas City, Mo., a monument to the city's money crisis is 6,000 dead elm trees. No funds were appropriated to replace them nor is there money to remove those killed by Dutch elm disease.

In Los Angeles, there is no money for several new station houses, scientific equipment, helicopters and a special department for police liaison with citizens.

¶Vacancies are not being filled. Mayor D'Alesandro of Baltimore ordered all city department heads to hold the line on planning, and to draw up an alternate set of figures 5 per cent below current spending. Denver will save $1.3-million by not filling vacancies this year. And several departments in Pittsburgh are operating far below strength. Kansas City is not filling police department vacancies.

¶Layoffs and dismissals are becoming common. In Cleveland, 89 police cadets were laid off. Mayor Peter F. Flaherty of Pittsburgh began an austerity drive by discharging 30 cleaning women and has dismissed a total of 350 since he took office last January. Another 300 city employes reportedly will be let go early next year.

Los Angeles has laid off 350 public works and water and power workers.

¶Almost all cities have increased taxes, but that is a step many politicians are reluctant to take, especially in an election year. Several elections will be held next year, and the money crisis is already a major political issue in many places.

In Seattle the City Council cut $1.5-million from Mayor Wes Uhlman's $88.8-million budget for the 1971 fiscal year. The Mayor branded the cut "a strange witches' brew of ineptitude and backroom politics," and the fight was on. The city, meanwhile, enacted increases in water and sewer rates. The theory is that if the council adopts the requested budget, there will be no cuts in city services.

Big Rise in Tax

In Los Angeles, Mayor Samuel W. Yorty complained that the tax on his home jumped from $1,408 in 1969 to $2,128 this year under a combined city-county rate schedule that rose this year to the highest level in history. Hartford's tax rate has nearly doubled since 1961, and the prospect is for further increases.

Kansas City's situation has been termed a near disaster. The voters rejected a 24-point revenue package last December that included a sales tax, a higher earnings tax and 17 bond propositions. A special election will be held Dec. 17 with only the earnings tax and a business profits tax on the ballot.

With the police department getting the biggest single share of the money, followed by the fire department, the drive to solicit support for the increased taxes has revolved around the "public safety" issue. However, the situation is complicated by the fact that a new city administration will be elected next March 30. Some citizens felt that the new administration should determine what kind of revenue package it wants and they recommended postponing the vote.

Slowdown by Firemen

The firemen have pressed demands for salary increases by engaging in a work slowdown. They are making only emergency repairs on their equipment and the fire alarm office will accept only emergency calls for resuscitators and actual fires.

Some cities' financial frustrations have been heightened by the loss of state and Federal aid because of declines in population. Some funds are granted on a per capita basis, and such cities as Cleveland, Baltimore, Chicago, New York, Los Angeles, Boston, San Francisco and Detroit will presumably lose some assistance. Some cities in Connecticut are considering asking the state General Assembly for massive fund increases.

Nevertheless, the National League of Cities has warned: "Central cities should not kid themselves that the state or Federal governments or the suburbs will come through with enough aid and relief to close the whole gap between local spending at the present rate of increase and local revenue from today's local tax practices."

"Once again the question is not whether, but how," the league says in its magazine, Nation's Cities. The question is not whether cities must do far more to help themselves financially, but how best the cities hold down their own local costs and step up their own local revenues."

"We were told by Mayor Flaherty to submit austerity budgets for 1971 and keep costs down," commented Joseph Cosetti, the city treasurer of Pittsburgh. "We are trying to apply new technology, new business machines and computers, but I think these just achieve better service without lowering costs.

"In February and March there were layoffs in every department. Lands and buildings[department] let out 30 cleaning women; the refuse department closed a city incinerator, resulting in 80 or 90 layoffs; cashiers, clerks, typists and appraisers have been laid off."

And, adding a political note similar to those that have kept a controversy going between Mayor Flaherty, who is politically independent, and other city officials, Mr. Cosetti said:

"We did that because in the past employment has been used by the Democratic organization. We asked 'Who do we need?' without regard to political consequences."

'Patchwork' Procedure

Mr. Clark, Denver's budget director, says the city gets by with a "patchwork" procedure that consists of "taking money from capital construction, increasing the rate of taxes or introducing new taxes. You can't continue to exist without doing something of this nature."

William G. Sage, auditor-controller of San Diego, said his city was in better condition than many others, but might be in real trouble next year.

"We have been about three years behind other states in reaching the crisis stage, but our reserves are just about used up and things are getting worse all along," Mr. Sage said. "We'll need new sources of revenue, or we'll have to cut back services."

Atlanta's finance director, Charles Davis, explained that state law required the city to plan its expenditures below the previous year's income. Thus, he said, Atlanta is in excellent shape."

In addition, the Federal Government contributes $50-million for urban renewal, the model cities program, the airport and other projects, as well as $50-million for pollution abatement. But Mr. Davis was concerned that if the Federal Government reduced its aid, the city would have to pay the tab.

Houston ended 1969 with a surplus of $14-million, and the healthy financial picture there is expected to continue because the tax bases have been broadened to include alcoholic beverages, tobacco products and building materials.

Credit for Houston's enviable financial situation is given to Mayor Louie Welch, who is regarded as an adept money manager.

November 27, 1970

Chicago and New York: Contrasts

By JOHN KIFNER

Special to The New York Times

CHICAGO, May 15—For 16 years, Richard J. Daley has run this city, and the marks of his tenure are everywhere: the big concrete expressways that speed commuter and commercial traffic in and out; O'Hare Airport, the world's busiest; city streets that are well swept and brilliantly lighted; the downtown building boom that is raising glistening commercial skyscrapers over the Loop's rackety el tracks; the luxury glass and steel high-rise apartments marching along the lakefront.

Because of such marks, the Mayor's legion of boosters, who have long smarted under Chicago's "second city" complex, have now been joined by some outsiders who are comparing this city to New York, with its fiscal crisis, strikes and threatened strikes, telephones that don't work, broken-down subways and general chaos.

Dick Daley's city works, they say, and John Lindsay's does not.

But the marks of Mayor Daley's tenure are there, too, in the towers of the ghetto housing projects that have become snipers' nests; the plywood-covered windows of a public school system that reading tests show to be one of the country's worst; an urban renewal program that has torn down three times as much housing as it has put up, and an infant mortality rate well above the national average.

The Mayor's boosters point out that Chicago's municipal bonds have a high AA rating by Standard & Poor's, while New York's are only BBB. But they do not mention that authorities say Chicago is perhaps the most racially segregated of the major cities and that whites are leaving it at a rate double that of New York.

Comparing New York and Chicago is difficult because the functions, the history, the traditions, the systems, the sizes and even the geography that have shaped the two cities are so different.

And while overburdened New York seems frequently on the edge of breakdown, the surface smoothness of Chicago may be deceptive. For while Mayor Daley has solidified traditional politics and tied it to the interests of the business community, there has been little benefit for the black community—nearly a third of the population—and his total control of the Democratic organization has come at the expense of the voice of individual citizens and community groups in what happens.

Chicago, unfettered by the geography that cramped New York's heart into a narrow, congested island, spread westward from Lake Michigan toward the flat prairies.

Today the cities cover about the same area—New York, 320 square miles; Chicago, 277—but there are 7,867,760 people in New York and 3,366,957 in Chicago.

More Light and Space

The differences show.

In most of Chicago, there are few buildings taller than three or four stories; there is more light, air and space. There are block after block of one- and two-family houses, and about half the city's families own their homes.

They show, too, in shorter lines for movies or restaurants, in telephones that produce an immediate dial tone and in the more relaxed air and slower pace of pedestrians who even wait for the "walk" signs on traffic lights.

To the eye of a New Yorker, the difference in population density shows most strikingly in streets that, even in ghetto neighborhoods, are cleaner than New York's. The efficiency of the street sweepers is one of the proud boasts among the municipal services, as is the system of bright lights in streets and alleys across the city that Mayor Daley initiated during his first term.

Commercial Center Still

Chicago began as a trading post and, while New York is a polyglot city of many functions, this has remained essentially a commercial center.

No longer a hog butcher, it is still Sandburg's "city of the big shoulders," and its diversified manufacturing, its transportation facilities, its central location and its trend toward corporate regionalization have put its economy on more stable footing.

Chicago's healthier business climate is reflected in figures from the Bureau of Labor Statistics that show a higher per capita income—$4,650 for the Chicago standard metropolitan statistical area in 1968 compared with New York's $4,439, and a lower rate of unemployment, 4 per cent, according to current figures, compared with New York's 4.7 per cent.

A Matter of Power

But, although the rates for Negroes are believed by statisticians to be grossly under-representative, there is a sharp difference in the ratio between black and white unemployment in the two cities. In New York, the rate for whites is 4.2 per cent; for Negroes and other races it is 5.4 per cent. In Chicago it is 3.5 per cent for whites and 5.3 per cent for Negroes and others.

Probably the most important difference between the two cities is political—the arrangement of power.

In New York, there is no power. Or, rather, the power is fragmented, scattered and diffused among often competing groups. There are the Mayor, the City Council, the upstate members of the Legislature, the Governor, the Board of Education, angry parents' groups, Democratic and Republican officials of varying stripes, municipal unions, civil servants, community organizations.

It's simply a case of frequently feuding baronies rather than a central seat of power.

Heading the government of New York City thus tends to be an exercise in juggling the demands of the competing groups.

It can be delicate. Observers agree that Mr. Lindsay's predecessor, Robert F. Wagner, was a successful juggler, although certain conditions were deteriorating beneath the surface. For example, transit workers' salaries remained low under Mr. Wagner, but then came Mr. Lindsay. Critics say it was his arrogance, coupled with rank and file pressure, that upset the juggling act and touched off Michael J. Quill's transit strike that inaugurated Mr.

Paul Conklin

Mayor Richard J. Daley

The New York Times/Gary Settle

Some of miles of two and three story, one and two family houses that stand behind Chicago's lakefront skyscrapers. Whites, many of whom have put their life savings into their houses, are being victimized by real estate agents.

Lindsay's first term.

Because of the city's dependence on the Legislature in many matters of fiscal aid, much of the power important to New York is held by two outsiders, Perry B. Duryea of Suffolk County and Earl W. Brydges of Niagara Falls, the leaders of the two houses of the Legislature. Within the city, too, there are clashes of power outside the formal political arena. This was shown in Mr. Lindsay's attempt to improve black schools through community control only to run into strife between the interests of the United Federation of Teachers and those of angry parents.

In Chicago, the lines of power are clearer, and most of them, sooner or later, end up in the hands of Richard J. Daley.

While Mr. Lindsay actually has more charter power—Chicago, on paper, has a "weak mayor, strong council" system—the reality is that there is simply no comparison between the "clout," a Chicago kind of word, wielded by the two men.

The base of Mayor Daley's power is his chairmanship of the Central Committee of the Cook County Democratic Organization, made up of the ward committeemen of the city's 50 wards and the 30 suburban township committeemen.

From his dual posts he controls about 34,000 city and county "temporary appointment" patronage jobs and the untold political favors that make the machine operate. And he controls the "slating" process, handpicking the candidates for city, county and statewide offices.

Of the 50 aldermanic seats, 37 are literally his, along with such crucial posts as State's Attorney, County Assessor, Clerk of the Circuit Court and the judgeships that are rewards to the faithful or resting places for the embarrassing. Then, through the slating process, he controls a large bloc of votes in the State Legislature, giving him important bargaining power even with a Republican Governor.

Further, at least when a Democrat is in the White House, his "kingmaker" reputation as head of the Illinois convention delegation and deliverer of the Cook County votes means special treatment.

Contrast that with a New York incumbent who cannot keep his own Republican party's nomination, who is at the mercy of the State Legislature, and who had urban renewal funds held up after he had criticized the policies of a Republican Administration.

Or, to make the contrast differently, if Mr. Lindsay had Mr. Daley's equivalent power, he would be able to name the city's Congressional delegation, most of the city's representatives in Albany, nearly all the local office holders and his party's candidate for Governor. And he would enjoy the cooperation and confidence of labor and business.

Some of the difference is attributable to the different political traditions of the two cities. While Mayor Daley inherited a long-standing powerful organization when he took over the old Kelly-Nash-Arvey machine, organization politics has steadily broken down in New York.

In New York, with its reform movement, its strong cultural community and its large Jewish population, there is a strong liberal caste to its decentralized politics, countered by small homeowners and ethnic groups in the outlying boroughs.

The Men Themselves

And, then, some of the difference is attributable to the two current Mayors themselves. Mayor Lindsay began his first term by insulting organized labor and few political critics have credited him with great political acumen since.

Mayor Daley, on the other hand, with his political organization, enjoys the loyalty of organized labor, which saluted him in the last campaign with a 10,000-person testimonial dinner at the new McCormick Place convention hall.

Mr. Daley grew up with many of the labor leaders; they serve on his prestigious boards and committees. And their membership enjoys the city's low unemployment rate, the overtime on construction projects rushed to provide ribbon cuttings skillfully timed just before elections, and the fact that the city pays its laborers construction rates, rather than the lower maintenance rates common to government.

A Business Alliance

But perhops the most remarkable and significant development during Mayor Daley's rule has been the alliance he has forged with the city's blue-blooded, traditionally Republican bankers, merchants and businessmen.

"I am not the candidate of State Street and LaSalle Street," the Mayor declared in his first race in 1955. But he immediately began efforts to revitalize the downtown area and direct the government to serve the interests of the financial community, which earned him a reputation as a builder.

By the end of his first term, the businessmen, most of them suburbanites, were lining up for a Nonpartisan Committe to Re-elect Mayor Daley, now a quadrennial tradition.

Donald M. Graham, chairman of the board of the Continental Illinois Bank and co-chairman of this year's Nonpartisan Committee, sat the other day in his spacious office, paneled in carved oak from an English manor house built in 1587, and spoke of his support for the Mayor.

"If a businessman went to [Martin] Kennelly [Mr.Daley's predecessor] for something he needed, like changing zoning to get a parking facility for his plant so he wouldn't have to move to the suburbs," he said, "well, he was a fine person individually, but he didn't deliver."

Among the things that have been delivered was an underassessment on the taxes of the city's five largest banks, which, for example, saved Mr. Graham's institution $1.8-million.

That disclosure a few weeks ago followed a major scandal last fall when it was discovered that Assessor P. J. (Parky) Cullerton had granted millions of dollars in tax breaks to real estate speculators and developers who were also big Democratic contributors.

In New York, major financial interests generally support Mayor Lindsay, but businessmen are not as concerned with daily political events as in Chicago. The boosterism that characterizes Chicago businessmen is absent in New York not only because of its immense size, but also because the most powerful businessmen have far-flung financial interests that carry their interest beyond New York.

In Chicago, urban renewal has helped make real estate speculation and development one of the city's most lucrative fields.

There is, for example, a big new Holiday Inn on Madison Street at the edge of the city's seamy skid row. It might seem an odd place to build a motel, but the area is to be renewed for a convention center. The contract for the renewal was granted without the customary delays to a company headed by two top executives of Holiday Inns of America and Charles R. Swibel, the chairman of the Chicago Housing Authority.

Mr. Swibel, who said he pledged only his credit, is receiving what amounts to a $1-million payment from the company.

There Are Other Chicagos

But, behind the expressways, the bustling Loop and the soaring buildings that are changing the skyline along the lakefront rim, there are other Chicagos

There is the Chicago of the white neighborhoods.

Although the pattern is breaking down somewhat, this has been traditionally a city of neighborhoods that were ethnic enclaves, close-knit, suspicious of strangers. Now there is resentment and fear, particularly in areas on the southwest side, that blacks will move in.

And the whites, many of whom have put their life savings into their small houses with the neat yards, are being victimized by real estate agents—"panic peddlers"—who are buying their houses at less than the assessed evaluation, then selling them to blacks at much higher prices.

The tensions are high. Last month, Mrs. Bernice Hight, a 39-year-old black woman, and her three teen-age daughters began to move into their new home on an all-white block on the southwest side. When they returned, they found part of the house in flames. There had been threats earlier. Afterward the police said they had found a gasoline can nearby.

The family moved into the damaged house anyway, but rocks and bullets have shattered some of the windows.

For such reasons as racial fear, poor schools and rising costs, white people are moving out of Chicago at a rate of 50,000 a year—505,000 in the last decade—a rate twice that of New York's.

The Negro Areas

And, then, there is the Chicago of the black neighborhoods.

These blacks' votes in the machine-dominated wards on the south and west sides are one of the mainstays of the Democratic party. The totals are slipping somewhat, but the votes are held in line by a kind of reverse patronage—by implied threats of being cut off from public housing or welfare (sometimes welfare checks are delivered, not by mail, but by the precinct captains), by smaller-scale patronage jobs, by precinct money poured in on election day.

Pierre de Vise, a DePaul University sociologist, has found that 77 per cent of Chicago's Negroes live in neighborhoods that are 90 per cent or more black, and only 2 per cent live in predominantly white neighborhoods. New York City's segregation is "considerably down the line" from that, he says, estimating that perhaps 55 to 60 per cent of that city's blacks are in such heavily black neighborhoods.

Aldermen Have Veto

The Chicago pattern is reinforced by the tradition of granting aldermen a veto over public housing in their wards. This has resulted in jamming giant, high-rise projects into ghetto areas, like the Robert Taylor Homes, whose grim buildings stretch like tombstones for nearly two miles along the Dan Ryan Expressway south of 35th Street.

Meanwhile, in other parts of the city, whole blocks leveled by urban renewal lie vacant, awaiting private speculators and high - income housing.

As the world knows, New York suffers from racial problems and tensions, too, exemplified by last week's rioting and looting in Brownsville, a devastated neighborhood that looks like the site of wartime bombing. And whites are fleeing many of their older neighborhoods, mainly from resentment and fear of the blacks.

But the city administration has directed much of its effort toward attempts to aid the poor. And Mayor Lindsay has gained a national reputation as an eloquent leader of the cause of the cities.

However, many critics contend that his performance has fallen short of his rhetoric in such matters as providing low-income housing or channeling money to reform the city's prison and court systems.

The Matter of Schools

As for public schools, Chicago's are predominantly terrible by all accounts; those in black neighborhoods are the worst. In 1968, some 85 per cent of the city's Negroes attended schools that were 95 per cent black, according to the Department of Health, Education and Welfare. In New York, the figure was 44 per cent attending 95 per cent black schools.

The average eighth-grader in Chicago is almost a year and a half behind in reading ability; in ghetto schools he is more than two years behind. In New York, the eighth-grader is just under a year behind in reading.

The difference in the proportion of white and black draftees rejected for mental reasons tells part of the story: In New York, two blacks are rejected for every white. In Chicago the figure is 5 to 1.

Chicago's otherwise healthy financial situation does not apply to the schools. State education superintendent Michael J. Bakalis told officials in Washington that Chicago schools might have to close down in the fall unless $58-million in Federal aid was forthcoming. New York's system is short $28-million in the current budget.

One of the major reasons for the Chicago government's fiscal stability and health—as reflected in its good bond ratings—is simply that the city does not spend for expensive services to the poor the way New York does.

One of eight Chicago citizens is on welfare (the New York ratio is one of seven), and they receive over $500-million a year in welfare, but most of it comes from Cook County. Only $14-million comes from the city. In New York, where the counties pay nothing to welfare, the city must contribute $700-million.

Objectors Unwelcome

The Cook County Democratic Central Committee, which runs the city all the way through to influencing judicial rulings in sensitive cases, does not suffer objections gladly.

When a priest declined to put a Daley poster on his parish bulletin board in Alderman Vito Marsulla's southwest side ward in the last election, he found the garbage piled up in the alley.

Or sometimes objectors are merely ignored — like the small band of aldermen in the City Council whose microphones are turned off when they protest too much.

The alderman who used to interrupt City Council meetings by crying, "God bless Mayor Daley" is dead now, but when the Mayor was sworn in last month, City Hall was flag-draped and flood-lit, there was a five-minute standing ovation, and Col. Jack Reilly, the city's director of special events, had 6,000 silver and bronze commemorative medals struck for distribution to precinct captains and other faithful, explaining: "I ordered them without consultation with the Mayor two months ago. I was that sure of the outcome of the election."

For the fifth time, Federal District Judge Abraham Lincoln Marovitz, an old friend from State Senate days, a West Side product who got his start as a lawyer for Capone gunmen, swore in the Mayor, adding the Gaelic benediction, "May the wind be always at your back."

It was a kind of summation of the Daley style—old-fashioned, hemi-regal, rooted in the Irish-tinted, neighborhood-based tradition, in sharp contrast to Mayor Lindsay's striped-shirt, Yale-trained, television-oriented smoothness.

But the long-unchallenged accrual of power by the Mayor and his Cook County Democratic organization has meant that Chicago government has taken on some of the classic qualities of a one-party state, including the use of the law enforcement and court apparatus for political purposes.

New York, meanwhile, seems to be completely lacking in the sort of centralized power that many observers believe is necessary to get things done in a huge city. It often seems absurdly ineficent with so many reins being pulled for attenion. And yet, despite its failures in things mechanical, the observers say, it has qualities in the human-relationships area that are real, although often difficult to define and control.

This example illustrates part of the difference:

The tenants of five apartment buildings facing Central Park in the 110th Street area of New York organized to fight a city plan to demolish the buildings for urban renewal. The plan was sponsored by the Housing Authority and endorsed by the Borough President. But the tenants, mostly black and poor, prevailed by convincing the Planning Commission that the buildings were structurally sound and that the families would be badly hurt by eviction.

In Chicago, the tenants of a roomy, old-fashioned building complex facing Lincoln Park were informed by letter last December that their building was to be razed. Some of the tenants met to see if anything could be done, and they learned that their building — operated by Arthur Rubloff, one of the city's biggest developers, a City Hall favorite and a major Democratic contributor—was to be replaced by a high-rise building.

At the third meeting, of about 20 people, a man knocked on the door, identified himself as the Democratic precinct captain, and demanded entrance. Three of the people at the meeting were city employes. They ran back into the kitchen and hid.

May 16, 1971

CITIES' EMPLOYES EARN TOP WAGES

Found Better Off Than U.S. or Private Counterparts

By PETER KIHSS

Federal studies of municipal jobs indicate that many workers in 11 cities surveyed earn more than Federal and private employes for comparable office jobs.

The reports indicate that New York, Chicago and Los Angeles lead the nation in wages for policemen, firemen and sanitation workers.

Chicago and New York have been paying the highest rates for city employes in building maintenance. Buffalo, Philadelphia and Los Angeles lead in earnings for municipal office workers.

One analysis by the regional Bureau of Labor Statistics office here compares 10 office jobs in eight cities. This indicates that New York, Chicago, Los Angeles and Philadelphia city employes' average earnings in office categories exceed the Federal Government's comparable nationwide fourth-year pay rates.

Cities Below U.S. Scale

This comparison indicates that only New Orleans and Kansas City, Mo., municipal office workers in the sampling are below the Federal scale, with the Boston and Atlanta patterns mixed.

Municipal Employes' Monthly Pay

(Averages, Generally 1970)

Category	N.Y.C.	Chi.	L.A.	Phil.	Bos.	N. Orl.	K.C.	Atl.	Buff.	Louis.	Hart.
Policemen	$895*	980	956	820	831	587	683	640	839	658	761
Firemen	907*	995	1,006	829	825	606	651	615	855	596	766
Sanitation drivers	798**	817	861	691	...	400	554	519	609.50	494	641
Sanitation collectors	798**	770	692	600	...	344	475	426	602	440	531
Janitorial	481	616	544	556	505	283	423	377	469.50	322	473
Auto mechanics	1,048	...	845	773	612	523	671	689	674.50	594	696
Carpenters	1,048	1,051	880	775	666	533	658	722	666.50	...	712
Electricians	1,041	1,247	992	778	...	600	691	702	659.50	...	753
Typists, B	444	441	522	528	396	329	366	412	495.50	336	365
Gen. stenogrs.	467	529	557	560	469	416	421	438	530	...	491
Sr. stenogrs.	543	652	657	653	533	504	495	506	676	344	570
Keypunch oprs.	460	464	588	598	438	363	406	460	511.50	312	459

Source: U. S. Bureau of Labor Statistics.

*Added to this have been retroactive increases of $100 a month.

**Added to this have been retroactive increases of $90 a month. New York sanitationmen have same scale for drivers and collectors.

Only in New Orleans and Kansas City do municipal office employes lag behind workers in private industries, the study indicates, and the other cities' workers fare better generally than the average private employe.

The Bureau of Labor Statistics has thus far completed studies of municipal wages and benefits for the nation's four largest cities and seven others. Seven more studies are under way in the bureau's first effort to develop nationwide data on the growing municipal labor forces and the issues coming up in their collective bargaining.

Mayor Lindsay's Labor Policy Committee said the bureau's latest report comparing New York earnings with private and suburban government pay here "confirms the city's position that municipal salaries are now generally equivalent to salaries for comparable jobs in the private sector, so that further pay increases may be justified only on the basis of increases in productivity or rises in the cost of living."

The city's Office of Labor Relations said that the city government's hourly rates for its building maintenance workers—reported by the Federal survey to run 36 to 64 per cent above private industry levels here—were set under a state law requiring payment of "prevailing" rates.

Separate Surveys

The city controller's office, which determines the rates to be paid under this law, said Mayor William F. O'Dwyer in the late nineteen-forties agreed with union leaders that the city's maintenance worker scale would be based on construction worker levels.

In its comparisons, the Bureau of Labor Statistics considers only private skilled craftsmen, such as carpenters and electricians, engaged solely in maintenance. It does not include those in construction.

The Federal surveys have been issued separately for each city by regional Bureau of Labor Statistics offices.

They cover New York City, initially in an April, 1970, sampling but with some updating to this year; Atlanta, Chicago, Kansas City, Mo., and New Orleans, as of May, 1970; Boston, as of June, 1970; Los Angeles and Philadelphia, as of July, 1970; Buffalo, as of last October; Hartford, as of last January, and Louisville, as of last April.

Samuel M. Ehrenhalt, assistant director of the Middle Atlantic regional office here, said a Newark survey was being completed and that offices elsewhere were studying Baltimore, Cincinnati, Houston, Denver, Seattle and Birmingham.

Annual surveys to compare Federal and private salaries have been made since a Federal Pay Reform Act of 1962, Mr. Ehrenhalt said.

In April, 1970, the bureau's national headquarters directed each of eight regional offices to make a "pilot survey" of municipal wages, each selecting a city. Since then, the project has been expanded.

The bureau sees the surveys as "useful as guides for salary administration purposes and for general economic analysis" but warns that they "do not supply mechanical answers to questions of pay policy."

In an interview, Mr. Ehrenhalt said comparisons among cities could be influenced by varying costs of living, with New York City considered the costliest.

August 28, 1971

CLEVELAND CUTS CITY EMPLOYE PAY

Police and Firemen to Lose a Day Every 2 Weeks

Special to The New York Times

CLEVELAND, Feb. 12—Mayor Ralph J. Perk has ordered all city employes to take an across-the-board 10 per cent cut in hours worked and in their pay.

The Mayor took the move in efforts to balance the city's proposed 1972 general fund budget of $89.3-million.

Effective immediately, the Mayor said earlier this week, all city employes including policemen and firemen will work only nine out of 10 days in each two-week pay period. Compensatory overtime cannot be substituted for the work reduction, his order said.

Administration sources said the action would save the city between $8-million and $9-million this year. Mayor Perk's action, in the form of an executive order, does not require approval of the City Council.

Council Backs Move

However, leaders of the City Council, notified in advance of the Mayor's decision, approved of it.

The council's Democratic majority leader, George L. Forbes, a black who had been a close supporter of former Mayor Carl B. Stokes, said he supported the order as a last resort.

"It does not solve the problems of the city," Mr. Forbes said. "Ironically, almost the same plan was offered in the previous administration and was turned down."

The City Council president, Edmund J. Turk, also a Democrat, said the work reduction was equitable and would spread the burden to all city employes.

Representatives of the Fraternal Order of Police filed a suit Thursday in Cuyahoga County Common Pleas Court seeking to have the Mayor's order declared "illegal, null and void." They say it is a violation of the City Charter. Representatives of the Fire Fighters Union indicated that they would file a similar action.

Mayor Perk, in explaining his action, said the cutback was one of two alternatives that members of his cabinet had considered. The other plan would have necessitated laying off 1,400 employes. The Mayor said this was ruled out because it would have curtailed city services.

The only city officials excluded from the order are elected officials — the 33 City Councilmen and the 13 judges of Cleveland Municipal Court.

Earlier in his three-month-old administration, the Mayor ordered his cabinet members to take a 10 per cent pay cut because of the budgetary difficulties. This order has now been canceled, but the Mayor said he would continue to take the 10 per cent cut in his $35,000 yearly salary.

The city's general fund budget is down $5.6-million from 1971 and down $16.5-million from the 1970 budget, because Cleveland voters twice failed to approve proposals to increase the city's 1 per cent income tax.

In 1970 when the first effort was made by the Stokes administration to raise the income tax, the city let a 5.8 mill real estate levy, which raised $17-million annually, expire.

During the campaign, Mayor Perk pledged not to seek new or increased taxes. He said recently that he intended to keep this pledge.

In the last year under the two city administrations, the city has laid off nearly 2,000 because of budget difficulties. Some 500 of these persons have lost their jobs since Mr. Perk took office in November as Cleveland's first Republican Mayor in more than 30 years.

Despite the cutback, Mayor Perk said an additional 175 persons might have to be laid off within the next month.

State law requires all cities to end the year with a balanced budget.

February 13, 1972

Many Cities to Cut Taxes Under Revenue Sharing

Special to The New York Times

WASHINGTON, Oct. 17 — Though that was not really the idea behind the whole thing, many communities around the country plan to use the money they get under the new Federal revenue-sharing program to reduce taxes—property taxes in almost all cases.

Elsewhere, where the money is to be spent, as intended, for public facilities and services, significant battles loom over the uses to be made of this windfall from the Federal Treasury. The issue appears likely to boil down to what one Texas official called "capital improvements vs. people needs."

Since the revenue-sharing legislation was finally passed by Congress only last week and will be signed by President Nixon Friday at a ceremony in Philadelphia, final decisions on the use of the money have not been made.

Some patterns emerge, however, in reports from 12 states, 19 large cities, and dozens of town and county governments across the nation.

Capital improvements, ranging from new city halls in Miami and Baldwin Park, Calif., to improved sewer and water facilities in dozens of communities, constitute the most commonly planned use of the funds.

Ranking second with city and suburban officials is some form of additional subsidy for public transit systems.

The third most frequently mentioned use—one that was hardly discussed as a possibility during the long Congressional debate over revenue sharing—is additional recreational facilities, ranging from tennis courts to parkland.

The reports also disclosed that the amount of money that will be received by state and local governments is significant in terms of their budgets and in terms of how much taxes would have to be increased to raise an equivalent amount of money locally.

For example, Boston, which already has one of the highest property taxes in the country, would have to increase the tax on a $25,000 house by $82.50 a year to equal the money it will receive this year from revenue sharing. The amount is somewhat smaller in most other places. The increase would be $26.32 on a $25,000 house in Dallas; $33.42 in Omaha; $37.50 in Allegheny County (Pittsburgh), Pa., and $47 in Chicago.

Pushes Sales Tax Up

Looked at in terms of the sales tax, the revenue-sharing money is also significant. New York City would have to increase its 3 per cent tax to 4.3 per cent to raise an amount equal to the $247.5-million it will get under revenue sharing; the sales tax in the state of Pennsylvania would have to go up from 6 to 6.8 per cent.

In Michigan, which has a flat-rate income tax, regardless of income level, the tax rate would have to rise from 3.9 to 4.2 per cent. Proportionally, an even greater rise, from 2.5 to almost 2.8 per cent, would be required in the Illinois income tax rate. That is an increase of 11 per cent.

The reports also showed that the complex formulas that Congress devised for distributing the money generally achieved the desired result of giving relatively more of the revenue-sharing funds to low-income areas than to high-income sections.

The financial fate of pairs of suburbs around major cities illustrates the point.

Less For Wealthy

Near Chicago, for example, the working-class suburb of Cicero will receive an amount equal to $9.10 for every resident, whereas Kenilworth, Ill., one of the wealthiest communities in the country, will receive $3.30. Working-class Everett, outside of Boston, will receive $22.33; wealthy Wellesley, $6. National City, a working-class suburb of San Diego, will receive $11.50 per capita, whereas wealthy Coronado will get $3.61.

Over-all, under the legislation, state and local governments will receive a total of $5.3-billion for the 1972 calendar year, with the amount rising somewhat over later years, to make up a total of $30.2-billion over the five years of the program.

All of the money will come on top of various other funds that state and local governments receive from the Federal Government under a vast array of aid programs. President Nixon's original idea of also transforming some of these old Federal aid programs into revenue sharing never received serious consideration by Congress.

One-third of the money will go to state governments, for which it generally represents something between 1 and 4 per cent of their total budgets, and two-thirds to local governments, for most of which it will apparently represent between 5 and 8 per cent of their budgets, although in some cases it rises to more than 30 per cent.

The basic idea behind the revenue-sharing legislation was to help state and local governments finance public services with Federal money, on the theory that the Federal Government can raise money more easily than state and local governments.

Rises With Incomes

This was thought to be the case primarily because the Federal Government raises so much of its money through the income tax, which automatically rises as incomes go up, whereas sales and property taxes do not go up so much or so automatically. The latter are the taxes on which state and local governments chiefly rely.

When the revenue-sharing bill was going through Congress, one of the main arguments that opponents made was that state and local governments were likely to use the money to reduce taxes. This was a particularly outrageous prospect, according to such opponents as Representative John W. Byrnes of Wisconsin, the ranking Republican on the House Ways and Means Committee, because the Federal Government is currently running a deficit in excess of $25-billion annually. Not only did the Federal Government have no surplus revenue to share, he argued but the states and localities ought to take care of their own fiscal problems by raising their own taxes.

The Times's check of 12 states, 19 large cities and dozens of county and town governments indicates that Representative Byrnes's expectations may be fulfilled.

In his home state of Wisconsin for example, Gov. Patrick J. Lucey is publicly committed to cut property taxes.

Wayne McGown, deputy director of the Wisconsin Department of Administration, said: "It is not a question of how the money will be used. It is a question of when we begin. The Governor has made it clear that he intends that it is all to go for local property tax relief in some form or other."

Political leaders and finance officials from Portland, Me., to San Diego also indicated that they expected to use all or part of the money for property tax reduction.

The only place checked where mention was made of the possibility of reducing some levy other than the property tax was Dallas. There, the lone black member of the City Council, George Allen, is fighting to use part of the revenue-sharing money to abolish the $1.50 per month garbage collection fee, which he argues is burdensome to the poor and especially to the elderly on fixed incomes.

The Dallas City Council is apparently one of the few local governmental units where the issue has been formally discussed. Other City Council members there are advocating uses ranging from taking over the city's financially troubled bus system to paying for capital improvements that have already been made.

In Phoenix, Ariz., for example, the two newspapers are leading the fight to have the money used for property tax reduction. But another faction is advocating use of the money for capital improvements and still a third group is struggling hard for a conservation objective—to have the city use the fund to buy the mountains around Phoenix and keep them as open-space parkland.

Another dispute going on in many places centers on the extent to which officials believe they are going to be able to count on receiving the revenue-sharing money, year after year.

If not, so the argument goes, the proper use for the money is capital improvements, a one-time nonrecurring item. That appears to be the predominant view of officials in Miami, for example, and of Mayor Sam Yorty of Los Angeles.

Little Talk By States

Discussions of what to do with the money appears to be less far advanced in most of the states surveyed than in the majority of the cities, towns and counties.

Jerry Bryan, administrative assistant to Gov. Warren E. Hearnes of Missouri, said he thought the funds "will come in and just sort of melt in with all the rest of the money." "Most people are thinking, thank God, at least we won't have to raise taxes," he added.

A few states face a problem in that the revenue-sharing bill will take away with one hand some of the money it grants with the other. This is because of restrictions in the legislation on Federal grants to the states for what are known as "social services" programs, which were supposed to help get families off welfare or keep them from going on.

Only New York State and Illinois will lose really sizable amounts of money because of this, but the way in which the new restrictions are written could cause some problems elsewhere, too. For example, under the revised social services program, day care centers for children constitute a priority use of the social services funds. Programs for the elderly do not.

Con Shea, director of the Colorado Department of Social Services, said he hoped the cities and counties in his state would use at least part of their revenue-sharing money to support programs for the aging.

"I want our elderly to be as important as roads and bridges," he said.

Elsewhere, strong feelings are expressed as to the importance of the money to fulfill all kinds of public needs.

McKeesport, Pa., a steel mill town, like many other cities, is going to use the money for "basic, traditional services.

Mayor Zoran Popovich enumerates the services:

"We've had to lay off some policemen and now we'll be able to hire some. We'll buy some much needed fire equipment. We'll spend some on recreation and on our water plant, which had been deteriorating. The problems are obvious. There won't be any frills."

"It's a godsend," Mayor Popovich added. "I feel like Ronald Colman walking out of the blizzard and walking into Shangri-La."

October 18, 1972

Fiscal Experts See the City In Severe Financial Crisis

By MICHAEL STERN

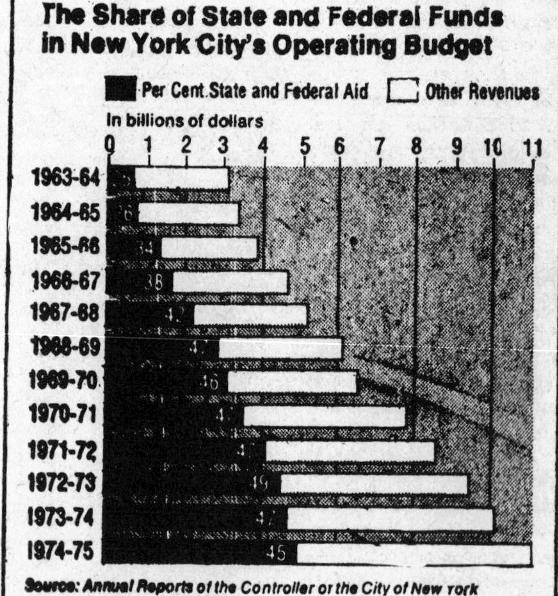

The New York Times/Oct. 27, 1974

The government of New York City is in deeper economic trouble today than it has been in at any time since the Great Depression of the nineteen-thirties.

That is the consensus of fiscal authorities interviewed in and out of government who assessed the city's economic situation after Mayor Beame's warning last month that inflation and the recession were putting his $11.1-billion budget for this year $200-million into the red.

The Mayor followed up that warning last week with a talk to the Chamber of Commerce and Industry in which he said that the same forces were opening an even larger gap between projected spending and income for the next budget year.

'Real, Not Phony'

Fiscal crises are annual events in New York, and Mayors have cried wolf so often that Mr. Beame felt compelled to tell his audience that "what I'm talking about is real—it's not phony."

But he is finding a ready credibility for his warnings. Indeed, the broad range of fiscal authorities who were interviewed agreed that the time of crisis really had arrived and that, if anything, Mr. Beame had understated the potential budget gaps, which could mount to more than $1-billion this year and even more next year.

Moreover, these experts add to the list of causes for the crisis budgetary gimmicks and borrowing for day-to-day expenses that were adopted to postpone the day of reckoning by the last three mayoral administrations, including Mr. Beame's, and that are now adding their own dynamic of increasing interest costs to the city's fiscal problems.

There also is broad agreement that the only ways out of the crisis are heroic austerities and belt tightenings that are unattractive both politically and economically and that may do permanent damage to the city's future.

Among these necessities are:

¶New and higher taxes.

¶Cuts in the Civil Service that would require layoffs as well as attrition reductions in staff.

¶Postponement of capital improvements that are needed to sustain the fabric of the city.

¶Reductions in both low-priority and high-priority services, from park maintenance and library staffing to policing and sanitation.

¶Slowing the seemingly inexorable rise in payroll, pension and fringe benefits costs that is thought to be a principal cause of the economic problem.

All of these measures would have the effect of making New York a less desirable place in which to live or do business, reinforcing the departure of productive people and enterprises that has been bleeding away the strength of the city for more than two decades.

Roderick L. O'Connor, president of the Citizens Budget Commission, the nonpartisan, business-oriented watchdog over New York's finances, assessed this situation this way:

"Everything we know about the city's budget problems leads us to believe that things cannot go on as they have been for very much longer. There will have to be some painful changes made soon or the city is going to go into a real decline."

Maintaining Political Base

The difficulty in making such changes, which is conceded by Mr. O'Connor and other critics of the way the city manages its purse, is that every municipal program and service has a political constituency. When a Mayor cuts a service, be it garbage pickups, police protection on the subways, maintenance of street trees or counseling of welfare clients, he also cuts off a bit of his political base.

In the current situation, Mr. Beame has given no clear indication of how much political capital he is willing to expend to put the city on a sounder financial basis. He has, however, given a few hints of what he will and will not do.

For the moment, he has rejected the possibility of new taxes, saying that this period of high unemployment and inflation in the city "is no time to think of taxes."

He also has said he will renege on his campaign pledge to begin phasing out one of the most widely criticized budgetary gimmicks used here—the shifting of such items as textbook buying and vocational training from the expense budget, which is financed through taxes, to the capital budget, which is financed through borrowing and therefore carries interest costs.

And he has rejected for the present dismissal of any of the city's 340,000 employes. Rather, he has ordered his Budget Director, Melvin N. Lechner, to reduce the staffs of city agencies by attrition.

Road to Economy

As a first step, Mr. Lechner has told the agencies not to fill 4,700 of the jobs that will become vacant this year. This is expected to save $29-million. However, this would be only 15 per cent of the estimated $200-million that the Mayor said was being added to the city's costs by inflation, high interest rates and high energy costs.

Moreover, there is doubt that these savings can be achieved since they come on top of unannounced mandatory cuts in payroll costs of $168,270,000 that the Budget Director has been requiring of the agencies since the 1974-75 budget year began on July 1.

These cuts are in the form of mandatory accruals—that is, orders that vacant jobs be left vacant until specified savings are made. The accrual rates vary from agency to agency, and range from 1.6 per cent in the Fire Department and 3.3 per cent in the Board of Education to 11.2 per cent in the Department of Correction and 14.8 per cent in the Controller's Office.

Mandatory accruals now are a standard budgetary practice in the city and are a principal means of helping the Mayor to provide funds for unanticipated needs or for higher payroll costs forced by new labor agreements.

The causes that led successive Mayors to go further and further down the road toward fiscal crisis are many and complex. But the basic cause is that the city's economy, which is bigger than the economies of all but the world's richest countries, has not been able to grow fast enough to sustain the rapid rise in the costs of city government.

When John V. Lindsay was Mayor, it was said that the fiscal problem of New York was that costs were rising 15 per cent a year while revenues were rising only 5 per cent a year.

Mayor Beame, in his budget message this year, put the problem this way: "During the last 10 years, normal growth in the city's tax revenues has never been sufficient to meet all its budget needs."

To close the gaps, the city raised taxes; it borrowed one year's revenues to pay another year's expenses; it shifted expense budget items to the capital budget and adopted other fiscal expedients, and it waged successful campaigns to get more aid from the Federal and state governments.

But now the options open to the city are running out, municipal fiscal experts say. Federal and state contributions to the costs of operating the city rose from less than 25 per cent of the budget in the early sixties to 48.7 per cent in 1972-73. However, the level of these contributions has fallen since then and this year represents only 44.5 per cent.

With President Ford committed to holding down the level of Government spending as the principal element in his war against inflation, it is unlikely that there will be any significant increases in Federal aid this year or next.

Similarly, with inflation and the economic slowdown likely to cut state tax receipts, there does not seem to be much chance that the city will be able to get new revenues from the state, either.

Even the compromise mass-transit aid bill, which has been endorsed by the President and which would give the city $175-million to help hold down the size of an impending increase in subway and bus fares, is in trouble in the Congress and may not pass.

Possibilities Run Out

The city's ability to shift expense budget items to the capital budget also is beginning to run out. The amount of money the city may borrow for capital spending is fixed by law. It may not exceed 10 per cent of the average assessed value of all the city's real estate over the previous five years.

Year by year, the city has been pushing its borrowing closer and closer to that limit, narrowing the margin it should be holding in reserve for emergencies. And year by year it has been taking more and more of that borrowing power to pay for current expenses rather than for financing such permanent improvements as firehouses, computer systems for the Police Department, sanitation trucks, schools, subway lines, street lights and small parks.

According to Controller Harrison J. Goldin, 53 per cent of the current capital budget of $1.7-billion — about $724-million—is being spent for current expenses. In 1972, expense items took only 20 per cent of the capital budget.

The growth of this practice has been condemned as wasteful by the city's business community. Frank A. Brady Jr., director of research for the Chamber of Commerce and Industry, likens it to "borrowing money to pay your laundry bills—you get deeper and deeper into debt while lessening your ability to climb out of the hole."

Even with the transfer of $724-million in expenses to the capital budget, Mayor Beame still did not have enough to cover the city's projected expenses this year. He provided almost $300-million more by one-shot devices. He advanced the date of sewer rental collections, took interest earned on pension-fund investments and got the state to advance payments of aid from next year to this year.

He also got the state to approve a device called the Stabilization Reserve Corporation, which is empowered to raise $520-million outside the debt limit to pay off deficits left over from the Lindsay administration and from the 1973-74 fiscal year.

How many more such devices are left in the City Hall cupboards? Aides to the Mayor say there are none, although they do not rule out the possibility that Mr. Beame and his fiscal advisers may invent some new ones.

This also was a year of new and higher taxes for the city. The real-estate tax was increased 45 cents to a rate of $7.34 for each $100 of assessed valuation. A penny was added to the combined city-state sales tax, raising it to eight cents on the dollar. A use tax of $15 a year was imposed on owners of automobiles. A 5 per cent tax was imposed on off-track betting. And the tax on banks' income was raised 20 per cent.

Taken together, these levies added an estimated $504-million to the tax burden of individuals and businesses here.

By all these devices, Mr. Beame was able to make projected revenues cover projected expenses of $11.1-billion. However, it is an open secret that many of the figures that went into making up these totals are fictions. They include hidden sums to pay salary increases for city employes and other anticipated expenses.

Inflated Figures Cited

According to the Citizens Budget Commission, the figures on the revenue side also were inflated to make the budget balance on paper. Herbert Ranschburg, the commission's director of research, said receipts from the stock-transfer tax, which gave the city $190-million in 1973-74, were projected to yield $233-million this year even though trading volume and the prices of stocks have been declining.

Similarly, Mr. Ranschburg said, the Mayor projected $814-million in receipts from the sales tax, compared with actual receipts of $575-million last year, allowing nothing for the loss in sales that always follows the imposition of higher taxes.

Mr. Beame has acknowledged that tax receipts so far this fiscal year have, indeed, fallen below his budget projections, but he has been blaming the slowdown in the economy rather than any fiscal trickery.

Figures compiled by the Controller's office show that in July and August, the first two months of the fiscal year, the city collected revenues from all sources of $309.8-million, $33.9-million less than the projected yield of $343.7-million.

Although it is too early in the fiscal year to predict how large the shortfall will be—collections may pick up later—aides to Controller Goldin say it will be "substantial." One said, "We'll be lucky if it is anywhere near as low as the $200-million predicted by the Mayor."

Mr. Goldin, who predicted before the budget was adopted that the 5 per cent levy on off-track betting would drive bets out of the city betting parlors, published figures last week to show that this is, indeed, happening. He again urged the Mayor to repeal this tax and asserted that its projected yield of about $30-million should be erased from the city's budget as unrealizable.

Shortfall in Realty Tax

One disquieting sign of the coming shortfall of revenues is the first quarter's return from the real-estate tax. As of the end of September, the arrears amounted to $79.5-million, or 6.45 per cent of the tax liability. This compares with a delinquency rate of 4.94 per cent in 1972-73 and of 5.59 per cent in 1973-74

The rate of deliquencies may fall later in the fiscal year, but if the first-quarter rate holds, the city will take in $318-million less in real-estate taxes than it had anticipated.

Similarly, the level of retail sales in the city apparently is not growing as fast as the Mayor hoped. United States Department of Commerce computations show that department store sales receipts in the city in June were only 2 per cent higher than in June, 1973, and in July only 4 per cent higher than in the previous July.

Since the city had predicted that sales receipts would grow at least as fast as the price level, which went up more than 10 per cent, the tax on these receipts consequently is going to fall short of expectations.

The impact of the 1 per cent rise in the sales tax is problematical; its effect cannot be isolated from other factors like unemployment and inflation. But the chief executive of one of the city's major department store chains said he expected the higher tax rate to drive a lot of business from his mid-town store to its New Jersey branches.

Lower Tax in Jersey

"The tax rate in New Jersey is only 5 per cent," he said, "and it does not apply to clothing, which is a large part of our business. With that kind of differential, anyone who lives in New Jersey and buys in New York has to be crazy."

When the Mayor said that inflation and recession were putting his budget into deficit, he referred specifically to higher energy costs, to higher rates of interest on borrowings and to the high rate of unemployment here—it was 7 per cent in August — which was increasing welfare costs and lowering revenues.

He did not mention the impact of inflation on the costs of paying city employes, however. Payroll, pension and fringe benefits take more than 60 per cent of the city's budget and even small increments in these costs have a huge impact.

In March, the Transport Workers Union, which represents subway and bus workers achieved a major breakthrough when it won a cost-of-living escalator in its new contract. The agreement provides an increase of 20 per cent over 15 months plus 2.5 cents for every rise of one per cent in the Consumer Price Index.

When the sanitationmen and firemen signed new agreements in July, they won a similar cost-of-living adjustment, and the expectation now is that the police and all other city employes will demand and get the same kind of inflation protection.

Labor Costs Ahead

Since the Consumer Price Index has shown no sign of slackening its monthly rises, the city is facing automatic wage increases that will further widen the budget deficit. Based on the formula won by the transit workers, an annual inflation rate of 15 per cent, somewhat lower than the actual rate in the last few months, would cost the city $233.7-million over a full year.

Taking all these factors into consideration, and adding in an anticipated need for a new transit subsidy to help keep the subway and bus fare from rising beyond 45 or 50 cents, Mr. Ranschburg, of the Citizens Budget Commission, said the city could easily wind up the 1974-75 fiscal year more than $1-billion in the red.

And with next year's budget already mortgaged through the one-time devices being used to help out this year's expenses, Mr. Ranschburg said the budget gap for 1975-76 could be even higher.

Economists who watch the city's fiscal affairs for some of the major banks here say those estimates may be a bit high. But they agree that the deficits for both years will be uncomfortably large and will require extraordinary remedies, including either new or higher taxes.

Mr. Brady, of the Chamber of Commerce and Industry, said of the problem:

"If a company was in that kind of situation, it would have no choice but to cut costs and practice some austerities until it got back into proper shape again. But the city refuses to do this. It goes on spending more and more every year."

In past years, city officials have pleaded helplessness in the face of mandatory increases in the budget. They cited, for example, the huge growth in welfare dependency here, which has forced up the costs of income maintenance for the poor from less than $500-million in 1964-65 to more than $2.5-billion this year.

Now, however, some economists are pointing out that since the Federal and state governments pay 75 per cent of the costs, welfare should be regarded as an income producer that adds to the city's economy.

By far the biggest reason for the constant rise in city budgets is the increase in municipal payroll costs. This rise is a result of the combined effects of growth in the workforce over the past 10 years from 220,000 to 340,000 and an increase in those years of '79 per cent in city wage and salary rates.

Rising expectations of the people who work for the city, along with increased militancy of their unions, have pushed pay and benefits so far that they have now surpassed what is offered in private industry for equivalent work.

Pension contributions alone now cost the city more than $1-billion a year and by 1980 they are expected to rise to more than $2-billion a year.

These benefits, paid for almost entirely by the city, now permit some categories of city workers, like Board of Education employes, to retire at age 65 after a lifetime career with combined pensions, annuity and Social Security payments that are higher than their salaries.

Publicly, city officials maintain that they fight the unions hard to hold down payroll costs. Privately, many concede that since the transit workers strike of 1966 at the start of the Lindsay administration, which paralyzed the city for 12 days, they go into every negotiation with the knowledge that no city administration will ever want to fight a union down to the mat again.

As one long-time aide to the Mayor put it: "That experience traumatized the city. It was a disaster. We can't let it happen again, with the subways, the police, the firemen, the sanitationmen or any other vital service. If it costs more money to keep the peace, well. . . ." And he shrugged his shoulders.

October 27, 1974

City Leads in Per Capita Expenditures

By PETER KIHSS

To provide services for New Yorkers, the city government spends nearly five times as much for each resident on operations and debt service as does Chicago, the country's next largest city — $1,233.68 compared wtih $267.29.

This is on the basis of data for the fiscal year 1973 derived from census reports and just published by the Tax Foundation here. Los Angeles, the third largest city, spent $241.78; Philadelphia, $415.15; Detroit, $356.94, and Houston, $161.54.

The comparison in the research group's newly published comprehensive biennial edition of "Facts and Figures on Government Finance" excludes pension costs. But a computation yesterday by Frank Fischer, research analyst for the foundation, showed a similar long lead here.

The cost of municipal-employe retirement here averaged $87.68 for each New Yorker, according to the computation. This compared with Chicago, $19.07; Los Angeles, $30.31; Philadelphia, $22.46; Detroit, $35.86, and Houston, $4.36.

The new publication showed Washington as the only one of the 48 largest cities whose per-capita spending on operations and debt service exceeds that of New York City, with $1,588.86. But Washington is a Federal district that does not have local costs shared with a state government.

The wide variations reflect the extent to which cities assume certain functions. In the published analysis of the 48 largest cities, the runners-up to New York City on over-all spending are Boston, $857.71; Baltimore, $806.14; San Francisco, $751.28 and Newark, $692.21.

The 48-city per-capita average is $525.71, with the lowest cost for El Paso, Tex., $133.49. Others at the low end include Miami, $173.15 and San Diego, Calif., $199. 31.

In an analysis of major functions, New York City is far ahead in public-welfare spending—$314.81, exceeding even Washington's $263.37.

Welfare is generally paid for by states, with the Federal Government sharing, and is rarely a municipal function in most of the country. In New York, the state requires the city to pay 25 per cent of the cost of welfare family cases and half the cost of home relief.

In the 48-city comparison, runners-up in welfare costs are San Francisco, $218.74; Baltimore, $157.35; Denver, $94.61; Norfolk, Va., $87.83, and Newark, $41.72. The average is as high as $78.95 largely because of New York City.

New York City is outranked on spending for education, police and firefighting programs. Washington's education spending is given as $333.44. Newark spends $325.04 compared with $295.63 for New York.

The 48-city per capita average on education spending is given as $90.27.

On police and fire expenditures, the foundation reports Washington as spending $152.30, followed by Boston, at $129.01, and Newark,

Spending by Ten Cities

Per-Capita Spending by 10 Largest Cities
(Fiscal 1973)

City	Population	Total Opg. & Debt Serv.	Police & Fire	Health & Hosp.	Education	Welfare	Employe Retirement
New York	7,895,563	$1,223.68	99.38	151.41	295.63	314.81	87.68
Chicago	3,369,359	267.29	85.51	12.60	6.53	3.23	19.07
Los Angeles	2,809,596	241.78	81.89	0.87	...	0.20	30.31
Philadelphia	1,950,098	415.15	88.99	46.95	12.61	17.72	22.46
Detroit	1,513,601	356.94	89.63	31.95	6.10	2.61	35.86
Houston	1,232,802	161.54	48.63	7.99	3.00	0.04	4.36
Baltimore	905,759	806.14	95.91	54.76	248.62	157.35	26.12
Dallas	844,401	218.30	58.02	4.02	...	...	7.82
Washington	756,410	1,588.86	152.30	183.81	333.44	263.37	73.66
Cleveland	750,879	233.72	81.96	7.19	0.09	0.01	0.52

$122.50, before New York's $99.38. The average is $77.42.

New York, with its network of municipal hospitals, is far ahead in cost of health and hospitals, at $151.41, again except for Washington, at $183.81. The average is $50.10.

New York is below average in spending on highways, with $20.42 compared with the 48-city figure of $22.01. This is a category with a wide range from Washington, at $68.79, and Baltimore, $61.47, to Miami, $7.77, and El Paso, Tex., $9.16.

A miscellaneous category covers such functions as sewerage and sanitation, housing and urban renewal, parks and recreation, libraries, debt service and public buildings. This puts New York far ahead at $314, except for Washington, with its different government structure, at $523.37.

The Tax Foundation's 288-page book, the 18th in a series begun in 1941, contains 213 tables of current and historical data on Federal, state and local taxes, expenditures and debts, and is available from the foundation at 50 Rockefeller Plaza at $5 a copy.

May 23, 1975

Many Cities in Crisis Cut Payrolls and Raise Taxes

By EILEEN SHANAHAN

Special to The New York Times

WASHINGTON, May 26—Like New York, many large cities across the nation are in financial trouble, but their troubles are generally much less severe.

The chief reasons, as disclosed by an examination of the budgets of other cities and by interviews with experts on municipal finance, are these:

¶Most other cities that were faced with a dramatically widening gap between expenditures and revenues made major cutbacks in city payrolls or raised taxes, or both. Cleveland appears to be a significant exception.

¶No other city has relied as heavily as New York on extremely short-term borrowing, particularly in the form of "anticipation" securities. These are bonds or notes that will be paid off out of revenues yet to be collected—that is, out of anticipated tax collections, state aid payments or specified fees. The holders of anticipation securities have the top priority claim to the proceeds of these future revenue collections.

Actually, New York City's financial troubles appear to have come as no surprise to students of municipal finance.

A study of "city financial emergencies," published in 1973 and based on data for 1971, identified five symptoms of unhealthy financial condition and found that New York City had four of them.

The study was done by the Advisory Commission on Intergovernmental Relations, a permanent organization whose members come from Federal and state and local governments.

The study, written in characteristically restrained bureaucratic prose, did not sound any alarms concerning New York or anywhere else. It merely recited the symptoms of vulnerability to financial emergency, and detailed which cities were displaying which ones.

Those exhibited by New York were the following:

¶Current expenditures that exceed receipts by more than 5 per cent.

¶Deficits in each of the preceding two years.

¶Deficit in the general fund under a uniform bookkeeping system known as the "cash basis."

¶Short-term loans outstanding at the end of the year.

The fifth symptom of financial ill health, which New York did not have, was a year-to-year decrease in assessed real estate values.

No city other than New York displayed as many as four of these symptoms, as of 1971. Two cities, Cleveland and Buffalo, each displayed three, and both of these cities are generally considered to be in shaky financial shape now.

It is difficult to use these measures of municipal financial distress to make an up-to-date assessment of the situation of New York or other cities, because different cities keep their books in such different ways that complex adjustments have to be made, by experts, in each city's published figures.

In addition, since most state constitutions forbid cities to run deficits, local officials will generally not admit a deficit is impending. They concede the fact only after the fiscal year has ended.

There is one readily available set of figures, however, that is published everywhere on about the same bookkeeping basis, that can be used as a uniform guide to the financial condition of cities.

This is the ratio of the city's "debt service"—that is, as most cities use the term, its interest payment plus its payments of principal on maturing long-term debt—to its current budget expenditures.

John E. Petersen, the Washington director of the Municipal Finance Officers Association, said in a recently published paper that the agencies that rate municipal bonds on their investment quality consider "a ratio of 10 per cent to be the separation between better and lesser creditworthiness."

A ratio of 15 per cent "warrants concern," Mr. Petersen's report continued, "and it should never exceed 20 to 25 per cent."

New York, as of the fiscal year now drawing to an end, had a ratio of debt service to current budget expenditures of 17.1 per cent. Only Cleveland among the major cities whose budgets were examined had a higher ratio.

Telephone interviews with budget officials in other cities disclosed that some of the criticisms made of New York and of how it got into its present financial difficulties may not be fair.

For example, it is commonly stated that New York is not only spending too much but also doing things that other cities do not do, such as subsidizing public transit.

Subsidized Elsewhere

But public transit is subsidized in many, perhaps most, other big-city areas. The money does not come out of the city budget, as such, because in most places there is a regional transit authority that handles the subsidy. But a significant share of the money—45 per cent, for example, in the case of Boston—comes out of the pockets of the taxpayers in the central city, often in the form of a special property tax levy.

Because New York is not part of any county government—on the contrary, five counties comprise the city—New York also pays much more of its own welfare and health bills than most cities.

On the other hand, the charges that New York has resisted the cutbacks in city services that might have ameliorated its financial troubles seem accurate. The layoffs of 1,941 city employes, scarcely one-half of 1 per cent of the total, are very small compared with those that have occurred in other places.

The principal city services that have been cut back because of layoffs include trash collections, street cleaning and maintenance and park maintenance. Buffalo has cut out one fire company and reduced the number of men in the remaining companies.

Here are brief sketches of the fiscal picture in some major cities:

CLEVELAND

Although Vincent Campanello, the budget director, will not admit to any such thing, a glance at the evidence puts Cleveland on the list of cities with serious financial problems. The ratio of the city's debt service to its current budget expenditures is 17.9 per cent, somewhat higher than New York's.

The report on "city financial emergencies" identified Cleveland as a problem city at least as far back as 1970 or 1971, when the voters refused to approve an income tax increase and, nearly simultaneously, let a special property tax levy expire.

Municipal services were cut—but not enough to avoid a deficit that required the city to get permission from the state legislature to issue a special type of debt security, similar to the widely criticized anticipation notes.

"Cleveland's financial emergency stemmed from its citizens' own choosing," the advisory commission report said, and continued deficits appear to be what Clevelanders are still choosing. Last November, the voters defeated a proposed increase in the city's income tax that would have applied to all who work in the city, resident and nonresident alike.

The defeat of the tax-increase proposal has led to layoffs of about 1,120 city workers, 10 per cent of the total, but that will save only $6-million or $9-million, not quite halving the prospective deficit.

Meanwhile, the city continues to issue new batches of the special 5-year notes in amounts that have been increasing by about $20-million a year. Mr. Campanella says they can be paid off at the present property tax rate.

MILWAUKEE

The residents of only two of the nation's 30 largest cities—Boston and Milwaukee—pay more in state and local taxes of all kinds than do the residents of New York. Yet despite its high tax rates, particularly for those with incomes of $15,000 or more, Milwaukee may be headed for financial problems.

The ratio of the city's debt service to its current budget expenditures is 15.2 per cent, into the range that "warrants concern" in the municipal bond markets.

Worse problems clearly loom ahead, according to Edwin C. Whitney, the city's director of budget and management. The firefighters just got a big raise and the issue of police salaries is now in arbitration.

State aid to the city is likely to be down because of the recession. Street-cleaning crews have been put on a shorter work year, as the only major economy so far. But Mr. Whitney believes the city "may face massive layoffs" of municipal workers next year.

DETROIT

Faced with a drastic decline in municipal revenues as a result of its unemployment rate—the highest, by far, for any major city—Detroit has responded with drastic layoffs of municipal workers and with other economies.

The city chronically runs a deficit—in fact, it has recorded only four years without a deficit in the last 25. It is somewhat surprising, therefore, that the ratio of the city's debt service payments to its budget expenditures is still under 8 per cent. However, the city looks less healthy financially by some other measurements used by financial analysts. Like New York, Detroit issues revenue-anticipation notes, though the amount is under stricter control by the state.

It is the reduction in personnel costs that constitutes the dramatic part of Detroit's response to its fiscal problems.

Some 1,980 workers, 10 per cent of the city payroll, will have been laid off between February and the end of the fiscal year, June 30. In addition, the city is trying to cut its payrolls by another 1,200 by not filling vacancies.

The city is trying to get its municipal employes unions to agree to cutbacks in work and pay, such as accepting straight time pay for holidays, that would reduce payroll costs by 8 per cent, which is the equivalent of 1,500 jobs. All these reductions would produce a cut of 24 per cent in city payrolls.

BUFFALO

With an unemployment rate close to 20 per cent, Buffalo is on everybody's list of cities in serious financial trouble. In the 1974-75 fiscal year, which ends June 30, the city will run a deficit of about $17-million in its $229-million current budget, mainly because it will collect considerably less revenue than it originally expected.

Philip Cook, the budget director, said that delinquencies in property tax collections, considered by some experts to be an unfailing sign of serious distress, amounted to more than 8 per cent and were "running higher now than at any time since the Great Depression and rising every month." The delinquency rate runs around 2 or 3 per cent in prosperous times.

The ratio of the city's debt service to its budget expenditures is 12.1 per cent and an unusually high proportion of its present and immediately prospective debt is short term.

Buffalo has moved against its financial problems on both the tax and the expenditure sides of its budget. An increase in the property tax rate was put into effect last year; layoffs totaling 16 per cent of the payroll have been made over the last four years.

BOSTON

The residents of Boston pay higher combined state and local taxes than the residents of any other of the nation's 30 largest cities. Of Boston's total revenue, 70 per cent comes from the property tax which is, by far, the highest in the nation, compared with something under 40 per cent for most cities. And property tax delinquencies in Boston have been creeping up to the point where Richard E. Wall, the budget director, thinks they may reach 10 per cent by the end of the fiscal year, June 30. The original budget estimates assumed a delinquency rate of 6 per cent—a $14-million difference.

The city has reduced payrolls by 10 per cent over the last two years, with the Hospital Department bearing about half the cut.

For the new fiscal year, spending is expected to rise by about $80-million to $600-million, and where the extra money is coming from is none too clear.

ST. LOUIS

In its new fiscal year that began May 1, St. Louis faced the prospect of a budget deficit of $20-million, which would have violated state law. To fill the gap, it has proposed a property tax increase, which the budget director, Jack A. Webber believes will not be approved, plus a 4 per cent cutback in city jobs, which comes on top of a 7 per cent cutback over the preceding four years. Street cleaning, recreation and services and park maintenance would be reduced.

In addition, St. Louis will juggle its payrolls to save $4.1-million that it would otherwise owe its workers, who are paid biweekly, because 1975-76 is a 27-payday year for people who are paid on Fridays. The payday will be slipped forward one day next year and in each of six succeeding years until, finally, there will actually be a 27-payday year. But by then there will be money in a special fund to take care of the extra payday.

SEATTLE

The current unemployment rate of 9 per cent looks good to Seattle, where almost 20 per cent of the working force were jobless only a few years ago after the collapse of the aerospace industry. That industry has recovered and Seattle is also benefiting from its position as a shipping point for the vast Alaska pipeline project.

The city raised its gross receipts tax on business and its excise levy on utility bills on Jan. 1. Both taxes are bringing in more money than estimated, with the result that the city may run a surplus this year. Contract negotiations with major groups of city employes and a possible resumption of deficit financing loom for next year, however.

Seattle's debt service payments are 9.4 per cent of its current budget expenses.

May 27, 1975

Control Over City Budgets Is Extensive in Some States

By EILEEN SHANAHAN
Special to The New York Times

WASHINGTON, June 7—The financial controls that Governor Carey wants to exert over New York City in return for helping it avert a financial crisis are quite limited compared with those that some other states have over their municipalities.

Under the criminal provisions of the New Jersey local budget law, a city official went to jail a few years ago for falsifying budget estimates so that his mayor, facing a tough re-election campaign, could increase spending without raising taxes.

The State of New Mexico has the authority—although it has never been used—to take over a municipal or county government whose financial affairs are not in order.

In Michigan, any type of borrowing by a local government, whether for operating or capital expenses, must be approved by the state's Municipal Finance Commission. And such borrowing is subject to strictly enforced limits.

In Arizona, the year-over-year increase in the spending of any local government may not exceed 10 per cent.

Only a minority of states exercise extensive control over the financial affairs of their local governments, however, according to information that has been compiled by the Advisory Commission on Intergovernmental Relations, a permanent advisory and research organization whose membership includes Federal, state and local officials.

Many states do no more than audit the books of counties and municipalities after the close of the fiscal year. And some states, including such large and wealthy ones as Ohio, do not even do that.

Many states do require local government budgets to be kept according to a uniform accounting system, and many offer technical system, and many offer technical help in budgeting and accounting to their local governments.

Where states do exercise considerable financial control over local governmental units, the laws creating the controls generally date to the nineteen-thirties or early forties. At that time, the laws were enacted in an effort to prevent a recurrence of the wave of defaults on municipal securities that occurred when overextended or mismanaged local governments were hit with the economic shock of the Depression.

By far, the most comprehensive local budget control law is New Jersey's. Michigan also has a strong law, and in both of these states there is a tradition that the office of local governments, whatever it is called, is staffed with professionals and reasonably free of politics.

In the opinion of such municipal finance experts as Philip M. Dearborn, executive director of the Municipal Research Bureau of Washington, this combination of a strong law and its administration by professionals goes a long way toward explaining how cities like Detroit and Newark, with extremely high unemployment rates, have nevertheless avoided the kind of fiscal emergency now confronting New York. They have been closely restricted in their spending and borrowing under the state laws.

John F. Laezza, director of New Jersey's Division of Local Government Services, sums up the results of the New Jersey law as follows:

"The state allows home rule just to a degree in financial affairs. The local governments don't like it, but they've grown up with it." New Jersey's law was enacted in 1938.

Like most states, New Jersey has a constitutional ban against deficit spending by local governments, but New Jersey, along with a few other states, takes steps in advance to prevent deficits.

Each of the state's 588 counties and municipalities must submit estimates to Mr. Laezza's office 40 days after the start of the fiscal year. He has the authority to reject any budget estimate he finds unrealistic and send it back to the local authorities for adjustment.

Just this year, Mr. Laezza said, he had "a concerted difference of opinion" with Hudson County officials who wanted to put the money they collect from motor vehicle fines, which is earmarked for road construction under state law, into the general fund. He told them they could not do that.

A more typical case, he said, is a simple overestimate by local authorities of the amount of revenue they will collect from the property tax—something New York City stands accused of — or an underestimate of outlays for a department or program.

New Jersey law also limits long-term and short-term borrowing by cities and counties. Borrowing against anticipated revenues—a procedure that has contributed heavily to New York City's cash shortage—is limited in New Jersey to 30 per cent of the total anticipated taxes.

Long-term borrowing is limited according to a formula based on total local property values.

Controls over borrowing constitute the main focus of Michigan's Municipal Finance Act of 1943. Long-term borrowing is limited, under a complicated formula, to approximately 5 per cent of the true market value of the property in the locality doing the borrowing.

Short-term borrowing is permitted against future tax collections and against future state aid payments, but only up to a ceiling of 50 per cent of the tax collections or state aid of the preceding year.

New Mexico emphasizes close controls over current spending. Counties have to report their revenue collections and their outlays every month, and municipalities every quarter; if spending exceeds one-twelfth of the year's estimate (or one-quarter, respectively), local officials have to be prepared to justify the deviation.

Albert Romero, chief of the Local Governments Division of the state Department of Finance and Administration, said that one reason for the inauguration of this type of control was that new county commissioners take office on Jan. 1, but the fiscal year runs until June 30.

"Sometimes," he said, "the old commissioners tried to spend more than their valid one-half of the year's appropriations."

The New Mexico state government also conducts public hearings on proposed local budgets that are aimed, among other things, at bringing to light any misrepresentations in the budget estimates.

Only last week, according to Mr. Romero, a hearing disclosed that the combined city and county government of Los Alamos was planning to issue a general obligation bond and that no provision had been made in the budget for paying the interest.

Despite the existence of some relatively strict state laws, no state comes close to imposing on its local governments all of the fiscal restrictions that were recommended by the Advisory Commission on Intergovernmental Relations in a 1973 study entitled "City Financial Emergencies."

Nor would the restrictions that would be imposed under the planned Municipal Assistance Corporation in New York come close to fulfilling all of these recommendations.

Among the dozens of proposals in the advisory commission report were the following:

¶Funds must automatically be included in the current year's budget for the payment of any short-term operating debt that was not liquidated at the end of the previous fiscal year.

¶States should enact laws that would establish, in advance, the conditions under which the state can move in and take over much of the financial management of a municipality or county.

Some of the conditions that might trigger such interventions would be default on debt payments, failure to pay taxes collected for other jurisdictions, failure to pay salaries or to fund pension obligations and the existence of unpaid obligations totaling 10 per cent or more of the total budget.

Once a state has interjected itself into local financial management under such a law, according to the advisory commission's recommendations, it should be allowed to approve or disapprove any specific expenditure or loan, any new hiring and even the filling of vacancies on the local payroll.

The commission also proposed that the state be permit in such circumstances "to act as an agent of the local governmental unit in collective bargaining with representatives of employes and to approve any agreement prior to its being effected."

The commission concluded that "there is no single standard pattern for the actions a state agency may be empowered to take when a city reaches a financial crisis.

"It must be emphasized, however, that it is essential for each state to know under what conditions a city will be deemed to have reached a financial crisis and exactly what steps it will take under those circumstances.

"Past experience, both in the Depression years and in more recent times, has shown that in the absence of stand-by legislative authority, both cities and states waste much valuable time debating the need to take action and in obtaining necessary legislative authority."

June 8, 1975

For Cities, No Single Problem or Solution

By Richard P. Nathan

WASHINGTON—There is a danger that the current, and justifiable, preoccupation with New York City finances by observers of the urban scene will cause them to overgeneralize. New York's fiscal ills have been chronicled in depth and classified in full. But New York's problems are not those of every city. For urban-policy-makers, the cardinal fact about United States cities is that they are different:

- Some central cities are well off —in fact, much better off than their suburbs.
- Some cities are served by region-wide governments; thus, the burden of serving poverty areas is reduced by being so widely shared.
- Other central cities with serious social and economic problems are, nevertheless, on the upswing because of economic and management reforms.
- A majority of urbanites live in small communities of under 50,000 people that are very different from New York City.

In a recent study of all central cities for urban areas of over 500,000 people done at The Brookings Institution, we examined six conditions of the central city — unemployment, dependency rates, low degree of education, income level, crowded housing, and poverty—and compared them with those of their own suburbs.

Using a common statistical technique, we standardized these comparisons, so that central cities ranking over 100 points are worse off than their suburbs on this combined measure, and those under 100 are better off.

Of the 58 central cities in the study, New York ranks tenth. Newark, N.J., is at the top of the list.

		City and Suburb Hardship Index
1.	Newark, N.J.	422
2.	Cleveland	331
3.	Hartford, Conn.	317
4.	Baltimore	256
5.	Chicago	245
6.	St. Louis	231
7.	Atlanta	226
8.	Rochester, N.Y.	215
9.	Gary, Ind.	213
10.	New York City	211

The single most important characteristic of these ten troubled central cities is their regional grouping. With the exception of Atlanta, the ten worst-off central cities are in the Northeast and North Central regions of the United States. In these regions we tend to find the most serious cases of city boundaries established in the late 19th century that at the time reflected the extent of urban settlement but now encase only the poverty-impacted core of a metropolitan area.

These old cities of the Northeast and North Central regions have very different political and economic characteristics from the newer, spread-out cities of the South and West.

We also found twelve central cities to be better off than their suburbs. Six are in the South; five in the West; one in the North Central region.

Houston, Phoenix and Dallas are the largest cities in this group. In all three, the central city's population accounts for more than half of that of the total population of the metropolitan area.

Important variations also occur in the layering of local government. Many central cities are served by overlying county governments that are geographically broader-based and that provide important central-city services. Los Angeles is the best case in point; the county government covers a population over three times larger than that of the central city and spends more money per capita than does the city government.

The 58 central cities in our analysis accounted for approximately one-fourth of the nation's population in 1970. In all, just under half of the nation's population lived in these largest central cities and their outlying suburban areas.

However, if we reduce the scope of analysis to central cities that themselves have over 500,000 people, then only 15 per cent of the nation's population lives in these very large central cities.

It is true that some of the nation's problem cities are like New York. Baltimore is the closest comparison. It too is a combined city-county with broad service responsibilities.

But if we were to design a large national spending program to help solve the problems of these troubled core cities, it undoubtedly would be very unfair to other cities that have made reforms to spread the burden of public services through consolidation (among them Jacksonville, Nashville and Indianapolis) or through the annexation of suburban territory (a widespread practice in the Southwest).

The problems of sick cities arise out of a complex web of structural, fiscal and social conditions. Efforts to deal with these conditions must take cognizance of the pluralistic character of state and local government.

Many domestic programs—Federal, state and local—are pertinent to the inner city. Federal revenue-sharing helps central cities to a greater extent than their suburbs. The new lump-sum grant to cities for community development legislated in 1974 is another means of getting at urban problems.

A bill recently passed in the Senate would provide emergency fiscal relief to hard-hit local governments in recession periods, essentially on a revenue-sharing basis. State financial-aid policies and the nation's welfare, health and mass-transit programs have important consequences for urban centers.

So do structural reforms like the recent establishment of a region-wide government for Indianapolis and the regional-cooperation arrangement to share social burdens in the Minneapolis-St. Paul metropolitan area.

It may belabor the obvious, but it must be stated that there can be no single solution for what above all is no single problem. If something we should label the "urban crisis" exists today, it is highly differentiated. This diagnosis is fundamental for those interested in solving the fiscal problems of New York City and other poverty-impacted, financially troubled core cities.

August 23, 1975

CAREY SIGNS $2.3-BILLION AID PLAN IMPOSING FINANCIAL CURBS ON CITY

NEGOTIATIONS ON

Albany Aides Moving to Provide the Cash Needed Monday

By FRANCIS X. CLINES

Special to The New York Times

ALBANY, Sept. 9—The emergency plan to hold off default in New York City through a $2.3-billion cash infusion and a state-mandated restructuring of the city's fiscal management was signed into law by Governor Carey this morning, in the latest attempt to deal with the city's continuing financial agony.

"We have begun a major effort to save a city and secure a state," the Governor declared in signing the complex measure, which all major state officials concede is highly risky but is the only immediate hope for containing the city's crisis.

The new law, designed to avert default for the next three months and to attempt to revive investor confidence so that the city might be able to resume borrowing on its own, was rushed through an all-night maze of legislative maneuvering and debate to the Governor's desk.

The measure had cleared the Assembly yesterday on a 80-70 vote, but the final Senate vote 33 to 26, did not come until shortly after 4 A.M.

$610-Million by Monday

Moving quickly, state officials already were negotiating for the first of three $250-million state loans for the city by tomorrow so that, in combination with other parts of the new law, the city will receive the $610-million in cash it must have by Monday to meet its current obligations.

The law—widely described in the special legislative session as a state "gamble" in behalf of the city — does the following:

¶Creates a seven-member Emergency Financial Control Board, dominated by state representatives, that will enforce austerity and control the city's revenue flow.

¶Pieces together three months' worth of needed cash from $750-million in state loans, from the tapping of public employe pension funds for $725-million, and from $800-million in other private and public sources.

¶Establishes a legal process to handle the feared, largely unknown prospect of default should an entity the size of the city government finally fail

The new law was designed by the Municipal Assistance Corporation, the agency created earlier this year by the state to sell bonds in behalf of the city. The M.A.C., after raising $2-billion, found investors cold to the city and demanding dramatic evidence that city officials would be forced to cut back severely.

"We have much to do," Mr. Carey said this evening as he made plans to fly to the city for private conferences relating to the crisis.

In short order, he must make three appointments to the new state emergency board to join the four elected officials — the Governor, Mayor Beame, State Controller Arthur Levitt, and City Controller Harrison J. Goldin. He also must see to a crucial piece in the financing plan — getting the final parts of a $250-million commitment from the financial community to help the city.

Meantime, Controller Levitt, who was busy today negotiating large-scale financing for both the state and city's needs, also will soon appoint a special deputy state controller, a job created under the new law to serve as a day-to-day auditor of the city's budget practices.

In the debate over the plan yesterday and early this morning, legislators who denounced it—mainly upstate Republicans — warned that default was inevitable and that the law would only plunge the state in behind the city.

But the Governor, who was strongly supported by the Senate majority leader, Warren M. Anderson, the Binghamton Republican, argued that the state's credit rating already was contaminated by the city's problem and that the only alternative to the emergency plan was certain default and widespread fiscal havoc for the state and municipalities.

Officials Lose Power

For the city, the new law means the shorning of much of the fiscal power of its elected officials as well as the certainty of additional austerities perhaps even more stringent than the wage freeze, transit fare rise and layoffs enacted in recent months.

In answering questions, the Governor again emphasized the psychological ramifications of the plan as much as its fiscal measures — noting the importance of quickly rebuilding a strong impression of the city in the minds of investors throughout the country. Accordingly, he said a long teachers' strike in the city would not help this effort.

He stressed, however, that whatever negotiators for the city and teachers agreed on, there was a wage freeze in place for city workers, including the teachers, under the new law

He offered a vivid description of the tight-fisted role to be played by the emergency board that will run the city's budget.

"The board is like the one who gives out the chips at the casino," he said. "You go to the window and get your chips and play the game."

The chips, he implied, would be far slower in coming than during the previous decade when the city government spent and borrowed itself into a deficit of $3.3-billion and the debilitating cycle of indebtedness that saw it forced to pay record interest, then be finally rebuffed by the money lenders this year.

In describing the desired attitude of the new emergency board, Mr. Carey spoke of members having "the guts" to make harsh decisions

Buck Stops in Albany

The politics of the new arrangement are dwarfed only by the financial stakes, for Mr. Carey will henceforth be prominently identified at the heart of the crisis, overshadowing his fellow Democrat, the Mayor, and presumably open to all the fiscal criticism the Mayor has been bearing in recent months.

The Governor was considered to have achieved a major victory in steering his program through the politically divided Legislature, but at the outset his victory has the same long-range uncertainties as the law's financial plan.

The announced goal of the program is to improve the city's fiscal health so rapidly that it will be able to borrow again by December, or at least find the M.A.C. able to borrow in its behalf again. The agency has an enlarged authorization under the new law, from the previous $3-billion to a total of $5-billion in financing.

Many legislators predicted they would be back before the end of the year for some additional hurried attempt at resuscitating the city. But the Governor and Senator Anderson, while offering no certainty of success, are emphasizing the original M.A.C. view that, if the city has not regained investor confidence by December, only Federal help can ultimately guarantee a halt in the city's slide toward default.

Thus far, the Democratic-controlled Congress has shown some sympathy, but President Ford and his Republican Administration have said repeatedly that it is up to the city to save itself.

All the questions and uncertainties of the emergency venture poured forth during the legislative debate.

To the legislators who argued that it was better to let default happen now because it could be contained, Senator Anderson, tired from a personal visit to Washington in search of help, declared: "I don't believe it. I go further, and I think it will have a serious impact on other communities throughout the nation."

In the final votes, proponents were stressing the inevitability of proceeding with the plan, emphasizing what default might mean in terms of human lives in the city through a curtailment of payroll and welfare checks.

The Governor took care of some members' political and neighborhood concerns, agreeing, for example, to study the plan of liberals and minority members that the state mandate that the investment community invest in the city. This let needed Democrats support the bill more easily, but privately many politicians saw no likelihood of any such financial mandate.

The Senate vote could be read as a casebook instance of the Republican majority opposition's facing an issue so towering that it blocked out room for the usual political maneuvering. Senator Anderson, who was privately pressed by bankers to accept the plan, was joined by nine other Republicans, mainly city representatives, in supporting the bill.

Two upstate Democrats sided with the rest of the Republican opponents in the 33-to-26 vote.

In the Democratic-controlled Assembly, the Republicans were more free to operate, and the minority leader, Perry B. Duryea of Montauk, L.I., kept his members entirely in opposition, even down to the city Republicans.

The Speaker, Stanley Steingut, Brooklyn Democrat, had enough room to let eight upstaters protect themselves by voting against the bill.

The 10 Republican Senators who voted for the bill were Mr. Anderson; John D. Calandra of the Bronx; William T. Conklin of Brooklyn; Leon Giuffreda of Suffolk; Roy M. Goodman of Manhattan; Martin Knorr and Frank Padavan, both of Queens; John J. Marchi of Staten Island; Joseph R. Pisani of New Rochelle, and Richard E. Schermerhorn of Cornwall-on-Hudson.

The two Democratic Senators who voted against the measure were James Griffin of Buffalo and John D. Perry of Rochester.

$610-Million First Goal

The immediate need of officials implementing the law is to assure the $610-million the city needs by Monday. This will hold off default for September, but comparably large packages of money must be delivered in the following two months.

The new emergency board, meantime, must begin the work to produce a detailed estimate of the city's revenues so the city can produce a financial plan by Oct. 20 for the remainder of the current fiscal year, as required by the law.

Preliminary estimates are that the city must own up to the need to cut more than $100-million and to face $3-billion more in credit demands by July. The fiscal plan is the attempt to detail the city's fiscal plight in as believable, if as harrowing, a form as possible to show a new mood of resolution to investors.

Like all the other major fiscal decisions, the emergency board will have the power to overrule the city on this, if necessary.

Governor Carey clearly had one of his more relaxed moments of recent days as he signed the law and pronounced the city and state a bit safer with "a bill that puts us on the threshold of tomorrow." "We can approach the period ahead with tempered optimism," he said.

By nightfall, the brief moment was forgotten and one of Mr. Carey's fiscal advisers, preparing the next steps, sounded like a weary Alpine climber. "Have you seen what we've got to do next?" he asked.

September 10, 1975

Highlights of Fiscal Plan

Special to The New York Times

ALBANY, Sept. 9—The act passed by the special session of the Legislature and signed into law early this morning by Governor Carey provides the city with $2.3-billion to stave off fiscal collapse at least until early December. But it transfers control of the city's budget from the local elected officials to a new state-dominated board.

And, if the city is unable to straighten out its fiscal affairs and regain access to the commercial money markets it will need later, the new law lays out the procedures to be followed in the event of default.

Following are the highlights of the new statutes:

Emergency Financial Control Board

The board is the key to the entire plan. The city must develop a three-year financial plan for itself and its independent agencies, and the board must make sure it is carried out. The board will take all city revenues into its own bank account and disburse those revenues only in accordance with the financial plan.

Members of the board will be the Governor, the State Controller, the Mayor, the City Controller and three persons appointed by the Governor with the advice and consent of the Senate.

Special Deputy State Controller

The act authorizes the State Controller to appoint a special deputy for New York City. He will function as the operating officer of the Emergency Financial Control Board and his principal task will be to monitor the city's compliance with the financial plan.

Default

The act provides the legal and administrative machinery for dealing with the city's obligations in the event of a default.

1. Creditors must give 30 days' notice before taking legal action against the city.
2. There would be a stay of at least 90 days of attempts by creditors to take action against the city.
3. The city and the control board would be authorized to submit a repayment plan to the state courts.
4. The city and the control board would be authorized to seek relief in the Federal courts under Federal bankruptcy law.

Wage Freeze

The act makes the wage increase imposed by the city in June a state law. It suspends all salary and wage increases for employes of the city and its independent agencies for one year. The control board can extend the freeze for the duration of the city's financial crisis.

Appropriations

Under the new law, the state will advance $250-million to the city and $500-million to the Municipal Assistance Corporation, but only after being assured that the rest of the $2.3-billion package will be forthcoming from sources other than the state, namely pension funds, and the financial community.

The state will advance $250-million to the M.A.C. this month, $250-million directly to the city next month and as much of the remaining $250-million to the M.A.C. in November as the city might need.

In addition, both the M.A.C. and the control board must certify before each monthly advance from the state that there is enough cash available for the city's needs for that month.

The appropriations to the city will be covered by short-term notes issued to the state and due Oct. 1, 1976. They will be backed by city-held mortgages on the so-called Mitchell-Lama housing projects. The appropriations to the M.A.C. will be covered by one-year M.A.C. notes for $250-million and M.A.C. bonds for $250-million, redeemable in 20 years.

Pension Funds

The city pension funds will buy M.A.C. bonds in the following amounts: Teachers' Retirement System, $200-million; Employes Retirement System, $225-million; Police Pension Fund, $55-million; Board of Education Retirement System, $10-million, and Fire Department Pension Fund, $10-million.

The state pension funds will buy M.A.C. bonds in the following amounts: Policemen's and Firemen's Retirement System and Employes Retirement System, $125-million; Teachers' Retirement System, $100-million. In addition, the State Insurance Fund will buy $100-million of M.A.C. bonds.

Under the act, none of these purchases will go through if the city defaults before the purchases can be made.

Trustee Responsibility

The act declares that M.A.C. securities are prudent and legal investments for a trustee of a public pension or retirement system. It releases such trustees from culpability in the event they lose money on their M.A.C. investments.

Also, the act makes M.A.C. bonds acceptable security for certificates of deposit and an acceptable investment for city sinking funds.

September 10, 1975

Crisis Is Believed to Cost Other Borrowers Billions

By MICHAEL C. JENSEN

When cities or states borrow money these days by selling securities in a tax-exempt bond market that has been staggered by New York City's financial crisis, it often means dollars and cents out of the pockets of the average American homeowner or taxpayer.

By some estimates, New York's financial debacle will cost municipal and state governmental units an extra $3-billion—spread over the life of newly issued notes and bonds—for a single year of borrowing money at swollen interest rates. That amounts to $14 for each man, woman and child in the United States.

The higher interest costs being paid by many cities and states are certain to be passed along to taxpayers and to customers of utilities and such services as water and sewage disposal. The ballooning costs will be reflected in higher property, income and sales taxes, and in costlier service rates.

The impact of New York's crisis is being felt in the far reaches of the nation—from East Millinocket, Me., to San Antonio, Tex., to Salem, Ore.

Murfreesboro, Tenn. (population 27,179), for example, had to borrow $3.8-million this month for a new fire station, a police building, airport hangars and school classrooms.

John Barber, the city recorder, said he agreed with estimates that New York City's financial difficulties were costing municipal bond issuers an average of at least half a percentage point in higher interest costs. On that basis, Murfreesboro is paying $20,000 a year extra—an average of about $1 on each local property assessment.

Murfreesboro's experience, multiplied by the thousands of issues that are floated each year to raise money for local or regional projects, is expected to result in a drain on taxpayers, and on a cutback in services and curtailment of capital projects.

While specific dollars and cents estimates of the impact of New York's financial difficulties have been hard to come by, Edward F. Renshaw, a professor of economics and finance at the State University of New York at Albany, recently estimated that the "spill-over" cost to the rest of the nation, in terms of added interest costs on bond issues, was already running at the rate of $2-billion a year.

Mr. Renshaw reached that conclusion by analyzing the narrowing gap between yields on corporate bonds and on state and local government bonds. Such a procedure helped to screen out other factors such as generally rising interest rates in all sectors of the economy.

Mr. Renshaw found that while the yields of both corporate and government bonds had been rising, the government bond yields had been rising more rapidly, indicating a skyrocketing of interest costs.

He also took into account the soaring cost of short-term borrowing by governmental units, and concluded that the "cumulative spill-over costs" to governmental units issuing bonds and notes was about $3-billion a year, or $14 a person on a population basis.

Costs Widespread

"The costs to other governmental units [outside New York] are really quite pervasive and extremely widespread," he said. "They are not confined solely to other large cities and communities with poor credit ratings."

Specialists at half a dozen Wall Street investment firms, asked for their own estimates, generally supported Mr. Renshaw's conclusions, although most of them warned that it was difficult to be too specific.

In addition, an inquiry by The New York Times into borrowing costs incurred by cities and states across the nation indicated that the impact of New York City's difficulties was indeed widespread, and that municipal and state fund raisers blamed much of their soaring costs on New York City.

The city of San Antonio, Tex., for example, had to pay an interest rate of almost 7.4 per cent early this month when it borrowed $50-million to help finance the construction of two new coal-powered electrical generating plants.

One Wall Street specialist familiar with the borrowing estimated that the city would pay an extra $4-million during the average 16-year life of the bonds that it issued as a direct result of New York's role in the deterioration of the bond market.

On that basis, San Antonio's 236,000 residential customers for gas and electricity (the city operates its own utility) would have to pay an additional 50 cents a year on the average to cover the higher borrowing costs.

"New York has undoubtedly had a negative influence," said Samuel E. Maclin, president of the Russ Securities Corporation in San Antonio, the city's financial consultant on borrowing.

Financial experts say much of the added cost in such borrowings is a direct result of investor reluctance to buy state and municipal securities.

Investors who traditionally buy such securities have been wary since New York City became mired in its well-publicized financial difficulties.

There is considerable uneasiness among investors over a possible default by New York City on some of its securities, and of a subsequent default by New York State, which has come to the financial rescue of the city.

Such defaults would weaken the tax-exempt market still further, experts believe, eroding the values of existing securities and making it more difficult for cities and states to borrow money at reasonable interest rates.

New York City has been hardest hit, and is currently unable to raise money by selling notes or bonds because investors simply will not buy them. Next hardest hit has been the State of New York and its various agencies and authorities such as the Housing Finance Agency. Other major cities like Detroit, Newark and Boston also have been severely affected.

Less highly publicized, but also in serious trouble, are smaller cities and towns in New York State. Poughkeepsie, for example, a small town 85 miles north of New York City that is best known as the home of Vassar College, recently had to borrow $3.5-million to finance a completed water-main-installation project and sewage-treatment plant.

The Case of Poughkeepsie

The town initially sought to borrow the money for a full year, but because it had to pay an interest rate of 8.9 per cent, it decided to borrow for only six months, and then return to the credit market in March, 1976, when rates might be lower.

Last March, when Poughkeepsie borrowed money for the same capital-improvement projects, it paid only 4.8 per cent interest. Edwin J. Stoll, the town's controller, estimated that aobut one-third of the increase was due to New York City's difficulties.

"We're paying the highest interest rate in our history," he said, as he sat in his small, modestly furnished office overlooking Route 44 in Poughkeepsie.

For Poughkeepsie residents who use town water, the increase in New York City-related interest costs amounts to about $4.50 per household. In Poughkeepsie, as in other cities and towns paying higher interest costs, reserve funds and other methods of cushioning the impact of the higher rates are being utilized. As a result, water fees in Poughkeepsie are not likely to rise immediately. In the long run, however, the money must come from the pockets of the townspeople.

Impact Not Understood

While New York's financial troubles have had a broad impact on taxpayers and homeowners throughout the country, that impact is little understood, partly because the subject is so arcane.

State and municipal bonds are sold primarily to raise money for long-term projects, and notes are sold largely to pay current expenses until anticipated taxes or other revenues can be collected. Interest on such loans is paid regularly to the investors who lend the money, and the bonds and notes are redeemed (paid off at face value) after a specified period of months or years.

The bonds and notes are usually sold to individual investors, or to banks, insurance companies and trustees or managers of other large pools of money. They are not generally sold directly to the public by the issuing body, but are sold to banks and brokerage houses, called underwriters, who then resell them to the public.

The borrowed money is used for public projects such as construction and repair of water and sewer systems, schools and playgrounds.

The government allows such securities to be sold on a "tax-exempt" basis, and therefore purchasers are not required to pay taxes on the interest they receive.

Because the bonds and notes are tax-exempt, they generally do not carry as high an interest rate as other types of securities like corporate bonds or United States Treasury bonds. As a result, state and municipal bodies selling tax-exempt securities have traditionally been able to borrow money relatively cheaply.

Most tax-exempt securities, once issued, are traded in an open market, and as their price fluctuates, their yield (the fixed annual interest expressed as a percentage of the current selling price) also fluctuates.

Thus, as prices drop, yields increase. For example, a bond with a face value of $1,000 that pays initial interest at 8 per cent, would have a current yield of over 10 per cent if it were selling for $750. Paradoxically, rising yields indicate that the market value of the security is deteriorating.

Borrowing Costs Soars

Moody's Bond Survey, an authoritative weekly review of the nation's bond markets, pointed out last week that the cost of borrowing in tax-exempt markets had soared to record levels in recent weeks. The highest-rated securities were approaching yields of 7 per cent, and less desirable bonds were commensurately higher.

"Unsettlement over the New York financial crisis, and concern over the Treasury's financing needs were two principal causative factors influencing the recent erosion of market confidence," Moody's said. "Tax-exempt rates reached unparalleled heights, with many issuers having difficulty marketing obligations."

Moody's added that the taxable-bond market also was feeling the impact.

"The tax-exempt sector and even the taxable side of the market were becoming increasingly uneasy over the potential consequences of a possible default by New York City and the impact that financial support to the city was having on the market for New York State debt," Moody's said.

Although warnings such as Moody's have been widespread in recent weeks, the government bond market has rebounded somewhat recently. Last week, for example, typical 20-year state and local government bonds gained an average of more than $23 for every $1,000 face amount. Bond experts said many high-quality issues continued to be offered at reasonable interest rates.

While most tax-exempt issues are for public projects, the law also allows corporations to borrow through cities and towns in tax-exempt markets for pollution-abatement equipment.

The Pain in Maine

The tiny town of East Millinocket, Me., recently floated an $8.25-million bond issue on behalf of the Great Northern Nekoosa Corporation, which has a local newsprint plant.

The company had to pay 8.3 per cent interest for the borrowing, which will be spread out over an average of 24 years.

Emery E. Allain, vice president of finance for Great Northern, said the interest rate probably would have been one-half a percentage point lower, if it had not been for New York City's difficulties.

The higher rate means Great Northern will pay close to $1-million extra in interest costs over the life of the bonds, and, according to Mr. Allain, "We'll have to pass it along in the price of the product."

At the state level, borrowed money has also become increasingly expensive. The State of Oregon, for example, sold $125-million worth of long-term bonds this month, paying a net interest cost of nearly 6.3 per cent for the money, which was earmarked for housing loans for veterans.

Oregon officials calculated that the interest rate was probably one-quarter of a percentage point higher than it would have been if New York City had not gotten into financial difficulties. That is equivalent to an out-of-pocket cost to the state's veterans' housing fund of over $300,000 a year, which ultimately must be reflected in higher interest rates than would otherwise be charged on loans made to veterans.

In some areas, the high cost of borrowed money has meant a deferral of projects. Buffalo, for instance, borrowed $24-million six months ago for new projects, and this month the city had difficulty raising money at reasonable rates to roll over or renew the loan. As a consequence, Buffalo borrowed less than $13-million from local banks and insurance companies, paying an average interest rate of about 10 per cent—nearly double what it paid last April.

The city also transferred more than $3-million out of its cash reserves and temporarily deferred projects involving improvements to the city water system and refurbishing of its parks and playgrounds.

Although the cost for the money that the city successfully borrowed was about $600,000 higher than the equivalent year-earlier cost (Buffalo attributes about half of the increase to New York City's difficulties), Buffalo residents will not be asked to pay more in taxes because the borrowing was cut in half. The impact they will feel is the deferral of the improvement projects.

"I'm not quarreling with what is happening in New York City, though," said George D. O'Connell, Buffalo's controller. "Except for the grace of God, there go I."

October 19, 1975

STATE UNIT BACKS CITY BUDGET PLAN, ORDERS NEW CUTS

Reductions of $700-Million and More Layoffs Approved Under 3-Year Program

SOME PROVISOS ADDED

Financial Control Board Asks Machinery to Monitor How Well City Complies

By FRANCIS X. CLINES

The state's Emergency Financial Control Board last night approved a three-year austerity plan for the city that will mean more than $700-million in budget cuts and additional thousands of layoffs whose total has not yet been determined.

The emergency board, fulfilling a legislative mandate, approved the basic proposals of Mayor Beame for cutting the expense budget for the next three years, but ordered that his planned cuts in the construction budget be increased by more than $100-million a year. In addition, the board ordered compliance machinery to monitor how well the city lives up to the avowed economies.

The action by the board, of which Governor Carey is chairman, represented the formal setting of a severe new course for the city. Officials said it would mean large-scale service cuts, an end to new municipal construction, a freeze on hiring and wages, and a payroll that would continue to shrink through attrition and layoffs.

The board accepted Mayor Beame's approach — that he must cut $200-million from the current expenditure budget as the first step in reducing a deficit estimated at $724-million in the next three years.

Construction Cuts

However, the board cut further into the city's separate construction budget, ordering $390-million more cut below what the Mayor intended to spend during the austerity period.

The austerity plan, mandated on the city in an attempt to repair its shattered credit standing, was described by one board official as, at best, a "Dunkirk" strategy — a large-scale retreat for the sake of the city's fiscal survival.

The approval by the seven-member board, which includes the Mayor, left numerous details still to be settled on the staff level. Various basic questions also remain to be answered, such the eventual numbe of additional layoffs to be required beyond the 21,000 city workers dismissed thus far in the crisis.

The city's Deputy Mayor for Financial Affairs, Kenneth S. Axelson, indicated that under the current highly uncertain outlook, the city would need Federal guarantees to get an estimated $6-billion to cover the city's current credit needs. This, he said, would be in addition to asking the major banking institutions to "roll over" their current short-term city obligations.

Beyond that, the city would eventually have to regain enough standing to borrow for its seasonal revenue adjustments.

Mr. Axelson said the three-year cut of $724-million from the city budget would be accomplished by a combination of program and personnel reductions. The latter would involve a still unknown mixture of actual layoffs and payroll attrition through such measures as retirements.

Before the board's approval was announced, Governor Carey stirred some confusion over the layoff-attrition question when he estimated in a speech to the City Club that the three-year plan would mean 55,000 "persons to be eliminated from the jobs."

Some officials said privately that the Governor seemed excessive in his numbers and vague in making distinctions between dismissals and attrition.

Mr. Axelson diplomatically put aside questions on this point, saying, "I don't know how he computed that figure."

Dollar-Cost Estimate

Privately, city and state officials emphasized that it was impossible at this time to state the exact dollar cost to the city of the plan's methods for extending the currently huge municipal debts into long-term financing. This is so because the plan is dependent on the city's hopes to get back into the borrowing market with Federal assistance, and there is no way of estimating what the interest rate and debt service might be.

Mayor Beame objected to the additional cuts in the construction budget, board sources said, but he was in the minority.

City officials, in their private negotiations with the control board, have contended that the construction, or capital, budget already had been severely cut, being almost halved in the next

The New York Times/Neal Boenzi

State Controller Arthur Levitt, left, and Governor Carey as meetings on finances went on at Mr. Carey's office here

three years from present levels.

The board's action will reduce it to the level of $930-million in 1978—a level of annual spending for the city's physical growth that was first passed by the city budget more than a decade ago.

As the board met privately to meet its deadline, related developments in the fiscal crisis included a speech by the Senate majority leader, Warren M. Anderson, Binghamton Republican. He used his strongest language yet in criticizing Ford Administration officials, as well as Congressional Democrats, for failing to help the city.

Senator Anderson, addressing the Union League Club here, was particularly critical of Treasury Secretary William E. Simon's view that whatever aid might be extended to the city should include a "punitive" approach to discourage future budget profligacy.

"I used to think 'Simon Says' was only a game they played up at the Borscht Belt hotels where you lose if you don't do what Simon says," the Senator declared. "These days I'm beginning to worry that 'Simon Says' is a game in which everybody loses. I suppose another solution would be to spank everybody in the city and send them to bed without police protection."

As the control board considered Mayor Beame's proposed budget cuts on a broad dollar basis, city and city-aided agencies were working out their own specific plans on how to enforce these same cuts.

Some traumatic plans were announced in the courts, where City Night Court is to be closed and more than 800 positions are to be closed out, including those of 19 senior Supreme Court justices who have been serving after reaching the age of 70.

In the schools, various economies were announced, including large increases in the cost of children's bus and subway passes.

Earlier in the day, City Controller Harrison J. Goldin journeyed to Washington with Governor Carey's secretary, David Burke, to confer with Congressional staff workers who have been preparing legislative proposals to help the city.

The basic goal of the Governor has been to achieve legislative approval of a plan whereby Federal guarantees of city borrowings would be extended as the way to attract investors back to city securities.

Felix G. Rohatyn, chairman of the Municipal Assistance Corporation, the state-created agency designed to float stronger bonds on behalf of the city, said he already was working on a plan under which, if Federal guarantees were given, the large institutional holders of M.A.C. bonds might agree to extend these obligations over longer periods, to lower the interest costs for the city.

As the board proceeded in private through the Mayor's figures, the earlier controversy over the city teachers' recent labor agreement resurfaced yesterday. Staff analysts for the emergency control board, which at first had rejected the agreement as too costly, now have concluded that the first year of the proposed settlement is within the austerity budget, according to board sources.

The only issue now holding up approval of the agreement is said to be the teachers' need to decide how much of the salary increase in the agreement they are willing to defer. The state emergency law provides, in effect, for a wage freeze during the coming three years.

The union leaders' hopes for easing the layoff threat were rooted in a presentation by the union consultant Jack Bigel, who pointed out in part that the new wage freeze was discouraging senior workers from staying on the job to enrich their pensions. As a result they are retiring at double and triple the usual rate lately.

No concrete plan for attrition has been set by the board, informed officials said last evening, but ways might eventually found to provide for attrition but fall back on dismissals if the payroll shrinkage proved too slow.

October 21, 1975

FORD, CASTIGATING CITY, ASSERTS HE'D VETO FUND GUARANTEE; OFFERS BANKRUPTCY BILL

'BAILOUT' BARRED

President's Plan Has Provision for Safety in Event of Default

By MARTIN TOLCHIN
Special to The New York Times

WASHINGTON, Oct. 29—President Ford said today that he was "prepared to veto" any bill that would rescue New York City by having the Federal Government guarantee the availability of funds to prevent a default.

"I can tell you—and tell you now—that I am prepared to veto any bill that has as its purpose a Federal bailout of New York City to prevent default," the President said.

Mr. Ford sent to the Congress, as an alternative, legislation to enable the city to file for bankruptcy and maintain essential services.

Congressional Democratic leaders indicated, however, that they would continue to pursue loan-guarantee legislation, which is expected to be reported out of the Senate Banking Committee tomorrow and the House Banking Committee within a week. House Democratic leaders met this afternoon to explore methods of linking the President's legislation to a loan-guarantee bill.

Officials Castigated

The President, who spoke slowly and deliberately, spent more than half of his 40-minute address at the National Press Club castigating the management and tactics of New York City and State officials. Even so, he hinted that Federal funds might be forthcoming if needed by the city after a default.

"In the event of default, the Federal Government will work with the [Federal] court to assure that police, fire and other essential services for the protection of life and property in New York are maintained," the President said.

L. William Seidman, one of the President's top economic advisers, who met with reporters before the speech, was asked if Federal cooperation with the courts could include financing.

"It could include money," Mr. Seidman said. "We don't foresee that possibility, but we don't preclude it."

Decries 'Scare Talk'

The President decried as "scare talk" warnings by city and state officials, and some bankers and economists who, he said, had predicted that a default by New York City could touch off a national and international "catastrophe." He added that New Yorkers themselves would suffer only "temporary inconveniences."

The President also said that the city had the capacity to avoid a default. "I don't assume that the city will default," he said in response to a question, "because I think the capacity of city and state is there to avoid default."

Mr. Seidman, asked to explain, said that the President was referring to the ability of both the city and state to invest $12-billion in pension funds in New York City obligations, the ability of the state to raise new taxes and earmark new revenues, and the ability of the city to reduce expenses.

Ford Sees No U. S. Loss

Mr. Ford responded to 10 minutes of questions submitted in writing, as is the National Press Club's custom. He thereby became the first President in memory to hold a news conference at the club.

Asked what a New York City default would cost the Federal Government, the President replied that "I foresee no loss to the Federal Government whatsoever."

Senator William Proxmire, Democrat of Wisconsin and chairman of the Senate banking committee, has said that a default would cost the Federal Government billions of dollars in long-term aid.

The President's promised veto contrasted with his statement at a news conference on Oct. 9, when he said that "I always consider any legislation passed by the Congress, but I certainly have to look at the small print on any legislation that is aimed at bailing New York City out when their financial or fiscal record has not been a good one."

Ten days ago, a high Administration official told The New York Times that the President would reluctantly approve legislation to ease the city's fiscal

The New York Times/Teresa Zabala

President Ford telling of his plans for New York City

The New York Times/William E. Sauro

Mayor Beame responding to the President's proposals

crisis, provided that it contained the stringent restrictions that Congress was likely to impose. In addition, Vice President Rockefeller also has been urging legislation to avert a New York default.

But the position the President stated today was consistent with his conservative Republican philosophy and with his view that the cities of the Northeast are not the base of his support.

The President's bankruptcy plan is similar to legislation now before the House Judiciary Committee, where it is stalled because the committee has been waiting for the approval of Mayor Beame.

The city, with state approval, would be authorized to file a petition with the Federal District Court in New York under a proposed new Chapter 15 of the Bankruptcy Act. Such a petition would not require the consent of a majority of the city's creditors, a provision of the present law, which is contained in Chapter 9.

The petition would state that the city was unable to pay its debts as they matured, and would be accompanied by a proposed way to work out an adjustment of its debts with its creditors.

The petition would lead to an automatic stay of suits by creditors so that the city's essential functions would not be disrupted. This would provide time for the city to work out arrangements with its creditors.

"The proposed legislation will include provision that as a condition of New York City petitioning the court the city must not only file a good-faith plan for payments to its creditors, but must also present a program for placing the fiscal affairs of the city on a sound basis," the President said.

The court would then determine if the city's plan was satisfactory — how many policemen, firemen and teachers the city needed and how much they should be paid—and would approve or disapprove each of these elements in the city's plan.

The President also said that "in order to meet the short-term needs of New York City, the court would be empowered to authorize debt certificates covering new loans to the city which would be paid out of future revenues ahead of other creditors."

Asked who would purchase the bonds of a defaulted city, Mr. Ford said that these certificates would have "top priority" and that "every other creditor stands in line."

Mr. Seidman, asked if it was contemplated that the Federal Government would be the purchaser of last resort of these debt certificates, replied that that had never been discussed and was not foreseen.

"I don't want anybody misled," the President said. "This proposed legislation will not, by itself, put the affairs of New York City in order. Some hard measures must be taken by the officials of New York City and New York State. They must either increase revenues or cut expenditures or devise some combination that will bring them to a sound financial position.

"Careful examination has convinced me that those measures are neither beyond the realm of possibility nor beyond the demands of reason," he continued. "If they are taken, New York City will, with the assistance of the legislation I am proposing, be able to restore itself as a fully solvent operation."

On Capitol Hill, however, some disagreed with his assessment. Speaker Carl Albert, Democrat of Oklahoma, said that he even doubted that the President would, in fact, veto loan-guarantee legislation.

"That might hurt him," Mr. Albert said. He said that although he had not studied the President's bankruptcy plan, "it is not enough."

Senator Mike Mansfield, Montana Democrat and Senate majority leader, said that a New York default "for one might prove the domino theory" because other cities were in deep financial trouble, but he said that he had not yet decided how to vote on any aid bill.

Senator Proxmire said that "in simple proposing to make it easier for New York City to go bankrupt, the President has chosen a course that would shove New York into a tin-cup status and onto the Federal Government's back for years to come."

Senator Hubert H. Humphrey, Minnesota Democrat and chairman of the Joint Economic Committee, said that the President's proposal "is nothing more or less than political quackery for a financial disease that goes far beyond New York City's boundaries."

Senator Hugh Scott, Republican of Pennsylvania and Senate minority leader, supported the President's proposal but said that he was maintaining "an absolutely open mind" on Federal loans or loan guarantees to aid New York City. "If more is needed, I would be prepared to judge it on the basis of what is fair and just," he said.

The Pesident concluded his speech by noting that Washington, like New York, was providing more benefits and services than it could afford. He said that if the practice continued "a day of reckoning will come to Washington and the whole country just as it has to New York."

"When the day of reckoning comes, who will bail out the United States of America?" he asked.

October 30, 1975

Study Finds Declining Cities Pay More for Services

By EILEEN SHANAHAN

Special to The New York Times

WASHINGTON, Nov. 16—Public services cost proportionally more in the largest cities and in those with declining populations, the very places that generally have a lessening ability to pay for them, according to a new study of the finances of urban areas.

The study, one of the most comprehensive of those recently published in the wake of the New York City financial crisis, was done by Thomas Muller, an economist with the Urban Institute.

It is entitled "Growing and Declining Urban Areas: A Fiscal Comparison," and was published by the institute today.

The study does not focus particularly on New York because its author found that New York does not fit clearly into either the "growing" or the "declining category. The city had a population decline of 1.8 percent from 1960 to 1973, but the 14 other cities in the over 500,000 population class that were labeled "declining" averaged a 12.5 percent population loss.

Mr. Muller's analysis shows that the services that local government must pay for generally cost more, both per capita and as a percentage of the money income of the city's residents, in the largest cities and in those that are losing population.

Traffic and Crime

All the reasons for this are not clear, he said, although some are. For example, traffic control costs proportionally more in the largest cities because traffic problems increase even faster than population does. The same is true of the rise in crime, or at least of the fear of crime, and thus the cost of police protection grows faster than the population.

As for the proportionally higher costs of local government in cities that are losing population, this may be traceable in part to the fact that declining cities are generally older and the older average age of buildings produces higher maintenance and fire-fighting costs, the study said.

Older cities, it said, also tend to have proportionally larger low-income populations that have an above-average need for public services, a situation that worsens with the continued outmigration of middle-income families from older cities.

The older, declining cities are also losing private jobs, especially in manufacturing, the study found, and though the number of persons on local government payrolls has been increasing, the increase is not big enough to offset the decline in private jobs.

Regional Patterns

Regional paterns of growth and decline are very pronounced, even among smaller cities, Mr. Muller found.

Among the cities with 500,000 or more population whose number has fallen since 1960, only San Francisco, Seattle and New Orleans were outside of the East or north central states. Of those that were growing, only Columbus, Ohio, and Indianapolis were in the East or north central area.

Even among cities in the 200,000 to 500,000 class this pattern held. All growing cities in this class except Toledo, Ohio, Wichita, Kan., and Yonkers are in the South or West. Conversely, only three of the declining cities—Birmingham, Ala., Oakland Calif., and Louisville Ky.—are in the South or West.

The problem for cities that are victims of outmigration is that population decline correlates with at least a relative fall in average income, Mr. Muller found. In other words, income per capita in these cities is rising more slowly than in growing cities.

Moreover, the number of jobs in growing cities tends to increase even faster than population growth, he said.

Most declining cities, except for Pittsburgh, St. Louis, and a few others, have tried to maintain public services at their previous levels, despite a lowered ability, at least relatively, to pay for them, Mr. Muller reported.

But there are strong pressures for reducing local government payrolls and denying wage increases to local government employees, and these will undoubtedly continue, he said.

He enumerated some dangers he saw in layoffs, particularly in police and fire departments, where he argued that dismissals according to seniority would increase the average age of policemen and firemen to the point where efficiency might be impaired. He also noted that a disproportionate number of minority workers would probably be laid off if strict seniority were followed.

However, Pittsburgh has cut its city payrolls by 18 percent since 1970, including a reduction in the police force, and there has been no general public disapproval, at least none that was registered at the polls, the study said.

To help declining cities pay for public services, Mr. Muller proposed a partial Federal guarantee for local government bonds that would be based on the loss of private jobs and population and the unemployment rate in a city.

He said that only bonds isued before 1975 should be guaranteed, because the objective of the guarantees would be to help finance previous capital outlays that a city could no longer support because of its declining condition.

His formula would produce guarantees for about $2 billion worth of New York City bonds or close to one-quarter of the city's "full faith and credit" bonds.

Mr. Muller also proposed that the Federal Government guarantee the pension payments of city workers who were retired early as a result of the need for local government economies. However, he said cities should be forced to move toward sounder funding of pension plans before such guarantees were given.

He also recommended changes in various Federal-aid formulas and a deliberate concentration of military procurement and other Federal contracts in declining areas.

At present both Federal military contracts and military bases are concentrated in growing areas, he said.

November 17, 1975

FORD ASKS $2.3 BILLION U.S. LOANS FOR CITY TO HELP FINANCE PLAN TO AVERT A DEFAULT

8% INTEREST RATE

Simon to Administer Seasonal Payments Made to the State

By MARTIN TOLCHIN

Special to The New York Times

WASHINGTON, Nov. 26—President Ford tonight dropped his opposition to Federal aid for New York City and proposed legislation for $2.3 billion in short-term seasonal loans that the city has said will enable it to avert default.

The President's action capped a turbulent eight-month campaign by city and state officials to obtain Federal funds, which they said were necessary to prevent insolvency, and an equally intensive White House campaign to compel the city and state to take "concrete actions" to put the city's fiscal house in order.

It also marked something of a political milestone, with the President choosing a course some conservative domestic advisers had told him would not be acceptable to many American voters. But it came only one day after the Legislature in Albany had enacted a package of taxes and other fiscal changes that also posed substantial political hazards.

Good Through June '78

The loans, which would be administered by Treasury Secretary William E. Simon, would extend through June 1978. The city would pay an interest rate of 1 point more than the Federal bill rate, which Administration officials said was now 7 percent.

Congressional leaders have said that they will accept the President's proposal as a substitute for pending loan-guarantee legislation, which was drafted following three months of Congressional hearings and intensive Congressional bargaining.

The House of Representatives is expected to approve the substitute legislation next Wednesday and the Senate a few days later.

The President, asked about his Oct. 29 pledge to veto any legislation whose purpose was to "bail out" New York City to prevent a default, replied, "New York has bailed itself out." [Question 3.]

"New York City, by what they have done in conjunction with New York State, in conjunction with the noteholders, pension fund people, they have bailed out themselves," he said.

He emphasized that the Federal Government would have a prior lien on all New York City income and said, "The Federal Government will be held harmless, and the taxpayers won't have to lose a penny." [Question 4.]

The President said that "we have always felt that they could do enough, but only because we were firm have they moved ahead to accomplish what they have done now." [Question 9.]

"If we had shown any give, I think they wouldn't have made the hard decision that they made in the last week or so," he added.

"There will be no cost to the rest of the taxpayers of the United States," he said.

L. William Seidman, one of the President's top economic advisers, told newsmen tonight that the city would receive its first loan, of $141 million, on Dec. 11.

The President, who had previously insisted that bankruptcy legislation was the only vehicle for Federal aid, took credit tonight for city and state fiscal changes that he said had led to tonight's action.

"Only a few months ago, we were told that all these reforms were impossible and could not be accomplished by New York alone," the President said. "Today they are being done."

"I have quite frankly been surprised that they have come as far as they have," Mr. Ford said, adding: "I doubted that they would act unless ordered to do so by a Federal court."

The President, asked if he feared political resentment because the Legislature had enacted new taxes, said, "The only requirement that I imposed was that the financial situation in New York City be such that we could handle the problem at the Federal level in the way in which we're doing it today." [Question 27.]

"As I understand it," he went on, "Governor Carey has taken the full responsibility for the total package. I think that's a very courageous stand by Governor Carey."

The President praised city and state officials "for their constructive efforts to date" but said that one problem remained: "In the next few months, New York City will still lack enough funds to cover its day-to-day operating expenses."

He said that he was proposing Federal aid because of the steps the city and state had taken and "because the private cerdit markets may remain closed to them."

"Lowest-Cost Way'

President Ford said: "The reason we made it a loan rather than a loan guarantee is very simple—it's a much cleaner transaction." [Question 1.]

"If you have a loan guarantee, you have other parties," he added.

The President's legislation, to be called "The New York City Seasonal Financing Act of 1975," envisions Federal aid of $1.3 billion in the current fiscal year and $2.1 billion in each of the following two fiscal years.

A loan may be made only if the Secretary of the Treasury determines that there is a reasonable prospect of repayment. Loans will bear such terms and conditions as the Secretary may deem necessary, and he would be authorized to withhold any Federal payments due the city due under the law if the loans are not repaid on time.

All loans will be made to the state, as the legal entity with which the Federal Government relates. The same provision is contained in the pending legislation.

President Ford had long insisted that the city and state were capable of solving their own problems and of preventing a default without Federal aid.

"I don't assume that the city will default because I think the capacity in the city and the capacity in the state is there to avoid default," the President said in response to a question after his speech at the National Press Club on Oct. 29.

The reaction to that speech, which was generally perceived as punitive, upset some persons close to the President. Especially unsettling, they said, was a New York Daily News front-page headline: "Ford to City: Drop Dead!"

Since last summer, the President's door has been open to New York officials and bankers, mayors, economists and others who pleaded their case. His position did not change, however.

The President and his economic advisers argued that aid for the beleaguered city would constitute a breach of Federal-state relations and an invitation to municipal excesses.

Precedent Feared

They had argued that such aid would be counterproductive because it would discourage the city from making fiscal reforms needed to restore its access to credit markets.

They said they felt that such aid could become a bottomless pit, and they questioned how the Federal Government could aid one city and not others. Finally, they had argued that a loan guarantee would actually make New York paper worth more than Federal paper because the New York paper would not be subject to Federal taxes.

The strongest counter to these arguments came from a procession of bankers, mayors, economists and at least one foreign leader — West Germany's Chancellor, Helmu Schmidt—who argued that the effect of default was unknowable and that it could trigger serious economic reversals of national and international proportions.

Some of those bankers, who represented the major New York banks, were not given much credence by the Administration, which viewed them as interested parties who had purchased city obligations in imprudent amounts.

The House Democratic leadership, however, immediately perceived that the issue had the makings of a national one that could appeal to voters in an election year; it seemed a classic confrontation between antiurban Middle-American Republicanism and activist Democrats.

If aid to New York was a no-win position for President Ford, the leaders felt, it was a no-lose position for the House Democratic leadership. Should the dire warnings prove to have been correct, they could always point to their efforts to head off the catastrophe.

Although many in Congress initially dismissed the prospects of Federal aid, the legislation showed surprising vitality in committees.

The day after the President had vowed in his National Press Club speech to veto "any bill that has as its purpose a Federal bailout of New York City to prevent default," the Senate Banking Committee approved $4 billion loan-guarantee legislation by an 8-5 vote.

The legislation had been drafted by Senator William Proxmire, Democrat of Wisconsin, chairman of the committee and the strongest proponent of the legislation, and Senator Adlai E. Stevenson 3d Democrat of Illinois, who proposed stringent provisions such as restructuring the debt and renegotiating labor contracts.

Four days later, on Nov. 3, the House Banking Committee approved, 23-16, legislation to authorize $7 billion in loan guarantees to New York City.

The following week Representative John J. Rhodes, Republican of Arizona and House minority leader, said that if the city put its fiscal house in order he would support short-term loan guarantees to assure the city's cash flow. Nonetheless, the threat of a Presidential veto continued to block floor action.

On Nov. 13, Ron Nessen, the Presidential press secretary, said that the city was in fact, if not legally, in default, and that the President would consider short-term assistance to ease its cash-flow problems once Governor Carey's fiscal plan was implemented.

During that period, four public opinion polls indicated that most Americans supported some form of Federal aid to New York to avert a default.

The only remaining hitch, then, was the enactment of a $200 million tax package by the Legislature, a restructuring of the debt and agreement on pensions, all of which fell into place in the last 24 hours.

November 27, 1975

For a National Urban Strategy

By Richard C. Wade

New York's fiscal crisis is far from over and the package put together by Gov. Hugh Carey needs nurture and good luck to succeed. But it is not too early to examine the deeper problems that occasioned the crisis, for they threaten nearly every major metropolis in the country. And unless there is a radical change in our national approach to this urban malaise there will be more New Yorks in the future of America's cities.

Historically, it is not difficult to explain the origins of this national urban crisis. Cities have always had trouble providing essential services to their residents. Cities grew with unprecedented speed, with staggering problems accompanying soaring population expansion. But until the years after World War II they had sufficient resources to handle the job. The wealthiest and best educated for the most part lived within municipal boundaries; the major industrial and commercial facilities were also there. Even when the built-up areas spilled beyond the municipal limits, the outlying areas could be annexed to the city, thus maintaining an expanding tax base.

This flexible historical casement, however, was shattered by the suburban explosion that followed World War II. Resistance in the new communities made annexation politically impossible except in the South and West. The middle class more and more abandoned the cities; commerce and industry inevitably followed the residential flight. As tax producers left the city, tax consumers—the poor and elderly—remained behind where they were joined by Southern and Hispanic migrants. This demographic revolution profoundly altered the nature of urban life everywhere.

The old self-sufficient metropolis required no national strategy. If left alone, it could take care of itself. Even the new breed of able postwar mayors discovered they could not maintain urban services on a stagnant tax base. Increasingly, they turned to Washington for help.

The Johnson Administration responded with compassion but bewilderment. No precedents, either here or abroad, seemed appropriate. Hence, Washington sponsored all kinds of studies, embraced numberless pilot projects, and dunned the cities with money, hoping to reduce tensions and to buy time until it developed a comprehensive scheme. Yet none emerged.

Part of the Johnson Administration's sensitivity to the problems of the cities was political; traditionally they provided Democratic Presidential candidates with crucial votes. The approach of Richard M. Nixon and President Ford has been no less political. The suburbs were to the Republicans what the cities were to the Democrats. Hence, the most important part of the Republican response was revenue-sharing. By spreading money among 39,000 communities, it ignored the disproportionate needs of the larger and older cities in favor of suburbs and small towns.

The second part of the Nixon-Ford suburban strategy was intellectual. Administration spokesmen simply announced that "the urban crisis" was over and then systematically dismantled or bureaucratically crippled programs of the "Great Society."

One might suppose that the New York crisis would have shaken this complacent policy. But Administration spokesmen quickly labeled it a mere fiscal problem. It was not until the banking community became nervous about the national—indeed international—consequences of a New York default that the Administration put aside its ideology and gave some grudging assistance.

Still, the Administration persists in its doctrine of "New York exceptionalism," contending that the rest of urban America is healthy and immune from those forces that brought the nation's largest city to its knees.

While New York tottered at the financial precipice, no one really discussed why the city had engaged in fancy fiscal flimflam in the first place. The simple fact was that the city could no longer afford to provide normal urban services with its present revenue.

Even after the return to solvency, there will still be a million poor New Yorkers, housing will be more desperate, schools will continue to decline, if not deteriorate, and the cost of medical care for the elderly and infirm will mount. And the flight of the white middle class will accelerate.

It is in this sense that New York's problems are part of a general national urban crisis. What is to be done? Clearly, neither the panicked policy of the Johnson Administration nor the suburban policy of the Nixon-Ford days has arrested the decline of our urban centers. Despite official optimism in Washington, every responsible municipal official realizes that the present fiscal solvency is illusory and the momentary social peace very fragile.

What is needed now is a new national urban strategy that will handle both the short-range financial crunch and the long-run deterioration of our metropolitan society. That policy should have, I think, at least these elements:

1. A new formula for revenue sharing that takes into account the disproportionate needs of the cities.

2. The federalization of welfare and health payments to remove a growing burden on municipalities.

3. Federal bonuses to metropolitan areas that combine suburban and urban services on a functional basis for greater efficiency.

4. A new housing policy that would require multi-unit developers receiving any public subsidy, overt or covert to provide 10 percent to 15 percent of those units for low- and moderate-income families.

5. Federal guarantees for municipal bonds.

Richard C. Wade is Distinguished Professor of Urban History at the Graduate Center of the City University of New York.

January 1, 1976

SUN BELT: WAVE OF THE FUTURE?

MAYORS IN SOUTH CONFER ON CITIES

'Wholesome Life' and Job Opportunities Studied

By WALTER RUGABER
Special to The New York Times

WILMINGTON ISLAND Ga., Nov. 16 — About 40 Southern mayors were soothed this week by a variety of experts on urban problems who suggested that the region's cities were much more pleasant than most places.

They are also richer than the country at large, the experts said. Their suburbs are less entrenched and less restricting. They have an apparent monopoly on the innovative consolidation of local governmental units.

But the leaders of the region's largest cities, who assembled for a two-day meeting arranged by the United States Conference of Mayors and financed by the Ford Foundation, also encountered many ominous signs.

Terry Sanford, the former Governor of North Carolina who is now president of Urban America, Inc., recalled waking up one morning as his train crossed northern New Jersey. He was on an industry-hunting trip to the North.

Great Industrial Area

"I looked out at the crowded tenements, the discolored streams, the smoggy atmosphere, the crowded, dingy living conditions, and realized that here was one of the great industrial sections of the country," he said.

"It was industry that I was seeking, and I wondered if all our efforts to bring new industry to North Carolina would mean only that we would destroy the climate of pleasant living, substituting that kind of unwholesome living."

Many of the mayors seemed haunted by the same fear as they met at informal discussions, cocktail parties and golfing foursomes at the Savannah Inn and Country Club.

Mr. Sanford said optimistically that the South, with some aggressive planning by the states, cities and the Federal Government, could provide the "wholesome life" as well as the job opportunities.

But widespread frustration was apparent among the mayors, who complained that their states had traditionally stymied development, with restrictions on taxing authority, annexation and other elements of development.

Mayors Not Surprised

Also, there was no surprise when John Feild, director of the community relations service detailed what he called the general indifference of Southern Congressmen to Federal programs designed for the cities.

Many of the mayors displayed enthusiasm but little hope for a proposal offered by Phillip Hammer of Washington, an economic consultant who is chairman of the National Capital Planning Commission.

He urged the assumption of all education and welfare burdens by a higher level of government in order to free municipal revenues for other pressing programs.

In another area, there was uneasiness when Vivian W. Henderson, president of Atlanta's predominantly Negro Clark College, called for steps to strengthen Negro communities with better housing and employment policies.

Despite the apprehensions that cropped up as the mayors studied their problems, the authorities who came here held out a hope that the South could avoid the crumbling, crisis-ridden cities of other regions.

For example, Mr. Feild said in an interview yesterday that the only city-county mergers or other forms of metropolitan consolidation in the nation had occurred in Jacksonville, Miami, Baton Rouge and Nashville.

Others pointed to imaginative activities by mayors such as Ralph Kelley of Chattanooga. He has put together various privately incorporated agencies to attract Federal money and large professional staffs.

On the other hand, many of the observers at this week's conference agreed that the advantages now apparent in most of the larger Southern cities were mainly the result of the region's agricultural past and its current economic boom.

Planning by political leaders has made few contributions in most cities, these observers said. In fact, they went on, urban growth has frequently occurred despite a failure to develop a fresh political outlook.

For example, the city of Jacksonville has recently completed the merger with surrounding Duval County that is considered one of the most aggressive developments anywhere in the country.

But many of the professional urbanologists here voiced sharp disappointment after the city's mayor, Hans G. Tanzler Jr., passed on one or two views developed in a discussion group he had led.

Mr. Tanzler asserted that the poor often just did not want to work, and that stiffer law enforcement should be imposed on slum neighborhoods to dry up "nefarious sources of income" in them.

"That's just a catchword that means, 'Niggers are shiftless,'" one of the mayor's listeners charged.

November 17, 1968

Phoenix Conflict: Rapid Growth of City vs. Good Life

People Find Quality and Quantity Are Not Synonymous

By STEVEN V. ROBERTS

Special to The New York Times

PHOENIX—"Mommy," says a local 2-year-old whenever he sees a vacant lot, "what are they going to build there?"

It is natural for anyone in Phoenix these days to assume that open space is for building, that the dusty cactus and chaparral will soon yield to brick and stone, to turquoise swimming pools and patches of lawn. The lawns are babied like children in the desert heat and are so intensely green they almost look painted on the arid earth.

The Talk of Phoenix

Today, almost one million people live in the Phoenix area, an increase of 45 per cent since 1960. They have come to escape the irritations and the agonies of city life elsewhere, but now they find that they are dragging their problems with them. Man, it seems, cannot escape himself.

The map looks as though someone put a juicy grapefruit down in the middle and squished it under a heavy boot. Spurts of urban sprawl extend into the desert as far as the Superstition Mountains, 30 miles from the downtown area. The site of the legendary Lost Dutchman gold mine is now virtually suburbia.

THIS did not happen by accident. The Chamber of Commerce, which must have a public relations department only slightly smaller than the Pentagon's, has pushed a tremendous campaign to attract tourists, residents and industry. For the last decade, anyway, the sacred value in Phoenix has been Growth.

There is another value here, however, one that is almost as important—"The Good Life." Those words have a certain mystique for Phoenix residents, who relish the warmth and dryness of desert life, the horses and orange trees in their backyards, the outdoor activity made possible by 300 days of sun every year.

Suddenly, however, these values seem to be in conflict. Growth is threatening The Good Life, and the civic psyche is deeply troubled. Bill Donaldson, the city manager of Scottsdale, a wealthy suburb, put it this way:

"People are starting to realize that quantity and quality are not synonymous. Of course, unless we station people on the border with shotguns, we'll continue to grow and grow rapidly. The problem is how to handle that growth in ways that improve the area and not destroy it."

THE clash between size and serenity has been best expressed in the current debate over smog. Dirty air has been an incipient problem here for years, but last December unusual climatic conditions caused an attack of noxious brown haze that blotted out the surrounding mountains for 11 days.

Residents realized that it could happen here. A specter was haunting Phoenix—Los Angeles.

The local newspapers, which are both owned by Eugene Pulliam, an outspoken conservative, immediately took up the cause. They ran pictures of industries belching smoke, and also ran editorials, cartoons and a series of articles called "It's Your Air."

Letters poured in. One contained a poem from Pamela L. Bostwick of Tempe, which included these lines:

Oh, see the poisons rising!
A patch of blue's surprising...
We may survive the day to rue
If as we do our little tasks
We all have on our little masks.

"I was really surprised at the papers," said one local Democratic politician. "They are taking on two sacred cows—the huge vested interests, like the mining companies, and tourism."

THE State Legislature opened a debate on a bill to impose stiffer control on polluters, but to some observers the results have been disappointing. Most of the time has been spent trying to place the blame on someone else. City representatives blame nearby copper smelters; legislators from the mining towns cite the cars of city dwellers.

"If we're not confused now," said State Senator Roy Goetze after several days of debate, "we just simply don't understand tne situation."

So far, the most decisive action has been taken by the Phoenix City Council—it banned smoking in its meeting room.

The difficulty in dealing with smog is compounded by the irrepressible individualism of many Phoenix residents, who include Senator Barry Goldwater. The city has no housing code, for example, because it would ostensibly limit "free enterprise."

One proposal to curb smog and the city's growing traffic problem calls for a mass transit system instead of a network of new freeways. But the plan is given little chance. Said one observer: "I just can't imagine people here giving up their own cars."

DESPITE what some critics call official footdragging at least one newcomer, a recent arrival from Indianapolis who sells nuts and candy in a big shopping center, thinks the debate is a healthy sign.

"The problem is still actually quite small," he said, "but it's great that they're so excited. They might be able to do something before the situation gets too serious. In some of those Eastern cities, it's already impossible."

In some ways, Phoenix is like those "Eastern cities," as are so many other urban areas in this country that seem to have become homogenized into a dispiriting sameness.

The franchise food shops, the gas stations, the ranch houses—to say nothing of the movies and the television programs—are identical from coast to coast. One bank here uses a brightly colored Indian doll as its symbol, and it stands out all over town.

Yet there is something special about Phoenix, something worth preserving from the evils of urbanness. Beyond the garish plastic signs hawking Kingaburgers and Big Whoppers you can still see graceful palms, stark mountains, brilliant skies—and it does the soul good. As a former hairdresser from New Jersey who now runs a cheese shop here said:

"It's just nice waking up to the sun. I come to work in a lighter mood. Back East, I would bundle up, and I felt the world closing in. When it rained for a few days my customers would get crabby, everything was oppressive. I feel lighter and happier here."

February 24, 1970

Scarlett O'Hara Might Like the New Atlanta

"Scarlett had always liked Atlanta. Like her, it was a mixture of the old and the new . . ." Margaret Mitchell's "Gone With the Wind."

By JAMES T. WOOTEN
Special to The New York Times

ATLANTA, Feb. 12—In her bonnet and veil and 12 flowing yards of flowered muslin hoopskirt, what would Miss O'Hara think now?

There are Yankees on Peachtree Street, Negroes in City Hall, hippies in the parks, crime in the streets, and last month, the schools were closed for a black Baptist preacher's birthday.

What is more, the Census Bureau announced this week that Atlanta's population was now more than half black, 51 per cent to be exact, making it the only major Southern city with that particular characteristic.

Suburbia's glories have overrun lovely Tara, gleaming skyscrapers loom over congested freeways, jetliners scream through dirty air shared by more than a million human lungs, and a former Grand Dragon of the Ku Klux Klan is now doing social work.

"I swear," Miss O'Hara could be expected to drawl, as she did when General Sherman's bombardment interrupted her afternoon nap, "it's just more than a civilized body can tolerate."

Still, all things considered, Scarlett might learn to like what Atlanta has become. Although it has emerged in the last decade as one of America's principal cities, it remains, like her, a mixture of the old and the new.

Its newness is as striking as the Regency Hyatt House Hotel, a 21-story combination of glass and steel and architectural innovation that has a revolving blue bubble of a restaurant on top and that has become a landmark on the city's changing skyline.

In the downtown area, new office buildings are rising and older ones are being remodeled and refurbished while on the fringes of the city office parks are being built for the convenience of suburbanites commuting from Sandy Springs or Chamblee or College Park or East Point.

In the last 10 years the economy has doubled and the population has increased by nearly one-third as the city has become a Mecca for young people from New Orleans to Richmond who come here with dreams of "making it."

Atlanta, in fact, has become the jangled nerve center of an entire region's commerce—a hustling, bustling, money-minded market place where most of the nation's 500 largest companies do big business every day.

Yet somehow, through it all, the old has not been displaced and its Southernness has survived.

"That's the remarkable thing about this place," said Lawrence F. Abingdon, a young sales executive who moved here from his native Boston two years ago. "You never quite get away from the idea that this is just a small Georgia town with a hell of a lot of people in it."

Another Northerner, transferred from Chicago, shares those views and has reaped a profit on their application. When visitors from the home office in Illinois come to Atlanta on business, he bets them $5 that when they go to lunch someone they don't know will speak to them on the street.

"In the last year, I've only lost once," William L. Botts, a marketing manager, said recently. "They can't believe you can have the size and scope of this city and still have the old charm and courtesy."

The New York Times Feb. 13, 1971

But Atlanta has, and in its blend of yesterday and today it has created a distinct, sometimes contradictory environment for its 1.3 million inhabitants.

It is, to be sure, an important regional hub for such companies as International Business Machines, Westinghouse and General Electric—the home of the Lockheed factory in nearby Marietta where the mammoth C-5A transport plane is produced, of satellite plants of General Motors and Ford, and of its

Photographs for The New York Times by JAY LEVITON

The bubble-shaped restaurant atop the Regency Hyatt House Hotel is a landmark on the changing skyline of downtown Atlanta and one product of a decade of growth that has seen city become the South's commercial capital.

own native giant, Coca Cola.

And yet it is also a place where a man who tips his hat is considered neither senile nor eccentric.

It is bright lights and traffic jams, air pollution and sidewalk muggings, downtown rot and suburban sprawl, luxury apartments and split-level homes, sirens and horns and grinding gears.

Yet it is also elegant old mansions and Sunday musicales and summer drinks on screened porches.

It is topless dancers and "nudy" films and pornography stalls, soul music and good jazz and picking and singing and sirens and horns and grinding gears.

Pace Slows After 5 P.M.

It is a place where the pace slows measurably after 5 o'clock and the double-time tempo of the day relaxes into an easy-going, leisurely stroll along Cain Street.

It is a kaleidoscope and cacophony of urban sights and sounds, all befitting its stature as the 20th largest metropolitan area in the country—but, in all of this, it is still Southern, as Southern as bourbon and branch water, as seersucker suits and segregation.

But the new nags at the old, and its native populace is down to 27 per cent of the total and decreasing every year.

Ten years ago it was nearly 40 per cent.

Many of its citizens wear its Southerness proudly, like a badge, including many Northerners who have converted. But there are thousands who regard it as a scar for it reminds them of a yesterday they prefer to forget: a past replete with the likes of Scarlett O'Hara ensconced at Tara with Prisse, her black slave, mouthing inane platitudes about the weather and the cotton.

"The old South mystique can be very comfortable for whites," said Julian Bond, the Negro legislator and lecturer who was denied a seat in the State House of Representatives after his first election four years ago. "But for the black people of Atlanta, it can be a cancerous impediment because it embodies not only charm but prejudice."

His indictment seems valid for in the last decade whites by the thousands have fled the city proper for the several suburbs surrounding it, an exodus that began when schools, neighborhoods and public facilities were desegregated. As a result, property values in the outer reaches of Atlanta soared beyond the reach of most Negro citizens.

For instance, a wealthy, middle-aged real estate broker readily concedes that

Vice Mayor Maynard Jackson, top left, presiding at a meeting of the Atlanta City Council. He is the first Negro elected to the post, in a city where black gains have been achieved with minimum of social upheaval as compared to other Southern towns.

houses he sold for $25,000 in 1960 are now going for between $40,000 and $45,000 in several of the suburbs.

Now, white immigrants to the city usually wind up in the suburbs with their children in all-white schools—if they can afford it. If they can't, their selection would include a number of transitional neighborhoods where real estate values have plummeted since integration began.

Many leaders, black and white, are now predicting that in a matter of a few years, the population of the inner city will be completely Negro.

Yet Atlanta has had many successes in solving its racial problems, a fact that Ivan Allen Jr., a former Mayor, attributes to the concern and cooperation of the business community and the presence and influence of Atlanta University, a nationally recognized center of Negro education.

The university, along with its Morris Brown College, Morehouse College, Clark College and Spelman College, now houses more than 20,000 students—a part of the nearly 80,000 collegians studying in the city at such schools as Georgia Tech, Georgia State, Emory University, Agnes Scott College and Oglethorpe College.

As the birthplace and burial ground for Martin Luther King Jr., Atlanta seemed destined for social changes, and they have occurred with a minimum of upheaval when compared with similar alterations in other Southern communities.

Now, slightly more than a decade after Dr. King was turned away from a restaurant at Rich's, a downtown department store world famous for its friendly service and liberal merchandise-return policies, Negroes and whites dine together in any restaurant in town.

In 1969, Maynard Jackson became the first Negro ever elected vice mayor of the city.

On Jan. 15, all city offices were closed to honor the birthday of Dr. King.

These, the city's boosters say, are signs of progress, and they are the kinds of things the Chamber of Commerce likes to tout in its brochures and advertising.

But this pronounced tendency toward boastfulness is not limited either to the Chamber of Commerce or to race relations as a subject matter. Even those transplanted to the city become adept at it. Visitors are told frequently that they are now driving past the largest or the smallest or the most expensive or the most unusual this or that east of the Mississippi.

"If Atlanta could suck as hard as it can blow, the Chattahoochee would run backward," a reporter from South Georgia complained not long ago. He was referring to the river that is now being polluted by sewage as it meanders through the city.

But the ado has paid off.

Since 1960, the metropolitan population, which includes parts of five counties, has increased by 330,000, a leap of 31.4 per cent. In the same period, retail sales more than doubled and nearly 400,000 motor vehicles were added to the city streets.

"If we could stop growing —not that I advocate that— but if we could, we could stop for a while and look around and maybe solve some of the things that are bothering us," said the city's youthful Mayor, Sam Massell Jr.

That a city official would concede that there are some bothersome aspects about life in Atlanta may be surprising, particularly in view of the fact that Atlanta has a reputation of accentuating the positive in national media advertising and other publicity.

But Mayor Massell, the first Jew to serve in that office here, is familiar with the proliferating problems of the city of his birth and he speaks frankly about them.

Transportation and traffic are major bugaboos. Those affluent whites who live in the suburbs can count on a drive of half-an-hour to an hour on jammed freeways going to and from their offices in the downtown sector.

Pollution is another. The city has been sternly warned by the new Environmental Protection Agency of the Federal Government that it must cease poisoning the Chattahoochee with raw sewage. And there are mornings when visibility in the city is nearly zero because of smoke.

These and all the other problems that inevitably afflict an urban area—an obsolete airport, a rising crime rate, public housing and education, disgruntled and underpaid policemen and fireman —all require money for solution and money is something Atlanta is running out of.

Many property owners here have watched and groaned as their land taxes increased between 500 and 800 per cent in the last decade. Other forms of municipal revenue are controlled by the state legislature, which in the past has been adamant in its refusal to allow the city to impose sales or income taxes on its citizens.

"But we cannot stop growing populationwise," the Mayor said, "because then our municipal revenue becomes stablized and the present income is already insufficient to fund present services."

Tersely, but thoroughly, Mayor Massell had summarized Atlanta's dilemma. It was a city obsessed by growth in the 'sixties. Nearly $4.5-million was spent in behalf of its growth in Chamber of Commerce programs— and now the problems of size are beginning to emerge.

Nevertheless, Mayor Massell, Vice Mayor Jackson and most of the city's leaders are optimistic.

"We survived Sherman's fire and we can survive getting big," a black alderman predicted last week. "We're going to make it and we're going to make it together, black and white, and we'll probably be better off than anybody around."

February 13, 1971

Vivien Leigh as Scarlett O'Hara and Thomas Mitchell as her father in a scene from "Gone With the Wind," a film that still evokes an image of old Atlanta that some cherish and others—particularly Negroes—want to forget.

Atlanta Elects a Black Mayor, First in a Major Southern City

By JON NORDHEIMER

Special to The New York Times

ATLANTA, Oct. 16—A black man was elected today as Mayor of Atlanta, the commercial and cultural center of the Old Confederacy that only a decade ago was quarreling over the admission of a handful of black children into the public schools.

Maynard Jackson, a 35-year-old black lawyer, defeated the white incumbent, Sam Massell, in a nonpartisan election that generated more racial acrimony than any Georgia election in recent years.

With all of the city's 193 precincts reporting, the unofficial vote count was:

Jackson 75,799
Massell 43,693

Mr. Jackson received 63 per cent of the vote. One of his aides estimated that he received about 30 per cent of the white vote.

Mr. Jackson, the present Vice Mayor, will become the first black mayor of a major Southern city when inaugurated in January. He will also be the first black politician to preside over a state capital anywhere in the United States.

He will run a city that now has blacks in control of the City Council and the Board of Education. Moreover, Atlanta is represented in Congress by a black man, Representative Andrew Young Jr., a former aide to the Rev. Dr. Martin Luther King Jr.

However, another former assistant to Dr. King, Hosea Williams, lost in a bid to become president of the Atlanta City Council, a powerful post created by the new city charter. He was defeated by a white liberal, Wyche Fowler, by a wide margin.

Mr. Massell, Atlanta's first Jewish mayor, had attempted to make Mr. Williams, a controversial figure who had been in the vanguard of many civil rights demonstrations in the city, an issue in the campaign. He told the white community that a city controlled by blacks in the two most powerful offices of government would lead to economic and social ruin.

Jesse L. Jackson of Chicago, one of several national civil rights figures here for the election, called Mr. Jackson's victory "the fruits of a political renaissance."

Another black leader, John Lewis, director of the nonpartisan Voter Education Project, hailed the vote as a "great victory" over the politics of race.

Mr. Jackson, who stands 6 feet 4 inches tall and weighs close to 300 pounds, had worked diligently to develop support in Atlanta's black community, which makes up 52 per cent of the city's population.

In the closing weeks of the campaign, particularly since the Oct. 2 election that narrowed the field of 11 mayoral candidates down to a contest betwee Mr. Massell and Mr. Jackson, the city has been lashed by the politics of race.

Each man labeled the other a "racist." In the balloting Oct. 2, Mr. Massell shared the white vote with other white candidates, and Mr. Jackson swept most black precincts by a 9-to-1 margin.

Since then, Mr. Massell has appealed for white support against what he declared was a black bloc vote for his opponent.

Consequently, this city, whic has the reputation of being the most liberal, cosmopolitan community in the Deep South, was exposed to direct appeals to racial solidarity.

The city, with 479,000 residents, is ringed by suburbs containing more than one million residents, including many middle-class whites who moved out of the city proper.

Atlanta's two major daily newspapers, which had harsh words for both candidates throughout the long campaign, grudgingly endorsed Mr. Jackson.

"Massell could not govern if he were elected after this campaign," The Atlanta Constitution said in this morning's editions.

The Atlanta Journal said yesterday that Mayor Massell had made a calculated attempt to divide the city along racial lines.

Mr. Massell was elected in 1969 to the $40,000-a-year post on the basis of support from a coalition of blacks and liberal whites. He was the first Atlanta Mayor to appoint blacks as department heads, and he clearly had planned to retain a measure of political support in the community.

But after the Oct. 2 election he concentrated his efforts in the runoff campaign in the white precincts.

While there was some white resentment at his tactics, the campaign was considered successful in making whites conscious about what Mr. Massell perceived as the inevitabe decline of property values and eocnomic collapse if the "Jackson-Williams team" came to power.

October 17, 1973

Amid Signs of Racial Division, Atlanta's Black Mayor Begins Second Year Under Fire

By B. DRUMMOND AYRES Jr.
Special to The New York Times

ATLANTA, Feb. 25—Little more than a year has passed since Maynard Jackson began his four-year term as the first black mayor of Atlanta, now a predominantly black city.

But already there is speculation about a successor, along with some delicate legislative maneuvering that could result in that successor's being white or more responsive to whites.

The General Assembly, which grants city charters in Georgia, has been asked to study the possibility of broadening Atlanta's inadequate tax base by annexing nearby suburbs, most of them predominantly white.

The legislature has also been asked to study whether governmental efficiency in the metropolitan area could be improved through merger of, say, city and suburban water and police departments.

Debate on the requests, submitted by a group of local legislators, is about to begin. A final vote is expected within a week or so.

Though the vote would do no more than authorize studies initially, it could be close because of the racial connotations and because of suburban antipathy toward the city.

Gusto and Rhetoric

Meanwhile, Maynard Jackson is beginning his second year in office, still presiding with great gusto and rich rhetoric over this booming city that has become the urban envy of much of the rest of the United States.

"Things are going pretty good," he says with a cheery smile.

But if Mr. Jackson's second year is anything like the first, things will be anything but smooth.

Like most fledgling mayors, Mr. Jackson was forced to spend an abnormal amount of his freshman year just learning the mayoral ropes.

That left little time for much concrete achievement. As a result, a goodly number of his half-million constituents were constantly sniping at him, egged on now and again by the million or so persons living in the suburbs.

Only a few weeks into his second year, the rotund, 36-year-old Mayor finds himself still under fire, facing other threats beside a legislative watering down of black power.

His council is growing increasingly independent, with its white president, Wyche Fowler, mentioned as a possible Jackson successor.

When the Mayor said a tax increase would be necessary if he was to govern the city properly, the Council turned him down.

Mr. Jackson is besieged daily by press charges of cronyism within his administration, many of them stemming from his appointment of Reginald Eaves, an old college friend, to the post of Public Safety Commissioner.

From the tightly knit Atlanta business community come blunt warnings that Mr. Jackson is letting one of the most dynamic cities in the country slip down the urban drain, a victim at last of white flight, bad schools, rampant crime and revenue squeezes that have crippled so many other metropolises.

From black leaders in other parts of the country come quiet warnings that Mr. Jackson's performance may hurt the overall image of black leadership in the country. Several of these leaders, some of them former Atlanta residents, have reportedly talked directly to the Mayor about this.

Mr. Jackson does not seem particularly worried.

"Nothing's so serious that we won't pull through in good shape," he says.

High-Rise Forest

A look at the Atlanta skyline, where construction cranes whirl and jerk atop a $1.5-billion forest of high-rise skeletons, tends to confirm his optimism and raise doubts about some of the charges and warnings leveled at him. This remains one of the healthiest cities in the United States, a town that has learned to conduct its commerce with Yankee briskness while retaining its Southern manners.

Still, Atlanta has some serious problems, perhaps more now than at any time since the tumultuous days of the civil rights movement. A number were present or in the making before Mr. Jackson took office, but others have cropped up since then.

The most pressing new problem is a disturbing division that has developed between the black political leadership, which has limited economic power, and the white economic leadership, which has limited political power.

The gap reached its widest point a few months ago when the businessmen, most of them members of a civic organization called Central Atlanta Progress, sent Mayor Jackson a report in which they asserted that the downtown's robust economic health was being threatened by crime, poor schools, racial polarization and white flight.

The New York Times/Bill Grimes

Mayor Maynard H. Jackson with city map in his office

A few days ago, when the Mayor spoke at the organization's annual breakfast gathering, he responded.

"What you should do," he told the businessmen, "is hold a press conference for all the world to see and hear, and you should stand up before the cameras and microphones—and I don't necessarily have to be there—and you should say: 'We live in Atlanta. We believe in Atlanta. We are going to stay in Atlanta.' "

The businessmen applauded the idea, though they have not yet held a press conference.

'We're Not Going to Leave'

However, Ivan Allen 3d, president of the Atlanta Chamber of Commerce, another of the men mentioned as a possible Jackson successor, subsequently told a gathering of leading Atlanta blacks:

"The simple fact is that Atlanta's business community is committed to the continued strength of the central core, more than is true in any other city in America. We're not going to leave it. I repeat, the business community has no intention of deserting Atlanta."

Mr. Allen, whose father was one of Atlanta's best known and most progressive Mayors, then warned his audience that Atlanta would not "work" unless the "politics of confrontation" was ended.

"It is time" he said, "to stop talking about 'we' in the white community and 'they' in the black community."

Finally, touching on the subject that seldom is talked about publicly in Atlanta, he called upon the city to solve its revenue shortage by looking for solutions "geographically, as well as methodologically."

To that end, a number of leading businessmen have been down to the state capitol to talk with Gov. George Busbee and members of the General Assembly about the need to study annexation and merger of services.

Most of those going to Capitol Hill have been white, but some have been black, for there is considerable feeling in Atlanta's substantial black business community that the city must do something about expanding its tax base.

Mayor Jackson himself acknowledges this need and says he would support "a certain enlargement, if it's done right."

"Which course to take is a very delicate matter," says Representative Grace Hamilton, a veteran black legislator who is one of the sponsors of the measure to set up the studies.

"As of now," she adds, "you can't rule out some sort of consolidation. Nor can you rule out merger of some city and county services. You just have to look at the whole situation and hope that nothing gets blown out of proportion or misinterpreted."

In recent years, as more and more whites have fled the inner core — Atlanta has gone from 38 per cent black in 1960 to 55 per cent black today—most of the growth has been to the north.

A few days ago, Governor Busbee warned that "this lopsided development threatens to sap the city's strength."

"It is," he continued, "a selfish cycle in which the wealthy, the white and the skilled huddle together in high-density enclaves, leaving behind them a dwindling tax digest and a host of problems they no longer feel any compunction to help solve."

This lack of compunction stems, in part, from a sense of helplessness and frustration. Racism on the part of both whites and blacks—the lack of it used to be one of Atlanta's strong points—also plays an ever larger role.

The Mayor has made several speeches about the danger of a resurgent racism, saying at one point:

"The bigots and fearmongers enter to sow confusion. I know that to many I represent a symbol that is distasteful because I am black. I'm not on a crusade to prove black people superior. Black people do not want to take over Atlanta."

Nevertheless, many whites feel the take-over has occurred. They remember when Atlanta was run by a white collection of merchants, bankers, lawyers and editors. Blacks had only a token say.

'All Gone Now'

"In the old days," one white businessman recalled recently in private conversation, "you could pick up the phone and dial the Mayor at his office or his home or his club—your club—or his friend's house—your friend's house—and you could get your business done, right there, first-name-basis, golfing buddies, on the spot.

"Well, that's all gone now. When George Busbee first got elected to the Governor's office, he called the Mayor's office and said he'd like to talk to the Mayor and somebody told him the Mayor was tied up for two weeks.

"What kind of city government is that?"

"A tragedy of absolutely unintentional errors," replies the Mayor's office.

Whatever the case, both races continue to eye one another warily in the city that once bragged it was "too busy to hate."

Panke Bradley, one of the more liberal whites on the City Council, says that "whenever you start to turn Maynard down on something, he tries to make you feel like you owe him something because of 350 years of repression that you didn't have anything to do with."

The other night, a dinner party attended by black and white couples—not an unusual gathering in Atlanta—broke up in anger when the conversation turned to city government.

"You're a damn racist," the black host called to a hastily departing white guest.

Carl Marshall, an urban consultant, says Atlanta is experiencing "an identity crisis."

Traditionally, Atlantans have been granite sure of who they were, bullish about their town, ready to boost it at every opportunity.

In the second year of Maynard Jackson's tenure, they seem not so cocksure. While their Chamber of Commerce continues its hard sell to businessmen elsewhere — "Atlanta, the world's next great city"—the Chamber now feels compelled to sell the town to local residents, too.

"Look up, Atlanta," the latest Chamber crusade implores the home folks.

February 26, 1975

Old New Orleans Weighing Future

By ROY REED

Special to The New York Times

NEW ORLEANS, Aug 1—A man here tells of a cousin, an educated, well-to-do woman now approaching middle age, who had never seen any part of the United States beyond a 40-mile radius of New Orleans until she was grown and married.

She had been to Paris and any number of other cities around the world, but, like many other people of this city in an earlier time, she had no curiosity about the United States outside New Orleans. The rest of the country was dismissed simply as "across the lake," meaning the region on the other side of Lake Pontchartrain, the 24-mile-wide body of water that separates New Orleans from an entire nation to the north.

Hers was probably the last generation of New Orleanians who were able to believe that nothing "across the lake" could match the glamor of their own creole gumbo of a city, one of the last American outposts of European culture.

An event that will take place Sunday illustrates how completely that heady insularity has disappeared. The Louisiana Superdome, a staggering symbol of the city's rush toward Americanization, will be opened to the public in an open house and dedication.

The construction of the dome, a sports and convention center, is not quite complete because of one more in a long series of delays. But it is near enough finished to be shown to the taxpayers who have bought it.

The dome is a monument to the American taste for big-time sports, big-time tourism and big-time bigness. It is the largest enclosed stadium-arena in the world. It is 630 feet across and 273 feet high. It has 125 million cubic feet of space, 9,600 tons of air-conditioning and 88 toilets. As of the last of numerous recalculations, it cost $178-million, not counting the interest on the bonds.

The opening of the dome has inspired a fit of introspection among Louisianians.

"If the French had kept the city," Walker Percy, the novelist, wrote in Harper's Magazine in 1968, "it would be today a Martinique, a Latin confection If the Americans had got there first, we'd have Houston or Jackson sitting athwart the great American watershed. As it happened, there may have occurred just enough of a cultural standoff to give one room to turn around in a public space which is delicately balanced between the Northern vacuum and the Southern pressure cooker."

Some here have decided that the delicate balance of Anglo-Saxon and Mediterranean cultures has been destroyed and that the Americanization of the city they love is now complete.

But others are not so sure. For even as they shake their heads over the look-alike suburbs that now make outer New Orleans look like Houston, and the Texas skyscrapers that compete with the dome for domination of the downtown, their eye lights on some pocket of the old city that the developers have not yet found.

Or their ear picks up an unfamiliar sound, a language that had not been heard here since creole days.

The most constant and diverting controversy here in recent years has been the change in the French Quarter, the original city built on the Mississippi River bank in the years after 1718.

Both New Orleanians and outsiders have been resourceful in mining the tourist dollar there. Trinket and antique shops are everywhere. Old houses have been converted to museums and businesses at such a rate that only a few well-heeled middle-class persons can still afford to live in the quarter.

Every street has two or three new hotels built to look old European with wrought-iron balconies and heavily planted patios that imitate, and frequently mock, the moldering French and Spanish residences of the 18th century.

The gritty old French Market by the river has been "renovated." The fish shops and vegetable vendors are giving way to boutiques and candle shops.

A letter writer to The Courier, a weekly newspaper published in the Quarter, complained recently that the developers were turning the Vieux Carre into "a homogenized, modern, urban Disneyland for tourists."

It may be too late for the French Quarter as anything but a tourist draw and museum piece. But New Orleanians know that the Quarter is not the end of interesting real estate in the old city.

Changing Neighborhoods

Young people with taste are moving into and fixing up half a dozen aged neighborhoods that lie between Canal Street and the colorless suburbs. They are restoring the old shotgun houses with the high ceilings and the carved facades.

One place the big money has not discovered is Old Algiers, which sits in a bend in the river across from the Quarter and is best reached by a 20-minute ferry ride. It is still possible in Old Algiers to find a bar without tourists, or a balcony from which one can look across the levee and watch the ships passing in front of St. Louis Louis Cathedral.

Then there is Magazine Street. Thousands of uptown people drive through Magazine Street every day and perhaps see nothing but a litter of a second-hand furniture stores and Pabst Blue Ribbon beer signs above the tiny bars and restaurants.

But if they look closely at the beer signs, they see that the names underneath have taken on a Latin-American lilt: La Caridad, Lempira, Chapinlandia. They have moved in quietly, unnoticed by many, during the last five years. These are the newest ingredient in the simmering, unceasing gumbo of New Orleans.

While the suburbs are being filled by immigrants from Anglo-Saxon Texas and Mississippi and northern Louisiana, bringing their Protestant ethic and their country music, the older city is being refilled by immigrants from Latin America. Some are Cubans, impelled here by their loathing of Fidel Castro. Many more are from Central America, especially from Honduras.

No one knows how many have come, partly because not all have entered the country legally. One can hear estimates as high as 100,000 from Honduras alone. They started coming years ago on the banana boats, and as a few settled and found work they sent for others.

As a consequence, old New Orleanians who were accustomed to broiled pompano accompanied by French wine have almost unawares developed a taste for fried rice with shrimp washed down by Carta Blanca beer.

The population of New Orleans, as in many other cities, dropped from 651,000 in 1964 to 568,700 last year while the population of its suburbs increased from 351,000 to 523,900 during the same period. Most of those moving to the suburbs are young whites, according to the Census Bureau.

Between 1960 and 1970, the black population inside the city rose 14.9 per cent, from 234,931 to 269,986, while the white population fell 17.6 per cent from 392,594 to 323,485.

Perhaps the most pressing question the city faces is how to provide a livelihood for all the disparate people who spice this urban gumbo.

That has always been a problem. The early settlers, who for some reason picked a site in the swamp that was trapped below sea level, ruled by mosquitoes and more or less permanently threatened by plague and hurricanes, decided that the only logical use of a city so situated was for shipping and trade. New Orleans became one of the world's leading ports.

But some time during this century the city's leaders found that easy money could be made by luring visitors here to get a glimpse of the past. Tourism has now become a rival of the port as the mainstay of the city's economy. And therein lies the cause of an increasingly bitter debate. Quo Vadis, New Orleans, the "city that care forgot?"

Mayor Moon Landrieu, a well-spoken moderate who is believed to aspire to a place on the Democratic party's national ticket, believes that the salvation of the city lies in the Superdome and the spirit of growth it represents.

He points to the spinoff of construction and service jobs that are being created as new hotels and office buildings rise around the dome. For a mile between the dome and the river, old faded Boydras Street is being changed to a glittering promenade of skyscrapers and high-rise hotels.

The dome and related construction have provided hundreds of jobs that have undoubtedly softened the impact of the national recession here. When the new hotels, restaurants and other tourist accommodations are opened, they will provide many more jobs.

But the critics of the dome mentality say the city has set itself on an irrevocable course of dependence on low-wage, no-advancement jobs for the masses of poor people who inhabit the city's quaint gingerbread slums.

One such critic is Bernard Marcus, a prominent lawyer who just finished a term as president of the Jewish Community Center. He deplores the tourist-based economy that the dome represents.

Instead of creating jobs for bellhops and waitresses, he said in an interview this week, the city should attract more manufacturing and train people in crafts and industrial skills.

That view is bolstered by a highly critical study of the New Orleans economy just completed by Dr. James R. Bobo, a professor of economics who is dean of the Graduate School at the University of New Orleans.

Dr. Bobo says the city's 7.2 per cent unemployment rate is misleading because there are 75,000 to 100,000 persons who rarely work or seek work and are not counted by the government statisticians. If these were counted, he told The New Orleans States-Item, the city's unemployment rate would be 24 or 25 per cent. Most in this "economic underworld" are black or female, he said.

Furthermore, he said, 21.6 per cent of the New Orleans population lives below the official government poverty level, compared to 9.1 per cent in Atlanta and 8.6 per cent in Dallas.

The Superdome will be an asset, he said.

"But service-industry jobs tend to be low-paying, require few skills and offer few opportunities for upward mobility," he added. "A amid or a car parker is likely to remain in that position." He continued:

Those who feel that New Orleans should tie its future to the port and related economic activities fear that it may be too late, that the dome has committed the city to an economy dominated by recreation and tourist businesses.

They note that the port of New Orleans lost two of its most prestigious shippers in recent months, United Fruit Company, the huge banana concern, and Volkswagen.

The losses were recorded without fanfare. The leaders of the city appeared to be preoccupied with opening the Superdome, planning its first event—a professional football game—and trying to persuade a baseball team to make its home there.

One prominent but not politically powerful citizen, who asked not to be identified, said the other day that he had changed his mind about the dome.

A few months ago, he said, he thought that even though it had been bad judgment to build it, the dome was a fact of life and should be put to its best use once it was finished.

He was mistaken, he said. "I now think that the best thing to do," he said, "is to call in Ed Levy Metals and say, 'Ed, will you take it down for nothing if you get all the salvage?'"

August 2, 1975

Influx of Population Down in Urban Areas

In New Trend, Only 3 of 8 Biggest Districts List Net Gain for '70 to '73

By WILLIAM E. FARRELL

The nation's eight biggest metropolitan areas have experienced since 1970 a sharp decline in the rate at which people are moving into them, a key measure of growth. Several demographers say the decline is without precedent since the first census in 1790.

Three of the eight areas—San Francisco, Boston and Washington — have been able to maintain small net balances of in-migration over out-migration: More people moved in than left.

But the five others — New York, Los Angeles, Chicago, Philadelphia and Detroit—have gone to the minus side. All of these but Chicago had shown migration gains during the nineteen-sixties. The turnabout in Los Angeles was particularly dramatic.

Projections made from the new data, gathered by the Census Bureau between 1970 and 1973, indicate that during the next 15 years there will be a pronounced shift of income away from the Northeast and North Central regions of the country to the Southern and Western regions. However, this study found, per capita incomes in the Northeast and North Central regions will continue to remain above the national average.

The expected shift in income along with the slowing growth rate in older urban areas will make the costs of providing essential municipal services increasingly onerous for wage earners, according to some urbanologists. It will be, according to this view, a bit like one person having to keep up all the rooms of an aging mansion whose inhabitants hav dwindled in numoer and affluence.

Precisely why the growth rate of the major metropolitan areas has tapered off is still under study. But census and demographic experts interviewed recently offered the following theories:

¶A slowdown in growth was inevitable, and it is finally coming to pass in aging American metropolitan areas, just as it is in Europe.

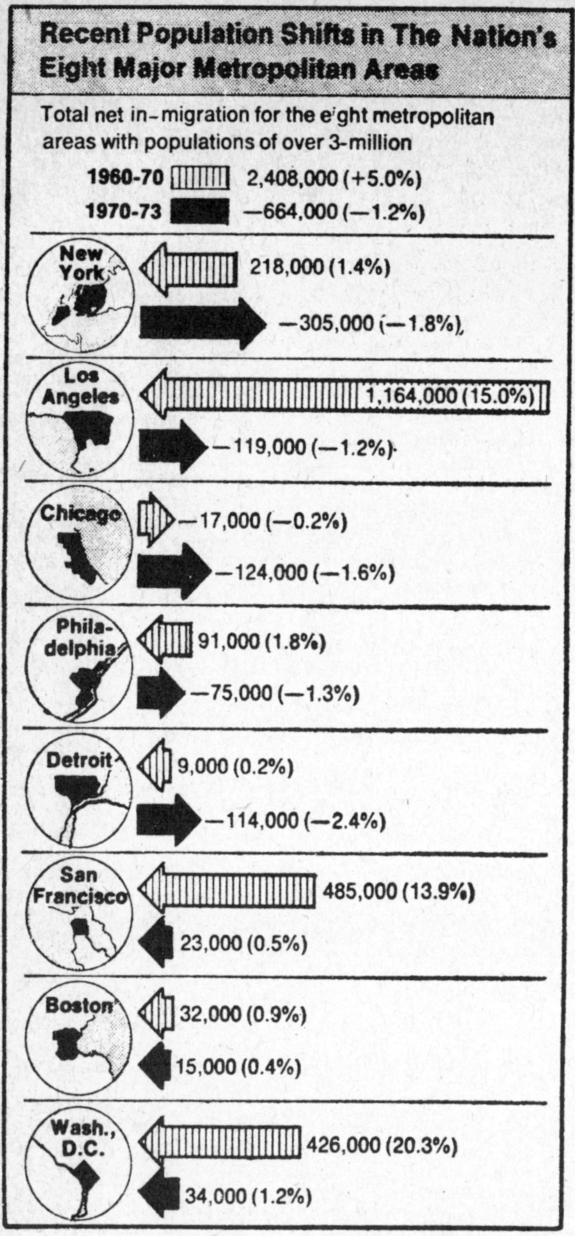

The New York Times/June 16, 1975

¶Large metropolitan areas, where big cities, particularly during the early and middle 20th century, often annexed land to meet their growth needs, have run out of space and the cities are left with nothing more to annex.

¶An "equaling out" is taking place with laggard regions like the South beginning to catch up to regions like the Northeast that have had a protracted period of constant growth.

¶The absence of a cohesive Federal urban policy is contributing to the aging of older cities because there is no national focus on the problems peculiar to them. New York City, with its fiscal crisis, is cited in this context.

In the nineteen-sixties, according to Richard L. Forstall, a Census Bureau demographic expert, the eight major metropolitan areas together "absorbed 2.4 million net in-migrants but, since 1970, in a particularly striking reversal of trend, they have lost 664,000 net migrants."

Over all, Mr. Forstall said, the eight areas, which include major cities and surrounding counties deemed part of the central city's economic and social patterns, gained 7.9-million persons in the nineteen-sixties through both migration and natural increase—that is, births.

This increase was nearly one-third of the nation's total gain during the decade, according to Mr. Forstall, who is chief of demographic statistics for the Census Bureau's Population Division.

But census data gathered between 1970 and 1973 show the over-all gain in the eight areas in that period to be fewer than 600,000 people.

In a study analyzing the new data, Mr. Forstall said that smaller metropolitan areas—those with populations between one and three million people—"have also experienced considerable reduction in growth since 1970."

Most of the in-migration in such areas has been in retirement centers in the areas of Phoenix, Ariz., Miami - Fort Lauderdale and Tampa-St. Petersburg in Florida.

Gains for Smaller Areas

Metropolitan areas of less than one million population, Mr. Forstall said, "have had a higher annual net in-migration rate since 1970 than they have had in the nineteen-sixties."

Census data showed also that the growth of rural areas was faster than that of metropolitan areas. The nation's nonmetropolitan counties—those with no population center of at least 50,000 persons—gained 4.2 per cent population between April, 1970, and July, 1973, while metropolitan counties, which include suburbs, gained 2.9 per cent.

Mr. Forstall noted that the slowing down in the United States paralleled a similar recent pattern in northwestern Europe.

"London's population growth largely ceased in the mid nineteen-sixties," he wrote. "Several, though not all, of the West German metropolitan areas have shown little recent growth, after 20 years of rapid recovery" following World War II.

Recent statistics for Amsterdam, Copenhagen and Stockholm, he said, "show a virtual halt to population growth in the metropolitan area."

The slowing down of the growth rate of heavily urban areas of the United States since 1970 while the nonurban growth rate speeded up was, Mr. Forstall said, "a development that stands in contrast with practically all preceding periods back to 1790."

"The more rapid growth of larger urban concentrations as compared to nonmetropolitan territory has been one of the most persistent of American demographic trends," he said.

Growth in Capital

Of the eight major metropolitan areas, only the Washington area — one with increasingly large numbers of Government workers—has grown since 1970 by as much as 1 per cent a year in net migration into the city.

The San Francisco area, which had 485,000 in-migrants during the nineteen-sixties, or 13.9 per cent, showed an increase of only 23,000 in the new survey, or 0.5 per cent.

The Boston area, which during the nineteen-sixties had 32,000 in-migrants, or 0.9 per cent, showed an increase of 15,000, or 0.4 per cent, in the 1970-73 study.

"The near cessation of growth has been especially dramatic for Los Angeles," Mr. Forstall said.

During the nineteen-sixties the Los Angeles area had net in-migration of almost 1.2-million people, but from 1970 through 1973 it had a net out-migration of 119,000.

The New York metropolitan area, which for purposes of the census survey included New York City, Nassau and Suffolk Counties and portions of New Jersey within commuting distance, had a net decrease of in-migrants during 1970-1973 of 305,000.

For the Chicago area the decrease was 124,000; for Philadelphia, 75,000, and for Detroit, 114,000.

In discussing possible reasons for the decline, Dr. Campbell Gibson, chief of the Census Bureau's National Population Estimates and Projection Branch, noted that in the past large cities often annexed adjacent territory, thus adding land that often took decades to fill up with people.

Now, he said in an interview, the era of annexation, particularly in the crowded northeastern United States, is over.

"Quite simply," he said, "the space is all filled up."

According to Mr. Forstall, the large gains made in the South during the nineteen-sixties—a rate of growth that has accelerated in the nineteen-seventies — is an "overdue catch-up" in an area that has traditionally lagged far behind the growth patterns of the Northeast and Midwest.

"What is really amazing is how the Northeast remained dominant so long," Dr. Gibson said. "What we're seeing now is a kind of equaling out."

Another possible factor, according to Mr. Forstall, is that a growing segment of the population is picking and choosing where it wants to live rather than letting the job market dictate location.

He said that this segment was probably quite small but that it nevertheless was larger than in the past, when "people didn't settle in Chicago necessarily because it was a desirable place to live. Jobs were there."

The new survey material showing a waning growth rate in the Northeast has raised questions about whether the Eastern Seaboard is "declining."

According to Prof. George Sternlieb, director of the Center

for Urban Policy Research at Rutgers University, the question is not so much one of "decline" but one of: "Can the Northeast age gracefully?"

Dying Gracefully

"Vienna is dying gracefully, but it has no competition," Professor Sternlieb said in an interview. "New York is in competition with the rest of the country.

In Mr. Sternlieb's view, the slowdown in the Northeast has been accentuated by a lack of Federal policy in the urban field.

He also said that while the Federal Government asserted it had no migration policy its investment in subsidized housing leaned heavily toward the South and Southwest.

The Northeast, with its heavy welfare caseloads, Professor Sternlieb said, is also "the victim" of the fact that the Federal Government has not enacted a national welfare program.

In addition, he said, the Northeast trails other areas of the country in receiving so-called "pork barrel" Government projects that provide many regional jobs.

"When was the last dam built in New York City?" he said.

Since there has been no national policy dealing with aging metropolises he said there is confusion at the local level.

"Nobody's guilty," Mr. Sternlieb remarked. "Everybody's acting in their own best interests."

A Federal policy is needed, he said, because the cumulative effect of piecemeal self-interest at the local level "can be disastrous."

Thomas Muller of the Rutgers urban center recently analyzed the fiscal characteristics of aging urban areas undergoing out-migration.

"The ability of local and state governments to provide public services can be severely constrained by out-migration," he said in a report. "The large New York, Pennsylvania or Ohio urban centers will have a smaller working population base to pay for capital outlays incurred in the past, while the demands for services to the elderly, underprivileged and minority low-income households will continue to increase."

Mr. Muller. who analyzed recent census data, said, "The number of municipal workers per 1,000 residents is 39 per cent higher in declining cities compared to those with rising populations. Houston has only 7.2 workers and San Diego 7.4 workers per 1,000 residents, while older cities such as Boston, New Orleans and Philadelphia have almost twice as many workers."

He did not include New York City in the report.

The Census Bureau's Regional Economic Analysis Division made projections of the new survey data to the year 1990. It foresaw a continuing trend of people and income into the South, but the report also said: "Despite the tendency for per capita income in low-income states to grow more rapidly than in high-income states, the gap remains wide.

"The national trend [in income] both historical and projected, is up strongly," the report said, "and all states and regions share in the gains—some more than others. A downward relative trend in a region, therefore, usually means less-than-average percentage growth; in only a few instances does it signify an absolute decline in the measure."

The report envisioned "a pronounced shift of income away from the Northeast and North Central parts of the country to the Southern and Western portions" and added: "The Far West and New England are exceptions to this generalization in the sense that they move at approximately the national rate."

The major reason given for the rapid expansion of income in the South, according to the projection, is manufacturing—both continuation of the already strong Southern textile industry and a rapid growth in chemicals, machinery, fabricated metals, paper and printing.

The projection foresees that the South will experience "an expansion in total manufacturing half again as fast as that in the nation as a whole."

Another impetus for the South is expected to come from a growing tourist and recreation industry.

The population shifts in larger, older metropolitan areas were analyzed recently by Vincent P. Barabba, director of the Census Bureau, in a talk he gave to a panel of urban experts. What little growth has been taking place in these metropolitan areas, he said, "has occurred only with the suburban areas."

"The central cities," he said, "have lost about 2 per cent of their populations since 1970."

"When we look at the suburbs on a regional basis," Mr. Barabba said, "we find that since 1970 they have accounted for all the growth in the North and the South. Only in the West has there been any measurable increase in the central-city population.

"So the suburbs continue to be the mainstay of metropolitan growth both regionally and nationally, just as they were during the nineteen-sixties."

June 16, 1975

Booming Houston Puts Its Faith in Unlimited Growth

By JAMES P. STERBA
Special to The New York Times

HOUSTON, Dec. 3—A young businessman here was asked recently to put Houston in perspective. He thought a while, then answered by recalling the first word that man uttered from another heavenly body. When Neil A. Armstrong set Apollo 11 on moon on July 20, 1969, the first word he said was "Houston." Then came, "Tranquility base here. The Eagle has landed."

It was no big deal, the businessman said, noting that Apollo's base, the Johnson Space Center, is on the edge of town. It was just a little something the rest of the world ought to keep in mind, he said.

The Chamber of Commerce proclaims Houston the city of the future. With its booming oil and petrochemical complexes, it is the fastest-growing major industrial center in America. A thousand new people move in each week. Its unemployment rate is the nation's lowest. And just as important, newcomers say, Houston has "the right attitude."

It is a young and raucous champion of unlimited growth, high flying capitalism, hard work and self reliance. And it tolerates neither big government nor loafers. Welfare is a dirty word.

The Answer Is Jobs

"Our answer to welfare is jobs," said Louie Welch, Chamber president and former Mayor. "And if people don't want to work, we don't want them here."

Promising more government programs and services to Houstonians, in fact, is not the way to win elections here. Mayor Fred Hofheinz, re-elected yesterday to his second two-year term, proudly noted on election eve that his administration had spent less money per capita on citizens than had the previous mayor's.

He promised more policemen and buses, but that was about all. His opponent, Frank Briscoe, promised even less.

According to Leonel Castillo the city comptroller, Houston, the nation's fifth largest city, spends less per capita on its citizens than any other big city in the country. Two years ago, when New York spent more than $1,200 per citizen, Houston spent $160.

"Nobody addresses the basic question of what we should be spending," he said. "If you're a young city like Houston, you don't have to spend a lot immediately, but things are going to come up later on, like maintaining the water system when it gets old.

"Neither candidate addressed himself to the fact that we're adding a thousand people a week here. That means you have to spend more money just to stay even."

Houston has no welfare program. Harris County, which includes the city, maintains a small emergency program to tide people over if, for example, they are burned out of their house.

"The State of Texas handles welfare, and it is almost punitive to our poor," Mr. Castillo said. "They barely survive."

According to the 1970 census, 11 percent of Houston's families had incomes below the national poverty level. For those qualified, the state provides child aid. A family with two children can receive only $86 per month, not including aid, through Federal programs such as food stamps and school lunches.

More aid to the poor and more city services in general mean more spending and higher taxes—all of which are anathema to Houston. This city lures corporations, professionals and skilled workers here by proclaiming that it has the lowest taxes of any major city in the nation. Mayor Hofheinz even lowered property taxes 3 percent this year, although he did raise water and sewer rates.

One reason for the low taxes is that a Texas law allows Houston to annex land by a simple vote of the City Council and regardless of the wishes of the land owners involved. Thus, unlike other cities hemmed in by incorporated suburban towns, Houston is constantly expanding its tax base.

Another reason for low city taxes is that many services are provided through the county or through special taxing districts. Houston, for example, does not pay for its own public school system out of city funds. Special independent school districts, with their own power to tax property, maintain the schools.

Similar taxing districts are also used to pay for the two public hospitals in town and for water, sewer and drain improvements.

Besides the City of Houston, there are more than 200 separate taxing units in Harris County, many of which newcomers are not aware of until they get here. Some tax experts say that this system amounts to a disguise of the area's mounting public indebtedness.

Under what looks to be a healthy economic climate, some of the districts are mounting billions of dollars in future indebtedness. They are formed to aid real estate developers by issuing government bonds to build streets, sewers, drainage and other land improvements. Instead of paying for these improvements in the price of their houses, homebuyers find themselves paying high property taxes.

When the city annexes the new development, it assumes the bond burden. In effect, city taxpayers end up paying for suburban sprawl.

Critics call it "boom by fiscal gimmickry," which they charge will over the next 20 years require soaring tax burdens.

Houstonians, however, do not seem to mind. To them, the consequences of growth and boom are readily apparent—jobs prosperity, new buildings, new people and few of the signs of decay that have sent people fleeing from other cities.

"Houston is a very growth-oriented city, and there is very little opposition to that proposition," said Mayor Hofheinz. In fact the growth issue was not even raised in the election campaign.

Houston's population is now 1.4 million, with 1.8 million more people in surrounding Harris County. That's roughly double what it was 15 years ago, and economic forecasters see no letup in growth.

"Cities tend to grow in curve patterns, building up, peaking and then declining," said an economic analyst for a Houston bank.

"We feel a lot of cities in this country have peaked and are declining, getting old and becoming overburdened. Not Houston. We're just beginning to build. We have the raw materials, the access to markets, the people and almost endless room for expansion."

December 4, 1975

Sunbelt Region Leads Nation in Growth of Population

Section's Cities Top Urban Expansion

By ROBERT REINHOLD
Special to The New York Times

WASHINGTON, Feb. 7—The Census Bureau reported today that the metropolitan areas of the South and Southwest were about the only ones experiencing any substantial growth in population since 1970. The urban centers of the North and Pacific Coast mostly either lost population or gained only marginally.

The new estimates, meant to update the 1970 census count to 1974, underscore a dramatic reversal in American population trends. After a generation in which Americans migrated by the millions into big cities and their surrounding suburbs, the rural and small-town areas are now growing faster than the urban areas.

The chief exceptions to this rule are in the South and Southwest. All but two of the 13 fastest-growing metropolitan areas are in Florida, Texas and Arizona—parts of the so-called Sunbelt. The two others are in Colorado, a Mountain State also attracting new population.

The new figures are based not on a census headcount but on estimates derived from birth and death statistics, income tax returns and other data thought to reflect shifts in population. The metropolitan population of the United States on July 1, 1974, was estimated to stand at 155 million, meaning that about three of every four Americans live in or around cities.

Topping the list in growth is Fort Myers, Fla., whose population is estimated to have swelled by 46.4 percent since 1970. The next two, also in Florida, are Sarasota (32 percent) and Fort Lauderdale-Hollywood (30 percent). By comparison, the population of the United States as a whole grew by 4 percent in the same period.

The other leaders were the areas of Fort Collins, Colo.; Orlando, Fla.; West Palm Beach-Boca Raton, Fla.; Killeen-Temple, Tex.; Tucson, Ariz.; Colorado Springs; Tampa-St. Petersburg, Fla.; Tallahassee, Fla.; Phoenix, Ariz.; and Austin, Tex. All expanded by more than 20 percent.

Drop in New York

At the same time, the estimates underline the contraction and stabilization of America's older cities and their suburbs. Even under a new definition, expanded to include the most distant suburbs, the New York area dropped by 313,600 persons, or 1.8 percent, in the four years.

Even Los Angeles, after decades of heady growth spurred by the glitter of California, showed clear signs that it had passed a peak. Since 1970 more people have moved out of the Los Angeles area than moved in, although births left the area with a small net growth of 2.5 percent.

Of the 21 largest metropolitan areas, only five—Houston, Miami-Fort Lauderdale, Dallas-Fort Worth, Atlanta and San Diego—grew faster than the national average. Five others lost population—New York, Cleveland, Seattle-Tacoma, St. Louis and Pittsburgh.

Census experts were cautious in interpreting the new estimates, saying they were complicated by declining birth rates, economic pressures and other subtle forces.

'A Slight Shift'

"It is possible to exaggerate the regional differences," said Richard L. Forstall, a demographer who specializes at the Census Bureau in questions of population distribution. "It's not a wholesale packing up and moving. There are a great many people moving in both directions. What we have is a slight shift in the balance."

Usually a metropolitan area has been defined as a "standard metropolitan statistics area," or S.M.S.A., consisting of a large city and its adjacent counties. However, demographers no longer consider this definition realistic in many areas of the country because of the relentless spread of suburbia into formerly rural areas and the merging of metropolitan areas.

Therefore, the government has devised a new entity called a "Standard Consolidated Statistics Area," or S.C.S.A., defined as "large metropolitan agglomerations consisting of

The New York Times/Teresa Zabala

A major factor in the emergence of the Sunbelt has been its ability to obtain defense contracts and space-exploration installations. The Redstone Arsenal was instrumental in transforming Huntsville, Ala., into a major urban center. Above, the nearby Marshall Space Flight Center.

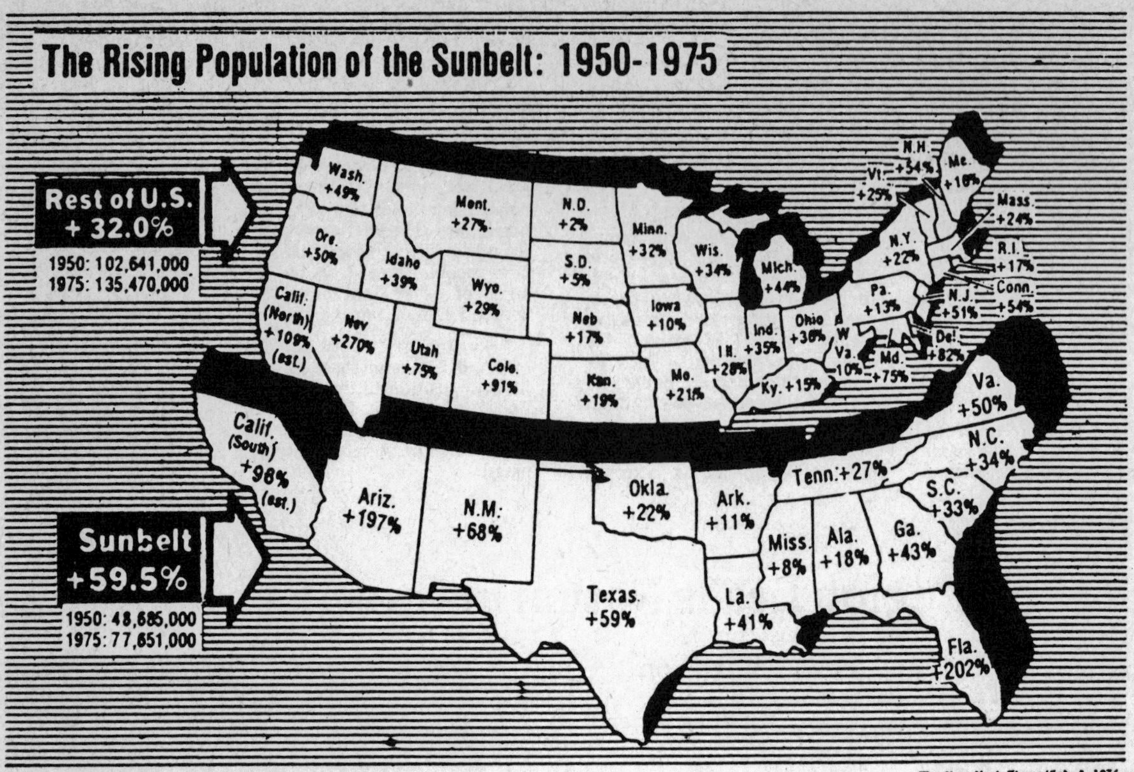

The New York Times/Feb. 8, 1976

groups of adjacent S.M.S.A.'s (1) having a certain level of intercommuting and (2) generally sharing a continuous urban mass as indicated by an overlapping urbanized area or adjacent urbanized area."

Three-State Area

Thus, the New York area is now expanded to include towns as distant as Asbury Park, N.J., and Norwalk, Conn., as well as all of Nassau and Suffolk Counties—an area with a total population of 17.2 million. Although births exceed deaths in the New York S.C.S.A. by 322,700, this was more than offset by the outmigration of more than 635,000 people.

Nearly every major Northern city suffered such losses in net migration. Both the Cleveland-Akron and the Seattle-Tacoma areas lost about 5 percent of their residents to other areas for example.

One of the biggest gainers of migrants was the Miami-Fort Lauderdale S.C.S.A., which absorbed 311,500 newcomers, or 16.5 percent of its 1970 population.

Taken together, the metropolitan areas of the Northeast and North Central regions gained a bare 0.4 percent in population, while those in the South and West grew by 7.1 percent.

Copies of the new report, titled "Estimates of the Population of Metropolitan Areas, 1973 and 1974, and Components of Change Since 1970," (Series P-25, No. 618), are available for 75 cents from the Government Printing Office, Washington, D.C., 20402.

February 8, 1976

AMERICANS VIEW THE CITY

Crowding to the Cities.

The new Governor of Virginia, in a late agricultural address, very earnestly urged the young men before him not to imitate those who had forsaken their "paternal acres" and gone to the large cities. This same point was enforced by our own Governor, HOFFMAN, and by Ex-Governor SEYMOUR, in their recent addresses on similar occasions. These dignitaries, Northern and Southern, all agree on the superior claims and advantages of agricultural life. The young men of every part of the country need such testimony, and we are glad to see it adduced.

The fact is undeniable that for some years farming pursuits throughout the country have been rather losing than gaining favor. The official returns show that agricultural production has not been keeping pace with the advancing population of the country, and alike demonstrate an increasing tendency to concentrate in large towns and cities. Farmers' sons have been moved by a spirit of adventure to turn their backs upon the steady occupation of their fathers, and betake themselves to speculation, or trade, or mechanical employments in town. The immense immigration into the country has by no means contributed its just proportion to the demands of agriculture. The last national census showed that nearly forty per cent. of the Irish of the country were living in the large cities, and thirty-six and a half per cent. of the Germans. If to these had been added those who were located in villages, and those who were scattered through the country employed in constructing railroads and other works of internal improvement, it would be seen at once that there were far more agricultural consumers among this great class of our population than agricultural producers. It is to be feared that the new census will show this disparity in a yet more marked degree. One thing is certain: that, taking the country at large, there will be shown an immense falling off of producers, to the extent of four millions at least, from the single event of emancipation.

Now, there can be no more fixed axiom in political economy than that agriculture must form the basis of the prosperity and power of the American people. It is the great foundation of our national wealth and consequence—the primary source of all our prosperity. It feeds us. To a great degree it clothes us. Without it we could not have manufactures, and should not have commerce. It furnishes our factories with their raw material, and it fills our ships with their cargoes. Social industry depends upon it; individual life depends upon it. There is no man in the country who is so wealthy as to be independent of the success of this great interest, nor any so poor as not to be affected by its prosperity or its decline. This country has peculiar facilities for advantageously prosecuting this great department of human labor. The variety of its climate, the abundance and cheapness of its fertile soil, are such as no other nation on the surface of the globe can boast. It is no credit to our vaunted enterprise that we have never yet made adequate use of these signal advantages—that the time has never yet been when the proportion of our farmers to the whole population was as large as it should have been—when the number of those engaged in professions and trades were not, at the very least, twice as great as the actual necessities of society required. There is reason to apprehend that this disproportion will increase. This restless, adventurous spirit is ever tending to take more complete possession of our people. Everybody is getting more infected with the eagerness to get rich in haste. There is a growing impatience of the good old plan of earning a competence by steady, persevering labor and frugal living. The young men of the day have tired of the isolation and monotony of agricultural life, and pant for something more stirring and exciting, and something that seems to promise quicker and more splendid returns. They have seized upon the first opportunity to launch away into the tide of trade and speculation. And that tide once embarked upon, it is very seldom that they find their way back again to the plowed fields. A large proportion of them have not succeeded in their new pursuits; tens of thousands of them have miserably failed, and become bankrupts and drones; and yet they have from the pure force of acquired habit clung to town life with all the greater tenacity.

It cannot be too well understood by these young malcontents in the country that failure there almost infallibly foretokens failure here. The same qualities and habits which stand in their way in the country will cause them to stumble in the city. It is everywhere the same all over the world: to fill any situation successfully, one must fill it as belonging to it. The man who feels above his business, let that business be what it may, is actually below any business. He is without anything to hold him up anywhere, and is bound to sink anyhow. The great work of life, whether in city or country, cannot be maintained by any such weaklings. Least of all is this tearing, grinding, crushing mart the place for them. We already have an over-production of incapables and drones. There is no room here for the drift of rural weakness and cowardice. Let the farmers' sons heed the counsels of their Governors and stay at home—holding fast to the oldest, happiest, most independent and most honorable of human occupations.

October 28, 1869

CITY AND WILDERNESS.

There can be no greater contrast between the city and the country than at this time of year. In Winter, a snow-fall paints the street and the plain with the same brush; and the city gains something over the country by the earliness of a Spring which compensates its scantiness. "The country ever has a lagging Spring," says BRYANT. But let one who is familiar with the beauty of natural solitudes walk through New-York now and his heart sinks within him. The streets of the better portions of the town, where rich people live, are a silent and stony desert. The house-fronts are closed, and as grim as the tombs of the Pharaohs. The angular façades of freestone, never cheerful, are now forbidding in their blankness. The gray-brown shutters are austerely shut; there is darkness within, while without the hot sunshine falls in sheets upon the cheerless walls and pavements. In the poorer parts of the city, say along the wards of our own East Side, there is more life, but even less comfort. At all times of day, knots of languid men and women lounge in the shade. Strapping young fellows doze idly in doorways or under the shelter of upturned wagons. Slatternly and dirty children, ragged and half-naked, swarm on the sidewalks. The sunlight rains hotly down into a street noisome with the refuse of poor kitchens. Indescribable smells arise on every hand. Everybody is sweltering in suffering silence, and the only sign of activity is the appearance of the huckster who drags his unwholesome load of garden-stuff through the hot street, howling his cry in answer to his sad brother who bewails "rags, bags, bottles," as he totters along the sidewalk. The whole picture is a striking illustration of the most abject misery of human civilization. Contemplating it, one can hardly realize that there anywhere exists on the same planet a barbaric wilderness unscarred by the hand of man.

And yet, somewhere in the woods of Maine or Northern New-York, or in the vast solitudes of Washington Territory and Oregon, some wanderer, too familiar with these artificial, stony ways of mankind, is wondering if it be possible that a cityful of miserable people anywhere exists. There the trees are huddled around in natural confusion; the ground is covered with a moss which springs ever upon decay, and the feet of the adventurous traveler sink among the dead leaves and twigs of many years' accumulation. Nature is untamed there, and the young trees contend with each other for the sunshine that sifts in through the screens of verdure overhead. Through occasional slits in the pillared forest one catches an occasional gleam of a silent stream, shut in from the world by masses of noble growths. A nameless fragrance of arboreal life and vegetable decay pervades the air. To the inattentive ear the silence is utter, save when some kingfisher whirrs away over the pond, or a cat-bird calls from the cedars, and the hollow boom of the bittern answers from a boggy glen as the night comes on. But below all these occasional notes, even in the solemn stillness of the virgin forest, continually arises the low hum of insect tribes, while overhead the leaves of the beeches and the birches are heard in their multitudinous rippling. No wonder the traveler, pausing in this wildness, thinks it impossible that anywhere there are hot and stony streets and over-governed people.

Of course, between these two extremes—city and wilderness—there are many gradations of social civilization. The monstrous caravansaries which infest the seashore and disfigure the mountains afford refuge to some. These may be the starting-places for people who desire to go into the wilderness alone. But, for the most part, with their telegraph wires, daily mails, and newspapers, they make a little city by themselves. The fugitive does not escape the worry and wrangle with the world's affairs, nor the cares of his own private business. In like manner, in the country boarding-house, even in the ideal and almost unattainable place where one has all the comforts of the country without the mean pretences of the city, one is environed with the things that drag people down to earth. Human association, incessant and entangling, must be escaped if we are to have perfect rest. The man, fatigued and worn, must go back to Nature if he would be healed and recuperated. A snatch at Nature from the window of a flying car, or from the balcony of a Summer hotel means nothing. The pure air and grassy ways of a New-Hampshire village will do much for the tired citizen who is "burning his candle at both ends." But even there he is pursued and devoured by the brood of cares, which leave him only in the pathless wilderness. He will find silence and oblivion for all his worries only in the untrodden ways of Nature.

We do not realize, until, in a fortunate hour, we find ourselves free, how much of our life is wasted in wrestling with impertinent things. We are neglecting ourselves while we do much for others, assimilating things which are only burdensome to us, oppressed with the cares of all Governments, and burdened with the great concerns of humanity. We throw ourselves into each day's news with an interest which is perpetually renewed, and is perpetually draining the life. The business of the world is always ours; and even in our recreations we take care that we shall not be lost to the mail-carrier and the telegraph wire, which pursue us with echoes of the world's work. As men, weary of the perpetual necessity for keeping up appearances, accounting for themselves, and doing what society demands they shall do, sometimes escape into the solitude of a great strange city, so others often flee into the wilderness. It is not surprising that hermits seclude themselves from the haunts of men without apparent reason. Lost to the world in the solitude of a trackless forest, they have revenged themselves for years of social tyranny and government by shirking all duties whatsoever.

A hermit's life is utterly selfish. But something like this is needed for the recuperation of men who habitually shoulder more than their share of the responsibilities of this world. The constant study of business, politics, art, philosophy, and the means of existence is fatiguing. There are few men who do not, sometimes, "hanker" after the wild freedom of the wilderness. We have within us a remnant of savage nature, and it is a good thing that we cherish it. Let us not be wholly given over to requirements of civilization. We may not subsist as amateur savages during the depths of a Northern Winter. But this is the season to forget in the primeval forest the arid and stony ways of the city.

July 1, 1877

THE DRIFT TO THE CITY.

The announcement of the Census Bureau that the urban population of the United States is approximately 54,796,100, as compared with a total rural population of 50,970,000, makes one wonder how much further the country would be behind in 1920 if free delivery routes had not been extended by the Post Office Department, if telephone exchanges had not been multiplied, and if the automobile had not taken the place of the buggy on the country roads. Community life in the rural regions was to banish loneliness by bringing the farm folk into intimate touch with the centres of population, and the comforts and luxuries of home were to be enjoyed on remote homesteads; yet the drift to the cities in the last ten years has not been stayed; on the contrary, country life is much less in favor than was the case in 1910, when the rural population exceeded the urban by almost 7,000,000, the totals being then, respectively, 49,348,883 and 42,623,383, although under the head of rural population were included the smaller towns and villages; in other words, townships. A change from almost 7,000,000 in the rear to about 4,000,000 in the lead for the urban population in ten years is significant.

It is easy to explain a conspicuous movement of population from the country to the cities and large towns by saying that four years of the World War were included in the decade, and that higher wages and a shorter working day were prime attractions to the country people; but the consequences may be serious. How long will the United States produce enough food for our own use if the farmers and the truck gardeners cannot plant and reap the old areas of cultivation for want of help? How long will the small towns and villages improve and prosper if the magnet of the city continues to draw their young people away? It may be asked whether a continuing urban growth at the expense of the country will not result in more or less physical deterioration of the American people, **and whether the old-fashioned virtues** are not likely to decline. It is certain that there will be more social discontent, and that political conditions will become more complicated. Back to the land is now a cry on many lips.

Doubtless industrial idleness would send numbers of people back to the farms, and a long period of peace would be favorable to a slackening of the tide moving toward the cities; but if the next census is to show a greater proportion of inhabitants in the country, something must be done to make living there more remunerative and satisfying. The farmer and gardener must have cheaper transportation and it must be made worth while for the residents of the townships to stay where they are. Evidently something is wrong with country life, its occupations and amusements, when so many cannot resist the " lure " of the city.

October 2, 1920

SOULS OF OUR CITIES

A Painter's Interpretation of the Expression of Civilization Through Machinery

By LOUIS RICH

CIVILIZATION, in the modern and stricter sense of the word, began with the building of towns and the founding of cities. Its spread and progress were synonymous with the spread and progress of communities. Studied from this angle, the history of mankind becomes chiefly a history of the development, rise and decline of centres of population. Cities assume the character of standpoints of history and at any given period furnish an index of the material and cultural advancement made by man.

The urbanization of life has been a particularly notable attendant of modern social progress. It has been made inevitable by the industrial revolution and the limitless capacity to use the products of mechanical arts. It has reached its highest development in America, where technical facilities and industrial enterprise have been greatest.

American cities, with their Cyclopean architecture, sky-piercing towers, monumental terminals, gigantic bridges, grain-gorged elevators, smoke and fire-belching factories, deep-cut defiles of streets teeming with people engaged in ceaseless, roaring, rushing movement, are staggering symbols of human power over space and matter. They represent the utmost that has been attained in the conquest and harnessing of mechanical forces. In them are seen the highest achievements of human will and effort. They provide a grandiose setting for man's most stupendous handiwork—the machine, which is visible life-energy, with man himself as its dynamic principle.

The machine-born and machine-intoxicated American city has its romance, likewise its poetry, its beauty. But these things are discernible only to those who can see the spiritual quality of the material, the ideal side of the practical. It is found in the achievement of the purposeful, in the triumph of organization. The soul of the American city is revealed in its anatomy. Its architecture is the ecstatic leap skyward of the ever young, the ever pressing. Its skyscrapers, warehouses, steel-mills and foundries are not monstrous cages where human thoughts and wishes are imprisoned. On the contrary, they are firmly founded and courageously built edifices expressive of the joy of will and action, of the joy of toil, which by penetrating life to its innermost secrets offers the only means of raising mankind to ever higher levels.

The Old World sees in America, i. e., in the American city and its characteristic features, the apogee of its own creative power, both actual and potential, the culmination of Occidental progress. Beyond that it can see nothing but decline, deterioration and destruction. The German philosopher Oswald Spengler in his book "Der Untergang des Abendlandes" predicts the downfall of Western civilization. But the prodigious vitality, the stupendous energy, the boundless faith and daring of America seem to confound even the most skeptical. In the rushing tempo of her cities, in the roar and clatter of their life, in the giddy flight of skyscrapers, the swoop of lifts and the thrilling swing of bridge-curves all elements of vision, sound and motion seem to blend into one triumphant outcry: "Here in our cities the world is just beginning!"

"He who makes the city makes the world," says Drummond. Life in an American city makes one feel that one is bearing a part in the work of the world. The world, as though conscious of the great work that is being carried on in America, is contributing its best workers, who come from every land and clime. The American city is still the great unifier of people of diverse races, creeds and views. The vast stream of its inhabitants hailing from every country of the globe amalgamates them all, fashioning them into a single people with a common aim.

Under Old World conditions they would have had one another by the throat, fighting like beasts of different species, as has been truthfully observed by some one. In the New World, however, with its incentives and opportunities, its lure of success and passionate rejections of failure, traditional animosities soon dissolve in the flux of doing and striving. New enmities and rivalries arise, of course. But these are merely clashes between equals. The will to achieve is the one common heart-beat pulsing in the amazing aggregate of bricks, beams and brains which the American city represents.

Thus has a young American artist, Louis Lozowick, conceived of our cities and proceeded to paint a series of them to give concrete form to his conception. His works have been exhibited in Berlin and have prompted some of the art critics to say that a new direction in the art of painting is being marked out by American artists. Perhaps more than any of his contemporaries, Lozowick has succeeded in drawing the attention of European artists and critics to America and opened up new possibilities of American influence on European art.

The cities which Lozowick paints are not realistic reproductions of places and views. Yet to one who is familiar with these cities the paintings will at once suggest the locale of their inspiration. They contain actual elements, such as buildings, bridges, wells, that form a significant part of the original location. But he employs these elements in a manner wholly subordinated to his aim. This aim is to paint the epic of the American city as it has impressed his lyrical self. To Lozowick there is a tremendous story in the American city, told not in words or written records, but in terms of structure, movement, color, mass. He paints the city not as it appears to the eye, but as it affects the mind, the soul, the imagination. He visualizes for us the meaning of the place we live in. For this reason his pictures are abstract. But their visionary truth, their fantastical consistency, is such as to suggest the distilled and concentrated essence of reality.

There are no people in Lozowick's metropolises, none of the rushing and chaotic life which we know to be a part of them. Streets and buildings are deserted. There are no signs, no advertisements, no traffic. The city has been reduced to the

"Pittsburgh." By Louis Lozowick.

"Chicago." By Louis Lozowick.

"New York." By Louis Lozowick.

prosaic elements of building-walls and roofs and smokestacks. But in the very strength of its structures there is evident the work of man. The steep towers, the piled up masses of office buildings, the abysses of streets and air passages, the viaducts, the blast furnaces, the rhythm, the precision, the co-ordination of it all suggests the forces and elements that have built the city.

Lozowick makes use of the many methods evolved by the various schools of art without adhering blindly to the creed of any one of them. He synthesizes them all into a technique adaptable to his subjects. He attains his effects by freely drawing upon the resources of both modernists and traditionalists. Design, composition, geometric arrangement, dissociation of movement, inverted perspective, logical structure, texture contrast—all enter into his workmanship.

The artist believes that there is no progress in art, but only change. This change is due to the changing conditions under which art is produced and to the infinite variety of elements of design and the possibilities of using them. No one school is preferable to another. Each reflects the period to which it belongs. What he has done with the cities can be done also with landscape. But in America the characteristic, the striking thing is not her landscape but her civilization. In America one is impressed by the preponderant rôle that science plays in the life of the nation, by the machine, by the phenomenal technical progress, by industrial activity and organization. All these things find their clearest expression in the American city. Therefore the city should be turned to artistic account.

Mr. Lozowick was graduated from the National Academy of Design New York.

February 17, 1924

CITY'S DOOM NEAR, HENRY FORD'S VIEW

The time is approaching, according to Henry Ford, when the big cities will disappear and there will be decentralization of industry as well as population, with industrial plants in country places and something like an exchange of labor between the farms and the factories.

This is the idea set forth in an interview with Mr. Ford, written by Drew Pearson for the current issue of Automotive Industries. Mr. Ford is quoted as believing that the passing of the big cities will mean less crime, poverty, unrest, nervous strain, and wealth. Mr. Pearson quotes Mr. Ford thus:

"The modern city has done its work and a change is coming. The city has taught us much, but the overhead expense of living in such places is becoming unbearable. The cost of maintaining interest on debts, of keeping up water supply, sewerage and sanitary systems, the cost of traffic control and of policing great masses of people are so great as to offset the benefits of the city. The cities are getting too heavy and are about doomed."

"Industry of the future will be organized on a big scale," Mr. Ford went on, "but competition will force it to move to parts of the country where labor is steady and overhead costs low." As an example, he mentioned what had been done in the making small parts for his cars.

"Instead of making the man come to the city," he said, "we take the work out to him in the country. The farm has its dull season, when the farmer can come into the factory, and the factory has its dull season, when the workmen can get out on the land and help produce food."

"Every man is better off for a period of work under the open sky, and while we cannot afford the time to go off for three or four months a year to dawdle around some fancy Summer resort, yet we can escape the routine of the factory and the monotony of the farm by an exchange of labor during the slack seasons."

August 28, 1924

"BROADACRE CITY": AN ARCHITECT'S VISION

Spread Wide and Integrated, It Will Solve the Traffic Problem and Make Life Richer, Says Frank Lloyd Wright

Recently in The New York Times Magazine the noted French architect Le Corbusier described the Green City which he has conceived as the solution of the modern urban problem—a substitute for the crowded centre. In the article that follows Frank Lloyd Wright, a pioneer American architect among moderns, presents another and diametrically opposed program — the Broadacre City, which he sees as the logical urban development of the machine age.

By FRANK LLOYD WRIGHT

LET us approach the traffic problem not as a tinker or garage mechanic, nor childishly try to tear the city down to get the green country in and set the city up in it again on its old site—feudal towers a little further apart. Vested interests, once invested, cannot be divested except by agreement. And they will not agree.

With an architect's vision, let us see the natural law of organic growth at work as change: seeking the sequence to provide for consequences. Enough blind-alley nonsense has been talked about congestion by skyscraperites—words obscuring the simple issue. Of what practical use is this skyscraperites' expedient imagery? Superspace making for rent, to enable super-landlords to have and to hold the super-millions in super-concentration to make super-millions of superfluous millions? For organic reasons the traffic problem is insoluble for the future on any basis satisfactory to human life within any busy city.

True, the herd-instinct grows with the swarm in the erstwhile village streets. But the swarm is taking to wings—or to wheels, which is much the same because increased facilities of lateral movement are almost equivalent to flight—a fond human dream about to be realized.

By means of the motor car and the inventions that are here with it, the horizon of the individual has immeasurably widened. A ride high into the air in any elevator today only shows the man how far he can go on the ground. And a view of the horizon gives him the desire to go. If he has the means, he goes, and his horizon widens as he goes. This physical release is at work upon his character.

His selfish interests might easily multiply and pile him up senselessly, in tiers of cells, ad infinitum, even after he got his release. These selfish interests may still turn the trick. He is still dazed by his new freedom. But, like a bird born in captivity, to whom the door of his cage has been opened, some time, soon, he will learn that he can fly. And when he learns that he is free, he is gone.

After all he himself is the city. The city is going where he goes and as he goes. When he goes he will be gone where he may enjoy all that the centralized city ever really gave him, plus the security, freedom and beauty of the ground that is his. That means he is going to the country with his machine by means of the machine, in larger sense, that is opening the way for him.

* * *

THE city is yet only about one-tenth the motor car city it will be if machine-made promises to the man are kept. Any dutiful devotion to the machine on man's part today should mean a motor car—comparative flight. The citizen and his increase either have a car or dream of having one, envying the neighbor the one or two or three which he already has.

If congestion is crucifixion now, what will congestion be within a few years when it is multiplied by "success" as many times as is inevitable?

Roughly calculate the mass of machines that machine-age "success" must mean to 6,000,000 people. More than several million private cars. Perhaps a quarter of a million trucks and as many delivery machines; a half million buses, displacing street-car tracks and unwholesome subways; hundreds of thousands of taxicabs, meantime. With room enough for each and for incidental transients to function at all, the mass would fill the busy city channels above the tenth story. Allowing for the criss-cross on the gridiron, it would double and pile up over the skyscrapers themselves. Call this exaggeration and cut it in two—then cut that in two again, to be rash. There will be enough left at the rate of increase "success" will bring, to bury Manhattan out of sight with its own cars and transients.

The motor car has just begun on the city. Why deck or double-deck or triple-deck the city streets at a cost of billions of dollars, only to invite increase and meet inevitable defeat? Why not allow the citizenship to keep the billions that decking would cost to buy more motor cars and get more out of living in a more natural and fruitful life, as freedom dawns on the citizen? The utility of the city as a form of centralization vanishes by way of the machine that built it.

Democracy means just that freedom for the citizen—if the machine is working for the citizen. Monarchy was the ideal of centralization—the unit compelled to revolve around about a common centre. Democracy is the ideal of integration—many units free in themselves functioning together in freedom.

Monarchy has fallen. Our capitalistic system, if it persists as a form of centralization, stands to fall. Electrified mechanical forces that are building our modern world now are, by nature, turning upon centralization to destroy it. That means that the city is destroying itself.

Drawn by Frank Lloyd Wright.

The Future—A Design for an Apartment Building in the "Broadacre City."

Centralization, whether expressed as the city, the factory, the school or the farm, now has the enormous power of the machine-age setting dead against it. It is in the nature of universal or ubiquitous mobilization that the city spreads out far away and thin. It is in the nature of flying that the city disappears. It is in the nature of universal electrification that the city is nowhere or it is everywhere.

Centralization by way of the city has had a big day and a long day. It is not dead yet. But it is no longer a necessity or a luxury. Mobilization of the human animal, volatilization of human thought, voice and vision make the city as troublesome an interference to life as "static" is troublesome to radio.

Once more humanity has overcome a physical disability with a mechanical appliance. The man may already get more out of his new release by way of increased facility for lateral movement than ever came to him before in the history of his race. Imagine then, what is coming to him in the next twenty-five years.

• • •

DEMOCRACY, as the systematized integration of small individual units, is a practical and rational ideal of freedom: machine in hand. Integration over the whole surface of the nation is ideal and is no less practical.

The Broadacre City is not merely the only democratic city. It is the only possible city, looking toward the future. Exaggerated vertical lanes of transport impinging upon congested, narrow horizontal lanes; tall channels, ruinous to privacy, to let light and air into offices or habitations; the shelf and the pigeon hole—all these are landlord expedients that it is high time to have done with. There is no life in them. There is only rent.

As for securing privacy by hermetically sealed and blinded buildings, hot air circulating between two glass surfaces opaque or transparent—that expedient means heating the inside and the outside impartially, 50-50, with no gratitude from the outside. And 1,000 people to the hectare (2.47 acres) is looking not so far ahead. It is 980 too many.

It has been discovered that severe standardization is no bar at all to even greater freedom in self-expression than was ever known before. Always providing we mean by self-expression genuine individuality—and not personal idiosyncrasy. These two discoveries are the Magna Carta of the new liberty into which the citizen may now go by way of machinery, and go in his own machine: to join the building of the Broadacre City of the twentieth century that, all unknown to him, has already begun to be built where he belongs.

The present-day city, in the light of our new opportunities, has become a stricture in distribution and transport; a handicap in production; an imposition upon family life.

• • •

THE present form of the automobile is crude and imitative compared to the varied forms it will soon take. The flying machine is only in a more or less experimental form, unwieldy in scale and a hostage to the elements. Teletransmissions of sight and sound are not only experimental; they are in their infancy, as is the intelligence to which their operation is entrusted.

We are proud of the great network of highways—the road systems of the country we are just beginning to build. And yet it requires but little imagination to see in all the power of these new resources, machines and materials, new release of human activity within reach of every one—the basis not only of adventure and romance with nature, but of a safer, saner, less anxious life for a free people; a longer, happier life wherein the man is sure of a living for himself and his own; sure also of some healthful association with beauty. Not only is the city itself a stricture, a handicap in production, but the contributing railroad is too limited in movement, too expensively clumsy and too slow in operation. The end of the day of the back-and-forth haul, long or short, demanded by centralization, is in sight; the end, too, of mass transport by iron rail.

No great flight of imagination is needed to see the coming highways as great architecture, the telephone and telegraph poles down. Poles and wires are already useless. Signboards down, too, as gratuitous insults to intelligence. Fine bridges and noble viaducts may be great architecture in great landscape, landscaping healing the cuts and fills of the construction of the roadbeds.

• • •

HIGHWAY travel is growing more and more interesting because, becoming as safe as the train, and swifter, it is more desirable because it is more spontaneous. Mobile, human transport is getting down within reach of every one at last: no waste time or waste motion to pay for.

Produce is fresh every hour because distribution is taking place where producer and consumer happen to stand or choose to live. No flight of immature imagination is needed to see these great highways with their tributaries and ramifications hooked up at intervals with safe systems of noiseless, compact air transport; to see the network of fine roads passing public-service stations that live up to all the name implies, passing roadside markets, integrated with groups of three, five and ten acre intensive farm units; diversified manufacturing units not far away; great automobile objectives as amusement resorts built on and with the natural features of environment; fine homes in parks and gardens that are small farms, too, all winding up the beautiful natural features of our great landscapes into the spacious broadacre cities of the near future: the greatest work of man for the liberation of mankind that has ever been realized.

Human environment on this soil of ours dedicated to human freedom may now be spacious and humane; life free as to individuality, yet integrated spontaneously, instantaneously as a whole with all life; the new cities affording each man and his family greater facility for culture, the amenities of life on a larger scale, human intercourse more liberal and healthy. Every home is a centre and a delightfully varied association with nature, the homemaker's birthright.

Not 1,000 to the hectare. No, nor space sold by the square foot. But space belonging to those who use it, by the acre. There is space enough for this "distribution"—good for nothing else.

Let us say, for the sake of argument, that the objectionable mechanical features of travel are removed, as they are rapidly being removed; that the utilitarian object of concentration in centralized cities is entirely gone, as it is indeed, or is fast going, hastened by the new leverage of the new power of a new life—we call it the machine for lack of a more comprehensive term. Suppose the motor bus is as comfortable and inviting to us as the Pullman never was and together with the low-gravity truck-train it takes to the right of way of the railroads; the average highway has four traffic lanes, the main arteries six or more.

These safe, broad traffic lanes—noble engineering in themselves — are thronged with life, moving not humdrum in standardized machines as we know them, but in many forms suited to many needs and individuals. Swift singles, doubles; safe quads and dignified sextets; safety and gayety now in the swift-moving fleet. Grade crossings eliminated. Charm returning to the road.

Self-contained mechanical units, as varied and well designed, are taking off into the air from plane stations at intervals—noiseless, compact and safe. Beguiling resorts, famous for hospitality, cuisine, entertainment, occur where the beautiful features of the land occur. Extensive, complete markets, with produce fresh every hour, are integrated with the intensive small farm units. Other markets pertain to manufacture or classified foreign products. These are scattered along the higways, but each series integrated as links in a great chain. Service stations that are hostelries and rendezvous for comfort and entertainment at strategic points are sightly features of the highway itself.

The farm units that produce and the factories, too, are within a ten-mile radius of the extensive roadside markets, integrated with them—and a ten-mile radius means within ten minutes of each other. The factories might be within walking distance of the acre home units of the workers; but why, when ten miles is ten minutes?

Interchange of products is by continuous movement in beautiful environment each way, spaciousness determined by the man in his machine and no traffic problem, because traffic is the norm of the new spacing or standard of measurement of the centring of all units.

As the citizen sits in his car, he may press a variety of buttons or turn an indicator and obtain any section he desires of the modern newspaper — the forests saved and millions of tons of waste paper eliminated. He picks up by sound and sight whatever he is interested in, learns by listening where the day's specialties are to be found; where events of interest are occurring or are going to occur, near or far away. All over the surface of the globe, in fact, if he pleases, he may listen in.

His home is now a centre to which all this comes and he is integrated with all other homes and forms of production or of distribution spontaneously and instantaneously. More, he has the means of easy, direct personal contact with all forms of production or distribution within a radius of 150 miles: two hours by wheeling or a half-hour by flying.

He can cross the continent, for conference or pleasure, within twenty-four hours. The home, you see, takes on a new significance. A fresh importance as the centre.

Business, too, takes on a different character. It is a form of freedom, not slavery. Anxiety is easier to bear. Individual initiative, in this new freedom, comes alive. Relieved of the inordinate, merciless pressure of centralization, architecture bursts into bloom. Hugo, the great modern of his time, said it might do so in the twentieth century. There is no prevailing style, but style is everywhere. The common sense of the age flowers into new forms born of new materials.

Better ideas of life take rational imaginative form. The garden as a park is normal to the "new" city. Play spaces for all the sports we have now and new ones to come. The integrated three, five and ten acre farm units are coveted things for beauty, and are a basis for a safe, rich life for the rearing of families: work to be done now with lessons to be learned. Man's relation to his animals takes on a better character in architecturally planned association, in surroundings where the nature of the association is recognized and provided for intelligently.

Spaciousness, transport, buildings, all of life intimate with the ground, appropriate to each other and to each and every one according to his need or the nature of his need and love of life. Woods, streams, mountains, ranges of hills, the great plains—all are shrines, beauty to be preserved.

Imagination is our human divinity. It alone is what the human herd needs to distinguish and save it from the fate that has overtaken all other herds, human or animal. In the nature of the traffic problem lies the liberation, and that soon, of such human enslavement as the city now stands to exploit. Or else in its nature lies the further degradation of humanity.

In this collision and irreconcilable war of mechanical factors which we call the traffic problem, an element of human freedom is caught and held against its larger interest—held to serve only the will and act of more or less gratuitous forms of fortune that function mostly as rent, in some guise—the will that built and maintains the city. The struggle is on.

* * *

THE traffic problem will be solved as architecture. But not by verticality. Narrow lanes of vertical transport impinging on inadequate horizontal alleys, narrow vertical channels destroying privacy to let light and air into dreary miles upon miles of shelving upon which human beings, by paying tribute, may perch or roost—this arrangement, however it may be rationalized or visualized, affords no measure of life to the man, such as was promised to him by our charter of freedom, the Declaration of Independence.

In this traffic problem our future as a nation is at stake. The problem will be solved as architecture, but the twentieth-century cities will be no scrap-pile or brick yard nor any standardized park with standardized colossi standing in it and scraping the sky. It will be solved by the horizontal line of the machine age, indefinitely extended as the great architectural highway and by the flat plane of the machine age expanded into the free acreage of the Broadacre City of free democracy: architecture and acreage seen as landscape. No power of man can long preserve any imposition reversing these new social forces when they are understood and put to work by man for man. No, not even if held by himself against himself.

March 20, 1932

A HISTORY OF THE URBAN LIFE

Mr. Mumford's "The Culture of Cities" Links Past, Present and Future

THE CULTURE OF CITIES. By Lewis Mumford. Illustrated. 598 pp. New York: Harcourt, Brace & Co. $5.

By R. L. DUFFUS

THOSE brought up in quieter times and places must have moments of dismay, and even of horror, at the sight and sound of the great modern city, of which New York is perhaps the most startling example. Its waste, its confusion, its denial of elemental human decencies—perhaps, worst of all, its complacency, as though it indeed represented the apex of 6,000 years of history—can be appalling. More shocking still is the thought that by means of great roads and eventually by airplanes it may be destined to invade, congest and vulgarize all the world's choice countrysides. Every one who has ever felt like this, who has ever had to brace himself against the city's barbaric thrust and has found it hard to give it due credit for its drama, its conquest of matter and its heroic marshaling of human energy, should read Lewis Mumford's new book.

It will not be altogether easy reading. One must bring some thought to Mr. Mumford's table if one wishes to carry away digestible ideas. He is now, even more than in his earlier writings, getting at fundamentals—at the vitamins, one may say, of the civilizing process. This is far more than a discussion of cities and city cultures. It is an attempt to analyze, historically and contemporaneously, the nature and trend of man's organized life. As in a previous work, "Technics and Civilization," which in some respects he admittedly parallels, Mr. Mumford "seeks to explore what the modern world may hold for mankind once men of good-will have learned to subdue the barbarous mechanisms and the mechanized barbarisms that now threaten the very existence of civilization." With barbarism so visibly on the march in many parts of the world and expressing itself in many outward aspects and many ways of thought, even in democratic and peaceful countries, the "culture of cities" is no academic abstraction. Only as we plan and build more perfect cities can any culture anywhere survive. The suburb and small town no longer provide escape. Only a few of us can get our mail at Mr. Smart's "R. F. D." Rousseau and Thoreau are dead. There are bats in the ivory tower. Our cities are our front line. If we are beaten there, we shall be harried and cut down in the deserts and on the mountain tops.

The city is undoubtedly the foremost expression of the dominant forces in any human culture. A society that has no cities can hardly be said to have a culture. "Here in the city," as Mr. Mumford says, "the goods of civilization are multiplied and manifolded; here is where human experience is transformed into viable signs, symbols, patterns of conduct, systems of order." A New Yorker may wonder why the root of the Latin word for city should appear in the adjective "urbane." But, urbane or not, these ganglia of human life are the centers of such creative forces as may be operating at a given time. To write of them, as Mr. Mumford shows, is to write man's history. In the present instance he begins with the medieval town, from which we have progressed or degenerated—don't be too sure which until you think it over.

Mr. Mumford is no homesick medievalist, retreating into the past because he cannot bear to face the present. He does think that the medieval city, at its best, did its job, for its time, within its cultural setting, better than New York or Chicago or London does its corresponding job today. The illusion of the dark, crowded, vile and unsanitary medieval town came partly out of the nineteenth-century (and earlier) illusion of automatic progress. If the lot of mankind had been steadily improving for several centuries, as we were not long ago taught to believe, and the end product was a modern city, how much worse, it was reasonably argued, must have been the medieval city. But consider the facts. Such a city would have been built first for a military or political purpose. It would naturally become a market. Its inhabitants would acquire rights and liberties beyond those of their rural brethren. There were narrower limits of wealth and power than under the feudal conditions outside—the towns were comparatively democratic. Sanitary conditions were bad, by good modern standards, but these were in part redeemed by the existence of "usable open spaces" and a closer relationship with nature than exists in communities of comparable importance today. The city was on a human scale, decentralized, not really overpowering, not dwarfing those who lived in it.

Deterioration arose from many causes. The Middle Ages closed in the rise of the centralized, warlike State with weapons of offense which enabled it to terrorize the masses, and paranoid rulers and ruling classes (strangely reborn in the totalitarian neurotics who are trying to make so much of today's world an annex to an insane asylum) had free rein. Their vagaries showed themselves in capital cities which sucked the life out of the countryside and which expressed themselves in bastard street plans and bastard architecture. The old freedom and the old free spaces vanished together. Into this picture entered the grim "coal and iron economy"—the paleotechnic era—with an attending army of economists to justify and bless the evil done by man to man. This economy was to give way, in the late nineteenth century, to the "neotechnic * * * based on the use of electricity," etc., and Mr. Mumford looks hopefully forward to the "biotechnic economy," in which "the biological sciences will be freely applied to technology, and in which technology itself will be oriented toward the culture of life."

The cities became, with an almost steady progression, less fit places for the happiness and well-being of most of those who had to live in them. The labor-saving machine seemed to damn the laborer. "The baroque conception of the despotic prince" gave way to that of "the untrammeled individual," who expressed his individuality by being a "despot in his own right." Population increased prodigiously and crowded into the cities. At the same time it came to be regarded as a raw material which favored "individuals" could employ for self-enrichment. As Mr. Mumford put it:

> The brakes of tradition and custom were lifted from the exploitation of land; there was no limit to congestion, no limit to rent-raising; there was no standard of order or decency or beauty to dictate the division and layout and building up of urban structures. Only one controlling agent remained: profit. * * * The two main elements in the new urban complex were the factory and the slum. By themselves they constituted what

was called the town. * * * Such urban masses could and did expand a hundred times without acquiring more than a shadow of the institutions that characterize a city in the sociological sense—that is, a place in which the social heritage is concentrated, and in which the possibilities of continual social intercourse and in-teraction raise to a higher potential the activities of men. * * * Never before in recorded history had such vast masses of people lived in such a savagely deteriorated environment.

For sensitive persons, anxious to save health and sanity, there was only one thing to do—run away, find privacy, shut the damned thing out. Hence "the romantic suburb," far from realities. The climax was Megalopolis, the shapeless, bloblike monster which occurs all over the Western World under various names. Mr. Mumford's chapter on the "Rise and Fall of Megalopolis" is a song of hate that stirs the blood.

Lewis Mumford

But unless something can be done about Megalopolis it is of no more use to hate it than it is to hate sickness and death. Far better to consult a psychiatrist and learn how to adapt ourselves to it. Our hope, as Mr. Mumford would see it, lies partly in the things that must happen, because this is a world of change, and partly in the things that can be made to happen. It is these things with which he deals in the latter two-thirds of his book—not the easier part to grasp or to summarize. One wonders, as one runs through the fifty-odd pages of bibliography which are visible evidences of his scholarship, if he hasn't attempted to get too much material—the precipitation of too much reading—into one volume. But the gist is clear. To get a new kind of city—indeed, to build real cities in the finer sense—we need, Mr. Mumford believes, a new type of civilization. We need to substitute for the "power state" the "service state." We need room to re-order our affairs in the interests of a richer life for all the people. We cannot have an orderly city, such would be the argument, unless we plan it for the people who live in it. It must exist for human development, not for exploitation. On this postulate hangs the whole doctrine, as Mr. Mumford elaborates it, of cities as centers of natural regions, of a complementary diffusion and centralization that come out of real cultural needs.

A New York Canyon.

From a Drawing by W. K. Oltar-Jevsky for "Contemporary Babylon."
(Architectural Book Publishing Company.)

Of course this is revolution, though perhaps not of the kind that need stir up the Red-baiters. Mr. Mumford has an amiable quarrel with Thomas Adams and the other city planners who made the regional plan and survey for the New York area. Their work seems to him already obsolescent. But the difference between their thinking and his is that they projected contemporary trend lines into the future, whereas he believes that trends alter and that the future can be controlled. They tried to provide for twenty million people in the New York region, because they saw no way of keeping the expected additional ten million out. He wishes to act dynamically upon the situation by changing the bases of our society. They didn't see their way clear to go so far, though some of them might have thought that it would be well if the growth of population in the area ceased as, let us say, of 1930.

But whether one goes in for caution or for the bold and hopeful adventure which Mr. Mumford contemplates one cannot help being stirred by Mr. Mumford's vision. A "city in which every quarter is ribboned with gardens and parks," a countryside intelligently used and not merely trampled over by those attempting to escape the intolerable conditions of the metropolis, a humanity-centered rather than a machine-centered, profit-centered society—this is a noble dream, and Mr. Mumford has written of it with scholarship, eloquence and profound sympathy.

April 17, 1938

Mr. Moses Dissects the 'Long-Haired Planners'

The Park Commissioner prefers common sense to their revolutionary theories.

By ROBERT MOSES
Commissioner of Parks

In municipal planning we must decide between revolution and common sense—between the subsidized lamas in their remote mountain temples and those who must work in the market place. It is a mistake to underestimate the revolutionaries. They do not reach the masses directly, but through familiar subsurface activities. They teach the teachers. They reach people in high places, who in turn influence the press, universities, societies learned and otherwise, radio networks, the stage, the screen, even churches. They make the TNT for those who throw the bombs. They have their own curious lingo and double talk, their cabalistic writings, secret passwords and abracadabra.

First, let's have a general look at the "Beiunskis." A Beiunski is usually a refugee whose critical faculties outrun his gratitude to the country which has given him a home. He is convinced that we are a pretty backward people and doesn't mind saying that they ordered things better in the old country. "Bei uns," he says, they did it this way. The fact that we happen to like our awkward and primitive ways will not turn any genuine Beiunski from the stern task of teaching us how really cultured folks should behave. You have to be quite humorless to be a good Beiunski.

Only the other day a famous Beiunski, author of God knows how many books, sufferer for years from logorrhea and now living in a hotel overlooking one of our New York parks, wrote this gem of advice and ponderous fun to the Mayor for transmission to the city Park Commissioner:

> My dear Mayor: As I know that you take small things as earnest as the so-called big things, I beg to communicate:
>
> Daily I enjoy the skating on the small lake at the south end of Central Park. By two small improvements many occasions for falls could be avoided:
>
> 1. The wood bridge leading from the dressing room to the ice is so overused that it should be renovated.
>
> 2. In Europe we used to spread water on the furrowed ice at night, so that it might freeze over until the morning, and therefore form a smooth surface again.*
>
> Hoping that you could find for me a quiet hour during the next month, I remain, dear Mr. La Guardia,
>
> Yours very sincerely—
>
> *If there is a lack of workmen, I would be glad to do it myself every evening with a watering can and a flashlight.

Let us look now at the writings of Eliel Saarinen, who was born, educated and practiced architecture at Helsingfors, Finland, came to the United States and founded the Cranbrook Academy of Art in Michigan. Saarinen is one of the really great architects of our time, who forsook his profession to become a revolutionary planner. He is bitter about our faults. Saarinen believes in what he calls "organic decentralization." Here are some of the things he says about it in "The City—Its Growth—Its Decay—Its Future":

> . . . concentration in the overgrown cities has caused compactness and disorder and, through these, deterioration and the spread of slums . . . the only remedy in such circumstances is a decisive surgery which can bring openness into the compact urban situation, and which—if executed gradually according to an organically comprehensive scheme—is the surest road . . . toward "organic decentralization." . . . It might be true, perhaps, that the most direct way of reaching this goal would be to try the decentralization principles on actual town-building, so as to gather experience through practical realities rather than through theoretical generalities. However logical such a thought may sound, it must be borne in mind that in "practical realities" organic decentralization is a slow process. . . . Matters being so, it is necessary for the time being to lean upon illuminating reasoning.

This "illuminating reasoning" leads Saarinen straight into communal land ownership. Here it is in the usual jargon:

> Transference of property rights is an essential part of the processes of organic decentralization. . . . This law is so much the more necessary because of the fact that transference of property rights to a considerable degree means a corresponding transference of people from one location in the city to another.

Obviously, Saarinen thinks he can apply Scandinavian experience to American conditions. This is the way they do it in Stockholm, according to John Graham Jr. in "Housing in Scandinavia":

> In the Inner City, property owned by the city is sold to private enterprise at prevailing market prices. The city may also sell its land in the Inner City area at a figure lower than the market value when the city is assured that the land will be put to a social use or, as expressed by the Stockholm authorities, "when the city is certain that the benefit of the low price of the land will actually redound to the good of the tenants and not to the advantage of the purchaser."

If this strikes you as pretty strong stuff, have a look at another distinguished foreign figure in our midst, Walter Gropius. In his biography in "Who's Who" Professor Gropius describes himself as born in Berlin, founder of the Bauhaus School of Architecture, which he moved from Weimar to Dessau in Germany and thence to Harvard and Chicago Universities. The Bauhaus School is known for functionalism, abstract art and other brilliant and revolutionary ideas.

Intelligent Americans are just beginning to realize that Gropius is hurting our architecture by advocating a philosophy which doesn't belong here and fundamentally offers nothing more novel than the lally column and the two-by-four timber. Here is a quotation from "The New Architecture and the Bauhaus":

> It was realized that the present plight of our cities was due to an alarmingly rapid increase of the kind of functional maladies to which it is only in the natural order of things for all aging bodies to be subject; and that these disorders urgently called for drastic surgical treatment. . . . Once the evils which produce the chaotic disorganization of our towns have been accurately diagnosed, and their endemic character demonstrated, we must see that they are permanently eradicated. The most propitious environment for propagating the New Architecture is obviously where a new way of thinking corresponding with it has already penetrated. It is only among intelligent, professional and public-spirited circles that we can hope to arouse a determination to have done with the noxious anarchy of our towns.

Still another prominent modernistic architect, Eric Mendelsohn, formerly practicing in Germany and now settled in this country, in a recent lecture at the University of California, contributed this little "ipse dixit" to the solution of the city traffic problem:

> In the master town plan motor traffic will by-pass the city area, or run as part of an independent speed network from end-stations and flying fields, underground, to the focal points of industrial, business and residential quarters, thus clearing the city of all surface mechanical traffic.

This certainly is a cute trick if you can do it.

A FEW months ago there appeared in Time an illustrated tabloid article under the heading "Science" about an engineer-architect, described as a widely famed city planner in Britain and on the Continent before the war, now studying United States city problems on a grant from the American Philosophical Society, with the help of his wife, a physicist teaching at Queens College, and a Harvard architect of the Bauhaus School.

The studies of this group convinced them that Manhattan's basic trouble is hardening of the arteries. It may be mentioned in passing that many radical planners habitually compare municipal diseases and cures to those of the human body. This little group of earnest thinkers begins by ripping up Manhattan's midriff. A belt highway is installed eighty feet high, with six separate levels for trucks, buses, passenger cars, etc., including two levels for parking. Avenues a century old are eliminated, together with 90 per cent of the present crosstown streets. Fifteen present blocks are thrown together into each of a group of separate villages. The estimated cost of $250,000,000—about one-fifth of the correct figure.

The British revolutionary planners have had great influence here. Let us, for example, take this description in The Architectural Forum of November, 1943, of the Uthwatt Report prepared by the Expert Committee on Compensation and Betterment and presented to the British Parliament in September, 1942, by the Minister of Works and Planning:

> . . . the committee proposed (1) immediate nationalization of all development rights by purchase for fair compensation in the name of the Authority; (2) all new development to be prohibited unless initiated or approved by the Authority; (3) all land to be used for new development to be acquired at fair value (less "development right") by the Authority and leased to the developer.

The Forum article did not exaggerate, if we judge by this direct quotation from Mr. Justice Uthwatt's committee, one of those little gems which blush unseen in the star-spangled galaxy lighting us from the midwife to the mortician:

> Immediate transfer to public ownership of all land would present the logical solution, but we have no doubt that land nationalization is not practicable as an immediate measure and we reject it on that ground alone.

Stalwarts who shudder at a 2-mill rise in the tax rate, who denounce post-war public works, who threaten the town with bankruptcy and ruin if municipal services are not drastically cut, demand that bureaucracy be curbed and howl dismally if zoning standards are raised sufficiently to insure light, air and decent living, praise Uthwatt and pass the dynamite.

SO intrigued were the Luce publications by the Uthwatt line of reasoning that they endorsed the entire revolutionary scheme of land expropriation and promptly developed the thesis that the revolutionaries are the true strategists while the practical planners and doers are merely tacticians. Fortune in a recent number, entitled "City Planning: Battle of the Approach," said:

> Another principle of modern planning, either ignored or shunned by the strictly tactical school, is that in order to be fully effective, city planning must be based on public control of the use of urban land. This means all the land without as well as within the city limits that is ever likely to become in fact a part of the urban community.
>
> During all the popular emphasis on beautification, spectacular piecemeal attacks on specific urban problems, and half-baked public works programs, there has been growing in the minds of a handful of thinkers and planners a real grasp of fundamentals.
>
> Vast and complicated as the whole job may appear, there is no good reason to look upon it as impossible. Strategy, to be sure, does demand a broader view of the problems of an urban community in its entirety than has been taken thus far anywhere in the world, except by the starry-eyed planners so unpopular with Commissioner Moses.

In metropolitan planning the tacticians, if that is to be our name, adapt, modify, improvise, improve, boldly but with some respect for our heritage. How often do we have the opportunity to work with the blank page, the untouched canvas, the raw land? Jones Beach and the Long Island parkway system were an exception. Why didn't the strategists seize this opportunity? Simply because it was too tough and long a fight with politics, local and big estate opposition, legislative ignorance and stubborn nature. And, as to things nearer home, where vested interests are really entrenched, what strategists in the Harvard Schools of Architecture, Regional Planning and Economics and in editorial sanctums have been seen on the side of the angels in the sweat and mud of battle?

IN a recent rather sour comment on the city's post-war program, as reflected in the exhibit recently opened to the public, a well-known New York daily newspaper made this editorial comment:

> But the beauties of a program like this (unsustained as yet on any considered financial foundation) should not blind one to the fact that it does not reach to those fundamental factors of land use, land values, tax assessments, rents and building costs which really determine the growth of a city. The program is a handsome poultice, standing ready to be slapped on the face of old New York when somebody provides the cash for the beauty treatment; it is in no sense a cure for the deeper problems which afflict her anatomy.

Let us see where this brilliant metaphor leads us. Poultices our plans may be, but is this editor really prepared to endorse the big surgical operation hinted at? Let's be sure of our diagnosis and not confuse the need of new plumbing with demands for a laparotomy. Let us remember that the surgeon is a bureaucratic government, reaching into our very vitals, and that the city might not recover from the shock of the operation. Moreover, who will pay the doctor's bill? Perhaps the patient isn't at death's door and merely needs a few vitamins. Would this paper support a program of Government ownership and control of land, drastic and arbitrary regulation of its use, complete deflation of the present real estate tax system and adoption of the foreign revolutionary program which obviously influenced its editor? You know the answer.

NOW for Frank Lloyd Wright of Wisconsin, another brilliant but erratic architect and planner. Regarded in Russia as our greatest builder, he has been enormously popular everywhere abroad. He is the author of "The Disappearing City" and founder of the Taliesian Fellowship, described as a cultural experiment in the arts. Here are a few samples from Frank Lloyd Wright's "Modern Architecture":

> Even the small town is too large. It will gradually merge into the general non-urban development. Ruralism as distinguished from Urbanism is American, and truly Democratic.

Last year I received from Mr. Wright a copy of his book "Taliesin" with a friendly note. The understanding was that the book would be passed around among the men upon whom I lean for advice. This reply summarizes their conclusions:

> While we were generally familiar with your publications and views, my little group of earnest thinkers, or rather constructors, have read the Taliesin Pamphlet and your more recent memorandum with considerable interest. The consensus of opinion is that we do not fully understand them. Some of the implications are most interesting, and, of course, we respect your accomplishments in the field of architecture, but it seems to us that you have taken on a little too much territory. Most of my boys feel that you would get further if you tried an experiment on a reasonable scale, frankly called it an experiment, and refrained from announcing that it was the pattern of all future American living.
>
> There it is. You can't expect anything better from moles who are blind, crawl short distances under the earth, and have only the most limited objectives.

THEN there is Lewis Mumford, lecturer on planning and author of "The Culture of Cities," an outspoken revolutionary, often quoted with approval by conservatives who obviously have no notion of the implications of his philosophy. Here are Mumford's Six Stages in the Cycle of the City:

> First Stage: Eopolis. Rise of the village community.
>
> Second Stage: Polis. An association of villages or blood-groups having a common site that lends itself to defense against depredation.
>
> Third Stage: Metropolis. Within the region one city emerges from the less differentiated groups of villages and country towns. . . . It becomes the . . . "mother-city."

Fourth Stage: Megalopolis. Beginning of the decline. The city under the influence of a capitalistic mythos concentrates upon bigness and power. The owners of the instruments of production and distribution subordinate every other fact in life to the achievement of riches and the display of wealth.

Fifth Stage: Tyrannopolis. Extensions of parasitism throughout the economic and social scene: the function of spending paralyzes all the higher activities of culture and no act of culture can be justified that does not involve display and expense.

Sixth and Final Stage: Nekropolis. War and famine and disease rack both city and countryside . . . the city of the dead; flesh turned to ashes; life turned into a meaningless pillar of salt.

The process is faintly reminiscent of the herpicide tragedy—"going, going, gone, too late for Mumford."

THIS brings us logically to my friend Rexford Guy Tugwell, professor, brain truster, former Under-Secretary of Agriculture and head of the Resettlement Administration, former chairman of the City Planning Commission of New York, now Governor of Puerto Rico, and author of "The Fourth Power," a book in which he advocates the establishment of a planning authority, with members chosen for life, wholly independent of and somewhat above the executive, legislative and judicial functions of the Government, as the last and absolute authority on all matters economic and physical.

Here is a revealing quotation from Dr. Tugwell's "The Principle of Planning and the Institution of Laissez Faire":

> The intention of eighteenth and nineteenth century law was to install and protect the principle of conflict; this, if we begin to plan, we shall be changing once for all, and it will require the laying of rough, unholy hands on many a sacred precedent, doubtless calling on an enlarged and nationalized police power for enforcement. We shall also have to give up a distinction of great consequence, and very dear to many a legalistic heart, but economically quite absurd, between private and public or quasi-public employments. There is no private business, if we mean by that one of no consequence to anyone but its proprietors; and so none exempt from compulsion to serve a planned public interest. Furthermore, we shall have to progress sufficiently far in elementary realism to recognize that only the Federal area, and often not even that, is large enough to be co-extensive with modern industry; and that consequently the States are wholly ineffective instruments for control. All three of these wholesale changes

are required by even a limited acceptance of the planning idea.

This is the way the Fourth Power Planning Commission, called by Dr. Tugwell "the directive," will proceed when they get control, as described by Dr. Tugwell:

> . . . evolution must necessarily be toward cooperative forms, collective customs, pragmatic morality and technically buttressed leadership; because this is what will give us the greatest product; and also because this is the only door to the future which is available to those who regard the avoidance of force as a necessity.

In December, 1940, Dr. Tugwell, as chairman of the New York City Planning Commission, proposed a new and revolutionary plan of land use. Boards of trade and real estate organizations, as well as civic groups whose tendency is to the left, fell for this green-belt plan. A handful of realists blew it up. At the public hearing before the Planning Commission, at which Dr. Tugwell presided, I made this statement:

> According to the figures in the staff report, you propose to increase the area of the "green belts" by about 48,000 acres. You propose, by the adoption of this plan, to notify the owners of one-third of all the taxable land in the city shown on the land-use map as "green belts" that they are foolish to continue paying their taxes and that it's just like throwing money in the sewer, since the land has no "economic future" for residence, business or industry. Just what do you expect this to do to property owners and to the city's financial structure?
>
> No one in this city has greater enthusiasm for the expansion of park and recreation areas than I have, and this applies with equal force to the city's State officials who for years have labored to develop and coordinate the city, suburban and State park and arterial program in New York. This group, as the result of long practical experience, has developed a healthy contempt for the kind of watercolor planning which consists of splashing green paint at a map and labeling the resulting blobs as "open areas," "green belts," "breathing spaces," etc.
>
> Actual accomplishments in New York City since 1934, and in the State and suburbs since 1924, were brought about by people who labored day and night for limited objectives in the face of great difficulties. These accomplishments were not brought about by itinerant carpetbag experts splashing at a ten-league canvas with brushes of comet's hair. I recommend that you file the "Master Plan of Land Use" and forget it.

That was the end of the green-belt scheme, and nothing has been heard of it since.

Adolf Berle, Dr. Tugwell's predecessor as chairman of the City Planning Commission, on the eve of his resignation to become Assistant Secretary of State lunched with me to talk over some details he was mopping up. As he struggled with his overcoat he left with me this farewell, which I hereby contribute to the growing collection of Berliana: "It's all very well for you, Bob, to spend your time on local street openings, but I'm off to Washington to solve the Chinese problem." You can't ask a global planner to waste his time on the sidewalks of New York.

THERE are too many people who not only lack the ability to work with others toward realizable objectives but who do not like the community and therefore want to tear it up by the roots, toss the pieces in the air and start afresh in the open country. The man who loves his city will recognize its faults and shortcomings, but will never damn it entirely out of hand and dismiss it as a monstrosity. It takes time to plan a city, as Vachel Lindsay said in his famous poem, "On the Building of Springfield":

Record it for the grandson of your son—
A city is not builded in a day.
Our little town cannot complete her soul
Till countless generations pass away.

The man who does not love his country and his own town can do nothing for them. It does not matter whether it be the land or place of his birth or of his adoption—so long as he becomes part and parcel of it. Carl Schurz did as much for the United States as any native son of no matter how deep and distinguished roots. The patriotic conservative will find plenty of faults at home. He should be eager to remedy them, but he must be loyal to the institutions and to the local scene in which his lot is cast. To revolutionary planning sophisticates this will seem simple to the point of imbecility, but truths, like ballads, are always simple.

June 25, 1944

Neighbors Are Needed

THE DEATH AND LIFE OF GREAT AMERICAN CITIES. By Jane Jacobs. 458 pp. New York: Random House. $5.95.

By LLOYD RODWIN

ONE of the most memorable caricatures by Max Beerbohm shows George Bernard Shaw's view of the world: it pictures the celebrated dramatist—his expression a cross between a scowl and an impish grin—standing gracefully on his head. In some cases, such views are rewarding; in others, unforgettable. In any event, one sees things somewhat differently, especially if the reporting is done with an irreverent eye, a waspish tongue and a "no holds barred" attitude to customary villains, heroes, strategy and tactics. By dint of these talents, Jane Jacobs achieves a brashly impressive tour de force in her reinterpretation of the problems and needs of the contemporary metropolis.

To the innocent onlooker, the drive for more comprehensive planning regions, low density suburbs, redevelopment of central areas, more parks, open space and highways, public housing, modern neighborhood design with superblocks facing interior lawns to reduce traffic hazards and achieve economies of scale—all these and more—suggest that we may yet make our cities more gracious and efficient. Contemplation of these prospects, however, only fills Jane Jacobs (an editor of Architectural Forum) with revulsion.

BIG cities, she says, are full of strangers. Citizens and strangers alike must enjoy security on city streets. This security, she insists, will never come just from a vigilant police force. It requires an intricate social system, which automatically achieves this effect. You get it from "public actors," from habitual street watchers, such as storekeepers, doormen and interested neighbors, and from more or less constant use at different hours, which is possible only if there is a rich mixture of activities in buildings of varying age and character.

Mrs. Jacobs' view is that people like to live, not just be, in such lively neighborhoods. Youngsters and elders alike need such surroundings. But she scoffs at our understanding of these requirements; for we continue to put up civic centers, low density residential areas and housing "projects" segregated by income. All these developments," she complains, combine to produce boring homogeneous cores which generate traffic for limited periods and then lapse afterward into dead or dangerous districts. Worse still, the new buildings with high rents squeeze out the marginal activities, the small business man just getting a start, the colorful shops with strange and exotic wares, the little restaurants and bars, almost everything deviant, bohemian, intellectual or bizarre—in other words, all that the author believes lends spice, charm and vigor to an area.

To brighten neighborhoods, "unslum" slums and reweave housing projects into the fabric of the city, Mrs. Jacobs proposes that we do most of the things urban experts tell us not to do: attract mixed activities which will generate active cross-use of land; cut the length of blocks; mingle buildings of varying size, type and condition; and encourage dense concentrations of people. Some of the most intriguing parts of this work involve the ingenuity with which she applies her ideas for enlivening districts such as Wall Street or Central Park after dark. Greenwich Village, where the author lives, is her model par excellence. A few other favorite examples include the North End of Boston, Georgetown in Washington, Rittenhouse Square in Philadelphia, the "Back of the Yards" in Chicago, and Telegraph Hill in San Francisco.

Reading this volume, one almost gets the impression of a golden age before the Garden City and the High Rise enthusiasts appeared on the scene. For Mrs. Jacobs mainly blames their ideas, or bastardized versions of them, for what is wrong with our cities. The irony is that most of the things she objects to are the effects of rising income and economies on parents hungry for more space for themselves and the kids. The reformers shared, perhaps even anticipated this hunger: so that in effect, what the author really resents is their failure to buck the trend or to provide more sophisticated living styles.

Whether Jane Jacobs is right or wrong, the first big efforts to do something about our cities are not conspicuously successful; and the reformers are already worrying about the reactions to the increasingly visible inadequacies. Her book is significant precisely for this reason. It fuses ineffectual elements of discontent into a program that can pack quite a wallop. It won't matter that, like the reformers she criticizes, she has little sympathy for persons who want to live differently from the way she thinks they ought to live; nor will it matter that some of her own proposals (on the planning process, for example) come straight from the planners she criticizes; and that some of her cherished reforms, however tentatively advanced, are as romantic and "utopian" as those she rejects. The same holds for transparent gaps and blind spots, such as her blasé misunderstandings of theory and her amiable preference for evidence congenial to her thesis. In short, except to the miscellaneous victims and the academic purists, it won't matter that what this author has to say isn't always fair or right or "scientific." Few significant works ever are.

Jane Jacobs' book should help to swing reformist zeal in favor of urbanity and the big city. If so, it might well become the most influential work on cities since Lewis Mumford's classic, "The Culture of Cities." It has somewhat comparable virtues and defects. Not quite as long or comprehensive, it is wittier, more optimistic, less scholarly and even more pontifical. The style is crisp, pungent and engaging; and like its illustrious predecessor, the book is crammed with arresting insights as well as with loose, sprightly generalizations.

A great book, like a great man, "is a strategic point in the campaign of history, and part of its greatness consists in being there." For all its weaknesses, Jane Jacobs has written such a book. Readers will vehemently agree and disagree with the views; but few of them will go through the volume without looking at their streets and neighborhoods a little differently, a little more sensitively. After all, it is the widespread lack of such sensitivity, especially among those who matter, which is perhaps what is most wrong with our cities today.

November 5, 1961

Cosmopolis: 'Too Big, Too Noisy, Too Bad'

THE INTELLECTUAL VERSUS THE CITY: From Thomas Jefferson to Frank Lloyd Wright. By Morton and Lucia White. 270 pp. Cambridge, Mass.: Harvard University Press and the M. I. T. Press. $5.50.

By CHRISTOPHER TUNNARD

EVER since Isaiah called down a curse on Babylon, the city has been blamed for the ills of society. When St. Augustine, the good Bishop of Hippo, told of a heavenly city he contrasted it with man's city, Rome, which had been punished for its sins by bloodshed and virtual annihilation. Cities were praised again in the Renaissance, but people fled them to escape the plague; and later, as the scene of rebellions and strikes, the city is chastised for mob rule and radical ideas. Only recently have the cities begun to fight back against sanctimonious upstate politicians, who use them as a scapegoat for their own ends. Rural corruption can be quite as noisome as the urban stench, but somehow in the city evils become magnified and crime statistics shout because there are more people to swell the numbers.

In the case of the American city, to which the present authors address a thesis suggested by others, we have the added detriments that it does not have a long tradition and has suffered from a good deal of neglect. It is called ugly, and a wasteland, which is not said of Paris, sinful though many would assume her to be. The visual appearance of the American city appeals mainly to self-confessed sophisticates or to beatniks, who profess to find affinities with jazz in the stepped-up skyline or who feel release in the anonymity of its repetitive street pattern.

It would be going too far to say that Americans have never liked their cities, and the authors, Morton and Lucia White, are careful not to do so. At best Americans have only tolerated their urban centers, and today the suburbanization of American life has come to dominate the thinking of a whole generation of the managerial class. This at a time when the central cities are in dire need of intellectual and moral leadership if they are to survive. The authors use the new crisis of the city as a peg on which to hang their examination of the ambivalent or antipathetic feelings of certain intellectuals as expressed in their writings. The book does not ask: Who is for Cosmopolis and who against? The protagonists of the city scarcely receive a hearing, and if one could make a generalization about their approach, it would be that the authors strain too hard to find the evidence and sometimes build a case on very little.

WHAT Henry James thought about the city in the morning, he may have forgiven after a good dinner. Many intellectuals can be repelled and fascinated by the city at the same time; few are as unequivocal as Emerson in his dislike of New York. That city, he noted in his journal, "would soon become intolerable, if it were not for a few friends—who, like women, tempered the acrid mass."

Mr. White is a philosopher at Harvard, and we can expect here to find a probing of the ideational sources of intellectual dislike, as distinct from the common forms of unreasoning bigotry. We cannot lay the blame on romanticism alone, he finds, because both in fact and in imagination the American city has provided such a variety of things to hate. He says the American city has been thought to be: "too big, too noisy, too dusky, too dirty, too smelly, too commercial, too crowded, too full of immigrants, too full of Jews, too full of Irishmen, Italians, Poles, too industrial, too pushing, too mobile, too fast, too artificial, destructive of conversation, destructive of communication, too greedy, too capitalistic, too full of automobiles, too full of smog, too full of dust, too heartless, too intellectual, too scientific, insufficiently poetic, too lacking in manners, too mechanical, destructive of family tribal and patriotic feeling."

Yet it is not necessarily viewed as inferior to wild nature, a romantic approach held by only a few intellectuals like Thoreau. Henry James and John Dewey had different motivations—the one perhaps because American cities did not measure up in social brilliance to some European ones, and the other because they seemed to him to lack opportunity for the face-to-face human relationships which he considered essential for living the good life. The authors conclude that the city is helplessly caught in the cross-fire between two powerful antagonists — "primitivists and sophisticates; and no mechanical recitation of the misleading aphorism that like effects are produced by like causes can gainsay this fact."

The book is excellently provided with quotations, and although the majority of intellectuals examined are literary figures, and well-known ones at that, the opinions of Jane Addams, Robert Park, Josiah Royce and Santayana are brought in for good measure. One may quarrel with interpretations occasionally — when Royce argues for a "higher provincialism" this does not imply an attack on the city but rather a plea for a more concious American loyalty. However, taken as a whole, the work is a revealing analysis of American attitudes toward urbanization and urban life.

Some important outside influences might have been given prominence: Spengler, who is mentioned, for the spread of 20th century pessimism, and Le Corbusier, who is not, for his animadversions on "the new slavery of tenacled cities" which have been as widely influential here as the jeremiads of Frank Lloyd Wright. If Theodore Dreiser, why not Sinclair Lewis?—and the powerful 19th-century voices of Dickens and Mrs. Trollope might surely have been paid some attention.

After this, somebody should write a book on the intellectuals who have praised the city. If, as the Whites suggest, we need the encouragement of an urban tradition to give us faith in our rebuilding operations, then it is to them that we should turn for new insights. There have always been those who would never exchange the grimy pavements of Gotham for Concord or Walden Pond. They are the urbane ones, and their leader is Samuel Johnson. "When a man is tired of London, he is tired of life; for there is in London all that life can afford," he told Boswell. Even today an effort to appreciate the good things that the city offers can be well worth while.

October 28, 1962

City Concept Criticized

Urban Renewal Commissioner Disputed on Plans

The writer of the following, Research Professor of Urban Studies at the University of Pennsylvania, is author of "The Twilight of Cities" and other works on city development.

TO THE EDITOR:

The talk by the Federal Urban Renewal Commissioner William L. Slayton which you reported on March 15 is of particular interest because he tried to defend something that cannot be defended in an age of growing mobility, increasing automation and rapidly rising population. He joins issue with the critics of the glorification of the central city who, in the opinion of the writer of this letter, justifiably ask: Why revitalize something that is dying and wait for a concept that is outmoded? Mr. Slayton admits that an outward trend is operative in many cities, but fails to draw the inevitable conclusions from this fact.

Instead of spending billions on slum clearance, these sums should be allocated to converting every slum, however small, into park land, thus gradually loosening up the congested city area and developing a continuous park system.

The idea of the city center as the physical and symbolic core of modern urban communities is a nostalgic and misguided attempt to save investments and to rescue a concept that was the idea of the Middle Ages. The present city centers are a dead weight on the cities and prevent a creative reorganization, long overdue, of the confused and decaying structure of the whole urban area. They have degenerated into executive ghettos and commercialized amusement compounds.

Meaningless Structure

The critics are not against cities as such, but merely against futile attempts to preserve a physical, economic and social structure that has become meaningless. Mr. Slayton believes that the facilities and services of the central cities depend on a citywide clientele. This statement cannot be maintained. These facilities are slipping away under our eyes from the congested areas.

What is basically wrong with all the proposals now enshrined in the propaganda slogan of city renewal is that they deal with symptoms, not with causes of the dilemma.

Nobody in his senses has ever suggested that "a suburban shopping center would be a place for Carnegie Hall." But Mr. Slayton uses this example as a serious argument against the critics of the ideas he defends. Suburbs and shopping centers are not the essential problem or the ultimate solution. They too are symptoms of a disease that has affected the bloodstream and the very existence of every city.

It is an uphill fight for city planners who want to investigate the genuine causes of the urban malady and to create dignified and viable urban communities. Our great foundations are firmly committed to the generalities of the city renewal program. No help can be expected fro' them. Nor can, for the time being, anything be hoped for from the Federal Renewal Administration. This may be a case for the personal intervention of the President.

E. A. GUTKIND.
Philadelphia, March 16, 1964.

March 29, 1964

Are Our Cities Doomed?

Yes

By EUGENE RASKIN
Adjutant Professor of Architecture, Columbia University

It does not take 20-20 vision to see that our big cities, such as New York are not merely in a state of crisis. They are dying. Inevitably.

They are physically obsolete, financially unworkable, crime-ridden, garbage-strewn, polluted, torn by racial conflicts, wallowing in welfare, unemployment, despair and official corruption. As they exist at present they are unsalvageable, destined to join the dinosaur in deserved extinction.

Urban planners and others who come up with temporary patchwork schemes and gimmicks to keep the cities going another year or two or three are as pathetic as the officers of the Titanic charting tomorrow's course while the water rises above their ears.

The idea should be easy enough to accept. In the million or so years that Man has puttered about this planet he has been at various times a tree-dweller, a cave-dweller, a cliff-dweller, a nomad, a farmer, and most latterly a denizen of cities. Each period came about in response to particular human needs. Each period developed, flourished and finally died away when it no longer met those needs, or the needs themselves changed.

In short, each phase (without benefit of planners) lasts until it has fulfilled its evolutionary role and is ripe for replacement by the next stage. This is what is happening now to our cities. New York, if anything, is overripe. You can tell by the smell.

What were the needs that gave birth to cities? In admittedly oversimplified terms they were three: Defense—stout walls, and many hands to build and guard them; Commerce—the exchange of goods, the gathering of artisans and professionals, the growth of industry; Excitement—the stimulation of varied contacts, new people and experiences, the lure of the bright lights and the glamour of the city's siren daughters.

Today, in the final decades of the 20th century, it is abundantly clear that cities can no longer meet these needs. Certainly New York can not. On the contrary, it is exactly in these main areas that the city fails most conspicuously.

Defense? A farce. In the era of intercontinental missiles defense is the last thing a city is good for. A city is a prime target, as was made entirely evident in World War II, when Londoners sent their wives and children out of town to escape the bombings.

Commerce? Laughter from the wings. It is hardly a secret that businesses and industries by the dozens are moving out of town as fast as they can go, accompanied by their technicians and executives, and followed by the anguished howls of the City Fathers watching their costs spiraling into the stratosphere while their coffers empty out like a bag of peanuts at the zoo. Meanwhile, office space, vastly overbuilt, goes begging for tenants.

Excitement? Too much, and of the wrong kind. The average city dweller hurries from his job (if he still has one) or from his rich, full day on the welfare line, happy if he makes it home to his police lock without being mugged and without finding his flat burglarized. He then anesthetizes himself with television so that he won't get ulcers thinking about dog dung, deviates, blackouts, brownouts and the myriad other joys of urban living.

Even the non-average person (the one with lots of money) is finding the city less rewarding each year His limousine can't get through the clogged streets; the once chic restaurants are deteriorating or closing; the night clubs are practically all gone. And the theater? We'll let Walter Kerr talk about that. As for the siren daughters, more often than not they turn out to be a pitiful row of hollow-eyed junkie prostitutes lined up along West 50th Street.

The finest values of the urban center are just beginning to be seen, after a long period of decline, as New York turns toward its next evolutionary stage, the one for which it is clearly destined—the place of Culture, of concerts, ballet, opera, museums, film festivals, of conventions and expositions, and of governmental facilities.

Witness the most impressive additions of the recent years: the Coliseum, Lincoln Center, the United Nations, the new Madison Square Garden. It is consistent, by the way, that the Lindsay administration, financial crisis and all, has just proposed a plan for a $100-million Convention Center on the West Side and a scheme for buying Yankee Stadium.

But "Exposition City" as one might name the urban center of the future is still merely in the earliest of stages. The thing to note is that the New York to be can be manned by a small fraction of the present teaming and miserable millions.

Where will the rest go? They will go where they are going already—those who can, that is—writers, artists, composers, white and blue collar workers, executives and professionals. That is, they go out of town, to live near their Industrial Parks, in their Adult Villages, their Young Ideas Towns, their Smoky Hills, their Retirement Communities, their Resorts, their Farms, and don't look now, yes, their Communes.

Note the ads in this very section of the newspaper. That's where people are going.

Manhattan, among several other large urban centers, recently reported a decreased population in the last census. Left behind, unhappily, are the impoverished — mainly blacks, Puerto Ricans and other disadvantaged groups. For the rich, the city, for all it is becoming a drag, is still quite lovely at dusk when the lights go on along Central Park South. For the poor it is a rat-infested hell, where one person in eight is on welfare, and the unemployment figures are staggering. The main point is that the movement is not into the city, as it has been for centuries, but out. Whoever can make it, gets out.

In short, the city is failing to fulfill those functions for which it came into being and is therefore dying. Its replacement, the new form of human organization which for the moment we can call the Post-Urban Society, is well under way and gathering speed—not in accordance with anyone's plan or theory, but simply as a result of thousands upon thousands of individual decisions arrived at by the force of circumstance. I submit that the Post-Urban Society—a variety of specialized nonurban communities relating to a scattering of much diminished "Exposition Cities"—is already so far realized that what we are dealing with is not urban prophecy, but solid, present fact.

Perhaps the best thing the planners could do would be to stand aside and keep out of the way of the Post-Urban Society. Actually, one can think of some useful things for them to do, if only to keep them from swelling the unemployment rolls:

1. Most important of all must come the *recognition* of the terminal nature of our present urban dilemma, so that the evolution and transition into the Post-Urban Society can be helped instead of hindered.

2. Rather than continue with their fruitless efforts to breathe life back into a dead horse, the planners could bend their energies toward devising new and better ways to get the crying poor out of the blighted center city ghettoes and out to where business and industry are moving and there is a possible chance of jobs. Or, if they must remain on welfare, they can at least be supported in humanly tolerable conditions. Meanwhile the old slums could be razed, and the ravaged and humiliated soil healed over with parks and gardens.

3. Another helpful task planners could perform might be to persuade the City Fathers not to place such projects as the World Trade Center, for instance, in the most densely used parts of the city, where the transit facilities are already so overburdened that practical approach seems only feasible by helicopter.

4. Every plan to "ease" traffic congestion by building more and wider approaches, underpasses, overpasses and similar anti-personnel devices must be scotched instantly, the proposers summarily shot and their estates used to help build blockades to keep autos out of the city.

Does all this seem a bit starry-eyed? Well, maybe it is, but I haven't heard anything from the urban planners that comes closer to the hard facts of what is going on. Mind you, I have nothing against the urban planners themselves. For the most part they are a cheery and harmless lot who throw delightful parties. I wish they would throw more in, oh, Colorado Springs, or Saratoga, or, well, almost anywhere, as long as it's out of town.

Professor Raskin is the author of "Sequel To Cities," published by Block Publishing Company.

May 2, 1971

Are Our Cities Doomed?

No

By SAMUEL TENENBAUM
Professor of Guidance and Counseling, Long Island University

The city nowadays has few defenders. It is being diagnosed, dissected—and found wanting. Some are saying that the city is so sick it will not survive, and if it does, it will continue on in a shriveled, pathological state. Nowhere at present do we hear of the grandeur of the city, its glory, its might, its beauty, its nobility. In our present view of the city, there is a contempt and a cynicism, an attitude hitherto unknown in history.

Through the centuries, even before the ancient Greeks and Romans, the city was an object of love, adoration and even worship. Around his city, a citizen sank his deepest spiritual self, his very religion. The sons of a city vied in serving it, in bringing to it glory and power and wealth. Caesars gladly went forth to conquer in its name. For power within it, men schemed, connived and murdered.

The city itself was regarded as a precious jewel, and its successful and powerful sons gave of their substance to embellish it and make it finer. Their handiwork remains to this day, for any tourist to see, in all its breathtaking beauty, the fountains, the temples, the cathedrals, the piazzas, the squares, the parks, the art treasures. Proudly, Augustus said: "I have found a Rome of bricks and left it marble."

At a time when there are so few defenders of the city, some observations about the city, some concept of its role in man's life, past and present, should be attempted, even if of a cursory and general nature.

From the outset, it should be said that the city and civilization go together, that cities are the breeding places of civilization. The very word "civilization" comes from the word

Ancient Pompeii

The Bettmann Archive

In the cities of ancient Rome, chariots undeterred by traffic lights ruled road, intimidating people and geese.

"civitas," the city. The story of ancient civilization is the story of its cities. When the cities of Greece and Rome fell, so fell the glory of Greece and Rome, for in their cities flourished the arts and the sciences, as also government, philosophy, law and ethics.

The Greek and Roman way of life was urban, and it was this urban way of life that gave rise to the power and the might of these ancient civilizations. The Greeks, already living in towns and cities in Homeric times, fearlessly roamed over the Black and Mediterranean Seas, and wherever they tarried they built cities.

"City and civilization go together . . . Talk about depopulated cities is idle . . . The present movement to cities is as strong as it ever was."

In our own times, it is difficult to conceive the devotion and passion that these ancient peoples felt for their thriving, bustling cities. Inhabitants of a city regarded themselves as bound together by the closest ties, almost mystic in concept. They thought of themselves as descendants of a common ancestor, and they thought of themselves as united in a common religion, worshiping the same protective god or hero.

Citizenship, hence, was a rare privilege, which came by birth. Outside of the city, the Greek was a foreigner without legal rights.

"To the freeborn inhabitant of Athens or Rome his city was at once his country, his state, his club and his home," Dr. Hutton Webster observed. "He shared in its government; he took part in the stately ceremonies that honored its patron god. In the city he could indulge his taste for talking and politics; here he found safety and society. No wonder that an Athenian or a Roman learned from early childhood to love his city with passionate devotion."

Both the Greeks and the Romans regarded banishment from the city as dire punishment.

When his disciples pleaded that Socrates save his life by fleeing Athens, he preferred death to exile.

By contrasting the words "urbane" and "rustic," we gain an insight into how the ancient Roman regarded the two ways of life. The word "urbane" means civilized (originally "citified"), polite, courteous, refined, elegant, agreeable, suave. "Rustic" means simple, artless, uncouth, rude, boorish, a country person.

By the fourth or fifth century, as its cities withered away and decayed, Europe went into a period of decline, popularly known as the Middle Ages and sometimes as the Dark Ages. Life during this period was rural. Concomitantly, it was chaotic, isolated, feudal. For several hundred years, ignorance prevailed in Europe, and the lamp of learning and scholarship was kept faintly lit in remote monasteries.

How bad conditions were can be fathomed from the fact that Rome's population at one time dropped to 17,000. Communications were slow. The roads were wretched and infested with bandits, while pirates endangered the sea lanes.

In the eleventh century cities began to revive, faintly at first, but by the end of the fourteenth century, they were vigorous and mighty, especially those in Italy. Even to mention these Italian cities brings back a glamorous and glorious past—Florence, Genoa, Venice, Milan. There was the Hanseatic League, which at its height had an association of 80 cities. There were the industrial cities of Flanders. As cities revived, so did the cultural, scholarly and artistic life of Europe.

To the great cities come, now as then, the intelligent, the able, the adventuresome, the talented, the enterprising—all those who want to live eventful, challenging lives. To it come merchants and traders, but also artists, poets, philosophers—all seeking an audience, appreciation and recognition. Also to it come the nonconformist, the rebellious, those who cannot conform or refuse to conform to local taboos and conventions, those who seek independence and wider intellectual horizons.

It is true that in a city live the disinherited and the poor. It is likewise true that the city attracts the eccentric, the queer, the unstable, the sexual deviate. To the city come the best and the worst. The contrasts stand out marked and stark—wealth and poverty, spiritual elevation and debasement, beauty and squalor. In a city, deviates become lost and anonymous, whereas in a small town they would be conspicuous and persecuted.

A city is like a magnet, and the bigger it is the stronger is its drawing power.

Sociologists will tell you that in a city there is a high social mobility. The small town tends to be static and conforming. A young man returns from the state university, having been graduated with the highest honors, but he finds that in his small community the social élite cannot forget that he is the son of the local garbage collector. So off he goes to the city, where it does not matter who his parents are, where he will be granted prestige and honor commensurate with his achievements.

The emphasis in a great city is on success and achievement and those who succeed win adulation and wealth. A great city is a dynamic place, ever seeking the new, ever restless, ever changing, ever discontented. In this respect, rural life is more secure and comfortable, especially for those who conform to local customs and dogmas.

Once a city becomes set and static in its ways, once it becomes inhospitable to youth, ambition and talent, once it enthrones the respectable and conventional, once it lays stress on position and family, rather than on ability and achievement—once that occurs, the city will wither away and lose its glory and its might.

Cities have been the natural enemies of restrictions, feudalism and royal power. They have fought for freedom and stood for freedom. They wanted safe roads, safe seas, and especially independence, and for this they fought heroically against the armies of kings and princes. In the medieval city, there was no place for serfs or slaves. "Town air renders free," went the expression.

"It is in the metropolitan communities," said Prof. William Anderson, "that the friends of civil liberty organize and carry on their work most effectively. . . . Great newspapers and printing houses, nonconformist economic, social and religious groups, find their most congenial habitat and their opportunity for greatest usefulness and influence and support to every sincere effort to protect civil liberties."

Racial and cultural heterogeneity is a mark of a great city. It is this heterogeneity of cultures—vying with one another, adding and enriching one another—that not only lends attractiveness and interest to the life of the city

19th-Century London

The Bettmann Archive

Pedestrians in Ludgate Hill section of London in the nineteenth century were better off not being in a hurry.

20th-Century New York

The New York Times

In the Garment District of New York a century later, the horses are gone but somehow familiar problem survives.

but also serves as the chief source of the city's growth and greatness. The influx of immigrants into a city, whether from its own hinterland or from foreign countries, generally comprise the disadvantaged groups who occupy menial jobs and live in the slums vacated by a preceding generation of immigrants who have elevated their position.

Historically, the city has been the great educator, the melting pot of races. The new group learns, acquires the ways of the older groups, and with new energy and spirit pushes ahead and challenges the older groups, stirring them. And if the older groups do not meet the challenge, if they remain static in their ways, the newer groups—they or their children—will take over.

Despite many dire predictions about the city's future, there should be no fear of such an outcome. Talk about depopulated cities is idle and without foundation. Cities are increasing at enormous bounds, and the present movement to cities is as strong as it ever was. Julian Huxley says categorically that all men, if given the choice, would prefer to live in the city. To what extent Huxley is right, one cannot say. But the indications are that the overwhelming number of people prefer to live in the city if they can manage to earn a livelihood there. When economic conditions are good, they flock to the city; when bad, as they were in the thirties, they swarm out, only to return in equal and larger numbers when urban conditions improve.

In America cities are about a century old. Before that, we hadn't sufficient surplus food to maintain a city. In olden days, it required nine farm families to feed one city family, so the bulk of the people had to work and live on farms. Modern mechanization has made it possible for a single farmer to feed in 1944 about 40 people. After the Civil War, the trek to the city began in earnest.

"We cannot all live in cities, yet nearly all seem determined to do so," said The New York Herald Tribune in 1867. They reject, the newspaper complained, the millions of acres of uncultivated farm land, "and rush into the city." The movement has never abated. In 1954, 168 metropolitan areas in the United States, comprising 7 per cent of its land surface, housed 57 per cent of its population. Three out of every five persons today are living in urban areas. The urban growth has been phenomenal. As recently as 1900, the urban population was 15 per cent; in 1950 it was 64 per cent, a total of 95,892,000 persons.

Anything that improves communication and transportation makes possible larger cities. Elevators increased enormously the theoretical possibility of growth in a city, as did railroads, automobiles and airplanes. As communications improve, cities will grow larger, not smaller. And if we follow the pattern of the past, the growth will pile up at the center, the central buildings becoming ever higher, the central population ever denser.

The growth will be stopped

only by the limitation set by transportation. The city is helpless without transportation, for it is not self-sufficient. It has to be maintained from the outside. For its food and for all else that it needs, the city must send out goods in trade, and that requires transportation. With every advance in transportation, the city theoretically can grow. All roads lead to Rome. All roads lead to the main cities.

We talk of traffic problems as if they had just come into existence. London was choked with the influx of horses, buses, trains. Our own big cities—New York, Boston and Philadelphia—were plagued by the same problem at that time. In order to relieve congestion, the big cities in America at the turn of the century began to build subway or elevated lines to thin out street traffic.

In ancient Rome, pedestrians in the crowded streets were pushed and bruised by objects being carted about. At one time, all wheeled traffic was prohibited from entering the heart of Rome by day and deliveries could be made only at night. But that did not prove an ideal solution, since residents complained of being disturbed while trying to sleep. Julius Caesar, besides battling armies, also battled traffic, and he introduced in Rome one-way traffic, parking lots for chariots, and pronibited trucks from loading and unloading during rush hours. He did not overcome the traffic problem, and no one since has done so. Taken in another light, traffic problems are only one of the signs of a city's growth.

Robert Moses, a great builder and a lover of his city on the style of the Greeks and the Romans, makes this prediction:

"Long after the last cowboy has disappeared into the sunset and the last cubic foot of natural gas has dried up in the bowels of the Panhandle, there will be cities with minarets and spires assaulting the heavens, gleaming in the dawn and beckoning to ambitious prairies youth. In them will survive the shrines of Molloch, the smithies of Vulcan, the faces that launched a thousand ships, the topless towers of commerce, the Helens who will make the country yokel immortal with a kiss."

What prompts the ordinary person to live in a man-made colossus? We have already in-

The Bettmann Archive

George Cruikshank, British artist of Victorian era, foresaw a touch of congestion in the future London.

dicated why the talented and the ambitious come to the city; also, why eccentrics and deviates seek it out. But most men, whether in the city or the country, live small, circumscribed lives.

Perhaps as insightful an answer as any was given by Justice Oliver Wendall Holmes. "Life," he said, "is an end in itself, and the only question as to whether it is worth living is whether you have enough of it."

In the city even those who live drab lives are less circumscribed. In countless ways, they cannot help being touched by the closeness of first-rate minds, whether directly or indirectly. In the daily newspaper, they have access to the best in journalism. On the stage, on the radio, on television, on lecture platforms, they are entertained, amused, instructed and inspired. Such influences enlarge an individual's horizons and uplift him spiritually.

By and large, in cities man lives with more ease, with more comfort, and probably with greater physical safety. Where can one duplicate the variety of foods available to him, or the purity of the city's milk and water supply; or the professional skills of its hospitals; or the multiplicity of institutions to serve his spiritual and cultural needs?

Pericles said of Athens: "The fruits of the whole world flow in upon us, so that we enjoy the goods of other countries as freely as own own." How much more so is this true of a great city today? Economically, there is no doubt that the urban dweller fares better than his country cousin; that he enjoys more of life's conveniences and necessities.

Emotionally, too, he lives a richer life. In a city, everything is felt more intensely, for here man truly throws in his lot with his fellow men. He lives close to them and feels their proximity and warmth, and shares with them the great moments that come to a people, whether in victory or defeat, triumph or despair. At such climactic moments, almost by instinct, the people stream out of their habitations, and, like a strong current, they flow into the main streets of the city. For a moment, this great conclave mingle their emotions, sharing them, fusing them in an unforgettable experience.

One cannot imagine a victorious army coming home from war being welcomed in a rural area. The city is the place for glitter, pomp and pageantry. The very size seems to augment the strength of the emotions, and it takes a great mass to lend emotions, dignity, force and sweep.

Speaking of the wonder that resides in a city, Richard Harding Davis said: "Any man who can afford a hall bedroom and a gas stove in New York City is better off than he would be as the owner of 160 acres on the prairie," Said Samuel Johnson: "When a man is tired of London, he is tired of living."

The city, unlike the village, allows each person the greatest privacy. It allows one to be alone. By the same token it permits differences much greater than in a small town. It allows the genius, the rebel; the non-conformist to work away undisturbed. It is this great concourse and variety of people working away in freedom, each stirring and influencing the other, that sets the atmosphere where great art, science and literature can flourish.

"Where should the scholar live?" asks Longfellow, "... in the green stillness of the country, or the dark, gray town, where he can hear and feel the throbbing heart of man? I will make answer for him and say, in the dark, gray town."

At present our cities are under severe attack from many sources. But what better than the city feeds the spirit of man? Where can he achieve better? What better place for the panoply of ceremony and high emotion? Where else can man better find congenial spirits to meet his social needs? Where else can he find more varied markets for his talents and abilities? Where else can he have such freedom to differ and not be a pariah?

And where else can he have the isolation and apartness that will permit him to labor in new fields. Where else can he better obtain the encouragement and the sense of personal triumph that come with success. Where else can he better find others to join him in common enterprise but in a city, built by man for man, the product of his intelligence, in which every part displays man's intelligence.

And what greater wonder is there than man's intelligence, as shown in his product? The city is that product.

May 2, 1971

NONURBAN LIVING IS GAINING FAVOR

2 Surveys Find That 8 of 10 Prefer Country or Suburb

By JACK ROSENTHAL
Special to The New York Times

WASHINGTON, Dec. 16—The once-magnetic appeal of great American cities has declined so steeply that, given a choice, about eight out of ten persons would prefer to live in suburban or rural areas, according to two new national public opinion surveys.

A new Gallup Poll issued today showed that only 13 per cent of a cross-section of Americans said that the city was an ideal place to live.

Even among those who now live in cities, only 20 per cent said they preferred city life. That is a striking change since 1966, when a similar survey found that 36 per cent of city residents preferred city life.

Similar questions were asked in a major national survey conducted for "The State of the Nation," a new social compendium to be published shortly by Potomac Associates of Washington.

This survey, conducted last summer, showed that 36 per cent of those interviewed lived in cities but that only 18 per cent would prefer to live in cities.

The findings for rural areas are nearly a reversal of these figures, according to the new publication. Only 18 per cent of the sample lives in rural areas but 38 per cent wished that it did.

Both surveys found that well over half the population would prefer to live outside cities and suburbs. But, in fact, about 70 per cent of Americans now live in these metropolitan areas and the percentage is growing.

The Gallup survey, conducted last August among 1,457 adults in 300 selected localities, found that the preference for nonurban life is strongest in the East, among blue-collar families with growing children.

Along with the positive attraction of more open areas, there may be negative factors in present city life, the Gallup organization suggested, citing a rising fear of urban crime.

The "State of the Nation" survey, of a cross-section sample of 1,806 adults, found the following contrasts between where people now live and where they would prefer to live:

	Present Residence	Preferred Residence
	(in percentages)	
City	36	18
Suburb	22	22
Town or Village	15	19
Rural Area	18	38
Unsure of Category	9	3

Parallel Findings

The findings of both the Gallup and the State of the Nation surveys paralleled research reported last spring by the Presidential Commission on Population Growth and the American Future.

This suggested that Americans want small town or countrified life, but within range of a large metropolitan area. This might well mean, the commission said in its final report, that:

"People want the best of both worlds—the serene and clean environment of rural areas and the opportunity and excitement of the metropolis. Ironically, people moving to such areas typically find that they soon lose their more desirable aspects—semi-rural areas rapidly become suburban."

December 17, 1972

The Power Broker

Robert Moses and The Fall of New York. By Robert A. Caro. Illustrated. 1246 pp. New York: Alfred A. Knopf. $17.95.

By RICHARD C. WADE

"The Power Broker: Robert Moses and the Fall of New York" has been launched with almost unparalleled fanfare, but even if it had been slipped quietly into the bookstores, its importance would have been quickly recognized, for it is the first extensive and comprehensive critique of one of the most powerful men of this—or any other—century. More than any other single man, Robert Moses laid his hand on New York City and State. For over 40 years he wielded more influence and naked power than any governor or mayor: indeed, in the area of public works, more than all of them combined. Through the control of public authorities and commissions he exercised unprecedented influence over the physical development of the entire state and especially its metropolis. Shielded from normal democratic accountability by independent agencies, working in almost total secrecy, sustained by a fawning press and generally grateful public, he wove a concrete web of parkways throughout the metropolitan area, soldered together the fractured boroughs of New York with bridges and tunnels, and surrounded the city with green parks and white beaches. The majesty and extent of his public works have no analogue anywhere in the world. For four decades he spent money on a scale that made city and state budgets look almost like statistical errors.

The author, Robert A. Caro, appreciates the scale of Moses's achievement in this exciting and well-written book; indeed, his prose is at its best when he describes the immensity of the Triboro Bridge complex, or the shimmering beauty of Jones Beach, or the transformation of New York's West Side from an unsightly assemblage of rotting wharfs, underused railroad tracks and scabrous industrial facilities into rolling parkland with breathtaking vistas for the motorist entering the city. There is also awesome respect, if not approval, for the speed with which Moses moved once a project got under way. Describing only a fraction of Moses's activity in the 1930's, Caro writes:

"In the five years after he became Park Commissioner, in a city in which the parks had been barren for decades, he made the parks bloom. In a city in which not a mile of new arterial highway had been built in fifteen years, he built fifty miles of arterial highway. In a city in which a new bridge had not been built in a quarter of a century, he built not only three new big bridges—Triborough, Henry Hudson, and the Marine Parkway—but 110 smaller ones to carry local streets across the parkways. *Si monumentum requiris, circumspice* reads the tomb of Sir Christopher Wren. If you want to see his monument, look around. By 1939, the same advice could have been given to a New Yorker asking to see the monuments of Robert Moses. They were everywhere in the great city." Not even Robert Moses himself in his autobiography, "Public Works: A Dangerous Trade" (1970), describes this physical achievement so glowingly.

But Moses is now finding out that the really dangerous part of the trade is not handling the opposition raised by projects as they are proposed or executed, but rather the judgment of history. Caro's book represents the beginning of this judgment. He questions almost everything about Moses—his strategy and tactics, his methods and ends, his vision and ideology, his honesty and integrity, his character and decency. Everything but his intelligence and self-discipline. These qualities Moses had in lavish amounts, and more than anything else they account for his spectacular success. Yet Caro sees this genius applied to destructive purposes, warped to undermine democratic process and turned unfairly, even viciously, on his adversaries.

The book is not, as Moses claimed in a pre-publication rebuttal, "full of mistakes, unsupported charges, nasty baseless personalities, and random haymakers thrown at just everybody in public life." There is, to be sure, some of that, but surprisingly little. And there could have been less if Moses had been more cooperative. After much resistance, he gave the author, a former reporter for Newsday, seven long interviews and for a while instructed intimates to be helpful. Then, suddenly, this arrangement broke down. For seven years Caro worked through public documents, agency records and newspaper files. He conducted interviews with 522 people directly involved in Moses's career, pored over maps and blueprints of numberless projects and read widely in planning literature. In short, this is no hit and run smear, though, as will be seen later, there are serious problems in Caro's methodology. Caro has tried to take seriously Moses's own admonition from his old friend

---

Richard C. Wade is Distinguished Professor of Urban History at the Graduate Center of the City University of New York and author of "Chicago: Growth of a Metropolis."

Al Smith, "Let's look at the record." Or at least as much as he was permitted to see.

Born in 1888, Robert Moses grew up in a well-to-do New York Jewish family with limitless opportunity and little hardship. His family and his schooling helped produce a man of burning idealism anxious for a career in public service. Tall, roughly handsome, well-bred, energetic and intelligent, young Bob Moses could have succeeded in almost anything he chose. Fresh from Yale (Class of 1909), and a little stung by its anti-Semitism, he joined the reform movement in New York City. Bored by research that provided no immediate results and feeling betrayed by elected liberals, he moved from the margins of power toward the center. He connected with Governor Al Smith in 1921 and, improbably, the King of Oliver Street hit it off with the aristocrat from uptown. Soon they were inseparable; soon, too, Bob Moses began to accumulate power that was independent of the Governor or any other elected official.

The source of that power rested in a device known as a public authority. Though not a new institution, it had been sparingly and narrowly used. Moses made it the principal vehicle for public improvements in New York. The Governor, of course, appointed its members, but their terms usually ran beyond his term. The authorities raised money by issuing bonds and by collecting tolls and fees. A public authority hence became a source of revenue and a well of patronage operating outside the electoral system and the direct control of elected officials. By 1959, Moses headed or controlled over a dozen of these commissions, presiding over parks, highways, bridges, tunnels, power plants, public housing and urban renewal. In short, the physical infrastructure of the nation's largest state lay essentially in the hands of one man.

And Moses used that power to its fullest extent. In its exercise he brooked no opposition, no matter how high the source. He tangled with six governors, seven mayors and three presidents; only at the end—in the 1960's—did he suffer significant defeat. Lesser opponents—state legislators, city councilmen, appointed bureaucrats and ordinary voters—he handled with haughty dispatch. Caro carefully reconstructs the way Moses dealt with those in his path. If they resisted, he called them enemies of the parks at a time when everyone supported parks. He linked them with special or private interests and held them up to public obloquy. A friendly, indeed supine, press would support him. If his adversaries persisted, he quickly abandoned the high road and bore in with a personal attack. Failing success there, Moses would not hesitate to tap his elaborate dossier for ammunition on an opponent's private affairs.

The last stage of the Moses technique, however, was even more harrowing. While "discussions" and "hearings" were going on, Moses would simply begin to build the project. While the normal adversary processes were underway, the issue would become moot. In the celebrated 1956 "battle of Central Park" he put his bulldozers through the contested glen in the dead of night while ostensibly negotiating with the disaffected mothers. When in 1934 he needed the land of the Columbia Yacht Club and the case was before a court, he sent his machines so near the clubhouse that the access roads became imperiled. A club official ruefully observed "they will have dug us out of here before the court can render its decision." Ordinary residents, with little capacity to resist, simply watched as the mixers laid a gash of cement through their neighborhood, destroying its cohesion and draining its vitality. Moses was undeterred by the complaints. "I raise my stein to the builder who can remove ghettos without moving people as I hail the chef who can make omelets without breaking eggs," he wrote in his recent rebuttal. "Those of us who engage in the dangerous trade of public works expect such pot shots and, short of libel, take them good-naturedly."

To Caro, however, Moses's methods were also symptoms of a deeper malaise. The master builder's arrogance (and that is the operative word throughout the book) reflected a contempt for democracy and for the opinions of plain citizens. Nor does Moses deny it. "The current fiction," he writes in his rebuttal, "is that any overnight ersatz bagel and lox boardwalk merchant, any down to earth commentator or barfly, any busy housewife who gets her expertise from newspapers, television, radio and telephone, is ipso facto endowed to plan in detail a huge metropolitan arterial complex good for a century." He gave similar short shrift to professional planners whom he thought excessively theoretical and idealistic, and hence, at best, useless. But people felt his arrogance even while they generally supported his projects and retaliated when they had a chance; in 1934 he ran for Governor of New York and lost by the largest margin in the state's history.

Caro's dislike for Moses's undemocratic methods is clear and eloquent; but what is not so clear in the book is another controversy that sits at the center of urban affairs today. For Caro is not only against Robert Moses of New York; he is against all the Robert Moseses of the country. He rejects the kind of planning—or perhaps better said, of building—that has governed American urban policy for the past two generations. This approach emphasized highways, the commercial reconstruction of central cities, urban renewal, high-rise public and luxury housing, and suburban growth. Caro's view stems from a newer perspective popularly associated with Jane Jacobs and most persuasively argued in her book "The Death and Life of Great American Cities" (the subtitle of "The Power Broker," significantly, is "The Fall of New York"). This view emphasizes decentralization of power and planning, neighborhood participation, smaller construction everywhere, and planned suburban communities. Caro's adherence to this school underlies his entire work and informs every episode, often overtly, but always subliminally. Hence, what seems on the surface to be a narrative biography is also a partisan discussion of one of the central questions of our time.

Two issues best illustrate this conflict. Moses was unbashedly a "rubber tire man," believing that the automobile had fundamentally and irrevocably transformed American society, especially its metropolitan areas. What was needed, he continually argued, was a transportation system appropriate to this new condition. Hence he developed a parkway and highway complex for New York to accommodate the burgeoning number of motorists. This was essentially a suburban strategy, and in the twenties and thirties he built a commuter's dream, with mile upon mile of landscaped parkways. In the forties, his belief led him to ram multilane highways through the city itself.

Caro's commitment however, is to mass transit and urban dwellers. He views the Moses program as destructive. It tore up city neighborhoods and old landmarks and soon became self-defeating because the new facilities only encouraged the inordinate growth of the automobile population. Hence every new bridge, tunnel or highway was overloaded from the day it opened, creating the modern traffic jam.

Caro gives the argument a class and race dimension as well, contending that Moses's programs favored white, middle-class suburbs over poor, minority urban neighborhoods. Indeed, some of the most bitter passages in the book deal with what Caro demonstrates to have been Moses's covert prejudice against the blacks.

The purpose of urban parks is another point of contention. Moses always viewed open spaces as areas for popular recreation. Hence he filled up his projects with tennis courts, swimming pools, playgrounds and restaurants. In addition, his designs always included spacious parking lots to accommodate patrons arriving by car. Caro, on the other hand, prefers parks that emphasize the conservation of rustic surroundings and the preservation of the natural environment; parks ought to be sanctuaries which permit a retreat from the noise, dirt and frenetic activity of the city. Any recreational park ought to be available to the poor by mass transit and not reserved for the middle-class automobile crowd. Because Moses built more parks than any other man since Frederick Law Olmsted, this controversy necessarily dominates a large portion of the book.

Thus "The Power Broker" is not simply a study of one man; it is also a polemic against the kind of planning that has shaped public policy in urban America throughout this century. This tendentiousness is the cause of the book's two major weaknesses. First, in building his case against Moses, Caro places too much emphasis on interviews and anonymous sources. Perhaps Moses, with his obsession for secrecy, deserves it, but the reader certainly does not. Sprinkled heavily throughout the 83 pages of notes in the rear of the book is the ominous phrase "confidential source," a device to cover the specific identity of a witness. More disturbingly, it appears at critical points in an episode or in the general analysis.

The burden of authenticity is thus shifted to Caro's use of identified sources. If he is accurate with these, then the presumption of credibility rests with the author. If not, then the reader must beware. This reviewer has talked with some of the people interviewed by the author. Not a large number but important ones and none who could be described as friends of Moses. They are all generally skeptical about the author's use of their recollection of events or his description of their views, and, in most cases, of the conclusions drawn about their relationship to Moses. The evidenciary problem is no doubt inherent in writing about a man still alive and depending so heavily on the memory of associates or enemies about remote events. But it is precisely this that separates journalism from history.

The second flaw in "The Power Broker" is no less important. The author has little historical perspective in which to place Moses and hence no way to assess his career in the broadest sense. Moses's great success lay in the fact that he was swimming with the tide of history. From 1924, when he began to work on Long Island, to the decline of his power in the 1960's, a massive urban explosion required public works on an unprecedented scale. A continuous boom characterized the four decades of his activity and sustained his ever-expanding programs. Moses perceived this historical surge and worked with its flow. But when conditions changed radically in the 1960's, it was inevitable that he would become obsolete. Elected officials, who had so often deferred to him, now found his policies politically impossible. They soon stripped him of one commission after another. Later they retired him altogether, giving him the 1964 World's Fair as a kind of gold watch for dedicated service.

Moses understood his relationship to history. "The time must be ripe," he wrote in his autobiography.

"The odds and Ides must be favorable, and we must live long and be fortunate." And he was also resigned to the ineluctable ending: "The armor plated rhino or crocodile is never quite invulnerable." But Caro attributes Moses's success largely to personal traits — intelligence, discipline, arrogance, energy and cunning. He leaves little to history. Nor does he explain why every major American city was doing much the same thing as New York at the same time without a Moses. Perhaps Moses pioneered; but the physical shape of urban America would no doubt look very much the same whether Moses had lived or not. In fact, chances are that even New York would not have been very different.

These two problems—the shortage of conventional, reliable documentation and the absence of an historical framework — explain the inordinate length of the book. The former led the author into excessive detail to establish credibility, and the latter prevented him from discriminating between the essential and the merely interesting. To be sure, reducing the size of "The Power Broker" would rob New York buffs of some singularly juicy items and perhaps eliminate some of the wonderful vignettes Caro provides of many of the state's major figures. But it would surely sharpen the focus, clarify central issues and give a scope to the book that sheer length can never provide.

There are serious criticisms, but they ought not deter the reader, for "The Power Broker" is the first successful entry to the highly guarded confines of the Robert Moses public works empire. Caro unravels the complicated legislation that created it, explains the expansion of its power, describes the unique life-style it bred and assesses its pervasive impact on the nation's largest metropolis. In the future, the scholar who writes the history of American cities in the 20th century will doubtless begin with this extraordinary effort. ■

September 15, 1974

Suggested Reading

General

Chudacoff, Howard P. *The Evolution of American Urban Society.* Englewood Cliffs, New Jersey: Prentice-Hall, 1975.

Gloat, Charles N. and A. Theodore Brown. *A History of Urban America.* 2nd ed. New York: Macmillan, 1976 [1967].

Green, Constance McLaughlin. *The Rise of Urban America.* New York: Harper and Row, 1965.

McKelvey, Blake. *The Emergence of Metropolitan America, 1915-1966.* New Brunswick, New Jersey: Rutgers University Press, 1968.

------------------. *The Urbanization of America, 1860-1915.* New Brunswick, New Jersey: Rutgers University Press, 1963.

Still, Bayard. *Urban America: A History with Documents.* Boston: Little, Brown and Co., 1974.

Warner, Sam Bass Jr. *The Urban Wilderness: A History of the American City.* New York: Harper and Row, 1972.

Weber, Adna Ferris. *The Growth of Cities in the Nineteenth Century: A Study in Statistics.* Ithaca, New York: Cornell University Press, 1965 [1899].

The Cities Mature

Atkins, Gordon. *Health, Housing and Poverty in New York City, 1865-1898.* Ann Arbor, Michigan: Edwards Brothers, Inc., 1947.

Blake, Nelson M. *Water for the Cities: A History of the Urban Water Problem in the United States.* Syracuse: Syracuse University Press, 1956.

Bremner, Robert H. *From the Depths: The Discovery of Poverty in the United States.* New York: New York University Press, 1956.

Hawes, Joseph M. *Children in Urban Society: Juvenile Delinquency in Nineteenth Century America.* New York: Oxford University Press, 1971.

Holli, Melvin G. *Reform in Detroit: Hazen Pingree and Urban Politics.* New York: Oxford University Press, 1969.

Mayer, Harold and Richard C. Wade. *Chicago: Growth of a Metropolis.* Chicago: University of Chicago Press, 1969.

Richardson, James F. *The New York Police: Colonial Times to 1901.* New York: Oxford University Press, 1970.

Schlesinger, Arthur M. *The Rise of the City, 1878-1898.* New York: Macmillan, 1933.

Steffins, Lincoln. *The Shame of the Cities.* New York: Hill and Wang, 1957 [1904].

Warner, Sam Bass Jr. *The Private City: Philadelphia in Three Periods of Its Growth.* Philadelphia: University of Pennsylvania Press, 1968.

The Modern Metropolis

Davies, Richard O. *The Age of Asphalt: The Automobile, The Freeway and the Condition of Metropolitan America.* Philadelphia: J. B. Lippincott Co., 1975.

DeForest, Robert and Lawrence Veiller. *The Tenement House Problem.* 2 vols. Arno Press and the New York Times, 1970 [1901].

Fein, Albert. *Frederick Law Olmsted and the American Environmental Tradition.* New York: George Braziller, 1972.

Gelfand, Mark I. *A Nation of Cities: The Federal Government and Urban America: 1933-1965.* New York: Oxford University Press, 1975.

Hines, Thomas S. *Burnham of Chicago: Architect and Planner.* New York: Oxford University Press, 1974.

Lubove, Roy. *Community Planning in the 1920's.* Pittsburgh: University of Pittsburgh Press, 1963.

------------------. *The Progressives and the Slums: Tenement House Reform in New York City, 1890-1917.* Pittsburgh: University of Pittsburgh Press, 1962.

Reps, John W. *The Making of Urban America: A History of City Planning in the United States.* Princeton: Princeton University Press, 1965.

Rodwin, Lloyd. *Housing and Economic Progress: A Study of the Housing Experience of Boston's Middle-Income Families.* Cambridge: Harvard University Press and the Technical Press, 1961.

Stave, Bruce M. *The New Deal and the Last Hurrah: Pittsburgh Machine Politics.* Pittsburgh: University of Pittsburgh Press, 1970.

Taylor, Graham R. *Satellite Cities: A Study of Industrial Suburbs.* New York: D. Appleton & Co., 1915.

Warner, Sam Bass Jr. *Streetcar Suburbs: The Process of Growth in Boston 1870-1900.* Cambridge: Harvard University Press and the MIT Press, 1962.

Big Cities, Big Problems

Banfield, Edward C. *The Unheavenly City.* Boston: Little, Brown and Co., 1970.

Boesel, David and Peter H. Rossi, eds. *Cities Under Siege: An Anatomy of the Ghetto Riots, 1964-1968.* New York: Basic Books, Inc., 1971.

Boskin, Joseph, ed. *Urban Racial Violence in the Twentieth Century.* Beverly Hills, California: Glencoe Press, 1969.

Gorham, William and Nathan Glazer, eds. *The Urban Predicament.* Washington, D. C.: The Urban Institute, 1976.

Lowe, Jeanne R. *Cities in a Race with Time.* New York: Random House, 1968 [c1967].

Massoth, Louis H. and Jeffrey K. Hadden, eds. *The Urbanization of the Suburbs.* Beverly Hills, California: Sage Publications, 1973.

Rae, John Bell. *The American Automobile: A Brief History.* Chicago: University of Chicago Press, 1965.

Weaver, Robert C. *The Negro Ghetto.* New York: Harcourt Brace, 1948.

Wilson, James Q., ed. *Urban Renewal: The Record and the Controversy.* Cambridge: MIT Press, 1966.

An Uncertain Future

Downs, Anthony. *Opening Up the Suburbs: An Urban Strategy for America.* New Haven: Yale University Press, 1973.

Ferrith, Fred. *The Year the Big Apple Went Bust.* New York: G. P. Putnam's Sons, 1976.

Starr, Roger. *The Living End: The City and its Critics.* New York: Conrad-McCann, 1966.

Index